P9-EDY-298

INTRODUCTION TO PSYCHOLOGY

INTRODUCTION

SECOND EDITION

TO PSYCHOLOGY

James W. Kalat

North Carolina State University

WADSWORTH PUBLISHING COMPANY
Belmont, California
A Division of Wadsworth, Inc.

PSYCHOLOGY EDITOR: Kenneth King
SENIOR DEVELOPMENT EDITOR: Mary Arbogast
EDITORIAL ASSISTANT: Michelle Palacio
PRODUCTION EDITOR: Sandra Craig
DESIGNER: MaryEllen Podgorski
PRINT BUYER: Karen Hunt
ART EDITOR: Donna Kalal
COPY EDITOR: Pat Tompkins
ART DEVELOPMENT: Audre Newman,
Martha Wiseman
PHOTO RESEARCH: Andromeda Oxford Ltd.,
Stephen Forsling
ILLUSTRATIONS: Graphic Typesetting Service,
John and Judy Waller, Carlyn Iverson, Beck Visual
Communications, Jeanne Schreiber,
Darwen Hennings
CAPTIONS: Pat Tompkins
COVER PHOTOGRAPH: Costa Manos/Magnum
COMPOSITION AND PREPRESS SERVICES: Graphic
Typesetting Service, Los Angeles

Credits appear on page 673.

Printed in the United States of America   55

2   3   4   5   6   7   8   9   10—94   93   92   91   90

LIBRARY OF CONGRESS
CATALOGING-IN-PUBLICATION DATA

Kalat, James W.
   Introduction to Psychology / James W. Kalat — 2nd ed.
      p.   cm.
   Includes bibliographical references.
   ISBN 0-534-12060-1
   1. Psychology.   I. Title.
BF121.K26   1990
150—dc20   89-29054
                  CIP

To my parents,
Edward and Rachael,
my wife, Ann,
and my children,
David, Sam, and Robin

A NOTE ABOUT THE AUTHOR

James W. Kalat (rhymes with ballot), born in 1946, received an A.B. degree summa cum laude from Duke University in 1968 and a Ph.D. in psychology from the University of Pennsylvania in 1971. He has been a member of the department of psychology at North Carolina State University since 1977 and is a Fellow of the American Association for the Advancement of Science, the American Psychological Society, and the American Psychological Association. Kalat is also the author of *Biological Psychology* (the third edition was published by Wadsworth in 1988).

CONTENTS IN BRIEF

CONTENTS

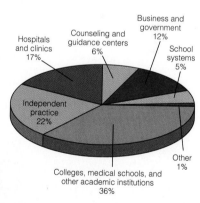

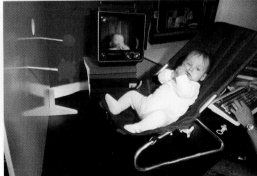

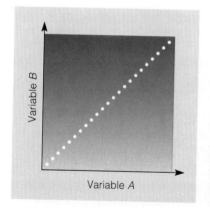

CHAPTER 3   Biological Psychology   54

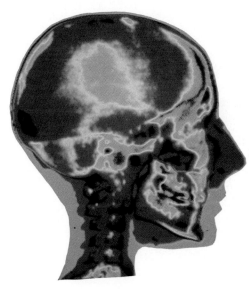

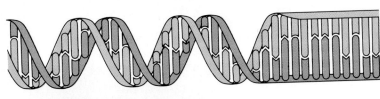

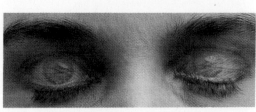

CHAPTER 7 Learning 236

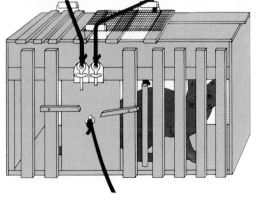

CHAPTER 8   Memory   276

THE STRUCTURE OF MEMORY   279

Ebbinghaus and the Associationist Approach to Memory   279

The Information-Processing Model of Memory   285

A Model of Retrieval from Memory   292

IMPROVEMENT, LOSS, AND DISTORTION OF MEMORY   295

Improving Memory by Improving Learning   295

Forgetting   301

■ The Suggestibility of Eyewitness Accounts: WHAT'S THE EVIDENCE?   305

Amnesia   307

xvi   CONTENTS

CHAPTER 9   Cognition   314

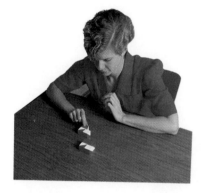

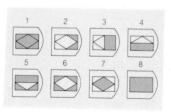

CHAPTER 10   Intelligence and Its Measurement   346

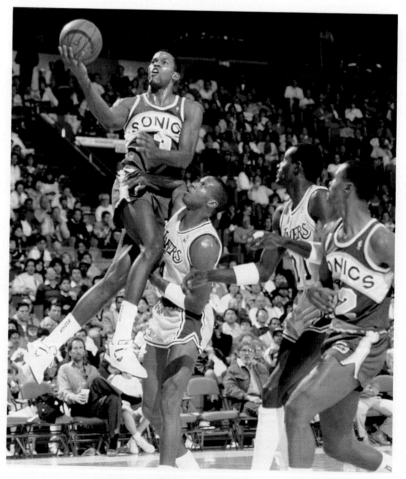

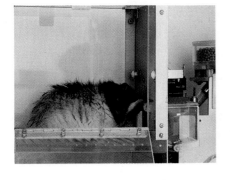

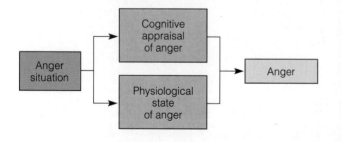

CHAPTER 12 Emotions, Health Psychology, and Stress 420

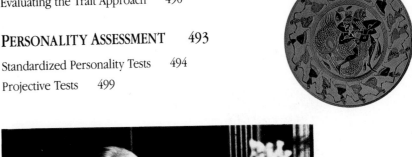

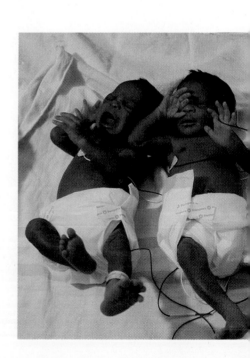

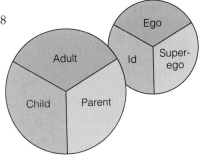

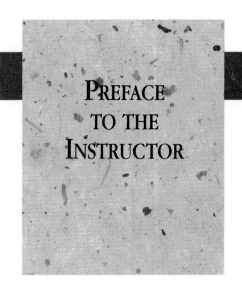

PREFACE TO THE INSTRUCTOR

A group of young people are deciding what to take with them on a backpacking trip through the mountains. They decide not to take a Swiss army knife: "After all, how often do we use a Swiss army knife?" They also decide against taking a map and compass: "We'll probably never need them." They leave behind a book on how to identify edible mushrooms: "Why should we take that? We hardly ever eat mushrooms." They also decide against taking a snake-bite kit: "Why carry that around? We'll probably never get bitten by a snake." They end up taking only their tent and a portable stereo, which is set to a decibel level that warrants an environmental impact statement.

We would like to say to them, "You're making a terrible mistake! Other people who have made this trip would urge you to take all the things you're leaving behind. It's a difficult trip. You should prepare yourselves for all contingencies."

We educators give this same advice to our students. We want to equip them with a rich supply of information before they set out on their backpacking trip of life. But they protest, "Why should we have to learn calculus, geography, and brain anatomy? We'll never use any of that." And we reply, "You're going to need more information than you realize. Get your equipment in order. Learn everything you can."

I do believe that students should learn calculus, geography, brain anatomy, and a great deal more. Still, more often than we care to admit, students are right. It is as if we were advising them, "On your backpacking trip take this electric waffle iron, this portable generator, this tank of fuel, this jumbo package of waffle mix, and place settings for twelve. Then you'll be able to have waffles any morning you want."

Not that the waffle iron and all the paraphernalia wouldn't be useful. It is simply too bulky. The same is true of education. There is an enormous amount of information that might turn out to be useful some day, but it is just too bulky to tote. The proper goal for educators, especially those who write textbooks, is to take the information we most want students to carry with them and try to make it portable. With this goal in mind, I have tried to include a good supply of potentially useful information in this second edition—more than I included in the first edition. But I have tried to make the information simple and clear and to add interesting examples that will make it easier to remember—easier to carry on the trip.

Moreover, there is an alternative to carrying with you everything you will need: As long as travelers know where to find additional supplies when they need them, they can keep their luggage down to manageable proportions. I have tried to prepare students to find additional supplies in psychology—and how to recognize which are good supplies and which are useless ones. My hope is that the students who use this book will continue to read in psychology for years to come, whether or not they take any further courses in the subject. Toward that end, I have tried to give them the background they will need to understand what they read and to evaluate evidence critically. In Chapter 2, I set forth the methods of investigation that psychologists use and the ways that scientists evaluate theories. With occasional questions titled "Something to Think About" and with an average of one section per chapter titled "What's the Evidence?" I try to motivate students to become actively engaged in evaluating evidence and pursuing questions on their own.

Finally, I have tried to nurture in students a love for the subject. Psychology is fun to talk about and fun to think about. I have tried to let students in on that fun.

SPECIAL FEATURES

Organization

The text consists of 16 chapters. Chapters 2–16 are each divided into two to five self-contained sections, each of which has its own introduction and its own summary. Instructors who wish to do so can easily omit certain sections or assign sections in an order of their own choosing. Instructors may also assign one or more parts of a chapter for each day of class, instead of assigning an entire chapter per week.

Coverage

For this edition, the content has been extensively revised and reorganized. More than half of the references cited in the first edition have been replaced with new ones, indicating the magnitude of the new research base. Most of the figures and illustrations are new as well. Some highlights of this text, particularly relating to how this edition differs from the first edition, are listed below:

- **Chapter 1, What Is Psychology?** is an intentionally brief introduction to what psychologists do. It introduces three of the most fundamental issues in psychology—free will and determinism, the mind-brain relationship, and the nature-nurture issue. The chapter briefly surveys the major subfields of psychology, concentrating on how each area deals with the question of the origin of individual differences. It includes a few highlights of the history of psychology, although it is not a history chapter per se. I believe in a short first chapter, because in my own course (and I presume in most courses), it is necessary to spend part of the first week explaining the organization of the course and waiting for the dust to settle.

- **Chapter 2, Scientific Methods in Psychology,** is, in my opinion, the most important chapter in the book. It deals not only with the procedures for conducting research but also with how scientists evaluate evidence, how they evaluate theories, and, in general, how they think. Chapter 2 includes the basic concepts of statistics in context. (A brief appendix to the chapter shows how to calculate a few representative statistics.) I do not think an instructor should have to choose between discussing statistics in detail and never mentioning them at all. I think all students should learn in general terms what statistical tests are and why it is important to use them.

- **Chapter 3, Biological Psychology,** contains a new section on genetics, evolution, and animal behavior. Several reviewers of the first edition recommended discussing genetics early in the text because it shows up again in many other contexts.

- **Chapter 4, Altered States,** deals mostly with sleep and hypnosis. It also includes a brief section on the effects of drugs. Note, however, that the main discussion of substance abuse is in Chapter 14.

- **Chapter 5, Sensation and Perception,** has about 50% more information than the first edition had. Note, for example, new coverage of dark adaptation, subliminal perception, attentive and preattentive processes, and movement perception.

- **Chapter 6, Development,** now appears earlier in the text. The first edition had one chapter on early development and one chapter on later development. This edition has one long chapter that deals with development by topic. It includes sections on early development, cognitive development, language development, and social development. The section on social development includes gender roles.

- **Chapter 7, Learning,** includes expanded coverage of social learning. (Some instructors may choose to assign this section when they discuss personality in Chapter 13.) This chapter also includes updated material on contemporary interpretations of classical conditioning and new examples of applications of operant conditioning.

- **Chapter 8, Memory,** has been extensively reorganized. It includes new information on amnesia, on the suggestibility of eyewitness accounts, and on self-monitoring of reading comprehension.

- **Chapter 9, Cognition,** is the most extensively revised chapter in the text. It includes new discussions of mental imagery, cognitive maps, categorization, problem solving, expertise and artificial intelligence, and the reasons behind illogical reasoning. Language, covered in the cognition chapter in the first edition, is now discussed in Chapter 6, Development.

- **Chapter 10, Intelligence,** is a new chapter. It includes an examination of some commonly used IQ tests, a discussion of how psychologists standardize and evaluate tests (including the concepts of reliability and validity), and a discussion of some controversial issues concerning intelligence.

- **Chapter 11, Motivation,** begins with general principles of motivation and then proceeds with three examples of motivated behavior: hunger, sex, and achievement. The section on hunger includes eating disorders.

- **Chapter 12, Emotions, Health Psychology, and Stress,** begins with general theories and principles of emotions, including two examples of emotions—anger and happiness. It continues with an expanded treatment of health psychology, followed by a discussion of coping with stress.

- **Chapter 13, Personality,** starts with the historically influential general theories of personality—those of Freud, Jung, Adler, Rogers, and Maslow. It then proceeds with personality traits, using new examples of personality traits: androgyny, locus of control, and self-monitoring.

- **Chapter 14, Abnormal Behavior,** has been reorganized in a number of ways. It begins with an overview of abnormal psychology based on DSM-III-R. The next three sections discuss in some detail the three most common types of psychological disorders—anxiety and avoidance disorders, substance abuse, and depression. The final section deals with schizophrenia, a less common but undeniably important disorder.

- **Chapter 15, Therapy,** collects material into one chapter that the first edition presented in two. It deals first with psychotherapy, then with medical therapies, and finally with some controversial social issues, such as the right to refuse treatment and the insanity defense.

- **Chapter 16, Social Psychology,** was written mostly by Richard Lippa from California State University, Fullerton, the author of a new social psychology textbook published by Wadsworth. This chapter offers much more extensive coverage than the first edition did, and it focuses on social perception and cognition, attitudes, interpersonal attraction, interpersonal influence, and applications of social psychology (and other fields of psychology) to industrial and organizational psychology.

Pedagogy

I think the best pedagogical device is clear, unambiguous writing. I have tried to give enough information on each topic to enable students to understand the topic even if the instructor does not elaborate on it in class. I have included certain special features to help the students who have difficulty understanding key points and certain other features to stimulate the best students:

1. Each chapter opens with an outline and a brief introduction intended to engage students' interest and to illustrate one of the fundamental issues of the chapter.

2. Each major section of the chapter begins with one or more questions and its own introduction. The questions are the ones that motivate research—the fundamental questions that psychologists ask. They are not always answerable, given our current knowledge. Each major section of the text concludes with a numbered list of summary points, with page numbers to refer students to the relevant parts of the text. The summary is followed by one or more suggestions for further reading.

3. Important terms appear in **boldface** where they are defined in the text. All the boldfaced terms are listed along with their definitions at the end of the chapter.

4. A combined Glossary/Subject Index appears at the end of the book. Anyone who wishes to check on a particular term can find the definition and the page reference at the same time.

5. Every so often—an average of eight or nine times per chapter—I present a "Concept Check." Concept Checks pose questions that a student who has read the section carefully should be able to answer. But they do not ask for simple repetition of some statements. Rather, the student needs to apply the information in some way or to draw a conclusion. The answers to all the Concept Checks are given at the end of the chapter in which they appear.

6. The "Something to Think About" sections invite students to go beyond the text and to consider questions that, in many cases, have no clear right or wrong answers. Some instructors may wish to use these questions as a basis for class discussion. I have sometimes invited students to write up answers to a set of "Something to Think About" questions as an extra-credit project. For whatever it may be worth, my own answers are available in the Instructor's Manual that accompanies this text.

7. Every chapter except Chapter 1 includes a "What's the Evidence?" section. (Chapter 14 includes two such sections.) "What's the Evidence?" sections describe the procedures and results of one or two experiments. In some cases the topic is an important, classic experiment. Other sections present less famous experiments that illustrate methodological points, sometimes even methodological difficulties. ("Evidence" does not always lead to firm conclusions.)

8. A number of supplements accompany the text. Art Kohn of Saint Andrews Presbyterian College has prepared a very thorough and creative Instructor's Manual. Ruth Maki of North Dakota State University has prepared a Study Guide (purchased separately) that provides study aids and practice test items. Roger Harnish of Rochester Institute of Technology has developed computer software to illustrate a number of important concepts. Additional supplements include Test Items (also available on computer disks) and overhead transparencies.

ACKNOWLEDGMENTS

A potential author needs self-confidence bordering on arrogance just to begin the job of writing a textbook. To complete it, the writer needs the humility to accept criticism of his or her favorite ideas and most carefully written prose. A great many people have provided helpful suggestions that have made this a far better text than it would have been otherwise.

I could not have started this book, much less completed it, without the constant support of my wife, Ann, my editor, Ken King, and my department head, Paul Thayer. To each of them: Thanks. You're the greatest.

Everett Sims, my writing consultant for both the first and second editions, has laboriously worked through at least two drafts of each chapter and has helped me to phrase each sentence as clearly as possible. Mary Arbogast, senior development editor, provided detailed and highly helpful suggestions on the organization and coverage of topics in each chapter. Maggie Murray, development manager, provided similar comments for Chapter 11. And Pat Tompkins carefully and thoroughly copyedited the final draft. If you like the way the book is written, each of these people deserves a good share of the credit.

Very special thanks to Richard Lippa of California State University, Fullerton, the primary author of Chapter 16, Social Psychology. In the summer of 1989 it became clear that I would not have time to bring the social psychology chapter up to the desired level. Lippa, who had just finished writing a social psychology textbook for Wadsworth, agreed to write a draft of what eventually became the first four sections of Chapter 16. I thank him deeply for making this a much better and more complete chapter than I could have written.

If you quickly thumb through this book you will begin to realize that coming up with all the illustrations and captions is an enormous task, almost like writing a separate text. I contributed a first suggestion for some of the figures, wrote a few captions and edited others, but other people did nearly all the work and should get the credit, including: Audré Newman and Martha Wiseman, art development; Andromeda Oxford Ltd. and Stephen Forsling, photo research; Donna Kalal, art supervision; and Pat Tompkins, captions. To each of these people, my sincere thanks.

I have had the great fortune to work with Sandra Craig, who has supervised the production of this book. A more dedicated worker would be hard to imagine. She and MaryEllen Podgorski, the book's designer, have been at work from early in the morning until late in the evening and on weekends, trying to get this book produced on time and trying to make it as good as possible. I deeply appreciate all they have done.

Still more people have my gratitude: Stacey Pollard, who has supervised the supplements; Robin Levy, who has directed the marketing campaign; and Art Kohn, Ruth Maki, and Roger Harnish, who have written the best supplements I have ever seen for a psychology text.

My colleagues at North Carolina State University provided me with encouragement, reprints and preprints, unpublished information, and free advice. I thank particularly Bruce Mallette, Don Mershon, Rupert Barnes-Nacoste, Slater Newman, Bob Pond, Paul Thayer, and Bert Westbrook.

Art Kohn has been the source of a number of creative ideas on how to approach certain topics; he has also been a stimulating person to talk to and a good friend. I also thank the following people for the information or suggestions they sent me: Garvin Chastain, Boise State University; Stephen S. Coccia, Orange County Community College; Cheryl-Anne Graham, a student at Kwantlen College; Sue Yin Hum, a student at Capital University; Jackie Ludel, Guilford College; William Moorcroft, Luther College; J. J. Turnage, University of Central Florida; and Michael Zeeky, Educational Testing Services.

I thank the following people for their helpful reviews on earlier drafts of all or part of the book: John Anson, Stephen F. Austin State University; Angela M. Bartoli, Shippensburg University of Pennsylvania; Johnston Beach, United States Military Academy; Dan Bellack, University of Kentucky; John B. Best, Eastern Illinois University; Pamela J. Birrell, University of Oregon; William H. Calhoun, University of Tennessee, Knoxville; Shelley B. Calisher, University of Colorado; D. Bruce Carter, Syracuse University; Samuel H. Clarke, North Adams State College; Sandra Schweighart Goss, University of Illinois; Gary Greenberg, Wichita State University; Donald M. Hall, Radford University; Anne E. Harris, Arizona State University; Melvyn B. King, State University of New York College at Cortland; Richard A. Kribs III, Motlow State Community College; Carlton Lints, Northern Illinois University; Dale McAdams, University of Rochester; Ruth H. Maki, North Dakota State University; Edward H. Matthei, University of California, Irvine; Sheryll Mennicke, Concordia College, St. Paul; Rowland Miller, Sam Houston State University; Michael Nedelsky, Augustana College, Sioux Falls; Ron Nowaczyk, Clemson University; Dawn R. Rager, State University of New York at Albany; Cynthia A. Rohrbeck, George Washington University; Joan A. Royce, Riverside City College; Virginia M. Scully, Towson State University; R. Lance Shotland, Pennsylvania State University; and Robert J. Wunderlin, Old Dominion University.

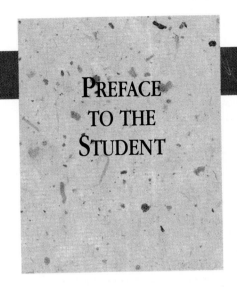

PREFACE TO THE STUDENT

Welcome to introductory psychology! I hope you will enjoy reading this text as much as I enjoyed writing it. When you finish, I hope you will write your comments on the last page of the text, tear the page out, and mail it to the publisher, who will pass it along to me. If you include your return address, I will send a reply.

The first time I taught introductory psychology, several students complained that the book we were using was interesting to read but impossible to study. What they meant was that they had trouble finding and remembering the main points. I have tried to make this book easy to study in many ways. I have tried to make sure my discussion of each point is as clear as possible. I have tried to select material that will be as interesting as possible to you.

In addition, I have included some special features to aid your study. Each chapter begins with an outline and a brief introduction to the topic. Every chapter except Chapter 1 is divided into two or more major sections. Each of those sections begins with one or more questions—the fundamental questions that psychologists are trying to answer, the questions that motivate research. In some cases you will be able to answer the question after you read the section; in other cases you will not, because psychologists themselves are not sure about the answers. At the end of each major section you will find a summary of some important points, wih page references. If you find one of the summary points unfamiliar, you should reread the appropriate section.

Throughout the text you will find certain words highlighted in **boldface**. These are important terms whose meaning you should understand. All the boldface terms in the text are listed with their definitions at the end of the chapter. They also appear in the Glossary/Subject Index at the end of the book. You might want to find the Glossary/Subject Index right now and familiarize yourself with it. Note that when you look up a term you find both its definition and page references to find it in the text. The Glossary/Subject Index also includes terms you might want to look up (such as *age differences)* that do not require definition.

At various points in the text you will find a question under the heading "Concept Check." These questions enable you to test your understanding. They do not ask you simply to recall what you have read but to use or apply the information in some way. Try to answer each of these questions, rereading the previous material if necessary. Then turn to the last page of the chapter to check your answers. If you cannot answer a Concept Check correctly, you probably have not been reading carefully enough, and you might want to reread the section in which the Concept Check occurs.

You will also find an occasional section marked "Something to Think About." These sections pose questions that require you to go beyond what is discussed in the text. In some cases there is no single right answer; there may be a number of reasonable ways to approach the question. I hope you will think about these questions, perhaps talk about them with fellow students, and maybe ask your instructor what he or she thinks.

I would like to deal with a few of the questions that students sometimes raise about their textbooks:

Do you have any useful suggestions on study habits? Whenever students ask me why they did so badly on the last test, I ask, "When did you read the assignment?" They often answer, "Well, I didn't exactly read *all* of the assignment," or "I read it the night before the test." To do your best, read each assignment *before the lecture.* Within 24 hours after the lecture, read over your lecture notes. Then, before you take the test, reread both the textbook assignment and your lecture notes. If you do not have time to reread everything, at least skim the text and reread the sections on which you need to refresh your memory.

As you read this book, try to think actively about what you are reading. One way to improve your studying is to read by the SPAR method: *S*urvey, *P*rocess meaningfully, *A*sk questions, *R*eview. The steps are as follows:

Survey: When you start a chapter, first look over the chapter outline to get a preview of the chapter's contents. When you start a major section of a chapter, turn to the end of the section and read the summary. When you begin to read the chapter you know what to expect and you can focus on the main points.

Process meaningfully: Read the chapter carefully. Stop to think from time to time. Tell your roommate some of the interesting things you learn. Think about how you might apply a certain concept in a real-life situation. Pause when you come to the Concept Checks and try to answer them.

Ask questions: When you finish the chapter, try to anticipate some of the questions you might be asked later. You can take questions from the Study Guide or you can compose your own questions. Write out your questions and think about them, but do not write your answers yet.

Review: Pause for a while—at least several hours, or, better yet, a day or two. If you first read a chapter before class, come back to the chapter the evening after class. Now write out the answers to the questions you wrote earlier. Check your answers against the text or against the answers given in the Study Guide. Reinforcing your memory a day or two after first reading the chapter will help you retain the material longer and with deeper understanding.

Is it worthwhile to buy and use the Study Guide? The Study Guide is designed to help students who have trouble studying, remembering the material, or answering multiple-choice questions. It is most likely to be helpful to freshmen, to students who have been away from college for a few years, and to students who have had trouble with similar courses in the past. It provides examples of multiple-choice questions, giving not only the correct answers but also explanations of why they are correct.

In the Study Guide for this text, written by Ruth Maki of North Dakota State University, you can work through each chapter in one or two hours. If you are willing to devote that much time to it, I believe the Study Guide will help you.

Does it help to underline or highlight key sentences while reading? Maybe, but don't overdo it. I have seen books in which a student underlined or highlighted more than half the sentences. What good that does, I have no idea.

What do those parentheses mean, as in "(Maki & Berry, 1984)"? Am I supposed to remember the names and dates? Psychologists generally cite references not by footnotes but in parentheses. "(Maki & Berry, 1984)" refers to a publication written by Maki and Berry and published in 1984. All the references cited are listed in alphabetical order according to the author's name in the References section at the back of the book.

No one expects you to memorize the names and dates in parentheses. They are there to enable you to look up the source of a statement in case you want more information. Some names *are* worth remembering, however. For instance, you will read about the research and theories of some famous psychologists, such as B. F. Skinner, Jean Piaget, and Sigmund Freud. You will certainly be expected to remember those names and a few others. But names that are important to remember are emphasized, not buried in parentheses.

Can you give me any help on how to read and understand graphs? The graphs in this book are easy to understand. Just take a minute or so to study them carefully. You will find four kinds: pie graphs, bar graphs, line graphs, and scatter plots. Let's look at each kind.

Pie graphs show how a whole is divided into parts. Figure 1 shows that more than one third of all psychologists take a starting job with a college or some other educational institution. Another one fifth to one fourth of psychologists work in independent practice. The total circle represents 100% of all psychologists.

Bar graphs show the frequency of events that fall into one category or another. Figure 2 shows that about one third of all adults in the United States suffer from some type of psychological disorder. The length of the bar represents the frequency of each disorder. A fairly large number of people have a problem of alcohol or drug abuse, phobia, or affective disorders; a relatively small number have schizophrenia or panic disorder.

Line graphs show how one variable is related to another variable. In Figure 3 you see that newborn infants spend about 16 hours a day asleep. As they grow older, the amount of time they spend in two types of sleep gradually decreases.

Scatter plots are similar to line graphs, with this difference: A line graph shows averages, whereas a scatter plot shows individual data points. By looking at a scatter plot, we can see how much variation occurs among individuals.

To prepare a scatter plot, we make two observations about each individual. In Figure 4 each student is represented by one point. If you take that point and scan down to the *x*-axis, you find that student's SAT score. If you then scan across to the *y*-axis, you find that student's grade average for the

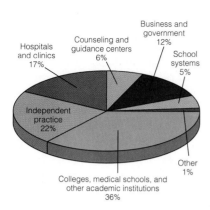

FIGURE 1

Pie graph.

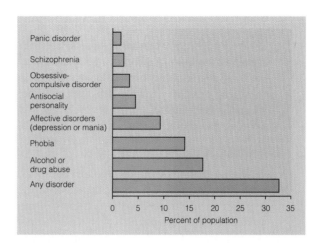

FIGURE 2

Bar graph.

freshman year. A scatter plot shows the relationship between two variables, but it also shows whether the variables are closely related or only loosely related.

We may have to take multiple-choice tests on this material. How can I do better on those tests?

1. Read all of the choices carefully. Do not choose an answer just because it looks correct; first make sure that the other answers are wrong. Sometimes you will find a second answer that also sounds correct; decide which of the two is better.

2. If you don't know the correct answer, make an educated guess. Start by eliminating any answer that you know cannot be right. Generally, an answer that includes words such as *always* and *never* is wrong. (Psychologists are seldom sure that something is always right or always wrong.) Also eliminate any answer that includes terms that are unfamiliar to you. (Correct choices use only terms that should be familiar to a reasonably conscientious student; incorrect choices may include obscure terms or even outright nonsense.)

3. After you finish a test, go back and check your answers and rethink them. Many students insist that it is a mistake to change an answer because they think their first impulse is usually right. J. J. Johnston (1975) tested this belief by looking through the answer sheets of a number of classes that had taken a multiple-choice test. He found that of all the students who changed one or more answers, 71 students improved their scores by doing so and only 31 lowered their scores. Similar results have been reported in a number of other studies. This does not mean that you should make changes just for the sake of making changes. But if you recon-

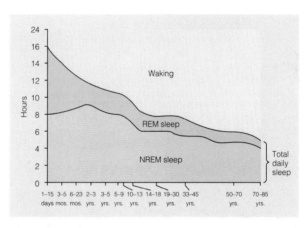

FIGURE 3

Line graph.

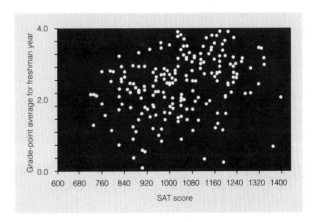

FIGURE 4

Scatter plot.

sider a question and change your mind about which answer is best, go ahead and change your answer.

Why, then, do so many students (and professors) believe that it is a mistake to change an answer? Imagine what happens when you take a test and get your paper back. When you look it over, which items do you pay attention to—the ones you got right or the ones you got wrong? The ones you got wrong, of course. You may notice three items that you originally answered correctly and then changed. You never notice the five other items you changed from incorrect to correct.

All right, so much for advice. Now let's talk about psychology.

INTRODUCTION TO PSYCHOLOGY

CHAPTER

1

WHAT IS
PSYCHOLOGY?

> "Let us, then, make a fresh start and try to determine what soul is and what will be its most comprehensive definition."
> ARISTOTLE
> (384–322 B.C.)

What is psychology and how did it originate?
What are some of its fundamental questions?
What are the principal theoretical approaches of psychology?
What are some of psychology's main areas of study?

As the space capsule opened, out sprang some little blue people. "We come from a nearby solar system," one of them said. "For years we have been listening to your radio and television programs. We have learned your language and your customs. We are very impressed with certain aspects of your science and we have come to learn from you. Take us to your scientists!"

"Glad to," said the earthling who greeted them. "There's a fine university just down the road. I can introduce you to some physicists, chemists . . ."

"Oh, no!" interrupted one little blue person. "Not that kind of scientist! Everything you know about the physical sciences is just common sense—to us, that is. We came here to learn about your amazing advances in psychology."

Had any psychologists been on hand to meet the little blue people, they would have been as surprised as anyone else. People sometimes charge that psychologists deal only in common sense. To be complimented on the amazing advances in psychology would be a novelty.

In many cases, we must concede, the charge that psychology deals with common sense is valid. For example, psychologists have conducted elaborate, careful studies demonstrating that people take longer to memorize a long list of words than they do to memorize a short list. And that students who spend more hours doing homework get better grades than those who study less. And that people are more likely to be influenced by a message from

an expert than by the same message from an ill-informed source.

Why would anyone spend so much effort to demonstrate facts that were obvious to anyone with a little common sense? The investigators could justify their experiments in two ways: (1) Any field makes progress by measuring. To a degree, even a fair amount of physics is common sense. After all, everyone knows that if you drop something, it will fall. Physics made progress by measuring exactly *how fast* a dropped object falls. Similarly, psychology can make progress by measuring *how much* longer it takes to learn a long list than a short list or *how much* more people are influenced by experts than by nonexperts. (2) We need to test common sense from time to time, because it occasionally turns out to be wrong.

Here is a test you can conduct yourself. Try to answer each of the following questions on the basis of common sense and then compare your answers with those on the last page of this chapter.

1. The workers at Consolidated Generic Manufacturing Company work on rotating shifts; each person works 8:00 A.M. to 4:00 P.M. for a few weeks, then midnight to 8:00 A.M., and then 4:00 P.M. to midnight. They complain of physical and mental distress, but the company insists on rotating shifts. What could be done to reduce the workers' distress?

2. Can hypnosis improve a person's memory of early childhood events or of a car accident?

3. You have just come out of the hospital; while still under the influence of strong medication you witness a crime. The police talk with you only briefly because you are still groggy. They come back two weeks later, but by then you have forgotten what you saw. What could you do to try to recover the memory?

4. At what age do children start using language in original ways, saying things they have never heard anyone else say?

5. You have just bought some new sandals, which you will not need until the next time you go to the beach, several months from now. Where should you store them so you will be sure to find them when you need them?

6. Do people with a high need for achievement set high goals, low goals, or intermediate goals for themselves?

7. After taking repeated injections of a drug, most people develop a tolerance to it and need stronger and stronger doses to get the same effect. What could be done to reduce their tolerance?

8. How well can a newborn infant see and hear?

9. What causes infants to develop a social attachment to their mothers?

10. How could you help someone who insists on acting "crazy" and resists all the usual forms of help?

11. You talk two people into doing an unpleasant chore. You give one a small bribe and the other a large bribe. Which one will enjoy the chore more?

THE PHILOSOPHICAL ORIGINS OF PSYCHOLOGY

In the late 1800s, a number of people, ranging from biologists to philosophers, decided not to rely on common sense but to collect and evaluate evidence. They founded the field of psychology as we know it today.

Psychology, broadly defined, is the systematic study of behavior and experience. The term *psychology* derives from the Greek roots *psyche,* meaning *soul* or *mind,* and *logos,* meaning *word* or *study.* Psychology began as the analysis of the mind or soul. As with most academic disciplines, it had its roots in philosophy. Although it has moved far away from philosophy in its methods, psychology continues to be motivated by some deep philosophical issues. Three of the most profound questions are free will versus determinism, the mind-brain problem, and the nature-nurture issue.

Free Will Versus Determinism

Physicists and chemists take for granted that everything that happens has a physical cause, except per-

Liberty includes the power to do as you please. This police officer risks his life to rescue someone who wants to kill himself. Are they free to do what they want? Are they acting on the basis of free will? Or are there causes controlling their behavior? According to determinism, all behavior has causes.

haps for certain random events at the subatomic level. If we have enough information about a physical object at any given time, then we can predict how that object will behave—at least in principle. (When a leaf falls from a tree, the complexity of its shape and the complexity of air currents make it impossible to calculate exactly where it will land. Still, we assume that its movement is determined by physical causes that we can identify.)

Does everything in human behavior also have a physical cause? According to a view known as **determinism**, the answer is *yes:* If we know enough about a person's heredity and environment and about all the influences acting on that person at any given moment, we should be able to predict what that person will do. In other words, everything people do has a physical cause.

Certain psychologists (and other people) deny that all human behavior is determined by some identifiable cause. They insist that human beings possess **free will**, the ability to make decisions that are not dictated by either nature or nurture and that cannot be predicted, no matter how much we know about an individual and regardless of how much we learn about human behavior. According to this view, people can decide voluntarily to change their own basic makeup.

In a sense, every psychological investigation is a test of determinism. An investigator tries to measure how some factor influences behavior. If the study shows that it does affect behavior, then the results are a point in favor of determinism.

In many cases we can see which factors control behavior and how. For example, if a fire breaks out in a building, everyone will try to get out. Free will *seems,* at least, to be more of a factor when the choices are about equal in importance. A woman is offered a choice between two scarves, a green one on her left and a blue one on her right. Is her choice between them determined in some way, or is it random and unpredictable?

Her decision may be unpredictable, in the same way that physicists cannot predict exactly where a leaf will fall in a backyard full of air currents. But being hard to predict does not make an event random. The factors that determine this woman's choice are fairly weak, like those acting on the leaf, but they exist nevertheless. First, other things being equal, most people tend to choose the object on the right. It is not obvious why we do so, but we do. (Perhaps the preference has something to do with the fact that we read left to right.) So the woman is more likely to select the blue scarf on her right. However, she may generally prefer green to blue, in which case she may choose the green scarf, unless she already has three green scarves and now prefers the blue one for variety. Or she may choose the scarf on the left because she just finished reading in her psychology text that people generally pick the object on the right, and she wants to prove that the text is wrong. In short, many factors act on a person even when it appears that a choice is utterly free.

No investigation of how people choose between one possibility and another can solve the free will versus determinism issue, of course. The philosophical question remains of how to reconcile the evidence for determinism with the strong private impression each of us has of making free choices. Still, the whole issue of free will versus determinism is one of the issues that sparks interest in psychological investigations.

Something to Think About

What kind of evidence, if any, would support the concept of free will? Demonstrating that a particular theory made incorrect predictions about behavior under given circumstances would not refute determinism. To support the concept of free will, you need to demonstrate that *no conceivable* theory would make correct predictions. Should a psychologist who believes in free will conduct the same kind of research that determinists conduct, or a different kind of research, or no research at all?

The Mind-Brain Problem

Every movement we make depends on muscle activity controlled by the nervous system, and every sensory experience depends on the activity of the nervous system. All activities of the nervous system follow the laws of physics and chemistry. What then is the role of the mind? We all believe that we have a conscious mind that makes decisions and controls behavior. So there must be a close relationship between the conscious mind and the physical nervous system, which includes the brain. But what is that relationship? The question of how they are related is the **mind-brain problem** (or mind-body problem). Does the brain produce the mind? If so, how and why? Or does the mind control the brain? If so, how could a nonphysical entity control a physical substance? Or are the mind and the brain just two names for the same thing? If so, what does it mean to say they are the same? (They certainly seem to be different.)

Although the mind-brain problem is a particularly difficult philosophical issue, it does lead to research. The research can determine links between brain activity on the one hand and behavior and experience on the other hand. For example, investigators have studied what happens as a result of electrical stimulation of the brain. Brief, mild stimulation of the brain can produce a variety of outcomes, depending on the location where the stimulation is applied. Those outcomes include eating, drinking, fighting, inhibition of fighting, and even falling asleep (see Figure 1.1). Stimulation of certain areas seems to provide pleasure. Rats and monkeys have sometimes pressed a lever thousands of times per hour to turn on a brief electrical shock to certain areas of their own brain (Olds, 1958, 1962). People who have received electrical stimulation to those same brain areas (as an experimental therapy for severe depression or chronic pain) have described the sensation as very pleasant, in many cases similar to sexual excitement (Delgado, 1969).

Again, research studies do not resolve the mind-brain problem of philosophy. They do shed light on it, however; they constrain the types of philosophical answers that we can seriously entertain.

FIGURE 1.1

(a) Electrically stimulating one area of the brain evokes an aggressive display in the cat on the left, although the stimulated cat does not act aggressively toward the other cat. (b) Electrical stimulation of a different area of the cat's brain elicits a different response—a directed attack.

Something to Think About

One way to think about the mind-brain relationship is to ask whether something other than a brain—a computer, for example—could have a mind. How would we know?

What if we built a computer that could perform all the same intellectual functions that humans perform? Could we then decide that the computer is conscious, as human beings are conscious? If we say the computer is *not* conscious, must we then conclude that consciousness is unnecessary, that a brain can get along just fine without it?

The movie *Star Wars* assumed the possibility of true consciousness in a computer by investing these characters with thoughts, feelings, and comic turns.

The hope of learning more about the mind-brain relationship is one of the ultimate goals behind many types of investigation.

The Nature-Nurture Issue

On the average, little boys spend more time than little girls do playing with toy guns and trucks and less time playing with dolls. Why? Are such behavioral differences the result of genetic differences between boys and girls, or are they the result of differences in the way society treats boys and girls?

In many countries, alcoholism is a serious problem. In other countries, people drink a lot of alcohol, but have less trouble with alcohol abuse. In still others—Turkey, for example—people drink very little alcohol. Why the differences? Are they entirely a matter of social custom, or do certain genes influence how much alcohol people consume?

Some psychological disorders are more common in large cities than in small towns and in the countryside. Does life in crowded cities somehow cause psychological disorders? Or do people develop such disorders because of some genetic predisposition and then move to a big city because that is the only place they can find jobs, housing, or welfare services?

Each of these questions is related to the **nature-nurture issue**, which shows up in various guises throughout psychology. Are differences in behavior due more to differences in heredity (nature) or more to differences in environment (nurture)?

The answer to that question varies from one instance to another. For example, one adolescent may have different interests than another because of differences in rate of biological maturation—an aspect of nature. But which one is better at chess will depend mostly on how much practice they have had—an aspect of nurture. Nearly always, the differences between two people are partly the product of heredity and partly the product of environment.

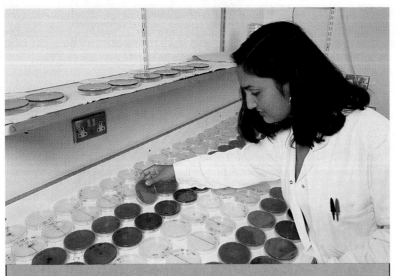

This scientist may have inherited her aptitude for research, but she also had support from her environment. Nature and nurture shaped her interests. The question is not "Which is more important?" but "How do differences in heredity or differences in environment affect differences in behaviors?"

- An animal-learning specialist investigates whether a rat that finds food in a particular place will remember the place and return to it later when it is hungry.

- A cognitive psychologist studies the performance of expert chess players and tries to write a computer program to mimic it.

- A comparative psychologist tries to determine whether chimpanzees, dolphins, and pigeons can learn to use symbols in a way that resembles the use of language by humans.

- A physiological psychologist compares the ability of infant and adult animals to recover behaviors impaired by brain damage.

Here are a few examples of more practical interests:

- A clinical psychologist tries to help a compulsive gambler stop gambling.

- An industrial psychologist helps a company devise a system for selecting among the many applicants for a given job.

- A school psychologist examines schoolchildren with academic difficulties to see why they are having trouble and what can be done about it.

- An ergonomist redesigns the cockpit of an airplane to make it easier for the pilot to find the controls.

THE RISE OF SCIENTIFIC PSYCHOLOGY

Today, people widely accept that collecting data is the best way to find out about the nature-nurture issue or any other issue in psychology. This approach was not always accepted. Noted philosophers used to argue that it was impossible to study the mind scientifically. Then, in 1879, an investigator named Wilhelm Wundt (pronounced "voont") set up the first psychology laboratory, in Leipzig, Germany, where he studied vision, hearing, and touch. The results of his studies were important in themselves, but the precedent he set was profound. Wundt demonstrated that it was indeed possible to measure psychological processes scientifically.

Today, the interests of psychologists range from social and cultural influences on human behavior to the effects of brain damage on animal behavior, from helping corporations select among job applicants to helping mentally retarded children walk and talk. Table 1.1 lists some of the common areas of psychological research and practice and shows the percentages of Ph.D. psychologists in each of those areas.

Some psychologists concentrate on theoretical issues. Others have more practical interests. The interests of most are somewhere in between. Here are a few examples of theoretical interests:

As Table 1.1 shows, more than 40% of all psychologists in this country are **clinical psychologists**, those who identify and treat people with psychological disorders. These are the professionals most people think of when they hear the word *psychologist*. Notice, however, that the majority of psychologists are *not* clinical psychologists.

Do not confuse psychologists with psychiatrists and psychoanalysts. Psychology is an academic discipline, as are chemistry, history, and economics. If you decide to become a psychologist, you must earn a Ph.D. degree or some other advanced degree in psychology. You will learn research methods and acquire expertise in one of the specialized subfields of psychology, such as learning, child development, perceptual processes, or psychological disorders. Your education will last at least four years, probably more, beyond your undergraduate education.

Psychiatry is a branch of medicine, as are dermatology, cardiology, and surgery. To become a psychiatrist, you must first earn an M.D. degree and then take an additional four years of residency training in psychiatry. Psychiatrists and clinical psychologists provide similar services for most clients: They listen, ask questions, and provide advice. For

TABLE 1.1 What Psychologists Do

Specialization	General Interest	Example of Specific Interest or Research Topic
Clinical psychologist	Emotional difficulties	How can people be helped to overcome severe anxiety?
Cognitive psychologist	Thinking, acquiring knowledge, remembering	How do the thought processes of experts and nonexperts differ?
Community psychologist	Organizations and social structures	Would improved job opportunities decrease certain types of psychological distress?
Comparative psychologist	Differences among animal species	How and why do humans differ from monkeys and monkeys from rats?
Counseling psychologist	Helping people to make important decisions and to achieve their potential	Should this person consider changing careers?
Developmental psychologist	Changes in behavior as people grow older	At what age can a child first distinguish between appearance and reality?
Educational psychologist	Improvement of learning in school	What is the best way to test a student's knowledge?
Environmental psychologist	The influence of noise, heat, crowding, and other environmental conditions on human behavior	How can a building be designed to maximize the comfort of the people who use it?
Ergonomist	Communication between person and machine	How can an airplane cockpit be redesigned to increase safety?
Industrial and organizational psychologist	People at work, production efficiency	Should jobs be made simple and foolproof or interesting and challenging?
Learning researcher	Principles of learning	How do reinforcement and punishment affect behavior?
Personality researcher	Personality differences among individuals	Why are certain people shy and others gregarious?
Physiological (or biological) psychologist	Relationship between brain and behavior	What body signals indicate hunger and satiety?
Psychometrician	Measurement of intelligence, personality, and interests	How fair or unfair are current IQ tests? Can we devise better tests?
School psychologist	Problems that affect schoolchildren	How should the school handle a child who regularly disrupts the classroom?
Sensation-perception researcher	Vision, hearing, other senses	Why does the moon look larger at the horizon than overhead?
Social psychologist	Group behavior, social influences	What methods of persuasion are most effective in changing attitudes?

Industrial-
organizational
6%

Developmental
4%

Experimental
9%

School
5%

Educational
6%

Social and
personality
4%

Other
11%

Counseling
11%

Clinical
44%

Specializations of Psychologists

TABLE 1.2 Psychologists, Psychiatrists, and Psychoanalysts

	Educational Degree	Prescribes Drugs?	Education Required After Undergraduate Degree	Number Practicing in United States*
Clinical psychologist	Ph.D. with clinical emphasis	No	4–5 years	17,000
Psychiatrist	M.D. plus psychiatric residency	Yes	8 years	25,000
Psychoanalyst	Psychiatry or clinical psychology plus training in psychoanalytic institute	Yes	14–16 years	3,000

*Figures are based on membership totals of professional organizations as of the mid-1980s. If practicing nonmembers were included, the totals would be higher.

clients with more serious problems, such as severe depression, psychiatrists are authorized to prescribe drugs such as tranquilizers and antidepressants. Psychologists cannot prescribe drugs, because they are not medical doctors. (Does that mean that psychiatrists have an advantage over psychologists? Not always. Ours is an overmedicated society. Some psychiatrists habitually treat anxiety and depression with drugs, while a psychologist would try to treat the problems by changing the person's way of living.)

Psychoanalysis, another mental-health profession, focuses on unconscious determinants of behavior, especially in psychological disorders. It was founded early in the 20th century by the Viennese physician Sigmund Freud, and to this day psychoanalysts adhere strongly to Freud's methods and theories. There is some question about who may rightly call themselves psychoanalysts. Some apply the term to any psychologist or psychiatrist who relies heavily on Freud's methods. Others apply the term only to graduates of an institute of psychoanalysis. Those institutes admitted only psychiatrists until 1988, when a court decision required U.S. institutes of psychoanalysis to begin admitting psychologists as well as psychiatrists. The training to become a psychoanalyst lasts six to eight years after one has become a psychologist or psychiatrist.

Table 1.2 summarizes the differences among psychologists, psychiatrists, and psychoanalysts.

Occupational Settings in Psychology

Psychologists work in many occupational settings, as shown in Figure 1.2. A little over one third work in academic institutions—colleges, universities, and medical schools. Almost 40% work in health-pro-

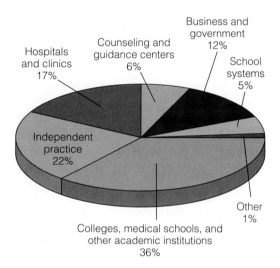

FIGURE 1.2

More than a third of psychologists work in academic institutions, with the remainder finding positions in a variety of settings.

vider settings—independent practices, hospitals, and clinics. Others work in business, government, guidance and counseling centers, and public school systems. Those who work in business help companies make decisions about hiring, promotions, training of workers, and job design. Those who work in school systems help teachers deal with discipline problems and with underachieving students.

Women and Minorities in Psychology

For a long time, academic psychology, like most other academic disciplines, was populated almost

Mary Calkins.

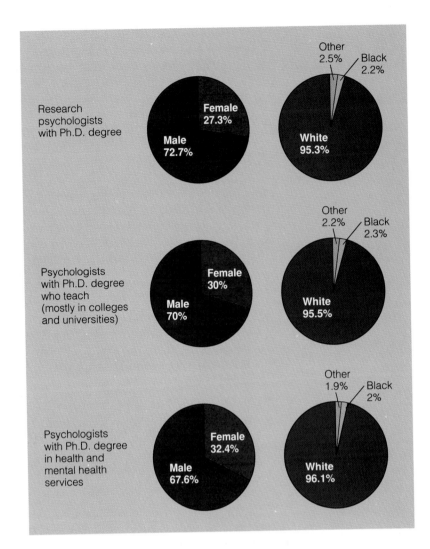

FIGURE 1.3

The number of female psychologists with a Ph.D. degree is growing —about half of current graduate students are women. Although the number of minority psychologists is small, it is also growing. (From Stapp, Tucker & VandenBos, 1985.)

entirely by men. Women students were not encouraged to seek a Ph.D. degree; those who did were rarely offered employment at the most prestigious colleges, universities, or research institutions.

One of the first women to make a career in psychology was Mary Calkins (Scarborough & Furomoto, 1987). When Henry Durant founded Wellesley College in 1870, he decided to hire only women to teach the all-female student body. But he could find no woman with an advanced degree in psychology. Finally, in 1890, he hired a bright young woman, Mary Calkins, who had a B.A. degree in classics, to teach psychology, promising that he would pay for her graduate education in psychology. Then the problem was to find a graduate program that would accept a female student. After much debate and stiff resistance, nearby Harvard University finally agreed to let her attend graduate classes, although at first it would not allow her to register officially as a student. In 1895, when she passed the final examination for the Ph.D. degree, one of her professors remarked that she had performed better on the examination than had any other student in the history of the department.

The Harvard administration, however, was still unwilling to grant a Ph.D. degree to a woman. It suggested a compromise: It would grant her a Ph.D. degree from Radcliffe College, the recently established women's undergraduate college associated with Harvard. She refused, declaring that to accept the compromise would violate the high ideals of education. She never gave in, and neither did Harvard. Although Mary Calkins never received a Ph.D. degree, she became a pioneer in psychological research, inventing a technique of studying memory, known as the paired-associates method, that is still used today.

The first woman to receive the Ph.D. degree in psychology was Margaret Washburn, who received the degree from Cornell University in 1894. She later wrote *The Animal Mind,* the first text on that topic, and served as president of the American Psychological Association. Christine Ladd-Franklin, another early psychologist, did outstanding research on vision.

According to a survey conducted in 1983, women hold more than 30% of all Ph.D. degrees in psychology in the United States (see Figure 1.3) and more than 50% of all master's degrees (Stapp, Tucker, & VandenBos, 1985). Both percentages are growing steadily. Just over 50% of all current graduate students in psychology are women.

Minorities also constitute a growing percentage of psychologists, though the total number is still small (see Figure 1.3). As of 1983, blacks, Hispanics, Asians, and other minorities together constituted about 5% of all American psychologists. Those numbers will grow as many graduate schools actively recruit qualified minority applicants.

SOME APPROACHES TO THE STUDY OF BEHAVIOR AND EXPERIENCE

Consider this question: Why are you reading this book right now? No doubt you could come up with a reason, but it would probably not tell the whole story. We rarely do anything for just one reason. Perhaps you are reading this book because:

- You are curious to learn something about psychology.

- You have found that reading your textbook assignments leads to better grades that will win you praise from your family and friends, increase your self-esteem, and bring you other rewards.

- You have nothing else to do right now.

- You know you will feel guilty if you spend a lot of money on a college education and then flunk out.

- Your roommate is reading a textbook, so you think you might as well do the same.

Notice that these reasons do not compete with each other. Several influences may combine and lead to a given behavior at a given time. Notice too that these reasons have to do with different things— your thoughts, your past learning, your emotions, and social influences.

Different psychologists explain the same behaviors in different ways and arrive at different answers to the same questions. In other words, they take different approaches to psychology.

In this chapter we look at a few of the most common and the most influential approaches. To compare them, we shall examine how each approach deals with the same psychological question of *individual differences*: Why does one individual behave differently from another?

I will discuss everything in this section in greater detail in later chapters. This is simply a preview of coming attractions.

The Quantitative Psychology Approach

Any useful study, in psychology or in any other discipline that deals with natural phenomena, must be based on careful measurements. **Quantitative psychologists** measure individual differences and apply statistical procedures to determine what their measurements indicate. In fact, nearly all psychologists take measurements and apply statistical procedures; quantitative psychologists are those who concentrate more on mathematics and generally give less attention to the theoretical interpretations.

To measure individual differences, psychologists have devised tests of IQ, personality, interests, and attitudes, most of them requiring pencil-and-paper answers. Once they have devised a test, they must determine whether or not it measures what it is supposed to measure.

Tests in psychology only measure; they do not explain. For example, once we determine that a particular child has a low IQ score, we can predict that the child will have trouble in school. The test score does not, however, tell us *why* the child is performing poorly—either on the test or in school. One child may perform poorly because of brain damage, another because of poor educational opportunities, yet another because he or she does not read or speak English. Measuring individual differences is a first step toward explaining them, but it is only a first step.

The Biological Approach

A **biological** (or **physiological**) **psychologist** tries to explain behavior in terms of the activity of the brain and other organs of the body. Such psychologists study the electrical and chemical activities in the nervous system and try to relate them to what a person or animal is doing. Biological processes contribute in several important ways to individual differences in behavior.

One biological variable that influences behavior is genetic makeup. For example, a single gene controls color blindness. Genes also determine the ability to taste certain bitter substances. Huntington's disease is a condition in which the person experiences movement disorders and eventually memory and thought disorders. This disease, too, is controlled by a gene (Chase, Wexler, & Barbeau, 1979). Although stressful experiences may hasten the onset of the disease, it appears that everyone with the disease-causing gene will eventually contract the disease.

Usually, however, psychologists deal with genes that merely increase the probability of a given behavior or condition, depending on a number of environmental circumstances. For example, there is evidence that certain genes increase the risk that a person may abuse alcohol or become depressed (Vaillant & Milofsky, 1982; Wender et al., 1986). How a person actually develops, however, depends on experiences and not just on genes.

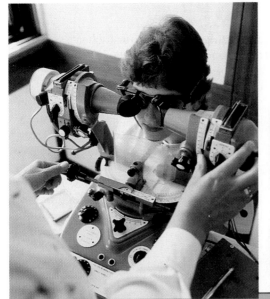

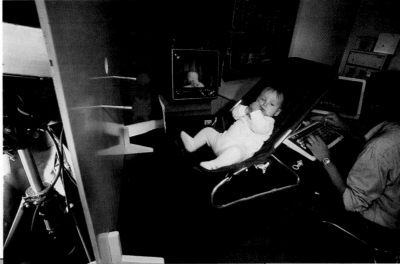

To study individual differences, some psychologists take a biological approach, looking for answers in genetics and the brain. This test for dyslexia (left) can identify the reading disorder, but not cure it. Other psychologists use tests that quantify abstract and subjective areas such as personality and intelligence. These tests, including this visual test of an infant, provide statistics about differences, but cannot explain why they occur.

A second biological factor that affects behavior is brain damage. Brain damage may result from such things as a sharp blow to the head, a ruptured blood vessel in the brain, an interruption of oxygen supply, prolonged malnutrition, or exposure to toxic chemicals. The effects on behavior vary enormously, depending on the location and extent of the damage. For example, people with damage to one area in the right half of the brain tend to ignore what they see in the left half of the world (Pierrot-Deseilligny, Gray, & Brunet, 1986). People with damage to another area may look at a single object from two angles and fail to recognize that it is the same object (Layman & Greene, 1988).

Variations in diet may also affect behavior, apparently more severely in some people than in others. The body uses the nutrients in food to synthesize the chemicals the brain uses. A habitual deficiency in certain vitamins and minerals may lead to serious memory and thought disorders (Brierley, 1977; Hoffer, 1973).

In short, the biological approach to the study of individual differences focuses on genetics, brain damage, diet, and other factors that alter the functioning of the body.

The Behavioral Approach

Another approach to psychology is the behavioral approach. A **behaviorist** is a psychologist who stud-

ies behaviors that can actually be observed instead of trying to analyze thought processes. Behaviorists concentrate on how behavior is learned. They believe that most behavior is influenced by the consequences of past behavior. How often we engage in a particular behavior depends on whether that behavior has usually led to positive, negative, or neutral outcomes in the past. Because many of the principles of learning are similar from one species to another, behaviorists often use animals in their investigations.

Consider a boy in the first grade who is constantly chattering, running around, and generally disrupting the class. The behaviorist wants to know why he is behaving that way. Although biological predisposition and emotional troubles are possible explanations, the behaviorist concentrates on the consequences of the child's disruptive behavior: Other children watch and giggle and the teacher stamps and yells. In other words, the child is attracting attention. He has learned that just sitting quietly and doing what is expected brings no response at all. How can the teacher get the child to behave better? One way is to praise him when he behaves in a quiet, cooperative manner. If that approach fails, the teacher can isolate him from the other children for a few minutes after misbehaviors.

Adult behavior is also governed by its consequences. Whether adults choose to spend their time studying or socializing, running in track meets or running for political office depends in part on the rewards and frustrations their choices produced in the past. Behaviorists try to relate individual differences to the individual's record of reward and punishment.

The Cognitive Approach

Cognition means thinking and acquiring knowledge. A **cognitive psychologist** studies those processes. (The root *cogn* also shows up in the word *recognize,* which literally means *to know again.*) Cognitive psychologists have learned much from the behaviorists. They do not simply ask people to describe their thought processes; they perform elaborate experiments to measure the consequences of those processes.

A cognitive psychologist who studies individual differences tries to identify the ways in which people think. For example, what do experts know or do that sets them apart from other people? One distinction is simply that the expert knows more facts. Consider a subject on which you are an expert: how to find your way around your college campus. A fellow student asks you, "How do I get from here to the biology building?" To answer, you can draw on the knowledge you share: "Go over toward the library. Then cut behind the library, between the library and the math building. The biology building will be right in front of you." Now a visitor who has never been on campus before asks you the same question. You say, "Go over toward the library. . . ." "Wait, where's the library?" "Well, go out this door, make a right, go to the next street. . . ." You will find that someone with little or no previous knowledge needs detailed and extensive instructions (Isaacs & Clark, 1987).

Another distinction between the expert and the nonexpert is that the expert can identify more categories. For example, a nonexpert might look at a group of birds on a beach and say, "Hey, look at all the sea gulls." An expert bird-watcher might reply, "There are three gull species and two tern species."

Moreover, the expert can identify the *right* categories. The inexperienced bird-watcher might say, sheepishly, "Oh, I see. Some of them have darker feathers than others." The expert would reply, "No, the ones with darker feathers are just younger. To tell one species from the other you have to check the color of the beak, the color of the legs, the size of the bird, the color of the eyes . . ." The expert knows what to look for—what is relevant and what is not (Murphy & Medin, 1985).

In short, a cognitive psychologist explains individual differences partly in terms of knowledge: People differ from one another because some of them know more than others do about a particular topic. Cognitive psychologists also study the ways in which people think and remember and how they use their knowledge.

The Social Psychology Approach

Social psychologists study how an individual's actions, attitudes, emotions, and thought processes are influenced by other people. They also study how people behave in groups. When we are with other people, we tend to take our cues from them on what we should do. You arrive at a party and notice that the other guests are walking around, helping themselves to snacks, and talking. You do the same. When you go to a religious service or an art museum, you notice how other people are acting and again conform your behavior to theirs.

According to social psychologists, one reason individuals behave differently is that other people *expect* them to behave differently and therefore treat them differently. For example, suppose a first-grade teacher believes, rightly or wrongly, that Johnny and Susie are particularly bright children who are likely to make good academic progress. The teacher gives a little more attention to those children than to the rest of the class. As a result, they may in fact make the progress the teacher expects (Rosenthal & Rubin, 1978).

Other predictions probably have similar effects. For example, a teacher expects a child to fail, and the child fails. (As you can imagine, no psychologist conducts studies to demonstrate this point!) Or a teacher knows that a child's parents have been in trouble with the law and predicts that sooner or later the child also will get into trouble. In one way or another, that prediction may affect the child's behavior.

Or consider sex differences. Rightly or wrongly, most people expect boys to behave differently from girls. From an early age, a child is told that little boys prefer certain toys and that little girls prefer others. Parents expect their sons to aspire to become doctors, or politicians, or professional athletes; they may or may not convey similarly high expectations to their daughters. The behavioral differences that subsequently emerge between boys and girls are partly the result of the different expectations that were conveyed to them. Social psychologists study such influences.

The Psychoanalytic Approach

Psychoanalysis, Sigmund Freud's method of treating psychological disorders, continues to exercise a strong influence on many psychologists. Psychoanalysts assume that people have unconscious thoughts and motives as well as conscious ones. The unconscious mind retains the memory of painful thoughts and experiences, often from early childhood, that the conscious mind ignores. The unconscious may make itself felt in dreams, physical complaints, slips of the tongue, and actions that a person performs for no apparent reason.

Why does one individual differ from another? Psychoanalysts hold that the source lies in the unconscious. For example, the parents of a teenage girl are constantly quarreling and sometimes physically attack each other. When they at last decide to divorce, the girl threatens to commit suicide. So they agree to stay together. The mother has a boyfriend who threatens to kill the father; the father threatens to kill the boyfriend. The girl feels threatened at home and insecure when she is away, because she never knows what she will find when she returns. Suddenly one of her legs becomes paralyzed, apparently for no medical reason. A psychoanalyst might say that the paralysis is neither imaginary nor pretended; it is a real symptom springing from the girl's unconscious desire to live in a happy, secure home where she would be cared for by her parents.

Psychoanalysis is a controversial approach. Many people who have gone through analysis are convinced that it has given them keen insight into their own behavior and the behavior of others. Still, claims about what is going on in the unconscious mind are almost impossible to test or confirm.

The Humanistic Approach

Humanistic psychology is a perspective that stresses conscious experience and deemphasizes the scientific analysis of behavior. (In theology, a *humanist* glorifies humans, generally denying or at least giving little attention to a supreme being. The term *humanistic psychologist* implies nothing about a person's religious beliefs.) This approach arose in the 1960s as a protest against both the behavioral approach and the psychoanalytic approach. **Humanistic psychologists** feel that to reduce human experience to the sum of many simple behaviors, or to explain human behavior in terms of forces beyond conscious control, is to underestimate human potential. Humanistic psychologists claim that people make deliberate, conscious decisions about what to do with their lives. People may decide to devote themselves to a great cause, to sacrifice their own well-being, and to risk their lives. To the humanistic psychologist, it is pointless to try to ascribe such behavior to past rewards and punishments or to unconscious thought processes.

An Oxford education, an arranged marriage: Benazir Bhutto, elected leader of Pakistan, has consolidated conflicting influences and fulfilled disparate expectations of her family's behavior. Social psychologists explore how people's expectations influence others.

Humanistic psychologists regard the individual as an integrated whole, rather than as an assemblage of parts. They insist that people are capable of altering their own behavior and deciding what kind of person they want to be.

Why does one individual differ from another? Humanistic psychologists have been vague in their answer to that question. They have produced little research and few theoretical explanations of behavior. It is one thing to say that each of us can decide what kind of person we are going to be. It is another to explain *why* different people make different decisions.

Overlap Among the Various Approaches

I have oversimplified the discussion of the approaches of psychology in several ways. First, it is only partly correct to refer to biological psychology, cognitive psychology, social psychology, and other types as approaches. True, each constitutes one way of approaching certain phenomena of interest to all psychologists. But each is also a separate field of study with its own special phenomena. Biological psychologists ask questions about how the brain works; social psychologists ask questions about group behavior. Second, the approaches just discussed are not the only approaches or the only major fields of study. In later chapters we shall consider additional approaches and topics. And third, the various approaches are not entirely distinct from one another. Nearly all psychologists combine insights and information gained from a variety of approaches. To understand why one person differs from another, we need to know about their biology, their past learning experiences, the social influences that have acted on them, and much more. Psychologists may use one approach at a time, but a person's behavior depends on many influences acting at once.

SUMMARY*

1.   Psychology is the systematic study of behavior and experience. Psychologists deal with theoretical questions, such as how experience relates to brain activity and how behavior relates to nature and nurture. Psychologists also deal with practical questions, such as selecting among applicants for a job or helping people to overcome bad habits. (page 5)

2.   Determinism is the view that everything that occurs, including human behavior, has a physical cause. That view is difficult to reconcile with the conviction that humans have free will—that we deliberately, consciously decide what to do. (page 5)

3.   The mind-brain problem is the question of how consciousness is related to the activity of the brain. (page 6)

4.   Behavior depends on both nature (heredity) and nurture (environment). Psychologists try to determine the influence of those two factors on differences in behavior. The relative contributions of nature and nurture vary from one behavior to another. (page 7)

5.   Psychology broke away from philosophy in the late 1800s. Although psychologists continue to be interested in many philosophical issues, they attempt to approach those questions with scientific methods. (page 8)

6.   Psychology is an academic field whereas psychiatry is a branch of medicine. Both clinical psychologists and psychiatrists treat people with emotional problems, but only psychiatrists can prescribe medicine and other medical treatments. (page 8)

7.   Psychologists take different approaches in trying to explain the origin of individual differences. Those following the quantitative approach focus on measuring individual differences through such devices as an IQ test. (page 12)

8.   Psychologists following the biological approach look for explanations of behavior in terms of genetics, brain damage, diet, and other biological factors. (page 12)

9.   Psychologists following the behavioral approach study only observable actions. They generally concentrate on the role of learning. (page 13)

10.   Psychologists using the cognitive approach concentrate on people's thought processes and knowledge. They demonstrate, for example, that people's performance on a given task depends largely on their factual knowledge. (page 14)

11.   Psychologists using the social approach study how people act in groups and how an individual's behavior is affected by other people. For example, when people expect a child to do well, they treat that child in a way that may increase the probability of success. (page 14)

12.   Psychologists following the psychoanalytic approach attempt to understand behavior in terms of unconscious thought processes and motives. (page 14)

13.   Psychologists guided by the humanistic approach concentrate on people's conscious, deliberate decisions. (page 15)

14.   The various approaches in psychology overlap partly in their interests, but not entirely. Each approach studies its own particular set of phenomena. (page 15)

SUGGESTIONS FOR FURTHER READING

Corsini, R. J. (1984). *Encyclopedia of psychology*. New York: Wiley. A useful reference source on all aspects of psychology.

Scarborough, E., & Furomoto, L. (1987). *Untold lives: The first generation of American women psychologists*. New York: Columbia University Press. A rich account of history and biography.

Sechenov, I. (1965). *Reflexes of the brain*. Cambridge, MA: MIT Press. (Original work published 1863.) One of the first attempts to deal with behavior scientifically and one of the clearest statements of the argument for determinism in psychology.

*The page numbers following each item indicate where you can look to review a topic.

Terms to Remember

behaviorist a psychologist who studies only observable behaviors rather than unobservable thought processes

biological (or **physiological**) **psychologist** a psychologist who tries to relate behavior to activities of the brain and other organs

clinical psychologists those who specialize in identifying and treating psychological disorders

cognition thinking and acquiring knowledge

cognitive psychologist a psychologist who studies thought processes and the acquisition of knowledge

determinism the view that all behavior has a physical cause

free will the alleged ability of an individual to make decisions that are not determined by heredity, past experience, or the environment

humanistic psychologist a psychologist who stresses the human potential to make conscious, deliberate decisions about one's life

mind-brain problem the philosophical question of how the conscious mind is related to the physical brain

nature-nurture issue the question of the relative roles played by heredity (nature) and environment (nurture) in determining differences in behavior

psychiatry the branch of medicine that specializes in identifying and treating psychological disorders

psychoanalysis a mental-health profession that treats psychological disorders by focusing on underlying, unconscious motives and thoughts

psychology the systematic study of behavior and experience

quantitative psychologist a psychologist who measures individual differences in behavior and applies statistical procedures to analyze those measurements

social psychologist a psychologist who considers how the behavior of the individual is influenced by other people and how people behave in groups

Answers to Questions in the Text*

1. Reversing the order of shifts will relieve the workers' distress. Instead of moving to an earlier shift each time, they should move to a later shift. (page 105)

2. No. Under hypnosis, people report old or forgotten memories in great detail but with low accuracy. Hypnosis stimulates acting ability more than it does memory. (page 117)

3. Take the same medications you took while in the hospital, even at the risk of feeling less alert. It is easiest to recall a memory if you are in the same physiological state as when you stored the memory. (page 298)

4. Children begin to make original and creative word combinations as soon as they start to link words together, around age 1½ to 2. (page 211)

5. Beware of storing an object in an unusual place just because the place is unusual. You will do better to find a meaningful place. In this case you might keep your sandals with your other shoes or with your swimming suit. (page 284)

6. People with a high need for achievement set their goals at an intermediate to high level. Those who set the highest goals for themselves are generally more interested in providing an excuse for failure than in trying to succeed. (page 412)

7. Simply going without the drug, even for long periods of time, has little effect on drug tolerance. Animal experiments suggest that the best way to reduce tolerance is to go through the usual drug-injection procedure using water or some other inactive substance instead of the drug itself. (page 528)

8. Infants can see and hear much better than was once assumed. Within several days after birth, infants can imitate facial expressions and recognize their mothers' voice. (page 187)

9. It is not a direct result of nursing or feeding. Apparently the main reason is the warm, cuddly feeling that goes with holding and being held, plus play and other social interactions. (page 220)

10. Some people seem to insist on acting "crazy" because it attracts attention. One effective way to reduce such behavior is to urge the person to keep on doing the same things he or she has been doing! (page 570)

11. The person who receives the small bribe will enjoy the task more. (page 613)

---

*These questions appear on pages 4–5. The page number following each item indicates the page in this text that provides a more detailed discussion of the topic.

CHAPTER
2

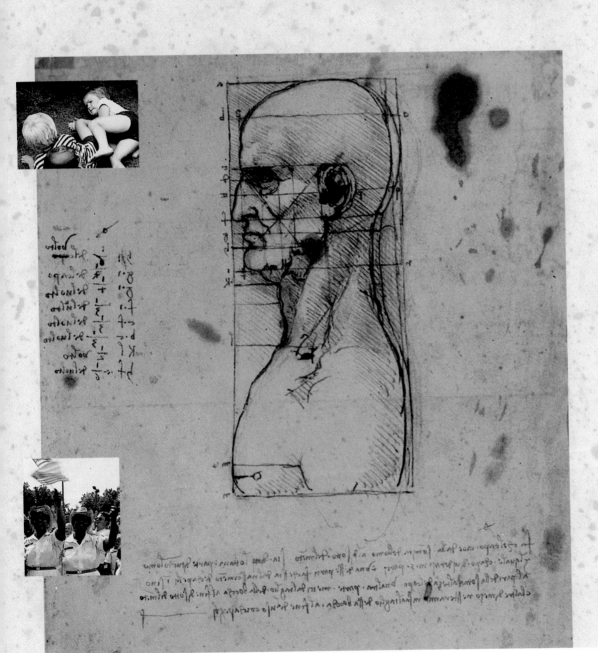

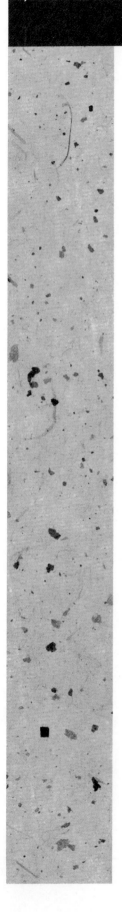

Every year spectacular claims are published about human behavior. Some of them receive wide publicity, even if there is little or no evidence to support them. Here are some examples:

- *Biorhythms.* Some people claim that your mood and your success on a given day depend on an intellectual cycle of 33 days, an emotional cycle of 28 days, and a physical cycle of 23 days, each cycle recurring regularly from the day of birth.

- *Age regression.* Some people say that under hypnosis and similar techniques, a person can recall in great detail what it was like to be a young child, a baby, an embryo, or even a sperm cell (Sadger, 1941). (One man said that he and his fellow sperm cells had resented their father because they knew he did not want them to fertilize the egg!)

- *Psychic communication.* In 1978 a man was killed when his car plunged off a cliff. Nearly three weeks later his body was found, partly eaten, with his pet dog nearby. The police were about to have the dog destroyed, but then a so-called psychic intervened. She claimed she could communicate with the dog, and the dog told her he had tried to defend the man's body from the coyotes and wild dogs that had eaten it. The police took her word for it and spared the dog's life (*Skeptical Inquirer,* 1978a).

- *The power of belief.* For a long time people were aware that the Earth had one moon and that Jupiter had at least four. They believed that Mars should have two, to fill out the mathematical progression. In 1877, two tiny moons appeared in a telescope for the first time. Why had no one seen them before? To most people the answer seemed obvious: Until 1877 there had been no telescopes powerful enough to detect such small and distant objects. But no, said one person: Those moons had not even existed before 1877! It was only because people had believed in them for so long that they had finally come into existence (*Skeptical Inquirer,* 1978b).

I could list hundreds of similar claims. Most of us dismiss the truly preposterous ones, such as the claim about the moons of Mars. The one about biorhythms is not so easy to dismiss. The idea is not utterly preposterous, though it conflicts with much of what we know about biology. Those who believe it cite isolated cases in which it seems to apply. To decide whether the idea is worthy of belief, we must evaluate the alleged evidence and collect additional, more reliable evidence.

We have to be especially careful to evaluate the evidence when someone proposes a theory that sounds plausible on first hearing. It is tempting then to accept the theory without noticing possible flaws in the evidence. Not all theories that sound reasonable turn out to be correct.

In short, *we must scrutinize carefully the evidence for every claim that is made, even those that strike us as reasonable.*

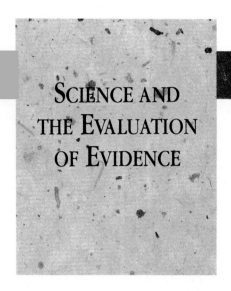

SCIENCE AND THE EVALUATION OF EVIDENCE

How do scientists decide which is a better theory and which is a worse theory?

Y ou will sometimes hear people say that something has been "scientifically proved." Scientists themselves seldom use the word *prove,* except when they are talking about a mathematical proof. They deal with probabilities, not certainties. In some cases they do not even agree with one another on what is probable. Still, even when they are uncertain about a given question, most scientists remain optimistic that further research will lead them closer to an answer.

A bold definition of science is this: *A science is a systematic study of natural phenomena in which investigators agree on how to evaluate competing theories.* Even when scientists disagree on which theory is best, they can still agree on what kinds of evidence they will accept in trying to decide.

Is psychology a science? By this definition, yes. Most psychologists are quick to concede that our knowledge of psychology is less complete and less systematic than our knowledge of physics, chemistry, and biology. But psychologists share the methods of physicists, chemists, and biologists. They all collect evidence and evaluate it.

Something to Think About

If we accept this definition of science, can we call the study of ethics a science? Does ethics deal with natural phenomena? Do ethicists agree with one another on how to evaluate competing theories? If ethics is not currently a science, could it be made into a science? How?

Similarly, is theology a science? Why or why not? If not, what would it take to convert it into a science, assuming that anyone wanted to do so?

STEPS IN GATHERING AND EVALUATING EVIDENCE

Above all, scientists want to know the evidence behind a given claim. To gather evidence, they conduct studies that go through a series of steps described in the following four paragraphs (see also Figure 2.1). Articles in scientific publications generally follow this sequence too. In each of the following chapters, you will find a section titled "What's the Evidence?" Those sections will go through one or more psychological investigations step by step, also in this order:

Hypothesis Any study begins with a **hypothesis**, which is a testable prediction of what will happen under certain conditions. In many cases the hypothesis is the product of someone's casual observations. For example, a psychologist might notice that children who like to watch violent television programs seem to be relatively violent themselves. So it seems, at any rate; we cannot always trust our impressions. The psychologist might then set out to test whether those children who watch the greatest amount of violence on television engage in the greatest amount of aggressive behavior.

Method Devising an appropriate method to test a hypothesis can be surprisingly difficult. For example, an investigator wants to measure how much violence each child watches on television. That may sound easy. But what counts as violence? Do we count minutes of violent programming or do we count violent acts? Do some types of violence count more than others? We encounter similar problems in measuring a child's aggressive behavior. The mark of a skillful investigator is the ability to find ways to measure something accurately.

Results Suppose the investigator somehow measures televised violence and aggressive behavior. Then the task is to determine the relationship between the two measures. Did the children who watched the greatest amount of violence also engage in the most aggressive behavior? If so, how strong was the relationship? Were the results convincing, or might they have arisen by accident? Here the investigator calls upon statistical techniques to evaluate the results.

FIGURE 2.1

Developing a theory
involves four steps to
test and confirm (or
disprove) a prediction.
Confidence in the
theory increases or
decreases with reports
of new experimental
results.

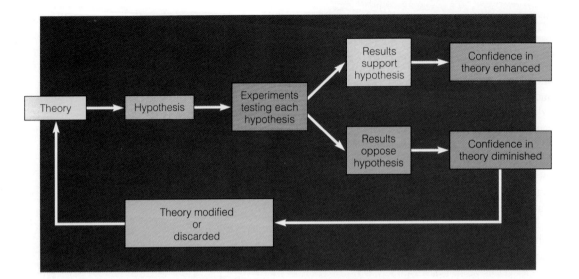

Interpretation Finally, the task is to determine what the results mean. Sometimes the results clearly contradict the hypothesis. For example, an investigator might find that children who watch a great deal of televised violence are no more aggressive than other children, in general. In that case we might abandon the hypothesis or we might modify it: Maybe it applies only to certain kinds of children or to certain kinds of violence.

If the results match the prediction, we would look for other possible explanations before we draw a conclusion. Suppose, for example, the investigator finds that the children who watched the most violence on television were also prone to the most aggressive behavior. We would not conclude that televised violence leads to aggressive behavior, because of an alternative interpretation: Perhaps aggressive children like to watch violent television!

It is almost always possible to suggest more than one interpretation of the results of a given study. At that point the investigator sets up a second study to follow up on the results of the first and tries to decide between the two interpretations. That study too may lead to further studies. Because almost any study has its limitations, the ultimate conclusion comes from a pattern of results from many studies.

Replicability

Before psychologists trust the results of a study, we like to have other investigators repeat the procedure. If they get similar results, then they have **replicable results**—that is, anyone who follows the same procedure can repeat them. If a result is replicable, we still may not be sure how to interpret it, but at least we think it is worthwhile to try. If the

results cannot be replicated, then perhaps there was some hidden flaw in the first study; we base no conclusions upon it.

What if a result can be replicated in some studies and not others? For example, when studying the effects of televised violence on children, certain investigators might find one set of results, while others find the opposite. Presuming that both sets of investigators conducted their studies equally well, what are we to believe?

Psychologists would look for some pattern in the results. Perhaps watching violence is associated with violent behavior only for children of a certain age or just for one sex. Or perhaps the results depend on the type of violent program or on the method of measuring aggressive behavior. If such a pattern emerges, we would accept a modified version of the hypothesis that fits the data. If no such pattern emerged, we would have to wait for further research before drawing any conclusion.

Note that a *replicable* result is not the same thing as a *replicated* result. Occasionally someone reports a spectacular result that a few investigators manage to replicate but most cannot. Such a result is not considered replicable. Presumably its occurrence depends on specific conditions that have not been determined. Until someone specifies those conditions, we cannot interpret the results.

The Problem of Selective Reporting

Even when a result appears to be replicable, we need to be cautious, because of the problem of **selective reporting**—the fact that investigators are more likely to publish findings when they match predictions than when they do not. For example, it is widely reported and widely believed that most males outperform most females on such spatial tasks as geometry and that males and females differ on numerous other tasks as well. What does a researcher do if he or she repeats one of the reported studies and finds no significant difference between males and females? The researcher might think, "Maybe I did the study wrong. Maybe I chose an unusual sample of males and females. I guess I'll either forget the whole thing or try again with a different procedure." Unfortunately, results that support established views are more likely to be published in the professional journals than those that do not (Fausto-Sterling, 1985; Greenwald, Pratkanis, Leippe, & Baumgardner, 1986). Consequently, the published literature tends to overstate the size and replicability of certain effects.

Up to this point I have alluded to research in psychology without much detail. I shall go into the details in the sections titled "Methods of Investigation in Psychology" and "Measuring and Reporting Results." Here, let's look at the big picture: After investigators collect mounds of evidence, what do they do with it? As part of the definition of *science* I said that investigators agree on how to evaluate competing theories. Exactly how do they decide what is a good theory?

CRITERIA FOR EVALUATING SCIENTIFIC THEORIES

The goal of scientific research is to establish **theories**, comprehensive explanations of natural phenomena. A good theory predicts many observations in terms of a few assumptions and reduces the amount of information we must keep available for reference. For example, without the theory of gravity, we would have to keep a set of detailed tables indicating how long it takes an object to fall to earth from various distances. With the formula for acceleration due to gravity, we can readily calculate the time required for any given distance.

A good theory reveals patterns in the observations we make. It enables us to reduce many complex facts to a few facts and to identify the interactions among them. To say that "the highest mountain in the world is in the Himalayas" does not state a theory, regardless of whether the statement is true. A theory is more general than the facts it explains.

When we are confronted with several competing theories, we must evaluate them to decide which is the most acceptable. Scientists use several criteria (Figure 2.2). First, *a theory should fit the known facts.* Second, *it should predict new discoveries.* We should not be impressed with a system that seems to explain why the stock market has risen and fallen in the past. The test is whether it also predicts when the market will rise or fall in the future.

Third, *a theory should not be so imprecise that it fits any and all observations.* It should be **falsifiable**. In other words, we should be able to imagine some occurrence that would contradict it. Consider a statement that is not falsifiable: "A dropped object will sometimes fall, sometimes rise, sometimes stand still, sometimes waver, and sometimes just disappear altogether." Because no conceivable observation could contradict this statement, its "correct" predictions count for nothing.

Another example is the 18th-century belief that drawing blood from a patient would cure every sort of ailment. If a physician drew blood and the patient recovered, the result was taken as support for the theory. If the patient died, the physician would explain, "The patient was so sick that it was too late to help." No possible outcome was taken as evidence against the theory (Stanovich, 1986).

Fourth, other things being equal, *scientists prefer the theory that explains matters in the simplest possible terms and makes the simplest assumptions.* That is often a difficult criterion to apply, but it is a most important one. We shall examine it in detail for the rest of this section on evaluating evidence.

THE PRINCIPLE OF PARSIMONY

According to the principle of **parsimony**, scientists prefer the theory that accounts for the results using the simplest assumptions. In other words, they prefer a theory that is consistent with theories they have already accepted. A theory that makes radically new assumptions is acceptable only after we have made every attempt to explain the results in a simpler way.

How do we decide what is a simpler assumption? If we have previously concluded that many animals solve problems by responding to what they see, then we may simply assume that another animal, solving a new problem, might also be responding to something it sees. It would be less simple (less parsimonious) to assume that the animal solves the problem by making mathematical calculations or by reading minds. That is, making simple assumptions is partly (though not entirely) a matter of sticking to the same assumptions we have already made. Consider the following three examples.

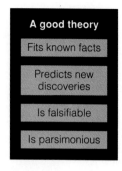

A good theory
Fits known facts
Predicts new discoveries
Is falsifiable
Is parsimonious

FIGURE 2.2

Scientists evaluate competing theories by these criteria and rank them as good or perhaps not so good.

These maharishis appear to levitate—in apparent defiance of physical laws. How would you explain this phenomenon? Scientists follow the principle of parsimony, also known as Occam's razor. They try to explain strange phenomena by using the most economical and familiar theories.

First Example:
Where Do Babies Come From?

Where babies come from is not obvious to everyone. I remember trying to explain it to my sons when they were young and getting reactions of amazement bordering on disbelief. And at least one human culture in modern times has rejected the theory that sexual intercourse causes babies.

According to Bronislaw Malinowski (1929), the Trobriand Islanders (near New Guinea) believed that the spirits of ancestors float in on the ocean tide; when they approach land, a special ghost takes one of the spirits and implants it in the head of a young woman. The young woman becomes pregnant, and the ancestral spirit becomes her baby. (Note that the theory suggests that young women can decrease their chance of pregnancy by staying far away from the ocean.)

Missionaries had repeatedly told the Trobrianders that sexual intercourse causes babies, but the Trobrianders had firmly rejected the idea. To try to convince them, Malinowski began, "Surely you must have noticed that virgins never have babies." The reply was, "Well, perhaps. But we don't have much experience with that sort of thing. There are practically no virgins around here."

While Malinowski was trying to think of other evidence that might make sense to a nonscientific people, one of the islanders said that he had evidence *against* the sex theory. "I was once away from the village on a journey for more than a year, and when I returned I found that my wife was pregnant. That proves that sex was not necessary."

Malinowski never did convince the Trobrianders of his theory, nor did they convince him of theirs. Why do we believe that sexual intercourse, rather than ancestral spirits floating on the water, causes babies? One reason is that to us the Trobrianders' theory is unfalsifiable. Because the supposed spirits are invisible, no one knows where they have been until after they have made a woman pregnant. Because no conceivable observation would contradict the theory, the theory is not scientific. Our other objection to the Trobriand Islanders' belief is that it is unparsimonious. It assumes that spirits float on water and enter a woman's head—an assumption that simply does not fit in with what we know or with what we think we know.

On their side, the Trobrianders rejected the sex theory because it seemed unparsimonious to them. They believed in spirits; they knew nothing of chemistry or biology. To explain to them about DNA and chromosomes and proteins would be like talking about zeta rays from outer space. For them to accept our view on where babies come from would not be a simple matter of exchanging one theory for another; they would have to change their entire view about the nature of the world.

Second Example:
Clever Hans, the Amazing Horse

Early in this century, Mr. von Osten, a German mathematics teacher, set out to prove that his horse, Hans, had great intellectual abilities, particularly in arithmetic (Figure 2.3). To teach Hans arithmetic, he first showed him a single object, said "One," and lifted Hans's foot once. Then he raised Hans's foot twice for two objects, and so on. Eventually, when von Osten presented a group of objects, Hans tapped his foot by himself, and with practice he managed to tap the correct number of times. With more practice, it was no longer necessary for Hans to see the objects. Von Osten would just call out a number, and Hans would tap the appropriate number of times.

Von Osten moved on to addition and then to subtraction, multiplication, and division. Hans seemed to catch on amazingly quickly, soon responding with 90–95% accuracy. Von Osten began touring Germany to exhibit Hans's abilities. He would

Figure 2.3

Clever Hans and his owner, Mr. von Osten, demonstrated that the horse could answer complex mathematical questions with great accuracy. The question was "How?" (After Pfungst, 1911, in Fernald, 1984.)

give Hans a question, either orally or in writing, and Hans would tap out the answer. As time passed, Hans's abilities grew, just from being around humans, without any special training. Soon he was able to add fractions, convert fractions to decimals or vice versa, do simple algebra, tell time to the minute, and give the values of all German coins. Using a letter-to-number code, he could spell out the names of objects and even identify musical notes, such as D or B-flat. (Hans, it seems, had perfect pitch.) Hans responded correctly even when questions were put to him by persons other than von Osten, in unfamiliar places with von Osten nowhere in sight.

Given this evidence, many people were ready to assume that Hans had great intellectual prowess. But others were not. Why not? Certainly the evidence was replicable. The problem was parsimony. No previous research had led us to assume that a nonhuman animal could perform complex mathematical calculations. Was there a simpler explanation?

Enter Oskar Pfungst. Pfungst (1911) discovered that Hans could not answer a question correctly if the questioner had not calculated the answer first. Evidently the horse was not actually doing the calculations, but was somehow getting the answers from the questioner. Next Pfungst learned that Hans had to *see* the experimenter. When the experimenter stood in plain sight, Hans's accuracy was 90% or better; when he could not see the experimenter, he either did not answer or made a wild guess.

Eventually Pfungst observed that any questioner who asked Hans a question would lean forward to watch Hans's foot. Hans had simply learned

to start tapping whenever someone stood next to his right forefoot and leaned forward. As soon as Hans had given the correct number of taps, the experimenter would give a slight upward jerk of the head and change facial expression in anticipation that this might be the last tap. (Even skeptical scientists who tested Hans did this involuntarily.) Hans simply continued tapping until he received that cue.

In short, Hans was indeed a clever horse. But what he did could be explained in simple terms that did not involve mathematical calculations or any other advanced cognitive process. We prefer the explanation in terms of facial expressions because it is more parsimonious.

Something to Think About

If Clever Hans had died before Pfungst had discovered his secret, we would never have known for sure how the horse was doing it. Would we be obliged to believe forever that this one horse could understand spoken language and could solve complex mathematical problems? How could we have evaluated such a hypothesis years later? (Hint: Would we have had to discover how Hans *did* answer the questions? Or would it be enough just to determine how he *could* have answered them?)

Third Example:
Extrasensory Perception

A highly controversial claim in psychology is the claim of extrasensory perception. Supporters of the idea of **extrasensory perception (ESP)** claim that certain people can acquire information without using *any* sense organ and without detecting *any* form of energy (Rhine, 1947). They claim, for instance, that a person gifted with ESP can read another person's mind (telepathy) even when the two are separated by a thick lead barrier that would block the transmission of almost any form of energy. They also claim that people who read minds can do so as accurately from a distance of a thousand kilometers as from an adjacent room, in apparent violation of the inverse-square law of physics.

Some ESP supporters also claim that certain people can perceive inanimate objects that are hidden from sight (clairvoyance), predict the future (precognition), and influence such physical events as the roll of dice by sheer mental concentration (psychokinesis). In other words, they claim it is possible to gain information or to influence physical events without transmitting any physical energy. If any of these claims were demonstrated to be valid, then we would have to restructure our entire

1. When the litters are overturned by the whirlwind and the faces are covered by cloaks, the new republic will be troubled by its people. At this time the reds and the whites will rule wrongly.

2. The great man will be struck down in the day by a thunderbolt. An evil deed, foretold by the bearer of a petition. According to the prediction another falls at night time. Conflict at Reims, London, and pestilence in Tuscany.

3. When the fish that travels over both land and sea is cast up on to the shore by a great wave, its shape foreign, smooth, and frightful. From the sea the enemies soon reach the walls.

4. The bird of prey flying to the left, before battle is joined with the French, he makes preparations. Some will regard him as good, others bad or uncertain. The weaker party will regard him as a good omen.

5. Shortly afterwards, not a very long interval, a great tumult will be raised by land and sea. The naval battles will be greater than ever. Fires, creatures which will make more tumult.

FIGURE 2.4

From these samples of the prophecies of Nostradamus (based on Cheetham, 1973), try to guess what events these statements are said to predict, according to those who believe Nostradamus was foretelling the future. See the answers on page 51 to check your "skills."

FIGURE 2.5

Can he read your mind? The Amazing Kreskin and other psychics perform surprising feats, but researchers have uncovered magicians' tricks, not special powers.

scientific view of nature, not just in psychology but in physics as well.

What evidence is there for ESP?

Anecdotes   One kind of evidence consists of anecdotes—people's reports of isolated events. Someone has a dream or a hunch that comes true or says something and someone else says, "I was just thinking exactly the same thing!" Such experiences may seem impressive when they occur, but they are meaningless as scientific evidence for several reasons. First, there is the possibility of coincidence. Of all the hunches and dreams that people have, eventually some are bound to come true by chance. Second, people tend to remember and talk about the hunches and dreams that *do* come true and to forget those that do not. They hardly ever say, "Strangest thing! I had a dream, but then nothing like it actually happened!" Third, people tend to exaggerate the coincidences that occur, both in their own memories and in the retelling.

We can evaluate anecdotal evidence only if people record their hunches and dreams *before* the predicted event. A few investigators have recorded people's predictions of future events and have checked later to see how accurate they were. Overall, very few predictions came true, and those that did come true were mostly vague and unspectacular (West, 1962).

You may have heard of the "prophet Nostra-

damus," a 16th-century French writer who allegedly predicted many events of later centuries. Figure 2.4 presents five samples of his writings. No one knows what his predictions mean until *after* the "predicted" events happen. At that point, people can imaginatively reinterpret his writings to fit whatever happened.

Concept Check

1. How could someone scientifically evaluate the accuracy of Nostradamus's predictions? (Check your answer on page 51.)

Professional Psychics   Many stage performers claim that they can read people's minds and perform other amazing mental feats. After closely observing such alleged psychics as Kreskin and Uri Geller, researchers David Marks and Richard Kammann (1980) concluded that they exhibited no special powers but only various kinds of deception commonly employed in magic shows.

For example, Kreskin (Figure 2.5) typically begins his act by asking the audience to read his mind. Let's try to duplicate this trick right now: Try to read my mind. I am thinking of a number between 1 and 50. Both digits are odd numbers, but they are not the same. That is, it could be 15 but it could not be 11. (These are the instructions Kreskin gives.)

Have you chosen a number?

All right, my number was 37. Did you think of 37? If not, how about 35? You see, I started to think 35 and then changed my mind, so you might have got 35.

Probably about half the readers "read my mind." If you were one of them, are you impressed? Don't be. There are not many numbers you could have chosen. The first digit had to be 1 or 3, and the second had to be 1, 3, 5, 7, or 9. You had to eliminate 11 and 33 because both digits are the same, and you probably eliminated 15 because I cited it as a possible example. That leaves only seven possibilities. Most people like to stay far away from the example given and tend to avoid the highest and lowest possible choices. That leaves 37 as the most likely choice and 35 as the second most likely.

Second act: Kreskin asks the audience to write down something they are thinking about while he walks along the aisles talking. Then, back on stage, he "reads people's minds." He might say something like, "Someone is thinking about their mother . . ." In any large crowd, someone is bound to stand up and shout, "Yes, that's me, you read my mind!" On occasion he describes something that someone has written out in great detail. That person generally turns out to be someone sitting along the aisle where Kreskin was walking.

After a variety of other tricks (see Marks & Kammann, 1980), Kreskin goes backstage while the local mayor or some other dignitary hides Kreskin's paycheck somewhere in the audience. Then Kreskin comes back, walks up and down the aisles and across the rows, and eventually shouts, "The check is here!" The rule is that if he guesses wrong, then he does not get paid. (But he seldom misses.)

How does he do that trick? Think for a moment before reading on.

Very simply, it is a Clever Hans trick. Kreskin studies people's faces. Most of the people are silently cheering for him to find the check. Their facial expression changes as he comes close to the check and then moves away. In effect, they are saying, "Now you're getting closer" and "Now you're moving away." At last he closes in on the check.

We can also explain the performances of many other stage performers in terms of simple tricks and illusions. Of course, someone always objects, "Well, maybe so. But there's this other guy you haven't investigated yet. Maybe he really does possess psychic powers." Until there is solid evidence to the contrary, it is simpler (more parsimonious) to assume that those other performers are also using illusion and deception.

Experiments Stage performances and anecdotal events always take place under uncontrolled con-

ditions. So we cannot determine the probability of coincidence or the possibility of deception. The only evidence worth serious consideration comes from laboratory experiments.

For example, an experimenter shuffles a special set of ESP cards (Figure 2.6) and then asks the subject to guess the order of the cards, from the top of the deck on down. Or the experimenter looks at a single card and asks the subject to name it. Because there are 25 cards in these decks, 5 each of 5 types, the subject should get about 5 correct just by guessing. If a subject does better than that, we can calculate the probability of accidentally doing that well. (Other experimental designs use the same basic idea.)

We can summarize the results of such experiments very simply: There is no replicable evidence that people can do better than chance (Druckman & Swets, 1988). Notice that word *replicable*. An occasional experiment does yield positive results. But of all the hundreds of experiments that have been conducted, a few are bound to show a positive result just by accident. No experiment is convincing unless other investigators, including skeptics, can repeat it and get similar results. No experiment in ESP meets the criterion of replicability.

A few people (very few) have reportedly done much better than chance in such experiments, some of the time and under certain conditions. For instance, one "star" subject averaged 8 correct calls out of 25 over more than 700 trials of 25 cards each (Rhine, 1947). The possibility of doing that well by chance is extremely low. But if the results are not due to chance, what are they due to? C. E. M. Hansel (1966) investigated the circumstances under which several "star" subjects performed; he concluded that in each case the subject could have obtained the information through the known senses. The subject could have seen a reflection on the experimenter's glasses, for example, or could have received signals from a friend peeking through the window, and so forth. It is difficult long after the event to determine what a subject actually did; all we can say is that

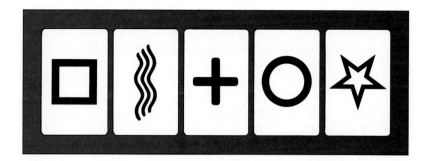

FIGURE 2.6

In a typical ESP experiment, a subject guesses the order of cards in a shuffled deck. The deck contains twenty-five cards, five each of the five types shown here.

these subjects *could* have gained the information through their senses. Why do scientists prefer to accept such an explanation instead of conceding that certain people may have special powers that violate the laws of physics? Quite simply, because it is more parsimonious to do so. We prefer the explanation that relies on simpler assumptions—that people use their known senses—unless the evidence absolutely forces us to a more complex explanation.

Evaluation   No evidence can disprove the existence of extrasensory perception—just as no evidence can disprove the existence of unicorns. But most psychologists remain skeptical of ESP for three basic reasons: (1) No experiment has yielded replicable positive results. (2) The history of ESP contains many known or strongly suspected frauds. Given that history, we insist on replicability even more strongly than usual. (3) Even if we had better evidence, we still could not explain how ESP could possibly take place. (Even its defenders offer no explanation.)

And yet many people still believe in extrasensory perception. Two California psychologists, Barry Singer and Victor Benassi, once put on a magic show resembling Kreskin's for a group of college students and asked them whether they thought ESP was at work. Seventy-five percent said yes. Singer and Benassi repeated the show for another group of students, announcing in advance that everything that happened would be the result of simple tricks. Fifty percent rejected that explanation and insisted that the psychologists were using psychic powers (Marks & Kammann, 1980). Apparently some people *want* to believe in extrasensory perception, even when the "psychics" themselves offer more parsimonious explanations.

What have we learned about science in general?

- Science does not deal with proof or certainty. All scientific conclusions are tentative and are subject to revision.

- Scientists always prefer the most parsimonious theory. They abandon accepted theories and assumptions only when better theories and assumptions become available.

- Scientists scrutinize any claim that violates the rule of parsimony. Before they will accept any such claim, they insist that it be supported by replicable experiments that rule out simpler explanations.

SUMMARY

1.   Although psychology does not have the same wealth of knowledge as other sciences have, it shares with those other fields a commitment to scientific methods, including a set of criteria for evaluating theories. (page 21)

2.   A scientific study goes through the following sequence of steps: hypothesis, methods, results, interpretation. Because almost any study is subject to more than one possible interpretation, we base conclusions on a pattern of results from many studies. The results of a given study are taken seriously only if other investigators can replicate them. (page 21)

3.   Scientists seek theories that account for large amounts of information. A good theory agrees with known facts and leads to correct predictions of new information. Its predictions are sufficiently precise so that we can imagine possible results that would falsify the theory. (page 23)

4.   Other things being equal, we prefer the theory that relies on simpler assumptions. (page 23)

5.   Claims of extrasensory perception are scrutinized very cautiously because evidence reported so far has been unreplicable and because careful investigation generally leads to more parsimonious explanations in terms of coincidence, magic tricks, or the use of the known senses. (page 25)

SUGGESTIONS FOR FURTHER READING

Alcock, J. E. (1987). Parapsychology: Science of the anomalous or search for the soul? *Behavioral and Brain Sciences, 10,* 553–565. An article outlining the reasons why most psychologists are skeptical of ESP. Accompanied by another article by K. R. Rao and J. Palmer favorable to ESP and 49 short commentaries by other investigators with a variety of viewpoints.

Kuhn, T. (1970). *The structure of scientific revolutions* (2nd ed.). Chicago: University of Chicago. An important book about what happens when scientists are forced to revise their basic assumptions and their way of thinking.

Marks, D., & Kammann, R. (1980). *The psychology of the psychic.* Buffalo, NY: Prometheus. A cogent scientific analysis of the exploits of alleged psychics.

Radner, D., & Radner, M. (1982). *Science and unreason.* Belmont, CA: Wadsworth. A critical survey of areas of pseudoscience and the fringes of science.

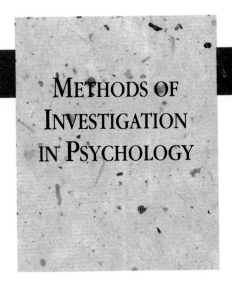

METHODS OF INVESTIGATION IN PSYCHOLOGY

How do psychologists design research studies?
What pitfalls should they try to avoid?

Psychologists try to approach questions scientifically, but they face some special problems that physicists and chemists do not face. Psychologists might ask, for example, "What is the effect of motivation on a worker's job performance?" Immediately they have to face some difficult questions: "What do we mean by motivation? How can we measure it or control it? And how should we measure job performance?" A physicist who wondered about the effect of temperature on the width of a steel bar would not have to ponder the meaning of the word *temperature* or the best way to measure a steel bar.

Here is a second major difference: When physicists study subatomic particles, they find that they cannot measure events without greatly affecting those events. Psychologists face that difficulty almost all the time. If you saw me watching you and taking notes on everything you did, would you continue acting the way you ordinarily do? Probably not. Psychologists have ways of overcoming this problem (see Figure 2.7), but they can seldom ignore it.

GENERAL PRINCIPLES OF CONDUCTING RESEARCH

This part of the chapter will trace some of the common methods of doing research in psychology. The goal is not primarily to prepare you to conduct psychological research, although I hope that at least a few readers will eventually do just that. The primary goal is to prepare you to be an intelligent interpreter of psychological research. When you hear about some new study in psychology, you should be able to ask a few pertinent questions and to decide how good the evidence is and what conclusion (if any) it justifies.

Defining the Variables

How could you determine how strong someone's motivation is? Or whether snails have emotions? Or whether IQ tests really measure intelligence? Before you could even begin to answer such questions, you would have to decide what the terms *motivation, emotion,* and *intelligence* mean.

What *do* they mean? As with any other words, they mean whatever we want them to mean. At one point in Lewis Carroll's *Through the Looking Glass,* Alice objects, "But 'glory' doesn't mean 'a nice knockdown argument.' " Humpty Dumpty replies, "When *I* use a word, it means just what I choose it to mean—neither more nor less."

Similarly, psychological terms mean whatever we choose them to mean. For many purposes, the most useful definition of a term is one that makes it measurable. Psychologists often insist on an **operational definition** of a term—a definition that specifies the operations (or procedures) used to measure some variable or to produce some phenomenon.

FIGURE 2.7

Observation through a one-way mirror enables psychologists to study subjects without making them self-conscious and influencing their behavior.

FIGURE 2.8

Aggressive behavior is difficult to define and measure. One psychologist might rate these boys' play as aggressive, while another might view the play as merely energetic, depending on each psychologist's definition of *aggression*.

An operational definition is not the same as a dictionary definition. A dictionary might define *motivation* as a desire, but that definition does not tell us how to measure motivation or how to produce it. Here is one possible operational definition: "The degree of motivation is the amount of work someone will do in order to obtain a particular outcome." That definition tells us how to measure motivation; it even suggests how to determine whether a person's motivation for a particular outcome is increasing or decreasing from one time to another.

Suppose someone wishes to investigate whether children who watch violence on television are likely to behave aggressively themselves. In that case the investigator needs operational definitions for both *televised violence* and *aggressive behavior.* No single definition is likely to be perfect. For example, the investigator might define *televised violence* as "the number of acts shown or described in which one person injures another." According to that definition, a 20-minute stalking scene counts the same as a quick attack, and a murder on screen counts the same as one that the characters just talk about. Cartoon violence does not count, because no "person" is injured. Similarly, an unsuccessful attempt to injure someone does not count. It is unclear from this definition whether we should count verbal insults. Another researcher might prefer a different operational definition.

Similarly, the investigator needs an operational definition of *aggressive behavior* (see Figure 2.8). To define it as "the number of acts of assault or

murder committed within 24 hours after watching a particular television program" probably would not be helpful. (Anyone who expected such a drastic response could not ethically perform the experiment.) A better operational definition of *aggressive behavior* specifies less extreme acts. For example, the experimenter might place a large plastic doll in front of a young child and record how often the child punches it. Again, other investigators might prefer some other operational definition. But as long as each researcher states his or her definition clearly and sticks to it, we have at least some idea what the results mean, and we know what procedure to follow if we want to try to replicate the study.

Concept Check

2. *Which of the following is an operational definition of* intelligence: *(a) the ability to comprehend relationships, (b) a score on an IQ test, (c) the ability to survive in the real world, or (d) the product of the cerebral cortex of the brain?*

What would you propose as an operational definition of hunger? *(Check your answers on page 51.)*

Random Samples and Representative Samples

In general, investigators examine the behavior of only a small number of individuals, but they want to draw conclusions about a large population, perhaps even about people in general. We say that the investigators studied a *sample* of the total population. Do the results from a limited sample really apply to the total population? The answer depends on how the sample is chosen.

Consider what can happen if the sample is greatly different from the total population: In 1936 the *Literary Digest* mailed 10 million postcards asking people their choice for president of the United States. Of the two million responses, 57% preferred the Republican candidate, Alfred Landon. As it turned out, Landon was soundly defeated by the Democratic candidate, Franklin Roosevelt. The reason for the misleading result was that the *Literary Digest* surveyed an unrepresentative sample. It selected names from the telephone and automobile registration lists. In 1936, at the end of the Great Depression, only fairly well-off people had telephones or cars, and most of them were Republicans. The sample included very few poor people, who voted overwhelmingly Democratic.

To conduct a meaningful study, we need either a representative sample or a random sample of the population. A **representative sample** closely resembles the entire population in its percentage of males and females, blacks and whites, young and old, Republicans and Democrats, or whatever other characteristics are likely to affect the results. To get a representative sample of the people in a given city, an investigator would first determine what percentage of the city's residents belong to each category and then select people to match those percentages. The disadvantage of this method is that a group may be representative with regard to sex, race, age, and political party and yet be unrepresentative with regard to some factor the investigators ignored, such as religious preference or level of education.

In a **random sample**, every individual in the population has an equal chance of being selected. To get a random sample of city residents, an investigator might select a certain number of households at random from the most recent census listing and then select one person at random from each of those households. The resulting sample probably will not match the population's percentages by sex, race, and age, at least not as closely as a representative sample does. Still, if the random sample is large enough, the percentages are likely to be close with regard to each of those variables, as well as others that the designers of a representative sample might have overlooked.

Concept Check

3. Suppose I compare the interests and abilities of men and women students at my university. If I find a consistent difference, can I assume that it represents a difference between men in general and women in general? If not, why not? (Check your answer on page 51.)

Single-Blind Studies and Double-Blind Studies

At some point in any psychological study, an investigator measures some aspect of behavior, perhaps by directly observing it and recording it. Imagine that you are the investigator and are recording acts of aggressive behavior by two groups of children. Imagine further that you are testing the hypothesis that Group A will be more aggressive than Group B (for whatever reason). You know that if the results support your hypothesis, then you can get your results published and you will be well on your way to becoming a famous psychologist. Now one child in Group A engages in some mildly aggressive act— a borderline case. You are not sure whether to count it or not. You want to be fair. You don't want your hypothesis to influence your decision of whether or not to count this act as aggression. Just try to ignore that hypothesis.

A representative sample requires carefully establishing the percentage of various characteristics in a group. With a valid sample, psychologists can apply their findings to a larger population. Could a random sample of these twins represent the general public?

To overcome the potential source of error in an investigator's bias, psychologists prefer to use a **blind observer**—that is, an observer who does not know which subjects are in which group and what is expected of each. Because blind observers do not know the hypothesis, they can be objective and record observations of behavior as fairly as possible.

A study conducted with a blind observer is known as a **single-blind study**, as is a study in which the observer knows which subjects received which treatment, but the subjects themselves do not.

In some experiments, researchers can conceal the independent variable—the factor that distinguishes one group from another—from both the observer and the subjects. For example, the experimenter could give one group a pill that might affect their behavior and give the other group an inactive pill (a **placebo**) that will have no biological effect on their behavior, without telling subjects which pill they are receiving. Then a blind observer records the effects on their behavior. Such a study is known as a **double-blind study**. (*Someone*, of course, would have to keep a record of which subjects took which pill; otherwise, the results could never be interpreted!)

VARIETIES OF RESEARCH DESIGN

The general principles I have just discussed apply to a variety of research studies. Psychologists use various methods of investigation, and each method

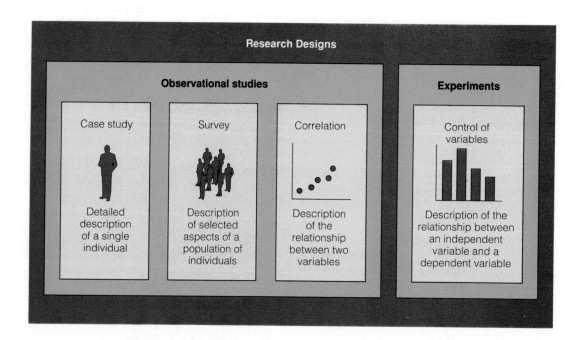

FIGURE 2.9

The findings of a case study, the simplest of the four types of research summarized here, may inspire further study with more complex investigations.

has its own advantages and disadvantages. Sometimes psychologists simply observe what one person does under certain conditions; on other occasions they perform complicated experiments on large groups. We shall begin with the simplest (and generally least conclusive) design—the case study—and progress to more complex designs—surveys, correlational studies, and experiments (see Figure 2.9).

Case Histories

Psychologists are sometimes interested in conditions that rarely appear. For example, some people can remember what they have seen or heard with amazing accuracy. Others show an amazing inability to remember what they have seen or heard. People with a rare condition called Cotard's syndrome believe they are dead. When we want to study such an unusual person, we may decide to put together a **case history**, which is a thorough study of a single individual. It may include information about the person's medical condition, family background, unusual experiences, and details on tasks the person can and cannot perform—in short, anything the investigator thinks might have some bearing on the person's unusual condition. On page 308 you will find an example of a case history of a brain-damaged man who lost his ability to learn facts. On pages 512–513 is a case history of a woman who periodically shifted from one personality to another.

A case history is well suited to exploring special, poorly understood conditions. Ideally, a series of case histories may reveal a pattern. If so, investigators may proceed to more elaborate research designs to test that apparent pattern more carefully.

Surveys

A **survey** is a study of the prevalence of certain beliefs, attitudes, or behaviors based on people's responses to specific questions. For example, in Chapter 11 we shall consider a couple of surveys of the prevalence of certain sexual behaviors. A survey is one of the most common methods of investigation in psychology, sociology, and political science. Conducting a survey is deceptively simple: Just draw up a list of questions, ask a number of people to answer them, and then report the results. If we are not very careful, however, the results may be misleading. We have already considered the problem of sampling; the results of a survey mean little unless we put the questions to a random or representative sample of people.

However, no matter how carefully we select the sample, the results can be meaningless if the questions are worded in a way that suggests a particular answer or if the interviewers drop hints that they are hoping for a particular answer. For example, if an interviewer mentions that the survey is sponsored by an organization dedicated to protecting the rights of mental patients, then people are likely to describe their attitudes as being highly favorable to that cause.

Even a survey based on a representative or random sample and containing unbiased questions may still produce misleading results. Before reading further, answer each of the following survey questions:

SURVEY

1. A new cable channel plans to rerun old TV programs. Please rank the following series from 1 (the program you would *most* like to see rerun) to 12 (the program you would *least* like to see rerun).

____ "Batman"

____ "Battlestar Galactica"

____ "Carol Burnett Show"

____ "I Love Lucy"

____ "Little House on the Prairie"

____ "Lone Ranger"

____ "Many Loves of Dobie Gillis"

____ "My Mother the Car"

____ "Smothers Brothers Variety Hour"

____ "Space Doctor"

____ "Superman"

____ "Wagon Train"

2. What do you think is the most important issue or problem facing our country today?

3. What do you think has been the most important event of the 20th century?

4. What do you think was the most important event in all of human history?

2. What do you think is the most important issue or problem facing our country today? (For example, the AIDS epidemic, the threat of nuclear war, conservation of natural resources, or whatever else you think is the most important issue.)

3. What do you think has been the most important event of the 20th century? (For example, the invention of nuclear power and nuclear weapons, the computer revolution, the civil-rights movement, changes in women's status, or whatever else you think was the most important event.)

4. What do you think was the most important event in all of human history? (For example, the invention of the alphabet, the invention of democracy by the Greeks, the introduction of monotheism by the Jews, the life of Jesus, or whatever else you think was the most important event.)

What did you base your opinions on in question 1? You have perhaps seen some of the programs and heard about others. But at least one of them is a series you have never even heard of: There never was a program called "Space Doctor." Did you assign a rating to "Space Doctor" and to any other programs you were unfamiliar with? Most people do.

The point is clear: *In examining the results of any survey, you should not assume that all the people who responded had a solid basis for their opinions.* (Keep that point in mind the next time you hear the results of a political survey.)

Now on to questions 2, 3, and 4. They are open-ended questions; you could answer them any way you wished. People come up with an enormous variety of answers to these questions. The results are different when we ask the same questions but suggest possible answers.

When people are offered such choices as these, a majority will select one of the suggested answers instead of entering a "whatever else" of their own—even if the suggestions are less reasonable than the ones just provided (Schuman & Scott, 1987). So how should the questions be phrased, with or without suggestions?

The purpose here is not to declare that one way of phrasing a question is right and the other is wrong. The point is simply this: *The results of a survey depend on how the questions are phrased.* (Whenever you hear that "54% of all Americans surveyed believe such and so," inquire how the question was phrased.)

Correlational Studies

A third kind of study is the *correlational study*. A **correlation** is a measure of the relationship between two variables, both of which are outside the investigator's control. Thus a correlational study is one in which the investigator examines the relationship between two variables, without actually manipulating either one of them.

For example, investigators have observed that people with a large number of alcoholic relatives are likely to develop alcohol problems themselves. In coming to that realization, no investigator controlled who was related to whom or how much alcohol anyone drank; the investigators merely observed a relationship that often occurs in nature. Another example: Students who do well on the first

FIGURE 2.10

All three graphs show correlation coefficients of +1.

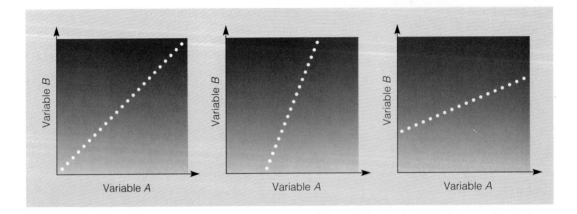

test they take in introductory psychology generally do well on the second test as well. Again, no investigators exert any control over the two events; they merely observe the relationship (or correlation) between them.

A survey can be considered a correlational study if the interviewers compare two or more groups. For example, the interviewers might compare the beliefs of men and women or of young people and old people. The interviewer could thereby measure a relationship between one variable (sex or age) and another variable (beliefs).

The Correlation Coefficient Some correlations are strong; some are weak. For example, there is probably a strong correlation between how much time various students spend studying French and the grades they get on their French tests. There is probably only a very weak correlation between how much time they spend studying French and the grades they get on their chemistry tests. In fact, it is possible that the students who spent the most time studying French may do worse than other students on chemistry tests.

To specify the strength and positive or negative direction of an observed correlation between variables, we use what is known as a correlation coefficient, which can range mathematically from +1 to −1. A **correlation coefficient** indicates how accurately we can use measurements of one variable to predict another. A correlation coefficient of +1, for example, means that we can make perfect predictions. Figure 2.10 shows the results of three hypothetical studies, all of which have a **positive correlation** of +1. Note that any increase in one variable is associated with an increase in the other variable.

A correlation coefficient of −1 also means that we can make perfect predictions. A **negative correlation** means that *increases* in one variable are associated with *decreases* in the other variable. Figure 2.11 illustrates a correlation of −1.

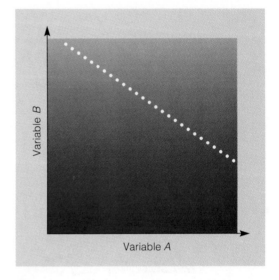

FIGURE 2.11

A negative correlation—in this graph a correlation coefficient of −1—indicates as strong a relationship between variables as a positive correlation does.

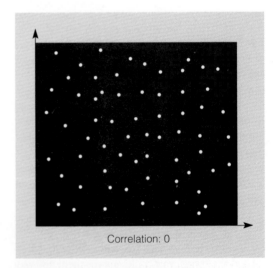

Correlation: 0

FIGURE 2.12

This scatterplot shows a correlation coefficient of 0, which means that knowing the value of one variable does not increase our accuracy of predicting the other variable.

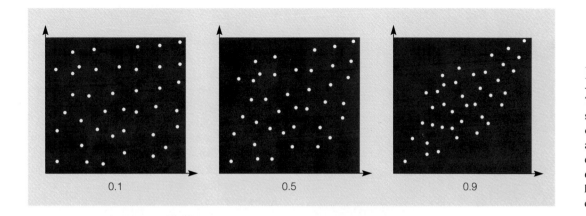

FIGURE 2.13

These three scatterplots show correlation coefficients of +0.1, +0.5, and +0.9. The appendix to this chapter explains how to calculate a correlation coefficient.

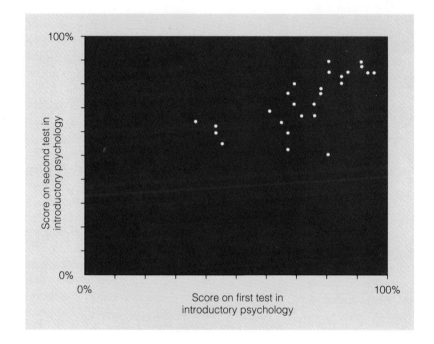

FIGURE 2.14

These plotted scores from two introductory psychology tests show a correlation coefficient of 0.7.

A correlation coefficient of zero indicates that an increase in one variable predicts neither an increase nor a decrease in the other variable. Figure 2.12 shows a graph of a zero correlation. (This kind of graph is called a *scatterplot*.)

In real life, psychologists seldom encounter a perfect +1, −1, or 0 correlation coefficient. Generally, correlation coefficients turn out to be some percentage of 1. The closer the correlation coefficient is to +1 or to −1, the closer the relationship between the two variables and the more accurately we can use one variable to predict the other. Figure 2.13 shows correlation coefficients of 0.1, 0.5, and 0.9. The graph in Figure 2.14 is based on real test scores of students in an introductory psychology class. (Note that in Figures 2.10 through 2.14, each point on the graphs represents two measurements for one person.)

Here are a few examples of the findings of correlational studies:

- The most crowded areas of a city are generally the most impoverished. (The correlation between crowdedness and poverty is positive.)
- The most crowded areas of a city are generally the least wealthy. (The correlation between crowdedness and wealth is negative.)
- People's telephone numbers have no relationship to their IQ scores. (The correlation between the two is zero.)
- Students who spend many hours doing their homework generally get higher grades than do students who neglect their homework. (Doing homework is positively correlated with getting good grades.)
- People who trust other people are unlikely to cheat other people. (Trusting is negatively correlated with cheating.)

Some of our beliefs reflect illusory correlations. For example, the roster of noteworthy scientists throughout history "proves" that men are better scientists than women are. What mistaken assumptions are behind this notion?

Concept Check

4. *Which indicates a stronger relationship between two variables, a +0.50 correlation between variables A and B or a −0.75 correlation between variables C and D? (Check your answer on page 51.)*

Illusory Correlations It is difficult to identify a correlation between two variables solely on the basis of casual observation. You might meet four women who mention that they really liked a particular movie, and then you overhear two men saying that they hated it. You start wondering why this film appeals more to women than to men. Well, maybe it does and maybe it doesn't. Those four women and two men may not be typical of all women and men. People sometimes think they see a correlation, even when none exists. An imagined or greatly exaggerated correlation is known as an **illusory correlation**. Much of what people believe about differences between women and men, or between blacks and whites, are examples of illusory correlations.

For another example of an illusory correlation, take the widely held belief that a full moon affects human behavior. For hundreds of years, many people have believed that crime and various kinds of mental disturbance are more common under a full moon than at other times. In fact, the term *lunacy* (from the Latin for *moon, luna*) originally meant mental illness caused by the full moon. Some police officers report that they receive more calls on nights of a full moon, and hospital workers report that more emergency cases turn up on such nights. However, those reports are based on people's memories over time rather than on carefully analyzed data. James Rotton and I. W. Kelly (1985) examined all available data relating crime, mental illness, and other phenomena to phases of the moon. They concluded that the phase of the moon has either no effect at all on human behavior, or so little effect that it is almost impossible to measure.

Why then does the belief persist? We do not know when or how it first arose. (It may have been true many years ago, before the widespread use of artificial lights.) But we can guess why it persists. Suppose, for example, you are working at a hospital and you expect to handle more emergencies on full-moon nights than at other times. Sooner or later, on a full-moon night, you encounter an unusually high number of accidents, assaults, and suicide attempts. You say, "See? There was a full moon and people just went crazy!" You tend to remember that night for a long time. You disregard all the other full-moon nights when nothing special happened and all the nights without a full moon when you were swamped with emergency cases.

That same selective memory might convince people that Friday the 13th brings bad luck, that dreams and hunches come true, or that people who live on the other side of the tracks are not to be trusted. The point is that an apparent correlation cannot be relied on until it has been carefully measured and confirmed by the data. The memory of a few events that seem to fit a pattern does not establish a correlation.

Correlation and Causation A correlational study tells us whether two variables are related to each other and, if so, how strongly. It does not tell us *why* they are related. *No matter how high the correlation coefficient between variables A and B, even if it is +1, it does not tell us whether A caused B, whether B caused A, or whether something else caused both A and B.*

Once in a while, we find a correlation in which one of the variables obviously causes changes in the other. For example, meteorologists have discovered that there is a positive correlation between the number of sunspots and winter temperatures in the stratosphere over the North Pole. Although we are not sure just how sunspots could affect the weather on Earth, it is far more likely that they do affect the weather rather than that the weather on Earth affects the sunspots.

Ordinarily, however, the direction of causation is far from obvious; for example:

TABLE 2.1 Comparison of Three Methods of Research

	Case History	Correlational Study	Experiment
Number of individuals studied	Usually one	Any number	Any number
Manipulated by investigator	Nothing	Nothing	Independent variable
Advantages	Ideal way to start when investigating rare condition	Easier to conduct than experiment, especially when studying effects of long-term experiences or anything else impractical to control in an experiment	Useful for determining cause-and-effect relationships
Possible ethical difficulties	None, because the investigator manipulates nothing	None, because the investigator controls nothing	Occasional need for deception; possibility of producing undesirable effects

- Unmarried men are more likely than married men are to wind up in a mental hospital or prison. So we can say that, for men, marriage is negatively correlated with mental illness and criminal activity. Does the correlation mean that marriage leads to mental health and good social adjustment? Or does it mean that men who are confined to mental hospitals or prisons are unlikely to marry?

- Most depressed people have trouble sleeping. Depression is negatively correlated with sleeping well. Does that mean depression causes poor sleep? Or does it mean that people who have difficulty sleeping become depressed? Or does something else, such as a dietary deficiency, lead to both depression and poor sleep?

Determining the size and direction of a correlation between two variables is an important first step in a study. But a correlation does not tell us about causation. To determine causation, an investigator needs to manipulate one of the variables directly, through a research design known as an *experiment*. When an investigator manipulates one variable and then observes changes in another variable, the causation is clear.

Methods of Conducting Experiments in Psychology

An experiment is a study in which the investigator manipulates at least one variable while measuring at least one other variable. The logic behind the simplest possible experiment is as follows: The investigator assembles a suitable sample of people (or animals), divides them randomly into two groups, and then administers some experimental procedure to one group and not to the other. Someone, preferably a blind observer, records the behavior of the two groups. If the behavior of the two groups differs in some consistent way, then the difference is presumably the result of the experimental procedure. Table 2.1 summarizes the ways in which experiments differ from case histories and correlational studies.

I shall describe psychological experiments and some of their special difficulties. For the sake of illustration, let's imagine that we are setting up an experiment to determine whether watching violent television programs leads to an increase in aggressive behavior. (We used this example in the discussion of operational definitions on pages 29–30.)

Independent Variables and Dependent Variables An experiment is an attempt to measure the effect of an independent variable, such as watching violent television programs, on a dependent variable, such as subsequent aggressive behavior. A *variable* is anything that can have more than one value. The **independent variable** is the variable the experimenter *manipulates* (see Figure 2.15); for example, the experimenter varies the amount of time the subjects in an experiment spend watching violent television. The **dependent variable** is the variable that changes in response to changes in the independent variable. The dependent variable is the variable the experimenter *measures*. In our example, the experimenter measures the amount of aggressive behavior the subjects exhibit.

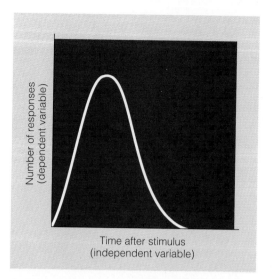

FIGURE 2.15

The independent variable is manipulated by the experimenter. The dependent variable is the measured outcome.

Pool of subjects	Condition	Independent variable	Dependent variable
Random assignment to groups	Experimental	3 hours per day watching *violent* TV programs	Violent behavior recorded by blind observer
	Control	3 hours per day watching *nonviolent* TV programs	Violent behavior recorded by blind observer

FIGURE 2.16

Once a researcher decides on the hypothesis she wants to test, she must design the experiment, such as these procedures for testing the effects of watching televised violence. An appropriate, accurate method of measurement is essential.

Concept Check

5. *An instructor wants to find out whether the frequency of tests in introductory psychology has any effect on students' final exam performance. The instructor gives weekly tests in one class, just three tests in a second class, and only a single mid-term exam in the third class. All three classes take the same final exam and the instructor compares their performances. Identify the independent variable and the dependent variable. (Check your answers on page 51.)*

Experimental Group and Control Group Here is more terminology you need to understand psychological experiments: The **experimental group** receives the treatment that the experiment is designed to test. In our example, the experimental group would watch televised violence for a specific length of time. The **control group** is treated in the same way as the experimental group *except* for the treatment the experiment is designed to test. In other words, the control group spends the same amount of time watching television but watches only nonviolent programs (see Figure 2.16).

In principle, that procedure sounds easy. In practice, a difficulty arises: We are conducting a study on a group of teenagers who have a history of violent behavior. The experimental group watches a good guys versus bad guys thriller with lots of action and violence. Exactly what do we ask the control group to watch? Can we find a program without violence that is just as exciting to watch? (It's not easy.)

Random Assignment The preferred way of assigning subjects to groups is **random assignment**: The experimenter uses some chance procedure such as drawing names out of a hat to make sure that every subject has the same probability as any other subject of being assigned to a given group. Imagine what could happen if the experimenter did not assign people at random. Suppose we let the subjects choose whether they want to be in the experimental group or the control group. The people most prone to aggressive behavior might generally choose to be in the experimental group (the one that watches violent programs). Or suppose we ask people to volunteer for the study, and the first 20 people who volunteer become the experimental group and the next 20 become the control group. Again, we will have trouble analyzing the results, because the people who are quickest to volunteer may be impulsive in other regards also.

Consider an animal example: We set up a rack of cages and put each rat in a cage by itself. The rack has five rows of six cages each, numbered from 1 in the upper-left corner to 30 in the lower right. Regardless of the procedures we use, we find that the rats with higher cage numbers are more aggressive than those with lower cage numbers. Why?

We might first guess that the difference has to do with location. The rats in the cages with high numbers are farthest from the lights and closest to the floor. They get fed last each day. To test the influence of these factors, we move some of the cages to different positions in the rack, leaving each rat in its own cage. To our surprise, the rats in cages 26–30 are still more aggressive than those in cages

1–5. Why? (How could they possibly know what number is on each cage, and even if they did know, why should they care?)

The answer has to do with how rats get assigned to cages. When an investigator buys a shipment of rats, which one goes into cage 1? The one that is easiest to catch! Which ones go into the last few cages? The vicious, ornery little critters that put up the greatest resistance to being picked up! The rats in the last few cages were already the most aggressive ones *before* they were put into those cages.

The point is that even with rats an experimenter must assign individuals to the experimental group and the control group at random. It would not be right to assign the first 15 rats to one group and the second 15 to another group. The same is true, only more so, with humans.

Studies of the Effects of Televised Violence on Aggressive Behavior: WHAT'S THE EVIDENCE?

We have talked in general terms about experiments on the effects of televised violence. Now let us consider some actual examples.

Part of the evidence regarding the effects of televised violence comes from correlational studies. Several such studies have found that people who watch a great deal of televised violence are more likely to engage in aggressive behavior than are people who do not (National Institute of Mental Health, 1982). Those results are suggestive but inconclusive. They do not tell us whether watching violence leads to aggressive behavior or whether people prone to aggressive behavior like to watch violence on television.

In another type of correlational study, investigators in the 1950s studied how viewers reacted when television first came to their region. Because the levels of violent behavior increased in many cities at about the time that television first appeared, some investigators suggested that violent television programs may have been responsible for the increased violent behavior (National Institute of Mental Health, 1982). Again the results are not decisive. The advent of television was hardly the only change taking place in those communities at the time, and we cannot assume it was responsible for the increase in violent behavior. To examine a possible cause-and-effect relationship, we must turn to experiments.

Hypothesis Children who watch violent television programs will engage in more acts of aggression

than will children who spend the same amount of time watching nonviolent programs.

Method One set of experimenters chose to study male juvenile delinquents (Parke, Berkowitz, Leyens, West, & Sebastian, 1977). The disadvantage was that the conclusions of the study might apply only to a limited group, not to young people in general. The advantage was that the experimenters could control the choice of television programs in a detention center much better than they could for youngsters living at home.

The boys were assigned randomly to two cottages. Those in one cottage watched violent films on five consecutive nights, while those in the other cottage watched nonviolent films. Throughout this period, "blind" observers recorded incidents of aggressive behavior by each boy. On the sixth day, each boy was put into an experimental setting in which he had an opportunity at certain times to press a button that would deliver an electric shock to another boy. (At least he thought he was delivering a shock. In fact, no shocks were given.) The experimenters recorded the frequency and intensity of shocks that each boy chose to deliver.

Results Compared to the boys who had watched nonviolent films, those who had watched the violent films engaged in more acts of aggression and pressed the button to deliver more frequent and more intense electric shocks.

Interpretation At least in this study, watching violent films led to increased violence. As with most studies, however, this one has its limitations. The boys in the experiment were not representative of boys in general, much less of people in general. Moreover, we cannot assume that we would get similar results with a different choice of violent films or a different method of measuring aggressive behavior. ■

The only way to get around the limitation of a given experiment is to conduct additional experiments, using different samples of people, different films, and different measures of aggressive behavior. A number of such experiments have been conducted; the results have been inconsistent. In some experiments, those who have watched violent films behave more aggressively; in others, the two groups behave about the same. In nearly all cases the difference between the two groups is small (Cook, Kendzierski, & Thomas, 1983; Freedman, 1984, 1986; Friedrich-Cofer & Huston, 1986).

Remember what I said about a result that is *replicated* but not consistently *replicable:* It suggests that an effect occurs under certain conditions but not under others. That seems to be the case for the effect of televised violence.

WHY EXPERIMENTS SOMETIMES GO WRONG

Research on human behavior poses some thorny problems that do not arise in other types of research. For example, a physicist studying the properties of a gas does not have to worry that some of the gas molecules might die, or quit the experiment, or might act strange because they know that they are in an experiment. Psychologists do have to worry about matters such as those.

Demand Characteristics

The subjects who take part in a psychological experiment often try to guess what the experimenter wants them to do and say. They feel that "good" results will help the experimenter succeed and will contribute to the advancement of knowledge. As a result, some experiments reveal more about the participants' expectations than about the phenomenon the experimenter is trying to study. Martin Orne (1969) defines **demand characteristics** as cues that tell a subject what is expected of him or her and what the experimenter hopes to find. In a well-conducted experiment such cues are held to a minimum.

One example of the effects of demand characteristics surfaced in an experiment on **sensory deprivation**. In experiments of this sort, subjects are placed in an apparatus that minimizes vision, hearing, touch, and other forms of sensory stimulation, as shown in Figure 2.17. After several hours, many subjects reported hallucinations, anxiety, and difficulty in concentrating; they exhibited impaired intellectual performance. M. T. Orne and K. E. Scheibe (1964) conducted an experiment to determine whether such effects might be related to the subjects' expectations.

College students participated in the experiment, which was described to them as a study on deprivation. The experimenter interrogated the students in the experimental group about their medical history and asked them to sign a form releasing the hospital in which the experiment took place from legal responsibility for the experiment's consequences. A prominently displayed "emergency tray" contained medicines and various instruments kept on hand "as a precaution." One subject per day entered an "isolation chamber," which was actually an ordinary room that con-

FIGURE 2.17

Experiments on sensory deprivation minimize stimulation from light, sound, smell, taste, and touch.

tained two chairs, a desk, a window, a mirror, a sandwich, and a glass of water. The subjects would never have guessed that the room had anything to do with sensory deprivation had they not been told so. Finally, the subjects were shown a microphone they could use to report any hallucinations or other distorted experiences and a "panic button" they could press to escape if the discomfort became unbearable. Students in the control group were led to the same room, but they were not shown the "emergency tray," they were not asked to sign a release form, and they were given no other indication that they were expected to have any unpleasant experiences.

Each subject was left alone in the room for 4 hours. Ordinarily, 4 hours by oneself is not a particularly disturbing experience. But everything the experimenter had said to the experimental group suggested that the experience would be dreadful, and the subjects acted as if it were. One pressed the panic button to demand release. Several others reported that they were hallucinating "multicolored spots on the wall," or that "the walls of the room are starting to waver," or that "the objects on the desk are becoming animated and moving about." Some complained of anxiety, restlessness, difficulty in concentrating, and spatial disorientation. At the end of the 4 hours, most of them showed impaired performance on a series of perceptual and intellectual tasks. The subjects in the control group reported no unusual experiences.

Sensory deprivation may very well have significant effects on behavior. But as this experiment illustrates, we must carefully distinguish between the effects of the independent variable and the effects of what the subjects *expect* of the experiment.

In a sense, demand characteristics set up *self-fulfilling prophecies*. In designing the experiment, the experimenter has a certain expectation in mind and then conducts the experiment in a way that may inadvertently convey that expectation to the subjects, thereby influencing them to behave as expected. To eliminate demand characteristics, many experimenters take elaborate steps to conceal the purpose of the experiment from the subjects. A double-blind study serves the purpose: If two groups share the same expectations but behave differently because of the treatment they receive, then the difference in behavior is presumably not the result of their expectations.

The Hawthorne Effect

Suppose you are sorting your laundry, when suddenly I enter the room, turn on a bright blue light, and explain that I am testing whether this bright blue light will cause you to finish your laundry faster than usual. Even if the light itself has no effect on your behavior, you might indeed work harder on your laundry and finish it faster for two reasons: (1) The sheer novelty of the situation increases your arousal, and (2) because you know I am watching you, you concentrate on your work instead of taking time out for various distractions. This tendency of people to work harder and perform better just because they know they are in an experiment is called the **Hawthorne effect**.

The Hawthorne effect has had a peculiar history. In the 1920s and 1930s some experimenters conducted a study of worker productivity at the Hawthorne plant of the Western Electric Company near Chicago. The experimenters variously increased and decreased the workers' rest periods and lengthened and shortened their work hours. They found that almost any change they made, in any direction, increased productivity. They concluded that productivity increased either because the workers were getting more attention than usual or simply because changes were taking place. That principle became known as the Hawthorne effect.

A reanalysis of the Hawthorne effect (Parsons, 1974), however, indicated that the workers had increased their productivity not because of the attention they got or the changes that took place but simply because they had improved their job skills during the many months over which the experiments took place. Their performance probably would have improved over time even if the experimenters had done nothing.

Still, the Hawthorne effect is a real factor. Sometimes any change in procedure seems to enhance performance. Change introduces variety and attracts attention to people's performance. For example, one experimenter gave a new drug to patients in a nursing home and found that it improved their memory. Later research revealed that the drug was incapable of even entering the brain cells. How could it have improved memory? The improvement was probably an example of the Hawthorne effect. The very fact that an experiment was underway may have prompted the nursing staff to be more attentive and the patients to make a greater effort.

Something to Think About

Your college tries an experiment: It announces that courses will last only a month, instead of the usual quarter or semester. During the first year under the new system, students and faculty alike agree that more learning is taking place than before. How could the college administration determine whether 1-month classes are really superior or whether the seeming improvement is just evidence of the Hawthorne effect? (Suggest an experiment for the college to try the following year.)

Differential Survival

At Generic State College, only 50% of all freshmen have decided on a career, while 90% of all seniors have decided. An observer concludes that between the freshman year and the senior year, most of the undecided students come to a decision. Sounds reasonable, right? But wait.

Suppose a creature from outer space is observing humans for the first time. He, she, or it discovers that about 50% of all human children are males but that only 10–20% of 90-year-olds are males. The creature concludes that as human males grow older, most of them change into females.

You see why that conclusion is wrong. Males—with a few exceptions—do not change into females. But they do die earlier, leaving a greater proportion of older females. So can we really say that a large percentage of undecided freshmen make career decisions by the time they become seniors? Perhaps undecided freshmen simply drop out of college before reaching their senior year.

This example represents the problem of **differential survival**: If some subjects drop out of a study (by dying, quitting, or moving away), then those who remain may be different from those who left. To avoid this problem, psychologists simply report the before-and-after data only for people who complete a study; they discard the data for those who leave.

Concept Check

6. *Decide which of the following examples represents demand characteristics, Hawthorne effect, or differential survival:*

a. *The Lizard Lick State College "Fighting Nematodes" lost 22 games in a row. When a new coach was hired, the team won 3 of its next 5 games.*

b. *Most of the first-year teachers in the Dismalville public school system complain about the school's policies. Teachers who have been at the school for 15 years or more rarely complain and seem quite satisfied.*

c. *A political survey reports one set of results when people are told, "This survey is sponsored by the Democratic party" and a different set of results when they are told, "This survey is sponsored by the Republican party."*

d. *A study of intelligence in one group of older people reports low performance among 70-year-olds, but (surprisingly) improved mean performance when those people reach age 80.*
(Check your answers on page 51.)

ETHICAL
CONSIDERATIONS
IN EXPERIMENTATION

In any experiment, psychologists manipulate some variable to see how it affects behavior. Perhaps the idea that someone might try to alter your behavior sounds objectionable. If so, bear in mind that every time you talk to other people, you are trying to alter their behavior at least in a slight way. Most experiments in psychology produce effects that are no more lasting than the effects of a conversation.

Still, some experiments do raise ethical issues. Psychologists are seriously concerned about ethical issues, both in the experiments they conduct with humans and those they conduct with animals.

Ethical Concerns in Experiments on Humans

Earlier in this chapter I discussed experiments on the effects of televised violence. If psychologists believed that watching violent programs on television would really transform viewers into murderers, then it would be unethical for them to conduct any experiment to find out for sure. Moreover, it would be unethical to perform any experimental procedure likely to cause serious depression, alcohol abuse, nightmares, suicidal tendencies, or other undesirable outcomes. It is also unethical to conduct any experiment that will cause the subject significant pain or embarrassment, unless perhaps the subject agrees to take part in the experiment in return for some reward. In short, it is unethical to conduct an experiment with subjects who would have refused to participate had they known what was going to happen.

To maintain high ethical standards in the conduct of experiments, psychologists ask prospective subjects to give their **informed consent** before proceeding. When they post a sign-up sheet asking for volunteers for an experiment, or at the start of the experiment itself, they explain that the subjects will receive electrical shocks, or that they will be required to drink concentrated sugar water, or that they will be asked to do something else they may not want to do. If any subjects object to the procedure, they can simply withdraw. The rest of the informed subjects agree to participate in the experiment.

In addition, experiments conducted at any college or at any other reputable institution must first be approved by a Human Subjects Committee at that institution. Such a committee judges whether or not the proposed experiments are ethical. For example, a committee would not approve an experiment that called for administering large doses of cocaine—even if some of the subjects were eager to give their informed consent. The committee also judges experiments in which the experimenters want to conceal certain procedures from the subjects. For example, suppose the experimenters plan to put subjects through a certain experience and then see whether they are more or less likely than others to obey instructions to pick up a live snake. If they were told in advance that they would be asked to pick up a snake, the experiment might be ruined. (Perhaps only people who liked to pick up snakes would agree to participate.) The committee would either approve or disapprove such an experiment.

Finally, the American Psychological Association, or APA (1982), publishes a booklet detailing the ethical treatment of volunteers in experiments. Any member who disregards the principles may be censured or expelled by the APA.

Ethical Concerns in Experiments on Animals

About 7–8% of all published studies in psychology use animals (Gallup & Suarez, 1980). Although some investigations require human subjects—for example, the effects of televised violence—psychologists can use animals to test the effects of certain drugs, prolonged sleeplessness, or brain damage (Figure 2.18).

Some people oppose the use of animals in any psychological experiment, regardless of the circumstances. Others urge that animals be used only in experiments that involve harmless procedures and that have a strong likelihood of generating important results. Those who defend the use of animals in research make the following replies:

- We certainly agree that animals should not be mistreated, but we also recognize "the right of the incurably ill to hope for cures or relief from suffering through research using animals" (Feeney, 1987). If animal experiments were abolished, certain areas of research, such as brain research, would be almost impossible to pursue.

- Research on animals has produced a wealth of valuable information leading to the development of antianxiety drugs, new methods of treating pain and depression, an understanding of how certain drugs impair the development of the fetus, insight into the effects of old age on memory, and methods of helping people to overcome neuromuscular disorders (N. E. Miller, 1985).

- Extremely painful experiments on animals are rare (Coile & Miller, 1984). Although they undeniably occur, their frequency has been greatly exaggerated.

- Although studies of plants, experiments with tissue cultures, and computer simulations provide useful information on a few issues, they are not acceptable substitutes for research on animals (Gallup & Suarez, 1985).

The debate continues. Meanwhile, colleges and other research institutions maintain Laboratory Animal Care Committees to ensure that laboratory animals are treated humanely, that their pain and discomfort are kept to a minimum, and that experimenters consider alternatives before they impose potentially painful procedures on animals. Because such committees have to deal with competing values, their decisions are never beyond dispute. How can anyone determine whether the value of the experimental results (which are hard to predict) will outweigh the pain the animals endure (which is hard

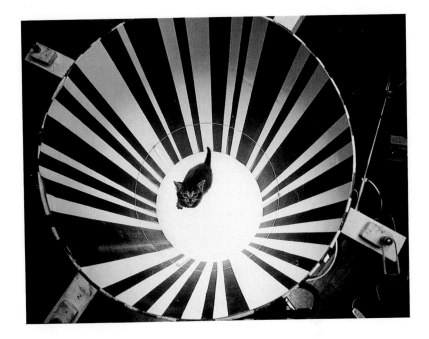

FIGURE 2.18

Although many people object to using animals in experiments, we have all benefited directly or indirectly from such experiments. To halt them now could handicap research on AIDS, Alzheimer's disease, and brain damage.

to measure)? As is often the case with ethical decisions, reasonable arguments can be raised on both sides of the question, and no compromise is fully satisfactory.

SUMMARY

1. Psychologists must begin any study by defining their terms. For many purposes they prefer operational definitions, which state how to measure a phenomenon or how to produce it. (page 29)

2. Because psychologists hope to draw conclusions that apply to a large population and not just to the small sample they have studied, they try to select a sample that resembles the total population. They may select either a representative sample or a random sample. (page 30)

3. To ensure objectivity, investigators use blind observers—observers who do not know how each individual has been treated or what results are expected. In a double-blind study, neither the observer nor the subjects know who has received which treatment. (page 31)

4. A case history is a detailed research study of a single individual. (page 32)

5. A survey is a report of people's answers to a questionnaire. Slight changes in the wording of a question may

significantly alter the responses people give. We should not assume that everyone who answers a question has a solid basis for an opinion. (page 32)

6. A correlational study is a study of the relationship between variables that are outside the investigator's control. The strength of the relationship is measured by a correlation coefficient. (page 33)

7. Beware of illusory correlations—relationships that people think they observe between variables after casual observation. (page 36)

8. A correlational study does not uncover cause-and-effect relationships, but an experiment can. (page 36)

9. Experiments are studies in which the investigator manipulates one variable to determine its effect on another variable. The manipulated variable is the independent variable. The one the experimenter measures to see how it was affected is the dependent variable. (page 37)

10. An experimenter should use random assignment of individuals in forming experimental and control groups.

That is, all individuals should have an equal probability of being chosen for the experimental group. (page 38)

11. Demand characteristics, the Hawthorne effect, or differential survival sometimes distort the results of an experiment. (page 40)

12. Experimentation on either humans or animals raises ethical questions. Psychologists try to minimize risk to their subjects, but they cannot avoid making difficult ethical decisions. (page 42)

SUGGESTION FOR FURTHER READING

Stanovich, K. E. (1986). *How to think straight about psychology.* Glenview, IL: Scott, Foresman. An excellent treatment of how to evaluate evidence in psychology and how to avoid pitfalls.

MEASURING AND REPORTING RESULTS

After psychologists have conducted a study, how can they determine whether the results are convincing or whether they demonstrate nothing but random fluctuations?

Some time ago, a television program about the alleged dangers of playing the game Dungeons and Dragons reported 28 known cases of D&D players who had committed suicide. Alarming, right?

Not necessarily. At least 3 million young people play the game regularly. The reported suicide rate among D&D players—28 per 3 million—is considerably *less* than the suicide rate among teenagers in general.

So do the results mean that playing D&D *prevents* suicide? Hardly. The 28 reported cases are probably not a complete count of all suicides by D&D players. Besides, the correlation between playing D&D and committing suicide, regardless of its direction and magnitude, could not possibly tell us about cause and effect.

Then what conclusion should we draw from these data? *None at all.* Sometimes, as in this case, the data are meaningless because of how they were collected. Even when the data are potentially meaningful, people sometimes present them in a confusing or misleading manner. Let's consider some of the proper ways of analyzing and interpreting results.

DESCRIPTIVE STATISTICS

To explain the meaning of a study, an investigator must summarize its results in some orderly fashion. When a researcher observes the behavior of 100 people, we have no interest in hearing all the details about every person observed. We want to know what the researcher found in general, on the average. We might also want to know whether most people were similar to the average or whether they varied a great deal. An investigator presents the answers to those questions through **descriptive statistics**, which are mathematical summaries of results, such as measures of the central score and the amount of variation. The correlation coefficient, discussed earlier in this chapter, is a descriptive statistic. (Descriptive statistics differ from inferential statistics, which I shall discuss later.)

Measurements of the Central Score: Mean, Median, and Mode

There are three ways of representing the average or the middle score: mean, median, and mode. The **mean** is the sum of all the scores divided by the number of scores. (Most people have the mean in mind when they say "average.") For example, the mean of 2, 10, and 3 is $15 \div 3 = 5$. The mean is a useful term, especially if we are dealing with a more or less normal distribution of scores, as shown in Figure 2.19a. A **normal distribution** (or normal curve) is a symmetrical distribution in which each of many independent factors produces a small amount of variation in whatever we are measuring. For example, suppose we measure how long various people take to memorize a poem. Their times might form an approximately normal distribution. If so, then more people will have times close to the mean than far from it and about as many people will have times below the mean as above it.

When the actual measurements in a study do not follow the normal distribution, such as in Figure 2.19b, the mean is less useful as an indication of what happened. Suppose 19 people memorize the poem in about 15 minutes each. But a 20th person falls asleep in the middle of the task and takes 8 hours to finish. Now the mean for the group of 20 is almost 40 minutes.

"Why not just ignore the one extreme individual?" you might ask. That could be a reasonable decision in this case, but not in others. Suppose most people solve a certain math problem in 2 to 4 minutes, a few solve it in a little more time, and about 20% fail to solve it at all, as shown in Figure 2.20. (Note that these scores definitely do not fall into the normal distribution.) While we might feel justified in ignoring the results of a single extreme

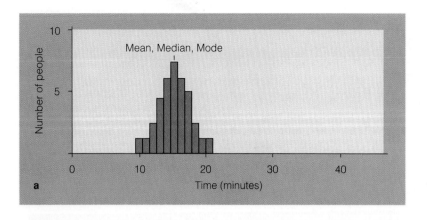

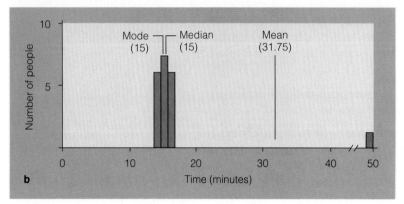

FIGURE 2.19

(a) A normal distribution. (b) The inclusion of one extreme score distorts the normal distribution and decreases the usefulness of the mean as a descriptive term.

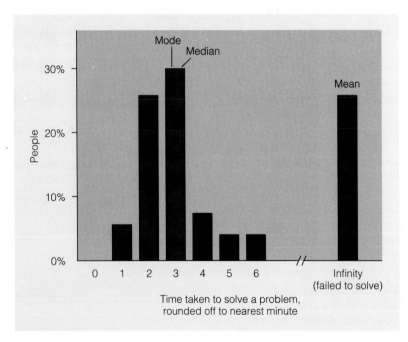

FIGURE 2.20

When a few scores are far from the rest of the distribution, the mean can be uninformative and misleading. In such cases the median (middle value) is more meaningful.

individual, we can hardly ignore 20%. If we assign a time of *infinity* to those who failed to solve the problem, the mean also comes to infinity. If we assign some arbitrary number to those who didn't solve the problem, then the resulting mean will be misleading.

When the distribution of scores in a study is far from the normal distribution, the mean may be a misleading indication of what happened. In such a case the median is a more reliable indication. To determine the **median**, we arrange all the scores in order from the highest score to the lowest score. The middle score is the median. For example, if the scores are 2, 10, and 3, the median is 3. In Figure 2.20 the median score is 3 minutes.

The third way to represent the central score is the **mode**, the score that occurs most frequently. For example, in the distribution of scores 2, 2, 3, 4, and 10, the mode is 2. The mode is not particularly useful for most purposes. Here is a case, however, in which we might want to use the mode: The bar graphs in Figure 2.21 illustrate how many times people attend religious services per month in two hypothetical communities. Here the mean and the median are useless for comparison purposes, because for both populations the mean happens to be 2.4 and the median is 2. It is of greater interest to note that the mode (the most common response) is zero times per month in one population and four times per month in the other.

Concept Check

7a. For the following distribution of scores, determine the mean, the median, and the mode: 5, 2, 2, 2, 8, 3, 1, 6, 7.
b. Determine the mean, median, and mode for this distribution: 5, 2, 2, 2, 35, 3, 1, 6, 7.
(Check your answers on page 51.)

Measures of Variation

Figure 2.22 shows two distributions of scores. Suppose they represent scores on two tests of knowledge about introductory psychology. Both tests have the same mean, median, and mode. But if you had a score of 80, then the meaning of that score would be different for the two tests. Such a score on the first test is above average, but nothing unusual. The same score on the second test would put you in the top 1% of your class.

To describe the difference between Figure 2.22a and b, we need a measurement of the variation (or spread) around the mean. The simplest such measurement is the **range** of a distribution, a statement of the highest and lowest scores. Thus the range in

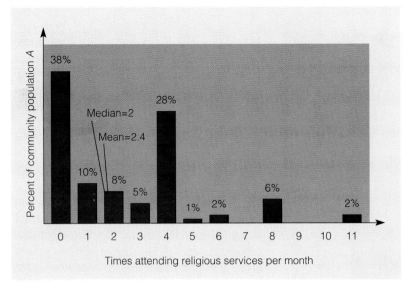

a

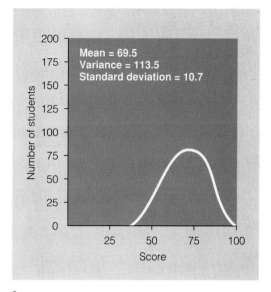

a

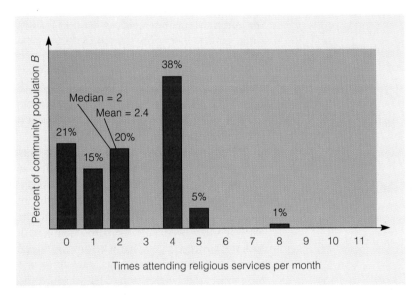

b

FIGURE 2.21

These two charts, which lack normal distributions, have the same median and mean. Here the difference in modes can be informative.

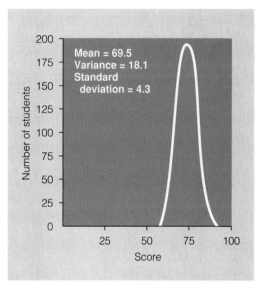

b

FIGURE 2.22

These two distributions of test scores have the same mean but different variances and different standard deviations.

Figure 2.22a is 39 to 100 and in Figure 2.22b it is 58 to 92.

The range is simple but not very useful, because it takes account of only two scores. For many purposes we would like to know whether nearly all the scores are clustered close to the mean or whether they are more diverse. One measure of variation that has important uses in statistics is the **standard deviation**, a measurement of the amount of variation of scores in a normal distribution. Figure 2.23 shows the relationship of the standard deviation to the mean and to the normal distribution. The stan-

dard deviation has this useful property: If we know that a certain score is a certain number of standard deviations above or below the mean, then we can consult statistical tables to determine what percentage of other scores it exceeds. For example, 68% of all the scores in a normal distribution fall within one standard deviation of the mean; 96% fall within two standard deviations. (The appendix at the end of this chapter explains how to calculate the standard deviation.)

For illustration, suppose the mean score on the verbal part of the Scholastic Aptitude Test is 500

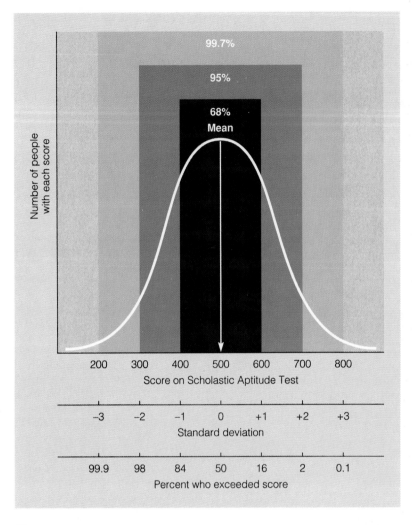

FIGURE 2.23

In a normal distribution, the amount of variation of scores from the mean can be measured in standard deviations.

but the standard deviation is 20. Compared to the other students in your class, did your performance improve, deteriorate, or stay the same? (Check your answer on page 51.)

EVALUATING RESULTS: INFERENTIAL STATISTICS

Suppose we conduct a study comparing the performances of first-graders and second-graders on a set of arithmetic problems. We would probably report the means and standard deviations for each group. But we are interested in not just the performances of the two groups but also the performances of first-graders and second-graders in general. When we talk about the entire population, we use **inferential statistics**, which are statements about large groups based on inferences from small samples.

There are, for example, procedures for estimating how much the mean of a sample differs from the mean of the total population. Take two extreme examples: First, physicians have reported that the mean body temperature of healthy humans is 37° C. That mean is based on measurements from so many people who differ from one another so slightly that we can be confident that we have determined the true mean with an error of no more than a small fraction of a degree. On the other extreme, one investigator measured how long it took three sheep to find their way through a maze once. One sheep took less than an hour; the second took about three hours; the third fell asleep repeatedly and took all day. We could determine a mean for the three sheep, but the probable error of the mean would be large.

The most common use of inferential statistics is to decide whether the difference observed between two groups is probably real or probably accidental. Suppose, for example, we discover that the members of an experimental group who watched a series of violent television programs committed a mean of 0.38 aggressive acts per person per day, while the members of a control group who did not watch violent programs committed a mean of 0.29 aggressive acts. Should we conclude that watching violent programs increases aggressive behavior? Or is it likely that two groups chosen at random might differ by 0.09 simply by accident?

To answer that question, we use statistical techniques. Different formulas are used for different purposes. The appendix at the end of this chapter gives an example of a statistical test. A statistical test determines the probability that a study may pro-

and the standard deviation is 100. (That was the original intention of the test's designers, although the results have not always turned out that way.) A score of 700 would be two standard deviations above the mean. Since 96% of all scores fall within two standard deviations of the mean, only 4% of all scores are more extreme than 700. Half of those (2%) are above 700; the other 2% are more extreme *on the other end* of the distribution—that is, less than 300. So a score of 700 would exceed the scores of 98% of all students taking the test.

Concept Check

8. *On your first psychology test, you get a score of 80. The mean for the class is 70 and the standard deviation is 5. On the second test, you get a score of 90. This time the mean for the class is again 70*

duce, *just by accident,* results as impressive as those that were actually obtained. If that probability is *low*, the results can be taken seriously.

In our example, we want to know how likely it is that two groups we chose at random might differ by accident in their level of aggressiveness by at least 0.38 to 0.29. That probability depends on several factors (see Figure 2.24):

1. The larger the difference between two groups, the less likely it is that the difference has arisen by accident.

2. Other things being equal, the more subjects each group has, the less likely that any difference observed between the groups is just an accident. If there are five subjects in the experimental group and five in the control group, the probability is fairly high that one group will accidentally include more aggressive people than the other. But if each group includes a thousand subjects, then the probability is slight that one group will accidentally include a much higher proportion of aggressive people than the other contains.

3. The more consistently the members of each group behave, the less likely it is that any difference between the groups has arisen through accident. For example, if almost everyone in the experimental group is found to commit about 0.38 aggressive acts per day, and if almost everyone in the control group is found to commit about 0.29 aggressive acts per day, then the difference between the two groups is probably not the result of accident. We would draw a different conclusion if we found that one extremely aggressive individual had single-handedly raised the mean for the experimental group.

To summarize the results of a statistical test, we use a value known as *p*. That value represents the probability of accidentally getting results at least as impressive as the reported results. If the value of *p* is low, the results are probably not due to accident. Psychologists usually regard a result as significant if the value of *p* is less than 5%, expressed as *p* < *.05*. A more cautious experimenter might insist on a stricter standard, such as *p* < .01. In any case, if the *p* value is lower than the standard chosen, then an experiment's results are said to be statistically significant. If the *p* value is higher than the standard chosen, the results are inconclusive.

Concept Check

9. *You compare the performance of women and men on 20 tasks. On one of the tasks, you find a significant difference (p < .01). How could you check against the possibility that this apparent difference is the result of accident? (Check your answer on page 51.)*

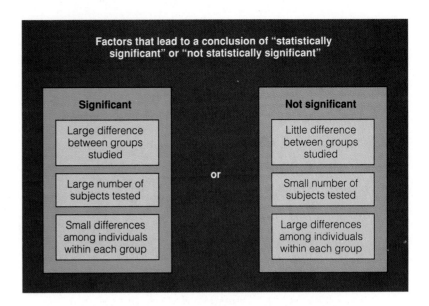

Factors that lead to a conclusion of "statistically significant" or "not statistically significant"

Significant		Not significant
Large difference between groups studied		Little difference between groups studied
Large number of subjects tested	or	Small number of subjects tested
Small differences among individuals within each group		Large differences among individuals within each group

FIGURE 2.24

We cannot draw conclusions from data until they are shown to be "statistically significant," which is why raw data must be subjected to appropriate statistical procedures. The appendix to this chapter describes some of these procedures.

Finding statistically significant results is only the first step toward drawing a conclusion. To say that an experiment has **statistically significant results** means only that the probability is low (though still greater than zero) that the effect arose by chance. The question remains, if not by chance, then what causes the difference? At that point psychologists call upon all their knowledge to try to determine the most likely interpretation of the results.

SUMMARY

1. Psychologists rely on descriptive statistics to summarize their results. Descriptive statistics include measures of central score, amount of variation, and correlation. (page 45)

2. One way of presenting the central score of a distribution is the mean, determined by adding all the scores and dividing by the number of individuals. Another way is the median, which is the score in the middle after all the scores have been arranged from highest to lowest. The mode is the score that occurs most frequently. (page 45)

3. To indicate whether most scores are clustered close to the mean or whether they are spread out, psychologists report the range of scores or the standard deviation. If we know that a given score is a certain number of standard deviations above or below the mean, then we can determine what percentage of other scores it exceeds. (page 46)

4. Inferential statistics are attempts to deduce the properties of a large population based on the results from a small sample. (page 48)

5. The most common use of inferential statistics is to calculate the probability that a given research result could

have arisen by chance. That probability is low if the difference between two groups is large, if the variability within each group is small, and if the number of individuals in each group is large. (page 48)

6. When psychologists say "$p < .05$," they mean that the probability that accidental fluctuations could produce the kind of results they obtained is less than 5%. They generally set a standard of 5% or less. If the results meet that standard, then they are said to be statistically significant. (page 49)

SUGGESTION FOR FURTHER READING

Agnew, N. M., & Pyke, S. W. (1987). *The science game* (4th ed.). Englewood Cliffs, NJ: Prentice-Hall. A discussion of all aspects of research, including both methods of conducting research and statistical analysis of results.

TERMS TO REMEMBER

blind observer an observer who does not know which subjects are in which group and what results are expected

case history a thorough description of a single individual, including information on both past experiences and current behavior

control group the group that is subjected to the same procedures as the experimental group *except* for the treatment that is being tested

correlation a measure of the relationship between two variables, neither of which is controlled by the investigator

correlation coefficient a mathematical estimate of the relationship between two variables, ranging from +1 (perfect positive relationship) to 0 (no linear relationship) to −1 (perfect negative relationship)

demand characteristics cues that reveal to the participants what results the experimenter expects

dependent variable the variable the experimenter measures to see how changes in the independent variable affect it

descriptive statistics mathematical summaries of results, such as measures of the central score and the amount of variation

differential survival the tendency for some people to remain in an experiment longer than others

double-blind study a study in which neither the observer nor the subjects know which subjects received which treatment

experimental group the group that receives the treatment that an experiment is designed to test

extrasensory perception (ESP) the alleged ability of certain people to obtain information without using any sense organ and without receiving any form of energy

falsifiable capable of being contradicted by imaginable evidence

Hawthorne effect the tendency for people's performance to improve not because of the independent variable but simply because they know a change has occurred in some procedure or because they know they are being observed

hypothesis a testable prediction of what will happen under certain conditions

illusory correlation an apparent relationship between two variables based on casual observation, even though the variables are actually unrelated

independent variable the variable the experimenter manipulates to see how it affects the dependent variable

inferential statistics statements about large groups based on inferences from small samples

informed consent a subject's agreement to take part in an experiment after being informed about what will happen

mean the sum of all the scores reported in a study divided by the number of scores

median the middle score in a list of scores arranged from highest to lowest

mode the score that occurs most frequently in a distribution of scores

negative correlation a relationship in which increases in one variable are associated with decreases in another variable

normal distribution a symmetrical frequency of scores produced by many factors, each of which produces small, random variations

operational definition a definition that specifies the procedures used to measure some variable or to produce some phenomenon

$p < .05$ an expression meaning that the probability of accidentally getting results equal to the reported results is less than 5%

parsimony literally, stinginess; the avoidance of new theoretical assumptions

placebo an inactive pill that has no known biological effect on the subjects in an experiment

positive correlation a relationship in which increases in one variable are associated with increases in another variable

random assignment assignment of subjects to groups by means of some chance procedure, to make sure that every subject has the same probability as any other subject of being assigned to a given group

random sample a group of people picked in such a way that every individual in the population has an equal chance of being selected

range a statement of the highest and lowest scores in a distribution of scores

replicable result a result that can be repeated (at least approximately) by any competent investigator who follows the original procedure

representative sample a selection of the population chosen to match the overall population with regard to specific variables

selective reporting publishing results that match researchers' expectations and neglecting results that do not match expectations

sensory deprivation temporary reduction of visual, auditory, and other stimulation of senses

single-blind study a study in which either the observer or the subjects are unaware of which subjects received one treatment and which received another treatment

standard deviation a measurement of the amount of variation among scores in a normal distribution

statistically significant results results that have a low probability of having arisen by chance

survey a study of the prevalence of certain beliefs, attitudes, or behaviors based on people's responses to specific questions

theory a comprehensive explanation of natural phenomena that leads to accurate predictions

ANSWERS TO CONCEPT CHECKS

1. To evaluate Nostradamus's predictions, we would have to ask someone to tell us precisely what his predictions mean *before* the events they supposedly predict. Then we would ask someone else to estimate the likelihood of those events. For example, if it is said that Nostradamus predicted violence in the Middle East next year, or a hurricane in the Gulf of Mexico between the years 2001 and 2011, we would estimate almost a 100% probability of those events. If there were a prediction that visitors from outer space will land in Greenland in March 2003, we would estimate a very low probability. Eventually we would compare the accuracy of the predictions to our advance estimates of their probability. (page 26)

2. The score on an IQ test is an operational definition of intelligence. (Whether it is a particularly *good* definition is another question.) None of the other definitions tells us how to measure or produce intelligence. One example of an operational definition of hunger is "the number of hours since one's last meal." Another is "the amount of food the individual eats when a certain type of food is available." (page 30)

3. Clearly not. It is unlikely that the men at a given college are typical of men in general or that the women are typical of women in general. Moreover, a given college may have set higher admissions standards for one sex than for the other, or it may have attracted mostly men who are interested in one major and mostly women who are interested in another. In that case, the men and women are almost certain to differ in ways that have no direct relationship to being male or female. (page 31)

4. The -0.75 correlation indicates a stronger relationship—that is, a greater accuracy of predicting one variable based on measurements of the other. A negative correlation is just as useful as a positive one. (page 36)

5. The independent variable is the frequency of tests during the semester. The dependent variable is the students' performance on the final exam. (page 38)

6. (a) Hawthorne effect. A change, perhaps any change, improves performance. (b) Differential survival. The least satisfied teachers do not spend 15 years at the school. (c) Demand characteristics. Telling people who sponsored the survey suggests they give answers favoring that sponsor. (d) Differential survival. Perhaps the more intelligent people were more likely to survive to age 80. (page 42)

7. (a) Mean = 4; median = 3; mode = 2. (b) Mean = 7; median = 3; mode = 2. Note that changing just one number in the distribution from 8 to 35 greatly altered the mean without affecting the median or the mode. (page 46)

8. Even though your score went up from 80 on the first test to 90 on the second, your performance actually deteriorated in comparison to other students' scores. An 80 on the first test was two standard deviations above the mean, a score better than 98% of all other students. A 90 on the second test was only one standard deviation above the mean, a score that beats only 84% of other students. (page 48)

9. The more comparisons one makes, the greater is the probability that at least one of them will appear to be statistically significant, just by chance. One way to avoid this difficulty would be to set a higher standard of statistical significance, such as $p < .001$, and to discount any difference that does not meet this high standard. Another way would be to repeat the study on a second population to see whether the difference is replicable. (page 49)

ANSWERS TO OTHER QUESTIONS IN THE TEXT

The prophecies of Nostradamus (see page 26), as interpreted by Cheetham (1973), refer to the following: (1) the French Revolution, (2) the assassinations of John F. Kennedy and Robert F. Kennedy, (3) Polaris ballistic missiles shot from submarines, (4) Hitler's invasion of France, and (5) World War II.

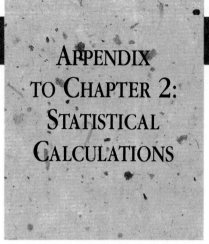

APPENDIX TO CHAPTER 2: STATISTICAL CALCULATIONS

This appendix shows how to calculate a few of the statistics mentioned in Chapter 2. It is intended primarily to satisfy your curiosity. Ask your instructor whether you should use this appendix for any other purpose.

Standard Deviation

To determine the standard deviation (SD):

1. Determine the mean of the scores.

2. Subtract the mean from each of the individual scores.

3. Square each of those results, add them together, and divide by the total number of scores.

The result is called the *variance*. The standard deviation is the square root of the variance. See Table 2.2 for examples.

TABLE 2.2

Individual Scores	Mean Minus the Individual Scores	Differences Squared
12.5	2.5	6.25
17.0	−2.0	4.00
11.0	4.0	16.00
14.5	0.5	0.25
16.0	−1.0	1.00
16.5	−1.5	2.25
17.5	−2.5	6.25
		36.00

Mean = 15.0
Variance = 36/7 = 5.143
Standard deviation = 2.268

Standard Error of the Mean

One way to infer whether the mean of a sample is close to the true mean of the population is to calculate the *standard error of the mean (SE)*. We calculate the standard error of the mean by dividing the standard deviation of the population by $\sqrt{N-1}$, where N is the number of individuals in the sample:

$$SE = SD/\sqrt{(N-1)}$$

If the sample includes many individuals who vary only slightly from one another, the standard deviation will be small, N will be large, and therefore the standard error of the mean will be small. On the other hand, if the sample includes few individuals who vary greatly from one another, the standard error will be large.

A Typical Statistical Test: The *t*-test

A number of statistical tests are available to suit different kinds of data and different kinds of experiments. For the simple case of comparing two groups, both of which show results that approximate the normal distribution, one of the most popular tests is the *t-test*. Assume that for two populations the means are $\bar{x}_1$ and $\bar{x}_2$, the numbers of individuals measured are n_1 and n_2, and the standard deviations are s_1 and s_2. We calculate t by using this formula:

$$t = \frac{(\bar{x}_2 - \bar{x}_1)\sqrt{n_1 \cdot n_2 \cdot (n_1 + n_2 - 2)}}{\sqrt{n_1 \cdot s_1^2 + n_2 \cdot s_2^2} \cdot \sqrt{n_1 + n_2}}$$

The larger the value of t, the more significant the difference between the two groups will be. The value of t will be high if the difference between the two means $(\bar{x}_2 - \bar{x}_1)$ is large, if the standard deviations (s_1 and s_2) are small relative to the means, and if the number of individuals is large. For example, if a group of 50 people has a mean of 81 and a standard deviation of 7, and a group of 150 people has a mean of 73 and a standard deviation of 9, then

$$t = \frac{(81 - 73)\sqrt{150 \cdot 50 \cdot 198}}{\sqrt{(150 \cdot 81 + 50 \cdot 49)}\sqrt{(200)}} = \frac{9748.8}{120.83 \times 14.14} = 5.71$$

The larger the value of t, the less likely it is that the results have arisen by accident. Statistics books contain tables that show the likelihood of a given t value. In this case, with 200 people in the two groups combined, a t value of 5.71 is highly significant ($p < .001$).

Correlation Coefficients

To determine the correlation coefficient, we designate one of the variables x and the other one y. We obtain pairs of measures, x_i and y_i. Then we use the following formula:

$$r = \frac{[(\Sigma x_i y_i) - n \cdot \bar{x} \cdot \bar{y}]}{n \cdot sx \cdot sy}$$

In this formula, $(\Sigma\, x_i\, y_i)$ is the sum of the products of x and y. For each pair of observations (x, y), we multiply x times y and then add together all the products. The term $n \cdot \bar{x} \cdot \bar{y}$ means n (the number of pairs) times the mean of x times the mean of y. The denominator, $n \cdot sx \cdot sy$, means n times the standard deviation of x times the standard deviation of y.

CHAPTER
3

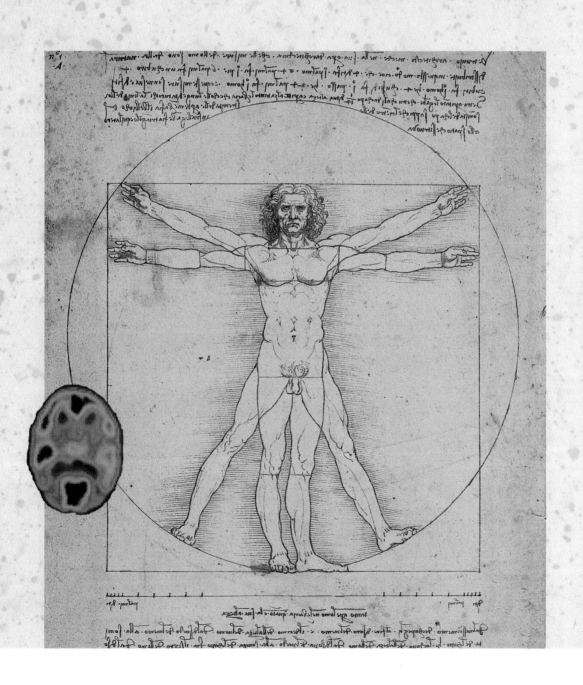

BIOLOGICAL PSYCHOLOGY

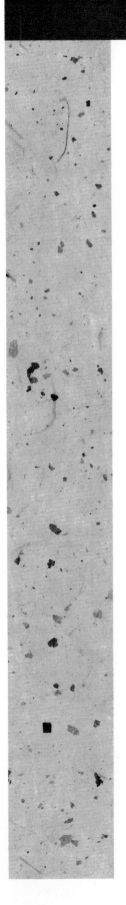

You have just found an ancient lamp in an old curiosity shop. You rub it and out pops the proverbial genie. The genie declares you will be granted a wish for almost anything you desire. There are just two restrictions: First, you cannot wish for more wishes. Second, you have to wish for something personal. You cannot wish for peace on earth, universal justice, or any other global change. What would you wish for? Think about it for a moment.

Some people say they would wish for millions of dollars. For someone deep in debt that might be a reasonable choice. But most people, especially bright young college students, are capable of earning a reasonable amount of money on their own. Why waste a magical opportunity on something you can get for yourself?

Other people say they would wish to live forever. But if you were to become very ill that might be a dreadful prospect. "Okay, then I'll wish to live forever and to remain healthy." Sorry, that's two wishes. (And it's no fair rephrasing your wish as "to live forever in good health." No matter how you put it, it's still two wishes.) You might wish for something of great value that you could not get otherwise—a particular power or skill, special knowledge, a certain opportunity or experience.

I know what I would wish for: the answer to the mind-body problem. I would like to know the relationship between the physical brain and conscious experience. How does consciousness arise? Why does it exist? Does the brain control conscious experience entirely, or does consciousness control the brain in some way? To understand that relationship would be to understand human experience at the deepest level and to understand a great deal about the nature of the universe.

In biological psychology, researchers study animal behavior, the anatomy of the brain, electrical currents in the nerves, and chemical interactions. But their most compelling interest is in the relationship between the mind and the brain.

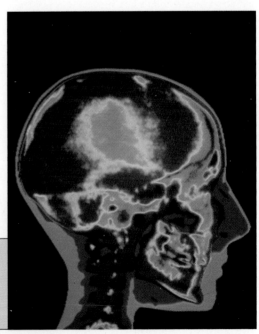

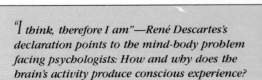

"I think, therefore I am"—René Descartes's declaration points to the mind-body problem facing psychologists: How and why does the brain's activity produce conscious experience?

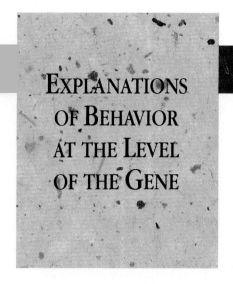

EXPLANATIONS OF BEHAVIOR AT THE LEVEL OF THE GENE

How does heredity affect behavior?
How does evolution influence behavior?

Everyone begins life as a fertilized egg. From then on, the way we develop is a combined product of our genes and our environment. If two people develop differently, that difference could be the result of a difference in their genes or in their environments or both.

In some cases a gene can make an enormous difference in behavior. One condition that apparently depends largely on one gene is **Alzheimer's disease**. People with a gene for Alzheimer's disease live a normal life until old age, when certain parts of the brain may gradually begin to deteriorate (Goldgaber, Lerman, McBride, Saffiotti, & Gajdusek, 1987; Tanzi et al., 1987). In the initial stages, people with Alzheimer's disease become forgetful. As a rule, they still remember their name and address and most of the other information they have known for years, but they have trouble remembering what they have just done and what has just happened. As the disease progresses, people grow confused, depressed, and unable to complete any train of thought (Schneck, Reisberg, & Ferris, 1982; Sinex & Myers, 1982). All that as the result of a single gene!

And yet the gene is not entirely responsible for the condition. Different people with the same gene have different outcomes. Whether they develop Alzheimer's disease at all, and how soon and how severely, apparently depends on many features in the environment. The same is true for many other genes of importance to psychology. Certain people have genes that make them more likely to become depressed, or to have an alcohol problem, or to develop numerous other conditions. None of those genes forces the person to develop such condi-

tions; the outcome always depends in part on everything else that happens in the person's life.

Often psychologists have trouble determining what behavior is due to the effects of genes and what to the effects of the environment. For example, are boys generally more aggressive than girls— at least in certain circumstances—because of certain genes that directly control aggressiveness? Or do they act more aggressively because parents and other people encourage such behavior more in boys than in girls?

And why do identical twins generally resemble each other in so many ways? Is it because they have the same genes or because they have shared the same environment?

These questions illustrate the *nature-nurture problem* mentioned in Chapter 1. It shows up in practically all fields of psychology. In this section I shall discuss what genes are, how they exert their effects, and how psychologists try to determine the role of genes in human behavior. I shall also discuss a few points about the evolution of behavior.

PRINCIPLES OF GENETICS

You may have studied genetics in a biology class, but here we will explore concepts of genetics from the viewpoint of psychology, as well as biology.

Nearly every cell of every plant and animal contains a *nucleus,* which in turn contains strands called **chromosomes** (see Figure 3.1). Chromosomes, which consist of the chemical **deoxyribonucleic acid,** or **DNA**, provide the chemical basis of heredity. Humans have 23 pairs of chromosomes; they receive one chromosome of each pair from the mother and one from the father (see Figure 3.2).

Sections along each chromosome are known as **genes**—DNA segments that exert an indirect control on development. The chemical structure of the DNA that makes up the chromosomes and genes controls the formation of another chemical, called *ribonucleic acid,* or *RNA,* which in turn controls the body's production of chemicals called *proteins.* Certain proteins serve as structural units in the body; others control chemical reactions that take place in the body. A change in the body's chemical reactions, especially a change that occurs early in development, can have a profound effect on an individual's structure and function. Figure 3.3 summarizes this chain of events.

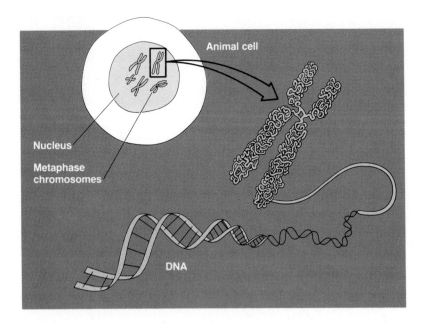

FIGURE 3.1

Chromosomes, which reside in the nucleus of animal cells, are made of helical DNA. During metaphase the DNA is very tightly coiled, but when the cell needs access to it during cell growth, the DNA unfolds into long, delicate strands.

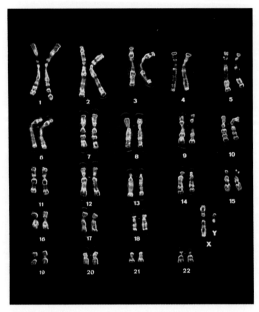

FIGURE 3.2

The nucleus of each human cell contains 46 chromosomes, 23 from the sperm and 23 from the ovum united in pairs.

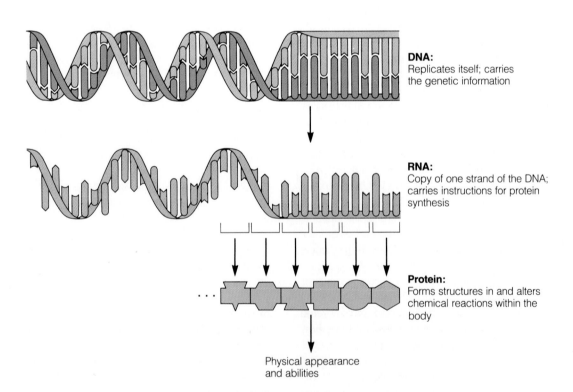

DNA:
Replicates itself; carries the genetic information

RNA:
Copy of one strand of the DNA; carries instructions for protein synthesis

Protein:
Forms structures in and alters chemical reactions within the body

Physical appearance and abilities

FIGURE 3.3

In the chemical chain of events that controls heredity, the information carried by DNA is transferred to RNA and then translated into proteins.

Occasionally a **mutation** (a random change) occurs in the structure of one of the genes, causing that gene to produce RNA molecules different from those the original gene produced. The ultimate result is an alteration in the appearance or activity of the organism. Most mutations are disadvantageous, although an occasional mutation will enable the body to produce proteins that are more advantageous than those it would otherwise have produced.

We can locate and identify certain genes by examining chromosomes under a microscope, though most genes cannot be located so readily. If we know that a particular gene is close to some other gene that we have already located on a chromosome, then we can use that other gene as a marker. For example, if you have a particular gene that we know your father and his mother also had, then you probably also have certain other genes that are close to that gene on their chromosomes. By using such reasoning, we can identify people who have a gene that predisposes them to a particular disease even before the symptoms have become evident (Gilliam et al., 1987).

The Transmission of Genes from One Generation to Another

Because people have two of each chromosome, they have two of each type of gene, one on each of the chromosomes. They have two genes for eye color, two for hair color, two for every characteristic. The two genes for hair color may be either the same or different. When both genes of a given pair are the same, the person is said to be **homozygous** (HO-mo-ZI-gus) for that gene. When the two genes are different, the person is **heterozygous** (HET-er-o-ZI-gus) for that gene (see Figure 3.4).

Certain genes are labeled **dominant genes** because they can mask the effects of other genes. Very few human behaviors depend on a single gene, but here is one example: The gene for the ability to curl the tongue lengthwise (Figure 3.5) is a dominant gene; all people who have that gene can curl their tongue, regardless of whether they are homozygous or heterozygous for that gene. The gene for the inability to curl the tongue is said to be a **recessive gene**. Only people who are homozygous for a recessive gene show its effects. In other words, if you cannot curl your tongue, you must be homozygous for the inability-to-curl gene (not exactly a serious handicap).

A person who is heterozygous for a particular gene will show the effects of the dominant gene, but may still pass the recessive gene to a son or a daughter. If parents who are heterozygous for the tongue-curling genes both pass the recessive gene

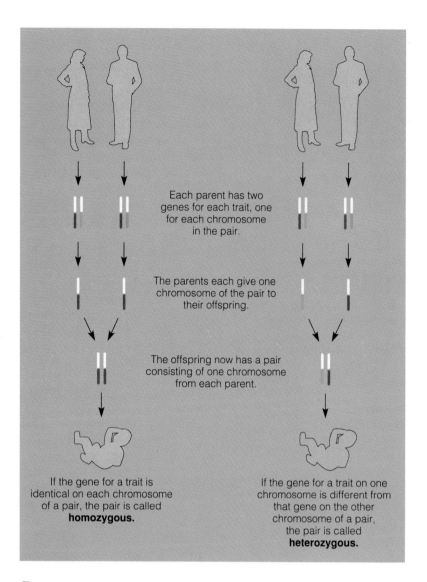

FIGURE 3.4

In a pair of homozygous chromosomes, the gene for a trait is identical on both chromosomes. In a heterozygous pair, the chromosomes contain different genes for a trait.

to a child, the child will not develop the ability to curl his or her tongue.

Concept Checks

***1.** The gene for tongue curling and the gene for the ability to taste the chemical phenylthiocarbamide, or PTC, are both dominant genes. (PTC tastes bitter to those who can taste it at all.) Suppose you can curl your tongue but cannot taste PTC. Are you homozygous or heterozygous for the tongue-curling gene, or is it impossible to say? Are you homozygous or heterozygous for the inability to taste PTC, or is it impossible to say? (Check your answers on page 97.)*
***2.** If two parents can curl their tongues but cannot taste PTC, what can you predict about their children? (Check your answer on page 97.)*

FIGURE 3.5

Curling the tongue lengthwise is a behavior that depends on a single gene.

FIGURE 3.6

An electron micrograph of X and Y chromosomes shows the difference in length. (From Ruch, 1984.)

Sex-Linked and Sex-Limited Genes

Some characteristics are more common in men; others are more common in women. Why? There can be many explanations, and a genetic explanation is not always a likely one. Still, genes do account for some of the differences, and it is valuable to know how genes could produce differences between the sexes.

One pair of human chromosomes are known as **sex chromosomes** because they determine whether a child will develop as a male or as a female. The other 22 pairs of chromosomes found in humans are known as **autosomal chromosomes**, from the Greek words *auto,* meaning "self," and *soma,* meaning "body." The autosomal chromosomes control the development of the body other than the genitals.

The sex chromosomes are of two types, known as X and Y (see Figure 3.6). A female has two **X chromosomes** in each cell; a male has one X chromosome and one **Y chromosome**. The female contributes one X chromosome to each child, and the male contributes either an X or a Y chromosome.

Genes located on the X chromosome are known as X-linked genes or as **sex-linked genes,** because the probability of their influence is linked to the sex of the individual. For example, the most common type of color blindness depends on a recessive gene the X chromosome carries. That gene is more likely to make its effects felt in males than in females. Why? Because every female has two X chromosomes, a female must be homozygous for this recessive gene in order for it to show its effects. A male, however, has only one X chromosome and consequently any gene on that chromosome exerts its effects; it cannot be overruled by a recessive gene on another chromosome.

Genetically controlled differences between the sexes do not necessarily depend on sex-linked genes. For example, adult men generally have deeper voices and more facial hair than women do. Those characteristics are not controlled by genes on the X or Y chromosome. They are controlled by genes that are present in women as well as men, but these genes are activated only in men. **Sex-limited genes** are those that affect one sex only or affect one sex more strongly than the other. The genes that control breast development in women are also sex-limited genes.

Why are men more likely to get into fistfights than women are? We do not have enough evidence to determine whether genes are responsible, but if the difference is because of their genes, the responsible genes are probably sex-limited genes rather than sex-linked genes. That is, males and females have the same genes that promote aggressive behavior, but male hormones activate those genes more strongly.

Concept Check

3. Suppose a color-blind man marries a woman who is homozygous for normal color vision. What sort of color vision will their offspring have? (Check your answer on page 97.)

THE EFFECTS OF GENES ON HUMAN BEHAVIOR: TYPES OF EVIDENCE

The ability to curl one's tongue lengthwise depends on the effects of a single gene and so does the ability to taste PTC. Most human behaviors, however, depend on the effects of several genes and on environmental influences as well. Researchers who study the effects of genes on human behavior concentrate on three sources of evidence: (1) the extent to which **monozygotic** (identical) **twins** resemble each other more closely than **dizygotic** (fraternal) **twins** do (see Figure 3.7); (2) the extent to which monozygotic twins who are separated at birth and reared in separate environments develop greater similarities than they would simply by chance; and (3) the extent to which adopted children resemble their adoptive relatives and their biological relatives.

Comparison of Monozygotic and Dizygotic Twins

Monozygotic twins resemble each other more closely than dizygotic twins in many behaviors, including anxiety, depression, aggression, assertiveness, shyness, and tendency toward alcoholism (Loehlin, Willerman, & Horn, 1988). They generally make similar scores on IQ tests, and they both do well or poorly on the same parts of the tests (Segal, 1985).

Something to Think About

One reason that monozygotic twins resemble each other more than dizygotic twins in, say, the tendency toward depression is that they have the same genes. Can you suggest another reason?

Monozygotic Twins Reared Apart

Only rarely are monozygotic twins separated at birth and reared in separate environments, but even those

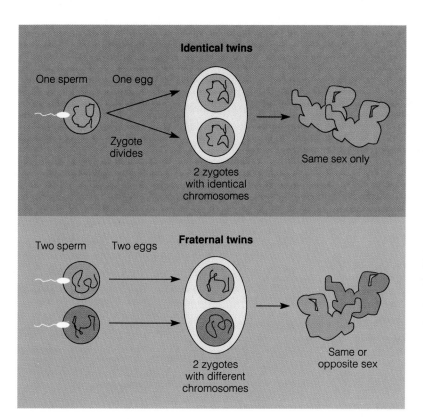

Identical twins

One sperm   One egg

Zygote divides

2 zygotes with identical chromosomes

Same sex only

Fraternal twins

Two sperm   Two eggs

2 zygotes with different chromosomes

Same or opposite sex

FIGURE 3.7

Identical (monozygotic) twins are produced from the same fertilized egg. Fraternal (dizygotic) twins grow from two eggs fertilized by two different sperm. The top photo shows two sets of identical twins. In the photo below are a pair of fraternal twins with their parents. The fact that the father is white and the mother is a woman of color led to the unusual occurrence of one dark-skinned twin and one lighter-skinned twin.

who are separated develop some striking similarities. One study revealed the following (Lykken, 1982):

- Twins who both wear seven rings on their fingers
- Twins who are both habitual gigglers
- Twins who both built a bench around a tree in their backyards
- Twins who are both extremely afraid of closed places, who are both compulsive counters of everything in sight, and who both walk into the ocean backward when they go swimming
- Twins who both amuse themselves by sneezing loudly in elevators, to watch how people react

We have no way of knowing how many of these similarities are the result of coincidence, but they surely are impressive. Dizygotic twins reared apart seldom show such similarities. (To see how many coincidences might arise, compare your history with that of some unrelated person your own age and see whether you discover any similarities.)

When identical twins Jim Lewis and Jim Springer first met, they discovered both had a wife named Betty, a son named James Allen, and a dog called Toy. A psychologist who studied their different backgrounds and similar interests and abilities said, "They were like bookends."

Adopted Children

Adopted children are more likely to resemble their biological parents than their adoptive parents. Several studies have shown that children of alcoholics, for example, are more likely to become alcoholics themselves even when they are adopted by people who are not alcoholics (Cloninger, Bohman, & Sigvardsson, 1981; Goodwin, 1978; Vaillant & Milofsky, 1982). The reason is probably genetic, although experience also contributes to alcoholic tendencies.

How Heredity Interacts with Environment

We sometimes speak of a gene for curly hair or a gene for the ability to curl the tongue. Actually, genes do not directly control hair curliness, tongue-curling ability, or any other observable characteristic. Rather, a particular gene facilitates a chemical reaction somewhere in the body. The effect of that reaction, and therefore the expression of the gene, depends on diet, on other chemical reactions in the body, and on environmental influences.

Because the ultimate effects of a gene depend on the environment, we distinguish between the genotype and the phenotype. The **genotype** is the entire set of genes within an individual; the **phenotype** is the actual appearance of that individual. For example, your genotype may contain only genes for straight hair, but, depending on your state of health, your diet, and your grooming habits, you may have straight hair, curly hair, or no hair at all.

In some cases, altering the environment counteracts the usual effects of a gene. For example, **phenylketonuria (PKU)** is an inherited condition in which a person lacks the chemical reactions that break down a substance called *phenylalanine* into other chemicals. On an ordinary diet, the affected person accumulates phenylalanine in the brain and becomes mentally retarded. However, an affected person who stays on a diet low in phenylalanine for at least the first 12 to 15 years of life does not become mentally retarded.

EVOLUTION

Our genes are a product of evolution. Evolution is more than a well-established theory supported by fossil evidence; it is a logical necessity based on what we know about genetics. The argument goes as follows:

1. The genes an organism inherits from its parents largely control its characteristics. In short, like begets like.

2. On occasion, genetic variations will cause an organism to differ from its parents. Such variations may arise from recombinations of genes (some from one parent and some from the other) or from mutations (random changes in the genes).

3. A particular gene may affect an individual's appearance, health, or behavior. If individuals with a certain gene reproduce more successfully than do those with other genes, they will spread their genes more widely. Over many generations, the frequency of that gene will increase while the frequency of others will decrease. Such changes in the gene frequencies of a species constitute **evolution**. Because we know that mutations sometimes occur in genes and that an occasional mutation may lead to greater success in reproduction, we can logically deduce that evolution *must* be taking place today. And we can infer that it must have occurred in the past as well, assuming that the principles of genetics and reproduction were the same then as they are now.

Animal and plant breeders discovered a long time ago that they could develop new strains through **artificial selection,** or selective breeding. By purposefully breeding only those animals with certain traits, breeders developed cocker spaniels, thoroughbred race horses, and chickens that lay enormous numbers of eggs. Charles Darwin's theory of evolution stated that **natural selection** can accomplish the same thing as selective breeding. If, in nature, individuals with certain genes reproduce more successfully than others do, then the species will come to resemble those individuals more and more as time passes.

Some people assume, mistakenly, that evolution means "the survival of the fittest." But what really matters in evolution is not survival but *reproduction* (see Figure 3.8). Someone who lives to the age of 100 without having a child has failed to spread his or her genes. Such a person has no more effect on the gene frequencies of the species than if he or she had died at birth. By contrast, a person who has five healthy children before dying at age 30 is a big success, evolutionarily speaking.

A gene that increases a person's chance of surviving long enough to reproduce will be favored over a gene that causes death in infancy. But genes that have no influence on the individual's survival may also be favored. For example, a gene that makes an individual more successful at attracting mates would certainly be favored, as would a gene that makes an individual more successful at protecting his or her offspring. (In fact, evolution would favor a gene that prompted individuals to risk their lives to defend their offspring, because it would help the offspring survive and eventually pass on the gene themselves.)

Concept Check

4. *Infertile worker bees are sisters of the queen bee, which lays all the eggs. In comparison with species in which all individuals are fertile, would you expect worker bees to be more likely or less likely to risk their lives to defend their sister? Would you expect a queen bee to be more or less likely than a worker bee to risk her life? (Check your answers on page 97.)*

ETHOLOGY AND COMPARATIVE PSYCHOLOGY

Psychologists learn about the genetics of behavior and the evolution of behavior largely through studies of animals. The study of animal behavior grew out of two separate pursuits: ethology and comparative psychology. **Ethology** is a branch of biology that studies animal behavior under natural or nearly natural conditions. Ethologists emphasize unlearned or **species-specific behaviors**—behaviors that are widespread in one animal species but not others. Species-specific behaviors are sometimes described as *instinctive,* although many investigators shun that term. (Many people use the term *instinct* as if it constituted an explanation. For example, they would say a mother squirrel takes care of her young because of her "maternal instinct." But simply naming what is happening is hardly an explanation.)

Comparative psychology is a branch of psychology that compares the behavior of various animal species. A comparative psychologist might study which species are best at localizing sounds or how species differ in their means of finding food. Comparative psychologists are more likely to study learned behaviors than species-specific behaviors. However, both ethologists and comparative psychologists study both types of behavior.

Both groups of scientists find that behavior is just as much a part of an animal's biology as its anatomy is. For example, the shortest possible definition of the family Columbidae (doves and pigeons) is "birds that can swallow with their heads down." All other birds must raise their heads to swallow. This behavior is a more consistent trait of doves and pigeons than is any single feature of their appearance.

The behavior of an animal, as with its anatomy, is adapted to its way of life. Consider the mating behavior of the kittiwake, a member of the gull

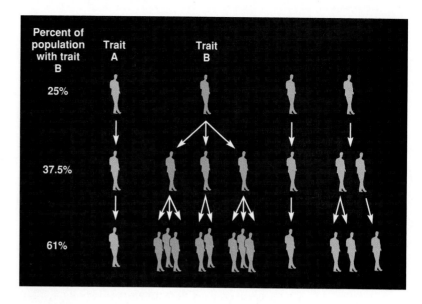

FIGURE 3.8

What's important in evolution is reproduction, not survival. Thus, in evolutionary terms, the person carrying trait B is the most successful.

FIGURE 3.9

The nesting behavior of kittiwakes is superbly adapted for their survival.

family (Tinbergen, 1958). Kittiwakes, unlike other gulls, nest on the ledges of steep cliffs (Figure 3.9). The ledge must be narrow, but not *too* narrow. Because there are just so many suitable ledges, kittiwakes fight ferociously to claim a territory. Herring gulls, which nest on the ground, rarely fight over territory, because for them one nesting site is about as good as any other. Kittiwakes use mud to build a hard nest with a barrier to prevent their eggs from rolling off the ledge. Herring gulls make no such effort. When kittiwake chicks hatch, they remain virtually motionless until they are old enough to fly. The ultimate cause of this behavior is clear: A chick that takes even a step or two may fall off

FIGURE 3.10

To ensure successful reproduction, male sticklebacks defend their territory against intruders and will even attack a model if the bottom of the model is painted red (the color of the male fish's belly during the mating season).

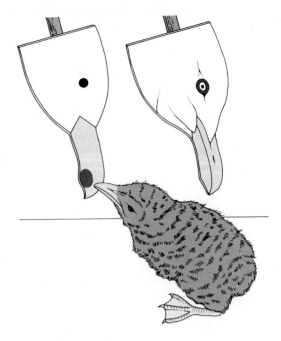

FIGURE 3.11

A herring gull chick will peck vigorously at a model of an adult's beak with a red spot near the tip but not at a "more realistic" model without a spot.

the ledge. Herring gull chicks, in contrast, begin to wander out of their nest long before they can fly.

Each of these kittiwake behaviors—fighting over territory, building secure nests, and remaining motionless—is well adapted to life on a narrow ledge. But have they been built into the animal by evolution, or are they learned anew by each individual? In the rare cases when kittiwakes nest on the ground, the chicks remain motionless anyway, even though they are in no danger of falling. When the egg of a gull species that does not nest on cliff ledges is placed in a kittiwake's nest, the kittiwakes accept the foreign egg and care for the chick after it hatches. But the chick invariably takes a few steps and falls to its death. Evidently some behavioral differences are a product of the evolution of each species rather than anything the individual learns.

SOCIOBIOLOGY

Sociobiology is a field that tries to relate the social behaviors of a species to its biology, particularly to its evolutionary history. According to sociobiologists, an animal interacts with others of its species in a particular way because doing so provides a survival or reproductive advantage. That is, behaving this way makes the animal more likely to spread its genes—or, to be more precise, because members of previous generations behaving this way succeeded in spreading *their* genes.

Animal Examples of Sociobiological Explanations

Sociobiologists try to understand how various social behaviors may have helped animals to survive and reproduce. Here are five examples (Tinbergen, 1958; Wilson, 1975):

- During the mating season, a male stickleback fish will attack anything with a red underside—even a piece of wood painted red underneath (see Figure 3.10). Why? Because during this season other male sticklebacks have a red belly. By driving other males out of its territory during the reproductive season, a male stickleback protects its reproductive opportunities. Over the evolutionary history of sticklebacks, those males that successfully defended their territory left more offspring than did those that did not.

- A herring gull chick will peck at any vertical sticklike object with a red spot near the tip (see Figure 3.11). Why? Because the parents' beaks have a red spot near the tip. A chick that pecks at red spots on vertical objects has a high probability of getting its parents to feed it.

- The largest males of the South American leaf fish build a nest and then try to attract females to deposit their eggs in it. Many of the smaller males, especially after being defeated in fights with larger males, change their appearance and behavior to resemble females. They enter the nests of the larger males and deposit their sperm, much as a female would deposit eggs. What is the reason for this unusual behavior? The smaller males are unable to defend a territory and attract females on their own. If they can fool a larger male into letting them deposit their sperm, however, some of those sperm might fertilize eggs when a female comes by.

- Lions generally live in groups made up of one adult male, several adult females, and their young. If a new male succeeds in driving off the old male, he is likely to kill all the young. Why? Female lions are not sexually receptive so long as they are nursing their young. By killing the young, the new male brings the females into sexual receptivity and increases the likelihood of spreading his genes.

- Starlings in flight flock tightly together when a hawk appears. Why? A hawk can descend on a lone starling at enormous speed and seize it with its talons. If a hawk descends on a dense flock, however, it may miss its prey and be jostled by the other birds, possibly sustaining a serious injury. The more tightly packed the flock, the less likely the hawk will attack.

Speculations on Human Sociobiology

Human social behavior also is partly the product of our evolutionary history. In principle that result is a logical necessity, yet citing precise examples is difficult because we are less certain about which human behaviors are strongly influenced by our genes and which ones are learned from our culture. Consider a couple of speculative, controversial examples:

- In most cultures throughout history, women have devoted more effort than men have to child care. Why? A sociobiologist might say the reason is that a woman knows for certain that a child is genetically her own. Because the man is less certain, excessive devotion to child care might serve to spread some other man's genes. Therefore evolution has more strongly favored genes that promote child care in women than in men. Perhaps humans have some genes for child care that are partly sex limited. Perhaps. However, human cultures begin teaching girls from an early age that they should want to take care of young children. The sociobiological explanation is at best only part of the story; at worst, it may be

Sociobiologists speculate that girls play with dolls because their genes program such action. A more plausible explanation: They simply imitate their mothers' behavior.

a means of maintaining the status quo and of telling women that they are biologically obligated to enjoy child care.

- Men are more likely than women are to seek multiple sexual partners. A sociobiological interpretation is that a man who impregnates several women is spreading his genes far and wide. A woman gains no such advantage in taking multiple sexual partners. Moreover, if she were to do so, she might have trouble getting any one of them to help her rear her children. Again, the sociobiological explanation sounds reasonable, but again it is difficult to separate the role of biology from the contributions of early experiences and cultural customs. As we shall see in Chapter 11, sexual customs vary significantly from one culture to another.

What then is the relationship between human behavior and human biology? Like other animals, we are the product of our evolutionary history. We must spend effort eating, drinking, regulating our body temperature, and dealing with other biological functions. We react to others of our species with interest. We react with fear to loud noises and other intense stimuli, even before we have learned what those stimuli mean. Our capacities for behavior are a product of our evolutionary history. But the actual behaviors are also a product of our experiences, including what we learn from our culture.

SUMMARY

1. Heredity may determine which people are most likely to develop a certain condition, although the actual outcome depends on the environment as well. (page 57)

2. Genes, which are segments of chromosomes, control heredity. Because chromosomes come in pairs, every person has two of each gene, one received from the father and one from the mother. (page 57)

3. A dominant gene exerts its effects even in people who have only one dominant gene. People must have two of a recessive gene, one on each chromosome, in order to show its effects. (page 59)

4. Genes on the X chromosome are sex linked. A sex-linked recessive will show its effects more frequently in males than in females. A sex-limited gene may be present in both sexes, but it exerts its effects more strongly in one than in the other. (page 60)

5. Most important human behaviors depend on many genes. We determine the contribution of genes by seeing whether monozygotic twins resemble each other more than dizygotic twins do, by comparing monozygotic twins reared in separate environments, and by examining how adopted children resemble their biological parents and their adoptive parents. (page 60)

6. Evolution by natural selection is a logical necessity, given the principles of heredity and the fact that individuals with certain genes leave more offspring than do individuals with other genes. (page 62)

7. Ethologists and comparative psychologists study animal behavior and try to understand how it evolved. (page 63)

8. Sociobiologists try to explain social behaviors in terms of the survival and reproductive advantages of those behaviors. Human social behaviors are difficult to interpret in those terms, however, because of the strong influence of tradition and culture. (page 64)

SUGGESTIONS FOR FURTHER READING

Crawford, C. B. (1989). The theory of evolution: Of what value to psychology? *Journal of Comparative Psychology, 103,* 4–22. Includes some thought-provoking suggestions about the evolution of human behavior.

Lorenz, K. (1949). *King Solomon's ring.* New York: Crowell. Delightful observations on animal behavior.

Tinbergen, N. (1958). *Curious naturalists.* New York: Basic Books. One of the best books for stimulating interest in animal behavior.

Explanations of Behavior at the Level of the Neuron

Is the brain the mind?
Can we explain our experiences and our behavior in terms of the actions of single cells in the nervous system?

Your brain, which controls everything you do, is composed of cells. Does this mean that every one of your experiences—every sight, every sound, every thought—represents the activity of cells in your brain?

A highly productive strategy in science is **reductionism**—the attempt to explain complex phenomena by reducing them to combinations of simpler components. Biologists explain breathing, blood circulation, and metabolism in terms of chemical reactions and physical forces. Chemists explain chemical reactions in terms of the properties of the 92 naturally occurring elements. Physicists explain the structure of the atom and the interactions among atoms in terms of a few fundamental forces.

Does reductionism apply to psychology? Can we explain human behavior and experience in terms of chemical and electrical events in the brain? Here we deal with attempts to answer those questions.

THE CELLS OF THE NERVOUS SYSTEM

The central nervous system—the brain and the spinal cord—contains two kinds of cells: neurons (NOO-rons) and glia (GLEE-uh). The glia are about one tenth the size of neurons but about ten times more numerous; thus the two kinds of cells occupy about the same total space. **Neurons**, or nerve cells, convey information from one part of the body to another by conducting electrochemical impulses. **Glia** have a variety of support functions, such as insulating the neurons and removing waste materials (such as dead cells) from the brain. They do not convey information.

Estimates of the number of neurons in the human central nervous system range from 30 billion to 100 billion (Black et al., 1984; Szentágothai, 1983). Counting them accurately is difficult because many of them are extremely small. Each neuron is connected to many others—some to well over a thousand. In other words, the total number of connections is enormous. Most neurons are almost constantly active. To understand the nervous system, we must understand the properties of both the individual neurons and the connections among them.

The basic function of any neuron is to receive information, process it in some way, and transmit impulses to other neurons, glands, or muscles. **Sensory neurons** convey information about lights, sounds, and other information from the sense organs to the central nervous system; **motor neurons** convey impulses from the central nervous system to the muscles and glands; **interneurons** simply convey information from one neuron to another. Neurons have a variety of shapes, depending on whether they receive information from a few sources or from many and whether they send impulses over a short distance or over a long distance (see Figure 3.12).

A neuron consists of three parts—a cell body, dendrites, and an axon (Figure 3.13a). The **cell body** contains the nucleus of the cell. The **dendrites** (from a Greek word meaning *tree*) are branching structures, usually short; they receive transmissions from other neurons. The **axon** is a single, long, thin, straight fiber with branches near its tip. As a rule, the axon transmits information to other cells; the tip of the axon releases a chemical that either excites or inhibits the dendrites or the cell body of another neuron.

The structure of the brain, unlike the structure of a computer, is not fixed throughout its life. Although the human brain gains no additional neurons after early infancy, the existing neurons frequently grow new branches of their axons and dendrites and retract other branches (Purves & Hadley, 1985). For example, an enriched social environment leads to increased branching of the dendrites. Rats kept in large cages with other rats and with a variety of objects to explore develop a wider pat-

FIGURE 3.12

The neurons in (a) and (b) receive input from many sources, the neuron in (c) from only a few sources, and the neuron in (d) from an intermediate number of sources. The neurons in (e) are sensory neurons, which carry messages from sensory receptors to the brain or spinal cord. Their cell bodies are on short stalks attached to long fibers traveling from the skin's touch receptors to the spinal cord. The axons are coded blue for easy identification. (Part b courtesy of Richard Coss.)

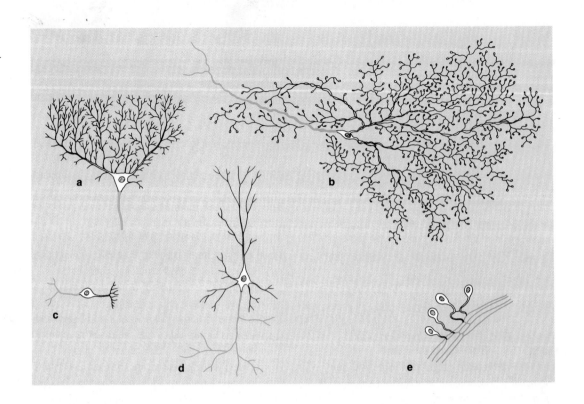

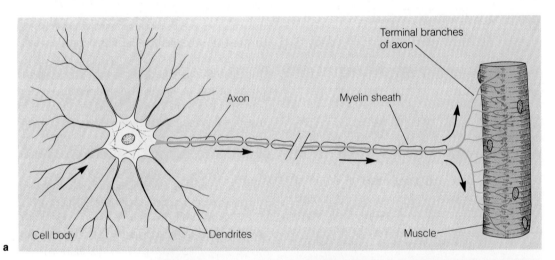

FIGURE 3.13

(a) The generalized structure of a motor neuron shows the dendrites, the branching structures that receive transmissions from other neurons; and the axon, a single, long, thin, straight fiber with branches near its tip. Axons, which range in length from 1 millimeter to more than a meter, carry information toward other cells. (b) A photomicrograph of a neuron.

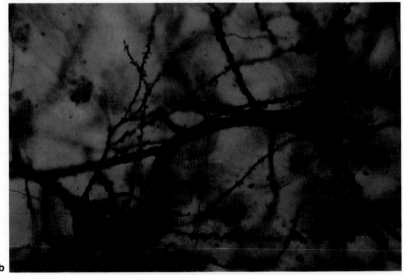

tern of dendritic branching than do rats kept in individual cages (Camel, Withers, & Greenough, 1986; Greenough, 1975). The increased branching enables each dendrite to integrate information from a greater number of sources. Animals with increased dendritic branching tend to perform better on a variety of learning and memory tasks.

Some environmental factors have the opposite effect: They *decrease* dendritic branching. For example, when rats and mice are exposed to alcohol over a period of time, their dendrites retract and respond to fewer incoming messages than before their exposure to alcohol (Riley & Walker, 1978; West, Hodges, & Black, 1981).

In humans, the dendritic branching changes with advancing age. Although the amount and type of change differ from person to person, nearly all people gradually lose some neurons as they grow older. In people who remain healthy and alert, the surviving neurons *increase* their branching pattern and tend to compensate for the neurons that have been lost. Each neuron that survives makes contact with so many other neurons that the total number of connections in the brain remains almost as high as before. In people who become senile, however, the surviving neurons fail to increase their branching; the branching may even decrease. As a result, the number of connections in the brain decreases and the capacity to process information declines (Buell & Coleman, 1981). (We do not know *why* neurons increase their branching pattern in some aging people and not in others.)

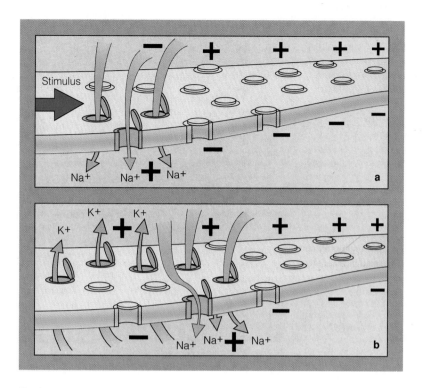

FIGURE 3.14

(a) During an action potential, sodium (Na) gates in the membrane open, and sodium ions enter the neuron, bringing a positive charge with them. (b) After an action potential occurs at one point along the axon, the sodium (Na) gates close at that point and open at the next point along the axon. When the sodium gates close, potassium gates open, and potassium ions flow out of the axon, carrying a positive charge with them. (From Starr & Taggert, 1989.)

THE ACTION POTENTIAL

An impulse travels down an axon by a process known as an action potential. Ordinarily, there is an electrical charge across the membrane (or covering) of an axon. The **action potential** is a sudden decrease or reversal in that charge, produced by the movement of sodium ions. An action potential travels at a rate of about 1–100 meters per second (varying from one neuron to another). That rate is slow compared to electrical conduction along a wire, which approaches the speed of light (300 million meters per second). However, an action potential has one advantage: It recharges at each point along the axon so that its strength does not decay over distance.

To understand the difference between the conduction of electricity and the transmission of the action potential, consider these two analogies: (1) If you heat one end of a metal bar, heat is conducted to the rest of the bar but the amount transmitted diminishes with distance from its source. The same

is true when electricity is conducted through metal. (2) If you set a string on fire, the fire passes along the string, consuming it at each point along the way. At the end of the string, the fire is just as intense as it was at the beginning. An action potential along an axon is like the movement of fire along a string, except that the axon is not destroyed and can function over and over again.

When the axon of a neuron is at rest, its interior has a negative electrical potential with respect to its exterior, because positively charged sodium ions are more concentrated outside the axon than inside it. When some stimulus excites the axon, small channels in its membrane open, enabling sodium ions to enter (Figure 3.14a), bringing with them their positive electrical charge. This flow of positive charge into the relatively negative interior of the axon constitutes the action potential. The action potential stimulates the next point along the membrane, causing sodium ions to enter at that point, as shown in Figure 3.14b. That entry recharges the action potential. The same procedure is repeated

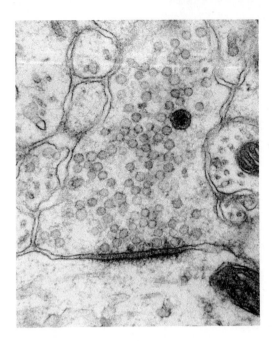

FIGURE 3.15

A synapse magnified thousands of times by an electron microscope. The small circular structures are synaptic vesicles.

at each point up to the end of the axon. Just after the sodium ions enter the membrane, potassium ions leave, thereby restoring the original charge across the membrane (see Figure 3.14b).

Because the transmission of information along an axon depends on the flow of sodium ions across its membrane, anything that blocks that flow will temporarily silence the neuron. For example, anesthetic drugs (such as Novocain) clog the channels through which sodium ions flow (van Dyke & Byck, 1982). When your dentist drills a tooth, the neurons in your tooth send out the message "Pain! Pain! Pain!" But the shot of Novocain given before the drilling blocks the messages along the axons before they reach your brain.

Concept Checks

5. What do you suppose happens to the sodium ions after they enter the axon or to the potassium ions after they leave? What can you infer must be true in order for the system to continue to work? (Check your answers on page 97.)

6. If you stub your toe, do you feel it immediately or is there a delay before you feel it? Why? (Check your answers on page 97.)

SYNAPSES: THE JUNCTIONS BETWEEN NEURONS

The transmission of information between one neuron and the next is different from the transmission along an axon within a given neuron. At a **synapse** (SIN-aps), the junction between one neuron and

another (Figure 3.15), one neuron releases a chemical that either excites or inhibits the next neuron. The following paragraph relates the process.

Each axon ends with a little bulge called a *presynaptic ending*, or a **terminal button** (see Figure 3.16). When an action potential reaches the terminal button, it causes the release of molecules of a **neurotransmitter**, a chemical that has been stored in packets called *synaptic vesicles* (Figure 3.16). Different neurons use different chemicals as their neurotransmitters. The neurotransmitter molecules then diffuse across a narrow gap called a *synaptic cleft* to the next neuron, the **postsynaptic neuron**, where the neurotransmitter molecules attach to receptors. Those receptors may be located on the neuron's dendrites or cell body or (for special purposes) on the tip of its axon. The neural communication process is summarized in Figure 3.17.

Depending on the chemical used as a neurotransmitter and on the type of receptor, the result may be either excitation or inhibition of the neuron. The postsynaptic neuron may be receiving nearly simultaneous excitation and inhibition from a great many other neurons. It produces an action potential of its own if the total amount of excitation outweighs the total amount of inhibition. If the inhibitory signals outweigh the excitatory signals, then the neuron is temporarily silent. This process resembles a decision. When you are trying to decide whether to do something, you weigh all the pros and cons and act if the pros outweigh the cons.

What would happen if the excitation and inhibition were equal, or if for a time the postsynaptic neuron received no excitation or inhibition at all? The outcome would vary. A few neurons would be silent; most would produce action potentials at a moderate rate. *Spontaneous firing* refers to the action potentials that occur under such conditions.

Note that inhibition is not just the absence of excitation; it is an active braking process. If one neuron sends a message to raise your arm, another neuron can cancel it. Inhibition has an important effect on behavior, because at any given time you may have reasons for doing something and reasons for not doing the same thing.

Concept Checks

7. As mentioned earlier, under some conditions the axons and dendrites of a neuron increase their branching. How will that affect the number of synapses? (Check your answer on page 97.)

8. Norepinephrine is a neurotransmitter that inhibits postsynaptic neurons. If a drug were injected that prevents norepinephrine from attaching to its receptors, what would happen to the postsynaptic neuron? (Check your answer on page 97.)

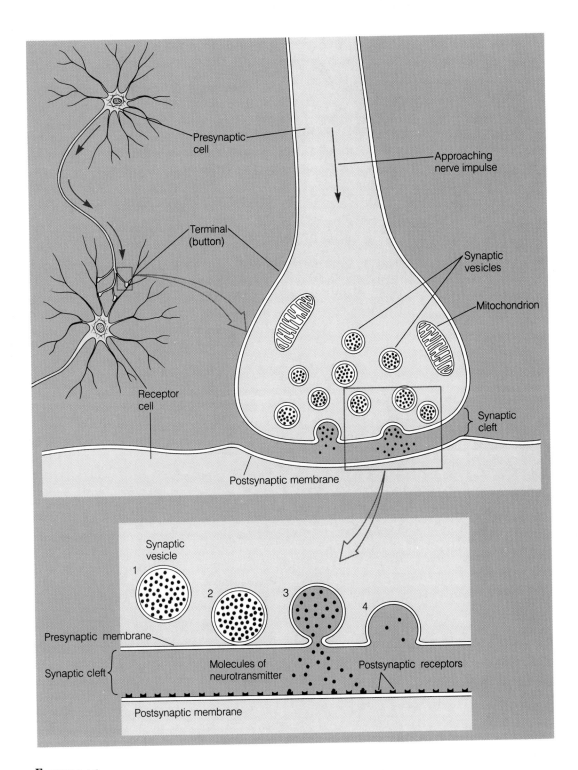

FIGURE 3.16

The synapse is the junction of the presynaptic (message-sending) cell and the postsynaptic (message-receiving) cell. At the end of the presynaptic axon is the terminal button, which contains synaptic vesicles filled with many molecules of the neurotransmitter.

FIGURE 3.17

The complex process of
neural communication
actually takes only 1 to
2 milliseconds.

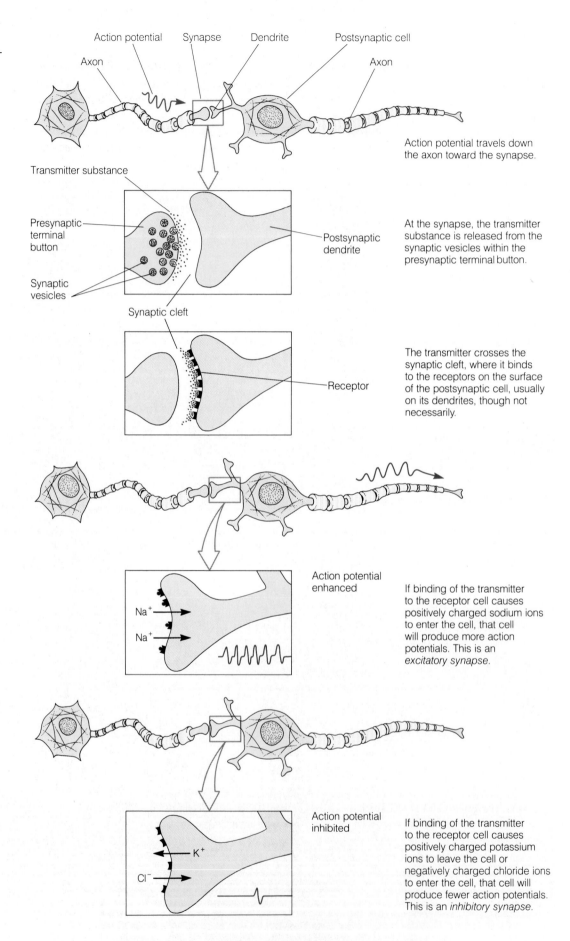

Action potential travels down
the axon toward the synapse.

At the synapse, the transmitter
substance is released from the
synaptic vesicles within the
presynaptic terminal button.

The transmitter crosses the
synaptic cleft, where it binds
to the receptors on the surface
of the postsynaptic cell, usually
on its dendrites, though not
necessarily.

If binding of the transmitter
to the receptor cell causes
positively charged sodium ions
to enter the cell, that cell
will produce more action
potentials. This is an
excitatory synapse.

If binding of the transmitter
to the receptor cell causes
positively charged potassium
ions to leave the cell or
negatively charged chloride ions
to enter the cell, that cell will
produce fewer action potentials.
This is an *inhibitory synapse*.

ROLE OF DIFFERENT NEUROTRANSMITTERS IN BEHAVIOR

Each neuron releases the same chemical or the same combination of chemicals at all branches of its axon. But different neurons release different chemicals. Investigators believe that dozens of chemicals serve as neurotransmitters (Snyder, 1984) and that different transmitters control different aspects of behavior (see Table 3.1). That likelihood has profound implications: If different transmitters control different aspects of behavior, then an excess or a deficit of a particular transmitter will cause some sort of abnormal behavior. Such imbalances may be caused by genetic factors, by brain damage, by drugs, and even by changes in the amount of some ingredient in a person's diet.

One example of a behavioral disorder related to a particular neurotransmitter is **Parkinson's disease**, a condition that affects many elderly people.

Its main symptoms are difficulty in initiating voluntary movement, slowness of movement, and tremors. It is accompanied by serious depression, which may be an effect of the disease rather than just a reaction to it. Without medical treatment, Parkinson's disease generally grows worse and worse as time passes, until the person dies. Parkinson's disease is not hereditary (Duvoisin, Eldridge, Williams, Nutt, & Calne, 1981).

In Parkinson's disease one path of axons in the brain gradually dies (Figure 3.18). All the axons in this particular path use the same neurotransmitter, a chemical known as **dopamine** (DOPE-uh-meen). Medical science has not, so far, discovered any way to halt the loss of axons containing dopamine, although furnishing extra dopamine to the brain does compensate somewhat for their loss. Dopamine, like many other chemicals, cannot cross directly from the blood into the brain. But another chemical, L-DOPA, taken in the form of pills, can enter the blood and cross into the brain, where it is converted into dopamine. This treatment does

TABLE 3.1 Important Neurotransmitters and Some of Their Functions

Neurotransmitter	Behavioral Consequences of Neurotransmitter Excess	Behavioral Consequences of Neurotransmitter Deficit	Comments
Acetylcholine		Memory impairment	Acetylcholine is also released at the junction between motor neuron and muscle.
Dopamine	Involuntary movements; schizophrenia?	Impaired movement (Parkinson's disease); memory impairment; depression?	The brain has several dopamine paths. Some are important for movement; others for thought and emotion.
Norepinephrine	Autonomic arousal; anxiety; symptoms resembling schizophrenia	Memory impairment; depression?	Several transmitters contribute to depression in complex ways not yet understood.
Serotonin		Increased aggressive behavior; sleeplessness; depression?	Serotonin synapses are disrupted or damaged by LSD, ecstasy, and several other abused drugs.
GABA (gamma-amino-butyric acid)		Anxiety	Tranquilizers facilitate GABA synapses and thereby reduce anxiety.
Glutamate; glycine; other amino acids			The most abundant transmitters in the central nervous system; their functions are poorly understood.
Endorphins	Inhibition of pain	Increased pain	The effects of endorphins are partly mimicked by morphine, heroin, and other opiates.
Neuropeptides			These are small chains of amino acids. The brain uses many neuropeptides; their functions vary and remain mostly unknown.

Sources: Kalat, 1988; Spring, Chiodo, & Bowen, 1987.

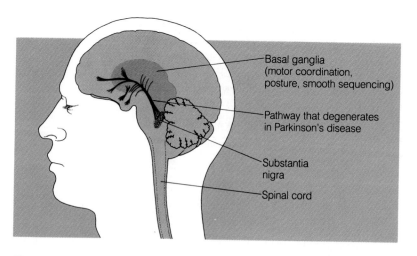

FIGURE 3.18

In Parkinson's disease one path of axons in the substantia nigra gradually dies. Patients can gain years of active life by taking a chemical called L-DOPA, which is converted to the neurotransmitter dopamine in the brain.

not reverse the disease; the axons continue to die. The extra dopamine does, however, reduce the symptoms of the disease and gives the victim additional years of normal, active life.

Although the cause of Parkinson's disease probably differs from one case to another, one possible cause is exposure to toxic substances. In 1982, several young adults (ages 22 to 42) developed Parkinson's disease after using illegal drugs that they had all bought from the same dealer. Investigators eventually identified the drug as a mixture of two chemicals known as MPPP and MPTP. Experiments with animals disclosed that MPTP causes damage to the substantia nigra, the same part of the brain known to be damaged in Parkinson's disease (Chiueh, 1988).

MPTP is occasionally released as an atmospheric pollutant by certain industrial and chemical processes. It is chemically similar to a number of herbicides and pesticides, including *paraquat*. Extensive exposure to such toxic substances may increase the risk of developing Parkinson's disease.

Concept Check

9. *People suffering from certain disorders are given* haloperidol, *a drug that blocks activity at dopamine synapses. How would haloperidol affect a person suffering from Parkinson's disease? (Check your answer on page 97.)*

CHEMICAL INTERFERENCE WITH THE FUNCTIONING OF NEURONS

Many factors can interfere with the healthy functioning of neurons. One is a lack of adequate vitamin B_1 (thiamine), a substance abundant in yeast, grain, beans, peas, liver, and pork. Although most other organs of the body can use a variety of fuels, most cells in the brain use only **glucose** (GLOO-kose), a sugar. However, for the brain to use glucose, it must have an adequate supply of vitamin B_1. If a person's diet is deficient in that vitamin over a period of weeks, parts of the brain deteriorate or die, and other parts function below their normal capacity. Vitamin B_1 deficiency is common among severe alcoholics and causes some of them gradually to develop a kind of brain damage known as Korsakoff's syndrome, characterized by severe memory loss.

A number of drugs can interfere with the activity of a particular type of synapse. Common cold remedies, for example, block the synapses that promote the flow of sinus fluids. Because the same neurotransmitter is used at other synapses as well, cold remedies have the side effects of increasing heart rate, decreasing salivation, and impeding sexual arousal.

Lysergic acid diethylamide (LSD) and most other hallucinogenic drugs (drugs that cause hallucinations) also are believed to act on the synapses. LSD is chemically similar to a neurotransmitter called **serotonin**, which plays an important role in sleep and mood changes. LSD attaches to the serotonin synapses, blocking their normal activity for about four hours and decreasing it for several days (Jacobs & Trulson, 1979). Mescaline (the active substance in peyote), "angel dust," and other hallucinogenic drugs resemble one or another of the neurotransmitters; they either block or stimulate various synapses in the brain. Heroin and morphine stimulate the synapses that normally respond to **endorphins** (en-DOR-fins), neurotransmitters that inhibit the sensation of pain, even though those drugs are not very similar to endorphins chemically.

A historical note: In the witchcraft trials in Salem, Massachusetts, in 1692, people suffering from nausea, muscle twitches, and hallucinations accused their neighbors of practicing witchcraft. The symptoms they complained of may not have been imaginary, as was long assumed. Evidence suggests that the rye grain that was commonly stored in New England at that time may have been covered with *ergot,* a fungus that sometimes produces LSD or similar chemicals. The symptoms of LSD ingestion often include nausea, muscle twitches, hallucinations, and all the other symptoms of which the "witchcraft" victims complained (Caporael, 1976; Matossian, 1982).

Concept Check

10. One way in which society could prevent Korsakoff's syndrome would be to prevent alcoholism. What would be another way? (Check your answer on page 97.)

SUMMARY

1. A neuron, or nerve cell, consists of a cell body, dendrites, and an axon. The axon conveys information to other neurons, where it is received by the dendrites or cell body or occasionally by another axon. (page 67)

2. The structure of a neuron may change as a result of experience, exposure to alcohol or other substances, or old age. (page 67)

3. Information is conveyed along an axon by an action potential, which is regenerated without loss of strength at each point along the axon. (page 69)

4. An action potential depends on the flow of sodium ions. Anything blocking that flow will block the action potential. (page 70)

5. A neuron communicates with another neuron by releasing a chemical called a neurotransmitter at a specialized junction called a synapse. A neurotransmitter can either excite or inhibit the next neuron. (page 70)

6. An excess or a deficit of a particular neurotransmitter may lead to abnormal behavior. (page 73)

7. The functioning of neurons may be impaired by a deficit of vitamin B_1 or by certain chemicals that resemble neurotransmitters. (page 74)

SUGGESTION FOR FURTHER READING

Kalat, J. W. (1988). *Biological psychology,* (3rd ed.). Belmont, CA: Wadsworth. Chapters 1 through 5 deal with the material discussed in this chapter, but in more detail.

Explanations of Behavior at the Level of the Nervous System

*What do different parts of the brain do?
Does a person who loses part of the brain also lose part of the mind?*

Every community has some division of labor among its members. Some people farm, some sell shoes, some build houses, some write psychology textbooks. Yet the division is not absolute. Many people who are not farmers grow a few vegetables in their backyard. And hardly anyone does only one job or does a job without the help of others.

The same is true of areas of the nervous system. Different areas contribute in different ways, but no one area is in complete control of any behavior. So even though we say that a particular structure is important for vision or for the control of movement, we know that it does not carry out that function without the participation of other areas.

Specialization by Areas of the Brain

Why should psychologists care what different parts of the brain do? There are at least two reasons, one practical and the other theoretical.

The practical reason is that we want to distinguish between people who act strangely because they have had bad experiences and people who act strangely because they have suffered brain damage. To do so, we have to know how brain damage affects behavior.

The theoretical reason is simply that the study of brain damage can help us understand the organization of behavior. In some manner or another, behavior must be made up of component parts. But what are those parts? Is behavior composed of ideas?

Sensations? Movements? Personality characteristics?

In the 1800s, people who called themselves "phrenologists" claimed to be able to measure a person's personality tendencies by feeling the bumps on his or her skull. According to their theory, every bump corresponded to an overgrown brain area; every depression corresponded to a deficient brain area. By feeling the scalp, the phrenologists claimed, they could determine that a person was particularly strong or weak in the behavior controlled by a certain area of the brain (see Figure 3.19).

Different parts of the brain do control different aspects of behavior, although those aspects have nothing to do with the phrenologists' maps. Depending on its location, brain damage may lead to impaired vision, faulty hearing, inability to perform certain movements, increased or decreased eating, fluctuations in body temperature, and a great variety of other outcomes. Each of those outcomes provides us with some clues as to how behavior is organized. Each outcome also helps to document the conclusion that *if part of the brain is lost, part of behavior and experience is lost as well.* Apparently the mind cannot function without the brain.

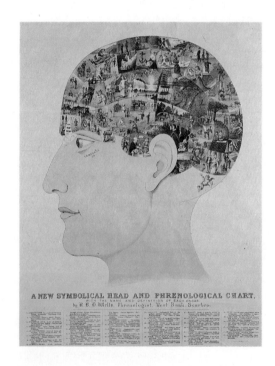

Figure 3.19

Phrenologists, or "mind scientists," felt the bumps on a person's skull to determine personality characteristics.

a

We can supplement the evidence from brain damage with studies of normal people. Investigators can measure brain activity in healthy, waking people through several techniques, including the monitoring of **regional cerebral blood flow (rCBF)**. To measure rCBF, investigators inject into the person's blood a small amount of radioactively labeled xenon, an inert gas. The more active a certain area of the brain is, the greater the amount of xenon-carrying blood that will enter that area. Measurements of the amount of radioactivity from various brain areas reveal which of those areas are most active at a given moment.

Figure 3.20a shows the apparatus used in measuring rCBF, and Figure 3.20b shows an example of the results. Reds and yellows indicate areas of high activity; greens, blues, and purples indicate progressively lower activity. This figure demonstrates that certain brain areas become highly active when a normal person (above) tries to solve a particular task and that those same areas fail to become active in mental patients (below) who perform poorly on the task.

So we can conclude that different parts of the brain make different contributions to behavior. That is at least a start toward understanding the mind-brain relationship. In the rest of this section we will explore some of those differences. Bear in mind, however, that the specializations are far from absolute. Although a given behavior may depend on certain areas more than on others, most areas contribute something to every complex behavior.

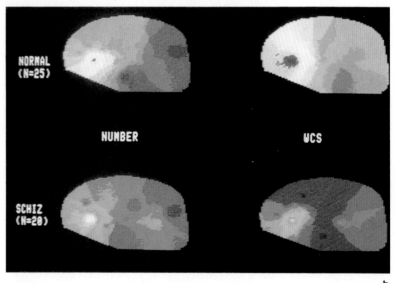

b

FIGURE 3.20

(a) This apparatus records regional cerebral blood flow (rCBF) in the brain, allowing investigators to measure activity in different parts of the brain. (b) For these recordings of regional cerebral blood flow, normal people (top) and patients with schizophrenia (bottom) performed two different tasks. While the views on the left were taken, the people were performing a simple numbers-matching task. When they performed a more complex task (right-hand views), different parts of the brain were activated. Note also that the results for patients are different from those for normal people.

An Overview of the Nervous System and Its Development

Psychologists and biologists distinguish between the central nervous system and the peripheral nervous system. The **central nervous system** consists of the brain and the spinal cord. The **peripheral nervous system** consists of the **nerves** (bundles of axons) that carry messages from the sense organs to the central nervous system and from the central nervous system to the muscles and glands. The peripheral nervous system has two divisions, the **somatic nervous system**, which controls the muscles, and the **autonomic nervous system**, which controls the organs. Figure 3.21 summarizes the major divisions of the nervous system.

Early in its embryological development, the central nervous system of vertebrates, including

FIGURE 3.21

The peripheral nerves carry messages back and forth between the central nervous system (the brain and spinal cord) and the rest of the body.

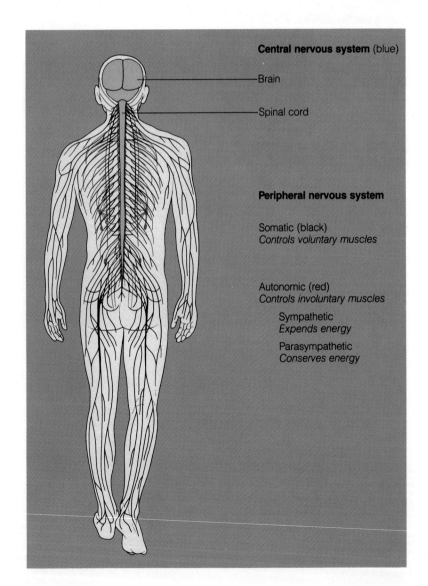

Central nervous system (blue)

— Brain

— Spinal cord

Peripheral nervous system

Somatic (black)
Controls voluntary muscles

Autonomic (red)
Controls involuntary muscles

Sympathetic
Expends energy

Parasympathetic
Conserves energy

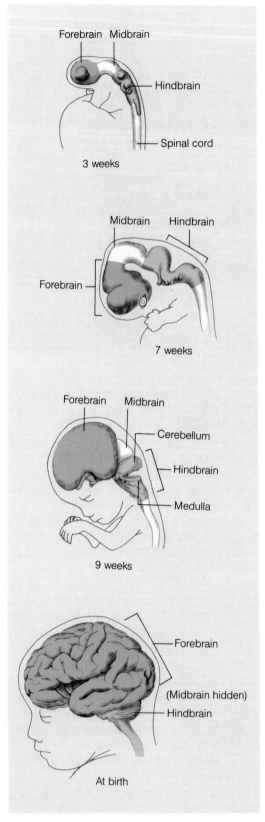

Forebrain Midbrain

— Hindbrain

— Spinal cord

3 weeks

Midbrain Hindbrain

Forebrain —

7 weeks

Forebrain Midbrain

— Cerebellum

— Hindbrain

— Medulla

9 weeks

— Forebrain

(Midbrain hidden)

— Hindbrain

At birth

FIGURE 3.22

The human brain at four stages of development, from three weeks after conception to birth.

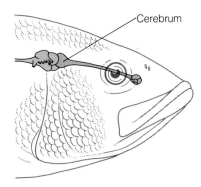

Striped bass

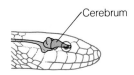

Grass snake

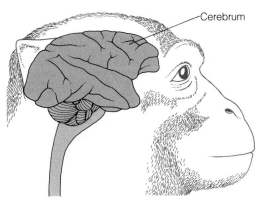

Macaque monkey

FIGURE 3.23

In mammals, such as macaque monkeys, the cerebral cortex is larger in proportion to the body and in proportion to the rest of the brain than it is in other vertebrates.

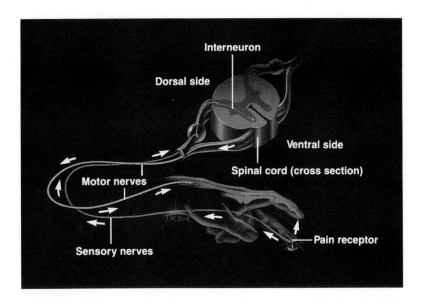

FIGURE 3.24

A cross section of the spinal cord showing the incoming (dorsal) sensory nerves and the outgoing (ventral) motor nerves.

The Spinal Cord

The **spinal cord** communicates with the rest of the body by means of sensory nerves and motor nerves. The **sensory nerves** carry information about touch, pain, and other senses from the periphery of the body to the spinal cord. Once the information reaches the spinal cord, it excites several types of neurons. Some of them send information to the brain, where it is experienced as a sensation. Other neurons connect directly to **motor nerves** in the spinal cord that send impulses to the muscles. Figure 3.24 illustrates the spinal cord. Note that all the sensory nerves enter on one side (the person's back); all the motor nerves leave on the other side (the stomach side).

Spinal injury is a common outcome of automobile accidents, other accidents, and certain diseases. If the spinal cord is completely cut, then the brain is separated from the part of the cord below the cut. The person then loses sensation and voluntary motor control in the part of the body served by the lower part of the spinal cord. If the cut is fairly low in the cord, then the person may lose control of only the legs and bowel and bladder control. If the cut is higher, then the person loses control of a greater area of the body. If the cord is cut near the top, then the person may lose control of the arms as well as the legs. And if a cut goes only part way through the cord, then a person may lose control of just the left side or just the right side.

humans, is a fluid-filled tube with three lumps, as shown in Figure 3.22. Those lumps develop into the forebrain, the midbrain, and the hindbrain; the rest of the tube develops into the spinal cord. The **hindbrain**, the most posterior (hind) part of the brain, includes the medulla, pons, and cerebellum. The **midbrain** is, as you might guess, the middle part of the brain. The hindbrain and the midbrain are more prominent in fish, reptiles, and birds than in mammals (Figure 3.23). The **forebrain**, the most anterior (forward) part of the brain, contains the cerebral cortex and other structures. It is by far the dominant portion of the brain in mammals, especially humans.

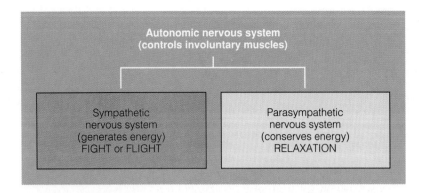

FIGURE 3.25

The autonomic nervous system, which controls the internal organs and involuntary actions, consists of the sympathetic nervous system (activated by adrenaline) and the parasympathetic nervous system.

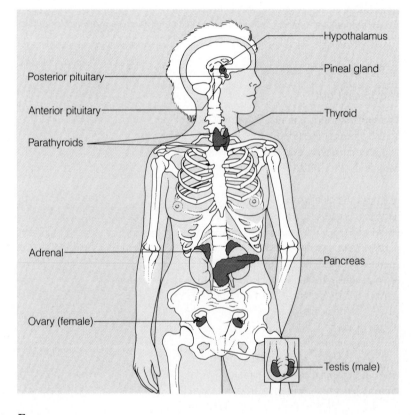

FIGURE 3.26

Glands in the endocrine system produce hormones and secrete them into the blood.

The Autonomic Nervous System

The autonomic nervous system, closely associated with the spinal cord, controls the internal organs such as the heart. The term *autonomic* means involuntary or automatic. The autonomic nervous system is partly, though not entirely, automatic. We are generally not aware of its activity, although it does receive information from, and send information to, the brain and spinal cord.

The autonomic nervous system consists of two parts: (1) The *sympathetic nervous system,* controlled by a chain of neurons lying just outside the spinal cord, increases heart rate and breathing rate and readies the body for vigorous "fight or flight" activities. (2) The *parasympathetic nervous system,* controlled by neurons in the very top and very bottom levels of the spinal cord, decreases heart rate, increases digestive activities, and in general promotes the body's activities that take place during rest (Figure 3.25).

The autonomic nervous system is particularly important for emotions. When you are nervous, your heart beats rapidly, you cannot catch your breath, and you feel "butterflies in the stomach." All those responses are the product of your autonomic nervous system. I shall return to this topic in more detail in the chapter about emotions (Chapter 12).

The Endocrine System

Although the endocrine system is not part of the nervous system, it is closely related to it, especially to the autonomic nervous system. The **endocrine system** is a set of glands that produces hormones and releases them into the blood. Figure 3.26 shows some of the major endocrine glands.

Hormones are chemicals released by a gland and conveyed by the blood to other parts of the body, where they alter activity. They are similar to neurotransmitters in that both affect the nervous system. The same chemical may be used both as a hormone and as a neurotransmitter. The difference is that when a chemical is used as a neurotransmitter, it is released immediately adjacent to the cell that it is to excite or inhibit. When it is used as a hormone, it is released into the blood, which diffuses it throughout the body. Neurotransmitters produce relatively rapid but brief effects. Because hormones take longer to reach the cells that respond to them, their effects are more gradual and in some cases last longer.

Some of the effects of hormones are nearly permanent. For example, the amount of the male sex hormone testosterone present during prenatal development determines whether an individual will develop as a male or as a female. Hormones also control the onset of puberty. Other effects of hormones are more temporary. For example, hormones control blood pressure, the rate of energy use, and the rate of urine production.

The autonomic nervous system exerts some control over the activity of the endocrine organs. When the sympathetic nervous system sends impulses to increase heart rate, it also sends impulses to activate the adrenal gland, which then releases the hormone epinephrine (also known as adrenalin), which produces a longer-lasting activation of the heart, as well as an increase in energy levels.

Concept Check

11. *Just after a meal, the pancreas produces increased amounts of the hormone* insulin, *which increases the conversion of the digested food into fats in many cells throughout the body. In what way is a hormone more effective for this purpose than a neurotransmitter would be? (Check your answer on page 97.)*

The Hindbrain

The **medulla** and **pons**, structures located in the hindbrain (Figure 3.27), are an elaboration of the spinal cord. Both structures receive sensory input from the head (taste, hearing, touch sensations on the scalp) and send impulses for motor control of the head (for example, chewing, swallowing, and breathing). The medulla and pons control so many life-preserving functions that almost any damage to them is fatal.

The **reticular formation** is a diffuse set of neurons that extends from the medulla into the forebrain. (The term *reticular* means "netlike.") As the name implies, neurons of the reticular formation are extensively interconnected with one another as well as with neurons that relay sensory information. Their role is mainly to govern arousal; they react to all types of sensory stimulation by sending impulses throughout much of the forebrain. After damage to the reticular formation, a person goes through a prolonged period of inactivity and unresponsiveness.

The **cerebellum** is active in the control of movement, especially for complex, rapid motor skills, such as playing the piano or dribbling a basketball (Kornhuber, 1974). A person who suffers damage to the cerebellum can still make muscular movements, but has to plan each series of movements slowly, one at a time, instead of executing them in a smooth sequence. Such a person has difficulty walking a straight line and speaks haltingly, slurring the words. (Words have to be planned as units; you cannot speak a word clearly by pronouncing one sound at a time.)

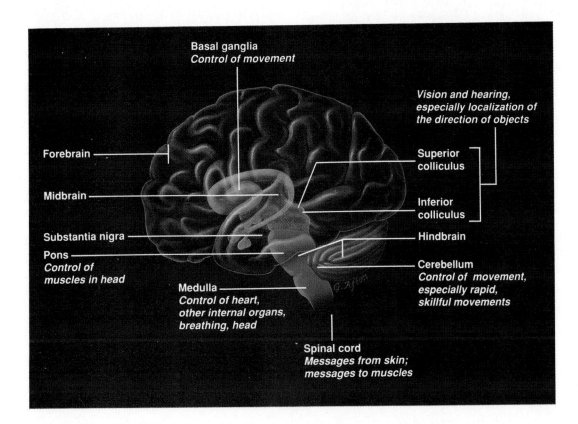

FIGURE 3.27

The human hindbrain and midbrain. The cerebellum regulates skilled movements. The medulla and pons control the head and many organs, including the heart.

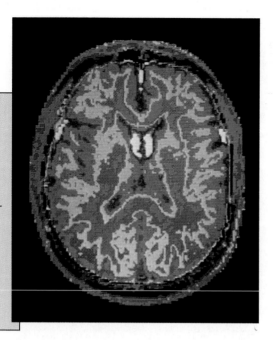

In this transverse section of the brain, the gray matter—the cerebral cortex—is red-brown; the white matter is yellow to blue-green. Shades of blue indicate the skull and fat under the scalp. Spinal fluid that bathes the brain is white.

One way of testing for damage to the cerebellum is the **finger-to-nose test**. A person is told to hold one arm out straight and then, with eyes closed, to touch the nose as quickly as possible. Although most people have little difficulty with this task, someone with a damaged cerebellum may move the finger slowly and haltingly or may miss the nose altogether.

The effects of damage to the cerebellum are similar to the effects of alcohol abuse. A person who has drunk too much alcohol generally has slow, slurred speech and cannot walk a straight line. The cerebellum is one of the first areas to be impaired by alcohol.

The Midbrain

In mammals, the midbrain is not a particularly prominent structure. In birds, reptiles, amphibians, and fish it is much larger and serves a wider variety of functions. The mammalian midbrain includes structures that contribute to certain aspects of hearing and vision, particularly for localizing auditory and visual stimuli, and to certain aspects of the control of movement. The substantia nigra is part of the midbrain. In Parkinson's disease, damage to the substantia nigra leads to an impairment of voluntary movement.

Central Parts of the Forebrain

The **cerebral cortex**, the outer surface of the forebrain, contains six distinct layers of cells and axons.

Beneath the cerebral cortex are several other structures, known as *subcortical areas* (Figure 3.28). One group of subcortical areas, including the hippocampus, amygdala, and hypothalamus, is known as the **limbic system**. (*Limbus* is Latin for "border"; the limbic system forms a border around the midbrain.) The structures of the limbic system are intricately linked with one another. They play an important role in motivated and emotional behaviors such as eating, drinking, social behaviors, and sexual responses (MacLean, 1977a). Damage or disorder in the limbic system leads to emotional reactions ranging from joy to disgust, from unprovoked violence to extreme calmness, and from indiscriminate sexual responsiveness to a lack of interest in sex. The hippocampus and amygdala in particular are also important for certain aspects of learning and memory.

Besides the limbic system, the other subcortical structures include the *thalamus,* which serves as an area of intermediate processing of sensory information on its way to the cerebral cortex. The *basal ganglia* are a group of fairly large structures that contribute to the control of movement. In contrast to the cerebellum, which is necessary for rapid movements such as talking, the basal ganglia are most active during periods of slower, more gradual movements such as walking.

THE CEREBRAL CORTEX

The cerebral cortex consists of two **hemispheres**, the left and the right. Each hemisphere is responsible for sensation and motor control on the opposite side of the body. The outer surface of the forebrain, the cerebral cortex, consists mostly of the cell bodies of neurons; its inner core consists of axons. You have probably heard people talk about "having a lot of gray matter." The *gray matter* of the forebrain is the cerebral cortex. It is called gray matter because it contains a great many cell bodies, which are grayer than the axons. The interior of the forebrain beneath the cerebral cortex contains large areas of *white matter,* composed entirely of axons. (Many axons are covered with *myelin,* a white insulation.)

The number of cell bodies in the cerebral cortex is proportional to the surface area. In humans, the cerebral cortex has a large number of folds and grooves (see Figure 3.29), which make its total surface area quite large. Although it is customary to divide each hemisphere of the cerebral cortex into four "lobes," as shown in Figure 3.29, the borders between the lobes are indistinct.

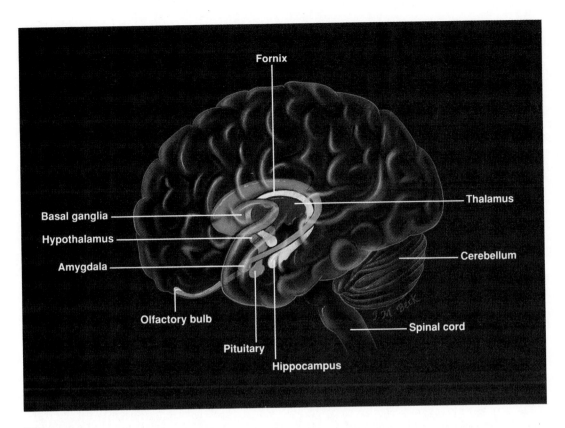

FIGURE 3.28

The human forebrain, showing the location of some subcortical structures. The hypothalamus, hippocampus, and several other subcortical structures compose the limbic system, which affects motivations and emotions.

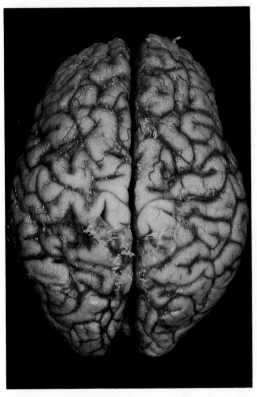

a

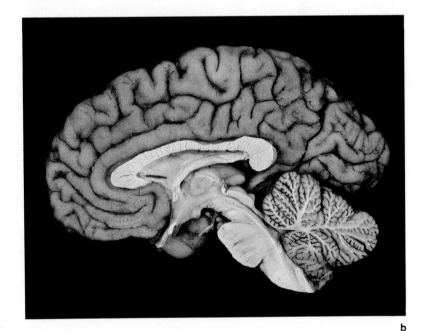

b

FIGURE 3.29

The human cerebral cortex: (a) top view shows left and right hemispheres; (b) side view of a complete hemisphere. The folds greatly extend its surface area.

The Occipital Lobe

The **occipital lobe**, at the rear of each hemisphere of the cerebral cortex, plays a critical role in vision. Damage to the occipital lobe results in loss of vision in part of the visual field, as if part of both eyes had been destroyed. (The **visual field** is the world as someone sees it. For example, your left visual field is what appears on your left.) Someone who suffers damage to the occipital lobe in the left hemisphere loses vision in the right half of the visual field. If the damage occurs in the right hemisphere, the loss is in the left half of the visual field. A person who suffers damage to the entire occipital lobe becomes essentially blind. At most, a slight ability to determine the direction of a source of light may remain (Campion, Latto, & Smith, 1983).

The Parietal Lobe

The **parietal** (puh-RIGH-eht-l) **lobe** is the main receiving area for the sense of touch. It is essential for body perception in general, including the perception of the location and movement of body parts and the orientation of the body in space. The parietal lobe also contributes to motor control, though to a lesser extent than does the frontal lobe.

A strip in the anterior (forward) part of the parietal lobe receives most touch sensation and other information about the body. This is the **somatosensory** (body-sensory) **cortex**. Damage to this strip in one hemisphere impairs perception on the opposite side of the body. Each location along the somatosensory cortex receives sensation from a different part of the body, as shown in Figure 3.30a.

Damage to an area in the parietal lobe just behind the somatosensory cortex disorganizes sensations of touch. A person with such damage can still feel objects but ignores what he or she is feeling. Such a person will neglect the side of the body opposite the damaged side of the brain (Heilman, 1979). For instance, if the parietal cortex in the right hemisphere is damaged, the person may fail to dress or groom the left side of the body, insisting that it is "someone else." Such people draw only the right side of an object, using only the right side of the paper (Figure 3.31).

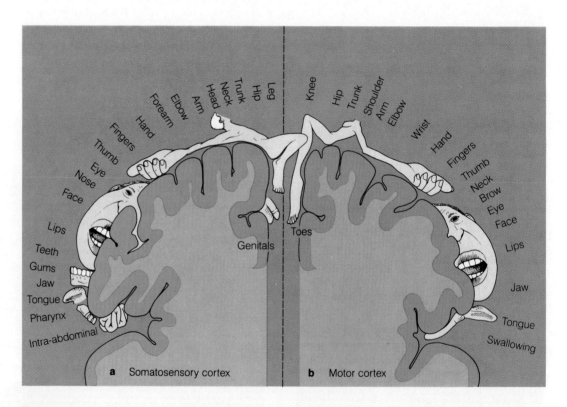

FIGURE 3.30

(a) The somatosensory cortex and (b) the motor cortex, illustrating which part of the body each brain area controls. Larger areas of the cortex are devoted to body parts that need to be controlled with great precision, such as the face and hands. The figure shows the left somatosensory cortex, which receives information from the right side of the body, and the right motor cortex, which controls the muscles on the left side of the body. (From Geschwind, 1979.)

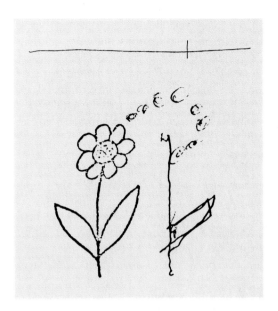

Figure 3.31

A person with damage to the right parietal lobe will draw only the right side of an object, using only the right side of the paper, as this attempt to copy a picture of a flower shows. (From Heilman, 1979.)

The Temporal Lobe

The **temporal lobe** of each hemisphere, located toward the temples, is the main processing area for hearing. It also plays an important role in some of the more complex aspects of vision. Damage to the temporal lobe does not leave a person blind, as damage to the occipital lobe does, but it does impair the ability to recognize complex patterns such as faces (Benton, 1980). Similarly, an irritation of the occipital lobe (from a brain tumor, for example) merely produces the experience of seeing flashing lights. But if the irritation occurs in the temporal lobe, then it may evoke elaborate, dreamlike hallucinations.

The temporal lobe has extensive connections with much of the limbic system and apparently plays an important role in emotional behavior. Tumors, epilepsy, or other abnormalities affecting the temporal lobe sometimes cause severe emotional outbursts. Some people, for example, exhibit unprovoked violent behavior (Mark & Ervin, 1970). Others suffer periods of uncontrollable laughter (Swash, 1972). Still others, including the Russian novelist Fyodor Dostoyevsky (who had temporal lobe epilepsy), experience periods of ecstatic pleasure and a feeling of "oneness with the universe" (Cirignotta, Todesco, & Lugaresi, 1980). Dostoyevsky declared that such experiences brought him the purest, most intense pleasure he ever had.

The Frontal Lobe

The **frontal lobe** is the large anterior portion of each cerebral hemisphere; it is apparently not necessary for any type of sensation, although it may be active in comparing information from different sensory systems that are active at the same time (Stuss & Benson, 1984). A strip along the rear portion of the frontal lobe, the **motor cortex** (Figure 3.30b), is important for the control of fine movements, such as moving one finger at a time. As with the somatosensory cortex, each part of the motor cortex controls a different part of the body. A person who suffers damage to the motor cortex of one hemisphere experiences weakness and an impairment of fine movements on the opposite side of the body.

Functions of the Prefrontal Cortex The prefrontal **cortex** (Figure 3.30b) is the portion of the frontal lobe in front of the motor cortex. The prefrontal cortex is critical for planning movements, for integrating movements with information that has just been received, for the inhibition of inappropriate behaviors, and for certain aspects of memory. For example, after damage to the prefrontal cortex, both humans and other species fail on tasks that require them to alternate between two movements (Freedman & Oscar-Berman, 1986; Sakurai & Sugimoto, 1986). Instead of alternating, they simply repeat one of the movements. They also fail on a task that requires them to keep track of objects they have just seen and to pick up any object they have not recently seen (Bachevalier & Mishkin, 1986). Again, they fail to inhibit one response and to substitute another. Evidently, the prefrontal cortex contributes in some way to the ability to keep track of recent memories and to plan actions based on them.

Prefrontal Lobotomies In the 1940s and early 1950s, an operation known as **prefrontal lobotomy** became a common treatment for depression, schizophrenia, and other disorders for which no other treatment was available at the time. This surgery damaged part of the prefrontal cortex or severed its connections with other areas of the brain. The operation was popularized by Dr. Walter Freeman, who performed more than a thousand lobotomies (Valenstein, 1986). The theoretical rationale behind the surgery was vague and ill founded, and the procedure itself was extremely crude, even by the standards of that time.

Did lobotomies help any mental patients? It is hard to say for sure. Prefrontal lobotomies did sometimes provide relief from anxiety and made some of the most agitated patients easier to handle. The surgeons themselves did some follow-up studies on limited aspects of the patients' behavior and pronounced most of the patients "improved."

Something to Think About

What reasons can you think of for regarding reports of this sort as scientifically unsatisfactory? (You may want to use some of the pointers in Chapter 2 as a checklist.)

However, the side effects of the surgery often included a loss of initiative, planning, and emotional expression, decreased ability to concentrate, confusion, loss of social skills, and certain defects of memory and cognition. We know, for example, that people with prefrontal damage lose the ability to inhibit one response and substitute another (Damasio, 1979). After they have learned to sort objects by color, for example, they find it difficult to switch to sorting them by shape. Because of these behavioral effects, lobotomies fell out of favor in the mid-1950s. After the introduction of drugs to control depression and schizophrenia, the use of lobotomies was almost immediately abandoned.

Concept Check

12. The following five people are known to have suffered damage to the cerebral cortex. From their behavioral symptoms, determine the probable location of the damage for each person: (a) impaired perception of the left half of the body and a tendency to ignore the left half of the body and the left half of the world, (b) impaired hearing and some changes in emotional experience, (c) inability to make fine movements with the right hand, (d) loss of vision in the left visual field, and (e) failure to inhibit inappropriate behaviors and difficulty remembering what has just happened. (Check your answers on page 97.)

THE CORPUS CALLOSUM AND THE SPLIT-BRAIN PHENOMENON

Visual information primarily stimulates the occipital lobes of the cerebral cortex. Auditory information primarily stimulates the temporal lobes. A touch on the left side of the body stimulates primarily the right parietal lobe; a touch on the right side of the body stimulates primarily the left parietal lobe. Although each of these sensory experiences takes place in a different location, the same "you" experiences them—or so it seems. But what would happen if one part of your brain was somehow disconnected from another part, so that the two parts could no longer communicate with each other? Might you then have two or more separate minds?

As we have seen, sensory information from each side of the body travels primarily to the opposite hemisphere of the cerebral cortex. The two hemispheres normally communicate with each other by means of a large set of axons called the **corpus callosum** (Figure 3.32). So ordinarily we can compare what is happening on one side of our body with what is happening on the other side. If the corpus callosum is cut, however, the hemispheres are almost completely isolated from each other.

Several teams of brain surgeons have disconnected the left hemisphere of the cerebral cortex from the right hemisphere. The purpose of such an operation is to relieve a condition called **epilepsy**, in which neurons somewhere in the brain begin to emit rhythmic, spontaneous impulses. Those impulses originate in different locations for different people. They quickly spread to other areas of the brain, including neurons in the opposite hemisphere. The effects on behavior can vary widely, depending on where the epilepsy originates in the brain and where it spreads. Most people with epilepsy respond well to antiepileptic drugs and live normal lives so long as they continue to take them. A few people, however, do not respond to any of the known drugs and continue to have major seizures so frequently that they cannot work, go to school, or travel far from medical help. Such people are willing to try almost anything to get relief.

And so surgeons decided to sever the corpus callosum of people with severe, otherwise untreatable epilepsy. The reasoning was that although the epileptic seizures would still occur, they would be prevented from spreading across the corpus callosum to the other hemisphere and so would be less severe, affecting only half of the body.

The operation was more successful than expected. Not only were the seizures limited to one side of the body but they also became far less frequent. A possible explanation is that the operation interrupted the feedback loop between the two hemispheres that allows an epileptic seizure to echo back and forth. These split-brain patients were able to return to work and to resume other normal activities. There were, however, some interesting behavioral side effects. But before I can discuss them, we need to consider the links between the eyes and the brain.

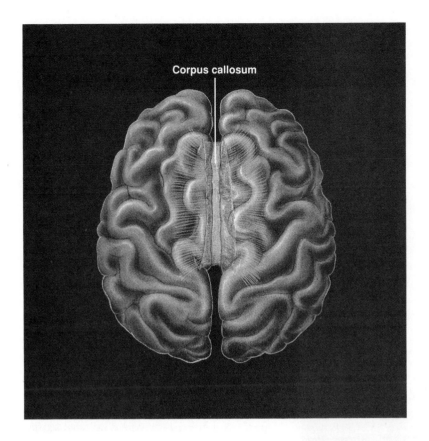

Corpus callosum

FIGURE 3.32

The corpus callosum is a large set of axons carrying information between the left and right hemispheres. If the corpus callosum is severed, the hemispheres are almost completely isolated from each other.

Connections Between the Eyes and the Brain

Note: This section presents a simple concept that is contrary to most people's expectations. Even when students are warned that this material will appear on a test and are practically told what the question will be, many of them still miss it. So pay attention!

Because each hemisphere of the brain controls the muscles on the opposite side of the body, it needs visual information from the opposite side of the world. If humans were built like rabbits or guinea pigs, which have eyes on the sides of their head (Figure 3.33), we could simply say that each hemisphere is connected to the eye on the opposite side. But our eyes are in front, both facing the same direction. So each eye sees both the left and the right halves of the visual world.

In order for the left hemisphere to control the right hand and the rest of the right side of the body, it needs to see the right side of the world. *This is not the same as seeing through the right eye:* Each eye sees both halves of the world. Rather, the left hemisphere has to be connected to *half of each eye,* so that it can know what both eyes are seeing in the right half of the world.

Figure 3.34 shows the connections between eye

FIGURE 3.33

Rabbit eyes are on the sides of the head, facing almost in opposite directions. In contrast, human eyes face in the same direction and thus see both the left and right halves of the visual world. We need this form of "double vision" for depth perception.

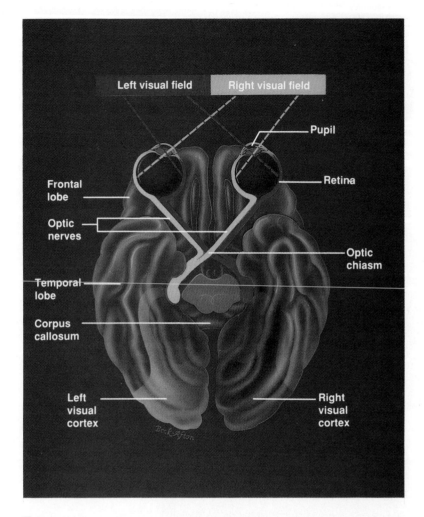

Left visual field | Right visual field

Pupil

Frontal lobe

Retina

Optic nerves

Optic chiasm

Temporal lobe

Corpus callosum

Left visual cortex

Right visual cortex

FIGURE 3.34

Axons from the retina form the optic nerve. At the base of the brain, the optic chiasm solves a transmission problem: Light from the left half of the world strikes receptors on the right sides of both retinas, and that information must be transmitted to the right side of the cerebral cortex. Light from the right side of the world, which strikes receptors on the left sides of both retinas, must be transmitted to the left half of the cerebral cortex.

and brain; it warrants careful study. Light rays from the visual world cross through the pupils and are focused on the **retina** (the visual receptors lining the back of the eyeball). Light from the *left* half of the world strikes receptors on the *right* sides of *both* retinas. Light from the *right* half of the world strikes receptors on the *left* sides of *both* retinas. Axons from the *left* sides of *both* retinas (which see the right side of the world) connect to the *left* hemisphere of the cerebral cortex. Axons from the *right* sides of *both* retinas (which see the left side of the world) connect to the *right* hemisphere of the cerebral cortex. The axons from the retina form the *optic nerve,* which travels to the **optic chiasm** (KI-az-m, from *chi,* the Greek name of the letter *X*)

or "optic cross," at the base of the brain; at that point half of the axons cross to the opposite side, as shown in Figure 3.34.

If you find it difficult to remember all this "left-right-left-right" business, think of it this way: Light from each side of the world strikes the opposite side of the retina. The brain is connected to the eyes in such a way that each hemisphere sees the opposite side of the world. If you remember those two statements, you will be able to sketch the connections shown in Figure 3.34.

What about the very center of the retina? Cells in a thin strip down the center of each retina send axons to both sides of the brain.

Behavioral Effects of Severing the Corpus Callosum

For almost all right-handed people and for about 60% of left-handed people, the brain area that controls speech is located in the left hemisphere of the brain. When visual or other information comes into your right hemisphere, you have no difficulty talking about it, because the corpus callosum readily transfers information between the hemispheres.

But what happens when the corpus callosum is severed? When a woman with a severed corpus callosum touches something with her right hand without looking at it, she can say what it is, because the touch information reaches her left hemisphere (Nebes, 1974; Sperry, 1967). However, if she touches something with her left hand, then she cannot say what it is, because the information reaches only her right hemisphere. If she is given several choices and is asked to point to what her left hand has felt, she can point to it correctly—but only with her left hand. In fact, she will sometimes point to the correct object with her left hand while saying, "I have no idea what it was. I didn't feel anything." Evidently, the right hemisphere can understand the instructions and answer with the hand it controls, but it cannot talk. Roger Sperry won a Nobel Prize for physiology and medicine in 1981 for these pioneering discoveries (Figure 3.35a).

Now consider what happens when this split-brain woman looks at something (Figure 3.35b). Under ordinary conditions, when her eyes are free to move about, she sees almost the same thing in both hemispheres. In the laboratory, however, it is possible to restrict information to one side or the other by presenting it faster than the eyes can move. The woman in Figure 3.35b focuses her eyes on a point in the middle of the screen. The investigator flashes a word such as *hatband* on the screen for

Left field:
    can't name or describe;
    can identify by touch with
    left hand

Right field:
    named with ease;
    can identify by touch with
    right hand

a

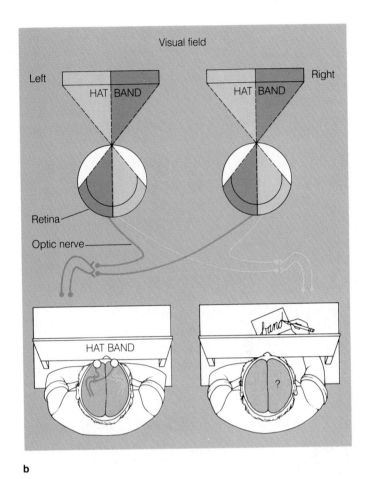

b

FIGURE 3.35

(a) A woman with a severed corpus callosum can name something she touches with her hidden right hand, but she cannot name an object that she feels with her left hand. Information from the left hemisphere goes to the right hemisphere, which cannot talk. (b) When the word *hatband* is flashed on a screen, a woman with a split brain can report only what her left hemisphere saw, *band*. However, with her left hand she can point to a hat, which is what the right hemisphere saw.

a split second, so that the woman does not have enough time to move her eyes. If she is asked what she saw, she replies, "*band*," which is what the left hemisphere saw. Information from the right side of the screen, you will recall, goes to the left side of each retina and from there to the left hemisphere. If she is asked what *kind* of band it might be, she is puzzled: "I don't know. Jazz band? Rubber band?" What the right hemisphere saw cannot get to the left hemisphere, which does the talking. However, if the investigator displays a set of objects and asks the woman to point to what she just saw, using her *left* hand, she points to a hat, which is what the right hemisphere saw! The left hemisphere and right hemisphere answer questions independently, as if they were separate people.

Split-brain people get along reasonably well in everyday life. Walking, for example, is no problem;

it is controlled largely by subcortical areas of the brain that exchange information through connections below the corpus callosum.

In special circumstances, the two hemispheres find clever ways to cooperate. In one experiment, a split-brain person was looking at pictures flashed on a screen, as in Figure 3.35b. He could not name most of the objects flashed in the left visual field, but after some delay, he could name such simple shapes as round, square, or triangular. Here is how he did it: After seeing the object (with the right hemisphere), he let his eyes move around the room. (Both hemispheres have control of the eye muscles.) When the right hemisphere saw something with the same shape as the object it had seen on the screen, it would stop moving the eyes. The left hemisphere just waited for the eyes to stop moving and then called out the shape of the object it saw.

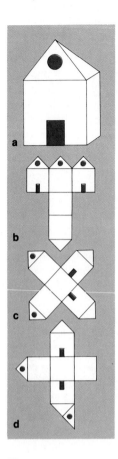

FIGURE 3.36

In one study, split-brain people were asked to feel an object (a) with one hand, without looking at it. Then they were asked to look at three drawings (b, c, d) and point to the one that could be folded to look like the object that they had felt. Most people pointed more accurately with the left hand (right hemisphere) than with the right hand (left hemisphere). (The correct answer is b.)

Concept Check

13. After damage to the corpus callosum, a person can describe some of what he or she sees, but not all. Where does the person have to see something in order to describe it in words? One eye or the other? One half of the retina? One visual field or the other? (Check your answer on page 97.)

Capacities of the Right Hemisphere

The left hemisphere of most people—almost all right-handers and more than half of left-handers—controls speech and writing. The right hemisphere of most people comprehends some language, but not so well as the left hemisphere does. The right side controls the left hand rather than the right hand, which is dominant for most people. For these reasons, scientists used to refer to the right hemisphere as the "minor" or the "nondominant" hemisphere.

However, observations have revealed that split-brain people can perform some tasks better with the left hand than with the right. For example, researchers asked split-brain people to feel various objects with one hand without looking at them (Levi-Agresti & Sperry, 1968). Thus only one hemisphere would receive the touch information. Then they were asked to look at some two-dimensional drawings, like those in Figure 3.36, and to point to the one that could be folded to look like the object they had felt. Most people pointed more accurately with the left hand (right hemisphere) than with the right hand (left hemisphere).

In another experiment, split-brain people were asked to copy simple drawings of objects such as a house, first with one hand and then with the other (Gazzaniga, 1970). Figure 3.37 shows some typical drawings by a right-handed split-brain person. Note that the left hand drew figures that were somewhat sloppy yet had their parts properly arranged with respect to one another. The right hand drew more neatly but confused the relationship of the parts.

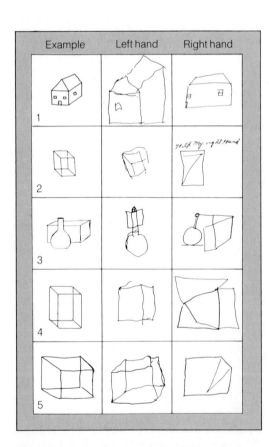

FIGURE 3.37

A right-handed split-brain person attempted to copy simple drawings with the left and right hands. The left hand was less coordinated but more accurate. (From Gazzaniga, 1970.)

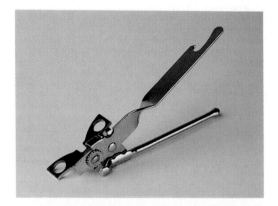

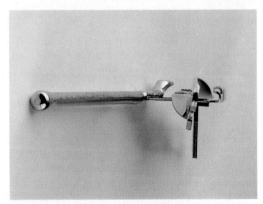

FIGURE 3.38

People who have had massive damage to the right hemisphere cannot always recognize a familiar object from an unusual angle.

Further information comes from studies of people with massive damage to the right hemisphere, generally as a result of a stroke. A normal person who can recognize a face or an object in its normal position can also recognize it from another angle (Figure 3.38). Many people with right-hemisphere damage can recognize faces and objects in their normal position, but only in that position (Layman & Greene, 1988). The right hemisphere is evidently critical for mentally manipulating visual information.

Hemispheric Differences in People Without Brain Damage: WHAT'S THE EVIDENCE?

Unless you are one of those rare people with a damaged corpus callosum, your corpus callosum provides constant, rapid communication between your two hemispheres. You can use either hand to point to what you have seen in either visual field. You—or more precisely your left hemisphere—can describe any information that enters either of your cerebral hemispheres. You can work puzzles and draw pictures accurately with either hand.

You may occasionally hear someone talk about the differences between "left-brained people and right-brained people," or say something like, "I failed introductory logic because it was a left-brained course and I'm a right-brained person." Presuming that the person is not *literally* half brained, you should be skeptical of such a claim. Still, we can demonstrate that certain tasks activate one hemisphere slightly more than the other in a normal person (see Figure 3.39). Let's look at an example.

Hypothesis Identification of the sounds of words depends mostly on the activity of the left hemisphere. Because gazing to the right tends to activate the left hemisphere (which sees the right visual field) and gazing to the left tends to activate the right hemisphere, a person should be able to identify the sound of a word more effectively when gazing to the right than when gazing to the left.

Method Jerre Levy and Linda Kueck (1986) asked 40 right-handed college students to look at arrays like the one in Figure 3.40. Half were told to scan left to right; the other half were told to scan right to left. The experimenter said a word such as *aid*. In the next 60 seconds, subjects tried to find words that rhymed with the word the experimenter had just spoken. (You might try finding words that rhyme with *aid* in Figure 3.40.) The number of available rhyming words was the same on the left side of the array as on the right side.

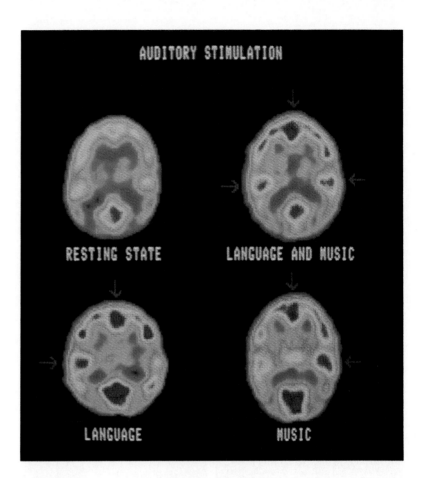

Results The subjects found a mean of 42.9% of the words on the right side and 37.9% of the words on the left side within the allotted 60 seconds. That difference is small but statistically significant.

Interpretation Subjects found more of the rhyming words on the right side than on the left side because the left hemisphere increases its activity when the person gazes to the right. And the left hemisphere is essential for this task. If the task had required skills present mostly in the right hemisphere, then the person would have performed better when gazing left.

Note that the effect was a fairly small one. Producing large effects in experiments like this is difficult with normal people (Hahn, 1987), presumably because the left hemisphere is only slightly more active when gazing right than when gazing left. In fact, both hemispheres are reasonably active at all times. ■

Concept Check

14. People with an intact brain and left-hemisphere control of language read a story and then listen to true-false questions. They answer by pressing one button for true *and another for* false. *Such people can answer equally accurately with either hand, but they respond slightly faster with the right hand. Explain. (Check your answer on page 97.)*

FIGURE 3.39

PET scans of the brain during four types of auditory stimulation. PET scans depend on the brain's use of glucose to fuel its activity. A volunteer is injected with a minute dose of a radioactive chemical closely related to glucose. That chemical, which tends to concentrate where there is increased activity, is detected by its emission of radioactivity. The resulting signals are processed by a computer to give these maps that show which parts of the brain are the most active. The highest concentration of radioactive chemical—and thus of brain activity—is indicated by the color red.

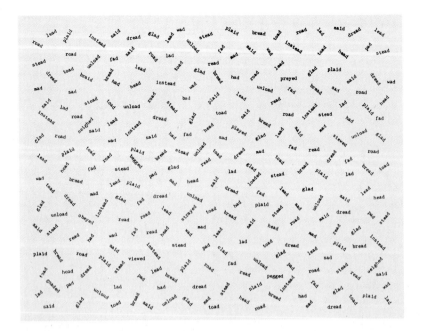

FIGURE 3.40

In one of the arrays used in the experiment by Jerre Levy and Linda Kueck (1986), subjects tried to find the words that rhyme with *aid* in 60 seconds.

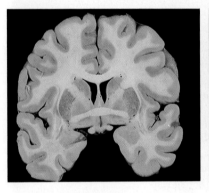
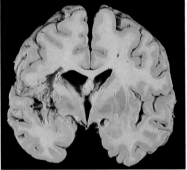

a   b

FIGURE 3.41

Comparison of a cross section through the brain of (a) a normal person and (b) a person who had had a stroke demonstrates the loss of cells in the brain of the stroke victim.

BRAIN DAMAGE AND BEHAVIORAL RECOVERY

You may have heard the expression, "They say we use only 10% of our brain." Stop and think about that for a moment. Who are "they"? No one who does research on the brain ever says anything of the sort. What does the statement really mean? Does it mean that someone could lose 90% of the brain and still function normally? If so, the statement is false. Does it mean that only 10% of the neurons in the brain are active at any given time? If so, false again. Perhaps it means simply that we could all know more and do more than we know and do now. That is undeniably true, though it has nothing to do with the estimated 10% (or any other numerical estimate). We all use all of our brain (even those who do not seem to be using their brains very well). Any loss of brain cells leads to some behavioral deficits or limitations.

Sooner or later, someone you know will probably suffer brain damage. The most common cause is a **stroke**, which is an interruption of the oxygen supply to the brain, caused by a blood clot in the brain or by some other interruption of the flow of blood. Because neurons cannot survive very long without oxygen, the result of a stroke is a loss of neurons. Figure 3.41 compares a normal brain with the brain of a stroke victim. Note the areas of lost cells in the stroke victim's brain.

A person who survives a stroke will suffer certain behavioral deficits, depending on the location of the damage. As time passes, however, the deficits usually decrease. For example, recall what happens after damage to the right parietal lobe: The person at first totally ignores the left side of the body and the left side of the world. If the damage is not too severe, however, the stroke victim gradually begins attending to stimuli on the left side, at least when there are no stimuli on the right side competing for attention. As recovery progresses over a period of weeks, the person comes to attend to both sides about equally, although he or she may still attend to stimuli on the right side first.

The reason for the recovery is not obvious. Dead neurons cannot be replaced by new ones, as dead skin cells can. A simple theory might be that one of the surviving brain areas takes over the functions of the damaged area. The evidence, however, contradicts that suggestion, except in children below the age of about 3–5, because their brains are not yet fully developed. After certain kinds of brain injury, children recover from the direct effects (such as loss of muscle control) better than adults do, although they suffer some generalized deficits (such as loss of intelligence) never seen in adults (Taylor, 1984). It is as if the undamaged areas assumed some of the functions of the damaged areas, but in so doing they lost certain functions of their own.

After damage to an adult brain, however, no area of the brain reorganizes its connections to assume a new function, any more than the right arm takes over the functions of a broken nose. How then does recovery take place?

Therapies for Brain Damage

After brain damage, certain structural changes occur within the brain (Finger & Stein, 1982). Glia remove dead cells and other toxic materials, and some of the surviving synapses in the affected area become more sensitive to neurotransmitters. In some cases, these and other structural changes contribute to recovery. Various therapies can aid this automatic recovery process. We shall look at two therapies, one structural and one behavioral.

Partial Brain Transplants Suppose you suffered damage to part of your brain. What would happen if a surgeon took the corresponding part of someone else's brain and transplanted it into yours? Never mind, for the moment, where the surgeon might find a donor or what kind of identity crisis you might experience. Let's just consider whether the operation might work.

If the surgeon took brain tissue from an adult donor, then the answer is simple: The operation would not work. Chances would be better if the donor was a **fetus** (an individual at an early stage of prenatal development). The neurons of a fetus are still growing and are primed to make connections with other neurons. In laboratory experiments, investigators have damaged part of a rat's brain, waited until the animal had recovered as much as it could by itself, and measured its behavioral deficits. Then they took the corresponding area from the brain of a fetal rat and transplanted it into the damaged brain of the adult. In a number of experiments, the rats that received the brain transplants showed substantial behavioral recovery (Gash, Collier, & Sladek, 1985).

Does this therapy have any potential for humans? The obvious problem is finding donors. One possibility is to transplant tissue from aborted fetuses. Although that procedure is theoretically the most likely to succeed, it arouses ethical objections and presents practical difficulties. For the transplant to succeed, the tissue would have to be taken at just the right stage of development and would have to be implanted almost immediately into the recipient's brain.

Another possibility is to take brain tissue from the fetus of a related species. Theoretically, such a procedure might work; brain tissue has been transplanted successfully from mice to rats (Bjorklund, Stenevi, Dunnett, & Gage, 1982).

Still another possibility has been tried as a treatment for Parkinson's patients—substituting adrenal gland tissue for brain tissue. Because adrenal gland cells produce dopamine, they can stand in for the lost neurons that released dopamine as

After a stroke at age 39, actress Patricia Neal had to learn how to walk and talk again. Dominoes and jigsaw puzzles were part of her therapy. Within three years she resumed her career.

their neurotransmitter. A few Parkinson's patients in Sweden, Mexico, and the United States have received adrenal gland transplants (Backlund et al., 1985; Lewin, 1988). Early reports seemed extremely promising, but long-term results have proved disappointing. Although the patients' condition generally improves after the transplant, it hardly returns to normal. Moreover, patients must continue to take medication.

Behavioral Therapies for Brain Damage If you suffered a deep cut on your right foot, you might still be able to hobble around by using your left foot as much as possible. You would be fully capable of walking on your right foot, but you would find it easier and less painful to rely on the left. However, heavy reliance on your left foot might sometimes be a hindrance. For example, you might choose to hop on one foot when it would be better to ignore the pain and run. Similarly, after brain damage, a patient often relies heavily on the undamaged parts of the brain just because it is easier to do so. Sometimes it is hard to tell whether a patient *cannot* do something or is simply not trying hard enough.

For example, someone whose vision or hearing has been impaired by brain damage may begin to rely more heavily on the other senses. As a result, the impaired sense may seem to be more impaired than it actually is. Rats with damage to their visual cortex can still learn (slowly) to respond to visual stimuli—*if* no other stimuli are present. If any other stimulus is changing—for example, if the floor is sometimes rough and sometimes smooth—the rats pay attention only to that other stimulus, even if it is irrelevant to the task (LeVere & LeVere, 1982). To find out what the rats can still do in response to visual stimuli, other forms of stimulation must be minimized.

By implication, some brain-damaged humans may be capable of doing more than they are doing, even shortly after they have suffered the damage. Recovery may depend less on structural changes in the brain than on learning to use what remains of the damaged areas. So the therapist should encourage such patients to tackle tasks that seem difficult for them to perform.

The Precarious Nature of Recovery

As we have seen, people can gradually recover some of the behaviors that are lost through brain damage. For example, a rat with damage to part of its hypothalamus at first neither eats nor drinks and seldom moves. If it is kept alive by tube feeding, it gradually begins to eat and drink a little of highly tasty substances, then a little more, and then begins to accept less tasty substances until eventually it eats enough of a normal diet to keep itself alive. Meanwhile, the rat begins to make a few simple movements and then more until eventually it has a full range of movements.

However, the recovered rat is still different from normal rats. Following sleep or any other period of inactivity, it needs a long warm-up period before it can move about normally (Golani, Wolgin, & Teitelbaum, 1979). If the room gets too cold, then the rat stops eating, drinking, and moving and returns to the behavior it exhibited just after the damage (Snyder & Stricker, 1985).

Similarly, many people who have recovered from a stroke deteriorate badly under conditions that a normal person tolerates with relative ease. A man who has recovered the ability to speak, for instance, may be able to utter only garbled nonsense after he has had a couple of alcoholic drinks.

Furthermore, long after people have recovered more or less normal behavior following brain damage, they may suffer a relapse in old age. An older person's behavior may deteriorate, eventually ending up about the same as it was just after the damage (Schallert, 1983).

This deterioration has interesting implications. If you suffer mild or gradual brain damage as a young adult—perhaps from a concussion, a brain infection, or the use of drugs—you may not notice any change in your behavior at the time. Your young brain compensates for the loss of neurons, and the surviving neurons may work a little harder to keep your behavior about the same. In old age, however, as natural processes lead to an additional loss of neurons and to less vigorous brain activity, the compensation begins to fail and the symptoms finally appear.

Something to Think About

Many young people who are exposed to toxins or brain infections show no symptoms at the time, but develop Parkinson's disease in old age. How might you explain this phenomenon, given what you have just learned about recovery from brain damage and deterioration in old age?

SUMMARY

1. Although nearly every structure of the brain contributes in some way to almost every behavior, each structure performs specialized functions. (page 76)

2. The central nervous system consists of the brain (forebrain, midbrain, and hindbrain) and the spinal cord. The peripheral nervous system consists of nerves that communicate between the central nervous system and the rest of the body. (page 78)

3. One division of the peripheral nervous system is the somatic nerves, which convey sensory information from the periphery to the central nervous system and which convey impulses from the central nervous system to the muscles. The other division of the peripheral nervous system is the autonomic nervous system, which regulates the activity of the internal organs. (page 78)

4. The autonomic nervous system is closely related to the endocrine system, organs that release hormones into the blood. (page 80)

5. The occipital lobe of the cerebral cortex is critical for vision. The parietal lobe is vital for touch and body sensations. The temporal lobe is essential for hearing, complex aspects of vision, and emotional behaviors. The frontal lobe contains the motor cortex, which controls fine movements. The anterior portion of the frontal lobe, the prefrontal cortex, is critical for planning movements and relating them to recent experiences. (page 84)

6. The corpus callosum is a set of axons through which the left and right hemispheres of the cortex communi-

cate. After it is damaged, information that reaches one hemisphere cannot be shared with the other. (page 86)

7. In humans, information from the left visual field strikes the right half of both retinas, from which it is sent to the right hemisphere of the brain. Information from the right visual field strikes the left half of both retinas, from which it is sent to the left hemisphere. (page 87)

8. The left hemisphere is specialized for language in most people. The right hemisphere is specialized to deal with visual and spatial relationships. (page 88)

9. Most brain-damaged people recover partly, although their behavioral capacities remain more precarious than those of people who have not suffered brain damage. Currently, the most successful therapy for brain damage is simply for the person to practice the impaired behaviors. (page 92)

SUGGESTIONS FOR FURTHER READING

Blakemore, C. (1977). *Mechanics of the mind*. New York: Cambridge University Press. A captivating, well-illustrated discussion of brain functioning.

Valenstein, E. S. (1986). *Great and desperate cures*. New York: Basic Books. A fascinating history of the rise and fall of prefrontal lobotomies.

TERMS TO REMEMBER

action potential a sudden decrease or reversal in electrical charge across the membrane of an axon

Alzheimer's disease a disease of old age marked by gradual damage to the brain leading to the gradual loss of memory and other abilities

artificial selection the purposeful selection, by humans, of certain animals for breeding purposes

autonomic nervous system a set of neurons lying in and alongside the spinal cord, which receives information from and sends information to the internal organs such as the heart

autosomal chromosomes the chromosomes other than the sex chromosomes

axon a single long, thin fiber that transmits impulses from a neuron to other neurons or to muscle cells

cell body the part of the neuron that includes the nucleus

central nervous system the brain and the spinal cord

cerebellum (Latin for *little brain*) a hindbrain structure

cerebral cortex the outer surface of the forebrain, consisting of six distinct layers of cells and fibers

chromosome a strand of hereditary material found in the nucleus of a cell

comparative psychology the branch of psychology that compares the behaviors of various animal species

corpus callosum a large set of axons connecting the left and right hemispheres of the cerebral cortex and enabling the two hemispheres to communicate with each other

dendrite one of the widely branching structures of a neuron that generally receive transmission from other neurons

deoxyribonucleic acid (DNA) the chemical that makes up a chromosome

dizygotic twins (literally two-egg twins) fraternal twins who develop from two ova fertilized by different sperm. Dizygotic twins are no more closely related than are any other children born to the same parents.

dominant gene a gene that will exert its effects on development even in a person who is heterozygous for that gene

dopamine a neurotransmitter that promotes activity levels and facilitates movement

endocrine system a set of glands producing hormones and releasing them into the blood

endorphin a neurotransmitter that inhibits the sensation of pain

epilepsy a disease characterized by abnormal rhythmic activity of some neurons in the brain

ethology the branch of biology that studies animal behavior under natural or nearly natural conditions

evolution a change in the gene frequencies of a species

fetus an individual at an early stage of prenatal development

finger-to-nose test a test to assess possible damage to the cerebellum in which a person is asked to hold one arm straight out and then touch the nose as quickly as possible

forebrain the most anterior (forward) part of the brain, including the cerebral cortex and the limbic system

frontal lobe the anterior portion of each hemisphere of the cerebral cortex, containing the motor cortex and the prefrontal cortex

gene a segment of a chromosome that indirectly controls development

genotype the entire set of genes within an individual

glia a cell of the nervous system that insulates neurons, removes waste materials (such as dead cells), and performs other supportive functions

glucose a sugar, the main source of nutrition for the brain

hemisphere in biology, the left or the right half of the brain

heterozygous having different genes on a pair of chromosomes

hindbrain the most posterior (hind) part of the brain, including the medulla, pons, and cerebellum

homozygous having the same gene on both members of a pair of chromosomes

hormone a chemical released by a gland and conveyed by the blood to other parts of the body, where it alters activity

interneuron a neuron that carries information from one neuron to another

limbic system forebrain structures below the cerebral cortex that are important for motivated and emotional behaviors such as eating, mating, and fighting

lysergic acid diethylamide (LSD) a chemical that can affect the brain, sometimes producing hallucinations

medulla a structure just above the spinal cord that controls many of the muscles of the head and several life-preserving functions such as breathing

midbrain the middle part of the brain, more prominent in birds and reptiles than in mammals

monozygotic twins (literally one-egg twins) identical twins who develop from a single fertilized ovum

motor cortex a strip of cerebral cortex in the rear of the frontal lobe, critical for fine control of the muscles

motor nerves nerves that convey impulses from the spinal cord to the muscles and glands

motor neuron a neuron that transmits impulses from the central nervous system to the muscles or glands

mutation a random change in the structure of a gene

natural selection the tendency, in nature, of individuals with certain genetically controlled characteristics to reproduce more successfully than others do

nerve a bundle of axons carrying messages from the sense organs to the central nervous system or from the central nervous system to the muscles and glands

neuron a cell of the nervous system that receives information and transmits it to other cells by conducting electrochemical impulses

neurotransmitter a chemical that is released by a neuron and then diffuses across a narrow gap to excite or inhibit another neuron

occipital lobe the rear portion of each hemisphere of the cerebral cortex, critical for vision

optic chiasm the location at which half of the axons from each eye cross to the opposite side of the brain

parietal lobe a portion of each hemisphere of the cerebral cortex that is essential for touch, for perception of one's own body, and to some extent for voluntary movement

Parkinson's disease a disease caused by the deterioration of a path of axons using dopamine as their neurotransmitter, characterized by difficulty in initiating voluntary movement

peripheral nervous system the nerves that convey messages from the sense organs to the central nervous system and from the central nervous system to the muscles and glands

phenotype the actual appearance of the individual, reflecting the way the genes have been expressed

phenylketonuria (PKU) an inherited disorder in which a person cannot break down phenylalanine, a common constituent of the diet; unless the diet is carefully controlled, the affected person becomes mentally retarded

pons a structure adjacent to the medulla that receives sensory input from the head and controls many muscles in the head

postsynaptic neuron a neuron on the receiving end of a synapse

prefrontal cortex the most anterior portion of the frontal lobe, critical for planning movements and for certain cognitive functions

prefrontal lobotomy an operation in which part of the prefrontal cortex is damaged or in which the connections are cut between the prefrontal cortex and other brain areas

recessive gene a gene that will affect development only in a person who is homozygous for that gene

reductionism the attempt to explain complex phenomena in terms of simpler components or events

regional cerebral blood flow technique (rCBF) a technique for estimating the level of activity in an area of the brain by dissolving radioactive xenon in the blood and measuring the radioactivity emitted in that area

reticular formation a diffuse set of neurons, extending from the medulla into the forebrain, that is largely responsible for variations in the level of arousal of the brain

retina the rear surface of the eye, lined with visual receptors

sensory nerves nerves that carry information from the sense organs to the spinal cord

sensory neuron a neuron that conveys sensory information to the central nervous system

serotonin a neurotransmitter that plays an important role in sleep and mood changes

sex chromosomes the chromosomes that determine whether an individual will develop as a female or as a male

sex-limited gene a gene that exerts its effects on one sex only or on one sex more than on the other, even though both sexes have the gene

sex-linked gene a gene situated on the X chromosome

sociobiology a field that tries to explain the social behaviors of animals in terms of their survival and reproductive advantages

somatic nervous system the nerves that control the muscles

somatosensory cortex a strip of cerebral cortex in the parietal lobe that is specialized for touch and related information

species-specific behavior a particular behavior that is widespread in one animal species but not in others

spinal cord the part of the central nervous system that communicates with sense organs and muscles below the level of the head

stroke an interruption of blood flow, and thus of oxygen supply, to part of the brain

synapse the specialized junction at which one neuron releases a neurotransmitter, which excites or inhibits another neuron

temporal lobe a portion of each hemisphere of the cerebral cortex that is critical for hearing, complex aspects of vision, and emotional behavior

terminal button a bulge at the end of an axon from which the axon releases a neurotransmitter

visual field what you see

X chromosome a sex chromosome of which females have two per cell and males have one

Y chromosome a sex chromosome found in males but not in females

ANSWERS TO CONCEPT CHECKS

1. It is impossible to say whether you are homozygous or heterozygous for the tongue-curling gene. Because that gene is a dominant gene, it produces the same effects in both the homozygous and the heterozygous conditions. If you cannot taste PTC, however, you must be homozygous for the nontasting gene. (page 59)

2. Because both of the parents must be homozygous for the inability to taste PTC, all their children will be unable to taste it also. Because both parents may be heterozygous for the tongue-curling gene, we cannot predict whether or not some of their children will be noncurlers. (page 59)

3. The woman will pass a dominant gene for normal color vision to all the children, so they will all have normal color vision. The man will pass a gene for deficient color vision on his X chromosome; the daughters will be carriers for color blindness. (page 60)

4. Because the infertile worker bees cannot reproduce, the only way they can pass on their genes is by helping the queen bee. Consequently, they will sacrifice their own lives to defend the queen. They will also risk their lives to defend other workers in the hive, because these workers also try to defend the queen. The queen, however, will do little to defend a worker, because doing so would not increase her probability of reproducing. (page 63)

5. The membrane gradually pumps the sodium ions out while simultaneously pumping potassium ions in. (page 70)

6. You will not feel the pain immediately because the action potential must travel from your foot to your brain. (If the action potentials travel at, say, 10 meters per second and your toe is about 1.5 meters from your brain, you will feel the pain about 0.15 second after you stub your toe.) (page 70)

7. Increased branching of the axons and dendrites will increase the number of synapses. (page 70)

8. Under the influence of a drug that prevents norepinephrine from attaching to its receptors, the postsynaptic neuron will receive less inhibition than usual. If we presume that the neuron continues to receive a certain amount of excitation, it will produce action potentials more frequently than usual. (page 70)

9. Haloperidol would increase the severity of Parkinson's disease. In fact, large doses of haloperidol can induce symptoms of Parkinson's disease in anyone. (page 74)

10. Another way to prevent Korsakoff's syndrome would be to require all alcoholic beverages to be fortified with vitamin B_1. (page 75)

11. The storage of fats takes place at many sites throughout the body. A hormone diffuses throughout the body; a neurotransmitter exerts its effects only on the neurons immediately adjacent to where it was released. (page 81)

12. The damage probably is in: (a) the right parietal lobe, (b) one of the temporal lobes, (c) the motor cortex in the left frontal lobe, (d) the right occipital lobe, and (e) at least part of the prefrontal cortex. (page 86)

13. To describe something, the person must see it with the left half of the retina of either eye. The left half of the retina sees the right visual field. (page 90)

14. Because they are responding to verbal questions, the left hemisphere must do the processing. They respond faster with the right hand because the left hemisphere controls it. Before they can answer with the left hand, the information has to cross the corpus callosum to the right hand. (That transit requires about 10 milliseconds.) (page 91)

CHAPTER

4

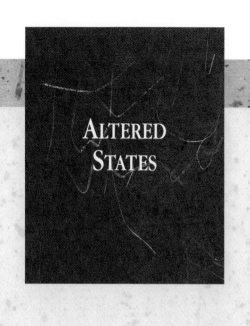

ALTERED
STATES

If I told you that you could flap your arms and fly, would you believe me? What if I told you that your cousin whom you have not seen in years is sitting in that empty chair in front of you? What if I said that as soon as you feel me tap your shoulder you will suddenly forget all your worries? Ordinarily you would not believe me for a second. You would wonder what was wrong with me that would make me say such ridiculous things.

And yet, if you had been hypnotized, you might accept my statements without even pausing to check whether they could be true. Similarly, in a dream you might find yourself flying, talking with famous people you have never met, or sitting in a classroom naked. You might ask yourself, "Is this really possible?" But you might not. In many dreams you simply accept what is happening as real.

People who take certain drugs also experience distortions of reality. They might see or hear things that no one else does. More frequently, they temporarily forget the serious problems that they will have to worry about when the drugs wear off.

Sleep, hypnosis, and drugs can produce altered states of awareness, altered states of interaction with the environment. The effects of sleep are distinctly different from those of hypnosis, and both differ sharply from the effects of drugs, and yet all three can enable people temporarily to believe in an altered reality that they would ordinarily reject as impossible.

Some 50,000 years ago, Australia's aborigines began interpreting their dreams through music, dance, and art about their Dreamtime, a mythical period when spirit ancestors created everything on the earth. The paintings, which were once done on the sandy soil of the desert, are now created on canvas, with dots of acrylic paint to reproduce the stones or clumps of plant matter that made up the traditional designs. Here a father is explaining his dreaming to his son.

Sleep
and
Dreams

Why do we sleep?
What accounts for the content of our dreams?

I have sometimes dreamed that I was flying or doing something else equally unlikely. After asking myself, in my dream, whether I was dreaming, I have sometimes decided that I was; at other times I have been uncertain; and a few times I have decided that I was really awake.

How do I know I am awake right now? Deciding that I am awake does not count for much, does it, if I have sometimes thought I was awake when I was really asleep?

Suppose you decide you are awake at this moment. How do you know that what you take to be the waking world is real and that the dream world you enter from time to time is unreal? You might say that the waking world lasts longer than dreams, contains more detail, and seems to follow laws of cause and effect. But there is no way for you to know for sure that your waking experiences are not illusions.

Even if we don't accept the idea of equating dreams with reality, we can identify an important similarity between dreaming and wakeful experience: Both are products of our brain. The difference is that wakeful experience is strongly influenced by external stimuli, whereas dreams are generated almost entirely from within. By studying dreams, we can learn some interesting things about the brain and about the dreamer.

Our 24-Hour Cycles

Humans and other animals that rely on vision for survival are active during the day and inactive at night (see Figure 4.1). Nothing could be more nat-

ural. But what happens to their day-night cycle if they are deprived of all external indicators of time? Two people spent a few weeks one summer in a remote part of Mammoth Cave in Kentucky, isolated from the outside world (Kleitman, 1963). For 24 hours a day, the temperature was a constant 12° Celsius and the relative humidity was a steady 100%. They saw no light except the light from lamps that they could control, and they heard no noises except the ones they made themselves. Nothing prevented them from staying awake all the time, from sleeping all the time, or from waking and sleeping by fits and starts. Yet, they went to sleep and awoke at about the same time every day. When they tried to adopt a different schedule, such as a 28-hour "day" (awake for 19 hours, asleep for 9), they found it difficult and unpleasant. Evidently, our daily rhythms depend on a built-in mechanism that continues to operate even in an unchanging environment.

We would not have been born with a mechanism that forces us to sleep for 8 hours or so out of every 24 unless sleep did us some good. But what good does it do? Scientists have proposed two theories.

Figure 4.1

An internal diurnal clock of 24 hours regulates your behavior. Even if you cannot find your watch, your body knows approximately what time it is. Its rhythmic changes in temperature and activity continue even if you have no external cues to time.

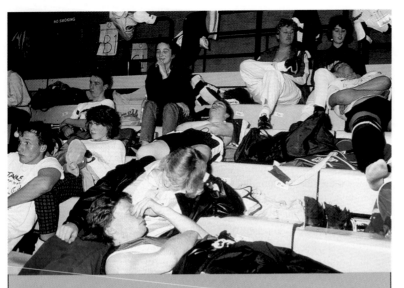

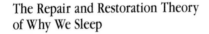

For every two hours awake, you spend one hour asleep—whether you've spent the day playing hockey or sitting at your desk. This need for periodic rest, regardless of your activity, suggests that sleep involves more than timeout to recuperate.

FIGURE 4.2

As a publicity stunt, disc jockey Peter Tripp stayed on the air for 10 days without sleep. After the first few days of his sleep-deprivation marathon, Tripp became increasingly irritable and irrational, particularly at night.

The Repair and Restoration Theory of Why We Sleep

According to the **repair and restoration theory**, the purpose of sleep is to enable the body to recover from the exertions of the day. During sleep the body increases its rate of cell division and the rate at which it produces new proteins (Adam, 1980). It also digests food. There is no doubt that these and perhaps other restorative processes do occur during sleep. But there are several reasons to doubt that we sleep only because of those processes.

First, if sleep were simply a means of recovering from the exertions of the day, it would resemble the rest periods we have after bouts of activity. But people need only a little more sleep after a day of extreme physical or mental activity than after a day of inactivity (Horne & Minard, 1985).

Second, some people get by with much less than the "normal" 7½ to 8 hours of sleep a day. An extreme case was a 70-year-old woman who claimed that she slept only about 1 hour a night. Researchers who observed her over a number of days confirmed her claim; some nights she did not sleep at all (Meddis, Pearson, & Langford, 1973). Nevertheless, she remained healthy.

Third, some people have intentionally gone without sleep for a week or more. The results have varied but have sometimes been milder than expected. In 1959, a New York disk jockey, Peter

Tripp, broadcast his radio show without sleeping for 10 consecutive days (see Figure 4.2). Toward the end, especially at night, he grew dizzy, irritable, and very unhappy. He experienced speech tremor, slurred speech, and gagging; he heard voices and "knew" that someone was trying to poison him. Yet when it was time to change a record or make an announcement he concentrated long enough to do his job properly, making only an occasional "strange" comment on the air (Johnson, 1969). After one night of sleep, his behavior returned nearly to normal.

In 1965 a San Diego high school student, Randy Gardner, stayed awake for 264 hours and 12 minutes in a project for a high school science fair. Unlike Tripp and most others with prolonged sleep deprivation, Gardner suffered no serious psychological consequences (Dement, 1972). On the last night of his ordeal he played about a hundred arcade games against psychologist William Dement and won every game. Just before the end of the 264 hours he held a television press conference and handled himself well. After sleeping 14 hours and 40 minutes, he awoke refreshed and apparently fully recovered.

Does this mean that it would be safe for you to go without sleep for 10 days? No. The reason we hear about Tripp and Gardner is that they were able to tolerate an unusually long sleep deprivation. Those who tried but failed to tolerate such deprivation are more common but less publicized.

If you go without any sleep some night—as

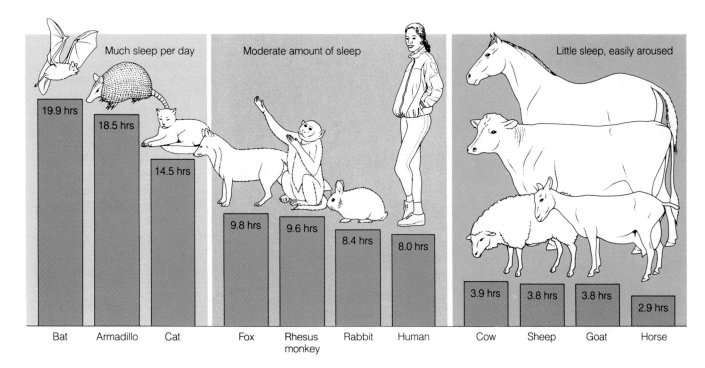

Much sleep per day			Moderate amount of sleep				Little sleep, easily aroused			
19.9 hrs	18.5 hrs	14.5 hrs	9.8 hrs	9.6 hrs	8.4 hrs	8.0 hrs	3.9 hrs	3.8 hrs	3.8 hrs	2.9 hrs
Bat	Armadillo	Cat	Fox	Rhesus monkey	Rabbit	Human	Cow	Sheep	Goat	Horse

FIGURE 4.3

Sleep time for mammals varies widely. Animals that are rarely attacked sleep a lot; those in danger of attack sleep only a few hours. Diet also relates to sleep. (Based on data from Zepelin & Rechtschaffen, 1974.)

most college students do at one time or another—you will probably grow very sleepy around 4:00 or 5:00 A.M. But if you are still awake later in the morning, you will feel much less sleepy than you did before. For the rest of the day you may feel a little strange, but you will probably have little difficulty staying awake and keeping reasonably alert. That night, however, you will feel very sleepy indeed. Apparently, the need to sleep is tied to particular time periods.

The Evolutionary Theory of Why We Sleep

Suppose we built a robot to explore the planet Mars. We provide the robot with visual detectors to help it explore the terrain and to steer it away from danger. It is fueled entirely by solar power. Should we program the robot to be equally active at all times?

No. The robot cannot see at night and might propel itself off a cliff or into rocks. Moreover, it would be using up energy at a time when it was not receiving any. So we would probably program it to cease its activity at night and to "awaken" at dawn the next morning.

According to the **evolutionary theory of sleep,** evolution equipped us with a regular pattern of sleeping and waking for the same reason (Kleitman, 1963; Webb, 1979). The theory does not deny

that sleep provides some important restorative functions. It merely says that evolution has programmed us to perform those functions at a time when activity would be inefficient and possibly dangerous. Note, however, that sleep protects us only from the sort of trouble we might walk into; it does not protect us from trouble that comes looking for us! So we sleep well when we are in a familiar, safe place, but we sleep lightly, if at all, when we fear that burglars will break into the room or that bears will nose into the tent.

The evolutionary theory accounts well for differences in sleep among species (Campbell & Tobler, 1984). Why do cats, for instance, sleep so much, while horses and sheep sleep so little? Surely cats do not need five times as much repair and restoration as horses do. But cats can afford to have long periods of inactivity because they spend little time eating and are unlikely to be attacked while they sleep. Horses and sheep must spend almost all their waking hours eating, because their diet is very low in calories (Figure 4.3). Moreover, they cannot afford to sleep too long or too soundly, because their survival depends on their ability to run away from attackers. (Woody Allen once said, "The lion and the calf shall lie down together, but the calf won't get much sleep.")

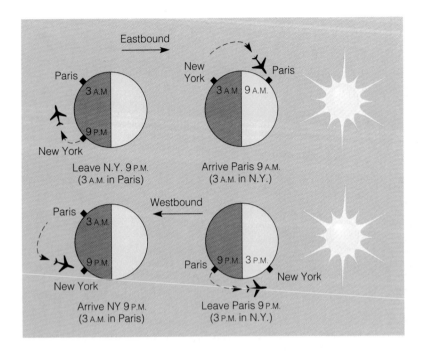

FIGURE 4.4

Direction and time differences influence jet lag. People traveling east "lose" time—and sleep—while those traveling west "gain" hours, helping them adjust to the new local time. When your flight leaves New York at 9:00 P.M., it's already 3:00 A.M. in your destination—Paris. When you arrive at 9:00 A.M., your body is still on schedule for 3:00 A.M. Later that night, when it is time to go to sleep, you may feel wide awake.

Shifting Sleep Schedules

When you travel across time zones, your internally generated cycles of waking and sleeping are thrown out of phase with the outside world. For example, if you travel from the west coast of North America to western Europe, it will be 7:00 A.M. (time to get up and go) when your body says it is 11:00 P.M. (time to go to bed). The resulting jet lag will make it difficult for you to fall asleep at night, to awaken in the morning, and to function during the day. Over days and weeks you will gradually adjust to your new schedule, but you will experience jet lag again when you return home. Back on the west coast, your body will scream, "Bedtime! Bedtime!" before anyone else thinks it is time for dinner.

Most people find it easier to adjust to a west-shifted time zone (where you go to bed later) than to an east-shifted time zone (where you go to bed earlier). East-coast people adjust to west-coast time more easily than west-coast people adjust to east-coast time (Figure 4.4). Adjusting to a new time zone is more difficult for some people than for others, and a few people find it almost impossible to adjust to an east-shifted time zone. If they have to move from the west coast to the east coast, they suffer **insomnia**, difficulty in getting to sleep or staying asleep. The same thing happens when they stay awake very late for a few nights in a row in

FIGURE 4.5

The graveyard shift is aptly named—serious industrial accidents, including those at nuclear power plants, usually occur at night, when workers are least alert. Night-shift jobs providing emergency services are essential. But few people want to work at night permanently, so workers rotate among three shifts. As in jet lag, the direction of change is critical. Moving forward—clockwise—is easier than going backward.

their own hometown. Their bodies cannot shift back to the earlier schedule once they have adjusted to the later schedule, and the result is insomnia.

Companies that want to keep their factories going nonstop run three work shifts: midnight to 8:00 A.M., 8:00 A.M. to 4:00 P.M., and 4:00 P.M. to midnight. Because it is difficult to find people to work regularly on the "graveyard shift" (midnight to 8:00 A.M.), many companies ask their workers to rotate among the three shifts. Depending on how the rotation is handled, the workers either adjust reasonably well or become unhappy, unhealthy, and inefficient.

Such companies should take two main considerations into account: First, workers should stay on one shift for a good stretch of time before being moved to another. If their schedule is changed every week, they will be unable to adjust well to any of the schedules. But if they stay on one shift for at least two or three weeks before moving to the next, they will adjust much better. Second, the direction of the rotation is important (Czeisler, Moore-Ede, & Coleman, 1982) (see Figure 4.5). A change from the 8:00 A.M. to 4:00 P.M. shift to the midnight to 8:00 A.M. shift is like traveling east; the adjustment is difficult. A change from the 8:00 A.M. to 4:00 P.M. shift to the 4:00 P.M. to midnight shift is like traveling west; the adjustment is easier. Workers in factories that use the clockwise, or "westward," shift have fewer health problems and are less likely to quit.

Concept Check

1. Suppose the leaders of the United States and the Soviet Union have agreed to meet for a summit conference halfway between Washington, DC, and Moscow. Should the United States prefer to meet in western Europe or on an island in the Pacific Ocean? (Check your answer on page 125.)

Something to Think About

What advice would you give someone who suffered severe, lasting insomnia because that person's body was not ready for sleep until 3:00 A.M.? Remember, the internal clock can shift more easily to a later time than to an earlier time. How could such a person reset his or her internal clock to the correct time?

STAGES OF SLEEP

In the mid-1950s, Michel Jouvet, a French scientist, discovered that brain activity and body activity vary from time to time during sleep. While trying to

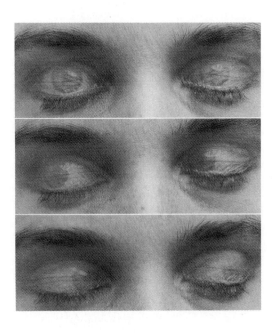

FIGURE 4.6

Rapid eye movements like those in this double-exposure photograph indicate when a sleeping person is dreaming.

record the very small head movements that a severely brain-damaged cat made while asleep, he found periods in which its brain was relatively active even though its muscles were completely relaxed. Further research indicated that such periods occur not only in brain-damaged cats but also in normal cats (Jouvet, Michel, & Courjon, 1959). Jouvet referred to these periods as *paradoxical sleep*. (A paradox is an apparent self-contradiction.) The paradox is that such sleep is very light in some respects but very deep in other ways. The brain is active, and the body's heart rate, breathing rate, and temperature fluctuate substantially (Parmeggiani, 1982). In these respects paradoxical sleep is very light. And yet most of the muscles, especially the large muscles involved in posture and locomotion, are very relaxed, and it is difficult to awaken someone during paradoxical sleep. In these respects paradoxical sleep is deep sleep.

At about the same time, American psychologists William Dement and Nathaniel Kleitman (1957a, 1957b) observed that in one stage of human sleep, the sleeper's eyes move rapidly back and forth under the closed lids (Figure 4.6). They referred to this stage as **rapid eye movement (REM) sleep**. (All other stages of sleep are known as **non-REM** or **NREM sleep**.) Almost at once investigators realized that REM sleep is the same as paradoxical sleep. When Dement and Kleitman awakened people during REM sleep, the sleepers usually reported that they had been dreaming. Apparently the rapid eye movements were external indications of an internal event; for the first time, it became possible to undertake scientific studies of dreaming.

FIGURE 4.7

These electrodes monitor the activity in a sleeper's brain, and an EEG then records and displays brain-wave patterns.

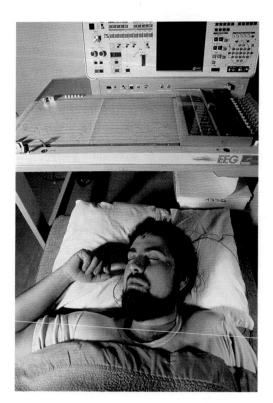

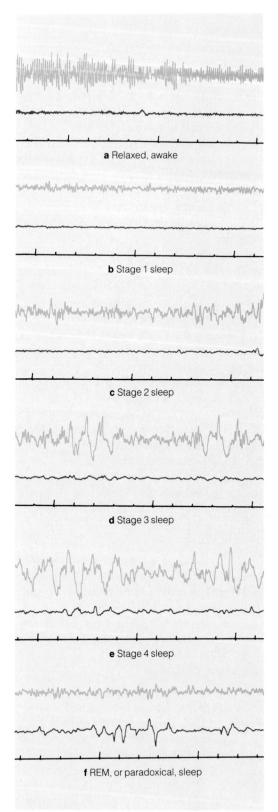

a Relaxed, awake

b Stage 1 sleep

c Stage 2 sleep

d Stage 3 sleep

e Stage 4 sleep

f REM, or paradoxical, sleep

Sleep Cycles During the Night

Sleep researchers have identified four stages of sleep: After we fall asleep, we progress from stage 1 sleep, in which the brain remains fairly active, through stages 2, 3, and 4. They can detect the stages by recording brain waves with electrodes attached to the scalp (Figure 4.7). A device called an **electroencephalograph**, abbreviated **EEG**, measures and amplifies slight electrical changes on the scalp that reflect patterns of activity in the brain. An awake, alert brain produces an EEG record with many short, choppy waves like the one shown in Figure 4.8a. In sleep stages 1 through 4, the brain produces an increasing number of long, slow waves, as shown in Figure 4.8b through e. These waves indicate *decreased* brain activity. They grow larger from one stage to the next because a larger proportion of the neurons are active at the same time. During wakefulness, by contrast, the neurons are out of synchrony and their activities nearly cancel each other out, rather like the voices of a crowd of people talking at the same time.

After we have reached stage 4 of sleep, we gradually move back through stages 3 and 2 to stage 1 again. A normal young adult cycles from stage 1 to stage 4 and back to stage 1 again in about 90 to 100 minutes. Then he or she repeats the sequence, again and again, all through the night (Figure 4.9). The first time through the cycle, stages 3 and 4 last the longest; later in the night the duration of stages 3 and 4 declines (and may disappear entirely), and

FIGURE 4.8

EEG recordings indicating wakefulness, stages 1 through 4 of sleep, and REM sleep. The blue line is the EEG from an electrode on the scalp. The red line records eye movements. And the black line indicates time in seconds. Over time, changes in these four stages and REM sleep will reflect changes in a sleeper's age and health.

the duration of stages 1 and 2 increases. Except for the first occurrence of stage 1 (when the person is just entering sleep), REM periods replace many or most of the stage 1 periods. Figure 4.8f shows a period of REM sleep. Note both the active EEG recordings and the eye movements.

Concept Check

2. *Would REM sleep and dreaming be more common toward the end of the night's sleep or toward the beginning? (Check your answer on page 125.)*

Sleep Stages and Dreaming

Dement's early research indicated that people who were awakened during REM sleep almost always reported they had been dreaming but that people who were awakened during any other period almost never reported dreaming. So, for a time, REM sleep was thought to be almost synonymous with dreaming. However, later studies found a fair amount of dreaming during non-REM sleep as well, although non-REM dreams are less vivid, less visual, less bizarre, and less likely to be experienced as something really happening.

The Function of REM Sleep: WHAT'S THE EVIDENCE?

What good is REM sleep? Or, as earlier researchers might have asked, what good is dreaming? There must be some reason why we evolved a tendency to go through cycles of REM and non-REM sleep. The most direct way to test the function of REM sleep is to deprive people of it.

Hypothesis   People who are deprived of REM sleep will show some sign of needing more REM sleep. At first, investigators did not know what sort of sign to expect.

Method   Dement (1960) monitored the sleep of eight young men for seven consecutive nights and awakened them for a few minutes whenever their EEG and eye movements indicated the onset of REM sleep. He awakened the members of a control group the same number of times but at random, so that he did not necessarily interrupt their REM sleep.

Results   Over the course of a week, Dement found it harder and harder to prevent REM sleep. On the first night the average subject in the experimental group had to be awakened 12 times. By the seventh night, the average subject had to be awakened 26 times, often with great difficulty. On the eighth night, all the subjects were permitted to sleep without

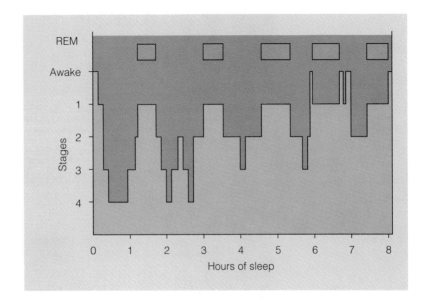

interruption. Most of them showed an "REM rebound," spending 29% of the night in REM sleep as compared with 19% before the experiment started. The subjects in the control group showed no such REM rebound because they had not been deprived of REM sleep.

Interpretation   REM sleep appears to satisfy some need, because the body tries to get more REM sleep after it has been deprived of it. This initial study led to a series of follow-up studies in which investigators measured the effects of REM deprivation on many aspects of behavior in humans and other species. Most people deprived of REM sleep report an increase in anxiety and irritability and some difficulty in concentrating (Ellman, Spielman, Steiner, & Halperin, 1978; Hoyt & Singer, 1978). Many report a ravenous appetite. Cats that have been deprived of REM sleep often engage in increased and indiscriminate sexual behavior, but this behavior has not been reported in humans.

In general, the effects of REM deprivation are not catastrophic and in some cases not even unpleasant. Selective deprivation of REM sleep may even bring about a striking improvement in the mood of some severely depressed people (Vogel, Thompson, Thurmond, & Rivers, 1973). Although REM-deprivation studies indicate that we do have a need for REM sleep, they tell us little about *why* we need it.

A second way to approach the question is to determine which people get more REM sleep than others. One clear pattern is that infants get more REM sleep than children do and that children get more than adults do (Figure 4.10).

From that observation, a number of people have inferred that REM sleep promotes brain development or serves some other function that is more

FIGURE 4.9

Condensing hundreds of pages of EEG recordings over a night, this graph shows that a person had five cycles of REM and non-REM sleep and woke up briefly three times. The large amount of stage 3 and 4 sleep early in the night is typical of most people. During such non-REM sleep, the body uses little energy. Brain activity, respiration, and temperature decrease. (From Dement, 1972.)

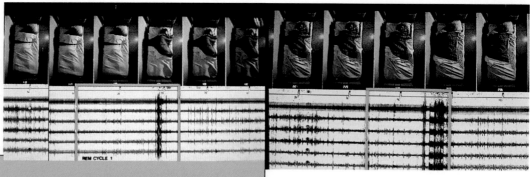

Monitoring the twilight zone: Below these pictures of a person in REM sleep are corresponding data reflecting physiological changes. An EEG records electrical activity in different parts of the brain, while other sensors detect muscle movement around the eyes and muscle tension under the chin. Through such research, psychologists hope to understand why we require REM sleep.

There is another way to study the function of REM sleep: Most people get less than 10% REM sleep during the first half of a night's sleep and more than 30% during the second half. Based on this fact, researchers have investigated whether the second half of a night's sleep gives us any special benefits that the first half does not. Let's examine another experiment in some depth.

Hypothesis   Psychologists have long known that learning something just before going to bed is a good way to strengthen a memory. Mary Fowler, Michael Sullivan, and Bruce Ekstrand (1973) tested whether REM sleep is particularly important in strengthening memories. They reasoned that if REM sleep promotes memory, then memory should improve more during the second half of a night's sleep, which includes a higher proportion of REM sleep.

Method   Three groups of 16 college students each tried to memorize a list of 15 words. The control group studied the list during the day and was tested 3½ hours later. The first experimental group was awakened soon after they went to sleep. They then studied the list and returned to sleep; 3½ hours later they were reawakened and tested. The second experimental group was awakened 4 hours after they went to sleep. They then studied the list and returned to sleep, to be reawakened and tested 3½ hours later. The difference among the three groups was whether their retention interval occurred during normal waking activities, the first half of a night's sleep, or the second half.

Results   The first experimental group, whose retention interval was the first half of their night's sleep, had the best memory of the word list. The second experimental group, whose retention interval was the second half of their night's sleep, had the second-best memory. The control group, whose retention interval was filled with normal waking activities, had the worst memory.

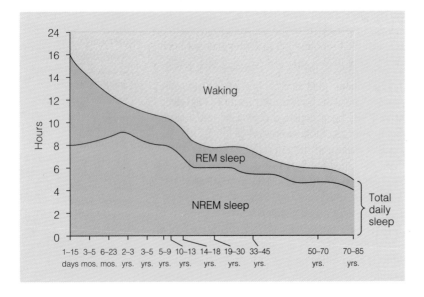

Figure 4.10

The percentage of time in REM and non-REM sleep varies with age. Most adults spend 75% of their sleep time in non-REM sleep. (From Roffwarg, Muzio, & Dement, 1966.)

acute in younger people. Maybe so, but we should be cautious about this evidence. Infants not only get more REM sleep but they also get more *total* sleep. If we compare species, we find that the species that get more total sleep (such as cats) have a greater percentage of REM sleep than those that get less total sleep (such as sheep). Among adult humans, those who sleep 9 or more hours per night spend much of that time in REM sleep; those who sleep 6 hours or less spend a smaller percentage of time in REM sleep. It is doubtful that cats gain more brain development than sheep, or that sleepy-head adult humans gain an unusual amount of brain growth. Perhaps infants get more REM sleep than adults simply because they get more total sleep.

Interpretation Evidently, REM sleep is not particularly beneficial to memory. Memory was better after 3½ hours of sleep than after 3½ hours of wakefulness, but it was better if that sleep included little REM sleep (the first half of the night) than if it included more than 30% REM sleep.

These results suggest that non-REM sleep is better for memory than REM sleep. But other interpretations are also possible: For example, maybe it is more difficult to store memories when one is awakened in the middle of the night than if one is awakened early in the night. Although the two groups were equally fast in memorizing the list, it is difficult to eliminate the possibility that they had not learned equally well.

Why then do we need REM sleep? At this point, we still do not know. We cannot rule out the possibility that it serves a function in brain maturation, although other hypotheses abound. Perhaps REM sleep is just a way of periodically arousing the brain without actually waking up. And perhaps it serves other functions not yet identified. ■

Insomnia can signal other disorders. Severely depressed people, for example, often have trouble falling asleep; they also wake up too early and then cannot return to sleep.

ABNORMALITIES OF SLEEP

The term *insomnia* refers to getting less sleep than one needs. Different people need different amounts of sleep. Sleeping 6 hours a night might constitute insomnia for one person; it might be normal for another. People who are tired and inefficient during the day are not getting enough sleep at night. Those who are alert and active during the day are sleeping enough, regardless of exactly how many hours they spend in bed at night.

It is convenient to distinguish three main types of insomnia: People with **onset insomnia** have trouble falling asleep. Those with **termination insomnia** awaken early and cannot get back to sleep. Those with **maintenance insomnia** awaken repeatedly during the night, though they get back to sleep each time. In many cases onset insomnia and termination insomnia are related to an internal biological rhythm that is out of synchrony with the outside world. At 11:00 P.M. a person with onset insomnia may feel as if it were still only 6:00 P.M. At 2:00 A.M. a person with termination insomnia may already feel as if it were 7:00 A.M. In such cases, therapy is a matter of trying to readjust the biological rhythms so the person can feel sleepy and wakeful at the normal times.

One cause of extremely poor sleep is known as **sleep apnea** (AP-nee-uh). (*Apnea* means "no breathing.") People with sleep apnea, many of whom are overweight middle-age men, have trouble breathing while they sleep (Weitzman, 1981), either because of damage to the medulla or because their breathing passages are obstructed when they are in a sleeping position. They fall asleep for a minute or two and then wake up gasping for breath. They may lie in bed for 8 to 10 hours a night but actually sleep less than half that time. During the following day they are likely to feel sleepy.

Some people suffer from **narcolepsy**, a medical condition that causes them to grow sleepy in the middle of the day. They may experience sleep as a sudden, irresistible "attack," generally triggered by a strong emotion. The causes are obscure, but stimulants and antidepressant drugs are moderately successful in controlling the condition. Affected people must learn to avoid situations that arouse strong emotions.

In a less spectacular but more common form of narcolepsy, affected people just feel drowsy much of the day and have trouble getting to sleep at night. Part of their problem is that their sleep cycle is out of phase with the outside world, and they seem unable to readjust it.

Sleep talking is another unusual event during sleep, although it is hardly abnormal. Most people talk in their sleep, at least once in a while (Arkin, 1978). The frequency with which sleep talking occurs is generally underestimated, because sleep talkers do not remember it themselves and usually no one else is awake to hear it. Sleep talking occurs in both REM sleep and non-REM sleep. It may range from

Centuries ago, nightmares (or bad dreams) were commonly thought to be the work of an incubus, an evil spirit or being who took advantage of people while they slept.

Concept Check

3. *Why would it be unlikely, if not impossible, for sleepwalking to occur during REM sleep? (Check your answer on page 125.)*

SOME QUESTIONS AND ANSWERS ABOUT SLEEP AND DREAMS

Are there differences between "good sleepers" and "poor sleepers"? Yes. "Good sleepers" fall asleep within 10 minutes after going to bed and seldom wake up without reason during the night. "Poor sleepers" take more than an hour to fall asleep and wake up one or more times during the night. About one fourth of all adults have some difficulty sleeping, and nearly three fourths of all psychiatric patients have difficulty sleeping (Soldatos & Kales, 1982). Whether sleep is good or poor has nothing to do with how long it lasts; 6 hours for one person may be more restful than 9 hours for another.

Good sleepers spend more time lying motionless (Hobson, Spagna, & Malenka, 1978). Poor sleepers change position more often and spend more time lying on their back (DeKoninck, Gagnon, & Lallier, 1983), though we cannot conclude that lying on one's back causes poor sleep. (Remember from Chapter 2 that correlation is not the same as causation.) Many overweight middle-age men sleep on their back because it is uncomfortable for them to lie on their stomach. They also have difficulty sleeping for reasons that are related to being overweight and not to sleeping position.

Is it possible to learn while asleep? Extravagant claims have been made about learning while asleep. Because the brain is relaxed and distractions are absent, the argument goes, people learn more efficiently from a tape recording while asleep than while awake.

However, learning during sleep is less effective than wakeful learning (Aarons, 1976). People who listen to tape-recorded information while asleep can recall little of it when they wake up, though they may learn the information more easily *after* they wake up.

Does everyone dream? Everyone studied in the laboratory has gone through normal REM periods. Even people who claim they never dream will say, if they are awakened during an REM period, "Well, I guess I was dreaming that time," and then proceed to describe a dream. Apparently such people do have dreams; they just fail to remember them.

a single, indistinct word or grunt to a clearly articulated paragraph. Sleep talkers sometimes pause between utterances, as if they were carrying on a conversation. In fact, you can sometimes engage them in a dialogue. Sleep talking is nothing to worry about. It is not related to any mental or emotional disorder, and sleep talkers rarely give away any secrets or say anything they would be embarrassed to say when awake.

Sleepwalking tends to run (walk?) in families. A person who appears to be sleepwalking may really be awake but confused. True sleepwalking occurs mostly in children during stage 4 sleep and lasts less than 15 minutes. Few children hurt themselves when sleepwalking, and most children outgrow it (Dement, 1972).

Finally, what about nightmares? Psychologists distinguish between nightmares and night terrors. A nightmare is simply an unpleasant dream that, except for the presence of anxiety, is much like any other dream. A night terror, however, creates a sudden arousal from sleep accompanied by extreme panic, including a heart rate three times the normal rate. Night terrors occur during stage 3 or stage 4, never during REM sleep. They are fairly common in young children, but their frequency declines with age (Salzarulo & Chevalier, 1983).

Rare cases have been reported of adults who experience both sleepwalking and night terrors, sometimes simultaneously (Hartmann, 1983). Some of them walk around flailing their arms wildly. One man is reported to have driven a car at high speed down the wrong side of the road while in a sleepwalking state.

However, their dreams are usually less intense and less emotional than most people's dreams are. Perhaps they forget their dreams because their dreams are, frankly, boring.

We all dream more than we remember. When people are awakened more than 5 minutes after the end of an REM period, they seldom report a dream. When we awake in the morning, the only dream we remember is the one that has just ended. And we quickly forget that dream unless we think or talk about it.

How long do dreams last? People once believed that dreams last only a second or so, but evidence indicates that dreams last about as long as they seem to last. William Dement and Edward Wolpert (1958) awakened people after varying periods of REM sleep and asked them to describe their dreams. A person awakened after 1 minute of REM sleep would usually tell a 1-minute story. A person awakened after 5 minutes of REM sleep would usually tell a 5-minute story—and so on, up to about 15 minutes. After more than 15 minutes of REM sleep, people would still tell only 15-minute stories, apparently forgetting the rest.

Occasionally a dream seems to last hours, even days. That is because of cuts and shifts in scenes. As in a play or a movie, a dream sometimes includes the transition, "Now it's the next day. . . ."

What do we dream about? The content of dreams comes from many sources, sometimes including the stimuli that happen to be acting on your body at the moment (Arkin & Antrobus, 1978; Dement, 1972). A sprinkle of water on your face may become a dream about rainfall, a leaky roof, or going swimming. A sudden loud noise may become a dream about an earthquake or a plane crash. A bright light may become a dream about flashes of lightning or a fire.

Some common motivations carry over from wakefulness into dreams (Arkin & Antrobus, 1978). People deprived of fluids frequently dream about drinking. People who have been kept in isolation dream about talking in groups. Several experiments have tested the effects of watching movies just before going to sleep. People who have watched violent movies tend to have unusually clear, vivid, and emotional dreams, though they are not necessarily violent. After watching movies with a great deal of explicit sexual content, people who are asked about their dreams frequently say, "I, uhh . . . forget what I was dreaming about."

To a large degree, dream content reflects spontaneous activity in the brain. During REM sleep, heightened activity occurs spontaneously in the cerebral cortex, especially in the areas responsible for vision, hearing, and movement. According to the **activation-synthesis theory of dreams**, the brain experiences this spontaneous activity as sensations, links the sensations together, and tries to synthesize them into a coherent pattern (Hobson, 1988). The product of that attempt is a dream. Because brain activity is spontaneous, the dream has a quality of "just happening." We do not decide to make a movement; the movement just happens. We do not decide to speak or to look to the left; the action just happens.

I sometimes dream that I am trying to move but I can't. Why is that? During REM sleep, one little section of the midbrain (the *caudal locus coeruleus*) sends messages to the nerves of the spinal cord causing the large muscles that control posture to relax completely. (Finger movements, twitches, and other small movements are unaffected.) Those messages make it almost impossible for you to move your muscles during REM sleep. Is that why we dream about an inability to move? Perhaps, although we cannot be sure.

Cats with damage to this section of the midbrain have nothing to inhibit their muscle activity; they become very active during REM sleep, running, jumping, pouncing, and giving every indication of acting out a dream (Jouvet & Delorme, 1965).

Why do I frequently dream that I am falling or flying? During sleep your head is in a different position from the position it is in when you are awake. Either for that reason, or just spontaneously, bursts of high activity occasionally occur in the part of the cerebral cortex responsible for *vestibular sensation* (sensation arising from the tilt of the head). Such sensations may get incorporated into dreams of flying, falling, twirling, and the like (Hobson & McCarley, 1977).

Do we dream in color? The very fact that people ask this question reveals why it is difficult to answer. People ask because they do not remember whether their dreams were in color. But how can an investigator determine whether people dream in color except by asking them? The best answer we have is that when people are awakened during REM sleep, when their recall is sharpest, they report color half the time or more (Herman, Roffwarg, & Tauber, 1968; Padgham, 1975). This does not mean that their other dreams are necessarily in black and white; it may mean only that the colors in those dreams are not bright, distinct, or memorable. Generally, dreams that occur toward the end of the night are the most visual, with the brightest colors.

"Even a saint is not responsible for what happens in his dreams."
ST. THOMAS AQUINAS

Joan Miró (here in his studio), Max Ernst, and other surrealist artists attempted to capture their dreams on canvas through automatic, or stream of unconsciousness, painting. The landscapes of their imaginations included such eerie scenes as Salvador Dalí's watches melting in a wasteland.

What do blind people dream about? A person who has had vision and then lost it because of damage to the eyes continues to see during dreams. But a person who has never had vision or who has lost it because of damage to the occipital cortex does not see during dreams. People with any degree of visual impairment are more likely than sighted people to dream about things that are experienced through touch—such as wood or bricks (Sabo & Kirtley, 1982).

What does it mean when I have the same dream over and over again? The content of such a dream is probably related to something you are concerned about or perhaps to something that worries you from time to time. People who have a single dream at least a few times a year tend to report more anxiety, depression, and stress in their waking lives than do other people (Brown & Donderi, 1986).

Do dreams ever give us creative ideas? Sometimes. Dreaming is less inhibited and restricted than wakeful thinking; it permits associations that you might abandon out of hand while awake. When you dream you accept anything as possible; you seldom

stop to test reality. Some people keep a pencil and paper next to their bed so they can jot down notes when they awaken from a dream in the middle of the night. In the light of day, they reject most of their dream "insights" as nonsense, though occasionally they find something of value.

Can psychologists learn about people's thoughts and personalities from the content of their dreams? People do dream about matters that concern them. Many psychotherapists rely on dream interpretations to learn about their clients' thoughts and problems. I shall discuss Sigmund Freud's approach to dream interpretation in Chapter 15. But be cautious about dream interpretations. Some therapists interpret dreams so imaginatively that the interpretations probably reveal more about the therapist than they do about the client. Most of their claims of dream interpretation have not been verified scientifically.

SUMMARY

1. Sleepiness depends on the time of day. Even in an unchanging environment, people become sleepy in cycles of approximately 24 hours. (page 101)

2. A number of repair and restoration functions take place during sleep. Sleep also serves to conserve energy at times of relative inefficiency. (page 102)

3. During sleep, people cycle through sleep stages 1 through 4 and back through stages 3 and 2 to 1 again. The cycle beginning and ending with stage 1 lasts about 90 to 100 minutes. (page 105)

4. A special stage known as REM sleep replaces many of the stage-1 periods. REM sleep is characterized by rapid eye movements, a high level of brain activity, and relaxed muscles. People usually dream during this stage. (page 105)

5. Insomnia—unsatisfactory sleep patterns resulting in daytime fatigue—may have many influences, including a biological rhythm that is out of phase with the outside world, sleep apnea, and narcolepsy. (page 109)

SUGGESTION FOR FURTHER READING

Moorcroft, W. (1989). *Sleep, dreaming, and sleep disorders: An introduction.* Lanham, MD: University Press of America. An excellent review of research on many aspects of sleep and dreams.

HYPNOSIS

his own hand, would work just as well. We would now conclude that his therapy, when it worked, did so through the power of suggestion on people whose problems were psychological in origin. But Mesmer clung to the conviction that it depended on an "animal magnetism" that came from his own body.

In his later years Mesmer grew stranger and stranger. After his death, his followers carried out serious studies of "animal magnetism" or "Mesmerism," eventually giving it the name "hypnotism." But by that time, many physicians and scientists associated hypnosis with eccentrics, charlatans, and other practitioners of hocus-pocus.

What can hypnosis do?
What are its limitations?

Ilf someone told you that you were 4 years old, and you believed it and started acting like a 4-year-old, or if someone told you that you could not move, and suddenly indeed you could not move, then psychologists would say that you had been hypnotized. If you decided *on your own* that you were only 4 years old or that you could not move, then psychologists would say that you were suffering from some psychological disorder—probably something fairly serious. Hypnosis induces a temporary state that is sometimes bizarre. No wonder we find it so fascinating.

Psychologists define **hypnosis** as a condition of increased suggestibility that occurs in the context of a special hypnotist-subject relationship. The term *hypnosis* comes from Hypnos, the Greek god of sleep. Although it has long been assumed that hypnosis is somehow related to sleep, the connection is rather superficial. It is true that in both states the eyes are usually closed and the person is without initiative. Moreover, both in hypnosis and in dreams, a person accepts contradictory information without protest. A hypnotized person resembles a waking person, however, in his or her ability to move about and to respond to stimuli.

Hypnosis was first practiced by an Austrian philosopher and physician, Franz Anton Mesmer (1734–1815). In treating certain medical problems, Mesmer would pass a magnet back and forth across the patient's body to redirect the flow of blood, nerve activity, and certain undefined "fluids." His novel form of therapy seemed to help some patients dramatically.

Later Mesmer discovered that he could dispense with the magnet; a piece of wood, or even

WAYS OF INDUCING HYPNOSIS

Mesmer thought that hypnosis was a power emanating from his own body, like the power a magnet exerts on metals. If so, only certain people would have the power to hypnotize others. Today we believe that becoming a successful hypnotist requires a certain amount of skill and training but no unusual personality traits.

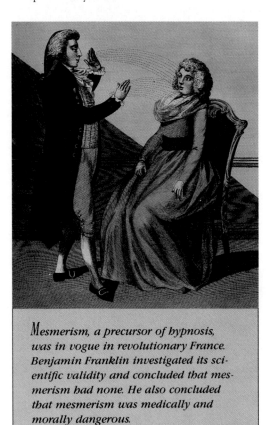

*M*esmerism, a precursor of hypnosis, was in vogue in revolutionary France. Benjamin Franklin investigated its scientific validity and concluded that mesmerism had none. He also concluded that mesmerism was medically and morally dangerous.

"Truth is nothing but a path traced between errors."*
FRANZ ANTON MESMER

*Don't ask me what this means.

FIGURE 4.11

The persuasive techniques of hypnotists include having subjects concentrate on the slow and monotonous rhythm of a pendulum or a metronome.

Hypnosis, which gets its name from a word for sleep, *resembles the suspended consciousness of sleep. When a novel draws you deeply into its world, you are entranced or "hypnotized" by it.*

There are several ways of inducing hypnosis. Typically, the hypnotist asks the subject to concentrate on something like a black dot on a white wall or on a swinging pendulum (see Figure 4.11). Meanwhile, the hypnotist repeats in a monotone: "You are starting to fall asleep. Your eyelids are getting heavy. Your eyelids are getting very heavy. They are starting to close. You are falling into a deep, deep sleep."

In another popular technique, described by R. Udolf (1981), the hypnotist suggests, "After you go under hypnosis, your arm will begin to rise automatically." (Some people, eager for the hypnosis to succeed, shoot their arm up immediately and have to be told, "No, not yet. Just relax; that will happen later.") Then the hypnotist encourages the subject to relax and suggests that the arm is starting to feel lighter, as if it were tied to a helium balloon. Later the hypnotist suggests that the arm is beginning to feel a little strange and is beginning to twitch. The timing of this suggestion is important, because after people stand or sit in one position long enough, their limbs really do begin to feel strange and twitch a bit. If the hypnotist's suggestion comes at just the right moment, the subject thinks, "Wow, that's right, my arm does feel a little strange. This is really starting to work!" Wanting to be hypnotized or believing that you are being hypnotized is a big step toward actually being hypnotized.

A little later the hypnotist may suggest that the subject's arm is starting to rise. If that fails, the suggestion may be revised a bit: "Your arm is so light

that when I push it upward a little, it will keep rising by itself." If the arm rises and then begins to waver and drop, a skilled hypnotist may say, "Now you can lower your arm." At some point along the way the subject's eyelids will close, even if the hypnotist has said nothing about closing them.

Gradually, the hypnotist brings the subject into a condition of heightened suggestibility. When people talk about the "depth" of hypnosis, they are making an estimate of how likely the subject is to do what the hypnotist suggests. A "deeply" hypnotized person will do what the hypnotist says to do and will experience (or at least will *report* experiencing) what the hypnotist says to experience.

What happens in hypnosis is not altogether different from what happens in ordinary experience. When you watch a good movie or play or read a good novel, you may become captivated by its "suggestions." You may focus your attention on the story and experience the emotions just as strongly as if you were one of the characters. Hypnosis has much the same effect (Barber, 1979).

Hypnosis can produce relaxation, concentration, temporary changes in behavior, and sometimes changes that persist beyond the end of the hypnotic state. There is no evidence, however, that it enables you to do anything you could not do ordinarily, with sufficient motivation.

DISTORTIONS OF PERCEPTION UNDER HYPNOSIS

One well-established effect of hypnosis on perception is the inhibition of pain. A hypnotic suggestion to feel no pain is sometimes so effective (with some people) that medical or dental surgery can be performed without anesthesia. Apparently, hypnosis has only a slight effect on the intensity of pain but a significant effect on the *distress* that accompanies pain (Hilgard, 1979). A hypnotized person may still feel the pain but simply "not care." That effect is particularly useful in certain kinds of surgery that are safer when performed without anesthetic drugs. Hypnosis also provides some relief for people who have developed a great tolerance to painkilling opiates or who for some reason cannot take opiates.

A few people report visual or auditory **hallucinations** (sensory experiences not corresponding to reality) under hypnosis; a larger number report touch hallucinations (Udolf, 1981). A hypnotist can bring about a touch hallucination by such suggestions as "Your nose itches" or "Your left hand feels numb."

When hypnotized people say that they see or hear something, or that they fail to see or hear something, are they telling the truth or are they just saying what the hypnotist wants them to say? There is no easy way to answer this question.

When a hypnotized person claims to feel no pain during abdominal surgery, we tend to take the person's word for it. Pretense can go only so far; surely the pain has been eased in one way or another. But visual and auditory hallucinations are another matter. In one experiment, people who were highly susceptible to hypnosis looked at the Ponzo illusion, shown in Figure 4.12a. Like other people, they reported that the top horizontal line looked longer than the bottom horizontal line. Then they were hypnotized and told not to see the radiating lines, just the two horizontal ones. Those who said that they no longer saw the radiating lines still perceived the top line as longer than the bottom one (Miller, Hennessy, & Leibowitz, 1973). If the radiating lines had truly disappeared, then the subjects would have seen something like Figure 4.12b, in which the horizontal lines look equal.

In another experiment, hypnotized subjects were told that they would hear nothing. From that point on, they appeared to be deaf, ignoring even shouts.

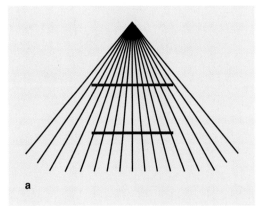

FIGURE 4.12

Horizontal lines of equal length in (a) the Ponzo illusion and (b) without the optical illusion. Researchers employ such visual stimuli to determine how hypnosis may alter sensory perception.

The experimenter spoke a word such as *dream*, showed the subjects four written words, and signaled for them to choose one—any way they wished. In each case, one of the words rhymed with the original word (such as *cream*) and one had a related meaning (such as *sleep*). The other two words were unrelated to the original word. A person who really did not hear the word *dream* would have a 50% chance of choosing one of the related words. The hypnotized subjects chose a related word 40% of the time (Nash, Lynn, Stanley, & Carlson, 1987). Evidently the hypnotized subjects did hear the word, but in some manner rejected it to make themselves appear to be deaf. (We cannot say whether they did so deliberately.)

So does hypnosis alter perception? Yes and no. Hypnosis does not screen out sensory information altogether, as if the sensory receptors had been destroyed. Evidently the information gets into the nervous system and persists long enough to exert some influence on behavior, even when people under hypnosis deny that they saw or heard anything.

Concept Check

4. In the experiment in which hypnotized people were told that they were deaf, what conclusion would we draw if they chose one of the related words more than 50% of the time? (Check your answer on page 125.)

SOME QUESTIONS AND ANSWERS ABOUT HYPNOSIS

Can everyone be hypnotized? Hypnotists claim that most people, except for young children and the mentally retarded, can be hypnotized "at least slightly" (whatever that means). Someone who wishes to can easily resist hypnosis, however; contrary to what you may have seen in movies or on

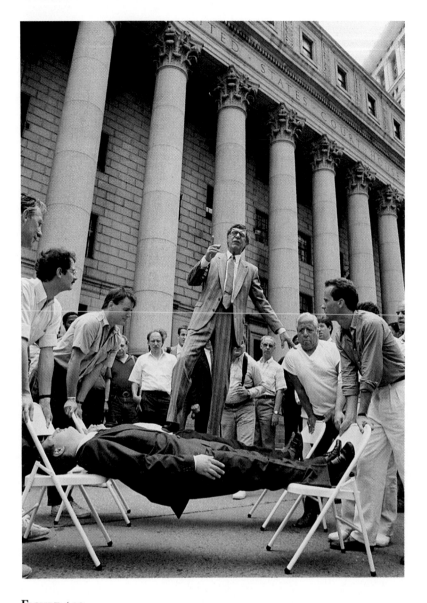

FIGURE 4.13

The U.S. Supreme Court ruled in 1987 that criminal defendants may testify about details they recalled under hypnosis. Its decision sparked this protest by the magician known as "the Amazing Kreskin." Kreskin borrowed a stunt usually used to demonstrate the power of hypnosis—standing on a person suspended between two chairs. Many psychologists and physicians doubt the accuracy of testimony obtained under hypnosis. Details reported with confidence under hypnosis often turn out to be factually inaccurate.

television, no one can hypnotize you if you do not want to be hypnotized. A hypnotist, like a teacher, can influence you only if you cooperate.

What happens if I go into a hypnotic state and can't wake up again? If the hypnotist dies or leaves, will I be stuck in some sort of trance forever? It is rare for anyone to experience any difficulty coming out of hypnosis. If the hypnotist leaves the room or stops talking, the hypnosis usually wears off in less than half an hour (Orne, 1979).

Do people under hypnosis show any special physical or mental powers they do not normally possess? Some spectacular claims have been made for the power of hypnotic suggestion, but on closer scrutiny most of them turn out to be less impressive. For instance, people under hypnosis can become as stiff as a board, so stiff that they can balance their head and neck on one chair and their feet on another chair and allow someone to stand on their body (Figure 4.13)! Amazing? Not really. You can probably do the same thing yourself without being hypnotized. (Do be careful about whom you invite to stand on you.)

Can a person fake the effects of hypnosis? In several experiments, one group (usually made up of college students) was "deeply" hypnotized while another group was told to pretend to be hypnotized. The pretenders were told that an experienced hypnotist would examine people from both groups and would try to determine which ones were really hypnotized.

Fooling the hypnotist turned out to be easier than expected. The pretenders were able to tolerate sharp pain without flinching and could recall or pretend to recall old memories. They could make their bodies as stiff as a board and lie rigid between two chairs. When told to sit down, they did so immediately (like hypnotized people) without first checking to make sure there was a chair behind them (Orne, 1959, 1979). When told to experience anger or some other emotion, they exhibited physiological changes such as increased heart rate and sweating, just like hypnotized people (Damaser, Shor, & Orne, 1963). Not even highly experienced hypnotists could identify the pretenders with confidence.

However, a few differences did emerge (Orne, 1979). The pretenders did certain things differently from the way the hypnotized subjects did them—not because they were unable to do them but because they did not know how a hypnotized subject would act. For instance, when the hypnotist suggested, "You see Professor Schmaltz sitting in that chair," people in both groups reported seeing the professor. Some of the hypnotized subjects, however, said they were puzzled. "How is it that I see the professor there, but I can also see the entire chair?" Pretenders never reported seeing this "double reality."

At that point in the experiment, Professor Schmaltz actually walked into the room. "Who is that entering the room?" asked the hypnotist. The pretenders would either say they saw no one or would identify Schmaltz as someone else. The hypnotized subjects would say, "That's Professor Schmaltz." Some of them said that they were confused by seeing the same person in two places at the same time. For some of them the hallucinated professor faded at that moment, whereas others continued to accept the double image.

Can a hypnotist get you to do anything that you would be unwilling to do ordinarily? "You don't have to worry," a hypnotist will reassure you. "People never do anything under hypnosis that would be against their morals or that they would consider offensive in everyday life." Although nearly all hypnotists seem to believe that statement is true, there is little solid evidence pro or con.

In one experiment (Orne & Evans, 1965), hypnotized college students were asked to perform three acts. First, they were told to go to a box in a corner of the room and pick up a poisonous snake. There actually was a poisonous, potentially deadly snake in the box. If a subject got too close to the snake, he or she was restrained at the last moment. Second, the hypnotist poured some highly concentrated, fuming nitric acid into a large container and said distinctly that it was nitric acid. To dispel any doubts, he threw a coin into the acid and let the subjects watch it as it started to dissolve. The hypnotist then told a subject to reach into the acid with bare hands and remove the coin. Here there was no last-second restraint. Anyone who followed the instructions was told to wash his or her hands in warm soapy water immediately afterward. (This was before procedures were adopted to protect subjects in psychological experiments.) Third, the hypnotist told a subject to throw the nitric acid into the face of the hypnotist's assistant. Unnoticed, the hypnotist had swapped the container of nitric acid for a container of water, but the hypnotized subject had no way of knowing that. The results: Five of the six hypnotized people followed all three directions.

Does this mean that you would do something under hypnosis that you would not ordinarily do? Before we can answer that, we need to know what people will do when they are *not* under hypnosis. M. T. Orne and F. J. Evans (1965) asked some subjects to pretend they were hypnotized and then asked them to pick up the snake, stick their hands into the fuming nitric acid, and throw the acid at an assistant. All six pretenders followed all three commands! Although they hesitated much longer than the hypnotized subjects, they still did as they were told. So did two of six people who were just told to take these actions as part of an experiment, with no mention of hypnosis. Why would they do such extraordinary things? They explained that they simply trusted the experimenter: "If he tells me to do something, it can't really be dangerous."

In short, people under hypnosis will do some strange things, but so will some people who are not *under hypnosis.*

Concept Check

5. *What can we conclude about the statement that "people under hypnosis will not do anything they would refuse to do otherwise"? Is the statement true or false, or is there too little evidence to decide? (Check your answer on page 125.)*

Are posthypnotic suggestions effective? A hypnotist may suggest to a subject under hypnosis that he or she will do or experience something after coming out of hypnosis. This **posthypnotic suggestion** may be to smile at the end of the hypnotic session, to dream about a certain topic that night, or to scratch the left ear whenever anyone says "ocean." Posthypnotic suggestions have been used to help people give up tobacco or alcohol, lose weight, stop nail biting, become more sexually responsive, stop having night terrors, or change some other behavior (Kihlstrom, 1979; Udolf, 1981). Such suggestions seem to be quite effective in helping people change their behavior, although the effects tend to wear off in a few days or weeks. The suggestions do not *force* any change in behavior; the people who agree to be hypnotized have already decided to try to quit smoking or to break some other habit. The hypnosis underscores that resolve.

Can hypnosis improve memory? A woman disappeared without a trace. When weeks passed with no word from her, the police became suspicious. None of her relatives could provide any information. So the police hypnotized her son. The son reported having seen his father murder his mother and then chop up her body and dispose of the pieces. On the basis of that testimony, the father was convicted and sentenced to life in prison. A few months later, the conviction was reversed when the woman turned up alive and well in another state. She had merely deserted her family.

Hypnotized people are highly suggestible. When told to recall something, they will almost surely report that they remember it. But what they report may be incorrect or may be a mixture of real memories and fantasies (Gibson, 1982). Even after they come out of hypnosis, they may continue to report the same memories, real or imagined, that they recalled under hypnosis.

In some laboratory experiments, hypnosis has improved memory (Stager & Lundy, 1985), but in most cases it has led to false reports. In one study (Dwyman & Bowers, 1983), researchers showed

FIGURE 4.14

Regression or role playing? One person made drawing a at age 6 and the other three drawings (b, c, d) as a college student under hypnosis. While under hypnosis, the person was asked to regress to age 6. The drawings under hypnosis are not like drawings done in childhood. Orne (1951) concluded that the hypnotized students played the role of a 6-year-old and drew as they thought a child would.

subjects photos and then asked them to recall as many as they could. After the subjects had done their best, they were hypnotized and asked to try again. Under hypnosis, the subjects recalled more items than before, though most of the additional items were wrong. Even so, they were just as sure about the additional wrong items as they were about the additional correct ones.

In response to such findings, a panel appointed by the American Medical Association (1986) concluded that testimony elicited under hypnosis should not be used in courts of law. This does not mean, however, that the police should never use hypnosis. If an investigation has reached a dead end, hypnotizing a witness may yield a useful lead, even though the witness's testimony itself is not admitted in court.

Can hypnosis help someone to recall memories from early childhood? A hypnotist might say, "You are getting younger. It is now the year _____; now it is _____; now you are only 6 years old." Under hypnosis a person may give a convincing performance of being a 10-year-old, a 6-year-old, or a 3-

year-old, even playing with teddy bears and blankets as a 3-year-old would (Nash, Johnson, & Tipton, 1979).

But does hypnosis actually aid in the recall of long-lost memories? Is the subject really reliving early childhood experiences? The evidence suggests that hypnosis is just making the person perform as a relaxed, confident actor. First, the childhood "memories" that the hypnotized subject so confidently recalls, such as the names of friends and teachers and the details of birthday parties, are generally inaccurate (Nash, 1987). Second, a person who has presumably regressed under hypnosis to early childhood retains spelling and other skills learned later in life. When asked to draw a picture, the subject does not draw as children draw but as adults imagine that children draw (Orne, 1951). (See Figure 4.14.) Finally, hypnotized subjects will respond to suggestions that they are growing older as well as to suggestions that they are growing younger. They give just as convincing a performance of being an older person (and "remembering" events in the future) as of being a younger person (Rubenstein & Newman, 1954). Because they must be acting out an imagined future, they are highly likely to be doing the same for the past.

Can hypnosis help someone to recall memories from a previous life? There are excellent reasons to be skeptical, to say the least (Spanos, 1987–88). People who claim to be recollecting a previous life generally describe the life of a person similar to themselves and married to someone who bears an uncanny resemblance to their current boyfriend or girlfriend. If subjects are asked whether their country (in their past life) is at war or what kind of money is in use, their guesses are seldom correct.

SUMMARY

1. Hypnosis is a condition of increased suggestibility that occurs in the context of a special hypnotist-subject relationship. Psychologists try to distinguish the genuine phenomenon, which deserves serious study, from exaggerated claims. (page 113)

2. To induce hypnosis, a hypnotist asks a person to concentrate and then makes repetitive suggestions. The first step toward being hypnotized is to desire to be hypnotized and to believe that the hypnosis is starting to succeed. (page 113)

3. Hypnosis can alleviate pain. It can also lead to reports of altered perception, although sensory information is rejected more than lost. (page 115)

4. Although hypnotists insist that a subject will never do anything under hypnosis that he or she would refuse to do otherwise, little solid evidence backs this claim. In experiments, it is difficult to find anything that either a hypnotized person or an unhypnotized person will refuse to do. (page 117)

5. Hypnosis does not reliably improve memory or confer any special physical or psychological abilities on the subject. The memories that people report under hypnosis are often inaccurate. No evidence indicates that it enables people to do anything they could not ordinarily do with sufficient motivation. (page 117)

SUGGESTIONS FOR FURTHER READING

Haley, J. (1967). *Advanced techniques of hypnosis and therapy.* New York: Grune and Stratton. Interesting description of techniques of inducing hypnosis and ways of using it.

Udolf, R. (1981). *Handbook of hypnosis for professionals.* New York: Van Nostrand Reinhold. A thorough review of research on all aspects of hypnosis.

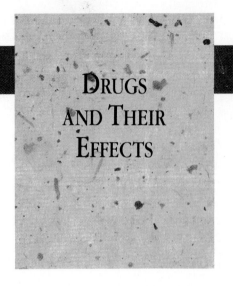

Drugs and Their Effects

What experiences do drugs of abuse produce? Why do people experiment with such drugs?

Alcohol and other drugs have been part of human experience throughout history. People sometimes experiment with unfamiliar drugs just to have new experiences. They may use drugs familiar to them because they like the experiences the drugs induce. In either case, they are trying to produce an altered state.

The abuse of alcohol and other drugs is a major concern in our society. In Chapter 14 I shall take up the question of addictions and what can be done about them. Here I briefly survey some common drugs of abuse, what experiences they produce, and why people use them.

A Survey of Abused Drugs and Their Effects

Many substances are used and abused because of their power to alter behavior and sensory experience. Although these substances have certain properties in common, their effects differ widely (see Table 4.1). Some—such as alcohol, tranquilizers, and opiates—have predominantly calming effects. Others—such as amphetamines and cocaine—have predominantly stimulating effects.

Alcohol

Alcohol is a class of carbon-based molecules that include an -OH group. Only one member of this class, *ethyl alcohol* or *ethanol,* can be consumed without severe toxic effects. Alcohol acts primarily as a relaxant (Sudzak et al., 1986), although it may

have certain stimulating effects as well. It leads to heightened aggressive, sexual, or playful behavior, mainly by depressing the brain areas that ordinarily inhibit such behaviors. Moderate use of alcohol serves as a tension reducer and a social lubricant. Excessive use impairs judgment, memory, and motor control (Hashtroudi & Parker, 1986; Hull & Bond, 1986). (See Figure 4.15.) After years of use, alcohol may lead to a long-lasting impairment of memory that persists even during periods of abstinence (Forsberg & Goldman, 1987). It can also lead to damage of the liver and other organs; it can aggravate and prolong many medical conditions.

Tranquilizers

Tranquilizers help people to relax and fall asleep. They are widely prescribed for medical reasons; sometimes people continue using them long after it is medically advisable. *Barbiturates* were once the most commonly used tranquilizing drug. When it turned out that they were habit forming, however, and that an overdose could easily be fatal, investigators looked for a substitute. Today the most commonly used tranquilizers are a class of chemicals called *benzodiazepines,* which include the drugs Valium, Librium, and Xanax (Tallman, Paul, Skolnick, & Gallager, 1980). Thousands of tons of benzodiazepines are taken in pill form every year in the United States. Benzodiazepines relieve anxiety, relax the muscles, and induce sleep. Although they are less habit forming than barbiturates, some people have trouble giving them up and use them in excess.

Opiates

Opiates are either natural drugs derived from the opium poppy or synthetic drugs with a chemical structure similar to the natural opiates. The most common opiate drugs—morphine and heroin—bind to a set of synapses in the brain that use endorphins as their neurotransmitter (see page 74). Once these drugs have left the brain, the affected synapses become understimulated. Shortly after taking an opiate drug, the user feels happy, is nearly insensitive to pain, and tends to ignore real-world stimuli; he or she feels warmth, contentment, and a loss of anxiety. A few hours later, the user enters withdrawal; elation gives way to anxiety, height-

TABLE 4.1 Commonly Abused Drugs and Their Effects

Drug Category	Effects on Behavior	Effects on Central Nervous System and Organs
Depressants		
Alcohol	Relaxant; relieves inhibitions; impairs memory and judgment	Widespread effects on membranes of neurons; facilitates activity at GABA synapses
Tranquilizers: barbiturates; benzodiazepines (Valium, Librium, Xanax)	Relieve anxiety; relax muscles; induce sleep	Facilitate activity at GABA synapses
Opiates: morphine; heroin	Decrease pain; decrease attention to real world; unpleasant withdrawal effects as drug leaves synapses	Stimulate endorphin synapses
Stimulants		
Caffeine	Increases energy, alertness	Increases heart rate; indirectly increases activity at dopamine synapses
Amphetamines; cocaine	Increase energy, alertness	Increase or prolong activity at dopamine synapses
Mixed Stimulant-Depressant		
Nicotine	Stimulates brain activity, but most smokers say cigarettes relax them	Stimulates activity at some (not all) acetylcholine synapses; increases heart rate
Distortion of Experience		
Marijuana (THC)	Intensifies sensory experiences; distorts perception of time; can relieve glaucoma, nausea; sometimes impairs learning, memory	Disrupts membranes; alters binding of many neurotransmitters; dissolves in body fats—traces persist for weeks
Hallucinogens		
LSD; mescaline	Cause hallucinations, sensory distortions, and occasionally panic	Alter pattern of release and binding of serotonin; stimulate dopamine synapses
Mixed Hallucinogen-Stimulant		
MDMA (ecstasy)	Causes hallucinations; increases energy	Stimulates and probably destroys serotonin synapses

ened sensitivity to pain, and acute sensitivity to external stimuli. Morphine (named after Morpheus, the Greek god of dreams) has medical use as a painkiller.

Marijuana

The active ingredient in marijuana (*Cannabis*) is THC, or tetrahydrocannabinol. It affects the brain by disrupting the membranes of neurons and by either facilitating or inhibiting the binding of a variety of neurotransmitters and hormones (Martin, 1986). Unlike opiates, marijuana does not bind to any single receptor.

People smoke marijuana because it produces a "high" and intensifies their sensory experiences (Weil, Zinberg, & Nelson, 1968). It also gives them the illusion that time is passing very slowly. Although its measurable effects on behavior wear off within three hours, more subtle effects may persist much longer. Marijuana dissolves in the fats of the body, and traces of it persist for weeks after it has been used (Dackis et al., 1982).

A number of early reports claimed that marijuana leads to brain damage, crime, mental illness, sexual debauchery, and a loss of motivation and ambition. It now appears, however, that those reports confused correlation with causation (see page 36).

FIGURE 4.15

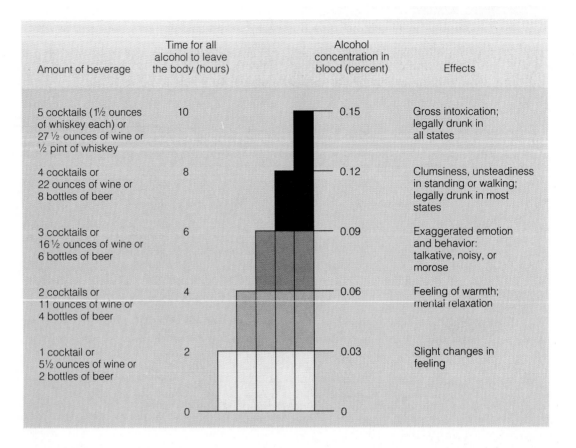

Amount of beverage	Time for all alcohol to leave the body (hours)	Alcohol concentration in blood (percent)	Effects
5 cocktails (1½ ounces of whiskey each) or 27 ½ ounces of wine or ½ pint of whiskey	10	0.15	Gross intoxication; legally drunk in all states
4 cocktails or 22 ounces of wine or 8 bottles of beer	8	0.12	Clumsiness, unsteadiness in standing or walking; legally drunk in most states
3 cocktails or 16 ½ ounces of wine or 6 bottles of beer	6	0.09	Exaggerated emotion and behavior: talkative, noisy, or morose
2 cocktails or 11 ounces of wine or 4 bottles of beer	4	0.06	Feeling of warmth; mental relaxation
1 cocktail or 5½ ounces of wine or 2 bottles of beer	2	0.03	Slight changes in feeling
	0	0	

It's not what you drink—beer, wine, or whiskey—but how much and how quickly you consume alcohol that determines your state of intoxication. What you eat before or while drinking and your physical size also influence alcohol's impact on you. This chart shows rising levels of alcohol in the bloodstream of a 150-lb person with an empty stomach. (Based on *Time*, 1974.)

Although marijuana use tends to be prevalent among people with a history of such behaviors, it does not cause them. Marijuana may, however, aggravate those behaviors in people who are already predisposed toward them (Hollister, 1986). By interfering with the ability to concentrate, it may also impair learning and memory (Miller & Branconnier, 1983), especially among people who are using marijuana for the first time. Some marijuana users experience a general loss of motivation. Marijuana does have certain medical uses. By reducing pressure in the eyes, it helps relieve glaucoma, a common cause of blindness. It also reduces nausea and acts as a weak painkiller.

Concept Check

6. Some employers conduct urine tests at random times to determine whether their employees have been taking drugs on the job. What special problem is likely to arise when they test for marijuana? (Check your answer on page 125.)

Stimulants

Stimulants are drugs that boost energy, heighten alertness, increase activity, and produce a pleasant feeling. Coffee, tea, and caffeinated soft drinks are mild stimulants. People drink these beverages partly for their taste and partly for their stimulant effects (Cines & Rozin, 1982). Amphetamine and cocaine are stronger stimulants. Amphetamine increases the release of the neurotransmitter dopamine, which increases activity levels and pleasure. Amphetamine and cocaine also prevent neurons from reabsorbing the dopamine they have released; they thereby prolong the effects of the dopamine (Ritz, Lamb, Goldberg, & Kuhar, 1987).

Prior to 1985, cocaine was available only in the form of cocaine hydrochloride, a chemical that can be sniffed or injected. Those who wanted to smoke it first had to treat the cocaine hydrochloride with ether to convert it into free-base cocaine—cocaine with the hydrochloride removed. Smoking free-base cocaine enables a high percentage of it to enter the body rapidly and thereby to enter the brain rapidly. The result is an intense, rapid feeling of pleasure and a craving for more of the drug.

The drug known as *crack* first became available in 1985. Crack is cocaine that has already been converted to the free-base form (Brower & Anglin, 1987; Kozel & Adams, 1986). It is not only ready to be smoked but also cheap enough to be popular. In this form, cocaine has become one of the most widely abused drugs. Because crack affects the brain more swiftly than other forms of cocaine, it is more likely to be addictive. Moreover, it is more likely to lead to heart attacks, other medical complications, and psychological disorders. Compared to other cocaine users, crack users experience more hallucinations, disordered thinking, and suicidal thoughts

Because crack is smoked, this form of cocaine reaches the brain in eight seconds, much faster—and in a more potent form—than most drugs, which is why it is so popular and addictive. An estimated 5,000 people try some form of cocaine for the first time every day.

Tablas, or yarn paintings, created by members of the Huichol tribe (Mexico), evoke the beautiful lights, vivid colors, and "peculiar creatures" experienced after the people eat the hallucinogenic peyote cactus in highly ritualized ceremonies.

and are more likely to attack other people violently (Honer, Gewirtz, & Turey, 1987).

Because selling crack is so lucrative, rival gangs in large cities compete with one another to control the sales. The resulting violence has created a problem for society that goes beyond the direct harm done by the drug itself.

Cigarettes

One reason people smoke cigarettes and other tobacco products is that smoking gives them something to do with their hands. Smoking is a finger habit, like fidgeting. A more compelling reason is that it lets them experience the effects of nicotine. Curiously, although nicotine stimulates the central nervous system, most smokers say that they find cigarettes relaxing (Gilbert, 1979).

The desire for nicotine probably is a major part of the motivation for cigarette smoking. Nontobacco cigarettes, which contain no nicotine, have never proved popular. Smokers who switch to low-nicotine cigarettes tend to increase the number of cigarettes they smoke, as if they were trying to maintain a constant level of nicotine in their body (Kumar, Cooke, Lader, & Russell, 1977; McMorrow

& Foxx, 1983). Moreover, many smokers who try to quit smoking find it easier to do so if they chew gum that contains nicotine (Fagerström, 1981; Jarvis, 1983; Lichtenstein, 1982).

Hallucinogens

Drugs that induce delusions or sensory distortions are **hallucinogens** (Jacobs, 1987). Most of them are derived from certain mushrooms or other plants; some are manufactured in chemistry laboratories. The hallucinogenic drugs LSD, PCP, and mescaline intensify sensations and sometimes produce a dreamlike state or an intense mystical experience. They occasionally prompt a panic response or violent behavior, and a few users report flashback experiences long after they have used the drugs.

The physiological action of the hallucinogens varies from drug to drug. LSD acts mainly on serotonin synapses in the brain, though it has some effect on dopamine synapses as well. It stimulates one type of serotonin receptors at irregular times and prevents serotonin from stimulating the receptors at the normal times. Repeated use of LSD may actually destroy some of the serotonin receptors and cause permanent changes in behavior (Jacobs, 1987).

"Ecstasy"

In the middle 1980s a new synthetic drug made its appearance on college campuses and elsewhere: MDMA, popularly known as "ecstasy." Ecstasy produces a mixture of stimulant and hallucinogenic effects. Unlike users of other drugs, ecstasy users do not crave frequent use, and after repeated use they lose interest in it. However, it is hardly a harmless drug. The limited research that has been conducted so far suggests that the drug produces permanent damage to brain cells containing serotonin (Price, Ricaurte, Krystal, & Heninger, 1989).

For many adults, a drink or two with friends after work—the "happy hour"—is a social ritual, Monday through Friday.

MOTIVES FOR USING ALCOHOL AND OTHER DRUGS

People usually take their first drink or their first cigarette in a group setting, almost as a social ritual. The motivation is *conformity,* the desire to be like other people. Young people are more likely to try alcohol or cigarettes if they see their friends or parents using them. Teenagers strongly resemble their parents in their use of coffee, cigarettes, and alcohol (Fawzy, Coombs, & Gerber, 1983).

After using alcohol or some other drug, some people experiment with the same drug and others in a quest for new sensations and new experiences. Adolescents who regularly drink alcohol, for example, are more likely than others are to try marijuana, and those who use marijuana are more likely to try LSD, heroin, and amphetamine (Kandel, 1975; Kandel, Davies, Karus, & Yamaguchi, 1986).

Many people in our society drink alcohol because it serves as a *social lubricant.* They have a drink or two before dinner and meet their friends at cocktail parties. Executives meet over drinks to discuss business. Alcohol makes them feel more relaxed and less self-conscious. It frees people to say and do things they would otherwise suppress. A friend of mine, after a few too many beers, once kissed a policeman for no apparent reason. (The policeman was still laughing as we walked away.) Even the *expectation* of becoming slightly intoxicated loosens people's inhibitions and helps them keep the conversation moving (Hull & VanTreuren, 1986). The prevalence of alcohol in so many settings is one reason that people with a drinking problem have trouble giving it up.

Alcohol serves a similar social function when it is used for *celebration.* Beer and stronger drinks often flow freely when friends get together to celebrate such happy events as winning a bowling tournament, completing a project, or just making it to Friday night.

Some people use alcohol or other drugs not only to celebrate the good times but also to escape the bad times. Their motive is *escape.* Many depressed people become alcohol abusers or drug addicts (Khantzian & Treece, 1985).

Young people, especially males, sometimes use drugs or alcohol to *attract attention,* to demonstrate to their friends how completely stoned or drunk they can get. They may even brag about how much damage they are doing to themselves.

A less common motivation for using alcohol or other drugs is *self-handicapping*—putting oneself at a disadvantage in order to have an excuse for failure (Jones & Berglas, 1978). One experiment was set up to make it appear that students had succeeded on a series of tasks, even though they themselves knew their success had been an accident. Then they were asked to choose between two drugs before continuing with a similar series of tasks. One drug, they were told, would improve their performance and the other would impair it. Most of the students opted for the drug that would impair their performance (Berglas & Jones, 1978). Apparently they expected to do poorly anyway (because their earlier success had been mostly a matter of luck), and they wanted to have a ready-made excuse for their failure. People who are doing poorly in their studies or in their work may turn to alcohol or other drugs for the same reason.

These are the principal motives for the experimental or occasional use of drugs. In Chapter 14 we shall consider the special motives associated with addiction.

SUMMARY

1. Alcohol, the most widely abused drug in our society, relaxes people and relieves their inhibitions. It can also impair judgment and reasoning. (page 120)

2. Benzodiazepine tranquilizers are widely used to relieve anxiety; they are also sometimes used to relax muscles or to promote sleep. (page 120)

3. Opiate drugs bind to endorphin receptors in the nervous system. The immediate effect of opiates is pleasure and relief from pain. As the drugs wear off, a withdrawal phase sets in, and the person experiences distress and increased sensitivity to pain. (page 120)

4. Marijuana acts by routes still poorly understood to intensify sensory experiences. Because it dissolves in the

body's fats, it can exert subtle effects over a period of days or weeks after use. (page 121)

5. Stimulant drugs such as amphetamine and cocaine increase activity levels and pleasure. Compared to other forms of cocaine, crack produces more rapid effects on behavior, greater risk of addiction, and greater risk of damage to the heart and other organs. (page 122)

6. Nicotine, found in cigarettes, is a stimulant to the brain, although smokers say they smoke to relax. (page 123)

7. Hallucinogens induce sensory distortions. Some hallucinogens are believed to lead to brain damage. (page 123)

8. People experiment with drugs for a variety of reasons, including conformity, a quest for new sensations, facilitation of social interactions, celebration, escape from worries, and self-handicapping. (page 124)

SUGGESTIONS FOR FURTHER READING

Hoffman, F. G. (1983). *A handbook on drug and alcohol abuse* (2nd ed.). New York: Oxford University Press. A description of the effects of commonly abused drugs.

Snyder, S. (Ed.) (1986). *The encyclopedia of psychoactive drugs*. New York: Chelsea House. A collection of volumes on all aspects of drugs and their effects.

TERMS TO REMEMBER

activation-synthesis theory of dreams the theory that parts of the brain are spontaneously activated during REM sleep and that a dream is the brain's attempt to synthesize that activation into a coherent pattern

alcohol a class of carbon-based molecules that include an -OH group, including ethanol

electroencephalograph (EEG) a device that measures and amplifies slight electrical changes on the scalp that reflect brain activity

evolutionary theory of sleep the theory that sleep evolved primarily as a means of forcing animals to conserve their energy when they are relatively inefficient

hallucination a sensory experience not corresponding to reality, such as seeing or hearing something that is not present or failing to see or hear something that is present

hallucinogens drugs that induce delusions or sensory distortions

hypnosis a condition of increased suggestibility that occurs in the context of a special hypnotist-subject relationship

insomnia difficulty in getting to sleep or in staying asleep

maintenance insomnia trouble staying asleep, with a tendency to awaken briefly but frequently

narcolepsy a condition characterized by sudden attacks of sleep

non-REM (NREM) sleep all stages of sleep other than REM sleep

onset insomnia trouble falling asleep

opiates drugs that are either derived from the opium poppy or that resemble drugs so derived

posthypnotic suggestion a suggestion made to hypnotized subjects that they will do something or experience something particular after coming out of hypnosis

rapid eye movement (REM) sleep a stage of sleep characterized by rapid eye movements, a high level of brain activity, and deep relaxation of the postural muscles; also known as paradoxical sleep

repair and restoration theory the theory that the purpose of sleep is to enable the body to recover from the wear and tear of the day

sleep apnea a condition in which a person has trouble breathing while asleep

termination insomnia a tendency to awaken early and to be unable to get back to sleep

tranquilizers drugs that help people to relax

ANSWERS TO CONCEPT CHECKS

1. The United States should prefer to schedule the meeting on a Pacific island so that its leader will travel west and the Soviet leader will travel east. (page 105)

2. REM sleep and dreaming are more common toward the end of the night's sleep. (page 107)

3. During REM sleep the major postural muscles of the body are completely relaxed. (page 110)

4. We would conclude that they really had heard the words. Note that this is the same conclusion we drew when people chose the related words *less* than 50% of the time. If they really did not hear anything, then they would choose a related word 50% of the time; any other result indicates that they heard. (page 115)

5. There is too little evidence to decide. People under hypnosis will do some strange and dangerous acts, but so will unhypnotized people who know they are participating in an experiment. (page 117)

6. Because marijuana dissolves in the fats and leaves the body very slowly, people may still test positive for the drug weeks after the last time they used it. (page 122)

CHAPTER

5

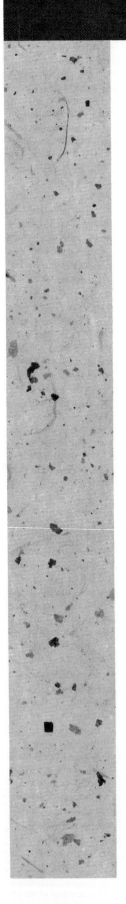

When my son Sam was 8 years old, he asked me, "If we went to some other planet, would we see different colors?" He did not mean just a new shade or a new mixture of familiar colors. He meant colors that were truly new, as different from familiar colors as yellow is from red or blue. I told him no, that would be impossible, and I tried to explain why. I am not sure he understood.

No matter where we might go in outer space, no matter what unfamiliar objects or atmospheres we might encounter, we could never experience a color, or a sound, or any other sensation that would be fundamentally different from what we experience on Earth. Different combinations, perhaps. But fundamentally different sensory experiences, no.

Three years later, Sam told me he was wondering whether people who look at the same thing are all having the same experience. When different people look at something and call it "green," how can we know whether they are all seeing the same "green"? I agreed that there was no sure way of knowing.

Why am I certain that colors on a different planet would look the same as they do on Earth and yet uncertain that colors look the same to different people here? You may find the answer obvious. If not, I hope it will be after you have read this chapter.

Sensation is the conversion of energy from the environment into a pattern of response by the nervous system. It is the registration of information. **Perception** is making sense of that information. Light rays striking your eyes or sound waves striking your ears give rise to sensation. When you say, "I see my roommate" or "I hear the call of a mourning dove," you are expressing your perception of what those sensations mean.

VISION

How do our eyes convert light energy into
something we can experience?
How do we perceive colors?

Suppose we were designing an all-purpose robot
to explore some alien terrain. We want it to be able
to avoid danger, look for fuel, and perhaps search
for other robots. So we equip it with devices to
detect and identify chemicals in the atmosphere
and in water (smell and taste), vibrations and other
mechanical pressures (touch and hearing), body
position (vestibular sensation), and various forms
of radiation (vision). We call those devices receptors. A **receptor** is a specialized cell that converts
energy from the environment into a form of energy
that an animal—or, in this case, a robot—can send
to its brain.

If cost were of no concern, we might design
the robot's receptors to register the exact intensity
and the directional source every time it encounters
a **stimulus**, an energy in the environment that can
influence action. But such refinements would be of
little use. What our robot needs to know is not the
exact dimensions of every stimulus but the answer
to this question: "What objects are out there and
what are they doing?" So then we might design our
robot to detect the outlines of objects (by comparing stimuli from adjacent directions) and to detect
movement (by comparing stimuli from one time to
another). We might as well let the robot ignore
information it cannot use, such as data about cosmic
rays.

Human beings are equipped with receptors that
are remarkably efficient at providing us with information that we can use. However, our receptors do
not report all the information available at any given
moment. We smell and taste some chemicals but
not others, we hear air vibrations at certain frequencies but not at others, and we see radiated
energy only in a narrow band of wavelengths. Other
species with different ways of life see, hear, and
smell many things that we are not aware of and
fail to detect many things that we are very much
aware of.

Back to our robot. Its receptors receive a stimulus—for instance, air vibrations at 3000 cycles per
second coming from the right. It records and stores
that information in some convenient way, perhaps
by flipping a switch or by entering a series of ones
and zeros on a magnetic disk. In any case, the internal representation of the information it receives is
physically very different from the original stimulus.
When it "hears" or "remembers" a tone of 3000
cycles per second, nothing inside the robot actually
vibrates 3000 times per second. Some change takes
place inside the robot (the robot's "experience")
that represents a change in the outside world, but
the two changes need not resemble each other in
any way.

The same is true for humans. For example, our
experience of a sound or a pattern of light is not
at all the same as the energy in the sound waves
or the light waves. Our experience does not grow
twice as strong when the stimulus grows twice as
strong. Our experience does not have to reproduce
the outside world; it just has to maintain a consistent relationship with it.

In short, *what we see, hear, and otherwise sense
is not what is really there in the outside world.* Our
experience is *lawfully related to* what is out there,
but it does not physically resemble the outside world
any more than a book about fire resembles crack-
ling flames.

Something to Think About

Why do you think animals have evolved receptors
that enable them to see light of certain wavelengths
and not others, to hear sounds of certain pitches
and not others, to taste and smell certain chemicals and not others?

THE DETECTION OF LIGHT

What we refer to as *light* is just one part of the
electromagnetic spectrum. As Figure 5.1 shows, the
electromagnetic spectrum is the continuum of all
the frequencies of radiated energy, from gamma

FIGURE 5.1

Visible light, what human eyes can see, is a small part of the electromagnetic spectrum. Experimenting with prisms, Isaac Newton discovered that white light is a mixture of all colors, and color is a property of light. A carrot looks orange because it reflects orange and absorbs all the other colors.

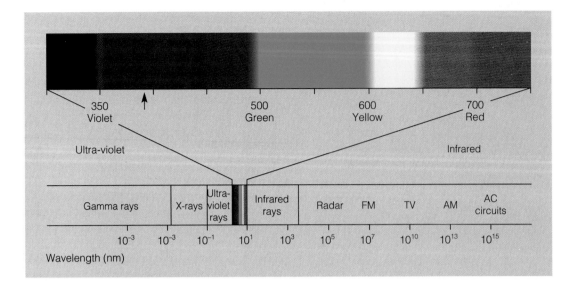

rays and X rays, which have very short wavelengths, through ultraviolet, visible light, and infrared to radio and TV transmissions, which have very long wavelengths. We use the term *visible light* to refer to what our eyes are equipped to receive—wavelengths from 400 nm to 700 nm. Some species—bees, for example—can see ultraviolet rays but cannot see the wavelengths we call "red." If a bee were writing this section, it would define visible light as wavelengths from perhaps 300 nm to 650 nm.

Structure of the Eye

When we see an object, light reflected from that object passes through an opening in the eye called the **pupil**. It then travels through the *vitreous humor* (a clear, jellylike substance) and strikes the **retina** at the back of the eyeball. The retina is lined with visual receptors (Figure 5.2). The image formed on the retina is upside down and backward with respect to its orientation in the outside world.

Early psychologists, puzzled by this inversion, proposed theories of where and how the brain flipped the image right-side up again. Today we no longer regard this as a problem. The bottom of the eye does not "know" it is the bottom, and the brain does not have to make little copies of everything we see—any more than a computer has to store a graphic screen by drawing a right-side up picture inside itself.

The light that enters through the pupil is focused by the cornea and the lens. The **cornea**, a rigid transparent structure, focuses light in the same way at all times. The **lens**, however, is a flexible structure that can vary in thickness, enabling the eye to focus on objects at different distances. When we

look at a distant object, for example, our eye muscles relax and let the lens become thinner and flatter, as shown in Figure 5.3. When we look at a close object, our eye muscles tighten and make the lens thicker and rounder. In old age the lens becomes less flexible. That is why many older people need eyeglasses, or corrective lenses, in order to focus on nearby objects.

The lens filters out some light, especially blue and ultraviolet light. A *cataract* is a disorder in which the lens becomes cloudy. People with severe cataracts may have a lens surgically removed and replaced with a contact lens. Sometimes they report seeing colors, especially blue, more clearly and distinctly than they did before the operation (Davenport & Foley, 1979). They do, however, suffer increased risk of damage to the retina from ultraviolet light.

Our vision is best when our eyeballs are nearly spherical. A person whose eyeballs are elongated, as shown in Figure 5.4a, can focus well on nearby objects but has difficulty focusing on distant objects. Such a person is said to be *nearsighted,* or to have **myopia** (mi-O-pea-ah). About half of all 20-year-olds are nearsighted and must wear glasses in order to see well at a distance. A person whose eyeballs are flattened, as shown in Figure 5.4b, is *farsighted.* Such a person can focus well on distant objects but has difficulty focusing on close objects. Farsightedness is less common than nearsightedness.

Some nearsighted people have undergone an experimental form of surgery known as *radial keratotomy* (CARE-ah-TOT-oh-mee). In this operation, the surgeon makes small incisions, generally 16 or fewer, in the eyeball (Bores, 1983). As the eyeball heals, it flexes and changes shape. If the surgery is

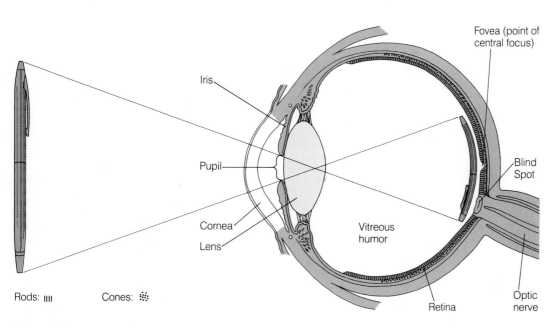

Iris

Pupil

Cornea

Lens

Fovea (point of central focus)

Blind Spot

Vitreous humor

Retina

Optic nerve

Rods: ⅠⅠⅠⅠ   Cones: ░

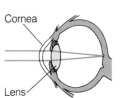

Cornea

Lens

Focus on distant object (lens thin)

Cornea

Lens

Focus on close object (lens thick)

FIGURE 5.2

The lens gets its name from Latin for *lentil,* referring to its shape—an appropriate choice, as this cross section of the eye shows. The names of other parts of the eye also refer to their appearance.

FIGURE 5.3

Changing shape so that objects near and far can come into focus, the flexible, transparent lens bends entering light rays so that they fall on the retina. In old age, the lens becomes rigid and people find it harder to focus on nearby objects.

Making things crystal clear: This scanning electron micrograph shows the fiberlike cells of the lens magnified 2,000 times. The precise arrangement of these cells in rows resembling zippers contributes to the transparency of the lens, which is 0.156 inch (4 millimeters) thick.

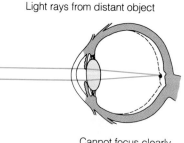

Light rays from distant object

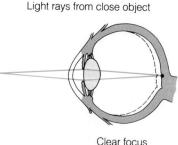

Light rays from close object

Cannot focus clearly

Clear focus

a

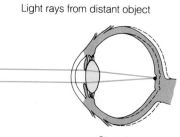

Light rays from distant object

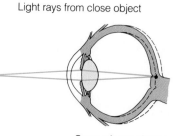

Light rays from close object

Clear focus

Cannot focus clearly

b

FIGURE 5.4

The structure of (a) nearsighted and (b) farsighted eyes distort vision. Because the nearsighted eye is elongated, light from a distant object focuses in front of the retina. Because the farsighted eye is flattened, light from a nearby object focuses behind the retina. (The dashed line shows the position of the normal retina in each case.)

What you see is what you get: These photographs simulate (a) nearsightedness and (b) farsightedness.

a

b

properly performed, the eye will more or less regain its normal shape. Most people experience an overall improvement of vision after the operation, although a few experience *overcorrection*—that is, they end up being farsighted instead of nearsighted (Waring et al., 1987).

The Visual Receptors

The visual receptors of the eye are specialized neurons that line the back of the retina. They are so

sensitive to light that they are capable of responding to a single photon, the smallest possible quantity of light.

These visual receptors are of two types: cones and rods. The two differ in appearance, as Figure 5.5 shows, and in function. The **cones** are adapted for color vision, for daytime vision, and for detailed vision. The **rods** are adapted for vision in dim light.

About 5 to 10% of all the visual receptors in the human retina are cones. Most birds have about the same proportion or a higher proportion of cones

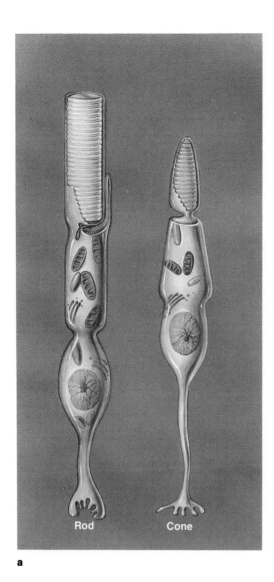

a

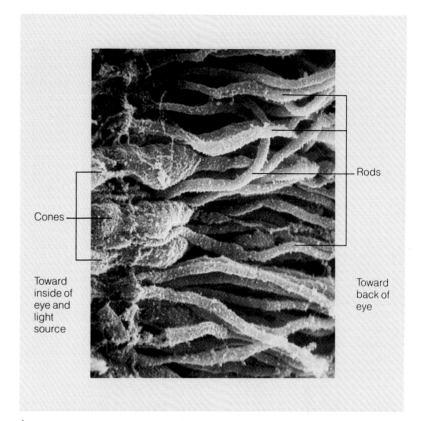

Cones

Rods

Toward
inside of
eye and
light
source

Toward
back of
eye

b

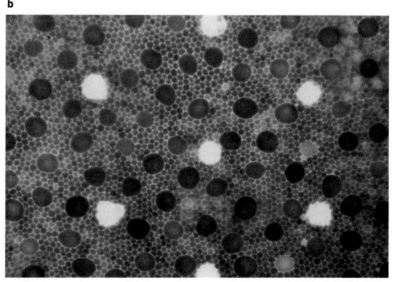

c

Rod   Cone

as humans have; they also have good color vision. Species with very few cones in their retina—rats, for example—make little use of color vision. Every species of mammal that has been tested has at least a small number of cones and at least a slight ability to respond to differences in color (Jacobs, 1981).

The proportion of cones is highest toward the center of the retina. The **fovea** (FOE-vee-uh), the central area of the human retina, is adapted for highly detailed vision and consists solely of cones. (See Figure 5.2.) Away from the fovea, the proportion of cones drops sharply. That is why you have poor color vision, or none at all, in the far periphery of your eye.

Try this experiment: Hold several pens or pencils of different colors behind your back. (Any objects will work so long as they have about the same size and shape and approximately the same brightness.) Pick one at random without looking at it. Hold it behind your head and bring it very slowly into your field of vision. When you just barely begin to see it, you will probably not be able to tell what color it is. (If glaucoma or some other medical problem

FIGURE 5.5

(a) A rod and a cone, the eye's two types of sensing cells. (b) Rods and cones seen through a scanning electron micrograph. (c) A fluorescence micrograph of a cross section of the retina. The large green or yellow cells are cones; the smaller ones are rods. The rods, which number over 120 million, help us see in dim light. The 6 million cones in the retina can distinguish gradations of color in bright light; they enable us to see that roses are red, magenta, ruby, carmine, cherry, vermilion, scarlet, and crimson—not to mention pink, yellow, orange, and white.

TABLE 5.1 Differences Between Rods and Cones

	Rods	Cones
Shape	Nearly cylindrical	Tapered at one end
Prevalence in human retina	90–95%	5–10%
Greatest incidence by species	In species that are active at night	In birds, primates, and other species that are active during the day
Area of the retina	Toward the periphery	Toward the fovea
Contribution to color vision	No direct contribution	Critical for color vision
Response to dim light	Strong	Weak
Contribution to perception of detail	Little	Much
Response to sudden change in visual stimulation	Slow	Rapid

has impaired your peripheral vision, you will have to bring the object closer to your fovea before you can see it at all.)

The rods are more effective than the cones in detecting dim light for two reasons: First, a rod is slightly more responsive to faint stimulation than a cone is. Second, the rods pool their resources. More than a hundred rods send messages to the next cell in the visual system, but only a few cones converge their messages onto a given cell.

There is another difference between rods and cones: When a light is suddenly turned off, the activity of the cones ceases almost immediately, whereas the activity of the rods declines more gradually (Jacobs, 1981). In other words, the cones give more accurate information about sudden changes in visual stimulation. Table 5.1 summarizes the key differences between rods and cones.

Concept Check

1. Why is it easier to see a faint star in the sky if you look slightly to the side of the star instead of straight at it? (Check your answer on page 178.)

Dark Adaptation

You go into a basement at night trying to find your flashlight. The only light in the basement is burned out. At first you can hardly see anything. A couple of minutes later, you are beginning to see well enough to find your way around. After 10 minutes, you can see well enough to find the flashlight. This

gradual improvement in the ability to see under dim light is called **dark adaptation**.

Here is how a psychologist could measure your dark adaptation (Goldstein, 1989): You are taken from a well-lit room into a room that is completely dark except for one tiny flashing light. You have a knob that controls the intensity of the light; you are told to make the light so dim that you can barely see it. Over the course of 3 or 4 minutes you will gradually decrease the intensity of the light, as shown in Figure 5.6a. Note that a decrease in the intensity of the light indicates an increase in the sensitivity of your eyes.

If you stared straight at the point of light, your results demonstrate the adaptation of your cones to the dim light. (You have been focusing the light on your fovea, which has no rods.) Now the psychologist repeats the study, with one change in procedure: You are told to stare at a very faint light while another light flashes in the periphery of your vision, where it stimulates rods as well as cones. You turn a control knob until the flashing light in the periphery is just barely visible. Figure 5.6b shows the results. During the first 7 to 10 minutes, the results are the same as before. But then your rods become more sensitive than your cones, and you begin to see even fainter lights. Your rods continue to adapt to the dark over the next 20 minutes or so.

Concept Check

2. You may have heard people say that cats can see in the dark. Is that possible? (Check your answer on page 178.)

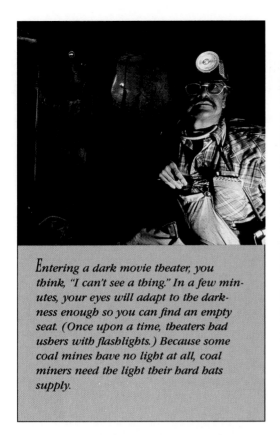

Entering a dark movie theater, you think, "I can't see a thing." In a few minutes, your eyes will adapt to the darkness enough so you can find an empty seat. (Once upon a time, theaters had ushers with flashlights.) Because some coal mines have no light at all, coal miners need the light their hard hats supply.

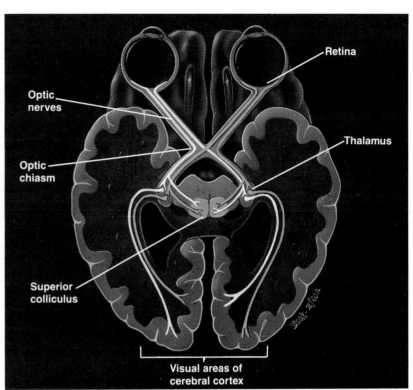

FIGURE 5.7

Considering the eye, Leonardo da Vinci wondered how something so small "could contain the images of all the universe." You may wonder how something so complex works well so often. From the retina, the optic nerves extend to the visual midbrain (superior colliculus) and thalamus, which in turn send messages to the visual cortex.

The Visual Pathway

If you were designing an eye, you would probably run the axons of the cones and rods straight to the brain. Nature chose a different method. The visual receptors send their impulses *away from* the brain, toward the center of the eye, where they make synaptic contacts with other neurons called *bipolar cells*. The bipolar cells in turn make contact with still other neurons, the **ganglion cells**. The axons from the ganglion cells join to form the **optic nerve**, which exits the eye, as Figure 5.7 shows. Half of each optic nerve crosses to the opposite side of the brain at the optic chiasm. (See Figure 3.34 on page 88.) Axons from the optic nerve separate and go to several locations in the brain. The largest number go to the thalamus, which then sends information to the occipital lobe, the primary area of the cortex for visual processing.

The area at which the optic nerve exits the retina is called the **blind spot**. There is no room for receptors here because the exiting axons take up all the space. You can find your own blind spot by covering your left eye and staring at the x or by

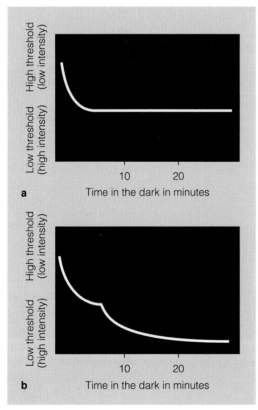

FIGURE 5.6

These graphs show dark adaptation to (a) a light you stare at directly, using only cones, and (b) a light in your peripheral vision, which you see with both cones and rods. (Based on Goldstein, 1989.)

covering your right eye and staring at the o below. Then slowly move the page forward and backward. At a certain distance the letter you are not staring at will disappear, because you focus that letter onto the blind spot of your eye.

x   o

Ordinarily we are unaware of our blind spot. Even people who have a very large blind spot as a result of damage to the retina are seldom aware of their loss. What accounts for this lack of awareness? Figure 5.8 may suggest an answer. Close one eye and focus the other eye on the x in the center of the figure. Then move the page forward and backward and look for your blind spot. You may be able to find it if you try hard enough, but it is much more difficult than with the preceding x-o exercise. Apparently when you look at a simple continuous pattern, the brain fills in the gap at the blind spot.

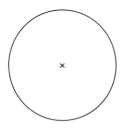

FIGURE 5.8

Can you find your blind spot using this figure?

Synchronizing Messages from Different Parts of the Retina

Suppose you have been hired to supervise the kitchen staff in a gourmet restaurant. Your job is to coordinate the activities of chef Charlotte, who is cooking the main dishes, with those of chef Charles, who is preparing the side dishes. Everything must be ready to serve at exactly the same time. You have two runners, Eric and Erin, who report to you periodically on the progress of the two chefs. If one chef gets ahead of the other, you send a message for that one to slow down and for the other one to speed up.

For some reason, however, Eric brings you news about Charles faster than Erin brings you news about Charlotte. When Eric tells you, "Charles just added the basil leaves," he is reporting on an event that happened 10 seconds ago. When Erin tells you, "Charlotte just started the hollandaise sauce," she is reporting on what happened 30 seconds ago. To synchronize the activities of the two chefs, you must synchronize the activities of the two runners. You might give Erin a pair of track shoes to speed her up and have Eric wear a pair of heavy boots and a 30-pound trench coat to slow him down.

We find a similar problem in the retina. Some receptors are located much closer to the optic nerve than others are (Figure 5.7). As a result, light that strikes the retina close to the optic nerve has a head start in traveling to the brain. Without some sort of compensation, we might experience events in one part of the visual field slightly sooner than we experience events in other parts.

The nervous system has a way of synchronizing those messages from the retina. The axons that make up the optic nerve vary in their velocity of conduction. Those that receive their input from receptors close to the optic nerve have a slower conduction velocity than those that receive their input from remoter areas of the retina (Stanford, 1987). The net result is that the information reaching the brain is fairly well synchronized, regardless of its point of origin in the retina.

COLOR VISION

As Figure 5.1 shows, different colors of light correspond to different wavelengths of electromagnetic energy. (White light consists of an equal mixture of all the visible wavelengths.) How does the visual system convert those wavelengths into our perception of color? Although no one theory answers all questions about color vision, we can account for the main phenomena of color vision with a combination of three theories—the trichromatic (or Young-Helmholtz) theory, the opponent-process theory, and the retinex theory.

The Trichromatic Theory

The **trichromatic theory**, also known as the **Young-Helmholtz theory**, was proposed by Thomas Young and modified by Hermann von Helmholtz in the 19th century. According to this theory, color vision depends on three types of cones, each of which is most sensitive to a particular range of light wavelengths (Figure 5.9). One type is most sensitive to short wavelengths, another to medium wavelengths, and another to long wavelengths. Each wavelength prompts varying levels of activity in the three types of cones. We perceive *blue* when the short-wavelength cones are more active than the other two. We see *green* when the medium-wavelength cones are the most active. We perceive *red* when the long-wavelength cones are the most active. When the long-wavelength and the medium-wavelength cones are equally active and the short-wavelength cones are less active, we see *yellow*. When all three types of cones are equally active, we see *white* or *gray*. Each color is the result of a unique ratio of responses. We perceive *black* when a group of cones is inactive and is bordered by an area where all three types of cones are active. The contrast is necessary for the perception of black.

Young and Helmholtz proposed their theory long before experiments had confirmed that people do indeed have three types of cones (Wald, 1968). They relied entirely on a behavioral obser-

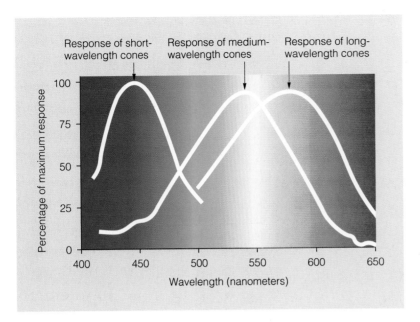

Response of short-wavelength cones   Response of medium-wavelength cones   Response of long-wavelength cones

FIGURE 5.9

Sensitivity of three types of cones to different wavelengths of light.

FIGURE 5.10

Black or blue? Blue spots look black unless they cover a sizable area. Count the red dots, then count the blue dots. Try again while standing father away from the page.

vation: They found that observers could choose three different colors of light and then, by mixing them in various proportions, match all other colors of light. (Note that mixing light of different colors is not the same as mixing paints of different colors. Mixing yellow and blue *paints* produces green; mixing yellow and blue *light* produces white.)

The short-wavelength cones, which respond most strongly to blue, are less numerous than the other two types, especially in the fovea. Consequently a tiny blue point may look black. In order for the retina to detect blueness, the blue must extend over a moderately large area. Figure 5.10 illustrates this effect. Count the red spots and then the blue spots. Then stand farther away and count the spots again. You will probably see as many red spots as before but fewer blue spots.

Concept Check

3. *According to the trichromatic theory, how do we tell the difference between bright yellow-green and dim yellow-green light? (Check your answer on page 178.)*

A century ago, Georges Seurat developed pointillism, applying paint to the canvas in dots rather than brush strokes. Looking at Sunday Afternoon on the Island of La Grande Jatte, *our eyes connect the dots to form larger shapes, yet the dots do not merge completely. In the close-up we see distinct points of red, yellow, and other colors. From a distance, they blend and appear to become other shades and colors.*

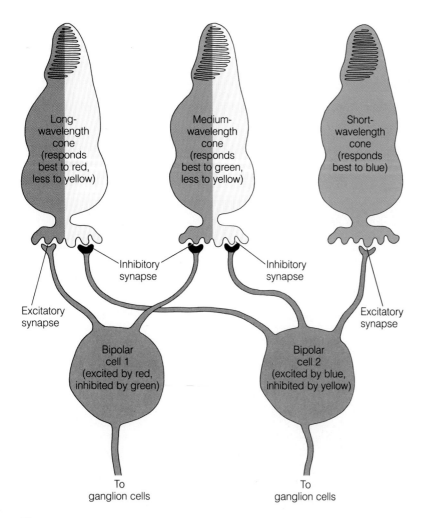

Figure 5.11

The connections between the cones and the bipolar cells of the retina produce opponent-process responses in the bipolar cells (and in all the other cells in the visual system of the brain). For example, bipolar cell 2 is excited when short-wavelength light strikes this group of cones, but it is inhibited when long-wavelength or medium-wavelength light strikes these cones.

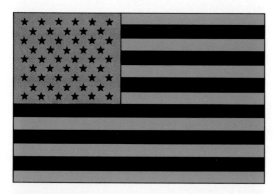

Figure 5.12

Seeing red, white, and blue: Use this flag to see the negative afterimages of opposite colors, which rebound after sufficient stimulation.

The Opponent-Process Theory of Color Vision

The trichromatic theory accounts for what happens at the level of the cones, but it fails to account for other phenomena of color vision. Another 19th-century scientist, Ewald Hering, having noticed that color perceptions seem to occur in pairs, proposed the **opponent-process theory** of color vision, which accounts for color vision at the level of the bipolar cells and ganglion cells.

According to this theory, we perceive color not in terms of independent colors but in terms of dimensions of red versus green, yellow versus blue, and white versus black. Any light stimulus leads to a perception somewhere along each of the three dimensions. Although Hering did not know it, the dimensions correspond to specific responses by ganglion cells in the eye. Some ganglion cells are excited when green light strikes the cones that connect to them and inhibited when red light strikes. Other ganglion cells are excited by red and inhibited by green. Still other cells are excited by yellow and inhibited by blue or excited by blue and inhibited by yellow. The white-black system is more complicated: If a cell is excited by white light, we cannot say exactly that it is inhibited by black. Rather, the cell is inhibited when the light on neighboring areas of the retina is brighter than the light in its own area.

For example, in Figure 5.11, bipolar cell 1 receives an excitatory synaptic message from the long-wavelength cone and an inhibitory synaptic message from the medium-wavelength cone. The cell increases its response in the presence of red light and decreases its response in the presence of green light. Bipolar cell 2 receives excitatory synaptic messages from the short-wavelength cone; it is therefore excited by blue light. Cell 2 receives inhibitory messages from both the long-wavelength cone and the medium-wavelength cone; it will be inhibited by either red light or green light, but it is most inhibited by yellow light, which activates both cones.

Figure 5.12 lends support to the opponent-process theory. Pick a point near the center of the figure and stare at it for a minute or so, preferably under a bright light, without moving your eyes or your head. Then look at a plain white or gray background. *Do this now.*

If you have normal or near-normal vision, you saw the United States flag. After the cells in your visual system have been activated in one direction long enough, removal of the stimulus makes them rebound in the opposite direction. Thus if you stare at something bright green and then look away, you will see red; if you stare at something yellow and then look away, you will see blue. The rebound colors are called **negative afterimages**.

Although Hering did not express his opponent-process theory in physiological terms, subsequent research has explained what actually happens in the nervous system (DeValois, 1965; Michael, 1978). At rest, when no light is shining on the retina, the bipolar cells of the retina spontaneously produce action potentials (page 69) at a moderate frequency. Consider bipolar cell 1 in Figure 5.11, which is excited when red light strikes a cone connected with it and is inhibited when green light strikes a cone connected with it. When bright red light first strikes the receptors, the frequency of action potentials in the bipolar cell increases sharply. As time passes, though, fatigue sets in, the frequency declines, and the sensation of color grows fainter. Suddenly the red light ceases. Now the activity of the bipolar cell drops below its usual spontaneous level to a level that generally occurs when it is inhibited by green light. So you see green.

Concept Checks

4. *How would bipolar cell 1 in Figure 5.11 respond to yellow light? Why? (Check your answers on page 178.)*
5. *The negative afterimage that you created by staring at Figure 5.12 may seem to move against the background. Why doesn't it stay in one place? (Check your answer on page 179.)*

The Retinex Theory

Even a combination of the trichromatic theory and the opponent-process theory does not explain color vision completely. Suppose you look at a full-color illustration in daylight; you see objects of all colors. Then you look at the same illustration under a mostly green light or while you are wearing green-tinted glasses. (See Figure 5.13.) Does everything look green to you? Undoubtedly the illustration looks greener than it used to, especially at first. And yet you still see objects as yellow, red, blue, or whatever color they were under normal lighting. This tendency of an object to appear nearly the same color under a variety of lighting conditions is called **color constancy**.

In response to such observations, Edwin Land (the inventor of the Polaroid Land camera) proposed what he calls the **retinex theory**. According to this theory, we perceive color through the combined contributions of the retina and the cortex (see Figure 5.14). (*Retinex* is a combination of *retina* and *cortex*.) The cerebral cortex compares the

FIGURE 5.13

If someone has an optimistic outlook, we say he views the world through rose-colored glasses. "She's green with envy," "I'm feeling blue," and "He saw red" express how feelings can color our overall outlook. Filters also can alter a scene without changing its various elements. As these photographs show, the colors remain identifiable, despite green and red filters. You experience this constancy when you wear sunglasses. Looking through dark-gray lenses, you see muted colors, but corn remains yellow and grass is still green, not gray.

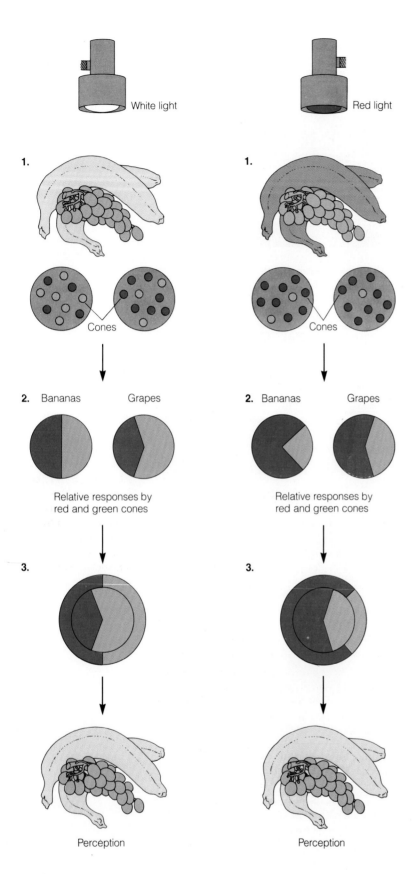

patterns of light coming from different areas of the retina and synthesizes a color perception for each area (Land, Hubel, Livingstone, Perry, & Burns, 1983; Land & McCann, 1971). Even when the light is mostly green, different objects reflect different amounts of green and other light; these differences enable the cortex to compare one object with another.

Two kinds of evidence support the retinex theory. First, if you look at a lemon under green light in a room full of objects, you see the lemon as yellow. But if you look at the same lemon under the same light against a totally black background, the lemon looks undeniably green. For color constancy to be maintained, the patterns of light coming from a variety of objects must somehow be compared and contrasted. Only the visual cortex is in a position to compare information from areas across the entire visual field.

Second, after monkeys suffer damage to an anterior portion of the occipital cortex, they no longer show color constancy (Wild, Butler, Carden, & Kulikowski, 1985). They still see colors, and they can still learn to pick up only orange objects, for example. But if the light is shifted from white to some other color, they no longer pick up the correct object. As the retinex theory predicts, the phenomenon of color constancy depends on the activity of the cerebral cortex.

The cerebral cortex deals with brightness in a similar way. The two gray areas in Figure 5.15 are of equal brightness, but to most viewers the area against the dark background looks much brighter. Brightness, like color, depends on comparison and contrast. The closer together two areas are, the greater the effect one area will have on the apparent color or brightness of the other (Gogel & Mershon, 1977).

Which of the three theories of color vision is correct? Each is correct up to a point, and they do not contradict one another directly. According to the trichromatic theory, color vision depends on three kinds of cones that respond differently to different wavelengths of light. According to the opponent-process theory, the nervous system con-

FIGURE 5.14

When bananas and grapes reflect red light, they excite a higher percentage of short-wavelength (red) cones than usual. According to the retinex theory, brain cells determine the red-green percentage for each fruit. Then cells in the visual cortex divide the "red-greenness" of the bananas by the "red-greenness" of the grapes to produce color sensations. In red and white light, the ratios between the fruits are nearly constant.

FIGURE 5.15

Brightness contrast. The two gray squares are equally bright. Do they look the same?

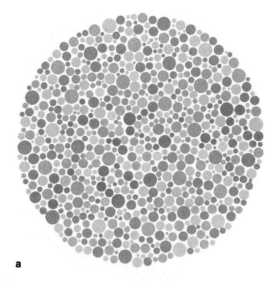

a

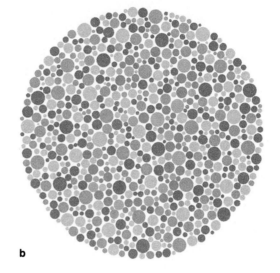

b

FIGURE 5.16

Items of a test for red-green color blindness, an inherited condition that affects mostly men. What do you see? Compare your answers to answer A, page 179.

verts those responses into a system of excitation and inhibition, in which one color excites a cell and an opposite color inhibits it. Finally, according to the retinex theory, certain parts of the cerebral cortex compare the patterns coming from different parts of the retina to determine the color in each.

Color Blindness

For a very long time, people apparently assumed that anyone with normal vision could see and recognize colors (Fletcher & Voke, 1985). Then, during the 1600s, the phenomenon of color blindness was unambiguously recognized. Here was the first clue that color vision is a function of our eyes and brains.

The total inability to distinguish one color from another is extremely rare, except as the result of certain kinds of brain damage. However, about 4% of all people are *partially* color-blind. Investigators believe that most cases of color blindness result from an abnormality of one of the three types of cones (Fletcher & Voke, 1985). For example, one type of cone may have less than the normal amount of **photopigment,** a chemical in the cones and rods that releases energy when it is struck by light. Depending on which type of cone is deficient, a person may be relatively insensitive to red light, green light, or blue light. When I say "relatively insensitive to green light," I do not mean that such a person is blind to green light; I mean rather that he or she has trouble discriminating green from other colors. Such people perceive a pure green patch as almost the same as gray, although to some of them a very large green patch may look almost the same as it does to a person with normal color vision (Boynton, 1988).

The most common type of color blindness is sometimes known as **red-green color blindness.** People with red-green color blindness have difficulty distinguishing red from green and either red or green from yellow. Actually, red-green color blindness has two forms, *protanopia* and *deuteranopia.* People with protanopia lack long-wavelength cones; people with deuteranopia lack medium-wavelength cones. People with the rare *yellow-blue color blindness* (also known as *tritanopia*) have trouble distinguishing yellows and blues. They are believed to lack short-wavelength cones.

Figure 5.16 gives a crude but usually satisfactory test for red-green color blindness. What do you see in each part of the figure? (To interpret your answers, refer to answer A on page 179.)

How does the world look to color-blind people? Their descriptions use all the usual color words: Roses are red, violets are blue, bananas are yellow, grass is green. But that does not mean that they

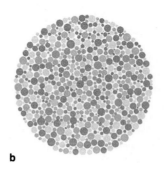

a   b   c

FIGURE 5.17

These stimuli induce temporary red-green color blindness and temporarily enhance color vision. First stare at pattern a under a bright light for about a minute, then look at b. What do you see? Next stare at c for a minute and look at b again. Now what do you see?

perceive red, green, or any other color the same way a person with normal color vision does. Can they tell us what the rose they say is *red* actually looks like to them? In most cases, they cannot. Certain rare individuals, however, are red-green color-blind in one eye but have normal vision in the other eye. Because they know what the color words really mean (from experience with their normal eye), they can tell us what their color-blind eye sees. They say that objects that look red or green to the normal eye look yellow or yellow-gray to the color-blind eye (Marriott, 1976).

If you have normal color vision, Figure 5.17 will show you what it is like to be red-green color-blind. First cover part b, a typical item from a color blindness test, and stare at part a, a red field, under a bright light for about a minute. Then look at part b. Staring at the red field has fatigued your red cones, and you now have only a weak sensation of red. As the red cones recover, you will see part b normally. If you are red-green color-blind, the effect will be weak.

Now stare at part c, a green field, for about a minute and look at part b again. Because you have fatigued your green cones, the figure in b will stand out even more strongly than usual. In fact, certain red-green color-blind people may be able to see the number in b only after staring at c. (Refer to answer B on page 179 if you need help.)

Something to Think About

The introduction to this chapter suggested that we would see no new colors on another planet and that we cannot be certain that different people on Earth really have the same color experiences. Try now to explain the reasons behind those statements.

SUMMARY

1. Our receptors gather only the most useful part of the information actually available in the environment and convert it into a form that can be transmitted to the brain. (page 129)

2. The cornea and lens focus the light that enters through the pupil of the eye. If the eye is not spherical or if the lens is not flexible, corrective eyeglasses may be needed. (page 130)

3. The retina contains two kinds of receptors: cones and rods. Cones are specialized for detailed vision and color perception. Rods detect dim light. (page 132)

4. The blind spot is the area of the retina through which the optic nerve exits; this area has no receptors and is therefore blind. (page 135)

5. Color vision depends on three types of cones, each most sensitive to a particular range of light wavelengths. The cones transmit messages so that the bipolar and ganglion cells in the visual system are excited by light of one color and inhibited by light of the opposite color. Then the cerebral cortex compares the responses from different parts of the retina to determine the color of light coming from each area of the visual field. (page 136)

6. Complete color blindness is rare. Certain people have difficulty distinguishing reds from greens; in rare cases, some have difficulty distinguishing yellows from blues. (page 141)

SUGGESTIONS FOR FURTHER READING

Goldstein, E. B. (1989). *Sensation and perception* (3rd ed.). Belmont, CA: Wadsworth. An excellent textbook covering sensory processes.

Hubel, D. H. (1988). *Eye, brain, and vision.* New York: Scientific American Library. A treatment by an investigator who shared the Nobel Prize in physiology and medicine for his research on the physiology of vision.

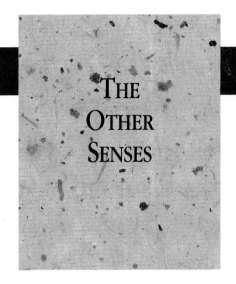

THE OTHER SENSES

How do hearing, the vestibular sense, skin senses, pain, taste, and olfaction— the nonvisual senses—work?

Consider these common expressions:

I *see* what you mean.

I *feel* sympathetic toward your plight.

I am deeply *touched* by everyone's support and concern.

The Senate will hold *hearings* on the budget proposal.

She is a person of great *taste*.

He was *dizzy* with success.

The policies of this company *stink*.

That *sounds* like a good job offer.

Each sentence expresses an idea in terms of sensation, though we know that the terms are not meant to be taken literally. When we say, "He has great taste," we are not talking about his tongue. Rather, we use such terms to describe a wide variety of concepts.

That usage is not accidental. Most of our thinking and brain activity is devoted to processing sensory stimuli. Sensations bring us in contact with the energies of the outside world. We have already considered the detection of light. Here we deal with the detection of mechanical energies such as touch and vibration and with the detection of chemicals (taste and smell).

HEARING

Fish detect vibrations in the water by means of a long row of touch receptors along their sides, called the *lateral line system.* The mammalian ear, which probably evolved as a modification of the lateral line system, converts sound waves into mechanical displacements of a membrane that a row of receptor cells can detect.

Sound waves are vibrations of the air or of some other medium. They vary both in frequency and in amplitude (see Figure 5.18). The *frequency* of a sound wave is the number of cycles (vibrations) it goes through per second. **Pitch** is a perception closely related to frequency. We perceive a high-frequency sound wave as high pitched and a low-frequency sound as low pitched. **Loudness** is our perception that depends on the *amplitude* of a sound wave—the vertical range of its cycles. Other things being equal, the greater the amplitude of a sound, the louder it sounds to us. Because pitch and loudness are psychological concepts, however, they can sometimes be influenced by factors other than the physical frequency and amplitude of sound waves.

The ear, a complicated organ, converts relatively weak sound waves into more intense waves

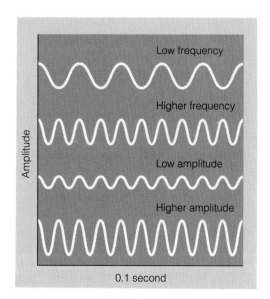

FIGURE 5.18

Four sound waves. The period (time) between the peaks determines the frequency of the sound; we experience frequencies as different pitches. The vertical range, or amplitude, of a wave determines the sound's intensity and loudness.

FIGURE 5.19

Hear here: When sound waves strike the eardrum (a), they cause it to vibrate. The eardrum is connected to three tiny bones—the hammer, anvil, and stirrup—that convert the sound wave into a series of strong vibrations in the fluid-filled cochlea (b). Those vibrations displace the hair cells along the basilar membrane in the cochlea, which is aptly named from the Greek word for *snail*. (c) A cross section through the cochlea. (d) A close-up of the hair cells.

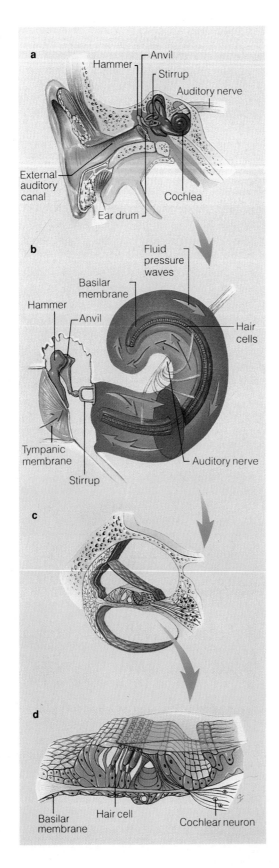

of pressure in the fluid-filled canals of the snail-shaped **cochlea** (KOCK-lee-uh) (Figure 5.19). When sound waves strike the eardrum, they cause it to vibrate. The eardrum is connected to three tiny bones: the hammer, the anvil, and the stirrup (also known by their Latin names: *malleus, incus,* and *stapes*). As the weak vibrations of the large eardrum travel through these bones, they are transformed into stronger vibrations of the much smaller stirrup. The stirrup in turn transmits the vibrations to the fluid-filled cochlea, where the vibrations displace hair cells along the **basilar membrane,** a thin structure within the cochlea. These hair cells, which act much like touch receptors on the skin, are connected to neurons whose axons form the auditory nerve. Impulses are transmitted along this pathway to the areas of the brain responsible for hearing.

A person can lose hearing in two ways. One is **conductive deafness,** which results if the bones connected to the eardrum fail to transmit sound waves properly to the cochlea. Sometimes surgery can correct conductive deafness by removing whatever is obstructing the movement of those bones. A person with conductive deafness can still hear his or her own voice, because it can be conducted through the skull bones to the cochlea, bypassing the eardrum altogether. The other type of hearing loss is **nerve deafness,** which results from damage to the cochlea, the hair cells, or the auditory nerve. Nerve deafness can result from heredity, from multiple sclerosis and other diseases, and from prolonged exposure to loud noises. Nerve deafness is permanent and cannot be corrected by surgery, although the use of hearing aids can compensate for the loss.

Pitch Perception

The adult human ear responds to sound waves from about 15–20 **hertz** to about 15,000–20,000 hertz (Hz). (A hertz, named for German physicist Heinrich Hertz, equals one cycle per second.) The low frequencies are perceived as deep tones of low pitch; the high frequencies are perceived as tones of high pitch. The upper limit of hearing declines suddenly after exposure to loud noises and declines steadily as a person grows older.

Other species can hear much higher pitches. Some whistles produce high pitches that are audible to dogs but not to humans. In general, animals with small heads, such as mice, can hear higher frequencies than humans can, sometimes as high as 100,000 Hz; animals with large heads, such as elephants, are limited to lower frequencies (Heffner & Heffner, 1982).

The ability to perceive pitch depends on three

Some loss of hearing is normal as people get older, but some people suffer hearing loss prematurely. The high-amplitude concert sounds rock musicians are exposed to can take a toll on their hearing; the damage to Peter Townshend's hearing includes tinnitus, ringing in the ear.

mechanisms. At low frequencies (up to about 100 Hz), the basilar membrane in the cochlea vibrates in synchrony with the sound waves; thus a sound with a frequency of 50 Hz excites each hair cell along the membrane 50 times per second, sending 50 impulses per second to the brain.

At intermediate frequencies (about 100–5000 Hz), the basilar membrane continues to vibrate in synchrony with the sound waves. However, the individual hair cells are unable to send an impulse to the brain every time the membrane vibrates. (A neuron cannot fire more than about 1,000 action potentials per second, and it cannot maintain that pace for long.) Even so, each vibration of the membrane excites at least a few hair cells, and groups of them (volleys) respond to each vibration by sending a message to the brain (Rose, Brugge, Anderson, & Hind, 1967). Thus a tone at 2000 Hz might send impulses to the brain 2,000 times per second, even though no neuron by itself could produce all those impulses.

At high frequencies, sound waves of different frequencies cause vibrations at different locations along the basilar membrane. The membrane is thin and stiff near the stirrup and wide and floppy at the other end. Consequently, high-frequency sounds cause maximum vibration near the stirrup end, and lower-frequency sounds cause maximum vibration at points farther along the membrane. During a high-frequency sound, hair cells near the stirrup become active; during a low-frequency sound, hair cells at the opposite end become active. The brain can identify the frequency by noting which cells are most active.

Our finely tuned hearing system perceives the different pitches that sophisticated musical instruments produce. The violin has seven dozen parts, and details as minor as its varnish can alter its sound. Perfect pitch—a talent Mozart had—is the ability to identify a single note.

The reason we can discriminate among pitches is that different pitches excite different hair cells along the basilar membrane (Zwislocki, 1981). Figure 5.20 shows how we perceive pitches of low, medium, and high frequency.

	Low frequency	Intermediate frequency	High frequency
Sound wave	∿∿∿∿∿	∿∿∿∿∿∿∿∿∿	∿∿∿∿∿∿∿∿∿∿∿∿∿

Response of four
cells at different
points along the
basilar membrane

Sum of response

       a   **b**   **c**

FIGURE 5.20

Synchronicity: How the ear responds to sounds of low, medium, and high frequency.
(a) At low frequencies, hair cells along the basilar membrane produce impulses in synchrony with the sound waves. (b) At medium frequencies, different cells produce
impulses in synchrony with different waves, but the group as a whole still produces one
or more impulses for each wave. (c) At high frequencies, only one point along the basilar membrane vibrates; hair cells produce impulses only at that point.

*Ventriloquists got their name from the
mistaken belief that they produced
voices from their stomachs. Our eyes tell
us that a dummy's moving mouth is the
source of sounds, although we know
this is impossible.*

FIGURE 5.21

The stereophonic hearing of our ears enables us to
determine where a sound is coming from. We can distinguish sounds that are just a thousandth of a second
apart. The ear located closest to the sound will receive
the sound waves first.

Concept Check

6. *When hair cells at one point along the basilar membrane produce 50 impulses per second, we hear a tone at 5000 Hz. What do we hear when those same hair cells produce 100 impulses per second? (Check your answer on page 179.)*

Localization of Sounds

When we taste, smell, or feel something, we experience it as being on the tongue, near the nose, or on the skin. When we see or hear something, the stimulus is on the retina of the eye or on the basilar membrane of the ear, but we do not experience it as such. We experience it as "out there." How do we know where a sound comes from?

Our auditory system determines the direction of a source of sound by comparing the messages coming from the two ears. If a sound is coming from a source directly in front, the messages will arrive at the two ears at the same time and will be equal in loudness. If the sound is coming from a source on the left, however, it will arrive at the left ear slightly before it arrives at the right ear, and it will be louder in the left ear (see Figure 5.21). Yet we do not hear two sounds; we have an experience of a single sound coming from the left. A difference between the messages in the two ears indicates how far the sound source is to the left or right of center.

Our auditory system also can detect the approximate distance of a sound source. In a closed room, we first hear the sound waves that come directly from the source and then, after a delay, we hear the waves that are reflected off the walls, floor, ceiling, and objects in the room. The more distant the source, the greater the percentage of reflected and delayed sound we hear. When we hear many reflected sounds (echoes), we judge the source of the sound to be far away.

We use visual cues as well as auditory cues in locating the source of a sound. If people see a loudspeaker in a room, they perceive the sound as coming from the loudspeaker even if it is really coming from somewhere else. The closer the actual source is to the loudspeaker, the greater this *visual capture effect* will be (Mershon, Desaulniers, Amerson, & Kiefer, 1980). The same effect comes into play when we "hear" a voice coming from a ventriloquist's dummy or from a movie or television screen.

Concept Check

7. *Why is it difficult to tell whether a sound is coming from directly in front of or from directly behind you? (Check your answer on page 179.)*

RECEPTORS OF MECHANICAL STIMULATION

Certain receptors, including the touch receptors, are called **mechanoreceptors** because they respond to mechanical stimulation like pressing and pulling. Pain, vestibular sensation, and hearing also detect mechanical stimulation.

The Vestibular Sense

In the inner ear on each side of the head, adjacent to the structures responsible for hearing, is a structure called the *vestibule*. The **vestibular sense** that it controls tells us the amount and direction of acceleration of our head and the position of our head with respect to gravity. It plays a key role in posture and balance and is responsible for the sensations we experience when we are riding on a roller coaster or sitting in an airplane during takeoff.

The vestibular sense also enables us to keep our eyes focused even when our head is moving. When you walk down the street, you can keep your eyes focused on a distant street sign even though your head is bobbing up and down. The vestibular sense detects each head movement and controls the movement of your eyes to compensate for it.

Do this experiment: Try to read this page while you are jiggling the book from side to side but keeping your head steady. Now hold the book steady and move your head from side to side. If you are like most people, you will find it much easier to read when you are moving your head than when you are jiggling the book. That is because your vestibular sense keeps your eyes focused on the print during head movements. People who have suffered injury to their vestibular sense report that they have to hold their head perfectly steady in order to read street signs or clocks. If they move their head even a bit, their vision becomes blurred.

The vestibular system is composed of three semicircular canals, oriented in three separate directions, and two otolith organs (Figure 5.22b). The *semicircular canals* are lined with hair cells and filled with a jellylike substance. When the body accelerates in any direction, the jellylike substance in the corresponding semicircular canal pushes against the hair cells, which send messages to the brain. The two *otolith organs* shown in Figure 5.22b also contain hair cells (see Figure 5.22c), which lie next to calcium carbonate particles. Depending on which way the head tilts, the particles move about in the direction of gravitational pull and excite different sets of hair cells. The otolith organs report the direction from which gravity is pulling and tell us which way is "up."

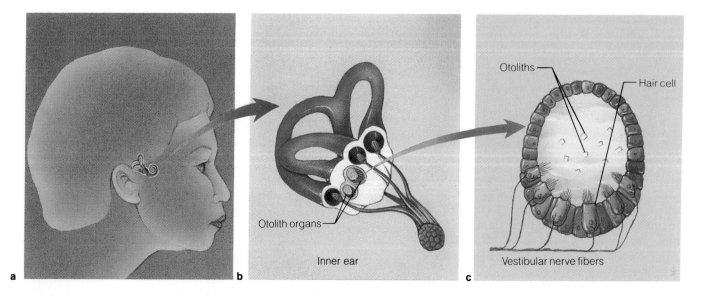

FIGURE 5.22

(a) Location of and (b) structures of the vestibule. (c) Moving your head or body displaces hair cells that maintain the vestibular sense by literally telling your brain "where your head is at."

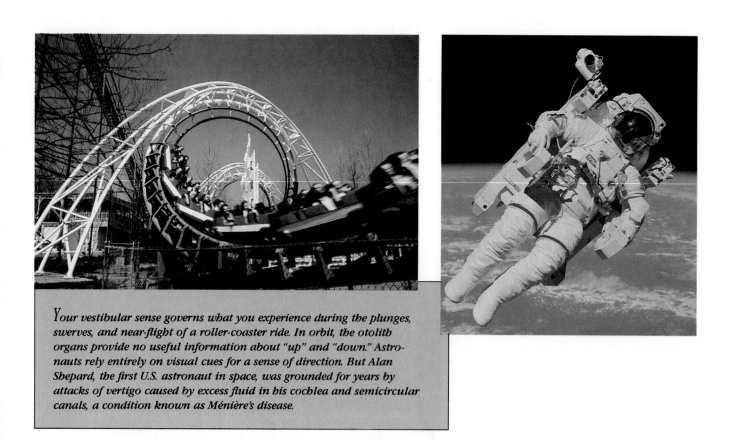

Your vestibular sense governs what you experience during the plunges, swerves, and near-flight of a roller-coaster ride. In orbit, the otolith organs provide no useful information about "up" and "down." Astronauts rely entirely on visual cues for a sense of direction. But Alan Shepard, the first U.S. astronaut in space, was grounded for years by attacks of vertigo caused by excess fluid in his cochlea and semicircular canals, a condition known as Ménière's disease.

At least that is true when the body is at rest. If you walk forward, inertia drags the calcium carbonate particles in your otolith organs backward. Yet you do not grow confused and think that "down" is behind you. How do you know which direction is up and which is down while you are moving?

Apparently, through a complex process, the brain integrates information from the vestibular system with information from the eyes and from the feet or from whatever other part of the body is in contact with the ground (Stoffregen & Riccio, 1988). When the rest of your body tells you that you are keeping your balance, you are likely to feel that your head is up and your feet are down, even if your otolith organs are telling you something else and even if you are not standing perpendicular to the Earth's gravity. For this reason, a pilot feels "right-side up" with respect to the airplane even when the airplane is executing a steep turn.

The Sense of Touch

What we commonly think of as the sense of touch actually consists of several partly independent senses. These are sometimes known as the **cutaneous senses** or the *somatosensory system*. Our senses of pressure on the skin, warmth, cold, pain, vibration, movement across the skin, and stretch of the skin all depend on different receptors in the skin (Iggo & Andres, 1982). (See Figure 5.23.) Those receptors send information to the brain along partly distinct, partly overlapping paths in the spinal cord, and they excite distinct, though neighboring, areas of the cerebral cortex (Kaas, 1983).

On the fingertips, the lips, and other highly sensitive areas of skin, the receptors are densely packed, and each receptor detects stimulation in only a small area of the skin. On the back and other less sensitive areas, the receptors are scattered more widely, and each one is responsible for detecting stimulation over a large surface. Similarly, much more of the parietal lobe is devoted to sensation from the lips and fingers than from the less sensitive areas, as shown in Figure 3.30a (page 84).

Humans are far better than most other species at identifying objects by touch, although raccoons provide some tough competition (Rensch & Dücker, 1963). Instead of trying to convert tactile sensations into a visual representation of an object—perhaps by tracing the outline of the object with a finger—humans identify objects by using hardness, texture, and other touch-related cues that do not have to be converted into visual representations (Klatzky, Lederman, & Reed, 1987).

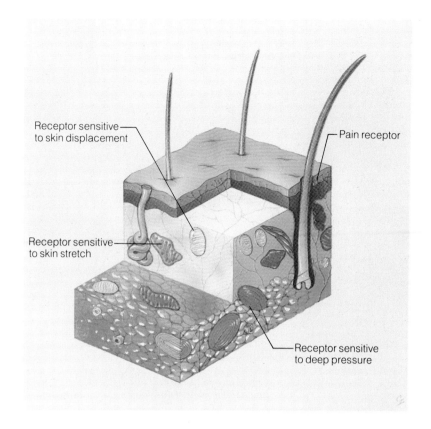

FIGURE 5.23

Some sensory receptors found in the skin, the human body's largest organ.

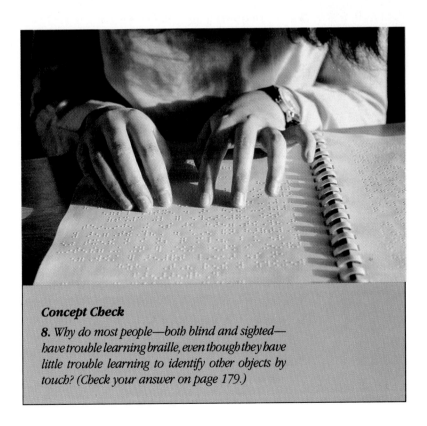

Concept Check

8. *Why do most people—both blind and sighted—have trouble learning braille, even though they have little trouble learning to identify other objects by touch? (Check your answer on page 179.)*

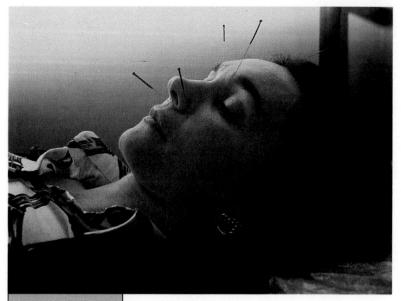

To prevent and control disease, the Chinese practice of acupuncture has traditionally been used to treat arthritis, malaria, and a wide range of other disorders. There are several speculations about how and why it is effective as an anesthetic during surgery. Some researchers think acupuncture's analgesic effects may be attributed to endorphins.

Pain

We experience pain in many ways: when we cut a finger, spill an irritating chemical on our skin, or suffer exposure to extreme heat or cold. Pain receptors are simple, bare nerve endings that send messages to the spinal cord. The sensation of pain, however, is far more complex than the simple relaying of stimulation from the skin to the central nervous system (Liebeskind & Paul, 1977; Melzack & Wall, 1983). Many people manage to carry on without complaint even after they have been severely injured. An injured athlete, for example, may show no signs of pain until the game is over. Other people report severe pain after what seems to be just a minor injury. And some people continue to feel pain long after an injury has healed, almost as if pain had become a learned habit. Because of observations such as these, R. Melzack and P. D. Wall (1965) proposed the **gate theory** of pain, the idea that pain messages have to pass through a gate in the spinal cord on their way to the brain. The brain can send messages down to the spinal cord to open or close that gate. Although some details of Melzack and Wall's theory are apparently wrong, their basic idea is valid: The activity of the rest of the brain can facilitate or inhibit the transmission of pain messages.

One way to reduce the sensation of pain is to provide some distraction. In terms of the gate theory, the distraction closes the pain gate. For example, surgery patients in a room with a pleasant view complain less about pain, take less painkilling medicine, and recover faster than do patients in a windowless room or a room with a poor view (Ulrich, 1984). Many people relieve their pain by listening to music, by playing games, or by recollecting some pleasant experience (Lavine, Buchsbaum, & Poncy, 1976; McCaul & Malott, 1984).

Several medical techniques are available for controlling pain. Many, if not all, of the axons transmitting pain messages in the spinal cord release a neurotransmitter called *substance P.* An injection of the chemical *capsaicin* into the spinal cord of a laboratory animal causes the pain axons suddenly to release large quantities of substance P. For a few minutes the animal shows signs of sharp pain, as if the axons had been activated by some painful stimulus. However, because the axons cannot replenish their supply of substance P nearly as fast as they release it, the animal becomes insensitive to pain for weeks. As the supply is restored, the pain returns (Yarsh, Farb, Leeman, & Jessell, 1979). This is a dangerous procedure, however, and unlikely to be used with humans because large doses of capsaicin damage neurons. (Capsaicin makes jalapeño peppers taste hot by releasing minute amounts of substance P from cells on the tongue. When you bite down on a hot pepper, you experience a temporary sensation of pain followed by a slight decrease in sensitivity to pain.)

A safer way of controlling pain is to take morphine or similar drugs that stimulate the **endorphin** synapses. The term *endorphin* is a combination of the terms *endogenous* and *morphine.* Endorphins are self-produced morphines; they act as neurotransmitters that inhibit the release of substance P, thus decreasing the sensation of pain and inducing pleasant feelings. They are generally found in the same areas of the brain as substance P is (McLean, Skirboll, & Pert, 1985). Endorphins may also be part of the system in the brain responsible for the experience of pleasure.

Pain alerts us to an injury. (People who are totally insensitive to pain have a short life expectancy!) However, once the brain has received a pain message, the prolonged sensation of pain can disrupt behavior. Presumably, endorphin synapses evolved as a means of reducing the pain signal after it has served its function.

A variety of stimuli can release endorphins. Under some circumstances a painful stimulus itself releases endorphins, so that exposure to one painful stimulus decreases sensitivity to the next painful stimulus. Pleasant stimuli may also release endorphins. (That may help explain why a pleasant view helps to ease postsurgical pain.)

Concept Check

9. Naloxone, *a drug used as an antidote for an overdose of morphine, is known to block the endorphin synapses. How could we use naloxone to determine whether a pleasant stimulus releases endorphins? (Check your answer on page 179.)*

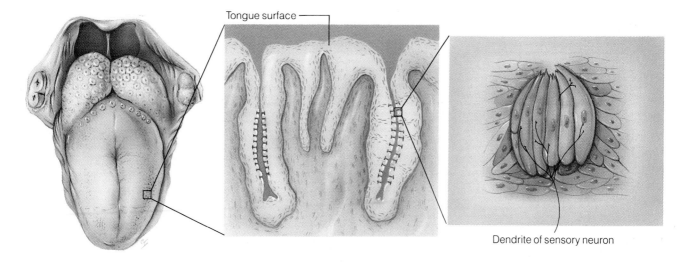

Tongue surface

Dendrite of sensory neuron

Figure 5.24

(a) The tongue, a powerful muscle used in speaking and eating. Taste buds, which react to chemicals dissolved in saliva, are located primarily on the tongue papillae (protuberances). (b) A cross section of one of the larger papillae, showing taste buds. (c) A cross section of one taste bud. Each taste bud has about 50 transducer cells within it that continuously replace others as they wear out; these cells last about 10 days. Taste buds are most concentrated at the tip and back of the tongue.

Chemical Receptors: Taste and Smell

The receptors for taste and smell distinguish among the various chemicals that come into contact with the nose and mouth. These **chemical receptors** have only meager connections to the cerebral cortex, but they have extensive connections to the subcortical areas associated with motivations and emotions. Consequently, tastes and smells tend to evoke strong emotional responses.

Taste

Vision and hearing enable us to do many different things: to find food and water, to avoid danger, to keep our balance, and to find suitable mates. But the sense of **taste** serves just one function: It tells us what to eat and drink. The cells in the brain that receive information from the taste receptors are closely related to the cells that control food intake (Yamamoto, 1987).

The taste receptors are located in **taste buds** found in tiny folds on the surface of the tongue (Figure 5.24). We can describe almost all tastes in terms of four qualities—sweet, sour, salty, and bitter—and we can match most tastes by combining those qualities in varying proportions. Among the possible exceptions are the taste of alkaline substances such as dilute sodium hydroxide (Schiffman & Erickson, 1971) and the taste of MSG, a seasoning used in certain Asian foods (Yamaguchi & Komata, 1988).

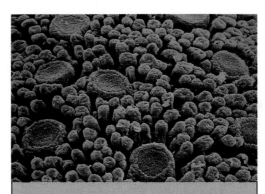

The tongue is one of the most sensitive parts of the body—something you may have discovered if you've accidentally bitten or burnt your tongue or eaten a potent chili pepper. This scanning electron micrograph of the tongue's surface shows the filiform (filamentlike) papillae, which help move food without tasting it. The circumvallate (round) papillae surround taste buds.

When we speak of the "taste of peppermint" or the "taste of curry," we are actually referring to a combination of three senses: taste, smell, and texture. The distinction between one food and another generally is based more on smell and texture than on taste. In discussing such a combination of sensations, the term flavor *is more appropriate than* taste.

Different Types of Taste Receptors

To date, no one has managed to isolate a taste receptor. It is generally believed, however, that the tongue has several distinct types of taste receptors, probably four or more. How can we infer that there are different types of receptors when we cannot isolate even one of them?

One basis for that inference is that we can match most tastes by mixing appropriate amounts of sweet, sour, salty, and bitter substances. Moreover, by following certain procedures, we can affect one taste without affecting others, presumably because the procedures act on only one type of receptors. Here are four examples:

- Cooling the tongue decreases one's sensitivity to the taste of sucrose and other sweet substances without affecting the taste of salty or sour substances and with only a slight effect on the taste of bitter substances (Frankmann & Green, 1988). This finding suggests that the receptors for sweet tastes have different properties from the receptors for other tastes. (It also implies that soft drinks will taste sweeter after a hot meal than after eating ice cream.)

- Have you ever drunk a glass of orange juice just after brushing your teeth? How can something that ordinarily tastes so good suddenly taste so bad? The reason is that most toothpastes contain sodium lauryl sulfate, a chemical that weakens our response to sweet tastes and intensifies our response to sour and bitter tastes (Schiffman, 1983). Again, the implication is that different taste receptors have different properties.

- The chemical amiloride prevents sodium ions from crossing the membrane of a cell. This chemical weakens the taste of sodium chloride (common table salt) and other salts as well as sugars but has no effect on the taste of bitter or sour substances (Schiffman, Simon, Gill, & Beeker, 1988). Evidently the salty receptor differs in some respects from the bitter and sour receptors.

- The artificial sweetener saccharin tastes both sweet and bitter, though some people experience one taste more strongly than the other. If you taste caffeine before tasting saccharin, both the sweet and the bitter tastes of saccharin will be intensified. Preexposure to caffeine has no effect, however, on substances that taste only sweet, such as sucrose, or on substances that taste only bitter, such as quinine (Schiffman, Diaz, & Beeker, 1986). Because we can affect the taste of saccharin without affecting the taste of sucrose or quinine, it seems likely that saccharin stimulates a separate receptor. In other words, we may have separate receptors for sweet, bitter, and sweet-bitter, as well as for salty and sour.

Olfaction

Olfaction is the sense of smell. The olfactory receptors, located on the mucous membrane in the rear air passages of the nose (Figure 5.25), detect the presence of certain airborne molecules. The axons of the olfactory receptors form the olfactory tract, which extends to the olfactory bulbs at the base of the brain (see Figure 5.26). The olfactory receptors contain proteins that react with chemicals that we inhale (Lancet et al., 1987). Depending on the type of molecule we have inhaled, different populations of olfactory receptors become active. Presumably, we recognize a smell on the basis of which cells become more active than others. Our understanding of olfactory receptors is primitive. We do not even know whether we have a few distinct types of olfactory receptors, as with the three types of cones responsible for color vision, or whether our olfactory receptors vary along some continuum, as with the hair cells along the basilar membrane of the ear.

The sense of smell is more acute in most other mammals than it is in humans. A single olfactory

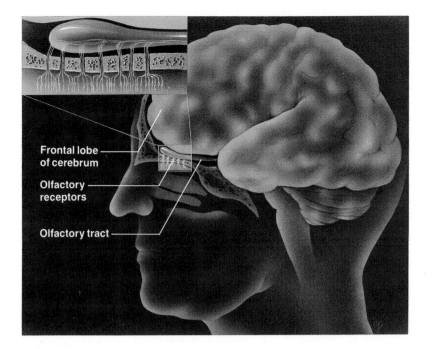

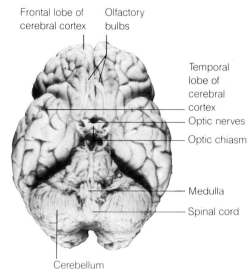

Frontal lobe of cerebral cortex
Olfactory bulbs
Temporal lobe of cerebral cortex
Optic nerves
Optic chiasm
Medulla
Spinal cord
Cerebellum

FIGURE 5.25

Location of the olfactory receptors and the olfactory tract, a set of axons carrying messages from the olfactory receptors to the brain.

FIGURE 5.26

The actual undersurface of the brain, showing the position of the olfactory bulbs above the nose.

receptor is probably about as sensitive in humans as it is in any other species, but other species have a greater number of receptors. Specially trained dogs can track a person's olfactory trail across fields and through woods. Dogs also recognize one another by odor. A male dog claims a territory by depositing a few drops of urine at key locations.

Many mammals identify one another by means of **pheromones**, odorous chemicals they release into the environment. In nearly all nonhuman mammals, the males rely on pheromones to distinguish sexually receptive females from unreceptive females.

Humans prefer *not* to recognize one another by smell. The deodorant and perfume industries exist for the sole purpose of removing and covering up human odors. But perhaps we respond to pheromones anyway, at least under certain conditions. For example, young women who are in frequent contact with one another, such as roommates in a college dormitory, tend to synchronize their menstrual cycles, probably as a result of pheromones they secrete. (If the women are taking birth-control pills, the synchronization does not occur.) In one experiment, women who were exposed daily to another woman's underarm secretions became synchronized to her menstrual cycle (Russell, Switz, & Thompson, 1980). (*Why* this occurs is not clear. Female dogs, cats, and rats do not synchronize their periods of fertility. Why should humans?)

Human males also secrete an odorous chemical in their sweat, in an amount proportional to the

Getting nosy: Secret, Ban, Arrid—as their names suggest, U.S. industries spend millions developing and promoting deodorants and antiperspirants so we can secretly banish sweat and have arid armpits. In the past, people used strong perfume to mask odors.

amount of testosterone in their blood. In one experiment, when samples of this chemical were placed in certain bathroom stalls, other men tended to avoid using those stalls (Gustavson, Dawson, & Bonett, 1987).

In addition to its role in responding to pheromones, olfaction plays a key role in food selection.

What we call the flavor of a food is produced by both its taste and its smell. When a meat or other food is spoiled, olfaction alerts us to that fact before we even try to taste it.

Something to Think About

Why might it be that humans as well as monkeys and chimpanzees are less sensitive to odors and more responsive to vision than are most other mammals? For an animal living in trees, which is more useful—vision or olfaction?

SUMMARY

1. At low frequencies of sound, we identify pitch by the frequency of vibrations on the basilar membrane. At intermediate frequencies, we identify pitch by volleys of responses from a number of neurons. At high frequencies, we identify pitch by the area of the basilar membrane that vibrates most strongly. (page 144)

2. We localize the source of a sound by detecting differences in the time and loudness of sounds our two ears receive. We also make use of echoes and visual cues in localizing sounds. (page 147)

3. The vestibular system tells us about the movement of the head and its position with respect to gravity. The vestibular system enables us to keep our eyes focused on an object while the rest of our body is in motion. (page 147)

4. We experience many types of sensation on the skin, each dependent on different receptors. The fingertips, lips, and face have especially rich supplies of such receptors. (page 149)

5. The sense of pain can be alleviated by a variety of events that release endorphins in the central nervous system. (page 150)

6. Our best evidence for the existence of several types of taste receptors is that certain procedures affect one taste quality (such as sweetness) without affecting the others. (page 152)

7. The olfactory system—the sense of smell—is still poorly understood. Other mammals and perhaps humans use odorous chemicals called pheromones for certain types of communication. (page 152)

SUGGESTIONS FOR FURTHER READING

Melzack, R., & Wall, P. D. (1983). *The challenge of pain*. New York: Basic Books. Discussion of factors that evoke and inhibit pain.

Zwislocki, J. J. (1981). Sound analysis in the ear: A history of discoveries. *American Scientist, 69,* 184–192. Review of research on the mechanisms of hearing.

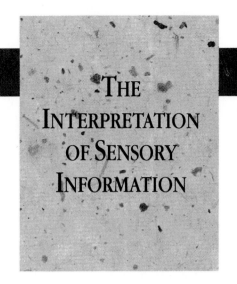

THE INTERPRETATION OF SENSORY INFORMATION

What is the relationship between the real world
and the way we perceive it?
How do we make sense of what we see?
Why are we sometimes wrong about what we
think we see?

W e send the robot we designed at the start of
this chapter to explore a planet in another solar
system. Just as the robot is about to relay messages
to us, something goes wrong and the transmission
fails. A second before the robot shuts down, however, it sends us two bits of information:

At time 0:00:01 it reports, "At a point 3 degrees
to the left of the center of vision and 1.5 degrees
below the center, light was recorded at a wavelength of 520 nanometers and an intensity of 8
lumens." (It tells us nothing about light from any
other location.)

At 0:11:08 it reports, "The sound detector on
the left recorded a vibration at 1 Hz." (It tells us
nothing about the sound detector on the right.)

What would these two tiny bits of information
tell us about this planet? A picture is worth a thousand words, but two thousandths of a picture are
worth only these two words: "practically nothing."
To learn anything useful, we would need to know
what objects lie on the surface of the planet, where
they are, whether they are moving (and, if so, how
fast and in which direction), what directions the
light is coming from and whether it changes intensity over time, and what kinds of sound are present
and where they originate and how long they last.
We could deduce none of that information from
reports about an isolated point of light and a single
sound.

What information do the visual, auditory, and
other receptors send to the brain of humans here

on Earth? A single visual receptor might send a
message like this: "light at intensity 8 lumens and
wavelength 520 nanometers at a particular point
on the retina at the current instant." By itself, such
a message would be utterly useless. Ordinarily, the
brain receives information from thousands of points
in each eye, hundreds of times per second. By comparing all these bits of information and by drawing
on past experience, the brain synthesizes a perception of the environment.

PSYCHOPHYSICS

Back in the late 1800s and early 1900s, when investigators were trying to establish a scientific basis
for psychology, many of them concentrated on the
relationship between the properties of physical
stimuli and our perception of those stimuli. That
study is known as **psychophysics**. The study of psychophysics has provided abundant evidence that
perception does not simply reproduce the physical
world.

The early psychophysicists discovered, for
example, that the *perceived* intensity of a stimulus
is not directly proportional to the actual physical
intensity of the stimulus. A light that is twice as
intense as another light does not *look* twice as bright.
Figure 5.27 shows the actual relationship between
the intensity of light and its perceived brightness.
The mathematical description of that relationship
is called the **psychophysical function**.

Those early investigators made another discovery: *The minimum detectable change in a stimulus
is a constant fraction of the original stimulus*. This

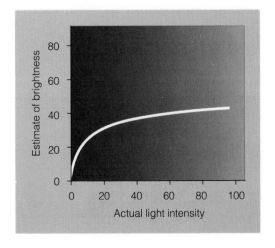

FIGURE 5.27

This graph of a psycho-
physical event shows the
perceived intensity ver-
sus its physical intensity.
When a light becomes
twice as intense physi-
cally, it does not seem
twice as bright.
(Adapted from Stevens,
1961.)

is known as *Weber's law,* after E. H. Weber, the 19th-century psychologist who discovered it. According to this law, if you can just barely tell the difference between a weight of 50 grams and a weight of 51 grams, you can also just barely tell the difference between 100 grams and 102 grams (2% in both cases). The minimum change in a physical stimulus that can be detected is known as the **just noticeable difference (JND)**. Mathematically, the JND equals the change in intensity divided by the original intensity.

The JND is larger for some sensory systems than for others, and it varies from one individual to another. Moreover, it changes drastically at very low and very high intensities. Still, it is a useful generalization. The general point is that we respond to the *percentage* change in any stimulus, not to the absolute change in its magnitude.

Concept Check

10. *Suppose you can just detect the difference between a tone of 4000 Hz and a tone of 4010 Hz. What would be the minimum frequency of a tone that you could just barely recognize as being higher in pitch than a tone of 8000 Hz? (Check your answer on page 179.)*

Sensory Thresholds

Under ideal circumstances, your sensory receptors can respond to extremely weak stimuli. Once your eyes have become adapted to darkness, the rods will respond to as little as a single photon of light (Baylor, Lamb, & Yau, 1979). An olfactory receptor can respond to a single molecule of an odorant. Human hearing is so acute that some people under certain conditions can hear the blood coursing through their ears.

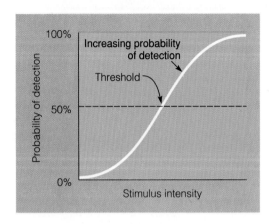

FIGURE 5.28

Typical results of an experiment to measure a sensory threshold. There is no sharp boundary between stimuli that you can perceive and stimuli that you cannot perceive.

How intense does a stimulus have to be for us to detect it under ordinary conditions? Many experiments have been conducted to determine the threshold of hearing—that is, the minimum intensity at which we can detect sound. Typically, subjects are presented with tones of varying intensity in random order; sometimes no tone at all is presented. On each trial the subjects are asked to say whether or not they heard a tone. Figure 5.28 presents some typical results. Notice that there is no precise dividing line between the tones that are heard and those that are not. Generally, as loudness increases, the probability of detection also increases. Still, over a certain range of loudness, we cannot be sure whether or not a person will report hearing a given tone on a given trial. A similar pattern of results applies to other sensory systems.

For this reason, perception researchers define a **sensory threshold** as the minimum intensity at which a given individual can detect a stimulus 50% of the time. Note, however, that on many occasions an individual can detect stimuli that are weaker than the threshold.

An individual's sensory threshold may change from time to time—perhaps as a result of **sensory adaptation**. The sensory threshold falls after a period when the sensory receptors have not been stimulated. A low threshold means you can detect faint stimuli. If you have seen nothing, heard nothing, tasted nothing, smelled nothing, or touched nothing for the past 30 minutes, your sensory threshold can fall to an extremely low level, as Table 5.2 shows. The sensory threshold at the time of maximum sensory adaptation is called the **absolute threshold**. The sensory threshold rises after the receptors have

TABLE 5.2 The Absolute Threshold in Five Sensory Systems	
Sense	Absolute Threshold
Vision	A candle flame seen at 30 miles on a dark, clear night
Hearing	The tick of a watch under quiet conditions at 20 feet
Taste	1 teaspoon of sugar in 2 gallons of water
Smell	1 drop of perfume diffused into the entire volume of a 6-room apartment
Touch	The wing of a fly falling on your cheek from a distance of 1 centimeter

Source: Galanter, 1962.

been exposed to intense stimuli. For example, after you spend time on a sunny beach, your ability to detect faint lights decreases. Similarly, after you taste a very sweet substance, your taste threshold for sweetness rises.

When people try to detect weak stimuli, they can make two kinds of error: They can fail to detect a stimulus (a "miss"), or they can say they detected a stimulus when none was present (a "false alarm"). **Signal-detection theory** is the study of people's tendencies to make correct judgments, misses, and false alarms. (Psychologists borrowed signal-detection theory from engineering, where this system is applied to such matters as detecting radio signals in the presence of interfering noise.) According to signal-detection theory, people's responses depend both on the ability of their senses to detect a stimulus and on their willingness to risk a miss or a false alarm. (When in doubt, they have to risk one or the other.)

Suppose we tell a subject that a 10-cent reward will be paid every time he or she correctly reports that a light is present, while a 1-cent penalty will be imposed for reporting that a light was present when it was not. Whenever the subject is not sure that a light is present, he or she will say yes, taking a risk of making a false alarm. The results will resemble those in Figure 5.29a. We inform other subjects that they will receive a 1-cent reward for correctly reporting that they saw a light and will suffer a 10-cent penalty *and* an electric shock for reporting that they saw a light when none was present. These subjects will say yes only when they are certain that a light was present. That is, they are more willing to risk a miss than a false alarm. The results will look like Figure 5.29b. *Clearly, if we want to determine which subjects are more sensitive to light, we have to take into account their misses and false alarms as well as their correct judgments.* Subjects whose measured thresholds are high may simply be exercising great caution in making their responses.

This same tendency toward caution shows up when subjects are tested to determine their threshold for recognizing words. For example, in one experiment the subjects were asked to try to read words that were flashed on a screen for just a split second. They performed well when ordinary words like *river* or *peach* were shown. For emotionally loaded words like *penis* or *bitch*, however, they performed poorly. In fact, the words had to be held on the screen for a substantially longer time before the subjects could identify them. These results suggest that some internal "censor" may actively impede perceptions that arouse anxiety (Blum & Barbour, 1979). It is also possible that the perceptions were

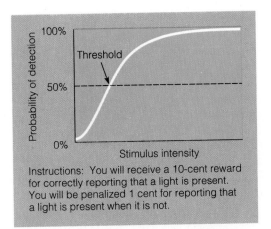

Instructions: You will receive a 10-cent reward for correctly reporting that a light is present. You will be penalized 1 cent for reporting that a light is present when it is not.

a

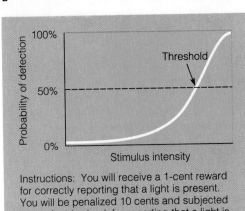

Instructions: You will receive a 1-cent reward for correctly reporting that a light is present. You will be penalized 10 cents and subjected to an electric shock for reporting that a light is present when it is not.

b

FIGURE 5.29

Results of experiments to measure a sensory threshold using two different sets of instructions.

normal but the subjects hesitated to blurt out the words unless they were absolutely certain they were right!

Concept Check

11. Someone turns on a flashlight, and its weak batteries make only a faint light. In a dark room you notice the light; in a well-lit room you do not. Why? One explanation is that in a dark room your sensory adaptation enables you to detect faint lights. Suggest another explanation that makes use of JNDs. (Check your answer on page 179.)

Subliminal Perception

You have probably heard of **subliminal perception**, the idea that a stimulus can influence us even when it is presented so faintly or briefly or along with such strong distractors that it is below the threshold for conscious perception. (*Limen* is Latin for "threshold"; thus subliminal means subthreshold.) Some people claim that subliminal perception can have a powerful, even manipulative, effect on human behavior. Allegedly, some advertisers use sublimi-

Although this family is playing Scrabble, someone is probably aware of what is happening on TV. If keeping the TV on is a household pattern, family members are less likely to be distracted—they have had lots of practice tuning out the background noise.

FIGURE 5.30

In this binaural test, the subject hears different tapes—one for the left ear, another for the right—playing at the same time. She is told to listen only to what one ear receives.

nal stimuli to coerce us into buying things we would not otherwise buy, and some storekeepers introduce whispered messages like "I will not shoplift" into their piped-in music.

Are such claims plausible or outright nonsense? As we have seen, stimuli that are just below the sensory threshold are perceived almost half the time. So they may affect behavior. What about stimuli that we just barely perceive for a fraction of a second but do not remember? Does the perception of such stimuli have some effect on behavior? To some extent, under certain circumstances, yes. The nervous system processes—at least briefly—a great deal of information that never makes its way into consciousness. Let's look at some examples.

Brief Attention to Stimuli We Seem to Ignore Under certain circumstances, we manage to focus our attention very sharply. When we are at a party, for example, we listen to one conversation and ignore the others. Neville Moray (1959) fitted some college students with earphones attached to a tape recorder that transmitted a different message to each ear, at a rate of 150 words per minute (see Figure 5.30). He asked each student to repeat, word for word, everything that came into one ear or the other. (To see how much attention this requires, turn on two radios tuned to different stations with someone talking. Choose one of the stations and try to repeat everything the announcer says.)

With a little practice, the students became reasonably adept at this task. Then the experimenter asked them some questions to see how much they remembered of what they had heard in the *other* ear. Most of them remembered almost nothing. They could remember whether they had heard a man's voice or a woman's voice or just a series of sounds, but they could not remember any of the content. They could not even say whether the voice had spoken English. Even when the announcer read a short list of simple words and repeated it 35 times, the students could neither recall the words nor pick them out from a list. They had apparently tuned out that ear so completely that nothing got through to their consciousness.

Was that information heard at all? To find out, Moray repeated the experiment, but this time, halfway through the tape, the voice in the tuned-out ear spoke the student's name: "You can quit this task now, Judy Callahan." About half the students remembered hearing the instruction, although most of them assumed that it was meant to be a distraction and ignored it. We might regard most of the information that reached the unattended ear as subliminal. Certainly none of it reached consciousness and none of it could be recalled. Yet it must have been perceived, at least for an instant.

Other Reported Examples of Subliminal Perception Several other experiments have reported that behavior may be influenced by stimuli so weak that people report no conscious awareness of them. Here are two examples (in Dixon, 1981):

A word such as PENCIL was flashed briefly on a screen cluttered with interfering stimuli. Then the subjects were shown a set of letters such as TERIW or WRITE and asked to say whether or not it was a word. Even though they had not reported seeing the word PENCIL, the fact that they had seen it even briefly increased the speed at which they identified the related word WRITE.

In another study, subjects were asked to listen to sentences they heard in one ear while ignoring what they heard in the other ear. At times, they would hear an ambiguous sentence in the attended ear (for example, "She was sitting by the bank") while a related word was played to the unattended ear (for example, *river* or *money*). Generally, they could not recall the word they had heard in the unattended ear. However, subjects who were exposed to the word *river* were more likely to interpret the ambiguous sentence in terms of sitting by a riverbank, while those who were exposed to the word *money* interpreted the sentence in terms of sitting near a financial institution.

What do such studies tell us about perception? Apparently, a subliminal stimulus can produce small effects, such as influencing how we perceive other stimuli. However, no reliable evidence indicates that subliminal stimuli can control people's buying behavior, enable them to break bad habits, or have any of the other dramatic effects that some people desire or fear (Balay & Shevrin, 1988; Creed, 1987; Wolitzky & Wachtel, 1973).

Something to Think About

What about those "subliminal perception tapes" you can buy that claim to help you quit smoking or overcome some other habit through subliminal suggestions? (The fact that people buy them does not mean that they do any good.) What evidence would we need to decide whether they work? If they do help some people, how could we determine whether they help because of the subliminal messages or just because people *believe* the tapes will help?

Farther Afield: Backward Subliminal Messages? One of the wilder claims about subliminal perception is that certain rock records contain satanic messages that have been recorded backward and superimposed on the songs. Some people allege that listeners unconsciously perceive the messages and are influenced to turn to drugs, devil worship, or some other vile act.

PEOPLE HAVE BEEN TRYING TO FIND THE BREASTS IN THESE ICE CUBES SINCE 1957.

The advertising industry is sometimes charged with sneaking seductive little pictures into ads.
    Supposedly, these pictures can get you to buy a product without your even seeing them.
    Consider the photograph above. According to some people, there's a pair of female breasts hidden in the patterns of light refracted by the ice cubes.
    Well, if you really searched, you probably *could* see the breasts. For that matter, you could also see Millard Fillmore, a stuffed pork chop and a 1946 Dodge.
    The point is that so-called "subliminal advertising" simply doesn't exist. Overactive imaginations, however, most certainly do.
    So if anyone claims to see breasts in that drink up there, they aren't in the ice cubes.
    They're in the eye of the beholder.

ADVERTISING
ANOTHER WORD FOR FREEDOM OF CHOICE.
American Association of Advertising Agencies

With a little imagination, people can "find" subliminal messages almost anywhere. However, research indicates that subliminal messages have only limited effects (if any) on behavior.

How could we test that claim? It would be useless to play a number of rock records backward and listen for a satanic message. Even if we listened to 100 records backward without hearing any message, we could not draw any conclusions about other records. And if we did hear something that sounded like a message, we could not be sure whether it was a real message or just a product of our imagination.

A more reliable approach would be to make a recording of our own and then to play it backward and ask people what they heard. People who listen to such recordings are totally unable to guess what the original (forward) message might have been (Vokey & Read, 1985). Furthermore, if the forward message tells people to do something, those who listen to it backward are not influenced in any way. In other words, even if certain records do contain backward messages, we have no reason to believe that listeners will be influenced by them.

Something to Think About

The fact remains that some people who play records backward claim to hear messages, satanic or otherwise, and assume that the messages must have been inserted intentionally. It is possible that a recording played backward may produce haphazard, nonsensical sounds that people with a little imagination "hear" as words. What sort of study could you set up to test that possibility?

In Spring in France *(1890), Robert Vonnoh follows the Impressionist style of using flickering patches of bright color. On one level the painter interprets a scene in terms of patterns of light and color, and the viewer then interprets those patterns in order to "see" the painting's content. In similar fashion, the brain interprets the sensory information it receives and transforms it into perception, which differs from the real physical world.*

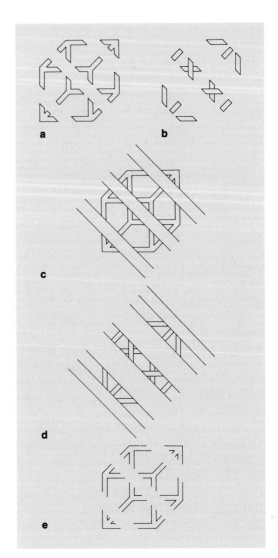

FIGURE 5.31

This picture is a puzzle until a context is introduced. Then a cube "emerges" from meaningless lines. (From Kanizsa, 1979.)

THE PERCEIVED WORLD AND THE REAL WORLD

As we have seen, perception is the process of drawing meaning from the stimuli that reach our sense receptors; perception does not *reproduce* the physical world. I have mentioned several examples of how the world we perceive differs from the real world. We have seen that when the physical intensity of a stimulus doubles, its perceived intensity does not double. And we have seen that, of all the possible wavelengths of electromagnetic radiation, we see only a narrow range of wavelengths as light. Moreover, although wavelength is a single continuous dimension (Figure 5.1), we perceive distinct reds, yellows, greens, and blues.

Figure 5.31 (based on Kanizsa, 1979) provides another example of how the perceived world differs from the real world. Parts a and b are composed of small geometric forms. Although we might guess that part a is made up of segments of a three-dimensional cube, we cannot "see" the cube. Part b does not even suggest a cube. In parts c and d, the added lines provide a context that enables us to see the cube. In part e, the deletion of short lines from a enables us to "see" imaginary lines that provide the same context. In c, d, and e, we have perceptually organized the meaningless forms of a and

b into a meaningful pattern; we are perceiving something that is not really there.

Similarly, in Figure 5.32a we see a series of meaningless patches. No matter how hard we try, we can perceive no real pattern. Yet in Figure 5.32b, the addition of some black glop immediately enables us to perceive those same patches as letter *B*s (Bregman, 1981). Note that the letters are not "there" in part b any more than they are in part a; we perceive them as being there only because we are imposing an active interpretation on the pattern.

Another example of our imposing an interpretation is an illusion known as the **autokinetic effect**: If you sit in a darkened room and stare at one small

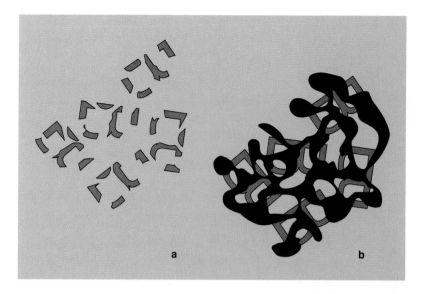

FIGURE 5.32

Someone familiar with only the Hebrew or Arabic alphabet would not "see" meaningful patterns emerge in part b. (From Bregman, 1981.)

stationary point of light, the point will eventually seem to move. Moreover, how much it appears to move and in which direction are subject to the power of suggestion. If someone says, "I see it moving in a zigzag manner" or "I see it moving slowly in a counterclockwise direction," you are likely to perceive it the same way. Because you expect to see it move, and because you have no frame of reference to show that it is not moving, you do see it move.

PERCEPTION AND THE RECOGNITION OF PATTERNS

Suppose you look at several photographs of faces you have never seen before (perhaps in the yearbook of a college you have never visited). Five days later, half of the photographs are shifted around and mixed with an equal number of new ones. Can you identify the faces you saw before? If you are like most people, you will get more than 90 percent correct (Galper & Hochberg, 1971; Hochberg & Galper, 1967). How do we do that? And how do we recognize familiar faces or even letters of the alphabet?

The Feature-Detector Approach

According to one explanation, we begin recognition by breaking a complex stimulus into its component parts. For example, when we look at the letter *K*, some part of the brain might identify a vertical line and two slanted lines on the right connected to the center of the vertical line. Another part of the brain might compare that analysis with information held in memory and say, "Oh. That combination of lines makes up the letter *K*." As we

shall see, investigators have identified neurons in the visual system of the brain that respond to particular lines or other features of a visual stimulus; these cells are **feature detectors**.

Investigators of artificial intelligence have tried to build machines that could recognize patterns by means of feature detectors. The task turns out to be more difficult than it sounds. Suppose we want to instruct such a machine to recognize the letter *A*. We have the machine scan a page of handwriting and break each character into points of light and dark, as in Figure 5.33. We then have it look for slanted lines meeting at a point at the top, with a horizontal line in the middle. If it finds all these characteristics, then it identifies the letter as an *A*.

So far, so good. But people's handwriting varies. The machine would have to identify each of the scrawls in Figure 5.34 as an *A*. Furthermore, humans learn to perceive things in context. We perceive the words in Figure 5.35 as CAT and HAT, even though the *A* in CAT is identical to the *H* in HAT. Apparently visual perception depends on something more than just feature detectors. Even so, feature detectors are probably an important part of visual perception, at least in the early stages of the process.

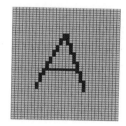

FIGURE 5.33

The letter *A* broken down into points of light and dark in the first stages of feature detection.

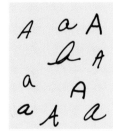

FIGURE 5.34

Legibility is in the eye of the beholder. Everyone's handwriting is distinctive. Could a machine be programmed to identify each of these (and more) as the letter *a*?

FIGURE 5.35

The influence of context on perception. The A in CAT is the same as the H in HAT, yet we interpret them differently.

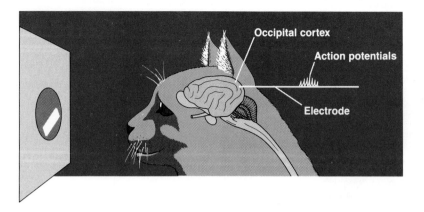

FIGURE 5.36

Electrodes implanted into the occipital cortex of a cat enable investigators to record a cell's response when various visual stimuli strike the eyes. Many cells respond vigorously only in the presence of a simple feature, such as a bar of light at a particular angle.

Feature Detectors in the Human Visual System: WHAT'S THE EVIDENCE?

We know that certain parts of the human brain, including the occipital cortex, contribute to vision. But what is the role of the individual neurons? And how could investigators determine that role? After all, they can hardly insert electrodes into the human brain. Let's look at two studies.

EXPERIMENT 1

Hypothesis Neurons in the visual cortex of cats and monkeys will respond specifically when light strikes the retina in a particular pattern, such as a line.

Method Two pioneers in the study of the visual cortex, David Hubel and Torsten Wiesel (1981 Nobel Prize winners in physiology and medicine), inserted thin electrodes into cells of the occipital cortex of cats and monkeys and then recorded the activity of those cells when various light patterns struck the animals' retina (see Figure 5.36).

Results They found that each cell has a preferred stimulus (Hubel & Wiesel, 1968). Some cells become active only when a vertical bar of light strikes a given portion of the retina. Others become active only when a horizontal bar or a bar tilted at a particular angle strikes the retina (Figure 5.37). In other words, the cells act as feature detectors.

In later experiments, Hubel and Wiesel and other investigators found a variety of other feature detectors, including some that respond to lines moving in a particular direction.

Interpretation Hubel and Wiesel found feature-detector cells in both cats and monkeys. If the organization of the occipital cortex is similar in species as distantly related as cats and monkeys, it is likely (though not certain) to be similar in humans as well.

A second line of evidence is based on the following reasoning: If the human cortex does contain feature-detector cells, one type of cell should become fatigued after we stare for a time at the features that excite it. When we look away, we should see an aftereffect created by the inactivity of that type of cell. (Recall the negative afterimage in color vision, as shown by Figure 5.12.)

One example of this phenomenon is the waterfall illusion: If you stare at a waterfall for a minute or more and then turn your eyes to nearby cliffs, the cliffs will appear to flow *upward*. In staring at the waterfall, you fatigue cells that respond to downward motion. When you look away those cells become inactive, but other cells that respond to upward motion continue their normal activity. Even though the motionless cliffs stimulate those cells only weakly, the stimulation is enough to produce an illusion of upward motion.

Here's a second example: If you stare at a pinwheel while it is rotating in a counterclockwise direction, you will fatigue the cells that respond to motion toward the center. After the pinwheel stops, it appears to be rotating in the opposite direction, with the lines apparently moving away from the center.

For another example, here is a demonstration you can perform yourself.

EXPERIMENT 2

Hypothesis After you stare at one set of vertical lines, you will fatigue the feature detectors that respond to lines of a particular width. If you then look at lines slightly wider or narrower than the original ones, they will appear to be even wider or narrower than they really are.

Method Cover the right half of Figure 5.38 and stare at the little rectangle in the middle of the left half for at least one minute. (The effect will grow stronger the longer you stare.) Do not stare at just one point; move your focus around within the rectangle. Then look at the square in the center of the right part of the figure and compare the spacing between the lines of the top and bottom gratings (Blakemore & Sutton, 1969).

Results What did you perceive in the right half of the figure? People generally report that the top set of lines look narrower than it really is and that the bottom set of lines looks wider.

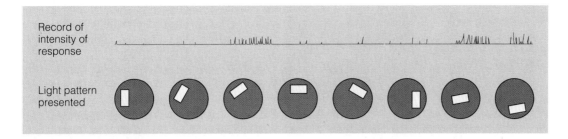

Record of intensity of response

Light pattern presented

FIGURE 5.37

Detecting feature detectors: response properties of one cell in the visual area of a monkey's cerebral cortex when light patterns oriented in various ways strike one part of the retina. Here the angle of the bar apparently determines the level of response.

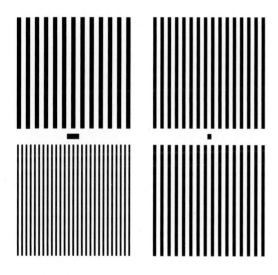

FIGURE 5.38

How to fatigue your feature detectors and create an afterimage. Follow the directions in Experiment 2 (page 162). (From Blakemore & Sutton, 1969.)

Interpretation Staring at the left part of the figure fatigues one set of cells sensitive to wide lines in the top part of the figure and another set sensitive to narrow lines in the bottom part. Then when you look at intermediate lines, the fatigued cells become inactive. Therefore, your perception is dominated by cells sensitive to narrower lines in the top part and to wider lines in the bottom part.

To summarize, two types of evidence suggest that the human brain contains visual feature detectors: (1) The brains of other species contain cells with the properties of feature detectors, and (2) after staring at certain patterns, we see aftereffects that can be explained as fatigue of feature-detector cells in the brain. ■

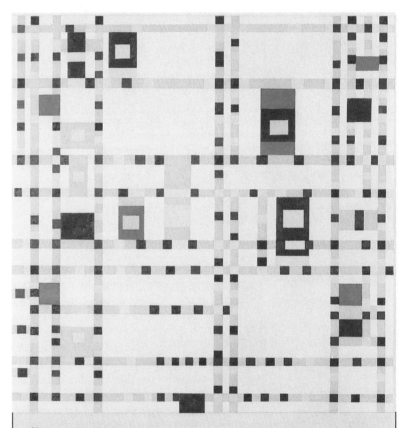

The Dutch painter Piet Mondrian developed a severe abstract style (known simply as de Stijl) relying on paint's primary colors, plus black and white. He aimed to capture reality through an equilibrium of asymmetrical balances. How does his Broadway Boogie-Woogie *(1942–1943) express Manhattan? (Oil on canvas, 50 × 50". Collection, The Museum of Modern Art, New York. Given anonymously.)*

Picasso with a Polaroid? No, this assemblage, Celia, Los Angeles, *is by the English artist David Hockney. According to Gestalt psychologists, the whole picture is more than its 32 parts together. Imagine these 32 photos jumbled together in a shoe box, like your vacation snapshots. Looked at individually and in random order, they would simply be 32 photos. Yet with the correct arrangement, they form a meaningful pattern. How do repetitions in* Celia *add to your information?*

Do Feature Detectors Explain Perception?

The feature detectors I have been describing are active during the early stages of visual processing. They detect lines of a certain width and angle and objects moving in a certain direction, for example. How do you perceive something more complicated, such as your grandmother's face, the Eiffel Tower, or even the letter *A*?

One possibility is that the brain contains increasingly complex feature detectors. One set of cells responds to single lines. Another set receives input from the first set and responds only to certain combinations of lines—such as the lines that make up the letter *A* (Selfridge, 1959). Still other cells respond to even more complex patterns, such as the pattern of a hand or a face (Desimone, Albright, Gross, & Bruce, 1984).

We run into problems, however, when we try to account for visual perception entirely in terms of feature detectors. For example, certain kinds of brain damage should destroy some pattern detectors but not others. A brain-damaged person should be able to perceive every letter *except F* or should be able to perceive all faces *except* those of her grandmother, her psychology professor, and the

prime minister of Great Britain. But such effects never occur. Either brain damage interferes equally with the perception of all visual patterns, or else it interferes with the perception of none of them. Apparently no neuron is involved in one and only one perception. Although feature detectors are active in the early stages of perception, something else must supplement their activity.

Gestalt Psychology

Can you recognize a face in Figure 5.39? If you have trouble, hold the page farther away, squint, or take your glasses off. Curiously, people with blurred vision "see" this face better than people with clear vision. If you still cannot see the face, refer to answer C on page 179.

The face in Figure 5.39 is made up of 226 squares of varying shades of gray. Does any one of those squares constitute 1/226 of the face? No. Out of context, any single square is no more a fraction of this face than of anything else. The face is not the sum of the 226 squares; the face is the overall pattern.

Such observations derive from **Gestalt psychology**. *Gestalt* (geh-SHTALT) is a German word

FIGURE 5.39

Do you see a face in this figure? (From Harmon & Julesz, 1973.)

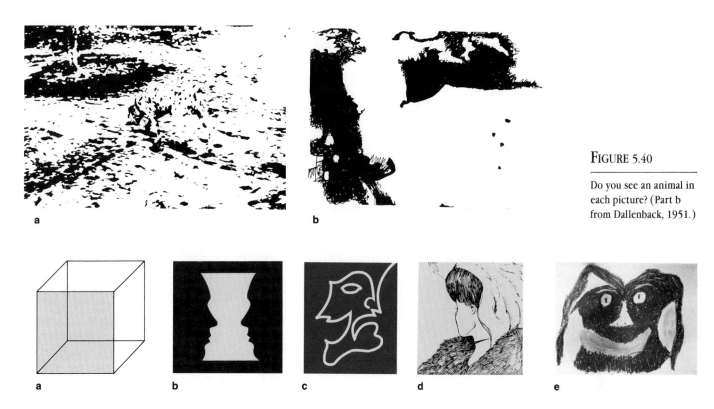

a

b

FIGURE 5.40

Do you see an animal in
each picture? (Part b
from Dallenback, 1951.)

a   b   c   d   e

FIGURE 5.41

Reversible figures. (a) The Necker cube. Which is the front face? (b) Faces or a vase.
(c) Comedy and tragedy. (d) An old woman and a young woman. (e) A face or what?
(Part d from Boring, 1930.)

for which there is no exact English equivalent; *con-figuration* and *overall pattern* come close. The founders of Gestalt psychology rejected the idea that a perception can be broken down into its component parts. If a melody is broken up into individual notes, the melody is lost. Their slogan was, "The whole is more than the sum of its parts."

According to Gestalt psychologists, visual perception is an active production, not just the passive reception of light. We considered examples of this principle in Figures 5.31 and 5.32. Here are some further examples:

Figure 5.40 shows a photo and a drawing of two animals. When you first look at these pictures, you will probably see nothing but meaningless black and white patches. As you continue to look at them, you may suddenly see the animals. (If you give up, check answer D, page 179.) And once you have seen them, you will see them again whenever you look at the pictures. To perceive the animals, you must separate **figure and ground**—that is, you must distinguish the object from the background. Ordinarily that process takes place almost instantaneously; only in special cases like this one do you become aware of the process.

Figure 5.41 contains five **reversible figures**, stimuli that may be perceived in more than one way. Part a is called the *Necker cube*, after the psychologist who first called attention to it. Which is the front face of the cube? If you look long enough, you will see it two ways. In fact, you can choose to see it one way or the other. You can see part b either as a vase or as two profiles. Part c combines the symbols of comedy and tragedy. Parts d and e are more difficult for most people to see two ways. Part d (from Boring, 1930) shows both an old woman and a young woman. Almost everyone sees one or the other immediately, but many people lock into one perception so tightly that they cannot see the other one. Part e was drawn by an 8-year-old girl who intended it as the picture of a face. Some people claim it looks like an apple. There is a third possibility. Can you find it? (If you have trouble with parts d or e, check answer E, page 179.)

It is difficult to explain in any scientific way *how* we perceive organized wholes, though the Gestalt psychologists offered a few principles of how we organize perceptions. Figure 5.42 gives examples of each principle. **Proximity** is the tendency to perceive objects that are close together as belonging

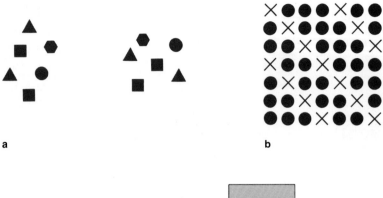

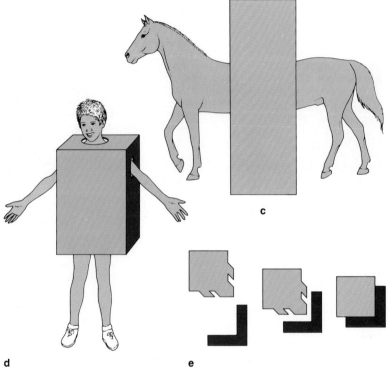

a   **b**

c

d   **e**

FIGURE 5.42

Gestalt principles of (a) proximity, (b) similarity, (c) continuation, (d) closure, and (e) good figure.

Finally, we tend to perceive a **good figure**—a simple symmetrical figure—even when the pattern can be perceived in some other way. In e, even after we see how the right-hand drawing was put together, we continue to perceive it as a red square overlapping a green square. In general, a good figure is a symmetrical figure or a figure composed of continuous lines.

Concept Check

12. *Which of the Gestalt principles were operating in your perception of Figures 5.31 and 5.32? (Check your answer on page 179.)*

Gestalt Principles in Hearing

The perceptual organization principles of Gestalt psychology apply to hearing as well as to vision (see Figure 5.43). College students in one experiment (Warren, 1970) listened to a tape recording in which the sound of the first *s* in the word *legislatures,* along with part of the adjacent *i* and *l,* had been replaced by a cough or a tone. The students were asked to listen to the recording and try to identify the location of the cough or tone. None of the 20 students identified the location correctly, and half thought the cough or tone interrupted one of the other words on the tape. They all claimed to have heard the *s* plainly. In fact, even those who had been told that the *s* sound was missing insisted that they had "heard" the sound. Apparently the brain had used the context to fill in the missing sounds. This is an example of the Gestalt principle of closure. Similar results have been reported in studies dating back to 1901 (Cole & Rudnicky, 1983).

There are reversible figures in sound, just as there are in vision. For instance, you can hear the sound of a clock as "tick, tock, tick, tock" or as "tock, tick, tock, tick." You can hear your windshield wipers going "dunga, dunga" or "gadung, gadung."

As with visual reversible figures, people occasionally get so locked into one interpretation of something they hear that they have trouble hearing it any other way. For example, read this sentence to a friend: "The matadors fish on Friday." Pause long enough to make sure your friend has understood the sentence. Then say: "The cat on the mat adores fish on Friday." If you read the second sentence normally, without pausing between *mat* and *adores,* your friend is likely to be puzzled. "Huh? The cat on the matadors? . . ." Had you not read the first sentence, your friend would not have had trouble understanding the second sentence.

to a group. The objects in part a form three groups because of proximity. The tendency to perceive objects that resemble each other as forming a group is called **similarity**. The objects in b group into Xs and Os because of similarity. When lines are interrupted, as in c, we may perceive a **continuation** of the lines. We can perceive this illustration as a black rectangle covering the front of one horse and the rear of another, but we can also perceive it as a rectangle covering the center of one very elongated horse.

When a familiar figure is interrupted, as in d, we perceive a **closure** of the figure—that is, we imagine the rest of the figure. (Because of closure you perceive the head, two arms, and two legs as belonging to the same woman. How might magicians use this principle?)

ants pawn term, dare worsted ladle gull hoe lift wetter murder inner ladle cordage, honor itch offer lodge, dock, florist. Disk ladle gull orphan worry putty ladle rat cluck wetter ladle rat hut, an fur disk raisin pimple colder Ladle Rat Rotten Hut.

Wan moaning, Ladle Rat Rotten Hut's murder colder inset. "Ladle Rat Rotten Hut, heresy ladle basking winsome burden barter an shirker cockles. Tick disk ladle basking tutor cordage offer groinmurder hoe lifts honor udder site offer florist. Shaker lake! Dun stopper laundry wrote! Dun stopper peck floors! Dun daily-doily inner florist, an yonder nor sorghumstenches, dun stopper torque wet strainers!"

FIGURE 5.43

When the nonsense words of "Ladle Rat Rotten Hut" are read aloud with the right inflections, listeners can usually make out the story of Little Red Riding Hood.

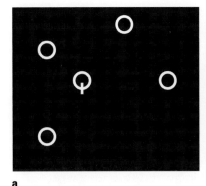

FIGURE 5.44

Demonstration of the preattentive processes. Find the vertical line in parts a and b. Most people find it about equally fast in both.

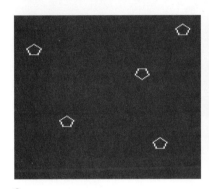

FIGURE 5.45

Demonstration of attentive processes. Find the pentagon pointing down in parts a and b. Most people take longer to find it in b.

Feature Detectors and Gestalt Psychology: Bottom-Up Versus Top-Down Processing

The Gestalt approach to perception does not conflict with the feature-detector approach. The two approaches merely describe perception in different ways. The feature-detector approach describes how perception, especially vision, develops from the bottom up. It takes the individual points of light identified by the receptors and connects them into lines and then connects lines into more complex features. According to the feature-detector approach, the brain says, "I see a point here and a point here and another point here, so there must be a line. I see a line here and another line connecting with it here, so there must be a letter *L*."

The Gestalt approach describes how perception develops from the top down. It starts with an overall expectation and then fits in the pieces. According to the Gestalt interpretation, the brain says, "I heard the word *legislature,* so there must have been an *s* sound. I see what looks like a circle, so the missing piece must be part of a circle too."

Which view is correct? Both, of course. Our perception has to assemble the individual points of light or bits of sound, but once it forms a tentative interpretation of the pattern, it uses that interpretation to organize the rest of the information.

Preattentive and Attentive Processes in Vision

When you look at a scene made up of many shapes and relationships among objects, you automatically notice certain details even if you are not intentionally looking for them. Consider Figures 5.44a and b. In each figure, find the circle that is intersected by a vertical line. Most people spot the vertical line in b about as quickly as the vertical line in a, even though b has far more distractors (circles without lines) (Treisman & Souther, 1985). The vertical line simply stands out in both figures. Apparently people examine all the circles *in parallel,* rather than attending to them one at a time. That is, they can look at all the circles at once. Their zeroing in on the vertical line does not require attention; it is the result of a **preattentive process**—a process that takes place automatically and simultaneously across a large portion of the visual field. Our preattentive processes probably use feature detectors to identify simple elements.

Now look at Figures 5.45a and b. Each part contains several pentagons, most of them pointing upward. Find the one pentagon in each part that points downward.

Most people take longer to find the pentagon pointing down in part b than in part a, because part

FIGURE 5.46

A photograph of a photo taken from the side appears distorted. Yet when you view a movie screen from an angle, you are seldom aware of the distortion.

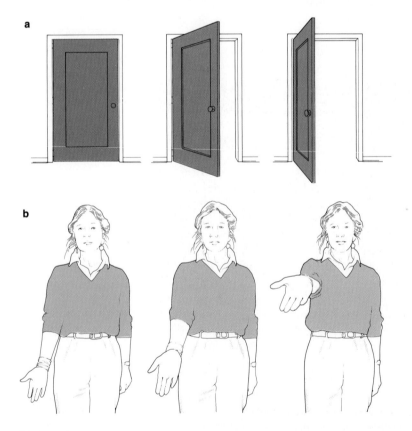

a

b

FIGURE 5.47

(a) Shape constancy. We perceive all three doors as rectangles. (b) Size constancy. We perceive all three hands as equal in size.

b contains more distractors. The greater the number of distractors, the longer it takes to find the pentagon that is different. People must turn their attention to one pentagon at a time until they come to the correct one. In contrast to the preceding example, this task requires an **attentive process**—that is, a procedure that considers only one part of the visual field at a time. An attentive process is a *serial* process because a person must pay attention to each part in the series. Under natural conditions our perception results from a mixture of preattentive processes and attentive processes.

PERCEPTION OF DEPTH AND MOVEMENT

As an automobile drives away from us, its image on the retina grows smaller, yet we perceive it as moving, not as shrinking. That perception illustrates **visual constancy**—our tendency to perceive objects as being constant in shape, size, and color, even though what actually strikes our retina may be something quite different. When we sit off to the side in a movie theater, for example, the images that strike our retina may be badly distorted (see Figure 5.46). And yet they seem almost normal (Cutting, 1987). Figure 5.47 shows examples of two visual constancies: shape constancy and size constancy. Constancies depend on our familiarity with objects. For example, we know that a door is still rectangular even when we view it from an odd angle. But to recognize that an object has kept its shape and size, we have to perceive movement or a change in distance. How do we do so?

Depth Perception

Depth perception is our perception of distance; it enables us to experience the world in three dimensions. Depth perception depends on several factors.

We use **retinal disparity**—the difference in apparent position of an object as seen by the left and right retinas—to compare the views the two eyes see. Try this: Hold one finger at arm's length. Focus on it with one eye and then with the other. Note that the apparent position of your finger shifts with respect to the background. Now hold your finger closer to your face and repeat the experiment. Notice that the apparent position of your finger shifts by a greater amount. *The discrepancy between the slightly different views the two eyes see becomes greater as the object comes closer.* We use the amount of discrepancy to gauge distance.

A second cue for depth perception is the **convergence** of our eyes—that is, the degree to which

FIGURE 5.48

Thanks to several cues, we can judge depth and distance with one eye as well as we do with both eyes. (1) Closer objects occupy more space on the retina (or on the photograph) than do distant objects of the same type. (2) Nearer objects show more detail. (3) Closer objects overlap certain distant objects. (4) Objects in the foreground look sharper than do objects on the horizon. These are known as monocular cues.

they turn in to focus on an object. When you focus on a distant object, your eyes are looking in almost parallel directions. When you focus on something close, your eyes turn in; you can sense the pulling in your muscles. The more the muscles pull, the closer the object must be.

Retinal disparity and convergence are called **binocular cues**, because they depend on the action of both eyes. **Monocular cues** enable a person to judge depth and distance just as effectively with one eye as with both. Several monocular cues help us judge the approximate distance of the objects in Figure 5.48. Knowing the true size of objects also helps us to estimate distance. For example, we know that the van in the middle distance in Figure 5.48d is really larger than the roller skater in the foreground. So we infer that the van is more distant. Shadows also provide visual cues (Figure 5.49).

Motion parallax, another monocular cue, helps us to perceive depth when we are actually looking at a scene, though it is of no help when we are looking at a photograph. When we are moving—riding along in a car, for example—close objects seem to pass by swiftly while distant objects seem to pass by very slowly. The faster an object passes by, the closer it must be.

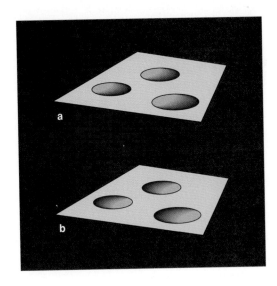

FIGURE 5.49

The direction of light and placement of shadow can create the illusion that objects are either (a) round objects sitting on a surface or (b) concave depressions in the surface. We are accustomed to seeing objects lit from above. Shadows therefore give us cues to "below." See what happens when you turn the book and look at this figure upside down.

On an Orient express. If you were a passenger on this train, the ground beside the tracks would appear to pass by more quickly than the more distant elements in the landscape. The photo's version of motion parallax is that the ground is blurred, the more distant objects crisp. Does this contradict another monocular cue telling us that objects near us look more distinct than do objects further away?

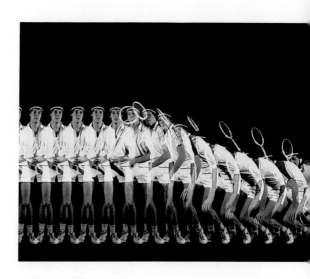

FIGURE 5.50

Motion pictures: When you watch a movie, you are unaware of its thousands of still photographs flickering by at a rate of 86,400 an hour. The sequence of photographs printed here conveys a sense of motion in another way.

Concept Check

13. In three-dimensional photography, cameras take two views of the same scene from different locations through lenses with different color filters or with different polarized-light filters. The two views are then superimposed. The viewer looks at the composite view through special glasses, so that one eye sees the view taken with one camera and the other eye sees the view taken with the other camera. Which depth cue is at work here? (Check your answer on page 179.)

Perception of Movement

Try this simple demonstration: Hold an object in front of your eyes and then move it to the right. Now hold the object in front of your eyes and move your eyes to the left. The image of the object moves across your retina in the same way, regardless of whether you move the object or move your eyes. Yet you perceive the object as moving in one case and not in the other. Why is that?

There are two reasons why the object does not appear to move when you move your eyes. One

reason is that the vestibular system constantly keeps the visual areas of the brain informed of movements of your head. Other systems keep the visual areas informed of eye movements. When your brain knows that your eyes have moved to the left, it interprets the change in what you see as being a result of that movement. In fact, when people are moving, they notice other moving objects *less* than when they are motionless. For example, you are more likely to notice a tree blowing in the wind when you are standing still than while you are driving a car (Probst, Krafczyk, Brandt, & Wist, 1984). (Under certain conditions, this tendency may be hazardous to drivers.)

The second reason is that we perceive motion when an object moves *relative to the background* (Gibson, 1968). When you walk forward, everything you see seems to be passing by. If certain objects pass by faster or slower than the objects around them, you perceive them as moving.

What do we perceive when an object is stationary and the background is moving? That hardly ever happens, but when it does, we incorrectly perceive the object as moving and the background as stationary. For example, when you watch clouds moving slowly across the moon from left to right, you generally perceive the clouds as a stationary background and the moon as an object moving from right to left. This perception, known as **induced movement**, is a form of *apparent movement,* as opposed to *real movement.*

I have already mentioned two other examples of apparent movement: the waterfall illusion and the autokinetic effect. Yet another example is **stroboscopic movement**. When a scene is flashed on a screen and is followed a split second later by a second scene slightly different from the first, you perceive the objects as having moved smoothly from their location in the first scene to their location in the second scene (see Figure 5.50). Motion pictures are actually a series of still photos flashed on the screen at a rate of 24 per second. Thus, the perceived movement is an illusion produced by the rapid succession of photos.

We also experience an illusion of movement when lights separated by a short distance blink on and off in a steady progression (see Figure 5.51). Your brain creates the sense of motion in what is called the **phi effect** or phi movement. You may have noticed signs in front of restaurants or motels that make use of this effect. As the lights blink on and off, an arrow seems to be moving and inviting you to come in.

Our perception of movement relies on a combination of preattentive and attentive processes (Dick, Ullman, & Sagi, 1987). When an object moves fairly slowly, we detect it at once by a preattentive process. If you are sitting outdoors you can immediately detect a squirrel running along the ground or a bird hopping through the tree tops, even if you are not particularly attending to it. However, if something jumps suddenly from one spot to another, such as a toad that hops quickly, you may not notice the movement unless you are paying attention. Similarly, if a squirrel goes behind a bush and later emerges on the other side, you can perceive it as a single squirrel that moved from one side of the bush to the other, but only if you are paying attention.

FIGURE 5.51

Gestalt psychology began in 1910 when Max Werthimer first used a stroboscope to study the phi phenomenon—the illusion of motion when similar objects appear in rapid succession, as in these blinking lights.

OPTICAL ILLUSIONS

Many people claim to have seen strange things: ghosts, flying saucers, the Loch Ness monster, Bigfoot, Santa's elves, or people floating in the air. Some of those people are probably lying, though others may have seen something extraordinary. Still others, however, may be misinterpreting something ordinary because their perception was distorted. An **optical illusion** is a misinterpretation of a visual stimulus as being larger or smaller or straighter or

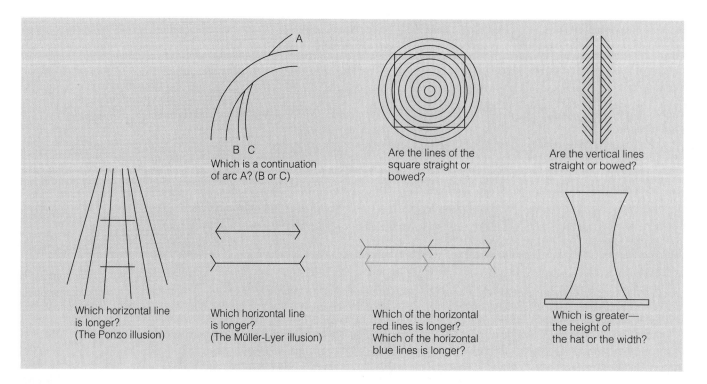

FIGURE 5.52

Most paintings rely on some optical illusion, but we are more aware of it in geometrical figures. (Check your answers with a ruler and a compass.)

Although this photo is not exactly an optical illusion, can you tell which objects are three-dimensional and which are two-dimensional?

more curved than it really is. Figure 5.52 shows some examples of optical illusions. Psychologists would like to come up with a single explanation for all optical illusions. (Remember the principle of parsimony from Chapter 2.) Although they have not fully succeeded, a fair number of optical illusions seem to depend on the relationship between size perception and depth perception.

The Relationship Between Depth Perception and Size Perception

If you can estimate the size of an object, you can deduce its distance. If you can estimate its distance, you can deduce its size. Figure 5.53 shows that an image of a given size on the retina may represent either a small, close object or a large, distant object. Watch what happens when you take a single image and change its apparent distance: Stare at Figure 5.12 again to form a negative afterimage. First examine the afterimage while you are looking at the wall across the room. Then look at the afterimage against the palm of your hand. The afterimage will look much larger against the wall than it does against your hand. Move your hand forward and backward. Does the size of the afterimage change?

In the real world, we seldom have trouble estimating the size and distance of objects. When you walk along the street, for instance, you never wonder whether the people you see are very far away or are only a few inches tall. Even so, judging size and distance is sometimes confusing (see Figure 5.54). I once saw an airplane overhead and for a minute or two was unsure whether it was a small, remote-controlled toy airplane or a distant, full-size airplane. Familiarity with the size of airplanes was

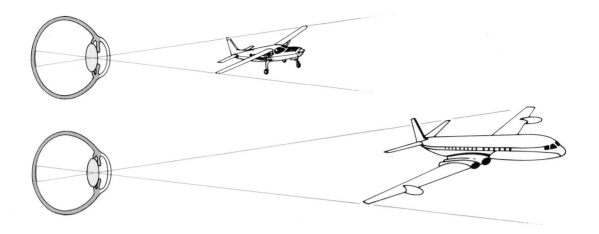

FIGURE 5.53

The tradeoff between size and distance. A given image on the retina may indicate either a small, close object or a large, distant object.

FIGURE 5.54

Because fish come in all sizes, we can estimate the size of a fish only if we know how far away it is or if we can compare its size to other nearby objects. See what happens when you cover the man and then cover the hand.

Although one of these clowns may be a midget or a giant, we are more likely to assume that this is some type of "trick" photograph. Part of that assumption comes from context—this section is about optical illusions. And part of it is based on our knowledge of clowns—it's natural for them to play a sight gag. As with a self-fulfilling prophecy, we tend to see what we want or expect to see.

a

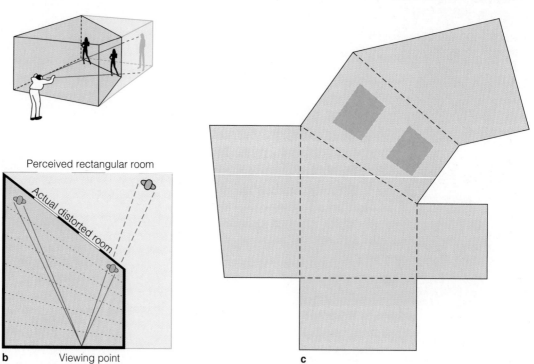

Perceived rectangular room

Actual distorted room

Viewing point

b

c

Figure 5.55

A room with a view: A study in deceptive perception, the Ames room is designed to be viewed through a peephole with one eye. (a) Both of these people are actually the same height. We are so accustomed to rooms with right angles that we can't imagine how this apparently ordinary room creates this optical illusion. (b) This diagram shows the positions of the people in the Ames room and demonstrates how the illusion of distance is created. (c) You can use this illustration to create a miniature Ames room. (Part b from Wilson et al., 1964.)

of no help to me, and in the sky there are few cues to distance.

The same difficulty arises in reported sightings of UFOs. When people see an unidentified object in the sky, there is usually nothing to help them estimate its distance. And if they overestimate its distance, they will also overestimate its size and speed.

What does all this have to do with optical illusions? Whenever we misjudge distance, we are likely to misjudge size as well. For example, Figure 5.55a shows people in the Ames room (named for its designer, Adelbert Ames). The room is designed to look like a normal rectangular room, though its true dimensions are as shown in Figure 5.55b. The two young women are actually the same height. If we eliminated all the background cues, then we would perceive the women as being the same size but at different distances. However, the apparently rectangular room provides such powerful (though misleading) cues to distance that the women appear to differ greatly in height. You can make your own model of the Ames room by copying Figure 5.55c, cutting it out and folding it.

Even a two-dimensional drawing on a flat surface may offer cues that lead to erroneous depth perception. Apparently we have a strong tendency to interpret two-dimensional drawings as if they were three-dimensional. Figure 5.56 shows a bewildering two-prong/three-prong device and a round staircase that seems to run uphill all the way clockwise or downhill all the way counterclockwise. Both drawings puzzle us because we try to interpret them as three-dimensional objects.

In Figure 5.57a, we interpret the railroad track as heading into the distance. Similarly, because the background cues in part b suggest that the upper line is farther away than the lower line, we perceive the upper line as being larger. The same is true of the right-hand cylinder in part c. Recall from Figure 5.53 that when two objects produce the same-size image on the retina, we perceive the more distant one as being larger. In short, by perceiving two-dimensional representations as if they were three-dimensional, we misjudge distance and consequently misjudge size. When we are somehow misled by the cues that ordinarily ensure constancy in size and shape, we end up experiencing an optical illusion (Day, 1972).

The Moon Illusion

The moon close to the horizon appears about 30% larger than it appears when higher in the sky (Figure 5.58). Some people try to explain this **moon illusion** by referring to the bending of light rays by

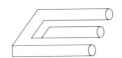

FIGURE 5.56

Expectations shape perceptions. These two-dimensional drawings puzzle us because we try to interpret them as three-dimensional objects.

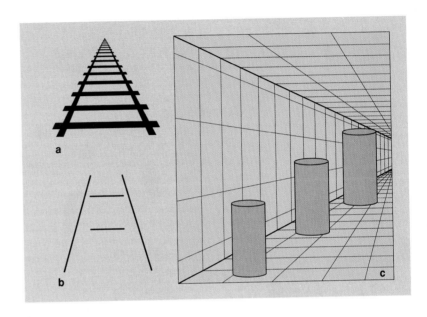

FIGURE 5.57

An interpretation of some optical illusions involving misjudgment of distances. In b, the top line looks longer because the perspective (resembling the railroad tracks in a) suggests a difference in distance. In c, the jar on the right seems larger because the context makes it appear farther away.

FIGURE 5.58

The moon illusion.

the atmosphere or to some other physical phenomenon. The seeming difference, however, is caused by a psychological rather than a physical phenomenon. If you actually measure the moon image with navigational or photographic equipment, you will find that its size is the same at the horizon as it is higher in the sky. (The atmosphere's bending of light rays makes the moon look orange near the horizon, but it does not increase the size of the image.)

One explanation of the moon illusion is that the many objects and land features we see as we look toward the horizon lead us to assume that the horizon is more distant than the sky. When the moon is near the horizon it looks far away; when it is high in the sky, we have few depth cues and the moon appears less distant. Consequently, we perceive the moon as being larger at the horizon (Rock & Kaufman, 1962).

According to a different explanation, we perceive the size of an object partly by comparing it to the size of everything else we see. When the moon is near the horizon, we compare it to the other objects we see at the horizon, all of which look small. We also compare the width of the moon to the small area of sky between the moon and the horizon. By comparison, the moon looks large. When the moon is surrounded by the vast, featureless sky, however, it appears small (Baird, 1982; Restle, 1970).

Both of these explanations may be partly correct. Apparently no single explanation can account for every optical illusion.

Optical illusions underscore a point that has arisen repeatedly in this chapter: Our perceptions are active processes that use all the knowledge we have, not just the sensory information striking our receptors at the moment. We are constantly estimating the sizes, distances, and speed of movement of everything we see. We interpret all that information together, so that everything we perceive (or misperceive) alters the way we interpret everything else.

SUMMARY

1. The perceived intensity of a sensory stimulus is not directly proportional to the intensity of the stimulus itself, because the brain alters the intensity of sensory stimuli as it processes them. (page 155)

2. There is no sharp dividing line between sensory stimuli that can be perceived and sensory stimuli that cannot be perceived. The sensory threshold is a stimulus intense enough to be perceived 50% of the time. (page 156)

3. Under some circumstances, a stimulus weaker than the sensory threshold may influence our perception of other stimuli, even though we do not consciously perceive the weak stimulus. It is doubtful, however, that subliminal perception has any powerful, irresistible effect on behavior. (page 157)

4. We interpret certain visual displays by referring to the context and other information we have about what is likely. (page 160)

5. In the first stages of the process of perception, feature-detector cells identify lines, points, and simple movement. (page 161)

6. According to Gestalt psychologists, we perceive an organized whole by identifying similarities and continuous patterns across a large area of the visual field. (page 164)

7. We can identify some features of the visual field immediately even without paying attention to them. We identify others only by attending to one part of the visual field at a time. (page 167)

8. We ordinarily perceive the shape, size, and color of objects as constant even though the pattern of light striking the retina varies from time to time. (page 168)

9. To perceive depth, we use retinal discrepancy between the views our two eyes see. We also use other cues that are just as effective with one eye as with two. (page 168)

10. We perceive an object as moving if it moves relative to its background. We can generally distinguish between an object that is actually moving and a similar pattern of retinal stimulation that results from our own movement. (page 170)

11. Our estimate of an object's size depends on our estimate of its distance from us. If we overestimate its distance, we will also overestimate its size. (page 172)

12. Many, but not all, optical illusions result from interpreting a two-dimensional display as three-dimensional or from other faulty estimates of depth. (page 175)

SUGGESTIONS FOR FURTHER READING

Gregory, R. L. (1978). *Eye and brain: The psychology of seeing*. New York: McGraw-Hill. Includes discussion of optical illusions.

Kanizsa, G. (1979). *Organization in vision*. New York: Praeger. Emphasizes the Gestalt approach to vision.

Rock, I. (1984). *Perception*. New York: Scientific American Books. Includes discussions of visual constancies, illusions, motion perception, and the relationship between perception and art.

TERMS TO REMEMBER

absolute threshold the sensory threshold at a time of maximum sensory adaptation

attentive process paying attention to only one part of a visual field at a time

autokinetic effect the illusory perception that a point of light in a darkened room is in motion

basilar membrane a thin membrane in the cochlea that vibrates after sound waves strike the eardrum

binocular cues visual cues that depend on the action of both eyes

blind spot the area of the retina through which the optic nerve exits

chemical receptors the receptors that respond to the chemicals that come into contact with the nose and mouth

closure in Gestalt psychology, the tendency to imagine the rest of an incomplete familiar figure

cochlea the snail-shaped, fluid-filled structure that contains the receptors for hearing

color constancy the tendency of an object to appear nearly the same color under a variety of lighting conditions

conductive deafness hearing loss that results if the bones connected to the eardrum fail to transmit sound waves properly to the cochlea

cone the type of visual receptor that is adapted for color vision, daytime vision, and detailed vision

continuation in Gestalt psychology, the tendency to fill in the gaps in an interrupted line

convergence the turning in of the eyes as they focus on close objects

cornea a rigid, transparent structure in the eye

cutaneous senses the skin senses, including pressure, warmth, cold, pain, vibration, movement across the skin, and stretch of the skin

dark adaptation a gradual improvement in the ability to see under dim light

depth perception the perception of distance

electromagnetic spectrum the continuum of all the frequencies of radiated energy

endorphin any of the neurotransmitters that decrease the perception of pain and induce pleasant feelings

feature detector a neuron in the visual system of the brain that responds to particular lines or other features of a visual stimulus

figure and ground an object and its background

fovea the central part of the retina that consists solely of cones

ganglion cells neurons in the eye that receive input from the visual receptors and send impulses via the optic nerve to the brain

gate theory a theory that pain messages have to pass through a gate in the spinal cord on their way to the brain and that messages from the brain can open or close that gate

Gestalt psychology an approach to psychology that seeks explanations of how we perceive overall patterns

good figure in Gestalt psychology, the tendency to perceive simple, symmetrical figures

hertz a unit of frequency representing one cycle per second

induced movement a perception that an object is moving and the background is stationary when in fact the object is stationary and the background is moving

just noticeable difference (JND) the minimum change that a person can detect in the intensity of a physical stimulus

lens a structure that varies its thickness to enable the eye to focus on objects at different distances

loudness a perception closely related to the amplitude of sound waves

mechanoreceptors receptors that respond to mechanical stimulation

monocular cues visual cues that are just as effective with one eye as with both

moon illusion the apparent difference between the size of the moon at the horizon and its size higher in the sky

motion parallax the apparently swift motion of objects close to a moving observer and the apparently slow motion of objects farther away

myopia nearsightedness, the inability to focus on distant objects

negative afterimage a color that a person sees after staring at its opposite color for a while

nerve deafness hearing loss that results from damage to the cochlea, the hair cells, or the auditory nerve

olfaction the sense of smell, the detection of chemicals in contact with the membranes inside the nose

opponent-process theory (of color vision) the theory that we perceive color in terms of a system of paired opposites: red versus green, yellow versus blue, and white versus black

optical illusion a misinterpretation of a visual stimulus as being larger or smaller or straighter or more curved than it really is

optic nerve a set of axons that extend from the ganglion cells of the eye to the thalamus and several other areas of the brain

perception the interpretation of the meaning of sensory information

pheromone an odorous chemical released by an animal that changes the way other members of its species respond to it socially

phi effect the illusion of movement created when two or more stationary lights flash on and off at regular intervals

photopigment a chemical that releases energy when struck by light and thereby enables rods and cones to respond to light

pitch a perception closely related to the frequency of sound waves

preattentive process a procedure that occurs automatically and simultaneously across a large portion of the visual field

proximity in Gestalt psychology, the tendency to perceive objects that are close together as belonging to a group

psychophysical function a mathematical function that relates the physical intensity of a stimulus to its perceived intensity—for example, luminous energy to brightness

psychophysics the study of the relationship between the properties of physical stimuli and our perception of those stimuli

pupil the opening in the eye through which light enters

receptor a specialized cell that responds to a particular form of energy and conveys its response to other cells in the nervous system

red-green color blindness the inability to distinguish between red and green

retina the rear surface of the eye, lined with visual receptors

retinal disparity the difference in the apparent position of an object as seen by the left retina and by the right retina

retinex theory the theory that color perception results from the cerebral cortex's comparison of various retinal patterns

reversible figure a stimulus that you can perceive in more than one way

rod the type of visual receptor that is adapted for dim light

sensation the conversion of energy from the environment into a pattern of response by the nervous system

sensory adaptation the tendency of a sensory threshold to fall after a period when the sensory receptors have not been stimulated and to rise after exposure to intense stimuli

sensory threshold the minimum intensity at which an individual can detect a sensory stimulus 50% of the time; a low threshold indicates ability to detect faint stimuli

signal-detection theory the study of people's tendencies to make correct judgments, misses, and false alarms

similarity in Gestalt psychology, the tendency to perceive related objects as belonging to a group

sound waves vibrations of the air or of some other medium

stimulus an energy in the environment that can influence action

stroboscopic movement an illusion of movement created by a rapid succession of stationary images

subliminal perception the alleged influence on behavior of a stimulus that is below the threshold for conscious recognition

taste the sensory system that responds to chemicals on the tongue

taste bud the site of the taste receptors, located in one of the folds on the surface of the tongue

trichromatic theory or **Young-Helmholtz theory** the theory that color vision depends on the relative rate of response of three types of cones

vestibular sense a specialized sense that detects the direction of tilt and amount of acceleration of the head

visual constancy the tendency to perceive objects as unchanging in shape, size, and color, despite variations in what actually reaches the retina

ANSWERS TO CONCEPT CHECKS

1. The center of the retina consists entirely of cones. If you look slightly to the side, the light falls on an area of the retina that consists partly of rods, which are more sensitive to faint light. (page 134)

2. As with people, cats can adapt well to dim light. No animal, however, can see in complete darkness. Vision is the detection of light that strikes the eye. (Similarly, the X-ray vision attributed to the comic book character Superman is impossible. Even if he could send out X rays, he would not see anything unless those X rays bounced off some object and back into his eyes. (page 134)

3. Although bright yellow-green and dim yellow-green light would evoke the same *ratio* of firing by the three cone types, the total *amount* of firing would be greater for the bright yellow-green light. (page 137)

4. Ganglion cell 1 would be almost unaffected by yellow light. Yellow light would stimulate the long-wavelength cone, which excites ganglion cell 1, but it would stimulate the medium-wavelength cone, which inhibits ganglion cell 1, about equally. (page 139)

5. The afterimage is on your eye, not on the background. When you try to focus on a different part of the afterimage, you move your eyes and the afterimage moves with them. (page 139)

6. We still hear a tone at 5000 Hz, but it is louder than before. For high-frequency tones, the pitch we hear depends on which hair cells are most active, not on how many impulses per second they fire. (page 147)

7. We localize sounds by comparing the input into the left ear with the input into the right ear. If a sound comes from straight ahead or from straight behind (or from straight above or below), the input into the left ear is identical with the input into the right ear. (page 147)

8. Braille images consist only of shape. They lack the variations in texture and hardness that are most helpful in identifying objects by touch. (page 149)

9. First determine how much the pleasant stimulus decreases the experience of pain for several people. Then give half of them naloxone and half of them a placebo. Again measure how much the pleasant stimulus decreases the pain. If the pleasant stimulus decreases pain by releasing endorphins, then naloxone should impair its pain-killing effects. (page 150)

10. 8020 Hz. (page 156)

11. In a dark room, even a small amount of light constitutes a large percentage of increase in the total amount of light—certainly more than one JND. The same amount of light increases the total amount of light in a well-lit room by a smaller percentage—less than one JND. (page 157)

12. In Figure 5.31, continuation, closure, and perhaps good figure; in Figure 5.32, closure. (page 166)

13. Retinal disparity. (page 170)

Answers to Other Questions in the Text

A. In Figure 5.16a, you should see the numeral 74; in Figure 5.16b, you should see the numeral 8.
B. In Figure 5.17b, you should see the numeral 29.

C.

a

b

Eye
Ear
Cheek
Jaw

d   Young woman

e

CHAPTER

6

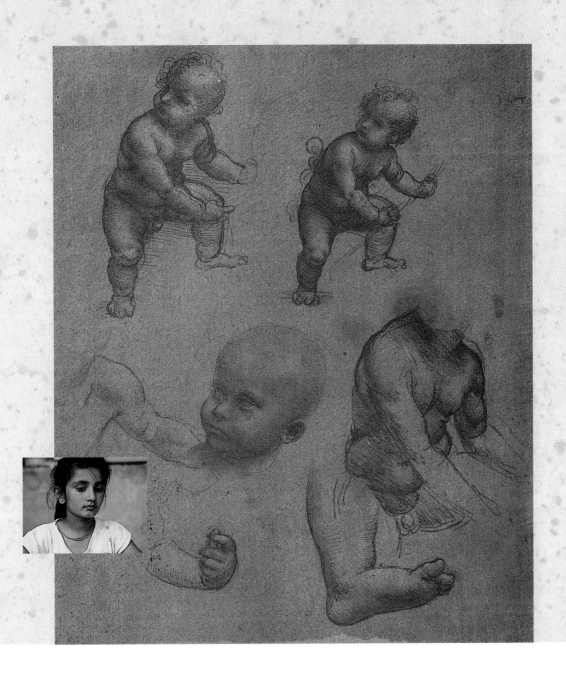

Suppose you buy a robot. When you get it home, you discover that it does nothing useful. It cannot even maintain its balance. It makes irritating, high-pitched noises, moves its limbs about haphazardly, and leaks. The store you bought it from refuses to take it back. And you discover that, for some reason, it is illegal to turn it off. So you are stuck with this useless machine.

Seven years later, your robot can walk and talk, read and write, draw pictures, and do arithmetic. It will follow your directions (most of the time), and sometimes it will even find useful things to do without being told. It beats you consistently at Chinese checkers.

How did all this happen? After all, you knew nothing about how to program a robot. Did your robot have some sort of built-in programming that simply took a long time to phase in? Or was it programmed to learn all these skills by imitating what it saw?

I know someone who is very much like that robot: my daughter, Robin. Nearly every parent wonders, "How did my children get to be the way they are?" The goal of developmental psychology is to understand everything that influences human behavior "from womb to tomb."

Methods of Studying Development and the Study of Early Development

What are the capacities of the newborn and the young infant?
How can psychologists determine those capacities?

An adult can do more than an infant can because of two influences: nature (heredity) and nurture (environment). Philosophers and psychologists have long debated which influence is more important. John Locke, a 17th-century English philosopher, insisted that the mind of a newborn child is a *tabula rasa* (Latin for "blank slate") that acquires content entirely through experience with the environment. Immanuel Kant, an 18th-century German philosopher, disagreed: He argued that the structure of the mind is fixed at birth and is independent of experience. In the 19th and early 20th centuries, some psychologists continued to believe that human behavior is mainly the result of heredity, while others maintained that it is strictly the result of experience. Today psychologists widely accept that both are essential, although the variations in certain behaviors may depend more on one influence than on the other.

One way to approach the nature-nurture issue is to study the behavior of newborns and very young infants. Such studies address the question, "What are we born with?" I shall deal with that question presently, but first let's examine the basic research designs for studying the development of behavior.

Research Designs for Studying Development

Suppose you wanted to study how some behavior develops. You could conduct the study in two ways.

You could observe different groups of children at different ages, say, from newborns to 10-year-olds, all at the same time. A **cross-sectional study** compares different groups of individuals of different ages all at the same time. Or you could observe a group of newborns and continue to observe those same children each year until they reached age 10. A **longitudinal study** follows a single group of individuals as they develop. Figure 6.1 contrasts the two kinds of study.

Example of a Cross-Sectional Study

When you walk into a first-grade classroom, the drawings you see tacked on the walls will probably look like those in Figure 6.2—not very neat but full of action and brimming with imagination. Now visit a fifth-grade classroom. The drawings there will look like those in Figure 6.3—neat, precise, and pretty boring (Winner, 1986). This is a cross-sectional study; you have compared the performances of different children at different ages.

The drawings of young children tend to be inaccurate and incomplete. When asked to draw a house, for example, many 4-year-old to 6-year-old children will draw something like Figure 6.4a. They may show only the front of the house, place the window up in the corner, and set the chimney perpendicular to the roof. Older children draw something like Figure 6.4b. They show the side in perspective, put the window in a reasonable location, and set the chimney perpendicular to the ground. When children are shown several such drawings and are asked which they like best, most 4- to 6-year-olds choose one that resembles their own drawings, even though it is crude by adult standards (Moore, 1986).

Examples of a Longitudinal Study

Children differ in their temperament from early infancy onward (Thomas & Chess, 1980; Thomas, Chess, & Birch, 1968). Some infants are "easy." They develop regular sleeping and eating habits, they show interest in new people and new objects, they seldom cry, and when they do cry they are easily comforted. Other infants are "difficult." Their eating and sleeping habits are irregular, they are easily frightened, they cry often, and they are hard to comfort. Still others are slow to "warm up" to new surroundings. They are shy and inhibited. They withdraw at first

a   3 months   3 years   5 years   11 years

b   2 years   2 years   5 years   5 years

7 years   7 years   11 years   11 years

FIGURE 6.1

Is there a "child prodigy," a "natural athlete," or a "born criminal" among these faces? And are such labels valid? To study how a certain behavior develops in people, psychologists can use two methods: (a) a longitudinal study, which follows one group over many years, and (b) a cross-sectional study, which compares different groups of different ages together at the same time. Which type of study is best depends on the purpose of the study.

FIGURE 6.2

It's cute, but is it art? Although the drawings by these first graders may strike you as charmingly clumsy or just inept, these children are proud of their work. From their perspective, their drawings are good art. Most adults agree that the drawings are interesting and original, even if the technical merit is low.

FIGURE 6.3

By the fifth grade, children can produce pictures that technically are more correct. But are they as interesting and original as the drawings of younger children? Are they as much fun?

a   b

FIGURE 6.4

Young childrens' drawings are usually simple and incomplete, so we assume that house
b is the work of someone older than the child who drew house a. Nevertheless, many
young children say they like picture a better than picture b.

from unfamiliar people and new experiences, but after repeated exposures they begin to react positively.

Are such differences in temperament consistent over time? Because we are interested in what happens to individuals, we need to conduct a longitudinal study. Longitudinal studies have found that difficult infants are more likely than are others to become difficult children and, eventually, troubled adults (Parke & Asher, 1983; Thomas & Chess, 1980). Easy infants tend to become easy children; shy and inhibited infants tend to become shy and inhibited children. In one study, infants who were identified as being highly inhibited at the age of 21 months ended up, with few exceptions, as shy, quiet, nervous, and fearful 7½-year-olds (Kagan, Reznick, & Snidman, 1988). Infants who were identified as uninhibited developed into socially interactive, highly talkative 7½-year-olds.

There are many exceptions, of course. We do not know *why* difficult infants tend to become difficult children and troubled adults. Is it just part of their nature to be difficult? Or do their parents treat them differently because they were such trouble as infants?

Advantages and Disadvantages of the Two Kinds of Study

Cross-sectional studies have obvious practical advantages. To conduct such a study, we simply assemble a group of children of, say, ages 2 through 15, and observe them all at the same time. To carry out a longitudinal study, however, we would have to study the 2-year-olds and then study them repeatedly until age 15. By that time many of them may have moved away. The problem becomes even more difficult when we try to make a longitudinal study of the elderly: Some of them will die or become seriously ill before we complete the study. (This is the problem of "differential survival" mentioned in Chapter 2.) By choosing a cross-sectional study, we avoid such problems.

A longitudinal study has another disadvantage: When we take repeated measures of the same people over time, we cannot separate the effects of age from the effects of historical time. Because current events influence the behavior of all individuals, some changes in behavior over time may be due to changes in society, not to aging.

Cross-sectional studies have disadvantages, too. Suppose we wanted to compare the IQ scores of young adults with the scores of older adults. If we found that the young adults scored significantly higher, we would have no way of knowing whether IQ actually declines with age or whether we just happened to sample a brighter group of 20-year-olds than 60-year-olds. Still another possibility is that the younger generation as a whole performed better than the older generation ever did, perhaps because of better health or better education. If that is the case, we would say that one **cohort** (a group of people born

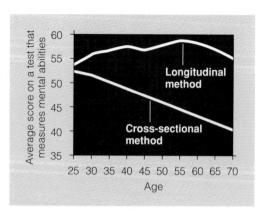

Figure 6.5

Results of a cross-sectional study suggest that mental performance declines with age, while a longitudinal study indicates that it improves with age (up to a point). The comparison suggests that factors other than age are at work; it also reminds us that no one method of study is foolproof.

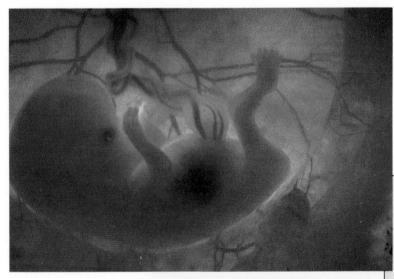

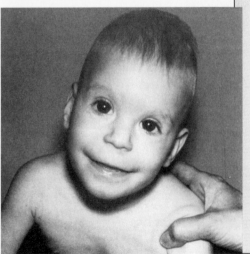

at a particular time) differs from another. The only way to be certain of the effect of age on IQ scores would be to test the same people repeatedly as they grew older. In this case, a longitudinal study would be the better choice, despite the inconvenience.

In many cases, the ideal solution is to use a combination of both cross-sectional and longitudinal studies (see Figure 6.5). When possible, psychologists do so.

Concept Checks

1. Suppose a longitudinal study of political attitudes reveals that people who were very liberal college students in 1970 had become more conservative by 1990. Could we conclude that people tend to grow more conservative as they grow older? Now suppose that a cross-sectional study conducted in 1990 reveals little difference in political attitudes between 20-year-olds and 40-year-olds. Would that finding change our interpretation of the longitudinal findings? (Check your answers on page 235.)
2. When we are studying the effect of aging on something like political attitudes, clothing styles, or tastes in music, which tend to change from year to year, should we use longitudinal studies or cross-sectional studies? (Check your answer on page 235.)

PRENATAL DEVELOPMENT

The development of the capacity for behavior begins before birth. In **prenatal** life, the environment consists of chemicals in the mother's bloodstream. If

During early months of development, the human fetus—especially its brain—is very susceptible to elements in the mother's blood. Proper nutrition and avoidance of cigarettes, alcohol, and other drugs (from cocaine to acne medication) will help provide a healthy environment. Despite growing awareness of substances potentially dangerous to the fetus, thousands of U.S. babies are born addicted to drugs or with fetal alcohol syndrome (FAS), which includes facial abnormalities—small head; low, prominent ears; poorly developed cheekbones; and a long, smooth upper lip—growth problems, and neurological abnormalities. These mental and physical distortions make the children difficult to rear and to educate. While FAS affects about 1% of children worldwide, some 5 to 25% of children on North American Indian reservations suffer from FAS (Kolata, 1989).

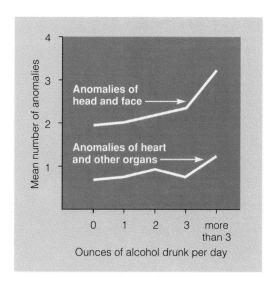

FIGURE 6.6

Physical evidence of a type of child abuse: Mean number of anomalies—such as a small head, folds around the eyes, malformed ears, and heart murmurs—in children born to mothers who drank different amounts of alcohol during pregnancy. (Modified from Ernhart et al., 1987.)

the mother is healthy and well-nourished throughout pregnancy, the **fetus** (a human offspring more than eight weeks after conception) will develop within a well-regulated, supportive environment.

A poor prenatal environment, however, may cause the fetus to develop abnormally. Throughout pregnancy, the fetus receives oxygen and nutrition from the mother along with whatever else is present in her blood. Early development is highly sensitive to some substances that have only minor or temporary effects on an adult. For example, if the mother drinks even small quantities of alcohol during pregnancy, the infant may show signs of the **fetal alcohol syndrome**, a condition marked by decreased alertness and other signs of impaired development after birth (Streissguth, Barr, & Martin, 1983). The more alcohol the mother drinks and the longer she drinks during pregnancy, the greater the risk to the fetus (see Figure 6.6). The fetus may also develop abnormally if the mother is malnourished, if she takes drugs, if she smokes cigarettes, or if she contracts *rubella* (German measles) or other diseases during pregnancy. Certain drugs and certain kinds of tumors may cause abnormal development of the infant's genitals (Money & Ehrhardt, 1972).

The brain in particular is more sensitive to certain chemicals during prenatal development and early infancy than it is later on. Drugs, poor nutrition, and hormonal abnormalities that would cause only tem-

porary problems for an adult may lead to permanent impairments of the brain during its early stages of development.

BEHAVIORAL CAPACITIES OF THE NEWBORN

Newborn horses and other hoofed animals are able to stand up, open their eyes, and follow their mother around within hours after birth. Capacities that emerge so rapidly, with almost no time for the animals to gain experience, presumably are built in genetically.

What capacities do human infants possess? Their capacities for action are highly limited. At first they cannot keep their head from flopping over, and they cannot coordinate their arm and leg movements. About the only useful movements they can make are mouth movements and eye movements. As the months pass, and as their control spreads from the head muscles downward, they are able to make progressively finer movements. After about a year they can move one finger at a time.

Because newborns have so little control over their muscles, it is easy to underestimate how much they can see or hear. Psychologists once doubted that infants could learn anything at all until they were about 3 weeks old (Lipsitt, 1963). Actually, though, infants are doing much more than waiting for their muscles to develop: They are learning a great deal about their body and about the environment, and they are developing their sensory responses at a rapid pace. How can we measure those emerging capacities when newborns are able to *do* so little?

Developmental psychologists concentrate on the few movements that *are* within the infant's control. One of those movements is sucking. They have discovered that a light or sound stimulus may increase the infant's sucking rate. In one study, 26 babies less than 3 days old could turn on a tape recording of their mother's voice by sucking on a nipple at certain times and at certain rates. By sucking at different times or at different rates, they could turn on a tape recording of some other woman's voice. When their manner of sucking produced their own mother's voice, their rate of sucking increased significantly (DeCasper & Fifer, 1980); it increased less when it produced a different voice. Apparently they recognized a voice they had become familiar with before birth.

In another study, the experimenters played a brief sound and noted how it affected the infant's

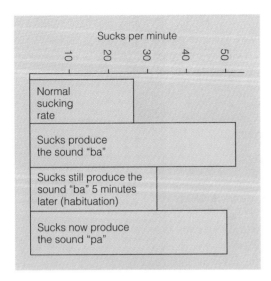

FIGURE 6.7

Sound effects: After 5 minutes of hearing the same sound, the infant's sucking habituates. When a new sound, *pa,* follows, the sucking rate increases, indication that infants hear a difference between the sounds *ba* and *pa.* (Based on results of Eimas, Siqueland, Juscyk, & Vigorito, 1971.)

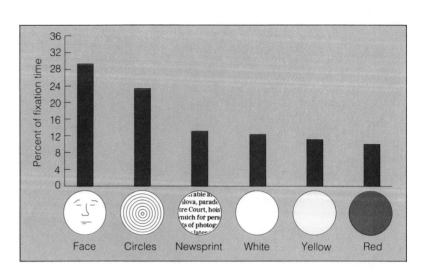

FIGURE 6.8

Face value: Infants pay more attention to faces than to other patterns—perhaps in part because faces offer variety. (Based on Fantz, 1963.) These results suggest that infants are born with certain visual preferences that do not depend on learned associations. The preference for faces facilitates the development of social attachments.

FIGURE 6.9

Infants 2 to 3 weeks old sometimes imitate adults' facial expressions without knowing what they express. (From Meltzoff & Moore, 1977.) Exchanging smiles with their parents strengthens the bond between them, although the infants may not yet understand who or what parents are.

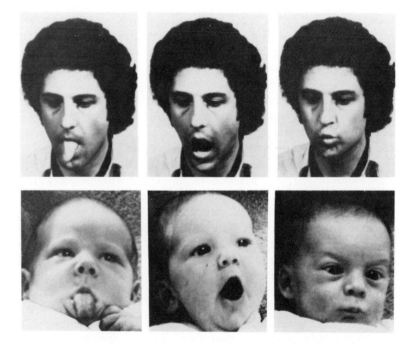

FIGURE 6.10

"Look, ma—no hands!": By the age of 8 weeks, infants can rapidly learn to kick one of their legs to activate a mobile attached to their ankle with a ribbon. After just a little practice, they can keep the mobile going for a full 45-minute session. In addition, these infants remember how to activate the mobile from one session to the next. (From Rovee-Collier, 1984.)

sucking rate (see Figure 6.7). For a time, the sucking rate increased. Then, after the sound had been played repeatedly, its effect grew weaker. The infant is said to have **habituated** to the sound. If a different sound is played, the sucking rate increases again. Psychologists use this technique to determine what the infant perceives as a "different" sound (Jusczyk, 1985). For example, an infant who has habituated to the sound *ba* will increase its sucking rate in response to the sound *pa* (Eimas, Siqueland, Jusczyk, & Vigorito, 1971). Apparently even month-old infants can tell the difference between *ba* and *pa*.

Another movement infants can control is turning their eyes toward an object that comes into their range of vision. Even at the age of 2 days infants pay more attention to drawings of human faces than to other patterns with similar areas of light and dark (Fantz, 1963). (See Figure 6.8.) They can also imitate facial expressions (Meltzoff & Moore, 1977), another indication of perception (Figure 6.9). (How and why they imitate, we do not know.) However, they have trouble keeping their eyes focused on a moving object. Infants can move their eyes quickly from one object to another, but they cannot move their eyes smoothly to follow a moving object until they are 2 to 3 months old (Aslin, 1985).

To demonstrate infant learning, one experimenter tickled an infant's cheek while sounding either a tone or a buzzer. A movement of the infant's head in the direction of the tickling after one sound (tone for half the infants, buzzer for the other half) brought a reward of sugar water; a movement after the other sound brought no reward. Newborns learned to turn their heads more often in response to whichever sound was paired with reward (Clifton, Siqueland, & Lipsitt, 1972; Siqueland & Lipsitt, 1966).

Rovee-Collier (1984) placed infants in a situation where they could activate mobiles and then observed evidence of lasting memory (Figure 6.10).

Concept Check

3. *Suppose a newborn sucks to turn on a tape recording of its father's voice. Eventually it habituates and the sucking rate decreases. Now the experimenters substitute the recording of a different man's voice for the father's. What would you conclude if the sucking rate increased? What would you conclude if it remained the same? What would you conclude if it decreased? (Check your answers on page 235.)*

THE ROLE OF EXPERIENCE IN EARLY DEVELOPMENT

In many respects, humans and other animal species develop according to a natural process controlled by instructions from the genes. They are born with certain capacities and additional capacities unfold as time passes. But experience modifies that process at every stage.

Environmental Enrichment

A varied and stimulating environment fosters brain development and prepares the individual to learn new behaviors. In a series of studies of the effect of environment on development, one group of rats was reared in an "impoverished environment," as Figure 6.11a shows. These rats were kept in small individual cages and were given only food and water. Another group was reared in an "enriched environment," as Figure 6.11b shows. These rats were kept in larger cages with several other rats and were provided with a variety of objects to explore, with new objects periodically replacing those that had become familiar.

The researchers found that the rats reared in the enriched environment were more active and learned more quickly, especially on complex tasks. They developed a 5% larger cerebral cortex than those reared in the impoverished environment. They also developed larger neurons, with wider-branching dendrites and a greater number of synapses (Renner & Rosenzweig, 1987).

a   b

FIGURE 6.11

Rats raised in solitary confinement in small, uninteresting cages (a) don't thrive as well as do rats raised in a stimulating environment with other rats (b). A stimulating environment affects the development of both the brain and behavior.

FIGURE 6.12

Don't look down: In a test of coordination between visual perception and motion, the optical illusion fooled most infants. Few of them could be lured across the "abyss" covered by clear glass.

The Role of Experience in the Development of Movement

Even capacities that emerge early in development must be strengthened by experience if they are to survive and improve. For example, some degree of coordination between vision and movement develops fairly quickly in infants. Richard Walk and Eleanor Gibson (1961) placed infants on the **visual cliff** shown in Figure 6.12. An infant who crawled down one side would crawl onto a colored board a couple of inches below. An infant who crawled down the other side would land on a clear plate of glass, also just a couple of inches below, although the drop *appeared* to be much greater than the drop on the other side. Even infants barely old enough to crawl chose the "shallow" side. When their mothers encouraged them to crawl the other way, many cried. Newborn goats and 10-day-old kittens were equally reluctant to move off the "deep" side.

In a study of early hand-eye coordination in human infants, researchers found that by age 5 months infants consistently reach for the closer of two objects (Yonas & Granrud, 1985). Infants begin to use various depth cues—such as binocular disparity, convergence, and motion parallax—at successive ages as each mechanism of depth perception matures. Evidently, infants do not need to learn much in order to coordinate their movements with what they see.

To maintain and improve that coordination, however, specific kinds of experience are necessary. Several studies have been made of kittens, which are ideal for such studies because kittens can move about quite well by the time they first open their eyes, about 10 days after birth. In one experiment, kittens were permitted to walk around in a dark room for 21 hours a day (Held & Hein, 1963). For the other 3 hours, half the kittens (the "active" group) were permitted to walk around in a well-lit cylindrical room, as Figure 6.13 shows. The other kittens (the "passive" group) were confined to boxes that were propelled around the room by the active kittens. Because the passive kittens could see out of the boxes, they had nearly the same visual experience the active kittens had; they also got regular exercise during the 21 hours of darkness each day. However, only the active kittens got a chance to see and walk at the same time and to learn the consequences of their movements.

The active kittens gradually developed good paw-eye coordination, but the passive kittens lagged far behind. In fact, the passive kittens apparently lost some of the abilities they had been born with: For example, they walked off the deep side on the visual cliff. Evidently kittens need to see and move at the same time in order to maintain and improve their visually guided behavior.

The general point is that experience contributes to development in a variety of ways. Even if a behavior is present soon after birth, experience may be necessary for the continued development of that behavior.

SUMMARY

1. Psychologists study development by means of cross-sectional studies, which examine people of different ages at the same time, and by means of longitudinal studies, which look at a single group of people at different times as they grow older. (page 183)

2. Cross-sectional studies have one major advantage: Because they examine people at the same time, they do not confuse the effects of age with the effects of historical time. (page 185)

3. Longitudinal studies have one major advantage: Because they examine the same people at all ages, they do not confuse the effects of age with differences among age cohorts. They also avoid the problem that an investigator may have selected different types of people for the different age groups. (page 185)

4. Behavioral development begins before birth. During prenatal development, an individual is especially vulnerable to the effects of alcohol and other drugs, toxic substances, and diseases. (page 186)

5. It is easy to underestimate the capacities of the newborn human infant because the infant has so little control over the muscles. A newborn can recognize his or her mother's voice and will pay more attention to pictures of faces than to other stimuli. A 1-month-old can notice the difference between the sounds *ba* and *pa*. (page 187)

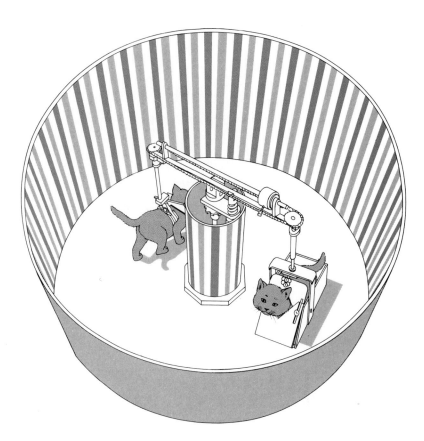

FIGURE 6.13

As the kitten carousel experiment demonstrates, experience influences development. These two kittens see the same thing, but only one can correlate what it sees with its own movements. Only the active kitten develops normal paw-eye coordination. (Modified from Held & Hein, 1963.)

6. In nonhuman animals, and presumably in humans as well, an enriched environment leads to enhanced development of the brain and behavior. (page 189)

7. Although a certain amount of hand-eye (or paw-eye) coordination may develop almost automatically at an early age, practice is necessary to maintain and improve that coordination. (page 190)

SUGGESTION FOR FURTHER READING

Horowitz, F. D. (Ed.) (1989). Special issue: Children and their development. *American Psychologist, 44* (2). A special issue devoted to all aspects of the development of behavior.

The Development of Thinking and Reasoning

What goes on in the mind of a small child?
How do the thought processes of children differ
from those of adults?

Preschool children ask some profound questions: "Why is the sky blue? What makes ice cubes cold? Why can't I stare at the sun when it's safe to look at a picture of the sun? Where does the sun go at night?" They are relentlessly curious about how things work and why. (Moreover, when you answer their questions, they never interrupt to ask, "Is this going to be on the test?")

These same budding little scientists also believe in Santa Claus, the Easter Bunny, and the Tooth Fairy. The child who asks "Why is there snow?" seems equally content with either an explanation of how moisture condenses in the upper atmosphere or with the simple reply, "So children can play in it."

Adults find it difficult to recapture what it was like to be a child. It is clear that children think differently from adults in a number of ways, but it is not easy to specify those ways. Here we examine several efforts to do so.

The Development of Thought and Knowledge: Piaget's Contributions

Attending a rousing political rally may have a profound effect on a young adult, much less effect on a preteen, and no effect at all on an infant. However, playing with a pile of blocks will be a more stimulating experience for a young child than for someone older. *The effect of a certain experience on a person's thinking processes and knowledge depends on that person's maturity and previous experiences.* The theorist who made this point most strongly and most influentially was Jean Piaget (peah-ZHAY) (1896–1980).

Early in his career, Piaget administered IQ tests to French-speaking children in Switzerland. He grew bored with the IQ tests because he felt he was not learning anything about intelligence, but he was fascinated by the incorrect answers that children consistently gave to certain questions. For example, when asked, "If you mix some water at a temperature of 50 degrees with an equal amount of water at 70 degrees, what temperature will the mixture be?" more than two thirds of all 9-year-olds answer, "120 degrees" (Jensen, 1980).

Unless someone was going around mischievously misinforming all the children in Switzerland, the children must be coming to some incorrect conclusions on their own. In other words—and this is one of Piaget's central insights—*children's thought processes are different from those of adults.* Children are not merely inexperienced adults, and they are not just less skillfully going through the same thought processes adults use. The difference between children's thought processes and those of adults is *qualitative* as well as *quantitative*—that is, it is a difference in kind and a difference in degree. Piaget supported this conclusion with extensive longitudinal studies of children, especially his own.

Characteristics of Children's Thought Processes

Piaget (1923) concluded that children's thought processes are *more intuitive* and *less logical* than those of adults. For example, assume that you put a boy doll and a girl doll behind a screen (Figure 6.14) and attach a green string to the boy doll and a red string to the girl doll. Then you ask a child, "If I pull the green string, which doll will come out?" The child correctly guesses the boy doll. You pull the string and indeed the boy doll appears. You repeat exactly the same procedure several times, until eventually when you ask which doll will come out the child guesses the *girl* doll. "Why do you think the girl doll will come out?" you ask. "Because it's her turn!" the child exclaims.

(Are adults ever guilty of the same thing? Alas, yes. When someone flips a coin and it comes up *heads* six times in a row, many people will bet that it will come up *tails* the next time, on the theory that *tails* is "due.")

FIGURE 6.14

Children rely more on intuition and less on logic than adults do, as this "guessing game" demonstrates. Based on what she thinks is right, or fair, this girl will eventually give the wrong answer.

"The child is father to the man," wrote the poet William Wordsworth. Jean Piaget (1896–1980), the most influential theorist on intellectual development in children, demonstrated that an experience's influence on a person's way of thinking depends on that person's age and previous experience.

Piaget also concluded that children's thought processes are **egocentric**. In using this term, Piaget did *not* mean that children are selfish; instead, he meant that the child sees the world as centered around himself or herself and is unable to take the perspective of another person. An egocentric point of view also assumes that everything has some purpose related to people. I remember once telling my 8-year-old son David that astronomers had found evidence that Pluto has a moon. "But Daddy," he replied, "I thought Pluto was too cold for anything to live there." I told him that was right. He asked, "Well, why would Pluto have a moon if there is no one there to see it?" In his view, moons existed only to entertain people.

As evidence that children's thought is egocentric, Piaget noted that children find it hard to take another person's point of view. If you and a preschool child sit on opposite sides of a pile of blocks and you ask the child to draw what the blocks would look like from your side, the child will draw them as they look from his or her own side.

When speaking, young children often omit the background information that a listener needs in order to understand what the child is talking about. At age 6, my daughter, Robin, told me that the children in her class liked their teacher so much that "she can't put her feet down." I eventually elicited the explanation that the teacher sometimes invited the chil-

dren to sit around her while she read a story, and they sat so close that she had nowhere to put her feet. At another time, Robin interrupted a conversation to tell me, "Imagination has five." I expressed puzzlement. A bit impatiently she replied, "Look, I'll show you: I-ma-gi-na-tion." With her hand she made one gesture with each syllable. Clearly, what she meant was that the word *imagination* has five syllables; the fact that she omitted that explanation at first is another example of egocentrism.

Later researchers have pointed out, however, that children's tendency to be egocentric is not absolute (Gelman & Baillargeon, 1983). If the pile-of-blocks task is greatly simplified, a child may accurately describe the other person's point of view. For instance, you show a child a card with one picture on the front and a different picture on the back, and then you sit across from the child and show the card again. Three-year-olds and even some 2-year-olds will describe what *they* see *and* what *you* see. When a child is looking at a card with a picture on only one side and you ask, "May I see it?" the child will turn it toward you. Apparently young children do recognize that perspectives differ.

Moreover, a 4-year-old will describe a scene differently depending on whether he or she is talking to a blindfolded adult, an adult who is not blindfolded, or a 2-year-old. When talking to a younger child, the 4-year-old will speak slowly and use sim-

FIGURE 6.15

A hands-on approach to exploration: This child assimilates the grasp response to different objects and accommodates that schema to fit them.

ple language. In other words, a child is more egocentric than an adult, but not completely egocentric, as Piaget claimed.

Concept Check

4. Which of the following is the clearest example of egocentric thinking?
a. A writer who uses someone else's words without giving credit
b. A politician who blames others for everything that goes wrong
c. A professor who gives the same complicated lecture to a freshman class that she gives to a convention of professionals
(Check your answer on page 235.)

How Thought Processes and Knowledge Grow: Some Piagetian Terminology

According to Piaget, a child's intellectual development is not merely an accumulation of experience or a maturational unfolding. Rather, the child constructs *new* mental processes as he or she interacts with the environment.

In Piaget's terminology, behavior is based on schemata. A **schema** is an organized way of interacting with objects in the world. For instance, infants have a grasping schema and a sucking schema. Older infants gradually add new schemata to their repertoire and adapt their old ones. This adaptation takes place through the processes of assimilation and accommodation.

In **assimilation** a person applies an old schema to new objects—for example, an infant may suck an unfamiliar object or use the grasp response in trying to manipulate it. In **accommodation** a person modifies an old schema to fit a new object—for example, an infant may suck a breast, a bottle, and a pacifier in different ways or may modify the grasp response to accommodate the size or shape of a new toy (see Figure 6.15).

Infants shift back and forth from assimilation to accommodation. For example, an infant who tries to suck on a rubber ball (assimilating it to her sucking schema) may find that she cannot fit it into her mouth. First she may try to accommodate her sucking schema to fit the ball; if that fails, she may try to shake the ball. She is assimilating her grasping schema to the new object—expanding her motor repertoire to include it—but at the same time she is accommodating that schema—changing it—to fit the ball.

Adults do much the same thing. You are given a new mathematical problem to solve. You try several of the methods you have already learned until you hit on the one schema that works. In other words, you assimilate your old schema to the new problem. If, however, the new problem is quite different from any problem you have ever solved before, you modify (accommodate) your schema until you work out a solution. Through processes like these, said Piaget, intellectual growth occurs.

Piaget's Stages of Intellectual Development

Piaget contended that children progress through four major stages of intellectual development:

1. The sensorimotor stage (from birth to about 1½ years)

2. The preoperational stage (from about 1½ to 7 years)

3. The concrete operations stage (from about 7 to 11 years)

4. The formal operations stage (from about 11 years onward)

The ages given here are approximate. Many people do not reach the stage of formal operations until well beyond age 11, if they reach it at all. Piaget recognized that some children develop at a faster rate than others, but he insisted that all children go through these four stages *in the same order*. Exactly how distinct the stages are is not clear (Keil, 1981).

The Sensorimotor Stage: Infancy Piaget called the first stage of intellectual development the **sensorimotor stage** because at this early age (birth to 1½ years) behavior consists mostly of simple motor responses to sensory stimuli—for example, the grasp reflex and the sucking reflex (Figure 6.16). Infants respond to what is present, rather than to what is remembered or imagined. Piaget concluded that infants in the sensorimotor stage are incapable of representational thought—that is, they do not think about objects they cannot see, hear, feel, or otherwise sense. Moreover, Piaget concluded that infants lack the concept of **object permanence**. They do not understand that an object continues to exist when they can no longer see it. (Not only is it "out of sight, out of mind," but "out of sight, out of existence" as well.)

How, you might ask, can we possibly know what a baby does or does not think? We cannot—at least, not for sure. Piaget was drawing inferences from the behavior he observed, though other people have drawn different inferences. After we review Piaget's observations, you can draw your own conclusions. (Better yet, study a baby to make your own observations.)

1. *Observation:* From age 3 months to age 6 to 9 months, an infant will reach out to grab a toy only if it is visible. If the toy is partially visible, the infant will reach for it; if it is fully hidden, however, the infant will not reach for it even after watching someone hide it (Piaget, 1937/1954). (See Figure 6.17.) *Piaget's interpretation:* An infant who does not see an object does not know it is there. *Other possible interpretations:* The infant may know the object still exists but may not remember *where* it is. Or the infant may be distracted by other objects that *are* visible.

2. *Observation:* If we hide a toy under a clear glass, most infants will lift the glass to get the toy; if we hide it under an opaque glass, most infants will make no effort to get it. *Possible interpretation:* Infants do not ignore a covered toy because they are unable to remove the cover. They ignore it because they do not see it.

3. *Observation:* If we show an infant a toy and then turn off the lights before the infant can grab it, the

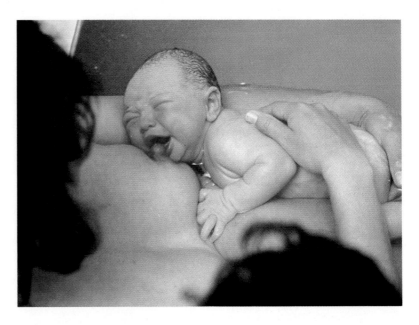

FIGURE 6.16

Although at birth babies suck at a breast, they have trouble drawing from it because they cannot coordinate sustained sucking, squeezing, swallowing, and breathing. A newborn needs practice to nurse efficiently.

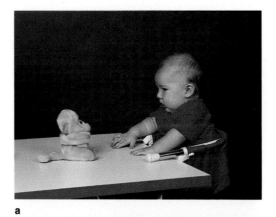

a

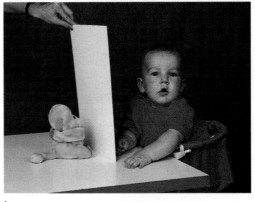

b

FIGURE 6.17

Now you see it, now you don't: During the sensorimotor period, a child will reach for a visible toy (a) but not one that is hidden behind a barrier (b)—even if he or she sees someone hide the toy. According to Piaget, this observation indicates the child lacks the concept of object permanence.

"*Having children is like having a bowling alley installed in your brain,*" *says Martin Mull. Bowling is an apt comparison—young children enjoy endlessly repeating simple games, long after they've driven their parents to distraction. As with adults, children learn through repeated experience. Peekaboo, a favorite game, is a way of learning about object permanence.*

infant will still reach out to grab it in the dark (Bower & Wishart, 1972). *Possible interpretation:* Contrary to the first two observations, this one seems to indicate that infants will reach for something they remember but cannot see, provided they can see nothing else. In the first two cases, objects that remain visible may distract the infant from objects that are no longer visible.

4. *Observation:* From about 9 to 11 months, an infant who watches you hide a toy will reach out to retrieve it. But if you hide the toy first on the right side and then on the left side, the infant will reach out both times to the right side. *One interpretation:* Even at this age, infants do not fully understand that an object remains where it was hidden. *Another interpretation:* Infants know the object has been hidden but cannot remember where.

Something to Think About

In performing certain tasks, infants resemble adults who have suffered damage to the corpus callosum. (Recall that those adults cannot coordinate the movements of either hand with what they see on the opposite side of the visual field; see page 88.) For example, before age 4 months, infants who have one hand secured behind their back will not reach out with the other hand to touch an object on the opposite side of their visual field (Provine & Westerman, 1979). Could immaturity of the corpus callosum explain observation 4? How might you test that explanation?

The Preoperational Stage: Early Childhood Around age 1½ years, children reach a landmark in their intellectual development: They begin to acquire language at a rapid rate. Susan Carey (1978) has estimated that children between the ages of 1½ and 6 learn an average of nine new words *per day*—almost one new word per hour—thereby increasing their ability to tell us what they know and think (see Table 6.1). The fact that they can now talk about the properties of unseen objects is evidence that they have acquired the concept of object permanence. But there remain many things they do not understand at this age. For example, they have difficulty understanding that a mother can be someone else's daughter. A boy with one brother will assert that his brother has no brother. A child may say that there are more girls in a class than there are children. Piaget refers to this period as the **preoperational stage**. The child is said to lack **operations**, which are reversible mental processes. For example, for a boy to understand that his brother has a brother, he must be able to reverse the concept "having a brother."

Children at this age generally accept their experiences at face value. A child who sees you put a white ball behind a blue filter will say that the ball is blue. When you ask, "Yes, I know the ball *looks* blue, but what color is it *really*?" the child grows confused. So far as the child is concerned, any ball that *looks* blue *is* blue (Flavell, 1986).

According to Piaget, preoperational children lack the concept of **conservation**. Just as they fail to understand that something can still be white even though it looks blue, they fail to understand that objects conserve such properties as number, length, volume, area, and mass after the shape or arrangement of the objects has changed. They cannot perform the mental operations necessary to understand such transformations. (Table 6.2 shows some typical conservation tasks.)

TABLE 6.2 Typical Tasks Used to Measure Conservation

Conservation of number

Preoperational children say that the two rows have the same number of pennies.

Preoperational children say that the second row has more pennies.

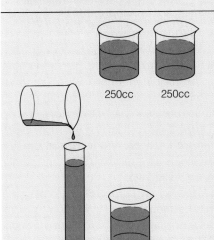

Conservation of volume

Preoperational children say that the two same-size containers have the same amount of water.

Preoperational children say that the taller, thinner container has more water.

Conservation of mass

Preoperational children say that the two same-size balls of clay have the same amount of clay.

Preoperational children say that a squashed ball of clay contains a different amount of clay from the same-size round ball of clay.

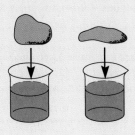

Conservation of mass—water displacement

A child in the early part of the concrete-operations stage may know that a round ball of clay and one that has been squashed contain the same amount of clay.

However, the same child may think that the round and the squashed balls of clay will displace different amounts of water.

For example, if we arrange two equal rows of pennies and ask which row contains more pennies, nearly all preoperational children will answer that the rows contain the same number of pennies. But if we spread one row out, they answer confidently that the longer row has more pennies. They do not even see a need to count the pennies to check their answer. Once we ask them to count the pennies, they discover that the number has remained the same (Gelman & Baillargeon, 1983). (Parents sometimes make use of a child's lack of conservation. A preoperational child has a cookie and asks for another one. The parent breaks the cookie in half and says, "Here. Now you have two cookies." At least some children seem satisfied.)

If we set up two glasses of the same size containing the same amount of water and then pour the contents of one glass into a different-shaped

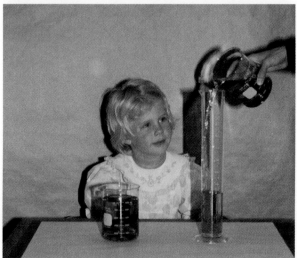

Looks can be deceptive: The conservation concept shows one way children think less logically than adults do. Preoperational children, up to about age 7 years, don't understand that some property of a substance—such as the volume of water—remains constant despite changes in its appearance.

glass, preoperational children will say that the taller, thinner glass contains more water.

I once doubted whether children really believed what they were saying in such a situation. Perhaps, I thought, the way the questions are phrased somehow tricks them into saying something they do not believe. Then something happened to convince me that preoperational children really believe their answers. One year, when I was discussing Piaget in my introductory psychology class, I invited my son Sam, then 5½ years old, to take part in a class demonstration. I started with two glasses of water, which he agreed contained equal amounts of water. Then I poured the water from one glass into a wider glass, lowering the water level. When I asked Sam which glass contained more water, he confidently pointed to the tall, thin one. After class he complained, "Daddy, why did you ask me such an easy question? Everyone could see that there was more water in that glass! You should have asked me something harder to show how smart I am!"

The following year I brought Sam to class again for the same demonstration. He was now 6½ years old, about the age at which children make the transition from preoperational thinking to the next stage. I again poured the water from one of the tall glasses into a wider one and asked him which glass contained more water. He looked and paused. His face got red. Finally he whispered, "Daddy, I don't know!" After class he complained, "Why did you ask me such a hard question? I'm never coming back to any of your classes again!" The question that was embarrassingly easy a year ago had become embarrassingly difficult.

The next year, when he was 7½, I tried again. This time he answered confidently, "Both glasses have the same amount of water, of course. Why? Is this some sort of trick question?"

The Concrete-Operations Stage: Later Childhood At about age 7, children enter the stage of concrete operations and begin to understand the conservation of physical properties. The transition is not sharp, however. The ability to understand the conservation of various properties emerges sequentially, at different ages. For instance, a 6-year-old child may understand that squashing a ball of clay will not change its weight but may not realize until years later that squashing the ball will not change the volume of water it displaces when it is dropped into a glass.

The **stage of concrete operations** is Piaget's term for the stage when children can perform mental operations on concrete objects. But they still have trouble with abstract or hypothetical ideas. For example, ask a child at this stage, "If you had five six-headed

"*Which tube is the longest?*" *Depending on the level of thinking a child has attained, he may consider the question easy or confusingly difficult.*

"*Which weighs more—a pound of feathers or a pound of bricks?*" *Many children would answer, "The bricks." They also think that a group spread over a larger area contains more items than a tightly arranged group.*

dogs, how many heads would there be?" Even a child who has no difficulty multiplying 5 times 6 is likely to object, "But there is no such thing as a six-headed dog!"

Or ask this question: "How could you move a 4-mile-high mountain of whipped cream from one side of the city to the other?" Older children find the question amusing and try to think of an imaginative answer. But children in the concrete-operations stage (or younger) are likely to complain that the question is silly or stupid.

Or ask, "If you could have a third eye anywhere on your body, where would you put it?" Children in this stage generally respond immediately that they would put it right between the other two, on their forehead. They seem to regard the question as not very interesting. Older children come up with more imaginative possibilities, such as on the back of their head or at the tip of a finger (so they could peek around corners).

The Formal-Operations Stage: Adolescence and Adulthood The **stage of formal operations** is Piaget's term referring to the mental processes used in dealing with abstract, hypothetical situations. Those processes demand logical, deductive reasoning and systematic planning.

Piaget set the beginning of the formal-operations stage at about age 11. He attributed some fairly sophisticated abilities to children in this stage, although later research indicates that many children take much longer to reach it and some people never do get there.

Suppose we ask three children, ages 6, 10, and 14, to arrange a set of 12 sticks in order from longest to shortest. The 6-year-old (preoperational) child fails to order the sticks correctly. The 10-year-old (concrete operations) eventually gets them in the right order, but only after a great deal of trial and error. The 14-year-old (formal operations) holds the sticks upright with their bottom ends on the table and then removes the longest one, the second-longest one, and so on.

A second example: We set up five bottles of clear liquid and explain that it is possible, by mixing the liquids together in a certain combination, to produce a yellow liquid. The task is to find the right combination. Children in the concrete-operations stage plunge right in with an unsystematic trial-and-error search. They try combining bottles A and B, then C and D, then perhaps A, C, and E, and so on. By the time they work through five or six combinations they forget which ones they have already tried. They may try one combination several times and others not at all; if and when they do stumble onto the correct combination, it is mostly a matter of luck.

Children in the formal-operations stage approach the problem more systematically. They may first try all the two-bottle combinations: AB, AC, AD, AE, BC, and so forth. If all those fail, they turn to three-bottle combinations: ABC, ABD, ABE, ACD, and so on. By adopting a strategy for trying every possible combination one time and one time only, they are bound to succeed.

Children do not reach the stage of formal oper-

TABLE 6.3 Summary of Piaget's Stages of Cognitive Development

Stage and Approximate Age	Achievements and Activities	Limitations
Sensorimotor (birth to 1½ years)	Reacts to sensory stimuli through reflexes and other responses	Little use of language; seems not to understand object permanence; does not distinguish appearance from reality
Preoperational (1½ to 7 years)	Develops language; can represent objects mentally by words and other symbols; can respond to objects that are remembered but not present at the moment	Lacks operations (reversible mental processes); lacks concept of conservation; focuses on one property at a time (such as length or width), not on both at once; still has some trouble distinguishing appearance from reality
Concrete operations (7 to 11 years)	Understands conservation of mass, number, and volume; can reason logically with regard to concrete objects that can be seen or touched	Has trouble reasoning about abstract concepts and hypothetical situations
Formal operations (11 years onward)	Can reason logically about abstract and hypothetical concepts; develops strategies; plans actions in advance	None beyond the occasional irrationalities of all human thought

ations any more suddenly than they reach the concrete-operations stage. Before they can reason logically about a particular problem, they must first have had a fair amount of experience in dealing with that problem. A 9-year-old who has spent a great deal of time playing chess reasons logically about chess problems and plans several moves ahead. The same child reverts to concrete reasoning when faced with an unfamiliar problem.

Table 6.3 summarizes Piaget's four stages.

Concept Check

5. *You are given the following information about four children. Assign each of them to one of Piaget's stages of intellectual development. (Check your answers on page 235.)*
a. Has mastered the concept of conservation; still has trouble with abstract and hypothetical questions
b. Performs well on tests of object permanence; still has trouble with conservation
c. Has schemata; does not speak in complete sentences; fails tests of object permanence
d. Performs well on tests of object permanence, conservation, and hypothetical questions

---

Piaget's Early Stages: Why Do Children Fail Certain Tasks? WHAT'S THE EVIDENCE?

According to Piaget, the four stages of intellectual development are distinct, and each transition from one stage to the next requires a major reorganization of the child's way of thinking. He contended that children in the sensorimotor stage fail certain tasks because they lack the concept of object permanence and that children in the preoperational stage fail conservation tasks because they lack the necessary mental processes.

Was Piaget right? One way to find out is to determine whether children who fail certain tasks can be taught to perform them correctly. If they lack the necessary capacities, as Piaget believed, such efforts will fail.

We might try, for example, to teach children under 7 years old to perform correctly on conservation tasks. Attempts to advance preoperational children to the concrete-operational stage simply by having them pour water or squash clay have met with little success (Cowan, 1978).

A more successful approach is to direct the children's attention to the aspects of the task that are most relevant. For example, a young child who judges that one row of pennies contains more pennies than another is simply observing that one row is *longer*

than the other. Might there be some way to get the child to pay attention to number instead of length?

EXPERIMENT 1

Hypothesis When given a task in which number is relevant and length is not, children in the preoperational period will pay attention to number.

Method In the so-called magic task, a cover is put over a small group of objects; when the cover is removed, the number of objects has changed (Gelman, 1982). The child's reaction is observed.

Results Even children who fail the conservation-of-number task immediately notice that something is wrong. They ask where the extra objects came from or what happened to the missing objects.

Interpretation The children obviously understand the concept of number, and they seem to know that the number cannot change without a reason. In the usual conservation of number task, preoperational children say that the stretched-out row of coins is "more." Apparently children make that judgment not because (as Piaget thought) they do not understand the constancy of a number but because they were attending to length instead of number.

EXPERIMENT 2

If that interpretation is correct, then it should be fairly simple to teach young children the concept of conservation of number: Just give the child practice on tasks that require the child to pay attention to number.

Hypothesis Children who are given simple number tasks will pay attention to number. After they have practiced such tasks for a while, they will show evidence of conservation of number on similar but more difficult tasks.

Method Rochelle Gelman (1982) gave preschool children a simplified version of the conservation-of-number task. Instead of asking the child to compare 2 rows of 7 or more objects, she presented 2 rows of just 3 objects each. After she spread out one of the rows, she asked which row had more. The children answered correctly that both rows were the same. (Most of the 3-year-olds counted first, to make sure.) After much practice with rows of 3 or 4 items each, she shifted to the standard conservation-of-number task shown in Table 6.2, using 8 to 10 items at a time.

Results A majority of 3-year-olds and 4-year-olds gave correct responses most of the time.

Future Newtons in action: At San Francisco's Exploratorium and other hands-on science "museums," kids get to learn concepts such as conservation on their own. Piaget considered this discover-it-yourself method essential for grasping basic principles.

Interpretation Even preschool children can give correct answers to conservation-of-number tasks if we get them to pay attention to number. Apparently they do understand the concept of number; they just do not realize at once that number is relevant to the question of which row of items has "more." ■

Evaluation of Piaget's Theories

Piaget's major contribution was to demonstrate that children's thinking differs from that of adults. Young children really do approach certain questions differently from adults and sometimes arrive at very different answers.

What is less certain is whether children go through distinct stages and whether children at higher stages

have capacities that children at lower stages lack altogether. As we have seen, depending on how someone poses the questions, infants may or may not show signs of understanding object permanence. Children less than about 7 years old are highly egocentric in some situations but less so in others. A child who fails the conservation-of-number task does nevertheless understand the concept of number; the same child can answer the questions correctly if we direct his or her attention to the key aspects. In short, Piaget seems to have underestimated the capacities of young children. They apparently have some fairly advanced capacities, even if they do not always use them. (And Piaget may have overestimated adolescents and adults. Even rather bright adults sometimes revert to egocentric and other illogical thinking.)

Moreover, children do not seem to pass suddenly from one stage of development to another. An 8-year-old child may give correct answers to some conservation tasks and not others. The same child may appear to be at the preoperational stage at some times, but at other times appear to be at the stage of concrete operations or even at the stage of formal operations. Although Piaget directed psychologists to some important aspects of how thinking develops, he may have overstated some of his conclusions.

Implications of Piaget's Findings for Education

One implication of Piaget's findings is that children have to discover certain concepts, such as the concept of conservation, mainly on their own. Teaching such concepts is mostly a matter of directing children's attention to the key aspects and then letting them discover the concepts for themselves.

A second implication is that teachers should be aware of each child's capacities and should work within them. Children in the lower grades can learn about concrete objects more easily than they can deal with symbolic and abstract concepts or with deductive logic. Recognizing a child's current stage of maturation and encouraging the child to go slightly beyond it is better than insisting that the child behave in a manner appropriate to a higher stage of development.

DEVELOPMENT OF MORAL REASONING

As children develop their reasoning powers, they apply their new reasoning abilities to moral issues. Just as 11-year-olds reason differently from 5-year-olds about what happens when water is poured from one beaker to another, they also reason differently about issues of right and wrong.

Kohlberg's Method of Evaluating Levels of Moral Reasoning

Morality used to be regarded as a set of arbitrary rules with no logical basis that people learn from their culture. Lawrence Kohlberg (1969; Kohlberg & Hersh, 1977) rejected that view, arguing instead that moral reasoning is the result of a reasoning process that resembles Piaget's stages of intellectual development. Young children equate "wrong" with "punished." Adults understand that certain acts are wrong even though they may never lead to punishment and that other acts are right even if they *do* lead to punishment. Kohlberg proposed that people pass through distinct stages as they develop moral reasoning. Although those stages are analogous to Piaget's stages, they do not follow the same time sequence. For example, an individual may progress rapidly through Piaget's stages while moving slowly through Kohlberg's stages.

Kohlberg suggested that moral reasoning should not be evaluated according to the decisions a person makes but according to the reasoning behind them. For example, in George Bernard Shaw's play *The Doctor's Dilemma,* two men are dying of tuberculosis. The doctor can save either one of them but not both. One man has little talent but is honest and decent. The other man, a young artistic genius, is dishonest, rude, and thoroughly disagreeable. Which one should the doctor save? According to Kohlberg, we cannot evaluate the doctor's moral reasoning by asking which man he decided to save. Instead, we should ask *on what basis* the doctor made his decision. In Shaw's play, the doctor saves the untalented man and lets the genius die in hopes that he can marry the widow. (You can evaluate the doctor's moral reasoning for yourself.)

Kohlberg believed that we all start with a low level of moral reasoning and mature through higher stages. (Shaw's doctor apparently did not get very far.) To measure the maturity of a person's moral judgments, Kohlberg devised a series of **moral dilemmas**—problems that pit one moral value against another. Each dilemma is accompanied by a question, such as "What should this person do?" or "Did this person do the right thing?" Actually, there is no one "right" answer to the questions. More revealing than the answer is the explanation and justification the respondent gives. The respondent's explanations are then matched to one of Kohlberg's six stages, which are grouped into three levels (see Table 6.4).

Something to Think About

Suppose a military junta overthrows a democratic government and sets up a dictatorship. In which of Kohlberg's stages of moral reasoning would you classify the members of the junta? Would your answer depend on the reasons they gave for setting up the dictatorship? In which stage would you classify a person who consistently based his or her decisions on the Ten Commandments?

The responses people make to Kohlberg's moral dilemmas suggest the level of moral reasoning at which they *usually* operate. Few people are absolutely consistent in their moral views, and their responses may differ from one time to another or even from one question to another. However, what does seem to be consistent in societies throughout the world is that people begin at the first stage and progress through the others in the order Kohlberg suggests, although they may not all reach the highest stages. (The order of progression is an important point. If people were as likely to progress in the order 3-5-4 as in the order 3-4-5, then we would have no justification for regarding stage 5 as higher than stage 4.) Apparently people do not skip a stage, and few revert to an earlier stage after reaching a higher one.

Figure 6.18 shows that most 10-year-olds' judgments are at Kohlberg's first or second stage, but that the mode of 16-year-olds' judgments is at stage 5. What accounts for this rather swift development of moral reasoning? Kohlberg suggests that it results from cognitive growth—16-year-olds are capable of more mature reasoning than are 10-year-olds. Rachael Henry (1983) proposes a different possibility: Adolescents reject parental authority. In stages 1 and 2, parents are the source of moral judgments, and what they say determines what is right and what is wrong. In stage 3, other people become the source of moral judgments. In stage 4, the source is the law; in stages 5 and 6, society as a whole or some abstract truth is the source of moral judgments. As adolescents continue to mature, they move farther and farther away from regarding their parents as the ultimate authority on questions of morality.

Criticisms of Kohlberg's Views of Moral Development

Although Kohlberg's theories have had an enormous impact on psychology, they do have certain limitations. Some critics point out that moral reasoning is just one part of moral behavior. James Rest (1983) divides moral behavior into four components:

TABLE 6.4 Responses to One of Kohlberg's Moral Dilemmas by People at Six Levels of Moral Reasoning

The dilemma: Heinz's wife was near death from a type of cancer. A druggist had recently discovered a drug that might be able to save her. The druggist was charging $2,000 for the drug, which cost him $200 to make. Heinz could not afford to pay for it, and he could borrow only $1,000 from friends. He offered to pay the rest later. The druggist refused to sell the drug for less than the full price paid in advance. "I discovered the drug and I'm going to make money from it." Late that night Heinz broke into the store to steal the drug for his wife. Did Heinz do the right thing?

Level/Stage	Typical Answer	Basis for Judging Right from Wrong	Description of Stage
The Level of Preconventional Morality			
1. Punishment and obedience orientation	"No. If he steals the drug he might go to jail." "Yes. If he can't afford the drug, he can't afford a funeral, either."	Wrong is equated with punished. What is good is whatever is in the man's immediate self-interest.	Decisions are based on their immediate consequences. Whatever is rewarded is "good" and whatever is punished is "bad." If you break something and are punished, then what you did was bad, regardless of whether it was intentional or accidental.
2. Instrumental relativist orientation	"He can steal the drug and save his wife, and he'll be with her when he gets out of jail."	Again, what is good is whatever is in the man's own best interests, but his interests include delayed benefits.	It is good to help other people, but only because they may one day return the favor: "You scratch my back and I'll scratch yours."
The Level of Conventional Morality			
3. Interpersonal concordance, or "good boy/nice girl" orientation	"People will understand if you steal the drug to save your wife, but they'll think you're cruel and a coward if you don't."	Public opinion is the main basis for judging what is good.	The "right" thing to do is whatever pleases others, especially those in authority. Be a good person so others will think you are good. Conformity to the dictates of public opinion is important. The intention of doing good is recognized as praiseworthy.
4. "Law and order" orientation	"No, because stealing is illegal." "It is the husband's duty to save his wife even if he feels guilty afterward for stealing the drug."	Right and wrong can be determined by duty, or by one's role in society.	You should respect the law—simply because it *is* the law—and should work to strengthen the social order that enforces it.
The Level of Postconventional or Principled Morality			
5. Social-contract legalistic orientation	"The husband has a right to the drug even if he can't pay now. If the druggist won't charge it, the government should look after it."	Laws are made for people's benefit. They should be flexible. If necessary, we may have to change certain laws or allow for exceptions to them.	The "right" thing to do is whatever people have agreed is best for society. As in stage 4, you respect the law, but in addition recognize that a majority of the people can agree to change the rules. Anyone who makes a promise is obligated to keep the promise.
6. Universal ethical principle orientation	"Although it is legally wrong to steal, the husband would be morally wrong not to steal to save his wife. A life is more precious than financial gain."	Right and wrong are based on absolute values such as human life. Sometimes these values take precedence over human laws.	In special cases it may be right to violate a law that conflicts with higher ethical principles, such as justice and respect for human life. Among those who have obeyed a "higher law" are Jesus, Mahatma Gandhi, and Martin Luther King, Jr. Few people act consistently on the basis of stage 6 moral reasoning.

Source: Kohlberg, 1981.

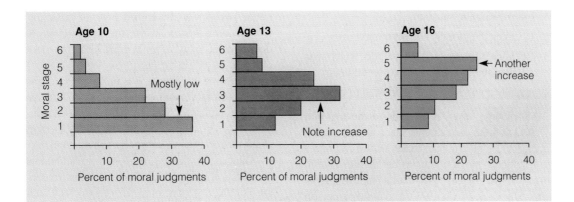

Age 10

Moral stage

6
5
4
3
2
1

Mostly low →

10   20   30   40

Percent of moral judgments

Age 13

6
5
4
3
2
1

← Note increase

10   20   30   40

Percent of moral judgments

Age 16

6
5
4
3
2
1

Another increase →

10   20   30   40

Percent of moral judgments

FIGURE 6.18

Distinguishing right from wrong: The development of moral reasoning. Most younger adolescents give answers corresponding to Kohlberg's earlier moral stages. By age 16, most are at Kohlberg's fourth and fifth stages. (Based on Kohlberg, 1969.)

People have strong moral responses to the question of abortion. With such a complex issue, people at the same level of moral development can come to opposite conclusions. An unwed teenage mother faces an additional difficult decision—whether to keep and raise her child or to give it up for adoption. Instead of having an anonymous transaction, this teen searched for a couple eager to adopt her baby. After interviewing potential parents, she chose this couple as the adoptive parents.

1. Interpreting the situation.

2. Deciding the morally correct thing to do.

3. Deciding what you actually will do, which may not be the same as the morally correct thing to do.

4. Actually doing what you've decided to do.

Kohlberg's stages relate only to the first and second of these components. Many juvenile delinquents and adult criminals make mature responses to Kohlberg's moral dilemmas but then engage in behavior that is anything but moral (Jurkovic, 1980; Link, Sherer, & Byrne, 1977). Apparently a person can distinguish between right and wrong in the abstract and then ignore that distinction in the way he or she behaves.

Another criticism is that Kohlberg's theories imply that moral reasoning is entirely a logical process. For example, we decide that it is wrong to hurt another person because human life and welfare are fundamentally valuable. But moral reasoning is partly an emotional process. We do not want to hurt other people because we feel bad when we see other people suffering (Kagan, 1984).

Still another criticism is that Kohlberg based his theory originally on studies of an all-male population. Carol Gilligan (1977, 1979) maintains that women and men approach moral decisions differently. Men focus mostly on rights and duties; women focus more on caring and relationships. When asked about the moral dilemma in Table 6.4, most men focus on rights, justice, and the relative values of human life and property values. Such answers may meet the criteria for stage 5 or 6. Many women respond to the same question in a different way: "If Heinz steals the drug, he will end up in jail, where he can no longer help his wife at all. Besides, the druggist will be angry and will never help them again. Couldn't Heinz talk to the druggist again or try to raise the money some other way?" Instead of citing an abstract principle, women consider how a particular act will affect each of the individuals. An answer based on how an act affects individuals is likely to be cate-

gorized as stage 3. But is men's way of reasoning, focusing on rights and justice, the only valid way to determine morality? Is it not equally valid to make decisions based on caring?

According to Gilligan, it is unfair to evaluate a woman's moral reasoning by the same method that we use to evaluate a man's. She has proposed alternative stages of moral development, which she claims characterize women's approaches (Table 6.5).

Gilligan's work has prompted much additional investigation into sex differences in moral reasoning. For the most part, studies have found that men and women do not differ greatly or consistently in their level of moral reasoning or in how they approach moral dilemmas (Brabeck, 1983). In general, women as well as men are concerned about justice; men as well as women are concerned about caring relationships. Still, even if the sexes do not differ significantly, individuals do. Some people focus mostly on abstract, general principles such as justice, while others focus mostly on how various decisions would affect individual people and their relationships. Even a given individual may approach some problems one way and other problems the other way.

SUMMARY

1. According to Jean Piaget, children's thought processes are more intuitive, less logical, and more egocentric than adults' thought processes are. (page 192)

2. Piaget described four stages of development of thought processes and knowledge. Children progress through those stages in order. (page 194)

3. We can teach children to give correct answers to questions that they ordinarily cannot answer until a later stage of development. (page 201)

4. Young children do not always use all the abilities they have. Although children in the preoperational stage ordinarily fail to demonstrate conservation of number, it is clear from other tasks that they do understand the concept of number. (page 201)

5. Lawrence Kohlberg contended that moral reasoning also can be described in terms of stages. According to Kohlberg, a person's moral reasoning should be evaluated on the basis of the reasons the person gives for a decision, rather than on the basis of the decision itself. (page 202)

SUGGESTION FOR FURTHER READING

Wadsworth, B. J. (1989). *Piaget's theory of cognitive and affective development* (4th ed.). White Plains, NY: Longman. A clear description of Piaget's main contributions.

TABLE 6.5 Carol Gilligan's Stages of Moral Development	
Stage	Basis for Deciding Right from Wrong
Preconventional	What is helpful or harmful to myself?
Conventional	What is helpful or harmful to other people?
Postconventional	What is helpful or harmful to myself as well as to others?

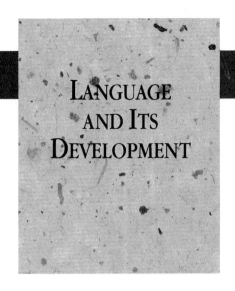

LANGUAGE AND ITS DEVELOPMENT

How do children learn language?
Do they just imitate people or do they learn the rules of language?

———————

Rats can learn mazes about as fast as humans can. Given enough practice, a chimpanzee or an elephant can learn to perform some rather complicated tasks. Apparently other species share the ability to reason—at least to some degree.

And yet the achievements of humans far surpass those of other species. We build bridges, discover cures for diseases, cultivate crops, write and read psychology textbooks, and put other species into zoos. What enables us to do so much more than other animals?

One answer to that question is language, a complex system that enables us to convert our thoughts into words and to convert other people's words into thoughts. By age 3, almost all children have learned language well enough to put it to some very important uses: They use it to acquire knowledge. ("Don't touch the stove!" "Stay away from the poi-

son ivy.") They use it to inform others. ("Swing me around some more, Daddy!" "*Not so fast,* Daddy!") A few years later they are using language to learn history, science, and the accumulated knowledge and wisdom of humanity.

THE COMPONENTS OF LANGUAGE

We can describe language, up to a point, in terms of simple elements: words and grammar. Words consist of units called phonemes and morphemes. A **phoneme** is a unit of sound. For example, *cat* has three phonemes (*c, a, t*); *breathe* has four (*b, r,* long *e, th*). A **morpheme** is the smallest unit of a word that has meaning. *Cat* has one morpheme (the whole word); *cats* has two morphemes (*cat* and *s*). (The final *s* is a unit of meaning because it indicates that the word is plural.)

Grammar is a system that enables us to use language. Grammar has two parts—semantics and syn-

In the form of print, hand signals, and talk, language touches nearly every aspect of our lives. Can you imagine what human life would be like without language?

Jazz improvisation is in some ways analogous to the productivity of everyday speech. Just as the jazz player improvises over the basic structure of a tune, and just as the player has almost limitless possibilities for varying that structure in improvising, there is also an unlimited variety of possible sentences in a language—countless ways we can vary the basic structure, content, and rules. The players pictured here are the Preservation Hall Jazz Band.

tax. **Semantics** is a set of rules for deriving meaning. For example, if someone shows you an odd-shaped thing and calls it a *wug,* you know at once that the word *wugs* means more than one of them. **Syntax** is a set of rules for linking words into sentences. For example, in English we typically arrange words in the order *noun—verb—direct object.*

Concept Check

6. *How many phonemes are in the word* thoughtfully? *How many morphemes? Is the English rule "add* -ed *to make a past tense" an example of semantics or syntax? Is the English rule "put the adjective before the noun" an example of semantics or syntax? (Check your answers on page 235.)*

Syntax and Sentence Formation

Syntax varies greatly from one language to another. English syntax relies heavily on rules of word order that we take for granted until we try to learn another language with different rules. For example, "Do your homework now" is a good English sentence because it follows the rules for word order. "Now do your homework" is also a good sentence. "Do now your homework" is awkward. "Now your homework do" is even more awkward. "Your now homework do" violates the rules for word order so thoroughly that

a listener is likely to regard it as a string of unrelated words.

Consider the following string of words: *Jeff, Susan, always, crazy, like, drove.* With just those six words, we can form sentences with entirely different meanings: Jeff drove Susan crazy like always. Jeff always drove like crazy Susan. Susan, like crazy Jeff, always drove.

Just how do people put words together into sentences? Before we start to speak, we ordinarily plan a group of words at a time, not just one word at a time. The simplest evidence for this conclusion comes from the phenomenon of Spoonerisms (Lashley, 1951). A **Spoonerism**, named after William Spooner, a professor at Oxford University, is an exchange of parts of two or more words, usually the initial sounds. For instance, Spooner is reported to have said "Our queer old dean" when he meant to say "Our dear old queen" and "You tasted the whole worm" when he meant "You wasted the whole term." The fact that people sometimes switch parts of words indicates that they plan the whole sequence of words together rather than one word at a time.

Not only do we say words as groups but we also hear and understand them as groups. When you hear a word in an ambiguous context, you may not know what meaning to give it. Was it *bred* or *bread*? But when you hear "butter and…," you hear the group as "butter and bread." When someone says, "Josephine had two jobs. She sold butter and _____ horses," you hear it as "…butter and bred.…"

The Productivity of Language

Language is *productive*—that is, we can use language to express a never-ending variety of new ideas. Every day we say and hear a few stock sentences, such as, "Nice weather we're having," "Have a nice day," and "Let's get something to eat." We also produce sentences that probably have never been said before, although we cannot specify *which* sentences those are.

The number of possible sentences in English alone is staggering—about 10^{30} sentences of 20 words or fewer. If every human on the planet produced a new sentence every second of every day for an entire century, they would come nowhere near reaching that total. Try this exercise (Slobin, 1979): Pick any sentence of 10 to 20 words from any book you choose. How long would you have to keep reading, in that book or any other, until you found exactly the same sentence again?

In short, it is impossible to imagine that we memorize all the sentences we will ever use. Instead, we must learn rules for making sentences and for interpreting other people's sentences. Noam Chomsky

(1980) has described those rules as a **transformational grammar**, which is a system for converting a deep structure into a surface structure. The **deep structure** is the underlying logic of the language. The **surface structure** is the sequence of words as they are actually spoken or written. According to this theory, whenever we speak we transform the deep structure of the language into a surface structure. Two surface structures may resemble each other without representing the same deep structure, or they may represent the same deep structure without resembling each other.

For example, "John is eager to please" has nearly the same surface structure as "John is easy to please." Yet the deep structures are quite different; in the first sentence John is doing the pleasing, and in the second sentence John is being pleased.

Transformational grammar consists of a set of rules for recognizing which surface structures are equivalent to one another—that is, which ones represent the same deep structure. The critical point about transformational grammar is the idea that we learn rules of how to make sentences and how to interpret them; we do not simply memorize all the sentences we shall ever use.

Ordinarily, when we listen to language, we process its deep structure—that is, its meaning—and only briefly attend to its surface structure (Sachs, 1967). To illustrate: One of the following sentences repeats a sentence you read a moment ago. Without peeking, can you remember which one it was?

1. Yet the deep structures are quite different; in the first sentence John is doing the pleasing, and in the second sentence John is being pleased.

2. Yet the deep structures are quite different; in one sentence John is being pleased and in the other John is doing the pleasing.

3. Yet the surface structures are quite different; in one sentence John is said to be eager, and in the other he is said to be easy.

If you are like most people, you had trouble remembering whether it was 1 or 2. (If you thought it was 3, you might want to read the last few paragraphs again.) Generally, once people understand a sentence, they remember its meaning, not its word-for-word sequence.

Understanding a sentence is a complex matter that requires knowledge about the world. For example, consider the following sentences:

1. I'm going to buy a pet hamster at the store, if it's open.

2. I'm going to buy a pet hamster at the store, if it's healthy.

You understand at once that *it* in the first sentence refers to the store and in the second sentence to the hamster. Nothing about the sentence structure tells you that. (If you were communicating with a computer or a being from another planet, you would have to specify what each *it* meant.) In short, language comprehension depends on assumptions that the speaker and the listener—or writer and reader—share.

HOW CHILDREN LEARN LANGUAGE

We seem to be born with some assumptions that simplify the task of learning a language. Consider how hard the task would be if we could make no assumptions about a language we were trying to learn: A creature from the planet Zipton is trying to teach you to speak Ziptonese. He/she/it points to your foot and says, "*GzmnUnkxl.*" Does that word mean *foot* in general, or does it mean your particular foot, some specific type of foot, or either a hand or a foot? Or does it refer to the color of your foot, its shape, or maybe its smell? Perhaps it refers to the relationship of your foot to the ground. Or maybe it is a command to do something (but what?) with your foot.

If you could make no assumptions whatever about the Ziptonese language, the task of learning to understand it would be almost hopeless. Yet almost all children manage to learn their parents' language reasonably well by the time they are 3 or 4. To account for that feat, many psychologists have suggested that children must begin with certain built-in assumptions that are not based entirely on experience—for instance, the distinction between nouns and verbs (Hoff-Ginsberg & Shatz, 1982).

Even young children have some general assumptions about their language. Ellen Markman and Jean Hutchinson (1984) showed 2-year-old and 3-year-old children pictures of common objects, gave the objects nonsense names, and then found out what other objects the children would apply those names to. For example, they called a birthday cake a *zig*. Then they showed pictures of a chocolate cake and a birthday present and asked which of them was another zig. Eighty-three percent of the children chose the chocolate cake. Evidently even children at this age know that a particular word applies to various objects in the same category.

Stages of Language Development

Language development in children follows a distinct sequence. It seems likely, though we have no

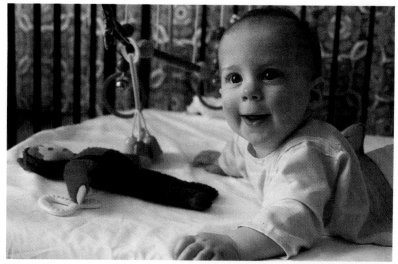

TABLE 6.6	Stages of Language Development in Children
Average Age	**Language Abilities**
3 months	Random vocalizations and cooing
6 months	Babbling
1 year	More babbling; some language comprehension; probably a few words, including "Mama"
1½ years	Some individual words, mostly nouns, but no phrases
2 years	Large vocabulary (more than 50 words); many 2-word phrases; no sentences
2½ years	Good language comprehension; longer phrases and short sentences; still many errors
3 years	Vocabulary around a thousand words; fewer errors; longer sentences
4 years	Close to basic adult speech competence

direct evidence, that this development reflects the gradual maturation of specialized areas of the brain.

Table 6.6 lists the average ages at which children reach various stages of language ability (Lenneberg, 1969; Moskowitz, 1978). Although there is great variation from one child to another, the rate of language development is not closely related to intelligence. A child who advances through these stages faster or slower than the average is not necessarily more intelligent or less intelligent than the average child.

Infants begin by babbling. For the first six months or so, there is no indication that their babbling is influenced by what they hear. Deaf infants babble as much as hearing infants do. Beyond about age 6 months, infants begin to modify their babbling to match what they hear. Hearing infants babble more, and deaf infants babble less.

By the time they are a year old, infants begin to understand language and most of them can say at least a word or two. One of the first sounds, for just about every infant anywhere in the world, is *muh*. Parents the world over have defined *muh-muh* (or something similar to it) as meaning "mother." Among the other early sounds common throughout the world are *duh, puh,* and *buh*. The sound of the letter *s* and certain other sounds are almost impossible for infants to pronounce at this stage. In many languages, the word for father is similar to *daddy* or *papa. Baba* is the word for grandmother in several languages.

In short, infants tell their parents what words to use for certain concepts as often as parents tell their infants.

By age 1½, most toddlers are speaking in 1-word sentences. Their vocabulary may be small or large—the average is about 50 words—but they almost never link words together. Thus a toddler might say "Daddy" or "bye-bye" but never "Bye-bye, Daddy." These 1-word utterances generally convey a great deal of information, however, and parents can usually make out their meaning from the context. "Mama" might mean "That's a picture of Mama," "Take me to Mama," "Mama went away and left me here," or "Mama, get me something to eat." Most of the words children use at this stage are nouns, along with a few verbs and still fewer adjectives. Their speech consists mostly of words for objects and actions, corresponding to what Piaget said was central to children's thinking at this age (Rice, 1989).

Some toddlers follow a pattern of language development different from the usual one (Nelson, 1981). Instead of speaking one word at a time and learning the names of objects, they speak poorly articulated, compressed sentences, such as "Do-it-again" or "I-like-read-Goodnight-Moon." At first these expressions are so poorly pronounced that adults, unless they listen carefully, may not realize that the child is doing anything but babbling. Children who start off by generating complex requests and phrases tend to do so consistently over much of the period of language development (Nelson, Baker, Denninger, Bonvillian, & Kaplan, 1985).

At about age 2, children start to produce many 2-word phrases (see examples in Table 6.7). Part of what children say at this age is imitative, and they pick up phrases very rapidly. In one study, a 20-month-old child asked the experimenter for an extra cookie and was teasingly told, "Okay, one for the road." On her next visit, the child ate one cookie and then asked, "One for the road?" (Nelson, 1985).

Still, even at this early stage, much of what children say is creative rather than just imitative. It is unlikely that they have ever heard their parents say, "More page," "Allgone sticky," or "Allgone outside." Such statements are contrary to adult speech habits and adult thought. A child who says "Allgone outside" seems to be saying that the outside is not there any more. (As Piaget said, young children do seem to think differently from adults.)

By age 2½ to 3 years, most children are generating full sentences. However, some peculiarities persist, varying from child to child. Many children have their own rules for making negative sentences. One of the most common is to add *no* or *not* to the beginning or end of a sentence, such as, "No I want to go to bed!" One little girl made her nega-

TABLE 6.7 Sample Two-Word Phrases Spoken by a 2-Year-Old Child

Phrase	Meaning
Mommy bath.	Mommy is taking a bath.
Throw Daddy.	Throw it to Daddy.
More page.	Don't stop reading.
More high.	More food is up there on top.
Allgone sticky.	My hands have been washed.
Allgone outside.	Someone closed the door.
No hug!	I'm angry at you!

tives just by saying something louder and at a higher pitch; for instance, if she shrieked, "I want to share my toys," she meant, "I do not want to share my toys." Presumably she had learned this "rule" by remembering that people screamed at her when they told her not to do something. My son Sam made negatives at this stage by adding the word *either* to the end of a sentence: "I want to eat lima beans *either*." Apparently he had heard people say, "I don't want to do that either," and had decided that an *either* at the end of the sentence made it an emphatic negative.

At this same age, children act as if they were applying grammatical rules. (I say "as if" because they cannot state the rules. By the same token, baseball players who anticipate exactly where a fly ball will come down act "as if" they understood complex physics and calculus.) For example, a child may learn the word *feet* at an early age and then, after learning other plurals, abandon it in favor of *foots*. Later, he or she begins to compromise by saying "feets," "footses," or "feetses" before eventually returning to "feet." Children at this stage say many things they have never heard anyone else say, such as "The mans comed" or "The womans goed and doed something." Clearly, they are applying rules of how to form plurals and past tenses, although they overgeneralize those rules. My son David invented the word *shis* to mean "belonging to a female." He had apparently generalized the rule "He—his, she—shis." My daughter, Robin, avoided the his/her problem for a long time by inventing the terms *hes* and *shes*.

Children gradually learn the rules of grammar even though most parents make little effort to correct their mistakes. In fact, many parents find their children's errors rather charming. One child once said, "Mommy, Tommy fall my truck down." The mother turned with a smile and said, "Tommy, did you fall Stevie's truck down?" By age 4, most children have nearly mastered the use of language. Their vocabulary is still limited, and they still make an occasional irregular statement, such as "Are we all out of cookies or are we still in them?" And adults can still confuse them by speaking in complex, compound, or passive sentences. For most purposes, however, these children are using language well.

Concept Check

7. *At what age do children begin to string words into novel combinations that they have never heard anyone say before? Why do psychologists believe that even very young children learn some of the rules of grammar? (Check your answers on page 235.)*

Language Development as Maturation

Language development depends largely on maturation rather than on the mere accumulation of experience. Lenneberg (1967, 1969) supports this conclusion with the following evidence:

- The sequence of stages outlined in Table 6.6 is about the same in all known cultures. The average ages differ a bit from one culture to another, but the various stages are easily recognizable worldwide, in all languages, at approximately the same ages.

- The speed at which children progress through the stages correlates poorly with their total exposure to language. When parents try to accelerate their children's progress by talking to them constantly, the children may acquire a slightly larger vocabulary than usual, but they still go through each stage at about the normal age. The hearing children of deaf parents are exposed to very little spoken language and fail to learn language at the normal pace. If they have some contact with relatives and neighbors, they progress through the various stages almost on schedule.

- Identical twins go through the stages at almost identical rates.

- Retarded children progress through the same stages as normal children do but at a slower rate. Once they reach puberty, their progress stops at whatever stage they have attained. Retarded children may still learn new words, but if they are at, say, the two-word stage, they will never advance to the sentence stage. The maturation of language ability seems to stop when physical maturation stops.

ATTEMPTS TO TEACH LANGUAGE TO CHIMPANZEES

Almost all human children, even many retarded children, acquire language skills in their first few years regardless of whether their parents make any real effort to teach them. Although closely related to humans genetically, chimpanzees have no language Why not? Researchers have tried to teach chimpanzees some approximation of human language, partly to discover the differences between chimpanzees and humans, partly to discover what learning a language requires, and partly to deepen their understanding of language itself.

Psychologists have alternated between two extreme views on whether it is possible to teach language to chimpanzees. During the 1920s and 1930s a number of psychologists were optimistic about the possibility. Winthrop Kellogg and Luella Kellogg (1933), psychologists at Florida State University, tried to rear a baby chimpanzee, Gua, in the same way as they were rearing their son Donald, who was about the same age. Gua did learn certain human habits, including drinking from a cup and eating with a spoon. She never learned to speak, however, although she seemed to understand a few spoken words.

Later, another couple (Hayes, 1951) reared a chimpanzee named Viki, giving her their undivided attention and free run of the house. (Imagine what their house looked like. Visitors sometimes asked whether the Hayeses lived there too or just the chimpanzee.) Viki, like Gua, learned a number of human habits and understood some spoken language, but her own speaking vocabulary was limited to some poorly articulated approximations to "cup," "up," and "mama."

With the failure of these and other attempts to teach chimpanzees to talk, most psychologists concluded that chimpanzees lack the necessary intelligence to learn to speak; they decided that speech requires a certain threshold size of brain, somewhere between that of a chimpanzee and that of a human.

Then in the 1960s and 1970s, opinion swung back the other way. Allen Gardner and Beatrice Gardner (1969), psychologists at the University of Nevada, tried to teach a chimpanzee, Washoe, to communicate by the sign language deaf people use. Sign language is closer to the hand gestures that chimpanzees use naturally, and it does not require them to imitate human voice sounds, for which their vocal tracts are poorly adapted. Washoe started slowly, but eventually she learned the symbols for about a hundred words. She occasionally linked symbols

a

b

c

d

Speaking is physically impossible for chimpanzees, but some psychologists have tried to teach them to communicate by gesture or symbols. (a) The Premacks' chimp uses a board to communicate. (b) Viki in her human home, helping with the housework. After years with the Hayeses, she could make only a few sounds similar to English words. (c) Kanzi, a pygmy chimp, presses symbols to indicate words. Pygmy chimps have shown the most promising ability to acquire language among the higher primates. (d) A chimp signing toothbrush. *(e) Roger Fouts with Alley the chimp, who is signing* lizard. *Sociologist Rodney Stark notes, "If we are the king of beasts, we talked our way into the title" (1989, page 141).*

e

together into meaningful combinations, such as "cry hurt food" for a radish, and "baby in my drink" when someone put a doll into her cup.

At about the same time, Ann Premack and David Premack (1972) taught chimpanzees to communicate by means of colored magnets that represented words, including such complex relational words as *same, if . . . then,* and *is the color of.* Other investigators reported success with similar systems. For a

while it appeared, at least to some observers, that chimpanzees could come very close to mastering human language when they were permitted to use visual symbols and hand gestures rather than spoken words.

Then skepticism set in once again. Careful analysis of the chimpanzees' use of sign language revealed that much of it was an imitation of symbols their human trainers had used recently (Terrace, Petitto,

Sanders, & Bever, 1979). Seldom did the chimpanzees string symbols together spontaneously to make a meaningful combination. There is no doubt that chimpanzees can learn the meaning of many symbols, including symbols for specific concepts like *banana* and for broader categories like *food* (Savage-Rumbaugh, Rumbaugh, Smith, & Lawson, 1980). However, they do not use those symbols in the same way a child does. A child with a large vocabulary strings words together to make original combinations and short sentences. Chimpanzees only occasionally put together original combinations (Pate & Rumbaugh, 1983; Terrace et al., 1979; Thompson & Church, 1980).

Researchers have reported spectacular results for the language abilities of another species of chimpanzee, the rare and endangered pygmy chimpanzee (Savage-Rumbaugh, McDonald, Sevcik, Hopkins, & Rubert, 1986). A few pygmy chimps have learned to press symbols to represent words. Unlike the common chimpanzees studied earlier, pygmy chimps learn a good deal just by watching others use the symbols. They frequently use the symbols to name objects they see, even when they are not making a request. They string symbols together into more original combinations than common chimpanzees typically do, and two of them seem to understand some spoken English even though they have never been instructed in it.

Although the controversy about whether or not chimpanzees can acquire language will probably continue, the research generated by that possibility has already led to a method of teaching language to people who would otherwise be unable to learn it. Many people who cannot speak for various reasons, including brain damage, can learn to communicate by using such visual symbols as colored magnets to represent words.

Concept Check

8. *Why are some psychologists hesitant to conclude that certain chimpanzees have been taught language? (Check your answer on page 235.)*

SOME QUESTIONS AND ANSWERS ABOUT LANGUAGE

Can any other animals besides chimpanzees and their relatives learn to use language symbols? Yes, at least to a limited extent. Dolphins have been taught to respond both to visual symbols and to computer-generated underwater sounds. They learned a number of words that could be combined into commands such as "bottom hoop fetch surface pipe," meaning go to the bottom, fetch the hoop, take it to the sur-

Learning a second language during childhood will have advantages and drawbacks for this Western child growing up in Indonesia.

face, and put it on the pipe (Herman, Richards, & Wolz, 1984). In one study, California sea lions learned the meaning of arm and hand gestures for such concepts as *large* and *small*. They would respond to the gesture *large-ball-mouth* by touching their mouth to the largest ball available (Schusterman & Krieger, 1986). Note that neither the dolphins nor the sea lions ever produced any symbols; they merely responded to symbols that humans presented.

Does that mean that dolphins and sea lions can comprehend language to some degree? That depends on how we define language *comprehension*. They learned the meaning of symbols and were able to respond correctly to a few novel combinations. Does that constitute language, or should we insist on a higher standard? (Depending on our definition, we can either affirm or deny that chimpanzees can learn language.)

If children weren't exposed to any language at all, would they make up one of their own? People have been puzzling over that question for centuries. Obviously, we cannot set up an experiment to find the answer.

Some parents, however, have unintentionally conducted such an experiment on their own children. Parents of deaf children, for example, sometimes fail to teach their children sign language, either because they are unaware that the children are deaf or because they try to teach the children spoken language despite their deafness. If, as often happens, the children fail to learn spoken language, they are effectively isolated from all exposure to language. The results are consistent: The children make up their own sign language (Goldin-Meadow, 1985). As they grow older, they make the system more complex, linking signs together into sentences with some consistency of word order. Most of the children manage to teach their system, or at least part of it, to one or both parents. Children who spend much time together adopt each other's signs and eventually develop a unified system.

Does learning a second language improve or impair one's use of the first language? Learning a second language during childhood slightly impairs performance on certain tasks, such as looking at an item in isolation and deciding whether it is a word or not (Ransdell & Fischler, 1987). Apparently, some nonwords resemble words in the second language and that resemblance causes confusion. But people who are fluent in two languages show increased flexibility in certain problem-solving tasks (Hakuta & Diaz, 1985).

Do children learn a second language faster than adults do? Although it is widely believed that children learn a second language faster than adults do, most studies suggest the opposite: Adults learn faster (Ekstrand, 1979; Rosenman, 1987). The advantage children have is that they may master the foreign pronunciation. Even when adults learn a language well, they generally continue to speak with a noticeable foreign accent.

Why do some people stutter? The causes of stuttering probably differ from one person to another, and in most cases the causes are simply unknown (Johanssen & Victor, 1986). Emotional stress generally aggravates stuttering, but it does not explain why certain people stutter and others do not. One possibility is that stuttering may be related to having control of speech by both hemispheres of the brain (Jones, 1966; Pinsky & McAdam, 1980; Sussman & MacNeilage, 1975). If both hemispheres control the speech muscles, then their messages may be out of synchrony and therefore impair the coordination of those muscles. Many stutterers stop stuttering when they sing; singing could be a way of synchronizing the two hemispheres.

Something to Think About

After many unsuccessful attempts to understand the chirping sounds dolphins produce, some investigators have concluded that the sounds do not really represent communication. On the assumption that the sounds *do* represent communication, suggest possible reasons why humans would have difficulty understanding them.

The sound spectrograph recordings show the repeated attempts of this stuttering child to vocalize a word. Stutterers have trouble controlling the muscles of speech, but the ultimate source of the problem lies in the brain, not the muscles.

2. Language is productive; we learn the rules for producing sentences and invent original sentences rather than attempting to memorize all the sentences we might need. (page 208)

3. Language comprehension depends on knowledge and assumptions the speaker and the listener share. (page 209)

4. Children progress through a sequence of stages of language capability. Most 1-year-olds can say a word or two and understand some of what is said to them. Most 4-year-olds can use language well for most purposes. (page 209)

5. As soon as children are capable of linking words together, they make new and creative combinations. They discover and apply some of the rules of the language such as the rules for making plurals. They often overgeneralize those rules and say such words as "womans." (page 211)

6. The development of the ability to learn language depends partly on biological maturation. (page 212)

7. Language is a human specialization, although chimpanzees can learn approximations of it. Chimpanzees can learn to use visual symbols for communication, though their performance does not match that of children. (page 212)

SUMMARY

1. Language consists of words and grammar. Words can be divided into parts: phonemes (units of sound) or morphemes (units of meaning). Grammar consists of semantics (rules of deriving meaning) and syntax (rules of how to string words into sentences). (page 207)

SUGGESTION FOR FURTHER READING

Slobin, D. I. (1979). *Psycholinguistics* (2nd ed.). Glenview, IL: Scott, Foresman. A review of how people learn and use language, with excellent and often entertaining examples.

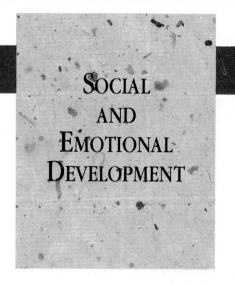

SOCIAL AND EMOTIONAL DEVELOPMENT

What are the special social and emotional problems that people face at different ages of life? What determines how we develop socially and emotionally?

You are a contestant on a new TV game show called "What's My Worry?" Behind the curtain is someone with an overriding concern. You are to identify that concern by questioning a psychologist who knows what it is. (You can neither see nor hear the person.) You must ask questions that can be answered with a single word or a short phrase. If you identify the concern correctly, you can win up to $50,000.

But there is one catch: The more questions you ask, the smaller your prize. If you guess correctly after one question, you win $50,000. After two questions, you win $25,000. And so on. It would be poor strategy to go on asking questions until you were sure of the answer; instead, you should ask one or two questions and then guess.

What would your first question be? Mine would be: "How old is this person?" Every age has its own characteristic worries, concerns, and decisions. Every age also brings its own special opportunities and pleasures. People of each age have their own ways of socializing with others and their own emotional needs.

ERIKSON'S AGES OF HUMAN DEVELOPMENT

How people spend their time and what they think about are largely determined by their current role in life—preschool child, student, worker, or retired person. And a person's role in life is determined largely, though not entirely, by his or her age. In many ways a 22-year-old parent with a full-time job has more in common with older people than with other 22-year-olds who are still students. To understand why people behave as they do, we need to know the decisions they are facing at their current stage of life.

Erik Erikson, a pioneer in child psychoanalysis, divided the human lifespan into eight *ages,* each with its own social and emotional conflicts. First is the age of the newborn infant, whose main conflict is **basic trust versus mistrust**. The infant asks, in effect, "Is my social world predictable and supportive?" The most significant step in the social development of a newborn infant is arriving at a basic trust that the parents will meet his or her needs. An infant whose early environment is supportive, nurturing, and loving will form an attachment to the parents that will also influence future relationships with other people (Erikson, 1963).

Erikson's second age is the age of the toddler, 1 to 3 years old, whose main conflict is **autonomy versus shame and doubt.** The toddler faces the issue, "Can I do things by myself or must I always rely on others?" Experiencing independence for the first

Erik H. Erikson.

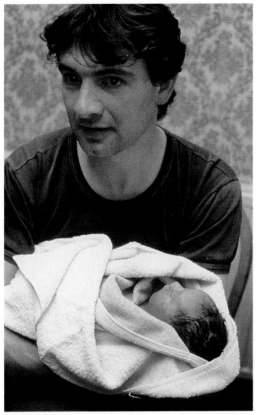

time, the toddler begins to walk and talk, to be toilet trained, to obey some instructions and defy others, and to make choices. Depending on how the parents react, children may develop a healthy feeling of autonomy (independence) or a self-critical sense of shame and doubt that they can accomplish things on their own.

Erikson's third age is the age of the preschool child, whose main conflict is **initiative versus guilt**. At ages 3 to 6, as children begin to broaden their horizons, their boundless energy comes into conflict with parental restrictions. Sooner or later the child breaks something or makes a big mess. The child faces the question, "Am I good or bad?" In contrast to the previous stage, where the child was concerned about what he or she is *capable* of doing, at this state the child is concerned about the morality or acceptability of his or her actions.

In the fourth age, preadolescence (about ages 6 to 12), **industry versus inferiority** is the main conflict. The question is, "Am I successful or worthless?" Children widen their focus from the immediate family to society at large and begin to prepare for adult roles. They fantasize about the great successes ahead, and they begin to compete with their peers in an effort to excel in the activities of their age. Children who feel that they are failing may be plagued with long-lasting feelings of inferiority.

*D*aughter or son, student, mother or father—your role usually reflects your age. In Erikson's eight ages of development, the infant's main concern is trust. In the second age, the toddler—able to talk and walk—faces the conflict of independence versus self-critical doubt. For preschool children, initiative versus guilt is the chief conflict.

Children who take pride in their accomplishments gain a long-lasting feeling of competence.

Erikson's fifth age is adolescence (the early teens), in which the main conflict is **identity versus role confusion**. Adolescents begin to seek independence from their parents and try to answer the question,

In grade school, children compete for recognition of their worth. During Erikson's fifth age, adolescence, concern shifts from what you can do to who you are. In the age of young adulthood, which often coincides with attending college, conflict centers on intimacy versus isolation.

TABLE 6.8 Erikson's Ages of Human Development

Age	Main Conflict	Typical Question
Infant	Basic trust versus mistrust	Is my social world predictable and supportive?
Toddler (ages 1–3)	Autonomy versus shame and doubt	Can I do things by myself or must I always rely on others?
Preschool child (ages 3–6)	Initiative versus guilt	Am I good or bad?
Preadolescent (ages 6–12)	Industry versus inferiority	Am I successful or worthless?
Adolescent (early teens)	Identity versus role confusion	Who am I?
Young adult (late teens and early 20s)	Intimacy versus isolation	Shall I share my life with another person or shall I live alone?
Middle adult (late 20s to retirement)	Generativity versus stagnation	Will I succeed in my life, both as a parent and as a worker?
Older adult (after retirement)	Ego integrity versus despair	Have I lived a full life or have I failed?

The often conflicting demands of family and work shape the central concern of midlife adults. Those who reach old age may avoid despair and achieve integrity (wisdom) by accepting their life.

"Who am I?" or "Who will I be?" They may eventually settle on a satisfactory answer—an identity—or they may continue to experiment with goals and life-styles—a state of role confusion.

Erikson's sixth age is young adulthood (the late teens and the 20s), in which **intimacy versus isolation** is the main conflict. Shall I share my life with another person or shall I live alone? Young adults who marry or who live with a friend find that they have to adjust their habits in order to make the relationship succeed. Those who choose to live alone may experience loneliness and pressure from their parents and friends to find a suitable partner.

Erikson's seventh age is middle adulthood (from the late 20s through retirement), in which the major conflict is **generativity versus stagnation.** Will I produce something of real value? Will I succeed in my life, both as a parent and as a worker? Or will the quality of my life simply dwindle with the years?

Erikson's eighth age is old age (the years after retirement), in which the main conflict is **ego integrity versus despair.** Have I lived a full life or have I failed? Integrity is a state of contentment about one's life, past, present, and future. Despair is a state of disappointment about the past and the present, coupled with fear of the future. Table 6.8 summarizes Erikson's ages.

Is Erikson's view of development correct? That is almost an unanswerable question. Some psychologists find Erikson's description of development a useful way to organize our thinking about human life; others find it less useful; almost no one

finds it easy to test scientifically. Erikson described development; he did not explain it. For example, he hardly addressed the question of how or why a person progresses from one stage to the next.

Still, Erikson called attention to the fact that the social and emotional concerns of one age differ from those of another, and his writings inspired interest in development across the entire lifespan.

Now let's take a closer look at selected issues in social and emotional development from infancy to old age. Beyond the primary conflicts that Erikson highlighted, development is marked by a succession of other significant problems.

Something to Think About

Suppose you disagreed with Erikson's analysis; for example, suppose you believed that the main concern of young adults was not "intimacy versus isolation" but "earning money versus not earning money" or "finding meaning in life versus meaninglessness." How might you determine whether your theory or Erikson's is more correct?

INFANCY: FORMING THE FIRST ATTACHMENTS

Before the late 1950s, if someone had asked, "What causes an infant to develop an attachment to its mother?" almost all psychologists would have replied, "Mother's milk." They were wrong.

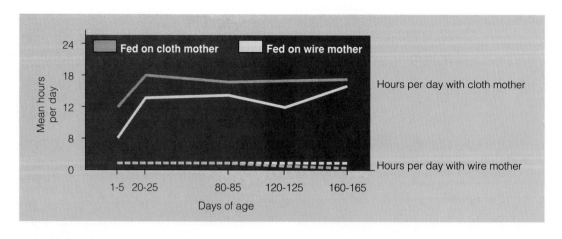

FIGURE 6.19

Regardless of which artificial mother fed them, all the baby monkeys preferred the cloth mothers; the bottom two lines show hours per day with the wire mothers.

Studies of Attachment Among Monkeys

Attachment—a long-term feeling of closeness between a child and a care giver—depends on more than just being fed. Attachment is part of trust, in Erikson's sense of "trust versus mistrust." That attachment or trust comes only partly from the satisfaction of biological needs. It also depends on the emotional responses provoked by such acts as hugging.

FIGURE 6.20

When a baby monkey has a choice between two artificial mothers, one made of wire and one covered with cloth, it prefers to cling to the cloth mother. (From Harlow, 1958.)

The most impressive evidence comes from an experiment that Harry Harlow conducted with monkeys. Harlow (1958) separated eight newborn rhesus monkeys from their mothers and isolated each of them in a room containing two artificial mothers. Four of the infant monkeys had a wire mother equipped with a milk bottle in the breast position and a cloth mother with no bottle; the other four had a cloth mother with a bottle and a wire mother with no bottle. Harlow wanted to find out how much time the baby monkeys would spend with the artificial mother that fed them.

Figure 6.19 shows the mean number of hours per day that the monkeys spent with the two kinds of mothers. Regardless of whether they got their milk from the cloth mother (Figure 6.20) or from the wire mother, they all spent more than half their time clinging to the cloth mother and very little time with the wire mother. Evidently their attachment depended more on *contact comfort*—comfortable skin sensations—than on the satisfaction of their hunger or sucking needs.

At first Harlow thought that the cloth mothers were serving the infants' emotional needs adequately. He discovered, however, that the monkeys failed to develop normal social and sexual behavior (Harlow, Harlow, & Suomi, 1971). (See Figure 6.21a.) When he put one of the artificially reared males together with a normal, sexually receptive female, the male would show interest but would approach the female in abnormal ways, such as trying to mount her from the side instead of from the rear, until eventually the female gave up and walked away. When he placed artificially reared females with a sexually experienced male, the male would strut around and go through his usual seduction act but the females did not respond.

Eventually, some of the artificially reared females did become pregnant despite their lack of cooperation. When their babies were born, however, the mothers rejected every attempt the babies made to cling to them or to be nursed. Clearly, the monkeys that had been reared by artificial mothers did not know how to react to other monkeys.

But the harmful effects of early social isolation proved to be reversible. For two hours a day, Harry Harlow and Margaret Harlow (1965) put 6-month-old monkeys that had been reared by artificial mothers together with normally reared 3-month-old monkeys (Figure 6.21b). Other 6-month-old monkeys would reject the isolated monkeys, but 3-month-olds did not. At first the isolates hid in a corner, but the 3-month-old monkeys kept running up to them and clinging to them. Within weeks they were all playing together (Figure 6.21c), and within 6 months the previously isolated monkeys were behaving almost normally. Apparently the experience of playing with younger monkeys largely compensated for the early lack of social development.

Similar Studies of Human Attachment

What do the Harlows' studies mean for humans? Do they mean that an infant needs a mother's personal attention during the early months? The most we can say for sure is that an infant—monkey or human—should not be entrusted to the care of inanimate objects.

Human infants thrive on personal attention. In the early 1900s, many foundling homes and orphanages raised infants under conditions that were little better than those of the Harlows' monkeys. The supervisors, trained to believe that unnecessary stimulation should be avoided, ruled that each infant be kept in a crib in a narrow cubicle. The nurses seldom cuddled the infants or played with them, and the infants rarely had an opportunity even to see other babies.

In various institutions, 30 to 100% of the babies died within one year (Spitz, 1945, 1946). Those who survived were retarded in physical growth and in language and intellectual development; they were socially inept and unresponsive to their environment (Bowlby, 1952). We cannot ascribe these results solely to early social isolation because many of the children were ill to begin with, and a number of those who survived continued to be reared under poor conditions (Clarke & Clarke, 1976). Still, severe deprivation of human contact early in life clearly can be extremely harmful.

a

b

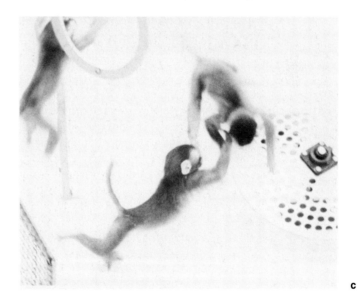

c

FIGURE 6.21

Much of what we learn and need depends on interaction with others. (a) This mother monkey reared in isolation ignores her baby. (b) A monkey reared with an artificial mother initially resists a younger monkey's attention. (c) After several weeks together, the older monkey plays with the younger one—a sign of recovery from its sterile upbringing. Monkeys, like humans, need much practice to develop normal social behaviors.

"Mommy" is a man: Today, as more mothers assume the role of family breadwinner, more fathers are staying home as the main care giver for their young children. Changing diapers is now an equal-opportunity occupation.

Concept Check

9. *In what way were the unstimulating institutions similar to the Harlows' artificial monkeys? (Check your answer on page 235.)*

CHILDHOOD: INFLUENCES ON SOCIAL DEVELOPMENT

Children develop in a social context made up of adults and other children. The family is particularly important. How children feel about themselves—good or bad, successful or worthless—depends to a large degree on their relationship with family members. Children in a loving family learn, "I am a lovable person." They also gain a sense of security. By playing with brothers, sisters, or other children, they begin to learn social skills. They also learn social skills by observation, especially by watching how their parents relate to each other. How do variations in early family environments affect a child's social and emotional development?

Development in a Nontraditional Family

For many years, psychologists assumed that most children grew up in a so-called traditional family, which consisted of a working father, a housekeeping mother, and one or more children. Today, only a small percentage of children in the United States and Canada grow up in such a family. An estimated 50% of all children eventually experience the divorce of their parents, a clear majority of mothers have at least a part-time job, and children grow up in a great variety of home environments.

Two-Paycheck Families In 1960, only one fifth of American mothers of preschool children had jobs outside the home. In the 1980s, half or more had jobs (Rubenstein, 1985). When both the father and the mother spend most of the day at work and have only a limited amount of time to spend with their children, how does that affect the child?

The results vary. Some mothers of young children work at unsatisfying jobs because they need the money. They tend to be unhappy about working; when they return home from work, they are not very cheerful or effective as mothers (Lamb, 1982). Other mothers work because they enjoy their careers. They return from work with high self-esteem; they make good use of the time they have available with their children. They become role models for their daughters, who are likely to develop career aspirations of their own (Hoffman, 1989).

Preschool children in two-paycheck families are left in various day-care arrangements. The effects on the children depend on the quality of the day care and the age of the child. When children less than a year old are entrusted to day-care centers where the staff is indifferent and unstable, the children are likely to feel insecure. When the day care is reasonably good, however, it is not clear whether the children are at a significant advantage or disadvantage compared to a child whose mother stays at home (Clarke-Stewart, 1989). Children who spend much of their first year of life in day care tend to be a bit "bossy," not very obedient to their mothers, and somewhat aggressive toward other children. They generally develop a number of social skills, however, and a good degree of self-confidence. The long-term consequences for their emotional development are unknown.

Fathers as Care Givers of Young Children Traditionally, mothers have spent more time than have fathers taking care of children, especially young children. But fathers have always played an important role (Lamb, 1974). They engage more often in vigorous, stimulating play with their children and serve as a role model for both sons and daughters. In homes where the father is absent or where the parents are hostile toward each other, the children often have difficulty relating to the opposite sex in later years.

More recently, some families have decided that the mother should work full time and that the father should be the primary caretaker for young children; other families have tried to divide the responsibilities equally. Fathers in such families resemble other fathers more than they resemble mothers. They are about as strict and punishing as more traditional fathers are (Radin, 1982). Although they play with their children more than the mothers do, they hug them less and talk to them less (Lamb, Frodi, Hwang, & Frodi, 1982). Generally, these untraditional fathers seem to make adequate parents, and their children seem to develop normally.

Parental Conflict and Divorce   Children who grow up in households where the parents are constantly fighting tend to develop anxiety and engage in emotional outbursts (Emery, 1982). If the parents stay together despite their hostility, the children's distress is long lasting. If they divorce, the children's distress is briefer but more intense.

Mavis Hetherington and her associates studied 72 middle-class, elementary-school children whose parents had been divorced and whose mothers had retained custody (Hetherington, Cox, & Cox, 1982). Hetherington found that both the children and the parents suffered considerable upheaval after the divorce, especially during the first year.

During this first year the children resorted to pouting and seeking attention. They were generally angry about their parents' divorce, and they let the parents know about it. One exasperated divorced mother said her relationship with her child was "like getting bitten to death by ducks." Boys in particular became very aggressive toward other children, and much of their aggressive behavior was unprovoked and ineffective. After two years they became better adjusted, but by then they had been rejected by their peers. Boys who changed schools after the first year managed to escape their reputation and make a fresh start.

The degree of distress varied from one child to another. Generally, a child's distress was greater if the mother had not worked before the divorce and had taken a job immediately afterward—often an economic necessity. The children in such families felt they had lost both their father and mother. In the studies by Hetherington and her associates, boys showed more distress and more negative behavior than girls did, partly because the mothers retained custody of the children. When the father had custody, the boys reacted better than the girls did (Santrock, Warshak, & Elliott, 1982). However, because many other factors are at work, we cannot conclude that a father should always be granted custody of sons or that a mother should always be granted custody of daughters.

In the long run, the effects of divorce on the children vary (Hetherington, Stanley-Hagan, &

Sticks and stones": Children use name-calling to ostracize those who are different—"four eyes," "teacher's pet," "cry-baby." How children get along with their peers significantly influences their social and emotional development.

Anderson, 1989). Some of the children show emotional distress for a year or two and then gradually feel better. Some become especially strong and emotionally resilient because of the experience. Others continue to act depressed 5 or 10 years after the divorce. A few seem to do well for a while and then show signs of distress years later, especially during adolescence.

The Influence of Other Children

The social and emotional development of children depends in part on how successful they are in forming friendships with other children. Children with few friends tend to suffer low self-esteem and to do poorly in both schoolwork and athletics. (But does the lack of friends lead to poor performance or does poor performance lead to the lack of friends?)

The behavior of brothers and sisters also influences a child's development. Siblings can exert a positive influence by acting as teachers and playmates or a negative influence by acting in a hostile or abusive manner. They may also exert an indirect effect by influencing the behavior of the parents. For example, when a brother or sister has a major physical handicap, the parents are likely to become distressed and overworked. The healthy child in the family may react by being aggressive, impulsive,

and self-destructive and engaging in other attention-getting behavior (Breslau & Prabucki, 1987).

Many studies have been made of the effects of being a firstborn child or being born later. A number of those birth-order studies report that firstborn children do better in school, are more ambitious, are more honest, and have a greater need to affiliate with others. Children born later tend to be more popular, more independent, less conforming, better adjusted emotionally, and possibly more creative. These tendencies are slight and inconsistent, however, and much of the evidence is based on poorly conducted studies (Ernst & Angst, 1983; Schooler, 1972). Be skeptical of recommendations that parents should space their children many years apart in order to give each of them the alleged benefits of the firstborn.

Something to Think About

Psychologists have offered two explanations for the effects of birth order on behavior: (1) Depending on whether there are older, younger, or no other children in the family, each child is subjected to different social influences. (2) Because the mother undergoes physical changes, such as changes in her hormones after giving birth, younger children experience different prenatal influences from those experienced by the firstborn child. What kind of evidence would you need to decide whether one of these explanations was more satisfactory than the other?

FIGURE 6.22

From carrying books to committing crimes, women and men do many things differently for reasons that remain uncertain.

The Development of Gender Roles

On the average, males behave differently from females in many ways. Men are more likely than women to hit one another (Eagly & Steffen, 1986) and to swear. Women tend to know more than men do about flowers. Men and women generally carry books and packages in different ways (Figure 6.22). No doubt you can add many other differences to these generalizations. What is the origin of these differences?

Although some of these differences may be based in part on biological differences between the sexes, they are at least fostered (if not caused) by **gender roles**, the different behaviors that society generally expects of men and women. A *gender role* is the psychological aspect of being male or female, as opposed to *sex,* which is the biological aspect.

Every society has some division of labor between the sexes and therefore different expectations of how women and men will behave. Different societies have different attitudes toward what is men's work and what is women's work. In some societies, for example, men do the hunting while women gather fruits and vegetables. In industrialized Western societies, men have traditionally held jobs away from

the home while women have cared for children and taken care of the home. To prepare people for their adult roles, a society teaches boys and girls what is expected of them, beginning at an early age.

Since about 1960, the trend has been for more women to work outside the home in our society. Still, society tends to teach children about the gender roles and expectations prevalent in the past. We have moved away from those expectations to some extent, but old traditions do not change rapidly.

Gender roles prescribe different behaviors for different situations (Deaux & Major, 1987). For example, society expects men to be more willing (and able) to help a stranger change a flat tire; it expects women to be more willing to help people who need long-term nurturing support (Eagly & Crowley, 1986).

In our society, females and males learn about gender roles in several ways (Frieze, Parsons, Johnson, Ruble, & Zellman, 1978). Parents begin to socialize their children into their male or female roles at an early age by according them different clothing, hair styles, and toys. Children learn "I'm a boy" or "I'm a girl" before they even know what the distinction means. Parents buy different kinds of toys for girls than for boys. Girls get more dolls; boys get more toy trucks and cars. The choice of toys in turn determines how much the parents talk with the children while they are playing. When parents and their children play with dolls, they talk a great deal; when

they play with cars and trucks, they talk less (O'Brien & Nagle, 1987).

Children also learn from role models. Boys tend to imitate their father, and girls tend to imitate their mother. Children also pay attention to role models outside the home. For instance, a girl who goes to a female pediatrician may think of becoming a doctor herself.

Finally, children learn about gender roles from other children. Even parents who try to avoid gender stereotypes find that their children come back from the playground or from school with strong prejudices about what boys do and what girls do.

Gender roles tend to limit the choices children feel will be open to them in later life. Deeply rooted stereotypes make life difficult for those who do not fit them. For example, a man who is more interested in the arts than in athletics may be made to feel that he is not a "real man." A woman whose strength lies in mathematics or who is more interested in building a career than in raising a family may be discouraged from developing her abilities.

Divorce, birth order, and gender-role influences are examples of the many and subtle factors that modify a child's social and emotional development. Even children reared in the same family, whose parents tried to treat all their children the same, may have experiences that differ in important ways. Psychologists are just beginning to understand all the ways children learn their social and emotional behaviors.

Concept Check

10. *Which of the following (if any) are examples of people following gender roles? (Check your answer on page 235.)*
a. A woman's ability to nurse a baby
b. A boy's interest in playing football
c. A girl's interest in ballet
d. A man's beard growth

ADOLESCENCE

Adolescence begins when the body shows signs of sexual maturation. In North America, the mean ages are around 12 to 13 in girls and about a year or two later in boys. It is more difficult to say when adolescence ends. Adolescence merges into adulthood, and adulthood is more a state of mind than a condition of the body. Some 12-year-olds act like adults, and some 30-year-olds act like adolescents.

Adolescence is a time of transition from childhood to adulthood. Children think of themselves as part of their parents' family; young adults are ready to start their own family. Adolescents are somewhere in between, still closely tied to their parents but spending more and more time with their peer group. Adolescence is a time of "finding yourself," of determining "Who am I?" or "Who will I be?" As Erikson said, identity is a major issue at this age.

Identity Crisis

In some societies, children are expected eventually to enter the same occupation as their parents and to live in the same town. The parents may even choose marriage partners for their children. In such societies, adolescents have few major choices to make.

Getting a driver's license and buying a car are early steps into the adult world. For teens, a car represents freedom; it's also a status symbol.

Our society offers young people a great many choices. They can decide how much education to get, what job to seek, and where to live. They can decide whether to marry and whom and when. They can choose their own political and religious affiliation. They can choose their own standards of behavior for sex, alcohol, and drugs. In making each of these choices, they may face conflicting pressures from peers, parents, and teachers.

Adolescents, realizing that they must make such decisions within a few years, face an **identity crisis**. The search for identity or self-understanding may lead an adolescent in several directions (Marcia, 1980). **Identity foreclosure**, for example, is the passive acceptance of a role defined by one's parents. An adolescent's father may declare, for example, "When you graduate from high school, you will go on to college and study electrical plumbing, just as I did when I was your age. Then you will go into the family business with me." Adolescents who accept such parental prescriptions enjoy at least one advantage: They avoid the uncertainty and anxiety that other adolescents endure while trying to "find themselves."

Until fairly recently, identity foreclosure was the norm for most young women. Parents and society both decreed, "You will be a full-time wife and mother." Today, young women have greater freedom to choose what to do with their life. That greater freedom has made it more likely that they will experience an identity crisis during adolescence.

The search for identity may also lead to **role diffusion**. The uncertain sense of identity and the low self-esteem that many adolescents experience may prompt them to experiment with a variety of roles, alternately playing the "party goer," the "rebel," the "serious student," the "loner," and the "class clown." Role diffusion is not necessarily a bad thing, at least as a temporary measure. It is natural to experiment with several roles before a person finds the one that seems most suitable.

Another possible outcome is a **moratorium**—a delay in resolving an identity crisis. The adolescent simply postpones making any lasting decision.

Finally, the search for identity may lead to **identity achievement**. Some adolescents deliberately decide what their values, goals, and place in society will be. That identity may or may not be permanent; we all continue to change in various ways throughout life, and from time to time we need to rethink our values and goals.

Self-Centeredness Among Teenagers

Respond to the following statements. Are they true or false?

- Other people will grow old and die, but I won't.
- Other people will fail to realize their life ambitions, but I will realize mine.
- I understand love and sex in a way my parents never did.
- Tragedy may strike other people, but it will never strike me.
- Everyone notices how I look and how I dress.

You know perfectly well that all these statements are false, and yet you may secretly believe them or act as if you did. According to David Elkind (1984), teenagers are particularly likely to harbor such beliefs. Taken together, he calls them the "personal fable," the conviction that "I am special; what is true for everyone else is not true for me." Up to a point, that fable may actually foster psychological well-being. It helps us to maintain a cheerful, optimistic outlook on life. It becomes dangerous when it leads people to take foolish chances: "I can drive when I'm drunk and never have an accident." "I won't get pregnant." "I'm going to be a success whether or not I study."

Teenage Sexuality

The decision about "Who am I?" or "What am I going to do with my life?" includes the question, "How shall I behave sexually?" Generally, sexual behavior is not an issue before **puberty**, the time of sexual maturation. Beginning at puberty, it suddenly becomes a very important issue indeed. A fairly high percentage of teenagers become sexually active, although the figures vary from year to year, as shown in Figure 6.23 (Brooks-Gunn & Furstenberg, 1989). Their motives for sex vary. It can be a search for pleasure, a way of strengthening a relationship with a boyfriend or girlfriend, a way of coping with frustrations, or a way of becoming accepted by a peer subculture.

When a young couple goes out on a first date, neither party can be sure what the other party has in mind. Some people look forward to sex on the first date; others are adamant about having no sex before marriage. F. Scott Christopher and Rodney Cate (1985) found that college-age couples progressed toward intimacy at vastly different rates. There probably is no one pattern of dating and intimacy that is best for all people. In Christopher and Cate's study, couples who were quick to reach sexual intimacy reported loving each other about the same amount as couples who were slower to become

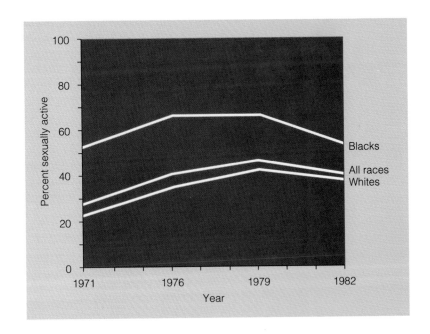

Figure 6.23

Sexual activity of adolescent girls ages 15 through 19, from 1971 to 1982. (From Brooks-Gunn & Furstenberg, 1989.) Do you think the risk of getting AIDS has changed the sexual behavior of teens? Or are they likely to consider themselves invincible—immune from a fatal disease?

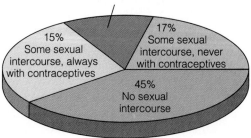

23%
Some sexual intercourse,
sometimes with contraceptives and
sometimes without

15%
Some sexual
intercourse, always
with contraceptives

17%
Some sexual
intercourse, never
with contraceptives

45%
No sexual
intercourse

FIGURE 6.24

Like playing Russian roulette: Sexual behavior and the use of contraceptives by teenage girls in the United States. (Based on data from Zelnik & Kantner, 1977, 1978.)

intimate. However, the rapid-involvement couples did report more conflict early in their relationship.

Perhaps the most important concern is that both members of a couple should be in agreement about what sex implies or does not imply about their relationship. In general, more men than women are willing to have sex casually with many partners (Hendrick, Hendrick, Slapion-Foote, & Foote, 1985). If a man regards intercourse as a casual act while his partner considers intercourse as an implied engagement to be married, then someone is headed for trouble.

Over the past several decades sexual activity among teenagers has grown increasingly common, in part because of the ready availability of birth-control pills and other contraceptive devices. And yet 10 to 15% of teenage girls have unwanted pregnancies (Zelnik & Kantner, 1977, 1978). Why? Because they do not *use* contraceptives. Fewer than one third use contraceptives the first time they have intercourse; even fewer use them consistently (Figure 6.24).

Despite the increase in teenage sexual activity, misinformation about sex still abounds (Morrison, 1985). Many sexually active teenagers mistakenly believe that:

- Young teenagers cannot get pregnant.

- It is impossible to get pregnant the first time you have sex.

- A woman must have sex frequently in order to become pregnant.

- Someone who has had sex several times without getting pregnant must be safe.

- A woman has to have an orgasm in order to get pregnant.

- A woman will not get pregnant unless she wants to.

Even teenagers who are better informed may fail to use contraceptives because they would be embarrassed to purchase them. Some believe that it is all right to have sex but wrong to *plan* for it. Still others fall victim to their "personal fables," as discussed earlier. They believe that "other people get pregnant, but it won't happen to me."

YOUNG ADULTHOOD

In young adulthood, marriage and career no longer lie in the future. Ready or not, the future has arrived. According to Erikson, the main concern at this age is "Shall I live by myself or share my life with another person?"

Attraction and Partner Selection

The custom of dating serves both short-term and long-term purposes. The short-term purpose is to have a pleasant time. The long-term purpose is to choose a marriage partner. The two are not always in harmony.

When people decide whom to date, one major determinant is familiarity. You are more likely to date someone you see frequently than someone you see rarely. The same is true when you choose friends. But extensive familiarity does not always lead to romantic attraction. In Israel, many children are reared in kibbutzim, collective farms, from infancy to adolescence. And yet young Israelis generally avoid dating people who grew up in the same kibbutz (Shepher, 1971). They regard one another almost like brother and sister.

Another major determinant of who dates whom is physical appearance. The best-looking girls tend to date the best-looking boys. Dating couples tend to resemble each other physically almost as much as married couples do (Plomin, DeFries, & Roberts, 1977). However, the superficial considerations that lead to casual dating are rarely substantial enough to sustain a lasting relationship. Couples who differ sharply in education and interests may date for a while, but they are not likely to marry (Plomin, DeFries, & Roberts, 1977).

Dating and Learning About Each Other

Dating couples gradually share a great deal of information about themselves, including their political and religious beliefs, their feelings toward their parents, and their deepest hopes and fears (Rubin, Hill, Peplau, & Dunkel-Schatter, 1980). Generally, women reveal more about themselves than men do—to friends

Arranged marriages involving dowries are still common in much of Asia and Africa. But most young American adults marry for love. Despite freedom in choosing a mate, about half of U.S. marriages split up. That does not mean half of all married Americans divorce. Some people divorce and marry two, three, or four times; these "repeat offenders" inflate the divorce rate.

TABLE 6.9 Premarital Questionnaire

1. After marriage, how often would you want to visit your parents? Your in-laws?

2. How many children do you want to have? How soon?

3. How do you want to raise your children? Should the mother stay home with the children full time while they are young? Or should the father and mother share the responsibility for child care? Or should the children be put in a day-care center?

4. Suppose the husband is offered a good job in one city and the wife is offered a good job in a city a hundred miles away. Neither spouse can find a satisfactory job in the other's city. How would you decide where to live?

5. Suppose a sudden financial crisis strikes. Where would you cut expenses to balance the budget? Clothes? Food? Housing? Entertainment?

6. How often do you plan to attend religious services?

7. Where and how do you like to spend your vacations?

8. How often would you expect to spend an evening with friends, apart from your spouse?

as well as to dating partners (Caltabiano & Smithson, 1983). Still, both men and women are generally reluctant at first to reveal themselves fully to a dating partner and to enter into intimate communication. What causes that reluctance?

As a rule, people exchange information about their private lives only after a long, gradual, give-and-take process. If an old friend opens up to you about his failure at work or tells you about his brother in jail, you may feel privileged. If the man who just moved in next door shares the same sort of information, you probably wonder what strange sort of person he is.

When people feel they have nothing to lose, they are more likely to reveal themselves. For instance,

couples who are facing serious difficulties in their marriage speak more candidly to each other than happily married couples do (Tolstedt & Stokes, 1984). Zick Rubin (1974) found that strangers who meet by accident on a train or a plane on their way to different destinations often reveal intimate information they would never reveal even to their closest friends. For example, "I'm on my way home from visiting my lover in Boston. My husband understands and doesn't object. He's impotent, you see."

Dating couples who have many acquaintances in common feel that they have a great deal to lose if they open up too freely or too quickly. Until they have actually decided to get married, many couples do not explore the matters that most often cause friction after marriage.

Answer the questions in Table 6.9 *as you think your boyfriend or girlfriend would answer them.*

Were you uncertain about how your boyfriend or girlfriend would answer any of the questions? If so, you are in the majority. And yet disagreements on such questions are among the most common reasons for divorce.

MIDDLE ADULTHOOD

From the 20s until retirement, the main concern of most adults is "What and how much will I produce? Will I make a valuable contribution and achieve significant success?"

These are generally highly productive years in which people take pride and satisfaction in their accomplishments. Middle adulthood lacks some of the excitement of young adulthood, but brings a greater sense of security and accomplishment. Middle-age adults generally have a good sense of how successful they are going to be in their marriage and career.

Job Satisfaction

Adults who are satisfied with their job are generally satisfied with their life, and people who like their life generally like their job (Keon & McDonald, 1982). Some adults manage to be happy even though they work at an unrewarding job, but the daily work routine is bound to have an enormous influence on their satisfaction.

How satisfied *are* most workers with their job? The answer depends on how we word the question. When pollsters ask simply, "Are you satisfied with your job?" about 85 to 90% say yes (Weaver, 1980). But when pollsters ask, "If you could start over, would you seek the same job you have now?" less than half of white-collar workers and only one fourth of blue-collar workers say yes. Although most workers say they are "satisfied" with their job, they could easily imagine being *more* satisfied.

The level of satisfaction is lower, on the average, among young workers than among long-term workers (Bass & Ryterband, 1979). (See Figure 6.25.) One explanation is that older workers have better, higher-paying jobs that offer greater responsibility and challenge. Another is that today's young people are harder to satisfy. But neither of those explanations accounts for all the results (Janson & Martin, 1982). Another possibility is that many young workers start in the wrong job and find a more suitable one later on. Yet another is that many young people are still considering the possibility of changing jobs; by age 40 it becomes more difficult to change, and people reconcile themselves to the job they have.

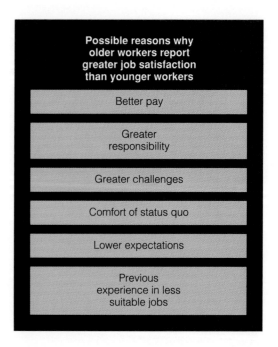

FIGURE 6.25

Nice work if you can get it: Summary of factors contributing to job satisfaction.

Your choice of career has a profound effect on the quality of your life. A student once told me that he found the courses in his major boring, but at least they were preparing him for a job. I cautioned him that he would probably find that job just as boring. Between the ages of 20 and 70 you will probably spend about half your waking hours on the job—a long time to live with work you find unsatisfying.

The Midlife Transition

People enter adulthood with a great many hopes and goals. Then as they settle into the daily round of activities, they tend to postpone their ambitions. Around age 40, some adults experience a **midlife transition**, a reassessment of their personal goals. Up to this point, they clung to the personal fable that their life would be a success in every way. There was always plenty of time to get that better job, start that family, write that great novel, take that trip up the Amazon, or get that graduate degree. But at some point they begin to realize that the opportunity to do all these things is rapidly fading.

Daniel Levinson (1977, 1978) reports that about 80% of all adults experience such a midlife transition. Other psychologists deny that the experience is anywhere near that common. The disagreement may be a matter of definition. Many middle-age adults go through a minor readjustment that is not traumatic. They review their successes and failures, examine the direction their life is taking, and set new, more realistic goals.

Some adults who go through a midlife transition accept their life as it is. Others refuse to abandon their early goals. Declaring "It's now or never," they train for a new job or take some other positive step—sometimes over the protests of family members who would prefer to play it safe. Still others become depressed and may turn to alcohol or some other means of escape.

Concept Check

11. In what way does a midlife transition resemble an adolescent identity crisis? (Check your answer on page 235.)

OLD AGE

The percentage of people who live into their 70s and 80s has grown steadily throughout the 20th century. An unprecedented number of them retire and remain healthy, active, and independent. Others live long after they are unable to care for themselves. One common concern of old age is to maintain a sense of dignity and self-esteem—to live with dignity and eventually die with dignity.

Many of the changes that people experience as they grow older are determined by society rather than by biology (Schlossberg, 1984). Our society expects that people will start their career and family in their 20s, achieve success during their 30s, continue to be productive throughout their 40s and 50s, and retire in their 60s.

Figure 6.26 shows the percentage of people in the United States employed at various ages (U.S. Department of Labor, 1989). For about 40 to 50 years of their life, people spend much of their time at work, taking pride in their accomplishments and enjoying their status. Then sometime between 60 and 70 they face voluntary or mandatory retirement. Many continue to be active, doing volunteer work, taking a part-time job, or serving as a U.S. senator.

People adjust to retirement in different ways (Atchley, 1980). Those who had a variety of interests and engaged in different activities before retirement usually find the adjustment easiest. Most retirees go through a "honeymoon" period at first, doing all the things they never had time to do before. However, their reborn hopes for great achievement soon fade. Just as many 20-year-olds start out with goals they can never achieve, many 65-year-olds enter

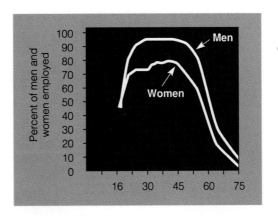

FIGURE 6.26

The percent of people employed as a function of age. These figures include students, patients in hospitals, and others who are not looking for a job. (Based on data from U.S. Department of Labor, 1989.)

retirement with hopes that are sure to be disappointed. Within a few months or a few years, they experience something similar to the midlife transition, review their prospects, and settle for more realistic goals.

Ultimately, people's health begins to fail and their activity declines. When that happens, most people are very concerned to maintain some control over their lives. Consider a person who has spent half a century managing a household or running a business. Now he or she may be living in a nursing home where staff members make all the decisions, from scheduling meals to choosing television programs. That person may deteriorate rapidly, both physically and intellectually. If the staff lets its residents make certain choices on their own and perform some tasks by themselves, their health, alertness, and memory tend to improve (Rodin, 1986; Rowe & Kahn, 1987).

THE PSYCHOLOGY OF FACING DEATH

We commonly associate death with old people, although a person can die at any age. But even a young person who expects to live many years must cope with anxiety about eventually dying. Not only do we have trouble dealing with the prospect of our own death but we also find it difficult to deal with the death of others. A dying person finds few listeners who are comfortable talking about death.

Most people deal with anxiety about death by

"A man who has not found something he is willing to die for is not fit to live."
MARTIN LUTHER KING, JR.

"This is perhaps the greatest lesson we learned from our patients: LIVE, so you do not have to look back and say, 'God, how I have wasted my life!'"
ELISABETH KÜBLER-ROSS (1975)

TABLE 6.10 Kübler-Ross's Five Stages of Adjustment to Death

Stage	Behavior or Experience of People Who Are Dying	Characteristic Expression
Denial	Refuse to acknowledge their condition; may visit several physicians or faith healers in search of someone to restore their health	"No, not me; it cannot be true"
Anger	Criticize and rage at doctors, nurses, and relatives	"Why me?"
Bargaining	Promise good behavior in exchange for the granting of a wish, usually the extension of life; those who do not believe in God may try to strike a bargain with the doctor	"Get me through this, God, and I'll give half my money to the church" or "Doc, give me some medicine that will make me well again, and here's what I'll do for you"
Depression	Sadness at losing what is past and sadness because of impending losses	"All I can do is wait for the bitter end"
Acceptance	Show little emotion of any sort; do not wish to be stirred up by news of the outside world, even by a potential new treatment to prolong life; psychologically ready to die	"The final rest before the long journey"

Source: Kübler-Ross, 1969.

telling themselves that their death is far in the future. When they learn they have a fatal disease, they react in special ways. In her book *On Death and Dying*, Elisabeth Kübler-Ross (1969) suggests that dying people go through five stages of adjustment (see Table 6.10).

Kübler-Ross suggests that all dying people progress through these five stages in the same order. Other observers, however, report that dying people may move from stage to stage in any order and may skip some stages altogether. In any case, these stages represent five common ways of coping with the imminent prospect of death.

Something to Think About

Do Kübler-Ross's stages apply only to people who are dying? Or do people react in similar fashion to lesser losses, such as a poor grade or the loss of a job? Have you ever had a personal experience in which you went through some of these same stages?

SUMMARY

1. Erik Erikson described the human lifespan as a series of eight ages, each with its own social and emotional conflicts. (page 216)

2. The attachment of an infant to his or her mother depends on the comfort of physical contact rather than on being fed. (page 220)

3. Both infant monkeys and infant humans need social contact and attention if they are to develop normal social behaviors. (page 221)

4. Children who grow up in two-paycheck families generally develop normal social and emotional behaviors if their day-care arrangements are pleasant and stable. Extensive experience in day care before an infant is 12 months old has complex effects that may combine good and bad elements. (page 222)

5. Parental conflict and divorce are emotionally upsetting to both the parents and the children. The emotional consequences for the children may be long lasting. (page 223)

6. Beginning at an early age, people learn what is expected of males and females. These expectations, called gender roles, are learned from parents, from role models, and from other children. (page 224)

7. Adolescents have to deal with an identity crisis, the question "Who am I?" Many experiment with several identities before deciding which one seems right. (page 226)

8. Adolescents also have to make decisions about sexual behavior. Dating couples vary to a great degree in how intimate they become sexually and how soon. (page 227)

9. One of the main concerns of young adults is the decision to marry or to establish some other lasting relationship. (page 228)

10. For most adults, satisfaction with life is closely linked with satisfaction on the job. Some adults experience a midlife transition in which they reevaluate their goals. (page 230)

11. In old age people make new adjustments, including the adjustment to retirement. (page 231)

12. People at all ages have to face the anxieties associated with the fact that we eventually die. People go through some characteristic reactions when they know that they are likely to die soon. (page 231)

SUGGESTIONS FOR FURTHER READING

Elkind, D. (1984). *All grown up and no place to go*. Reading, MA: Addison-Wesley. An account of the problems teenagers and young adults face.

Sheehy, G. (1977). *Passages*. New York: Bantam. Describes the problems and crises that people face from young adulthood through old age.

Tavris, C., & Offir, C. (1977). *The longest war*. New York: Harcourt Brace Jovanovich. A highly engaging account of sex roles, the differences between women and men, and the relationships that form between women and men.

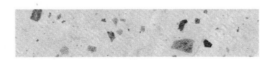

TERMS TO REMEMBER

accommodation Piaget's term for the modification of an established schema to fit new objects

assimilation Piaget's term for the application of an established schema to new objects

attachment a long-term feeling of closeness between people, such as a child and a care giver

autonomy versus shame and doubt the conflict between independence and doubt about one's abilities

basic trust versus mistrust the conflict between trusting and mistrusting that one's parents and other key figures will meet one's basic needs; first conflict in Erikson's eight ages of human development

cohort a group of people born at a particular time (as compared to people born at a different time)

conservation the concept that objects retain their weight, volume, and certain other properties in spite of changes in their shape or arrangement

cross-sectional study a study of individuals of different ages all at the same time

deep structure the logic of the language underlying a sentence

egocentric an inability to take the perspective of another person, a tendency to view the world as centered around oneself

ego integrity versus despair the conflict between satisfaction and dissatisfaction with one's life; final conflict in Erikson's eight ages of human development

fetal alcohol syndrome a condition marked by decreased alertness and other signs of impaired development, caused by exposure to alcohol prior to birth

fetus a human offspring more than 8 weeks after conception

gender roles the different behaviors that society generally expects of women and men

generativity versus stagnation the conflict between a productive life and an unproductive life

habituate to decrease a person's response to a stimulus when it is presented repeatedly

identity achievement the deliberate choice of a role or identity

identity crisis the search for self-understanding

identity foreclosure the acceptance of a role that a person's parents prescribe

identity versus role confusion the conflict between the sense of self and confusion over one's identity

industry versus inferiority the conflict between feelings of accomplishment and feelings of worthlessness

initiative versus guilt the conflict between independent behavior and behavior inhibited by guilt

intimacy versus isolation the conflict between establishing a long-term relationship with another person and remaining alone

longitudinal study a study of a single group of individuals over time

midlife transition a time of reassessment of one's goals

moral dilemma a problem that pits one moral value against another

moratorium a delay in resolving an identity crisis

morpheme a unit of meaning

object permanence the concept that an object continues to exist even when one does not see, hear, or otherwise sense it

operation according to Piaget, a mental process that can be reversed

phoneme a unit of sound

prenatal before birth

preoperational stage according to Piaget, the second stage of intellectual development, in which children lack the concept of conservation

puberty the time of onset of sexual maturation

role diffusion experimentation with various roles or identities

schema (plural: schemata) an organized way of interacting with objects in the world

semantics a set of rules for deriving meaning

sensorimotor stage according to Piaget, the first stage of intellectual development, in which an infant's behavior is limited to making simple motor responses to sensory stimuli

Spoonerism an exchange of parts of two or more words, usually the initial sounds

stage of concrete operations according to Piaget, the third stage of intellectual development, in which children can deal with the properties of concrete objects but cannot readily deal with hypothetical or abstract questions

stage of formal operations according to Piaget, the fourth and final stage of intellectual development, in which people use logical, deductive reasoning and systematic planning

surface structure the structure of a sentence as it is actually spoken or written

syntax a set of rules for linking words into sentences

transformational grammar the theory that we transform the underlying logic of the language, the deep structure, into a spoken surface structure

visual cliff an apparatus that makes one side of a table appear to drop sharply in depth, as if off a cliff

ANSWERS TO CONCEPT CHECKS

1. We could not conclude from those results that people grow more conservative as they grow older, because it is possible (even likely) that the nation as a whole had become more conservative during that period. A cross-sectional study showing no difference between 20-year-olds and 40-year-olds would confirm that the change in political opinions was probably not due to age. (The fact that 20-year-olds in 1990 are more conservative than 20-year-olds in 1970 is a difference in cohorts.) (page 186)

2. When studying the development of a behavior in which styles or fashions change from year to year, you should use a cross-sectional study, so that you can compare people of different ages at the same point in time. (page 186)

3. If the rate increased, we would conclude that the infant recognizes the difference between the father's voice and the other voice. If it remained the same, we would conclude that the infant did not notice a difference. If it decreased, we would assume that the infant for some reason preferred the sound of the father's voice to that of the other man. (That would be a puzzler, because it is difficult to imagine how a newborn would recognize his or her father's voice.) (page 189)

4. (c) is the clearest case of egocentric thought, a failure to recognize another person's point of view. It is not the same thing as selfishness. (page 194)

5. (a) Stage of concrete operations; (b) preoperational stage; (c) sensorimotor stage; (d) stage of formal operations. (page 201)

6. *Thoughtfully* has 7 phonemes: th-ough-t-f-u-ll-y. (A phoneme is a unit of sound, not necessarily a letter of the alphabet.) It has 3 morphemes: thought-ful-ly. (Each morpheme has a distinct meaning.) The rule "add -*ed* to make past tense" is an example of semantics. The rule "put the adjective before the noun" is an example of syntax. (page 208)

7. Children begin to string words into novel combinations as soon as they begin to speak two words at a time. We believe that they learn rules of grammar because they overgeneralize those rules, saying such "words" as *womans* and *goed*. (page 212)

8. Although the chimpanzees have learned the meanings of many symbols, they seldom string them together into novel combinations (sentences), the way children with a similar vocabulary do. (page 214)

9. Both the institutions and the Harlows' monkeys failed to provide the social contact necessary for infants to learn how to relate to others. (page 222)

10. A boy who becomes interested in football and a girl who becomes interested in ballet are examples of people following gender roles. The other two are not. (Gender roles are psychological, not physical.) (page 226)

11. In both a midlife transition and an adolescent identity crisis, people reexamine their goals, plan for the future, and decide who they are or who they want to be. (page 231)

LEARNING

Some psychologists from outer space land on Earth. Their first task is to determine whether humans are capable of learning. They arbitrarily choose a response—going to sleep—and reward humans whenever they make that response. The psychologists try various rewards, including food and water, but the humans keep sleeping at their same old rate. Maybe humans are just incapable of learning, they surmise.

Well, the psychologists decide, let's work with a different response—breathing. And let's try punishment instead of reward. So every time the human subjects take a breath, they are given an electric shock. But again they seem incapable of learning. They keep right on breathing. So the psychologists try stronger shocks, then stronger and stronger, until finally the humans seem to have learned. The psychologists conclude: If given strong enough shocks, humans will learn to stop breathing.

Human psychologists sometimes make similar mistakes when they study the learning abilities of animals—especially when they study animals whose way of life is very different from our own. We cannot study learning in isolation from the rest of behavior.

Under what circumstances do animals (including human beings) learn? And exactly what is learned? Is learning simply a matter of changing one's responses and the rate at which one responds? Or is it a matter of recognizing the relationships among events?

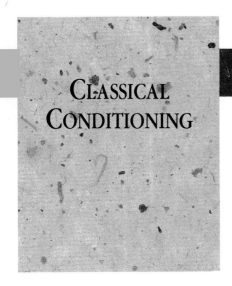

CLASSICAL CONDITIONING

When we learn a relationship between two stimuli, what happens?
Do we start responding to one stimulus as if it were the other?
Or do we learn how to use information from one stimulus to predict something about the other?

You are sitting alone in your room when you hear the doorknob turn. You look up because you know your roommate is about to enter the room. A few moments later you can see from a facial expression that your roommate is in a foul mood, so you say nothing. Your roommate flicks a switch on the stereo and you flinch because you know the stereo is set to a deafening noise level.

Note that you are responding to sensory stimuli. You respond to the sound of the turning doorknob, to your roommate's expression, and to the flick of a switch on a stereo. Note also that your responses are based on your previous experiences. At some point you learned what each of these stimuli means.

Much of our behavior consists of learned responses to simple signals. Can all behavior be analyzed into such simple units? Some psychologists have said yes: Behavior is the sum of many simple stimulus-response connections.

Other psychologists have said that even those apparently simple responses to simple stimuli are not so simple as they seem. To explain even the simplest learned responses, we have to give the individual credit for having paid attention to a vast amount of information.

In their efforts to discover what takes place during learning, psychologists have conducted thousands of experiments, many of them on nonhuman animals. The underlying idea is that the behavior of a rat or a fish is likely to be easier to understand than that of a human. Furthermore, if we discover that the learned behavior of, say, a rat is highly complex, then it is safe to assume that the learned behavior of a human is at least that complex.

ANIMAL INTELLIGENCE: THE LEGACY OF DARWIN

The study of animal learning arose from attempts to understand animal intelligence. In *Descent of Man* (1871), Charles Darwin proposed that humans and other species share a remote common ancestor. That proposal has two somewhat contradictory implications about animal intelligence:

1. All animal species should exhibit at least some trace of intelligence similar to human intelligence.
2. Because each species has evolved certain specializations that help it to cope with its natural way of life, animals should exhibit differences in intelligence as well as similarities.

At first, Darwin's fellow scientists were more interested in the first of these implications than in the second. After centuries of assuming that nonhuman animals were mindless beasts governed solely by instinct, they now had reason to look for intelligence in animals.

Soon a new field of study emerged: comparative psychology, which compares the behavior of different animal species. (Comparative psychology is analogous to comparative anatomy, which compares the anatomy of different species.) Early in the 20th century, comparative psychologists set about trying to demonstrate and measure animal intelligence. One of their goals was to rank various animals, so that they could say that the smartest nonhuman animal is, say, the chimpanzee, followed by the dolphin, the elephant, and so on—however the order might turn out. To do so, they compared the rates at which different animals learn when faced with various problems. Here are some of the problems the psychologists designed:

- *The delayed-response problem.* An animal was given a signal indicating where it could find food. Then the animal was delayed in its movement toward the food (Figure 7.1a). The question: Over how long a delay can each species remember where to find the food?

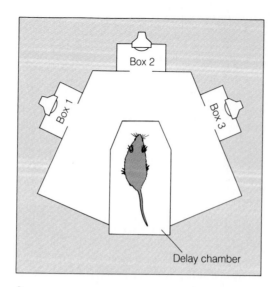

a

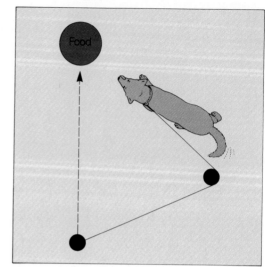

b

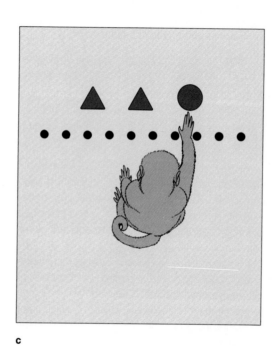

c

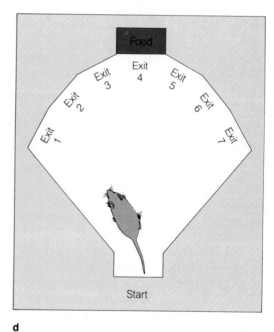

d

FIGURE 7.1

Fast food: several tests that were used to assess animal intelligence. (a) The delayed-response problem and (b) the detour problem tested reactions to different types of interference—preventing direct access to food. (c) The oddity problem tested linking an abstract concept with perception of concrete differences, as did the more sophisticated many-door or multiple-choice problem (d). The results, however, were found to depend on differences in activity level, feeding habits, and other factors—not just on "intelligence."

The researchers assumed that the "smarter" animals could remember longer.

- *The detour problem.* An animal was separated from food by a barrier (Figure 7.1b). The question: Will the animal get the idea of taking a detour away from the food at first in order to get to it? The researchers assumed that the smarter species would be quicker to grasp the idea.

- *The oddity problem.* An animal was given a choice among three objects, two of which looked alike (Figure 7.1c). Food was always hidden under the object that looked different,

and a new set of objects was used for each trial. The questions: Will the animal get the idea of picking the odd object? How rapidly will it do so?

- *The many-door or multiple-choice problem.* An animal was placed successively in a variety of boxes equipped with three to nine doors (Figure 7.1d). The question: Will the animal learn to respond according to some abstract rule, such as always go to the door farthest to the left, always go to the middle door, or alternate between the left door and the right door (Cook, 1953)?

Comparative psychologists set their animals to other tasks as well (Maier & Schneirla, 1964). In every task, however, they discovered that factors other than intelligence had some bearing on how well each species performed. For example, rats can learn that foods with one flavor are high in calories while foods with another flavor are low in calories. (They demonstrate their learning by developing a preference for the high-calorie flavor.) Hamsters fail to learn the preference, not because they are less intelligent but because they stuff the food into their cheek pouches and do not swallow it until hours later. When hamsters are fed liquids, which they have to swallow at once, they learn just as well as rats (Arbour & Wilkie, 1988).

The researchers came up with another puzzling discovery: A species that seemed smarter on one task sometimes turned out to be less smart on other tasks. For example, horses learn faster than zebras on many tasks, but zebras learn faster on tasks that require them to compare one stripe pattern with another (Giebel, 1958). (See Figure 7.2.)

Apparently an animal's speed of learning a given task depends on its sensory and motor capacities, its motivations, and its natural behaviors. If that is the case, differences in performance from one species to another may be unrelated to differences in intelligence (MacPhail, 1987).

THE RISE OF BEHAVIORISM

Around 1920, psychologists began to lose interest in comparing intelligence from one species to another, partly because of the difficulties just mentioned (Kalat, 1983). However, they were still interested in the nature of learning, and they continued to assume that all species possess some capacity to learn. If learning and intelligence differ only in degree, they reasoned, then it should be possible to discover the basic laws of learning by studying the behavior of any species in any convenient laboratory task. The psychologists who take this approach to the study of learning refer to themselves as **behaviorists** (Watson, 1913). Behaviorists try to explain the causes of behavior by studying only those behaviors that scientists can observe and measure, without reference to unobservable mental processes.

The original behaviorists were, in part, protesting against the views of earlier psychologists who had tried to study the psychological processes of humans by asking people to *introspect,* to look within themselves. Those psychologists had asked questions like these: "How clear and intense is your idea of roundness? Is it stronger or weaker than

FIGURE 7.2

In an experiment by Giebel (1958), zebras compared stripe patterns. How "smart" a species is depends in part on what ability or skill is tested.

your idea of color? Does the idea get stronger or weaker when you close your eyes?" The behaviorists pointed out that it was useless to ask people for reports on their own experience, because there is no way to check on the accuracy of such reports. If someone says, "I hear singing," or "I see the moon," we can check the reports against our own observations. But if someone sits calmly and says, "I feel angry," we have no way of verifying the report. And if someone says, "My idea of roundness is stronger than my idea of color," we can hardly even guess what is meant, much less whether it is correct. *If psychology is to be a scientific enterprise, behaviorists insist, it must deal only with behaviors that can be observed and measured.*

Behaviorists make several assumptions:

1. *All behavior is caused or determined in some way.* (Recall the discussion of free will and determinism in Chapter 1.) In other words, all behavior obeys certain laws. The reason psychologists cannot always predict what you will do is that they do not know enough about you and about the stimuli that are acting upon you. Moreover, their theories of behavior are not yet sufficiently well developed for them to make full, comprehensive predictions.

2. *Explanations of behavior based on internal causes and mental states are generally useless.* We commonly "explain" people's behavior in terms of their motivations, or emotions, or mental state. However, behaviorists insist that such explanations explain nothing:

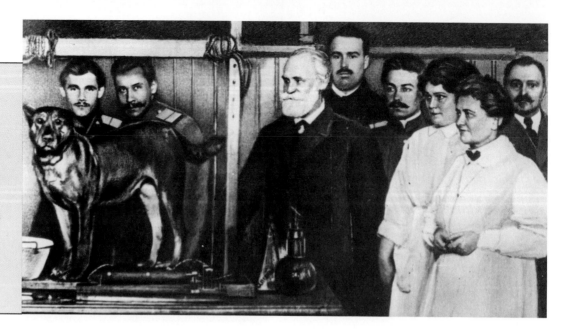

Ivan P. Pavlov (with the white beard) with students and an experimental dog. Pavlov focused on limited aspects of the dog's behavior—mostly salivation—and found some apparently simple principles to describe that behavior.

Q. Why is she studying so hard?
A. Because she is highly motivated to get good grades.
Q. How do you know she is highly motivated to get good grades?
A. We can see that she is highly motivated because she studies so hard.

Q. Why did she yell at that man?
A. She yelled because she was angry.
Q. How do you know she was angry?
A. We can tell she was angry because she was yelling.

Behaviorists today are a little more willing than those of the past to talk about anger, hope, motivation levels, and other internal states. But before they will do so, they insist on a precise operational definition of the terms (page 29), and they insist that we have some solid evidence for the internal state other than the behavior it is supposed to explain.

3. *The environment molds behavior.* Each sensory stimulus gives rise to a response. Learning consists of a change in the connections between stimuli and responses. For this reason, behaviorism is sometimes referred to as *stimulus-response psychology,* or *S-R psychology.* Much of the rest of this chapter elaborates on what stimulus-response psychology means.

PAVLOV AND CLASSICAL CONDITIONING

Suppose you always feed your cat at 4:00 P.M. with food you keep in the refrigerator. As 4:00 P.M. approaches, your cat goes to the kitchen, claws at the refrigerator, meows, and salivates. You might explain the cat's behavior by saying that it "expects" food, that it "knows" there is food in the refrigerator, or that it is "trying to get someone to feed it." Behaviorists reject such explanations in favor of a more mechanical interpretation based on stimuli and responses. When Ivan P. Pavlov proposed a simple, highly mechanical theory of learning, it was widely accepted almost overnight.

Pavlov, a Russian physiologist, won a Nobel Prize in physiology in 1904 for his research on digestion (Gantt, 1973). He continued his research by measuring the secretion of digestive juices in a dog's stomach when food was placed in its mouth or in its stomach. One day he noticed that a dog would salivate or secrete digestive juices as soon as it saw or smelled food. Because this secretion presumably depended on the dog's previous experiences with food, Pavlov called it a "psychological" secretion.

Pavlov's Procedures

Pavlov guessed that animals are born with certain automatic connections—he called them **unconditioned reflexes**—between a stimulus such as food and a response such as secreting digestive juices in the digestive system. He conjectured that animals also acquire certain reflexes as a result of experience. If so, he reasoned, it might be possible to transfer a reflex from one stimulus to another. For example, if a certain sight—say, a flashing light—always preceded food, an animal might begin to make the same digestive response to the light that it would make if food were already in its mouth. Thus the flashing light would also produce digestive secretions, as would a buzzer or any other originally neutral stimulus that regularly preceded food.

The process by which an organism learns a new association between two stimuli—a neutral one and one that already evokes a reflexive response—has come to be known as **classical conditioning** or **Pavlovian conditioning**. (It is called *classical* simply because it has been known and studied for a long time.)

Pavlov used an experimental setup like the one Figure 7.3 shows. First he strapped a dog into the harness. (He had to choose his dogs carefully. Excitable dogs would fight and try to escape; docile dogs would fall asleep in the harness.) Then he attached a tube to one of the salivary ducts in the dog's mouth to measure salivation. He could have measured stomach secretions, but it was easier to measure salivation.

Pavlov found that whenever he gave the dog food, saliva flowed into the dog's mouth. This happened automatically; no training was required. He referred to the food as the **unconditioned stimulus (US)** and to the salivation as the **unconditioned response (UR)**. (You will need to master many terms in this section.) In other words, before Pavlov started to train the dog, the unconditioned stimulus (US) elicited the unconditioned response (UR) consistently and automatically.

Next, Pavlov introduced a new stimulus, a buzzer. On hearing the tone, the dog made certain orienting responses: It got up, lifted its ears, and looked around. It did not salivate, however, so the stimulus was essentially neutral initially. Pavlov sounded the buzzer a few seconds before giving food to the dog and did this over and over again; after enough repetitions, the dog would salivate as soon as it heard the buzzer (Pavlov, 1927/1960).

Pavlov called the buzzer the **conditioned stimulus (CS)**, because the dog's response to it depended on the preceding conditions. He called the salivation that followed the sounding of the buzzer the **conditioned response (CR)**. In situations like the ones Pavlov studied, the conditioned response is very similar to the unconditioned response; the only difference is that the UR is evoked by one stimulus and the CR is evoked by a different stimulus.

To summarize: The *unconditioned stimulus* (US) is the stimulus that automatically elicits the *unconditioned response* (UR) before the experiment begins. Once the experiment has begun, the *conditioned stimulus* (CS) at first elicits either no response at all or some irrelevant response, such as just looking around. After one or more repetitions, the *conditioned stimulus* elicits the *conditioned response,* which ordinarily resembles the unconditioned response. Figure 7.4 diagrams these relationships.

Here is another example of classical condition-

FIGURE 7.3

A dog strapped into a harness for an experiment on classical conditioning of salivation. The experimenter can ring a bell (CS), present food (US), and measure the response (CR and UR) without direct contact with the animal. If the aroma of bread baking makes your mouth water, is your response conditioned or unconditioned?

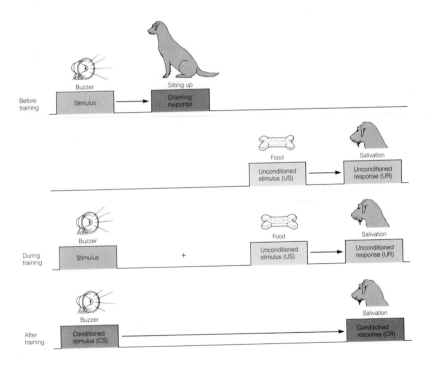

FIGURE 7.4

A summary of classical conditioning.

ing: We sound a tone and then puff some air directly into a person's eye. The person blinks automatically. After we repeat this combination a few times, the tone by itself causes the person to blink (Figure 7.5). In this example, the tone is the CS, the air puff is the US, and the blink is both the CR and the UR.

The unconditioned stimulus may be almost any stimulus that evokes an automatic response. The

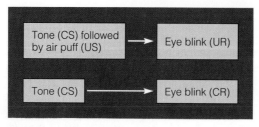

| Tone (CS) followed by air puff (US) | → | Eye blink (UR) |

| Tone (CS) | → | Eye blink (CR) |

a   b

FIGURE 7.5

The procedure for classical conditioning of the eyeblink response.

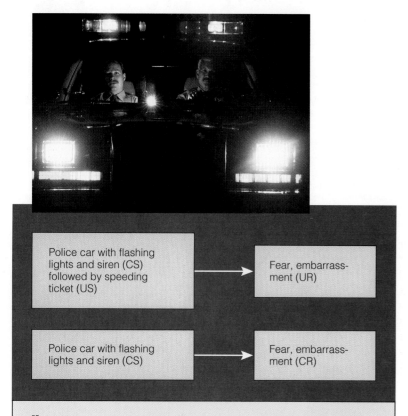

| Police car with flashing lights and siren (CS) followed by speeding ticket (US) | → | Fear, embarrassment (UR) |

| Police car with flashing lights and siren (CS) | → | Fear, embarrassment (CR) |

How and why do we learn? The theory of classical conditioning maintains that learning occurs when we modify our behavior because of certain stimuli. Acquisition—establishing or reinforcing a conditioned response (CR)—connects a conditioned stimulus (CS) and an unconditioned stimulus (US). Do the flashing lights and siren of a police car evoke a conditioned response in you? What about the ringing of a telephone?

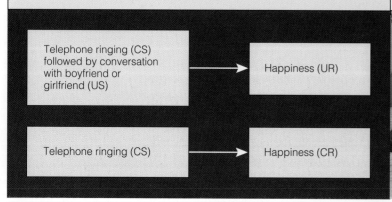

| Telephone ringing (CS) followed by conversation with boyfriend or girlfriend (US) | → | Happiness (UR) |

| Telephone ringing (CS) | → | Happiness (CR) |

conditioned stimulus may be almost any detectable stimulus—a light, a sound, the interruption of a constant light or sound, a touch, a smell, or some combination of stimuli. In general, conditioning occurs more rapidly when the conditioned stimulus is unfamiliar than when it is familiar. For example, if someone hears a tone a thousand times before the first time it is paired with a puff of air, the person will take a long time to show any signs of conditioning. The person has difficulty learning that the tone predicts the air puff because it has never predicted anything in the past (Kalat, 1977; Mackintosh, 1973). Similarly, imagine two people who are bitten by a snake. The one who has never been close to a snake before may develop an intense fear of snakes; the one who has spent the past five years tending snakes at the zoo will develop little if any fear. In both cases the snake is a CS and the bite is a US, but the familiarity of the CS determines whether the person will develop a strong association or a weak one.

This section deals mostly with laboratory examples. Later chapters will show that classical conditioning is relevant to such human behaviors as drug tolerance and phobias (Chapter 14).

Concept Check

1. A nursing mother consistently responds to her baby's crying by putting the baby to her breast. The baby's sucking causes the release of milk. Within a few days, as soon as the mother hears the baby crying, the milk starts to flow, even before she puts the baby to her breast. What is the CS? The CR? The US? The UR? (Check your answers on page 274.)

The Phenomena of Classical Conditioning

The process that establishes or strengthens a conditioned response is known as **acquisition**. Figure 7.6a shows how the strength of a conditioned

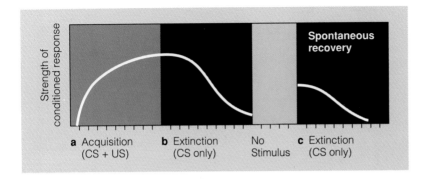

FIGURE 7.6

The strength of a conditioned response increases during acquisition (a) and decreases during extinction (b). After a period of no stimulus followed by renewed testing with the CS, spontaneous recovery of the CR may be observed temporarily (c); the extinguished CR returns without positive reinforcement. However, unless the CS is again paired with the US, spontaneous recovery is only temporary.

response increases as the conditioned and unconditioned stimuli are repeatedly presented together. However, acquisition is not the end of the story, because any response that can be learned can also be unlearned or changed.

Once Pavlov had demonstrated the manner in which classical conditioning occurs, inquisitive psychologists began to ask, "What would happen if we changed the experiment like this?" Their investigations, prompted by either practical or theoretical concerns, or by mere curiosity, have revealed many phenomena that are related to classical conditioning.

Extinction   Suppose I sound a buzzer and then blow a puff of air into your eyes. After a few repetitions you start closing your eyes as soon as you hear the buzzer. Now I sound the buzzer repeatedly without puffing any air. What do you do?

If you are like most people, you will blink your eyes the first time and perhaps the second and third times, but before long you will stop blinking. This dying out of the conditioned response is called **extinction** (Figure 7.6b). *To extinguish a classically conditioned response, repeatedly present the CS without the US.*

As with acquisition, extinction involves learning; just as acquisition establishes a connection between the CS and the US, extinction establishes a connection between the CS and the *absence* of the US. The factors that facilitate or impair acquisition have similar effects on extinction. For example, a loud noise that is paired with a CS will interfere with a recently acquired conditioned response. After extinction has taken place, however, the same loud noise paired with the CS actually restores the conditioned response (Pavlov, 1927). Apparently, a distracting stimulus interferes with whatever has been recently learned, which might be either a conditioned response or the *extinction* of the conditioned response.

Extinction is not the same as forgetting. Both serve to weaken a learned response, but they arise from different sources. Forgetting occurs when we have no opportunity to practice a certain behavior over a long time. Extinction occurs as the result of a specific experience—namely, perceiving that the CS is not followed by the US.

Spontaneous Recovery   Suppose we classically condition a response and then extinguish it. Several hours or days later, we present the CS again. In many cases, the CR will reappear. But unless we present the US as well, the CR will rapidly be extinguished. **Spontaneous recovery** refers to this temporary return of an extinguished response after a delay (Figure 7.6c). For example, the sound of a buzzer (CS) is followed by a puff of air blown into the eyes (US) many times until the person blinks at the sound of the buzzer. Then the buzzer is presented repeatedly by itself until the person stops blinking. Neither the buzzer nor the puff of air is presented for the next few hours. Then the buzzer is sounded again and the person blinks—not strongly, perhaps, but more than at the end of the extinction training.

Why does spontaneous recovery take place? Think of it this way: At first, the buzzer predicted a puff of air blown into the eyes. Then it predicted nothing. The two sets of experiences conflict with each other, but the more recent one predominates and the person stops blinking. Hours later, neither experience is much more recent than the other and the effects of the original acquisition are almost as strong as the effects of the extinction.

Concept Check

2. In Pavlov's experiment on conditioned salivation in response to a buzzer, what procedure could you use to produce extinction? What procedure could you use to produce spontaneous recovery? (Check your answers on page 274.)

Stimulus Generalization   Suppose I play a note or tone—say, middle C—and then blow a puff of air into your eyes. After a few repetitions you start to

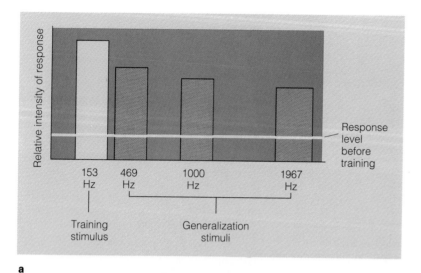

a

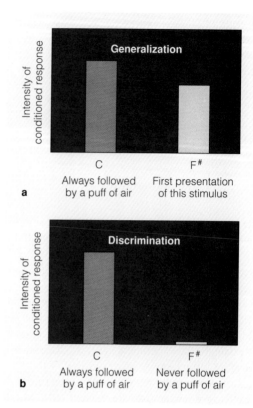

a

Always followed   First presentation
by a puff of air   of this stimulus

b

Always followed   Never followed
by a puff of air   by a puff of air

FIGURE 7.8

(a) A similar stimulus, such as the note F, will produce a generalized response. (b) But when F is repeatedly presented without the air puff, an individual learns to discriminate.

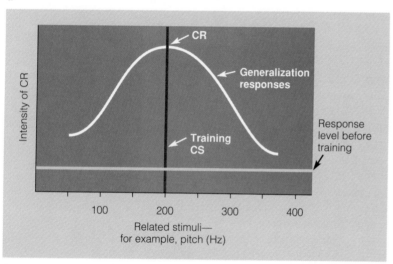

b

FIGURE 7.7

Stimulus generalization. (a) People who were trained to respond to a tone of 153 hertz (Hz) were tested on that tone and three others. In this experiment (Hovland, 1937), the response generalized most strongly to the tones closest to the training tones. (b) This curve shows the typical results that researchers would expect in a stimulus generalization experiment. According to classical conditioning theory, these results should be about the same no matter what stimulus we choose.

blink your eyes as soon as you hear middle C. What happens if I play some other note?

You will probably blink your eyes in response to the new tone as well. The closer the new tone is to the training note (middle C), the more likely you will be to blink (Figure 7.7). **Stimulus generalization** is the extension of a conditioned response from the training stimulus to other, similar stimuli.

Although I have described the CS simply as the note middle C, the CS actually includes the entire set of sensory stimuli impinging on you at the time—the tone itself, the lab room, the presence of the experimenter, and any other background stimuli. Thus, a minor change in the tone or in any of the background stimuli will decrease the conditioned response. If the changes are drastic enough, the conditioned response will disappear altogether (Pearce, 1987). For example, if a middle C is always paired with a puff of air in a psychology lab room, you will blink your eyes when you hear the tone in that setting but not when you hear it at a piano recital.

Discrimination Now suppose I always follow middle C with a puff of air but never follow F-sharp with a puff of air. Eventually you will use **discrimination**—that is, you will respond differently to the two stimuli because different outcomes followed them. You will blink your eyes when you hear middle C but not when you hear F-sharp. We rely constantly on discrimination in everyday life: We learn that one bell signals that it is time for class to start and a different bell signals a fire (Figure 7.8).

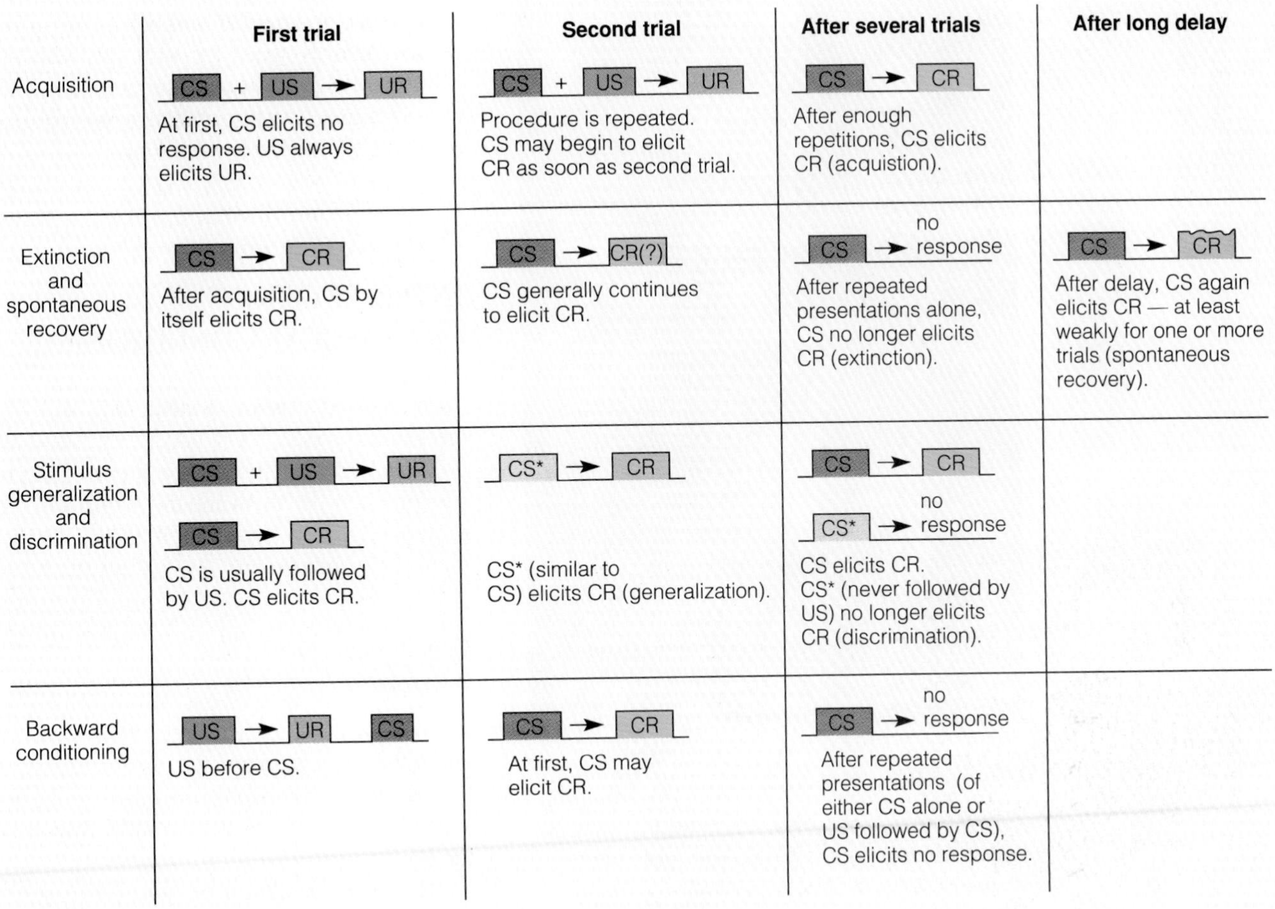

	First trial	Second trial	After several trials	After long delay
Acquisition	CS + US → UR At first, CS elicits no response. US always elicits UR.	CS + US → UR Procedure is repeated. CS may begin to elicit CR as soon as second trial.	CS → CR After enough repetitions, CS elicits CR (acquistion).	
Extinction and spontaneous recovery	CS → CR After acquisition, CS by itself elicits CR.	CS → CR(?) CS generally continues to elicit CR.	CS → no response After repeated presentations alone, CS no longer elicits CR (extinction).	CS → CR After delay, CS again elicits CR — at least weakly for one or more trials (spontaneous recovery).
Stimulus generalization and discrimination	CS + US → UR CS → CR CS is usually followed by US. CS elicits CR.	CS* → CR CS* (similar to CS) elicits CR (generalization).	CS → CR CS* → no response CS elicits CR. CS* (never followed by US) no longer elicits CR (discrimination).	
Backward conditioning	US → UR CS US before CS.	CS → CR At first, CS may elicit CR.	CS → no response After repeated presentations (of either CS alone or US followed by CS), CS elicits no response.	

FIGURE 7.9

The phenomena of classical conditioning. These and other phenomena were discovered by psychologists who tried to use Pavlov's methods to investigate basic and (they hoped) simple principles of learning.

Something to Think About

We can easily determine how well human subjects discriminate between two stimuli. We can simply ask, "Which note has the higher pitch?" or "Which light is brighter?" How could we determine how well an animal can discriminate between these stimuli?

Backward Conditioning In Pavlov's experiments on salivation, as in most classical conditioning experiments, learning occurred only if the CS (buzzer) came before the US (food). If the CS continues until the US begins, we refer to the training as *delayed conditioning;* if the CS stops before the US begins, we refer to it as *trace conditioning,* because the individual has to store a memory trace of the CS until the US begins. Occasionally, however, **backward conditioning** occurs, in which the US comes *before* the CS.

If backward conditioning occurs at all, it will occur rapidly. For example, in one experiment rats received a painful electric shock. Just after the shock, a plastic toy hedgehog was lowered into the cage.

From then on, the rats showed an intense fear of the plastic hedgehog. It was as if, after experiencing the shock, they had asked, "What hit me?" and then had looked around and blamed it on the first suspicious-looking stimulus they saw (Keith-Lucas & Guttman, 1975). When the procedure was repeated many times, however, the rats learned that the hedgehog appeared only *after* the shock, and their fear declined. A stimulus that consistently appears just after the US becomes a **conditioned inhibitor**—a stimulus that inhibits the conditioned response because of past experiences in which it predicted the absence of the unconditioned stimulus (Miller & Spear, 1985). If a conditioned inhibitor is presented at the same time as a conditioned stimulus, then it greatly weakens the conditioned response.

Figure 7.9 summarizes the phenomena of classical conditioning.

Pavlov's Theory of the Causes of Classical Conditioning

Pavlov believed that in order for classical condi-

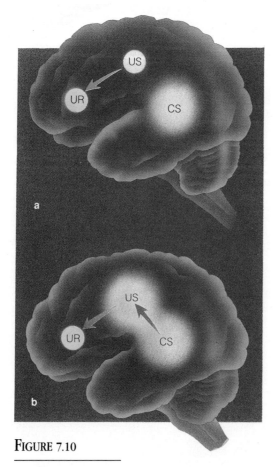

FIGURE 7.10

A conditional time frame: Pavlov believed that when the conditioned stimulus and the unconditioned stimulus are presented too far apart, no association, and therefore no conditioning, occurs (a). When the CS and the US are presented close together in time (temporal contiguity), the interaction between the activated areas creates a connection, and therefore conditioning occurs (b).

tioning to occur temporal contiguity must be present between the CS and the US. **Temporal contiguity** means being close together in time. With rare exceptions, the CS must be presented first, followed quickly by the US. All other things being equal, the longer the delay between CS and US, the weaker the conditioning will be.

Pavlov believed not only that temporal contiguity facilitated conditioning but also that temporal contiguity actually *caused* it. According to his theory, every stimulus excites a specific area of the brain. A buzzer excites a "buzzer center" and meat excites a "meat center." Exciting both centers at the same time establishes and strengthens a connection between them. From then on, any excitation of the buzzer center (CS) also excites the meat center (US) and evokes salivation (Figure 7.10).

Pavlov's theory appealed to behaviorists at the time because it offered a simple, mechanical expla-

nation of learning. It still appeals to those who study the physiological mechanisms of learning in invertebrate animals (see, for example, Kandel & Schwartz, 1982). However, most current investigators of learning have turned to more complex interpretations of classical conditioning.

CONTEMPORARY INTERPRETATIONS OF CLASSICAL CONDITIONING

Pavlov viewed classical conditioning as a rigid mechanical process. If a CS and a US are repeatedly presented close together in time, then a connection will form between them and the animal will come to respond to the CS as if it were the US. Is that all there is to conditioning?

Conditioning: More Than a Transfer of Responses

In Pavlov's experiments, in which the CR was similar to the UR, it was natural to assume that conditioning consisted of shifting connections in the brain so that the CS could evoke the same response as the US.

However, the CR can be quite different from the UR. For example, most animals respond to an electric shock by running around and making a lot of noise. But they respond to a buzzer (CS) that signals a forthcoming shock (US) by becoming inactive and quiet. They do not treat the buzzer as if it were a shock. They react to it more or less as they would to signals of possible danger in the real world.

Temporal Contiguity Is Not Enough: WHAT'S THE EVIDENCE?

Contrary to what Pavlov believed, a CS followed immediately and repeatedly by a US may, under certain conditions, establish very little connection between the two stimuli. Here are two examples:

EXPERIMENT 1

Hypothesis If classical conditioning depends on temporal contiguity, then an animal should associate a US with any suitable CS that preceded it. But if animals respond only to an informative stimulus, then they should not associate a new CS with a US if some other CS had already told them the US was coming.

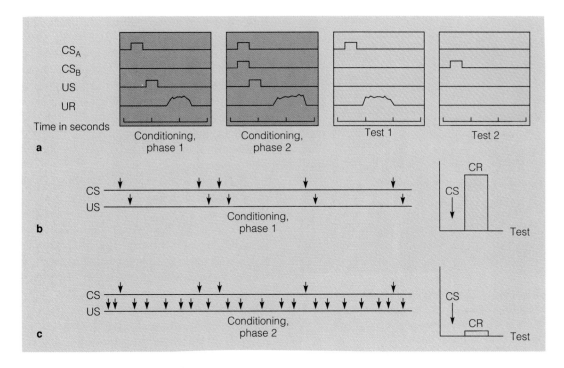

Figure 7.11

Procedures and results of two experiments that demonstrate how classical conditioning depends on contingency, not contiguity. (a) First, one stimulus is paired with a US until animals respond to it consistently; then that stimulus and another are presented just before the US. Even after many pairings, animals respond to the original (informative) stimulus and hardly at all to the added (redundant) stimulus (Kamin, 1969). (b) For two sets of animals, the CS is always followed by the US. For the first group, the CS has predictive value, and animals come to respond to it. For the second group, the US occurs so frequently that the CS has no predictive value; the CS elicits no response despite the many pairings between the CS and the US (Rescorla, 1968).

Method Stimulus A (either a light or a sound) was repeatedly followed by a US (shock) until rats showed a clear, consistent response to stimulus A (Kamin, 1969). Then the experimenter presented stimulus A and stimulus B (also either a light or a sound) simultaneously, followed by the same shock. Later the experimenter tested rats' reactions to stimulus A and stimulus B, each presented separately.

Results The rats continued to respond to stimulus A, as expected. However, they responded very weakly to stimulus B. Figure 7.11a diagrams the results.

Interpretation If temporal contiguity were the main factor responsible for learning, the rats should have learned a strong response to stimulus B as well as to stimulus A because both were always followed promptly by the US. However, stimulus B was uninformative. Stimulus A predicted the US, but stimulus B added nothing whatever to that prediction.

Experiment 2

Hypothesis A CS that immediately precedes a US may or may not be a useful predictor of the US,

depending on how often the US occurs without the CS. If the US occurs only after a CS, then animals will associate the CS with the US. If the US occurs frequently in the absence of the CS, then animals will not associate the CS with the US even though they are linked by temporal contiguity.

Method For some rats, CS and US were presented in the sequence shown in the top part of Figure 7.11b. The horizontal lines represent time; the vertical spikes represent times of presentation of the stimuli. For other rats, CS and US were presented in the sequence shown in the bottom part of Figure 7.11b. In both cases, the CS was followed immediately by the US every time. But in the second case the US occurred so frequently in the *absence* of the CS that the CS was a poor predictor of the US (Rescorla, 1968, 1988).

Results Rats given the first sequence of stimuli formed a strong association between CS and US. Those given the second sequence of stimuli formed little or no association between CS and US and failed to respond to the CS (Rescorla, 1968, 1988). Figure 7.11b diagrams the results.

It must have been the sushi: When you feel ill (US), you probably blame your nausea on something you ate (CS), particularly if it was something unfamiliar. You make this connection even if you begin feeling ill more than an hour after the meal.

Interpretation   The results support the same conclusion as the first experiment: *Animals (including humans) associate a CS with a US only when the CS predicts the occurrence of the US.* A CS that comes just before the US is generally a good predictor, but not in all cases. If the CS comes immediately before the US but provides no new information, the animal will not associate the CS with the US. In other words, conditioning depends not on contiguity but on **contingency**, or predictability. ■

Concept Check

3. If temporal contiguity were the main factor responsible for classical conditioning, what result should the experimenters have obtained in Experiment 2? (Check your answer on page 274.)

Situational Specializations of Learning

For some kinds of conditioned responses, such as salivating and blinking, learning is greatest if the delay between the CS and the US is less than 2 seconds (all other things being equal). Under ordinary conditions, no evidence of learning occurs if the delay is greater than 20 seconds (Kimble, 1961). Thus when Pavlov and others referred to temporal contiguity, they were referring to CS-US delays of a matter of seconds.

In certain special situations, however, learning

surely occurs even when the delay is longer. John Garcia and his colleagues (Garcia, Ervin, & Koelling, 1966) demonstrated that rats can associate food with illness over delays much longer than 20 seconds. They gave rats a saccharin solution that the rats had never tasted before. Ordinarily, rats will readily drink saccharin and show a strong preference for it. But 15 minutes or more *after* the rats had stopped drinking, the experimenters injected mild poisons to make them slightly ill. When the rats had recovered, the experimenters again offered them a saccharin solution. None of them would drink it, even though they readily drank water. Evidently the rats had learned a connection between taste and illness, in spite of the long delay and after only a single pairing. **Conditioned taste aversion**, or **bait shyness**, is the phenomenon of avoiding eating something that has been followed by illness when eaten in the past.

Research has shown that taste aversion is not the result of a lingering aftertaste of the food but is truly the result of an association between events separated by a long delay. For example, rats can learn that drinking one concentration of a solution will make them sick and that another will not, even though both concentrations leave the same aftertaste (Rozin, 1969).

J. Garcia and R. A. Koelling (1966) demonstrated another specialization of learning: Animals are predisposed to associate poison with foods but not with lights and sounds. They are also predisposed to associate shocks with lights and sounds but not with foods. In Garcia and Koelling's experiment, rats were allowed to drink saccharin-flavored water from tubes that were set up so that whenever the rats licked the water a bright light flashed and a loud noise sounded. Some of the rats were exposed to X rays (which can induce nausea) while they drank. Others were given electric shocks to their feet 2 seconds after they had begun to drink. After the training was complete, each rat was tested separately with a tube of saccharin-flavored water and with a tube of unflavored water that produced lights and noises. Figure 7.12 illustrates the experiment.

The rats that had been exposed to X rays avoided only the flavored water. The rats that had received shocks while drinking avoided only the tube that produced lights and noises. Evidently rats (and other species) have a built-in predisposition to associate illness mostly with what they have eaten or drunk and to associate skin pain mostly with what they have seen or heard. Such predispositions are presumably beneficial because foods are more likely to cause internal events, and lights and sounds are more likely to signal external events.

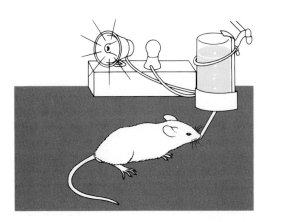

Rats drink saccharin-flavored water. Whenever they make contact with the tube, they turn on a bright light and a noisy buzzer.

Afterward:

Some rats get electric shock.

Some rats are made nauseated by X-rays.

Next day: Rats are given a choice between a tube of saccharin-flavored water and a tube of unflavored water hooked up to the light and the buzzer.

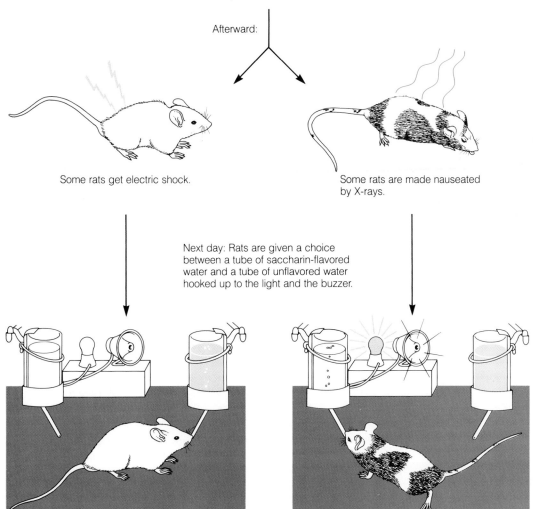

Rats that had been shocked avoided the tube with the lights and noises but drank the saccharin-flavored water.

Rats that had been made nauseated by X-rays avoided the saccharin-flavored water but drank the water with the lights and the buzzer.

FIGURE 7.12

The experiment by Garcia and Koelling (1966). Rats "blame" tastes for their illness, lights and sounds for their pain.

Classical Conditioning as Information Processing

According to the current view of classical conditioning, the learner is an active processor of information. Conditioning is no longer seen as the passive connection of two stimuli, just because they come close together in time. Each individual enters the world with certain predispositions—such as the predisposition to associate illness with what it eats instead of what it sees or hears. When it experiences a series of stimuli, it determines what each predicts. If a given stimulus provides reliable information about what is about to happen, the animal learns to respond to that stimulus. Otherwise, it does not. In a sense, an individual undergoing classical conditioning resembles a scientist who is trying to figure out what causes what (Rescorla, 1985).

SUMMARY

1. The scientific study of learning grew out of attempts to compare the intelligence of various animal species. (page 239)

2. Behaviorism is an attempt to explain behavior without reference to unobservable mental processes. Behaviorists assume that all behavior is caused in some way, that mental states do not explain behavior, and that behavior is molded by sensory stimuli. (page 241)

3. Ivan Pavlov discovered classical conditioning, the process by which an organism learns a new association between two stimuli that have been paired with each other—a neutral stimulus (the conditioned stimulus) and one that already evokes a reflexive response (the unconditioned stimulus). The organism displays this association by responding in a new way (the conditioned response) to the conditioned stimulus. (page 242)

4. After classical conditioning has established a conditioned response to a stimulus, the response can be extinguished by presenting that stimulus repeatedly by itself. (page 245)

5. If the conditioned stimulus is not presented at all for some time after extinction and then is presented again, the conditioned response may return to some degree. That return is called spontaneous recovery. (page 245)

6. An animal or person who has been trained to respond to one stimulus will respond similarly to similar stimuli. However, if one stimulus is followed by an unconditioned stimulus and another is not, the individual will come to discriminate between them. (page 245)

7. As a rule, people and animals develop conditioned responses only if the conditioned stimulus is presented before the unconditioned stimulus. In exceptional circumstances, an unconditioned stimulus can be associated with a conditioned stimulus that follows it. (page 246)

8. Pavlov believed that temporal contiguity between two stimuli caused classical conditioning. We now believe that conditioning is caused by contingency, or the extent to which the occurrence of the first stimulus predicts the occurrence of the second. (page 248)

9. Conditioning is based on certain predispositions, such as the predisposition to associate illness with foods rather than with other events. (page 250)

SUGGESTION FOR FURTHER READING

Rescorla, R. A. (1988). Pavlovian conditioning: It's not what you think it is. *American Psychologist, 43,* 151–160. A theoretical review by an investigator who has contributed significantly to changing views of classical conditioning.

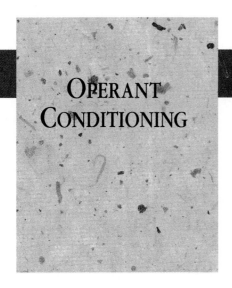

OPERANT CONDITIONING

How do rewards and punishments guide
our behavior?
How can we most effectively use rewards
and punishments to guide
the behavior of others?

John B. Watson, one of the founders of behaviorism, once said, "Give me a dozen healthy infants, well-formed, and my own specified world to bring them up in and I'll guarantee to take any one at random and train him to become any type of specialist I might select—doctor, lawyer, artist, merchant-chief, and yes, even beggar-man thief, regardless of his talents, penchants, tendencies, abilities, vocations, and race of his ancestors" (1925, p. 82).

We shall never know whether Watson was right, because no one ever gave him a dozen healthy infants and let him specify the world in which they would be raised. Today, few psychologists share Watson's conviction that differences in experience are responsible for virtually all differences in behavior. Still, experience clearly has a strong influence on behavior. Whether we choose to do something is largely determined by whether we have been rewarded or punished for doing it in the past.

THORNDIKE AND OPERANT CONDITIONING

Shortly before Pavlov performed his innovative experiments, Edward L. Thorndike (1911/1970), a Harvard graduate student, had begun to train and test some cats in his basement. Saying that earlier experiments had dealt only with animal intelligence, never with animal stupidity, he devised a simple, behavioristic explanation of learning.

Thorndike put cats into puzzle boxes (Figure 7.13) from which they could escape by pressing a lever, pulling a string, or tilting a pole. Sometimes he placed a food reward outside the box. (Usually, though, just escaping from a small box seemed reward enough.) The cats learned to make whatever response led to the reward. Thorndike discovered that they learned faster if they got the reward immediately after making the response. The longer the delay between response and reward, the less improvement there was in the rate of response.

When the cat had to tilt a pole in order to escape, it would first paw or gnaw at the door, scratch the walls, or pace back and forth. Eventually, by accident, it would bump against the pole and open the door. The next time, the cat would go through the same repertoire of behaviors but might bump against the pole a little sooner. Over many trials, the time it took the cat to escape grew shorter, in a gradual and irregular fashion. Figure 7.14 shows a learning curve to represent this behavior. A *learning curve* is a graph of the changes in behavior that occur over successive trials in a learning experiment.

Had the cat "figured out" how to escape? Had it come to "understand" the connection between bumping against the pole and opening the door? No, said Thorndike, a true behaviorist. If the cat had gained some new insight at some point along the way, he explained, its speed of escaping would have increased suddenly and would have remained constant for all later trials. Actually, the cat's performance improved only slowly and gradually.

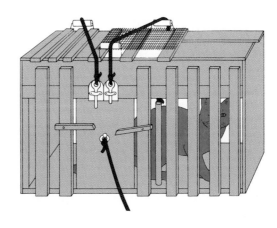

FIGURE 7.13

Thorndike said, "Learning is connecting." Here's one of his puzzle boxes. (Based on Thorndike, 1911.)

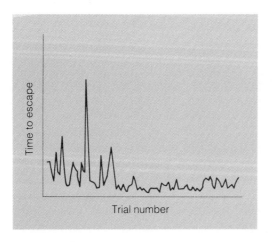

FIGURE 7.14

Trial and error or insight? As data from one of Thorndike's experiments show, the time a cat needs to escape from a puzzle box gradually grows shorter, but in an irregular manner.

Clearly, something other than understanding must have been at work.

Thorndike concluded that learning occurs only as certain behaviors are strengthened at the expense of others. An animal enters a given situation with a certain repertoire of responses (labeled R_1, R_2, R_3 ... R_N, in Figure 7.15a). First, it engages in its most probable response for this situation (response R_1 in the figure). If nothing special happens, it proceeds to other responses. Eventually, it gets to a lower-probability response—for example, bumping against the pole that opens the door (response R_7 in the figure). The opening of the door serves as a reinforcement.

A **reinforcement** is an event that increases the probability that the response that preceded it will be repeated in the future. In other words, it "stamps in," or strengthens, the response. The next time Thorndike's cat is in the puzzle box, its response may have a .04 probability instead of a .03 probability of occurrence, and after another reinforcement the probability may go up to .05. Eventually, the pole-bumping response has a greater probability than any other response, and the cat escapes quickly (Figure 7.15c).

Thorndike summarized his views in the **law of effect** (Thorndike, 1911/1970, p. 244): "Of several responses made to the same situation, those which are accompanied or closely followed by satisfaction to the animal will, other things being equal, be more firmly connected with the situation, so that, when it recurs, they will be more likely to recur." In other words, a response followed by favorable consequences becomes more probable, and a response followed by unfavorable consequences becomes less probable. This process does not require that the animal "think" or "understand."

Changing behavior by following a response with reinforcement is known as **operant conditioning** (because the subject *operates* on the environment to produce an outcome) or **instrumental conditioning** (because the subject's behavior is *instrumental* in producing the outcome). The difference between operant conditioning and classical conditioning is one of procedure: In operant conditioning, the subject's behavior determines what the outcome will be and when it will occur. In classical conditioning, the subject's behavior has no effect

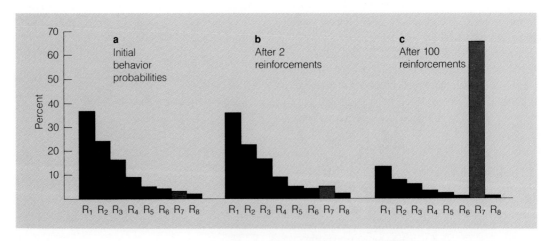

FIGURE 7.15

Thorndike's theory of learning. According to Thorndike, an animal enters any situation with a repertoire of responses (R_1 through R_N, with R_1 representing its mostly likely response). If reinforcement always follows R_7, the probability steadily increases that the animal will make that response in that situation.

on the outcome (the presentation of either the CS or the US).

Some psychologists have suggested that classical conditioning and operant conditioning may differ in other ways as well. For example, they have suggested that classical conditioning applies only to **visceral** responses, such as salivation and digestion, which involve the internal organs. In this view, operant conditioning applies only to **skeletal** responses—that is, movements of muscles such as those of the legs. But this distinction is cloudy. If a tone is followed by an electric shock in classical conditioning, the tone will come to control the animal's skeletal movements as well as its heart rate. And a few investigators have reported that reinforcement in operant conditioning can increase the frequency of heart rate, intestinal contractions, and other visceral responses (Miller, 1969); later studies have failed to replicate those results (Dworkin & Miller, 1986).

Concept Check

4. *When I ring a bell, an animal sits up on its hind legs and drools; then I give it some food. Is that an example of classical conditioning or of operant conditioning?*

Well, actually this is a trick question; you do not have enough information to answer it. What else would you have to know before you could answer? (Check your answer on page 274.)

Why Are Certain Responses Learned More Easily Than Others?

Thorndike's cats quickly learned to push and pull various devices in their efforts to escape from his puzzle boxes. But when Thorndike tried to teach them to scratch themselves or lick themselves to receive the same reinforcement, they learned slowly and never performed at a high level. Why not?

One possible reason is **belongingness**, the concept that certain stimuli "belong" together, or that a given response might be more readily associated with certain outcomes than with others (Seligman, 1970). I mentioned one example of this principle in the discussion of classical conditioning: Rats are predisposed to associate illness with something they ate rather than with something they saw or heard. Another example: Dogs can readily learn that a sound coming from one location means "raise your left leg," while a sound coming from another location means "raise your right leg." But it takes them virtually forever to learn that a ticking metronome means raise the left leg while a buzzer means raise

the right leg (Dobrzecka, Szwejkowska, & Konorski, 1966). Somehow the location of a sound and a location on the body "belong" together; a type of sound does not belong with a location on the body.

Presumably Thorndike's cats were slow to associate scratching themselves with escaping from a box because the two activities do not "belong" together. (In the entire history of the cat species, this was probably the first time that scratching oneself had caused a door to open!) But there is another possible explanation for why cats have trouble learning to scratch themselves for reinforcement: A cat can scratch itself only when it itches (Charlton, 1983). Consider what would happen if you knew that you would be handsomely reinforced for swallowing rapidly and repeatedly. Your response rate might remain low even if you had learned the association well. Some behaviors are just not easy to produce on command.

Extinction, Generalization, and Discrimination

As in classical conditioning, operant conditioning is subject to extinction, stimulus generalization, and discrimination. In operant conditioning, we achieve **extinction** by omitting the reinforcement after a subject has made a response. For example, you have been in the habit of asking your roommate to join you for supper. The last five times you asked, your roommate said no. You stop asking. (In classical conditioning, you will recall, extinction is achieved by presenting the CS without the US.)

If a subject receives reinforcement for making a particular response in the presence of a certain stimulus, the subject will make the same response in the presence of a similar stimulus. The greater the difference between the original stimulus and the new stimulus, however, the less vigorously the subject is likely to respond. This phenomenon is known as **stimulus generalization**. For example, you might smile at a stranger who reminds you of an old friend. Or you might reach for the turn signal in a rented car in the place you would find it in your own car. In both cases you are responding to a new stimulus in the same way you have learned to respond to an old stimulus.

If a subject is reinforced for responding to one stimulus and is reinforced less strongly (or not at all) for responding to another stimulus, then the subject will learn to use **discrimination** between them and will respond more vigorously to one than to the other. For example, you walk toward a parked car you think is yours and then you realize it is not. After several such experiences you learn to identify your own car from a distance.

TABLE 7.1 Comparison of Classical Conditioning and Operant Conditioning

	Classical Conditioning	Operant Conditioning
Terminology	CS, US, CR, UR	Response, reinforcement
Subject's behavior...	Does not control US	Controls reinforcement
Paired during acquisition	Two stimuli (CS and US)	Response and reinforcement (in the presence of certain stimuli)
Responses studied	Mostly visceral	Mostly skeletal
Extinction procedure	CS without US	Response without reinforcement
Generalization	Stimulus similar to CS evokes CR to some degree	Some degree of responding in the presence of stimuli similar to those that have been present during reinforcement
Discrimination	One stimulus is followed by US; a similar stimulus is not	Responses are reinforced in the presence of one stimulus, but not in the presence of another

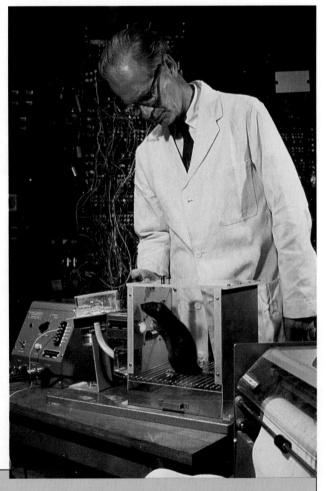

B. F. Skinner with one of his laboratory animals. Of nonrat subjects, Skinner said, "Education is what survives when what has been learnt has been forgotten."

Table 7.1 compares operant conditioning and classical conditioning.

B. F. SKINNER AND THE SHAPING OF RESPONSES

The most influential behaviorist of recent times has been B. F. Skinner, who demonstrated many uses of operant conditioning.

Although we ordinarily expect scientific progress to emerge from a logical sequence of experiments designed to test certain hypotheses, it sometimes results from simple accident. For example, in one of Skinner's (1956) early experiments, he arranged for rats to run down an 8-foot-long alley to get food. But after a while he grew tired of picking the rats up every time and returning them to the starting position. So he built a circular runway. Now the rats, after getting the food, could run around the circle and back to the start box on their own. But Skinner still had to replenish the food in the goal box each time. He rigged it so the rats could do that too. Eventually he decided there was no need for the alley to be 8 feet long. In fact, he dispensed with the alley altogether. What was left was a simple box, now called the *Skinner box* (Figure 7.16), in which a rat presses a lever or a pigeon pecks an illuminated disk (or "key") to receive food.

Shaping Behavior

Suppose we want to train a rat to press a lever. We could simply put the rat in the box and wait, just

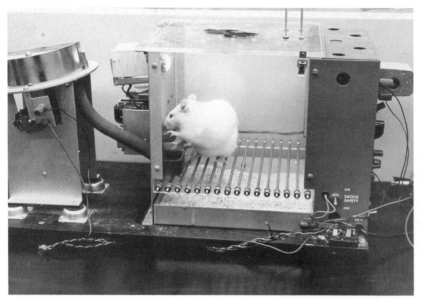

FIGURE 7.16

Form follows function: An operant conditioning chamber, or "Skinner box." When the light above the bar is on, pressing the bar is reinforced. A food pellet rolls out of the storage device (left) and down the tube into the cage.

as Thorndike waited for cats to find their way out of his puzzle boxes. However, the rat might never press that lever. To avoid interminable waits, Skinner devised a powerful technique, called **shaping**, for establishing a new response by reinforcing successive approximations to it.

We might begin by reinforcing the rat for standing up. Because that is a common behavior for rats, the rat soon gets its first reinforcement. Before long the rat has received several reinforcements and is beginning to stand up more frequently. Now we change the rules. We give the rat food only when it stands up while facing in the general direction of the lever. Soon the rat spends much of its time standing up and facing the lever. Now we provide reinforcement only when the rat stands in the part of the cage nearest the lever. Gradually the rat moves closer and closer to the wall on which the lever is mounted, until it is touching the wall. Then the rat must touch the lever and finally apply weight to it. This whole shaping of behavior can sometimes be completed in minutes. The rat learns to make the response through a series of short, easy steps.

Chaining Behavior

To produce more complex sequences of behavior, psychologists use a procedure called **chaining**. Assume that we want an animal to engage in a specified sequence (or chain) of responses. We reinforce each response by giving the animal the opportunity to make the next response. The final response in the chain leads to food or some other reinforcer.

Squirrels on vacation? These water-skiers learned to ski through shaping and chaining, methods of reinforcing desired behavior and building on it. Standing still would be just the first of many steps in gradually training these animals to ski.

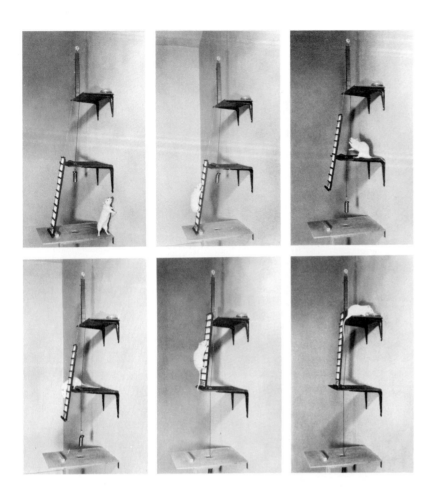

which produces a sound that tells you to put the car into gear and step on the accelerator. You drive forward until you reach a certain street, where you turn and proceed until you reach your destination. Each behavior is reinforced by the opportunity to engage in the next behavior.

To show how effective shaping and chaining can be, Skinner sometimes performed this demonstration: First, he trained a rat to go to the center of a cage. Then he trained it to do so only when he was playing a certain record. Then he trained it to wait for the record to start, go to the center of the cage, and sit up on its hind legs. Step by step Skinner eventually trained the rat to wait for the record to start (which happened to be of the "Star Spangled Banner"), move to the center of the cage, sit up on its hind legs, put its claws on a string next to a pole, pull the string to hoist a flag, and then salute the flag until the record had finished. Only then did it get its food reinforcement. Needless to say, a show of patriotism is not part of a rat's natural repertoire of behavior; it learns to go through the motions only by successive approximations.

INCREASING AND DECREASING THE FREQUENCY OF RESPONSES

To a large extent our behavior is governed by its consequences. We engage in acts that increase the number of good things that happen to us and decrease the number of bad things. Investigators of operant conditioning try to determine in detail how those good things and bad things change our behavior.

Reinforcement and Punishment

A few pages back, I defined *reinforcement* as an event that increases the probability that the preceding response will be repeated in the future. Psychologists distinguish two kinds of reinforcement: positive reinforcement and negative reinforcement. *Both* kinds of reinforcement *increase* the responses they are paired with. **Positive reinforcement** is the presentation of a favorable event, such as food, water, or access to a sexual partner. **Negative reinforcement** is an escape from an unfavorable event. Although this terminology tends to be confusing (Kimble, 1981), the logic behind it is straightforward. Just remember that reinforcement always strengthens a response; the terms *positive* and *negative* refer to whether something is presented or removed. Food is a positive reinforcer;

FIGURE 7.17

Nobody said this would be easy: Chained behavior. To reach food on the top platform, this rat must climb a ladder and pull a string to raise the ladder so it can climb up again. Behavior chains longer than this can be sustained by one reward at the end.

For example, a rat might first be placed on the top platform in Figure 7.17, where it eats food. Then it is placed on the intermediate platform with a ladder in place to the top platform. It learns to climb the ladder. After it has done so repeatedly, it is placed on the intermediate platform but the ladder is not present. The rat has to learn to pull a string to raise the ladder so it can climb to the top platform. Finally the rat is put on the bottom platform. It has to learn to climb the ladder to the intermediate platform, pull a string to raise the ladder, and then climb the ladder again. For each response in the chain, the reinforcement is the opportunity to engage in the next behavior, until the final response in the chain leads to a primary reinforcement.

Humans learn to make chains of responses, too. When you drive a car, you turn on the ignition,

turning off an electric shock is a negative reinforcer. If you turn off a dripping faucet, the end of the "drip drip drip" sound serves as a negative reinforcement.

Punishment, the opposite of reinforcement, is an event that decreases the probability that the preceding response will be repeated. Inhibiting a response in order to avoid punishment is known as *passive avoidance*. For example, we avoid jumping off cliffs in order to avoid injury; we do not steal because we would expect to be punished if we did.

Negative punishment is the weakening of a response by the omission of a favorable stimulus. For example, a teenager who drives recklessly loses the privilege of driving the family car. The loss of a favorable opportunity suppresses the tendency toward reckless driving.

Figure 7.18 summarizes the four varieties of operant conditioning. Remember this key point: All reinforcement increases a behavior; all punishment decreases it.

How effective is punishment? Should children sometimes be spanked? Should retarded people be punished for engaging in dangerous behaviors? Psychologists are not in full agreement on these matters.

If an individual has a strong motivation to engage in a certain behavior and has no other way to satisfy that motivation, punishment is generally ineffective. In one experiment, B. F. Skinner (1938) first trained some rats to press a bar to get food and then switched procedures so that pressing the bar no longer produced food. For some of the rats, Skinner arranged the apparatus so that the bar slapped their paws every time they pressed it during the first 10 minutes. The other rats received no punishment. For the first 10 minutes, the punished rats lowered their response rate. In the long run, however, they made as many total responses as the unpunished rats did.

Skinner concluded that punishment temporarily suppresses a behavior but does not permanently weaken it. Later research, however, indicates that under certain circumstances punishment exerts lasting effects on behavior. The problem with Skinner's study is that the hungry rats had no alternative response available for obtaining food. If you got a shock every time you touched the refrigerator door but knew there was no food available elsewhere, you would go on trying to open the door. Psychologists now believe that punishment can be effective so long as it is delivered promptly and consistently after a response is made and so long as some alternative response is available (Walters & Grusec, 1977). Even so, the effectiveness of pun-

	Pleasant stimulus	Unpleasant stimulus
Presented	Positive reinforcement (increases response frequency)	Punishment (decreases response frequency)
Removed	Negative punishment (decreases response frequency)	Negative reinforcement (increases response frequency)

FIGURE 7.18

The four categories of operant conditioning.

ishment depends on many factors. For example, children respond more readily to mild punishment accompanied by a parent's explanation of why they were punished than they do to more intense punishment without an explanation. Punishment is ineffective if children learn that they can get more attention for "bad" behavior than for "good" behavior. It may even stimulate the very behaviors it is meant to discourage. For example, a parent who spanks a child for nervous fidgeting may find that the spanking makes the child even more nervous and fidgety.

In practical situations, the question is not whether punishment will work but whether it is the best way to achieve the desired results. If you want to teach your young son or daughter not to touch a hot stove, you may get good results from a swift but gentle slap on the wrist or even a sharp NO! A few years later, if you want to teach the same child to speak politely to others, an occasional reinforcement for politeness is likely to work better than punishment for rudeness. The government has found that it can elicit more cooperation from business firms by granting them tax credits for desirable actions than by fining them for undesirable actions.

Something to Think About

Your local school board proposes to improve class attendance by failing any student who misses a certain number of classes. How might it achieve the same goal through positive reinforcement?

"*You can catch more flies with honey than with vinegar.*" *That old maxim expresses a problem-solving procedure that may apply to the following question: For the government to reduce environmental pollution, which approach would be more effective—to offer tax incentives to corporations that clean up their manufacturing methods or to penalize companies that pollute?*

David Nathanson, a psychologist in Florida, uses the Premack principle in teaching children with Downs syndrome or other mental disabilities. The goal is to improve their ability to learn by increasing their short attention spans; the positive reinforcement is the opportunity to "play" with a dolphin. The children, ranging in age from 2 to 10, first receive individual instruction in a classroomlike setting. Then the teacher takes a child to the pool to meet the dolphin. A card with a picture and word on it is shown to the child and then thrown into the water; the dolphin pushes it back to the child with its nose. If the child identifies the picture with the correct word, he or she gets a "kiss" from the dolphin or gets to throw the card back in the water. The children tend to give correct answers more often with the dolphins than in the classroom.

What Constitutes Reinforcement?

Generally, an event that serves as a positive reinforcer for one response also will serve as a positive reinforcer for other responses. In fact, Thorndike put together a list of positive reinforcers simply by testing various events to see which worked and which did not. If an event increased the probability that the preceding response would be repeated, he identified that event as a positive reinforcer.

The Premack Principle David Premack (1965) proposed a more theoretical approach to reinforcement. He suggested that if an animal, on its own, is more likely to make response A than response B, then giving the animal the opportunity to make response A will positively reinforce response B. This relationship is known as the **Premack principle**. For example, if, under certain circumstances, an animal ordinarily drinks more than it eats, then giving it the opportunity to drink will be a positive reinforcer for eating. By giving it water as a reinforcer, we can get the animal to eat more. If you would ordinarily spend more time playing video games than studying French grammar, then someone could use the opportunity to play video games as a reinforcement, or incentive, for finishing your French assignment. However, if you would ordinarily spend more time studying French grammar than playing video games, then someone could get you to play more video games by offering a French grammar book as a reinforcement.

Psychologists have to find appropriate measures of how frequent or how likely a response is. For example, sexual behavior in some species occurs only once or twice a year. But during a short time it may take priority over everything else. Consequently, the opportunity to engage in sexual behavior may serve as a powerful reinforcer at certain times but have no effect as a reinforcer at other times.

Concept Check

5. Suppose you are trying to teach a socially withdrawn child to interact with others by means of positive reinforcement. According to the Premack principle, how should you begin? (Check your answer on page 274.)

Primary and Secondary Reinforcement We can easily see why food and water are reinforcers; we all need to eat and drink in order to survive. But we will also work for a dollar bill or a college diploma. We distinguish between **primary reinforcers** such as food and water, which satisfy biological needs, and **secondary reinforcers** such as dollar bills, which become reinforcing because of their association with a primary reinforcer in the past. Dollar bills have no value to us at first, but become reinforcing once we learn that we can exchange them for food or other primary reinforcers. A student learns that good grades will win the approval of parents and teachers; an employee learns that increased sales will win the approval of the employer. We spend most of our time working for secondary reinforcers.

Reinforcement as Learning What Leads to What

Thorndike, you will recall, held that reinforcement strengthens the response that preceded it. According to that view, reinforcement is a mechanical process; the person who experiences reinforcement simply engages in the response more frequently, without understanding *why*.

According to another view that E. C. Tolman (1932) first proposed, individuals learn what leads to what. A rat may learn that running down an alley leads to food. Having learned that, the rat does not automatically go running down the alley all the time. It runs down the alley only when it needs food.

For example, suppose an animal has managed to find its way through a maze. We reward it by giving it something it may not need at the moment, such as food just after it has eaten a meal. Despite this reinforcement, the animal does not repeat the behavior, at least not right away. But if we retest the animal several hours later, we find that it suddenly increases the frequency of the behavior (Tolman & Honzik, 1930).

Another example: A rat is reinforced with sugar water for making response A and is reinforced with food pellets for making response B. After both responses have become well established, the rat is made ill after consuming, say, the sugar water and quickly learns to avoid it. Now the rat is put in a cage where it can make both response A and response B, although neither response produces any reinforcement. The rat spends most of its time making response B and seldom, if ever, makes response A (Colwill & Rescorla, 1985). Clearly something more is at work here than reinforcement increasing the frequency of responses. Evidently the rat has learned which response produced which outcome.

In other words, we must distinguish between learning and performance. Whether or not the subject makes a response depends on what outcome is associated with that response and on how strongly motivated the subject is to achieve that outcome.

Some secondary reinforcers are surprisingly powerful. Consider, for example, how hard some first-graders work for a little gold star that the teacher pastes on an assignment.

The Cumulative Record

In operant-conditioning experiments, the frequency of a response is usually depicted on a **cumulative record**. Imagine a recording device in which a pen moves along a line at a steady rate of, say, 10 centimeters per minute. Every time the animal makes the desired response, the pen records a little blip, as shown in Figure 7.19a. But counting all the responses recorded over a period of time would be a slow, tedious, and probably inaccurate procedure. So the recorder is designed to accumulate the responses. Every time the pen blips one notch upward, it stays at the higher level until it records the next response. Then it moves up another notch, and so on. The result is a cumulative record (Figure 7.19b).

Just by glancing at the record and observing the slope of the line, we can determine the rate of response. If the line rises sharply, we know that the subject is responding rapidly. If the line is flat, we know that the subject is not responding at all. The line *never* slopes downward. (However, when the line reaches the top of the page, the recorder resets itself to zero.) Figure 7.19 shows the cumulative

FIGURE 7.19

Ways of recording the rate of response in operant conditioning. (a) The pen returns to the starting point after each response. (b) A cumulative record. The pen begins at the right edge of a roll of paper and moves to the left edge. After each response, the pen remains at the new elevation. The line's slope indicates the rate of response. When the pen reaches the left edge, it automatically returns to the paper's right edge. The final record on paper is turned sideways so the right edge becomes the bottom and the response line slopes up.

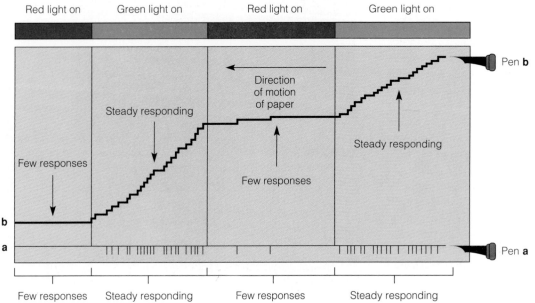

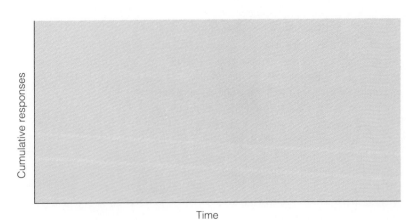

FIGURE 7.20

record for a pigeon that has learned to respond to a green light but not to a red light. (This is an example of discrimination, discussed on page 255.)

Concept Check

6. *What would the cumulative record look like for a subject that has been responding at a high rate and then goes through extinction? Pencil in your answer on Figure 7.20. (Check your answer on page 274.)*

Schedules of Reinforcement

The simplest procedure in operant conditioning is to provide reinforcement every time the correct response occurs. **Continuous reinforcement** refers to reinforcement for every correct response. As you know, not every response in the real world leads to reinforcement. Reinforcement for some responses and not others is known as **partial reinforcement**. We behave differently when we know that only some of our responses will be reinforced. Psychologists have investigated the effects of many **schedules of reinforcement**, which are rules for the delivery of reinforcement. Continuous reinforcement is the simplest schedule of reinforcement. Four schedules for partial reinforcement are fixed ratio, fixed interval, variable ratio, and variable interval.

Fixed-Ratio Schedule A fixed-ratio schedule provides reinforcement only after a certain number of correct responses have been made—after every fifth response, for example. Even with a fixed-ratio schedule that calls for hundreds of responses, some animals will continue to respond until they get reinforcement. We see similar behavior among pieceworkers in a factory, whose pay depends on how many pieces they turn out or among fruit pickers who get paid by the bushel.

The response rate on a fixed-ratio schedule tends to be rapid and steady. However, if the schedule requires a large number of responses for a reinforcement, there may be a temporary interruption. For example, an animal that has just finished pressing a lever 50 times to get a piece of food will pause for a while before starting to press again. The more responses that are required, the longer the pause will be. The same is true of humans. A student who has just completed 10 calculus problems may pause briefly before starting her French assignment; after completing 100 problems, she will pause even longer.

Fixed-Interval Schedule A fixed-interval schedule provides reinforcement for the first response made after a specific time has passed. For instance, an animal might get food only for the first response it makes after each 2-minute interval. Then it would have to wait another 2 minutes before another response would count. Animals (including humans) on such a schedule usually learn to pause after each reinforcement and begin to respond again only as the end of the time interval approaches.

Checking your mailbox is an example of behavior on a fixed-interval schedule. If your mail is delivered at about 3 P.M., you will get no reinforcement for checking your mailbox at 2:00 P.M. If you are eagerly awaiting an important letter, you will begin to check around 2:30 and continue checking every few minutes until it arrives.

Variable-Ratio Schedule A variable-ratio schedule is the same as a fixed-ratio schedule except that the number of responses necessary for reinforcement

*R*einforcements—*continuous or partial—encourage us to continue trying. Whatever the job, all employees are on a schedule of reinforcement. This factory worker is paid on a fixed-ratio schedule— her wages depend on the number of items she produces. Businesses that adopt incentive-pay systems usually increase productivity. Gambling offers reinforcement on a variable-ratio schedule. Some people play blackjack or roulette for hours at a time with few rewards for their efforts. The unpredictability is part of the appeal to gamblers. But never knowing whether or not the next bet will be the big payoff makes it hard to quit. "Just one more" may become one more hour.*

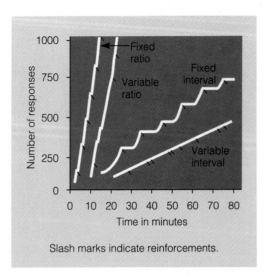

Slash marks indicate reinforcements.

FIGURE 7.21

Variations on a theme: Partial reinforcements follow schedules based on a variable of either time or number. The steepness of these four lines indicates the rates of responding. The rate of responding generally is higher with ratio schedules than with interval schedules. Fixed-interval schedules lead to bursts of rapid responding followed by a reinforcement, then a pause in responding. (Adapted from Skinner, 1961.)

varies from time to time. Reinforcement may come after 10 responses, then after 17 more responses, then after another 9. Variable-ratio schedules generate steady response rates. Gambling is reinforced on a variable-ratio schedule, because the gambler receives payment for some responses and not others on an irregular basis.

Much of our day-to-day behavior is reinforced on a variable-ratio schedule. For example, a radio station announces it will give free concert tickets to the next 40 people who call. When you call, you find that the line is busy. The more times you try dialing the station, the greater your chance of eventually getting answered. Similarly, when you go out on a date, you have some chance of having a good time. The more dates you go on, the more frequent your reinforcements will be. Both your calls to the radio station and your dating behavior are maintained by a variable-ratio schedule.

Variable-Interval Schedule In a **variable-interval schedule**, the time interval varies between one reinforcement opportunity and the next. For example, reinforcement may come for the first response after 2 minutes, then for the first response after 7 seconds, then for the first response after 3 minutes 20 seconds, and so forth. There is no way of know-

ing how long it will be before the next response is reinforced. Consequently, animals usually respond to a variable-interval schedule at a slow but steady rate. In an office where employees are rewarded if they are at work when the boss appears, they will work steadily but not necessarily vigorously so long as the boss's appearances are irregular and unpredictable.

Stargazing is another example of a response reinforced on a variable-interval schedule. The reinforcement for stargazing—seeing a comet, a nova, or some other unusual phenomenon—appears at irregular, unpredictable intervals. Consequently, both professional and amateur astronomers scan the skies regularly.

Figure 7.21 includes cumulative records for responding on four schedules of reinforcement. Note the long pause after each reinforcement in a fixed-interval schedule. If a fixed-ratio schedule requires a very large number of responses per reinforcement, it too has a long pause after each reinforcement.

Extinction of Responses Maintained by Ratio or Interval Reinforcement After a schedule of partial reinforcement (either a ratio schedule or an interval schedule), the extinction of responses tends to be slower than it is after a schedule of continuous reinforcement (reinforcement for every response). That tendency is known as the **partial-reinforcement extinction effect**. If a subject has become accustomed to reinforcement for every response it makes, a sudden cessation of reinforcement is very noticeable and extinction sets in rapidly. On a ratio or an interval schedule, however, the subject learns that it may have to respond many times before getting reinforcement. Consequently, a long time may pass before it discovers that its responses will never be reinforced again. So extinction occurs slowly.

Concept Checks

7. The reinforcement for studying hard is getting a good score on a test. Which schedule of reinforcement is in force in each of the following situations? When will students study in each case? (Check your answers on pages 274–275.)

a. The professor gives unannounced tests ("pop quizzes") at unpredictable times.

b. The professor gives a test on the last day of every month.

c. Students work at their own pace and take a test as soon as they finish a chapter.

8. A novice gambler and a longtime gambler both lose 20 bets in a row. Which is more likely to continue betting? Why? (Check your answer on page 275.)

Some Practical Applications of Operant Conditioning

Although operant conditioning arose from purely theoretical concerns, it has had a long history of practical applications. Here are four examples.

Animal Training

Most animal acts today are based on training methods similar to Skinner's. To get an animal to perform a trick, the trainer first trains it to perform some simple act that is similar to its natural behavior. Then the trainer shapes the animal, step by step, to perform progressively more complex behaviors. Most animal trainers rely on positive reinforcement rather than on punishment.

During the Second World War, Skinner proposed a military application of his training methods (Skinner, 1960). The military was having trouble designing a guidance system for its air-to-ground missiles. It needed apparatus that could recognize a target and guide a missile toward it but that would be compact enough to leave room for explosives. Skinner said that he could teach pigeons to recognize a target and peck in its direction. If pigeons were placed in the nose cone of a missile, the direction of their pecking would guide the missile to the target. Skinner demonstrated that pigeons would do the job more cheaply and more accurately than the apparatus then in use and would take up less space. But the military laughed off the whole idea.

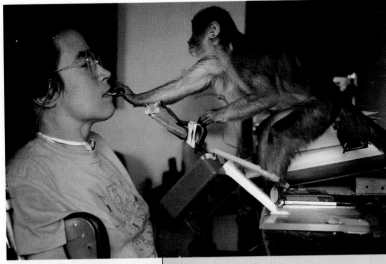

The high-tech hope of robots handling housekeeping chores has yet to materialize, but in the meantime, simian aides—trained monkeys—are helping the disabled. Monkeys are proving useful for doing indoor tasks for people with limited mobility—such as the simian aide above with a quadriplegic man. The monkey at left is being trained to retrieve objects identified with a laser beam. Such training relies on shaping behavior Skinner-style—building a new response by reinforcing sequential approximations to it.

Behavior Modification

Say what you will about ethics, we often try to change people's behavior—in prisons, for example, and mental hospitals and schools. The principles of operant conditioning have proved very useful in efforts to modify behavior.

In **behavior modification**, a psychologist sets a specific behavior goal and then systematically reinforces the subject's successive approximations to it. For example, Donald Whaley and Richard Malott (1971) describe a 9-year-old boy who would talk loudly and rapidly for more than 10 minutes at a time without ever pausing long enough for others to get a word in. As you might imagine, the boy's parents, teachers, and indeed everyone who knew him were eager to modify his behavior.

A psychologist began by searching out a behavior that the boy preferred even to talking (recall the Premack principle). That turned out to be firing a cap pistol. (Perhaps because it made even more noise than talking?) Whenever the boy paused for at least 3 seconds, he earned some caps. In the first session, he earned only 20 reinforcements in 90 minutes (see Figure 7.22). (He was silent for only 60 seconds during those 90 minutes!) Over successive sessions, he earned more reinforcements. Then the psychologist shifted to a fixed-ratio schedule, reinforcing only every fifth pause. By the sixth session, the boy was pausing about once per minute. He was still gabby, but at least other people were getting some chance to talk.

Concept Check

9. Which type of operant conditioning was used in the preceding example of the gabby boy: positive reinforcement, negative reinforcement (active avoidance), punishment (passive avoidance), or negative punishment (omission training)? (Check your answer on page 275.)

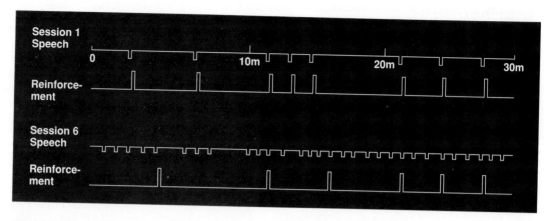

FIGURE 7.22

This boy talked too fast, too loud, and too much until a psychologist helped him shift his motor mouth to idle occasionally. To modify the boy's behavior, pauses were rewarded with caps. (The boy liked firing a cap pistol even more than talking.) After starting with continuous reinforcement—awarding caps for every 3-second pause—the psychologist switched to a fixed-ratio schedule of reinforcement.

```
                                    Date:   January 1, 1990


Goal:   To cut down on my smoking


What I will do:  For the first month I will smoke
  no more than one cigarette per hour.  I will not
  smoke immediately after meals.  I will not smoke
  in bed.   In February I will cut back to one every
  other hour.


What others will do:  My roommate Joe will keep
  track of how many cigarettes I smoke by counting
  cigarettes in the pack each night.  He will
  keep records of any cigarettes I smoke after
  meals or in bed.


Rewards if contract is kept:  I will treat myself
  to a movie every week if I stick to the contract.


Consequences if contract is broken:  If I break the
  contract, I have to clean the room by myself on
  the weekend.


Signatures:

              Steve Self
              Joe Roommate
```

FIGURE 7.23

Self-contract.

Breaking Bad Habits

Some people learn to conquer their own bad habits by means of reinforcements, with a little outside help. Nathan Azrin and Robert Nunn (1973) devised this three-step method:

1. Make the person more aware of the habit. Encourage him or her to interrupt the behavior and to isolate it from the chain of normal activities. As an extension of this step, Brian Yates (1985) suggests asking the person to imagine an association between the behavior and something repulsive. For example, someone who is trying to break a fingernail-biting habit might imagine that the fingernails are covered with sewage.

2. Show approval to reinforce progress. Give the person a sense of accomplishment. Some people provide their own reinforcement, perhaps by buying a special treat after they have abandoned the habit for a certain period of time.

3. Encourage the person to engage in some behavior that is incompatible with the offending habit. For example, if a person has the nervous habit of hunching up his or her shoulders, suggest depressing the shoulders.

People can learn to control their own behavior by administering reinforcements and punishments, in much the way an experimenter controls an animal's behavior. Figure 7.23 shows one example, in which a college student set a specific goal for himself (to decrease his smoking) and a list of reinforcements and punishments. If he successfully limited his smoking, he would treat himself to a movie. If he exceeded the limit he had set for himself, he would have to clean the room by himself on the weekend, and he would not go to a movie. Many people set up similar patterns of reinforcement and punishment for themselves, generally without a written contract.

Persuasion

How could you get someone to do something he or she did not want to do? To take an extreme example, how could you convince a prisoner of war to cooperate with the enemy?

The best way is to start by reinforcing a very small degree of cooperation and then working up from there. This principle has been applied by people who had probably never heard of B. F. Skinner, positive reinforcement, or shaping. During the Korean War, for example, the Chinese Communists forwarded some of the letters written home by prisoners of war but intercepted others. (The prisoners could tell from the replies which letters had been forwarded.) The prisoners began to suspect they would have better luck getting their letters through if they said something mildly favorable about their captors. So from time to time they would include a brief remark that the Communists were not really so bad, or that certain aspects of the Chinese system seemed to work pretty well, or that they hoped the war would end soon. After a while the Chinese captors ran essay contests in which the soldier who wrote the best essay (in the captors' opinion) would win a little extra food or some other privilege. Most of the winning essays contained a statement or two that complimented the Communists on some minor matter or that admitted "the United States is not perfect." Gradually more and more soldiers started to include such statements in their essays. Occasionally the Chinese might ask one of them, "You said the United States is not perfect. We wonder whether you could tell us some of the ways in which it is not perfect, so that we can better understand your system." Then they would ask the soldiers who cooperated to read aloud their lists of what was wrong with the United States. And so on. Gradually, without torture or coercion, and with only modest reinforcements, the Chinese induced many prisoners to make public statements denouncing the United States, to make false confessions, to inform on fellow prisoners, and even to reveal military secrets (Cialdini, 1985).

The point is clear: Whether we want to get rats to salute the flag or soldiers to denounce it, the most effective training technique is to start with natural behaviors, to reinforce those behaviors, and then gradually to shape more complex behaviors.

SUMMARY

1. Edward Thorndike introduced the concept of reinforcement. A reinforcement increases the probability that the preceding response will be repeated. (page 253)

2. Operant conditioning is the process of controlling the rate of a behavior through reinforcement. (page 254)

3. In operant conditioning, a response becomes extinguished if it is no longer followed by reinforcement. (page 255)

4. Shaping is a technique for training subjects to perform acts that are remote from their natural behavior by reinforcing them for successive approximations to the desired behavior. (page 256)

5. Punishment, the omission of a reinforcement, or the omission of a punishment also will change the rate of a behavior. (page 258)

6. The opportunity to engage in a frequent behavior will reinforce a less frequent behavior. Something that an individual can exchange for a reinforcer becomes a reinforcer itself. (page 260)

7. Animals (and people) learn which reinforcement is associated with which behavior. The frequency with which they repeat a given behavior depends on the strength of their motivation to receive the associated reinforcement at the moment. (page 261)

8. The timing of a response depends on the schedule of reinforcement. In a ratio schedule of reinforcement, an individual is given reinforcement after a fixed or variable number of responses. In an interval schedule of reinforcement, an individual is given reinforcement after a fixed or variable period of time. (page 262)

9. People have applied operant conditioning to animal training, education, behavior modification, habit breaking, and persuasion. (page 265)

SUGGESTIONS FOR FURTHER READING

Schwartz, B. (1988). *Psychology of learning and behavior,* 3rd ed. New York: Norton. An excellent comprehensive text on learning.

Skinner, B. F. (1948). *Walden two.* New York: Macmillan. A novel about an attempt to devise an ideal society according to the principles of operant conditioning.

SOCIAL LEARNING

How do we learn from the successes and failures of others without trying every response ourselves?

Hºw do you learn how fast you should drive your car? Classical conditioning plays a role: You notice that your speedometer has hit 70 and a few seconds later you hear a police siren, which you perceive as an unpleasant sound. The next time you notice your speedometer hitting 70, you experience a conditioned response: nervousness.

Reinforcement too plays a role in your behavior: When you drive at a steady 55 mph, the fact that you reach your destination sooner than if you had driven at 45 provides positive reinforcement.

Wannabes: Teens are prone to identifying themselves with a favorite celebrity. Imitating superficial characteristics is easy; many people copy the hair and clothing styles of popular rock stars, actors, and athletes. Copying their talent is harder.

When you drive at 70, reaching your destination even sooner will provide further reinforcement. But it may also bring punishment, causing you to reach your destination both later and poorer.

You also learn from observing the behavior of others. You read that the police plan to enforce the speed laws more rigorously than usual during a holiday weekend, so you stay within the limit. But you notice that everyone is passing you, so you speed up. Then you pass a three-car wreck and recognize some of the cars that had passed you a minute before, so you slow down again. Note that you speed up and slow down even though you are experiencing no direct reinforcement or punishment. You learn about the reinforcements and punishments that your own behavior is likely to provoke by observing what happens to others. Social learning is learning by observation and imitation of others and by imagining what would happen to us if we imitated that behavior.

SOCIAL-LEARNING THEORY

According to **social-learning theory** (Bandura, 1977, 1986), just about everything we do is learned, even what we call "personality." And yet we learn about many behaviors even before we engage in them, before they have been reinforced in any way. How does that learning come about? It results from observing the behavior of others and from imagining the consequences of our own behavior.

Although psychologists speak of "social-learning theory," it is not a theory in the sense described in Chapter 2. It does not lead to predictions that can be rigorously tested, and there is no evidence that will directly confirm or refute it. Social-learning theory is more a point of view than it is a formal theory. It focuses on the effects of observation, imitation, setting goals, and self-reinforcement.

Modeling and Imitation

When you join a religious organization, a fraternity, or a sorority or when you start a new job, you discover that the people already there observe certain customs. They will explain some of those customs to you, but the only way you will learn about others is by watching. Those who already know the customs serve as models (or examples) for you; when you copy their example, we say that you are **mod-**

According to social learning theory, imitation is especially significant in human behavior. Children need role models to learn how to act in society—how to cross the street safely, for example. Do you do anything in public that is not based on imitation?

eling your behavior after theirs, or that you are **imitating**.

We are selective in choosing whom to imitate. We imitate people we regard as successful, people with whom we identify, people we want to be like. Advertisers are keenly aware of this tendency. They try to identify the consumers who are most likely to buy their products and the people those consumers are most likely to admire and imitate. Cereal and candy advertisements feature happy, healthy children; soft-drink ads feature attractive young adults; ads for luxury cars feature wealthy executives and their impeccably groomed spouses.

The advertisers of Miller's Lite beer have used this approach in a particularly effective manner. Earlier attempts to market a low-calorie beer had all failed. Beer drinkers perceived low-calorie beer as "diet beer" or "sissy beer." So Miller's ads featured well-known, middle-aged former athletes drinking Lite beer and getting into he-man disputes about *why* people should drink Lite beer—because it tastes great or because it is less filling. The campaign was so successful that the demand for *all* low-calorie beers, not just Miller's, skyrocketed.

This tendency to identify with role models is especially powerful among children. Parents who want to teach their children to cooperate and share with others get better results by setting an example of cooperation than by simply telling the children to cooperate (Young-Ok & Stevens, 1987). Children also take behavioral cues from other adults and

from television characters. They tend to imitate adults of their own sex more than adults of the opposite sex, even when the behaviors are fairly trivial. In one experiment, children watched adults choose between an apple and a banana. If all the men chose one and all the women chose the other, the boys who were watching wanted what the men had chosen and the girls wanted what the women had chosen (Perry & Bussey, 1979). In other words, children learn about gender roles and sex stereotypes by observation.

Albert Bandura, Dorothea Ross, and Sheila Ross (1963) studied the role of imitation in learning aggressive behavior. They had two groups of children watch films in which an adult or a cartoon character violently attacked an inflated doll. They had another group watch a film in which the characters did not attack the doll. Then they left the children in a room with an inflated doll. The children who had watched films showing attacks on the doll (and *only* those children) attacked the doll vigorously, using many of the same movements they had just seen (Figure 7.24).

Concept Check

10. *Many people complain that they cannot tell much difference between the two major political parties in the United States. Why do most American politicians campaign in similar styles and take similar stands on the issues? (Check your answer on page 275.)*

FIGURE 7.24

A child will mimic an adult's behavior even when neither one is rewarded or reinforced for the behavior. This girl attacks a doll after seeing a film of a woman hitting it. These results suggest that people who watch much violence may begin to imitate it. Think of Saturday morning cartoons: A mouse bonks another mouse with a frying pan, a coyote tries to crush a roadrunner with a boulder. Is watching hours of bopping and bashing harmless because the violence involves nonhuman characters? Or might some viewers copy what they have seen?

Ignorance is bliss? Fortunately, we don't have to directly experience danger to know that we should avoid it. We can learn from the experience of others. In the case of an infectious disease, this substitution is known as vicarious punishment.

Imitation also plays a role in learning the habits of using alcohol (Collins & Marlatt, 1981) and tobacco. It is hard to imagine how anyone who had never seen others smoke cigarettes could have invented the habit. ("Hey, that's an interesting-looking weed. I think I'll wrap it up in a piece of paper, set it on fire, and stick it in my mouth.") Few people enjoy their first use of alcohol or tobacco, but they keep trying it so they can be like the people whose approval they desire. Belief in the power of role models' persuasion is such that cigarette and whiskey ads are banned from TV. In the hundreds of beer commercials you've seen, everyone is always having a good time, but no one is drinking beer.

Vicarious Reinforcement and Punishment

Six months ago your best friend quit a job with Consolidated Generic Products in order to open a restaurant. Now you are considering whether you should quit your own job with Consolidated Generic and open your own restaurant in a different part of town. How do you decide whether or not to take this step?

Perhaps the first thing you do is to find out how successful your friend has been. You do not automatically imitate the behavior of someone else, even someone you admire. Rather, you imitate behavior that has proved reinforcing for that person. In other words, you learn by **vicarious reinforcement** or **punishment**—that is, by substituting someone else's experience for your own.

When a new business venture succeeds, other companies try to figure out the reasons for that success and try to follow the same course. When a venture fails, other companies try to learn the reasons for that failure and try to avoid making the same mistakes. When a football team wins consistently, other teams copy its style of play. And when a television program wins high ratings, other producers are sure to present look-alikes the following year.

Something to Think About

Might vicarious learning lead to a certain monotony of behavior? Might it contribute to the lack of variety in the television programs and movies that are offered to the public? How can we learn vicariously without becoming like everyone else?

Vicarious punishment seems to affect behavior less than vicarious reinforcement does. We are bombarded by reminders that failure to wear seat belts will lead to injury or death, and yet many of us fail to buckle up, even though failure to use seat belts is illegal in some states. Despite widespread publicity about the consequences of using addictive drugs or of engaging in "unsafe sex," many people ignore the danger. Even the death penalty, an extreme example of vicarious punishment, seems to have little effect on the murder rate.

The Role of Self-Efficacy in Social Learning

You watch an Olympic diver win a gold medal for a superb display of physical control. Do you go out and try to do the same? Probably not. Why? After all, you admire the diver and you see that his or her behavior met with strong positive reinforcement. Why does that vicarious reinforcement fail to motivate you to engage in imitative behavior?

If you are like most people, the reason is that you doubt you are capable of duplicating the diver's performance. People imitate someone else's behavior only if they have a sense of **self-efficacy**—the perception that they themselves could perform the task successfully.

We achieve or fail to achieve a sense of self-efficacy in two ways. One way is by observing ourselves. If I have tried and failed to develop even simple athletic skills, I will have no sense of self-efficacy when I think of trying to duplicate the behavior of an Olympic medalist. A student who

We spend our time on things that we do well and avoid doing things that we do poorly. This pattern often creates self-fulfilling prophecies. For example, if you play tennis well, you are likely to have the self-confidence—a sense of self-efficacy—to play against other good players and the motivation to practice your backhand. A strong sense of self-efficacy enables dancers to follow a rigorous schedule of exercise and rehearsal. Basketball player Ralph Sampson and other professional athletes work out to improve skills that are already highly developed.

Wanting to lose weight is a first step, but actually doing it requires more than wishful thinking. These people are being weighed in a Kansas City supermarket as part of a program called the Great American Shape-Up. Dieters who fail with self-reinforcement may find that going public with their weight-loss goal helps them succeed. Weight Watchers and Overeaters Anonymous offer support from people sharing a common problem.

has studied hard and has done well on several exams will have a strong sense of self-efficacy when faced with the next exam. We also learn about self-efficacy from role models. If your older cousin has studied hard and has gained admission to medical school, you may believe that you can do the same.

People's persistence or lack of persistence in coping with a difficult task is strongly influenced by their sense of self-efficacy. Kidney patients under dialysis treatment are advised to curtail their fluid intake sharply. Patients who are confident they can follow the instructions generally restrict their intake and respond well to the treatment. Those who confess that they "can't tolerate frustration" generally yield to temptation, go on drinking fluids, and soon die (Rosenbaum & Smira, 1986).

Similarly, people who believe they can quit smoking have a reasonable chance of succeeding. People who doubt their ability to quit may try hard at first, but sooner or later they have one cigarette, decide they are a hopeless case, and give up (Curry, Marlatt, & Gordon, 1987).

The Role of Self-Reinforcement in Social Learning

We learn by observing others who are doing what we would like to do. If our sense of self-efficacy is strong enough, we decide to imitate their behavior.

But *actually* doing it is another matter. People typically set a goal for themselves and monitor their progress toward it. They even provide reinforcement or punishment for themselves just as if they were training someone else. They say to themselves, "If I finish this math assignment on time, I'll treat myself to a movie and a new magazine."

People who have never learned to use self-reinforcement can be taught to do so. Donald Meichenbaum and Joseph Goodman (1971) worked with a group of elementary-school children who acted impulsively, blurting out answers and failing to consider the consequences of their actions. To encourage them to set appropriate goals for themselves and to practice self-reinforcement in achieving them, Meichenbaum and Goodman taught the children to talk to themselves while working on a task. For example, a child might say, "Okay, what do I have to do? You want me to copy the picture. . . . Okay, draw the line down, down, good; then to the right, that's it; now down some more and to the left. Good, I'm doing fine so far. Remember, go slowly. Now back up again. No, I was supposed to go down. That's okay. Just erase the line carefully. . . ." After only four training sessions, the children had learned to pause before answering questions and were answering more questions correctly.

Unfortunately, self-reinforcement does not always work. One psychologist, Ron Ash (1986), tried to teach himself to stop smoking by means of punishment. He decided to smoke only while he was reading *Psychological Bulletin* and other professional publications that are respected but dull. By associating smoking with boredom, he hoped to eliminate his desire to smoke. Two months later he was smoking as much as ever, but he was starting to *enjoy* reading *Psychological Bulletin*!

Sometimes outside help contributes to our efforts at self-reinforcement. A wholesale bakery once called on some psychologists to help reduce the rate of injury among employees. The workers had set their own safety goals, but their efforts at self-reinforcement were apparently faltering. The psychologists set about identifying the right and wrong ways to perform certain acts. For example: Workers should not leave cardboard lying on the floor. At least one person must always be stationed at each end of the conveyor belt. Pans should not be stacked above the rear rail of the pan rack. The psychologists then helped the company set up a system for keeping track of the number of times the workers committed unsafe acts. The record was shared with the workers at frequent intervals. Over time, the injury rate declined considerably (Komaki, Barwick, & Scott, 1978).

SUMMARY

1. We learn much by observing what other people do and what consequences they experience. (page 268)

2. We are more likely to imitate the actions of people we admire and people with whom we identify. (page 269)

3. We tend to imitate behaviors that have led to reinforcement for other people. We are less consistent in avoiding behaviors that have led to punishment. (page 270)

4. Whether or not we decide to imitate a behavior that has led to reinforcement for others depends on whether we believe we are capable of duplicating that behavior. (page 271)

5. Once people have decided to try to imitate a certain behavior, they set goals for themselves and may even provide their own reinforcements and punishments. (page 272)

6. Psychologists use various techniques to help people set goals and find ways to achieve them. (page 272)

SUGGESTION FOR FURTHER READING

Bandura, A. (1986). *Social foundations of thought and action.* Englewood Cliffs, NJ: Prentice-Hall. A review of social learning by its most influential investigator.

TERMS TO REMEMBER

acquisition the process by which a conditioned response is established or strengthened

backward conditioning presenting the unconditioned stimulus before the conditioned stimulus

behaviorist a psychologist who tries to explain the causes of behavior by studying only those behaviors that he or she can observe and measure, without reference to unobservable mental processes

behavior modification a procedure for modifying behavior by setting specific behavior goals and reinforcing the subject for successive approximations to those goals

belongingness the concept that certain stimuli are readily associated with each other and that certain responses are readily associated with certain outcomes

chaining a procedure for developing a sequence of behaviors in which the reinforcement for one response is the opportunity to engage in the next response

classical conditioning or **Pavlovian conditioning** the process by which an organism learns a new association between two stimuli paired with each other—a neutral stimulus and one that already evokes a reflexive response

conditioned inhibitor a stimulus that inhibits the conditioned response because of past experiences in which it predicted the absence of the unconditioned stimulus

conditioned response (CR) a response that the conditioned stimulus elicits only because it has previously been paired with the unconditioned stimulus

conditioned stimulus (CS) a stimulus that comes to evoke a particular response after being paired with the unconditioned stimulus

conditioned taste aversion or **bait shyness** the tendency to avoid eating a substance that has been followed by illness when eaten in the past

contingency the degree to which the occurrence of one stimulus predicts the occurrence of a second stimulus

continuous reinforcement reinforcement for every response

cumulative record a method of recording responses in which a recording pen moves up one notch for each response

discrimination making different responses to different stimuli that have been followed by different outcomes; in operant conditioning, the learning of different behaviors in response to stimuli associated with different levels of reinforcement

extinction in classical conditioning, the dying out of the conditioned response after repeated presentations of the conditioned stimulus unaccompanied by the unconditioned stimulus

extinction in operant conditioning, the weakening of a response after a period of no reinforcement

fixed-interval schedule a rule for delivering reinforcement for the first response the subject makes after a specified period of time has passed

fixed-ratio schedule a rule for delivering reinforcement only after the subject has made a certain number of responses

law of effect Thorndike's theory that a response that is followed by favorable consequences becomes more probable and a response that is followed by unfavorable consequences becomes less probable

modeling or **imitating** copying a behavior or custom

negative punishment the weakening of a response by the omission of a favorable stimulus

negative reinforcement escape from an unfavorable event

operant conditioning or **instrumental conditioning** the process of changing behavior by following a response with reinforcement

partial reinforcement reinforcement for some responses and not others

partial-reinforcement extinction effect the tendency for extinction to occur more slowly on either a ratio or an interval schedule than on a schedule of continuous reinforcement

positive reinforcement the presentation of a favorable event

Premack principle the principle that the opportunity to engage in a frequent behavior will reinforce a less frequent behavior

primary reinforcer an event that satisfies a biological need

punishment an event that decreases the probability that the preceding response will be repeated in the future

reinforcement an event that increases the probability that the response that preceded it will be repeated in the future

schedule of reinforcement a rule for the delivery of reinforcement following various patterns of responding

secondary reinforcer an event that becomes reinforcing when it is associated with a primary reinforcer

self-efficacy the perception of one's own ability to perform a task successfully

shaping a technique for establishing a new response by reinforcing successive approximations to it

skeletal pertaining to the muscles that move the limbs, trunk, and head

social-learning theory the view that people learn by observing and imitating the behavior of others and by imagining the consequences of their own behavior

spontaneous recovery the return of an extinguished response after a delay

stimulus generalization the extension of a learned response from the training stimulus to similar stimuli; in operant conditioning, the tendency to make a similar response to a stimulus that resembles one that has been associated with reinforcement

temporal contiguity being close together in time

unconditioned reflex an automatic connection between a stimulus and a response

unconditioned response (UR) an automatic response to an unconditioned stimulus

unconditioned stimulus (US) a stimulus that automatically elicits an unconditioned response

variable-interval schedule a rule for delivering reinforcement after varying amounts of time

variable-ratio schedule a rule for delivering reinforcement after varying numbers of responses

vicarious reinforcement or **punishment** reinforcement or punishment observed to have been experienced by someone else

visceral pertaining to the internal organs

ANSWERS TO CONCEPT CHECKS

1. The CS is the baby's crying. The US is the baby's sucking at the breast. Both the CR and the UR are the release of milk. Many nursing mothers experience this classically conditioned reflex. (page 244)

2. To bring about extinction, present the buzzer repeatedly without presenting any food. To bring about spontaneous recovery, first bring about extinction and then wait hours or days and present the buzzer again. (page 245)

3. If temporal contiguity were the main factor responsible for classical conditioning, rats exposed to the first sequence of stimuli should have responded the same as those exposed to the second sequence of stimuli. (page 250)

4. You would have to know whether the bell was always followed by food (classical conditioning) or whether food was presented only if the animal sat up on its hind legs (operant conditioning). (page 255)

5. Begin by determining the child's dominant or most preferred activity. Perhaps the child likes to play with a favorite toy or visit a favorite place. Use those activities to reinforce the behavior you want to encourage. (page 260)

6.

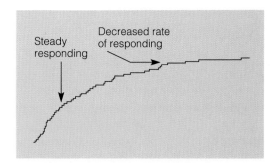

A cumulative record showing extinction. As the rate of response decreases, the slope of the line becomes less steep, until at last the line becomes horizontal. Compare with your graph in Figure 7.20 (page 262). If you drew a line sloping downward, reread the description of cumulative records on page 261. Remember, a high rate of responding is shown by a line sloping upward; a horizontal line shows no response. (page 262)

7. (a) Variable interval; students will study at a steady rate each day. (b) Fixed interval; students will study vig-

orously as they get close to the end of the month and will pause for some time after each test. (c) Fixed ratio; students will study at a steady pace (except for interruptions from other courses and other commitments). (page 264)

8. The habitual gambler will continue longer, because he or she has a history of being reinforced for gambling on a variable-ratio schedule, which retards extinction. For the same reason, an alcoholic who has had both good experiences and bad experiences while drunk is likely to keep on drinking even after several consecutive bad experiences. (page 264)

9. If you consider "silence" an active response, you could regard this as an example of positive reinforcement for silence. Otherwise, it is an example of negative punishment for the response of talking. The response (talking) is decreased because its occurrence leads to the omission of the reinforcer (the caps). (page 265)

10. One reason why most American politicians run similar campaigns and take similar stands is that they all tend to copy the same models—candidates who have won elections in the past. One other reason is that they all pay attention to the same public-opinion polls. (page 269)

CHAPTER

8

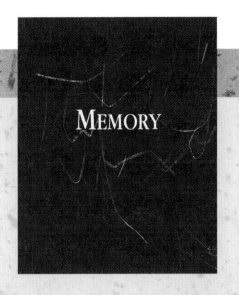

MEMORY

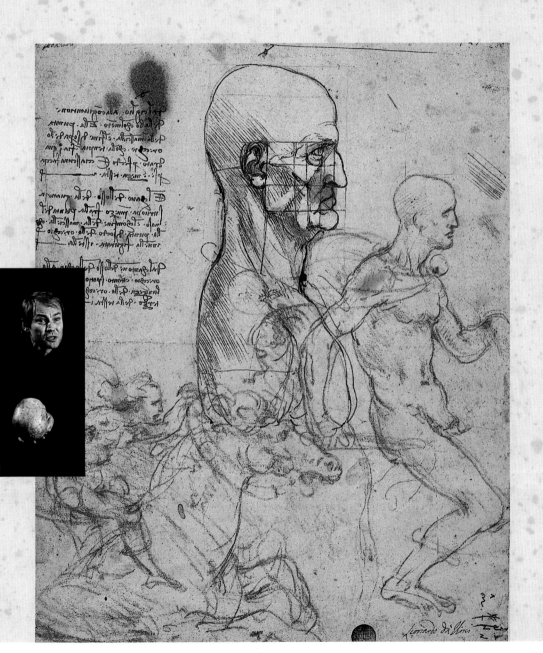

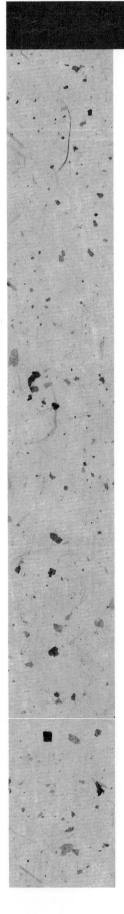

Suppose I offer you—for a price—an opportunity to do absolutely anything you want to do for one day. You will not be limited by any of the usual constraints on what is possible. You can travel in a flash from one place on Earth to another, visiting as many places as you care to crowd into that single day. You can even travel into outer space, exploring other worlds and observing life (if any) on other planets. You can travel forward and backward through time, finding out what the future holds in store and witnessing the great events of history— or even of prehistoric times. (But you will not be able to alter history.) Anything you want to do— just name it and it is yours. Furthermore, I guarantee your safety: No matter what time and place you choose to visit or what you choose to do, you will not be killed or injured.

Now, how much would you be willing to pay for this once-in-a-lifetime opportunity? Oh, yes, I should mention ... there is one catch. When the day is over, you will forget everything that happened. You will never be able to recover your memory of that day, even slightly. Any notes or photos you might have made will vanish. And anyone else who takes part in your special day will forget it, too.

Now how much would you be willing to pay? Much less, I am sure. Perhaps nothing. Living without remembering is hardly living at all. Our memories are almost the same thing as our "selves."

Interpreting the past: Do photographs distort and erase memory or do they preserve it? Some say the camera has made most representational art obsolete, but modern artists such as Robert Rauschenberg have incorporated photos and other famous images in their paintings and collages, using reminders of our cultural memory to shape that memory. [Robert Rauschenberg (American, 1925–), Retroactive I, 1964. Oil on canvas, 84 × 60 inches. Wadsworth Atheneum, Hartford. Gift of Susan Morse Hilles.]

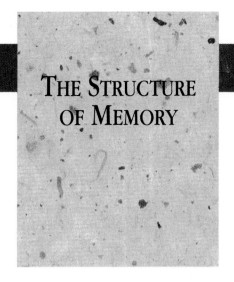

THE STRUCTURE
OF MEMORY

Are there different types of memory?
Do we remember some types of material better
than others?

"Memory is a record of past events." That definition sounds reasonable enough, though it includes far more than what we usually mean when we speak of memory. The rings of a tree provide a record of the rainfall and other weather conditions in past years. The dirt on the soles of your shoes provides a record of where you were this morning. If you fold a sheet of paper, the crease provides a permanent record of the event. All these are *records* of past events, but none of them is a memory.

Can you explain why they are not memories? "Well, for one thing," you may reply, "the paper cannot describe the occasion on which the crease was made." True, but the same holds true for much of human memory as well. Even though you remember how to tie your shoes, you probably cannot describe the occasion when you first formed that memory.

So what is memory? How can we define it to include all of human memory without including tree rings, the dirt on your shoes, or the crease in a sheet of paper? Defining *memory* is not easy. We need to know more about memory before we can say precisely what it is or is not. This section describes what we have discovered so far.

EBBINGHAUS AND
THE ASSOCIATIONIST
APPROACH TO MEMORY

Since the time of John Locke, David Hume, David Hartley, and other British philosophers of the 1600s

and 1700s, *association* (the linking of sensations or ideas) has been regarded as central to all thought processes. By the 1800s, associationism had become the dominant view of memory and related processes. Its influence is evident in the 20th-century writings of Pavlov, Thorndike, and the other researchers mentioned in Chapter 7. According to associationism in its original form, all experience consists of simple sensations or other psychological "elements." Similarity or contiguity in time and space links those simple elements together—"associates" them—into more complex assemblages, much as chemical bonds associate atoms into compounds.

Such was the theoretical environment in which the German psychologist Hermann Ebbinghaus (1850–1909) undertook his study of memory. Like many other psychologists of his time, Ebbinghaus began by interpreting memory in terms of association. Unlike the others, however, he devised a way of studying memory experimentally. Previously, when investigators asked people to describe their memories, they had no way of determining whether the descriptions were accurate.

Ebbinghaus simply taught a person something new and then tested the person's memory of it. This procedure enabled him to control certain variables (such as amount of practice and delay before testing) and to determine whether the person's memories were accurate. His method gradually became the dominant approach to the study of memory (Newman, 1987).

To make sure that the material to be memorized would be unfamiliar to his subjects, Ebbinghaus invented the **nonsense syllable**, a meaningless three-letter combination such as REK or JID. He wrote out 2,300 such syllables and arranged them in random lists (see Figure 8.1). His goal was to

FIGURE 8.1

Hermann Ebbinghaus significantly contributed to the study of memory by observing his own capacity for memorizing lists of nonsense syllables.

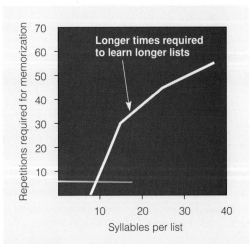

FIGURE 8.2

Say it again, Hermann: The number of repetitions that Ebbinghaus needed to memorize lists of various lengths.

When this you see, remember me: Could you recall the names of the students in your third-grade class? Trying to remember without any hints is recall. Using a photo or a list of initials is cued recall. If you tried to choose the correct names from a list, you would be engaged in recognition. If you compared how fast you relearned the correct names and how fast you learned another list, you would be using the savings (or relearning) method.

determine how rapidly people could memorize such lists and how long they could remember them. He had no cooperative introductory psychology students to draw on for his study, so he ran all the tests on himself. Over the course of about six years he memorized nearly 10,000 lists of nonsense syllables. (He must have been unusually dedicated to his science or uncommonly tolerant of boredom.)

One of Ebbinghaus's first discoveries was that it takes longer to memorize a long list than it takes to memorize a short one. That may strike you as obvious, but Ebbinghaus was able to measure *how much* longer it takes to memorize longer lists. Fig-

ure 8.2 gives the results. Note that he was able to memorize a list of up to seven syllables in a single reading, but each additional syllable increased the number of repetitions required to recall the list.

Serial Learning, Paired-Associates Learning, and Free Recall

Over the years many other psychologists have conducted similar experiments. Some of them used **serial learning**, the method Ebbinghaus had used, in which a person tries to memorize a series of items in order (such as BIX, YUR, NOL, GEF, PAK). In serial learning, each item serves as a stimulus for the recall of the next item. Other psychologists, beginning with Mary Calkins (page 11), used **paired-associates learning**, in which a person tries to memorize pairs of items, such as:

ZIK—TUV

MEL—RAB

REK—JID

GAK—HUZ

BEX—DOF

To test your memory of paired items, the investigator might give you the first item of each pair and ask you to supply the second item.

A third method of studying memory is **free recall**, in which a person reads or hears a list of individual (unpaired) items and then tries to recall the items in any order. For example, you might try to name the seven dwarfs (from *Snow White*), the five Great Lakes, or the current residents of your dormitory. Your answers would be considered free recall because you could name items in any order.

If you use the serial-learning method to memorize material, you may actually *remember* more than you can *recall* at any given moment (Rubin, 1977). For example, suppose you memorize the Preamble to the U.S. Constitution. You memorize it by the serial method. (It is difficult to imagine learning it any other way.) Months later, you try writing it out. You start writing and continue until you reach a stumbling block, and then you stop. If you could remember the words you had forgotten, they would probably remind you of the next words, which would lead to the next words, and so on. By contrast, when you use the paired-associates or free-recall method, the failure to remember one word need not interfere with your memory of any other word. For example, you might memorize the nicknames of 200 college teams. When you try to recall them later, you might forget "Heidelberg College: Student Princes" and "University of Southeast Alaska:

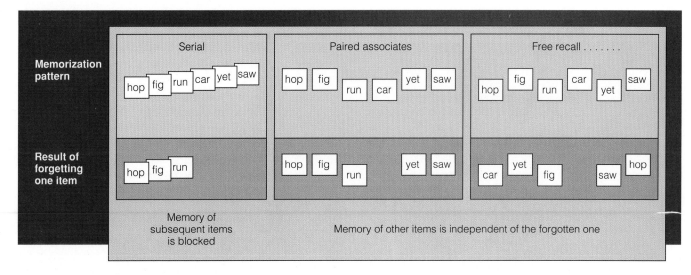

	Serial	Paired associates	Free recall . . . .
Memorization pattern	hop fig run car yet saw	hop fig run car yet saw	hop fig run car yet saw
Result of forgetting one item	hop fig run	hop fig run yet saw	car yet fig saw hop
	Memory of subsequent items is blocked	Memory of other items is independent of the forgotten one	

FIGURE 8.3

Three ways of testing memory. When someone tries to recite something memorized by the serial method, in which each item prompts recall of the next one, the failure to remember one word usually makes it impossible to recall the rest of the words.

Humpback Whales," but forgetting those items would not interfere with your remembering "University of California, Santa Cruz: Banana Slugs."

These three ways of testing memory are summarized in Figure 8.3.

Concept Check

1. *Which type of memorization (serial, paired associates, or free recall) is used in each of the following?*
a. *Memorizing a grocery list*
b. *Memorizing the English meanings of several French words*
c. *Learning the words to a new song*
d. *Memorizing which name goes with which face in a group of new acquaintances*
(Check your answers on page 312.)

Ways to Measure the Persistence of a Memory

Have you ever had trouble finding your keys because you were not sure where you left them? In a sense you have lost them, though they are probably not gone forever. Similarly, when you forget a fact, the memory of that fact is probably not gone forever; it is just hard to find at the moment. We have several ways to measure the persistence of a memory—that is, how strongly it is available after various delays.

The simplest way is to ask for **recall**. To recall something is to produce it. For instance, I might ask you, "Please name all the children in your second-grade class." To get a perfect score you have to come up with all the names. Yet even if you cannot recall any of the names, the memory of them

may not have disappeared completely. Essay tests require recall.

We can demonstrate that the memory persists by using **cued recall**. I still want you to come up with all the names, but this time I give you a hint. I might show you a photograph of all the children in your second-grade class or I might give you a list of their initials. Try this: Cover the right side of Table 8.1 with a piece of paper and try to identify each of the people described. (This is the recall method.) Then uncover the right side, revealing each person's initials, and try again. (This is cued recall.)

In **recognition**, a third method of testing the persistence of memory, a person is asked to choose the correct item from among several items. This way, we can detect memories that are too weak to be produced with either the recall method or the cued-recall method. Suppose you are still unable to name some of the children in your second-grade class even when you have their initials. If I give you a choice of several names, you may be able to recognize the right ones. Multiple-choice tests use the recognition method to test memory.

A fourth method, the **savings**, or **relearning**, **method**, will sometimes detect weaker memories than any of the other methods. Suppose you cannot name some of the children in your second-grade class (recall method) and cannot pick out their names from a list of choices (recognition method). If I presented you with the correct list of names, you might learn it faster than you would learn an unfamiliar list of names. The fact that you *relearn* something more quickly than you learn something new is evidence that some memory has persisted

TABLE 8.1 Illustration of the Difference Between Recall and Cued Recall

Instructions: First try to identify each person in the left column while covering the right column (recall method). Then expose the right column, which gives each person's initials, and try again (cued recall).

Author of *Moby Dick*	H. M.
Only woman with face on a U.S. coin ($1)	S. B. A.
Author of Hercule Poirot stories	A. C.
Vice president in Nixon's first term	S. A.
Discoverer of classical conditioning	I. P.
Baseball's all-time career home-run leader	H. A.
Author of Sherlock Holmes stories	A. C. D.
First U.S. woman astronaut	S. R.
Author of this book	J. K.
Author of *Gone with the Wind*	M. M.
First names of the Wright brothers (airplane inventors)	W. & O.
Democratic nominee for vice president in 1984	G. F.

For answers, see answer A on page 313.

Se habla español? If you studied Spanish in school and then years later took a trip to Peru, you would find that your Spanish would come back fairly easily, thanks to the phenomenon of relearning.

(MacLeod, 1988). In other words, you *save time* when you relearn material that you learned in the past. The amount of time saved (time needed for original learning minus the time for relearning) is a measure of memory.

All these methods of testing the persistence of memory call for what are known as *explicit* or *direct* tests, because the subjects know that they are trying to produce something from memory. Other methods call for *implicit,* or *indirect,* tests in which the subjects may not realize that their memory is being tested.

Some people show evidence of memory on an implicit test, even while insisting that they remember nothing (Richardson-Klavehn & Bjork, 1988). For example, brain-damaged people are asked to read a list of words, such as DEFEND, TINSEL, and BATHED. When they are tested later, they are unable to remember any of the words on the list. Then they are given three-letter combinations and asked to complete each stem to make a complete word, any word:

DEF—

TIN—

BAT—

Instead of coming up with other words that could be built on the stems, they generally fill in the letters that will form the words on the original list. Moreover, when the experimenter flashes a series of blurred words on a screen, the brain-damaged people can read and identify the words DEFEND, TINSEL, and BATHED more easily than they can recognize other six-letter words. In some way these words are "activated." The people are likely to see them and say them even though they say they do not remember seeing them on the original list. (Some people do not even remember that there *was* a list.)

People without brain damage also sometimes show evidence of implicit memory when they have no explicit memory (Graf & Mandler, 1984; Schacter, 1987a). First you might read a list of words, including CHAIRMAN, LECTURES, PENDULUM, and DONATION. You read them just once, and when you are asked to repeat the list a few minutes later, you cannot. Then you are asked to fill in the missing letters to make words from the following:

__HA__R____N
M____N__T__C
__E__D__L__M
__EC____R__S
A____A____IN

You will probably find it easy to fill in the letters for the words you had read (CHAIRMAN, PENDU-

LUM, and LECTURES) but more difficult for the other words (MAGNETIC and ASSASSIN). Reading a word temporarily primes the word and increases the chance that people will recognize it from a word fragment.

Concept Check

2. Each of the following is an example of one method of testing the persistence of memory. Identify each method.

a. Although you thought you had completely forgotten your high-school French, you do much better in your college French course than does your roommate, who never had French in high school.

b. You don't have a telephone directory and are trying to remember the phone number of the local pizza parlor.

c. After witnessing a robbery, you have trouble describing the thief. The police show you several photographs and ask whether any of them was the guilty party.

d. You go to a restaurant that you say you do not remember, although you went there in early childhood. To your surprise, you find your way to the restroom without directions.

e. Your friend asks, "What's the name of our chemistry lab instructor? I think it's Julie or Judy something."

(Check your answers on page 312.)

Some Basic Phenomena of Memory

Ebbinghaus and others discovered that several factors influence the ease with which we memorize both meaningful material and nonsense syllables. The *length of the list* is one factor, as we have seen. People memorize short lists faster than longer lists.

Serial-Order Effect

A second factor affecting memory is the order in which items appear on the list—their serial order. For example, suppose you are trying to memorize an alphabetical list of animals. According to the **serial-order-effect**, the names you will probably learn first and retain best are those at the beginning and end of the list—aardvark and zebra. The *primacy effect* is the tendency to remember the first items; the *recency effect* refers to the tendency to remember the last items. Try to write the names of all the presidents of the United States (or any similar list). If you are like most people, you will have no difficulty naming the first few or the last few, but you will falter on many of the names near the middle of the list. Figure 8.4 shows the percentage of people who recalled each of the presidents up to Gerald Ford, using the free-recall method (Roediger & Crowder, 1976).

The first few items in a list are easy to remem-

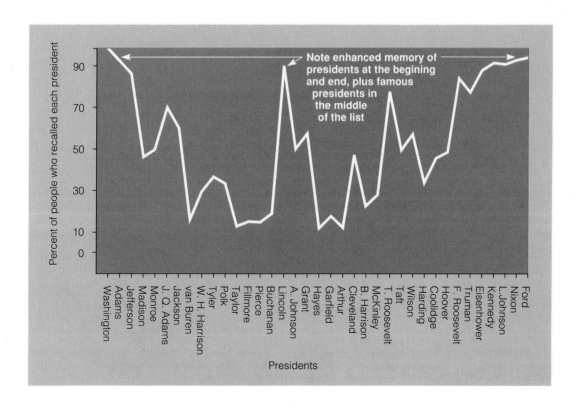

FIGURE 8.4

Arthur who? The percentage of students who, using the free-recall method, recalled the names of the first 37 presidents. Note the increased recall near the beginning and end of the list. (Based on Roediger & Crowder, 1976.)

ber because we can rehearse them by themselves for a time without any interference from other items. The last item on a list stands out simply because it is the last. Suppose you listen to a list of words that ends "... KNIFE, HORSE, LEAF." Then you are asked to recall as many words as possible in any order (the free-recall method). You are very likely to remember LEAF. Next you are told that you will hear a list of words followed by the word BEGIN. When you hear BEGIN, you are to recall as many words as you can, but not the word BEGIN itself. The list ends "... SPOON, GOAT, ROOT, BEGIN." You are much less likely to remember ROOT in the second list than LEAF in the first. You will remember hearing BEGIN, although you know it is not one of the words you are supposed to recall. Even if the experiment is repeated many times, always ending with the word BEGIN, your memory of the word before BEGIN will never be as good as it would be had BEGIN not been included. Evidently you attend to and store the last word you hear, even when you try not to (Frick, 1988; Greene, 1988).

Distinctiveness

A third factor that affects the ease of memorization is **distinctiveness**, the quality of being different from other elements in a list. Read the following list and then recall immediately, in any order, as many items as you can:

> potato, asparagus, cauliflower, turnip, broccoli, Alabama, beans, corn, peas, rutabaga, squash, cabbage

One of the items you are most likely to recall is *Alabama,* even though it is near the middle of the list. *Alabama* is the only word beginning with a capital letter and the only word that refers to something other than a vegetable. We tend to learn and remember unusual, distinctive items better than we do less distinctive items.

If you join a group that includes 30 men and only 2 women, you will probably learn the women's names faster than the men's. If you meet several men with rather ordinary appearances and similar names, like John Stevens, Steve Johnson, and Joe Stevenson, it may take you a long time to get their names straight. But if you meet a seven-foot-tall red-headed man named Stinky Rockefeller, you will have no trouble remembering his name. (The influence of distinctiveness on memory is sometimes known as the **von Restorff effect**, after the psychologist who first demonstrated it.)

Moreover, you are likely to remember an experience that occurs when you are in an intensely emotional state even though the experience is not very distinctive in itself. For instance, a large percentage of the people who are old enough to remember the assassination of John F. Kennedy, the assassination of Martin Luther King, Jr., or the explosion of the *Challenger* spacecraft can recall a wealth of unimportant details associated with the event, such as exactly where they were when they first heard the news, who they were with, what they said, and what the weather was like (Brown & Kulik, 1977). You may remember a number of details from your first day at college.

Meaningfulness

A fourth factor that affects the ease of memorization is **meaningfulness**, the ability of an item to fit into a known pattern of information. A list of paired associates such as BOY—DOG is much easier to remember than a list of paired associates such as VEK—ZUP. You may have noticed in Figure 8.4 that people remembered not only the U.S. presidents near the beginning and end of the list but also a few from the middle, such as Abraham Lincoln. The reason is that those few are highly meaningful. We could also say that they are highly distinctive.

J. D. Bransford and M. K. Johnson (1972) described one clever experiment illustrating the influence of meaningfulness. After looking at either picture a or picture b in Figure 8.5, two groups of people listened to the paragraph in part c (Bransford & Johnson, 1972, page 131). Note that the paragraph makes sense if you have seen picture a but is nearly incomprehensible if you have seen only picture b.

As you might expect, the people who had seen picture a remembered about twice as much of the paragraph as those who had seen only picture b. You may have noticed the same thing in class. Students with enough background to understand a topic remember more from a lecture or from a book than do students to whom the topic makes little sense.

Under most circumstances, meaningfulness is a greater aid to memory than is distinctiveness. People sometimes try to help themselves remember where they put something by placing it in a distinctive, unusual place: "I won't need this plane ticket for two months. So I'll put it in this really unusual place so I'll be sure to remember it—right under my stereo set." Two months later it is easy to remember that the ticket is tucked away in some unusual place. But *which* unusual place? That may be forgotten (Winograd & Soloway, 1986). It would be better to put the ticket in a meaningful place somehow related to travel—in a suitcase, inside a travel book, under a globe of the world, or with

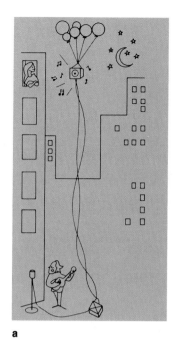

a

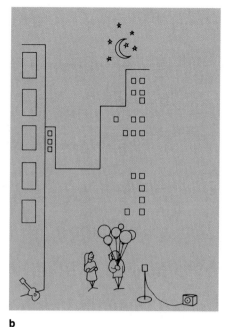

b

c

If the balloons popped, the sound would not be able to carry since everything would be too far away from the correct floor. A closed window would also prevent the sound from carrying since most buildings tend to be well insulated. Since the whole operation depends on a steady flow of electricity, a break in the middle of the wire would also cause problems. Of course, the fellow could shout, but the human voice is not loud enough to carry that far. An additional problem is that a string could break on the instrument. Then there could be no accompaniment to the message. It is clear that the best situation would involve less distance. Then there would be fewer potential problems. With face to face contact, the least number of things could go wrong.

FIGURE 8.5

In an experiment by Bransford and Johnson (1972), one group of people looked at picture a and another group looked at picture b. Then both groups heard the paragraph in part c. The paragraph is meaningful only if you have seen picture a.

the swimsuit you plan to take on the trip (see Figure 8.6).

THE INFORMATION-PROCESSING MODEL OF MEMORY

So far I have mentioned a number of observations *about* memory. But exactly what *is* memory and how does it work?

The simple truth is that psychologists do not know for sure. According to one view, the **information-processing model** of memory, human memory is analogous to the memory system of a computer: Information enters the system, is processed and coded in various ways, and is then stored (see Figure 8.7). It may first enter temporary storage (as when information is typed into a computer) and then enter permanent storage (as when information is entered onto a disk). Later, in response to a *retrieval cue,* a person can recover the information.

Investigators who use the information-processing approach generally distinguish among several types of memory: a very brief sensory store, short-term memory, and long-term memory.

The Sensory Store

Every memory begins as an exposure to a sensory stimulus. After you see or hear something for even a split second, you can report minor details about it briefly before the memory vanishes. This recall is possible because it has been temporarily entered into the **sensory store**, a very brief storage of sensory information. However, unless you immediately and actively attend to this sensory information, it will fade in less than a second as new information replaces it in the sensory store.

George Sperling (1960) tested how much information people can retain in the sensory store. He flashed an array like the one shown in Figure 8.8 onto a screen for 50 milliseconds (1/20 of a second). When he asked viewers to report as much of the whole array as they could, he found that they could recall a mean of only about four items. If he had stopped at that point, he might have concluded that viewers could store only a small fraction of an array.

But Sperling knew that it takes several seconds for a person to report even a few items, and he knew it was likely that memories in the sensory store would fade over those seconds. In other words, much of the array, perhaps even all of it, may have entered the sensory store but may have faded in the time it took to report more than a few items.

Factors affecting ease of memorization

First

Distinctiveness

Meaningfulness

Last

FIGURE 8.6

These four factors affect memorization of items on a list, as Figure 8.4 shows. For long-term recall, meaningfulness is usually the most helpful factor.

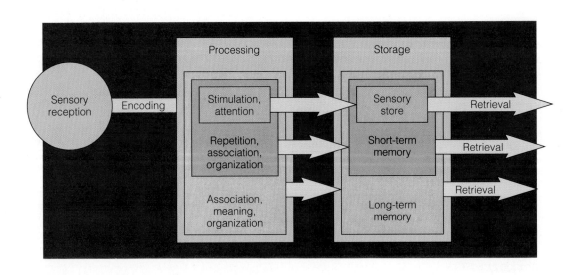

FIGURE 8.7

FIGURE 8.7

The information-processing model of memory resembles a computer's memory system, including temporary and permanent memory. As with a computer, the quality of the memory depends on the input: garbage in, garbage out.

Cruising past memory lane: How much of the passing scene do you notice as you drive by? Many images (and sounds) enter your sensory register and fade almost immediately, unprocessed and therefore unavailable to any longer-term memory. If you choose to pay attention, or if you have a particular motivation (such as hunger, which makes you search for a restaurant), you can fix a number of things in at least your short-term memory.

FIGURE 8.8

The type of array that George Sperling flashed on a screen for 50 milliseconds. After the display went off, a signal told the viewer which row to recite.

To test that possibility, he told viewers he would ask them to report only one row of the array, but he did not tell them *which* row. After flashing the array on the screen, he immediately used a high, medium, or low tone to signal which row the viewers were to recall. Most people could name all of the items in that row, regardless of which row he indicated. Evidently, nearly all of the information in the array was available to them for a split second. When he waited for even a second before signaling which row to recall, viewers could recall few, if any, of the items in that row.

Something to Think About

Sperling demonstrated the capacity of the sensory store for visual information. How could you demonstrate the capacity of the sensory store for *auditory* information?

Unless the information that enters the sensory store is immediately used in some way, it fades rapidly. In fact, the same information may enter the sensory store repeatedly without ever forming a permanent memory. Someone once told me he worked at the Wardlaw Building. "Where's that?" I asked. When he explained, I realized I had driven past that clearly marked building on my way to work every day for the past 11 years. Although I had seen the sign thousands of times, it had never remained in my memory.

Here is an exercise you can try on yourself: Figure 8.9 shows a real U.S. penny and 14 fakes. Can you identify the real one? Are you sure? In one study (Nickerson & Adams, 1979), only 15 of 36 U.S. citizens chose the correct coin. (If you do not have a penny in your pocket, check your answer on page 313, answer B.) Now try drawing (from memory) a nickel or the back of a penny. (If you are not from the United States, draw a coin common in your own country.) If you are like most people, the detailed appearance of the coin has passed through your sensory store repeatedly but has never entered your lasting memory.

Short-Term Memory
Versus Long-Term Memory

The information in the sensory store may activate representations in memory. Psychologists distinguish two types of representation, according to duration. **Long-term memory** is a relatively permanent store of (mostly) meaningful information. **Short-term memory** is the particular subset of information a person is dealing with at the moment. (Figure 8.10 compares the rates of decay of the sensory store and short- and long-term memory.) For many years, psychologists thought of short-term memory and long-term memory as separate stages: Information first enters short-term memory and stays there a while. Some but not all of the information in short-term memory eventually enters a separate long-term memory. That view is simple and appealing, but it does not answer all questions about memory. For example, how could information enter short-term memory independently of long-term memory? If I ask you to repeat "dog, cat, horse," you store those words in your short-term memory long enough to repeat them, but you used your long-term memory just to understand the words I spoke. Many psychologists therefore think of short-term memory not as a separate, independent kind of storage but as an activated subset of the material stored in long-term memory (Cowan, 1988).

Information in short-term memory is available only temporarily. After attention is distracted, the information is difficult to find, though perhaps not lost altogether. Someone comes up to you at a party and says, "Hello, I'm Sally Brown." "I'm pleased to

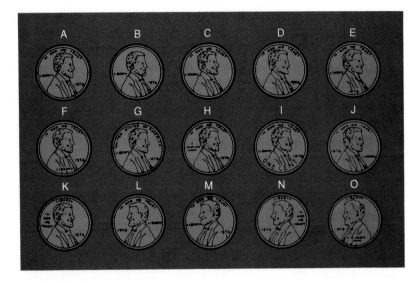

FIGURE 8.9

Where's Honest Abe? Can you spot the genuine penny among 14 fakes? (Based on Nickerson & Adams, 1979.) And can you recall what's on the back of a $10 bill?

meet you, Sally," you reply. Two minutes later you want to introduce her to someone else, but you have already forgotten her name. (Curiously, although you have forgotten the name, you are not completely in the dark as if you had never heard it. For example, you feel certain that it was *not* "Myrtle McGillicudy" or "Desira LaMore.")

In contrast, the information stored in long-term memory can be available at any time. To get information from long-term memory, a person needs a *retrieval cue*, an association that facilitates retrieval.

FIGURE 8.10

After about 1 second, you cannot recall information from the sensory store. Short-term memories can be recalled up to about 20 seconds without rehearsal—much longer if you keep rehearsing them. Long-term memories decline somewhat, especially at first, but you may be able to retrieve them for a lifetime. Your address from years ago is probably in your long-term memory and will continue to be for the rest of your life.

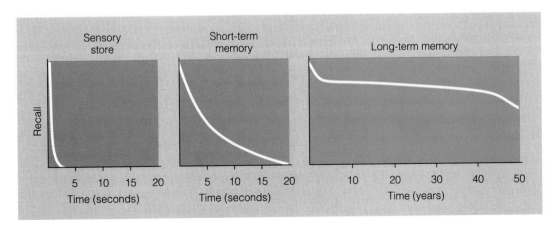

Few American women can match the memories of Eleanor Roosevelt (1884–1962), the activist First Lady during the turbulent years of the Depression and World War II. When she put her remembrances on paper, she filled three volumes. In This I Remember *(1949), covering events from 1921 to 1945, she states the importance of returning to the family home at Hyde Park: "Had I not stayed here it would have been far more difficult to write it and I might never have done so." In other words, the familiar setting provided for cued recall; her long-term memory was stimulated by retrieval cues. History—personal or public—consists largely of who remembers what.*

A retrieval cue serves as a reminder. Some retrieval cues work better than others. For example, the retrieval cue "the city you were born in" should enable you to retrieve the name of one city from your long-term memory. The retrieval cue "U.S. city whose name is also the name of a type of animal" probably does not enable you to retrieve anything quickly. You laboriously go through all the cities (or animals) you can think of until eventually you come upon an answer, most likely Buffalo, New York. (Conceivably, you might think of Caribou, Maine, or Duck, North Carolina, or Deadhorse, Alaska.) Retrieving long-term memories is sometimes a difficult, effortful task.

Capacity Difference Between Short-Term Memory and Long-Term Memory Short-term memory and long-term memory differ sharply in their *capacity* to store information. When you read or listen to sev-

eral items and then try to recite them from memory (short-term memory), you discover that you can recall very few of them. Read each of the following sequences of letters and then look away and try to repeat them from memory. Or read each aloud and ask a friend to repeat it.

EHGPH
JROZNQ
SRBWRCN
MPDIWFBS
ZYBPIAFMO
BOJFKFLTRC
XUGJDPFSVCL

Most normal adults can repeat a list of seven letters or numbers, about the same length as Ebbinghaus managed to memorize after reading a list once (Figure 8.2). George Miller (1956) referred to this as "the magical number seven, plus or minus two." When people try to repeat a longer list, however, they may fail to remember even the first seven items. It is somewhat like trying to hold several books in one hand: You can hold a certain number, depending on their size, but if you try to hold too many you may drop them all.

By contrast, long-term memory has a vast capacity with a limit that is difficult to estimate. Storing something in long-term memory is like putting books on the shelves of a library; you need not discard an old book to make room for a new one. Some people find room for an amazing amount of information in their long-term memories. The musical conductor Arturo Toscanini knew every note for every instrument for 250 symphonies, 100 operas, and many other compositions (Marek, 1975).

Although we know of no way to expand the capacity of our short-term memory, certain strategies help us to use it more effectively. Read this sequence of numbers once, then try to repeat it:

3141627182814141732

Could you do it? Most people cannot even come close to repeating all 19 digits. If you have a strong background in mathematics, however, you may have recognized this sequence as the approximate values of four mathematical constants (π, 3.1416 . . . ; e, 2.71828 . . . ; the square root of two, 1.414 . . . ; and the square root of three, 1.732). If you recognized those constants, you had only 4 items to store instead of 19, and the capacity of your short-term memory was more than adequate.

Here is an easier example that illustrates the same point. Try to repeat the following sequence of 12 digits:

106614921776

If you recognized that this sequence consists of three important dates (the Norman invasion of England in 1066, Columbus's arrival in America in 1492, and the Declaration of Independence in 1776), then you could repeat all 12 digits. You stored the sequence as 3 items (years) instead of 12 items (digits). The process of grouping digits or letters into meaningful sequences is known as **chunking**. Note that chunking uses knowledge previously stored in long-term memory.

Although practice will not expand the capacity of your short-term memory, it can improve your ability to chunk information. One student from Carnegie-Mellon University, described only as a "typical male undergraduate" (Ericsson, Chase, & Falcon, 1980), volunteered for an experiment on the memorization of digits. At the beginning, he could repeat only about 7 digits at a time. Over the course of a year and a half, working 3 to 5 hours a week, he gradually improved his ability, as shown in Figure 8.11, until he could repeat a sequence of up to 80 digits.

However, he had not expanded his short-term memory capacity. When tested with letters instead of numbers, his capacity was still 7. Instead, he had developed some extraordinary strategies for chunking, many of which were useful to him but would not be to most people. For instance, he would store a sequence beginning "3492 . . ." as "3 minutes, 49.2 seconds, a near world-record time for running a mile," followed by another four-digit sequence that he might recognize as a good time for running a kilometer, then a mediocre marathon time, then someone's age and a date in history. (He was himself a competitive runner.) He had organized his memory in such a way that he could fit an impressive amount of information into each chunk.

Difference in Decay over Time   Well-established long-term memories are virtually permanent. They do fade a little over time; certainly your memories for the events of last week are clearer than for those of a year ago. Still, with proper reminders even people 70 and 80 years old can remember many childhood experiences.

By definition, short-term memories fade much faster. Every day, we enter many facts into our short-term memory—an address, a telephone number, the price of something at a store—that we use briefly and then forget.

Lloyd Peterson and Margaret Peterson (1959) demonstrated that decay with a simple experiment that you can repeat for yourself if you can trap some friend into volunteering. First read aloud a meaningless sequence of letters, such as HOZDF. Then

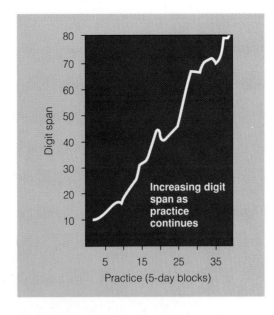

FIGURE 8.11

One student's ability to memorize a sequence of numbers, over 18 months. With practice, he greatly expanded his short-term memory for digits but not for letters or words. (From Ericsson, Chase, & Falcon, 1980.)

wait for a bit and ask your friend to repeat it. He or she will have no difficulty doing so. The reason is that your friend suspected you would ask for a recall of the letters and spent the delay rehearsing, "H-O-Z-D-F, H-O-Z-D-F, . . ." A 5-year-old child might forget the letters within 10 to 20 seconds because young children do not routinely rehearse material.

If you prevent rehearsal during the delay period, however, your adult friend will forget just as quickly as a child will. Say, "I am going to read you a list of letters, such as HOZDF. Then I'm going to tell you a number, such as 231. When you hear the number, begin counting backward by threes: 231, 228, 225,

"What novel—or what else in the world—can have the epic scope of a photograph album?" asked Günter Grass, a German novelist. As a physical record of past events, a scrapbook or photo album cues memories, helping parents and grandparents share their family history with their children.

TABLE 8.2

Letter Sequence	Starting Number	Delay in Seconds	Correct Recall?
BKLRE	712	5	
ZIWOJ	380	10	
CNVIU	416	15	
DSJGT	289	20	
NFMXS	601	25	

FIGURE 8.12

Recall of letters after delays of up to 18 seconds when subjects counted backward during the delays. (Based on data of Peterson & Peterson, 1959.)

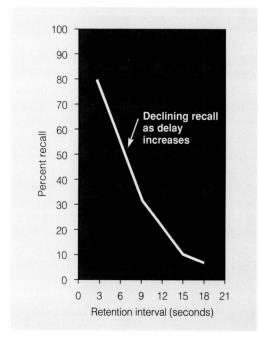

Declining recall as delay increases

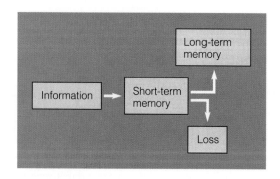

FIGURE 8.13

According to the original conception of the relationship between short-term and long-term memory, if a short-term memory is rehearsed long enough, it becomes a long-term memory. Without consolidation, it is lost. This view is now considered oversimplified.

threes from 231. Highly meaningful material enters long-term memory quickly and does not rapidly decay.

The Transfer from Short-Term Memory to Long-Term Memory

Originally, short-term memory and long-term memory were thought of as containers. New information went first into the short-term container; if it stayed there long enough (through rehearsal), it might be transferred into the long-term container (see Figure 8.13). The transfer was referred to as **consolidation.**

According to this hypothesis, all we must do to form a long-term memory is to hold something in short-term memory long enough for it to be transferred into long-term memory. But the data contradict this simple view. Simply holding an item in short-term memory does not make it highly available for recall later, and how long it stays in short-term memory does not, by itself, make much difference. In one experiment (Craik & Watkins, 1973), college students were asked to listen to a long list of words and then to report the last word on the list that began with the letter *g.* For example, in the list *table, giraffe, frog, key, banana, pencil, spoon, grass, garden, house,* the correct answer would be *garden.* Note what the students had to do: When they heard the first *g* word, *giraffe,* they had to hold it in short-term memory until they heard *grass,* six words later. At that point they replaced the word *giraffe* in short-term memory with the word *grass,* which they immediately replaced with the next word, *garden.* After students had given the correct answer (*garden*), the experimenter asked (to the students'

222, 219, and so on. When I tell you to stop, I'll ask you to repeat the sequence of letters." You can record your data as in Table 8.2.

Try this experiment with several friends and compute the percentage of those who recalled the letters correctly after various delays. Figure 8.12 gives the results Peterson and Peterson obtained. Note that only about 10% of their subjects could recall the letters correctly after a delay of 18 seconds. In other words, if we fail to rehearse something that has entered short-term memory, it will generally fade away within 20 seconds or less.

This demonstration works well, however, only when the person is trying to memorize something fairly meaningless, like HOZDF. If you ask your friend to memorize "I love you" or "There is a poisonous snake under your chair," he or she is likely to remember it well even after counting backward by

In fourteen hundred ninety-two,
Columbus sailed the ocean blue.

How to ride a bicycle.

Your factual memory contains information about Columbus and his voyage; your procedural memory comes to your aid when you hop on a bicycle to go to school. Note that the first illustration offers a visual and an aural reminder: the image of the ships, posted on bulletin boards in countless grade school classrooms, and the rhythm and rhyme of the verse, which help the facts stick in the mind. (We use rhyme to remember other facts—"Thirty days hath September, April, June, and November.") As for bike riding, could you describe the individual steps it involves, explaining exactly how to do it?

surprise) for all the words on the list that began with *g*. The students remembered *grass* and *giraffe* about equally well (or equally poorly) even though they had stored *giraffe* in short-term memory six times as long as they had stored *grass*. Evidently, how long a word stays in short-term memory has little to do with whether it moves into long-term memory.

Types of Long-Term Memory

Your memory of how to ride a bicycle, your memory of where you parked your bicycle this morning, and your memory of the physical principles that explain how a bicycle works are all long-term memories, but are they really the same kind of memory? Maybe not. Psychologists draw several distinctions among types of long-term memory.

Factual Memory Versus Procedural Memory One distinction is between factual memory and procedural memory (Tulving, 1985). **Factual memory** (or declarative memory) is the ability to remember information. It includes everything from remembering

your name to remembering the last word you heard. **Procedural memory** is the ability to remember *how* to perform an acquired skill. Examples include remembering how to use a typewriter, how to play tennis, how to ride a bicycle, and how to use a knife and fork.

Procedural memories differ from factual memories in several ways. First, humans begin to acquire procedural memories at an earlier age. We all retain many skills that we learned early in life, such as how to walk and how to pick up objects. Before the age of 5, however, our memory for facts, especially our memory for specific events, is poor. Second, factual memory is apparently more vulnerable. People may suffer *amnesia* (memory loss) after certain kinds of brain damage or as a result of serious emotional difficulties, as we shall see later in this chapter. Such people lose much of their factual memory, but they seldom forget how to walk or how to use a fork.

Episodic Memory Versus Semantic Memory Psychologists distinguish two kinds of factual memory: episodic memory and semantic memory (Tulving,

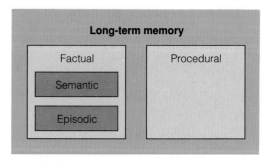

FIGURE 8.14

Classifications of long-term memory.

of a continuum rather than totally separate categories. For example, your memory of what tests and papers are required this semester is a semantic memory. But when you try to recall that memory, you may think back to the first day of class when the requirements were announced. That is, you recall an episodic memory. You start to describe the rules of basketball—a semantic memory—and then you remember that last month someone told you about a change in one of the rules for this year. Figure 8.14 summarizes the various categories of memory.

Concept Check

3a. You remember how to tie your shoes. Is that a procedural memory or a factual memory?
b. Someone asks you what time it is. You check your watch and say 12:30. A few seconds later, after you have been distracted, someone asks what time you said it was. You have forgotten. Was your memory short-term or long-term?
c. You remember how a clock works. Is that a semantic memory or an episodic memory?
d. You remember an event that happened to you the first day of high school. Is that a short-term memory or a long-term memory? Semantic or episodic?
(Check your answers on page 312.)

A MODEL OF RETRIEVAL FROM MEMORY

Psychologists often talk about retrieving something from memory as if that were a matter to take for granted: The memory is there somewhere; all the person has to do is to find it. But what does it mean to say that the memory is "there"? And what does it mean to "find it"?

Psychologists have barely begun to address those questions seriously. One approach that has attracted much attention is the **connectionist model.** Actually,

This toddler will remember how to use chopsticks all her life, but she is unlikely to recall many facts about her early years. Because of a phenomenon known as infant amnesia (see page 310), we normally remember only a few facts or events from the first four or five years of life.

1972). **Episodic memory** is the memory of particular events in your life; **semantic memory** is the memory of general principles—such as traffic laws, the formula for finding the area of a circle, and the instructions for operating a stereo. When you recall an episodic memory, you recall when the event occurred, what people were present, what they said, and other details. When you recall a semantic memory, you recall a general concept rather than a specific event.

Episodic memory includes memory of key events in your life; it also includes memory of what has happened most recently. For example, you remember where you parked your car this morning, whether or not you have read the morning newspaper, and when and where you promised you would meet your roommate for supper. For purposes such as these, we generally remember only the most recent information. There is little point in remembering where you parked your car yesterday or where you met your roommate for supper last Wednesday. Only a small percentage of our episodic memories are worth retaining permanently.

Episodic and semantic memory are two ends

psychologists have proposed several connectionist models. Although the models differ in various details, their underlying idea is the same: A memory is stored by means of linkages among units.

According to one connectionist model, our perceptions and our memories are represented by vast numbers of connections among "units" (McClelland, 1988; Rumelhart, McClelland, & the PDP Research Group, 1986). These are described in hypothetical terms, although they presumably correspond to neurons. Each unit is connected to other units, and the connections can have a variety of positive and negative weights (see Figure 8.15).

At any given moment, a certain number of units are active. Each unit excites some of its neighbors and inhibits others, to varying degrees. We might think of a given unit as a "reminder" or a "retrieval cue" for certain of its neighbors, but no one unit by itself can activate another unit very much. The representation of a word in memory is distributed over many units; the representation of a concept is distributed over even more units. To activate a unit, many other units must send it excitatory messages.

Figure 8.16 is an example of the kind of phenomenon this model attempts to explain. Why do you see the top word in that figure as RED instead of PFB? In fact, in the other three letters of that figure, you *do* see those letters as P, F, and B. But in the top word, one ambiguous figure activates some P units and some R units; the next figure activates E and F units, and the third figure activates D and B units. All those units in turn activate other more complex units corresponding to RFB, PFB, PFD, and RED. Because RED is the only English word in the group, the units that correspond to RED are easier to activate than those for PFB and the others. Consequently, you perceive the word as RED. As the RED unit becomes active, it in turn provides feedback to strengthen the activity of the R, E, and D units.

Here is a more complex example (based on Winograd & Church, 1988). Professor Wonderful is trying to remember the names of the students in her class. Jeff Noyes is sitting in the front row, where he has sat every day since the beginning of the semester. The perception of his face activates a unit that is connected with the name Jeff Noyes. His seating location activates another unit that is connected with that same name. Moreover, the professor has just been thinking about all the noise out in the hall. "Noise" is also connected to "Noyes." All these units acting in combination retrieve the name from memory.

Note that this model clearly does *not* imagine a "little person in the head" who finds memories and retrieves them. Rather, a variety of activated

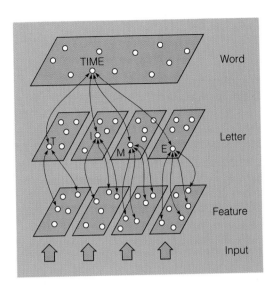

FIGURE 8.15

One example of the connectionist approach to retrieval from memory. Sensory information activates many units, each corresponding to a visual feature. Those units activate units corresponding to letters; they in turn activate a word unit. A great many other units, not shown here, would also be activated to a lesser degree. The word TIME is retrieved because it is the best match to the sensory input. In other cases, a word may be retrieved because of activity in other kinds of units, including units corresponding to what a person has heard or has been thinking about. (From McClelland, 1985.)

FIGURE 8.16

Demonstration that a word is recognized from a pattern across all the letters. Although each of the letters in the top word is ambiguous, a whole word—RED—is perceived. (From Rumelhart, McClelland, & the PDP Research Group, 1986, page 8, Figure 2.)

units working together call another unit into activity. Although at the moment connectionist models are somewhat vague and difficult to test rigorously (Massaro, 1988), they are being elaborated and modified by continuing research.

SUMMARY

1. Hermann Ebbinghaus pioneered the scientific study of human memory by examining his own ability to memorize lists of nonsense syllables under various conditions. (page 279)

2. Four explicit methods of testing memory are recall, cued recall, recognition, and savings. The savings method is the method best able to detect a weak memory; the recall method is the least able. We can also test memory by implicit tests, in which the person is unaware that memory is being tested. (page 281)

3. People are most likely to remember the items at the beginning and end of a list, the unusual items, and the most meaningful items. (page 283)

4. According to the information-processing model of memory, the manner in which we enter memories is like the manner in which we enter information into a computer. (page 285)

5. Psychologists distinguish among sensory store, short-term memory, and long-term memory, between factual memory and procedural memory, and between episodic memory and semantic memory. (page 285)

6. The connectionist model of memory represents each memory as a series of connections among items. (page 292)

SUGGESTION FOR FURTHER READING

Rubin, D. C. (Ed.). (1986). *Autobiographical memory.* Cambridge, England: Cambridge University. A collection of articles on the memories of one's own experiences.

IMPROVEMENT, LOSS, AND DISTORTION OF MEMORY

How can we improve memory?
Why do we sometimes forget?
Why do we sometimes think we remember something, when in fact we are wrong?

At one point while I was doing the research for this book, I went to find an article that I remembered reading, which I thought would very nicely illustrate a particular point I wanted to make. I was pretty sure I remembered the author, the name of the journal, and the date of the article within a year. So I was certain it would not take me long to find the article.

About four hours later I finally located it. I was right about the author, but I was wrong about the journal and the year. Worst of all, I discovered that the results the article reported were quite different from what I remembered. (The way I *remembered* the results made a lot more sense than the *actual* results!)

Why does my memory—and probably yours as well—make mistakes like this? And is there any way to improve memory?

IMPROVING MEMORY BY IMPROVING LEARNING

"I'm sorry. I don't remember your name. I just don't have a good memory for names." "I went to class regularly and did all the reading, but I couldn't remember all those facts when it came time for the test."

When people cannot remember names or facts, the reason is generally that they did not learn them very well in the first place. To improve your ability

to remember something, be very careful about how you learn it.

Distribution of Practice

You want to memorize a part for a play. Should you sit down and study your lines in one long marathon session until you know them? Or should you spread your study sessions over several days? Research indicates that **distributed practice**—that is, a little at a time over many days—is generally better than **massed practice**, the same number of repetitions over a short time. One reason is that it is hard to maintain full attention when you repeat the same thing over and over at one sitting. Another is that studying something at different times links it to a wider variety of associations.

Depth of Processing

Once again, how well you will remember something depends on how well you understood it when

"*Alas! poor Yorick. I knew him, Horatio.*" *Hamlet delivers some two dozen soliloquies (solo speeches) of hundreds of words each. (In comparison, the Gettysburg Address is 266 words.) Actors generally use distribution of practice to learn their parts, memorizing a little daily over weeks. They also associate their lines with emotional motivations, physical movements, cues from other actors, and their own memories to help them remember.*

you learned it and how much you thought about it at the time. According to the **depth-of-processing principle** (Craik & Lockhart, 1972), information may be stored at various levels, either superficially or deeply, depending on the number and type of associations formed with it.

At the most superficial level, a person merely focuses on the words and how they sound. If you try to memorize a list by simply repeating it over and over, you may recognize it when you see or hear it again, but you may have trouble recalling it (Greene, 1987). Actors and public speakers who have to memorize lengthy passages soon discover that mere repetition is an inefficient method.

A more efficient way to memorize is to deal actively with the material and to form associations with it. For example, you read a list of 20 words. At a slightly deeper level of processing than mere repetition, you might count the number of letters in each word, think of a rhyming word, or note whether the word contains the letter *e*. Such activities require a more active involvement on your part and establish more connections among the words on the list and other items in your experience. At a still deeper level of processing, you might consider the meaning of each word and try to think of a synonym for it. According to this theory (and according to many experimental results), the deeper the level of processing, the more you will remember. *(How can you use this principle to develop good study habits?)*

The depth-of-processing principle resembles what happens when a librarian files a new book in the library. Simply to place the book somewhere on the shelves without recording its location would be a very low level of processing, and the librarian's chances of ever finding it again would be slight. So the librarian fills out file cards for the book and puts them into the card catalog. To fill out just a title card for the book would be an intermediate level of processing. To fill out several cards—one for title, one for author, and one or more for subject matter—would be a deeper level of processing. Someone who came to the library later looking for that book would have an excellent chance of finding it. Similarly, when you are trying to memorize something, the more "cards" you fill out (that is, the more ways you link it to other information), the greater your chances of finding the memory when you want it.

You can improve your memorization of a list by attending to two types of processing that are largely independent of each other (Einstein & Hunt, 1980; McDaniel, Einstein, & Lollis, 1988). First, you can go through the list thinking about how much you like or dislike each item or trying to recall the last time you had a personal experience with it. That will enhance your processing of *individual items*. Second, you can go through the list and look for relationships among the items. That will enhance your processing of the *organization* of the list. You might notice, for example, that the list you are trying to memorize consists of five animals, six foods, four methods of transportation, and five objects made of wood. Even sorting items into such simple categories as "words that apply to me" and "words that do not apply to me" will enhance your sense of how the list is organized and therefore your ability to recall it (Klein & Kihlstrom, 1986).

Concept Check

4. *Here are two arrangements of the same words:* **a.** *Be a room age to the attend hall will over party across be there 18 you after wild in the class must.* **b.** *There will be a wild party in the room across the hall after class; you must be over age 18 to attend. Why is it easier to remember b than a—because of processing of individual items or because of processing of organization? (Check your answer on page 312.)*

Self-Monitoring of Reading Comprehension

What is the difference between good readers (those who remember what they read) and poor readers (those who do not)? One difference is that good readers process what they read more deeply. But how do readers know when they have processed deeply enough? How do they know whether they need to slow down and read more carefully?

Good readers monitor their own reading comprehension; that is, they keep track of whether or not they understand what they are reading. Occasionally in reading, you come across a sentence that is complicated, confusing, or just badly written. Here is an example from the student newspaper at North Carolina State University:

He said Harris told him she and Brothers told French that grades had been changed.

What do you do when you come across a sentence like that? If you are monitoring your own understanding, you notice that you are confused. Good readers generally stop and reread the confusing sentence or, if necessary, the whole paragraph. As a result, they improve their understanding and their ability to remember the material. When poor readers come to something they do not understand, they generally just keep on reading. Either they do not notice their lack of understanding or they do not care.

The same is true for whole sections of a book. A student who is studying a textbook should read quickly when he or she understands a section well but should slow down when the text is more complicated. To do so, the student has to monitor his or her own understanding. Above-average students can generally identify which sections they understand best; they single out the sections they need to reread. Below-average students have more trouble picking out which sections they understand well and which ones they understand poorly (Maki & Berry, 1984).

Actually, most people—including bright college students who get good grades—could improve their comprehension through better self-monitoring (Glenberg, Sanocki, Epstein, & Morris, 1987; Zabrucky, Moore, & Schultz, 1987). Many educators recommend that a reader pause at regular intervals to check his or her understanding. The Concept Checks in this text are intended to encourage you to pause and check your understanding from time to time.

A self-monitoring system you can use with any text is the **SQ3R method:** Survey, Question, Read, Recite, and Review.

- *Survey.* Read the outline of a new chapter and skim through the chapter itself to get a feeling for what the chapter covers. (Skimming a mystery novel would ruin the suspense. Textbooks, however, are not meant to create suspense.)

- *Question.* Write a list of what you expect to learn from the chapter. You might include the review questions in the chapter, questions from the Study Guide, or questions of your own.

- *Read.* Study the text carefully, take brief notes, and stop to think about key points. (The more you stop and think, the more retrieval cues you form.)

- *Recite.* Reciting does not mean simply repeating without thinking. It means producing correct answers. Use what you have read to answer the questions you listed.

- *Review.* Read the chapter summary, skim through the chapter again, and look over your notes.

A similar system is the **SPAR method:** Survey, Process meaningfully, Ask questions, and Review and test yourself. Both SQ3R and SPAR rest on the principle that readers should pause periodically to check their understanding. Start with an overview of what a passage is about, read it, and then see whether you can answer questions about the passage or explain it to others. If not, go back and reread.

Encoding Specificity

A new book titled *Brain Mechanisms in Mental Retardation* arrives in the library. The librarian places it on the appropriate shelf and fills out three cards for the card catalog: one for the author, one for the title, and one for the subject, *mental retardation.* I happen to read a section in this book on the physiological basis of learning. Three years later I want to find the book again, but I cannot remember the author or title. I go to the card catalog and look under the subject headings *physiology* and *learning.* But the book I want is not listed. Why not? Simply because the librarian filed the book under a different heading. Unless I use the same subject heading the librarian used, I cannot find the book. (Had the librarian filled out several subject cards instead of just one, I would have had a better chance of finding it.)

A similar principle applies to human memory. (Note that I say *similar.* Your brain does not actually store each memory in a separate place, as a librarian stores books.) When you store a memory, you attach to it certain retrieval cues, like file cards. These retrieval cues are the associations you use both when you store a memory and when you try to recall it. Depending on your depth of processing, you may set up many retrieval cues or only one or two. No matter how many cues you set up, however, it helps if you use those same cues when you try to find the memory again.

The **encoding specificity principle** states that your memory will be more reliable if you use the same cue when you try to retrieve a memory as you used when you stored it (Tulving & Thomson, 1973). Although cues that were not present when you stored the memory may help somewhat to evoke the memory (Newman et al., 1982), they are less effective than cues that were present at the time of storage.

Here is an example of encoding specificity (modified from Thieman, 1984). First, read the list of paired associates in Table 8.3. Then turn to Table 8.5 on page 301. For each of the words on the list there, try to recall a related word on the list you just read. *Do this now.*

The answers are on page 313, answer C. Most people find this task difficult and make only a few of the correct pairings. Because they initially coded the word *cardinal* as a type of clergyman, for example, the retrieval cue *bird* does not remind them of the word *cardinal.* The cue *bird* is effective only if

Table 8.3

Clergyman	—	Cardinal
Trinket	—	Charm
Social event	—	Ball
Shrubbery	—	Bush
Inches	—	Feet
Take a test	—	Pass
Baseball	—	Pitcher
Geometry	—	Plane
Tennis	—	Racket
Stone	—	Rock
Magic	—	Spell
Envelope	—	Seal
Cashiers	—	Checkers

cardinal is somehow associated with that cue at the time of storage. In short, you can improve your memory by storing information in terms of retrieval cues and by using the same retrieval cues when you try to recall the information.

Encoding Specificity: Context-Dependent and State-Dependent Memory

Almost anything that happens during an experience may serve as a retrieval cue for that memory. The environment at the time is likely to be associated with the experience and thus to become a retrieval cue. It may then be easier to remember the event in the same environment than in some other environment—an instance of **context-dependent memory**. For example, Duncan Godden and Alan Baddeley (1975) found that divers who learn a word list while 4.5 meters underwater remember the list much better when they are tested at the same depth underwater than when they are tested on the beach.

One's physiological condition at the time can also serve as a potent retrieval cue. A **state-dependent memory** is a memory that is easier to recall if a person is in the same physiological state he or she was in when the event occurred. Someone who has an experience while under the influence of alcohol, nicotine, or some other drug will remember that event more easily when under the influence of the same drug again (Lowe, 1986; Warburton, Wesnes, Shergold, & James, 1986).

All sorts of influence may lead to state-depen-

dent memories. For example, the physiological condition of your body is different at different times of day. Other things being equal, your memory is slightly better when you try to recall an event at the same time of day at which it occurred (Infurna, 1981). (You may have noticed that when you wake up in the morning you sometimes start to think about the same thing you were thinking about the morning before.)

A person's mood may also contribute to state-dependent memory, although the evidence for mood-dependent memory is weak. Evidence is stronger for a related phenomenon: When someone is happy, he or she is more likely to think of happy events and words associated with happiness; a person who is sad is more likely to think of unhappy events and words associated with sadness (Blaney, 1986).

When you are trying to recall an event that happened first thing in the morning or when you were sick or when you were in some other distinct physiological state, trying to reconstruct how you felt at the time may strengthen your memory by opening up your access to state-dependent memories.

Mnemonic Devices

When you know that you will have to remember certain information at a future time—such as tasks you must tend to on Thursday or items you need to buy at the grocery store—what can you do to make sure you will remember?

One strategy is to repeat the list over and over again. That is the way Ebbinghaus memorized his lists of nonsense syllables. It may work fairly well for you, though you will probably forget at least part of the list.

A better strategy is to write out the list. Unless you lose the list, you need not worry about forgetting any of the items. Even if you do lose the list, you are likely to remember more items than if you had never written it out (Intons-Peterson & Fournier, 1986). (This is one reason it pays to take notes during a lecture.)

But what if you have no pencil and paper handy? Someone says, "Quick, we need supplies for the party. Go to the store and bring back ginger ale, ice, cups, instant coffee, napkins, hot dogs, paper plates, and nacho chips." One way to remember is to take the initials of those items—GICINHPN—and rearrange them into the word PINCHING. Now you just have to remember PINCHING and each letter will remind you of one item you need to get.

Any memory aid that is based on encoding each item in some special way is known as a **mnemonic device**; the word *mnemonic* ("nee-MAHN-ik") comes from a Greek root meaning memory. (The same root appears in the word *amnesia,* lack of memory.) A mnemonic device is a method for creating systematic retrieval cues.

Mnemonic devices come in many varieties. Some are simple, as in my example of arranging the initials of words in a memorable order or thinking up a little story that includes each item to be remembered (such as "Every good boy does fine" to remember the notes EGBDF). Others are more elaborate. One of the oldest and most effective is the **method of loci** (method of places). First you memorize a series of places and then you use some vivid image to associate each of these locations with something you want to remember.

You and your roommate have just registered for a course called "History of Psychology." On the first day of class, your instructor announces that on the mid-term exam you will have to write from memory a list of all the presidents of the American Psychological Association (Figure 8.17a). Unfortunately, this association has elected a new president every year since 1892. This may not strike you as an educationally sound assignment, but you are stuck with it.

Your roommate says, "Wow, that's a lot to memorize!" So she sits down and starts reading the list to herself. But you remember something you learned from your introductory psychology book. You look back at Figure 8.2 and estimate that learning a list of about 100 names will take over 200 repetitions. You procrastinate, hoping that it will be easier to memorize the list later in the semester, after the names have become familiar and meaningful.

Unfortunately, neither your textbook nor your professor says a single word about any of those people. Now it is a week before the mid-term exam, and you have not even looked at the list. Your roommate has been dutifully reading the list every night and is feeling very smug. What do you do? Fortunately, you remember one more thing from your textbook: mnemonic devices, particularly the method of loci.

You start by walking the entire route from your desk to your psychology classroom. You repeat the trip until you have memorized every location along the way. Then you link the locations, in order, to the names.

For example, suppose the first six locations you pass are the desk in your room, your bookcase, the door to your room, the corridor, a restroom along the way, and the stairs. The first six presidents of the APA were Hall, Ladd, James, Cattell, Fullerton, and Baldwin. This method works best if you make up your own images, but Table 8.4 provides some examples.

You could go on for as long as necessary to complete the list, but let's check your progress so far. Look away from this page, imagining (in order) your desk, the bookcase, the door, the corridor, the restroom, and the stairs (see Figure 8.17b). Can you recite the names of the first six presidents of the American Psychological Association?

With a little ingenuity, you can modify this technique to suit your own purposes. For example, instead of memorizing a sequence of 100 places to fit the 100 names, you might memorize 25 places and use each of them four times: for the front of the place, the back, the left side, and the right side.

Exceptional Memory

A few people develop extraordinary abilities to memorize. Several people who achieved fame for their extraordinary memory were not much good at anything else; they merely showed off their memorizing the way other people juggle or perform magic tricks.

But one person with an exceptional memory, the mathematician Alexander Aitken, excelled in logical reasoning, mathematics, and many other skills (Hunter, 1977). A few examples of his memory: As a schoolboy, he was once told to work out the decimal for 1/97; he noticed that it had an interesting repeating pattern and from then on could recite it from memory. He memorized whole books of Virgil (in Latin) and *Paradise Lost.* His memory for detail was so good that committees often used him as a walking record book of all their past deliberations and decisions. As part of an experiment, a psychologist once asked him to memorize a list of 25 words. After reading them once, he was able to recite the first 12. After reading them four times, he recited them all. He was tested four more times over the next 15 months; three of those four times he got all 25 correct. Twenty-seven years later, he wondered whether he could still remember the list, not having thought about it during all that time. It took him a few minutes, but he got all 25.

Whenever he wanted to memorize something, he did not concentrate; he relaxed. "One must be relaxed, yet possessed, in order to do this well.... Interest is the thing. Interest focuses the attention.... The thing to do is to learn by heart, not because one has to, but because one loves the thing and is interested in it. Then one has moved away from concentration to relaxation."

Another special type of memory is **eidetic imagery** (i-DET-ik). (*Eidetic* derives from the Greek word "eidos," meaning shape.) People with eidetic imagery can look briefly at a large, complicated picture or pattern and later recall its contents in

FIGURE 8.17

One cue is better than none: (a) A fascinating list of APA presidents. If you had to memorize this list, you could use the method of loci (b). Start with nearby locations and "decorate" them with items on your list in the order in which you pass by. Through this use of visual imagery, you can create cues where none existed.

TABLE 8.4

Location	President	Image to Link Them
1. Desk	Hall	Someone named *Hall* standing there, ready to *haul* your desk
2. Bookcase	Ladd	A little *lad* sitting on the bookcase, reading *Aladdin*
3. Door	James	Someone named *James* standing in the doorway or a bluejay making a mess (a *jay-mess*) on the door
4. Corridor	Cattell	A *cat* in the corridor *tell*-ing you where to go or yourself in the corridor tripping over a *cat's tail*
5. Restroom	Fullerton	people crowding into the restroom, filling it *fuller* than a *ton*
6. Stairs	Baldwin	a bald-headed man (a *bald one*) coming up the stairs

TABLE 8.5

Instructions: For each of these words, write a related word that you remember from the second column of the list in Table 8.3.

Pottery	_____
Animal	_____
Part of body	_____
Transportation	_____
Football	_____
Crime	_____
U.S. politician	_____
Music	_____
Personality	_____
Write	_____
Bird	_____
Board game	_____
Sports	_____

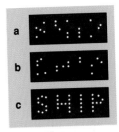

FIGURE 8.18

Dot patterns used to test eidetic imagery. Some eidetikers form an eidetic image of a and superimpose it on b to "see" c. (From Miller & Peacock, 1982.)

detail. They speak of "seeing" an image that they can scan by moving their eyes back and forth, as if it were still "out there" (Haber, 1979).

Eidetic imagery is sometimes called "photographic memory," although the image usually lacks both the detail and the accuracy of a photograph. According to Ralph Haber (1979), about 5 to 10% of elementary-school children have some degree of eidetic imagery; the ability fades during adolescence and rarely persists into adulthood.

Among "eidetikers," the clarity and detail of the image vary greatly. Some really seem to "see" an image but can identify no more detail than other people can retrieve from their visual memories. Here we have the same problem we have with all self-reports—we cannot know what the eidetikers mean when they say they "see" an image. A few eidetikers, however, can perform some impressive feats to back up their self-reports.

The most spectacular eidetiker was a woman who could look at a patternless array of dots and then, a day later, superimpose her memory of that array onto a second patternless array and perceive a pattern that emerged only when the two arrays were combined (Stromeyer, 1970). Some other eidetikers can do the same thing if the dot pattern is simple and the delay is very short (Miller & Peacock, 1982). For example, they can look at the dot pattern in Figure 8.18a, then quickly superimpose an eidetic image of it onto Figure 8.18b to see the result shown in Figure 8.18c (Miller & Peacock,

1982). Very few people without eidetic imagery can look at the two dot patterns, one at a time, and then correctly guess what will happen when one is superimposed on the other.

Eidetic imagery is a mixed blessing. Some eidetikers complain that they have trouble reading because unwanted images get in the way. They also find that after they lose an eidetic image (through interference from seeing something else), they forget it more completely than other people forget their visual memories.

FORGETTING

Quickly now, what is the capital of Missouri? What was the name of your seventh-grade English teacher? What is the formula for finding the volume of a sphere? To whom did you last write a check, and what was the amount? What is the correct definition of the term *demand characteristics*?

We all have difficulty recalling facts we once knew perfectly well. Why? And why do we sometimes think we remember something well, when in fact we are wrong? Finally, why do some people seem to forget nearly everything?

Short-term memories fade unless we rehearse them. When you look up a telephone number, you can remember it long enough to dial it. When you try to dial that number later the same day, however, you will probably have to look it up again.

Long-term memories also fade, but much more slowly. When people are given a series of words and asked to recall a personal experience connected with each of them, they recall recent events more readily than they recall events from the remote past (Crovitz & Schiffman, 1974; Rubin, Wetzler, & Nebes, 1986). That finding suggests that memories grow weaker over time. But are they really lost?

Perhaps not. Marigold Linton (1982) wrote notes about at least two important personal events each day for six years and recorded the date on the back of each note. At various times she drew notes at random from the pile and tested her ability to recall the approximate date of each event. She found that she remembered the dates of about 95% of events a year old and a slightly lower percentage of older events. Similarly, Willem Wagenaar (1986) made cards recording 2,400 personal events over six years. At the end of the six years he tested himself by reading part of each card (for example, "what happened") and trying to recall the rest (for example, who, where, and when). Although he remembered the recent events more clearly than the older events, he was able to recall at least a little information about almost every event.

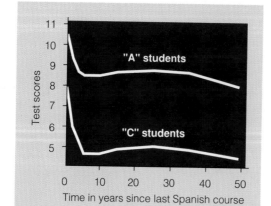

FIGURE 8.19

Spanish vocabulary as measured by a recognition test at various times since people last studied Spanish. (From Bahrick, 1984.)

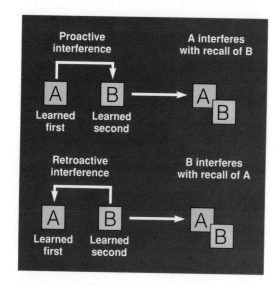

FIGURE 8.20

The difference between proactive interference and retroactive interference. Actually, both occur together.

Harry Bahrick (1984) tested people who had studied Spanish in school 1 to 50 years previously on their current memory of Spanish. Nearly all agreed that they had rarely used Spanish and had not refreshed their memories at all since their school days. (That is a disturbing comment, but beside the point.) Their retention of Spanish dropped noticeably in the first 3 to 6 years, but remained fairly stable from then on (Figure 8.19). In other words, we do not completely forget even very old memories that we seldom use.

Concept Check

5. *The results shown in Figure 8.19 are for* recall. *How might you determine whether people remember even more than the figure shows? (Check your answer on page 312.)*

The Role of Interference

One of the main reasons we forget is **interference**, or competition among related memories. If you have trouble remembering the name of your acquaintance John Stevenson, it may well be because of interference from the memory of a similar-looking acquaintance named Steve Johnson. Finding a pearl in a bucket of white marbles is harder than finding a pearl in a bucket of black marbles.

For convenience, psychologists distinguish between two types of interference: proactive interference and retroactive interference. **Proactive interference** is the hindrance an older memory produces on a newer one. **Retroactive interference** is the impairment a newer memory produces on an older one. Figure 8.20 shows the difference.

Here is an example: Oblivia Sue memorizes a list of the 20 main products of India. Later she memorizes similar lists for Pakistan, Afghanistan, Egypt, and Thailand. Then both Oblivia Sue and her twin sister, Perplexity Jean, memorize a list of the 20 main products of Burma. Which sister will remember the Burma list longer? Perplexity Jean will, because it is the only such list she has memorized. Her sister will have trouble keeping the Burma list distinct from the other five lists she has memorized.

Oblivia Sue's problem is *proactive interference;* the earlier material increases the rate at which she forgets the later material. How great the effect will be depends on how similar the two sets of material are. Although memorizing the products of several countries will interfere with the memory of the products of yet another country, it will not interfere with the memory of something unrelated, such as an airline schedule.

Here is another example: Amorfus and his twin brother, Equivocus, both memorize a long poem. Then Amorfus memorizes seven more long poems, while Equivocus plays in a bridge tournament. Afterward, we test their memory of the first poem and find that Equivocus remembers it much better than Amorfus does. The reason is that *retroactive interference* hindered Amorfus. The seven poems he memorized interfered with his recall of the first poem.

Actually, proactive interference and retroactive interference always occur simultaneously. Whenever you memorize two sets of material, the first interferes with the memory of the second by proactive interference; the second interferes with the memory of the first by retroactive interference.

Here is a real example with historical significance. In trying to measure how long a memory lasts, Hermann Ebbinghaus memorized several lists of 13 nonsense syllables each and then tested his memory after various delays. The results appear in

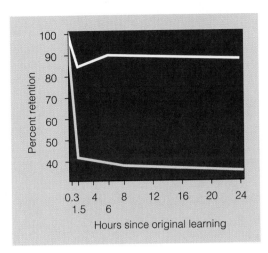

FIGURE 8.21

Yellow line: Recall of lists of syllables by Ebbinghaus after delays of various lengths (Ebbinghaus, 1913).
White line: Recall of lists of words by college students after delays of various lengths. (Based on Koppenaal, 1963.)

Figure 8.21. He forgot a mean of more than half of each list after an hour and still more after 24 hours.

In themselves, these results are rather depressing. Think of it from the standpoint of an educator: If students forget most of what they learn in one day, how much will they remember a year from now? Fortunately, later research has been more encouraging. Psychologists have conducted several similar experiments, using either nonsense syllables or real words, with college students as their subjects. The results, in sharp contrast to those of Ebbinghaus, showed very little forgetting over a 24-hour period.

What do you suppose accounts for the difference in results? It is not so much the extraordinary intelligence of college students as it is something special about Ebbinghaus's experience. In the process of memorizing thousands of lists of nonsense syllables, he had subjected himself to an enormous degree of proactive interference. Although he could still memorize new lists, the interference from earlier lists led to unusually rapid forgetting.

One moral of the story is this: When you want to memorize something, avoid studying anything else too similar too soon. Many people find that they can remember material best if they study it just before going to sleep.

Concept Check

6. *Professor Tryhard learns the names of his students every semester. After a number of years, he finds that he learns them as quickly as ever but forgets them faster. Is that an example of retroactive interference or proactive interference? (Check your answer on page 312.)*

Something to Think About

Remember spontaneous recovery from Chapter 7, page 245? Can you explain it in terms of proactive interference? (What is learned first? What is learned second? What would happen if the first interfered with the second?)

An Impediment to Retrieval: The Tip-of-the-Tongue Phenomenon

Sometimes you may experience the so-called **tip-of-the-tongue phenomenon**. You are trying to recall a word or name, you know that you know it, and yet you cannot retrieve it. Even so, you can usually come up with a fair amount of information about the word you are trying to produce. You can often give the first letter of the word, approximately how many syllables it has, and perhaps a word that sounds like it (Brown & McNeill, 1966).

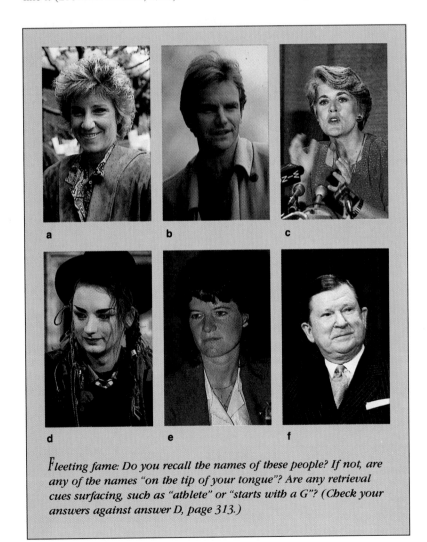

Fleeting fame: Do you recall the names of these people? If not, are any of the names "on the tip of your tongue"? Are any retrieval cues surfacing, such as "athlete" or "starts with a G"? (Check your answers against answer D, page 313.)

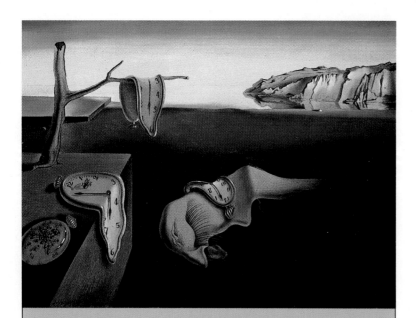

Salvador Dalí was 27 when he painted The Persistence of Memory *in 1931. Do the soft watches in this barren landscape represent time's distortion of memory? A Surrealist, Dalí was interested in mysterious and disturbing dream images. He described these watches as "like fillets of sole destined to be swallowed by the sharks of mechanical time." If that sounds fishy, feel free to interpret the surreal according to your own reality.*

If you know so much about the word, why can't you remember it? Often it is because of interference from a similar word. I once had a tip-of-the-tongue experience about a week after listening to a particularly interesting speech. I was trying to remember the speaker's name, but all I could say was that it was something like "Bhagavad Gita," the name of the Hindu holy writings. I asked a friend who had heard the same speech; he too said it was on the tip of his tongue, but all he could remember was that it was something like "Rita Levi-Montalcini," another noted researcher. Eventually we recalled the correct name: Paul Bach-y-Rita.

When you have a tip-of-the-tongue experience, irrelevant associations may lead you to a word that is similar but not quite right. I had difficulty thinking of "Bach-y-Rita" because something in me kept saying "Bhagavad Gita." When that happens, it is best to turn your attention to something else until the competing association fades.

A similar block occurs when someone is trying to remember a list of items and is presented with an incomplete list. Suppose you are trying to remember the names of all 30 members of a club you belonged to in high school. Before you start, a friend who was also a member hands you a list of

the 15 she can remember. Will her list help you to recall the others? No, actually it will impair your memory (Roediger & Neely, 1982; Slamecka, 1968). You will tend to concentrate on the 15 names on your friend's list and, as in a tip-of-the-tongue experience, your memory of the other names will be blocked.

Selective Memory and Distortions

Your memory of the events of the last day or two includes precise details, even unimportant ones. If you studied in the library last night, you may remember where you sat, what you were reading, who sat down next to you, and where you went for a snack afterward. As time passes, many of those details, perhaps all of them, will fade like an old photo. However, if you happen to fall in love with the person who sat down next to you, you may remember the experience forever. (Recall from page 284 that the events surrounding an emotionally charged experience become highly memorable.) Even in that case, however, you will remember only certain details (such as meeting that person) and will forget or distort less important details.

When we try to recall an event after some of the details have faded, we tend to fill in the gaps with what seems most reasonable—a **reconstruction** of our memories. (During an original experience we *construct* a memory. When we try to retrieve that memory, we *reconstruct* it from what survives.) If you forget what you were reading in the library the night you met your true love, you might reconstruct the memory this way: "I must have been reading something, or I wouldn't have been in the library. Let's see, that semester I was taking a chemistry course that took a lot of study, so maybe I was reading a chemistry book. No, wait, I remember that when we went out for a snack we talked about politics. So maybe I was reading a political science text."

We also reconstruct the time and circumstances of a particular experience: "That happened while I was still in high school. I remember talking about it with the other guys working at the Burger Hut, so it must have been before I quit my job there. And it was before I started dating Carla. So it must have been about October of my senior year." We use political landmarks for the same purpose, such as, "I think that happened during the latter part of the Reagan administration, so it must have been about 1987 or 1988" (Brown, Shevell, & Rips, 1986).

Sometimes what we call a memory is just a reasonable guess. In answering the question "How many hours did you spend studying last month?"

very few students will try to remember all the hours and count them up. They recall a day they consider "typical," estimate how long they studied that day, and then multiply by 30 to get the number of hours they studied in a month (Bradburn, Rips, & Shevell, 1987).

Such guesses work reasonably well most of the time, but they sometimes lead to error or distortion. In one study (Brewer & Treyens, 1981), students waited in a room described as "the experimenter's office," without any instruction to pay attention to anything in the room or to try to remember it. After leaving, they were asked to describe the room. Most of them described the desk, chair, walls, and other items that are ordinarily found in an office. They generally failed to mention the skull that was there. And about a third of them described a bookcase, which was not there. Clearly, what they reported as memory was a mixture of actual experiences with inferences of "what must have been there."

In another experiment, two groups of college students were asked to read a story about a woman named Betty (Snyder & Uranowitz, 1978). The first part of the story, about Betty's early years, was the same for both groups. One key sentence in that section stated that Betty dated during high school but never had a steady boyfriend. For Betty's adult life, the two groups were given different versions. One group was told that Betty got married; the other group was told that Betty became a lesbian. When the two groups tried to recall the story, they emphasized differing aspects of Betty's early life. Those who had read that Betty got married were more likely to recall, "In high school, she dated." Those who had read that Betty became a lesbian were more likely to recall, "In high school, she never had a boyfriend." Apparently, people remember what best fits their memory of the rest of the story or what best fits their preconceptions. Distortions of this sort are so common that we should be skeptical when someone tells about an amazing experience, especially if it happened years ago.

The Suggestibility of Eyewitness Accounts: WHAT'S THE EVIDENCE?

When someone distorts a story in a psychologist's laboratory, no harm is done. But sometimes a great deal is riding on the accuracy of someone's memory.

You have just watched a robbery committed by someone you had never seen before. You were the only witness. When the police ask you to describe

In recalling an event from our past, we reconstruct our memories, using the details we do remember. The person here might eventually make this reconstruction: "Let's see. That was when Dad took me to New Hampshire for a glider ride. We were living in Boston then. Oh, those are the sandals I got for my first year at summer camp, so I must have been 8. That would make it the summer of 1976.

the thief, you do your best, but you saw him for only a few seconds and cannot recall many details. The police ask, "Did he have a mustache? Did he have a tattoo on his right hand? Two other robberies were pulled off around here in the last few days by a man with a mustache and a tattoo on his right hand." Suddenly it comes back to you: "Yes, he definitely had a mustache. And I'm almost sure he had a tattoo." Did the suggestion help you to recall those details? Or did it prompt you to reconstruct details that you never actually saw?

EXPERIMENT 1

Hypothesis If people are asked questions that suggest or presuppose a certain fact, many people will later report remembering that "fact," even if it never happened.

Method Elizabeth Loftus (1975) asked two groups of students to watch a videotape of an automobile accident. Then she asked one group, "Did you see the children getting on the school bus?" She did not ask the other group that question. In fact, there was no school bus in the videotape. A week later, she asked both groups 20 new questions about the accident, including this one: "Did you see a school bus in the film?"

When an eyewitness fails to recall an important point, a lawyer may ask a leading question designed to refresh his memory—or plant an idea in jurors' minds. Some witnesses, especially children, may be so eager to cooperate that they will "remember" whatever seems helpful.

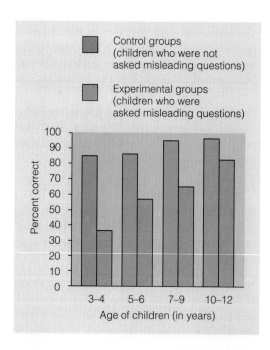

Control groups
(children who were not
asked misleading questions)

Experimental groups
(children who were
asked misleading questions)

FIGURE 8.22

Children who were asked misleading questions were less likely than other children were to give correct answers later. The effect of misleading questions was greater on younger children than on older children. (From Ceci, Ross, & Toglia, 1987.)

Results   Of the first group (those who were asked about seeing children get on a school bus), 26% reported they had seen a school bus; of the second group, only 6% said they had seen a school bus.

Interpretation   The question "Did you see the children getting on the school bus?" presupposes that there was a school bus. Some of the people who heard that question added a school bus to their memory of the event. The students reconstructed what happened by combining what they actually saw with what they believed might reasonably have happened and with what someone suggested to them afterward.

Special problems arise when a child is the witness to a crime. A child claims to have been sexually molested, for example, or a child is the only witness to a murder. How trustworthy is the child's testimony, especially when the case comes to trial many months later, after parents and police have asked who-knows-what kinds of questions?

In one experiment, children listened as an adult read a short story about a girl who got a stomachache from eating eggs too fast. When the children were later asked simple questions about the story, children at all ages from 3 through 12 replied correctly about 90% of the time. But some of the children were first asked, "Do you remember the story about Loren, who had a headache because she ate her cereal too fast?" After hearing this question, younger children were more heavily influenced than were older children, as shown in Figure 8.22. They reported remembering headaches instead of stomachaches and cereal instead of eggs (Ceci, Ross, & Toglia, 1987). Such results do not mean that we should discount the testimony of young children. (To do so would virtually legalize crimes against children!) But they do mean that anyone who questions young children must be especially careful not to word the questions in a way that will suggest one answer or another.

What do results of this type mean? Suppose experimenters ask you whether you remembered the girl who had a headache because she ate her cereal too fast. Later they ask whether she ate eggs or cereal. When you say you think she ate cereal, that might mean that the suggestion changed your memory. But it might also mean that you have no idea what she ate, so you are willing to go along with the experimenters' claim that it was cereal. Or you might think, "Hmm ... I thought it was eggs, but the experimenters said cereal, and I suppose they should know. So I'll say cereal, too." When the experimenters' suggestion leads you to give the wrong answer, does it actually weaken your original memory?

Hypothesis When people are given a misleading suggestion and then asked about what they saw, they may give answers that follow the suggestion. But if they are asked questions that eliminate the suggested information as a possible answer, they will return to the original information.

Method College students saw a series of slides about a man who entered a room, stole some money and a calculator, and left. One of the slides showed a coffee jar on a file cabinet. At the end of the slides, the students were asked a series of questions. Some were asked a question designed to mislead them: They were asked whether they saw a jar of sugar on the file cabinet. Others were just asked about a jar. Later, some students were asked what kind of jar they saw on the file cabinet, a jar of coffee or a jar of sugar. Others were asked what brand of coffee they saw on the file cabinet (Zaragoza, McCloskey, & Jamis, 1987).

Results The suggestion had an effect on students who were asked which they saw, coffee or sugar. Of those who had heard the misleading question about a jar of sugar, 39% said they remembered a jar of sugar. Of those who had not heard the misleading question, only 18% said they remembered a jar of sugar.

However, the suggestion had no effect on students who were asked what brand of coffee they saw. Regardless of whether or not they had heard a misleading question about a jar of sugar, about 60% reported the correct brand of coffee.

Interpretation A misleading suggestion does sometimes lead people to answer a question incorrectly by substituting the suggested information for the original information. But evidently the suggestion does not impair the original memory. If someone asks a question that excludes the suggested information, people remember the original information as well as if the suggestion had never been made. ■

There is a message in all this about how psychologists do research: What seems like the obvious interpretation for a given set of results may not be the only one and perhaps not even the best one. The psychologists who conducted experiment 1 proposed what seemed a reasonable interpretation—that the misleading suggestions had actually changed people's memories. But other psychologists doubted that interpretation and conducted their own study, which led to a different interpretation.

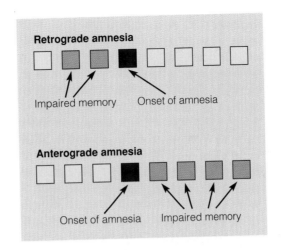

FIGURE 8.23

Who am I? In retrograde amnesia, memories immediately prior to the start of amnesia are obliterated. In anterograde amnesia, memories that form after a traumatic event are difficult to recall.

AMNESIA

So far, I have been discussing kinds of memory loss and distortion that we all experience. Some people, however, experience **amnesia** (am-NEE-zha), a profound loss of memory resulting from brain damage or a severe emotional crisis.

Psychologists distinguish between retrograde (RE-tro-grade) amnesia and anterograde (ANT-uh-ro-grade) amnesia (see Figure 8.23). **Retrograde amnesia** is a loss of memory for events that occurred just before the onset of amnesia. A person who suffers a blow to the head and loses consciousness generally forgets what happened during the few minutes just before the injury, but depending on the severity of the injury, this retrograde amnesia may extend over a period of months or years. Some people who suffer retrograde amnesia for emotional reasons may forget who they are, where they live, and everything that has ever happened to them. Such amnesia is generally a temporary memory loss, whereas amnesia caused by head trauma can last indefinitely.

Anterograde amnesia is an inability to form new long-term memories. People with certain kinds of brain damage can recall what happened prior to the damage, but forget a new event almost as soon as their attention is distracted.

In both retrograde amnesia and anterograde amnesia, the loss is usually limited to factual memory; procedural memory remains largely intact. A person who forgets everything that happened before last Tuesday (retrograde amnesia) will still remember how to walk, talk, drive a car, and tie shoelaces. Similarly, a person who suffers anterograde amnesia may be incapable of learning new facts yet moderately adept at learning new motor skills.

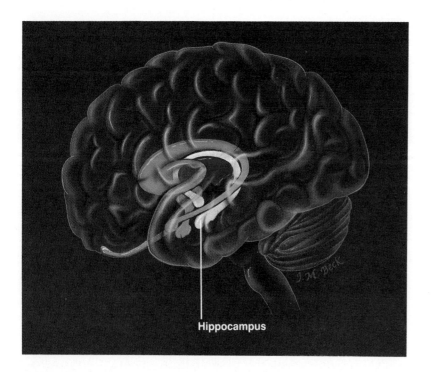

FIGURE 8.24

Location of the hippocampus, the area of brain damage in the famous patient H. M. The hippocampus, just inside the posterior part of the cerebral cortex, gets its name from its curved shape; *hippocampus* is Greek for "sea horse."

Amnesia Caused by Brain Damage

In 1953, a man with the initials H. M. was subjected to unusual brain surgery in an attempt to control his extreme epilepsy. H. M. had suffered such frequent and severe seizures that he was unable to keep a job or live a normal life; he had failed to respond to any of the drugs used to control epilepsy. In desperation, surgeons removed an area of his brain called the **hippocampus** (see Figure 8.24), which they believed was the area where his epileptic seizures originated.

The surgery did control H. M.'s epilepsy, but it led to an unexpected and very severe memory problem (Corkin, 1984; Milner, 1959). H. M. could still form normal short-term memories, such as repeating a brief list of items. With constant rehearsal, he could even retain those memories for several minutes. Moreover, he could still recall long-term memories from the time before his operation. He had great difficulty, however, forming new long-term memories. For years after the operation, he gave the year as 1953 and his own age as 27. Later, he took wild guesses. He would read the same issue of a magazine repeatedly without realizing that he had read it before. He could not even remember where he had lived for the last few years.

H. M. is a modern Rip van Winkle who becomes more and more out of date with each passing year (Gabrieli, Cohen, & Corkin, 1988; Smith, 1988). He does not recognize the names or faces of people who became famous after the mid-1950s. He could not name the president of the United States even when Ronald Reagan became president, though he remembered Reagan as an actor from before 1953. He does not understand the meaning of words that entered the English language after the time of his surgery. For example, he guessed that *biodegradable* means "two grades," that *soul food* means "forgiveness," and that a *closet queen* is a "moth." For H. M., watching the evening news is like visiting another planet.

Although H. M. has learned few new facts since 1953, he *has* learned that his memory is poor. Curiously, although he has great difficulty learning new facts, he is able to acquire new skills, such as learning to read material written in mirror fashion (Cohen & Squire, 1980):

with the words reversed like this

Although he has learned to read mirror writing, he does not remember having learned it. He is always a bit surprised by his success.

A condition with somewhat similar symptoms, known as **Korsakoff's syndrome**, is caused by a prolonged deficiency of vitamin B_1, usually as a result of chronic alcoholism. The deficiency leads to widespread brain damage and to multiple impairments of memory (Oscar-Berman, 1980; Squire, 1982). Patients with Korsakoff's syndrome suffer varying degrees of retrograde amnesia, although many of them can recall a fair number of details about their past (Baddeley & Wilson, 1986). Their main trouble is anterograde amnesia. Although they can memorize a list of paired associates, they forget the list rapidly, especially if they are tested in a room different from the room in which they learned it (Winocur, Moscovitch, & Witherspoon, 1987). They have particular trouble remembering *when* various events took place (Schacter, 1987b). For example, if asked what they ate this morning or what they did last night, they describe something they did some time in the past.

A final example of amnesia caused by brain damage is **Alzheimer's disease**, a degenerative condition that generally occurs in old age (Coyle, Price, & DeLong, 1983). (See Figure 8.25.) People suffering from Alzheimer's disease can (in the early stages of the disease) recall events from long ago, but they have trouble remembering new information. When an investigator played a round of golf with an Alzheimer's patient (Schacter, 1983), the patient could remember the rules and terminology of golf per-

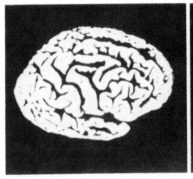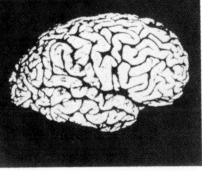

FIGURE 8.25

The brain on the left, from an Alzheimer's disease patient, is noticeably smaller compared to the normal brain on the right. With this disease, the central nervous system degenerates.

fectly well but could never remember how many strokes he had taken on a hole. He often forgot whether he had already teed off or was still waiting his turn. During later stages of the disease, the person suffers impairments of all aspects of memory and many motor skills.

Concept Check

7. Is H. M.'s problem retrograde amnesia or anterograde amnesia? (Check your answer on page 312.)

Amnesia Caused by Emotional Troubles

Some people who suffer severe retrograde amnesia show no indication of brain damage. Because the onset of their amnesia often coincided with a traumatic emotional experience, psychologists believe that the amnesia may be a means of escape from memories too unpleasant to deal with. In some cases, however, the cause cannot be determined.

One patient who was suffering severe retrograde amnesia for no apparent biological reason was still able to learn and remember new material. He was asked to memorize a list of paired associates in which famous people were paired with professions other than their own, such as the one in Table 8.6. He actually learned a list similar to this *faster* than normal people did. Most people are hindered by proactive interference, but this patient had completely forgotten what various people were really famous for and had no trouble remembering the new pairings (Kapur, Heath, Meudell, & Kennedy, 1986).

Accused criminals frequently claim that they are suffering emotionally induced amnesia. From one fourth to more than half of all convicted murderers claim they cannot remember the crime they are accused of; some say they cannot remember anything that happened that entire day. Because it is likely that committing a murder would be associated with intense, unpleasant emotions, some of them may in fact be experiencing emotionally

To remember what you need at a supermarket, you may take a list along, but people with Alzheimer's disease may need reminders to buy food and to eat it. With such people, factual memory fades. Procedural memory is less impaired; those with the disease forget to do things more than they forget how *to do them. Posting reminders to turn off appliances is often useful.*

TABLE 8.6

Oliver North	singer
PeeWee Herman	tennis player
Michael Jordan	politician
Margaret Thatcher	actress
Dan Rather	standup comic
Steven Spielberg	owner of fried-chicken chain
Mary Lou Retton	televangelist
Whitney Houston	inventor
Donna Rice	movie critic
Tammy Faye Bakker	medical researcher
Ayatollah Khomeini	talk-show host

induced amnesia. Others—those who were on drugs or alcohol at the time—may have forgotten because their memories are state dependent (page 298).

But what about the possibility that some of these accused criminals are faking amnesia? Occasionally a claim of amnesia is made to support a plea of not guilty by reason of insanity. Suppose a psychologist or a psychiatrist is asked to determine whether such a person is truly suffering amnesia or is just faking it. How accurately can an expert distinguish the real thing from an imitation?

Daniel Schacter (1986a, 1986b) devised an experiment to answer that question. He had one group of students read a passage or watch a videotape that included many details that most people do not notice. When they were asked what certain people in the story were wearing or exactly what they said at certain times, the subjects replied that they did not remember. A second group read the same material or watched the same videotape after being instructed to watch for those details but to *pretend* to forget them. Schacter then brought in a number of psychologists and psychiatrists who were frequently called as expert witnesses in court to determine which subjects had really forgotten and which ones were only pretending. None of the experts showed much more than 50-50 accuracy, even in those cases on which they felt most certain. The moral of the story: *If someone claims to know whether a person is suffering amnesia or faking it, be skeptical. At least ask that person to explain how he or she knows.*

Amnesia of Infancy and Old Age

Most adults can recall very few experiences from before the age of 5. That relative lack of memories is known as **infant amnesia** or *childhood amnesia*. Memories from that period are forgotten, but not just because they are old (Wetzer & Sweeney, 1986). After all, a 60-year-old can remember more from age 20 than a 20-year-old can remember from age 3.

Psychologists have proposed a number of theories to explain why our early memories are so vulnerable. The explanation probably goes beyond the maturation of language ability or any other uniquely human developmental process, because nonhumans also forget most of what they learned as infants (Bachevalier & Mishkin, 1984).

One possible explanation is that young children fail to organize their memories as adults do. Most adults, when given a list of items to remember, sort them into groups or look for patterns that will

aid recall. Preschool children almost never use such aids (Kail & Strauss, 1984; Moely, Olson, Halwes, & Flavell, 1969).

Another possibility is that infant amnesia may be related to the slow maturation of the hippocampus (Moscovitch, 1985). Although we recall few factual memories from before age 5, we retain an enormous number of procedural memories from that time—how to walk, talk, put on clothing, keep ourselves clean, and conduct other daily activities. That pattern of retaining procedural memories while losing factual memories is characteristic of H. M. and of other humans and animals with damage to the hippocampus.

Something to Think About

Does the encoding specificity principle (page 298) suggest another possible explanation for infant amnesia? (*Hint:* Your physiological condition always differs somewhat at the time of attempted recall from what it was at the time of original learning.)

A certain amount of memory loss also is common in old age. The degree of loss varies from one person to another and from one time to another for a given individual. What is most likely to suffer is memory for context and time. Older people may wonder, "Did I already tell this story to my daughter, or was it someone else?" "Where did I park my car today?" "Is my appointment for today or for tomorrow?" Again, one possible explanation for such memory failure is a loss of neurons in the hippocampus (Barnes & McNaughton, 1985).

B. F. Skinner (1983) has devised various techniques to compensate for the memory decline he experienced as he grew older. Skinner trusts as little as possible to memory. He writes notes to himself whenever he wants to remember something. If he decides he should take an umbrella when he leaves the house, he immediately places an umbrella near the front door. He avoids launching into long, complex sentences, lest he forget where he was going before he reaches the end. He is alert to signs of fatigue. When he senses that he is engaging in unnecessary delay, feeling sorry for himself, blaming others, losing his appetite, or using profanity, he takes a vacation.

Skinner and his wife have worked out certain cooperative strategies to cope with failing memory. When they meet someone whose name they cannot remember, he begins, "Of course, dear, you remember. . . ." Then she interrupts, "Why, of course! How good to see you again."

SUMMARY

1. Memory can be improved through distributed practice. (page 295)

2. People can process information at various depths, depending on the number of meaningful associations they form. Processing information deeply makes it easier to recall later. (page 295)

3. Good readers monitor their own reading comprehension and reread the material they do not understand at first. The result is to improve their understanding and, eventually, their memory of the material. (page 296)

4. At the time of learning one establishes retrieval cues related to the material learned. It is easiest to recall a memory if one uses the same retrieval cues at the time of recall as at the time of learning. (page 297)

5. Mnemonic devices such as the method of loci enable people to store and retrieve memories in a highly reliable manner. (page 298)

6. Long-term memories fade very slowly over time. Much of the difficulty in retrieving long-term memories is due to interference from similar memories. (page 302)

7. After the details of a memory fade, we fill in the gaps based on what seems reasonable. Sometimes suggestions from other people lead us to distort our memories. (page 304)

8. Amnesia is of two types—loss of old memories and difficulty establishing new memories. In both types, factual memories are more likely to suffer than are procedural memories. (page 307)

9. Some people suffer amnesia as a result of emotional trauma. It is difficult to distinguish between someone who is suffering from real amnesia and someone who is just pretending. (page 309)

10. Most people remember little of what happened to them before the age of 5. Several theories have been proposed to account for that loss of early memory. (page 310)

SUGGESTIONS FOR FURTHER READING

Cermak, L. S. (1975). *Improving your memory.* New York: McGraw-Hill. A lively book about mnemonic devices and other ways to improve memory.

Squire, L. R. (1987). *Memory and brain.* New York: Oxford University. An excellent review focusing on amnesia and the biological foundations of memory.

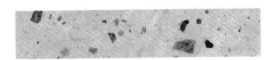

TERMS TO REMEMBER

Alzheimer's disease a degenerative condition of the brain that results in memory impairments, especially anterograde amnesia

amnesia a severe loss of memory

anterograde amnesia the inability to form new long-term memories

chunking the process of grouping letters or digits into meaningful sequences that can be easily remembered

connectionist model a model that represents memory as a set of links among units

consolidation the transfer of information from short-term memory to long-term memory

context-dependent memory a memory that is easier to recall in the environment in which it was formed than in some other environment

cued recall a method of testing the persistence of memory by asking someone to remember a certain item after being given a hint

depth-of-processing principle the principle that a memory can be stored either superficially or at various depths, depending on how deeply a person thinks about it and how many associations he or she forms with it

distinctiveness the quality of being different from other elements in a list

distributed practice practice of something one is trying to learn spread over a period of time

eidetic imagery the ability to look at a large, complicated picture or pattern and later recall its contents in detail

encoding specificity principle the principle that memory is strengthened by using the same retrieval cues when recovering a memory as when storing it

episodic memory a person's memory of particular events in his or her life

factual memory the ability to remember facts

free recall remembering a list of items in any order

hippocampus a forebrain structure believed to be important for certain aspects of memory

infant amnesia the relative lack of memory for experiences that occurred before the age of 5

information processing model the procedure by which either a computer or a person codes, stores, and retrieves information

interference competition among related memories

Korsakoff's syndrome a condition caused by prolonged deficiency of vitamin B_1, which results in a combination of both retrograde amnesia and anterograde amnesia

long-term memory memory that lasts indefinitely

massed practice practice of something one is trying to learn by means of many repetitions in a short time

meaningfulness the ability of a person to fit a given item into a known pattern of information

method of loci a mnemonic device that calls for linking the items on a list with a memorized list of places

mnemonic device any technique for aiding memory by encoding each item in some special way

nonsense syllable a meaningless syllable, such as JID, sometimes used in studies of memory

paired-associates learning memorization of pairs of items

proactive interference the interference produced by an older memory on a newer one

procedural memory the ability to remember how to perform acquired skills

recall a method of testing the persistence of memory by asking someone to produce a certain item (such as a word)

recognition a method of testing the persistence of memory by asking someone to choose the correct item from several items

reconstruction filling in the gaps in a memory with what seems reasonable

retrieval cue an association that facilitates retrieval of information from long-term memory

retroactive interference the interference produced by a newer memory on an older one

retrograde amnesia loss of memory for events that occurred during a time just prior to the onset of the amnesia

savings method or **relearning method** a method of testing the persistence of memory by measuring how much faster someone can relearn something learned in the past than something being learned for the first time

semantic memory memory of facts, ideas, or general principles

sensory store the very brief storage of information derived from the senses

serial learning memorization of a series of items in order

serial-order effect the tendency of people to remember items at the beginning and the end of a list better than those in the middle

short-term memory memory that forms instantaneously but lasts only until a person's attention is distracted

SPAR method a self-monitoring method of study based on these steps: survey, process meaningfully, ask questions, review, and self-test

SQ3R method a self-monitoring method of study based on these five steps: survey, question, read, recite, review

state-dependent memory a memory that is easiest to recall when a person is in the same physiological state as when the memory was formed

tip-of-the-tongue phenomenon the experience of knowing something but being unable to produce it

von Restorff effect the tendency to remember the most unusual items on a list better than other items

ANSWERS TO CONCEPT CHECKS

1. (a) Free recall, because you do not care whether you recall the items in any particular order; (b) paired-associates learning; (c) serial learning, because you must remember the words in the correct order; (d) paired-associates learning. (page 281)

2. (a) Savings; (b) recall; (c) recognition; (d) implicit or indirect; (e) cued recall. (page 283)

3. (a) Procedural; (b) short-term; (c) semantic; (d) long-term, episodic. (page 292)

4. The arrangement of words in b promotes organizational processing. A relationship among the words is evident in b but not in a. (page 296)

5. People would remember even more if they were tested by the recognition method, as Bahrick (1984) demonstrated. They would probably show even greater retention if they were tested by the savings method. (page 302)

6. Proactive interference; old memories are interfering with retention of new ones. (page 303)

7. Anterograde amnesia. (page 309)

ANSWERS TO OTHER QUESTIONS IN THE TEXT

A. Herman Melville, Susan B. Anthony, Agatha Christie, Spiro Agnew, Ivan Pavlov, Henry Aaron, Arthur Conan Doyle, Sally Ride, James Kalat, Margaret Mitchell, Wilbur and Orville, Geraldine Ferraro. (page 282)

B. The correct coin is A. (page 286)

C. (page 297)

Pottery	Pitcher
Animal	Seal
Part of body	Feet
Transportation	Plane
Football	Pass
Crime	Racket
U.S. politician	Bush
Music	Rock
Personality	Charm
Write	Spell
Bird	Cardinal
Board game	Checkers
Sports	Ball

D. (a) Chris Evert, (b) Sting, (c) Geraldine Ferraro, (d) Boy George, (e) Sally Ride, (f) John Tower.

CHAPTER

9

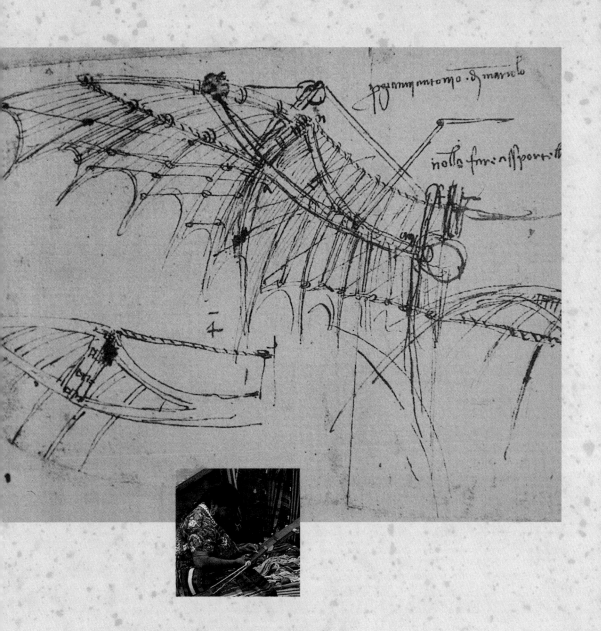

How does a television set work? We can answer that question in two ways: One way is to describe the internal wiring and what each electronic device does. The other way is to describe how the set as a whole operates. (For example, if I flip a certain switch, the set comes on. If I turn a dial, the channel changes.)

How does a human work—that is, behave? We can also answer that question in two ways: One way is to describe what each neuron does and how the various neurons communicate with one another. The other way is to describe the behavior of the person as a whole. (For example, when the weather turns cold or rainy, I go indoors. At certain times of day I walk toward a restaurant.)

Do we need a third way of describing behavior? Might we describe behavior as something caused by thoughts, knowledge, expectations, and desires?

As we saw in Chapter 7, behaviorists say no. We do not need such terms to describe how a television works or to describe human behavior. Moreover, neurons and behavior are easily observed and measured. Thoughts and knowledge are not. A scientific study, say the behaviorists, should deal only with what can be observed and measured.

And yet each of us is directly aware of our own thoughts. Even if we cannot observe or measure other people's thoughts directly, we are sure of the reality of our own. In fact, my own conscious mind is the thing I am *most* sure of. (After all, the external world might be just an illusion.)

Granting that thoughts exist, we ask what are they? Even if we cannot observe them directly, can we measure them indirectly through their effects on behavior? This chapter deals with the attempts of psychologists to grapple with these questions.

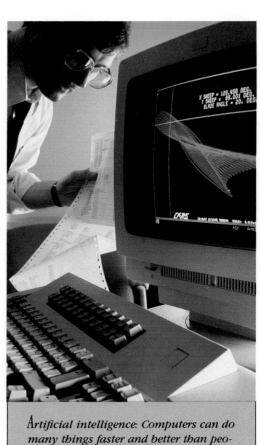

Artificial intelligence: Computers can do many things faster and better than people can, but can they think? According to Pablo Picasso, "Computers are useless. They can only give you answers." What's wrong with only giving answers? How do people give answers? How do they come up with questions? In short, what does thinking *mean?*

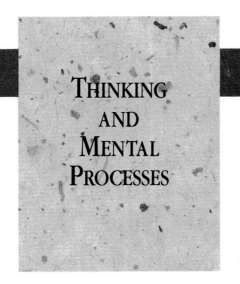

THINKING AND MENTAL PROCESSES

How is it possible to measure thought processes? Are mental images similar to visual images?

In 1986, investigators located the remains of the luxury liner *Titanic*, which had sunk in 1912. With great expense and effort they maneuvered a remote-control device to photograph various parts of the ship. Why did they bother? Did they plan to recover valuable cargo from the ship? No. Did they expect to learn anything about why the ship sank? Maybe, although the causes of the disaster were already well established. Actually, the investigators did not expect to learn anything especially useful. They wanted to know more about the ship just because they wanted to know. And so did all the rest of us who eagerly pored over the pictures.

Once we saw the pictures, we knew something that we had not known before. But was that the end of it? Hardly. The pictures started us thinking. We imagined what the ship must have looked like in 1912 and how we would have felt if we had been on board when it sank. Those thoughts led to other thoughts. Perhaps this is why we seek new information about the *Titanic* or about anything else: The new information gives us something new to think about.

Cognition means thought. It refers to all those processes that enable us to imagine, to gain knowledge, to reason about that knowledge, and to judge what it means. Cognitive psychology is the study of how people think, how they acquire knowledge, how they plan, and how they solve problems. In short, it deals with some of the most complex and most interesting processes in psychology.

WHY STUDY COGNITION?

"Why," you might ask, "do psychologists bother conducting experiments on how people think and what they know? Why not just ask them?" Because people do not always know the answer. Sometimes something influences their thoughts and actions without their being aware of the influence.

Consider, for example, an experiment in which a psychologist establishes that a certain variable has demonstrably affected the subjects' behavior and then discovers that the subjects were unaware that the variable had affected them. In one such experiment (Nisbett & Schachter, 1966), two groups of college students were told that the experiment was designed to discover how much electric shock a person can stand before finding the pain unbearable. This sounds like a study Nazi doctors might have undertaken, but the students accepted it as a routine psychological experiment.

First the experimenters asked the students to take a pill so they could measure how the pill affected reactions to shock. Actually, the pill was a placebo

"Now the *immediate* fact which psychology, the science of mind, has to study is also the most general fact. It is the fact that in each of us, when awake (and often when asleep) *some kind of consciousness is always going on.* There is a stream, a succession of states, or waves, or fields (or of whatever you please to call them), of knowledge, of feeling, of desire, of deliberation, etc., that constantly pass and repass, and that constitute our inner life. The existence of this stream is the primal fact, the nature and origin of it form the essential problem, of our science."

WILLIAM JAMES
(1899)

"*Because it's there*": *Searching for the* Titanic *led to the development of a submersible robot camera, which took this photo. No one aboard anticipated—"thought of"—an accident; with lifeboats for only half the passengers, 1,522 died.*

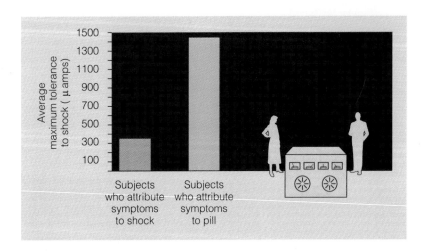

FIGURE 9.1

Different reactions to shock, depending on the instructions about a pill—a placebo—that the students took. (*Placebo* comes from Latin for "I shall please.")

containing an inactive substance. Students in one group were told, incorrectly, that the pill would cause a faster heart rate, irregular breathing, trembling hands, and butterflies in the stomach. (These are in fact the effects of electric shock.) Students in the other group were told, correctly, that the pill would not affect their reactions to the shock. Then each student was strapped into a device and the shocks were administered. They started at a low level of intensity, 20 microamperes, and were gradually stepped up until the student said, "That's as much as I can take. Let me out."

The students who were told that the pill would increase their heart rate and breathing rate endured, on the average, more than four times as strong a shock as the students who had been told that the pill would have no effect. Why? As the shocks grew stronger, both groups began to experience changes in heart rate, breathing rate, and hand tremors. The group that expected the pill to produce those effects apparently thought, "Aha! The pill is taking effect, just as they said it would!" (Figure 9.1). The other group, told that the pill would have no effect, knew the shocks were causing the increased heart rate and breathing rate. Afraid that they were being seriously hurt, they demanded to be let out.

Afterward, the experimenters told the students who had been misled about the pill's effects that they had withstood a very heavy shock and asked them, "Why do you suppose you were able to take more shock than the others?" Most of the students said something about being tough or about having gotten used to pain at some time in the past (Nisbett & Wilson, 1977). Very few of them even mentioned

the pill. The experimenters then suggested that the reason the students had endured the shock may have been that they attributed their physiological reactions to the pill. Even then, most of the students said, "That's very interesting. But that's not why I took so much shock. I wasn't even thinking about the pill. I took all that shock because I'm so tough."

As in many other cases, the subjects did not know why they were behaving as they did. So asking them to describe their thought processes or the reasons for their behavior would not lead to the correct answers. Cognitive psychologists have had to develop clever methods to infer what and how people think, without asking them directly.

MEASURING MENTAL ACTIVITY

For years, many psychologists, especially behaviorists, paid no attention to the study of mental activity because, they claimed, there was no way of observing or measuring it. True, we cannot observe mental activity directly—just as physicists cannot observe magnetic fields directly. We can, however, measure the *effects* of mental activity. Recently, investigators have devised several ways of measuring mental activity, generally by measuring the time it takes people to answer certain questions.

For example, subjects in one experiment watched a number flashed on a screen (Sternberg, 1967). They were told to pull one lever if the number was, say, either 3 or 7, and a different lever if it was any other number. To make the correct response, the subjects had to go through three steps: First, they had to perceive what number was being flashed on the screen. Second, they had to compare that number to the numbers they had memorized (3 and 7) to determine whether it was one of them. Third, they had to pull a lever.

How did they perform that second step, the step that requires thinking rather than perception or action? Did they test the number against each of the numbers they had memorized, one at a time? ("Is it a 3? Is it a 7?") Or did they somehow test it against both the 3 and the 7 simultaneously?

Saul Sternberg (1967) answered that question not by asking the subjects how they did it but by measuring their **reaction times** under various conditions. Sometimes the subjects had to decide whether the number on the screen was a single number, such as 3. Sometimes they had to decide whether it was either of two numbers, such as 3 or 7. Sometimes they had to decide whether it was one of four numbers, such as 3, 4, 6, or 7. Sternberg measured how long subjects took to respond to each stimulus. Figure 9.2 gives the results.

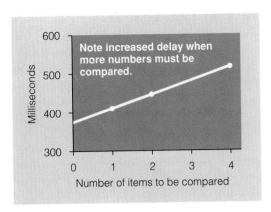

FIGURE 9.2

Split-second decisions: Mean reaction time for subjects who had to compare the number they saw on a screen to one, two, or four numbers they had memorized. Note that the reaction time increases when more numbers must be compared. (Based on Sternberg, 1967.)

When the subjects had to compare the number on the screen to four numbers they had memorized, they took 71 milliseconds longer to respond than when they had to compare it to two. Their response took 35 milliseconds longer when they had to compare the number to two than when they had to compare it to a single number. Because the relationship was so regular, Sternberg concluded that the subjects were comparing the number on the screen to each of the numbers they had memorized, one at a time. Apparently, they took 35 milliseconds to compare the displayed number to each of the memorized numbers.

In Figure 9.2, a straight line connects the points for one, two, and four numbers held in memory. If we extend the line back to *zero* numbers, as shown in the figure, we find a reaction time of only 372 milliseconds. Theoretically, that is what the reaction time would be if subjects did not have to compare the number on the screen to any other number. Presumably, 372 milliseconds represents the combined time required for step 1 (perceiving the number) and step 3 (pulling the lever).

Studies of reaction times have also led researchers to identify previously unrecognized mental activities. In one study, subjects were shown a series of shapes arranged in pairs such as a circle and a triangle. They were asked to press one button if the shapes were the same and a second button if they were different. We might suppose that people go through the same processes to decide that the shapes are the same as to decide that they are different; therefore it should take the same time to give either answer. However, subjects consistently responded more rapidly when they indicated *same*

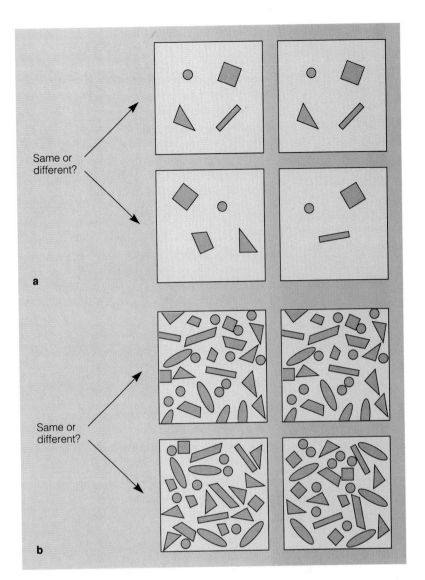

FIGURE 9.3

(a) With relatively simple figures, most people say "same" faster than they say "different," perhaps because they see the sameness at once. (b) With complex figures, people say "different" faster than they say "same," apparently because they must carefully double-check all parts of the identical figures to be sure they are the same.

than when they indicated *different* (Farell, 1985). In most experiments of this type, people have taken longer to say that two items are different than to say that they are the same; they have also taken longer to answer a question *no* than to answer *yes*.

So far, psychologists are not sure why it takes longer to answer *no* or *different* than to answer *yes* or *same*. Perhaps negative answers require an additional mental activity that positive answers do not require. Or perhaps in most experiments it is just easier to see that two items are the same than to see that they are different. For example, in Figure 9.3a we can see at a glance that the top two items are the same, while it may take longer to determine that the bottom two are different. If the experimenter uses complex items like those in Figure 9.3b, however, subjects take a long time to say that the bottom two items are different, but take even longer to say that the top two items are the same (Ratcliff, 1985). In any case, the reaction times indicate how much mental processing is necessary to answer a question; further research will tell us more about what those mental processes are.

Psychologists have used similar measurements of reaction time to study a variety of mental processes that could otherwise be described only by people's self-reports. We shall consider three examples to which researchers give substantial attention: mental imagery, cognitive maps, and categorization of objects.

Concept Check

1. In studies similar to Sternberg's, experimenters made it harder to perceive the numbers on the screen by making them blurry. The results were similar to those shown in Figure 9.2, except that the line in the graph moved upward. The slope of the line was the same. Which step in a subject's response was affected by the blurred letters: perceiving the number, comparing it to the numbers in memory, or pulling the lever? (Check your answer on page 344.)

MENTAL IMAGERY

Figure 9.4 represents a three-dimensional object. Start at any corner, move your pencil along the edge to another corner, then along another edge, and so forth. Can you trace every edge of the figure without touching any edge twice and without jumping from one point to another?

After you have solved that problem, try this one: Without drawing anything, imagine a simple cube. Start at any corner and see whether you can move from corner to corner, covering every edge only once without jumping from one point to another. Can you do it? (Check both answers on page 345, answer A.)

How did you try to solve the problem with the imaginary cube? If you are like most people, you "pictured" a cube in your mind as if you were actually seeing it. You answered the question by using a "mental image."

Suppose you went out your front door, turned left, went to the next corner and turned right, and then alternated left and right turns at every succeeding corner for four more turns. Where would you be? Most people say that they relied on mental images to answer this question, picturing every turn in their mind.

FIGURE 9.4

Trace element: Can you move your pencil along all the edges without jumping from one point to another and without tracing any edge more than once?

FIGURE 9.5

Julia used a magnet to maneuver a metal ring through a maze. Her actions indicated that she used mental images to imagine movements before she tried them. (From Döhl, 1970.)

A *square peg in a square hole: Fair Isle sweaters, Islamic mosaics, aboriginal sand paintings, medieval illuminated manuscripts, oriental rugs—throughout history, people have used their imaginations to create intricate patterns that first existed in the mind. Imagining involves making a mental image and imitating it to solve a problem or form a pattern. Novelist D. H. Lawrence wrote, "You can't* invent *design. You recognize it, in a fourth dimension. That is, with your blood and bones, as well as with your eyes." Does his notion apply to this Guatemalan weaver?*

Do nonhuman animals use mental images too? One study suggests that chimpanzees do. A chimpanzee named Julia was confronted with a series of mazes. By using a magnet to pull a metal ring through the maze, as in Figure 9.5 (Döhl, 1970; Rensch & Döhl, 1968), she could then insert the ring into a vending machine and get some food. The experimenters tested Julia hundreds of times. To minimize the possibility that she would simply memorize the sequence of correct turns, the experimenters used 69 complicated mazes and never used the same one twice in succession.

How would you solve such a problem? If you simply started pulling the ring by trial and error, you would make a mistake on your first move 50% of the time. Five or 10 moves later you would realize you were on the wrong track, and you would have to retrace your steps to the beginning before you could head in the correct direction. It would be better to plan your moves before you begin, probably by mentally tracing a path from the exit of the maze backwards to the beginning. That is apparently what Julia did as well. She focused her eyes on the exit and then moved back step by step to the start. By the time she first touched the mag-

net, she had apparently planned all her moves. Without delay she pulled the ring through the maze, turning the wrong way at only 5% of all the points where she had to make a choice. She apparently had used some form of visual imagery to plan her moves.

So people and chimpanzees see mental images, right? But wait a minute: Computers can solve the same questions without drawing little pictures inside themselves. Thus it is at least possible to solve the questions without using mental images; maybe we are fooling ourselves when we say that we see mental images. Even if we do have mental images, what are they, anyway? Are they like an actual visual experience? We cannot get very far just by asking people to describe their images. Psychologists have found several ways of measuring the effects of mental images on people's behavior.

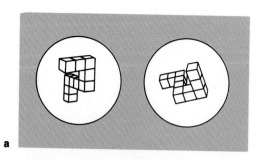

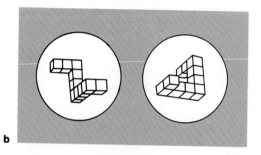

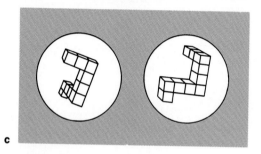

FIGURE 9.6

Cubism? Examples of pairs of drawings used in an experiment by Shepard and Metzler (1971). Do the drawings for each pair represent the same object being rotated, or are they different objects? (See answer B on page 345.)

Mental Imagery:
WHAT'S THE EVIDENCE?

Roger Shepard and Jacqueline Metzler (1971) conducted a classic study of how humans solve visual problems. They reasoned that if people actually visualize mental images, then the time it takes them to rotate a mental image should be similar to the time it takes to rotate a real object.

Hypothesis When people have to rotate a mental image to answer a question, the farther they have to rotate it, the longer it will take them to answer the question.

Method The experimenters showed subjects pairs of two-dimensional drawings of three-dimensional objects, as in Figure 9.6, and asked whether the

drawings in each pair represented the same object rotated in different directions or whether they represented different objects. (Try to answer this question yourself before reading further. Then check answer B, page 345.)

The subjects could answer by pulling one lever to indicate *same* and another lever to indicate *different*. When the correct answer was *same*, a subject might determine that answer by rotating a mental image of the first picture until it matched the second. If so, the delay should depend on how far the image had to be rotated.

The delays before answering *different* were generally longer and less consistent than those for answering *same*—as is generally the case. Subjects could answer *same* as soon as they found a way to rotate the first object to match the second. However, to be sure that the objects were different, they might have to double-check several times and imagine more than one way of rotating the object.

Results Subjects were almost 97% accurate in determining both *same* and *different*. As predicted, their reaction time for responding *same* depended on the angular difference in orientation between the two views. For example, if the first image of a pair had to be rotated 30 degrees to match the second image, the subject took a certain amount of time to pull the *same* lever. If the two images looked the same after the first one had been rotated 60 degrees, the subject took twice as long to pull the lever. In other words, the subjects reacted as if they were actually watching a little model of the object rotate in their head; the more the object needed to be rotated, the longer they took to determine the answer.

Interpretation Viewing a mental image is at least partly like real vision. ■

In a related experiment, subjects were shown pairs of cubes. Each face of a particular cube was labeled with a different letter or number. For each pair, subjects were asked whether it was possible that the two cubes were identical. To answer, they had to imagine the rotation of one of the cubes. The rotation could be completed either by two 90-degree turns, as Figure 9.7a shows, or by one turn through an oblique angle, as Figure 9.7b shows. Those who reported that they could imagine turns through oblique angles answered the questions more accurately even though they answered faster than other subjects did (Just & Carpenter, 1985). An experiment such as this helps us to understand why certain people answer a problem faster or more accurately than others do: They go through different identifiable mental processes.

In another study of mental images, college students looked at a drawing of a face—one of those in Figure 9.8—for five seconds (Kosslyn, Ball, & Reiser, 1978). They were then told to form a mental image of the face in one of three sizes: *overflow* (so large that they could "see" only the mouth), *full size* (as large as possible while still "seeing" the whole face), and *half size* (about half as large as full size). Regardless of the size of the face, subjects were to focus on the mouth. Then the experimenters asked whether the eyes were light or dark. Subjects were told to glance up to see the eyes in the image before answering. Subjects took longer to answer with an overflow image than with a full-size image and longer with a full-size image than with a half-size image. For an image of a given size, subjects who had seen face a or d took longer than those who had seen face b or e, and those subjects in turn took longer than those who had seen face c or f. In short, how long subjects took to answer depended on how far the eyes of the mental image were from the mouth. The results support the interpretation that people consult a mental image to answer the question.

Something to Think About

Some people report that they have auditory images as well as visual images. They "hear" words or songs "in their head." What kind of evidence would we need to test that claim?

Has the evidence I've presented so far convinced you that people really do experience mental images? Most psychologists are convinced, though a few of them say that people might *behave as if* they were visualizing something in their mind without *actually* experiencing a mental image. Here is one final line of evidence: When people say they are experiencing mental images, the parts of their brain that are responsible for vision become more active (Farah, 1988). Subjects have been asked such questions as: "What color is a football?" "Are the hind legs of a kangaroo shorter than its front legs?" In those subjects who say that they are relying on visual images to answer these questions, the blood flow increases to the occipital cortex (the visual area of the cortex). People who have suffered damage to that area cannot answer such questions.

Note an important point about scientific procedure: We almost never base a conclusion on just one experiment. Although the experiment on rotating mental images is a classic, we look for additional evidence that points to the same conclusion.

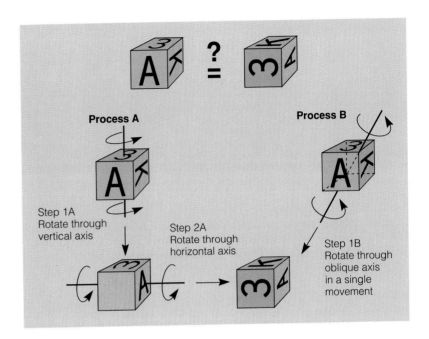

FIGURE 9.7

Two ways to solve the problem of the identity of the two cubes. Process A requires two steps, and process B requires one step. Those who used process B solved the problem more quickly—and more accurately.

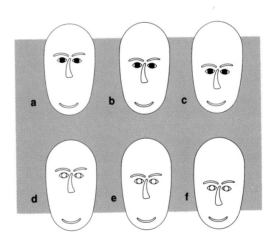

FIGURE 9.8

Subjects looked at one of these faces for five seconds and then formed an overflow, full-size, or half-size mental image of it, focusing on the mouth. When they were asked whether the eyes were light or dark, the delay of their answers depended on the distance from the mouth to the eyes in the mental images. (From Kosslyn, Ball, & Reiser, 1978.)

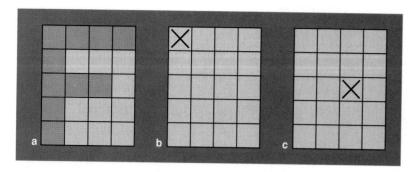

FIGURE 9.9

X marks the spot: Measuring how mental images form. After subjects memorize block letters like the one in a, they are shown a pattern such as b or c and then asked whether the letter *F* would cover the *x*.

The Piecemeal Formation of Mental Images

We have just considered evidence to demonstrate the existence of mental images—a point that may have struck you as obvious from the start. The experimental evidence is nevertheless valuable for two reasons.

First, it reassures us that our intuitions were correct. (Common sense is not always right, after all.) Second, in the process of conducting the experiments we have just described, psychologists developed methods that they can employ to address other questions—questions whose answers are far from obvious. For example, when you form a mental image of, say, your house, does it appear all at once or bit by bit?

Subjects in one experiment first memorized a series of block letters, like the letter shown in Figure 9.9a. Then they were shown a grid with an *x* on one spot and were asked whether or not a given letter—in this case, *F*—would cover the *x*. When the *x* was in the upper left-hand corner of the grid, as in Figure 9.9b, the subjects answered quickly. If they were drawing the letter *F*, that is the position they would fill in first. When the *x* was in some other position farther from the upper left, as in Figure 9.9c, they took longer to answer. Evidently they formed a mental image of the letter gradually, starting in the upper left where they would start to draw it and then proceeding to the rest of the letter (Kosslyn, 1988). That is, the image forms piece by piece, not all at once.

Try this demonstration of the same point: Form a mental image of a dog. Once you have formed it, does it seem complete? If so, answer two questions: First, what breed of dog is it? Second, does it have a collar? Most people have little hesitation in identifying the breed; the breed was part of their initial image. But most people pause before saying whether

they saw a collar. The dog in the initial image neither had a collar nor lacked a collar; that part of the image was simply unformed. When asked about a collar, people have to add another feature to the image.

COGNITIVE MAPS

We use mental images to help us find our way about. You are staying at a hotel in an unfamiliar city. You walk a few blocks to get to a museum; then you turn and walk in another direction to get to a restaurant; after dinner you turn again and walk to a theater. After the performance, how do you get back to the hotel? Do you retrace all your steps? Can you find a shorter route? Or do you give up and hail a cab?

If you can find your way back, you do so by using a **cognitive map**, a mental representation of a spatial arrangement. One way to measure the accuracy of people's cognitive maps is to test how well they can find the route from one place to another. Another way is to ask them to draw a map. As you might expect, people draw a more complete map of the areas they are most familiar with. When students try to draw a map of their college campus, they generally include the central buildings on campus and the buildings they enter most frequently (Saarinen, 1973). The longer students have been on campus, the more detail they include (Cohen & Cohen, 1985).

The errors people make in their cognitive maps follow three regular patterns. First, they tend to remember street angles as being close to 90 degrees, even when they are not (Moar & Bower, 1983). We can easily understand that error. For practical purposes, all we need to remember is "go three blocks and turn left" or "go two blocks and turn right"; we do not burden our memory by recalling "turn 72 degrees to the right."

Second, people tend to overestimate the distance between two cities if there are several other cities between them; they underestimate the distance if there are no other cities between them (Thorndyke, 1981). This error reflects a reasonable guess, because cities are likely to be far apart if they have many other cities between them.

Third, people generally imagine geographical areas as being aligned neatly along a north-to-south axis and an east-to-west axis (Stevens & Coupe, 1978; B. Tversky, 1981). Try these questions, for example: Which city is farthest west—Reno, Nevada; Los Angeles, California; or Denver, Colorado? And which is farther north—Philadelphia, Pennsylvania; or Rome, Italy? Most people reason that, because

FIGURE 9.10

Logical versus actual: Location of Reno, Los Angeles, and Denver. Most people imagine that Los Angeles is the farthest west because California is west of Nevada.

California is west of Nevada, Los Angeles is "obviously" west of Reno. (Figure 9.10 shows the true position of the cities.) Rome is in southern Europe and Philadelphia is in the northern part of the United States; therefore Philadelphia should be north of Rome. In fact, Rome is north of Philadelphia.

You see now the differences between a cognitive map and a real map: Cognitive maps, like other mental images, highlight some details and omit others. They distort the actual relationships among geographical locations in regular and predictable ways. Nevertheless, they are accurate enough for most practical purposes.

CATEGORIZATION

Categorization is another mental process that cognitive psychologists study. According to an alleged listing in an ancient Chinese encyclopedia, animals can be divided into the following categories: those that belong to the emperor, embalmed ones, trained animals, suckling pigs, mermaids, fabulous ones, stray dogs, those that are included in this classification, those that tremble as if they were mad, innumerable ones, those drawn with a very fine camel's hair brush, others, those that have just broken a flower vase, and those that resemble flies from a distance (Rosch, 1978).

We generally rely on more useful groupings than this. For example, we learn to categorize certain objects as "cars." When we recognize a new object as a member of the category "car," we know what to expect of it and how to operate it. If we also recognize the object as a member of a subcategory—say, "1990 Ford"—we may know where to find the controls for the lights, the windshield wipers, and the defrost.

Do you have a good sense of direction, or do you rely on printed maps when you're in an unfamiliar place? A cognitive map, a visual picture in your mind, lacks the detail and accuracy of paper maps but is often adequate for your purposes. You might, for example, find your way in a European city by using a cathedral as your reference point.

The Australian aboriginal language Dyirbal has a word—balan—which refers to the category composed of women, fire, dangerous things, birds, and unusual animals, such as the platypus.

We often take our categories for granted, as if our way of categorizing objects were the only possible way. But people in other cultures sometimes make use of categories that seem strange to us (Lakoff, 1987). The Japanese word *hon* refers to long,

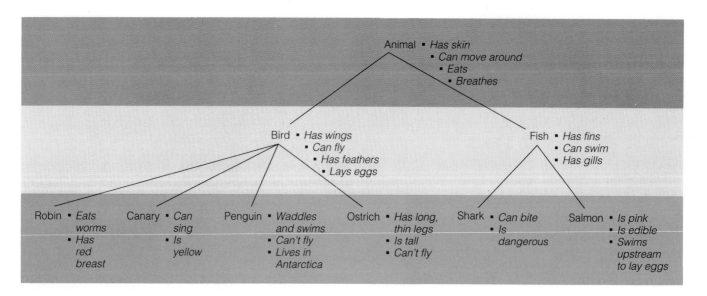

FIGURE 9.11

Categorization of objects by levels. (Modified from Collins & Quillian, 1969, Figure 1.)

When we categorize things, we move from the general to the specific or from the specific to the general. To babies, parents are part of a group of large people. Later, they realize that some people are male, some female, and they see that people come in different shapes and colors. Children eventually learn that each person is unique and has a name, although Aunt Louise and Aunt Sarah look similar and share many traits. Aristotle was the first to organize nature—from rocks to humans—in a classification scheme to better understand common attributes and distinct features. Over the centuries, these schemas became more elaborate.

thin things, including sticks, pencils, trees, hair, and snakes. It also includes items that do not strike Americans as obvious examples of long, thin things: hits in baseball, shots in basketball, telephone calls, television programs, a mental contest between a Zen master and a student, and medical injections. Clearly, people from different cultures categorize objects in different ways.

How do people decide how to categorize objects? That question is part of the more basic question, "How do we think?" Psychologists have developed several views of how we categorize.

Categorization by Levels

According to one view (Collins & Quillian, 1969, 1970), we categorize items at various levels, with several categories at one level combining into a single category at the next higher level, as in Figure 9.11. For example, *salmon* and *shark* are both fish; *fish* and *bird* are both *animals*. Each lower-level category has all the defining features of the higher-level category plus certain distinctive features of its own. For example, *canary* has the distinctive features *can sing* and *is yellow*; it also necessarily has all the features of the higher-level category *bird*, such as *has wings* and *can fly*.

Categorizing objects in this way simplifies our memory task. Once we learn, for example, that a yellow warbler is a kind of bird, we do not have to memorize that it has wings and feathers, lays eggs, and can fly. We can assume all those facts. When necessary, we memorize any exceptions that arise

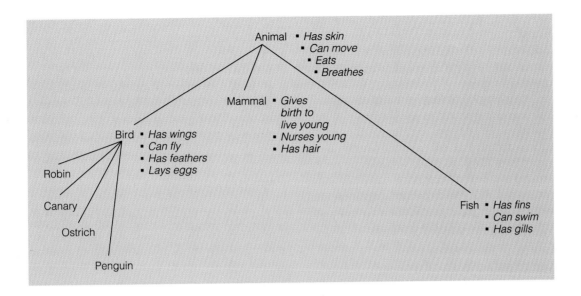

FIGURE 9.12

Categorization of objects by features. In this type of classification, distances between items depend on how many features the two items share. (Based on Collins & Loftus, 1975.)

in the lower categories, such as the fact that ostriches and penguins, unlike most birds, cannot fly.

The evidence for this view of how we organize mental categories comes from measurements of reaction times. Suppose you are asked several true-false questions about canaries. To the statement "A canary is yellow," you respond rapidly, because *yellow* is a distinctive feature of *canary*. To the statement "A canary lays eggs," you respond more slowly. According to the categorization by levels approach, you are slow because laying eggs is not a particularly distinctive feature of canaries. Before you can respond to that statement, you have to reason, "Canaries are birds, and birds lay eggs. So canaries lay eggs." Your reaction time is slower, because it takes time to go from the canary level to the bird level. Finally, to the statement "Canaries have skin," your reaction time is slower yet. *Skin* is not a distinctive feature of either canaries or birds. So you have to go from the canary level to the bird level to the animal level before you find the distinctive feature *skin*.

Most cognitive psychologists regard the approach of categorization by levels as only partly satisfactory. Robins, canaries, and penguins are all birds; therefore, according to this approach, they should all be at the same level. And yet people are quicker to agree that robins and canaries lay eggs than they are to agree that penguins lay eggs. Evidently we do not classify all birds in the same way. Nor do we classify all members of any other category in exactly the same way. Cognitive psychologists have looked for a better way to explain categorization.

Concept Check

2. Which would take you longer to decide: whether Eskimos wear parkas or whether Eskimos wear clothes? Why? (Check your answer on page 345.)

Categorization by Features

Do robins have feathers? Do penguins have feathers? Almost everyone answers both questions correctly, but the reaction time is longer when people are asked about penguins. Why? Perhaps because it also takes longer to decide whether penguins are birds than to decide whether robins are birds (Rips, Shoben, & Smith, 1973; Smith, Shoben, & Rips, 1974). Robins are "typical" birds; they share a great many features with other common, familiar birds. Penguins differ in many ways from other birds. Indeed, you might say, "Technically, penguins are considered birds," but it would be bizarre to say, "Technically, robins are considered birds." Perhaps we define a category, such as *bird*, in terms of certain important features. According to categorization by features, we define the category *bird* in terms of wings, feathers, flight, egg laying, and a certain typical size and shape. We decide whether something fits that category by determining how many of those features it has. Robins have all the defining features of birds; penguins lack flight and stand in an odd, unbirdlike posture.

Figure 9.12 illustrates categorization by features. In this figure, the distances between items depend on how many features the items share in common. For example, the distance from *robin* to *bird* is short, but the distance from *penguin* to *bird* is long. The distance from *canary* to *bird* is a little longer than the distance from *robin* to *bird* because we generally see canaries only in cages, where they cannot fly very far.

Categorization by features is a better explanation than categorization by levels is, but it still has limitations. We often deal with loosely defined categories, such as "interesting novels," "embarrassing experiences," and "tasty meals." Could you list the features that define "interesting novel"? Probably not. To deal with loosely defined categories—and most of the categories people deal with are loosely defined—we need another approach.

Categorization by Prototypes

Five-year-old children can easily recognize what is and what is not a bird, although they might guess wrong about penguins (which are odd birds) and bats (which are mammals that fly like birds). And yet none of them probably could define the term *bird*. They probably think of birds as "robins and sparrows and things like that." That is, their concept of the word is based on the examples they know.

Adults also deal with categories that they cannot rigorously define. We refer to certain foods as fruits or vegetables without being able to define either *fruit* or *vegetable*. We classify certain people as *smart, liberal,* or *athletic* without being able to define those terms precisely.

According to Eleanor Rosch (1978; Rosch & Mervis, 1975; see also Nosofsky, 1986), most categories have no firm boundaries; instead, they are defined by the members that belong to them, especially by the most familiar and most typical members. The most typical members are **prototypes**. According to the categorization-by-prototypes approach, we decide whether an object belongs to a category by determining how well it resembles the prototypical members of the category.

For example, we define the category *vehicle* by giving examples: car, bus, train, airplane, boat. To decide whether some other object is a vehicle, we compare it to these examples. Because a truck has much in common with them, we consider it a typical vehicle. Because a blimp has less in common with them, we consider it an atypical vehicle. Because water skis and elevators have even less in common with our examples, we might consider them as borderline examples of vehicles. The more an object differs from the prototypes, the longer people take to decide whether the object belongs to the category.

The main point of Rosch's prototype approach is that category membership is sometimes a matter of degree. When we are asked whether a penguin is a bird, we can answer *yes* or *no*. When we are asked whether an elevator is a vehicle or whether the man next door is intelligent, we have to answer in terms of degree.

What does this research tell us about how we think? It says that when we use a category term, we are often thinking about a set of prototypical examples, not about a term that can be defined rigorously.

SUMMARY

1. Psychologists perform experiments on cognition because people are not always aware of all their own mental processes or the reasons behind their behaviors. (page 317)

2. Psychologists make inferences about mental processes by measuring reaction times. For example, they find that it takes people one period of time to decide whether a number is a 3, and a longer time to decide whether it is either a 3 or a 7. Such studies indicate that people test possibilities in sequence rather than simultaneously. (page 318)

3. Measurements of reaction times indicate that mental images are similar to vision. When people report that they are using mental images to imagine a moving object, their reaction times and errors are similar to those that would occur if they were seeing an actual moving object. (page 320)

4. Mental images form one piece at a time, not all at once. (page 324)

5. People find their way from place to place partly by consulting a cognitive map of the locations. Cognitive maps resemble the actual spatial layout well enough to be useful, although they also tend to be distorted in several ways. (page 324)

6. We think of objects in terms of categories, such as birds. When we learn that some new object is a member of a certain category, we assume that it possesses the basic features shared by other members of that category. (page 325)

7. Many categories, such as *vehicle*, have no precise definition or boundaries. When we use such a category, we think in terms of prototypes (typical examples) of the category. (page 328)

SUGGESTIONS FOR FURTHER READING

Gardner, H. (1987). *The mind's new science*. New York: Basic Books. An easily read review of the history of cognitive psychology.

Lakoff, G. (1987). *Women, fire, and dangerous things*. Chicago: University of Chicago. A discussion of how we conceptualize categories.

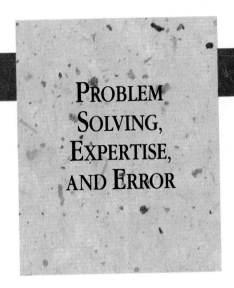

PROBLEM SOLVING, EXPERTISE, AND ERROR

Why do people sometimes reason illogically? How can we improve our ability to solve problems?
What do experts know or do that sets them apart from other people?

On a college physics exam, a student was once asked how to use a barometer to determine the height of a building. He answered that he would tie a long string to the barometer, go to the top of the building, and carefully lower the barometer until it reached the ground. Then he would cut the string and measure its length.

When the professor marked this answer incorrect, the student asked why. "Well," said the professor, "your method would work, but it's not the method I wanted you to use." The student protested that he had no way of reading the professor's mind. The professor then offered, as a compromise, to let the student try again.

"All right," the student said. "Take the barometer to the top of the building, drop it, and measure the time it takes to hit the ground. Then from the formula for the speed of a falling object, using the gravitational constant, calculate the height of the building."

"Hmmm," replied the professor. "That too would work. And it does make use of physical principles. But it still isn't the answer I had in mind. Can you think of another way to use the barometer to determine the height of the building?"

"Another way? Sure," replied the student. "Place the barometer next to the building on a sunny day. Measure the height of the barometer and the length of its shadow. Also measure the length of the building's shadow. Then use the formula

$$\frac{\text{height of barometer}}{\text{length of barometer's shadow}} = \frac{\text{height of building}}{\text{length of building's shadow}}$$

The professor was becoming more and more impressed with the student, but he was still reluctant to give credit for the answer. He asked for yet another way.

The student suggested, "Measure the barometer's height. Then walk up the stairs of the building, marking it off in units of the barometer's height. At the top, take the number of barometer units and multiply by the height of the barometer to get the height of the building."

The professor sighed. "Just give me one more way—any other way—and I'll give you credit, even if it's not the answer I wanted."

"Really?" asked the student with a smile. "Any other way?"

"Yes, any other way."

"All right," said the student. "Go to the man who owns the building and say, 'Hey, buddy, if you tell

Post-it power: Once in a while, a new product proves so useful that you wonder how you ever did without it. From invention to marketing, Post-its were six years in the making at 3M, the Minnesota corporation famous for Scotch tape. Known for innovation, 3M spends twice as much on research and development as does the average U.S. manufacturer. Its researchers are encouraged to spend 15% of their time on personal projects that may be potential money-makers. Some 60% of the ideas don't pan out, yet 3M makes 200 new products a year. By fostering exploration, 3M sometimes hits the jackpot—as with Post-its (Knowlton, 1988).

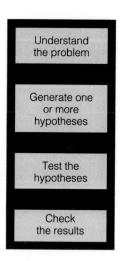

FIGURE 9.13

The four steps in solving problems.

me how tall this building is, I'll give you this neat barometer!' "

We sometimes face a logical or practical problem that we have never tried to solve before. Perhaps no one has ever dealt with it before. In any case, we have to devise a new solution; we cannot rely on a memorized or practiced solution. Sometimes people develop creative, imaginative solutions, like the ones the physics student proposed. Sometimes they offer less imaginative, but still reasonable, solutions. Sometimes they suggest something quite illogical, and sometimes they cannot think of any solution at all. Psychologists study problem-solving behavior partly to understand the thought processes behind it and partly to look for ways to help people reason more effectively.

PROBLEM SOLVING

Generally we go through four phases when we set about solving a problem (Polya, 1957): (1) understanding the problem, (2) generating one or more hypotheses, (3) testing the hypotheses, and (4) checking the result (Figure 9.13). A scientist goes through those four phases in approaching a new, complex phenomenon, and you would probably go through them in trying to assemble a bicycle that came with garbled instructions. To at least a small extent, people can be trained to solve problems more successfully (Bransford & Stein, 1984). We shall go through the four phases of problem solving, with advice on how to handle each phase.

Understanding and Simplifying a Difficult Problem

You are facing a question or a problem, and you have no idea how to begin. You may even think the problem is unsolvable. Then someone shows you how to solve it and you realize, "I could have done that, if I had only thought of trying it that way."

When you do not see how to solve a problem, try starting with a simpler version of it. For example, here is what may appear to be a difficult, even an impossible, problem: A professor hands back students' test papers at random. On the average, how many students will accidentally receive their own paper? (Note that the problem fails to specify how many students are in the class.)

At first the problem sounds impossible, but see what happens if we start with simpler cases: How many students will get their own paper back if there is only one student in the class? One, of course.

What if there are two students? There is a 50% chance that both will get their own paper back and a 50% chance that neither will. On the average, one student will get the correct paper. What if there are three students? Each student has one chance in three of getting his or her own paper. One-third chance times three students means that, on the average, one student will get the correct paper. We begin to see a pattern. Having worked through a few simple examples, we realize that the number of students in the class does not matter; on the average, one student will get his or her own paper back.

Here is another way to approach a seemingly impossible problem: *If you do not see how to answer the question, answer a related question.* For example, try the following problem (Figure 9.14): Train A goes from Baltimore to Washington at 25 miles per hour. Train B travels from Washington to Baltimore at the same speed. Baltimore and Washington are 50 miles apart. A bird leaves Baltimore at the same time as the trains, flying 60 miles per hour. It flies until it reaches train B and then instantly reverses direction and flies back until it reaches train A. Then it flies back to train B, and so forth. By the time the two trains and the bird meet at the center, how far will the bird have traveled?

If you start by calculating how far the bird will travel by the time it meets train B for the first time, then how far it travels to meet train A again, you quickly become discouraged. A better solution is to begin by answering an easier question: How much time will it take for the two trains to meet? That is the same period of time the bird will fly. At 60 miles per hour, how far will the bird have flown during that time? (You can check your answer on page 345, answer C.) Note how the answer to the easy question enabled us to answer the difficult question.

Finally, *if you do not know the answer to a factual question, see whether you know enough to make a decent estimate.* The physicist Enrico Fermi posed questions to his students that they could answer in this manner (von Baeyer, 1988). For example, what is the circumference of the Earth? Even if you do not know the answer, you might know the distance from New York to Los Angeles—about 3,000 miles (4,800 km). The distance from New York to Los Angeles is also a change of three time zones. How many time zones would a traveler cross in going completely around the Earth? Twenty-four. So the distance from New York is $\frac{3}{24}$ (or one eighth) of the distance around the Earth. Eight times the distance from New York to Los Angeles is 8 × 3,000 miles (4,800 km) = 24,000 miles (38,400 km). That is a decent approximation of the actual circumference of the Earth, 24,902.4 miles (40,068 km).

Generating Hypotheses

Suppose that after simplifying a problem as well as we can, we realize that many answers are possible. At that point we need to generate **hypotheses**—preliminary interpretations that we can evaluate or test.

In some cases, we can generate more hypotheses than we can test. Consider the traveling salesperson problem in Figure 9.15. Starting and finishing at the place marked HOME, how could you travel through each of the marked cities while keeping your total travel distance to a minimum? We could set up an algorithm to solve the problem. An **algorithm** is a mechanical, repetitive mathematical procedure for solving a problem such as "Calculate the distance from HOME to a first city, then to a second city, and so on through all cities and back to HOME again. Repeat the same procedure for all possible orders of the cities. Compare the distances of all the possible routes."

That algorithm tests all the possible hypotheses (routes) and is sure to lead us to the best. But even with just 10 cities to visit there are nearly 2 million possible routes (10 factorial divided by 2). As the number of cities increases, the task becomes unmanageable even for large computers. To make the problem manageable, we must narrow the number of hypotheses. We do so by resorting to **heuristics**, strategies for simplifying a problem or for guiding an investigation. For instance, we might decide to test only those routes in which each move takes us to one of the four closest cities or only those routes that do not cross an earlier route.

For other problems, we find that we have too few hypotheses rather than too many. Consider the following: Take any 3-digit number, such as 427, and then repeat it: 427427. Whatever number you choose, the resulting 6-digit number will be evenly divisible by 13. Why?

You might begin by testing several such numbers to see whether they are in fact evenly divisible by 13, but that would not be the same as testing a hypothesis. The difficulty here is generating *any* hypothesis at all. Try for a while. (If you give up, see answer D on page 345.) Sometimes people who cannot generate a hypothesis, or who find themselves generating the same few hypotheses again and again, find it helpful to do something else for a while and then return to the problem afresh.

Here is another example of a task for which it is difficult to generate a hypothesis (Gardner, 1978): Figure 9.16 shows an object that was made by cutting and bending an ordinary piece of cardboard. How was it made? If you think you know, take a piece of paper and try to make it yourself.

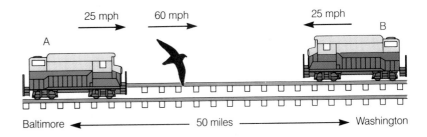

FIGURE 9.14

As the crow flies: A bird flies back and forth between two trains traveling at the speeds indicated. When it meets one train, it reverses direction instantaneously and flies toward the other. How far will the bird have traveled when the two trains meet at the halfway point?

FIGURE 9.15

What is the shortest route from home through each of the other cities and back again? In this problem, we can generate more hypotheses than we can easily test.

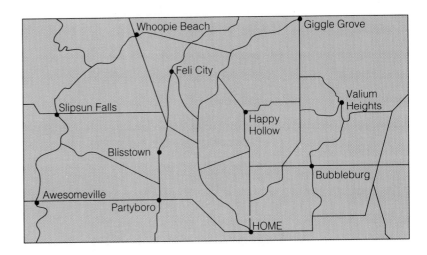

FIGURE 9.16

An object made by cutting and folding an ordinary piece of cardboard. How was it done?

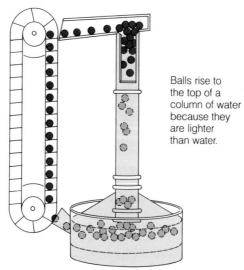

Balls overflow onto conveyor belt and pull it down because they are heavier than air.

Balls rise to the top of a column of water because they are lighter than water.

Balls reenter column of water.

FIGURE 9.17

What is wrong with this perpetual motion machine?

People react to this problem in different ways. Some see the solution almost at once; others take a long time before insight suddenly strikes them; still others never figure it out. Some people have looked at this illustration and told me that it was impossible, that I must have pasted two pieces together or bought a custom-made piece of "trick" cardboard.

Give it a try. When you discover the answer, you will see how your thinking was at first limited by certain habits and assumptions. The correct answer is on page 345, answer E.)

Solving problems of this type differs from solving, say, algebra problems. Most people can look at an algebra problem and reasonably predict whether or not they will be able to solve it. As they work on it, they can estimate how close they are to reaching a solution. On **insight** problems, however, such as the cardboard-folding problem, the answer comes either suddenly and unpredictably ("Aha!") or not at all (Metcalfe & Wiebe, 1987).

Concept Check

3. The government wants to know how much the average citizen pays for groceries each week. So it finds a city with only one grocery store, asks the store manager how much money he or she receives for sales in a given week, and divides that amount by the number of people who live in the city. Is that approach to the problem an example of an algorithm or an example of heuristics? (Check your answer on page 345.)

Testing Hypotheses

If you think you have solved a problem, test your idea to see whether it will work. Many people who think they have a great idea never bother to try it out, even on a small scale. One inventor applied for a patent on the "perpetual motion machine" shown in Figure 9.17. Rubber balls, being lighter than water, rise in a column of water and overflow the top. Being heavier than air, they fall, moving a belt and thereby generating energy. At the bottom, they reenter the water column. Do you see why this system could never work? You would if you tried to build it. (Check your answer on page 345, answer F.)

Checking the Results

The final step in solving a problem is to check the results. You think you have the solution; you think your hypothesis works. Fine, but to make sure, check it again. In scientific research, checking may mean repeating an experiment to see whether the results are replicable. In mathematics, checking may be a matter of repeating the calculations or at least of thinking about whether the answer you calculated is plausible. For example, if you have calculated that the answer to some question is "40 square IQ points per cubic second," you might realize that the answer is inherently meaningless and that something must have gone wrong.

Generalizing Solutions to Similar Problems

After laboriously solving one problem, can people then solve a related problem more easily? Can they at least recognize that the new problem is related to the old problem, so they know where to start?

Sometimes yes, but all too frequently no. For example: You just flipped a coin 10 times and got *heads* all 10 times. You are going to flip it 10 more times. How many heads should you *expect* to get?

Most people know that, according to probability theory, the answer is 5. Getting 10 heads in the first 10 tries was a matter of chance. There is no reason to expect that the next 10 tries will be mostly heads or that they will be mostly tails to "make up for" the string of heads.

Now consider a related question: Your basketball team has won its first 10 games. How many of its next 10 games is it likely to win? Here 5 may be the wrong answer, but 10 is also a wrong answer. A 10-game winning streak is partly a matter of skill but also partly a matter of chance. In its first 10 games, your team probably enjoyed some good breaks and some helpful calls by the referees on close plays. It may not be so lucky with the next 10.

a

b

Figure 9.18

Around the bend? (a) Draw the trajectory of water as it flows out of a coiled garden hose. (b) Draw the trajectory of a bullet as it leaves a coiled gun barrel.

A reasonable prediction is that your team will win 7 or 8 of its next 10 games, even if it plays as well as it did before.

Most people who apply the laws of probability to the first question fail to apply them to the second question. They understand statistical reasoning, but they fail to see its relevance to familiar situations (Nisbett, Fong, Lehman, & Cheng, 1987).

In other situations as well, people who have solved one problem correctly fail to solve a second problem that is basically similar. Figure 9.18a shows a coiled garden hose. When the water spurts out, what path will it take? (Draw it.) Figure 9.18b shows a curved gun barrel. When the bullet comes out, what path will it take? (Draw it.)

Almost everyone draws the water coming out of the garden hose in a straight path. Even after doing so, however, many people draw a bullet coming out of the gun in a curved path, as if the bullet remembered the curved path it had just taken (Kaiser, Jonides, & Alexander, 1986). The physics is the same in both situations: Both the water and the bullet will follow a straight path (except for the effects of gravity).

Sometimes we recognize similar problems and use our solution to an old problem as a guide to solving a new one; sometimes we do not. What accounts for the difference? One reason is it is easier to generalize a solution after we have seen several examples of it; if we have seen only a single

a An arithmetic-progression problem in algebra:

Q: A boy was given an allowance of 50 cents a week beginning on his sixth birthday. On each birthday following this, the weekly allowance was increased 25 cents. What is the weekly allowance beginning on his 15th birthday?

Solution: Let a_n = allowance beginning on nth birthday.
d = difference added on each birthday

$$a_{15} = a_6 + (9)d$$

↖ Number of birthdays from age 6 to 15

$$= \$.50 + (9) \times .25 = \$2.75$$

b A constant-acceleration problem in physics:

Q: An express train, traveling at 30 meters per second at the start of the third second of its travel, uniformly accelerates increasing in speed 5 meters per second each succeeding second. What is its final speed at the end of the 9th second?

Solution: Let s_n = speed at beginning of nth second
d = difference added each second

$$s_{10} = s_3 + (7)d$$

Speed at beginning of 10th second (end of 9th)
↘ Number of seconds from the start of 3rd second to end of the 9th

$$= 30 + (7) \times 5 = 65 \text{ mph}$$

Figure 9.19

Recognizing old wine in new bottles: An arithmetic-progression problem in algebra (a) and a constant-acceleration problem in physics (b). Students who had learned to solve the algebra problem recognized the physics problem as similar and solved it successfully. Most students who had learned to solve the physics problem, however, failed to recognize the algebra problem as similar and failed to solve it. (From Bassok and Holyoak, 1989.)

example, we may think of the solution in only that one context (Gick & Holyoak, 1983). For example, one group of high school students had learned to solve arithmetic-progression problems in algebra, practicing on a variety of problems. When they were given a fundamentally similar problem in physics, they recognized the similarity and solved it (Figure 9.19). A different group of students had been taught to solve the physics problem; when they were given the related problem in algebra, most of them failed to recognize the similarity (Bassok & Holyoak, 1989). Apparently the physics students associated the solution entirely with physics, and they failed to see it as a general principle that could be applied more widely.

Let's try a series of problems that are fundamentally similar and see whether after solving one or more of them you can transfer the solution to other problems.

First: Last summer Lisa traveled from Toronto to Miami. David traveled from New York to Los Angeles (see Figure 9.20). Both took a route that was approximately, but not exactly, straight. Lisa says, "There must be some point on the map that we both passed through last summer." She does not know *where* that point was, and Lisa and David

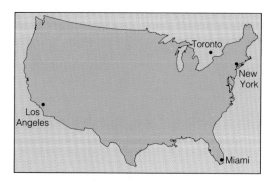

FIGURE 9.20

Going my way? Lisa traveled from Toronto to Miami. David traveled from New York to Los Angeles. Both must have traveled through at least one point in common on the map—though not necessarily at the same time. How do we know that?

FIGURE 19.21

Down south and down under: Lisa traveled from Anchorage to Miami; David traveled from Madagascar to New Zealand. Lisa must have passed through at least one point that was exactly on the opposite side of the world from a point that David passed through (not necessarily at the same time). How do we know that?

need not have passed through it at the same time. Still, there must be some point that they both passed through. How does Lisa know that? (Be sure to ponder this before reading on. If you get discouraged, check answer G, page 345, which provides a good hint but not the answer.)

Second problem: This summer Lisa traveled from Anchorage, Alaska, to Miami. David traveled across the South Pacific from Madagascar to New Zealand (see Figure 9.21). Both followed paths that

were only approximately straight. David says, "You must have passed through some point on the globe that is *exactly* opposite to some point I passed through." Again, there is no way to know which points those were. How does David know he is right? (If you need a hint, check answer H, page 345.)

Third problem: Joan says, "I have been at two points on the Earth's surface that are *exactly* opposite each other. I know I am right about that, even though I do not know which points they were." How does she know that? (No additional hints are given. If you give up, check answer I, page 345.)

Almost no one who *begins* with the third problem gets the right answer. But after working through the first two problems, you may have succeeded in transferring your solution to the third problem.

Creativity and Problem Solving

Solving a problem is always to some extent a creative activity. The problem solver must come up with a solution which is, at least for that person, new and unfamiliar. A higher degree of creativity is represented when someone finds a solution or makes a product that no one has ever achieved before. Psychologists define **creativity** as the development of novel, socially valued products (Mumford & Gustafson, 1988). Note that the product must be "socially valued." I once watched the premiere performance of a new ballet that I could describe only as "odd." At the end, I joined a few others in the audience in polite applause, but no one seemed to enjoy the performance. Even though the ballet was novel, most people would not consider it creative.

Some people consistently produce more creative ideas and products than others, although they may be more creative in one situation than in another (Barron & Harrington, 1981). That is, someone who thinks of creative solutions to mathematical or engineering problems may show little creativity as a poet or a painter.

Still, psychologists have tried to identify whatever it is that all forms of creativity have in common. The Torrance Tests of Creative Thinking use items similar to the one shown in Figure 9.22 to measure creativity. Scores on these tests provide a reasonably good prediction of long-term creative performance. Children who score high are more likely than others to make creative achievements as adults, including inventions, publications, artistic and musical compositions, and clothing designs (Torrance, 1980, 1981, 1982).

Although psychologists can measure creativity, they have made little progress in explaining what

FIGURE 9.22

A "what-is-it?" picture similar to those in one part of the Torrance Tests of Creative Thinking.

causes it or why some people are more creative than others. The causes of "major" creative contributions may differ from those of "minor" contributions. Major contributions are those that reorganize a body of information; minor contributions are those that apply known methods to new examples. For example, Pavlov's theory of classical conditioning is a major contribution, whereas a new study of the classical conditioning of fears is a minor contribution. In fields ranging from science to the arts, young adults make a disproportionate number of major contributions, while middle-age adults are responsible for the greatest share of minor (though still important) contributions (Mumford & Gustafson, 1988; Simonton, 1988).

HUMAN EXPERTISE AND ARTIFICIAL INTELLIGENCE

Experts in a given field quickly solve problems that baffle other people. After learning to solve a new kind of problem, they quickly recognize other problems of the same type. They seem to understand their field better than other people do.

But what do we mean when we say "understand"? How could we determine whether someone understands, say, algebra? We would need an operational definition of *understand*. Suppose we adopt this one: Understanding is measured by how accurately someone can solve problems. That is, anyone who can solve algebra problems accurately must understand algebra.

Let's try an algebra problem: A board was sawed into two pieces. One piece was ¾ as long as the whole board. It exceeded the length of the second

board by 2 meters. What was the length of the whole board? (Pause to calculate the answer.)

If your algebra is not too rusty, you quickly calculated that the answer is 4 meters. If you now enter the appropriate information into a computer, it too will report an answer of 4 meters. So, according to our definition of *understand*, the computer "understands."

But is the computer's understanding the same as yours? Let's try another problem similar to the first: A board was sawed into two pieces. One piece was ⅔ as long as the whole board. The second piece exceeded it in length by 2 meters. What was the length of the whole board? (Pause to calculate your answer.)

Many people answer 6 meters (Larkin, McDermott, Simon, & Simon, 1980). A computer invariably comes up with the correct answer—which is *minus* 6 meters. If you said 6 meters, does your answer mean that the computer understands better than you do? The computer seems to understand algebra, but you understand something the computer does not: the real world. Your semantic memory tells you that boards cannot have negative lengths and that (contrary to what the problem said) the piece that constitutes ⅔ of the whole must be the longer of the two.

How could a computer convince you that it understands problems the way you do? Certainly it would help if the computer replied to the second problem, "Do you really mean that the ⅔ piece is shorter than the other piece? A real board must have a positive length, and therefore the ⅔ piece must be longer than the other piece."

Suppose the computer does say something along those lines. Would you then concede that the computer understands?

Human Expertise

Before we can even try to answer questions about computer intelligence and understanding, we have to find out something about human intelligence. One task of cognitive psychologists is to determine what it means to be an expert on a subject. Once we know exactly what an expert does, we may be able to design a computer that can mimic that performance—and perhaps even improve upon it.

Expert Pattern Recognition

One distinction between a person who is an expert and one who is not is that an expert can look at a pattern and identify its important features almost at once. In a typical experiment (De Groot, 1966), people were shown pieces on a chessboard, as in

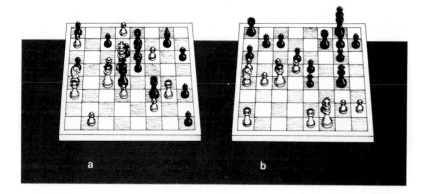

FIGURE 9.23

Pieces arranged on a chessboard in a way that might actually occur in a game (a) and in a random manner (b). Master chess players can memorize the realistic pattern much better than average players can, but they are no better than average at memorizing the random pattern.

For children learning to read, parents are expert readers, thanks to years of experience. Perhaps kids like to hear stories repeated so they can pretend they can read, too.

Figure 9.23, for 5 seconds. Then they were asked to recall the position of all the pieces. When the pieces were arranged as they might occur in an actual game, expert players could recall the position of 91% of them, while novices could recall only 41%. When the pieces were arranged randomly, however, the expert players did no better than the nonexperts. Although expert chess players do not have a superior memory in general, they recognize familiar chessboard patterns far better than other people do.

Similarly, expert radiologists can recognize X-ray patterns, especially abnormal ones, about as well as they can recognize faces (Myles-Worsley, Johnston, & Simons, 1988). They have learned to attend to the relevant features and to ignore the rest.

Almost all well-educated people achieve that level of expertise in at least one domain: reading. You may not think of yourself as an expert reader, because we usually reserve the word *expert* for the rare few who stand out from all the rest. Yet the difference between your ability to read and that of a child who is just starting to read is enormous and comparable to the difference between an expert chess player and someone who is just learning how to play. You or I can look at a printed page and tell at a glance whether the words are in English. In a few seconds we can identify the topic and say something about the writing style.

We also show our expertise when we read a single word. We may have to sound out an unfamiliar word, but we recognize a familiar word as a whole, much as an expert chess player or X-ray specialist recognizes a familiar pattern.

In one experiment, the experimenter flashed a single letter on a screen for less than a quarter of a second and then flashed an interfering pattern on the screen and asked, "What was the letter, C or J?" Then the experimenter flashed a whole word on the screen for the same length of time and asked, "What was the first letter of the word, C or J?" (see Figure 9.24). Which question do you think the subjects answered more correctly? Most of them identified the letter more accurately when it was part of a whole word than when it was presented by itself (Reicher, 1969; Wheeler, 1970). This is known as the **word-superiority effect**.

In a follow-up experiment, James Johnston and James McClelland (1974) briefly flashed words on the screen and asked students to identify one letter (whose position was marked) in each word (see Figure 9.25). On some trials they told the students to focus on the center of the area where the word would appear and to try to see the whole word. On other trials they showed the students exactly where the critical letter would appear on the screen and told them to focus on that spot and ignore the rest of the screen. Most students did better at identifying the critical letter when they were told to look at the whole word than when they focused on just the letter itself!

The context of other letters aids recognition only if the combination is a word or something close to a word. For example, it is easier to recognize the difference between COIN and JOIN than the difference between C and J. But it is easier to recognize the difference between C and J than the difference between XQCF and XQJF (Rumelhart & McClelland, 1982).

You may have experienced the word-superiority effect yourself. A common game on long car trips is to try to find every letter of the alphabet on the billboards along the way. Many people find it easier to spot a particular letter by reading whole words than by checking each word letter by letter.

What accounts for the word-superiority effect? It may be that the recognition of letters interacts with the recognition of words (McClelland & Rumelhart, 1981). Perhaps certain systems in the brain tentatively identify the letters of a word all at once: "I think this is a C, I think this is an O, I think this is an I, I think this is an N . . . ." And some other system may say, "Oh, I guess that's the word COIN." This higher-level decision then feeds back to the letter-identifying systems and confirms their tentative decisions because they make sense in the context. In short, once people become expert readers, they can immediately recognize many patterns and deal with them as wholes.

Experienced readers identify familiar words almost without effort. It is difficult for us to *avoid* reading them as words, even if we try. For example, read the following instructions and then turn to Figure 9.26 on page 338 and follow them:

Notice the blocks of color at the top of the figure. Reading from left to right, give the name of each color as fast as you can. Then, in the center of the figure notice the nonsense syllables printed in different colors. Don't try to pronounce them; just say the color of each one as fast as possible. Then turn to the real words at the bottom. Don't read them; just say the color of each one as fast as possible. Now turn to page 338 and follow the instructions just given.

If you are like most people, you found it very difficult not to read the words at the bottom of the figure. After all the practice you have had reading English, you can hardly bring yourself to look at the word RED, written in yellow letters, and say "yellow." (This is known as the **Stroop effect**, after the psychologist who discovered it.) It is very dif-

Did you see C or J?

Was the first letter C or J?

FIGURE 9.24

Do you C a J? (a, b) A student watches either a word or a single letter flashed on a screen. (c, d) An interfering pattern is then flashed on the screen and the student is asked, "Which was presented, C or J?" More students were able to identify the letter correctly when it was part of a word.

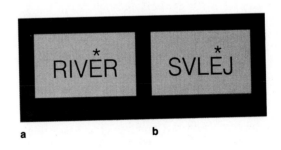

a   b

FIGURE 9.25

Students were better at identifying an indicated letter when they focused on an entire word (a) than when they were asked to remember a single letter in a designated spot among random letters (b). We readily recognize familiar words even when they're misspelled.

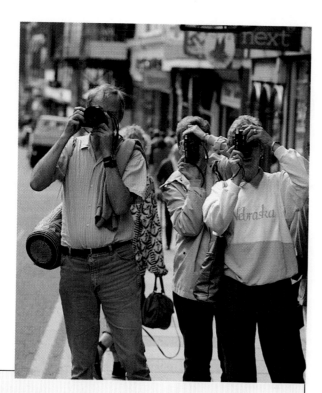

ZYK TUV MRK VLB YIU   GAK NYL WVB

ACJ BDC DSR   CAJ KFI NOZ RFL

XNE PZQ   RBY SOV ALA GNT URF PNR

RED YELLOW   BLUE GREEN RED YELLOW

     RED RED YELLOW BLUE YELLOW   GREEN BLUE

YELLOW   RED GREEN   GREEN YELLOW RED BLUE

FIGURE 9.26

Seeing red: The Stroop effect. Read (left to right) the color of the ink in each part. Try to ignore the words themselves.

Anyone who can press a button can take a picture. Some snap-happy tourists assume that if they take enough pictures or use an expensive camera, then at least some are bound to be good. Shooting the same subject—say a cable car in San Francisco—a professional photographer would likely produce a superior photo because of learning from experience. Having shot far more rolls of film than amateurs have, the professional considers composition and knows how to use the capabilities of various cameras, films, and filters to achieve the desired effect.

ficult to suppress your habit of reading words even when you know you are not supposed to read them. (One way to suppress the habit, reported by bilingual students, is to name the colors in a language other than English. Another way is to blur your vision intentionally so that you cannot make out the letters.)

Expert Problem Solving   Some people manage to solve unfamiliar problems, while other people, who possess all the information they need, fail to do so. For example, try this problem: Given a triangle, as shown in Figure 9.27, find the line parallel to the base that will divide the area of the triangle in half.

Alan Schoenfeld (1985) observed the steps people went through as they tried to solve this problem. One pair of college students who had just completed a calculus course began by guessing that the line should be drawn halfway between the base and the vertex of the triangle. After carefully drawing that line, they realized it was wrong. Then they drew a line from the vertex to the midpoint of the base, forgetting that the line had to be parallel to the base. One of them suggested that they go back to the problem and "underline the important parts." When the allotted 30 minutes expired, they were no closer to a solution than when they began.

By contrast, one professional mathematician noticed that any line drawn parallel to the base will create a small triangle Xyz *similar* to the large triangle XYZ, as shown in Figure 9.28. Because the angles of the two triangles are the same, the height-to-base ratio of the small triangle (h/b) must be the

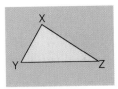

FIGURE 9.27

A question to test mathematical problem-solving skills: What line drawn parallel to the base of the triangle will divide the area in half?

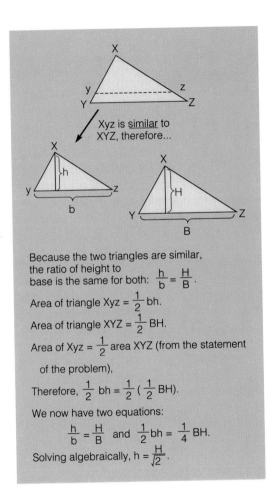

Xyz is _similar_ to XYZ, therefore...

Because the two triangles are similar, the ratio of height to base is the same for both: $\frac{h}{b} = \frac{H}{B}$.

Area of triangle Xyz = $\frac{1}{2}$ bh.

Area of triangle XYZ = $\frac{1}{2}$ BH.

Area of Xyz = $\frac{1}{2}$ area XYZ (from the statement of the problem),

Therefore, $\frac{1}{2}$ bh = $\frac{1}{2}$ ($\frac{1}{2}$ BH).

We now have two equations:

$\frac{h}{b} = \frac{H}{B}$ and $\frac{1}{2}$ bh = $\frac{1}{4}$ BH.

Solving algebraically, h = $\frac{H}{\sqrt{2}}$.

FIGURE 9.28

An expert solution for how to divide the area of a triangle in half by a line drawn parallel to the base. The impossible may seem easy once you see the answer.

same as the height-to-base ratio of the large triangle (H/B). Because the problem specified that the area of the small triangle is half the area of the large triangle, he concluded that the ratio of h to H must be the ratio of 1 to the square root of 2 (see Figure 9.28).

The two students knew how to do everything the professional mathematician did. What then

accounts for the difference in performance? The expert almost immediately picked out the relevant information and plotted a direct route to the solution. The nonexperts wasted time on wild-goose chases without realizing that what they were doing was irrelevant to the task. Evidently expertise is a matter not just of having the right tools but also of knowing which tools to use and when. (Exactly _how_ an expert recognizes the correct tool is a matter for future research.)

Artificial Intelligence

One way to find out what constitutes understanding or expertise is to equip a computer with certain skills and observe its performance. From the mistakes it makes we can discover what was missing and what we need to add to improve its understanding.

One computer, described by Roger Schank (1984, p. 83), was programmed to write children's stories. Here is one of its first short stories:

One day Joe Bear was hungry. He asked his friend Irving Bird where some honey was. Irving told him there was a beehive in the oak tree. Joe threatened to hit Irving if he didn't tell him where some honey was.

The computer was not trying to be funny; it simply did not know that honey could be found in a beehive. So the programmers added that information. The computer's second story came out as follows:

One day Joe Bear was hungry. He asked his friend Irving Bird where some honey was. Irving told him there was a beehive in the oak tree. Joe walked to the oak tree. He ate the beehive.

These two little stories demonstrate a fundamental point: _Intelligence, whether natural or artificial, requires a vast supply of factual information._

Another computer took a stab at more grown-up fiction: A woman gets on a bus. She sits next to a man who tells her that he is a waiter. She says, "Bring me a liverwurst and swiss cheese sandwich on rye, heavy on the mayonnaise, hold the mustard."

What went wrong? The computer "knew" that a person can ask a waiter to bring food, but it didn't know that one can do so only in a restaurant. To overcome this problem, a programmer has to equip the computer with **scripts**—outlines of what people do in certain settings. For example, when a woman goes into a restaurant, she waits to be seated, reads the menu, orders food, waits, receives the food and eats it, takes the check, leaves a tip, pays the check, and departs. At a fast-food outlet, the script is different. A ride on a bus has still another script. And so on. In the process of programming the computer, we discover, if we had not discovered it before, that learning scripts is as essential to human understanding as it is to programming a computer.

Some computers have been programmed to perform more practical functions—medical diagnosis, for example. A patient complains to a physician about being tired, gaining weight, and feeling cold. Even well-trained physicians sometimes commit themselves to a hypothesis prematurely (for example, "chronic fatigue") without considering other possibilities. A computer can help. The physician enters the patient's ailments and medical history into a computer. The computer consults its memory bank for a few seconds and then reports a variety of possibilities, including depression and hypothyroidism in addition to chronic fatigue. It might also note that the patient has previously been medicated for some other complaint and that the prescribed pills sometimes produce fatigue and weight gain as side effects. Finally, the computer might recommend tests to determine which of the diagnoses is correct.

Computers are particularly helpful in suggesting uncommon diagnoses that a physician might otherwise overlook. To do so, of course, they must be fed an enormous amount of information, including data and diagnostic strategies (Duda & Shortliffe, 1983). Their diagnosis is only as good as this information.

Something to Think About

The *Turing Test*, suggested by computer pioneer Alan Turing, proposes the following operational definition of artificial intelligence: A person poses questions to a human source and to a computer, both in another room. The human and the computer send back typewritten replies, which are identified only as coming from "source A" or "source B." The questioner can ask any number of questions before guessing whether the computer is source A or source B. If the questioner cannot determine which replies are coming from the computer, then the computer is credited with having passed a significant test of understanding.

Suppose a computer did pass the Turing Test. Would we then say that the computer "understands," just as a human does? Or would we say that it is merely *mimicking* human understanding? Is there any way to be sure?

REASONS BEHIND ILLOGICAL REASONING

Although we humans pride ourselves on our intelligence and on our ability to solve problems, we sometimes err on fairly simple problems. After someone points out the correct answer, we are surprised at our own mistake. Sometimes we err because we relied on inappropriate heuristics. Recall that heuristics are methods for simplifying a problem and facilitating an investigation. Ordinarily, relying on heuristics enables us to find a reasonable, if not perfect, answer. Occasionally, however, heuristics can lead us astray. Let's now consider several reasons why people sometimes arrive at illogical conclusions.

Premature Commitment to a Hypothesis

Sometimes we make mistakes because we commit ourselves prematurely to a particular hypothesis and fail to consider other possibilities. Suppose a psychologist asks subjects to look at a photo way out of focus, as in Figure 9.29a, and asks them what they think the photo shows. Then the psychologist shows them a series of photos, each one in slightly sharper focus, until they correctly identify what is shown in the photos. Some people try to simplify the task by forming a hypothesis such as, "Maybe it's a picture of the Statue of Liberty." That is a heuristic of sorts; it guides further exploration of the photos. However, if the initial hypothesis is wrong, it can mislead.

Peter Wason (1960) asked students to discover a certain rule he had in mind for generating sequences of numbers. One example of the numbers the rule might generate, he explained, was "2, 4, 6." He told the students that they could ask about other sequences, and he would tell them whether or not those sequences fit the rule. As soon as they thought they had enough evidence, they could guess what the rule was.

Most students started by asking, "8, 10, 12?" When told "yes," they proceeded with, "14, 16, 18?" Each time, they were told, yes, that sequence fits the rule. Soon most of them guessed, "The rule is three consecutive even numbers."

"No," came the reply. "That is not the rule."

Many students persisted, trying "20, 22, 24?" "26, 28, 30?" "250, 252, 254?" And so forth. Eventually they would say, "Three even numbers in which the second is two more than the first and the third is two more than the second." Again, they were told that the guess was wrong. "But how can it be wrong?" they complained. "It always works!"

The rule Wason had in mind was, "Any three

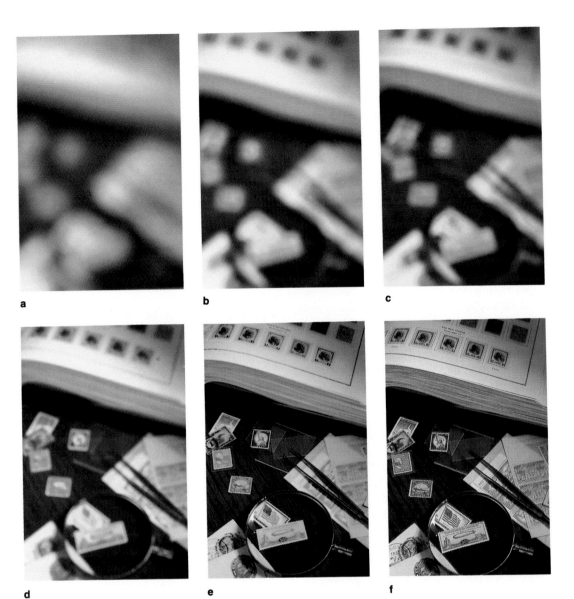

a   **b**   **c**

d   **e**   **f**

FIGURE 9.29

Guesstimating: People who form a hypothesis based on the first photo look at succeeding photos trying to find evidence that they are right. Because their first guess is generally wrong, they do less well than do people who look at the later photos before making any preliminary guesses.

positive numbers of increasing magnitude." For instance, 1, 2, 3 would be acceptable; so would 4, 19, 22, or 3, 76, 9 million. Where the students went wrong was in testing only the cases that their hypothesis said would fit the rule. One must also examine the cases that the hypothesis says will *not* fit the rule (Klayman & Ha, 1987).

Many scientists make the same mistake by pursuing a single hypothesis to the exclusion of all others. They repeat a single type of experiment that always supports that hypothesis, without considering other possible explanations of the results (Frishhoff & Beyth-Marom, 1983).

Base-Rate Information and the Representativeness Heuristic

We often have to make decisions on the basis of probabilities and incomplete information. Is that blip on the radar screen an enemy missile, a passenger plane, or a large bird? Is this applicant the kind of person our company should hire? Is this patient suffering from cancer or from something else?

When we have to decide whether something belongs in category A or category B, we should consider three questions: (1) How closely does it resemble the items in category A? (2) How closely does it resemble the items in category B? (3) Which is more common, category A or category B? The answer to the third question is known as **base-rate information**—that is, data about the frequency or probability of a given item, how rare or how common it is.

People frequently overlook the third question and base their judgments solely on the first two: how representative the item is of category A and of category B. This is known as the **representative-**

ness heuristic, which is the tendency to assume that if an item is similar to members of a particular category, it is probably a member of that category itself. That is a reasonable assumption if the category itself is common, but not if it is rare.

For example, consider the following question (modified from Kahneman & Tversky, 1973):

Psychologists have interviewed 30 engineers and 70 lawyers. One of them is Jack, a 45-year-old married man with four children. He is generally conservative, careful, and ambitious. He shows no interest in political and social issues and spends most of his free time on home carpentry, sailing, and mathematical puzzles. What is the probability that Jack is one of the 30 engineers in the sample of 100?

Most people think the description is more representative of engineers than of lawyers. Based on representativeness, they estimate that Jack is probably an engineer. But what about the fact that the sample includes more than twice as many lawyers as engineers? That base-rate information should influence their estimates. In fact, however, most people pay little attention to the base-rate information. They make about the same estimates of how likely Jack is to be an engineer, regardless of whether the sample includes 30% engineers or 70% engineers (Kahneman & Tversky, 1973). However, people do use the base-rate information if they have paid attention to it. If people actually count out cards saying "engineer" or "lawyer," they use that information in estimating how likely it is that Jack is an engineer (Gigerenzer, Hell, & Blank, 1988).

Here is another example of the importance of base-rate information: Suppose (contrary to fact) that someone has invented a miraculous, painless, and harmless way of testing brain waves that will reveal whether or not a person is a criminal. When all the people who have committed felonies are tested, 99% of them show a positive result. When innocent people are tested, 1% of them show a positive result. Would it be reasonable to administer the test to everyone in the country and then throw into prison all those who show a positive result?

You may object that the test is not perfect because it makes an error once out of every hundred times. True, but that by itself is not a strong objection. (Do you believe that our current legal system makes an error *less* than 1% of the time?) Do you have any other objection?

The problem is that this test would throw more innocent people than guilty people into prison (Hogarth, 1981; Kahneman & Tversky, 1973). Suppose a city has 150,000 law-abiding citizens and 1,000 criminals. The test would convict 990 of the criminals (99% of 1,000 individuals) *plus* 1,500 of the noncriminals (1% of 150,000). So most of the people who landed in jail would be innocent! We make this sort of error when we overlook base-rate information, such as the fact that innocent people are more numerous than criminals or that hawks are more numerous than enemy missiles.

Concept Check

4. *Suppose an improved lie-detector test can determine with 90% accuracy whether people are telling the truth. An employer proposes to administer the test to all employees, asking them whether they have ever stolen from the company and firing everyone who fails the test. Is that policy reasonable? Assume that the company has 1,000 employees, of whom only 20 have ever stolen anything. (Check your answer on page 345.)*

The Availability Heuristic

When asked how common something is, or how often something happens, we generally start by trying to think of examples. Try this question: In the English language, are there more words that start with *k* or words that have *k* as the third letter? If you are like most people, you guessed that there are more words that start with *k*. How did you decide that? You tried to think of words that start with *k*: "king, kitchen, kangaroo, key, knowledge. . . ." Then you tried to think of words that have *k* as the third letter: "ask, ink, elk, . . . uh. . . ." You were relying on the **availability heuristic**, the strategy of assuming that how many memories of an event are available indicates how common the event actually is. Because it was easier to think of words that start with *k* than words with *k* as the third letter, you assumed that there really are more words that start with *k*. In fact, however, words with *k* as the third letter are considerably more common.

The availability heuristic leads to illusory correlations, as we saw in Chapter 2. Someone asks, "Do people act strange on nights of a full moon?" If you have always expected people to act strange on such nights, you may be able to remember more examples when they did act strange than examples when they did not.

The availability heuristic can also lead to stereotypes. Someone tells you that "Dallonians" are tall, lazy, and prone to crime. Now that you are alert to the possibility of tall, lazy, criminal Dallonians, you notice examples that fit the stereotype. Later you find it easier to remember examples that fit the stereotype than examples that do not fit. You particularly remember the most extreme examples—the tallest, laziest, and most criminal Dallonians you have met. Perhaps you begin to believe that many, even most, Dallonians are similar to the ones you remember most clearly (R. A. Jones et al., 1977; Rothbart, Fulero, Jensen, Howard, & Birrell, 1978).

You can guard against overuse of the availability heuristic. When you try to estimate whether one type of event is more common than another, look for systematic data. Don't just trust your memory of how often various events occur.

The Framing of Questions

If we were truly logical beings, we would give the same answer to a question no matter how it was reworded. In fact, we do not. Most people give one answer to a question that is phrased in terms of gain and give a different answer to the same question when it is phrased in terms of loss.

For example: You have just been appointed head of the Public Health Service and you have to make a decision: A new contagious disease has been detected, and you have to choose between two plans for combating it. If you do nothing, 600 people will die. If you adopt Plan A, you will save the lives of 200 people. If you adopt Plan B, there is a 33% chance that you will save all 600 and a 67% chance that you will save no one. (Choose one of the plans before reading further.)

Now another contagious disease breaks out; you must again choose between two plans. If you adopt Plan C, 400 people will die. If you adopt Plan D, there is a 33% chance that no one will die and a 67% chance that 600 will die. (Choose one now, then compare your choices with the results in Figure 9.30.)

Consider another example, this one dealing with money instead of lives. Which would you rather have?

    W. A gain of $240

or X. A 25% chance to win $1,000

Now you have to make another decision. You have just received an outright gift of $1,000, but you must choose between two unpleasant alternatives:

    Y. A loss of $750

or Z. A 75% chance of losing the whole
        $1,000 (a 25% chance of losing nothing)

Tversky and Kahneman found that 84% of all people chose W over X (avoiding risk), whereas 87% chose Z over Y (taking a risk). Note that W is actually $10 less than choice Y and that X is the same as Z. Again, people generally avoid taking a

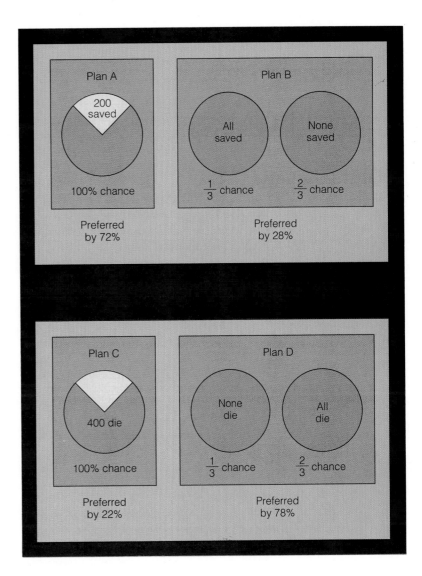

FIGURE 9.30

Built-in bias? When Amos Tversky and Daniel Kahneman (1981) offered these choices to more than 150 people, 72% chose A over B and 78% chose D over C. However, Plan A is exactly the same as Plan C (200 live, 400 die), and Plan B is exactly the same as Plan D. Why then did so many people choose both A and D? The reason, according to Tversky and Kahneman, is that most people avoid taking a risk when a question is phrased in terms of gain, but they are willing to take a risk when a question is phrased in terms of loss.

risk when considering gains but accept the risk when considering losses. Put another way, people try to avoid losses. Apparently the pain associated with a loss is much greater than the pleasure associated with a gain of the same size.

This tendency has several consequences. For example, suppose a service station offers gas at a price of $1 per gallon but charges 5 cents extra for using a credit card. Many people will object to the extra charge. But if the service station sets the price at $1.05 per gallon, with a 5-cent discount for paying cash, most customers will still use their credit cards and pay the $1.05 without protest.

Concept Check

5a. *Someone says, "More than 90% of all college students like to watch late-late night television, while only 20% of older adults do. Therefore most watchers of late-late night television are college students." What error in thinking has this person made?*

b. *Someone tells me that if I say "abracadabra" every morning I will stay healthy. I say it daily, and, sure enough, I stay healthy. I conclude that saying this magic word really does ensure health. What error of thinking have I made?*
(Check your answers on page 345.)

SUMMARY

1. People go through four steps in solving a problem: understanding and simplifying the problem, generating hypotheses, testing hypotheses, and checking the results. (page 330)

2. People who have solved a problem of a particular type may or may not recognize that another problem is similar. They are more likely to do so if they have seen a variety of examples of that type of problem. (page 332)

3. Experts can recognize complex but familiar patterns at a glance. Most of us achieve that level of expertise in reading. (page 335)

4. Experts solve problems better than nonexperts do because experts recognize quickly which tools or approaches to use. (page 338)

5. For a computer to produce artificial intelligence, it must be programmed with vast stores of factual knowledge. (page 339)

6. People sometimes make mistakes in their reasoning because they commit themselves to a hypothesis prematurely or because they ignore base-rate information. (page 340)

7. People often assume that the events they remember easily are typical of other events as well. As a result, they overestimate the frequency of some events and underestimate the frequency of others. (page 341)

8. People tend to take more risks to avoid a loss than to win a gain. Consequently, they make different choices depending on how a question is phrased. (page 343)

SUGGESTIONS FOR FURTHER READING

Bransford, J. B., & Stein, B. S. (1984). *The ideal problem solver.* New York: Freeman. Advice on how to approach and solve both "mind-bender" problems and practical problems.

Schank, R. C. (1984). *The cognitive computer.* Reading, MA: Addison-Wesley. A discussion of artificial intelligence.

TERMS TO REMEMBER

algorithm a mechanical, repetitive mathematical procedure for solving a problem

availability heuristic the strategy of assuming that the number of available memories of an event indicates how common the event actually is

base-rate information information about the frequency or probability of a given item

cognition the processes that enable us to imagine, to gain knowledge, to reason about knowledge, and to judge its meaning

cognitive map a mental representation of a spatial arrangement

creativity the development of novel, socially valued products

heuristics strategies for simplifying a problem or for guiding an investigation

hypothesis a preliminary interpretation that has not yet been sufficiently tested

insight thinking of an answer suddenly and unpredictably

prototype a highly typical member of a category

reaction time the delay between a stimulus and the subject's response to it

representativeness heuristic the tendency to assume that if an item is similar to members of a particular category, it is probably a member of that category itself

script an outline of what people do in a certain setting

Stroop effect the difficulty of naming the colors in which words are written instead of reading the words themselves

word-superiority effect greater ease of identifying a letter when it is part of a whole word than when it is presented by itself

ANSWERS TO CONCEPT CHECKS

1. Making the letters blurry slowed the perception of the number. If it had slowed the process of comparing a number to the numbers in memory, the slope of the line would have become steeper. (page 320)

2. It should take longer to respond that Eskimos wear clothes. Wearing parkas is a distinctive feature of Eskimos, along with living in igloos. To answer whether Eskimos wear clothes we have to go a level up, either to "Eskimos are humans; humans wear clothes" or to "parkas are clothes." (page 327)

3. It is an example of heuristics; someone has devised a simple way to obtain an approximate answer. A possible example of an algorithm would be to collect grocery receipts from a random sample of all the people in the country and then divide the total of the receipts by the number of people sampled. (page 332)

4. The employer would fire 18 dishonest employees (90% of the 20 who had stolen). The employer would also fire 98 honest employees (10% of the 980 who had not stolen). Because the base-rate of dishonesty is low, a clear majority of those identified as dishonest are actually honest. (page 342)

5. (a) Failure to consider the base rate: 20% of all older adults is a larger number than 90% of all college students; (b) Premature commitment to one hypothesis without considering other hypotheses (such as that one could stay healthy without any magic words). (page 344)

ANSWERS TO OTHER QUESTIONS IN THE TEXT

A. One solution is given here. The imaginary cube problem is impossible. (page 320)

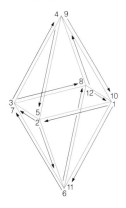

B. The objects in pair a are the same; in b they are the same; and in c they are different. (page 322)

C. Sixty miles. The trains meet in 1 hour, and the bird flies 60 miles per hour. (page 330)

D. All numbers of the form XYZXYZ are integral multiples of 1,001. You can get any of these numbers by multiplying XYZ times 1,001. Because 1,001 is evenly divisible by 13, every number that is evenly divisible by 1,001 is also evenly divisible by 13. (If you did not think of this idea, do not be discouraged. Most people take a long time to think of it, if they get it at all.) (page 331)

E. The illustration here shows how to cut and fold an ordinary piece of paper or cardboard to match the figure. (page 332)

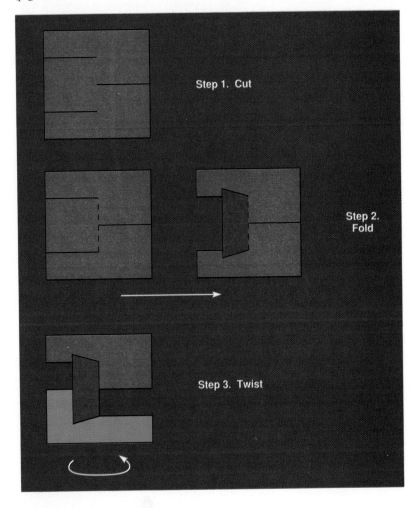

Step 1. Cut

Step 2. Fold

Step 3. Twist

F. The water in the tube would leak out of the hole in the bottom. Any membrane heavy enough to keep the water in would also keep the rubber balls out. (page 332)

G. *Hint:* Sketch a possible path that David might have taken—not necessarily a straight line. Is there any way for Lisa to get from Toronto to Miami without crossing that line? (page 334)

H. *Hint:* Draw a possible path for Lisa. On David's side of the globe, draw a line that represents the opposite of every point on Lisa's line. Can David get from Madagascar to New Zealand without crossing that line? (page 334)

I. She traveled between two points, such as Anchorage to Miami, and between two other points, such as Madagascar and New Zealand. One path intersects the opposite of the other path. (page 334)

CHAPTER

10

INTELLIGENCE AND ITS MEASUREMENT

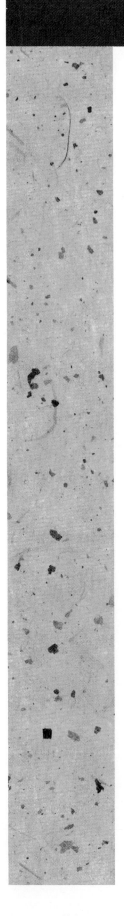

Let's consider three questions:

1. Were the people of prehistoric times as intelligent, in general, as the people of today?

2. Which is the most intelligent: a chimpanzee, a dolphin, or an elephant?

3. What is the probability of finding intelligent life on other planets?

The mere fact that we ask such questions—and sometimes argue about the answers—implies that we think we know what *intelligent* means. To some extent we do; at least we can generally agree on what is or is not an example of intelligent behavior. And yet psychologists find it difficult to specify the precise meaning of *intelligence* even for living people—much less for prehistoric people, dolphins, or extraterrestrials. Here are some of the ways that psychologists have defined *intelligence* (Wolman, 1989):

- The ability to cope with the environment through learning

- The ability to judge, comprehend, and reason

- The ability to understand and deal with people, objects, and symbols

- The ability to act purposefully, think rationally, and deal effectively with the environment

Note that these definitions use such terms as *judge, comprehend, understand,* and *think rationally*—terms that are themselves poorly defined. Psychologists are still trying to determine what intelligence is.

Meanwhile, some psychologists are busy administering IQ tests, attempting to measure people's intelligence. How can anyone measure intelligence without knowing exactly what it is? The idea may be less preposterous than it sounds. Physicists measured light intensity and electric current long before they had any clear understanding of what light and electricity really are. Maybe psychologists can do the same with intelligence.

Ah, but then again, maybe not. The fact that physicists measured electricity before they understood it does not guarantee that we can always measure something we do not understand. Hardly anyone is completely satisfied with our measurements of intelligence today, and hardly anyone thinks we understand intelligence well at a theoretical level. Psychologists are doing their best, but even they are not sure how good "their best" is.

The psychology of intelligence is an area of both serious controversy and serious research, some of it rather complex and sophisticated. It is also the area in which psychologists first developed many of their tools of measurement and investigation.

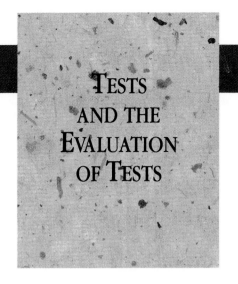

TESTS AND THE EVALUATION OF TESTS

What is the purpose of IQ tests?
How can we measure the usefulness of such tests?

Intelligence testing has a long history of controversy, partly because of misconceptions about its purpose. Consider this analogy:

You and I have just been put in charge of choosing members of the next U.S. Olympic team. To choose the best-qualified people, we decide to hold tryouts in basketball, gymnastics, high jumping, and all the other events. Suddenly the Olympic rules are changed: Each country can send only 30 men and 30 women and each athlete must compete in every event. Furthermore, the competitive events will be new ones, not exactly like any of the familiar events, and the Olympic Committee will not publish the rules for any of the new events until all of our athletes have arrived at the Olympic site. Clearly, we cannot hold regular tryouts. How shall we choose the team?

Our best bet would be to devise a test of general "athletic ability." We would measure the abilities of all the applicants to run, jump, change direction, maintain balance, throw and catch, kick, lift weights, respond rapidly to signals, and perform other athletic feats. Then we would choose the applicants with the best scores.

That might not be the best possible test, and we would no doubt make some mistakes in our selection of athletes. But if we must choose 60 athletes, and if we want to maximize their chances of winning, we certainly have to use some sort of test. So we go ahead with our Test of General Athletic Ability.

As time passes, other people begin to use our test. It becomes well accepted and widely used.

Does its acceptance imply that athletic ability is a single quantity, like speed or weight? No. When we devised the test, it merely suited our purposes to combine various scores of skills as if athletic ability were a single quantity, even though we knew it was not. (Some athletes are good at one sport but not at others.)

IQ Tests

Intelligence tests resemble our imaginary test of athletic ability. If we have to choose from among applicants to a school or college, we want to select those who will profit most from the experience. Because students may be studying subjects that they have never studied before, we want to measure their general ability to profit from education rather than any specific knowledge or specialized ability. By the same token, if we want to identify children who belong in a special education program for retarded children, we need to measure their general ability to handle schoolwork. Regardless of whether we are trying to identify the best students or the worst, we should base our judgments on accurate, objective, fair information. We look at the students' grades and the recommendations of their teachers, even though we know that such evidence can be inaccurate and unfair. (Some schools are better than others; some teachers grade harder than others.) We also look at students' scores on standardized tests.

Intelligence quotient (IQ) tests attempt to measure an individual's probable performance in school and similar settings. The first IQ tests were devised for a practical purpose by two French psychologists, Alfred Binet and Theophile Simon (1905). The French Ministry of Public Instruction wanted a fair way to identify children who had such serious intellectual deficiencies that they could not succeed in the public school system of Paris. Those children were to be put into special classes for the retarded. Formerly, the task of identifying retarded children had been left entirely to medical doctors. But different doctors had different standards for judging retardation, and there was no way to resolve their disagreements. An equitable, impartial test of some sort was needed. Binet and Simon produced a test to measure the skills that children need for success in school, such as understanding and using

TABLE 10.1 Examples of the Types of Items on the Stanford-Binet Test

Age	Sample Test Item
2	Test administrator points at pictures of everyday objects and asks, "What is this?" "Here are some pegs of different sizes and shapes. See whether you can put each one into the correct hole."
4	"Why do people live in houses?" "Birds fly in the air; fish swim in the _____."
6	"Here is a picture of a horse. Do you see what part of the horse is missing?" "Here are some candies. Can you count how many there are?"
8	"What should you do if you find a lost puppy?" "Stephanie can't write today because she twisted her ankle. What is wrong with that?"
10	"Why should people be quiet in a library?" "Repeat after me: 4 8 3 7 1 4."
12	"What does *regret* mean?" "Here is a picture. Can you tell me what is wrong with it?"
14	"What is the similarity between *high* and *low*?" "Watch me fold this paper and cut it. Now, when I unfold it, how many holes will there be?"
Adult	"Make up a sentence using the words *celebrate*, *reverse*, and *appointment*." "What do people mean when they say, 'People who live in glass houses should not throw stones?'"

Source: Modified from Nietzel and Bernstein, 1987.

language, computational skills, memory, and the ability to follow instructions.

Such a test can make useful predictions. It can tell us that Susie is likely to do well in school but that Nancy is not. But suppose Susie does well and Nancy does poorly. Can we say that Susie does better in school because she has a higher IQ score?

No. Consider this analogy: Suppose we ask why a certain baseball player strikes out so often. Someone answers, "Because he has a low batting average." Clearly, that explains nothing. (The reason for the low batting average is that he strikes out so often.) Similarly, saying that a student does poorly in school because he or she does poorly on an IQ test isn't much of an explanation; after all, the IQ test was designed to measure the very skills schoolwork requires. *An IQ score is like any other score: It measures current performance. A test measures differences among people; it does not explain the differences.*

IQ tests have gained a special mystique in our society. Many schools routinely administer IQ tests to all their students, but few ever tell the students the results. Why not? School administrators say that they fear the students will compare scores with one another and that those who made lower scores will feel discouraged. Maybe so, but the main point of IQ tests is to predict how well students will perform in school, and schools always tell students their grades. Students can compare grades and make one another feel just as bad as if they were comparing IQ scores. Perhaps the secrecy surrounding IQ scores makes them seem more important than they really are.

The Stanford-Binet Test

The test Binet and Simon designed was later modified for English speakers as the **Stanford-Binet IQ test**. This test is administered to individual students by someone who has been carefully trained in how to present each item and how to score each answer. It contains items that range in difficulty, as designated by age (see Table 10.1). An item designated as "age 8," for example, will be answered correctly by 60 to 90% of all 8-year-olds. (A higher percentage of older children will answer it correctly, as will a lower percentage of younger children.) Those who take the test are asked to answer only those items that are pegged at or near their level of functioning. For example, the psychologist testing an 8-year-old might start with the items designated for 6- or 7-year-olds. If the child missed many of them, the psychologist would go back to the items for 5-year-olds. But if the child answered all or nearly all of the 6- and 7-year-old items correctly, the psychologist would proceed to the items for 8-year-olds, 9-year-olds, and so forth. When the child begins to miss item after item, the test is over. Ordinarily, the entire test lasts no more than an hour to an hour and a half.

In its original form, the Stanford-Binet test produced a **mental age** (MA) for each child. A child who performed as well on the test as the average 8-year-old was said to have a mental age of 8. To determine the child's "intelligence quotient," the child's mental age was divided by his or her actual chronological age (CA), and the result was multiplied by 100.

$$IQ = (MA/CA) \times 100$$

However, that formula has its limitations. First, children can achieve a given IQ score more easily at certain ages than at others. (A 5-year-old with a mental age of 6 is not exactly as outstanding as a 10-year-old with a mental age of 12, even though the formula gives them both an IQ score of 120.) Second, the formula cannot be used for teenagers or adults, because test scores do not change much beyond about age 14. (The average 14-year-old has the same mental age as the average 35-year-old.)

Consequently, IQ scores are now computed from tables set up to ensure that a given IQ score will mean the same thing at different ages. A 6-year-old with an IQ score of, say, 116 has performed better on the test than 84% of other 6-year-olds. A 9-year-old with an IQ score of 116 has performed better than 84% of other 9-year-olds. An adult with an IQ score of 116 has performed better than . . . you get the point. The mean IQ for all ages is 100.

In Table 10.1 notice that the Stanford-Binet test includes questions designated for ages as low as 2 years. It is possible to make rough estimates of intelligence in infants as young as 6 months, mostly by determining whether they pay more attention to a changing visual stimulus than to a stimulus that remains constant (Bornstein & Sigman, 1986; Rose & Wallace, 1985). Nevertheless, estimates of intelligence are relatively unstable for children under the age of 4 or 5. Before 4 or 5, scores are likely to fluctuate more widely than scores obtained at later ages (Honzik, 1974; Morrow & Morrow, 1974).

Concept Check

***1.** Given the initial formula for calculating IQ— (MA/CA) × 100—the mean IQ had to be 100. Do you see why? (Check your answer on page 373.)*

The Wechsler Tests

Two IQ tests devised by David Wechsler are now more commonly used than the Stanford-Binet. Known as the **Wechsler Adult Intelligence Scale— Revised (WAIS-R)** and the **Wechsler Intelligence Scale for Children—Revised (WISC-R)**, these tests produce the same average, 100, and almost the same distribution of scores as the Stanford-Binet produces. As with the Stanford-Binet, the Wechsler tests are administered to one individual at a time. The main advantage of the Wechsler tests is that in addition to an overall score, they provide scores in two major categories (verbal and performance), each of which is divided into component abilities. (Table 10.2 shows examples of test items, and Figure 10.1 shows one individual's test profile.) Thus the Wechsler tests may reveal that someone is particularly strong or particularly weak in a specific ability.

Each of the 12 parts of the WISC-R and the WAIS-R begins with very simple questions that almost everyone answers correctly; each part then progresses slowly to increasingly difficult items. Six of the 12 parts constitute the Verbal Scale of the test; these parts require the use of spoken or written language. The other 6 parts constitute the Perfor-

*M*uch of the WAIS-R involves nonverbal tests in which a person is asked to perform certain tasks. Here, to evaluate visual-spatial organization, a woman arranges colored blocks according to a specified pattern while a psychologist times her. Although playing with blocks may seem odd for measuring an adult's intelligence, Wechsler originally developed his tests in part because the Stanford-Binet was geared toward children. As he said, asking "an ex-Army sergeant to give you a sentence with the words 'boy,' 'river,' [and] 'ball' is not particularly apt to evoke either interest or respect" (Wilson et al., 1964, page 132).

mance Scale. Although a person must know English well enough to understand the instructions, the answers are nonverbal.

The inclusion of questions that ask for factual information (such as "From what animal do we get milk?") has caused much controversy. Critics complain that such items measure knowledge, not ability. Defenders reply, first, that "intelligent" people tend to learn more facts than others do, even if they have had no more exposure to the information. Furthermore, as we saw in Chapter 9, expertise and problem-solving ability require a substantial amount of factual knowledge. Finally, the purpose of the test is to predict performance in school, and in that respect it works. Granted, the test measures current performance rather than raw ability. But no one knows how to measure ability independent of performance.

TABLE 10.2 Items from the Wechsler Intelligence Scale for Children (WISC)

Test	Example
Verbal Scale	
Information	From what animal do we get milk? (Either "cow" or "goat" is an acceptable answer.)
Similarities	How are a plum and a peach similar? (Correct answer: "They are both fruits." Half credit is given for "Both are food" or "Both are round.")
Arithmetic	Count these blocks: ■ ■ ■ ■ ■ ■ ■ ■ ■
Vocabulary	Define the word *letter*.
Comprehension	What should you do if you see a train approaching a broken track? (A correct answer is "Stand safely out of the way and wave something to warn the train." Half credit is given for "Tell someone at the railroad station." *No* credit is given for "I would try to fix the track.")
Digit Span	Repeat these numbers after I say them: 3 6 2.
Performance Scale	
Picture completion	What parts are missing from this picture?
Picture arrangement	Here are some cards with a gardener on them. Can you put them in order?
Block design	See how I have arranged these four blocks? Here are four more blocks. Can you arrange your blocks like mine?
Object assembly	Can you put these five puzzle pieces together to make a dog?
Coding	Here is a page full of shapes. Put a slash (/) through all the circles and an **X** through all the squares.
Mazes	Here is a maze. Start with your pencil here and trace a path to the other end of the maze without crossing any lines.

Source: Based on Wechsler, 1949.

WISC-R PROFILE

Clinicians who wish to draw a profile should first transfer the child's *scaled scores* to the row of boxes below. Then mark an X on the dot corresponding to the scaled score for each test, and draw a line connecting the X's.*

VERBAL TESTS

	Information	Similarities	Arithmetic	Vocabulary	Comprehension	Digit Span
Scaled Score	7	11	9	10	10	—

PERFORMANCE TESTS

	Picture Completion	Picture Arrangement	Block Design	Object Assembly	Coding	Mazes
Scaled Score	8	7	6	6	11	—

*See Chapter 4 in the manual for a discussion of the significance of differences between scores on the tests.

FIGURE 10.1

A WISC-R score profile for an overall IQ score of 89. Note that the WISC-R identifies a person's areas of strength as well as his or her areas of weakness. The range of abilities evaluated include memory, abstract reasoning, logic, and using arithmetic. (WISC-R Profile from the Psychological Corporation; data supplied by William Erchul.)

Raven's Progressive Matrices

The Stanford-Binet and Wechsler tests, though useful for many purposes, have certain limitations. First, because they require comprehension and use of the English language, they are unfair to people who do not speak English well, including immigrants and hearing-impaired people. Even the performance items on the Wechsler test pose problems; people with an imperfect command of English sometimes misunderstand the instructions. A second limitation is that these tests ask for specific information that may be unfamiliar to many people.

To overcome such problems, psychologists have tried to devise a culture-fair or a culture-reduced test that would make minimal use of language and would not ask for any specific facts. One example of a culture-reduced test is the **Progressive Matrices** test devised by John C. Raven. Figure 10.2 presents matrices of the type this test uses. The matrices, which "progress" gradually from easy items to difficult items, attempt to measure "abstract reasoning"; they call for no verbal responses and no specific information. The instructions are simple enough to be explained to a person who does not speak English or to a preschool child. Spanish-speaking immigrants to the United States score about the same, on the average, as the rest of the U.S.

Binet and Simon began developing an intelligence test so they could impartially identify mentally retarded children, such as the girl being tested here. An American who takes a standard IQ test but lacks fluency in English will not be accurately assessed. Similarly, someone without normal fluency in any spoken language should be evaluated with tests that "speak"—perhaps by color or shape—in a language she can comprehend. People may seem only as "smart" or as "dumb" as the IQ tests are.

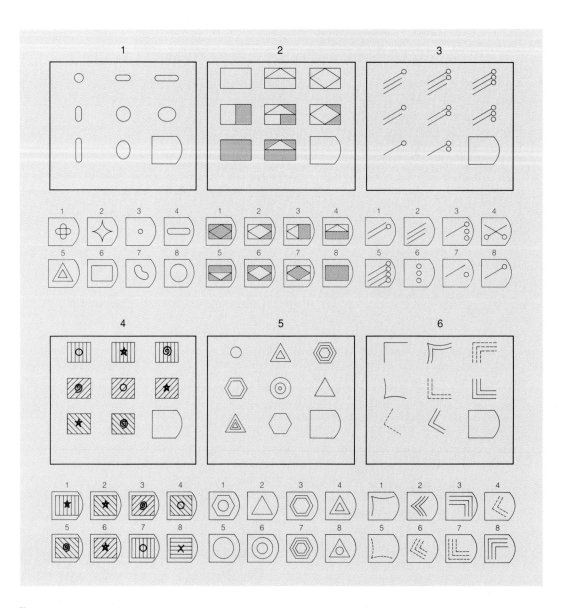

Figure 10.2

Items similar to those in Raven's Progressive Matrices test. The instructions are: "Each pattern has a piece missing. From the eight choices provided, select the one that completes the pattern, both going across and going down." (You can check your answers against answer A, page 373.)

population (Powers, Barken, & Jones, 1986). The test comes in various forms, for people who are retarded, average, or above average. It can be given either with or without time limits. Naturally, people are expected to score higher when no time limits are imposed.

The Progressive Matrices test cannot be used with blind people. Moreover, it provides only a single score, whereas the Wechsler test provides scores on several distinct abilities.

Something to Think About

Is the Progressive Matrices test truly "culture fair"? That is, would it be equally fair to people from all societies on Earth? If not, is it at least likely to be fairer than other IQ tests?

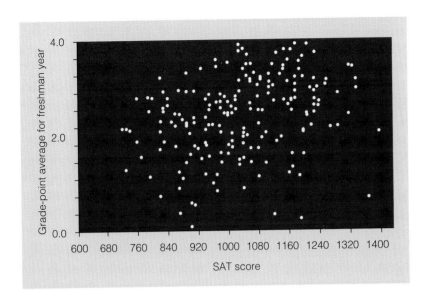

FIGURE 10.3

The relationship between total SAT score and college grades for the freshman year. The correlation between the two variables here is 0.3, which means that SAT scores do predict college grades, but with only moderate accuracy.

The Scholastic Aptitude Test

Although most people do not regard the **Scholastic Aptitude Test (SAT)** as an intelligence test, it serves the same function: It predicts performance in college. (Figure 10.3 shows the relationship between SAT scores and grade point average during the freshman year in college.) Administered to large groups of students at one time, the SAT consists of multiple-choice items divided into two sets, verbal and quantitative. Each set is scored on a scale from 200 to 800. The designers of the test intended that the mean score would be 500 on each scale. Now that a higher percentage of high school students take the test, the mean score is actually about 450. Figure 10.4 presents examples of the types of items found on the SAT. As college students, you are probably familiar with the SAT or with the similar American College Test (ACT).

The SAT was designed to help colleges select among applicants for admission. The best predictor of college success is success in high school. But high school grades by themselves are not entirely satisfactory. Some high schools set higher standards than others and may give lower grades for work that would receive higher grades elsewhere. Even within a given school, some students take more challenging courses than others do. One student's B− average may indicate higher academic accomplishment than another student's A average. The SAT offers a way to compare students who have attended different high schools and taken different

FIGURE 10.4

Look familiar? These two sample items from the Scholastic Aptitude Test reflect its two parts, which measure mathematical and verbal skills, and the different abilities needed to answer them. (From The College Entrance Examination Board and the Educational Testing Service.)

A.

5. In the figure above, what is the area of the shaded region?

(A) 21 (B) 24 (C) 25 (D) 28 (E) 32

B.

25. LINGUISTICS: LANGUAGE::
(A) statistics: sociology
(B) ceramics: clay
(C) gymnastics: health
(D) dynamics: motion
(E) economics: warfare

Unlike the SAT, high school grades vary according to the teacher, subject, and school. A student who took calculus, Latin, and physics, played varsity basketball, and worked part-time on weekends may graduate with a B average, while a student with easier courses may have higher grades but less ability.

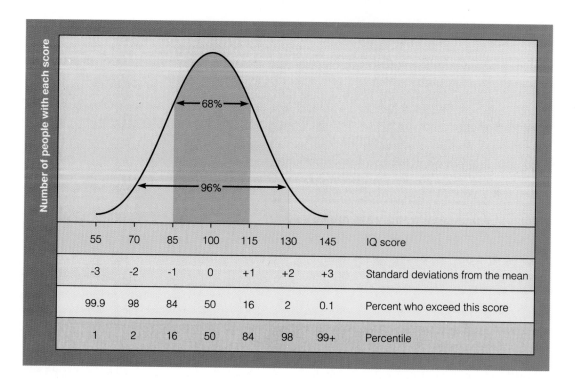

FIGURE 10.5

The distribution of IQ scores. About 1% of people have an IQ of more than 140. Each score has some error of measurement, and a person's IQ score typically fluctuates by a few points—sometimes more—from one test session to another.

55	70	85	100	115	130	145	IQ score
-3	-2	-1	0	+1	+2	+3	Standard deviations from the mean
99.9	98	84	50	16	2	0.1	Percent who exceed this score
1	2	16	50	84	98	99+	Percentile

courses. As a predictor of college success, the SAT by itself is even less satisfactory than high school grades by themselves. When combined with high school grades, however, SAT scores significantly improve the prediction of college success (Weitzman, 1982).

Because many students worry about doing well on the SAT, a coaching industry has developed. Students can pay to attend sessions after school or on weekends. If you attended such sessions, did you get your money's worth? If you did not attend them, did you miss a chance for a much higher SAT score? Researchers have attempted to answer these questions.

Several studies have compared the SAT scores of students who attended coaching sessions to the scores of students of similar ability who did not. The results have been consistent: On the average, participation in SAT-coaching sessions raises a student's score by about 10 to 20 points (on a scale from 200 to 800). Students who attend longer, more intensive coaching sessions score only slightly higher than those who attend briefer sessions. To improve scores by more than about 30 points, a student has to spend almost as much time in the coaching sessions as in school (Kulik, Bangert-Drowns, & Kulik, 1984; Messick & Jungeblut, 1981).

THE STANDARDIZATION OF IQ TESTS

Binet, Wechsler, and the other pioneers who devised the first IQ tests set the mean score at 100. They selected items that would produce a standard deviation of 15 for the Wechsler test and 16 for the Stanford-Binet, as Figure 10.5 shows. (The standard deviation, you may recall from Chapter 2, is a measure of the degree of variability of performance. If most scores are close to the mean, the standard deviation is small; if scores vary widely, the standard deviation is larger.)

In any normal distribution, 68% of all people are within 1 standard deviation above or below the mean; 96% are within 2 standard deviations. Thus someone with a score of 115 on the Wechsler test exceeds the scores of 84% of other people of the same age—the 50% at or below the mean plus the 34% within 1 standard deviation above it. We say that such a person is "in the 84th percentile." Someone with an IQ score of 130 is in the 98th percentile, which means that his or her score is higher than the scores of 98% of others of the same age. Psychologists sometimes refer to people more than 2 standard deviations above the mean as "gifted." Those more than 2 standard deviations below the mean are said to be "retarded." The designations are arbitrary. There is not much difference between an allegedly "gifted" child with an IQ of 130 and an allegedly "nongifted" child with an IQ of 129.

The process of selecting items and determining the meaning of scores is known as **standardization**. Standardization sets **norms**, which are descriptions of the frequencies at which particular scores occur. For example, the mean performance of a population is the norm for an IQ of 100. A level of performance 1 standard deviation above the mean is the norm for an IQ of 115.

Psychologists try to standardize a test on a large, representative population. For example, if a test is to be used with children throughout the United States and Canada, it would be a mistake to standardize it using a group of children from just one school system; those children might be better acquainted or less acquainted with certain materials than are children in some other region. When a new test is created, or an old one revised, the test's authors try it out on a mixture of children from different geographical regions, some rural and some urban.

Selection of Items for an IQ Test

The authors of IQ tests select items with a range of difficulty so that some people will get high scores, others will get low scores, and most will get scores somewhere in the middle. Ideally, all the items should have something in common with one another. Yet they should not be *too* similar. Consider the following items:

If it takes three workers two days to complete a job, how long will it take six workers?

If it takes four workers two days to complete a job, how long will it take eight workers?

Either question might well be included on an IQ test but not both. Anyone who gets one right will probably also get the other one right.

To make sure that all the items are testing approximately the same thing—intelligence—the authors of IQ tests find the correlation between performance on each item and performance on the test as a whole. A positive correlation between a given item and the test as a whole means that people who answer that item correctly tend to do well on the rest of the test. A negative correlation or a correlation near zero indicates that the item is measuring something unrelated to the rest of the test. Such items are discarded or reworded.

Restandardization of IQ Tests

Over the years, the standardization of any IQ test becomes obsolete. In 1920 a question that asked people to identify "Mars" was fairly difficult, because most people knew little about the planets. Today, in an era of space exploration, the same question is easy for most people. Periodically, the publishers of each IQ test update it, reword the questions, and change the scoring standards.

The result has been to make IQ tests harder. To keep the mean score at 100, items that were

How well would you do on a test covering Native American myths, ceremonies, and history? If you live near a reservation, you may know a little about one tribe; otherwise, what you know may be limited to movie westerns. Tests that aim to be culture-fair avoid asking for facts and relying on language skills.

once considered difficult but that have since become easy have been replaced with more difficult items (Flynn, 1984, 1987). In other words, people are doing better and better at answering the questions that used to appear in IQ tests. Why? No one knows. Evolution is not a plausible explanation for such a rapid change. The explanation may lie in improved education, in better health and nutrition, in exposure to a wider range of information via television, or in other changes in the environment.

EVALUATION OF TESTS

At some point in your academic career, you probably complained that a test was unfair. You were sure you knew the important material, but the test concentrated on minor details or penalized you for not saying something in quite the right way. Your instructor may have replied that what you considered "minor" details were actually important or that the way you worded your answers suggested that you did not really understand the material. You and your instructor may not have come to any agreement on what was important and on how to determine whether the test measured it.

Similarly, many people complain about intelligence tests. They charge that instead of measuring intelligence, all the tests measure is whether or not someone has been exposed to certain facts and certain experiences. Much is at stake in this dispute.

"If something exists, it exists in some amount. If it exists in some amount, it can be measured."
EDWARD L. THORNDIKE

"Anything which exists can be measured incorrectly."
DOUGLAS K. DETTERMAN (1979)

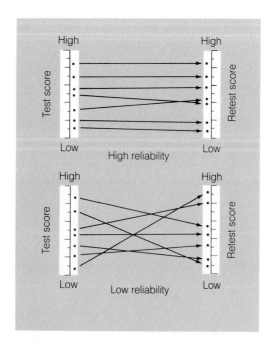

FIGURE 10.6

Test reliability: Each dot in the left column indicates a score on the first test; each dot in the right column represents a score on a retest. On a test with high reliability, the order of scores is similar on both tests. On a test with low reliability, scores on the retest may vary considerably from those on the first test. (From *Psychology Today*, 1979.)

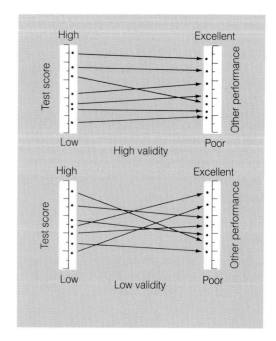

FIGURE 10.7

Predictive validity: For each person, we obtain a test score (left column) and a measurement of performance on some other task outside the test (right column). If the test has high predictive validity, then people with high test scores generally perform well on the other task. If the predictive validity is low, then people with high scores may or may not do well on the other task. As with reliability, a correlation coefficient measures predictive validity. (From *Psychology Today*, 1979.)

Unlike a test given at the end of a course, intelligence tests substantially influence the future of millions of people. Along with school grades, test scores help to determine which children will attend regular classes, which will be placed in special classes for slow learners, and which will attend courses designed for gifted students.

Because intelligence tests are administered repeatedly, the authors have a wealth of experience to draw on when they revise their tests. If a given item proves to be too hard or too easy, they can discard it. If an item proves to be confusing, they can reword it. They evaluate how well the test achieves what it is intended to achieve. The two basic ways of evaluating any test are to check its reliability and to examine its validity.

Reliability

The **reliability** of a test is defined as the repeatability of its scores (Anastasi, 1988). A reliable test measures something consistently. When we give a test once and then give the same test, or an equivalent version of it, a second time, people should get approximately the same score as they did the first time or at least should retain approximately the same rank within the group. (If everyone's score went up by 10 points, the test would still be reliable.) Figure 10.6 illustrates **test-retest reliability**.

To measure the reliability of a test, psychologists use a correlation coefficient. They may test the same people twice, either with the same test or with equivalent versions of it, and compare the two sets of scores. Or they may compare the scores on the first and second halves of the test or the scores on the test's odd-numbered and even-numbered items. If all the items measure approximately the same abilities, the scores on one set of items should be highly correlated with the scores on the other set of items. As with any other correlation coefficient, the reliability of a test can (theoretically) range from +1 to −1. In the real world, however, negative reliabilities never occur on tests. (A negative reliability would mean that people who do better than average the first time they take a test will do worse than average the next time. That simply never happens.)

If a test's reliability is perfect ($+1$), the person who scores the highest on the first test will also score highest on the retest, and the person who receives the 127th-best score will again make the 127th-best score. If the reliability is 0, scores will vary randomly, like the scores on a coin-flipping "test." In that case, someone who makes a very high score the first time is neither more likely nor less likely than anyone else to make a high score the second time. The reliability of psychological tests is always reported as a correlation coefficient between 0 and 1. The reliability of the WISC-R has been measured at about .95; the reliabilities of the Stanford-Binet, Progressive Matrices, and SAT are also in the range of about .90 to .95 (Anastasi, 1988; Burke, 1985; Siegler & Richards, 1982). These figures indicate that the tests are measuring whatever they measure in a consistent, repeatable manner.

Concept Checks

2. I have just devised a new "intelligence test." I measure your intelligence by dividing the length of your head by its width and then multiplying by 100. Would that be a reliable test? (Check your answer on page 373.)

3. Most students find that if they retake the SAT, their scores increase the second time. Does that improvement indicate that the test is unreliable? (Check your answer on page 373.)

Validity

A test's **validity** is a determination of how well it measures what it claims to measure. One type of validity is **content validity**. We say that a test has high content validity if its items accurately represent the information the test is meant to measure. For example, a licensing examination for psychologists would have high content validity if it tested all the major points a practicing psychologist is expected to know. A test for a driver's license has content validity if it includes all the important laws and regulations that pertain to driving.

A second type of validity is **construct validity**. A test has construct validity if what it measures corresponds to a theoretical construct. For example, intelligence is a theoretical construct. Psychologists expect it to have certain properties, such as increasing as a child grows older. They also expect it to include several component abilities, such as mathematics, memorization, and verbal reasoning. For

an IQ test to have construct validity, it must reflect those properties. For example, older children should, as a rule, perform better on the test than younger children do. And the test should include items relating to a variety of abilities.

Predictive validity, a third type of validity, means that a test's scores accurately predict a certain behavior in some setting outside the test. For example, an interest test that accurately predicts what courses a student will like has predictive validity. Similarly, an IQ test that accurately predicts how well a student will perform in school has predictive validity. Figure 10.7 illustrates predictive validity.

If a test's scores correlate well with academic performance at the time the test is given, then we say the test has **concurrent validity**. For example, we could demonstrate the concurrent validity of an IQ test by showing that students with high test scores are also getting high grades in their courses.

As with reliability, a correlation coefficient measures predictive validity and concurrent validity. To measure validity, we compare test scores against some measure of behavior. For instance, we might compare scores on an IQ test to grades in school or scores on an aggression test to the frequency of arrests for violent crimes. A validity of $+1$ would mean that the scores perfectly predicted the behavior in question. A validity of 0 would mean that the scores had no relationship to that behavior. The predictive validity of such tests as the WISC-R, Stanford-Binet, Progressive Matrices, and SAT generally range from about 0.3 to 0.6, varying from one school to another (Anastasi, 1988; Siegler & Richards, 1982). (Given the erratic nature of grading systems, it would be hard to devise a test that correlated much better than 0.6.)

Concept Check

4. Can a test have high reliability and low validity? Can a test have low reliability and high validity? (Check your answers on page 373.)

Utility

In addition to reliability and validity, a good test should have utility. **Utility** is defined as usefulness for a practical purpose. Not every test that is reliable and valid is also useful. For example, psychologists are making progress toward a reliable, valid test of intelligence for infants (Bornstein & Sigman, 1986). But if we had such a test, what would we do with it? With most infants, nothing at all. Because no infants are ready to go to school, such an intelligence test would have very limited utility.

(That conclusion does not imply that psychologists who are studying infant intelligence are wasting their time. Their research may lead to an understanding of the causes of retardation, how to prevent it, and how giftedness develops.)

Similarly, some psychologists have questioned the utility of the SAT (for example, Gottfredson & Crouse, 1986). We can predict students' college grades moderately well by means of high school grades alone. Adding SAT scores improves the prediction, but does it improve the prediction enough to be worth the cost, the time, and the anxiety? That is, even if the test has respectable reliability and validity, does it have enough utility to justify requiring it? Psychologists have different points of view on this question.

Interpreting Fluctuations in Scores

Suppose you make a score of 94% correct on the first test in your psychology course. On the second test (which was equally difficult), you make a score of 88%. Does that score indicate that you studied harder for the first test than for the second test? Not necessarily. Whenever you take tests that are not perfectly reliable, your scores are likely to fluctuate. The lower the reliability, the greater the fluctuation.

When people lose sight of that fact, they sometimes try to explain apparent fluctuations in performance that are really due to the unreliability of the test. In one well-known study, Harold M. Skeels (1966) identified a group of low-IQ infants in an orphanage and then placed them in an institution where they received more personal attention. Several years later, most of those infants showed great increases in their IQ scores. Should we conclude, as many psychologists did, that the extra attention improved the children's performances? Not necessarily (Longstreth, 1981). IQ tests for infants have low reliabilities—in other words, the scores fluctuate widely from one time to another. If someone selects a group of infants with low IQ scores and retests them a few years later, the mean IQ score is almost certain to improve, simply because the early scores were poor estimates of the children's abilities. Or, to put it another way, the scores had nowhere to go but up.

Summary

1. The Stanford-Binet and other IQ tests were devised to predict the level of performance in school. (page 349)

2. The Wechsler IQ tests measure 12 separate abilities, grouped into a Verbal Scale of 6 parts and a Performance Scale of 6 parts. (page 351)

3. Culture-reduced tests such as Raven's Progressive Matrices can be used with people who are unfamiliar with English. (page 353)

4. The Scholastic Aptitude Test is similar to IQ tests because it predicts performance in school, specifically in college. (page 355)

5. IQ tests have a mean of 100 and a standard deviation of about 15 or 16, depending on the test. Items are carefully selected so that performance on each item correlates positively with performance on the test as a whole. (page 356)

6. IQ tests are restandardized periodically. To keep the same mean, test authors have made the tests more difficult from time to time. (page 357)

7. Tests are evaluated in terms of reliability and validity. Reliability is a measure of a test's consistency, or the repeatability of its scores. Validity is a determination of how well a test measures what it claims to measure. (page 358)

Suggestions for Further Reading

Anastasi, A. (1988). *Psychological testing* (6th ed.). New York: Macmillan. A thorough treatment of the design and interpretation of IQ tests and other psychological tests.

Sternberg, R. J. (Ed.) (1982). *Handbook of human intelligence.* Cambridge, England: Cambridge University. A collection of articles on topics ranging from the evolution of intelligence to artificial intelligence.

CONTROVERSIAL ISSUES IN THE STUDY OF INTELLIGENCE

What is intelligence?
What do the scores on IQ tests mean?
Are variations in intelligence between groups of people the result of differences in genes?

Clams, oysters, limpets, and starfish are very inactive animals with a relatively simple nervous system. Their lack of activity has much to do with their lack of an elaborate nervous system. If you aren't going to do much, you don't need much of a brain. And if you don't have much in the way of brains, it would be a mistake to move around a lot. (If you do, you're probably going to get yourself into trouble!)

When we think of human intelligence, we may have an image of students sitting quietly in a classroom and occasionally writing answers on a sheet of paper—not much more active than the average clam. But the value of intelligence is that it leads to the possibility of purposeful action.

WHAT IS INTELLIGENCE?

As we saw in the preceding section, IQ tests were developed for the practical function of selecting students for special classes. They were not based on any theory of intelligence, and those who administer them are usually content to define intelligence as the ability to do well in school. Given that definition, IQ tests do measure intelligence.

For theoretical purposes, however, that definition is not satisfactory. But what is a good definition? We cannot determine whether IQ tests measure intelligence unless we agree on what intelligence is.

One survey of over a thousand specialists in intelligence testing found that 53% believed that a consensus exists on what *intelligent* means (Snyderman & Rothman, 1987). (Think about that: A consensus is a general agreement. Here, a bare majority, just over 50%, says that a "general agreement" exists. How general can it be?)

That agreement, such as it is, says that intelligence includes abstract thinking, problem solving, knowledge and the capacity to acquire more knowledge, memory, adaptation to the environment, mental speed, linguistic and mathematical competence, and creativity. Some psychologists draw up somewhat different lists of what intelligence includes. Robert Sternberg (1985) and Richard Weinberg (1989), for example, include social and practical intelligence, the ability to:

- Respond to facial cues and gestures that mean "I'd like to talk to you" or "Please don't bother me"

- Watch two people at work and figure out which one is the supervisor

- Look at a couple and tell whether they have an ongoing relationship or whether they have just met

- Figure out what is most important for success on a job

Reading comprehension: Do you know how to "read" people? Are you adept at interpreting body language? Some psychologists include the concept of social intelligence as part of intelligence. Without such an ability, door-to-door salesmen or office managers may have trouble meeting productivity goals.

Although they are worlds apart in terms of culture and education, these Micronesian sailors and the crew of a British ship have to solve similar problems in navigating precisely to distant locations. They resolve the problems in different ways. The Micronesian sailors follow a familiar route, navigating by the sun and stars. The British crew travels along familiar or unfamiliar routes by using complex instruments. Is one solution more "intelligent" than the other?

Psychologists would like to organize this list of intelligent abilities more intelligently. Intelligence should not consist of a haphazard set of unrelated abilities; the list should have some structure or organization. Just as all the objects in the world are composed of compounds of 92 elements, most psychologists expect to find that all the kinds of intelligence are compounds of a few basic abilities. They have proposed several models of how intelligence is organized.

Spearman's Psychometric Approach and the *g* Factor

Charles Spearman (1904) took a **psychometric** approach to intelligence. Psychometric means the measurement (*metric*) of individual differences in behaviors and capacities. Spearman began by measuring how well a variety of people performed a variety of tasks, such as following complex directions, judging musical pitch, matching colors, and performing arithmetic calculations. He then found that their performance on each task correlated positively with their performance on all the other tasks. He deduced that all the tasks must have something in common. To perform well on any test of mental ability, Spearman argued, people need a certain general ability, which he called *g*. The *g* factor has to do with perceiving and manipulating relationships; it relates to abstract reasoning rather than to the recall of factual information. For example, the Progressive Matrices test is regarded as a good measure of *g*.

To account for the fact that performance on various tasks does not correlate perfectly, Spearman suggested that each task requires the use of a "specific" ability, *s*, in addition to the general ability *g* that all tasks require. Thus intelligence consists of a general ability plus an unknown number of specific abilities, such as mechanical, musical, arithmetical, logical, and spatial. Spearman called his theory a "monarchic" theory of intelligence because it included a dominant ability, or monarch, which ruled over the lesser abilities.

Later, Spearman discovered that some of the specific abilities he had identified correlated fairly highly with one another. So he proposed that in addition to the general factor and the specific factors, intelligence included "group" factors that were broader than the specific factors, but not so broad as the *g* factor.

Most, but not all, investigators of intelligence have accepted the concept of a *g* factor. J. P. Guilford (1973), for example, has argued that people have many independent mental abilities that do not necessarily correlate significantly with one another.

Cattell's Distinction Between Fluid Intelligence and Crystallized Intelligence

Raymond Cattell followed Spearman's psychometric approach but proposed a major modification of Spearman's concept of *g*. According to Cattell (1987), the *g* factor has two components: fluid intelligence and crystallized intelligence. The analogy is to water: Fluid water can take any shape, whereas ice crystals are rigid. **Fluid intelligence** is the power of reasoning and using information. It includes the ability to perceive relationships, deal with unfamiliar problems, and gain new types of knowledge. **Crystallized intelligence** consists of acquired skills and knowledge and the application of that knowledge to specific content in a person's experience. Crystallized intelligence includes the skills of a good auto mechanic, salesperson, or accountant.

Fluid intelligence, according to Cattell and his colleagues, reaches its peak well before age 20; beyond that age it may either remain constant or begin to decline. Crystallized intelligence, on the other hand, continues to increase as long as a person remains active (Cattell, 1987; Horn & Donaldson, 1976). A 20-year-old may be more successful than a 65-year-old at solving some problem that is unfamiliar to both of them, but the 65-year-old will excel in solving problems in his or her area of specialization.

In some cases, people can solve a problem only by thinking about it in familiar terms—that is, by using crystallized intelligence. In one study, for example, workers at a dairy plant were relatively poor at solving such simple multiplication problems as 17 × 68. Those same workers, however, could quickly calculate the price of 17 quarts of milk at 68 cents a quart, without even using pencil and paper (Scribner, 1986).

While the distinction between crystallized intelligence and fluid intelligence is appealing, it is not always easy to apply in practice. We ordinarily rely on a combination of the two though we may rely more on one than on the other.

Sternberg's Triarchic Theory of Intelligence

Whereas Spearman and Cattell concentrated on the number of abilities that together constitute intelligence, Robert Sternberg has been interested in a different question: What is the nature of the mental abilities that constitute intelligence? When people do something intelligent, exactly what are they doing? That question brings the study of intelligence into the realm of cognitive psychology.

In contrast to Spearman's monarchic theory, Sternberg (1985) has proposed a "triarchic" theory of intelligence. As its name suggests, the **triarchic theory** posits that intelligence is governed by three types of process, which he refers to as metacomponents, performance components, and knowledge-acquisition components.

Metacomponents *Metacomponents* are the mental abilities we use in planning an approach to a prob-

lem. In Chapter 9 we considered the problem of "What line parallel to the base of a triangle divides the area of the triangle in half?" Your first response to such a question is, "Where do I begin?" When you map out a strategy for solving a problem and decide which skills to employ, you choose the relevant performance components and knowledge-acquisition components and regulate their use in solving a problem.

Performance Components *Performance components* are the mental abilities we actually use in solving a problem or completing a task. These are the abilities that IQ tests measure. Suppose you are asked to complete the following analogy:

Washington is to 1 as Lincoln is to:

(a) 5, (b) 10, (c) 20, (d) 50.

To find the answer, you must use several performance components. The first is to encode the information, to decide what it means. For example, you will presumably encode Washington and Lincoln as George Washington and Abraham Lincoln (or, conceivably, as Washington, DC, and Lincoln, NE). The second performance component is to combine and compare information: "What is the relationship between Washington and 1? Well, let's see.... Washington was the 1st president. But Lincoln was the 16th president, and that isn't one of the choices, so that can't be the right relationship. Washington's picture is on the $1 bill. Maybe that's it. Lincoln's is on the $5 bill, and 5 is one of the choices. So I'll answer 5." Finally, you make a response—say a word, circle an answer, or do whatever else is required. The act of responding is another performance component.

Knowledge-Acquisition Components *Knowledge-acquisition components* are the mental abilities we use in gaining new knowledge. For example, if you are reading the instructions for operating a new computer program, you will stop to think about various sections, reread parts that were not immediately clear, try out certain instructions, and imagine trying out others. Each step is a knowledge-acquisition component of intelligence.

Evaluation of the Triarchic Theory Sternberg's triarchic theory is not simple to test. Sternberg (1985) himself has conducted experiments to determine what components are required for solving various problems and to describe some of the differences among the three types of components. And in doing so he has focused attention on the processes people go through when exercising their intelligence.

Intelligence *literally means understanding by gathering and selecting words and reason, but what is it specifically? Gardner's theory of multiple intelligences identifies abilities and their relationship—or lack of relatedness. Various kinds of intelligence may exist in isolation. Or one person may have several different abilities. A Renaissance man is someone with diverse interests and expertise—Benjamin Franklin, for example. Do you know anyone who is a Renaissance man or woman?*

CHAPTER 10: INTELLIGENCE AND ITS MEASUREMENT

Still, more research needs to be done before we know how well his theory accounts for intelligence.

Gardner's Theory of Multiple Intelligences

We began this section with a list of several types of intelligent behavior. Then we saw how Spearman simplified the list by assuming that all kinds of intelligence share one major factor in common. Cattell divided that one factor into two, and Sternberg proposed three components of intelligence.

We come full circle with Howard Gardner's (1985) proposal that people have **multiple intelligences**—numerous unrelated forms of intelligence.

Gardner defines intelligence as the ability to do something that other people value within one's culture. Given that definition, intelligence is not a single process, and various types of intelligence may not even be related to one another. Gardner distinguishes language abilities, musical abilities, logical and mathematical reasoning, spatial reasoning, body movement skills, and social sensitivity. He points out that people may be outstanding in one type of intelligence but not in others. For example, a *savant* (literally, "learned one") is a person who has an outstanding ability in one area such as music or calendar calculations but poor abilities in other areas. (The movie *Rain Man* depicted one such person.) These people demonstrate that various kinds of intelligence do not necessarily depend on one or a few general abilities; each can occur in isolation. If that is true, you might ask, how did Spearman find evidence for a *g* factor that contributes to all types of intelligent performance? Gardner replies that Spearman confined his attention to a limited set of abilities and ignored the types of intelligence that correlate poorly with the ones he measured.

Note the difference between Sternberg's approach and Gardner's approach: Sternberg focuses on the separate mental abilities people use when they approach a problem but assumes that they use the same abilities for different problems. Gardner assumes that people use different abilities for different kinds of problems and tasks.

The Relationship Between Theories of Intelligence and Tests of Intelligence

The psychometric theories of intelligence proposed by Spearman and Cattell are derived directly from current IQ tests; they describe how many abilities a person needs in order to perform well on the items included in the tests. The psychometric

theories offer little guidance on what items *should* be included in IQ tests.

Neither Sternberg's triarchic theory nor Gardner's multiple intelligences theory has so far led to a new IQ test, although either one might. Both theories have been directed toward understanding what intelligence really is and what abilities it includes. As future research defines those abilities better, it may lead to new and improved methods of testing intelligence.

In the meantime, psychologists will have to get by with their current, incomplete understanding of intelligence and with the IQ tests currently available. Those tests are useful from a practical standpoint but not very appealing from a theoretical standpoint. We turn now to some of the controversies surrounding those tests and what they measure.

ARE IQ TESTS BIASED?

If a test is meant to measure intelligence (or anything else), then it should measure it accurately no matter who is taking the test. Do IQ tests meet that standard? On the average, blacks make lower IQ scores than whites do. Can we then say that the tests are biased against blacks? On the average, women make lower scores than men do on the quantitative section of the SAT. Does that mean that the SAT is biased against women?

To determine whether any test is biased against a group, psychologists must look at more than just the group's mean score on the test. Psychological testing specialists do not regard an IQ test as being "biased" against a group if it *correctly* predicts that the group will perform poorly in whatever activity the test is intended to measure. A test is **biased** against a group only if it *systematically underestimates* the group's performance. (A test can be biased in favor of a group if it systematically overestimates the group's performance.) Psychologists try first to determine whether particular items on a test are biased against one group or another and then whether the test as a whole is biased.

Evaluating Possible Bias in Single Test Items

To determine whether a particular item is biased, psychologists have to go beyond an "armchair analysis" that says "this item looks as if it might be unfair." For example, in a 1980 court case, a group of parents challenged the use of IQ tests by school systems in the Chicago area because they believed the tests were biased against black children. Although the judge ruled that the tests were not biased, he

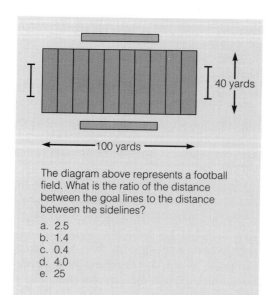

The diagram above represents a football field. What is the ratio of the distance between the goal lines to the distance between the sidelines?

a. 2.5
b. 1.4
c. 0.4
d. 4.0
e. 25

FIGURE 10.8

Offside penalty: An item formerly included on the SAT until psychologists determined that it was biased against women.

suggested that certain individual items might be biased. For example, one item on the WISC-R asks what you should do if a smaller child starts a fight with you. The correct answer, according to the test manual, is that you should show restraint. The judge suggested that some black children might be taught always to strike back, even against a smaller child, so that item might be biased against blacks.

Although the judge's suggestion sounds reasonable, it is based on an armchair analysis rather than data. The data, it turns out, reveal that the "fight with a smaller child" item is slightly easier for black children than for white children (Koh, Abbatiello, & McLoughlin, 1984).

To determine whether a particular item is biased, psychologists ask two questions: Is the item significantly more difficult for one group than for another? And does the item correlate more highly with the total test score for one group than for another?

Figure 10.8 presents an item that psychologists have determined is biased against women. This item, which once appeared on the SAT, shows a diagram of a football field and asks for the ratio of the distance between the goal lines to the distance between the sidelines. For men, this was one of the easiest items on the test, and their performance on it correlated highly with their performance on the rest of the test. That is, nearly all the men who missed it did poorly on the rest of the test as well. However, this item was more difficult for women than for men. A higher percentage of women missed it, and some women who did very well on the rest of the test missed it. The reason was that a number of women did not know which were the goal lines and which were the sidelines. Some of them left the item blank; others answered 0.4 instead of the

correct answer, 2.5. When the publishers of the SAT realized that this item was biased against women, they replaced it with one that had nothing to do with football.

Evaluating Possible Bias in a Test as a Whole

As we have seen, a biased test is one that systematically underestimates the performance of a group. If an IQ test is indeed biased against blacks, for example, then blacks with an IQ score of, say, 100 are really more intelligent than whites with the same score.

In that sense, the Stanford-Binet and Wechsler tests are undeniably biased against people who do not speak or understand English well, including the foreign born and many deaf people. Such people do much better in school and on the job than their scores predict, especially in the long run. Most immigrant children with an IQ score of, say, 70 do poorly in school at first, but as they master the English language, their performance improves far more than we would expect of most children with an IQ of 70. In fact, on a nonverbal test such as the Progressive Matrices, immigrant children and deaf children get normal IQ scores (Vernon, 1967). (Note that when I say that the Stanford-Binet and Wechsler tests are "biased" against the deaf or the foreign born, I do not mean that the authors intentionally built in any bias. All I mean is that the tests make inaccurate predictions for those people.)

Psychologists, unfortunately, have not always been sensitive to the problem of test bias. In the late 1910s and early 1920s, hostility toward immigrants was widespread among U.S. citizens, including many psychologists. One prominent psychologist claimed that the results of IQ tests showed that over 80% of recent Russian, Jewish, Polish, and Hungarian immigrants were "feebleminded" (Gelb, 1986). Today it seems obvious that those immigrants were greatly impaired by their lack of familiarity with the English language and with U.S. culture and that the tests were heavily biased against them. At the time, though, many Americans were prepared to believe the worst about immigrants, and the test results were widely accepted. Laws enacted in 1924 greatly restricted immigration. It is difficult to reconstruct exactly how much influence psychologists had on the passage of that law (Snyderman & Herrnstein, 1983), but they certainly contributed to the regrettable climate of the time.

However, there is no solid evidence that IQ tests in current use are biased against racial minorities within the United States. Minority group students with a given IQ score generally do about as well in school and at other tasks as do middle-class whites with the same score (Cole, 1981; Lambert, 1981; Svanum & Bringle, 1982). Minority group students with a given SAT score generally do about as well in college as do white students with the same scores (McCornack, 1983). Because the tests are fairly accurate in predicting the performance of each group, they are not "biased" in the technical sense of that word.

One could still argue that our measures of school performance—that is, classroom grading—penalize blacks and other students who are unfamiliar with the vocabulary and experiences of the majority culture. By that reasoning, IQ tests give an "unbiased" prediction of school grades, but the grades themselves are unsatisfactory.

What about the fact that most of the psychologists who administer IQ tests are white? Does that fact constitute bias against blacks? Would black children score higher if the tests were administered by a black psychologist? That suggestion sounds reasonable, but the data do not support it. One review of 27 experiments found that the race of the psychologist administering the test had no consistent effect on the scores of either black or white children (Sattler & Gwynne, 1982).

Note that when I say the IQ tests show no demonstrable bias against minority groups, I am *not* saying that the differences in scores are due to differences in innate ability. In fact, we do not know why the races differ in their performance on IQ tests. We shall return to this question later in this section.

"*Students will rise to your level of expectation,*" says Jaime Escalante, the high school teacher portrayed by Edward James Olmos in Stand and Deliver. *The movie chronicles his talent for inspiring average students to excel in calculus. School counselors warned that he was asking too much of his students; parents said their kids didn't need calculus. And when his students first passed the advanced placement test in calculus, they were accused of cheating, a charge that seemed to reflect bias against the students, who were not white, middle-class, college-prep types. Since 1982, when his students first surprised his critics, the number of the school's students passing the test has increased each year. What does this success suggest about intelligence?*

Concept Checks

5. *A test of driving skills includes items requiring people to describe what they see. People with visual impairments score lower than do people with good vision. Is the test therefore biased against people with visual impairments? (Check your answer on page 373.)*

6. *Some police departments refuse to hire anyone who is shorter than a certain height. Does that rule produce a hiring bias against short people and against women (who tend to be shorter than men)? (Check your answer on page 373.)*

GROUP DIFFERENCES IN IQ SCORES

Binet and the other pioneers in IQ testing discovered that girls tend to do better than boys on language tasks, while boys tend to do better than girls on some visual-spatial and mathematical tasks. By

loading the test with one type of item, they could have "demonstrated" that girls are smarter than boys or that boys are smarter than girls. Instead, they carefully balanced the two types of items to ensure that the mean score of both girls and boys would be 100.

Girls' mean performance continues to be better than boys' on certain verbal tasks, especially those that depend on speech fluency. Similarly, on the average, boys still do better than girls in certain areas of mathematics, such as geometry. Over the second half of the 20th century, however, the differences between the sexes in both verbal and mathematical tasks have been gradually decreasing (Feingold, 1988; Hyde & Linn, 1988). (Why they are decreasing is unknown, as is the reason for their existence in the first place.)

Whites and blacks in the United States also differ in their mean performance on IQ tests. The mean score of whites is 100. The mean score of blacks is generally said to be 85, although that fig-

The question is not do heredity and environment affect intelligence but how do they affect it? In the Kennedy family, running for office (and winning) is like going into the family business. They have had the privileged upbringing of the very wealthy, but they have also shared a nurturing of ability and ambition and a zeal to compete. In a case such as this, we cannot separate the contributions of heredity from those of environment.

ure is based largely on old studies. The gap between blacks and whites on the SAT has been slightly but steadily decreasing over the years (Jones, 1984); the gap on the Stanford-Binet and Wechsler tests may also be decreasing. The reasons for the differences have proved hard to identify and consequently have become the subject of much controversy. We shall return to this question in a moment; first we shall consider the general question of how heredity and environment contribute to performance on IQ tests.

How Do Heredity and Environment Affect IQ Scores?

The British scholar Francis Galton (1869/1978) was the first to offer evidence that a tendency toward high intelligence is hereditary. As evidence, he simply pointed out that eminent and distinguished men—politicians, judges, and the like—generally had a number of distinguished relatives. We no longer consider that evidence convincing, because distinguished people share environment as well as genes with their relatives. Besides, becoming distinguished is only partly a matter of intelligence.

The question of how heredity affects intelligence has persisted to this day and has turned out to be difficult to answer to everyone's satisfaction. If we could control people as we control experimental animals, we could answer the question con-

clusively. We could take hundreds of babies from high-IQ parents and hundreds from low-IQ parents and then randomly assign half of each group to either high-IQ or low-IQ adoptive parents, as Figure 10.9 shows. We could see to it that none of the parents would "adopt" their own child and that none would know whether their adoptive child was from high-IQ or low-IQ parents. A few years later we could test the children to see whether their IQs matched those of their biological parents or those

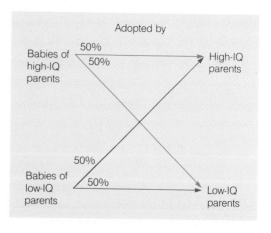

FIGURE 10.9

Effects of adoption: Design for an ideal but impossible experiment to determine the influence of heredity and environment on IQ scores.

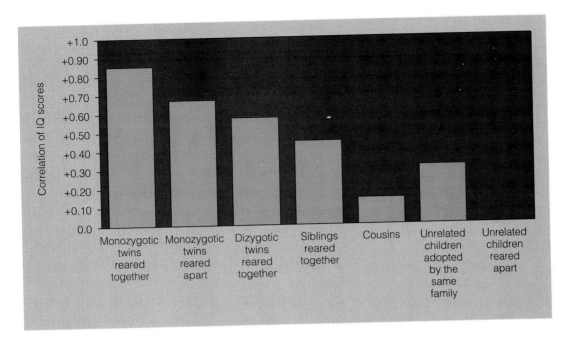

FIGURE 10.10

Mean correlations for the IQs of children with various degrees of genetic and environmental similarity. (Adapted from Bouchard & McGue, 1981.)

of their adoptive parents. Of course, we cannot conduct any such experiment.

For many years an extensive study of British twins reported by Cyril Burt seemed to provide decisive evidence. Burt's data conformed almost perfectly to the hypothesis that genetic differences are responsible for differences in IQ. Suspicious because the data conformed too perfectly, Leon Kamin (1974) carefully reexamined Burt's publications and uncovered numerous instances of vague procedures and some extremely unlikely patterns in the results. For instance, over a period of decades, as Burt added more and more children to his studies, he continued to get exactly the same correlation coefficients between the IQ scores of twins, even to the third decimal place! Moreover, he published some papers with two "coworkers" who were unknown to his university and to his colleagues. Burt died before the controversy arose, so we shall never know exactly what happened. The suspicion is strong, however, that he either distorted or fabricated much or all of his data. At any rate, we no longer take his reported findings seriously.

A number of other investigators (whose honesty is not in doubt) have also looked at the relationship of heredity and environment to intelligence. We shall consider the various types of evidence they have produced and note the strengths and weaknesses of each. The issues here are not limited to studies of IQ tests; they extend to any discussion of the influence of human heredity and environment.

Identical and Fraternal Twins Identical, or monozygotic, twins develop from a single fertilized egg;

consequently their heredity is identical (see Chapter 3). Fraternal, or dizygotic, twins develop from separate eggs; they are no more closely related than are a brother and sister. Figure 10.10, which is based on a review of the literature by Thomas Bouchard and Matthew McGue (1981), shows the correlations of IQ scores for monozygotic twins, dizygotic twins, and individuals with several other degrees of relationship. Note the stronger correlation between monozygotic twins than between dizygotic twins. The correlation in IQ scores is high for monozygotic twins even if they are reared in separate environments.

A single individual will usually get somewhat different scores on two successive tries at any IQ test, because no IQ test is perfectly reliable. On the average, that difference is about 6 points. Identical twins who take the same test at the same time differ from each other by about that same amount, and therefore their IQ scores correlate highly (Plomin & DeFries, 1980). Fraternal twins differ by a larger amount and nontwins by a still larger amount. Remoter relatives, such as cousins, have IQ scores that correlate positively, but not strongly.

These results are usually interpreted to mean that identical twins resemble each other more in IQ scores than fraternal twins do because their heredity is the same. Fraternal twins resemble each other more than nontwins resemble each other because the fraternal twins are the same age and have shared the same environment. In short, both heredity and environment have a significant influence on IQ scores.

Some psychologists have challenged this interpretation, saying that identical twins resemble each

Studies of adopted children indicate that their IQs resemble those of their biological parents more than those of their adoptive parents. Many psychologists think differences in heredity explain some variance in IQ scores, but how much remains unclear. One key factor is prenatal care—or the lack of it.

other more than fraternal twins only because their experiences are more similar. That is, parents and others may treat identical twins more similarly than they treat fraternal twins. However, researchers have found that identical twins who always *thought* they were fraternal twins resemble each other as much as other identical twins; fraternal twins who always *thought* they were identical twins resemble each other only as much as other fraternal twins, not as much as identical twins (Scarr, 1968; Scarr & Carter-Saltzman, 1979). That is, the main determinant of similarity in IQ is whether twins are actually identical, not whether they think they are identical. The reason for the similarity is more likely genetic than environmental.

Identical Twins Reared Apart   Several studies have reported that identical twins who have been adopted by different parents and reared in separate environments strongly resemble each other in IQ scores (Bouchard & McGue, 1981; Farber, 1981). That resemblance seems to suggest a strong genetic contribution to IQ. What happens, however, is that the "separate" environments have often been very similar (Farber, 1981; Kamin, 1974). In some cases the biological parents raised one twin and close relatives or next-door neighbors raised the other twin. Consequently, these results are difficult to interpret.

A further complication: The IQ scores of children are significantly affected by small differences

in age, and "8-year-old children" vary in age from exactly 8 years to 8 years and 11 + months. So twins, who are exactly the same age, will almost certainly resemble each other more than will two children "of the same age" chosen at random.

Adopted Children   Many psychologists believe that the most convincing evidence for a genetic influence comes from studies of adopted children. The IQ scores of children who are reared by their biological parents closely resemble their parents' IQ scores. The IQ scores of children who are reared by adoptive parents have less resemblance to their adoptive parents' IQ scores. In fact, the IQs of adopted children resemble the IQs of their biological parents more than they resemble the IQs of their adoptive parents (Scarr & Carter-Saltzman, 1982). Furthermore, the IQs of unrelated children adopted by the same family resemble each other less closely than the IQs of related children who are adopted by separate families (Teasdale & Owen, 1984).

The interpretation of these results is confounded to some extent by the policies of adoption agencies. Most adoption agencies place children of high-IQ parents with high-IQ adoptive parents. Thus, adopted children with high-IQ parents may develop high IQs themselves not just because of their heredity but also because of their environment. Still, the fact that adopted children resemble their biological parents *more* than they resemble their adoptive parents implies a significant role of heredity in IQ scores.

More than 90% of psychologists who specialize in testing believe that differences in heredity account for at least part of the variation in IQ scores (Snyderman & Rothman, 1987). They are in less agreement *how much* of the variation is due to heredity. Indeed, a few authorities remain unconvinced that heredity accounts for *any* of the variation (Kamin, 1974). Before we can draw firm conclusions, we will need more extensive research.

Note that even if we did conclude that heredity contributes to variation in IQ scores, we could not conclude that people are somehow stuck with the IQ they were born with. "Hereditary" does not mean "unmodifiable" (Angoff, 1988). Heredity does not control IQ (or anything else) directly; it controls how the individual reacts to the environment, sometimes in highly complex ways. It is possible that the environment that enables one group of children to achieve their full potential may not be the best for other children. Conceivably, some special environment may put children with a particular set of genes at an advantage, even though they are at a disadvantage in other environments. Again, we need more research.

Race and IQ Scores: WHAT'S THE EVIDENCE?

On the average, blacks in the United States score about 85 on IQ tests, 15 points lower than the average for whites. The difference is fairly constant on a variety of IQ tests. But measuring the difference does not explain its origin. Arthur Jensen (1969) argued that the difference is due largely to hereditary differences between the races. That was a highly controversial suggestion, to say the least, and a difficult one to test. Most of Jensen's data had to do with the contribution of heredity to IQ differences among whites; he argued that if hereditary differences are responsible for much of the variation in IQ within a race, they are likely to be responsible for part of the difference between races as well. However, the validity of that point is far from certain. It is generally agreed that differences in environment are larger between the average white family and the average black family than between two randomly chosen white families.

How could we test the contributions of heredity and environment to the race differences? One way would be to trade environments—have some black families raise white children and white families raise black children. Psychologists cannot conduct such an experiment, but they have examined what happens when white families adopt black children. (Black families seldom adopt white children.) They have also looked for a relationship between the IQs of black children and the relative degrees of their European and African ancestry. Let's examine two of the most carefully conducted studies.

STUDY 1

Hypothesis   If the IQ difference between the races is due partly to early experiences, then black children reared by white families will perform better on IQ tests than do most other black children.

Method   Sandra Scarr and Richard Weinberg (1976) located black children who had been adopted by white families in Minnesota. Many of these families also had adopted white children, and many had biological children of their own. IQ tests were administered to all the adopting parents and all the children.

Results   The mean IQ scores are shown in Figure 10.11.

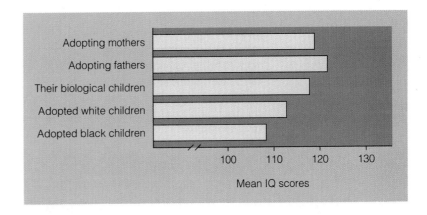

FIGURE 10.11

Results of the Scarr-Weinberg (1976) study. Black children and white children reared under similar conditions had similar, though not identical, IQ scores.

Interpretation   The mean IQ score of the adopted black children was not only higher than the mean of other black children (85) but also higher than the mean for the white population (100). This result provides impressive support for the idea that the difference in IQ between the races is due largely to environmental differences. The results, however, also suggest a possible role for heredity because both sets of adopted children scored lower than the adopting parents and their biological children scored. To test the possibilities further, Scarr and her colleagues conducted a second study.

STUDY 2

Hypothesis   If heredity is responsible for even part of the difference between the races in IQ performance, then blacks with a high percentage of European ancestry should obtain higher IQ scores than blacks with a lower percentage. (The mean for the U.S. black population is about 75 to 80% African ancestry and 20 to 25% European ancestry. Few U.S. blacks have 100% African ancestry.)

Method   The investigators (Scarr, Pakstis, Katz, & Barker, 1977) estimated the percentage of African ancestry for 362 black children in Philadelphia by means of blood typing. They examined 14 different blood factors—the familiar ABO blood types, the Rh factor, the Duffy factor, and 11 others. Some blood factors are more common in Europe than in Africa and vice versa. For example, type B blood is present in only 9% of Europeans but in 21% of Africans. No Europeans have Duffy type A-B- blood, while 94% of Africans do. By comparing each child's blood factors to the frequency of those blood factors in both Europe and Africa, the investigators estimated the degree of European ancestry for each child. They were under no illusion that their estimates were highly precise, but that was of no great concern. All that mattered was that, in general, children with higher estimated European ancestry had more actual European ancestry. Then they correlated their estimates of European ancestry with performance on Raven's Progressive Matrices and four other tests of intellectual performance.

Results The investigators tried several methods of weighting the importance of various blood factors to estimate European and African ancestry. Regardless of which method they used, they found virtually no correlation between the estimates of European ancestry and measures of performance.

Interpretation No one or two studies can ever resolve a question like this completely, and additional research would be helpful. (For example, as with any study, the investigators may have used a sample of children that was not representative of the entire population.) Still, we can safely say that the best available evidence indicates that hereditary factors account for little if any of the race differences in IQ. ■

SUMMARY

1. The designers of the standard IQ tests defined intelligence simply as the ability to do well in school. Psychologists with a more theoretical interest have defined intelligence by listing the abilities it includes. (page 361)

2. Different psychologists have drawn up different lists of the abilities that make up intelligence. Some define intelligence fairly narrowly; others include such abilities as social attentiveness, musical abilities, and motor skills. (page 361)

3. A number of "intelligent" abilities share a common element, known as the *g* factor, which is closely related to abstract reasoning and the perception of relationships. (page 362)

4. Psychologists distinguish between fluid intelligence (a basic reasoning ability that a person can apply to any problem, including unfamiliar types) and crystallized intelligence (acquired abilities to solve familiar types of problems). (page 362)

5. According to the triarchic theory of intelligence, intelligence has three types of components: metacomponents (which guide the planning of an approach to a problem), performance components (which guide the actual solving of a problem), and knowledge-acquisition components (which guide the acquisition of new knowledge). (page 363)

6. According to the multiple intelligences view, people possess many types of intelligence that are independent of one another. (page 365)

7. IQ tests have been accused of being biased against blacks and certain other minorities. Bias is defined as a systematic underestimation or overestimation of the performance of a group. By that definition, IQ tests are apparently not biased; they predict the school performance of blacks about as accurately as that of whites. (page 365)

8. To determine the contribution of heredity to the variation in scores on IQ tests, investigators consider three types of evidence: comparison of identical twins and fraternal twins, studies of identical twins reared apart, and studies of adopted children. Based on the available evidence, the role heredity plays in variations in intelligence is still debatable. (page 368)

9. Black children with a higher percentage of European ancestry have about the same mean IQ score as do black children with a lower percentage of European ancestry. These results suggest that heredity is not responsible for the difference in IQ scores between blacks and whites. (page 371)

SUGGESTIONS FOR FURTHER READING

Gardner, H. (1985). *Frames of mind.* New York: Basic Books. A theoretical description of separate "intelligences."

Sternberg, R. J. (Ed.). (1982). *Beyond IQ.* Cambridge, England: Cambridge University. An influential effort to describe the mental abilities that constitute intelligence

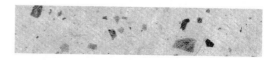

TERMS TO REMEMBER

bias a systematic underestimation or overestimation of the performance of a given group in a certain activity

concurrent validity the relationship between a test's scores and performances outside the test at approximately the same time

construct validity the degree to which the properties of a test correspond to a theoretical concept

content validity the degree to which the questions on a test represent the information that the test is meant to measure

crystallized intelligence acquired skills and knowledge and the application of that knowledge to specific content in a person's experience

fluid intelligence the basic power of reasoning and using information, including the ability to perceive relationships, deal with unfamiliar problems, and gain new types of knowledge

g Spearman's "general" factor that all IQ tests and all parts of an IQ test are believed to have in common

intelligence quotient (IQ) a measure of an individual's probable performance in school and in similar settings

mental age a measurement of an individual's intelligence, expressed as an age. Someone who performs as well as the average child of age *x* has a mental age of *x* years.

multiple intelligences Gardner's theory that intelligence is composed of numerous unrelated forms of intelligent behavior

norms descriptions of the frequencies at which particular scores occur

predictive validity the ability of a test's scores to predict behavior in another setting

Progressive Matrices an IQ test that attempts to measure abstract reasoning and is designed to be as fair as possible to people from a variety of cultures and backgrounds

psychometric the measurement of individual differences in abilities and behaviors

reliability the repeatability of a set of test scores

Scholastic Aptitude Test (SAT) a test of students' likelihood of performing well in college

standardization the process of selecting items for a test, determining its mean and standard deviation, and determining what various scores on the test mean

Stanford-Binet IQ test a test of intelligence, the first important IQ test in the English language

test-retest reliability the reliability of a test, as determined by comparing scores on an initial test with scores on a retest

triarchic theory Sternberg's theory that intelligence is governed by three types of process, which he refers to as metacomponents, performance components, and knowledge-acquisition components

utility usefulness of a test for a practical purpose

validity the degree to which a test measures what it is intended to measure

Wechsler Adult Intelligence Scale—Revised (WAIS-R) an IQ test commonly used with adults

Wechsler Intelligence Scale for Children—Revised (WISC-R) an IQ test commonly used with children, which yields a verbal score and a performance score as well as an overall IQ

Answers to Concept Checks

1. By definition, an average child has a mental age equal to his or her chronological age. For example, an average child of age 8 has a mental age of 8. Therefore, MA/CA = 1 for the average child. Because IQ = (MA/CA) × 100, such a child has an IQ of 100. (page 351)

2. Yes! To say that a test is "reliable" is simply to say that its scores are *repeatable*—that and *only* that. My test would give perfectly reliable (repeatable) measurements. True, they would be utterly useless, but that is beside the point. Reliability is not a measure of usefulness. (page 359)

3. No. An individual's score may be higher on the retest, either because of the practice at taking the test or because of the additional months of education. But the rank order of scores does not change much. That is, if a number of people retake the test, all of them are likely to improve their scores, but those who had the highest scores the first time will probably have the highest scores the second time. (page 359)

4. Yes, a test can have high reliability and low validity. A measure of intelligence determined by dividing head length by head width has high reliability (repeatability) but presumably no validity. A test with low reliability cannot have high validity, however. Low reliability means that the scores fluctuate randomly. If the test scores cannot even predict a later score on the same test, then they can hardly predict anything else. (page 359)

5. No, this test is not biased against people with visual impairments. It correctly determines that they are likely to be poor drivers. (page 367)

6. It is not obvious whether the height rule would create hiring bias against short people. To answer this, we would have to find out whether tall people make consistently better police officers than short people do. If they do, then using height as a test would not be biased; it would correctly predict a difference in performance. If short people perform police duties just as well as tall people do, then the rule would be biased. (page 367)

Answers to Other Questions in the Text

A. (p. 354)
1. (8) 2. (6)
3. (3) 4. (4)
5. (6) 6. (2)

CHAPTER

11

MOTIVATION

NASA is searching for a volunteer to make a solo trip to Mars. If you volunteer, you will journey for two or three years in a small, uncomfortable spacecraft, eating monotonous food and having no human companionship. You will have about a 20% chance of coming back to Earth alive. What you are offered in return is a chance to be the first human being to set foot on Mars. How would you respond to this opportunity? When I pose this question to large groups of students, most decline, but at least a few say they are ready to volunteer.

Nonhuman animals would respond more predictably. Although many animals display curiosity from time to time, they are mostly guided by their needs for food, water, sexual partners, and comfortable shelter. They also work to avoid pain and to protect their young. No rat would sacrifice its comfort or risk its life just to be the first rat on Mars.

Why do people devote so much of their time and energy, sometimes even risking their lives, for scientific, political, religious, or other abstract goals? Psychologists are still searching for an answer to that question; instead of attempting to answer it, we shall deal in this chapter with some aspects of motivation that are better understood.

We begin with an overview of some general principles of motivation. Then we shall explore three examples of motivated behaviors: hunger, sexual activity, and striving for achievement. I have selected these examples for emphasis largely because they are an important part of human life but also because they illustrate how our biology interacts with the social setting. Hunger is based on a biological need, but what, when, and how much we eat also depends on what we learn from other people. Sexual motivation also serves a biological need, but the search for a suitable partner is fundamentally a social behavior. Striving for achievement is learned as a method of pleasing and impressing others. Although it is primarily a social motivation, it is an outgrowth of the competition for dominance that we can observe throughout the animal kingdom.

What moves people to risk their lives scaling cliffs or sky diving? Some say they feel most alive when courting danger.

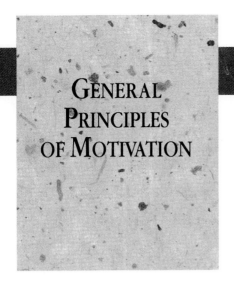

GENERAL PRINCIPLES OF MOTIVATION

What is motivation?
How could a psychologist determine whether an act is motivated or not?

Y‌ou are sitting quietly, reading a book, when suddenly you hear a loud noise. You jump a little and gasp. Was that action motivated? "No," you say. "I jumped involuntarily." Now I tell you that I want to do a little experiment. I shall tap my pencil; as soon as you hear it, you should try to jump and gasp just as you did the first time. I tap my pencil and, sure enough, you jump and gasp—not exactly as you did the first time, but approximately so. Was that action motivated? "Yes," you reply.

In both cases, I accept your answer. But we cannot always trust people's self-reports. Someone accused of murder says, "I didn't mean to kill. It was an accident." Your friend, who promised to drive you somewhere and then left without you, says, "I didn't do it on purpose. I just forgot." Maybe so and maybe not. How do we decide whether or not a behavior is motivated? We need a clear understanding of how motivated behaviors differ from unmotivated behaviors.

CHANGING VIEWS OF MOTIVATION

What is motivation? Let's try some definitions: "Motivation is what activates and directs behavior." Will that do? Light activates and directs the growth of plants, but we would hardly say that light "motivates" plants.

"Motivation is what makes our behavior more vigorous and energetic." That definition is no bet-

ter. Some people are strongly motivated to lie motionless for hours on end.

How about this: "Motivation is what changes one's preferences or choices"? That might do, except that we would first have to define *preference* and *choice*.

To be honest, it is hard to state precisely what we mean by motivation. Psychologists have repeatedly altered their views of motivation. By considering one theory after another, they have seen the shortcomings of each and have developed some idea of what is and is not motivation.

Motivation as an Instinctive Energy

Motivation, which comes from the same root as *motion*, is literally something that "moves" a person. So we might think of it as a type of energy. Sigmund Freud, the founder of psychoanalysis, proposed that the human nervous system is a reservoir of **libido**, a kind of sexual energy. As libido builds up, it demands an outlet, like air in an over-inflated balloon or hot water trapped under a geyser. If its normal outlet is blocked, it will discharge itself through some other channel. Freud used this concept to explain why people who are unable to release their libido in a normal way sometimes engage in irrational, self-defeating behaviors. If, for example, you had an impulse or an energy for engaging in some forbidden sex act, it might manifest itself in the form of nervous twitches (Freud, 1908/1963).

Konrad Lorenz, a pioneer in the field of ethology (the study of animal behavior under natural conditions), proposed a similar theory. According to Lorenz (1950), animals engage in instinctive acts when specific energies reach a critical level. For example, a male stickleback fish outside the breeding season has no specific energy for mating, and it will not respond sexually. At the start of the breeding season, it has a small amount of mating energy and it will court female stickleback fish (as we saw in Chapter 3). At the height of the breeding season, it has a great amount of mating energy and it will court females vigorously; it may even respond sexually to a piece of wood painted to resemble a female of its species.

Figure 11.1 illustrates Lorenz's model. A specific kind of energy builds up in the reservoir and flows into the tray below. The outlets in that tray represent ways of releasing the energy. If condi-

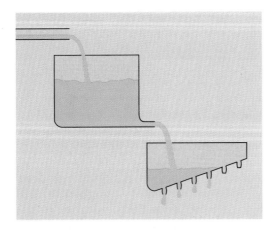

FIGURE 11.1

Motivation and frustration: Lorenz's model of displacement behavior. As energy (represented as a fluid) builds up in a "reservoir" in the brain, it needs to be discharged. Ordinarily, an instinct is released through natural or preferred outlets. If those are blocked, however, energy spills into another outlet, and the animal engages in an irrelevant behavior. (After Lorenz, 1950.)

tions are right, the energy is released through the lowest outlet—for example, mating with a normal partner. If that outlet is blocked and energy continues to build up, the energy will spill through one of the higher, less preferred outlets.

Both Freud and Lorenz based their theories on a conception of the nervous system that is now obsolete. They believed that every impulse to action had to be carried out in one way or another. We now know that under certain circumstances an impulse for a given behavior can simply be canceled or inhibited. (Recall that some synapses in the nervous system are excitatory and others are inhibitory.)

Drive Theories

Closely related to the instinctive energy theories, such as those of Freud and Lorenz, are theories that describe motivation as a **drive**, an internal state of unrest that energizes learned behaviors. According to Clark Hull (1943), drives arise from biological needs. Motivated behaviors reduce those needs and thereby reduce drives. Motivation, according to Hull's theory, is a kind of irritation that leads to one behavior after another until one of them reduces the irritation. For example, when you get a splinter in your finger, the discomfort motivates you to engage in various actions until you get rid of the splinter. The greater the irritation, the more vigorous your behavior.

Note the contrast: According to Freud and Lorenz, motivation leads to a particular kind of action, such as mating or fighting. According to Hull's drive theory, a motivation does not specify any particular action; it merely energizes whatever response will decrease the need or the drive. For example, Hull would say that if you could satisfy your hunger by pumping food directly into your stomach, without chewing it or tasting it, you would be willing to do so. Or if you could reduce your sexual urges by some means other than sexual activity, you would be satisfied to do so.

The principal shortcoming of Hull's theory is that it implies that people (and other animals) always try to reduce their drives and thereby their level of stimulation. In fact, we all seek variety and stimulation in our lives, some of us more than others. People who are described as high in *sensation seeking* are more attracted than most people are to parachute jumping, skiing, gambling, using drugs, trying foreign foods, and associating with unusual people (Zuckerman, Buchsbaum, & Murphy, 1980). It is difficult to think of their constant craving for variety and stimulation in terms of drive reduction.

Most psychologists today consider Hull's drive theory too narrow. It ignores the fact that a person's interest in food, for example, depends not only on hunger (an internal drive) but also on what foods are available. Similarly, interest in sex depends partly on an internal drive and partly on the presence or absence of a suitable partner.

Homeostasis

Beginning with the works of Walter Cannon (1929), psychologists have identified certain drives as homeostatic. **Homeostasis** is the maintenance of biological conditions within an organism—such as body temperature and weight and the amount of water in the body—at a state of equilibrium. For life to continue, each of these variables must remain within certain limits. Unlike a rock, which remains static only because nothing is acting on it, the homeostasis of the body is more like a spinning top; someone has to apply additional energy from time to time to keep it spinning. Homeostasis is maintained partly by physiological processes and partly by behavior. For example, we maintain constant body temperature partly by shivering, sweating, and other involuntary physiological responses and partly by putting on extra clothing, taking off excess clothing, or finding a more comfortable location. Many of our basic biological motivations, such as hunger and thirst, are homeostatic.

However, our behavior does not keep internal conditions completely constant (Hogan, 1980;

Satinoff, 1983). People eat more when they find tasty foods than when they find unappetizing foods; they eat and drink to be sociable even when they do not need food or water. Homeostatic drives contribute to our behavior, but they do not fully control any behavior.

Incentive Theories

Why do people ride roller coasters? It is doubtful that they have any drive or need to go thundering down a steep decline. Or suppose you have just finished a big meal and someone offers you a slice of a very special cake. If you are like most people, you eat it but hardly because you need it. Evidently, motivation is something more than an internal force that pushes us toward certain behaviors; it is also an **incentive**—an external stimulus that *pulls* us toward certain actions.

The distinction between a drive and an incentive is not clear cut. Jumping into a swimming pool on a hot summer day may satisfy your biological drive to maintain normal body temperature, but the prospect of splashing around in the water may serve as a strong incentive as well.

Most motivated behaviors are controlled by a combination of drives and incentives. You eat because you are hungry (a drive) and because you see appealing food in front of you (an incentive). How much you eat depends on both the strength of the drive and the appeal of the incentive.

Intrinsic and Extrinsic Motivations

Parallel to the distinction between drives and incentives is a distinction between intrinsic motivations and extrinsic motivations. An **intrinsic motivation** is a motivation to engage in an act for its own sake; an **extrinsic motivation** is based on the rewards and punishments the act may bring. For example, if you eat because you are hungry, you are following an intrinsic motivation; if you eat something you don't like in order to please the cook, you are following an extrinsic motivation. Most of our behavior is motivated by a combination of intrinsic and extrinsic motivations. An artist paints partly for the joy of creation (intrinsic) and partly for the eventual profit (extrinsic). You read this book partly because you enjoy reading it (I hope) and partly because you want to get a good grade on a test.

Does a combination of intrinsic and extrinsic motivations lead to more persistent and effective performance than, say, an intrinsic motivation alone? Not always. In a classic study, researchers gave four monkeys a device like the one in Figure 11.2 to

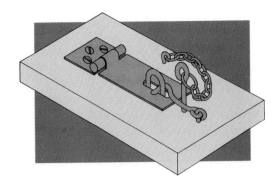

FIGURE 11.2

A device offered to monkeys—first as play and later as a way of getting food. (From Harlow, Harlow, & Meyer, 1950.)

play with. To open it, a monkey had to remove the pin, lift the hook, and lift the hasp, in that order. The monkeys played with the device from time to time over a period of 10 days. They received no reinforcements; they played with it apparently just for the fun of it (an intrinsic motivation). By the end of the 10 days, each monkey was able to open the device quickly, almost never getting the steps out of order. Then the device was placed over a food well in a place where the monkeys were accustomed to finding a raisin (an extrinsic motivation). If they opened the device they could get it. Suddenly their ability to open the device deteriorated. Instead of patiently removing the pin, the hook, and the hasp as they had done before, they attacked the hasp forcefully. They took longer to open the device for food than they had for play. Later, when they were given the device by itself with no food available, they opened it less frequently than before and made more errors in their attempts (Harlow, Harlow, & Meyer, 1950). Evidently, opening the device for food had become work, and the monkeys no longer saw it as play.

The same principle applies to human behavior: If people are given extrinsic reinforcements just for participating in an interesting activity, they become *less* interested in that activity, at least temporarily (Bates, 1979). For example, college students in one experiment were asked to try to arrange seven plastic pieces with complex shapes to match figures in a drawing. At one point halfway through the experiment, students in the experimental group were paid one dollar for each correct match. (Students in the control group did not know that the experimental group was being paid.) Then the experiment continued without pay for anyone. So long as the students in the experimental group were being paid, they worked harder than the students in the control group. After pay was suspended, the experimental group worked less than the control group did (Deci, 1971). Results such as these illustrate the **overjustification effect**: When people are given more extrinsic motivation than necessary to perform a task, their intrinsic motivation declines. According to one interpretation, people ask themselves, "Why am I doing this task?" They answer, "It's not because I enjoy the task. It's because I'm being paid." Once the extrinsic motivation is removed, the task seems uninteresting. The overjustification effect has been reported in a variety of settings, among both children and adults (Kassin & Lepper, 1984).

Does the overjustification effect imply that workers would enjoy their job more and work harder if they were not paid? Of course not. On the job, extrinsic motivators such as salary and bonuses are essential for good performance (Scott, 1976). But people do sometimes stay at a job for intrinsic reasons. A number of people who have won a million dollars or more in a state lottery have kept their jobs even after becoming financially secure (LeBlanc & LeBlanc, 1978).

Does the overjustification effect imply that children should not be rewarded for doing their homework? Maybe, maybe not. Faced with a page of addition or subtraction problems, most children have so little intrinsic motivation that an extrinsic motivation could do no harm. They may have to be bribed to complete such tedious arithmetic until they can get to the kinds of mathematics that are intrinsically more interesting. However, there may be some harm in rewarding children for reading stories or for performing any other task that they find reasonably interesting.

Concept Check

1. Many college students play tennis in their spare time. Are they following an intrinsic motivation or an extrinsic motivation? One student practices especially hard in hopes of becoming a professional player. Is that student following an intrinsic motivation or an extrinsic motivation? Given the overjustification effect, would you expect retired professional players to enjoy playing tennis more or less than other people do? (Check your answers on page 419.)

TYPES OF MOTIVATION

How many motivations do people have? They are motivated to obtain food, water, shelter, clothing, companionship, sexual activity. . . . The list could go

on. Can we group these into a few coherent categories?

Primary and Secondary Motivations

One way to categorize motivations is to distinguish primary motivations from secondary motivations. **Primary motivations**—such as the desire for food and water—serve obvious biological needs. **Secondary motivations** develop as a result of specific experiences; they do not serve any biological need directly, although they may lead indirectly to the satisfaction of primary motivations. For example, some people collect coins or stamps; they will go to great efforts to obtain a rare specimen that would motivate no more than a shrug from other people. A collector has learned to value these rare specimens because they may lead to recognition from fellow collectors and eventually to financial gain. (Primary motivations and secondary motivations are analogous to primary reinforcers and secondary reinforcers, discussed in Chapter 7. In both cases, *primary* implies the satisfaction of a biological need. *Secondary* implies learned.)

People can have an unlimited number of secondary motivations. Because the biological needs of the body are limited, psychologists expect to find only a limited number of primary motivations. Table 11.1 presents four examples of psychologists' attempts to list all the primary motivations.

If you study the lists closely you may see the complexity of the task. Each list includes one or more debatable entries, and none of them seems complete. All of them have omitted certain specialized motivations, such as the motivation to obtain vitamins and minerals. Moreover, none of these lists has any structure or organization. Each implies that all motivations are equally important and that every motivation is independent of the others. Wouldn't it make sense to group certain motivations together, such as urinating and defecating or the several kinds of avoidance? And shouldn't some motivations be distinguished as more important, or at least more urgent, than others?

Concept Check

2. Is your interest in graduating from college a primary motivation or a secondary motivation? (Check your answer on page 419.)

Maslow's Hierarchy of Needs

Abraham Maslow (1970) listed human motivations in an organized, structured way. His influential

TABLE 11.1 Four Lists of Primary Motivations

W. McDougall (1932)	P. T. Young (1936)	H. A. Murray (1938)	K. B. Madsen (1959)
Food seeking	Hunger	Inspiration	Hunger
Disgust	Nausea	Water	Thirst
Sex	Thirst	Food	Sex
Fear	Sex	Sentience	Nursing
Curiosity	Nursing	Sex	Temperature
Protective/parental	Urinating	Lactation	Pain avoidance
Gregarious	Defecating	Expiration	Excretion
Self-assertive	Avoiding heat	Urination	Oxygen
Submissive	Avoiding cold	Defecation	Rest/sleep
Anger	Avoiding pain	Pain avoidance	Activity
Appeal	Air	Heat avoidance	Security
Constructive	Fear/anger	Cold avoidance	Aggression
Acquisitive	Fatigue	Harm avoidance	
Laughter	Sleep		
Comfort	Curiosity		
Rest/sleep	Social instinct		
Migratory	Tickle		
Coughing/breathing			

Note: I have rephrased some of the words in more familiar language—for example, *pain avoidance* instead of *noxavoidance*.

proposal includes both primary motivations and secondary motivations. According to Maslow, our behavior is governed by a **hierarchy of needs**. The most basic are the physiological needs for food, drink, oxygen, and warmth, as shown at the bottom level of Figure 11.3. Maslow holds that these basic needs ordinarily take priority over all others. For example, people who are gasping for breath will do nothing else until they have satisfied their need for oxygen. Once they have satisfied their physiological needs, they seek to satisfy their safety needs, such as security from attack and avoidance of pain. When those needs are satisfied, they proceed to the needs for love and belonging—making friends and socializing with them. Next come the needs for esteem, such as gaining prestige and a feeling of accomplishment. At the apex of Maslow's hierarchy is the need for **self-actualization**, the need to achieve one's full potential.

Maslow's theory is appealing because it recognizes a wide range of human motivations—from satisfying our biological needs to savoring the joy of accomplishment. Moreover, it suggests that the various motivations are not equal. When they conflict, the basic physiological needs take priority over safety needs, which take priority over the need for love, and so on.

Maslow's hierarchy has been widely accepted, although it has inspired little research, and what research has been done has often failed to support the theory (Wahba & Bridwell, 1976). No evidence supports the idea that motivations fall into five distinct categories. That is, the differences between the need for oxygen and the need for food (both basic physiological needs) are as great as the differences between the need for love and the need for self-esteem. More importantly, people sometimes work to satisfy higher-level needs before they satisfy lower-level needs. Even when you are ravenously hungry, you might skip a meal to be with someone you love, or to study for a test, or to accept an award. Martyrs have willingly sacrificed their lives to advance some political or religious cause. Depending on the circumstances, almost any motivation may take priority over the others, at least temporarily.

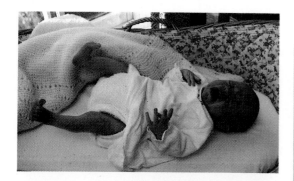

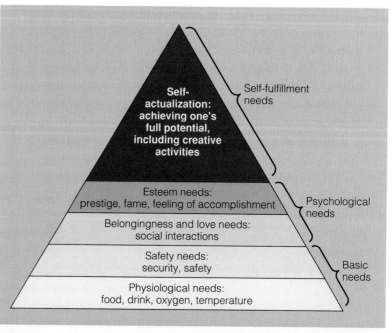

Self-fulfillment needs

Self-actualization: achieving one's full potential, including creative activities

Esteem needs: prestige, fame, feeling of accomplishment

Psychological needs

Belongingness and love needs: social interactions

Safety needs: security, safety

Basic needs

Physiological needs: food, drink, oxygen, temperature

FIGURE 11.3

Maslow's hierarchy of needs imposes an appealing, commonsensical order to human behavior: If you are thirsty, you will want to drink something to meet that basic need. If your primary physical needs are met, you can focus on meeting psychological needs for companionship and achievement. Your final efforts will be devoted to reaching your potential. But do all people follow this principle? Some people, including Olympic performers, sacrifice eating, drinking, and companionship to strive toward athletic accomplishment and prestige. Artists might also give up some physical comforts and social pleasures to focus on an inner vision and to realize their creative potential.

GENERAL PROPERTIES OF MOTIVATED BEHAVIOR

What, if anything, do various types of motivated behavior have in common? The foremost characteristic of motivated behaviors is that they are goal directed (Pervin, 1983). They have a quality of "persistence until." A person or animal engages in one behavior after another until reaching the goal. When you feel cold, you do not always do one particular thing. You may go inside, put on a sweater, huddle with others, run around, or just stand and shiver, depending on the circumstances. Similarly, when you are hungry, you may act in a number of ways to obtain food. To determine whether a particular behavior is motivated, as opposed to automatic or reflexive, an observer needs to watch the individual over a period of time in a variety of circumstances. If the individual varies the behavior at different times and persists until reaching a goal, then the behavior is motivated, or intentional.

Something to Think About

A frog flicks its tongue at a passing insect, captures it, and swallows it. The behavior serves to satisfy the frog's need for food, so we might guess that it is motivated. However, the behavior appears to be as constant as a reflex. How might you determine whether or not the behavior is motivated?

A second characteristic of motivated behaviors is that they vary from time to time, under the influence of both internal (biological) and external (social) controls (Pervin, 1983). For example, you wear clothes to keep yourself warm, to look attractive, to display your exquisite taste, and to avoid arrest for indecent exposure. Exactly what clothing and how much clothing you wear depends on what you feel like doing, today's weather, and the people you expect to see. We have more than one motivation for almost everything we do.

Motivated behaviors vary from person to person as well as from situation to situation. People do not differ much in their drive for oxygen, but they differ significantly in their search for food, still more in their motivation for sexual activity, self-esteem, and self-fulfillment—the needs near the top of Maslow's hierarchy. In the rest of this chapter, we shall return periodically to the ways in which people differ in their motivations.

SUMMARY

1. Sigmund Freud and Konrad Lorenz viewed motivated behaviors as outlets for instinctive energies. They believed that specific energies accumulated in the nervous system and had to be released in one way or another. Their theories were based on a now-obsolete concept of the nervous system. (page 377)

2. Clark Hull described motivation as a drive that could energize learned behaviors. According to this view, motivated behavior persists until it reduces the drive. The weaknesses of this theory: It implies that people always wish to decrease their level of stimulation, and it ignores the importance of external stimuli in the formation of motivations. (page 378)

3. Many motivations are at least partly homeostatic; that is, they tend to maintain internal conditions in a nearly constant state. (page 378)

4. Motivations are partly under the control of incentives—external stimuli that pull us toward certain actions. Both drives and incentives control most motivated behaviors. (page 379)

5. People and animals engage in some actions because the actions themselves are interesting or pleasing. Providing an external reinforcement for the actions may actually reduce the interest or pleasure they provide. (page 379)

6. Psychologists have made several attempts to list or categorize various motivations. One prominent attempt, offered by Abraham Maslow, arranged needs in a hierarchy ranging from basic biological needs at the bottom to the need for self-actualization at the top. His claim that people satisfy their lower needs before their higher needs does not apply in all cases. (page 380)

7. Motivated behaviors persist until the individual reaches a goal. They are controlled by internal and external forces and by biological and social forces. Motivated behaviors vary from time to time, from situation to situation, and from person to person. (page 383)

SUGGESTION FOR FURTHER READING

Mook, D. G. (1987). *Motivation: The organization of action.* New York: Norton. A theoretical treatment of the basic principles of motivation.

MOTIVATION AND BIOLOGICAL STATES: THE CASE OF HUNGER

What causes us to feel hungry?
How do we choose which foods to eat?
Why do some people gain excessive weight
and others deliberately lose weight
to a dangerous level?

In the 1970s, the United States suffered a gasoline shortage. Sometimes drivers found that every service station in their area was out of gas. After a few such experiences, they stopped taking chances. Whenever they saw a station with gas, they would stop and fill their tank, even if it was already more than half full.

If you expect to have trouble finding food from time to time, a good strategy is to fill up your "tank" whenever you can. Throughout most of human existence, people have had to contend with periodic food shortages and famines. To many of our ancestors, the idea of going on a diet to lose weight would have made no sense at all.

Today, most people in the United States, Canada, and Europe have more than enough to eat at all times. The strategy of filling the tank as often as possible is no longer helpful, and many people habitually overeat.

Social pressures make matters even worse. When you visit friends or relatives, they may offer you food as a gesture of affection, and they may act hurt if you refuse their hospitality. Say you visit the family of your boyfriend or girlfriend, and you want to make a good impression. "Dinner's ready!" someone calls. You go into the dining room and find a huge meal, which your hosts clearly expect you to enjoy. Do you explain that you are not hungry because you already made a pig of yourself at lunch? Probably not.

Eating is controlled by many motives, both physiological and social. We eat to get needed nutrition but also to experience tastes and to socialize.

PHYSIOLOGICAL MECHANISMS OF HUNGER

Hunger is a homeostatic drive that serves to keep fuel available for the body to use. Specialized mechanisms in the brain monitor how much fuel is available; when supplies begin to drop, the brain triggers behaviors that lead to eating. But how does the brain know how much fuel is available and therefore how much a person should eat and how often?

The problem is far more complex than keeping enough fuel in a car's gas tank. When the fuel gauge shows that the tank is running low, you fill it with gas. Your body cannot simply keep track of how much fuel is in your stomach. Right now, in addition to the fuel in your stomach and intestines, a fair amount of fuel is present in every cell of your body, ready to be used. Additional fuel is circulating in your blood, ready to enter cells that need it. Still more fuel is stored in fat cells, available to be converted into a form that can enter the blood. If necessary, your body can break down muscle tissues to provide additional fuel. Whereas your car will stop within seconds after it uses all the fuel in the gas tank, your body can keep going for days, even weeks, after your stomach is empty.

Unlike your car, which uses only gas, your body needs a complex mixture of proteins, fats, and carbohydrates, plus assorted vitamins and minerals. How much you should eat at a given meal depends both on how much nutrition you need and on exactly what combination of nutrients is present in the foods you are eating. How can your brain possibly get it right?

Fortunately, it doesn't need to. The brain monitors how much fuel you need, based on the fuel available in your cells and circulating in your blood. When the need for more fuel is great enough, you feel hungry. How much you eat in your next meal corresponds only loosely to how much you need. If you eat too little, you will feel hungry again soon. If you eat too much, part of the excess will be temporarily stored as fat and later converted from fat to sugars that can enter your bloodstream. As a result, you won't feel hungry again as soon as usual. You do not have to eat exactly the correct amount in a given meal; you can correct your errors over the next few meals.

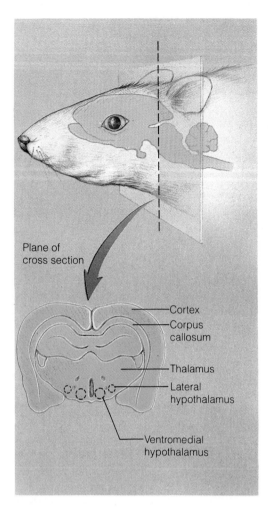

FIGURE 11.4

The lateral (side) and ventromedial (lower-middle) regions of the hypothalamus, which regulates internal organs—such as the stomach—and influences behavior related to them—such as eating. This side view of a rat's head (above) indicates the plane of the ear-to-ear section (below) of the brain that shows the two regions. (After Hart, 1976.)

The Short-Term Regulation of Hunger

To determine how much fuel your body needs at a given moment, your brain keeps track of several factors (Friedman & Stricker, 1976). One of the most important factors is **glucose**, the most abundant sugar in your blood. Many of the foods you eat can be converted into glucose; so can your body's fats. An important source of energy for all parts of the body, glucose is the main source of energy for the brain. The brain monitors the amount of glucose and other fuels that enters the cells. If the amount is insufficient, certain parts of the brain produce the sensation of hunger. One part of the brain, the **lateral hypothalamus** (Figure 11.4), plays an impor-

tant role in this process, although it is hardly the only important area. After damage to the lateral hypothalamus, individuals eat less and lose weight; some starve to death in the presence of good food.

The amount of glucose entering the cells at any given time depends partly on the amount of glucose present in the blood, but that amount does not fluctuate widely under normal circumstances (LeMagnen, 1981). How much glucose enters the cells depends mainly on the hormone **insulin**, which the pancreas releases to increase the entry of glucose into the cells. It also increases the amount of a meal that is stored as fats. Figure 11.5 shows its effect on hunger and eating. When insulin levels are very low, as in the medical condition diabetes, little glucose enters the cells and the person feels hungry. People with diabetes may eat a great deal without gaining weight because the food they eat cannot enter the cells—not even the fat cells (Lindberg, Coburn, & Stricker, 1984). They simply excrete much of what they eat.

At medium levels of insulin, enough glucose enters the cells to satisfy hunger. As glucose goes from the blood to the cells, stored fats are converted to glucose to replenish the blood's supply. With medium levels of insulin, glucose can enter the cells, but the body does not store much of the circulating glucose as fats. In fact, some of the body's fats are converted to glucose that enters the blood. As a result, the person does not feel hungry. When insulin levels are high, glucose continues to enter the cells easily, but a high percentage of it is converted to fats and stored in fat cells. The glucose level in the blood begins to drop, and hunger increases. (Figure 11.6 shows the relationship between glucose level and food intake.) People with constantly high insulin levels gain weight yet feel starved (Johnson & Wildman, 1983). Most of what they eat is stored as fat, and little of it is reconverted to glucose (LeMagnen, 1981). For most people, insulin levels fluctuate from the medium range to the high range.

Damage to the **ventromedial hypothalamus** in the brain raises the insulin level and leads to weight gain (Figure 11.7). No matter how much the person or animal eats, most of it is converted to fats and stored in the cells. Glucose levels in the blood stay low, and hunger is high (Friedman & Stricker, 1976; King, Smith, & Frohman, 1984).

Concept Checks

3. Insulin levels fluctuate cyclically over the course of a day. Would you guess that they are higher in the middle of the day, when hunger is high, or late at night, when hunger is generally low? (Check your answer on page 419.)

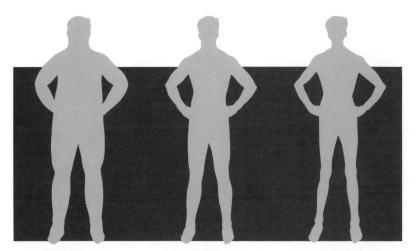

High insulin
Food is stored as fat. Little glucose in blood. Appetite increases; Weight increases.

Lower insulin
Fat supplies are converted to glucose. Appetite is lower.

Very low insulin
Glucose cannot enter cells. Appetite is high but much of nutrition is excreted. Weight decreases.

FIGURE 11.5

How insulin affects glucose, appetite, and weight.

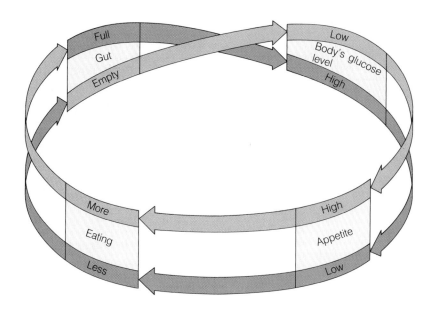

FIGURE 11.6

To maintain equilibrium, homeostatic regulating systems, such as the one for food intake shown here, provide a feedback mechanism. Low levels of glucose—the brain's primary energy source—stimulate the hypothalamus, which prompts the pancreas to release insulin and raise the levels of glucose. Once the glucose reaches a certain level, control mechanisms act to lower it.

The guinea pig is so commonly used in experiments that its name is synonymous with research subject. *By conducting animal research, researchers studying obesity can explore disorders in human metabolism.*

FIGURE 11.7

An obese rat with a damaged ventromedial hypothalamus compared with a normal rat. Because of its brain damage, the overweight rat can eat less than an ordinary rat does and still gain weight. Yet the brain damage also makes the rat hungrier—a no-win situation. This rat's excess fat prevents it from grooming its fur.

Burger binge: We say we are "full" when we're no longer hungry. That feeling is satiety. We all sometimes eat when we aren't hungry. For example, many people automatically munch snacks while watching TV. And as TV commercials for indigestion indicate, some people don't know when to stop eating.

4. Does damage to the lateral hypothalamus lead to weight gain or weight loss? Does damage to the ventromedial hypothalamus lead to weight gain or weight loss? (Check your answers on page 419.)

Satiety

The brain monitors the levels of glucose and other nutrients in the cells to determine when the body needs more fuel. But when you start to eat, how does your brain know when you should stop?

Satiety (sah-TI-uht-ee) is the experience of being full, of feeling no more hunger. Ordinarily, satiety depends mostly on stomach distention. When the stomach is full, you feel sated (Deutsch, Young, & Kalogeris, 1978). Food entering the small intestine may also contribute to the feeling of satiety, possibly by causing the intestine to release a certain hormone (Smith & Gibbs, 1987). Moreover, if you are eating a familiar, calorie-rich diet, you may stop eating long before your stomach is full because you have learned how much energy to expect from the food (Deutsch, 1983).

The Long-Term Regulation of Hunger

You eat some meals that are rich in calories and some that are low in calories. You probably never eat a meal that contains exactly the number of calories you have burned since your last meal. What would happen if you made a slight but consistent error in the size of each meal? If you consistently ate just 5% more than you needed, you would gain 15 pounds (7 kilograms) per year (Jéquier, 1987). If you consistently ate 5% less than you needed, you would eventually starve to death.

The brain prevents this kind of error by monitoring body weight over time. That long-term mechanism compensates for errors made by the short-term mechanisms of hunger and satiety. When you lose weight, for whatever reason, you feel hungrier and eat more until you gain the weight back. Conversely, when you gain weight, you feel less hungry and cut back on your eating until you lose the weight again. All this happens automatically; you do not need to check the scales each day. Over the course of months, most people maintain a nearly constant body weight. That weight is referred to as a **set point**—a level that the body attempts to maintain.

When someone eats less food than usual for a few days, appetite increases during the next few days; conversely, after a huge meal (Thanksgiving dinner, for example), appetite decreases. Note that the physiological regulators maintain a *constant* weight, but not necessarily a normal or healthy weight. Some people fluctuate around a low weight; others fluctuate around a much higher weight. Most adults maintain almost the same weight year after year, unless they become ill, change their way of life, or make a deliberate effort to lose weight.

Concept Check

5. After damage to the ventromedial hypothalamus, an animal's weight eventually reaches a higher than usual level and then fluctuates around that amount. What has happened to the set point? (Check your answer on page 419.)

MOTIVES IN FOOD SELECTIONS

So far I have discussed how you determine when and how much to eat. A separate issue, just as important, is how you determine which foods to eat. Within a fairly wide range, you can vary your choices from day to day without noticing much effect. Consider the following analogy.

One day the chef made soup out of nothing but

An adventure in fine dining: Very young children will try eating almost anything—dirt, cigarette butts, lipstick—at least once. Later they may become finicky eaters and refuse to even try certain vegetables and other foods.

vegetables: broccoli, potatoes, carrots, peas, beans, onions, corn, a pinch of salt, and lots of water. The next day the chef used chicken, beef, tomatoes, cheese, spices, and some fruit. Surprisingly, the soup turned out almost the same as it did the day before. It filled up the pot a bit more, but it was basically the same soup. In fact, no matter how exotic the ingredients the chef added, the soup always ended up about the same.

That "soup" is your body. The chef (your hand) throws in different ingredients every day, and sometimes you fill up the pot a little more than usual. But your body stays about the same. The human digestive system has an amazing ability to turn almost any food into tissues and energy.

But not all ingredients are acceptable. Sand and furniture polish are definitely out. And the system needs some variety. If you eat just one food day after day, you are likely to end up ill. Yet, within a fairly wide range, you can exert much freedom in your choice of foods.

Nevertheless, most people acquire strong food preferences. How do we decide what to eat? Mainly we learn what *not* to eat. Toddlers around the age of 1½ will put almost anything into their mouth and try to eat it. Gradually they learn to avoid insects, hair, soap, paper, leaves, and other items that adults consider inedible (Rozin, Hammer, Oster, Horowitz, & Marmora, 1986). Up to age 7 or 8, almost the only reason children give for refusing to eat something is that they think it would taste bad (Rozin, Fallon, & Augustoni-Ziskind, 1986). As they grow older, they give a wider variety of reasons for accepting certain foods and rejecting others, ranging from the taste of the food to the associations it arouses. Food selection is a complex matter; as with other motivations, it depends on a combination of physiological, social, and cognitive factors. Let's consider some of the most important factors.

Acceptance or Rejection of Foods Based on Taste

Some taste preferences are present at birth. Infants readily consume sweet liquids; when they taste something bitter or sour, they turn their head and spit it out.

At least one taste preference can be triggered by an abnormal condition within the body. One boy showed a strong craving for salt. As an infant, he licked the salt off crackers and bacon but refused to eat the food itself. One of the first words he learned was *salt*. He put a thick layer of salt on everything he ate and sometimes he ate salt by itself. When deprived of salt, he ate almost nothing and began to waste away. At the age of 3½, he was taken to the hospital and fed the usual hospital fare. He soon died of salt deficiency (Wilkins & Richter, 1940).

It turned out that the boy's adrenal glands were defective (Figure 11.8). These glands secrete hormones that enable the body to retain salt. The boy craved such great amounts of salt because salt was being excreted so rapidly from his body. (We are often told to limit our salt intake for health reasons, but too little salt can also be dangerous.)

Research on animals confirms that a deficiency of salt in the body triggers an immediate craving for salty foods. As soon as animals, including humans, become salt deficient, they show a heightened preference for salty tastes (Rozin & Kalat, 1971). People who have lost large quantities of salt as a result of bleeding or heavy sweating often express a craving for salt. In short, changes in body chemistry can alter a person's motivation to choose a particular food.

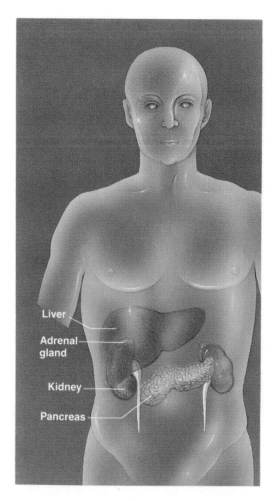

FIGURE 11.8

Location of the adrenal glands in the human body.

You eat what you are: Most of us prefer to eat food we're well acquainted with. We eat turkey and pumpkin pie on Thanksgiving because our ancestors did. These Hmong refugees from Laos live in California; they could have turkey on the fourth Thursday of November, but that holiday is not part of their heritage, and they prefer preparing foods familiar to them. If you have enjoyed trying novel dishes, you may explore menus at different restaurants. But if you've stung your tongue eating hot peppers, gotten nauseous noshing knishes, and had hives after sampling shellfish, you may decide to stick to meat and potatoes.

Restaurant listings in the Yellow Pages reflect the ethnic makeup of a city. San Francisco, for example, has several Burmese and Cambodian restaurants and dozens of places specializing in Chinese cuisine, while Miami has many Cuban restaurants.

Preference for Familiar Foods

Although people eat a wide variety of foods, they are cautious about eating foods they have never eaten before. Think about the first time you tried artichokes, jalapeño peppers, or coffee, for example. Although you probably enjoy new combinations of familiar ingredients, you tend to be wary of a new food or drink. If you ever become ill after eating something, you are likely to be even more cautious about eating something new (Rozin, 1968).

Members of every culture and every ethnic group become familiar with its preferred ways of preparing and seasoning foods. Children who grow up in Italian families come to prefer foods flavored with tomato, garlic, and olive oil. Mexican children at first dislike jalapeños as much as any other children do, but by the time they reach adulthood, they insist on having them with almost every meal. Cuisine is one of the most stable features of human cultures. In the United States, for example, the children and grandchildren of immigrants tend to follow the food choices of their forebears long after they have discarded other old-country customs.

People can also acquire a taste for a given amount of a flavor. For example, they may grow accustomed to a high-salt diet or a low-salt diet (Beauchamp, 1987). If they use a great deal of salt on their food, they may come to prefer salty tastes more than other people do; once they reduce their salt intake, their preference for salty tastes gradually declines. In short, food preferences depend largely on familiarity.

Learned Associations with Foods

As mentioned in Chapter 7, animals associate foods with the gastrointestinal consequences of eating them. The same is true of humans. When you eat something and later get sick, you may form a strong aversion to that food, especially if it was unfamiliar. Ordinarily, that aversion occurs because something in the food made you ill, but the same learning takes place even if something else caused the illness. A person who eats a greasy corn dog at an amusement park and then goes on a wild ride and gets sick may find corn dogs repulsive from then on. The person may "know" the ride was at fault, but somehow an area deep in the brain associates the food with the sickness.

This tendency to associate certain foods with sickness usually is an aid to survival. It helps us to learn which substances are safe and which are harmful. For cancer patients, however, the tendency creates a special problem: Patients undergoing certain kinds of chemotherapy feel nauseated after every treatment. Over time, they may learn an aversion to every food they ate before every treatment (Bernstein, 1985; Bernstein & Borson, 1986). They may end up eating almost nothing.

One way to avoid that danger is for a cancer patient to be given the same food before every chemotherapy session. The patient makes that one food the scapegoat and associates it strongly with the ensuing nausea. No such association is made with foods eaten at other times (Mattes, 1988).

Moreover, people sometimes reject safe, nutritious foods because they have learned to associate them with something that evokes repulsive associations (Rozin & Fallon, 1987; Rozin, Millman, & Nemeroff, 1986). In our society, most people refuse to eat brains or any part of a dog, cat, or horse. Most Americans are repelled by the very thought of eating an insect. Insects are quite nutritious; many

Since you got sick after riding a roller coaster, you've avoided the cotton candy and chili dogs you ate just before riding the roller coaster. Learned associations with food can also be positive. The aroma of a barbecue may recall summer weekends at home. Or you may find comfort in gravy and mashed potatoes fixed just like Mom used to make.

Just seeing this aborigine eating a grub may make you feel queasy. In every culture, people enjoy foods that others find repulsive: snails, tripe, grasshoppers, eel, sweetbreads, raw oysters, fish roe, beef tongue. To many Europeans, for example, corn on the cob is barnyard feed, not something for people to eat.

As Orson Welles noted, "Gluttony is not a secret vice." But obesity isn't necessarily a sign of gluttony; some overweight people eat less than some thin people do. Besides, saying people are fat because they eat too much is like saying alcoholics drink too much—a self-evident answer that fails to explain why the disorder occurs.

birds eat nothing else. Why then do people refuse to eat them? Apparently it is not because the insect might be carrying germs; most people say they would refuse to eat even a *sterilized* cockroach (Rozin & Fallon, 1987). They also say they would refuse to drink a glass of apple juice after a dead, sterilized cockroach had been dipped into it. After seeing a cockroach dipped into a glass of apple juice, some people even refuse to drink other apple juice poured into a different glass (Rozin, Millman, & Nemeroff, 1986).

EATING DISORDERS

The mechanisms I have discussed so far enable most people to select a reasonable, well-balanced diet and to maintain their weight within normal limits. In some individuals, the motivational mechanisms go awry. They feel hungry all the time and eat too much, or they alternate between stuffing themselves and starving themselves, or they feel hungry but refuse to eat. Some of these disorders result from physiological abnormalities; others result from social and cognitive influences that compete with the normal physiological mechanisms.

Obesity

Obesity is the excessive accumulation of body fat. A body weight 20 to 40% above the standard for a person's height is considered mild obesity. Weight 41 to 100% above the standard is considered mod-

erate obesity. Weight more than 100% above the standard is considered severe obesity (Berkow, 1987). Why do some people become seriously overweight? Obviously because they take in more calories than they use up. But *why* do they do that? One reason, as we have seen, is that some people have high levels of insulin, which causes much of the food they eat to be stored as fats. Let's consider some other possible reasons.

Emotional Disturbances   One prevalent idea is that people overeat in response to anxiety, depression, or some other emotional problem. Carbohydrate snacks act like tranquilizers through a complex mechanism. The carbohydrates raise the body's levels of insulin, which in turn facilitates the entry of glucose into the cells, as mentioned earlier. Insulin also helps several amino acids enter the cells. As those amino acids leave the blood, the relative proportion of other amino acids in the blood increases. One of those is the amino acid *tryptophan*; the brain converts it into the neurotransmitter serotonin, which promotes relaxation. In essence, carbohydrates set in motion a chain of events that leads to a feeling of calmness (Wurtman, 1985). When some people feel low, they try to cheer themselves up by overeating. In one survey of 100 adults (Edelman, 1981), 40 said that they overeat three or more times a month when they fall into an unpleasant mood. When they feel nervous, tired, lonely, or sorry for themselves, they set out on a binge of eating. Afterward, they feel bloated and regret having eaten so much, but they also feel calm and relaxed.

Is there any evidence that emotional problems cause *permanent* overweight? No. Edelman's study revealed that as many normal-weight people as overweight people engage in eating binges. Moreover, other evidence indicates that overweight people, on the average, experience about the same emotional problems as other people do. The prevalence of anxiety, depression, and other psychological concerns is no greater among obese people than among other people of the same age and the same overall health (Wadden & Stunkard, 1987). Apparently, the only difference is that severely overweight people feel lonely and depressed *as a result* of being overweight.

Overresponsiveness to the Taste of Foods   Like humans, rats will become obese under certain conditions. We can make a rat obese either by damaging parts of its brain or by feeding it a diet rich in sweet and fatty foods (Blundell, 1987). As rats grow more and more obese, they become increasingly finicky about their food. They overeat when

*P*arents sometimes use food as a reward or consolation prize. Bribing with sweets is common: "If you put all your toys away, you can have some cookies." Such practices may encourage eating patterns that later lead to obesity.

"*Y*our eyes are bigger than your stomach": Schachter's externality hypothesis maintains that overweight people are guided by taste, sight, and smell rather than by need. French haute cuisine devotes much attention to the appearance of food, and nouvelle cuisine is largely the art of arrangement. As Julia Child said, "It's so beautifully arranged on the plate—you know someone's fingers have been all over it."

they are offered highly palatable foods, but they undereat when they are offered less tasty foods (Sclafani & Springer, 1976; Teitelbaum, 1955). Apparently their eating is guided more by incentives (the taste of food) than by drives (the body's need for food).

Might the same be true of overweight people? According to the **externality hypothesis** (Schachter, 1971; Schachter & Rodin, 1974), overweight people are motivated more strongly by external cues (such as the taste and appearance of food) than by internal cues (the physiological mechanisms that control hunger). Perhaps the tendency to overeat tasty foods leads people to gain weight.

Stanley Schachter (1968, 1971) supported this hypothesis with some very simple experiments. In one case, college students were told they were taking part in a taste experiment. They were all given a milkshake and were told to drink as much of it as they wanted. Then they were asked to rate its flavor. Overweight students drank more than the normal-weight students when the milkshake tasted good, but less when it tasted bad (Figure 11.9).

Does this result indicate that people become overweight *because* they are motivated more strongly by taste than by the need for food? Maybe, maybe not. It is equally plausible that they respond more strongly to external cues *after* becoming overweight.

Decreased Energy Output The common assumption is that overweight people overeat. That is often true, but not always. Many overweight people consistently eat normal or even small meals and still fail to lose weight (DeLuise, Blackburn, & Flier, 1980).

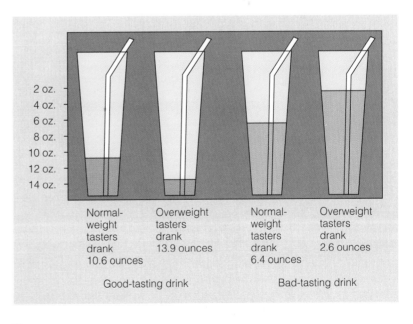

2 oz.			
4 oz.			
6 oz.			
8 oz.			
10 oz.			
12 oz.			
14 oz.			

Normal-weight tasters drank 10.6 ounces

Overweight tasters drank 13.9 ounces

Normal-weight tasters drank 6.4 ounces

Overweight tasters drank 2.6 ounces

Good-tasting drink

Bad-tasting drink

FIGURE 11.9

Good taste: Results of Schachter's experiments. Overweight tasters drank more of the good-tasting milkshake but less of the bad-tasting drink than their normal-weight counterparts did. What do these findings tell us about the taste sensitivity of overweight people?

Obesity runs in families, partly because of low energy expenditure. Even in the first year of life, infants born to overweight mothers tend to be less active and to burn off less energy than the infants of normal-weight mothers.

This patient is having her oxygen consumption measured. This measure of physical fitness, along with cholesterol counts and fat-to-body-weight ratios, may help people identify bad eating habits. But many nutritional uncertainties remain about how consuming or avoiding different foods affects human health.

They become and remain overweight not because they take in too much energy but because they expend too little.

Obesity tends to run in families (Stunkard et al., 1986). By studying infants born to obese parents, we may be able to learn something about what predisposes individuals to obesity. One group of investigators compared the infants of 12 overweight mothers and 6 normal-weight mothers over their first year of life. All the babies weighed about the same at birth, but 6 of the babies of the overweight mothers had become overweight by the end of the year. Those babies also had been relatively inactive since birth. During the first three months they had expended about 20% less energy per day than had the babies who maintained normal weight (Roberts, Savage, Coward, Chew, & Lucas, 1988).

Low energy expenditure is a good predictor of weight gain in adults as well. Eric Ravussin and his associates (1988) found that the adults with the lowest energy expenditure over a 24-hour period were the most likely to gain weight over the next 2 to 4 years.

Losing Weight

Seriously overweight people sometimes become so desperate to lose weight that they will try almost anything—including surgery to remove fat, implanting a balloon in the stomach (to reduce its capacity), taking drugs that suppress appetite, and having the jaws wired shut (Munro, Stewart, Seidelin, Mackenzie, & Dewhurst, 1987). Clearly, these people's efforts are goal directed; they will take whatever measures necessary to lose weight. However, many of these determined people fail to achieve their goal of permanent weight loss.

The best way to lose weight is simply to eat less—except that it is not simple to eat less. If it were, no one would resort to implanting a balloon in the stomach or having the jaws wired shut. For people who cannot stick to a diet by themselves, therapists have devised programs based on the belief that people have multiple motivations for most behaviors. People who enter a weight-loss program want to feel healthier and look more attractive. The therapist provides additional motivations, including praise and support from other members of the weight-loss group. The therapist also tries to make clients more aware that their eating is controlled by external cues, such as the aroma and appearance of foods. Sometimes simply getting snack foods out of sight helps people stick to a diet. Because weight is based on long-established eating habits, dieters are advised to learn new habits of eating in mod-

Expending calories in aerobic exercise helps dieters lose weight. Exercise doesn't change fat into muscle; it develops muscles, which burn more calories than fat does.

eration, not to starve themselves temporarily and become "gluttons in reverse" (Cummings, 1979).

Dieters are also advised to get regular exercise. Exercise plus dieting helps people maintain a lower weight than does dieting by itself (Epstein & Wing, 1987; Epstein, Wing, Koeske, & Valoski, 1984; Pi-Sunyer, 1987). The difficulty is that most obese people have trouble sticking to a regular exercise program, as many other people do as well.

Unfortunately, supervised weight-loss programs usually produce disappointing results (Brownell, 1982). One reason is that only people who have serious trouble losing weight are likely to join the programs. If you decided today that you wanted to lose weight, you would first try to lose weight on your own. According to Schachter (1982), more than half of all dieters manage to lose weight on their own, some of them permanently. The people who enter weight-loss programs have tried to lose weight time after time and have always failed. By the time they enter a program, they are discouraged and pessimistic about their chances of success. Perhaps we should be impressed by even

the modest successes that weight-loss programs achieve.

The Effect of Intentional Weight Loss on Appetite

Many people in our society, especially women, believe they should lose weight even though their weight is already well within normal limits. The motivation to lose weight is a product of cultural standards that depict thin women as especially attractive. April Fallon and Paul Rozin (1985) asked women to indicate on a diagram which body figure they thought men considered most attractive. The investigators also asked men which female figure they considered most attractive. As Figure 11.10 shows, women thought that men preferred thinner women than most men actually do. (Curiously, the same study found that men thought women preferred heavier men than most women actually do.)

Given the social pressure to be thin, many people deprive themselves of food they would like to

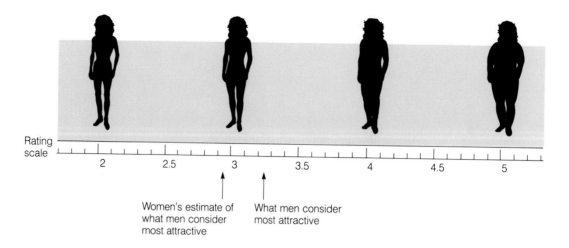

Rating scale

2   2.5   3   3.5   4   4.5   5

Women's estimate of what men consider most attractive

What men consider most attractive

FIGURE 11.10

"Beauty is in the eye of the beholder"—here science backs up a time-honored observation: Mean results of a study by Fallon and Rozin (1985). Women and men were asked which figure they considered most attractive in the opposite sex and which figure they thought the opposite sex considered most attractive.

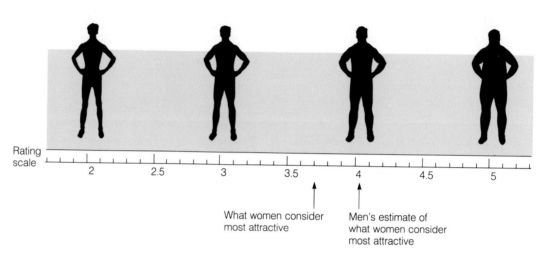

Rating scale

2   2.5   3   3.5   4   4.5   5

What women consider most attractive

Men's estimate of what women consider most attractive

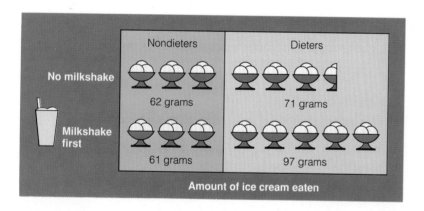

	Nondieters	Dieters
No milkshake	62 grams	71 grams
Milkshake first	61 grams	97 grams

Amount of ice cream eaten

FIGURE 11.11

The "what-the-heck effect": Dieters who drank a milkshake before tasting ice cream ate more ice cream than did dieters who had not drunk a milkshake. Apparently those who drank a milkshake thought, "I've broken my diet anyway, so I may as well eat all I want." (Data from Ruderman & Christensen, 1983.)

eat (Polivy & Herman, 1987). By consistently depriving themselves of food, normal-weight dieters hold their weight below the set point that is natural for their body. Despite their determination, however, nature drives normal-weight dieters to increase their intake. When they fall off their diet at one meal, for whatever reason, they are likely to indulge themselves on the next as well. (This is known as the "what-the-heck effect.") They say to themselves, "I've already broken my diet. I know I'll gain weight anyway, so why not live it up tonight?"

In one experiment, normal-weight subjects were told that they were taking part in market research on the flavors of ice creams. Some of them were first asked to drink a milkshake, while others were not. Then they were all asked to taste three flavors of ice cream. (The dependent variable was how much ice cream they ate.) When this experiment was conducted with people who were not dieting, the ones who had first drunk a milkshake ate *less* ice cream than those who had not (Figure 11.11). No surprise here; those who had drunk a milkshake were simply feeling less hungry. But when the experiment was conducted with normal-weight people who were dieting, those who had first drunk a milkshake ate just as much ice cream and sometimes even *more* than those who had not drunk a milkshake (Ruderman, 1986; Ruderman & Christensen, 1983). The tendency was particularly pronounced among dieters with low self-esteem (Polivy, Heatherton, & Herman, 1988). Apparently the dieters said to themselves, "What the heck. As long as I've already eaten more than I should have, I may as well eat all I want."

The research on weight loss underscores an important point about motivation in general: Our motivations are controlled by a complex mixture of physiological, social, and cognitive forces. People become overweight in the first place for a variety of reasons, including high insulin levels and low rates of using energy. They try to lose weight mostly for social reasons, such as trying to look attractive. Sometimes the physiological factors and the social factors collide, as when normal-weight people try to make themselves thinner and thinner.

Anorexia Nervosa

Some people go beyond reasonable limits in their passion to lose weight. The Duchess of Windsor once said, "You can't be too rich or too thin." That may be true about being too rich, but it is definitely wrong about being too thin. Some people are so strongly motivated to be thin (for social and cognitive reasons) that they manage to overrule their physiological drives almost completely.

A rather chubby 11-year-old girl, who weighed 118 pounds (53 kilograms), was told to watch her weight (Bachrach, Erwin, & Mohr, 1965). She did

so all through her teens. Along the way she suffered certain hormonal difficulties, including menstrual irregularity, heavy menstrual bleeding, and deficient activity of her thyroid gland. At age 18 she still weighed 118 pounds (53 kg), but with her taller frame that weight was normal for her (Figure 11.12a).

After she was married, she moved from her home in Virginia to her husband's place of employment in California. She immediately became homesick. Because the couple could afford only a small apartment with no cooking facilities, they ate most of their meals at a very cheap restaurant. Soon she began to lose weight and stopped menstruating. Sexual relations were painful and unpleasant for her. Her physician warned her that she was losing far too much weight and said that if she did not start regaining some of it he would be forced to send her home to her parents. He intended this as a threat, but she took it as a promise. By the time she visited the physician again, she had lost even more weight. She went back to Virginia.

Even after returning to familiar surroundings and home cooking, however, she continued to lose weight. The weight loss seemed to have developed a momentum of its own, and she continued to get thinner, eventually reaching a weight of only 47 pounds (21 kilograms)). Figure 11.12b shows her at age 21.

This is a typical case of **anorexia nervosa**, a condition in which a person refuses to eat adequate food and steadily loses weight. (*Anorexia* means "loss of appetite." *Nervosa* means "for nervous reasons," as opposed to organic reasons.) At the outset, the person may have decided to lose weight for health reasons, or to become a dancer, or for some

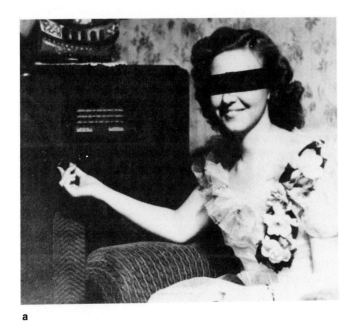

a

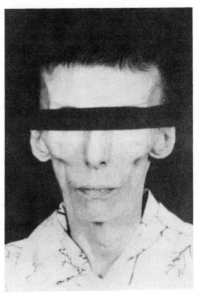

b

FIGURE 11.12

(a) An 18-year-old woman. (b) The same woman at age 21, a victim of anorexia nervosa. (From Bachrach, Erwin, & Mohr, 1965.)

Ballet dancers exercise daily, so you might think they eat heartily without worrying about gaining weight. But ballerinas are notorious for bulimic behavior—perhaps in part because they face constant pressure to remain thin. Moreover, ballet demands great physical control and precision; those good enough to dance professionally apply that discipline to staying thin.

are so seriously afflicted that they consult a physician, about 5 to 10% die of starvation. The prevalence of anorexia has been gradually increasing over the past several decades (Mitchell & Eckert, 1987), perhaps because of society's increasing pressure on women to be thin.

Anorexia nervosa has been described as a "pathological fear of fatness." Even when anorexic women become painfully thin, they often describe themselves as "looking fat" and "needing to lose weight." However, women with anorexia nervosa continue to feel hungry, even though they eat almost nothing. Some of them show a lively interest in cooking and in talking about food. Anorexia might be described as a special case of Maslow's hierarchy of needs: An anorexic woman manages to suppress her lower-level hunger needs in order to pursue higher level goals of self-esteem. But her biology does not give up; even while she refuses to eat, her thoughts may be preoccupied with food.

Surprisingly, even when they are on the verge of starvation, anorexic women have unusually high energy levels (Falk, Halmi, & Tryon, 1985). They run long distances, engage in sports, work diligently on their school assignments, and sleep very little.

What motivates someone to become anorexic? First, many women who become anorexic have always prized self-control. Their extreme weight loss demonstrates extreme self-control and thereby raises their self-esteem.

Second, by becoming so thin that they lose their secondary sexual characteristics, including breast development, they stop being attractive to men. At least some young women with anorexia have a fear of sex and a fear of accepting an adult role. By becoming extremely thin, they can retreat into looking like, acting like, and being treated like little girls again.

Third, maintaining a dangerously low weight is a way of rebelling quietly and of attracting attention. Before the onset of the disorder, most anorexic girls are described as having been obedient, conforming, and highly intelligent perfectionists—girls who never gave their parents or teachers any trouble (Bruch, 1980; Goldstein, 1981; Rowland, 1970). Perhaps as a result, their parents and others took them for granted and gave them little attention. Their severe weight loss makes the parents and friends suddenly attentive and concerned. The anorexic girl comes to enjoy the attention; she becomes reluctant to lose it by gaining weight.

There are probably other reasons behind anorexia. As with most complex human behaviors, anorexia is based on a combination of motivations, not just one.

other reason. But the weight loss continues long after the original motivation has vanished.

Anorexia nervosa occurs in about 0.5% of white teenage girls. It is generally preceded by or accompanied by hormonal abnormalities, including a cessation of menstruation. Anorexia is almost unheard of before the teens; it is rare in boys and uncommon in black girls. Although the problem seldom arises later than the early 20s, it may persist through the 20s and beyond. Because relatively little is known about males with anorexia, our discussion here will focus entirely on females.

As with other psychological conditions, anorexia nervosa comes in all degrees. Of those who

Bulimia

Other people, again mostly young women, starve themselves at times but occasionally throw themselves into an eating binge. They may consume up to 20,000 calories at a time (Schlesier-Stropp, 1984)—the equivalent of about 30 Big Macs, 10 helpings of french fries, and 10 chocolate milkshakes. Some, but not all, force themselves to vomit or use laxatives after gorging on these enormous meals. People who alternate between self-starvation and excessive eating are said to suffer from **bulimia**. Like anorexic women, they are preoccupied with food and show an exaggerated fear of growing fat (Striegel-Moore, Silberstein, & Rodin, 1986). Unlike anorexic women, they do not necessarily remain thin.

We might imagine that people who go on eating binges might starve themselves for a while to make up for it. According to Janet Polivy and Peter Herman (1985), however, the causation goes in the other direction: A bulimic person who diets until falling far below the body's normal weight has an overwhelming urge to eat. It is the dieting that causes the binges. Bulimia is an extreme case of the what-the-heck effect: Bulimic people starve themselves far below their normal weight, violate their diet a bit, and then go on an eating binge. Again, a conflict between physiological motivations and social or cognitive motivations can lead to drastic fluctuations in behavior.

SUMMARY

1. Mechanisms that monitor the amount of glucose and other fuels in the cells regulate hunger. The availability of glucose depends on the hormone insulin, which facilitates the entry of glucose into the cells. (page 386)

2. We stop eating when food distends the stomach, if not before. With familiar foods, we can learn how much to eat, based on the number of calories in the food. (page 388)

3. An individual meal may be larger or smaller than necessary to provide the energy the body needs. In the long run, a person compensates for such fluctuations by regulating body weight. When weight increases, hunger decreases; when weight decreases, hunger increases. (page 388)

4. Food preferences can be altered by changes in body chemistry, such as a deficiency of salt. Other things being equal, we tend to prefer familiar foods. We avoid foods that have been followed by illness and foods that we associate with something repulsive, even if the food itself is harmless. (page 388)

5. Several factors contribute to a person becoming overweight. High levels of insulin increase weight by causing blood glucose to be stored as fats. People who are motivated more by the tastes of foods than by the need for nutrition may be likely to gain weight. Inactive people are more likely to gain weight than active people. (page 392)

6. People in our society resort to a variety of strategies to lose weight, with varying degrees of success. Regular exercise can help severely overweight people to lose weight. (page 394)

7. Normal-weight people who follow a strict diet have a strong desire to eat more than they do. On occasion, they abandon their diet and indulge in eating binges. (page 395)

8. Young women suffering from anorexia nervosa deprive themselves of food, sometimes to the point of starvation. They suppress their physiological drives to satisfy other motivations, including self-esteem. People suffering from bulimia alternate between periods of strict dieting and brief but spectacular eating binges. (page 397)

SUGGESTIONS FOR FURTHER READING

Rozin, P., & Vollmecke, T. A. (1986). Food likes and dislikes. *Annual Review of Nutrition, 6,* 433–456. A review of the factors that influence our choice of foods.

Stellar, J. R., & Stellar, E. (1985). *The neurobiology of motivation and reward.* New York: Springer Verlag. A general treatment emphasizing hunger and thirst.

Wilson, C. P. (1983). *Fear of being fat: The treatment of anorexia nervosa and bulimia.* New York: J. Aronson. An excellent review of eating disorders.

Wurtman, R. J. (1987). Human obesity [Special issue]. *Annals of the New York Academy of Sciences, 499.* A collection of articles by specialists in research and therapy with severely overweight people.

SEXUAL MOTIVATION

What causes sexual arousal?
What sexual customs are prevalent in our society?
What accounts for some of the variations in
sexual practices?

In most mammalian species, male and female come together just long enough to mate; then they go their separate ways. In other species, male and female stay together after mating to care for the young. With few exceptions, however, the sex act occurs only when the female is fertile. When she is incapable of becoming pregnant, she does not give off the odors that attract males, and even if a male approaches her sexually, she rejects his advances. Although neither male nor female knows the relationship between mating and pregnancy, their sexual motivations serve the purpose of reproduction.

Humans are exceptions in this regard. We are interested in sex even at times of the month when a woman is unlikely to get pregnant; in fact, we often take measures to prevent pregnancy. Couples sometimes stick together not only long enough to rear children but also long after the children are grown up. Sexual motivation is a force that binds people together in powerful and intimate relationships. Jealousy based on sex drives people apart; it is one of the leading causes of murder (Daly, Wilson, & Weghorst, 1982). In one way or another, our sexual motivation influences many of the social customs that define our civilization.

Sexual motivation, like hunger, depends on both a physiological drive and available incentives. Again as with hunger, the sex drive increases during a time of deprivation, at least up to a point, and it can be inhibited for social and symbolic reasons, including religious vows.

However, the sex drive differs from hunger in important ways. Many people experience little sex drive in the absence of such incentives as a loving partner or erotic stimuli. Moreover, people differ greatly in the incentives that arouse them sexually. Some people are aroused by the sight of shoes or undergarments, the feel of rubber or leather, the experience of inflicting or receiving pain, and other preferences that most people do not share and find hard to understand.

THE VARIABILITY OF HUMAN SEXUALITY

Sexual motivation varies enormously from one person to another. This point was first demonstrated by Alfred C. Kinsey, who was in many ways an unlikely person to become a sex expert. Kinsey, shy and studious, went through high school, college, and graduate school without ever having had a date (Pomeroy, 1972). After earning a Ph.D. degree in zoology, he met a young woman who shared his

Kissing is an expression of mutual sexual attraction. When his wife caught him with a chorus girl, Chico Marx said, "I wasn't kissing her. I was whispering into her mouth."

interest in the study of insects. They were married the following year.

Some years later, Indiana University persuaded Kinsey to coordinate a new course on marriage. Faculty members from other departments were to participate in the course, but Kinsey, being a biologist, was to teach the section on sexual relations. Finding little useful information in the library, he set out to interview people about their sexual behavior. Within a few years, what began as a modest effort had become a substantial research program involving lengthy interviews with 18,000 people from all walks of life throughout the United States.

Kinsey conducted all his interviews face to face. To put people at ease, he assured them that everything they said would be kept confidential and that nothing they said would shock him. To describe the sex organs and sex acts, he used whatever words, technical or slang, that the other person used. Most people said that he enabled them to relax and to talk more freely about sex than they ever had to anyone else.

Kinsey published tables reporting the frequencies of various sex acts among people in the United States in the 1940s. Unfortunately, he made no effort to obtain a random or representative sample to ensure that the people he interviewed were representative of the population as a whole in age, race, education, and other characteristics. He obtained most of his interviews by going to organizations and trying to get everyone in the organization to talk to him. The organizations ranged from college fraternities to nunneries, and he certainly obtained a wide range of responses. His sampling of organizations was neither representative nor random, and the statistical data he reported may have been far from accurate. For example, 37% of the men he interviewed reported having at least one homosexual experience. More recent studies with more representative samples have reported percentages around 20% (for example, Fay, Turner, Klassen, & Gagnon, 1989). Even if some of Kinsey's data were inaccurate, his studies paved the way for other surveys and scientific studies of sex.

One of Kinsey's undisputed findings was that human sexual behavior is highly variable (Kinsey, Pomeroy, & Martin, 1948; Kinsey, Pomeroy, Martin, & Gebbard, 1953). Figure 11.13a shows the reported frequencies of orgasm per week by males from adolescence to age 30. Although Kinsey's percentages may not be exactly accurate, the enormous range is clear. While most men were having orgasms zero to four times a week, others were averaging two or three times a day. At the extremes, one 30-year-old man reported that he had experienced

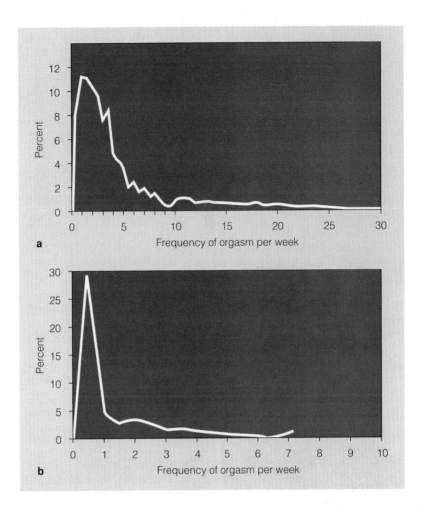

a Frequency of orgasm per week

b Frequency of orgasm per week

FIGURE 11.13

Frequency of orgasm per week in (a) adolescent to 30-year-old males and (b) single females age 16–20 (Kinsey, Pomeroy, & Martin, 1948; Kinsey, Pomeroy, Martin, & Gebbard, 1953. The actual percentages may be inaccurate, but the frequency of sexual outlets clearly is highly variable.

orgasm only once in his life, while another man had an average of four to five orgasms a day over the preceding 30 years.

The range of variation was equally great among females. For example, Figure 11.13b shows the reported frequencies of orgasm in single women age 16 to 20. About 10% of the adult women Kinsey and his colleagues interviewed had never had an orgasm, whereas a few said they had had 50 or more orgasms within 20 minutes.

The mean frequency of orgasm gradually declines as one grows older, as Figure 11.14 shows. But these figures can be very misleading for several reasons. First, Kinsey lacked a random sample. Second, these are the results of a cross-sectional study; the results of a longitudinal study might well be different. Third, the data in Figure 11.14 represent

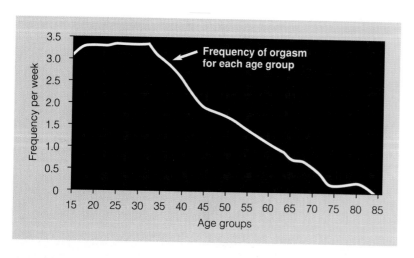

Figure 11.14

Mean frequency of orgasm, or climax, in men of different ages. (From Kinsey, Pomeroy, & Martin, 1948.) *Climax* is from the Greek word for *ladder;* a sexual climax is like reaching the top of a ladder.

means of large groups; the behavior of a given individual may be very different from that of the group mean. Some older people remain almost as active sexually as they ever were, while others become almost completely inactive (Martin, 1981).

Something to Think About

Why is it likely that the results of a longitudinal study of aging and sexual activity might be different from those of a cross-sectional study? Think about the possibilities of sampling error and of cohort effects. (Review page 185 if necessary.)

Kinsey found that very few people were aware of the great variation in sexual behavior in the population at large. For example, when he asked people whether they believed that "excessive masturbation" causes physical and mental illness, most said they did. (We now know it does not.) He then asked what would constitute "excessive." For each person, "excessive" meant a little more than what he or she did. One young man who masturbated about once a month said he thought three times a month would be excessive and would cause mental illness. Another man, who masturbated three times a day, said he thought five times a day would be excessive. (In reaction to these findings, Kinsey once defined *nymphomaniac* as "someone who wants sex more than *you* do.")

Cultural Variations

Sexual behaviors that are considered acceptable or even normal in one society may be regarded as strange, deviant, or even criminal in another. How-

ever, we must approach comparative studies of sexual practices with caution. Imagine what would happen if an anthropologist from New Guinea spent a few months talking to people in a single city of the United States and then wrote a book about the sexual customs of American society. The possibilities for distortion and error are obvious. Although reports about sex in other societies may not be altogether reliable, we know that sexual customs differ strikingly from one society to another.

At one extreme are certain societies in Polynesia that encourage premarital sex, sometimes at an early age, on the theory that intercourse is necessary for sexual maturation (Davenport, 1977). The rules about who are acceptable partners for premarital sex differ from one island to another. On some islands, only potential marriage partners are acceptable. On other islands, only someone who *cannot be* a marriage partner is acceptable, such as an uncle or an aunt. On some islands, extramarital sex is routinely accepted.

At the opposite extreme, some societies actively discourage sexual activity. On a small island off the coast of Ireland, for example, the average age of marriage for men is 36 and for women is 25 (Messenger, 1971). There is no sexual activity before marriage; even after marriage, it is brief and infrequent. Nudity is strictly forbidden, and people cannot even bare their legs or shoulders in public. After early childhood, people do not undress completely even to take a bath. No one on the island knows how to swim. (Swimming would require removing too much clothing.) Their attitudes toward sex are an outgrowth of the economics and religion of the island. Because farm land is limited, they cannot afford to allow population growth. Because their Roman Catholic religion forbids the use of contraceptives, they must hold sexual activity to a minimum. The islanders have had to constrain their sexual motivation in order to satisfy their other needs.

Anthropological studies of this sort imply that sexual customs are not the direct result of any biological necessity. Human societies can survive with a vast variety of sexual customs; as economic conditions and other circumstances change, attitudes toward sex are likely to change as well.

Sexual Behavior and Customs in the United States

In most Judeo-Christian societies, the standard teaching (if not always the standard practice) has long been "no premarital or extramarital sex, especially for women." Centuries ago, when people married younger than they do today, that teaching may have been easier to follow. Today, the mean age at first marriage is almost 23 for women and 25 for men (National Center for Health Statistics, 1988). The mean age of reaching puberty is about 13 or 14 (Kumar, 1975). A delay of 10 years (often more) between puberty and marriage makes the prohibition against premarital sex a more serious strain than it used to be.

Young people have sometimes been told to abstain from masturbation as well as from intercourse. In the late 1800s, Graham's crackers and Kellogg's cornflakes were created to provide intentionally bland foods that would help young people suppress their sexual desires (Money, 1983). The theory was that if people don't enjoy their food very much, then they won't crave other pleasures, either. (Can you imagine an advertisement today, "Buy our cereal; it will lower your sex drive"?)

One reason for the rule of no sex before marriage was society's desire to avoid the birth of fatherless children. Today the availability of contraceptive devices has made it possible to reduce the number of unwanted pregnancies. Moreover, the manner in which sex is treated in the movies and other media has encouraged people to engage in premarital intercourse with greater freedom than before.

Not everyone in the United States is sexually permissive, of course (Brooks-Gunn & Furstenberg, 1989). Some people have their first sexual experience at an early age; others wait until much later. Some have sex on the first date; others have sex only with someone they plan to marry (Christopher & Cate, 1985). The rules governing sexual activity in our society are uncertain at the moment; we live in an age of experimentation.

Something to Think About

Experimentation is desirable in some matters, such as choice of reading material, but not so desirable in other matters, such as highway driving practices. Do you think experimentation in sexual practices is desirable or undesirable? Would society be better off or worse off if we all agreed on one set of sexual customs?

Sexual Behavior in the AIDS Era

During the 1980s, a new factor entered into people's sexual motivations: the fear of **acquired immune deficiency syndrome (AIDS)**, a new and deadly sexually transmitted, or venereal, disease.

For the AIDS virus to spread from one person to another, it must enter the second person's blood. (Outside the blood or the body's cells, the virus

For years, the news about AIDS often went from bad to worse. For those anxious and uncertain about how the disease could affect them, this AIDS hotline provides a service that's cheap, readily available, and—perhaps most important—anonymous. People too intimidated or uncomfortable to discuss sexual practices with a physician can ask about such matters in a phone call.

"If you think education is expensive, try ignorance," observed one college president. With a deadly disease such as AIDS, ignorance is very dangerous. These teens are learning about AIDS, but as noted in Chapter 6, teens sometimes consider themselves invincible. Is AIDS education changing behavior? A recent study reports that more male teens are sexually active now than in 1979, but more of them, 57%, are also using condoms (Sonenstein, Pleck, & Ku, 1989).

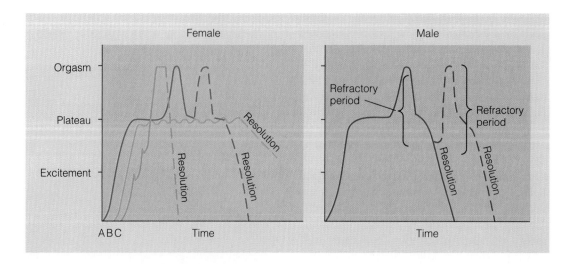

FIGURE 11.15

Stages of sexual arousal. Each line represents the response of a different individual. (After Masters & Johnson, 1966.)

cannot survive.) There are three common routes of transmission: transfusions of contaminated blood, sharing needles used for intravenous injections, and sexual contact.

In vaginal intercourse, there is an estimated 3% chance that the virus will be transmitted by an infected male to the female, and no more than a 2% chance that it will be transmitted by an infected female to the male (Kaplan, 1988). The likelihood increases if either partner has an open wound on the genitals or if the woman is menstruating. The virus spreads much more readily during anal intercourse, because the lining of the rectum is likely to be torn. There is an estimated 7 to 10% chance that the virus will be transmitted through anal intercourse (Kaplan, 1988). These estimates are uncertain, as researchers have had only a limited time to study this disease.

For generations, people have known how to avoid contracting syphilis, gonorrhea, and other **venereal diseases**: Don't have sex with someone who might be infected, or when in doubt, use a condom. To be really safe, don't have sex at all. Because AIDS is life-threatening and (so far) incurable, it has had a greater impact on sexual customs than other venereal diseases have had. Since the advent of AIDS, many people, especially homosexual men, have grown more cautious. More homosexual males are choosing long-term sexual partners, and more are using condoms to reduce the likelihood of transmitting the virus (William, 1984). One study of men leaving a homosexual bathhouse found that only 10% were engaging in anal sex without a condom—a far lower percentage than was common prior to the AIDS crisis (Richwald et al., 1988).

Some heterosexual couples also have become more cautious. As in other areas of life, some people habitually take greater risks than others, either because they do not think about the risks or because they think "it can't happen to me." People who take risks with sex tend to take risks in other areas as well; people who are cautious in their sexual behavior are mostly cautious in other activities as well. For example, students who report that they use condoms also say that they habitually wear seat belts (Baldwin & Baldwin, 1988).

SEXUAL AROUSAL

Sexual motivation depends on both physiological and cognitive influences. William Masters and Virginia Johnson (1966), who pioneered the study of human sexual response, discovered that physiological arousal during the sex act is about the same in men and women. They observed people engaging in masturbation and sexual intercourse in a laboratory and monitored their physiological responses. Masters and Johnson identified four physiological stages in sexual arousal (Figure 11.15). During the first stage, *excitement*, a man's penis becomes erect and a woman's vagina becomes lubricated. Breathing grows rapid and deep. Heart rate and blood pressure increase. Many people experience a sex flush of the skin, which sometimes resembles a measles rash. Women's nipples become erect, and, if they have never nursed a baby, their breasts swell slightly. Although this stage is referred to as excitement, it actually requires some level of relaxation. Feeling nervous or tense interferes with sexual excitement; so do stimulant drugs (even coffee).

During the second stage, called the *plateau*, excitement remains fairly constant. This stage lasts for varying lengths of time, depending on the person's age and on the intensity of the stimulation. During the third stage, excitement becomes intense and is followed by a sudden relief of tension known as *climax* or *orgasm*, which is felt throughout the entire body. During the fourth and final stage, *resolution*, the person returns to an unaroused state.

As Figure 11.15 shows, the pattern of excitation varies from one person to another. Some women experience no orgasm at all; others experience a single orgasm or multiple orgasms consecutively. Men do not experience multiple orgasms, although they may achieve orgasm again following a rest (or refractory) period. In both sexes the intensity of orgasm ranges from something like a sigh to something like an epileptic seizure.

At any rate, that is the normal pattern. Some people are unable to complete the four stages of arousal. Some men cannot get or maintain an erection. Others have premature ejaculations; they advance from excitement to orgasm sooner than they or their partners wish. A substantial number of women, perhaps as many as 10%, and relatively few men advance to the plateau stage but seldom or never experience orgasm. The reasons for such sexual dysfunctions include both physiological disorders and competing motivations. For example, some people are inhibited in their sexual arousal because they have been taught that sex is shameful. When the problems are motivational rather than physiological, a therapist can work with people to reduce their anxieties or to learn new patterns of sexual activity more satisfactory to both themselves and their partners (Andersen, 1983).

Sexual Identity and Orientation

Just as hunger includes two major aspects—how much food to eat and which foods to choose—sexual motivation includes two aspects—how frequently to have sex and with whom. Sexual intercourse is a social experience; while masturbation can be done alone, intercourse requires a partner. For most of us, not just any partner will do. Each of us chooses a specific individual as a partner. We begin by developing a clear preference for male or female partners. What is responsible for that preference?

Psychologists distinguish two aspects of being male or female: sexual identity and sexual orientation. **Sexual identity** is the sex the person regards himself or herself as being. That is, people think of themselves as being men or women, and they identify with others of that sex. **Sexual orientation** is the person's preference for male or female sex partners. Someone who thinks of himself as a man and

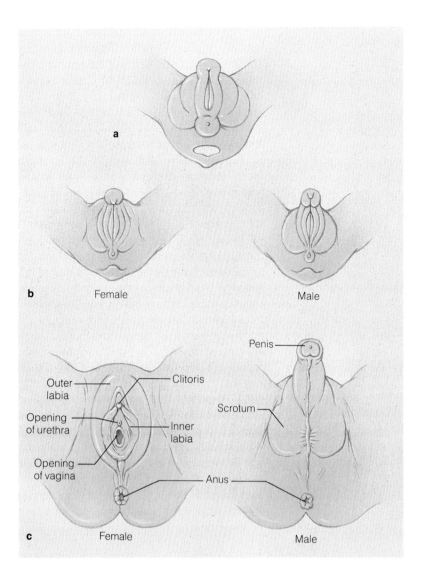

Figure 11.16

Development of genitals: (a) one set of structures in early embryological development; in the first six weeks, reproductive organs look identical in human embryos. (b) Second trimester. (c) At birth. (Based on Netter, 1965.)

who prefers other men as sex partners has a male sexual identity and a homosexual sex orientation. Sexual orientation is based partly on anatomical and physiological factors, partly on social influences. Psychologists do not yet fully understand the causes of sexual orientation.

Influences on Sexual Anatomy

In the earliest stages of development, the human fetus has a "unisex" appearance (Figure 11.16). One structure subsequently develops into either a penis or a clitoris; another structure develops into either a scrotum or labia. The direction that development takes depends on hormonal influences during prenatal development. Genetic male fetuses generally secrete relatively high levels of the hormone **testosterone**, and their structures develop into a penis and a scrotum. Genetic female fetuses generally secrete lower levels of testosterone, and their structures develop into a clitoris and labia. High levels of the hormone **estrogen** are present in the mother at this time, and some of that hormone enters the circulation of the fetus. However, because sexual development depends mostly on the testosterone levels, the mother's hormones do not alter the appearance of either male or female fetuses.

In rare cases, the fetus may secrete an intermediate level of testosterone early in development, or the mother may take medications similar to testosterone. The structures may then develop into something about halfway between male and female (Money & Ehrhardt, 1972).

Some psychologists believe that the psychological makeup of adults reflects this early bisexuality. According to this view, we go through life with the potential to adopt either the male or the female role in our relationships with others and to respond sexually to either male or female partners. For most people, only half of that potential expresses itself. What activates one half or the other—or both? It may be that hormonal levels in the fetus influence subsequent sexual behavior, as they influence sexual anatomy. However, the evidence is not conclusive (Hines, 1982). I shall discuss some of it later in this section.

Concept Check

6. If a human fetus were exposed to very low levels of both testosterone and estrogen throughout prenatal development, how would the sexual anatomy appear? (Check your answer on page 419.)

Influences on Sexual Orientation

In nearly all cases, sexual anatomy matches sexual identity. Your parents told you that you were a boy or a girl on the basis of your anatomy. Before long, you identified yourself as being what they said you were. Occasionally, someone with a male anatomy insists, "I am a woman in a man's body," or someone with a female anatomy claims, "I am really a man."

Sexual anatomy is a less certain determinant of sexual orientation. While most people feel sexual attraction to members of the opposite sex (heterosexuality), a significant number are sexually attracted to members of their own sex (homosexuality). A national survey of 1,450 adult men indi-

cated that at least 20% had had at least one sexual contact to orgasm with another male (Fay, Turner, Klassen, & Gagnon, 1989). For a majority of those men, however, their only such experience was some adolescent sex play, such as teenage boys masturbating together. A little more than 3% said they had "occasionally" or "often" had sexual contact with other males after the age of 19.

Adult homosexuals often report that their sexual preference was apparent to them from as early an age as they can remember. They do not choose it voluntarily, and they could not change it easily. What causes some people to develop a heterosexual preference and others to develop a homosexual preference? There probably are several contributing factors. I shall deal here only with males, partly because homosexuality is more common among males than among females and partly because most of the research has been done with males.

At one time, most psychologists regarded homosexuality as a mental illness caused by a family background in which a domineering or rejecting mother lived in conflict with a detached, indifferent father. Many studies supported that causal linkage (Wakeling, 1979). Those studies, however, were based mainly on the reports of therapists, who treated a number of homosexual men for a variety of psychological troubles. Homosexual men without psychological problems never consulted therapists, and therefore the therapists did not know that such men existed (Hoffman, 1977). Studies of homosexual men who have never gone to a therapist conflict with the view that homosexuality is a psychological disorder; many homosexual men are content and well adjusted (Siegelman, 1974). Furthermore, many homosexual men who do suffer anxiety and other problems may simply be responding to the manner in which society treats them.

Hormonal Influences on Sexual Orientation: WHAT'S THE EVIDENCE?

A possible contributor to homosexual preferences is the influence of hormones on the development of the brain prior to birth. Hormonal influences at certain stages of pregnancy can alter the anatomy of the genitals; perhaps hormonal influences at other stages can alter the brain in ways that eventually influence sexual orientation.

In an area such as this, laboratory experiments on humans are out of the question. Investigators combine experiments on animals and correlational studies with humans. Let's begin with an animal study.

AN EXPERIMENT WITH RATS

Hypothesis Because the hormones of a pregnant rat pass through her blood into the blood of her fetuses, hormonal changes in the mother might alter the brain development of the fetuses. Based on previous studies measuring the times that certain parts of the brain develop, Ingeborg Ward (1972, 1977) proposed that an alteration of the rat mother's hormones during the last week of her pregnancy might lead to long-term changes in the sexual orientation of her offspring.

Method Ward confined pregnant rats in a small, tight, brightly lighted Plexiglas enclosure for three 45-minute periods per day on days 14 through 21 of the rats' 23-day pregnancy. This procedure produced a stress response, which increased the release of adrenal hormones by the mother. After the babies were born, Ward let them develop without any further stress. She observed their sexual behavior in adulthood toward both males and females.

Results The female offspring developed the same as other female rats do. Although the males developed nearly normal sexual anatomy and nearly normal adult testosterone levels, they responded sexually to male partners more than they did to female partners. In the presence of females, they showed few sexual responses. In the presence of males, they arched their backs in the position a female rat takes to invite a male to mount her.

Interpretation In response to the stressful experience, the mother rats' adrenal glands secreted high levels of adrenal hormones, which apparently competed with the male hormone testosterone for entry to the brain. The adrenal hormones also temporarily suppressed the males' testosterone production. In the presence of low levels of testosterone, the hypothalamus (part of the brain) developed in a manner that increased the probability of a sexual interest in males.

Even in rats, sexual orientation depends on experiences and not just on brain anatomy. In a later study, Ingeborg Ward and Jonathan Reed (1985) found that a prenatally stressed male that shared a cage with a female for the first two months of life was likely to develop a stronger sexual interest in female partners than in male partners. A prenatally stressed male caged with a male was likely to respond sexually either to other males or equally to both males and females. (Males that had not been exposed to prenatal stress were more interested in females

According to one survey, at least 20% of all men in the United States have had at least one homosexual contact. A smaller percentage, 3%, have had occasional or frequent homosexual contacts after age 19. Those percentages are merely estimates for the total population. (From Fay, Turner, Klassen, & Gagnon, 1989.)

than in other males, regardless of their early experiences.) Prenatal stress does not necessarily cause a male rat to develop a sexual interest in males; it just increases the probability, depending on experiences after birth.

A CORRELATIONAL STUDY WITH HUMANS

Although prenatal hormones influence sexual orientation in rats, we cannot assume that human development depends on the same factors as rat development does. Still, the rat experiment shows us something to look for in humans.

Hypothesis Perhaps women whose adrenal glands are highly activated by stress during some stage of pregnancy give birth to sons with a preference for male sexual partners.

Method Investigators asked 283 mothers of adult sons and daughters to recall any stressful experiences they had before or during pregnancy (Ellis, Ames, Peckham, & Burke, 1988). The investigators sent a separate questionnaire to the sons and daughters to determine their sexual orientation.

Results On a scale of stress severity ranging from a low of 1 to a high of 4, the mothers of male homosexuals rated the middle third of their pregnancy at 2.3. The mean for the other mothers was 1.5. There were no significant differences among the mothers of heterosexual men, bisexual men, heterosexual women, and homosexual women.

Interpretation These results support the hypothesis that prenatal stress increases the probability that a male will develop a homosexual orientation. They do not suggest any relationship between prenatal stress and bisexuality or lesbianism. At most, prenatal hormones increase the probability of a given sexual orientation; sexual orientation develops through a person's experiences as well, in ways that psychologists do not yet clearly understand (Ellis & Ames, 1987).

Although mothers of homosexual men recalled more stress during pregnancy than most other mothers do, psychologists have to be cautious about drawing a firm conclusion. First, the mothers of homosexual men reported only slightly more prenatal stress than did the other mothers. Second, it is difficult to reconstruct accurate memories of pregnancy 20 years or more after the fact.

So does prenatal stress predispose some men to homosexuality? Maybe. If you decide to become a psychologist, you will have to get used to the word *maybe*—and *probably*. In the present case, the experiment with rats tells us that prenatal hormones *can* influence sexual orientation, but we do not know whether they *do* influence sexual orientation in humans. The survey of mothers' recollections supports the suggestion that prenatal stress influences sexual orientation. Combined, the two studies lead us to a louder "maybe" than either study would by itself, but the conclusion is still "maybe." As I pointed out in Chapter 2, psychologists rarely talk about "proving" a conclusion. As they collect more and more evidence that supports a conclusion, they feel greater and greater confidence in it, but the conclusion remains tentative, subject to revision in light of new evidence. ■

Concept Check

7. *Most studies find that adult homosexual men have approximately the same levels of testosterone in their blood as heterosexual men of the same age have. Do such results conflict with the suggestion that prenatal hormonal conditions predispose certain men to homosexuality? (Check your answer on page 419.)*

MOTIVATION AND RAPE

Up to this point we have been considering sexual behavior among consenting adults. Not all behavior meets that description. **Rape** is sexual contact obtained through violence, threats, or intimidation.

Only a small proportion of raped women report

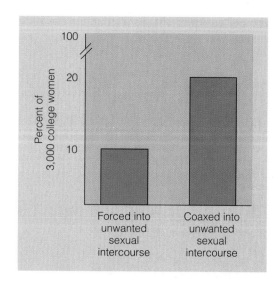

FIGURE 11.17

Date rape is prevalent among college students. Knowing the assailant doesn't mean it isn't rape.

the rape to the police; consequently, police statistics vastly understate the prevalence of rape. Women who are forced into sex by a date may not even perceive the event as rape (Allgeier, 1987). In a survey of more than 3,000 women at 32 colleges, 9% reported that they had been forced into unwanted sexual intercourse, and 25% said they had participated in unwanted intercourse in response to verbal coaxing or while under the influence of alcohol (Koss, Gidycz, & Wisniewski, 1987; see Figure 11.17). Most cases were date rapes, rather than assaults by strangers.

In a survey of men at the same colleges, 4.4% admitted that they had forced themselves sexually on a woman at least once, and an additional 3.3% said they had attempted to do so (Koss & Dinero, 1988). Perhaps these 4.4% of the men were responsible for the rapes reported by 25% of the women. But it is more likely that many of the men understated the sexual coercion they had used. Some men convince themselves that the woman they raped did not really mean it when she said no.

What motivates men to rape? That is a hard question to answer, because most of our data are based on men who have been actually *convicted* of rape. Most of the rapes that come to the attention of the police and the public are violent attacks by strangers. The men most likely to be convicted are repeat offenders. Those who commit repeated, violent attacks are probably not representative of other rapists; indeed, it is hard to imagine how researchers could obtain a representative sample. Based on an admittedly unrepresentative sample, psychologists' tentative assessment is that rapists feel anger toward women and a need to dominate or control them. Some rapists feel that they have been hurt or belittled by women in the past. Although much less is known about date rapists, one survey of admitted date rapists found that they also reported anger toward women and a drive to dominate them (Lisak & Roth, 1988).

Some psychologists distinguish between rapists who intended to humiliate and injure their victims and those who used only enough force to subdue their victims. However, there is no way to determine for sure whether a rapist is using force just to obtain compliance or is indulging in violence for its own sake (Prentky, Knight, & Rosenberg, 1988).

We do know that most convicted rapists have a long history of hostility and violence toward both men and women (Gebhard, Gagnon, Pomeroy, & Christenson, 1965; Groth, 1979). Many of them were sexually abused in childhood; in committing their assaults, they may be reenacting their own experiences, sometimes more closely than they realize (Burgess, Hazelwood, Rokous, Hartman, & Burgess, 1988).

Some rapists have a weak sex drive or are almost impotent; they hope to find sexual satisfaction by being "completely in charge," something they cannot manage with a willing partner. They are sexually aroused by photos and audiotapes of rape, whereas most other men are either unaroused or repulsed (Earls, 1988). To judge whether a convicted rapist is still dangerous, measurements of his sexual arousal are sometimes made while he listens to tapes. Men who develop erections while listening to descriptions of rape are considered to be still dangerous.

Something to Think About

Rapists and child molesters sometimes pore over sexually explicit magazines and videotapes just before committing an offense (Malamuth & Donnerstein, 1982; Marshall, 1988). Can we conclude that such materials lead to the offenses? (Remember, correlation does not mean causation.) What kind of evidence would we need to determine whether sexually explicit materials lead to sex offenses?

Rape is a complex matter, and, like other motivated behaviors, it has a variety of causes. While a rapist may have been an abused child or may feel anger toward women, these circumstances do not explain why he commits an attack at a particular

Is she "asking for trouble"? This young woman is trying to look like a movie star. If she were raped, some people would say it was her fault. But blaming a rape victim for being attractive is like blaming a robbery victim for owning a stereo system.

moment. In many cases, he is so intoxicated from alcohol or other drugs that he sheds the inhibitions that would ordinarily prevent such an attack (Lisak & Roth, 1988). Psychologists have much to learn before they can understand rape and contribute to its prevention.

SUMMARY

1. Alfred Kinsey, who conducted the first extensive survey of human sexual behavior, found that sexual activity varies more widely than most people realize. (page 400)

2. Some societies are highly permissive in their attitudes toward sexual practices; others are extremely restrictive. In the United States, sexual freedom has been on the rise throughout much of the 20th century, although the AIDS epidemic has made some people more cautious in their sexual activities. (page 402)

3. Sexual arousal proceeds through four stages: excitement, plateau, orgasm, and resolution. For a combination of physiological and motivational reasons, some people fail to pass through all four stages or pass through them more quickly than they wish. (page 404)

4. In the early stages of development, the human fetus possesses anatomical structures that may develop into either male genitalia (if testosterone levels are high enough) or female genitalia (if testosterone levels are lower). How much prenatal hormones affect human sexual behavior is uncertain. (page 405)

5. Homosexuality is no longer regarded as a mental illness. One possible determinant of homosexuality is stress experienced by the mother during pregnancy. Such stress may interfere with the expression of certain hormones at certain stages of brain development in the fetus. (page 406)

6. Rape, especially date rape, and other sex offenses occur far more often than police records indicate. Convicted rapists generally have a long history of violence; for many of them, the motivation seems to be more aggressive than sexual. Many rapists were sexually abused as children. (page 408)

SUGGESTION FOR FURTHER READING

Hyde, J. S. (1989). *Understanding human sexuality* (2nd ed.). New York: McGraw-Hill. A comprehensive textbook on human sexual behavior.

ACHIEVEMENT MOTIVATION

What motivates some people to work
harder than others?
How do we learn an achievement motivation?
How do people with a strong achievement
motivation differ from others?

Your 2-year-old nephew is building a stack of blocks. You say, "Here, let me help you," and you finish stacking the blocks. Will he smile and thank you? Hardly. He is more likely to cry, "I wanted to do it myself!" His goal was not to *have* a tall stack, but to *build* a tall stack.

Now you are doing something creative yourself—painting a picture, writing a story, playing chess perhaps—something you do moderately well. Someone more expert than you says, "Here, let me help you. I see you're having a little trouble, and I think I can fix it." How do you react? You might not burst into tears, but you probably resent the help. You are more interested in completing the task yourself than in having a perfect final product.

Most of us strive for the joy of accomplishment, some more than others. What occupation do you hope to enter after graduation? Have you chosen it because it is your surest way to earn a lot of money? Or have you chosen it because it will enable you to take pride in your achievements? Many people forgo a better-paying job to take one that gives them a greater opportunity to achieve. (I bet your psychology professor is one such person.)

THE MEASUREMENT OF NEED FOR ACHIEVEMENT

The **need for achievement** is a striving for competitive success and excellence. It includes both a component of intrinsic motivation (accomplishing

goals for their own sake) and a component of extrinsic motivation (accomplishing goals in order to impress others and to receive rewards). This motivation has much in common with other culture-dependent, cognitive goals such as striving for affiliation (being with other people), for power, and for theoretical knowledge: The striving for such goals is not necessary for immediate survival, although it may promote a person's long-range welfare. For some people these goals take precedence over hunger and other physiological needs.

The need for achievement was first inferred from the performance of schoolchildren. Some children are much more successful in school than are others who, so far as we can tell, are equal in ability. The same is true in athletics, business, and other aspects of life. Apparently, some people simply try harder than others. If that is true, then we

Tennis champions such as Martina Navratilova and Steffi Graf need more than athletic skill to win tournaments—they need to put great effort and many hours into their practice and preparation. But why do some people and not others develop such a strong motivation for achievement?

FIGURE 11.18

Every picture tells a story: A stimulus picture similar to those used in the Thematic Apperception Test.

should be able to measure and study this tendency as a personality variable.

But how? If you wanted to determine which workers or schoolchildren were most highly motivated to achieve, what would you measure and how? You could not simply measure how much people achieve because you are trying to explain *why* some people achieve more than others. You would need some measure of the need for achievement that is separate from the achievements themselves.

Another way *not* to measure the need for achievement is to ask people whether they are strongly motivated for success. Many people say yes because they believe it is socially desirable to do so. Psychologists measure achievement motivation indirectly, perhaps without even telling people what they are measuring.

One of the most popular methods of measuring need for achievement makes use of the *Thematic Apperception Test*, which we shall look at again in Chapter 13. Investigators show people pictures like the one in Figure 11.18 and ask them to tell a story about each picture, including what is going on, what led up to this scene, and what will happen next (McClelland, Atkinson, Clark, & Lowell, 1953). The investigators then count the number of times each person mentions striving for goals and achievements.

For example, this story would score high:

This girl is taking an important test. First she went through the test and answered all the items she knew well. Now she is trying to remember the answer to one of the more difficult questions. She

gazes off into the distance, trying to remember everything she has read about this topic. She finally remembers, writes down the correct answer, and gets a perfect score. Later she goes on to college, becomes a Rhodes scholar, and eventually becomes a famous inventor.

Contrast that story with this one:

This girl is sitting through a very boring class. She is gazing off into the distance, thinking about the party she went to last weekend. As soon as class is over, she goes out and has a good time with her friends.

Such a story would rate a zero on need for achievement.

Need for Achievement and Setting Goals

Suppose you have a choice of three video games to play. One game is easy; you know you can get a high score on it, but so could anyone else. The second game is more difficult; you are not sure how well you would do. The third is the most difficult; you would expect to lose quickly, as most people do. Which do you choose? Most people prefer the game of intermediate difficulty, especially people with a strong need for achievement (Atkinson & Birch, 1978).

For example, in one study, children were asked to throw 10 rings to try to hit a peg from any distance they chose, from 1 to 15 feet (0.3 to 4.6 meters). Because the others stood around watching as each child threw the rings, there was an element of competition even though no one was keeping score. Children who had scored high on need for achievement generally chose intermediate distances and managed to hit the peg a little less than half the time (McClelland, 1958).

According to one interpretation of these results, the value of a goal is a product of its expectancy and its value (Atkinson, 1957). The **expectancy** is the perceived probability of achieving a goal, such as 50% or 99%. The value is, simply, what the goal would be worth. Easy goals have a high expectancy but a low value. The most difficult goals have a high value but almost zero expectancy. Intermediate goals have a fairly high expectancy and a fairly high value; the product of multiplying the two is also high (Figure 11.19).

Many psychologists doubt that this *expectancy-value interpretation* applies in all cases. It assumes that people mentally calculate the probability of success and multiply by the pride they would feel in success—hardly a simple undertaking. Even preschool children usually prefer tasks of intermediate difficulty, even though they have trouble estimating how well they will do on the task and even though they do not seem to value accomplishing difficult tasks much more than accomplishing simple tasks (Schneider, 1984).

According to an alternative explanation, the *competency interpretation*, people prefer intermediate tasks because the results are more informative (Heckhausen, 1984; Schneider, 1984). According to that explanation, even preschool children want to know their own competence. People who attempt a task that is too easy or too difficult learn little about their competence. They learn about their competence by attempting an intermediate task, one on which they might or might not succeed. The competence interpretation is not necessarily inconsistent with the expectancy-value interpretation; as is often the case in psychology, both theories may be valid, perhaps for different people or under different circumstances.

Most people, not just people with a strong need for achievement, prefer tasks with intermediate difficulty. However, people with a strong need for achievement show an even stronger preference than other people do (Schneider, 1984). A few people prefer especially easy or especially difficult tasks. Such people are dominated by a **fear of failure**. By adopting a strategy of taking no risks and setting low goals, they avoid failure, although they never achieve any remarkable success. When they set extremely high goals for themselves, at least they have an excuse for failure. Apparently, they would rather fail at an impossible task than run the risk of failing at a realistic task.

People with a strong fear of failure make a normal effort, or even an extraordinary effort, on an easy task or in a relaxed, low-pressure situation. But if they are told, "This is an important test; you are going to be evaluated, so do your best," they lower their effort. (Fear of failure is closely related to test anxiety.) By contrast, people with a strong need for achievement make little effort on an easy task or when the situation puts little pressure on them. When they are told that they are going to be evaluated, they try harder (Nygard, 1982).

When people receive feedback on their performance, such as "You got 82% correct on the first test," those with a strong need for achievement usually increase their efforts, whereas those with a lower need do not increase their efforts and sometimes decrease them. Apparently those with a strong need for achievement set such high goals that they interpret almost any feedback as meaning that they are behind schedule and need to try harder. People with a low need for achievement set lower goals,

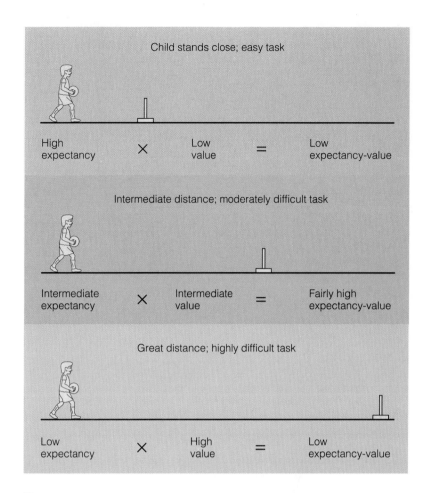

FIGURE 11.19

Children are asked to toss rings at a target from whatever distance they choose. Those with a high need for achievement select an intermediate distance (McClelland, 1958). According to the expectancy-value theory, people seek the highest possible product of expectancy times value (Atkinson, 1957).

and almost any feedback they receive reassures them that they are doing all right (Matsui, Okada, & Kakuyama, 1982).

Something to Think About

Some people have suggested that our society has become less ambitious and less motivated by achievement than it once was. How could we test that hypothesis?

Concept Check

8. The new football coach at Generic Tech has set up a schedule for next year. The team will play only opponents that had a won-lost record of 5-6 or 6-5 last year. Does this coach have a high need for achievement or a high fear of failure? (Check your answer on page 419.)

Working smarter, working harder: How does goal setting influence behavior? According to Edwin Locke and his associates (1981), setting a goal focuses workers' attention on the task at hand and thereby reduces distraction. It fosters a high level of effort and persistence and motivates workers to develop new strategies for performing the task. They ask, "How can we reorganize our efforts to reach our goal? How can we cooperate more effectively? What can we do differently?"

Setting goals leads to vigorous activity if:
The goal is realistic.
A serious commitment is made, especially if it is made publicly.
Feedback is received.

FIGURE 11.20

Conditions for high activity toward achieving goals.

Effective and Ineffective Goals

High but realistic goals are especially effective in motivating people with a strong need for achievement. To a lesser degree, they can motivate almost anyone. At the start of the college semester, four young women are asked to state their goals. One is aiming for a straight-A average. Another hopes to get at least a C average. A third plans to "do as well as I can." A fourth has no set goals. Which student will work hardest and get the best grades?

The student aiming for a straight-A average will do the best, under certain circumstances:

- She must have enough ability for the goal to be realistic. If she has always had to struggle just to get a passing grade, she will quickly become discouraged.

- She must take her goal seriously. If she only *says* she is aiming for straight A's and then never thinks about it again, it will make no

difference to her. She can increase her commitment to the goal by stating it publicly. The more people who know about her goal, the harder it will be for her to ignore it.

- She must get some feedback from periodic test scores and grades on assignments to tell her what she needs to study harder (Figure 11.20).

The same conditions hold for workers (Locke, Shaw, Saari, & Latham, 1981). A high yet realistic goal leads to better performance than an easy goal. A vague "do your best" goal is no better than no goal at all. For a goal to be effective, workers must be committed to achieving it and must receive periodic feedback on their progress. Once they reach their goal, they must be rewarded; otherwise, they will be indifferent toward setting goals later on.

Concept Check

9. *Under what conditions would people be most likely to keep their New Year's resolutions? (Check your answer on page 419.)*

AGE AND SEX DIFFERENCES IN NEED FOR ACHIEVEMENT

Some people have such a strong need for achievement that they will devote every available moment to an ambitious task they have set for themselves. They are so highly motivated by achievement for its own sake that they need no other reward. An extrinsic incentive, such as extra pay for high accomplishment, does not enhance their performance (McClelland, 1985). The challenge itself is all the motivation they need. Others place a lower value on achievement. How does the need for achievement develop, and why does it become stronger in some people than in others?

The Development of Need for Achievement in Childhood

Given that the need for achievement is a secondary motivation (one that is learned) rather than a primary motivation (one that serves a direct biological need), we might imagine that people would take a long time to develop it. In fact, children 18 months old clearly show pride in their accomplishments, such as building a tall stack of blocks. By age 2½, they understand the idea of competition; they show pleasure at beating someone else, disappointment at losing (Heckhausen, 1984).

Although preschool children show great plea-

Does school take the joy out of learning? Many students might say yes. In school, children discover that some of their peers handle tasks better than they do. Poor grades and public comparisons may make a once-optimistic child feel like a failure, especially if the teacher favors the best students.

sure at completing a task, they seldom appear distressed by their inability to complete it. Heinz Heckhausen (1984) tried to find out how children less than 4 years old would react to failure. He rigged up various contraptions so that a child's stack of blocks would topple or fall through a trap door. He often managed to arouse the children's curiosity, never their discouragement. Eventually he began to suspect that children learn the experience of success long before they understand failure.

Preschool children are highly optimistic about their own abilities. Even if they have failed a task repeatedly, they announce confidently that they will succeed the next time. An adult asks, "Who is going to win this game the next time we play?" Most preschool children shout "Me!" even if they have lost time after time in the past (Stipek, 1984).

Perhaps optimism comes naturally to humans. We quickly learn how it feels to succeed; we learn more slowly what it means to fail. When children enter school, their teachers force them to compare themselves to one another. Within a few years, some children approach tasks with a fear of failure instead of a joyful striving for success (Stipek, 1984).

Psychologists have not yet determined when and why children change their attitudes toward success and failure, but they suspect teachers unintentionally convey the message, "You probably aren't going to like this or do it very well, but you have to do it anyway." Jere Brophy (1987, page 190) reports the following quotes from junior high teachers:

- "If you get done by ten o'clock, you can go outside."

- "This penmanship assignment means that sometimes in life you just can't do what you want to do. The next time you have to do something you don't want to do, just think: 'Well, that's part of life.'"

- "You'll have to work real quietly, otherwise you'll have to do more assignments."

- "This test is to see who the really smart ones are."

Sex Differences in Need for Achievement

According to some reports, women score lower than men do on need for achievement as measured by the Thematic Apperception Test. The difference is subject to both biological and environmental interpretations. Male hormones may encourage aggressiveness and competition in humans, as they clearly do in other species. Aggressiveness and competition are not the same as striving for achievement, but they may facilitate it. In addition, our society encourages boys to set high goals and to begin competing at an early age, while it encourages girls to concentrate more on being sensitive to the needs of others (Honig, 1983).

Perhaps the reason for the sex difference in need for achievement has to do with neither hor-

Does society value men's achievements more than women's? If so, does that tendency lead women to set different goals from men or to value achievement less highly? In recent years women have begun to reach high levels of achievement in areas previously dominated by men, such as politics. Supreme Court Justice Sandra Day O'Connor is one such example.

mones nor early experiences but with social influences in adolescence and later life. The goals that high school girls set for themselves are about as high as those of high school boys (Farmer, 1983). Within several years after high school, many women lower their goals. Why?

In one study, a group of adult women filled out a job-interest questionnaire. The interests they checked most frequently included secretary, elementary teacher, home economics teacher, and dietician. Two weeks later they filled out the questionnaire again, but this time they were given these instructions:

I want you to pretend with me that men have come of age and that: (1) Men like intelligent women; (2) Men and women are promoted equally in business and the professions; and (3) Raising a family well is very possible for a career woman. [Farmer & Bohn, 1970, page 229].

After hearing these instructions, the women showed a significantly increased interest in becoming an author, psychologist, lawyer, insurance salesperson, or physician. They largely lost interest in becoming a secretary, teacher, or dietician (Farmer & Bohn, 1970). Evidently, women lower their career aspirations because they fear that high ambitions

will scare men away, or because they believe businesses will not promote them fairly, or because they fear that a full-time career will interfere with raising a family (Farmer, 1987).

Women have often been led to believe, perhaps correctly, that men resent and dislike highly successful women. Matina Horner (1972) proposed that women have low motivation for achievement because they have a *fear of success*. She did not mean that women try to fail, but merely that they might try to avoid high, conspicuous levels of success. Horner asked 90 college women to complete a story beginning, "After the first-term finals, Anne finds herself at the top of her medical school class." She asked 88 men to do the same, except that she substituted "John" for "Anne." Almost two thirds of the women told stories in which Anne quit medical school or suffered social rejection or other misfortunes. Less than one tenth of the men said that anything unpleasant happened to John. Horner concluded that women have been taught that high levels of achievement are unfeminine; once they approach those levels, they begin to fear the consequences.

However, these results have been difficult to replicate. They have a "now you see it, now you don't" quality. In most later studies, about an equal percentage of men and women raised concerns about fear of success (Zuckerman & Wheeler, 1975). Was Horner therefore wrong? Not necessarily. The results could have differed because of changes in procedure, including slight changes in instructions. They could also have differed because of a change in society. Since the late 1960s, when Horner collected her first results, our society has developed a more supportive attitude toward women with career aspirations. Perhaps women today have less reason to fear success than women of the past had.

Are women right in believing that businesses will not promote them fairly? It is difficult to say. On the one hand, many businesses are making a deliberate effort to recruit and promote women, partly in response to court rulings that require equal treatment of women. On the other hand, "Two facts matter to business: Only women have babies and only men make rules" (Schwartz, 1989, page 65). Although many women want to take an extended leave from a job after they give birth, many employers prefer that they quit altogether. The result is that everyone loses: The woman leaves a promising career and later returns to the work force with much lower aspirations. The company loses a talented worker permanently. And observers conclude that it is a mistake to hire women for top jobs, because they are likely to quit (Schwartz, 1989). Perhaps our society will find better ways to enable women (and men) to combine career ambitions with family commitments.

SUMMARY

1. Some people work harder than others because of their strong need for achievement. Need for achievement can be measured by the stories a person tells when looking at a picture in the Thematic Apperception Test. (page 411)

2. People with a strong need for achievement prefer to set goals that are high but realistic. Given such a goal, they will work as hard as possible. (page 412)

3. In contrast, people with a low need for achievement or a strong fear of failure prefer goals that are either easy to achieve or so difficult that they provide a ready excuse for failure. (page 413)

4. Almost everyone is motivated to achieve a goal if the goal is realistic, if the person makes a serious commitment to achieving it, and if the person gets feedback on his or her efforts to reach the goal. (page 414)

5. Children begin showing delight in their accomplishments by age 1½. Preschool children are highly optimistic about their own abilities. After they enter school, they learn the meaning of failure and start to show discouragement. (page 414)

6. According to some reports, men have, on the average, a stronger need for achievement than women have, although some of the results are difficult to replicate. To some extent, women lower their aspirations because they fear that their high success may displease men or because they believe that employers will not promote them fairly. Studies in the 1960s indicated that women were inhibited by a fear of success, but that fear is no longer evident. (page 415)

SUGGESTION FOR FURTHER READING

McClelland, D. C. (1985). *Human motivation.* Glenview, IL: Scott, Foresman. A text by one of the pioneers in the study of achievement motivation.

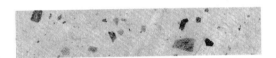

TERMS TO REMEMBER

acquired immune deficiency syndrome (AIDS) a disease often transmitted sexually that gradually destroys the body's immune system

anorexia nervosa a condition in which a person refuses to eat adequate food and steadily loses weight

bulimia a condition in which people have periods of excessive eating

drive an internal state of unrest that energizes learned behaviors

estrogen a hormone present in higher quantities in females than in males

expectancy the perceived probability of achieving a goal

externality hypothesis hypothesis that overweight people are motivated more strongly by external cues (such as the aroma and taste of food) than by internal cues (the physiological mechanisms that control hunger)

extrinsic motivation a motivation based on rewards and punishments separate from the act itself

fear of failure a preoccupation with avoiding failure, rather than taking risks in order to succeed

glucose the most abundant sugar in the blood

hierarchy of needs Maslow's categorization of human motivations, ranging from basic physiological needs at the bottom to the need for self-actualization at the top

homeostasis the maintenance of biological conditions within an organism in a state of equilibrium

incentive an external stimulus that pulls people toward certain actions

insulin a hormone released by the pancreas that increases the entry of glucose into the cells and increases the amount of food that is stored as fats

intrinsic motivation a motivation to engage in an act for its own sake

lateral hypothalamus an area of the brain that contributes to the control of hunger

libido according to Sigmund Freud, sexual energy

need for achievement a striving for competitive success and accomplishment

obesity the excessive accumulation of body fat

overjustification effect the tendency for intrinsic motivation to decline after people have been given more extrinsic motivation than necessary to perform a task

primary motivations motivations that serve obvious biological needs

rape sexual contact obtained through violence, threats, or intimidation

satiety the experience of being full, of feeling no hunger

secondary motivations motivations that develop as a result of specific experiences and that do not directly serve any biological need

self-actualization the need to achieve one's full potential

set point a level (such as a weight level) that the body attempts to maintain

sexual identity the sex a person regards himself or herself as being

sexual orientation a person's preference for male or female sex partners

testosterone a hormone present in higher quantities in males than in females

venereal disease a disease that is spread through sexual contact

ventromedial hypothalamus an area of the brain, in which damage leads to weight gain via an increase in the secretion of insulin

Answers to Concept Checks

1. College students who play tennis for recreation are following an intrinsic motivation. A student who practices tennis in hopes of a professional career is following an extrinsic motivation. According to the overjustification effect, you should expect a retired professional tennis player to enjoy playing tennis less than other people do—at least less than other players of high ability. (page 380)

2. Your interest in graduating from college is a secondary motivation, because it is something you had to learn to value. Such secondary motivations can become very strong. (page 380)

3. Insulin levels are higher in the middle of the day. As a result, much of the food you eat is stored as fats and you become hungry again soon. Late at night, when insulin levels are lower, some of your fat supplies are converted to glucose, which enters the blood. (page 386)

4. Damage to the lateral hypothalamus leads to weight loss. Damage to the ventromedial hypothalamus leads to weight gain. (page 388)

5. The set point has increased. (page 388)

6. A fetus exposed to very low levels of both testosterone and estrogen throughout prenatal development would develop a normal female appearance. High levels of testosterone lead to male anatomy; low levels lead to female anatomy. The level of estrogen does not play a decisive role. (page 406)

7. Not necessarily. The suggestion is that prenatal stress (or any other condition with equivalent effects) may interfere with the effect of testosterone on the brain during a critical stage of its development, even though the testosterone levels may be within the normal range. After the stress is removed, the testosterone levels remain normal, but certain aspects of brain development have already been determined. (page 408)

8. You were right if you said the coach has a high need for achievement, because he chose a schedule that will pose an intermediate challenge—not too easy, not too difficult.

   You were also right if you objected that I did not give you enough information to answer the question. I did not tell you how Generic Tech's team fared last season. If they went undefeated last year, then the new schedule may be too easy. If Tech has not won a game in years, then the schedule is too difficult. If the schedule is either too easy or too difficult, then the coach probably has a fear of failure. (page 413)

9. A New Year's resolution is like any other goal: People are more likely to keep it if it is realistic, if they state the resolution publicly, and if they receive feedback on how well they are achieving it. (page 414)

CHAPTER

12

EMOTIONS, HEALTH PSYCHOLOGY, AND STRESS

The *Star Trek* character Mr. Spock is reputed to feel very little emotion because he is half Vulcan—and people from the planet Vulcan feel no emotions at all. Suppose you are the first astronaut to land on Vulcan. The Vulcans gather around and ask you, their first visitor from Earth, what *emotion* is. What do you tell them?

"Well," you might say, "emotion is how you feel when something surprisingly good or surprisingly bad happens to you."

"Wait a minute," they reply. "We don't understand these words *feel* and *surprisingly.*"

"All right, how about this: Emotions are experiences like anger, fear, happiness, sadness. . . ."

"Anger, fear—what do those terms mean?" the Vulcans ask.

Defining such terms would be like trying to explain *color* to a blind person—maybe harder. Even though blind people cannot experience color, they can determine whether someone else has color vision by showing cards like the ones in Chapter 5. Anyone who reports seeing one pattern in the cards has color vision; anyone who reports seeing another pattern does not. Could you set up a similar test that would let the Vulcans determine whether someone was experiencing an emotion? Perhaps, but what sort of test could you use? The problem is clear: *Color vision* has a well-established meaning; *emotion* has an imprecise meaning that is defined mostly by example.

Although we might not be able to explain emotion to the Vulcans, we might learn something about emotions from them: What is the function of emotions? Could we get by without them? Might we sometimes be better off without them? By studying beings who experience no emotion, we might come to understand the role of emotions in our own behavior.

In this chapter we shall consider what psychologists have learned so far about emotions, which still leaves some major questions unanswered. We begin with general theories and principles. Then we turn to the role of emotions in health and the ways in which people cope with the emotions associated with stress.

When we experience emotions, we are in some way moved. (Movement is the root of emotion.) Our feeling of disturbance is a positive or negative excitement; sometimes we cry for joy, sometimes for grief. Although emotions are hard to define, we know what others mean when they say, "I'm angry," "He feels embarrassed," or "She's really happy."

EMOTIONAL BEHAVIORS

What causes us to feel one emotion or another?
What determines the intensity of the emotion?
What causes anger?
What causes happiness?

———————————

You may have heard the expression "as happy as a clam." How happy *is* a clam? More to the point, how could anyone *know* whether a clam was happy (or sad or anything else)?

Let's take something easier: How can we tell whether a dog feels emotions? "Simple," you may answer. "We can tell from its facial expression, whether it barks or whines, whether it charges forward or backs off, and whether it wags its tail." Because all these behaviors—except tail-wagging—resemble the way we ourselves express emotions, we assume that dogs experience emotions similar to ours.

What about fish? Do they have emotions too? Fish never change their facial expression, they do not make sounds, and they wag their tail only to propel themselves through the water. They do not *express* emotion the same as we do or even as dogs do. But expressing emotion is not the same thing as feeling emotion. To decide whether a fish (or a clam) experiences emotion, we need some way to measure or infer emotion from the animal's behavior. For example, fish attack intruders, swim away from danger, mate, and engage in other behaviors that humans find highly emotional. So we might say that fish engage in certain "emotional behaviors," even though we have no way to determine whether they *experience* emotions the same way we do.

As these examples suggest, we cannot be sure what emotional experiences dogs, clams, or even other humans have. For that reason, any scientific study of emotion must begin with systematic studies of the observable aspects of emotion—its physiology, expressions, and effect on behavior.

EMOTION AND PHYSIOLOGICAL AROUSAL

Originally, the word *emotion* was a general term for any sort of turbulent movement. People used to talk about thunder as an "emotion of the atmosphere." Eventually, the word came to refer only to feelings that give rise to vigorous motion of the body, such as fear, anger, and joy.

In contemporary terms, an emotion is "an inferred complex sequence of reactions to a stimulus [including] cognitive evaluations, subjective changes, autonomic and neural arousal, impulses to action, and behavior designed to have an effect upon the stimulus that initiated the complex sequence" (Plutchik, 1982, page 551). According to that definition, emotion has many aspects, presumably linked to one another. One aspect—autonomic and neural arousal—is relatively easy to investigate scientifically. Most emotional states include increased arousal of the autonomic nervous system, which prepares the body for vigorous action.

We experience emotional arousal when we have a strong tendency either to approach or to avoid something, generally in an energetic way (Arnold, 1970). For example, love includes a strong drive to come close to another person. Anger includes a tendency to charge toward someone and to attack either through speech or action. Fear and disgust are associated with a tendency to escape. All emotions share certain features related to physiological arousal. So although anger, fear, and happiness are very different emotional states, we may express any one of them by screaming or by engaging in frenzied activity.

"But wait," you say. "Sometimes when I feel highly emotional I can hardly do anything at all. Like the time I borrowed a friend's car and then wrecked it. When I had to explain what had happened to the car, I could hardly speak." True, but even then your emotion was associated with a tendency to take vigorous action. While you were reporting the wreck to your friend, you undoubtedly felt a strong urge to run away. Although you

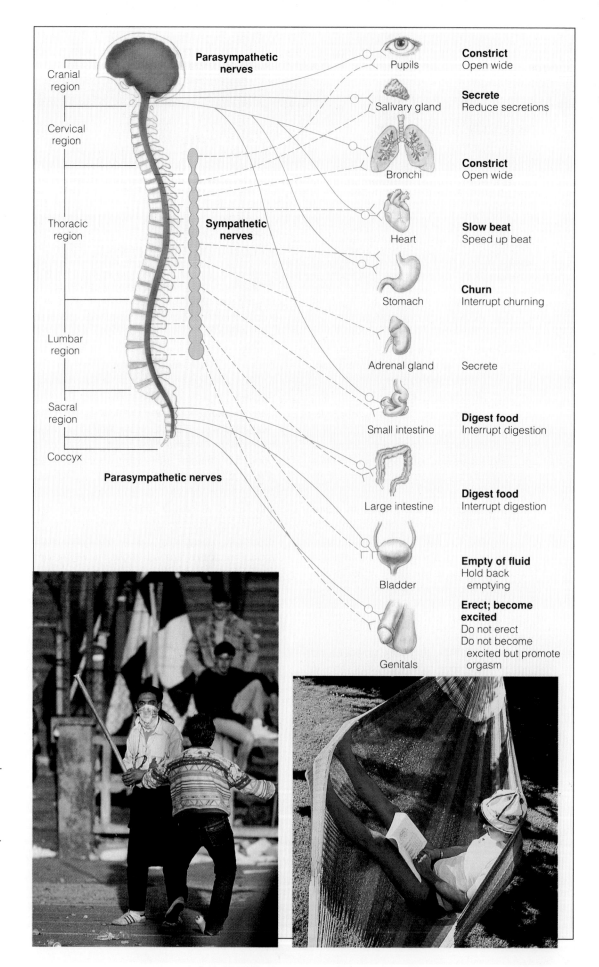

The sympathetic and parasympathetic nervous systems.

Parasympathetic nerves		
Cranial region	Pupils	**Constrict** Open wide
	Salivary gland	**Secrete** Reduce secretions
Cervical region	Bronchi	**Constrict** Open wide
Thoracic region	**Sympathetic nerves**	
	Heart	**Slow beat** Speed up beat
	Stomach	**Churn** Interrupt churning
Lumbar region	Adrenal gland	Secrete
	Small intestine	**Digest food** Interrupt digestion
Sacral region	Large intestine	**Digest food** Interrupt digestion
Coccyx	Bladder	**Empty of fluid** Hold back emptying
Parasympathetic nerves	Genitals	**Erect; become excited** Do not erect Do not become excited but promote orgasm

FIGURE 12.1

The sympathetic and parasympathetic nervous systems. Which system is at work in each of the photos? *Sympathetic,* sharing a common feeling, comes from the Greek *syn-* ("with") and *pathos* ("emotion"); the prefix *para-* here means "closely related to."

suppressed that urge, it made itself apparent in your trembling voice and shaking hands.

The intensity of emotional behaviors is strongly influenced by the autonomic nervous system, a good place to begin our study of emotion.

The Autonomic Nervous System

Any stimulus that arouses an emotion—such as a hug, a fire alarm, or a slap on the face—alters the activity of the **autonomic nervous system**, the section of the nervous system that controls the internal organs. The word *autonomic* means independent; biologists once believed that the autonomic nervous system operated independently of the brain and the spinal cord. We now know that the brain and the spinal cord send messages to alter the activity of the autonomic nervous system, but we continue to use the term *autonomic*.

The autonomic nervous system consists of the sympathetic nervous system and the parasympathetic nervous system (Figure 12.1). Two chains of neuron clusters just to the left and right of the spinal cord make up the **sympathetic nervous system**. These clusters are richly interconnected and tend to respond as a unit. Thus a stimulus that arouses any part of the sympathetic nervous system arouses the rest of it as well. Its axons extend to the heart, intestines, and other internal organs. The **parasympathetic nervous system** consists of neurons whose axons extend from the medulla and the lower part of the spinal cord to neuron clusters near the internal organs. These clusters are not directly interconnected; they essentially operate independently.

The *sympathetic* nervous system arouses the body for "fight or flight" (see Figure 12.2). For example, if someone charges at you, you may have to choose between fighting and running away; in either case, your sympathetic nervous system prepares you for a burst of vigorous activity. It does so by increasing your heart rate, breathing rate, production of sweat, and flow of epinephrine (EP-i-NEF-rin; also known as adrenaline). The *parasympathetic* nervous system decreases the heart rate and promotes digestion.

Both systems are constantly active, though one may be more active than the other at any given time. An emergency that demands a vigorous response increases the activity of the sympathetic system; a situation that demands no vigorous response increases the activity of the parasympathetic system. Once the stimulus that has excited sympathetic activity ceases, there is a "rebound" of increased parasympathetic activity (Gellhorn, 1970). (See Figure 12.3.) For example, while you are running away from an attacker, your sympathetic ner-

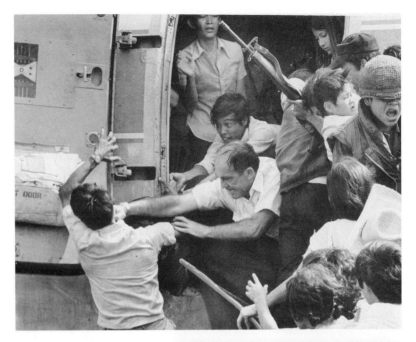

FIGURE 12.2

The fight-or-flight response. When a cougar charges a grizzly cub, the cub runs (if a place of safety is nearby) or fights. Only by mobilizing as much energy as possible does the cub have any chance for survival. During the fall of Saigon at the end of the Vietnam War, those already on an evacuation helicopter beat back others who wanted to climb aboard; there wasn't room for everyone who wanted to escape. As their postures and expressions show, this life-or-death situation aroused the fight-or-flight response in everyone.

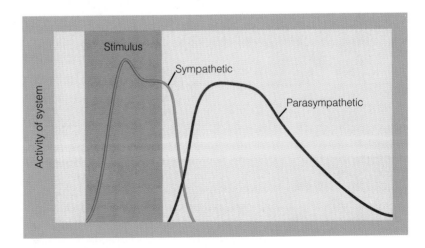

FIGURE 12.3

The autonomic rebound phenomenon. After removal of the stimulus eliciting the sympathetic response, the sympathetic response is reduced, while the opposing parasympathetic response is enhanced. This is why a "crash" follows a cocaine "high."

a

FIGURE 12.4

Emotion and the polygraph: Taking appropriate measures? The polygraph measures several variables at the same time (*poly-* meaning "many"). (a) A lie detector graphs the autonomic arousal that people usually experience when they lie. After posing unthreatening questions to establish a baseline, the examiner asks questions that may cause signs of arousal, as in the change in GSR (b).

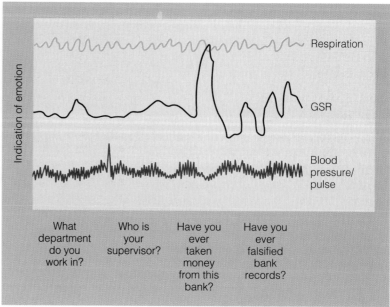

b

vous system increases your heart rate and your breathing rate. If the police suddenly intercept your attacker, your sympathetic arousal ceases, and your parasympathetic system becomes highly activated as a rebound. If the rebound is great enough, a person who has just escaped from danger may faint because of the sudden decrease in heart rate.

Concept Check

1. When you ride a roller coaster, does your heart rate increase or decrease? What happens after you get off? (Check your answers on page 463.)

Measuring the Activity of the Sympathetic Nervous System

Any new stimulus, such as a sudden flash of light or an unexpected loud noise, briefly activates the sympathetic nervous system. One way to measure this activation is to check the **galvanic skin response** (GSR)—that is, the electrical conductance of the skin. An investigator may place two electrodes on the skin, pass a weak, even imperceptible current between them, and measure changes in the flow of the current. Any activation of the sympathetic nervous system causes a slight sweat that moistens the skin and increases its ability to conduct electricity (Richter, 1929).

A more elaborate way of measuring activation of the sympathetic nervous system is by means of

a **polygraph**, a special instrument for recording physiological changes including blood pressure, heart rate, breathing rate, and GSR (see Figure 12.4).

The polygraph is occasionally used in psychological research, but its most common use is as a so-called lie detector. The assumption is that people feel anxious when they lie—especially when they are hooked up to a lie detector—and consequently their sympathetic nervous system will show more arousal than when they are telling the truth.

But does lying really produce more arousal than telling the truth does? Not necessarily. Some honest people become anxious and tense when they are asked about possible wrongdoing, even though they answer all questions truthfully. Other people, especially those who do not believe the polygraph test can catch them in a lie, manage to remain calm when they are lying (Waid & Orne, 1982).

People who try to detect lying without using a polygraph are correct only slightly more than half the time (Zuckerman, Koestner, & Alton, 1984). The polygraph detects lying more accurately than that, but not *much* more accurately. Typically, a polygraph examiner will mistakenly identify about one third of innocent, honest people as liars (Kleinmuntz & Szucko, 1984).

In the past, many employers relied on polygraph tests to screen job applicants or current employees, asking such questions as "Have you ever stolen from your employer?" Many honest people get nervous when asked such a question; conse-

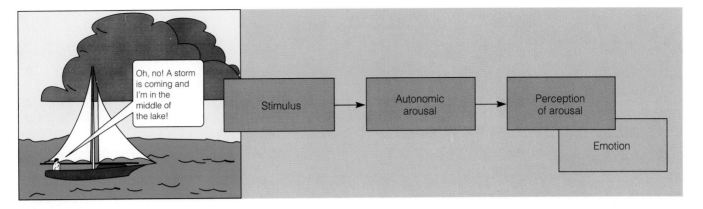

FIGURE 12.5

Which came first, the chicken or the egg? That is, do we tremble because we are afraid or do we feel afraid because we tremble? The James-Lange theory of emotions says the emotion follows arousal instead of sparking it. Here, the sudden realization that a storm is approaching arouses the sailor's autonomic system. The perception of this arousal leads to the experience of fear.

quently, employers who used polygraph tests rejected many worthy applicants and cast suspicion on many honest employees. In 1988 the U.S. Congress passed a law prohibiting private employers from using polygraph tests except under special circumstances (Camara, 1988). And courts of law rarely admit the results of polygraph tests.

The **guilty-knowledge test**, a modified version of the polygraph test, produces more accurate results by asking a different type of question (Lykken, 1974). Instead of asking, "Did you rob the gas station?" the interrogator asks, "Was the gas station robbed at 8 o'clock? At 10:30? At midnight? At 1:30 in the morning? Did the robber carry a gun? A knife? A club?" So long as the questions deal with facts that have not yet been publicized, innocent people should be no more nervous about one question than about another. A person who shows greater arousal when asked about the correct details of the crime than when asked other questions must have "guilty knowledge"—knowledge that only someone who had committed the crime or had talked to the person who committed it could possess. The guilty-knowledge test, when properly administered, almost never identifies an innocent person as guilty, though it sometimes identifies a guilty person as innocent.

Something to Think About

How might the results of the guilty-knowledge test be biased by a questioner who knows the correct details of the crime? How could the test be administered to minimize that bias?

The James-Lange Theory of Emotions

We have seen that any emotion triggers arousal of the autonomic nervous system. In 1884, William James and Carl Lange independently proposed that autonomic arousal is more than just an *indication* of emotion—in their view, it *is* the emotion (Figure 12.5).

Common sense suggests that an outside stimulus causes an emotion and that the emotion in turn causes autonomic changes and body movements: We cry because we are sad, we tremble because we are afraid, we attack because we are angry. James and Lange turned this concept around. According to the **James-Lange theory**, a stimulus evokes autonomic changes and body movements *directly,* and what we call an emotion is merely our perception of those changes and movements. We decide we are sad *because* we cry, we feel afraid *because* we tremble, we feel angry *because* we attack. Similarly, the act of smiling makes us happy and frowning makes us unhappy.

But what about the emotions people feel when they are not doing anything active? If you are attacking or running away, the emotion you are experiencing is clear, both to an observer and to yourself. But sometimes you feel angry, frightened, happy, or sad when you are just sitting still. How do you know which emotion you are experiencing? According to the James-Lange theory, you can tell by your autonomic state. You feel one way when you are angry, another way when you are happy, another way when you are frightened or sad. (Remember, according to this theory, an emotion

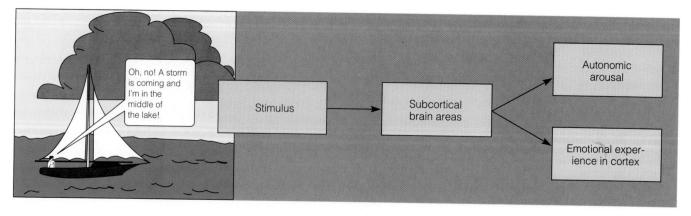

FIGURE 12.6

According to the Cannon-Bard theory of emotions, the cognitive experience of emotions—knowing you are afraid, say—is independent from the physiological response, such as breaking into a cold sweat. According to this theory, emotion occurs directly in the central nervous system. The sailor's brain becomes aware of fear even before feedback from the autonomic nervous system reaches the brain.

is the *perception* of what is happening in your body, not the *cause* of that change.) But is the autonomic state associated with anger noticeably different from the state associated with anxiety or any other emotion?

Heart rate and respiration increase during almost any emotion. Beyond that basic similarity, each emotional state has certain distinguishing physiological features (Davidson, 1978, 1984; Ekman, Levenson, & Friesen, 1983). With its "butterflies in the stomach" sensation, anxiety is probably the most distinctive emotional experience (Neiss, 1988). Your heart rate increases a little more when you are angry or frightened than when you are happy; the temperature of your hands increases more when you are angry than when you feel any other emotion. Your facial muscles respond in different ways when you experience different emotions, even though you are not actually smiling or frowning or making any other observable expression (Schwartz, 1982).

Granted that emotional states produce different physiological states, do those differences account for the differences in emotions, as James and Lange proposed? If you begin to breathe rapidly and your heart begins to race, do you decide whether you are angry or frightened by checking the temperature of your hands—or any other physiological indicator? Or do you decide you are afraid because you see a tiger charging at you? If the tiger influences your decision, then James and Lange underestimated the importance of cognition in determining emotions. Several other psychologists have tried to clarify the role of cognition with other theories of emotions.

The Cannon-Bard Theory of Emotions

Walter Cannon (1927), a prominent American physiologist, proposed that an emotional state consists of autonomic changes and cognitions, which arise independently of the autonomic changes. This view, as modified by Philip Bard (1934), is known as the **Cannon-Bard theory of emotions** (see Figure 12.6). According to this theory, certain areas of the brain evaluate sensory information and, when appropriate, send one set of impulses to the autonomic nervous system and another set to the forebrain, which is responsible for the subjective and cognitive aspects of emotion.

Cannon and Bard were wrong in some of their notions about the anatomy of the system. For example, they suggested that the thalamus plays a key role in the cognitive interpretation of emotions; today psychologists assign this role to the limbic system, discussed in Chapter 3 (MacLean, 1970, 1980).

A more serious drawback to the Cannon-Bard theory is its insistence that the cognitive aspect of emotions is independent of the autonomic aspect. When tranquilizing drugs decrease the arousal of the sympathetic nervous system, they also decrease the intensity of emotions, especially anxiety. When people suffer damage to the spinal cord, and therefore lose sensations arising from the stomach, intestines, and other organs, they continue to feel emotions but less intensely than before (Jasnos & Hakmiller, 1975; Lowe & Carroll, 1985). In short, the cognitive experience of emotion does not appear

FIGURE 12.7

Testing a theory: Results of the Schachter and Singer experiment.

to be independent of the physiological changes, as Cannon and Bard suggested.

Schachter and Singer's Theory of Emotions

Suppose we wire you to another person in such a way that you share the other person's heart rate, breathing rate, skin temperature, and muscle tension. When the other person feels a particular emotion, will you feel it too? (If so, the results would strongly support the James-Lange theory.)

We cannot perform that experiment, but we can do the next best thing: We can use a drug to induce nearly the same physiological state in two people and then see whether they both report the same emotion. To make things a little more interesting, we can put them in different situations. If emotion depends only on a person's physiological state, as the James-Lange theory says, then both people will report the same emotion, even if they happen to be in different situations. Stanley Schachter and Jerome Singer (1962) put these ideas to a test in a now-famous experiment.

Schachter and Singer gave injections of the hormone epinephrine to a group of college students who agreed to participate in their experiment. (Epinephrine mimics the effects of arousal of the sympathetic nervous system for about 20 to 30 minutes.) The experimenters told some of the subjects that the injections were vitamins; they did not warn them about the likely autonomic effects. The subjects were then placed in different situations. Some were placed, one at a time, in a situation designed

to arouse euphoria, or excited happiness. The others were placed in a situation designed to arouse anger.

Each student in the euphoria situation was asked to wait in a room with a very playful confederate, or accomplice, of the experimenter. The confederate flipped wads of paper into a trash can, sailed paper airplanes, built a tower with manila folders, shot paper wads at the tower with a rubber band, and played with a Hula-Hoop. He encouraged the subject to join him in play.

Each subject in the anger situation was put in a waiting room with an angry confederate and asked to fill out an insulting questionnaire that included such items as these:

Which member of your immediate family does not bathe or wash regularly?

With how many men (other than your father) has your mother had extramarital relationships?

4 or fewer _____ 5–9 _____ 10 or more _____

Most students in the euphoria situation showed strong emotional responses. Some joined the confederate in his play (Figure 12.7), and some of them initiated play of their own. (One jumped up and down on the desk, and another opened a window and threw paper wads at passersby.) The students in the anger situation responded with different emotions; some muttered angry comments, and some refused to complete the questionnaire.

But another factor was important in this experiment. Some of the subjects had been informed

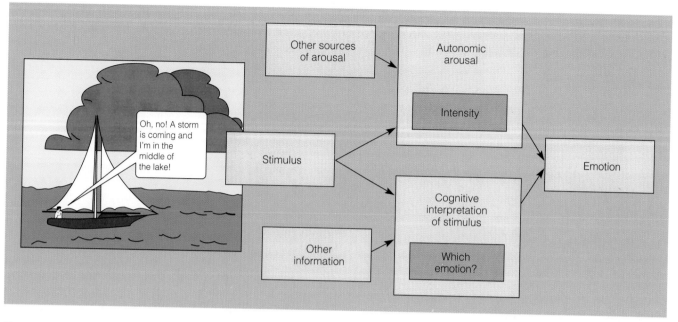

FIGURE 12.8

Schachter and Singer's theory of emotions says there is no one-to-one correspondence between a physiological state and an emotion. For example, if your face feels hot after someone says something to you, your feeling could be interpreted as shame, anger, embarrassment, or pleasure—or a combination of emotions. The storm stimulates the sailor, who may fear it or find it an exhilarating challenge.

To frighten people, today's horror movies rely on guts 'n' gore, the demented and deformed. But the sophisticated suspense films of Alfred Hitchcock reveal a genius for manipulating audiences; his movies are, says Pauline Kael, "a source of perverse pleasure." Perhaps psychologists could learn about inducing emotions from studying Rear Window, The Birds, *and* Notorious.

beforehand that the injections would produce certain autonomic effects, including hand tremor and increased heart rate. No matter which situation they were in, those subjects showed only slight emotional responses. When they felt themselves sweating and their hands trembling, they said to themselves, "Aha! I'm getting the side effects, just as they said I would."

What can we conclude from this experiment? According to **Schachter and Singer's theory**, a given physiological state is not the same thing as an emotion (see Figure 12.8). The intensity of the physiological state—that is, the degree of sympathetic nervous system arousal—determines the intensity of the emotion. But that physiological state could be perceived as any of several emotions. Depending on all the information people have about themselves and the situation, they could interpret a particular type of arousal as anger, as euphoria, or just as an interesting side effect of taking a pill. Table 12.1 contrasts Schachter and Singer's theory with the James-Lange and Cannon-Bard theories.

Unfortunately, these conclusions neglect another group of subjects—subjects whose results raise problems for Schachter and Singer's theory. These subjects were given placebo injections and then placed in the euphoria situation or the anger situation. According to the theory, these subjects should have experienced little emotion, because they had not been given any treatment to increase their autonomic arousal. However, they showed about as much euphoria in the euphoria situation and as much anger in the anger situation as did the subjects injected with epinephrine. Therefore, critics argue,

TABLE 12.1 Three Theories of Emotion

Theory		Comment
James-Lange theory	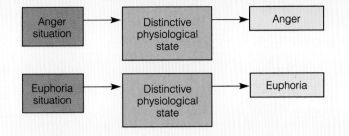	The situation determines the physiological state, and the physiological state completely determines the emotion.
Cannon-Bard theory	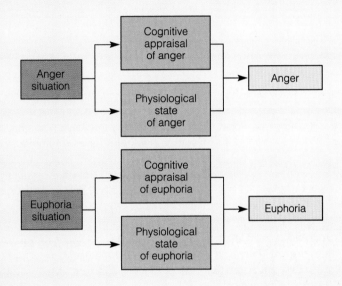	The situation determines the cognitive state and the physiological state independently.
Schachter-Singer theory	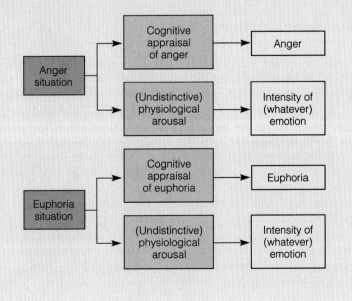	The situation determines the cognitive appraisal, which determines the emotion. All emotions are presumed to be physiologically indistinguishable; the physiological arousal determines the intensity of emotion but not the type of emotion.

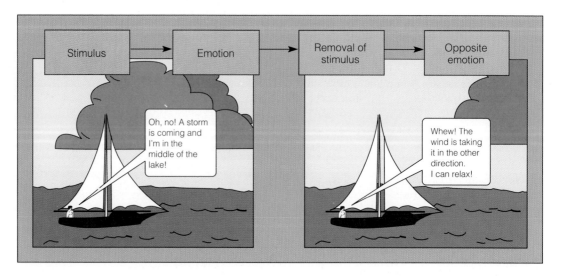

FIGURE 12.9

In the opponent-process principle of emotions, the opposite emotion replaces the initial one. When the storm disappears, the sailor's fear turns to relief.

the epinephrine injections may have had nothing to do with the results. If we accept that possibility, we are left with this summary of Schachter and Singer's experiment: People in a euphoria situation act happy; people in an anger situation act angry. That result is neither surprising nor theoretically important (Plutchik & Ax, 1967).

A further problem: Two separate studies failed to replicate Schachter and Singer's results. When students in those experiments were given a treatment to increase their arousal (either an epinephrine injection or a posthypnotic suggestion) and were then placed in a euphoria situation, they did not label their arousal as euphoria. Most of them identified it as anger (Marshall & Zimbardo, 1979; Maslach, 1979). Contrary to Schachter and Singer, we have no solid evidence that a given physiological state can be identified as different emotions at different times.

Schachter and Singer were right in calling attention to the importance of cognition, but they may have gone too far. In emphasizing how cognition determines our emotions, they downplayed the contributions of physiological states. To some extent, fear, anger, and happiness really do feel different physiologically, and those physiological differences contribute to emotions. Cognitions also contribute to emotions but not just as a way of labeling the physiological arousal.

So where are we in our quest for an understanding of emotions? None of the three theories is convincing at this point. While all three continue to be influential, especially Schachter and Singer's

theory, none is well established or widely accepted. The basis of emotions may be more complex: Cognitions influence physiological arousal and physiological arousal influences cognitions.

Concept Check

2. *You are in a small boat far from shore, and you see a storm approaching. You feel frightened and start to tremble. According to the James-Lange theory, which came first, the fright or the trembling? According to Schachter and Singer's theory, which came first? (Check your answers on page 463.)*

The Opponent-Process Principle of Emotions

Earlier I mentioned that the removal of a stimulus that activates the sympathetic nervous system leads to a rebound activation of the parasympathetic nervous system. That fact is related to a larger, general principle, the **opponent-process principle of emotions** (Solomon, 1980; Solomon & Corbit, 1974). According to this principle, the removal of a stimulus that excites one emotion causes a swing to an opposite emotion (see Figure 12.9). This principle is closely related to the opponent-process principle of color vision (discussed in Chapter 5). Recall that when you stare for a long time at one color and then look away, you see its opposite. (After staring at yellow, you see blue.) Solomon and Corbit suggest that the same principle holds for emotional states.

Suppose you make a parachute jump for the first time. As you start to fall, you experience an emotional state akin to terror. As you continue to fall and your parachute opens, your terror begins to subside. When you land safely, your emotional state does not simply return to normal; it rebounds in the opposite direction. You experience relief. As time passes, your relief gradually fades until at last you return to a normal state. Figure 12.10 shows these changes in emotional response over time. Solomon and Corbit refer to the initial emotion as the A state and the opposite, rebound emotion as the B state.

Here is another example: You hear on the radio that you have just won a million dollars in a lottery. You immediately experience elation and joy. Later you discover that you are not the winner after all. Someone with a similar name has won. Now you feel sad, even though you lost something you never had and never expected to have.

Solomon and Corbit further propose that repetition of an experience strengthens the B state but not the A state. For example, after you have made several parachute jumps, your rebound pleasure becomes greater and starts to occur earlier and earlier. Over time, you may not be aware of any initial terror at all; the entire experience becomes pleasant. In a less dramatic context, people find their first roller-coaster ride less pleasant than later rides.

Figure 12.10 illustrates the changes in emotional response that occur when the experience-and-rebound cycle is repeated many times. Note that the A state has become weaker and the B state has become stronger and more prolonged.

The opponent-process principle offers a link between emotions and motivations. As I mentioned briefly in Chapter 11, people sometimes seek stimulation and excitement for their own sake. Some people learn to enjoy parachuting and other thrill sports because of the emotions they produce. Those emotions are largely a product of the opponent-process principle; the B state that initially occurs as a relief at the end of the experience becomes more and more prominent with each repetition.

Concept Check

***3.** If we apply the opponent-process principle to the experiences drugs produce, we can describe the initial "high" as the A state and the subsequent unpleasant withdrawal experience as the B state. If someone takes a drug repeatedly, how will the A state and the B state change? (Check your answer on page 463.)*

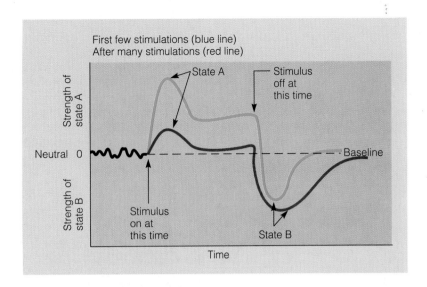

FIGURE 12.10

The opponent-process principle of emotions. The blue line shows emotional responses to a stimulus that is introduced and then withdrawn. The red line shows emotional responses to a stimulus that has been introduced and withdrawn repeatedly. Note how the intensity of the responses alters over time. (Based on Solomon & Corbit, 1974.)

THE EXPRESSION OF EMOTIONS

We experience certain emotions—anger, for example—primarily in the presence of other people. Embarrassment occurs almost exclusively in the presence of an audience, at least an imagined audience (Miller, 1986). We laugh louder when we laugh with others. Emotions in general are enhanced by having other people around, and we have many facial expressions and gestures for communicating our emotions.

I started this chapter by asking how you could tell whether a clam was feeling an emotion. That is difficult, because clams have no facial expressions. But with people we can study facial expressions and discern fairly accurately what emotions they are feeling and whether those emotions are growing more intense or are decreasing (Ekman, Friesen, & Ancoli, 1980). Some people are better at this than others. For reasons unknown, women tend to be somewhat more accurate than men are at detecting people's emotions in a variety of situations (Hall, 1978).

Can you make yourself happy by smiling or sad by frowning? James Laird (1974) molded people's faces into a smile or a frown by telling them to contract first this muscle, then that one, without ever using the words *smile* or *frown*. He found that

This symbol, by now the universal "cheer up" sign, is based on the notion explored by psychologists that your facial expression can influence your mood and emotions. Put on a happy face and you're bound to feel happier.

 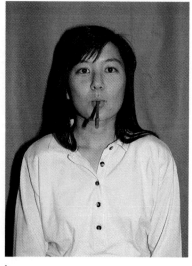

a   **b**

FIGURE 12.11

Funny faces and funny papers: When people hold a pen with their teeth (a), they rate cartoons as funnier than when they hold a pen with their protruded lips (b).

an induced smile made people more likely to feel happy, and that an induced frown made them more likely to feel sad or angry.

But remember the problem of *demand characteristics*: Subjects in an experiment often report what they think the experimenter expects them to report. Even though Laird never used the words *smile* or *frown,* the subjects may have identified their expressions and guessed that they were supposed to be related to their mood.

In another study, the experimenters found a clever way to conceal their purpose. They told subjects that the experiment had to do with how people with disabilities learn to write after losing control of their arms. The subjects were told to hold a pen either with their teeth or with their protruded lips, as Figure 12.11 shows. Then they were to use the pen in various ways, such as drawing lines between dots, underlining words on a page, and making checkmarks to rate the funniness of cartoons. When they held the pen with their teeth, their face was forced into a near-smile and they rated the cartoons as very funny. When they held the pen with protruded lips, they rated the cartoons as significantly less funny (Strack, Martin, & Stepper, 1988). (You might try holding a pen in one way and then the other while reading newspaper cartoons. Do you notice any difference?)

Cross-Cultural Similarities in Facial Expressions of Emotions

If we assume that the ancient ancestors of humans had anything in common with today's monkeys, then we can assume that they communicated their emotional states through gestures, facial expressions, and tone of voice (Redican, 1982). (See Figure 12.12.) When we evolved spoken language, we

FIGURE 12.12

Monkey see, monkey do? The facial expressions of chimpanzees are similar to those of humans.

FIGURE 12.13

The eyebrow-raising greeting by a man from New Guinea. (From Eibl-Eibesfeldt, 1973.) Traveling around the world, you could communicate anywhere by using such universal facial expressions of emotion as smiling and frowning. But you might give the wrong message if you didn't know that nodding your head in some cultures means "no" or which hand and foot gestures are insulting.

superimposed that upon the previous system without replacing it. We still use facial expressions to communicate our emotions more often than we use words. You wink, nod, or smile to show a romantic interest; you withhold such expressions to indicate a lack of interest. You signal your eagerness to end a conversation by checking your watch, by edging toward the door, or by some other nonverbal means. To *say* you are bored would be considered rude.

Many common facial expressions of emotions are similar throughout the world. Charles Darwin (1872/1965) asked missionaries and other people stationed in remote parts of the world to describe the facial expressions of the people who lived there. He found that people everywhere laugh, cry, smile, and frown and use similar facial expressions to pout, sneer, and blush and to express grief, determination, anger, surprise, terror, and disgust. Although the frequency and the circumstances in which people used those expressions varied, the expressions themselves were about the same.

A century later, Irenäus Eibl-Eibesfeldt (1973, 1974) photographed people in different cultures to document the similarities in their facial expressions. He confirmed that people throughout the world laugh, cry, smile, and frown; he also found that people in nearly all cultures wink, kiss, and stick out their tongue, although again the frequencies and the circumstances vary. He found that to express a friendly greeting, people raise their eyebrows briefly (Figure 12.13). The mean duration of that expression is the same in all cultures: one third of a second from start to finish, including one sixth of a second in the fully elevated position.

People in various cultures also interpret the meaning of facial expressions in much the same way. Paul Ekman and his associates (Ekman, 1972; Ekman, Sorenson, & Friesen, 1969) took photographs of Americans whose faces were showing happiness, anger, fear, disgust, surprise, and sadness and then asked people in the United States, Japan, Brazil, Chile, and Argentina to name the emotion that each face displayed (Figure 12.14). People in all these countries identified the expressions with greater than 80% accuracy.

In a later study, people from 10 cultures were shown photographs of faces and were asked to identify both the primary emotion in each case (the emotion expressed most strongly) and the secondary emotion that might also be present—for example, mostly anger plus a little disgust. People in all 10 cultures generally agreed on both the primary and the secondary emotion and on the intensity of the emotion in each case (Ekman et al., 1987). People are even better at identifying emotions when they can observe body position, voice quality, and speech content in addition to facial expressions (O'Sullivan, Ekman, Friesen, & Scherer, 1985).

Each culture has its own special expressions and gestures, as well as special rules that govern the use of facial expressions (Klineberg, 1938). For example, although people in all cultures laugh, they laugh at different things. The Chinese have elaborate rules on how to display grief. The Japanese are taught to smile when scolded by a superior. The Maori of New Zealand cry when they meet a friend after a long absence.

The Origin of Expressions and Gestures

The universality of any behavior may be the result of genetic similarities, learned responses to similar experiences, or both. For example, the reason people throughout the world are afraid of the dark may be that we all have genes favoring fear of the dark or that we have all learned that dark places really are dangerous.

Either explanation—similar genes or similar learning—seems to account for the origin of certain expressions and gestures. The best evidence for a genetic influence is that children who are born deaf and blind quickly develop normal expressions of smiling, frowning, laughing, and crying, even though they have had little or no opportunity to learn such expressions (Figure 12.15). The blind boy in Figure 12.16 covers his face in embarrassment just as a sighted person would. This response is particularly striking because the boy does not know what it means to see or to be seen.

Many common gestures are probably learned

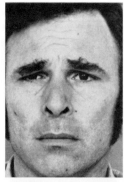

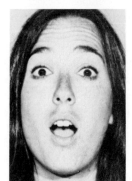

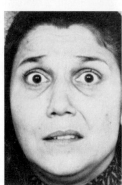

FIGURE 12.14

Face value: Faces expressing six emotions, used in experiments by Ekman. Can you identify which face conveys anger, disgust, fear, happiness, sadness, and surprise? Check your answers on page 463. (From Ekman & Friesen, 1984.)

FIGURE 12.15

This laughing girl was born deaf and blind. (From Eibl-Eibesfeldt, 1973.)

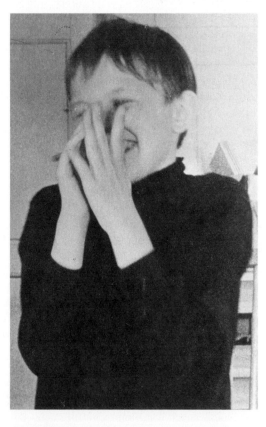

FIGURE 12.16

A boy, blind since birth, covering his face in embarrassment. (From Eibl-Eibesfeldt, 1973.) Does he share our sense of the notion of "looking foolish"?

modifications or extensions of built-in behaviors. For example, people in many, but not all, parts of the world shake their head to indicate "no." The origin of this gesture may be the infant's unlearned response of turning away from unwanted food. Later, a child learns to shake his or her head as a general indication of rejection.

Once the meaning of a gesture or an expression has become well established, people may use an opposite expression to convey the opposite meaning. Darwin called this the "principle of antithesis." For example, Eibl-Eibesfeldt (1973, 1974) has observed that some cultures use an "antigreeting" expression that is the opposite of the eyebrow-raising greeting. Instead of raising their eyebrows and slightly opening their mouth, these people close their eyes, lower their eyebrows, and tighten their lips. The message: "I close you out."

EXPERIENCING EMOTIONS

How many different emotions do humans experience? Carroll Izard (1977) distinguishes 10: interest, joy, surprise, distress, anger, disgust, contempt, fear, shame, and guilt. We could shorten this list by, for example, combining shame and guilt. Or we could expand the list by distinguishing between different degrees of an emotion such as distress versus anguish or fear versus terror. Should we add embarrassment to the list, or is that the same as shame? Some cultures identify emotions for which there are no words in the English language; for example, the Japanese identify a special emotion *amae,* "the need to be loved" (Lazarus, Averill, & Opton, 1970). Instead of trying to discuss each type of emotion, I shall focus on two common emotions, anger and happiness.

Anger and Aggressive Behavior

Anger is experienced as a desire to hurt another person or to drive another person away. It is a familiar and normal human emotion that can be destructive, either by leading to violent behavior or, if suppressed, by undermining relationships between people.

Most people become angry far more often than they become physically aggressive. In one study, some people were asked to describe their most recent experience of anger; others kept an "anger diary" for a week (Averill, 1983). They reported that in more than half their experiences of anger, their anger was directed against family or friends. They usually dealt with their anger by saying something to the person who had aroused it or by talking about the experience to someone else. Very rarely did they physically attack the person who had provoked their anger.

The Functions of Aggressive Behavior When anger does lead to aggressive behavior, what does the aggressive behavior *accomplish*? It must serve some adaptive purpose, or else it would not have evolved as a widespread behavior in so many species.

In both human and nonhuman animals, one of the main functions of aggressive behavior is **territoriality.** For example, during the reproductive season, pigeons and many other birds defend their nesting site and drive away any intruder that comes too close. That aggressive behavior enables them to keep competitors away from their mates and their food supplies. People too may respond aggressively to an invasion of their territory. (Imagine the reaction if you sat inches away from a stranger in an uncrowded library or stood very close to the only other person in an elevator.) Competition for a girlfriend or a boyfriend may also provoke aggressive behavior. About 20% of murders not committed in the act of robbery or other crimes are provoked by sexual jealousy (Daly, Wilson, & Weghorst, 1982).

However, there is an important difference between aggressive behavior in animals and in humans: Humans sometimes attack when they are not angry. Soldiers, for example, often fight because they are obeying orders even though they feel little or no hostility toward their enemies.

When soldiers are sent to fight in distant wars, they may not be motivated initially by hatred of the enemy. They fight only because they must follow orders.

When a riot erupts in America, as in the Liberty City section of Miami in 1980 or Detroit in 1967, reactions express either surprise that it happened or surprise that it didn't happen sooner. Martin Luther King, Jr., the civil rights leader who advocated nonviolent protest, said, "Riots are the language of the unheard." And in riots, the message of fury from frustration is loud and clear.

"An eye for an eye...": The problem of how to reduce violent behavior is ancient, while efforts to predict it are a modern development. Some solutions to the first problem—such as hanging or castrating a rapist—are no longer acceptable to many people, while success in prediction as a form of prevention has generally been limited.

Arousal of Anger and Aggression A rat in a cage or a human on the street may display anger that leads to aggressive behavior even in the absence of threats to territory or to mate selection. For example, you may get angry when a storekeeper sells you shoddy merchandise or when your boss denies you a promotion you think you deserve. According to the **frustration-aggression hypothesis**, all aggressive behavior is caused by "frustration" (Dollard, Miller, Doob, Mowrer, & Sears, 1939). You experience frustration when a motivated behavior is interrupted or when an expected reinforcement is withheld. Frustration can arise when a barking dog interferes with your sleep or when a drought prevents a good harvest. Although this hypothesis is phrased in terms of aggression, it applies to anger as well. A person who feels frustrated is likely to feel angry; if you waited in line for an hour only to discover that you were in the wrong line, you are likely to snap angrily at any convenient target.

However, the frustration-aggression hypothesis appears to be an oversimplification. Unpleasant events that do not cause frustration sometimes lead to aggressive behavior. For example, when two rats confined to a small cage receive shocks to their feet, they strike at each other as if they were defending themselves against an attack (Blanchard & Blanchard, 1984; Ulrich, Wolff, & Azrin, 1964).

Leonard Berkowitz (1983) has proposed a more comprehensive theory: All unpleasant events— including frustration, pain, foul odors, a hot environment, and frightening information—give rise to both the impulse to fight and the impulse to flee. Which impulse dominates depends on the circumstances, such as the availability of avoidance responses, the targets available for attack, and the individual's previous experiences with fighting and fleeing. For example, if someone bumps into you and spills hot coffee all over you, do you scream angrily? Perhaps. But if that person is your boss, or the loan and scholarship officer at your college, or the biggest and meanest-looking person you have ever seen, you may smile and apologize for being in the way.

Prediction and Control of Violent Behavior People who cannot control their anger sometimes commit acts of violence, even criminal acts. Anger is hardly the only cause of violence, but because it is one primary cause, let's now consider how psychologists try to predict violent behavior.

A parole board is trying to decide whether or not to release a prisoner who is eligible for parole. The staff of a mental hospital is debating whether or not to discharge a patient with a history of violent behavior. A judge is trying to decide whether or not to send a first-time offender to jail. In each case, the authorities ask a psychologist or a psychiatrist for a professional opinion on whether the person is dangerous.

How accurate are such opinions? If they are based mainly on interviews, they are accurate only a little more often than they would be by chance (Monahan, 1984). Some dangerous people manage to convince others that they are harmless.

The most accurate predictions are those based on biographical information. People who were physically abused as children and who witnessed violence between their parents are more likely than others are to commit repeated acts of violence, including murder (Eron, 1987; Lewis et al., 1983, 1985, 1987). The physical pain of being beaten may provoke future violence, and a violent parent provides a model for the child eventually to imitate. (Recall the principles of social learning from Chapter 7.)

Many other biographical factors increase the likelihood of violent behavior (Eron, 1987; Lewis et al., 1983, 1985):

- A history of acting violently during childhood
- Not feeling guilty after hurting someone
- Symptoms of brain damage or of major psychological disorders
- Being closely related to someone who has been committed to a psychiatric hospital

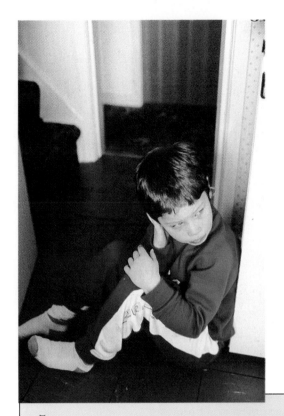

Time out: Some violent behavior is learned and can be extinguished. One technique is a form of deprivation, isolating a child after he or she hits others. Another method reinforces good behavior—an approach used for the chatterbox in Chapter 1.

- A history of suicide attempts
- Watching a great deal of violence on television

How can anyone help people to control their violent behavior? Punishment is sometimes effective and may be necessary in extreme cases, but it is often counterproductive. Excessively painful punishment actually triggers aggressive behavior.

Sometimes cognitive approaches are effective. People can be taught to stop making unrealistic, perfectionistic demands on themselves and others. They can be taught to tolerate frustration.

Encouraging people to learn new behaviors is another way to control violent behavior (Fehrenbach & Thelen, 1982). Eliminating reinforcement may extinguish or reduce the offensive behavior. If a child has learned to win attention by throwing temper tantrums, for example, then parents and teachers should ignore the tantrums. Or they can impose "time-out" periods after an episode of violent behavior, perhaps by temporarily isolating a child who regularly attacks other children. Finally, they can reinforce acceptable behavior, perhaps by giving points toward a reward for every hour spent in calm conversation.

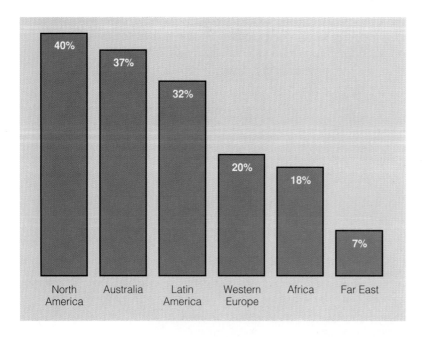

FIGURE 12.17

Percentages of people in different regions who responded "very happy" to the question, "Generally speaking, how happy would you say you are—very happy, fairly happy, or not too happy?" (Based on data from Gallup, 1976–1977.)

Happiness

What makes people happy? The answer is more elusive than you might expect. Common sense tells us that people are happy when more good things than bad things happen to them. You are happy when you earn a promotion at work or a good grade at school, when you win an award, or when you receive a compliment. You are also happy when you rid yourself of a worry that made you unhappy—remember the opponent-process principle. For example, you become happy when you discover that the $500 fine you received for overdue library books was a mistake.

However, such events make people happy only for a little while. Most people do not become permanently depressed because of a single tragic event, and hardly anyone becomes permanently happy because of a single good event. A person who won a lottery a few years ago is not significantly happier than most other people are; a person whose spinal cord was badly injured a few years ago is only a little less happy than others are (Brickman, Coates, & Janoff-Bulman, 1978). As the novelist Fyodor Dostoyevsky (1862/1986, page 29) wrote concerning his years in prison, "Man is a creature that can get used to anything, and I think that is the best definition of him!"

The events of the day may account for the fact

that you are a little happier than usual today or will be a little less happy tomorrow, but they do not account for long-term happiness. Why are some people happy just about all the time, while others are almost never cheerful? Are certain kinds of people consistently happier than others?

Perhaps so, but measuring and comparing happiness is difficult. In the case of anger, an observer can at least occasionally observe behaviors associated with the emotion. An angry person sometimes attacks. What does a happy person do? Because happiness is not consistently linked to any particular type of behavior, the main way for psychologists to measure happiness is to ask people how happy they are.

That method is suitable for some purposes but not all. Suppose I rate how happy I am on a scale from 0 ("totally unhappy") to 7 ("as happy as I could be"). Last Tuesday I checked 3; today I check 5. A reasonable conclusion is that I am happier today than I was last Tuesday. But suppose you check 7. Does that mean that you are happier than I am? Perhaps your 7 is no happier than my 5.

Figure 12.17 shows the percentages of people in different parts of the world who rate themselves as "very happy." Are there really that many more happy people in Latin America than in Europe? Are there really so few happy people in the Far East? Or does the expression "very happy" mean different things to different people (and in different languages)? Until psychologists find better ways to measure happiness, such questions will be difficult to answer.

The other major problem in studying happiness is that investigators must rely mostly on correlational data. They find, for example, that wealthy people tend to be happier than poor people are. Does that mean that money buys happiness or that happy people are likely to succeed at their jobs and become wealthy? Married people are generally happier than unmarried people. Is that because marriage makes people happy or because no one wants to marry an unhappy person? Employed people are happier than unemployed people are. Undeniably, losing a job makes a person unhappy, but perhaps people with a happy attitude hold onto their jobs longer than others do.

Religious people tend to be happier than people with no religious faith. People with close family ties and many friends tend to be happier than are people with few social contacts. People who are healthy, who love someone, and who are achieving their goals also tend to be happy. In each case, the results are clear, but the explanation is not. We know what is correlated with happiness; we cannot say what causes happiness (Diener, 1984).

Within a given country, at a given time, wealthy people tend to be happier than poor people are. However, people in wealthy countries do not seem to be much happier than people in poor countries. Moreover, as a given country—the United States, for example—becomes wealthier and wealthier, the average person in that country does not become happier and happier (Diener, 1984). Apparently happiness is related not to having a certain absolute amount of wealth but to having *more* wealth than other people have.

Do you make happiness happen—or is it something that happens to you? Most of us would agree that birthday parties, weddings, and other celebrations are happy occasions, but we would have trouble describing our happiness at such events. According to novelist Aleksandr Solzhenitsyn, imprisoned for years in a Soviet labor camp, "It is not the level of prosperity that makes for happiness but the kinship of heart to heart and the way we look at the world.... A man is happy so long as he chooses to be happy, and no one can stop him."

Summary

1. Emotions are generally associated with arousal of the sympathetic or parasympathetic branch of the autonomic nervous system. The sympathetic nervous system readies the body for emergency action. The parasympathetic nervous system promotes digestion and other less vigorous activities. It also becomes highly active immediately after the cessation of strong sympathetic arousal. (page 423)

2. The polygraph measures the activity of the sympathetic nervous system through such variables as heart rate, breathing rate, blood pressure, and electrical conductance of the skin. The polygraph is sometimes used as a "lie-detector," although its accuracy for that purpose is low. (page 426)

3. According to the James-Lange theory of emotions, an emotion is the perception of a change in the body's physiological state. (page 427)

4. According to the the Cannon-Bard theory, the cognitive experience of an emotion is independent of physiological arousal. (page 428)

5. According to Schachter and Singer's theory, autonomic arousal determines the intensity of an emotion, but does not determine what that emotion will be. We identify an emotion on the basis of how we perceive the situation. (page 429)

6. None of these three theories of emotion is fully satisfactory. Physiological and cognitive influences interact in complex ways to produce emotional experiences. (page 432)

7. As the opponent-process principle of emotions points out, the removal of the impetus for a given emotion brings about a sudden swing to the opposite emotion. (page 432)

8. Facial expressions are closely tied to emotions. When people move their facial muscles into something that resembles a smile, they are more likely to be happy or amused than if they maintain other expressions. (page 433)

9. Many human facial expressions are largely the same for cultures throughout the world. (page 434)

10. People experience anger frequently, although it seldom leads to violent acts. Aggressive behavior often occurs in defense of territory or in competition for a mate. Frustration or other unpleasant experiences often prompt aggressive behavior. (page 437)

11. Psychologists and psychiatrists find it difficult to predict whether a particular prisoner would be dangerous if released. Currently, the best way to make such predictions is to review the prisoner's biographical information, especially the history of violent behavior. (page 439)

12. Happiness is difficult to measure, and most of what we know about it is based on correlational data. People are likely to be happy if they are wealthy, married, employed, healthy, and religious and if they have close ties to family and friends. The causes of happiness remain uncertain. (page 440)

Suggestions for Further Reading

Jones, W., Cheek, J., & Briggs, S. (Eds.) (1986). *Shyness: Perspectives on research and treatment.* New York: Plenum. See especially R. S. Miller's chapter on embarrassment.

Mandler, G. (1984). *Mind and body: Psychology of emotion and stress.* New York: Norton. Perhaps the best scholarly work on the emotions.

HEALTH PSYCHOLOGY

How do our emotions affect our health?

Bobby Boozer lives on high-fat foods. He smokes a pack of cigarettes every day and drinks a case and a half of beer every week. He sleeps irregular hours and rarely exercises. He has unsafe sex with partners he hardly knows. He worries all the time. He is angry with his boss, his neighbors, and the salesman who sold him a lemon of a car. And he still carries a grudge against Suzie Jones, who once embarrassed him in front of his friends back in the seventh grade. What are his chances of living a healthy life?

You know the answer. And no doubt so does he. Our health—good, bad, or in between—depends largely on how we live. But this does *not* mean that you are responsible for every illness you get. Even if you follow all the advice your physician gives you, you may be jogging home from the health food store one day when a stranger bumps into you, coughs in your face, and gives you pneumonia. We do not have complete control over our health. But we do have some control.

Health psychology deals with the ways in which people's behavior can enhance health and prevent illness and how behavior contributes to recovery from illness (Feist & Brannon, 1988). It deals with such issues as why people smoke, why they may ignore their physician's advice, and how to reduce pain. In this section, we shall focus mainly on how stress and other emotional conditions and situations affect health.

STRESS

Have you ever gone without sleep several nights in a row trying to finish an assignment before a deadline? Or waited what seemed like forever for some-

one who was supposed to pick you up? Or had a close friend suddenly not want to see you anymore? Or tried to explain why you no longer want to date someone? Each of these experiences provokes an emotional response and causes stress.

Selye's Concept of Stress

According to Hans Selye (1979), an Austrian-born physician who worked at McGill University in Montreal, **stress** is "the nonspecific response of the body to any demand made upon it." Every demand on the body evokes certain *specific* responses as well. The body responds in one way to the loss of blood, in another way to the lack of sleep. But *all* demands on the body evoke generalized, nonspecific responses. For example, they all activate the sympathetic nervous system, increase the release of the hormone epinephrine, and interfere with your ability to concentrate.

When people say, "I've been under a lot of stress lately," they are generally referring to a string of unpleasant experiences. Selye's concept of stress is broader than that: He includes any experience that brings about some change in a person's life. For example, getting married or being promoted is presumably a pleasant experience, but it also demands that you make a number of changes in the way you live, and so in Selye's sense it produces stress. It is unclear, however, whether a favorable stressor makes the same demands on the body as does an unfavorable stressor.

According to Selye, the body goes through three stages in its response to a stressor: The first is *alarm,* a brief period of high arousal of the sympathetic nervous system. However, the body cannot maintain a high level of arousal indefinitely. If the stressor persists, the body enters into *resistance,* a stage of moderate arousal and adaptation to the stressor. If that stage is too intense or lasts too long, the body enters the third stage, *exhaustion,* in which the sympathetic nervous system no longer responds and the parasympathetic system takes over. The end result is what Selye calls the **general adaptation syndrome**, which is characterized by weakness, fatigue, loss of appetite, and a general lack of interest. This condition may even weaken the immune system and make the body vulnerable to sickness (Riley, 1981). (See Figure 12.18.)

Prolonged exposure to stress produces more severe effects than short-term stress does (Fran-

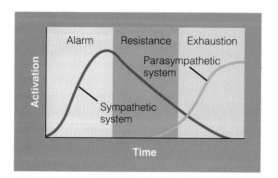

FIGURE 12.18

The three stages of the
stress reaction.

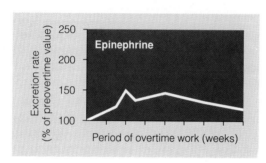

FIGURE 12.19

Stressed out: Epinephrine levels of a group of women before, during, and after a long
period of working overtime. To establish a baseline, each woman's epinephrine level
prior to the overtime period was taken as 100%; thus any number above 100% represents an increase. (From Frankenhaeuser, 1980.)

*In recent years, stress management has become a growth industry.
Some stress is inevitable and appropriate, but too much for too
long can be dangerous. In this measurement of stress, blood samples are taken from this subject before he begins a video game
designed to reduce emotional stress. Once he finishes the game, a
second blood sample will be taken to compare levels of epinephrine in his blood before and after the game.*

kenhaeuser, 1980). When factory workers perform
repetitive, physically difficult work, their epinephrine levels rise steadily throughout the working day.
In one group of women who had to work overtime
for several weeks, epinephrine levels rose throughout the entire period and remained elevated even
after their work hours returned to normal (Figure
12.19).

The mere threat of danger can have similar
effects. In a highly publicized accident at the nuclear
power plant at Three Mile Island, Pennsylvania,
people who lived nearby were in serious danger
but experienced no actual harm. A year later, they
still had elevated epinephrine levels, complained
of emotional distress, and showed impaired performance on a proofreading task (Baum, Gatchel,
& Schaeffer, 1983).

The effects of prolonged exposure to a stressor
depend on the nature of the stressor. Some Vietnam veterans, for example, experience **posttraumatic stress disorder**, a special kind of general
adaptation syndrome caused by prolonged exposure to combat or other traumatic experiences (Pitman, Orr, Forgue, deJong, & Claiborn, 1987). This
condition has been recognized after wars throughout history, under such names as "battle fatigue"
or "shell shock."

Years after returning to civilian life, someone
with posttraumatic stress disorder may suffer from
anxiety, depression, nightmares, guilt, and outbursts of anger. He or she may have difficulty concentrating or relating emotionally to other people
(Keane, Wolfe, & Taylor, 1987). A brief reminder of
war experiences can trigger a flashback that borders on panic.

One nationwide survey reported posttraumatic
stress disorder in 20% of the American veterans
who were wounded in Vietnam (Helzer, Robins, &
McEnvoy, 1987). The disorder occurs in about 3.5%
of veterans who were not wounded. It can also
occur in victims of rape and other violent attacks
and people who have watched someone get killed.

People with posttraumatic stress disorder are
likely to find day-to-day events stressful. During the
first year after their return to civilian life, veterans
with posttraumatic stress disorder report many
stressful events in their lives (Solomon, Mikulincer,
& Flum, 1988). They are more sensitive to new
stressors, which prolong the effect of the war trau-
mas, sometimes for years.

An Alternative to
Selye's View of Stress

Almost everyone reacts vigorously to certain kinds
of stressors, such as being bitten by a snake. But

This group of Vietnam vets met regularly for a year to work on problems related to post-traumatic stress. Since the group disbanded, one member has had a show of his hand-colored photographs (this group portrait is a sample of his work). Another member has started his own company. Some members have created new careers; some have been in and out of substance-abuse programs. Most continue to experience vivid dreams full of war images.

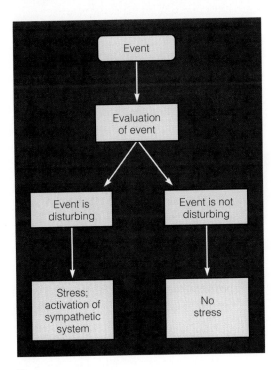

FIGURE 12.20

Do we assess stress? Lazarus believes that evaluation of some kind, conscious or unconscious, always precedes emotion.

common everyday events are clearly more stressful to some people than to others. Why?

An alternative to Selye's view holds that the amount of stress a person experiences depends on how the person interprets the stressful event rather than on the event itself (Lazarus, 1977). (See Figure 12.20.) Two men are bitten by a snake. The first man panics; the second man remains calm, because

he recognizes the snake as a harmless variety. Two women are criticized by their boss. One is deeply hurt; the other shrugs and says, "Wow, the boss is in a foul mood today!"

To the extent that stress depends on our interpretation of an event, not simply on the event itself, people can learn to cope with potentially stressful events, as we shall see later in this chapter. They can learn to deal with events actively instead of feeling threatened by them.

Measuring Stress and Its Effect on Health

Most investigators agree that severe stress can endanger a person's health. For example, prolonged job stress is significantly correlated with anxiety and depression (deWolff, 1985). People who experience severe stress on the job report frequent illnesses as well. (At least they often call in sick and stay home from work!)

How much stress is injurious to one's health? Is it true that the more stress a person experiences, the more that person's health suffers?

To answer such questions, we need to measure both stress and health. Measuring health is tough enough; measuring stress is even more difficult. One approach is to give people a checklist of stressful experiences. For example, Thomas Holmes and Richard Rahe (1967) devised a Social Readjustment Rating Scale that lists both desirable and undesirable events. (They were following Selye's idea that any event that forces a change in a person's life is stressful.) Each event has a point value indicating the effort a person would presumably need to adjust to it. For example, a person receives 100 points for the death of a spouse, 73 points for divorce, 50

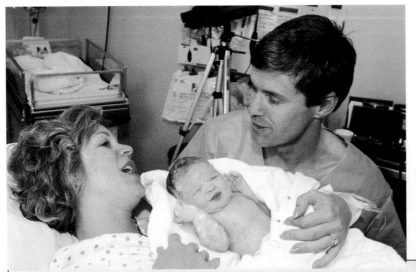

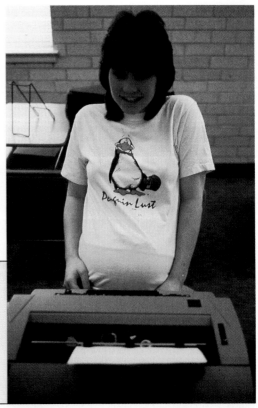

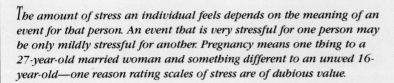

The amount of stress an individual feels depends on the meaning of an event for that person. An event that is very stressful for one person may be only mildly stressful for another. Pregnancy means one thing to a 27-year-old married woman and something different to an unwed 16-year-old—one reason rating scales of stress are of dubious value.

TABLE 12.2 Readjustment Rating Scale

Rank	Life Event	Point Value	Rank	Life Event	Point Value
1	Death of spouse	100	22	Change in responsibilities at work	29
2	Divorce	73	23	Son or daughter leaving home	29
3	Marital separation	65	24	Trouble with in-laws	29
4	Jail term	63	25	Outstanding personal achievement	28
5	Death of close family member	63	26	Wife begin or stop work	26
6	Personal injury or illness	53	27	Begin or end school	26
7	Marriage	50	28	Change in living conditions	25
8	Fired at work	47	29	Revision of personal habits	24
9	Marital reconciliation	45	30	Trouble with boss	23
10	Retirement	45	31	Change in work hours or conditions	20
11	Change in health of family member	44	32	Change in residence	20
12	Pregnancy	40	33	Change in schools	20
13	Sex difficulties	39	34	Change in recreation	19
14	Gain of new family member	39	35	Change in church activities	19
15	Business readjustment	39	36	Change in social activities	18
16	Change in financial state	38	37	Mortgage or loan less than $10,000	17
17	Death of close friend	37	38	Change in sleeping habits	16
18	Change to different line of work	36	39	Change in number of family get-togethers	15
19	Change in number of arguments with spouse	35	40	Change in eating habits	15
20	Mortgage over $10,000	31	41	Vacation	13
21	Foreclosure of mortgage or loan	30	42	Christmas	12
			43	Minor violations of the law	11

Source: Holmes & Rahe, 1967.

points for marriage, 47 points for getting fired, 40 points for pregnancy, and so on down through 12 points for surviving Christmas and 11 points for getting a traffic ticket. A person's points are added, and the total is assumed to reflect the amount of stress a person has experienced within a given time (see Table 12.2).

This scale has been widely criticized. For one reason, it includes 53 points for suffering the stress associated with "personal injury or illness." It also ascribes points for sex difficulties, change in sleeping habits, and change in eating habits—all symptoms of illness. So it is not very impressive to find that people with high stress scores have an increased probability of being ill.

The scale also fails to measure some important stressors. It takes no account of constant day-to-day problems such as coping with racism, sexism, or poverty. It also ignores the stress we experience from events that do *not* happen. For example, all year long you expect to be laid off from your job. You keep waiting, but the rumored plant closing never happens. Or you have been counting on a promotion at work, and you have told all your friends that you are expecting it, but then you do not get promoted. You get no points on the rating scale for "not getting fired" or "not being promoted." In fact, your experience does not count as stress according to Selye's definition of stress (a response to changes in your life). And yet anyone who has lived through such an experience can tell you that it was very stressful.

Aside from the problems with this particular scale, however, the whole approach of using a checklist to measure stress presents problems. As Richard Lazarus (1977) pointed out, the stress evoked by an event depends on how people interpret the event and what they do about it. An event that is highly stressful for one person may be only slightly stressful for another (Theorell, 1985). Being fired may be a disaster for a 50-year-old who is discharged for mismanaging company funds but only a minor annoyance to a 19-year-old who is released from a summer sales job because business is slow.

Something to Think About

Can you think of a better way to measure stress? Some psychologists have given people a list of events and have asked them to assign a value to each event they have experienced on the basis of how stressful they found it. Is that an improvement, or does it introduce problems of its own?

Another possibility is to measure the changes an event evokes in heart rate and other body indi-

cators. What difficulties can you see with that approach?

Because stress is so difficult to measure, it is obviously difficult to measure the effect of stress on overall health. Psychologists can, however, study the relationship between specific experiences and specific disorders.

STRESS AND PSYCHOSOMATIC ILLNESS

A **psychosomatic illness** is an illness that is influenced by a person's experiences—particularly stressful experiences—or by his or her reactions to those experiences. It is *not* an imagined or a pretended illness. And it is not entirely the result of psychological factors. High blood pressure, for example, is caused by a combination of a genetic predisposition, stress, and salt in the diet (Friedman & Iwai, 1976).

For many years physicians looking for the sources of illness concentrated on physical agents such as germs or injuries, giving no thought to the possibility of a psychosomatic influence. Then, in the early 1800s, they found soldiers who were suffering from what we would now call posttraumatic stress disorder. Some of the soldiers showed serious (though temporary) physical ailments, including blindness or paralysis, even though they had never been hit by a bullet or shrapnel. A few even died on the battlefield when a cannon ball landed nearby without striking them. Physicians of the time suggested that the soldiers were injured by the wind of the cannon ball passing by, or by atmospheric electricity stirred up by the wind, or by the heat or the temporary vacuum it left in its wake. Even these far-fetched hypotheses seemed more parsimonious at the time than the idea that fear and stress could lead to illness (McMahon, 1975).

Physicians and psychologists still have trouble explaining how emotional states affect the body. They do not assume that emotions lead directly to illness. They know, however, that people who have certain emotional experiences are more likely than others to overeat, to smoke, or to engage in other habits that increase the risk of illness. Certain behaviors and experiences can damage the immune system and increase a person's vulnerability to a variety of disorders ranging from minor infections to cancer (Shavit et al., 1985).

One young woman died of fear in a most peculiar way: When she was born, on Friday the 13th, the midwife who delivered her and two other babies that day announced that all three were hexed and would die before their 23rd birthday. The other two did die young. As the third woman approached her 23rd birthday, she checked into a hospital and informed the staff of her fears. The staff noted that she dealt with her anxiety by extreme hyperventilation (deep breathing). Shortly before her birthday, she hyperventilated to death.

How did that happen? Ordinarily, when people do not breathe voluntarily they breathe reflexively; the reflex is triggered by carbon dioxide in the blood. By extreme hyperventilation, this woman had exhaled so much carbon dioxide that she did not have enough left to trigger reflexive breathing. When she stopped breathing voluntarily, she stopped breathing altogether ("Clinicopathologic conference," 1967). This is a clear example of a self-fulfilling prophecy: The fact that the woman believed in the hex caused its fulfillment. It is also a clear example of an indirect influence of emotions on health.

We shall examine three examples of well-investigated diseases that may be linked to particular emotional experiences or personality types: ulcers, heart disease, and cancer.

Ulcers and Stress:
WHAT'S THE EVIDENCE?

An **ulcer** is an open sore on the lining of the stomach or duodenum (the upper part of the small intestine) that is usually caused by excess digestive secretions. People who experience severe work-related stress are believed to be especially vulnerable to ulcers.

How could we test the relationship between stress and ulcers, and, if possible, determine which aspect of stress is responsible for ulcers? Because of the manifest difficulties of conducting such studies with humans, Joseph Brady, Robert Porter, Donald Conrad, and John Mason (1958) used monkeys.

Hypothesis Monkeys that are responsible for turning off shocks for both themselves and their partners will get ulcers. Monkeys that get the same number of shocks without having any control over them will be less likely to get ulcers.

Method The experimenters fastened two monkeys into chairs. One of the monkeys, the so-called executive monkey, could prevent electric shock by pressing a lever at least once every 20 seconds. If it failed to do so, *both* monkeys would receive a shock to their feet once every 20 seconds until the

executive monkey pressed the lever again. Both monkeys got the same shock, but only the executive monkey had to cope with the work and worry. The shock-avoidance sessions lasted for six hours, twice a day, seven days a week, until one monkey or the other showed signs of illness.

Results Four pairs of monkeys were used over the course of the experiment. Within the first hour or two of the first session, every executive monkey became highly adept at pressing the lever; neither monkey received many shocks after that. All four executive monkeys developed severe ulcers, and three of them died. None of the passive partners developed ulcers.

Interpretation Actually, it is not easy to draw any firm conclusion. First, the design of the experiment was flawed: Instead of assigning monkeys randomly to the executive and passive roles, the experimenters put all the monkeys through a brief training period and then chose the fastest learners to be the executives. Conceivably, fast learners may be more likely than slow learners to get ulcers. It is even remotely conceivable that the fast-learning monkeys would have developed ulcers without being put into the shock apparatus. That suggestion may or may not strike you as plausible, but it illustrates the importance of proper control groups: When experimenters use inadequate control groups, they cannot eliminate alternative explanations of the results.

Why did the executive monkeys get ulcers? The experimenters' hypothesis was that being in a position of responsibility leads to ulcers. Yet the executive monkeys faced not only responsibility but also relentless physical activity. The results of this experiment do not tell us whether the ulcers formed because of the responsibility or because of the physical work.

Later studies with both humans and rats found that having control over unpleasant events generally *decreases* the stress they evoke. A passive individual who has no control over shocks is highly vulnerable to ulcers. The only reason that the passive monkeys in the original experiment did not get ulcers was that the executive monkeys were so good at avoiding shocks. The passive monkeys did no work and received no shocks. All they did was sit for six hours at a time, watching their hard-working partner press a lever. The ulcers of the executive monkeys probably formed as a result of the work itself rather than from any sense of responsibility.

We have here a good example of how the scientific method proceeds: The results of a single experiment may be interpreted in more than one

No time for salads: For busy businesspeople, weekday meals are often hurried and unbalanced—coffee and orange juice (a stomach acid bath) for breakfast; coffee, a cheeseburger, and a bag of chips (for midday heartburn); more coffee and a candy bar ("quick energy"); and a microwave-zapped frozen "entrée" (tomato sauce as dinner's vegetable). Such eating habits may promote formation of an ulcer.

way. And one experiment's results often lead to further experiments that help us to interpret the first experiment. ■

How does stress cause ulcers? A stressful experience activates the sympathetic nervous system, causing heart rate, breathing rate, and epinephrine secretions to increase. However, ulcers do not form during the stress session itself; they form afterward during the rest period (Desiderato, MacKinnon, & Hissom, 1974). Once the stress session is over, the autonomic nervous system rebounds from a state of high sympathetic arousal to a state of high parasympathetic arousal that produces an increase in digestive secretions, even when there is no food in the digestive system. Those excess secretions eat away at the lining of the stomach and intestines and produce an ulcer.

A rat's chance of getting ulcers decreases if it can take some action, such as pressing a lever to avoid the shock. Even an *ineffective* response sometimes helps rats to cope with the stress of shocks. When two rats confined to a small cage receive shocks, they generally attack each other. Although they suffer cuts and bruises in the fray, they develop fewer ulcers than do rats that have no opponent to fight (Weiss, Pohorecky, Salman, & Gruenthal, 1976). Similarly, people who take action of almost any sort during times of stress feel better as a result.

Concept Check

4. Last week your physician told you that you are prone to ulcers. You have just completed three midterm exams in one day, an experience you found very stressful. What could you do to guard against

developing an ulcer? Should you go to bed? Exercise? Eat something? If you had a choice between taking a drug that would slightly stimulate your sympathetic nervous system and a drug that would slightly stimulate your parasympathetic nervous system, which one, if either, would you take? (Check your answers on page 463.)

Heart Disease

The upholsterer repairing the chairs in a physician's waiting room once noticed that the fronts of the chairs wore out before the backs. To figure out why, the physician began watching patients in the waiting room. He noticed that his heart patients habitually sat on the front edges of their seats, waiting impatiently to be called in for their appointments. This observation led the physician to hypothesize a link between heart disease and an impatient, success-driven personality, now known as the Type A personality (Friedman & Rosenman, 1974).

People with a **Type A personality** are highly competitive; they must always win. They are impatient, always in a hurry, and often angry and hostile. By contrast, people with a **Type B personality** are relatively easygoing, less hurried, and less hostile. They may be just as successful as the Type As, but they do not let the drive for achievement dominate their lives. (Are you a Type A or a Type B? Check yourself by answering the questions in Figure 12.21.)

Apparently some association exists between Type A personality and susceptibility to heart disease, although psychologists are not sure how strong that association is or under what circumstances it occurs

Measuring the Type A Personality
_____ 1. Do you find it difficult to restrain yourself from hurrying others' speech (finishing their sentences for them)?
_____ 2. Do you often try to do more than one thing at a time (such as eat and read simultaneously)?
_____ 3. Do you often feel guilty if you use extra time to relax?
_____ 4. Do you tend to get involved in a great number of projects at once?
_____ 5. Do you find yourself racing through yellow lights when you drive?
_____ 6. Do you need to win in order to derive enjoyment from games and sports?
_____ 7. Do you generally move, walk, and eat rapidly?
_____ 8. Do you agree to take on too many responsibilities?
_____ 9. Do you detest waiting in lines?
_____ 10. Do you have an intense desire to better your position in life and impress others?

FIGURE 12.21

If you answer yes to a majority of these items, Friedman and Rosenman (1974) would say you probably have a Type A personality. But they would also consider your explanation of your answers, so this questionnaire gives only a rough estimate of your personality. Friedman and Rosenman classified everyone as either Type A or Type B, but most psychologists believe people can have any degree of Type A traits from low to high. Describing himself as "a classic Type A personality" with a history of heart disease, Friedman says, "You can't change your fundamental personality. But you _can_ change your behavior." He has by setting priorities, learning to say no, and trying to see himself as a stranger would (Castleman, 1989, pages 19–20).

(Booth-Kewley & Friedman, 1987; Friedman & Booth-Kewley, 1988; Matthews, 1988). How might we account for such a linkage? At first, psychologists focused on the role of impatience and competitiveness. When Type A people perform competitive tasks, their muscle tension increases and their sympathetic nervous system is aroused (Williams et al., 1982). Because they seek competitive tasks, their hearts are working hard much of the time.

However, later evidence has indicated that impatience and competition by themselves do not greatly increase the risk of heart disease. Heart disease correlates more strongly with unpleasant emotions, especially depression and anger (Booth-Kewley & Friedman, 1987). Future research will tell us more about how depression and anger contribute to heart disease.

Concept Check

5. _People with a Type A personality are likely to develop stress-related heart disease. Yet when they fill out the Social Readjustment Rating Scale, mentioned earlier, their scores are often low. Why might that scale understate the stress levels of Type A people? (Check your answer on page 463.)_

Cancer

Among the causes of cancer are genetics and exposure to toxic substances. Behavior can influence the onset and spread of cancer, at least indirectly. For example, people who smoke cigarettes increase their risk of cancer. Women who examine their breasts regularly can detect breast cancer at an early, treatable stage. Do emotions contribute directly to cancer? Because the brain influences the immune system, which fights cancer, an emotional experience might lead to an impairment of the immune system and therefore to a greater risk of cancer.

The two emotional states most likely to lead to cancer are depression and stress. Many cancer patients are depressed (Weinstock, 1984), and many of them report that they were depressed, often following the death of a loved one, long before they knew they had cancer. Severe depression suppresses the activity of the immune system and leaves a person more vulnerable than usual to all sorts of infection and disease, including the spread of certain types of tumors (Anisman & Zacharko, 1983; Baker, 1987).

In research on the effects of stress in animals, investigators have found that stress increases the spread of cancer and shortens the animal's survival. But it is difficult to generalize those results to humans. First, the results vary from one study to another, depending on the duration and type of stress and the genetic makeup of the animals. Second, nearly all the animal studies deal with cancers caused by viruses, and viruses cause fewer than 5% of human cancers (Fox, 1983).

Depression, stress, and severe emotional problems probably do increase the risk of cancer in humans. Still, the influence is minor; emotional factors are far less important in causing cancer than are genes and toxic substances (Anisman & Zacharko, 1983; Derogatis, 1986; Fox, 1983).

Psychological factors may exert a stronger influence on what happens after the onset of cancer. People who receive steady support from their family and friends have a better chance of recovery. People who decide to fight the disease have a better chance than do those who take a resigned, helpless attitude that "what will be, will be" (Geer, Morris,

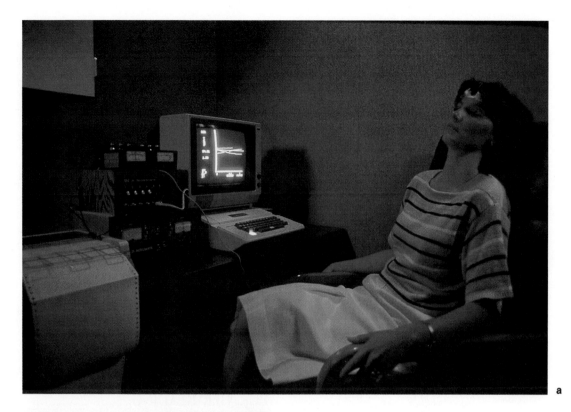

a

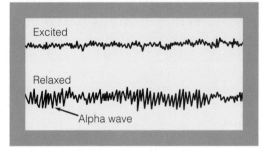

Excited

Relaxed

Alpha wave

b

FIGURE 12.22

Alpha better: (a) To aid mental fitness, people may calm themselves using biofeedback machines. Brain researcher James Hardt helped develop a computerized biofeedback program, Mind Fitness, which translates brain waves into musical tones; a person "hears" his alpha waves (Hollandsworth, 1989, page 24). Although biofeedback helps people control their arousal, its long-term medical value is still uncertain for most purposes. (b) EEG patterns corresponding to excited (beta) and relaxed (alpha) states.

& Pettingale, 1979). Exactly how the patient's attitude contributes to survival we do not know, but again it probably relates to enhancing or impairing the functions of the immune system.

BIOFEEDBACK: A BEHAVIORAL METHOD OF CONTROLLING BODY FUNCTIONS

As we have seen, stress, depression, hostility, and other unpleasant emotional states can make people more vulnerable to illness. Is there anything we can do to make ourselves less vulnerable or to improve our health?

Maybe. **Biofeedback**, for example, is a method for gaining voluntary control over physiological processes that we cannot ordinarily control. Recording devices are attached to the body to monitor heart rate, blood pressure, brain waves, or other body activities (Figure 12.22). The person is given constant information ("feedback") about the activity and instructions to try to control it. For example, to reduce the effects of stress, we might monitor the person's blood pressure and the electrical activity of the brain. We could sound a tone whenever the person's blood pressure dropped below a certain level or whenever the brain began to emit *alpha waves*. (These brain waves occur at a rate of 8 to 12 per second; they generally indicate a state of relaxation.) So long as the person remains calm and relaxed, the tone sounds continuously (Schwartz, 1975). As soon as the person tenses up, the tone ceases.

Biofeedback has proved effective in certain specific applications, such as control of pain, gaining certain motor skills, and increasing relaxation (Schneider, 1987). But its effectiveness is more difficult to evaluate in other instances. Most practitioners use biofeedback in combination with other techniques, so it is difficult to determine the contribution of biofeedback itself. Many common applications of biofeedback provide only doubtful medical benefits (Roberts, 1985). For example, the lowered blood pressure and other effects produced by biofeedback generally do not persist after the monitoring devices have been detached (Blanchard & Young, 1973, 1974).

SUMMARY

1. According to Hans Selye, stress is "the nonspecific response of the body to any demand made upon it." Any event, pleasant or unpleasant, that brings about some change in a person's life produces some measure of stress. (page 443)

2. The body goes through three stages in response to a stressful experience: alarm, resistance, and exhaustion. (page 443)

3. The degree of stress an event evokes depends not only on the event itself but also on the person's interpretation of the event. People with posttraumatic stress disorder react strongly to daily events because of their previous experiences with war, rape, or other deeply upsetting events. (page 444)

4. The stress an individual experiences is difficult to measure. Two people who have gone through similar experiences may show different levels of stress. (page 445)

5. Stress, hostility, and other emotional experiences may increase the probability of certain illnesses. A psychoso-

matic illness is somehow related to a person's experiences or to his or her reactions to those experiences. (page 447)

6. Ulcers form because of excess digestive secretions that can be produced by the parasympathetic rebound following a period of excess sympathetic nervous system activity. (page 448)

7. People with a Type A personality are competitive, impatient, and hostile. They are more likely than others to suffer heart disease, although the strength of that relationship and the reasons behind it are still in dispute. The emotional states of depression and hostility pose a greater risk than do competitiveness and impatience. (page 449)

8. Depression and stress may increase the risk of cancer, at least slightly. People who take a fighting attitude toward their cancer generally survive longer than do those with a helpless attitude. (page 450)

9. Biofeedback is a method of trying to gain control over such physiological processes as heart rate and blood pressure. Some of its common uses have not been demonstrated to be medically useful. (page 451)

SUGGESTION FOR FURTHER READING

Feist, J., & Brannon, L. (1988). *Health psychology*. Belmont, CA: Wadsworth. A textbook that surveys the relationship between behavior and health.

COPING WITH STRESS

How can we reduce the harmful effects of stress on the body? How can we learn to cope with stress?

$\mathbf{A}$n eccentric millionaire whom you have never met before hands you a $10 bill for no apparent reason, no strings attached. How do you feel? Happy, I presume.

Now let's change the circumstances a bit: That generous person had been handing out $100 bills until it was your turn. Then the millionaire said, "Sorry, I just ran out of $100 bills. So I'll have to give you a $10 bill instead." Now how do you feel? Disappointed, sad, angry? You may even feel *cheated,* although you have just received something for nothing.

Just as your reaction to a free $10 bill depends on the circumstances, so does your reaction to bad news. How would you feel if you had studied hard for a test and then got a C−? Unhappy, I presume. But if you then discovered that everyone around you had failed the test, your C− would seem good by comparison. You would begin to feel much better.

How you feel about an event depends not just on the event itself but also on how you interpret it (Frijda, 1988; Lazarus, Averill, & Opton, 1970). Was it better or worse than you had expected? Better or worse than what happened to someone else? Was it a one-time event, or did it carry some hint of what might happen in the future? How you feel about an event also depends on your personality. Some people manage to keep their spirits high even in the face of tragedy while others are devastated by lesser setbacks. How do people cope with disappointments, anxieties, and stress? And can we learn to cope more successfully?

RELAXATION

As we have seen, the sympathetic nervous system prepares us to respond vigorously to emergencies. But sometimes it gets aroused when there is no call for action. We become angry at someone we have no intention of fighting. We worry about something that will happen tomorrow or next week, or about something that *may* happen. At such times, the arousal of our sympathetic nervous system intensifies our stress without accomplishing anything useful.

Obviously, then, one way of coping with stress is simply to relax. But for some people that is more easily said than done. Even when they go fishing, they remain tense, concentrating on fishing as if it were some sort of life-and-death competition (Schwartz, 1987).

If you want to relax, here are some suggestions that may help (Benson, 1985):

1. Find a quiet place. Do not insist on absolute silence; just find a spot where the noise is least disturbing.

2. Adopt a comfortable position, relaxing your muscles. If you are not sure how to do so, start with the opposite: *Tense* all your muscles so you become

$erene in a beginner's lotus position, this woman relaxes while exercising. In yoga's many positions, or postures, emphasis is on gradually increasing flexibility and strength through slow stretches paired with rhythmic breathing exercises.

More sweat, less stress: Whether competing against yourself or someone else, strenuous exercise is a good way to reduce stress. Stress is a cousin of distress, Latin for "taking apart." With a daily run or a few weekly games of raquetball or tennis, you'll be better prepared to pull yourself together.

fully aware of how they feel. Then relax them one by one, starting from your toes and working systematically toward your head.

3. Reduce all sources of stimulation, including your own thoughts. Focus your eyes on some simple, unexciting object. Or repeat something over and over—a sentence, a phrase, a prayer, or even a meaningless sound like "om"—whatever feels comfortable to you.

4. Don't worry about anything, not even about relaxing. If worrisome thoughts keep popping into your head, dismiss them with an "Oh, well."

Some people call this practice meditation. People who spend a little time each day practicing this technique report that they feel less stress. Many of them also lower their blood pressure and improve their overall health (Benson, 1977, 1985).

EXERCISE

Exercise also can help to reduce stress. It may seem contradictory to say that both relaxation and exercise reduce stress, but exercise helps people relax. Exercise is a particularly helpful way to deal with nervousness about an anticipated stressful event (Mobily, 1982). Suppose you are tense about something you have to do tomorrow. Your sympathetic nervous system becomes highly aroused in preparation for that event, yet there is nothing you can do about it. Under those conditions, the best approach may be to work off some of your excess energy through exercise and relax afterward.

Regular exercise also prepares people for the unexpected. People in good physical condition react less strongly than other people to stressful events (Crews & Landers, 1987). An event that would elevate the heart rate enormously in other people elevates it only moderately in a person who has been exercising regularly.

PREDICTING AND CONTROLLING EVENTS

Another way of coping with stress is to try to gain some sense of control over events or at least a feeling that you know what is likely to happen next. In the winter of 1988, an unusually severe snowstorm hit my hometown of Raleigh, North Carolina. Because the city had little snow-clearing equipment, and because most residents had scant experience driving through snow, the schools and many businesses closed down for five days. By the end of the fifth day, many people were complaining of "cabin fever": "I can't stand being cooped up in this house another day! I've got to get out!" Staying at home, in itself, was not the problem. The problem was that people had no way of knowing whether they would be staying home the next day or going to school or work. And the answer was beyond their control.

In general, an event is less stressful if we can predict or control it than if we cannot (Thompson, 1981). For example, repeated electric shocks cause rats to develop ulcers. If they hear a warning signal before each shock, however, they do not necessarily develop ulcers (Weiss, 1970). Rats that learn how to make a response that will produce a "safety signal" (indicating that the shocks will cease temporarily) are also less likely to develop ulcers, even if they do not make the response consistently enough to avoid the shocks altogether (Weiss, 1972).

Prediction and control also help humans to cope with stress. In several experiments, people were asked to perform difficult tasks while listening to loud bursts of noise that might impair their performance. Some subjects were shown a switch and were told that they could cut off the noise if they chose to, although the experimenters preferred that they leave it on. Even though none of the subjects flipped the switch, simply knowing that they *could* turn off the noise made it less disturbing to them. They performed better on a proofreading task than did subjects who had no control over the noise (Glass, Singer, & Pennebaker, 1977; Sherrod, Hage, Halpern, & Moore, 1977).

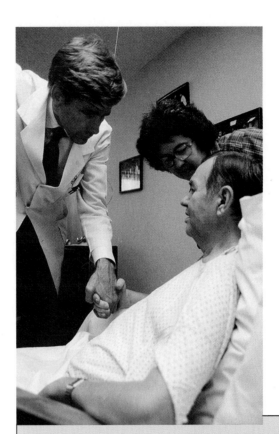

*S*urgical patients recover more quickly when they are told what is going to happen. They are better able to cope with pain if they are told what to do when it arises (Ludwick-Rosenthal & Neufeld, 1988). Such information gives them a slight feeling of control.

Concept Check

6. Which would disrupt your studying more, your own radio or your roommate's radio? Why? (Check your answers on page 463.)

Coping with the Effects of Crowding

Do you become uneasy when you are caught in a crowd? It probably depends on the circumstances. Being part of the crowd at a theater or at a ballgame is a pleasant and exciting experience. Encountering the same crowd in a traffic jam after the performance is annoying. A study was made of five married couples, all Peace Corps volunteers, who decided to share a one-room apartment to prepare themselves for the lack of privacy they would face in the field. The couples all reported that they regarded the experience as positive (MacDonald & Oden, 1973). The crowding of inmates in a prison, however, triggers both physical and psychiatric

Is a crowded environment stressful? Yes and no, reports sociologist Rodney Stark (1989). Studies of high-density neighborhoods (blocks packed with apartments, for example) don't support the notion of psychic overload—that life in cities like Chicago promotes mental and physical illness. But people who live in crowded homes do have more family fights.

complaints (Epstein, 1982). Prison inmates have little sense of control. Moreover, being in prison is stressful with or without crowding.

People who know they must live in crowded conditions tend to modify their behavior in some way, depending on the means available to them. For example, college students assigned three to a dormitory room may decide to do most of their studying in the library (Karlin, Rosen, & Epstein, 1979).

People who have no way of escaping crowded conditions find it harder to cope with the resulting stress. Seward Smith and William Haythorn (1972) studied Navy men who were confined to a small space in groups of 2 or 3 for 21 days in a simulated deep-sea exploration. Many of them experienced anxiety and grew annoyed with their companions, but they suppressed their reactions and told themselves "I can take anything for 21 days." As soon as they were released, however, they showed anxiety, short tempers, and other mild disturbances.

How Do Predictability and Controllability Help?

Why does a predictable or controllable event produce less stress than an unpredictable or uncontrollable event does? One possibility is that we fear that an unpredictable, uncontrollable event may

grow so intense that it will eventually become unbearable (Thompson, 1981). So long as we know what will probably happen next, we assume that things won't get any worse. And so long as we have some measure of control over an event, we tell ourselves that we can take some action if the situation becomes unbearable.

A second possibility is that when an event is predictable we have a chance to prepare ourselves for it. In animal experiments, a signal that warns of an imminent shock enables a rat to adopt a protective posture that will reduce the pain.

There is a third possibility: When we have no way of predicting or controlling a stressful event, we have to keep ourselves in a constant state of arousal. Suppose you dread being called on in class to answer questions. If your professor calls on students at random, you have no way of predicting when your name will be called. You must stay ready and alert every minute. If your professor calls out names in alphabetic order, however, you can relax until just before your turn comes.

Is Predictability Always Helpful?

As a general rule, knowing what to expect reduces the stressfulness of an experience. But if you are not likely to face the experience for some time, and if there is nothing you can do about it anyway, then just knowing about it may not be helpful. If someone could tell you when and how you were going to die—and you knew you could do nothing to avoid it—would you want to know? Maybe you would, on the grounds that you could make better decisions about how to live whatever life was left to you. But you might prefer not to know.

People with a family history of Huntington's disease are faced with precisely that decision. Huntington's disease is an uncommon, inherited disorder that typically strikes at about age 40. People with the disease undergo a gradual deterioration in their muscle control and mental functioning until they die about 15 years later. If your father or mother had the disease, you would have a 50% chance of getting it yourself.

Before the 1980s, people with a family history of Huntington's disease had to live with uncertainty until they either got the disease themselves or grew old without getting it. Today, medical technicians can examine an individual's chromosomes, compare them to the chromosomes of relatives with and without Huntington's disease, and determine with up to 95% accuracy whether the individual will fall victim to the disease (Gusella et al., 1983). That information, however it turns out, helps people to make important decisions about their future, particularly about whether or not to have children. But they have no way of preventing or delaying the onset of the disease. Some people who know they are at risk decide to have their chromosomes examined. Others choose to remain uncertain. In short, people are not always sure they want to know what to expect if they can do nothing about it.

INOCULATION

Any stressful experience is less disturbing if you know what to expect, but it is hard to know what to expect if you have not been through the experience before. Sometimes a good solution is to provide people with a small-scale preview of a stressful experience they may have to face later.

In other words, we can **inoculate** or immunize someone against certain kinds of stressful experience (Burchfield, 1979). For example, a medical school may show students films of surgical operations before they watch live operations. Even painful electric shocks cause less distress if they are preceded by milder shocks (Sines, 1979).

One way to inoculate people against stressful events is to have them practice ways of dealing with such events beforehand (Janis, 1983; Meichenbaum, 1985; Meichenbaum & Cameron, 1983). For example, the army has soldiers practice combat skills under realistic conditions, sometimes under actual gunfire. Another way is through role playing. A police trainee might pretend to intervene while two people act like a husband and wife engaged in a violent quarrel. If you are nervous about going to your landlord with a complaint, you might get a friend to play the part of the landlord and then practice what you plan to say.

Inoculation has proved successful with young people suffering from "dating anxiety." Some young people are so nervous about saying or doing the wrong thing that they avoid all opportunities to go out on a date. By means of role playing, in which they practice dating behaviors with assigned partners, they can be helped to feel less apprehensive (Jaremko, 1983).

Concept Check

7. *Suppose you are nervous about giving a speech before a group of 200 strangers. How could you inoculate yourself to reduce the stress? (Check your answer on page 463.)*

SOCIAL SUPPORT

When people are trying to cope with a physical illness, the loss of a job, depression, alcoholism, or any other long-term problem, they often turn to friends and family for support. They may want help in getting through the day or just encouragement and a shoulder to cry on. People who receive support of this kind generally handle their problems more successfully than do people who have to struggle on their own.

Often the best support comes from others who have gone through a similar experience. Alcoholics Anonymous, for example, is composed of recovering alcoholics who try to help one another. For another example, the nurses who work in the intensive care units of hospitals undergo constant, often severe stress (Hay & Oken, 1977). Their duties are physically exhausting and highly demanding. The unspoken (but rigidly obeyed) rule is never to refuse help to either a patient or a fellow nurse. They are surrounded by the sight, sound, and smell

In Northern Ireland, these boys are growing up familiar with murder and mayhem. For them, guns are weapons, not playthings, and they learn early who the enemy is. Perhaps this boy with a gun is being coached by an older brother. Does this "survival training," a form of inoculation, have drawbacks and benefits? Does it make fighting less stressful?

Someone to talk to: During a Saturday get-together, these women unwind, sharing good news and bad. Because they have similar jobs, they discuss concerns about work, knowing that the others will understand them. People with specific, overwhelming problems—alcoholism, the death of a child, an incurable disease— often find relief in talking with others in similar straits. The growing number of support groups suggests they fill a need. Today, even relatively rare diseases such as lupus and Reye's syndrome have information services and support groups.

Trying to ignore pain won't eliminate it, but distractions can make it more tolerable—as with this boy recovering from heart surgery. Most adults develop distractions: playing cards, reading mysteries, knitting.

of patients who are suffering and dying. When a patient dies, it is often the nurse, not the doctor, who has to inform the relatives. At the end of the day, the nurses cannot simply go home and resume life as usual. They have to unwind, and they often do so by sharing their experiences with other nurses.

Social support also helps people to cope with the common, everyday situations that all of us experience. Married people tend to be healthier than unmarried people, better adjusted psychologically, less likely to use drugs, less likely to be convicted of crimes, and less likely to commit suicide. That tendency is, of course, a correlation, not evidence of causation. To measure whether marriage helps people cope with stress, we must do more than compare married people with unmarried people. We need a longitudinal study examining the same people before and after they marry. According to one such study, medical students who married while they were in school reported a sharp drop in stress levels (Coombs & Fawzy, 1982). They said that their spouse provided care, concern, and reaffirmation of their self-esteem when it was threatened.

DISTRACTION

People who are trying to cope with stress caused by mild but persistent pain often resort to some sort of distraction. Pain includes the emotional response to an injury as well as the sensation of the injury, and one way to reduce that response is to concentrate on something unrelated to the pain. Many people find they can reduce dental or post-surgical pain by playing video games, watching comedies on television, imagining that they are arguing with someone, or thinking about some meaningful event in their lives (McCaul & Malott, 1984). The Lamaze method teaches women to cope with the pain of childbirth by concentrating on breathing exercises. One reason hypnosis tends to reduce pain may be that it distracts the sufferer's attention.

How effective a distraction is depends partly on whether or not a person believes that it will help. In one experiment, college students were asked to hold their fingers in ice water until the sensation became too painful to endure (Melzack, Weisz, & Sprague, 1963). Some of them listened to music of their own choice and were told that listening to music would lessen the pain. Others also listened to music but were given no suggestion that it would ease the pain. Still others heard nothing but were told that a special "ultrasonic sound" was being transmitted that would lessen the pain. The group that heard music and expected it to lessen the pain tolerated the pain better than the other two groups did. Evidently, neither the music nor the suggestion of reduced pain is as effective as both are together.

Does distraction really reduce pain, or do people just report that it does because they think they are expected to? We know that music sometimes acts like a pain-killing drug: It causes certain pathways in the nervous system to release neurotransmitters known as endorphins, which excite the same receptors that heroin and morphine excite (Goldstein, 1980). Recordings of brain activity show less response to electric shock while music is playing than during silence (Lavine, Buchsbaum, & Poncy, 1976).

Distraction also helps us to cope with stress that is not painful. People who are concentrating on a difficult task find it helpful to take a break once in a while. They may go to a movie, read something entertaining, play a round of golf, or just daydream. Finally, trying to find the humor in a stressful situation often provides an effective distraction.

Something to Think About

Many experiments report that a placebo by itself serves as an effective pain-killer for certain patients. Why might that be?

COPING BY MEANS OF ILLUSIONS

- In the long run, I shall be more successful than most other people are.

- Sure I have my strengths and weaknesses, but my strengths are in areas that are important; my weaknesses are in areas that don't really matter.

- When I fail, it is because I didn't try hard enough or because I got some bad breaks. It is not because of any lack of ability.

- No matter how bad (or good) things are, they are going to get better.

- Right now I'm sad that my wife (husband) left me, but in the long run I'll be better off without her (him).

- I lost my job, but in many ways it was a crummy job. The more I think about it, the happier I am that I lost it. I can get a better one.

Remember the "personal fable" of adolescence in Chapter 6? Most normal, happy people nurture various versions of that fable throughout their life.

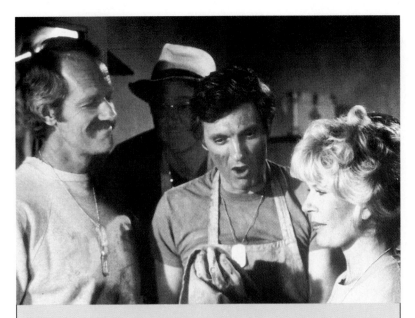

Life in a mobile army surgical hospital doesn't seem a likely setting for comedy, but humor acts as a safety valve in stressful circumstances. Humor may be grim, "sick," or absurd, reflecting the situation it aims to alleviate. Just as playing practical jokes distracts Hawkeye, watching "M.A.S.H." relieves our stress by offering escape from our own problems for a while.

They believe that they are and will be happier and more successful than most other people are. They exaggerate their strengths, downplay their weaknesses, and distort bad news to make it seem less bad, maybe even good (Taylor & Brown, 1988).

When a situation is undeniably bad, people may still find ways to deny it. Medics serving in the Vietnam War knew they were risking their lives every time they boarded a helicopter to go to the aid of wounded soldiers. Because they had no way to predict or control the enemy's actions, we might expect that they would have experienced extreme stress. In general, however, measurements of the activity of their autonomic nervous system showed low levels of arousal on both flight days and nonflight days (Bourne, 1971). Why? They had managed to convince themselves of their own invulnerability. They even told exaggerated stories about their close brushes with death as evidence to prove that they led a charmed life.

One study of 78 women who had surgery for the removal of breast cancer found that they coped with their stress and anxiety in three ways (Taylor, 1983):

First, they searched for some meaning in the experience. Many of them said they had become better people and had developed a new attitude toward life.

Their belief that they could make it to the Olympics supported this relay team through hours of grueling training. Here a prerace moment of concentration helps them focus on the illusion that they can win. If they are disappointed, they may take refuge in yet another illusion—returning to the next Olympic games or setting a new record.

Second, they tried to regain a feeling of mastery over their lives. They wanted to believe that they knew why they had developed cancer and that they knew how to avoid a recurrence. Many asserted with confidence (but without evidence) that they had developed cancer because of an unhappy marriage, or because of a bad diet, or because they had been taking birth-control pills, or because of something else that they had stopped doing after surgery.

Third, they all sought to boost their self-esteem by comparing themselves with someone else. Most of them thought they were doing better than average for cancer patients, or knew someone who was worse off. Others *imagined* someone in a worse situation: "I'm glad I had only one breast removed instead of both, like some other women." "Sure, I had both breasts removed, but at least I was 70 years old at the time. It would have been worse if it happened when I was young." "It was terrible to have both breasts removed at age 25, but I was already married, and my husband has been sympathetic and supportive." "Well, at least I'm still alive."

All these responses were based on *illusions.* Many of the women clung to uncertain theories of

why they had the disease in the first place and how they could control it in the future. And it obviously could not be true that almost all of them were doing "better than average." What happened to such women if and when something destroyed their illusions?

Not much, in most cases. Eventually, many of them were forced to abandon one or more of their illusions. At first they were disappointed or somewhat depressed, but they were not devastated. Most of them soon came up with a new illusion to take its place.

Such reactions are not surprising. Most of us harbor illusions about our own abilities and future achievements, even though they are regularly disproven. A student expects to get better grades this year than ever before. An athletic coach predicts that the team will win the league championship this year. A senator expects to get elected president. When we fail to live up to our expectations, do we become severely depressed? No. We just say, "Wait till next time."

Is it a mistake to rely on illusions? Not at all. Illusions sometimes turn into reality. The student

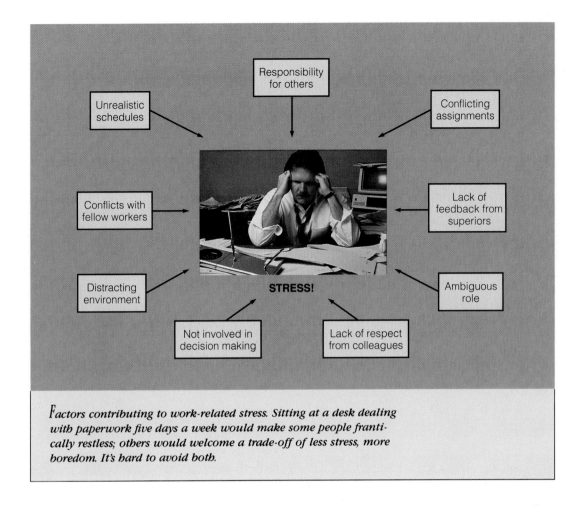

Factors contributing to work-related stress. Sitting at a desk dealing with paperwork five days a week would make some people frantically restless; others would welcome a trade-off of less stress, more boredom. It's hard to avoid both.

may get better grades, the team may win the championship, and the senator may be elected president. Moreover, a certain amount of hope and optimism promotes mental health.

Psychologists sometimes try to help people develop a more optimistic self-image, even if that image is partly illusion (Försterling, 1985). They encourage people to think of their successes as an indication of ability and to think of their failures as an indication of lack of effort. An improved self-image helps some people to feel less depressed and more in control of their lives.

ORGANIZATIONAL INTERVENTIONS

Up to this point I have talked about ways in which people can overcome stress on their own or with the help of their friends and family. Sometimes circumstances make it difficult for people to cope with stress by themselves. Employers, for example, may unintentionally cause stress for their employees

through incessant time pressure, demanding standards of performance, and too many complaints and too few compliments (Parker & DeCotiis, 1983). Many employers feel that their employees should learn to cope with the stress. But what if an employee can't cope? Might it not be better to change certain aspects of the job than to keep firing employees? Even when the job itself is not the source of stress, an employer can be sensitive to the special needs an employee may have at a particular time.

Some jobs seem stressful for some people and not for others, but for practically everyone certain jobs are highly stressful—for example, nurses on an intensive care ward or air traffic controllers. People with such jobs struggle to complete difficult tasks quickly and worry about what will happen if they make an error. Such people can learn to cope with their daily stress through relaxation, distraction, and the like. But a more effective approach is to try to reduce the stress in the job itself, by providing more help, longer breaks, and occasional opportunities to work at less strenuous tasks.

Our society is becoming more aware of the special stresses people face at certain times. One

Having a disability is tough enough without the additional obstacles in the paths of the disabled. In recent years, many businesses and communities have attempted to make the normal comings and goings of daily life less stressful for those with disabilities. Are the buildings you live, work, and study in accessible by wheelchair? Are the restrooms? The Center for Independent Living in Berkeley, California, is a leader in advocating such improvements.

example is the stress placed on working women who have children. Permitting a longer maternity leave would reduce that stress.

Society has taken some steps to reduce the stress and improve the lives of people with disabilities by providing special parking places, wheelchair access to buildings, braille instructions on elevators, and closed-captioned television programming for the deaf. But we can do much more.

SUMMARY

1. How successfully we cope with a stressful event depends largely on how we interpret the event. (page 453)

2. One way of coping with stress is to find a quiet place, relax the muscles, and eliminate distracting stimuli. (page 453)

3. Events are generally less stressful when people think they can predict or control them. (page 455)

4. Being able to predict a stressful event without being able to control it does little to reduce stress. (page 456)

5. Someone who has experienced a mild sample of a stressful experience is less stressed than are other people by a later, more intense version of the same experience. (page 457)

6. Support and encouragement from friends and family help to alleviate stress. (page 457)

7. Distracting a person's attention from the source of stress helps to reduce the stress. (page 458)

8. Many people reduce their stress by means of illusions. (page 459)

9. Society can take effective steps to reduce stress. (page 461)

SUGGESTION FOR FURTHER READING

Lazarus, R. S., & Folkman, S. (1984). *Stress, appraisal, and coping.* New York: Springer. A theoretical treatment of coping responses with an extensive review of the literature.

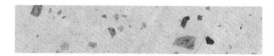

TERMS TO REMEMBER

autonomic nervous system a section of the nervous system that controls the functioning of the internal organs

biofeedback a method for providing constant information about physiological processes in order to gain voluntary control over processes that people cannot ordinarily control

Cannon-Bard theory of emotions theory that certain areas of the brain evaluate sensory information and, when appropriate, send one set of impulses to the autonomic nervous system and another set to the forebrain, which is responsible for the subjective and cognitive aspects of emotion

frustration-aggression hypothesis the theory that frustration leads to aggressive behavior

galvanic skin response (GSR) a brief increase in the electrical conductivity of the skin, indicating increased arousal of the sympathetic nervous system

general adaptation syndrome a reaction to severe and prolonged stress, marked by fatigue, loss of interest, and increased vulnerability to illness

guilty-knowledge test a test that uses the polygraph to measure whether a person has information that only someone guilty of a certain crime could know

health psychology a field of psychology that deals with how people's behavior can enhance health and prevent illness and how behavior contributes to recovery from illness

inoculation protection against the harmful effects of stress (or an infectious agent) by earlier exposure to a small amount of it

James-Lange theory the theory that emotion is merely our perception of autonomic changes and movements evoked directly by various stimuli

opponent-process principle of emotions principle that the removal of a stimulus that excites one emotion causes a swing to an opposite emotion

parasympathetic nervous system a system of neurons located at the top and bottom of the spinal cord; the neurons send messages to the internal organs that prepare the body for digestion and related processes

polygraph a machine that simultaneously measures heart rate, breathing rate, blood pressure, and galvanic skin response

posttraumatic stress disorder a condition characterized by periodic outbursts of anxiety, panic, or depression provoked by reminders of war or other traumatic experiences

psychosomatic illness an illness that is influenced by a person's experiences or reactions to experiences

Schachter and Singer's theory of emotions theory that emotions are our interpretation of autonomic arousal in light of all the information we have about ourselves and the situation

stress according to Selye, the nonspecific response of the body to any demand made upon it

sympathetic nervous system a system composed of two chains of neuron clusters lying just to the left and right of the spinal cord; the neurons send messages to the internal organs to prepare them for a burst of vigorous activity

territoriality the tendency to fight to defend the area where one builds a nest and raises young

Type A personality a personality characterized by impatience, hostility, and intense striving for achievement

Type B personality a personality characterized by less impatience, less hostility, and less competitiveness than a Type A personality

ulcer an open sore on the lining of the stomach or duodenum

ANSWERS TO CONCEPT CHECKS

1. When you ride a roller coaster, your heart rate increases (sympathetic activity). After you get off, your heart rate falls to lower than usual (rebound increase in parasympathetic activity). (page 426)

2. According to the James-Lange theory, the trembling and shaking came first. Schachter and Singer's theory agrees. However, according to the James-Lange theory, your perception of the trembling and shaking leads immediately and automatically to the experience of fear. According to Schachter and Singer's theory, you first interpret your trembling on the basis of circumstances before you experience fear: "Am I shaking because of that pill I took? Because someone made me angry? Because I'm excited? Because I'm frightened?" (page 432)

3. After someone takes a drug repeatedly, the A state becomes weaker. (That is known as tolerance, a phenomenon we shall consider in Chapter 14.) The B state (withdrawal) becomes stronger. (page 433)

4. To avoid an ulcer, try to calm down gradually after your stressful experience. Exercise for a while instead of going straight to bed. Eat something to absorb the excess stomach acids. If you choose to take a drug, take the one that slightly stimulates the sympathetic nervous system and thereby blocks the excess rebound of the parasympathetic nervous system. (page 449)

5. The Social Readjustment Rating Scale measures events that change a person's life; it does not measure constant sources of stress such as the pressures of work. It also fails to measure how people react to events, such as impatience, competitiveness, and hostility. (page 450)

6. Your roommate's radio would be more disruptive. You can turn your own radio on or off, switch stations, or reduce the volume. You have no such control over your roommate's radio (unless your roommate happens to be very cooperative). (page 455)

7. Practice giving your speech to a small group of friends. If possible, practice giving it in the room where you are to deliver it. (page 457)

ANSWERS TO OTHER QUESTIONS IN THE TEXT

Figure 12.14, page 436: From left to right, top to bottom, the faces express happiness, anger, sadness, surprise, disgust, and fear.

PERSONALITY

Several thousand people have the task of assembling the world's largest jigsaw puzzle, which contains over a trillion pieces. Connie Conclusionjumper examines 20 pieces very closely, stares off into the distance, and announces, "When the puzzle is fully assembled, it will be a picture of the Houston Astrodome!" Prudence Plodder says, "Well, I don't know what the whole puzzle will look like, but I think I've found two little pieces that fit together."

Which of the two is making the greater contribution to completing the puzzle? We could argue either way. Clearly the task will require an enormous number of little, unglamorous accomplishments like Prudence's. But if Connie is right, her flash of insight will be extremely valuable in assembling all the little pieces. Of course, if the puzzle turns out to be a picture of two sailboats on Lake Erie, then Connie will have made us waste time looking for connections that are not there.

Some psychologists have offered grand theories about the nature of personality. Others have investigated why people with a certain type of personality act the way they do in a specific situation. We need both contributions. We begin with the grand, overall theories of personality. Then we turn to investigations of more limited aspects of personality. Finally, we consider methods of measuring personality characteristics.

In Geronimo with His Spirit *(1984), the artist, Frederick Brown, implies that each of us has a "true self" that differs from the self we show to the world. Brown's interpretation of this Apache chief tells us something about both the painter and the painted. The word* personality *is derived from a Latin word meaning "mask," implying that your personality is what you show to the world. The term gradually came to mean the true self—even the aspects you try to conceal from other people.*

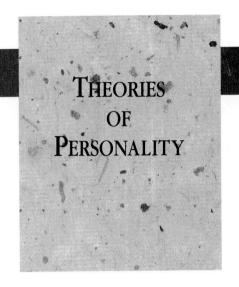

THEORIES OF PERSONALITY

Is personality rooted in one or two dominant motivations, such as sexuality or the desire for superiority?
Is personality influenced by unconscious motivations and thoughts?
What is a "healthy" personality?

What makes us tick? What makes us the way we are? Way down deep, are humans good, bad, or somewhere in between?

The 17th-century philosopher Thomas Hobbes argued that humans are by nature selfish. Life in a state of nature, he said, is "nasty, brutish, and short." To protect ourselves from one another, we must be restrained by a watchful government.

The 18th-century political philosopher Jean-Jacques Rousseau disagreed. He maintained that humans are good by nature but have been corrupted by "civilized" governments. Although he conceded that society could never return to "noble savagery," he believed that education and government should promote the freedom of the individual. Rational people acting freely, he maintained, would advance the welfare of all.

The debate between those two viewpoints survives in modern theories of personality (see Figure 13.1). Some theorists, including Sigmund Freud, have held that people are born with sexual and destructive impulses that must be held in check if civilization is to survive. Others, including Carl Rogers, have held that people will achieve good and noble goals once they have been freed from unnecessary restraints.

Which point of view is correct? Do not decide too quickly. Many people reject Freud's theory without having read any of his works. Others embrace it without fully understanding it and then proceed to "analyze" the behavior of their friends.

The personality theories we shall consider are complex, and we cannot do them full justice in just a few pages. For a deeper understanding, read the books listed under "Suggestions for Further Reading" at the end of this section on personality theories.

PERSONALITY AND CONCEPTIONS OF ITS ORIGIN

The term *personality* comes from the Latin word *persona,* meaning "mask." In the plays of ancient Greece and Rome, actors wore masks to indicate whether they were happy, sad, or angry. Unlike a mask that one can put on or take off, however, the term *personality* implies something stable. **Personality** consists of all the consistent ways in which the behavior of one person differs from that of others.

The ancient Greeks believed that personality depended on which of four different "humors" (chemicals) predominated in a person's body (Figure 13.2). A predominance of yellow bile made people hot tempered. A predominance of black bile made people depressed. An excess of phlegm made people sluggish and apathetic. An excess of blood made people courageous, hopeful, and amorous. The ancient Greek theory persists in the English language in such terms as *phlegmatic* and *melancholic* (literally, "black-bile-ic").

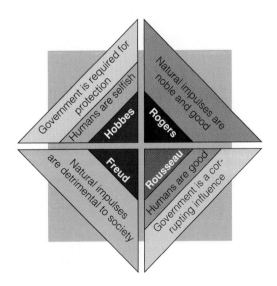

FIGURE 13.1

Opposing views of human nature.

"Every individual is virtually an enemy of civilization. . . . Thus civilization has to be defended against the individual. . . . For the masses are lazy and unintelligent . . . and the individuals composing them support one another in giving free rein to their indiscipline."
SIGMUND FREUD
(1927/1953)

"There is in every organism, at whatever level, an underlying flow of movement toward constructive fulfillment of its inherent possibilities. There is a natural tendency toward complete fulfillment in man."
CARL ROGERS
(1977)

FIGURE 13.2

According to the second-century Greek physician Galen, people's personalities depended on four humors. From left to right: Someone with an abundance of blood, or sanguine, has a changeable temperament. Someone with an excess of black bile is melancholy. A person with too much yellow bile, or choleric, is easily angered. And someone with too much phlegm is generally inactive. Accepted in Europe and the Arab world, Galen's theory remained popular throughout the Renaissance. Scholars were thought those most prone to melancholy, and an Oxford scholar, Robert Burton, wrote a large volume on it, *The Anatomy of Melancholy,* first published in 1621.

Today, although we no longer believe in the four humors, we do believe that personality is influenced by such physical factors as hormones and neurotransmitters. It is also influenced by our experiences, including our observation and imitation of other people's behavior.

According to some historically influential theories of personality, differences in personality arise from the different ways in which people try to satisfy one central motive, such as the sex drive, the desire for superiority, or the drive to achieve one's full potential. We begin with Sigmund Freud, who concentrated on the sex drive.

Frida Kahlo (1910–1954), a self-taught artist, said, "I paint because I need to," beginning at age 18 when she spent a year bedridden, recovering from an accident that smashed her spine, pelvis, and foot. In her many relentlessly intense self-portraits, Kahlo presents a similar masklike face. But her works are filled with symbols—the hummingbird here, a Mexican love charm aimed at her wandering husband (Diego Rivera), is just one element drawing on her Mexican heritage. Blood red is a primary color in paintings about the pain dozens of operations failed to relieve. Yet her friends said she never complained about her poor health.

SIGMUND FREUD AND PSYCHOANALYSIS

Sigmund Freud (1856–1939), a medical doctor, developed theories on personality development that have had an enormous influence on psychologists and other students of human behavior. Freud's theory was the first of several psychodynamic theories. A **psychodynamic theory** relates personality to the interplay of conflicting forces within the individual, including some that the individual may not recognize consciously.

Freud's main interests were cultural history and anthropology, and he wrote several books and articles about those topics in his later years. As a Jew in late 19th-century Austria, however, he knew he had little chance of becoming a university professor. The only professional careers open to Jews in his time and place were in law, business, and medicine.

Freud chose to study medicine, though he was never deeply committed to it. He took over seven years to complete medical school because he spent much of his time taking elective courses in biology and philosophy. After receiving his medical degree, he worked in brain research and began to practice medicine only when it became financially necessary. His interest in theory persisted throughout his life. Even the methods he devised for treating psychological disorders had more to do with *understanding* the disorders than with *relieving* them.

Freud's Concept of the Unconscious

Early in his career, Freud worked with the psychiatrist Josef Breuer, who had been treating a young woman with physical complaints that seemed to have no medical basis. As she talked with Breuer about her past and recalled various traumatic, or emotionally damaging, experiences, her symptoms gradually subsided. Breuer proposed that the memory of those experiences was somehow associated with tension and that recalling the experiences released the tension. He called this release of pent-up tension **catharsis**, a term Freud adopted in his own theory.

Freud began to apply Breuer's "talking cure" to some of his own emotionally disturbed patients. He referred to his method of explaining and dealing with personality as **psychoanalysis**, and to this day psychoanalysts remain loyal to that method and to the theories behind it.

Psychoanalysis is based on the assumption that each of us has an unconscious mind as well as a conscious mind (Figure 13.3). The **unconscious** has

*J*ust as Sigmund Freud interpreted other people's personalities, his biographers have tried to understand his personality and the influence it had on his theories. Freud had a close relationship with his mother and a colder, more distant relationship with his father. Was his conception of the Oedipus complex a product of his own childhood experiences? In that case and others, Freud based his theories partly on his dialogue with his clients and partly on his own introspection.

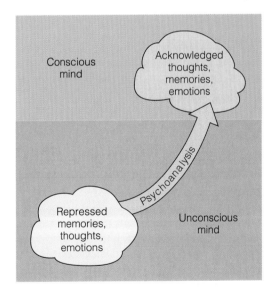

FIGURE 13.3

Freud believed that through psychoanalysis parts of the unconscious could be brought into the conscious mind, where a person could deal with them.

The paintings of Jackson Pollock (1912–1956) were influenced by Freudian and Jungian conceptions of the unconscious, by the Surrealist idea of painting from the unconscious, and by Native American art and culture. Pollock believed that Native American pictographs (rock paintings or drawings) and Surrealist art both found their imagery in the unconscious mind. In earlier paintings and drawings he used a primitive style similar to that of pictographs in an effort to explore his own unconscious symbols. Later, in the drip paintings, he used the information he had discovered about himself. The drip paintings also functioned as a sort of therapy. Pollock had observed Navajo sand painting, which was done as part of ceremonies to cure illnesses. For his own creations, he placed his canvas on the floor, then walked around it, working from all four sides to drip and splatter the paint, experiencing what was for him a healing process that culminated in a symbolic work (Rushing, 1986).

thoughts, memories, and emotions just as the conscious mind does, though it acts in a less logical fashion. Even though we are not directly aware of the unconscious, it has a profound influence on our behavior.

Psychoanalysis started out as a fairly simple theory: The unconscious contains memories of traumatic experiences, and the goal of psychoanalysts is to bring those memories to consciousness. That effort produces catharsis and relieves the patient of irrational and self-defeating impulses.

As Freud listened to his patients, however, he became convinced that the traumatic events they recalled were not sufficient to account for their abnormal behavior. Some patients reacted strongly to past events that others took in stride. Why? He concluded that still earlier traumatic events, which were even harder to recall, predisposed certain patients to overreact.

Freud urged his patients to recall ever-earlier experiences. When many of them reported experiences of sexual abuse in early childhood, he pro-

posed that *all* emotionally disturbed behavior could be traced to such experiences.

Over the next few years, as Freud analyzed himself and others, he changed his mind: Sexual abuse of children, he decided, was not common enough to account for all the disturbed behavior he observed. When his patients reported that they had been sexually abused as children, he concluded that they were reporting fantasies.

Regardless of whether the recollections of sexual abuse were real or fantasy, they were clearly disturbing to Freud's patients. So he modified his theory: The ultimate cause of a disturbed personality is the *sexual fantasies* of young children, including imagined sexual abuse.

That revision of Freud's original theory made it very difficult to test the theory scientifically. It is possible to test the effects of early experiences on subsequent behavior, but it is almost impossible to test the effects of early fantasies.

Was Freud correct in changing his mind? Maybe not. Today we recognize that sexual abuse of children occurs far more often than it is reported and that it can leave long-lasting psychological scars. In some ways Freud's earlier writings now sound more up-to-date than his later ones. Historians are not sure why Freud changed his mind. Jeffrey Masson (1984) suggests that Freud simply lost the courage to defend his earlier views and that for a long time he nurtured doubts about whether he had been right to abandon them.

Stages of Psychosexual Development in Freud's Theory of Personality

Freud believed that psychosexual interest and pleasure begin long before the individual achieves sexual maturity. He used the term **psychosexual pleasure** in a broad sense to include the good feelings arising from the stimulation of parts of the body. He maintained that the way we deal with psychosexual development influences nearly all aspects of our personality.

Freud proposed that young children have sexual tendencies that resemble those of more primitive mammals. Just as nonhuman mammals respond sexually to stimuli that do not excite most adult humans, children respond "sexually" to stimulation of the mouth, the anus, and other body zones. Freud collected no direct evidence for this view and in fact made no extensive observations of children. Rather, he reconstructed childhood experiences from the memories of his patients and other adults.

According to Freud (1905), people have a psychosexual energy, which he called **libido** (lih-BEE-doh), from a Latin word meaning "desire." The libido provides the energy for much behavior throughout life, as I mentioned in Chapter 11. At different ages it focuses on different parts of the body. Normally, it starts in the mouth and "flows" to other parts as the child grows older. Children go through five stages of **psychosexual development**, each with a characteristic sexual focus that leaves its mark on adult personality. If normal sexual development is blocked or frustrated at any stage, Freud said, a **fixation** occurs. Part of the libido becomes fixated at that stage; that is, it continues to be preoccupied with the pleasure area associated with that stage. Table 13.1 summarizes the stages.

The Oral Stage   In the **oral stage**, from birth through the first year or so (Freud was vague about the age limits of all his stages), the infant derives intense psychosexual pleasure from stimulation of the mouth, particularly while sucking at the mother's breast. In the later part of the oral stage, the infant begins to bite as well as suck.

According to Freud, an infant who receives either

TABLE 13.1   Freud's Stages of Psychosexual Development

Stage (approximate ages)	Sexual Interests	Effect of Fixation at This Stage
Oral stage (birth to 1 year)	Sucking, swallowing, biting	Lasting concerns with dependence and independence; pleasure from eating, drinking, other oral activities
Anal stage (1–3 years)	Expelling feces, retaining feces	Orderliness, stinginess, stubbornness
Phallic stage (3–5 or 6 years)	Touching penis or clitoris; Oedipus complex or Electra complex	Difficulty feeling closeness; males: fear of castration; females: penis envy
Latency period (5 or 6 to puberty)	Sexual interests suppressed	—
Genital period (puberty onward)	Sexual contact with other people	—

The beginning of psychosexual development is the oral stage, in which infants enjoy stimulation of their mouth—which for them means sucking, swallowing, and biting. They like putting things in their mouth and gnawing on them; this seems understandable, given the limited things infants can do. According to Freud, if normal sexual development is blocked at this stage, the child will grow up continuing to get much pleasure from drinking and eating, as well as kissing and smoking. Perhaps this pipe smoker's mother weaned him too quickly—or let him nurse too long. And perhaps such an explanation is wrong. Like many of Freud's ideas, this one is difficult to test.

From one extreme to another: In Freud's anal stage, from age 1 to 3, children's psychosexual pleasure centers on defecation, one of the few activities they have some control over. In theory, people with an anal fixation are messy and wasteful or very neat and miserly—so one explanation supposedly covers those who are sloppy and those who are fastidious. One problem in assessing such notions is that few adults have a clear memory of their toilet training.

too little or too much opportunity to suck can become fixated at the oral stage. The consequence is that much libido remains attached to the mouth; throughout life the person may continue to receive great pleasure from eating, drinking, smoking, and kissing. He or she may also take pleasure from being "fed" information. Someone who is fixated at the later part of the oral stage may be inclined to "biting" sarcasm and ridicule. People with an oral fixation have lasting concerns with dependence and independence, according to Freud.

The Anal Stage   Around one to three years of age, children enter the **anal stage**. At this time they get psychosexual pleasure from their bowel movements. They may enjoy either the sensation of excreting feces or the sensation of holding them back.

A child can develop a fixation at the anal stage if toilet training is too strict or if it starts too early

or too late. People with an anal fixation either go through life "holding things back"—being orderly, stingy, and stubborn—or, less commonly, they may go to the opposite extreme and become wasteful, messy, and destructive.

The Phallic Stage   Beginning at about age three, in the **phallic stage**, children begin to play with their genitals. They become more aware of what it means to be male or female. If parents teach children that touching their genitals is shameful, the children may become fixated at the phallic stage. According to Freud, boys with a phallic fixation are afraid of being castrated; girls with such a fixation develop "penis envy." Both males and females with a phallic fixation may find it difficult to experience closeness and love.

According to Freud, boys in the phallic stage experience an **Oedipus complex**. (Oedipus—EHD-ah-puhs—was a figure in a play by Sophocles. Oedipus unknowingly murdered his father and married his mother.) Freud claimed that a boy develops a sexual interest in his mother and competitive aggression toward his father. But the boy realizes that his father is larger and stronger; he learns to identify with his father and to shift his own sexual interests to someone other than his mother. A boy who fails to resolve the Oedipus complex may forever feel anxiety and hostility toward other men.

Similarly, Freud asserted, little girls experience an **Electra complex**, named after a character in an ancient Greek play who persuades her brother to kill their mother, who had murdered their father. A girl with an Electra complex feels a romantic attraction toward her father and hostility toward her mother. Freud was vague about how girls resolve the Electra complex; he implied that they never resolve it completely and therefore remain partly fixated at the phallic stage.

Freud's writings about boys' fear of castration, girls' penis envy, the Oedipus complex, and the Electra complex have long been controversial. In most children it is difficult to observe anything that resembles the Oedipus complex or the Electra complex.

The Latent Period From about age 5 or 6 until adolescence, Freud said that most children suppress their sexual interest. They enter a **latent period**, a time when they play mostly with peers of their own sex. Most psychologists call this a "period" instead of a "stage of development" because psychosexual interest is not developing (changing); it is just waiting. According to Freud, no one becomes fixated at the latent period.

Apparently a product of the way we rear children in Europe and North America, the latent period may not occur in certain unindustrialized societies.

The Genital Stage Beginning at puberty, young people take a strong sexual interest in other people. This is known as the **genital stage**. According to Freud, anyone who has fixated a great deal of libido at earlier stages has little libido left for the genital stage. But people who have successfully negotiated the earlier stages can now derive primary satisfaction from sexual intercourse; other types of stimulation reinforce this primary source of pleasure.

Evaluation of Freud's Stages Was Freud right about these stages and about the consequences of fixation? Many psychologists are uncertain about whether his views can even be tested. Recall from Chapter 2 that a good scientific theory is falsifiable—that is, its predictions should be clear enough

for us to imagine data that would contradict them. Freud's theory makes such vague predictions that psychologists are not sure what results would contradict them (Grünbaum, 1986; Popper, 1986).

For example, consider Freud's views concerning anal fixation: If the parents are too strict in their toilet training, or if they begin it too early or too late, the child will become either orderly, stingy, and stubborn *or* messy and wasteful. That is hardly a precise prediction.

Suppose we make the prediction more precise, concentrating on what Freud considered the most common result of anal fixation: Does strict toilet training lead to a combination of orderly, stingy, and stubborn behavior? Phrasing the question in that way at least makes it scientifically testable. Most of the studies that have tested that hypothesis fail to support it; strict toilet training is not consistently related to orderly, stingy, or stubborn behavior (Fisher & Greenberg, 1977). The evidence relating early oral experience (such as duration of breastfeeding) to a later "oral personality" (characterized by dependence and a craving for eating, drinking, and smoking) is slightly stronger (Fisher & Greenberg, 1977). Even so, many psychologists are skeptical of the relationship because many of the studies that report it were poorly designed. To the extent that Freud's theory of psychosexual development is testable, the evidence is as yet unconvincing.

Defense Mechanisms Against Anxiety

According to Freud, an individual's personality is determined to a large degree by the way the unconscious mind deals with anxiety. To reduce the anxiety that certain thoughts and motivations cause, Freud said, we reject highly unpleasant thoughts from the conscious mind and force them into the unconscious.

Personality, Freud claimed, consists of three aspects: the id, the ego, and the superego. (Actually, he used German words that mean *it, I,* and *over-I.* A translator used Latin equivalents instead of English words.) The **id** consists of all our biological drives, such as sex and hunger. It seeks immediate gratification. The **ego** is the rational, decision-making aspect of the personality. The **superego** contains the memory of our parents' rules and prohibitions, such as, "Nice little boys and girls don't do that." Sometimes the id produces sexual or other motivations that the superego considers repugnant, evoking feelings of guilt. The ego may side with either the id or the superego; if it sides with the superego, it tries to avoid even thinking about the id's unacceptable impulses.

Figure 13.4

I versus anxiety: The ego—the rational I—has numerous ways of defending itself against anxiety, that apprehensive state named for the Latin word meaning "to strangle." These defense mechanisms try to ignore or avoid facing unpleasant reality, and they are part of an internal battle in which you fight against yourself.

To defend itself against anxiety caused by the conflict between the id's demands and the superego's constraints, the ego may exclude certain thoughts and impulses and relegate them to the unconscious. Among the **defense mechanisms** that the ego employs are repression, denial, rationalization, displacement, regression, projection, reaction formation, and sublimation (Figure 13.4). Defense mechanisms are normal ways of suppressing anxiety and are often adaptive. They become a problem only if they are carried to extremes, or if they prevent a person from dealing with reality.

Most psychologists today find it difficult to imagine the mind in terms of three warring factions. They regard Freud's description as an occasionally useful metaphor at best.

Concept Check

1. *What kind of behavior would you expect of someone with a strong id and a weak superego? What behavior would you expect of someone with an unusually strong superego? (Check your answers on page 503.)*

Repression   The defense mechanism of **repression** is motivated forgetting—the active rejection of unacceptable thoughts, desires, and memories and their relegation to the unconscious. Repression is perhaps the most central concept in Freud's theory.

For example, a woman sees someone beating another person to death. Later she cannot remember what she saw. She has repressed the painful memory. Another example: A man gives a speech and several members of the audience raise serious objections to what he says. Later he forgets their objections. People sometimes repress their own unacceptable thoughts as well.

Denial The refusal to believe information that provokes anxiety is called **denial**. Whereas repression is the motivated forgetting of certain information, denial is an assertion that the information is incorrect.

For example, a doctor tells a woman that her child is mentally retarded. She refuses to accept this opinion and shops around for another doctor who will tell her the child is not retarded.

Rationalization When people attempt to prove that their actions are rational and justifiable and thus worthy of approval, they are using **rationalization**. For example, a student who wants to go to the movies instead of studying says, "More studying won't do me any good anyway." Someone who misses a deadline to apply for a job says, "I didn't really want that job anyway."

Displacement By diverting a behavior or a thought away from its natural target toward a less threatening target, **displacement** lets people engage in the behavior they prefer without experiencing severe anxiety.

For example, a man who is angry at his boss comes home and kicks his dog. He really wants to kick his boss, but that would cause him too much anxiety. Or a student who fails an examination blames her professor for giving an unfair test and her roommate for distracting her when she was trying to study. To admit that the fault was her own would cause anxiety.

Regression A return to a more juvenile level of functioning, **regression** is an effort to avoid the anxiety of facing one's current role in life. By adopting a childish role, a person can escape responsibility and return to an earlier, perhaps more secure way of life. A person may also regress to an earlier stage of psychosexual development in response to emotionally trying circumstances.

For example, after a new sibling is born, a 5-year-old child may start wetting the bed again. Following a divorce or a business setback, a man may resort to daydreaming, getting drunk, or other immature behaviors.

Projection The attribution of one's own undesirable characteristics to other people is known as

John McEnroe comments on a referee's call in a juvenile manner. Which defense mechanisms are athletes using in the following comments: "The umpire's blind," "They had the home-field advantage," "The referees sided against us," "You gotta play rough to win"?

projection. When people project their own faults onto others, they generally do not deny that they themselves possess those faults (Holmes, 1978; Sherwood, 1981). However, by suggesting that the faults are widespread, they make them more acceptable and less anxiety provoking.

For example, someone says, "Everyone cheats on their income taxes," or "Every student cheats on a test now and then." People who make such statements probably cheat a little themselves.

Reaction Formation In an effort to reduce anxiety and to keep undesirable characteristics repressed, people may use **reaction formation** to present themselves as the opposite of what they really are. In Shakespeare's play *Hamlet,* Gertrude says, "The lady doth protest too much, methinks." People who insist too vehemently that something is "absolutely" true often harbor secret doubts about whether it really is true.

For example, someone with strong deviant sexual impulses may become a crusader against pornography. Someone who feels deep hostility toward other people may join a campaign against cruelty to animals. In each case the person is saying, "See? I was afraid I might have this terrible fault, but that can't be true because I'm working for the exact opposite."

Sublimation The transformation of an unacceptable impulse into an acceptable, even an admirable, behavior is **sublimation**. According to Freud, sublimation enables a person to express the impulse without admitting its existence. For example, painting and sculpture may represent a sublimation of sexual impulses. Someone with unacceptable aggressive impulses may sublimate them by becoming a surgeon. Whether Freud is correct about sublimation is difficult to say; if the true motives of a painter are sexual, they are hidden well indeed. However, if Freud is correct, sublimation is the one defense mechanism that leads to socially constructive behavior.

Concept Check

2. Which of the following descriptions is an example of repression, denial, rationalization, displacement, regression, projection, reaction formation, or sublimation?

a. A man who is angry with his neighbor goes hunting and kills a deer.

b. Someone with a smoking habit insists that there is no convincing evidence that smoking impairs health.

c. A woman with doubts about her religious faith tries to convert others to her religion.

d. A man who beats his wife writes a book arguing that people have an instinctive need for aggressive behavior.

e. A woman forgets a doctor's appointment for a test for cancer.

f. Someone who has difficulty dealing with certain people resorts to pouting, crying, and throwing tantrums.

g. A boss takes credit for a good idea suggested by an employee because, "It's better for me to take the credit so that our department will look good and all the employees will benefit."

h. Someone with an unacceptable impulse to shout obscenities becomes a writer of novels.
(Check your answers on page 503.)

Manifestations of the Unconscious in Everyday Life

Freud believed that the unconscious made itself felt in nearly all aspects of ordinary life. Even an act that may be explained as "just a meaningless accident" reflects an unconscious motivation. For example, when one of Freud's patients "forgot" an appointment, Freud assumed the patient did not want to keep it. When a patient left something behind in Freud's office and had to come back to get it, Freud assumed that the patient enjoyed being with him and was unconsciously planting an excuse to return. Much of people's personality, Freud said, was based on unconscious motivations.

Freud also interpreted *slips of the tongue,* or what have come to be called "Freudian slips," as revelations of unconscious thoughts and motives. If you said "I leave you" when you intended to say "I love you," Freud would assume that your error revealed an unconscious rejection of your professed love.

Today, psychologists believe that most slips of the tongue and other such errors have multiple causes (Norman, 1981). For example, President Jimmy Carter once introduced former Vice President Hubert Horatio Humphrey as "Hubert Horatio Hornblower." Perhaps Carter thought of Humphrey as someone who "blows his own horn" too much. But even if we accept this as a Freudian slip, that is not the whole explanation. Horatio Hornblower was a character in a series of novels. Carter may have referred to Horatio Hornblower many times before, and after saying "Hubert Horatio" it would have been easy for him to substitute Hornblower for Humphrey.

Freudian Slips:
WHAT'S THE EVIDENCE?

Freud claimed that what we say "by accident" reveals hidden motives. How can we test that claim?

We could follow people around and record all their slips of the tongue, or we could ask them to record all their own slips. But we would still have to guess or infer the hidden motives of the people we were following. And the people who were recording their own slips would have to decide which slips to record. If they were familiar with Freud's theory, they might record only the errors that seemed to fit the theory and ignore those that did not.

A second method would be to induce a motive—hunger, for example—for the purposes of an experiment. Then we could ask the hungry subjects to read a certain passage, and we could count how many of their slips of the tongue had something to do with eating. We could repeat the experiment with people in whom we had induced a different motive, to see whether they made different slips.

But most people make so few slips of the tongue that the experiment might go on for months without yielding significant results. To test Freud's theory, we need a procedure that increases the frequency of slips of the tongue. Michael Motley and Bernard Baars (1979) devised such a procedure.

Hypothesis When people are performing a difficult task on which they are likely to make slips of the tongue, the kinds of slips they make will depend on the kinds of motivations they are feeling at the moment.

Method The experimenters divided 90 male college students into three groups: a "sex" group, a "shock" group, and a control group. Those in the sex group were greeted by a very attractive female experimenter dressed in a sexy outfit and behaving in a seductive manner. Those in the shock group were met by a male experimenter who attached electrodes to their arms and told them the electrodes were connected to a "random shock generator" that might or might not give them one or more painful shocks at unpredictable times during the experiment. (No shocks were actually given.) Those in the control group were met by a male experimenter who attached no electrodes to them and made no mention of shocks. Thus one group should have a heightened sexual motivation, one group should have a strong fear of shock, and one group should be concerned with neither sex nor shock during the experiment.

The students watched a screen on which the experimenters flashed pairs of words or nonsense syllables, such as "HAT-RAM" and "PIG-BIT." Each pair was flashed for one second. A buzzer sounded 0.4 second after each pair appeared, telling the students to speak aloud the *previous* pair. So, for example, after seeing "PIG-BIT," they would have to say "HAT-RAM" (the previous pair), and remember "PIG-BIT" to say after the next pair. About 30% of the time students made slips of the tongue. For example, they would say "HAT-RAM" as "RAT-HAM" and "PIG-BIT" as "BIG-PIT."

Some of the syllable pairs were designed to promote sex-related slips. For example, "GOXI-FURL" and "LOOD-GEGS" might be pronounced as "FOXY GIRL" and "GOOD-LEGS." Other pairs were designed to promote shock-related slips. For example, "SHAD-BOCK" and "WOT-HIRE" might be pronounced as "BAD-SHOCK" and "HOT-WIRE." Still other pairs did not suggest any slips related to either sex or shock.

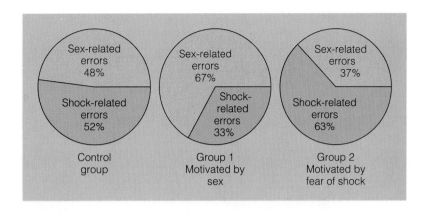

FIGURE 13.5

Your Freudian slip is showing: The frequency of sex-related and shock-related slips of the tongue by men who were motivated by sex, fear of shock, or neither. (Based on results of Motley & Baars, 1979.)

Results The men in the sex group made more than twice as many sex-related slips as shock-related slips. The opposite was true for the men in the shock group. Those in the control group made both types of error about equally. Figure 13.5 illustrates the results.

Interpretation The results support Freud's claim that a strong motivation can increase the frequency of slips of the tongue related to that motivation. Slips of the tongue may indeed tell us something about a person's thoughts and desires.

But the results do not support Freud's contention that hidden motivations are the *main* cause of slips of the tongue. Slips were common in this experiment because the task was so difficult. Having to say one pair while preparing to say another produced conflict between the two pairs that a subject was trying to remember. ■

The Legacy of Freud

Among Freud's contributions to the study of personality were his recognition of the importance of childhood experiences and the sex drive. His methods of treating psychological disorders led to the whole range of psychotherapeutic techniques, which we shall consider in Chapter 15. Still, it is difficult to evaluate how much of his theory is correct. Psychologists today express a wide range of opinions about Freud. Some follow his ideas closely, and others reject almost all his ideas as pseudoscience.

Some psychologists, known as **neo-Freudians**, have remained faithful to parts of Freud's theory while modifying other parts. One of the most influential neo-Freudians was Karen Horney (HOR-nigh;

Karen Horney, a major neo-Freudian, revised some of Freud's theories, while Carl G. Jung rejected some, including Freud's concept of dreams hiding their meaning from the conscious mind: "To me dreams are a part of nature which harbors no intention to deceive but expresses something as best it can" (Jung, 1965).

1885–1952), who believed that Freud had exaggerated the role of the sex drive in human behavior and had misunderstood the sexual motivations of women. Horney contended that Freud had slighted the importance of cultural influences on personality and was more interested in tracing the childhood sources of anxiety than he was in helping people deal with current problems. Still, Horney's views were more a revision than a rejection of Freud's theories. Other theorists, including Carl Jung and Alfred Adler, broke more sharply with Freud.

CARL G. JUNG AND THE COLLECTIVE UNCONSCIOUS

Carl G. Jung (YOONG; 1875–1961) was an early member of Freud's inner circle. Freud regarded Jung as a son, the "heir apparent" or "crown prince" of the psychoanalytic movement. But their father-son relationship gradually deteriorated (Alexander, 1982). At one point, Freud and Jung agreed to analyze each other's dreams. Freud described one of his dreams, but then refused to provide the personal associations that would enable Jung to interpret it, insisting that "I cannot risk my authority."

Jung was more forthcoming. He described a dream in which he explored the upper stories of a house, then explored its basement, and finally, discovering that the house had a subbasement, began to explore that. Jung thought the dream referred to his explorations of the mind. The top floor was the conscious; the basement was the unconscious; and the subbasement was a still deeper level of the unconscious, yet to be explored. Freud, however, insisted that the dream referred to Jung's personal experiences and frustrations (Hannah, 1976).

Jung's own theory of personality incorporated many of Freud's insights, but put greater emphasis on people's search for a spiritual meaning in life and on the continuity of human experience, past and present. Jung believed that every person has a conscious mind, a "personal unconscious" (equivalent to Freud's "unconscious"), and a collective unconscious. The personal unconscious represents a person's own experience. The **collective unconscious**, which is present at birth, represents the cumulative experience of preceding generations. Because all humans share a common ancestry, all have nearly the same collective unconscious. (Jung never explained how the collective unconscious might develop biologically.)

Jung drew his evidence for the collective unconscious from observations of various cultures. He pointed out that similar images emerge in the

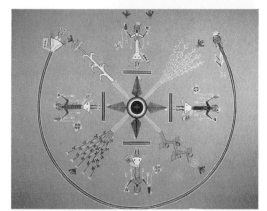

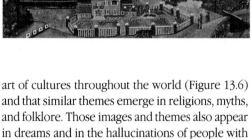

art of cultures throughout the world (Figure 13.6) and that similar themes emerge in religions, myths, and folklore. Those images and themes also appear in dreams and in the hallucinations of people with severe psychological disorders.

Jung's impact on contemporary psychology is hard to judge. Some psychotherapists make extensive use of his ideas, and most are at least aware of them. Many of his ideas are vague and mystical, however, and difficult to deal with scientifically.

FIGURE 13.6

The mandala, or magic circle, is an image common to many cultures throughout history as a representation of the self. It symbolizes the self's striving for unity and wholeness. These mandalas (clockwise from upper left) are a rose window from Chartres cathedral, France (circa 1200); a Hindu painting; the work of Jung's patient Kristine Mann, who founded the New York Jung Institute; a Greek ceramic (circa 550 B.C.); a mosaic from Beth Alpha Synagogue, Israel (circa A.D. 500); Jung's painting of the sacred in a ring of flames above a world of war and technology (1920); and a Navajo sand painting, Southwest United States.

Like Horney, Alfred Adler thought Freud put too much stress on the sex drive; Adler was very interested in feelings of self-esteem. How does his notion of striving for superiority compare with Maslow's goal of self-actualization (discussed in Chapter 11)?

ALFRED ADLER AND INDIVIDUAL PSYCHOLOGY

Alfred Adler (1870–1937), a physician who, like Jung, had been one of Freud's early followers, broke with Freud because he believed Freud was overemphasizing the sex drive and neglecting other, more important influences on personality. Their disagreement reached a peak in 1911, with Freud insisting that women experience "penis envy" and with Adler contending that women were more likely to envy men's status and power. The two were never reconciled.

Adler founded a rival school of thought, which he called **individual psychology**. To Adler this term did not mean "psychology of the individual." Rather, it meant "indivisible psychology," a psychology of the person as a whole rather than a psychology of parts, such as id, ego, and superego. Adler agreed with Freud that childhood experiences have a crucial effect on personality, that many motives are outside conscious awareness, and that people can be helped to overcome their problems through a "talking cure." He put far more emphasis, however, on conscious, goal-directed behavior.

Adler's Description of Personality

Several of Adler's early patients were acrobats who had had an arm or a leg damaged by a childhood illness or injury. Determined to overcome their handicaps, they had worked hard to develop the strength and coordination they needed to perform as acrobats. Perhaps, Adler surmised, people in general try to overcome their weaknesses and transform them into strengths (Adler, 1932/1964).

As infants, Adler pointed out, we are small, dependent creatures; we strive to overcome our inferiority. Some people never succeed, however, and go through life with an **inferiority complex**, an exaggerated feeling of weakness, inadequacy, and helplessness. Even those who do manage to overcome their feelings of inferiority persist in their efforts to achieve.

According to Adler, everyone has a natural **striving for superiority**, a desire to seek personal excellence and fulfillment. Each person creates a **style of life**, or "master plan," for achieving a sense of superiority. That style of life may be directed toward success in business, sports, politics, or some other competitive activity. Or it may be directed toward "success" of a different sort: For example, someone who withdraws from life may gain a sense of accomplishment or superiority from being uncommonly self-sacrificing. Someone who constantly complains about real or imagined illnesses or handicaps may, by demanding help from friends and family, win a measure of control or superiority over them. Or someone may commit crimes in order to savor the attention they bring.

Adler recognized that people may not be aware of their own style of life and the assumptions behind it and may fail to realize that the real motive behind some word or action is to manipulate others. They may engage in self-defeating behavior because they have not admitted to themselves what their goals really are. Adler tried to determine people's real motives. For example, he would ask someone who complained of a backache, "How would your life be different if you could get rid of your backache?" Those who said they would become more active were presumably suffering from real ailments that they were trying to overcome. Those who said they could think of no way in which their life would change, or said only that they would get less sympathy from others, were presumably suffering from psychologically caused ailments or at least were exaggerating their discomfort.

Concept Check

3. In Adler's theory, what is the relationship between striving for superiority and style of life? (Check your answer on page 503.)

Adler's View of Psychological Disorders

Any personality based on a selfish style of life is unhealthy, Adler (1928) said. People's need for one another requires that they develop a **social interest**, a sense of solidarity and identification with other people. People with a strong social interest strive for superiority in a way that contributes to the welfare of the whole human race, not just to their own welfare. In equating mental health with a strong social interest, Adler saw mental health as a positive state, not just the absence of impairments.

In Adler's view, people with psychological disorders are not suffering from an "illness." Rather, they have set immature goals, are following a faulty style of life, and show little social interest. Their response to new opportunity is "Yes, but . . ." (Adler, 1932). They are striving for superiority in ways that are useless to themselves and to others.

For example, one of Adler's patients was a man who lived in conflict with his wife because he was constantly trying to impress her and dominate her (Adler, 1927). In discussing his problems, the man revealed that he had been very slow to mature physically and had not reached puberty until he was 17 years old. Other teenagers had ignored him and had treated him like a child. He was now a physically normal adult, but he was overcompensating for those years of feeling inferior by trying to seem bigger and more important than he really was.

Adler tried to get patients to understand their own style of life and to correct the faulty assumptions on which it rested. He urged them to strengthen their social interest and to strive for superiority in ways that would benefit both themselves and others.

Adler's Legacy

Adler's influence on psychology exceeds his fame. His concept of the "inferiority complex" has become part of the common culture. He was the first to talk about mental health as a positive state rather than as merely the absence of impairments. Many later forms of therapy drew on Adler's innovations, especially his emphasis on the assumptions underlying a patient's behavior. Humanistic psychologists followed Adler in urging people to take responsibility for their own behavior and for modifying their style of life.

HUMANISTIC PSYCHOLOGY

In the 1950s and 1960s humanistic psychology emerged as a protest against both behaviorism and psychoanalysis, the dominant viewpoints in psy-

To Adler, a key element for mental health is having a social interest—an active concern for the welfare of society, not just your own welfare. Noting the failure of many to become involved in the well-being of others, Martin Luther King, Jr., said, "We shall have to repent in this generation . . . for the appalling silence of the good people."

chology at that time (Berlyne, 1981). Those two approaches, despite their many differences, are both rooted in *determinism* (the belief that every behavior has a cause) and in *reductionism* (the attempt to explain behavior in terms of its component elements). **Humanistic psychology** affirms the capacity of humans to determine their own course in life. Humanistic psychologists believe that personality can be understood only as a whole, not as an assemblage of parts. They also oppose the tendency of psychoanalysts to concentrate on people's problems and weaknesses. Humanistic psychologists prefer to emphasize people's potential, the "higher" side of human nature.

Humanistic psychologists deal with consciousness, values, and abstract beliefs, including the spir-

In search of excellence: Carl Rogers maintained that striving for excellence through self-actualization is a natural human goal. Scores of best-selling self-help books support this idea.

itual experiences and the beliefs that people live by and die for. According to humanistic psychologists, personality depends on what people believe and how they perceive the world. If you believe that a particular experience was highly meaningful, then it *was* highly meaningful. A psychologist can understand your behavior only by asking you for your own evaluations and interpretations of the events in your life. Consequently, humanistic psychologists have little interest in reporting the means and medians for large groups of people. In spite of the risks of relying on anecdotal evidence, they prefer to study unique individuals and unique experiences—the exceptions to the rule, not just the rule itself.

For example, humanistic psychologists study growth experiences—the moments that people identify as points of transition, when they may say, "Aha! Now I have become an adult," or "Now I have truly committed my life to this goal" (Frick, 1983). They also study **peak experiences,** moments in which a person feels truly fulfilled, content, and at peace. Some people report that they "feel at one with the universe" when they hear "thrilling" music, or take part in an emotional religious ceremony, or achieve some great accomplishment. Some mountain-climbers who have scaled Mount Everest report what is literally a "peak" experience (Lester, 1983).

Carl Rogers and the Goal of Self-Actualization

Carl Rogers, one of the founders of humanistic psychology, studied theology before turning to psychology, and the influence of those early studies is apparent in his view of human nature.

Rogers (1980) holds that human nature is basically good. People have a natural drive toward **self-actualization,** which means the achievement of their full potential. According to Rogers, it is as natural for people to strive for excellence as it is for a plant to grow. The drive for self-actualization is the basic drive behind the development of personality. (To some extent, Rogers's concept of self-actualization is similar to Adler's concept of striving for superiority.)

Beginning at an early age, children evaluate themselves and their actions. They learn that what they do is sometimes good and sometimes bad. They develop a **self-concept,** an image of what they really are, and an **ideal self,** an image of what they wish they were. Rogers measured a person's self-concept and ideal self by handing the person a stack of cards containing statements such as "I am honest" and "I am suspicious of others." The person would then sort the statements into two piles: *true of me* and *not true of me.* Then Rogers would provide an identical stack of cards and ask the person to sort them into two piles: *true of my ideal self* and *not true of my ideal self.* In this manner he could determine whether someone's self-concept was similar to his or her ideal self. People who perceive a great discrepancy between the two generally experience distress. Humanistic psychologists try to help people overcome that distress, either by improving their self-concept or by changing their ideal self.

To promote human welfare, Rogers maintains, people should relate to one another with **unconditional positive regard,** a relationship that Thomas Harris (1967) has described with the phrase "I'm OK, you're OK." Unconditional positive regard is the complete, unqualified acceptance of another person as he or she is, much like the love of a parent for a child. If someone expresses anger, or even a desire to kill, the listener should accept that as an understandable feeling, even while discouraging the other person from acting on the impulse. This view resembles the Christian admonition to "hate the sin but love the sinner."

Abraham Maslow and the Self-Actualized Personality

Abraham Maslow, another of the founders of humanistic psychology, proposed that people have a hierarchy of needs, an idea we considered in Chapter 11. The highest of those needs is self-actualization, the fulfillment of a person's potential. What kind of person achieves self-actualization, and what is the result of achieving it? Maslow (1962, 1971) sought to describe the self-actualized per-

sonality. He complained that psychologists concentrate on disordered personalities, reflecting the medical view that health is merely the absence of disease. They seem to assume that all personality is either "normal" (that is, bland) or undesirable. Maslow insisted, as Adler had, that personality may differ from the "normal" in positive, desirable ways.

To determine the characteristics of the self-actualized personality, Maslow made a list of people who in his opinion had achieved their full potential. His list included people he knew personally as well as figures from history (Figure 13.7). He then sought to discover what they had in common.

According to Maslow (1962, 1971), people with a self-actualized personality show the following characteristics:

1. An accurate perception of reality. They perceive the world as it is, not as they would like it to be. They are willing to accept uncertainty and ambiguity when necessary.

2. Independence, creativity, and spontaneity. They follow their own impulses.

3. Acceptance of themselves and others. They treat people with unconditional positive regard.

4. A problem-centered outlook, rather than a self-centered outlook. They think about how best to solve a problem, not how to make themselves look good.

5. Enjoyment of life. They are open to positive experiences, including "peak experiences."

6. A good sense of humor.

Critics have attacked Maslow's description on the grounds that, because it is based on his own choice of subjects, it may simply reflect the char-

FIGURE 13.7

Humanistic psychologist Abraham Maslow (left) and two people he considered self-actualized: Jane Addams and Albert Schweitzer. In *Motivation and Personality,* Maslow (1970) listed people who he thought lived up to their full potential, among them William James, Eleanor Roosevelt, and Thomas Jefferson. His longer list of "potential or possible cases" includes poets and other writers, artists in several fields, philosophers, and social leaders: John Keats, Ralph W. Emerson, Ida Tarbell, Pierre Renoir, Pablo Casals, Joseph Haydn, Thomas More, John Muir, Harriet Tubman, and Eugene Debs. Addams (1860–1935), a social worker and leading suffragette, founded Chicago's Hull House, a settlement providing community services for the poor. Schweitzer (1875–1965) practiced his concept of ethics as "reverence for life" as a physician and missionary in central Africa. Both Addams and Schweitzer received the Nobel Peace Prize.

acteristics he himself admired. In any case, Maslow set a precedent for other attempts to define a healthy personality as something more than personality without disorder.

SUMMARY

1.   Personality consists of all the stable, consistent ways in which the behavior of one person differs from that of others. Theories of personality are closely related to conceptions of human nature. Some observers believe that human beings are basically hostile and need to be restrained (Hobbes, Freud). Others believe that human beings are basically good and are hampered by restraints (Rousseau, Rogers). (page 467)

2.   Sigmund Freud, the founder of psychoanalysis, proposed that human behavior is greatly influenced by unconscious thoughts and motives. (page 469)

3.   Freud believed that many unconscious thoughts and motives are sexual in nature. He proposed that people progress through stages or periods of psychosexual development—oral, anal, phallic, latent, and genital—and that frustration at any one stage can lead to a lasting fixation of libido at that stage. (page 471)

4.   According to Freud, unacceptable thoughts and impulses are relegated to the unconscious because they are threatening or anxiety provoking. People engage in repression and other defense mechanisms to exclude such thoughts and impulses from the conscious mind. (page 473)

5.   Unconscious thoughts influence many aspects of everyday life, including slips of the tongue, although other influences may be more important. (page 476)

6.   Carl Jung believed that all people share a "collective unconscious" that represents the entire experience of humanity. (page 478)

7.   Alfred Adler proposed that people's primary motivation is a striving for superiority. Each person adopts his or her own "style of life," or method of striving for superiority. (page 480)

8.   According to Adler, the healthiest style of life is one that emphasizes "social interest"—that is, concern for the welfare of others. (page 481)

9.   Humanistic psychologists emphasize conscious, deliberate decision making and the capacity to achieve one's full potential. (page 481)

10.   Carl Rogers focused attention on the discrepancies between a person's self-concept and his or her ideal self. He recommended that people relate to one another with unconditional positive regard. (page 482)

11.   Abraham Maslow described a self-actualized personality, which he said was characteristic of people who achieve their full potential. (page 482)

SUGGESTIONS FOR FURTHER READING

Adler, A. (1954). *Understanding human nature.* Greenwich, CT: Fawcett. (Original work published 1927.) Adler's most general and most popular book.

Freud, S. (1924). *Introductory lectures on psychoanalysis.* New York: Boni & Liveright. Available in various paperback editions, this is Freud's attempt to describe the fundamentals of his theory to a general audience.

Maslow, A. H. (1962). *Toward a psychology of being.* Princeton, NJ: Van Nostrand. A good introduction to humanistic psychology.

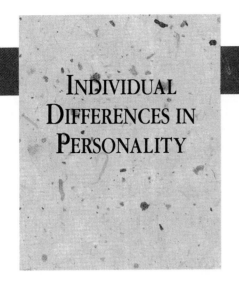

INDIVIDUAL
DIFFERENCES IN
PERSONALITY

Is personality consistent over time and from one
situation to another?
What are personality traits?

In many ways all rocks are the same. If you plan
to drop a rock and you want to predict when it will
hit the ground, you do not need to know what kind
of rock it is. If you skip a rock across a lake, throw
it against a window, or use it to crack open a coco-
nut, you can pretty well predict what will happen.

For other purposes, however, you need to know
something about the rock. If you want to predict
what will happen if you run an electric current
through it, you have to know what kind of rock it
is. If you want to determine a fair sale price for the
rock, you need to know whether it is a diamond or
a piece of granite.

Similarly, nearly all people behave the same in
some ways and differ in other ways. Most people
grow sleepy about once every 24 hours. When people sweat, they feel thirsty. When they escape from
pain or danger, they feel happy. Statements of this
type, which apply to nearly everyone, are sometimes referred to as **nomothetic** (NAHM-uh-THEHT-
ick) **laws** (from the Greek *nomothetes,* meaning
legislator). Up to this point, most of this book has
dealt with such universal statements.

But psychologists are also interested in the ways
in which people differ. If we want to predict how
someone will spend a Saturday afternoon, or how
that person will react to being with others, to being
alone, to succeeding, or to failing, we need to know
much about that person. We need to know what
makes that one individual different from others.
Statements that apply to individual differences are
known as **idiographic laws** (Silverstein, 1988). (The
prefix *idio-* means "individual.")

PERSONALITY TRAITS
AND STATES

Personality includes all the characteristics that define
the individual from one time to another and from
one situation to another. Is personality really as
consistent as we ordinarily assume? Some personality researchers claim that people have fairly broad
personality characteristics that are generally stable
over time and from one situation to another. Others
claim that people learn how to behave in specific
situations and that the apparent consistency of their
personality is mostly an illusion.

Both of these positions may be partly correct.
A person may exhibit characteristics that are consistent over a variety of appropriate circumstances,
though not at all times or in all situations (Alston,
1970). A consistent tendency in behavior, such as
shyness, hostility, or talkativeness, is known as a
trait. In contrast, a **state** is a temporary activation
of a particular behavior. People's behavior varies
from time to time because they are in different
states. For example, Don, who has a trait of being
highly talkative, talks in a discussion group but not
in a library, because the library induces a state of
silence. Donna, who has a trait of being reticent, is
quiet most of the time, but talks a great deal while
she is working at an information booth. Although
Don and Donna's behavior changes drastically from
one situation to another, they still have consistent
traits that would become apparent, for example, if
they both attended the same dinner party.

Note that both traits and states are just descriptions of behavior, not explanations. Suppose Susan
sits next to Steve and Steve says hardly anything to
her. We ask why. Perhaps Steve has been quiet all
afternoon (a state) or perhaps he is always shy
around women (a trait). Neither statement *explains*
his behavior (Briggs, 1985). Still, it would tell us
what we should *try* to explain: Are we trying to
explain why Steve has been quiet all afternoon? Or
why he is always shy around women?

Concept Check

*4. Two psychologists agree that a particular person
is showing anxiety, but they argue about whether
the anxiety is "trait anxiety" or "state anxiety." What
do they mean by that distinction? How could they
settle their argument? (Check your answers on
page 503.)*

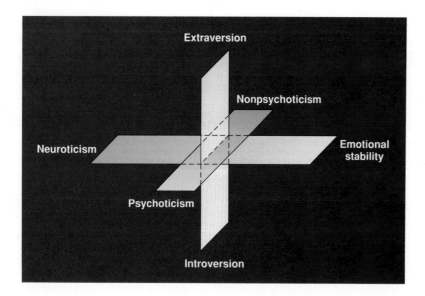

FIGURE 13.8

In this model of personality structure, any personality can be represented as one point in the three-dimensional space. (After Eysenck, 1952.) According to Eysenck, once we have described how neurotic, how psychotic, and how introverted or extraverted a person is, we have described the main features of that individual's personality.

TABLE 13.2 Five Traits That Account for Variations in Personality

Trait	Description
Neuroticism	Anxious, insecure, guilt prone, self-conscious
Extraversion	Talkative, sociable, fun loving, affectionate
Openness to new experience	Daring, nonconforming, enjoying new experiences, imaginative
Agreeableness	Sympathetic, warm, trusting, cooperative
Conscientiousness	Dependable, ethical, productive

Source: Based on McCrae and Costa, 1987.

EXAMPLES OF PERSONALITY TRAITS

How many personality traits are there? Gordon Allport and H. S. Odbert (1936) plodded through a dictionary and found almost 18,000 words that might be used to describe personality traits. Even after we eliminate synonyms, we still face a very long list. By one count, psychologists had identified 153 personality traits by the year 1983 (Royce & Powell, 1983).

Depending on our purpose, we can classify personalities in different ways. To return to our rock analogy, how could we decide how many kinds of rocks there are? A geologist might draw up a list based on chemical composition—granite, quartz, and feldspar, for example. A landscape architect might draw up a list based on size or color, ignoring chemical composition. Someone else might classify rocks in terms of where they were found. The "right" way to classify rocks depends on how we plan to use the classification.

Similarly, we can identify either several thousand personality traits or just a few, depending on our purpose. In general, psychologists prefer the simplest classification. If "shyness" means about the same thing as "timidity," we do not need to measure both traits. Psychologists use a method called *factor analysis* to find which traits correlate with one another and which ones do not.

Using that method, Hans Eysenck (1952a) proposed that psychologists could explain personality by using just three sets of traits: extraversion versus introversion, neuroticism versus emotional stability, and psychoticism versus nonpsychoticism (normal thinking), as shown in Figure 13.8. *Extraversion* means a directing of interest toward other people; *introversion* means a turning of interest inward, toward oneself. *Neuroticism* means easy arousal of anxiety and emotional distress; *psychoticism* means disordered thinking.

More recent research has favored a model that includes these five traits: neuroticism, extraversion, openness to new experiences, agreeableness, and conscientiousness (McCrae & Costa, 1987). (See Table 13.2.) Most other traits overlap one of these five or combine two or more of them. These five traits do not account for all aspects of personality, but they describe behavior in most situations.

Still, psychologists continue to study other personality traits that describe behavior in specialized situations. We shall discuss three examples of personality traits—androgyny, locus of control, and self-monitoring—which are among the most popular topics of contemporary research.

Masculinity, Femininity, and Androgyny

Two of the most obvious personality traits are masculinity and femininity, which are not the same as being biologically male or female. Not all males are equally masculine; not all females are equally feminine.

a

b

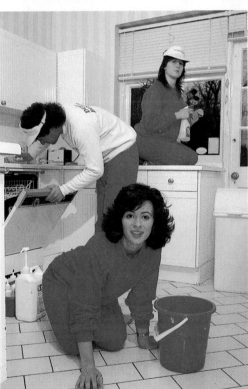

d

c

e

How would you define the traits masculine and feminine? Most people have trouble giving many characteristics; you may not consider any of them essential. But think how our words reflect attitudes. How do you use the term househusband? Do you call women "cooks" but men "chefs"? We speak of "career women," but businessmen are never "career men." If you say female sports fans are less feminine than these house cleaners (c), you need to clarify feminine. These cleaners do traditional "women's work," but they run a company to clean others' homes.

TABLE 13.3 Sample Items from the Bem Sex-Role Inventory

Masculine Items	Feminine Items
Ambitious	Affectionate
Assertive	Cheerful
Competitive	Compassionate
Makes decisions easily	Loves children
Self-reliant	Loyal
Willing to take risks	Sympathetic

Source: Bem, 1974, page 156.

According to society's definition of these terms, it is masculine to be ambitious, to be self-assertive, and to be interested in sports. It is feminine to enjoy caring for children, to be sympathetic and understanding, and to enjoy beautifying the house and garden.

Is it healthy to accept these roles wholeheartedly? Not entirely, perhaps—at least not if they limit one's choices. A man who loves taking care of children and who hates sports may worry that he is not very masculine. A highly assertive woman may be told that she is unfeminine. Perhaps people would be healthier and happier if they felt free to combine masculinity and femininity in whatever way they like—to be, for example, ambitious, assertive, interested in children, *and* sympathetic to the needs of others.

Reasoning along these lines led Sandra Bem (1974) to identify a psychological trait called **androgyny** (from the Greek roots *andr-* meaning man and *gyne-* meaning woman). According to Bem, androgynous people, as she originally conceptualized the trait, are equally masculine and feminine. They are not limited by one stereotype or the other; they can display masculine or feminine traits with equal ease, depending on what the situation requires.

Table 13.3 presents part of a checklist of masculine and feminine traits. To measure your degree of androgyny, check all the items that apply to yourself. If you check about the same number of masculine and feminine items, you are said to be androgynous. Such people, Bem predicted, are more likely to be mentally healthy and flexible in their behavior than are other people.

Bem's original method of measuring androgyny is probably not the best (Spence, 1984). The checklist does not measure all aspects of masculinity or femininity. It tends, in fact, to focus heavily on self-assertiveness and sympathy with other people.

Moreover, a person can make a score that is *equal* in masculinity and femininity either by scoring high in both or by scoring low in both. Someone who is assertive, self-reliant, cheerful, and compassionate has the advantages of both masculinity and femininity; such a person is likely to have high self-esteem and a good ability to get along with others. Someone who is unassertive, highly dependent, gloomy, and indifferent to others is also considered androgynous because the masculinity and femininity scores are equal (at zero). But such a person is at a disadvantage in many regards. For this reason, most investigators now define androgyny as a personality high in both masculinity and femininity.

Does androgyny confer any benefits that are greater than the sum of the benefits provided by masculinity and the benefits provided by femininity? So far, the research has failed to document any such additional benefits (Spence, 1984). Yet many psychologists believe that the idea of androgyny is a sound one and that the lack of research support is due to our current inability to measure androgyny properly.

Locus of Control

Do you think your success in life will depend mostly on your own efforts or mostly on circumstances beyond your control? People who believe they are largely in control of their lives are said to have an **internal locus of control**. Those who believe they are controlled mostly by external forces are said to have an **external locus of control** (Rotter, 1966). Table 13.4 lists some items from a questionnaire designed to measure locus of control. Many personality researchers and clinical psychologists use this questionnaire.

People's perception of their locus of control tends to be fairly consistent from one situation to another (Lefcourt, 1976). Those with an internal locus of control tend to take responsibility for their own behavior—for both their successes and failures (see Figure 13.9). When someone of the opposite sex finds them attractive, they assume it is because of their charm. By contrast, people with an external locus of control assume that the other person was just easy to please.

People with an internal locus of control know that they are not *always* in control. If they buy a lottery ticket or play a game of chance, they realize that they have no control over the outcome. In fact, they tend to be less interested in games of chance than people with an external locus of control are (Lefcourt, 1976). They not only *believe* they are generally in control but also *like* to be in control.

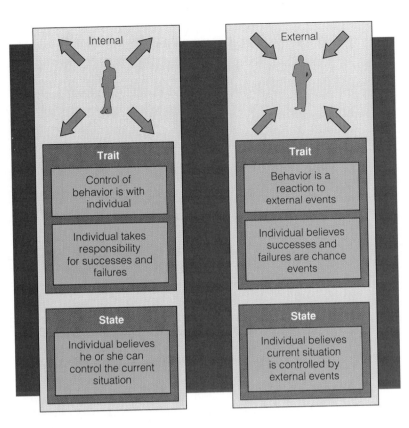

FIGURE 13.9

Locus of control can exist either as a lasting personality trait or as a temporary state of behavior.

Locus of control correlates with a number of other personality traits (Lefcourt, 1976). For example, people with an internal locus of control tend to work longer on a problem before giving up. They are more likely to choose a larger reward next week over a smaller reward today. People with an external locus of control are more likely to feel depressed and helpless.

Locus of control may show itself as a temporary state as well as a lasting trait. In other words, we may display an internal locus of control under certain circumstances and an external locus of control under others. For example, people generally display an internal locus of control when they are engaged in tasks that require skill, when they make choices, and when they are competing against others.

Even in a pure-chance situation, an opportunity to make a choice induces many people to exhibit an internal locus of control (Burger, 1986). For example, in one study, people were given a chance to buy $1 lottery tickets for a $50 prize (Langer, 1975). Some of them were simply handed a ticket,

Regardless of whether people have an internal or an external locus of control, some people's ability to control events is limited. These Catholic refugees have fled the North Vietnamese army. They cannot defeat the army, but rather than live in the communist state it supports, they have chosen to leave. Would you guess that people who take such risky actions have an internal locus of control or an external one?

while others were permitted to choose their own ticket. Those who chose their own ticket thought they had a better chance of winning. Days later, all the ticket holders were asked whether they were willing to sell their ticket to someone else. Those who had been handed a ticket agreed to sell for a mean price of less than $2. Those who had chosen their own ticket asked a mean price of more than $8 per ticket, and some held out for the full $50!

Self-Monitoring

You may know some people who seem to be consistently inconsistent: Whenever they face an unfamiliar situation, the first thing they do is determine what is expected of them and what everyone else is doing. Mark Snyder (1979) refers to such people as **high self-monitors** because they are constantly monitoring their own behavior to make sure that they are making the right impression (Figure 13.10). They may be quiet and reserved in one setting, outgoing and adventuresome in another. Their personality seems to be constantly changing.

In contrast, people who are **low self-monitors** pay little attention to what is expected of them or what impression they are making. If they are outgoing in one setting, they will be outgoing in other settings as well. Their personality seems to be consistent over time and from situation to situation.

High self-monitors and low self-monitors differ in their relationships with other people. For example, low self-monitors typically spend their time with a small group of friends and choose the same people to be their chemistry lab partners or their tennis partners. In contrast, high self-monitors look around for someone who is good at chemistry or good at tennis (Snyder, Gangestad, & Simpson, 1983). A low self-monitor is likely to establish a strong relationship with a dating partner, while a high self-monitor is more likely to break off a relationship with one partner in favor of a new partner who will make a better impression on others (Gangestad & Snyder, 1985).

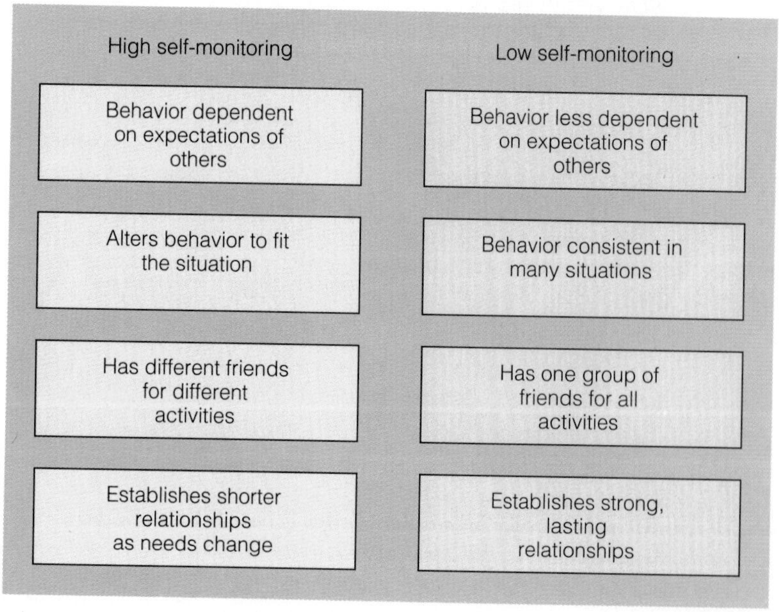

Concept Check

5. *Suppose we ask several people to express their attitudes on a variety of issues, such as drinking alcohol, cleaning up the environment, and improving race relations. Then we look for a correspondence between their attitudes and their actual behavior. Whose behavior is more likely to match their attitudes—low self-monitors or high self-monitors? (Check your answer on page 503.)*

EVALUATING THE TRAIT APPROACH

Most psychologists agree that traits show reasonable consistency from one time to another. A person who is talkative at a party tonight will probably be talkative at a party tomorrow night. Someone who returns a lost wallet to its owner one time will probably do the same thing the next time. According to the results of one questionnaire, traits are reasonably consistent over as long as eight years (Stein, Newcomb, & Bentler, 1986).

Psychologists share less agreement on how consistent traits are across situations. Does a student who talks a lot at parties also speak up during class discussions? If someone is honest about returning a lost wallet, will the same person be honest in filing an income tax return? Is a "friendly" person friendly to chance acquaintances, or just toward a few close friends?

Criticisms of the Trait Approach

Walter Mischel (1981) has been the leader of those who believe that such general traits as honesty and friendliness have only a weak carryover from one situation to another. Instead of talking about "friendliness," he suggests we should specify "friendliness to next-door neighbors" or "friendliness to store clerks." Narrowly defined traits are more likely to show consistency than are broadly defined traits. According to Mischel (1973), people

High self-monitoring	Low self-monitoring
Behavior dependent on expectations of others	Behavior less dependent on expectations of others
Alters behavior to fit the situation	Behavior consistent in many situations
Has different friends for different activities	Has one group of friends for all activities
Establishes shorter relationships as needs change	Establishes strong, lasting relationships

FIGURE 13.10

Making an impression: High and low self-monitoring.

"I'm shy," you say, but are you equally shy in class, with friends, and at a party where you know few of the guests? Those who are critical of the trait approach question whether shyness is a trait or a response occurring only in certain situations.

In short, Mischel and others believe that broad personality traits, such as talkativeness or honesty, have little to do with variations in human behavior. They hold that behavior depends more on states than on traits and that, in any case, traits are usually specific to given situations.

Why then do most of the people we know *seem* to have a consistent personality? One possibility is that the apparent consistency is mostly an illusion (Schweder, 1982). When we see someone behaving in a friendly way in a certain situation, we may assume that he or she is friendly in other situations as well. When someone is shy in our presence, we may assume that the person is shy with other people as well.

Distortions of memory may strengthen such illusions. We tend to remember those occasions when people behave in a way that fits our image of them. When someone who is usually outgoing behaves in a quiet, withdrawn manner, we dismiss the behavior as uncharacteristic (Hamilton, 1979).

Concept Check

6. *Given the ways in which people distort their memories of others, why does a person have a hard time trying to escape his or her reputation? (Check your answer on page 503.)*

Defense of the Trait Approach

Other psychologists insist that personality traits are more consistent than Mischel and other critics claim. Granted, a person who is friendly or talkative in one situation may not be equally so in every situation. (We would think something was wrong with a person who always acted the same way.) But people do show considerable consistency in their personality, and it is hard to believe that our perception of that consistency is just an illusion (Allport, 1966; McGowan & Gormly, 1976).

Defenders of the trait approach suggest several reasons for regarding personality traits as more consistent than the critics claim. First, *because of the demands of certain scripts, we cannot expect personality traits to be consistent across all situations.* For example, a person who is friendly and talkative at a party sits quietly during a lecture. Is that a sign of an inconsistent personality? Hardly. The script for a lecture class is so tightly defined that all the students are locked into the same behavioral state. In situations that are governed by more loosely defined scripts, such as a get-together over lunch, a person's behavior is a more accurate reflection of personality traits.

Second, *people sometimes seem to be inconsistent in one personality trait only because they*

have different personalities only because each person has learned a unique set of responses to each of the situations he or she faces.

In familiar situations, we learn to follow **scripts**—the rules governing who will do what and when (Abelson, 1981). The script for a lecture class, a religious service, or a round of golf specifies who will do what and when. Because nearly everyone who has learned the appropriate script will behave in about the same way, Mischel suggests that scripts and situations influence behavior more than any broad personality trait does.

Of course, people sometimes behave differently in the same situation. One reason is that they may differ in their personality traits. Another reason is that the script may assign different roles to different people. For example, the college-lecture script prescribes that the professor stand in front of the class and either talk or control the discussion. The same script prescribes that the students sit, take notes, and talk when called upon. It may even imply that seniors who are majoring in the field should participate more actively in class discussion than sophomores or juniors do.

are being consistent in some other trait (Bem & Allen, 1974). For example, a woman has always been honest in filling out her tax returns and in returning lost wallets. Now her neighbor asks, "Why didn't you invite me to your party next Saturday?" The woman replies, "Oh, it's just a party for people from my office." That is a lie; the real reason is that the neighbor always starts arguments. Why has this otherwise honest woman told a lie? Is it because of some inconsistency in her trait of honesty? Perhaps, but only because she is even more consistent in being tactful and friendly (Kenrick & Stringfield, 1980). A person can be consistent in one or several traits, but no one can be entirely consistent in all traits.

Third, *personality traits sometimes appear to be inconsistent only because of inadequate measurements* (Epstein & O'Brien, 1985). Suppose we want to study "interest in sports" as a personality trait. We find that the correlation between "interest in basketball" and "interest in hockey" is relatively low, because many people follow one sport closely and pay little attention to the other. So we might conclude that "interest in sports" is not much of a personality trait, given its inconsistency from one measure to another.

Would that be a sound conclusion? No, because neither "interest in basketball" nor "interest in hockey" is by itself a good indicator of "interest in sports" as a general trait. People can be either interested or uninterested in a particular sport for reasons that have little to do with sports in general. Many sports fans in the southern states, for example, follow every sport *except* hockey.

Watch what happens when we take a different approach: This time we ask people how closely they follow basketball, hockey, football, baseball, and the Olympics. For those who report that they follow most of those sports closely, we conclude that "interest in sports" is a strong trait. For those who report that they follow no more than one of the sports, we conclude that "interest in sports" is a relatively weak trait. The trait as measured in this more elaborate way will prove to be reasonably stable across situations and a good predictor of how people spend their spare time, what they like to talk about, and what they watch on television.

Similarly, when psychologists observe other traits in a variety of situations, they can measure them more accurately than if they measure them just once or twice. The resulting measures correlate strongly with additional measurements of behavior (Epstein, 1979; Moskowitz, 1982).

SUMMARY

1. Psychologists seek both nomothetic laws, which apply to all people, and idiographic laws, which apply to individual differences. (page 485)

2. Traits are personality characteristics that persist over time; states are temporary changes in behavior in response to particular situations. (page 485)

3. Psychologists seek a short list of traits that describes as much of behavior as possible. Much can be explained by these five traits: neuroticism, extraversion, openness to new experiences, agreeableness, and conscientiousness. (page 486)

4. Androgyny is a trait that combines the features of masculinity and femininity. Psychologists are not sure whether it confers any special benefits beyond the separate benefits of its two components. (page 488)

5. People with an internal locus of control believe that for the most part they are in control of their lives. People with an external locus of control believe that their lives are controlled mostly by outside forces. (page 488)

6. High self-monitors mold their behavior to the demands of the situation in an effort to make a good impression. Consequently, their behavior tends to be inconsistent across situations. Low self-monitors tend to be less concerned about the impression they are making; consequently, their behavior tends to be more consistent. (page 490)

7. Some personality theorists have criticized the trait concept on the grounds that behavior seems to be inconsistent from one situation to another. (page 490)

8. Defenders of the trait concept point out that (1) we should not expect traits to be apparent at all times or in all situations, (2) people sometimes appear to be inconsistent in one trait only because they are more consistent in some other trait, and (3) traits sometimes appear to be inconsistent only because they have been measured inadequately. (page 491)

SUGGESTION FOR FURTHER READING

Liebert, R. M., & Spiegler, M. D. (1987). *Personality: Strategies and issues*. Chicago: Dorsey. A textbook that covers the major approaches to the study of personality.

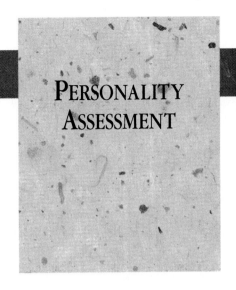

PERSONALITY ASSESSMENT

How can we measure personality?
How can we use measurements of personality?

A new P. T. Barnum Psychology Clinic has just opened at your local shopping mall and is offering a Grand Opening Special on personality tests. You have always wanted to know more about yourself, so you sign up. Here is Barnum's true-false test.

Questionnaire for Universal Assessment of Zealous Youth (QUAZY)

1. I have never met a cannibal I didn't like.   T F
2. Robbery is the only major felony I have ever committed.   T F
3. I eat "funny mushrooms" less frequently than I used to.   T F
4. I don't care what people say about my nose-picking habit.   T F
5. Sex with vegetables no longer disgusts me.   T F
6. This time I am quitting glue-sniffing for good.   T F
7. I generally lie on questions like this one.   T F
8. I spent much of my childhood sucking on telephone cords.   T F
9. I find it impossible to sleep if I think my bed might be clean.   T F
10. Naked bus drivers make me nervous.   T F
11. Some of my friends don't know what a rotten person I am.   T F
12. I usually find laxatives unsatisfying.   T F
13. I spend my spare time playing strip solitaire.   T F

You turn in your answers. A few minutes later a computer prints out your individual personality profile:

You have a need for other people to like and admire you, and yet you tend to be critical of yourself. While you have some personality weaknesses, you are generally able to compensate for them. You have considerable unused capacity that you have not turned to your advantage. Disciplined and self-controlled on the outside, you tend to be worrisome and insecure on the inside. At times, you have serious doubts as to whether you have made the right decision or done the right thing. You prefer a certain amount of change and variety and become dissatisfied when hemmed in by restrictions and limitations. You also pride yourself as an independent thinker and do not accept others' statements without satisfactory proof. But you have found it unwise to be too frank in revealing yourself to others. At times you are extraverted, affable, and sociable, while at other times you are introverted, wary, and reserved. Some of your aspirations tend to be rather unrealistic [Forer, 1949, page 120].

Do you agree with this assessment?

This experiment has been conducted several times with psychology classes (Forer, 1949; Marks & Kammann, 1980; Ulrich, Stachnik, & Stainton, 1963). The questionnaire was a little less preposterous than the QUAZY, but everyone received exactly the same personality profile you did. The students were asked, "How accurately does this profile describe you?" About 90% rated it good or excellent. Some expressed amazement at its accuracy: "I didn't realize until now that psychology was an exact science."

The students accepted this personality profile partly because it vaguely and generally describes almost everyone and partly because people tend to accept almost *any* statement that an "expert" makes about them. Richard Kammann repeated the experiment, but substituted a strange, unflattering personality profile that included statements like "Your boundless energy is a little wearisome to your friends" and "You seem to find it impossible to work out a satisfactory adjustment to your problems." More than 20% of the students rated this unlikely assortment of statements a "good to excellent" description of their own personality (Marks & Kammann, 1980).

The moral of the story is this: Psychological testing is tricky. If we want to know whether a particular test measures a particular person's personality, we cannot simply ask whether or not that person thinks it does. Even if a test is totally worthless—horoscopes, palm reading, or the QUAZY—many people will describe its results as a "highly accurate" description of themselves. To devise a psychological test that not only *appears* to work but also actually *does* work, we need to go through some elaborate procedures to design the test carefully and to determine its reliability and validity.

STANDARDIZED PERSONALITY TESTS

Psychologists have devised a great variety of standardized tests to measure personality. A **standardized test** is one that is administered according to specified rules and whose scores are interpreted in a prescribed fashion. An important step in standardizing a test is to determine the distribution of scores for a large number of people. We need to know the mean score and the range of scores for people in general and the mean and the range for various special populations, such as severely depressed people. Given such information, we can determine whether a given individual's score on the test is within the normal range or whether it is more typical of people with some disorder.

Most of the tests published in popular magazines have never been standardized. A magazine may herald its article, "Test Yourself: How Good Is Your Marriage?" or "Test Yourself: How Well Do You Control the Stress in Your Life?" After you have taken the test and compared your answers to the scoring key, the article may tell you that "if your score is greater than 80, you are doing very well . . . if it is below 20, you need to work on improving yourself!"—or some such nonsense. Unless the magazine states otherwise, you can take it for granted that the author pulled the scoring norms out of thin air and never even bothered to make sure that the items were clear and unambiguous.

We shall begin with two examples of standardized tests of personality and later consider a less objective method of assessing personality—projective tests.

The Minnesota Multiphasic Personality Inventory (MMPI)

The **Minnesota Multiphasic Personality Inventory** (mercifully abbreviated **MMPI**) consists of about 550 true-false questions. (Alternative versions vary in number.) Typical items are "My mother never loved me" and "I think I would like the work of a pharmacist." (All the items given here have been reworded.) The MMPI was originally designed to measure the 10 personality traits listed in Table 13.5. Figure 13.11 shows a profile of one individual's test scores. The items relating to each trait were scattered throughout the test, rather than clustered. Over the years, psychologists have used other combinations of MMPI questions to measure hundreds of personality dimensions.

Construction of the MMPI In choosing the MMPI questions, the original authors relied strictly on trial and error (Hathaway & McKinley, 1940). They asked hundreds of people of both sexes and all ages to answer hundreds of true-false questions about themselves. Then they posed the same questions to groups of depressed people, paranoid people, and people with other clinical disorders. They selected those items that most of the people in a given clinical group answered differently from the way most other people answered them. Their assumption was that if you answer the way depressed people usually answer, you may be depressed too.

The result was a test that works in practice. Most people with a high score on the depression scale are depressed; most people with a high score on the hypochondriasis scale complain of constant ailments.

Some of the MMPI test items fit popular theories and expectations, and some do not. For example, one question on the schizophrenia scale is "Sometimes I hear voices even though no one else is around." That item makes good sense theoretically, because "hearing things" is considered to be characteristic of schizophrenia. Not all schizophrenic people hear things, but most people who do are suffering from schizophrenia. (We shall discuss schizophrenia, a serious mental disturbance, in Chapter 14.)

However, two items on the depression scale are "I attend church regularly" and "Occasionally I tease animals." If you answer *false* to either of those items, you get a point on the depression scale! The authors of the MMPI had no theoretical reason to expect that depression would have any relationship, one way or the other, with church attendance or animal teasing. It was simply a fact that significantly more depressed people than normal people answered false to those two items. (A possible explanation is that many depressed people don't do much of *anything*; attending church and teasing animals are only two of many possible activities.)

TABLE 13.5 The Ten Original MMPI Scales

Scale	Typical Item
Hypochondria	I have chest pains several times a week. (T)
Depression	I am glad that I am alive. (F)
Hysteria	My heart frequently pounds so hard I can hear it. (T)
Psychopathic deviation	I get a fair deal from most people. (F)
Masculinity-femininity	I like to arrange flowers. (T = female)
Paranoia	There are evil people trying to influence my mind. (T)
Psychasthenia (obsessive-compulsive)	I save nearly everything I buy, even after I have no use for it. (T)
Schizophrenia	Sometimes I hear voices even though no one else is around. (T)
Hypomania	When things are dull I try to get some excitement started. (T)
Social introversion	I have the time of my life at parties. (F)

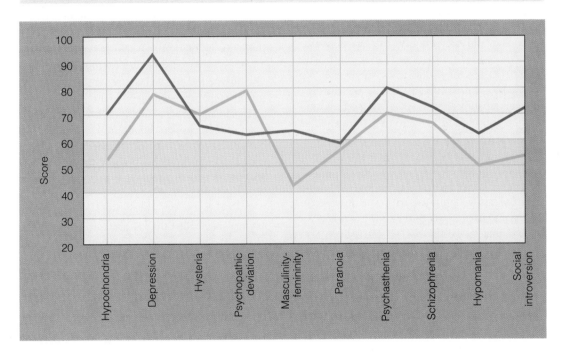

FIGURE 13.11

Profile of a personality: For the MMPI's 10 clinical scales, a score is plotted to profile an individual, as shown here. For each scale, such as hysteria and paranoia, the normal range is 40 to 60. Scores above 70 suggest disorders. The red line is the profile of a 27-year-old man with moderate to severe depression and anxiety (Graham, 1977). The green line is the profile of a 28-year-old woman with moderate depression and a tendency toward impulsive behavior (Anastasi, 1988).

Concept Check

7. If you never go to church and never tease animals, are you on your way to becoming depressed? (Check your answer on page 503.)

Revision of the MMPI   The MMPI was standardized in the 1940s. As time passed, the meaning of certain items, or at least of certain answers to them, changed. For example, how would you respond to the following item?

I am an important person.   T   F

In the 1940s, fewer than 10% of all people marked this item *true*. At the time, "important person" meant about the same as "famous person," and people who called themselves important were thought to have an inflated view of themselves. Today a majority of people mark this item *true*. After all, we now believe that every person is important.

What about this item?

I like to play drop the handkerchief.   T   F

Drop the handkerchief is a game similar to tag. It dropped out of popularity in the 1950s, and most people born since then have never even heard of the game, much less played it.

To bring the MMPI up to date, a group of psychologists rephrased some of the items (Butcher,

1989; Holden, 1986). A different game was substituted for drop the handkerchief, and the "important person" item was rephrased to mean what it used to mean. New items were added to deal with alcohol and drug abuse, Type A behavior, stress, and marriage troubles. Moreover, the revised test has been administered to over 2,500 adults in the United States, including all ethnic groups, to determine what scores are typical of people today. In other words, the test has been restandardized. (Any test has to be restandardized from time to time. You may recall from the discussion of IQ tests that certain items once considered difficult are now considered relatively easy.)

Detection of Deception The designers of the MMPI built some very sophisticated innovations into their test. They realized that people who take personality tests sometimes lie to make themselves look good, thereby rendering their test scores invalid. How could psychologists tell whether someone was lying?

To measure that possibility, they included a "lie scale." They did not, of course, ask questions like "Sometimes I lie to make myself look good. True or false?" Rather, they included such items as "I like every person I have ever met" and "Occasionally I get angry at someone." If you answer true to the first question and false to the second, you are either a saint or a liar. The test authors, convinced that there are more liars than saints, would give you two points on the "lie scale." Almost everyone gets a few points on the lie scale, but if you get too many a psychologist will refuse to trust your answers on the other items and will throw your test away.

A similar method is used to detect deception on other types of tests. For example, many employers ask job applicants to fill out a questionnaire that asks them how much experience they have had with certain job-related skills. What is to prevent eager applicants from exaggerating or even lying about their experience? To find out whether applicants are lying, some employers include among the authentic items a few bogus items referring to nonexistent tasks:

How much experience have you had at:	None	A Little	Much
Matrixing solvency files?	—		
Typing from audio-fortran reports?	—	—	—
Determining myopic weights for periodic tables?	—	—	
Resolving disputes by isometric analysis?	—	—	—
Stocking solubility product constants?	—	—	—
Planning basic entropy programs?	—	—	—
Operating a matriculation machine?	—	—	—

According to the results of one study, almost half of all job applicants claimed experience at one or more nonexistent tasks (Anderson, Warner, & Spencer, 1984). Moreover, applicants who claimed a great deal of experience at nonexistent tasks also overstated their ability on real tasks. An employer can use answers on bogus items as a correction factor. The more skill an applicant claims to have on a nonexistent task, the more the employer discounts that applicant's claims of skill on real tasks.

Something to Think About

Could you use this strategy in other situations? Suppose a political candidate promises to increase aid to college students. You are skeptical. How could you use the candidate's statements on other issues to help you decide whether or not to believe this promise?

Detection of Errors in Answering Questions If someone answered the MMPI carelessly or misnumbered the answers, the resulting pattern of scores might be very misleading. How could a psychologist tell whether people had been careless in taking the test? One way would be to have them take the test again and check to see whether they changed many of their answers. But doing so would be time consuming and perhaps inconclusive. Many people change their answers not because they were careless the first time but because they have trouble deciding how to answer (Bond, 1986).

To cope with this problem, the test authors built in what they called the "F" scale, which includes items that almost everyone answers the same way. (It is called "F" for *feigning*, because it catches people who are faking, as well as people who answer carelessly.) Examples are "I never smell anything," and "I spent last week in Tibet." Very few people can honestly say "true" to either of those items. It is possible that you have a defective sense of smell and that you spent last week in Tibet; two points on the F scale would not disqualify your answer sheet. But if you give a number of highly unusual answers, a psychologist will assume either that you misnumbered your answer sheet or that you were clowning around. In either case, your answer sheet is worthless for assessing your personality.

Proper and Improper Uses of the MMPI The MMPI is useful to researchers who want to measure personality traits to see how they correlate with other traits or to test a theory of personality development. It is also useful to clinical psychologists who want to learn something about a client before beginning therapy or who want an independent measure of how much a client's personality has changed during the course of therapy (McReynolds, 1985).

By itself, however, the MMPI does not provide enough information for a psychologist to decide whether or not someone has a mental or an emotional problem. Its validity is not high enough for that purpose. In fact, apparently well-adjusted people produce a wide distribution of scores on each of the MMPI scales. Occasionally, an apparently well-adjusted person scores higher on the depression or the schizophrenia scale than do most people who are actually depressed or schizophrenic. Identifying a person with schizophrenia or any other unusual condition is a signal-detection problem, as we discussed in Chapter 5. Suppose that people without schizophrenia outnumber people with schizophrenia by 100 to 1. Suppose further that 95% of the schizophrenic people scored above 50 on the MMPI schizophrenia scale and only 5% of the normal people scored that high. As Figure 13.12 shows, 5% of the normal population is a *larger* group than 95% of the schizophrenic population. Thus, if we called everyone "schizophrenic" who scored above 50, we would be wrong more often than right.

Even so, some people use the MMPI as if its validity were high enough to base firm conclusions on its results. Some employers use it to screen job applicants, selecting only those who have the "right" personality. Some companies want to hire only people with an "aggressive" personality for sales jobs. Others want to eliminate anyone who shows signs of any psychological abnormality. The test was not designed for selection among job applicants, and many psychologists question both the accuracy and the ethics of using it for such purposes.

If you were to take the MMPI, how much would you learn about yourself? Suppose you gave the following answers:

I doubt that I will ever be successful.	True
I often wake up in the middle of the night.	True
I am glad that I am alive.	False
I have thoughts about suicide.	True
I am helpless to control the important events in my life.	True

A psychologist analyzes your answer sheet and tells you, "Your results show signs of possible depression." How impressive is that analysis? Chances are, you were already well aware of feeling depressed. In most cases, the MMPI does little more than restate what you have already said about yourself. It might be news to hear that you are "schizophrenic" or

	Scores above 50 on new test	Scores below 50 on new test
People with schizophrenia (100 people)	95 (95% of 100)	5 (5% of 100)
People without schizophrenia (10,000 people)	500 (5% of 10,000)	9,500 (95% of 10,000)

FIGURE 13.12

Results of a hypothetical test that is 95% accurate in identifying schizophrenia. Because schizophrenia is uncommon, most of the people with high scores on the schizophrenia test do *not* have schizophrenia. Personality tests can be used to suggest a possible diagnosis of a person's problem, but by themselves they cannot establish a diagnosis with sufficient accuracy.

"obsessive-compulsive" but only because you were not familiar with those terms. However, this is not to say that the MMPI is useless. It can be quite informative to the psychologist, even when the results are not particularly surprising to the client.

The 16-PF Test

The **16-PF Test** is another widely used standardized personality test. The term "PF" stands for personality factors. The test measures 16 factors, or traits, of personality. Unlike the MMPI, which was intended primarily to identify abnormal personalities, the 16-PF Test was devised to assess various aspects of normal personality. Raymond Cattell (1965) used factor analysis to identify the traits that contribute most significantly to personality. As we saw earlier in this chapter, other psychologists using factor analysis identified 3 or 5 major traits; Cattell found 16. He then devised a test to measure each of those traits. Because of the large number of factors, the results of his test apply to a rather wide range of behaviors (Krug, 1978).

When someone takes the 16-PF Test, the results are printed out as a **personality profile**, as Figure 13.13 shows. By examining such a profile, an experienced psychologist can determine the person's dominant personality traits.

Although the 16-PF Test was originally designed to assess normal personality, it does enable clinicians to identify various abnormalities, such as schizophrenia, depression, and alcoholism (Kerzendorfer, 1977). Each disorder is associated with a characteristic personality profile (see Figure 13.14).

FIGURE 13.13

Personality profiles on the 16-PF test for airline pilots, creative artists, and writers. A personality profile shows whether people are high or low on a given trait. In this sample, writers were the most imaginative group. (Adapted from *Handbook for the Sixteen Personality Factors,* copyright 1970 by the Institute for Personality and Ability Testing, Inc. Reproduced by permission of the copyright owners.)

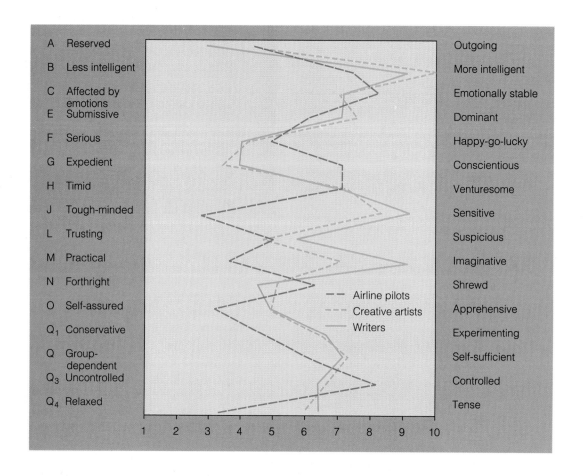

FIGURE 13.14

A personality profile for a person with severe anxiety, based on the 16-PF test. The profile shows that this person is high in guilt, low in "ego strength." Cattell made up his own words for familiar concepts so that he could provide a precise definition that would not be confused with the everyday and vague meaning of a term such as *depression.* For example, *surgency* means something similar to cheerfulness and sociability. *Parmia* resembles adventurousness or boldness. (From Cattell, 1965.)

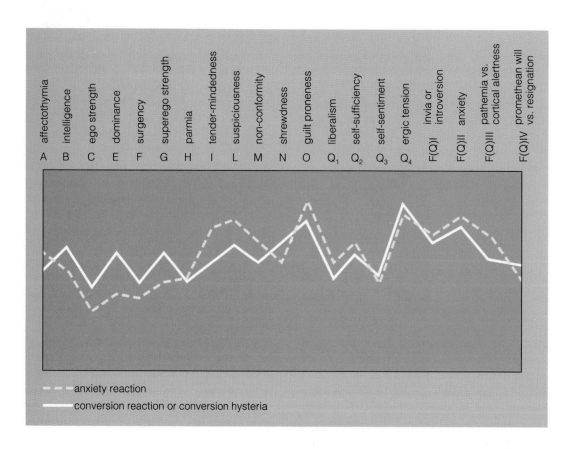

PROJECTIVE TESTS

The MMPI, the 16-PF, and other standardized personality tests are easy to score and easy to handle statistically, but they restrict how a person can respond to a question. To find out more, we need to ask open-ended questions that permit an unlimited range of responses.

Simply to say "Tell me about yourself" rarely evokes much information. In fact, most people find such invitations threatening. They may not be fully honest even with themselves, much less with a psychologist they have just met. To prompt people to describe themselves freely, we need to ask questions that are open ended but not threatening.

Many people find it easier to discuss their problems in the abstract than in the first person. For instance, they might say, "I have a friend with this problem. Let me tell you my friend's problem and ask what my friend should do." They then describe their own problem. They are "projecting" their problem onto someone else, in Freud's sense of the word.

Rather than discouraging projection, psychologists often make use of it. They use **projective tests**, which are designed to encourage people to project their personality characteristics onto ambiguous stimuli. This strategy helps people reveal themselves more fully than they normally would to a stranger, or even to themselves. Let's consider two of the best-known projective tests.

Rorschach Inkblot Test

The **Rorschach Inkblot Test** is probably the most famous projective test of personality. It was created by Hermann Rorschach, a Swiss psychiatrist, who was interested in art and the occult. He read a book of poems by Justinus Kerner, a mystic writer, who had made a series of random inkblots and had then written a poem about each one. Kerner believed that anything that happens at random reveals the influence of occult, supernatural forces.

Rorschach made his own inkblots, but put them to a different use. He was familiar with a word-association test then in use in which a person was given a word and was asked to say the first word that came to mind. Rorschach combined this approach with his inkblots: He showed people an inkblot and then asked them to say what came to mind (Pichot, 1984).

After testing a series of inkblots on his patients, Rorschach noticed that they reported seeing different things in the inkblots. In a book published in 1921 (English translation, 1942) he presented the

"*This looks like an inkblot*": In the Rorschach Inkblot Test, there are no wrong or right answers. The psychologist records the client's visual associations and behavior and later interprets them.

10 inkblots that still constitute the Rorschach Inkblot Test. He invited other researchers to determine whether people's responses to his inkblots revealed anything important about their personality. Long before adequate research had been done, however, many psychologists had already begun to use the inkblots with their patients.

The Rorschach Inkblot Test consists of 10 cards like the one in Figure 13.15. Five are black and white; five are in color. If you take this test, a psychologist will hand you a card and ask, "What might this be?" The instructions are intentionally vague. The assumption is that everything you do in an ill-defined situation will reveal something significant about your personality to the psychologist—and the more poorly defined the situation, the better. The psychologist may keep a record of almost everything you do: what you say you see, how you explain your remarks, where you hold the cards, whether you rotate them, how long you take to make your first response, how long you study each card, and the length of any pauses between your responses.

Because everything you do, down to blinking your eyes, is considered significant, the psychologist avoids suggesting what you should do. If you want to get a psychologist really flustered, say that you do not understand what is expected but that you would be glad to cooperate if only the psychologist would give you an example of what to say. The one thing a psychologist can *never* do with the Rorschach is to give an example.

What does a psychologist look for in your responses? One thing is the number of responses you make. An average person gives about two to

FIGURE 13.15

A Rorschach Inkblot.

five responses per card. Anyone who averages fewer than two per card may be depressed, unimaginative, uncooperative, or perfectionistic (wanting to give only "the best possible answer" each time). Anyone who makes many more than five responses per card may be bright and imaginative or a dull-witted person who enjoys this "easy" test. Emotionally disturbed people may see absolutely nothing in some of the cards, or may give an extremely long list of replies. People are permitted to talk as long as they want. Boris Semeonoff (1976) reports an adolescent boy who once gave an average of 14 responses per card. (The rules for administering the test prohibited the psychologist from telling him to stop!)

Psychologists are also interested in whether the person taking the test responds to the whole blot, a large part of it, a minor detail, the white spaces, or other features. They also note whether the person says anything about the color of the blot or describes any movement.

Finally, psychologists are interested in the content of the responses. For example, one woman, who was having serious marital difficulties, gave the following responses:

(Card 1) Outer looks like wings of a butterfly . . . and inner details, a stolid woman. Butterfly may in a sense be pulling at the woman in two different directions. One is responsibility and obligation, and the other direction is pursuit of a [long pause] well, love, selfish but satisfying.

(Card 3) Seems to suggest two human forms . . . facing each other. . . . Myself, both myself . . . one part tells me one way; another portion, a completely contradictory way. . . . Red in center seems to suggest . . . almost in a romantic sense . . . the heart. . . . This is feminine form, and they are connected to this, the right and the left of it. Therefore, two sides. The right meaning which is right or constructive, the left which would be the destructive or the short-sighted way. The immediate impact was two figures facing each other. Both emanate from one female form and it seemed to be concerned with the romantic affair of the heart. I'm all three" [Beck, 1960, pages 58–59].

Although the Rorschach Inkblot Test is widely used, its reliability and validity are not impressive. To determine its validity, psychologists check to see whether the test distinguishes between normal people and people with various disorders and whether it predicts whether a patient is likely to improve or to deteriorate. The test has reasonable validity for discriminating between normal people and severely disordered people. According to one review, its reliability is about .83 and its predictive validity is about .45 to .50 (Parker, 1983). That validity is not high enough to support clinical judgments; a psychologist needs to have greater certainty before deciding how to treat a patient (Shields, 1978).

What is worse, different psychologists examining the same responses sometimes draw entirely different conclusions (Squyres & Craddick, 1982). Consequently, the reliability and validity of the test vary from one psychologist to another. The usefulness (validity) of a baseball bat in hitting a ball depends on who is swinging the bat; similarly, the usefulness of the Rorschach depends on who is giving the test and interpreting the results. Interpreting the Rorschach is more an art than a science.

Concept Check

8. *Why would it be impossible to receive a copy of the Rorschach Inkblot Test by mail, fill it out, and mail it back to a psychologist to evaluate your answers? (Check your answer on page 503.)*

The Thematic Apperception Test

The **Thematic Apperception Test (TAT)** consists of 20 pictures like the one shown in Figure 13.16. It was devised by Christiana Morgan and Henry Murray as a means of measuring people's needs; it was revised and published by Murray (1943). Different sets of pictures are used for women, men, boys, and girls. The subject is asked to make up a story for each picture, describing what is happening, what events led up to the scene, and what will happen in the future. The pictures are all somewhat ambiguous but, except for the 20th card (which is blank!), they provide a better-defined stimulus than does the Rorschach.

People who take the TAT are expected to identify with the people shown in the pictures. That is why men are given pictures showing mostly men, and women are given pictures showing mostly women. The stories people tell usually relate to recent events and concerns in their own lives, possibly including concerns they would be reluctant to talk about openly.

For example, one young man told the following story about a picture of a man clinging to a rope:

This man is escaping. Several months ago he was beat up and shanghaied and taken aboard ship. Since then, he has been mistreated and unhappy and has been looking for a way to escape. Now the ship is anchored near a tropical island and he is climbing down a rope to the water. He will get away successfully and swim to shore. When he gets there, he will be met by a group of beautiful native women with whom he will live the rest of his life in luxury and never tell anyone what happened. Sometimes he will feel that he should go back to his old life; but he will never do it [Kimble & Garmezy, 1968].

This young man had entered divinity school, mainly to please his parents, but was quite unhappy there. He was wrestling with a secret desire to "escape" to a new life with greater worldly pleasures. In his story, he described someone doing what he really wanted to do but could not openly admit.

The TAT is often used in a clinical setting to get clients to speak freely about their problems. It is also used for research purposes. For instance, an investigator might measure someone's "need for achievement" by counting all the stories he or she tells about achievement. The same might be done for aggression, passivity, control of outside events, or dominance. The investigator could use the findings to study the forces that strengthen or weaken various needs and why certain groups of people express different needs.

Standards for interpreting the TAT are clearer than are those for the Rorschach; two psychologists listening to the same answers generally come to the same conclusions (Lundy, 1985; Sutton & Swensen, 1983). To find the reliability of the TAT, investigators determine the correlation between its results and other measures of personality, including interviews and observations of behavior under natural conditions (Suinn & Oskamp, 1969). The validity varies from one application to another and from one study to another. Most psychologists agree that the test has high enough validity for research purposes but not high enough for making clinical judgments. In other words, the results do not enable a psychologist to diagnose an individual's problems or to decide what to do about them.

A person's responses on the TAT may vary considerably from time to time because the test measures "current concerns" (which change over time) rather than fixed personality traits (Lundy, 1985). Generally, TAT results correspond better to what a person *has done recently* than to what he or she *will do in the future* (Anastasi, 1988). For that reason, it might be better to say that the TAT measures "current concerns" rather than "needs."

Evaluation of Personality Tests

The popularity of certain personality tests is largely the result of habit and inertia. Many psychologists have had years of experience with the MMPI and have assembled exhaustive data about the meaning of every possible pattern of results. They may concede that it would be possible to devise a better test or even that better tests are already available. But they are so familiar with the MMPI that they are reluctant to switch. (For the same reason, the United States has been slow to shift to the metric system.)

Given the generally modest validity of projective tests, why do many psychologists continue using them? Some say that using them is like listening to faint radio signals from outer space or like reading faded documents written thousands of years ago: To get certain kinds of information, they are willing to tolerate some ambiguity about what the signals mean. Others say that they use the tests as "interviewing techniques" rather than as measuring devices. The tests help to "break the ice," to give the psychologist and the client a starting point for discussion. When the tests are used for that purpose, their low validity is not a serious problem.

FIGURE 13.16

Picture this: An item from the Thematic Apperception Test.

SUMMARY

1. Because most people are inclined to accept almost any interpretation of their personality based on a personality test, tests must be carefully scrutinized to ensure that they are measuring what they claim to measure. (page 493)

2. A standardized test is one that is administered according to explicit rules and whose results are interpreted in a prescribed fashion. Standards are based on the scores of people who have already taken the test. (page 494)

3. The MMPI, a widely used personality test, consists of a series of true-false questions selected by trial and error in an effort to distinguish among various personality types. (page 494)

4. The MMPI and certain other tests guard against lying by including items on which nearly all honest people will give the same answer. Any other answer is probably a lie. An unusual number of "lying" answers will invalidate the results. (page 496)

5. The MMPI reveals information about personality, but its results do not by themselves justify a diagnosis of psychological disturbance. (page 497)

6. The 16-PF Test, another standardized personality test, measures 16 personality traits. Although it was designed primarily to measure normal personality, its results do distinguish between normal and abnormal personalities. (page 497)

7. A projective test—such as the Rorschach Inkblot Test or the Thematic Apperception Test—lets people describe their concerns indirectly while talking about "the person in the picture" or about some other ambiguous stimulus. (page 499)

8. Although the reliability and validity of projective tests are generally unimpressive, their results can be useful in

getting a conversation started between a therapist and a client. (page 501)

SUGGESTIONS FOR FURTHER READING

Alex, C. (1965). *How to beat personality tests*. New York: Arc. Though intended for amusement, this book contains useful information about personality tests.

Anastasi, A. (1988). *Psychological testing* (6th ed.). New York: Macmillan. A good textbook on both personality testing and IQ testing.

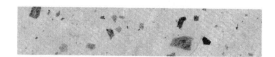

TERMS TO REMEMBER

anal stage Freud's second stage of psychosexual development, in which psychosexual pleasure is focused on the anus

androgyny a combination of the features of masculinity and femininity

catharsis the release of pent-up tension

collective unconscious according to Jung, an inborn level of the unconscious that symbolizes the collective experience of the human species

defense mechanism a method of protecting oneself against anxiety caused by conflict between the id's demands and the superego's constraints

denial the refusal to believe information that provokes anxiety

displacement the diversion of a thought or an action away from its natural target toward a less threatening target

ego according to Freud, the rational, decision-making aspect of personality

Electra complex according to Freud, a young girl's romantic attraction toward her father and hostility toward her mother

external locus of control belief that outside forces are responsible for most of the important events in one's life

fixation in Freud's theory, a persisting preoccupation with an immature psychosexual interest as a result of frustration at that stage of psychosexual development

genital stage Freud's final stage of psychosexual development, in which sexual pleasure is focused on sexual intimacy with others

high self-monitors people who constantly monitor their own behavior and change it readily to make a good impression

humanistic psychology a branch of psychology that emphasizes the capacity of people to make conscious decisions about their own lives

id according to Freud, the aspect of personality that consists of biological drives and demands for immediate gratification

ideal self a person's image of what he or she would like to be

idiographic laws laws that apply to individual differences

individual psychology the psychology of the person as an indivisible whole, as formulated by Adler

inferiority complex an exaggerated feeling of weakness, inadequacy, and helplessness

internal locus of control belief that one's own efforts control most of the important events in one's life

latent period according to Freud, a period in which psychosexual interest is suppressed or dormant

libido in Freud's theory, a sexual energy

low self-monitors people who make relatively little effort to mold their behavior to the expectations of others

Minnesota Multiphasic Personality Inventory (MMPI) a true-false standardized personality test

neo-Freudians personality theorists who have remained faithful to parts of Freud's theory while modifying other parts

nomothetic laws laws intended to apply to all individuals

Oedipus complex according to Freud, a young boy's sexual interest in his mother accompanied by competitive aggression toward his father

oral stage Freud's first stage of psychosexual development, in which psychosexual pleasure is focused on the mouth

peak experience an experience that brings fulfillment, contentment, and peace

personality all the stable, consistent ways in which the behavior of one person differs from that of others

personality profile a graph that shows an individual's scores on scales measuring a number of personality traits

phallic stage Freud's third stage of psychosexual development, in which psychosexual interest is focused on the penis or clitoris

projection the attribution of one's own undesirable characteristics to other people

projective test a test designed to encourage people to project their personality characteristics onto ambiguous stimuli

psychoanalysis Freud's approach to personality, based on the interplay of conscious and unconscious forces

psychodynamic theory a theory that relates personality to the interplay of conflicting forces within the individual, including some that are unconscious

psychosexual development in Freud's theory, progression through a series of developmental periods, each with a characteristic psychosexual focus that leaves its mark on adult personality

psychosexual pleasure according to Freud, any enjoyment arising from stimulation of part of the body

rationalization attempting to prove that one's actions are rational and justifiable and thus worthy of approval

reaction formation presenting oneself as the opposite of what one really is in an effort to reduce anxiety

regression the return to a more juvenile level of functioning as a means of reducing anxiety or in response to emotionally trying circumstances

repression motivated forgetting; the relegation of unacceptable impulses or memories to the unconscious

Rorschach Inkblot Test a set of 10 inkblots used as a projective test of personality

script a set of rules governing behavior in a particular situation

self-actualization the achievement of one's full potential

self-concept a person's image of what he or she really is

16-PF Test a standardized personality test that measures 16 personality traits

social interest a sense of solidarity and identification with other people

standardized test a test that is administered according to specified rules and whose scores are interpreted in a prescribed fashion

state a temporary activation of a particular personality tendency

striving for superiority according to Adler, a universal desire to seek a personal feeling of excellence and fulfillment

style of life according to Adler, a person's master plan for achieving a sense of superiority

sublimation the transformation of an unacceptable impulse into an acceptable, even an admirable, behavior

superego according to Freud, the aspect of personality that consists of memories of rules put forth by one's parents

Thematic Apperception Test (TAT) a projective personality test in which people are asked to make up stories about a series of pictures

trait a relatively permanent personality tendency

unconditional positive regard complete, unqualified acceptance of another person as he or she is

unconscious according to Freud, an aspect of the mind that influences behavior, although we are not directly aware of it

ANSWERS TO CONCEPT CHECKS

1. Someone with a strong id and a weak superego would be expected to give in to a variety of sexual and other impulses that other people would inhibit. Someone with an unusually strong superego would be unusually inhibited and dominated by feelings of guilt. (page 474)

2. a. Displacement; b. denial; c. reaction formation; d. projection; e. repression; f. regression; g. rationalization; h. sublimation. (page 476)

3. In Adler's theory, a person's style of life is his or her method of striving for superiority. (page 480)

4. "Trait anxiety" is a tendency to experience anxiety in a wide variety of settings. "State anxiety" is anxiety evoked by a particular situation. Psychologists could observe whether this person's anxiety declines sharply when the situation changes. If it does, it is state anxiety. If not, it is trait anxiety. (page 485)

5. The correlation between expressed attitudes and actual behavior is likely to be higher among low self-monitors than among high self-monitors. The behavior of high self-monitors depends more on the situation than on enduring traits. (page 490)

6. People tend to remember the occasions when someone's behavior matches his or her reputation. They regard occasions when behavior does not match the reputation as exceptions. (page 491)

7. Probably not. Everyone is expected to agree with at least a few of the items on the depression scale. A suspicion of depression arises only when someone agrees with substantially more of these items than most other people do. (page 495)

8. The Rorschach Inkblot Test must be administered in person by a psychologist who observes how you hold the cards, whether you rotate them, and anything else you do. The psychologist may also ask you to explain where you see something or why it looks the way you say it does. (page 500)

CHAPTER

14

504

ABNORMAL
BEHAVIOR

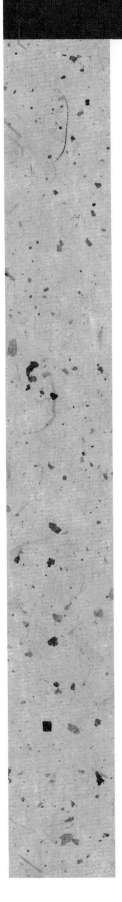

O ver the past four months, George has struck and injured several dozen people, most of whom he hardly knew. Two of them had to be sent to the hospital. George expresses no guilt, no regrets. He says he would attack every one of them again if he got the chance. What should society do with George?

1. Send him to jail?

2. Commit him to a mental hospital?

3. Give him an award for being the best defensive lineman in the league?

Before you can answer, you must know the context of George's behavior. Behavior that seems normal at a party might seem bizarre at a business meeting. Behavior that earns millions for a rock singer might earn a trip to the mental hospital for a college professor. Behavior that is perfectly routine in one culture might be considered criminal in another.

Even when we know the context of someone's behavior, we may wonder whether it is "normal." Suppose your rich Aunt Tillie starts to pass out $5 bills to strangers on the street corner and vows that she will keep on doing so until she has exhausted her entire fortune. Is she mentally ill? Should the court commit her to a mental hospital and turn her fortune over to you as her trustee?

A man claims to be Jesus Christ and asks permission to appear before the United Nations to announce God's message to the world. A psychiatrist is sure that he can relieve this man of his disordered thinking by giving him antipsychotic drugs, but the man refuses to take them and insists that his thinking is perfectly normal. Should we force him to take the drugs, just ignore him, or put his address on the agenda of the United Nations?

What is normal? Rock musicians can earn fortunes from behavior that would get most people fired. Groups like the Plasmatics vie for attention by deliberately looking provocatively strange.

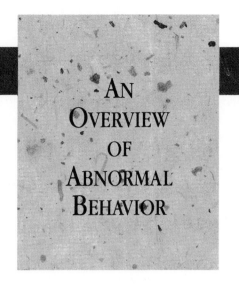

AN OVERVIEW OF ABNORMAL BEHAVIOR

Why do some people behave abnormally?
What are the most common kinds of abnormal
behavior?

Psychological abnormalities come in many forms. Some are difficult to recognize, because "abnormal" behaviors are just exaggerations of normal ones. Students in medical school often contract what is known as "medical students' disease." Imagine that you are just beginning your training in medicine. One of your textbooks describes "Cryptic Ruminating Umbilicus Disorder":

"The symptoms are very minor until the condition becomes hopeless. The first symptom is a pale tongue." (You go to the mirror. You can't remember what your tongue is supposed to look like, but it *does* look a little pale.) "Later a hard spot forms in the neck." (You feel your neck. "Wait! I never felt *this* before! I think it's something hard!") "Just before the arms and legs fall off, there is shortness of breath, increased heart rate, and sweating." (Already distressed, you *do* have shortness of breath, your heart *is* racing, and you *are* sweating profusely.)

Sooner or later, most medical students decide they have some dreaded illness. The problem is imaginary; they merely confuse the description of some disease with their own normal condition. When my brother was in medical school, he diagnosed himself as having a rare, fatal illness, checked himself into a hospital, and wrote a will. (Today he is a successful physician.)

"Medical students' disease" is even more common among students of psychological disorders. As you read this chapter and the next, you may decide that you are suffering from some such disorder: "That sounds exactly like me! I must have Deteriorating Raving Odd Omnivorous Lycanthropy!"

Well, maybe you do. But more likely you do not. Psychological disorders are just exaggerations of tendencies that nearly all of us have; we simply recognize ourselves in the descriptions of the disorders. The difference between "normal" and "psychologically disordered" is a matter of degree.

CONCEPTS OF ABNORMAL BEHAVIOR

What constitutes abnormal behavior or psychological disorder? In a descriptive sense, "normal" is average, and anything that differs very much from the average is said to be abnormal. But by that definition, unusually happy or unusually successful people would be considered abnormal.

We might define abnormal behavior as any behavior that distresses a person, any behavior that a person wants to escape from. But some people say they are doing just fine, even though their behavior strikes everyone else as bizarre.

The American Psychiatric Association (1987) has defined psychological disorders as patterns of behavior associated with distress (pain) or disability (impaired functioning) or with an increased risk of death, pain, or loss of freedom. We can question that definition as well. For example, when Martin Luther King, Jr., fought for the rights of black Americans, he engaged in behaviors that brought the risk of death, pain, and loss of freedom. But we regard his acts as heroic, not abnormal.

Another definition is that abnormal behavior is behavior that a particular culture regards as troublesome or unacceptable. For example, someone who is frequently intoxicated with alcohol may be considered normal in one society, abnormal in another. People whose only problem is that they see things and hear things that no one else does may be put into a mental hospital, or they may be revered as visionaries, depending on the beliefs of their society (Leff, 1981). The difficulty with defining abnormal behavior as a behavior a society does not accept is that it does not tell us what behavior a society *should* accept. Some totalitarian governments have classed all political dissidents as "mentally ill."

In short, there may be no simple way to define abnormal behavior or psychological disorder. In some cases we cannot be sure that a given behavior

*P*eculiar behavior was once explained as demon possession. Here St. Zenobius exorcises devils, fleeing from the mouths of the possessed. At the time of this late 15th-century work, attributed to Botticelli, the religious fanatic Savonarola was exorcising the city with public burnings of luxury goods—bonfires of vanities.

Today, *one influential point of view is that some psychological disorders are the result of biological disorders,* including brain damage, chemical imbalances in the brain, hormonal abnormalities, poor nutrition, inadequate sleep, and various diseases. Drugs and even over-the-counter medications can trigger abnormal behavior, especially in people who fail to follow the instructions for taking the medicine (Hall, Gardner, Perl, Stickney, & Pfefferbaum, 1978).

A second point of view is that some psychological disorders are the result of disordered thinking caused by early experiences. That is essentially the Freudian point of view. Even many theorists who disagree with Freud believe that traumatic experiences early in life may later distort people's thinking.

Both of these points of view regard psychological disorders as something "wrong" with the person. *A third point of view is that some psychological disorders are reactions to a stressful or unsupportive environment* that the person is trying to cope with as well as possible.

Consider alcohol abuse. Many people think of alcohol abuse as a disease, and perhaps it is—in some ways, for some people. But as soon as we label it a "disease," we begin to look for causes within the person. But what if the person is drinking excessively as a reaction to something in the environment? Might it be more appropriate to try to change the environment than to try to change the person?

Each of these three viewpoints may be correct for certain people and for certain disorders. Behavior can go awry in a great many ways.

THE PREVALENCE OF PSYCHOLOGICAL DISORDERS

It is difficult to estimate how widespread psychological disorders are because only about one third of all people suffering from them seek professional help, and even those who do seek help are as likely to go to their family doctor as to a psychiatrist or a psychologist (Shapiro et al., 1984). The only way to assemble accurate data on the prevalence of various disorders is to survey a large random sample of people over a wide geographical area.

Such a survey, of about 20,000 people, was conducted in Baltimore, St. Louis, and New Haven (Eaton et al., 1984; Regier et al., 1984). Trained interviewers tried to reach all the "usual residents" of each selected neighborhood, including those who lived at home and those who lived in institutions such as prisons, mental hospitals, and nursing homes.

is abnormal and in need of treatment. Still, when a person's distress is obvious, we can at least identify the existence of a problem, even if we are not sure what the problem is.

Abnormal behavior has been known in all cultures throughout history. Each time and place has interpreted such behavior according to its own worldview. People in the Middle Ages, for example, regarded bizarre behavior as a sign that the disturbed person was possessed by a demon. To exorcise the demon, priests resorted to prescribed religious rituals. During the 1800s, when the "germ" theory of illness was popular and people sought a scientific explanation for everything they observed, physicians interpreted abnormal behavior as "mental illness." They tried to find its cause and a way to cure it, just as they did in treating other illnesses.

They found that about one fifth of all adults were suffering from a psychological disorder of some sort (as defined by the American Psychiatric Association) and that close to one third had suffered from such a disorder at some time during their life (Myers et al., 1984; Robins et al., 1984).

The most common psychological disorders are anxiety disorders, alcohol and drug abuse, and depression. As Figure 14.1 shows, each of these "big three" problems affects about 5 to 10 percent of all people at any given time and a higher percentage at some time during their lives. That figure is only approximate because each disorder occurs in varying degrees and because different psychologists set different cutoffs for what constitutes a "disorder."

THE CLASSIFICATION OF PSYCHOLOGICAL DISORDERS

Any scientific study must be based on some accepted method for classifying information. Imagine what biology would be like if biologists had no systematic way of classifying animals: Someone publishes an article about the mating behavior of a "black bird." You try to replicate the study, but you get different results. Then you discover that the black bird the first researcher studied was a crow, while you have been studying a raven. Or worse yet, that other researcher was studying a haphazard mixture of crows, juncos, and starlings. To avoid such confusion, biologists use a system of classification in which each term refers to one and only one species.

Similarly, we need a clear, unambiguous system of classifying psychological disorders. Psychiatrists and clinical psychologists have been trying for years to devise such a system of classification, though they have not yet fully succeeded. One difficulty is that many psychological disorders are poorly understood, and it is difficult to classify items that we do not understand. A second difficulty is that many people have more than one disorder or what seems to be a mixture of disorders.

Currently, the most widely used classification scheme is the one adopted by the American Psychiatric Association (1987) in its *Diagnostic and statistical manual of mental disorders, third edition—Revised, commonly known as* **DSM III-R**. It lists the acceptable labels for all psychological disorders (alcohol intoxication, exhibitionism, pathological gambling, anorexia nervosa, sleepwalking disorder, stuttering, and hundreds of others), with a description of each and guidelines on how to distinguish it from similar disorders. DSM III-R describes disorders as they appear in North Amer-

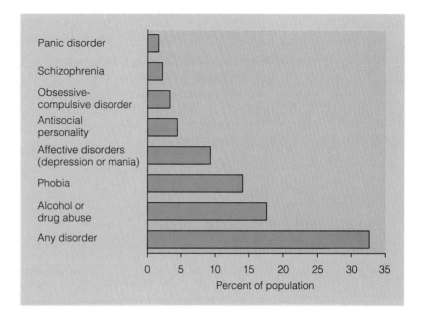

FIGURE 14.1

Prevalence of mental disorders: Almost 20% of the people surveyed in three U.S. cities had some psychological disorder at some time during their lifetime (Myers et al., 1984; Robins et al., 1984). These figures—a combination of self-reports and the assessment of trained interviewers—are estimates that do not indicate the severity of the disorder in individuals. The total percentage for disorders (32%) is less than the total of the seven categories (49%) because some people had two or more disorders. The homeless were not surveyed.

ica and Europe; other societies have variations on these disorders and additional disorders that we do not see (Leff, 1981). I shall use the terminology of DSM III-R in this chapter. The American Psychiatric Association plans to publish a new edition, DSM IV, in the early 1990s.

The clinicians and researchers who use DSM III-R classify each client along five separate axes. Axes 1 to 3 categorize specific disorders. Axis 1 lists disorders that have a particular time of onset and a realistic probability of recovery. These are the disorders that psychologists and psychiatrists deal with most frequently. Table 14.1 lists some of the categories of disorder on Axis 1.

Axis 2 iists disorders that generally persist throughout life, such as mental retardation and personality disorders (see Table 14.2). A **personality disorder** is a maladaptive, inflexible way of dealing with the environment and other people, such as antisocial behavior or an avoidance of other people. While many other psychological disorders resemble medical disease to some extent, personality disorders clearly do not. They seem to be an integral part of the person, like being tall, or left handed, or red headed. People with personality disorders seldom complain about their condition.

Disorders usually first evident in childhood or adolescence	**Examples:**
	attention-deficit hyperactivity disorder Impulsivity; hyperactivity; inability to pay attention to school or work
	anorexia nervosa Abnormal fear of fatness; voluntary starvation
	pica The eating of inedible objects such as hair or dirt
	gender identity disorders Rejection of one's own sex; insistence that one is, or wants to be, a member of the opposite sex (*not* homosexuality)
	Tourette's disorder Repetitive movements, such as blinking an eyelid or twitching a hand; chanted sounds—in many cases, obscene words
	elimination disorders Bed-wetting; urinating or defecating in one's clothes
	stuttering Frequent repetition or prolongation of sounds, interfering with speech
Organic mental disorders	The result of deterioration of the brain or of temporary interference with brain functioning, as in opiate intoxication or opiate withdrawal
Psychoactive substance use disorders	Alcohol abuse, cocaine abuse, opiate abuse, and abuse of other mind-altering substances
Schizophrenia	Deterioration of everyday functioning, along with either a lack of emotional response, or thought disorders, or hallucinations or delusions
Delusional (paranoid) disorder	Irrational beliefs, such as the belief that "everyone is talking about me behind my back" or that "I have discovered the secret that will solve all the world's problems if I can just get people to listen to me"
Mood disorders	Periods of depression serious enough to interfere with daily life, sometimes alternating with periods of mania, which is the opposite of depression
Anxiety disorders	Lingering anxiety at almost all times, unpredictable attacks of severe anxiety, or periods of anxiety that regularly occur when the person is confronted with a particular object or thought
Somatoform disorders	**Examples:**
	conversion disorder One or more physical ailments, such as blindness or paralysis, that are caused at least in part by psychological factors, but are not intentionally produced
	hypochondriasis Repetitive, exaggerated complaints of illness
	somatization disorder Recurrent, multiple complaints of pain and other ailments that are apparently not due to any physical disorder
Dissociative disorders	Loss of the memory of a person's own identity or the memory of past events, not caused by brain damage
Sexual disorders	**Examples:**
	pedophilia Sexual attraction to children
	exhibitionism Sexual pleasure from exposing oneself in public
	voyeurism Sexual arousal primarily from watching other people undressing or engaging in sexual intercourse
	fetishism Sexual arousal primarily from leather or other inanimate objects
Sleep disorders	**Examples:**
	insomnia Frequent feeling of not being rested after a night's sleep
	sleep terror disorder Repeated periods of awakening suddenly in an experience of panic
	sleepwalking disorder Repeated episodes of leaving the bed, walking about, and not remembering the episode later
Impulse control disorders	A tendency to act on impulses that other people usually inhibit, such as the urge to gamble large amounts of money foolishly, the urge to steal something, or the urge to strike someone

Developmental disorders	**Examples:**
	mental retardation Intellectual functioning significantly below average; significant deficits in adaptive behavior
	autistic disorder Lack of social behavior; impaired communication; restricted repertoire of activities and interests
Personality disorders	Maladaptive personalities
	Examples:
	paranoid personality disorder Suspiciousness; habitual interpretation of other people's acts as threatening
	schizotypal personality disorder Poor relationships with other people; odd thinking; neglect of normal grooming. This disorder is similar to schizophrenia but less extreme
	antisocial personality disorder Lack of affection for other people; tendency to manipulate other people without feeling guilty; high probability of getting into trouble with the law; low probability of keeping a job
	borderline personality disorder Lack of a stable self-image; trouble establishing lasting relationships with other people or making lasting decisions about values, career choice, even sexual orientation; repeated self-endangering behaviors, such as drug abuse, reckless driving, casual sex, binge eating, shoplifting, and running up large debts
	histrionic personality disorder Excessive emotionality and attention-seeking; constant demand for praise
	narcissistic personality disorder Exaggerated opinion of one's own importance and a lack of regard for others. (Narcissus was a figure in Greek mythology who fell in love with himself.)
	avoidant personality disorder Avoidance of social contact; lack of friends
	dependent personality disorder Preference for letting other people make decisions; lack of initiative and self-confidence

When they seek treatment, it is generally at the insistence of their family, acquaintances, or employer.

Axis 3 lists physical disorders, such as diabetes or alcoholic cirrhosis of the liver, that may affect a person's behavior. A person may have more than one disorder on a given axis—for example, alcohol abuse and depression—or may have none at all.

Stress may intensify a psychological disorder and may affect the course of treatment. Axis 4 indicates how much stress the person has had to endure, on a scale from 0 (almost no stress) to 6 (stress equivalent to being held hostage or to the death of one's child).

Some people with a psychological disorder are able to go on with their normal work and social activities; others are not. Axis 5 evaluates a person's overall level of functioning, on a scale from 1 (serious attempt at suicide or complete inability to take care of oneself) to 90 (happy, productive, with many interests).

Concept Check

***1.** Earlier I suggested three definitions of abnormal behavior: (1) behavior that gives a person discomfort, (2) behavior that leads to distress, disability, or an increased risk of pain or loss of freedom, and (3) behavior that society finds troublesome or unacceptable. By which of those definitions does a personality disorder qualify as an abnormal behavior? (Check your answer on page 554.)*

EXAMPLES OF AXIS 1 DISORDERS

Later in this chapter we shall consider in detail the three most common Axis 1 disorders—anxiety disorders and phobias, alcohol and drug abuse, and mood disorders—as well as schizophrenia, which can be especially disabling. At this point, we will consider somatoform disorders and dissociative disorders. (These are interesting, important Axis 1 disorders that we do not consider elsewhere.)

Somatoform Disorders

The term *somatoform* is derived from the Greek root *soma,* meaning body. **Somatoform disorders** are disorders in which a person has physical symptoms that seem to have no medical cause. The person is not pretending or imagining the symptoms; they are real, but they result from psychological rather than medical problems.

Somatoform disorders affect only about one person in a thousand (Myers et al., 1984; Robins et al., 1984). For unknown reasons, they tend to be more common in females than in males, possibly because they are a reaction to the dominating behavior of men toward women (Chodoff, 1982).

Hypochondriasis (HI-po-KON-DRI-ah-sis) is a type of somatoform disorder in which a person exaggerates physical complaints or complains of ailments that a physician cannot detect. In **conversion disorder**, a person, for no apparent medical reason, exhibits such symptoms as paralysis, blindness, deafness, dizziness, or an inability to speak. Some women (and, rarely, men too!) show symptoms of pregnancy, complete with "morning sickness" and a swollen abdomen, although they are not pregnant. Such symptoms are clearly not imaginary.

Many of Sigmund Freud's patients suffered from conversion disorders, which at the time were known as *hysteria.* The term *conversion* implies that the person has "converted" an anxiety-producing conflict into a physical symptom. For example, a person who is anxious about the possibility of hitting someone might develop a paralysis of the arm. Someone who has watched a highly distressing event might become blind.

A person who experiences a long series of ailments that seem to have no medical basis is said to be suffering from **somatization disorder**. The common symptoms are nausea and vomiting, pain, shortness of breath, difficulty swallowing, and a burning sensation in the genitals or rectum. People with somatization disorder generally experience anxiety and depression as well.

Many theorists believe that somatoform disorders develop and persist because they bring the sufferer two advantages. First, they enable the person to avoid facing a serious emotional conflict by converting it into a physical symptom. Second, they bring **secondary gain**—indirect benefits such as the attention and sympathy of others and an excuse for avoiding unpleasant activities.

Dissociative Disorders

Dissociation is the separation of one set of memories from another for no discernible medical reason. For instance, a person suffering from amnesia may forget only a particularly traumatic set of memories, such as being sexually molested, observing wartime atrocities, or committing a violent act in a moment of rage. Or the amnesia may be more general, extending to the person's identity and past experiences or to the person's entire store of factual information. Such global amnesia usually lasts only a few days.

In a state known as **psychogenic fugue** (FYOOG), people wander about, sometimes over great distances, lose track of their identity, and perhaps assume a new name. They are generally disoriented and fail to respond appropriately to their surroundings. The fugue state usually ends abruptly; the person "wakes up" mystified at being in a strange place and generally unaware of what happened during the fugue.

In the most extreme type of dissociation, the personality separates into several identities, a condition known as **multiple personality disorder** (Solomon & Solomon, 1982). The person may shift abruptly from one personality to another, each with its own behavioral patterns, memories, and even name, almost as if each personality were really a different person.

Many people, including some who should know better, describe multiple personality as "schizophrenia." They are wrong. People with multiple personality disorder have several personalities, any one of which by itself might be considered normal, whereas people suffering from schizophrenia have just one seriously disordered personality. Multiple personality is rare; schizophrenia affects about 1% of all people.

One famous case of multiple personality was Chris Costner White Sizemore, who was described in the book and the movie *The Three Faces of Eve* (Thigpen & Cleckley, 1957) and who eventually told her own story in the book *I'm Eve* (Sizemore & Pittillo, 1977). (See Figure 14.2.) Chris Sizemore is not sure how her problem began but, so far as she can recall, it started during early childhood. As a 2-year-old, she had seen the dead body of a man and had been told that a "monster" had killed him. She felt that it was some other girl in her body who was seeing the dead man, and not she herself. Soon after, she saw a man at a sawmill who had accidentally been sawed into three pieces. Then, when Chris was 6, her grandmother died. At the funeral, when her aunt tried to get her to kiss her dead grandmother, she reacted with horror. Faced with this

FIGURE 14.2

Chris Sizemore, the real "Eve," and one of her paintings. She exhibited a total of 22 personalities, including her final, permanent identity.

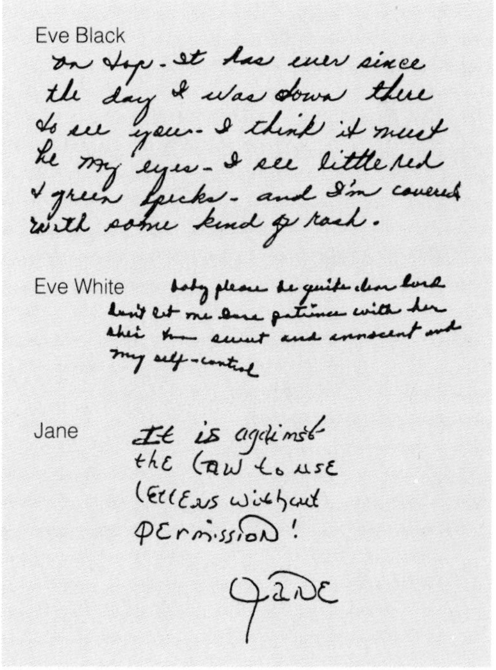

FIGURE 14.3

Handwriting samples from three of Chris Sizemore's personalities.

series of traumatic experiences, she dissociated herself from them. From her perspective, another girl simply took over her body at various times.

The psychiatrist who treated Chris in adulthood described her 10th, 11th, and 12th personalities in *The Three Faces of Eve.* One, whom he called "Eve White," was a shy, inhibited woman. Another, "Eve Black," was a fun-loving party-goer, who once "came out" just long enough to leave poor Eve White in a sexy dress, drunk, in a bar surrounded by soldiers who wondered why she suddenly seemed not to know them. Yet another was "Jane," a calm, intelligent woman who claimed to have a college education. At the end of treatment, the psychiatrist believed that Jane would emerge as the single, permanent personality. She divorced and remarried, and at first her difficulties seemed to be over.

In fact, 10 more personalities were yet to emerge—in groups of 3, except for the final personality. Each had some memory of past personalities but little or no knowledge of her current "selves." Sometimes one self would write notes to the other selves. Each had a different handwriting (Figure 14.3). One of them was mute and left handed. Two had allergies that the others did not have. Chris's daughter became fairly adept at identifying and dealing with the separate personalities, but occa-

sionally she would have to ask, "Who are you today, Mommy?"

Many psychiatrists' bills later, a single personality emerged that has remained Chris's only personality since the mid-1970s. Today Chris is a healthy, pleasant woman and a talented painter. She remembers each of her past selves. Curiously, she does not remember how to sew—a skill some of her previous personalities had learned.

Multiple personality appears to be a means of coping with an intolerable reality. We do not know why a few people resort to this means of coping while others do not. As we shall see in Chapter 15, psychologists and psychiatrists sometimes find it difficult to distinguish between true cases of multiple personality and people who pretend to have multiple personalities, including criminals seeking to use an insanity defense.

Concept Check

2. People with Alzheimer's disease forget most of their factual memories. Why then is Alzheimer's disease not considered a dissociative disorder? (Check your answer on page 554.)

Summary

1. Abnormal behavior is the result of various combinations of biological factors, early experiences, and learned responses to a stressful or unsupportive environment. (page 507)

2. Psychological disorders are classified in the *Diagnostic and statistical manual of mental disorders,* third edition-revised (DSM III-R). This manual classifies disorders along five axes. Axis 1 and Axis 2 deal with psychological disorders; Axis 3 deals with physical ailments that may affect behavior; Axes 4 and 5 provide means for evaluating a person's stress level and overall functioning. (page 509)

3. Axis 1 of DSM III-R lists disorders that usually begin after infancy and that have at least some likelihood of recovery. The three most common disorders of this sort are anxiety disorders, substance abuse, and depression. (page 509)

4. Axis 2 of DSM III-R lists conditions that arise early and persist throughout a lifetime such as mental retardation and personality disorders. (page 509)

5. Personality disorders are stable characteristics that impair a person's effectiveness or ability to get along with others. Examples of personality disorders are excessive dependence on others and excessive self-centeredness. (page 509)

6. Somatoform disorders are conditions in which a person has physical ailments that have no apparent organic basis but are in some way based on psychological problems. (page 512)

7. People with dissociative disorders lose access to a particular set of memories. One type of dissociative disorder is multiple personality, in which a person alternates among two or more personalities, each with its own set of memories. (page 512)

Suggestion for Further Reading

American Psychiatric Association. (1987). *Diagnostic and statistical manual of mental disorders* (3rd ed.-rev.). Washington, DC: Author. The standard guide to the classification and description of psychological disorders.

ANXIETY AND AVOIDANCE DISORDERS

Why do some people take extreme measures
to avoid something that is harmless or only
slightly dangerous?
Why do some people develop strange habits
and rituals?

Y ou go to the beach, looking forward to an after-noon of swimming and surfing. Someone tells you that a shark attacked two swimmers yesterday and has just been sighted close to shore. Do you venture into the water? What if the shark attack occurred a month ago, and no shark has been seen in the area since then? Now would you go in? What if no shark has attacked anyone in this area, but someone saw a small shark there a few days ago?

What if no shark has ever been seen within 50 miles of this particular beach, but recently you read a magazine story about shark attacks?

How much fear and caution is normal? Staying out of the water because you see a shark is perfectly reasonable. Staying out of the water because of sharks you have read about is, by most people's standards, excessively cautious. If you refuse even to look at photographs of the ocean because they might *remind* you of sharks, you have a serious problem indeed.

It is normal to have a certain amount of fear and to avoid situations that might provoke fear. But excessive fear and caution are linked to some of the most common psychological disorders.

ANXIETY DISORDERS

Many psychological disorders are marked by a combination of fear, anxiety, and attempts to avoid anxiety. Anxiety, unlike fear, is generally not asso-ciated with a specific situation. We feel fear in the presence of a hungry tiger, but our fear passes as soon as we get away. But we cannot escape the anxiety we experience about dying or about our personal inadequacies. Some degree of anxiety is normal; it becomes a problem only when it inter-feres with our ability to cope with everyday life.

Generalized Anxiety Disorder

People with **generalized anxiety disorder** are con-stantly plagued by exaggerated worries. They worry that "I might get sick," "My daughter might get sick," "I might lose my job," or "I might not be able to pay my bills." Although these people have no real-istic reason for such worries—at least no more rea-son than anyone else—their worries persist and interfere with daily life. They grow tense, restless, irritable, and fatigued.

Panic Disorder

Panic disorder is an emotional disturbance found in about 1% of all American adults and among very few children (Myers et al., 1984; Robins et al., 1984). People with this disorder experience a fairly con-stant state of moderate anxiety, along with occa-sional panic attacks, accompanied by chest pains, difficulty in breathing, increased heart rate, sweat-ing, faintness, and shaking (see Figure 14.4). A panic attack generally lasts only a few minutes, although it may last an hour or more. During an attack, most people worry about fainting, dying, or going crazy (Argyle, 1988). After a few such attacks, those wor-ries may grow more intense and may even trigger further attacks.

Panic disorder can become self-perpetuating (Figure 14.5). Many people deal with anxiety by taking a deep breath or two, to help calm them-selves down. On the theory that "if a little is good, a whole lot will be better," they may continue breathing deeply, or hyperventilating. **Hyperven-tilation** expels carbon dioxide and therefore low-ers the carbon dioxide level in the blood. Then if something happens that increases the carbon diox-ide level, such as sudden physical activity or an experience that excites the sympathetic nervous system, the carbon dioxide level in the blood increases by a large percentage and stimulates an increased heart rate, trembling, and other symp-toms of a panic attack—the very thing the person

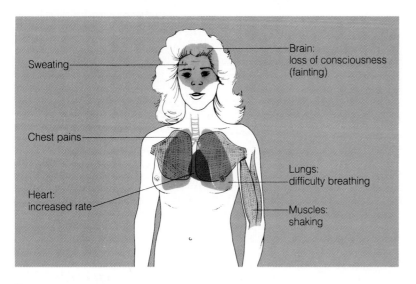

FIGURE 14.4

Hitting the panic button: Physical manifestations of a severe anxiety attack.

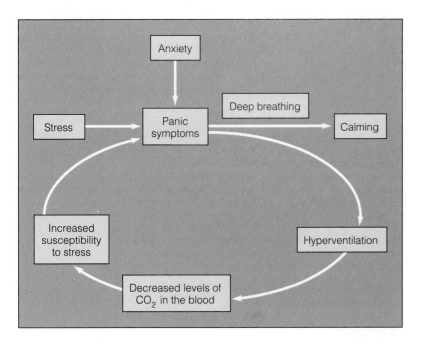

FIGURE 14.5

Deep breathing helps to calm a person, but extreme deep breathing increases the probability of another panic attack.

was trying to avoid (Gorman et al., 1986; Woods et al., 1986). After a few such episodes, the likelihood of further attacks increases. One treatment for panic attacks is to teach the person to avoid hyperventilating (Wolpe & Rowan, 1988).

When people discover that physical exertion sometimes triggers a panic attack, they may decide to avoid any sort of physical activity. As a result, they grow even more sensitive to the effects of physical activity; even slight exertion will raise the level of carbon dioxide in their blood. Consequently, some authorities recommend regular exercise as a treatment for panic attacks (Ledwidge, 1980).

Concept Check

3. Why might mild exertion trigger a panic attack, especially in someone who is in poor physical condition? (Check your answer on page 554.)

DISORDERS RELATED TO AVOIDANCE LEARNING

People learn to avoid punishment, as we saw in Chapter 7. In some cases, their efforts to avoid punishment become so extreme and persistent that they begin to interfere with daily activities. They develop phobias (extreme fears) and compulsions (rituals designed to avoid unpleasant thoughts or events).

We begin with superstitions, which are usually intended as ways of avoiding bad luck. Although superstition is not listed in DSM III-R and is not generally considered a psychological disorder, it is nevertheless closely related to phobias and obsessive-compulsive disorder, and it sheds light on how they develop.

Superstitions and Avoidance Learning

A **superstition** is a behavior that someone engages in regularly as a way of gaining good luck or (more frequently) avoiding bad luck. Wearing green shoes for good luck is a superstition. Taking a useless pill that your doctor has prescribed is not a superstition because you have good reason to believe it will be effective. If people in an agricultural society follow a witch doctor's advice to bury a cat under the full moon to ward off evil spirits representing bad weather, should we consider that act a superstition? The answer is debatable; their behavior may be comparable to that of people in our society who follow a physician's incorrect advice.

Something to Think About

Someone you respect tells you that unless you take part in a certain ritual you will be punished *after death*. If you engage in that ritual, are you acting out of superstition? People who are not religious tend to dismiss all religious practices as superstition, and many religious people tend to dismiss everyone else's religious practices as superstition. Try to put your own beliefs aside for a moment and look at both sides of the question. How could you decide whether a certain ritual was based on superstition?

Superstitions are remarkably persistent. The superstition that one should "knock on wood" after talking about good luck has persisted for so long that no one is sure where or how it originated. One theory is that it began in ancient times when people believed that demons inhabited trees. Saying that you had been having good luck would let the demons know that they had not been giving you your fair share of bad luck lately. To escape their efforts to even things out, you would pound on the wood to scare them away. Most people who knock on wood today have never heard of that theory (or any other) and certainly would not take it seriously. Why then does the superstition persist?

Animals that have learned to avoid shocks sometimes develop behaviors that resemble superstitions. Suppose a monkey learns to press a lever to avoid shocks; then the experimenter disconnects the shock generator so that the response is unnecessary. The monkey continues responding indefinitely; so far as it can tell, nothing has changed. The response still "works." If the monkey could tell us why it pressed the lever every few seconds, it would say that it does so to prevent electric shocks. In many ways the behavior of a person who knocks on wood to avoid bad luck is similar.

What would happen if the monkey continued to press the lever but got an occasional shock anyway? You might assume that the shocks would weaken its lever-pressing behavior. Actually, the shocks *strengthen* the behavior, at least temporarily (Kadden, 1973; Sidman, Herrnstein, & Conrad, 1957). The occasional shock seems to tell the monkey that it has not been pressing fast enough.

Compare these results to human superstitions: Suppose you believe that Friday the 13th is a dangerous day. You are very cautious every Friday the 13th, but occasionally some misfortune happens anyway. On any other day, you would think nothing of it, but because you were expecting bad luck, the misfortune confirms your belief that Friday the 13th

*M*any movies exploit fears of three types: (1) the fantastic that could not occur (Aliens), (2) those horrors that actually could occur (Jaws), and (3) those that did occur (The Killing Fields). Perhaps the most frightening are those that could happen. The Indiana Jones movies make the most of common fears involving caverns full of snakes, insects, and rats. In this flashback, the young Indy encounters masses of snakes as he attempts to escape from the bad guys—the beginning of the snake phobia Jones displays throughout the series? We enjoy this controlled access to danger because, after all, it's only a movie.

is dangerous. The next Friday the 13th nothing goes wrong. Do you conclude that the day is not dangerous? No, you conclude, "It helps to be careful on Friday the 13th. I was cautious all day long, and I avoided bad luck."

In other words, so long as you engage in avoidance behavior, you will never find out that your behavior is useless. The only way to learn that a superstitious behavior is useless is to try doing without it, though you might be unwilling to take that chance.

Phobias

Terror is the only thing that comes close to how I feel when I think of moths. Their willowy, see-through wings always seem filthy. I remember being stuck in a car with a huge moth and my date, not knowing how terrified I was of moths, thought I was kidding when I told him I was afraid. It was terrible! I can feel it right now . . . the . . . feeling trapped and the moth with its ugly body flitting around so quickly, I couldn't anticipate where it would go next. Finally that creature hit me in the arm and I screamed—it felt dirty and sleazy and then it hit me in the face and I began to scream uncontrollably. I had the terrible feeling it was going to fly into my mouth while I was screaming, but I couldn't stop [Duke & Nowicki, 1979, page 244].

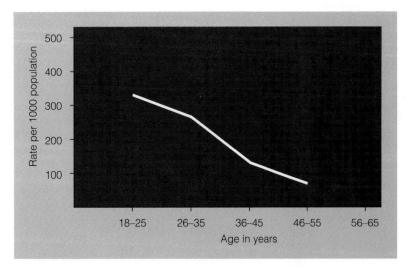

FIGURE 14.6

The prevalence of phobias as a function of age.

Phobias are sometimes defined as "irrational fears," but that definition is inadequate. A fear of snakes or spiders is not irrational—some of them are dangerous. Yet such a fear is often regarded as a phobia. Some people have such a strong fear of these creatures that they keep away from fields in which they might be lurking, stay away from unfamiliar buildings, avoid books that might have pictures of snakes or spiders, and don't talk to strangers who, after all, might like to *talk* about snakes or spiders.

A **phobia** is best defined as *a fear so extreme that it interferes with normal living*. Confronting the object of the phobia may lead to sweating, trembling, and rapid breathing and heart rate. Often fear of the object is compounded by a fear that the fear itself will provoke a heart attack.

Because most people with phobias are well aware that their fears are exaggerated, it does no good to tell them not to be afraid. In fact, attempts to reduce phobias by providing information sometimes backfire. One city tried to combat the phobia of elevators by posting signs on elevators throughout the city: "There is no reason to be afraid of elevators. There is almost no chance at all that the cable will break or that you will suffocate." The signs actually *increased* the phobia of elevators.

The Prevalence of Phobias   How many people suffer from phobias? As with most other psychological disorders, phobias are exaggerations of normal behaviors. Depending on where we draw the line between phobias and normal fears, estimates of the prevalence of phobias range from 5 to 13% of the population (Myers et al., 1984). About twice as many

women as men experience phobias. Figure 14.6 shows the prevalence of phobias by age.

The most common phobia is **agoraphobia**—a fear of open places or public places, from *agora,* the ancient Greek word for marketplace (Reich, 1986). People with agoraphobia sometimes become so distressed about being alone in a public place that they experience heart palpitations, lose bowel and bladder control, or vomit. To avoid both the misery and the embarrassment, they stay home as much as possible and almost never go out alone. Many people suffer from both panic disorder and agoraphobia (Margraf, Ehlers, & Roth, 1986; Noyes et al., 1986). They suffer attacks of panic in almost any situation, but especially in open, public places. In many ways, phobias are like panic disorder, except that phobias are aroused by a specific object.

The Learning of Phobias   Although people seem to be born with certain fears, such as fear of loud noises, phobias and extreme fears are learned. John B. Watson, one of the founders of behaviorism, was the first to demonstrate the possibility of learning a fear through classical conditioning (Watson & Rayner, 1920). Today, we would consider it unethical to try to create a fear, especially in humans, but in 1920 such restraint was less common. Watson and Rosalie Rayner studied an 11-month-old child, "Albert B.," who had previously shown no fear of white rats or other animals. They set a white rat down in front of Albert, and then, just behind him, they struck a large steel bar with a hammer. The sudden sound made Albert whimper and cover his face. After seven repetitions, the mere sight of the rat would make Albert cry and crawl away (Figure 14.7). Watson and Rayner declared that they had created a strong fear and that phobias in general might develop along similar lines. Unfortunately, they did not try to "cure" the "phobia" through extinction procedures. So far as they knew, Albert may have gone through life terrified of white rats.

Although Watson and Rayner's study is open to several methodological criticisms (Harris, 1979; Samelson, 1980), it led the way for later interpretations of phobias as learned responses. Their explanation of phobias fails to answer some important questions: Why do people develop phobias toward objects that have never injured them? Why are some phobias much more common than others? And why are phobias so persistent?

Concept Check

4. In classical-conditioning terms, what was the CS in this experiment? The US? The CR? The UR? (Check your answers on page 554.)

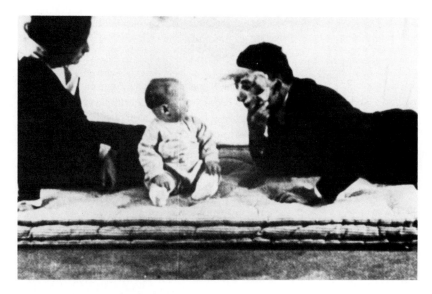

FIGURE 14.7

Little Albert with John Watson (in Santa mask) and his assistant, Rosalie Rayner. The photo is from a film Watson made. Watson and Rayner's study is flawed in being based on results with just one person, but psychologists today would not try to replicate it with additional children. (Courtesy of Professor Benjamin Harris.)

Learning Fear by Observation: What's the Evidence?

Contrary to Watson and Rayner's explanation, almost half of all people with phobias have never had a painful experience with the object they fear (Öst & Hugdahl, 1981). Are you afraid of snakes? Most people have at least a moderate fear of snakes, and a fair number have phobias about them. Have you ever been injured by a snake? Chances are, no. Why do so many people fear snakes when so few have ever been injured by one?

As noted in our consideration of social learning in Chapter 7, we learn many things by watching or listening to others. Perhaps we hear that someone has been injured by a snake, and we become afraid too.

That hypothesis is probably correct, but how can we demonstrate it? Susan Mineka and her colleagues demonstrated how monkeys can learn fear by observing other monkeys (Mineka, 1987; Mineka, Davidson, Cook, & Keir, 1984).

EXPERIMENT 1

Hypothesis Monkeys that have seen other monkeys show fear of a snake will develop such a fear themselves.

Method Monkeys that live in the wild generally show a strong fear of snakes. They are not born with that fear, however; monkeys reared in a laboratory show no fear of snakes. Mineka put a laboratory-reared monkey together with a wild-born monkey and let them both see a snake. The lab monkey watched the wild monkey show signs of fear. Later she tested the lab monkey by itself to see whether it had acquired a fear of snakes.

Results When the lab monkey saw how frightened its partner was of the snake, it became frightened too. It continued to be afraid of the snake when tested by itself even months later.

Interpretation The lab monkey may have learned a fear of snakes because it saw that its partner was afraid of snakes. But Mineka considered another possible, though less likely, interpretation: The lab-reared monkey may have become fearful simply because it observed the other monkey's fear. That is, maybe it did not matter *what* the wild-reared monkey was afraid of. To test this possibility, Mineka conducted a second experiment.

EXPERIMENT 2

Hypothesis A monkey that sees another monkey show fear but does not know what the second monkey is afraid of will not develop the same fear itself.

Method A monkey reared in a lab watched a monkey reared in the wild through a plate of glass. The wild monkey could see a snake through a window that the lab monkey could not see. Thus the lab monkey saw the wild monkey show fear, but did not know what it was afraid of. Later the lab monkey was put close to a snake to see whether it would show fear.

Results The lab monkey showed no fear of the snake.

Interpretation To develop a fear of snakes, the observer monkey had to see that the other monkey

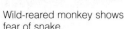

Wild-reared monkey   Lab-reared monkey

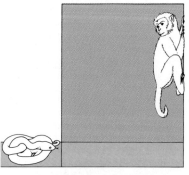
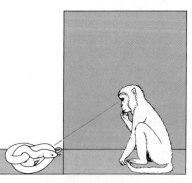

Wild-reared monkey shows   Lab-reared monkey shows
fear of snake.   no fear of snake.

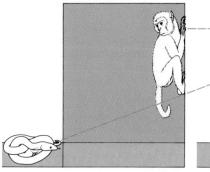
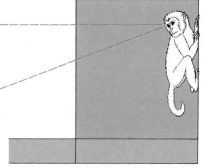

Lab-reared monkey learns
fear of snake by observing
wild-reared monkey and snake.

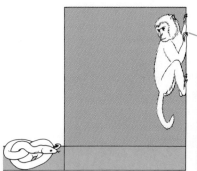
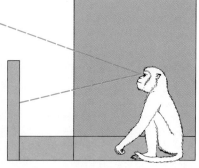

Barrier masks   Lab-reared monkey does not
snake from   learn fear when snake is not
view of lab-   visible.
reared monkey.

FIGURE 14.8

A laboratory-reared monkey learns to fear snakes from the reaction of a monkey reared in the wild. But when the snake is not visible, the lab-reared monkey fails to learn fear.

was frightened of snakes, not just that it was frightened (Figure 14.8).

Note that although the observer monkey had to see *what* the other monkey was afraid of, it did not have to see *why* it was afraid. Just seeing the other monkey's fear of the snake in Experiment 1 was enough. Humans not only observe other peo-

ple's fears but also can tell one another what we are afraid of and why. ■

Why Some Phobias Are More Common Than Others
Suppose you are moderately afraid of snakes even though you have never been bitten. If hearing that snakes bite people is enough to produce a fear, why aren't you absolutely terrified of cars? You have heard about automobile accidents in which people were injured or killed. You may have witnessed such an accident or have been injured in one yourself. Yet you are not afraid of cars. Nor do you have a phobia of guns or tools or electric outlets. Why not?

The most common phobias are of closed spaces, public places, heights, lightning and thunder, animals, and illness. Why are these phobias so common while phobias of cars and guns and tools are almost unheard of? One explanation is that the objects of these common phobias have always been dangerous to humans. Martin Seligman (1971) suggested that people are inherently "prepared" to learn certain phobias. For millions of years people who quickly learned to avoid snakes, heights, and lightning have probably had a better chance to survive and to transmit their genes than people who are slow to learn those fears. We have not had enough time to evolve a tendency to fear cars and guns.

To test this hypothesis, Susan Mineka (1987) let one group of monkeys watch a videotape of a monkey showing fear of a snake and let another group watch a videotape of a monkey showing fear of flowers. (It was actually the same videotape except that the snake was electronically erased and some flowers were substituted.) The observer monkeys learned a strong fear of snakes but not of flowers. Evidently it is easier to learn fear of snakes than to learn fear of flowers.

There may be other reasons why some phobias are more common than others. One is that we have many safe experiences with cars and tools to outweigh any bad experiences. We have few safe experiences with snakes or with falling from high places. Monkeys that had had previous experience with snakes or that had observed monkeys that were unafraid of snakes were less likely to develop a fear by watching a monkey that showed fear of snakes (Mineka & Cook, 1986).

Another possibility is that people generally develop phobias for objects they cannot predict or control. Danger is more stressful when it takes us by surprise (Mineka, 1985; Mineka, Cook, & Miller, 1984). If you are afraid of spiders, for example, you have to be constantly on the alert for those tiny, unpredictable critters. Lightning is also unpredictable and uncontrollable. You don't have to worry that electric outlets will take you by surprise. You have to be on the alert for cars when you are near a road, but not the rest of the day.

The Persistence of Phobias   Well-established phobias can last a lifetime. And yet, if phobias are the result of classical conditioning, they should be easy to extinguish. You see a white rat and something happens to frighten you. After a few repetitions, you become afraid of white rats. But if you later see a white rat many times and nothing alarming happens, your fear should be extinguished. So why do phobias last so long?

The answer is that phobias, like superstitions, are the result of avoidance learning. If you avoid all black cats, you will never discover that they do not bring bad luck. Similarly, if you stay away from snakes or heights or closed places because you are afraid of them (a phobia), you will never learn that your fear is exaggerated. In other words, extinction never takes place.

Therapies for Phobias   We shall consider therapies in Chapter 15. Here, however, let us examine two therapies that are intended specifically for phobias—systematic desensitization and flooding.

A monkey that learns to press a lever to avoid shocks keeps on pressing long after the shock device has been unplugged. The best way to teach it to stop is to prevent it from making the response. When we do that, it reacts with terror at first but gradually calms down. Similarly, the best way to eliminate a superstition is to prevent the avoidance response. A person who frequently confronts black cats eventually learns that they do not bring bad luck. The same is true of phobias. The best way to eliminate a phobia is to expose a person to the object that arouses the fear. When nothing bad happens, the phobia fades.

The most common and most successful treatment for phobia is **systematic desensitization**, a method of reducing fear by gradually exposing people to the object of their fear (Wolpe, 1961). Someone with a phobia of dogs, for example, is first given training in methods of relaxation. Then the patient is asked to lie on a comfortable couch with relaxing music playing in the background and with the therapist nearby (Figure 14.9). The therapist asks the patient to imagine a small black-and-white photo of a dog. Next the patient is asked to imagine a full-color photo and then to imagine a real dog. After the patient has handled all those images without distress, the same sequence is repeated with real photos and eventually with a real dog.

The process resembles Skinner's shaping pro-

FIGURE 14.9

Facing phobias: If you avoid dogs because you think they will attack you, you'll never discover that most aren't vicious. These phobic people are being treated by systematic desensitization using pictures of dogs.

cedure (page 256): The patient is given time to master one step before going on to the next. The patient can say stop if the distress becomes too severe; the therapist then goes back several steps and repeats the sequence. Some people get through the whole procedure in a single, one-hour session; others need weekly sessions for two or three months.

A related treatment for phobias is known as **flooding** or **implosion** (Hogan & Kirchner, 1967; Rachman, 1969). Again the fear is extinguished by exposing the patient to the object of the phobia, but in this treatment the object is presented suddenly rather than gradually. (It is called "flooding" because the patient is "flooded" with fear.) If you had a phobia of rats, for example, you might be told to imagine that you were locked in a room full of rats crawling all over you and viciously attacking you. The image arouses your sympathetic nervous system enormously, and your heart rate and breathing rate soar to high levels (Lande, 1982).

The human sympathetic nervous system is not capable of maintaining extreme arousal for very long, however, and within a few minutes your heart rate and breathing rate begin to decline. A little later, you report that you feel more relaxed, even though the therapist continues to suggest images of rats chewing your eyeballs and intestines. Once you have reached this point, the battle is half won.

Concept Checks

5. *In what way does systematic desensitization resemble extinction of a learned shock-avoidance response? (Check your answer on page 554.)*

6. *How is the flooding procedure related to the*

James-Lange theory of emotions, discussed in Chapter 12? (Check your answer on page 555.)

Obsessive-Compulsive Disorder

People with **obsessive-compulsive disorder** have two kinds of problems: An **obsession** is a repetitive, unwelcome stream of thought. Sometimes after listening to the radio, I find myself humming a tune or hearing a tune playing over and over "in my mind" for hours, even though I may not even like the tune. A more serious obsession may haunt a person for months or years; a single train of thought repeats itself over and over despite all attempts to stop it. A **compulsion** is a repetitive, almost irresistible action. Obsessions generally lead to compulsions, as an itching sensation leads to scratching.

The Origin of Obsessions People with obsessive-compulsive disorder feel a combination of guilt and anxiety over certain thoughts or impulses. They may have felt an impulse to engage in some sexual act they consider shameful or an impulse to hurt someone they love. They decide, "Oh, what a terrible thing to think. I don't want to think such a thing ever again." And so they resolve to shut the thought or impulse out of their consciousness.

We do sometimes manage to repress thoughts from our consciousness. Strangely, though, the harder we try, the more difficult it becomes.

As a child, the Russian novelist Leo Tolstoy once organized a club with a most unusual qualification for membership: A prospective member had to stand alone in a corner *without thinking about a white bear* (Simmons, 1949). If you think that sounds easy, try it. You probably go months at a time without thinking about polar bears, but when you try *not* to think about them, you can think of nothing else.

In one experiment, college students were asked to tape record everything that came to mind during five minutes but to try not to think about white bears. If they did, they were to mention it and ring a bell. Subjects reported thinking about a bear a mean of more than six times during the five minutes (Wegner, Schneider, Carter, & White, 1987).

They were then told to continue recording their thoughts for the next five minutes, but this time they should *try* to think about white bears. On the average, they reported about 22 white-bear thoughts over that period. Other subjects, who had not first tried to avoid thinking about white bears, were also told to try to think about white bears. They reported only about 16 white-bear thoughts over five minutes. In other words, the students who had first tried to avoid thinking about white bears now found it especially easy to think about white bears (Figure

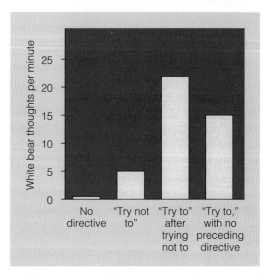

FIGURE 14.10

A one-track mind: People who were asked not to think of something thought about it far more than usual. When they were told to try to think about it, those who had previously suppressed the thoughts then thought about it more than other people did.

14.10)! Why? Very simply: The subjects who were trying to suppress white-bear thoughts looked around the room, deliberately thinking about the walls, the floor, the light switch ... anything they could find. When the white-bear thoughts intruded anyway, those thoughts became associated with all these objects. So now the walls, the floor, and the light switch reminded the subjects of white bears! Apparently once an obsessive train of thought has set in, attempts to fight it are likely to backfire.

One Type of Compulsion: Cleaning Obsessions give rise to two major compulsions: cleaning and checking. Obsessive-compulsive cleaning is similar to a phobia of dirt. Here is a description of a severe cleaning compulsion (Nagera, 1976):

"R.," a 12-year-old boy, had a long-standing habit of prolonged bathing and hand washing, dating from a film about germs he had seen in the second grade. At about age 12, he started to complain about "being dirty" and having "bad thoughts," but he would not elaborate. His hand washing and bathing became longer and more frequent. When he bathed, he carefully washed himself with soap and washcloth all over, including the inside of his mouth and the inside of each nostril. He even opened his eyes in the soapy water and carefully washed his eyeballs. The only part he did not wash was his penis, which he covered with a washcloth as soon as he entered the tub.

Coupled with his strange bathing habits, he developed some original superstitions. Whenever he did anything with one hand, he immediately did the same thing with the other hand. Whenever anyone mentioned a member of R.'s family, he would mention the corresponding member of the other person's family. He always walked to school by the same route, being careful never to step on any spot he had ever stepped on before. (After a while this became a serious strain on his memory.) At school, he would wipe the palm of his hand on his pants after any "good" thought; at home, he would wipe his hand on his pants after any "bad" thought.

R.'s problems were traced to a single event. Just before the onset of his exaggerated behaviors, R. and another boy had pulled down their pants and looked at each other. Afterward he felt guilty and full of anxiety that he might do the same thing again. The constant bathing was apparently an attempt to wash away his feelings of "dirtiness." The superstitious rituals were an attempt to impose rigid self-control. His underlying reasoning could be described as, "If I can keep myself under perfect control at all times, even following these rigid and pointless rules, I will never again lose control and do something shameful."

Another Type of Compulsion: Checking An obsessive-compulsive checker "double-checks" everything. Before going to bed at night, he or she checks to make sure that all the doors and windows are locked and that all the water taps and gas outlets are turned off. But then the question arises, "Did I *really* check them all or did I only imagine it?" So everything has to be checked again. And again. "After all, I may accidentally have unlocked one of the doors when I was checking it." Obsessive-compulsive checkers can never decide when to stop checking; they may go on for hours, and even then not be satisfied.

Obsessive-compulsive checkers have been known to check every door they pass to see whether anyone has been locked in, to check trash containers and bushes to see whether anyone has abandoned a baby, to call the police every day to ask whether they have committed a crime that they have forgotten, and to drive back and forth along a street to see whether they ran over anyone the last time through (Pollak, 1979; Rachman & Hodgson, 1980).

Why do checkers go on checking? According to some reports, they do not trust their memory of what they have done (Sher, Frost, Kushner, Crews, & Alexander, 1989). In one study, the experimenters asked several people—among them some obsessive-compulsive checkers—to read a list of words and to think their opposites. (For instance, when they saw "NORTH-S . . . ," they would think

south.) Then the experimenters combined the two sets of words—the words on the list and their opposites—and asked the subjects to identify which words they had read and which ones they had only thought. The obsessive-compulsive checkers did about as well as the control group in identifying which words they had read, but their confidence in their answers was significantly lower. Compared to the control group, the checkers were less confident of their ability to distinguish between what had actually happened and what they had just imagined (Sher, Frost, & Otto, 1983).

Comparing Cleaners and Checkers Obsessive-compulsive cleaners and checkers have many characteristics in common. Many of them have an obsessive impulse to commit some vile deed, such as shouting an obscenity, pushing a stranger in front of a subway train, or committing suicide. They worry that they may someday commit the deed, although very few of them ever do. Nearly all have some insight into their own behavior and realize that their rituals are inappropriate. Obsessive-compulsive cleaners and checkers differ in certain respects, however, as Table 14.3 shows.

About 2 to 3% of all people in the U.S. suffer from obsessive-compulsive disorder at some time during their life (Karno, Golding, Sorenson, & Burnam, 1988). The disorder occurs most frequently among hard-working, perfectionistic people of average or above-average intelligence. It may develop either suddenly or gradually. Sometimes the disorder develops gradually and then suddenly grows worse after some precipitating event. Although the onset may occur in early childhood, the disorder is usually first recognized between ages 10 and 25.

Table 14.4 lists some items from a questionnaire on obsessive-compulsive tendencies (Rachman & Hodgson, 1980). Try answering these questions yourself, or try guessing how an obsessive-compulsive person would answer them. The most common obsessive-compulsive answers are given on page 555. (The few items listed here are not sufficient to diagnose someone as obsessive compulsive. So don't worry if you give all the obsessive-compulsive answers.)

Therapies for Obsessive-Compulsive Disorder Most obsessive-compulsive people simply live with their disorder. Only a few ever seek professional help. Obsessive-compulsive disorder can sometimes be treated successfully by a therapy similar to systematic desensitization. Like people with superstitions or phobias, people with obsessive-compulsive disorder try to avoid some distressing thought or

TABLE 14.3 Obsessive-Compulsive Cleaners and Checkers

	Cleaners	Checkers
Sex distribution	Mostly female	About equally male and female
Dominant emotion	Anxiety, similar to phobia	Guilt, shame
Speed of onset	Usually rapid	More often gradual
Life disruption	Dominates life	Usually does not disrupt job and family life
Ritual length	Less than 1 hour at a time	Some go on indefinitely
Feel better after rituals?	Yes	Usually not
Response to treatment	Fair	Poor

Source: Rachman & Hodgson, 1980.

TABLE 14.4 Questionnaire for Obsessive-Compulsive Tendencies

1. I avoid using public telephones because of possible contamination.   T F

2. I frequently get nasty thoughts and have difficulty in getting rid of them.   T F

3. I usually have serious doubts about the simple everyday things I do.   T F

4. Neither of my parents was very strict during my childhood.   T F

5. I do not take a long time to dress in the morning.   T F

6. One of my major problems is that I pay too much attention to detail.   T F

7. I do not stick to a very strict routine when doing ordinary things.   T F

8. I do not usually count when doing a routine task.   T F

9. Even when I do something very carefully, I often feel that it is not quite right.   T F

Source: Rachman & Hodgson, 1980.

impulse and never learn that the avoidance is unnecessary. Therapists expose the obsessive-compulsive patient to the distressing thought while physically preventing the compulsive behavior. This treatment sometimes leads to the eventual "extinction" of the behavior, although it seldom eliminates the problem altogether, and it usually fails with the most severely impaired patients (Beech & Vaughan, 1978; Marks, 1981).

SUMMARY

1. People with generalized anxiety disorder or panic disorder experience extreme anxiety. Panic disorder is characterized by episodes of disabling anxiety, some of which may be triggered by hyperventilation. (page 515)

2. Once an individual has learned a shock-avoidance response, the response may persist long after the possibility of shock has been removed. Superstitions, phobias, and obsessive-compulsive disorder are also avoidance behaviors; as with shock-avoidance responses, they persist because people do not discover that they are unnecessary. (page 516)

3. A phobia is a fear so extreme that it interferes with normal living. Phobias are learned through observation as well as through experience. (page 517)

4. People are more likely to develop phobias of certain objects than of others; for example, snake phobias are more common than car phobias. The objects of the most common phobias have menaced humans throughout evolutionary history. They pose dangers that are difficult to predict or control, and they are generally objects with which we have had few safe experiences. (page 519)

5. A common therapy for phobia is systematic desensitization, in which the patient is taught to relax and is then gradually exposed to the object of the phobia. Flooding is similar except that the person is exposed to the object suddenly. (page 521)

6. People with obsessive-compulsive disorder try to avoid certain thoughts or impulses that cause anxiety or guilt. (page 522)

7. The two types of compulsion are cleaning and checking. Cleaners try to avoid any type of contamination. Checkers constantly double-check themselves and invent elaborate rituals. (page 522)

SUGGESTION FOR FURTHER READING

Wegner, D. (1989). *White bears and other unwanted thoughts*. New York: Viking Penguin. An account of experiments on obsessive thinking.

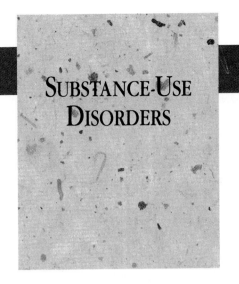

SUBSTANCE-USE DISORDERS

unteers. And yet if I change the term *brain device* to *drug* and change *experimenter* to *drug peddler,* it is amazing how many volunteers come forward.

For some people, using alcohol or drugs is apparently a harmless pleasure. For others, it is extremely destructive. In Chapter 4 we examined the effects of several drugs on behavior. Instead of reviewing all those drugs again here, we shall focus on addictions, principally to alcohol and opiates—addictions that have been familiar to humans for centuries and which continue to be major problems today.

Why do people sometimes abuse alcohol and
other drugs?
What can be done to help them quit?

How would you like to volunteer for a little experiment? I want to implant a device in your head to control your brain activity—something that will automatically lift your mood and bring you happiness. There are still a few kinks in it, but most of the people who have tried it say it makes them feel good at least some of the time, and some people say it makes them feel "very happy."

I should tell you about the possible risks: My device will endanger your health and will reduce your life expectancy by, oh, 10 years or so. Some people think it may cause permanent brain damage, but they have not proved that charge, so I don't think you should worry about it. Your behavior will change a good bit, though. You may have difficulty concentrating, for example. The device affects some people more than others. If you happen to be one of those it affects strongly, you will have difficulty completing your education, getting or keeping a job, and carrying on a satisfactory family life. But if you are lucky, you may avoid all that. Anyway, you can quit the experiment any time you want to. You should know, though, that the longer the device remains in your brain, the harder it is to get it out.

I cannot pay you for taking part in the experiment. In fact, *you* will have to pay *me.* But I'll give you a bargain rate: only $5 for the first week and then a little more each week as time passes. One other thing: Technically speaking, this experiment is illegal. We probably won't get caught, but if we do, we could both go to jail.

What do you say? Is it a deal?

I presume you will say no. I get very few vol-

Actress Tallulah Bankhead (1903–1968) said, "Cocaine isn't habit-forming. I should know—I've been using it for years." The use and abuse of drugs is nothing new in the United States, although crack, which this dealer is packaging, is. This smokable form of cocaine is popular because it's cheap and potent.

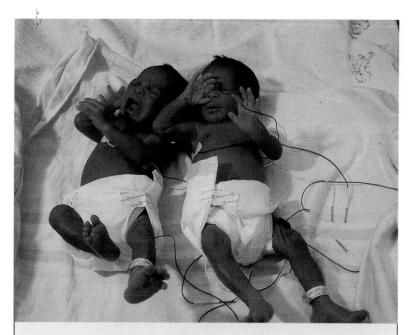

*I*nnocent victims: *Two of a rapidly growing population of "crack babies," born addicted because of their mothers' drug use during pregnancy. Because crack is relatively new, data on the long-term effects on such infants are incomplete but indicate that they will be badly handicapped in many ways for years, perhaps for life. Of those who choose to use drugs, no one basic personality type seems more susceptible to addiction than another, but there seems to be greater cocaine abuse among those suffering from bipolar disorder and hyperactivity than in people with other disorders. The mood swings of these two conditions may increase vulnerability (Kolata, 1989b).*

PSYCHOACTIVE SUBSTANCE DEPENDENCE (ADDICTION)

Most people who drink alcohol or experiment with marijuana and other drugs do so in moderation. But some people are such heavy users that they jeopardize their health, their work or education, and the welfare of their family. They may use the substance daily, only on weekends, or only during sporadic binges; whatever the pattern, they know they are consuming too much. They may decide again and again to quit or cut down, but they find it impossible to change their behavior. Those who cannot quit a self-destructive habit are said to have a **dependence** on a substance or **addiction** to it.

A common estimate is that about 10% of all people in the United States and Canada have a substance dependence. Depending on where we draw the line between those with a problem and those without a problem, the estimate might be either higher or lower. But without question, the problem is widespread.

Some substances are much more likely than others are to be addictive. Other things being equal, the more rapidly a substance enters the brain, the more likely it is to be addictive. Cigarettes are more addictive than cigars, for example, because smokers inhale cigarette smoke more deeply, allowing the nicotine to enter the bloodstream and reach the brain more quickly (Bennett, 1980). Similarly, gulped alcohol is more addictive than sipped alcohol, injected cocaine is more addictive than sniffed cocaine, and crack cocaine is more addictive than injected cocaine.

Roy Wise and Michael Bozarth (1987) have proposed that all addictive substances have one property in common: They activate the dopamine synapses responsible for locomotion. Even opiates, barbiturates, and alcohol—which act mainly as depressants—stimulate movement, especially in small doses.

Almost any substance, however, can be addictive under certain circumstances. In one hospital ward where alcoholics were being treated, one of the patients moved his bed into the men's room (Cummings, 1979). At first the hospital staff ignored this curious behavior. Then, one by one, other patients moved their beds into the men's room. Eventually the staff realized what was going on. These men, deprived of alcohol, had discovered that they could get a "high" by drinking enormous amounts of water! By drinking about 7.5 gallons (30 liters) of water a day and urinating the same amount (which was why they moved into the men's room), they managed to alter the acid-to-base balance of their blood enough to produce something like drunkenness. They had become "water addicts." Is water addictive? *The addiction is not in the drug but in the user.*

Something to Think About

Are any addictive behaviors beneficial? (What about jogging?)

WITHDRAWAL AND TOLERANCE

The human body adjusts both physiologically and psychologically after repeated use of alcohol and other drugs. Physiologically, the body chemistry changes. Psychologically, people experience unpleasant effects as the drugs wear off but learn to counteract some of the effects of the drugs the next time they take them.

Drug Withdrawal

When habitual users suddenly stop using alcohol or opiate drugs (such as morphine or heroin), they gradually enter a state of **withdrawal** (Gawin & Kleber, 1986). With alcohol, the typical withdrawal symptoms are sweating, nausea, sleeplessness, and, in severe cases, hallucinations and seizures (Mello & Mendelson, 1978a). With opiate drugs, the typical withdrawal symptoms are anxiety, restlessness, loss of appetite, vomiting, diarrhea, sweating, and gagging (Mansky, 1978). Users who quit tranquilizers may also experience withdrawal symptoms; those who quit stimulants or marijuana generally report only mild withdrawal symptoms or none at all.

Some researchers explain drug withdrawal as a special case of the opponent-process theory of emotions, in which removing the stimulus for one emotion causes a rebound to the opposite emotion, as discussed in Chapter 12 (Solomon, 1980; Solomon & Corbit, 1974). A drug provides the stimulus for a mostly pleasant emotional state. As the drug wears off, however, the user rebounds to the opposite emotional state. Opiates, for example, overstimulate certain brain receptors and cause them to become fatigued (Herz & Schulz, 1978). The overstimulation produces one effect; the fatigue afterwards produces the opposite effect.

After many repetitions, the initial high grows weaker and the withdrawal grows more intense and more unpleasant. To escape the withdrawal symptoms, users are compelled to take the drug again. The desire to avoid the withdrawal symptoms sustains the addiction.

Drug Tolerance

After someone has taken a drug repeatedly, it produces less effect. To achieve the desired high, drug users have to increase the dose. Some users inject three or four times more heroin or morphine into their veins than it would take to kill a nonuser. **Tolerance** refers to the weakened effect of a drug after repeated use.

What brings about drug tolerance? It may result in part from automatic chemical changes that occur in cells throughout the body to counteract the drug's effects (Baker & Tiffany, 1985). It may also result in part from psychological causes. For example, alcohol impairs the coordination of rats as well as humans. If rats are simply injected with alcohol every day for 24 days and then tested, the results show that their coordination has been seriously impaired. Apparently they have developed no tolerance to the alcohol. However, if their coordination is tested after each of the 24 injections, their

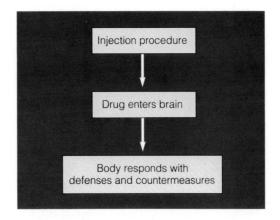

FIGURE 14.11

The development of drug tolerance.

performance steadily improves (Wenger, Tiffany, Bombardier, Nicholls, & Woods, 1981). In other words, by practicing coordination while under the influence of the alcohol, the rats develop a tolerance to alcohol. Similarly, though amphetamine suppresses appetite, rats that eat a little food after each amphetamine injection gradually develop tolerance to the drug's effects (Streather & Hinson, 1985).

Concept Check

7. *People who use amphetamines or related drugs as appetite suppressants generally find that the effect wears off after a week or two. How could they prolong the effect? (Check your answer on page 555.)*

Drug Tolerance as Classical Conditioning

Psychologists can describe the development of tolerance in terms of classical conditioning. When drug users inject themselves with morphine or heroin, the injection procedure is the initial stimulus. Within seconds, the drug enters the brain and begins to affect experience. It also triggers a response: The brain and other parts of the body mobilize various defenses and countermeasures against the changes the drug is evoking—for example, changes in hormone secretions, heart rate, and breathing rate. Figure 14.11 shows the sequence.

Whenever one stimulus predicts another stimulus that produces a response, we have the conditions necessary for classical conditioning. Shepard Siegel (1977, 1983) has demonstrated that classical conditioning does indeed take place under these circumstances. Initially, the injection ritual is

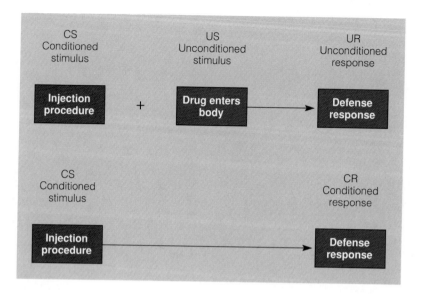

FIGURE 14.12

Classical conditioning: After repeated injections, the injection procedure elicits defense responses against the drug as a conditioned response. That conditioned response produces tolerance to the drug.

a neutral stimulus that gives rise to no relevant response. After many pairings of that stimulus with the entry of the drug into the brain, however, the injection procedure by itself is able to evoke the defensive response (Figure 14.12).

How might classical conditioning contribute to drug tolerance? The first time one takes a drug, there is a certain delay between the time the drug enters the brain and the time the brain mobilizes its defenses. After classical conditioning has taken place, the injection procedure, acting as a CS (conditioned stimulus), may itself trigger the defense reactions, even before the drug has entered the brain. As the defense reactions are aroused earlier and earlier, the effects of the drug grow weaker and the user can tolerate heavier and heavier doses.

Here is an example of the evidence that supports the classical-conditioning interpretation of drug tolerance. If we assume that the injection procedure serves as a conditioned stimulus, then the body's defense reactions should be stronger when the drug is given through the usual injection procedure (with the CS) than when it is given by some other means (without the CS). In other words, an experienced drug user should show more tolerance when the drug is administered under familiar circumstances, with the usual preparation (CS). The evidence strongly supports this prediction (Eikelboom & Stewart, 1982; Lê, Poulos, & Cappell, 1979; Poulos, Wilkinson, & Cappell, 1981; Siegel, 1983; Tiffany & Baker, 1981). *To show strong tolerance in*

a particular environment, the individual must have previously received the drug in that environment.

Why do some people die of a drug overdose that is no greater than the dose they normally tolerated? According to the classical-conditioning interpretation, they probably took the fatal overdose in an unfamiliar setting. Because that setting did not serve as a CS, it failed to trigger the usual tolerance.

Something to Think About

If a drug user regularly takes a drug in a particular environment, that environment will tend to maintain tolerance at a high level. And if the person has abstained from taking the drug for several months, simply returning to that familiar environment will trigger a craving for the drug. What is likely to happen to people who return home after having been cured of their drug habit at a distant treatment center? How could they avoid a renewed craving for the drug?

Concept Checks

8. *Using the classical-conditioning terminology introduced in Chapter 7, what are the CS, US, CR, and UR in the development of tolerance to a drug? (Check your answers on page 555.)*

9. *Within the classical-conditioning interpretation of drug tolerance, what procedure should extinguish tolerance? (Check your answer on page 555.)*

PREDISPOSITION TO ADDICTION

Although only a minority of alcohol drinkers become alcoholics, many alcoholics become addicted before they reach the age of 25 (Cloninger, 1987). Some people try heroin once or twice and then quit; others inject themselves so frequently they eventually destroy every vein they can find (Dole, 1978). Why do some people become addicted while others do not?

Most of the research has dealt with alcoholism, the most common addiction, so we shall focus on predisposition to alcoholism. Might it be possible to determine in advance which people are most likely to develop into alcoholics? If we could identify those people early enough, we might be able to train them to drink in moderation or to abstain altogether.

Genetics and Family Background

There is convincing evidence that genetics plays a role in predisposition to alcoholism. The close bio-

One temperance group used to post signs reading: "Liquor means alcohol. Alcohol means poison. Why drink poison?" Most people don't think of alcohol as poison and don't give much thought to why they drink, perhaps because most drinkers do not become alcoholics. Those who do often don't fit the stereotype of derelicts. These women appear to be social drinkers, but maybe one of them frequently drinks to excess. If so, even some of her close friends may not know.

logical relatives of alcoholics are more likely to become alcoholics themselves than are the relatives of nonalcoholics (Gabrielli & Plomin, 1985). That holds true even when the children of alcoholics are adopted by people who are not alcoholics (Cloninger, Bohman, & Sigvardsson, 1981; Vaillant & Milofsky, 1982).

The incidence of alcoholism is greater than average among adults who have grown up in families marked by conflict between the parents, poor relationships between parents and children, and inadequate parental supervision of the children (Maddahian, Newcomb, & Bentler, 1988; Schulsinger et al., 1986; Zucker & Gomberg, 1986). Once they reach adolescence, many children who grow up in such an environment respond by missing school, engaging in impulsive behaviors, and experimenting with alcohol and other drugs. As adults, they are vulnerable to both alcoholism and drug addiction.

The culture in which children are raised also plays a role. For example, most Jewish families emphasize drinking in moderation, and relatively few Jews who drink become alcoholics (Cahalan, 1978). That is more or less true of Italians as well. By contrast, the Irish tend to be more tolerant of heavy drinking, and alcoholism is more prevalent among people of Irish background (Vaillant & Milofsky, 1982).

Still, individuals differ. Not all children of alcoholic parents become alcoholics themselves, and not all children who grow up in a culture that tolerates heavy drinking become alcoholics. Again, how can we predict which people are most vulnerable to alcoholism?

Ways of Predicting Alcoholism: WHAT'S THE EVIDENCE?

Perhaps a person's early behavior might offer some indicator of who is more likely or less likely to become an alcoholic. One way to find such a clue would be to record the presence or absence of various behaviors in hundreds of young people. Twenty years later we find out which of them have become alcoholics and determine which early behaviors would have predicted those outcomes. Such a study would take 20 years. Moreover, it might be difficult to find some of the subjects after that time, especially the alcoholics.

A more feasible approach would be to compare children of an alcoholic parent with children of parents who are not alcoholics. From previous studies, we know that more children of alcoholics will become alcoholics. Therefore, behaviors that are significantly more prevalent among the children of alcoholics may predict vulnerability to alcoholism.

In the first of the following studies, experimenters tested whether alcohol might be more rewarding to the sons of alcoholics than to the sons of nonalcoholics (Levenson, Oyama, & Meek, 1987).

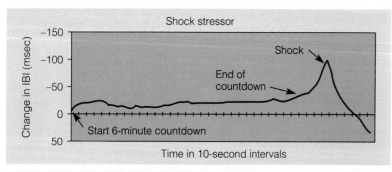

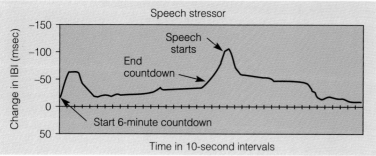

FIGURE 14.13

Changes in stress over time for a typical subject. The line goes up to indicate a decrease in the interval between heartbeats—an increase in heart rate. Note that heart rate increased as soon as the countdown began and then remained stable. It rose toward the end of the countdown and again at the time of the shock or speech. Alcohol suppressed these signs of stress, especially for the sons of alcoholics. (From Levenson, Oyama, & Meek, 1987.)

EXPERIMENT 1

Hypothesis When people are put into a stressful situation, an opportunity to drink alcohol will reduce that stress for almost everyone, but it will have a greater effect on the adult sons of an alcoholic parent than on other men the same age.

Method The experiment was conducted on young men, half of them sons of an alcoholic father and half of them sons of nonalcoholic parents. (The study focused on men because alcoholism is about twice as common in men as in women.) The men were told that at a certain time they would receive an electric shock and at another time they would have to give a three-minute speech on "What I like and dislike about my body." They watched a clock tick off the waiting time. Half of each group were given alcohol to drink at the start of the waiting period, and everyone who was offered alcohol drank it.

Results All the men showed considerable stress, as measured by heart rate, pulse rate, restlessness, and self-reports of emotions. All those who drank alcohol showed a lower heart rate and reported less anxiety. The easing of stress was more pronounced in those who had an alcoholic father (see Figure 14.13.)

Interpretation Men who are genetically vulnerable to alcoholism experience greater stress-reducing effects from alcohol than other men the same age. Perhaps the degree to which alcohol relieves stress may provide a measure of vulnerability to alcoholism.

Two other experiments examined the possibility that young men who are vulnerable to alcoholism might have trouble estimating their own degree of intoxication (O'Malley & Maisto, 1985; Schuckit, 1985). Because these two experiments used practically the same method and reported the same pattern of results, I shall report them as one.

EXPERIMENT 2

Hypothesis Sons of an alcoholic father will underestimate how much they have been affected by the alcohol they have drunk.

Method Young men, some sons of alcoholic fathers and some sons of nonalcoholic parents, consumed drinks containing various amounts of vodka. None of them knew how much vodka was in the drinks. (Vodka has virtually no taste or smell.) After consuming the drinks, they performed various motor and cognitive tasks. They also estimated how much vodka they had drunk and how intoxicated they were.

Results The sons of alcoholic fathers were just as much affected as the sons of nonalcoholics were in their motor and cognitive performance. However, they consistently underestimated how much vodka they had drunk and how intoxicated they were.

Interpretation Men who are not especially vulnerable to alcoholism are quick to recognize when they have started to become tipsy and generally stop drinking at that time. Men who are genetically more vulnerable to alcoholism are slower to recognize the signs of intoxication and continue drinking. Again, it may be possible to identify individuals who are particularly prone to alcoholism by testing their ability to monitor their own level of intoxication. ■

TREATMENTS FOR ALCOHOLISM AND DRUG ADDICTION

At some point, most alcoholics and drug addicts decide that the occasional pleasures the drugs give them are not worth all the pain they bring. So they decide to quit. But quitting is difficult.

Nicholas Cummings (1979) estimates that clinical psychologists spend one fifth to one fourth of their time with patients suffering from alcohol and drug-abuse problems. Of those who seek professional help, more than half drop out along the way and only about 20% manage to quit their habit for a full year. Addicts who check into a hospital for treatment can be supervised 24 hours a day to ensure full abstinence. **Detoxification** refers to a supervised period to remove drugs from the body. In the long run, however, most addicts respond no better to hospital treatment than they do to out-patient treatment (Miller & Hester, 1986).

One explanation for these disappointing results is that only the most severe cases tend to seek professional help. Most people who want to overcome an addiction manage to do so on their own. Those who have the greatest trouble quitting are the most likely to seek professional help (Schachter, 1982).

Actually, the statistics on the success or failure of treatment programs seem more discouraging than they should be. True, most addicts who overcome their addiction suffer a relapse and return to their addiction. But it is also true that most of them manage to quit again (Brownell, Marlatt, Lichtenstein, & Wilson, 1986). A relapse after a period of abstention is not necessarily a failure; it may provide the addict with "practice" toward long-term abstention.

Therapists use many methods for helping people overcome substance abuse disorders. In Chapter 15 we shall consider methods of therapy in general, as they apply to all types of disorders. Here we focus on methods that apply exclusively to substance abuse.

Treating Alcoholism

Alcoholism, the habitual overuse of alcohol, is the most common and most costly form of drug abuse in the United States and Europe. An estimated 25 to 40% of all hospital patients suffer from complications caused by alcohol abuse (Holden, 1987).

Alcoholics Anonymous The most widespread treatment for alcoholism in North America is **Alcoholics Anonymous (AA)**, a self-help group of people who are trying to abstain from alcohol use and help others do the same. In all large cities, and in many smaller cities and towns, AA meetings are held regularly in community halls, church basements, and other available spaces. New members are asked to commit themselves to attend 90 meetings during the first 90 days. (Those who miss a meeting can compensate by attending two or more meetings another day.) From then on, they can attend as often as they like.

In 1935, two alcoholics—a stockbroker and a physician—founded Alcoholics Anonymous. This pioneering self-help group stresses abstinence from drinking, mutual support from peers, and a twelve-step recovery program. The first step is an admission of powerlessness over alcohol. The final step includes sharing the program's message. Other support groups include Alateen, Women for Sobriety, and Narcotics Anonymous.

Millions of people worldwide have participated in the AA program. One reason for its appeal is that all the members have gone through similar experiences and are willing to share their advice. A member who feels the urge to take a drink, or who has already had one, can call a fellow member day or night for support. There is no charge for attendance at meetings; members simply contribute what they can toward the cost of the meeting place. AA has inspired other "anonymous" self-help groups whose purpose is to help drug addicts, compulsive gamblers, compulsive eaters, and the relatives of alcoholics and drug addicts.

Although AA members themselves have no doubt about the value of the program, the organization has never encouraged research to measure its effectiveness. Moreover, investigators would find it difficult (and ethically questionable) to assign people randomly to AA membership and a control group.

About 50% of AA members abstain from alcohol altogether for at least a year and a half after joining; others try to abstain but suffer occasional relapses (Emrick, 1987; Thurstin, Alfano, & Nerviano, 1987). Those results compare favorably to the results for alcoholics in programs other than AA and alcoholics who try to quit on their own. Still, because assignment to groups is not random, we cannot draw a firm conclusion. (Perhaps those who join AA are more highly motivated to quit than other alcoholics are.)

"If, when you honestly want to, you find you cannot quit entirely, or if when drinking, you have little control over the amount you take, you are probably alcoholic."
ANONYMOUS
(1955)

Antabuse In addition to or instead of attendance at AA meetings, many alcoholics seek medical treatment. Many years ago, investigators noticed that the workers in a certain rubber-manufacturing plant drank very little alcohol. The investigators eventually linked this behavior to disulfiram, a chemical that was used in the manufacturing process. Ordinarily, the liver converts alcohol into a toxic substance, acetaldehyde (ASS-eh-TAL-de-HIDE), and then converts acetaldehyde into a harmless substance, acetic acid. Disulfiram, however, blocks the conversion of acetaldehyde to acetic acid. Whenever the workers drank alcohol, acetaldehyde accumulated in their body and they became ill. Over time, they learned to avoid alcohol.

Disulfiram, under the trade name **Antabuse**, is now commonly used in the treatment of alcoholism (Peachey & Naranjo, 1983). Alcoholics who take a daily Antabuse pill become very sick whenever they have a drink. They develop a sensation of heat in the face, a headache, nausea, blurred vision, and anxiety. The threat of sickness is probably more effective than the sickness itself (Fuller & Roth, 1979). By taking a daily pill, a recovering alcoholic renews a decision not to drink. Those who actually do take a drink in spite of the threat get quite ill, at which point they may decide not to drink again, or they may decide not to take the pill again!

Concept Check

10. *About 50% of Asians have a gene that makes them unable to convert acetaldehyde to acetic acid. Would such people be more likely or less likely than others to become alcoholics? (Check your answer on page 555.)*

Controversy:
Is Alcoholism a "Disease"?

Some people regard alcoholism as an indication of a weak will or low morality. Psychoanalysts interpret it as a manifestation of deeper, underlying psychological conflicts. Alcoholics Anonymous, on the contrary, maintains that alcoholism is a disease. What that means is not exactly clear, because the medical profession makes no precise definition of disease, and neither does AA. Apparently, AA means that alcoholism is the problem itself, not just a sign of some other psychological or moral weakness, and that alcoholics should feel no guiltier about their alcoholism than they would about having pneumonia.

Labeling something as a disease has consequences, both intended and unintended. First, it implies that alcoholics should be entitled to the same benefits as people with other diseases. Not everyone concedes that point. In 1988, a case was brought to the U.S. Supreme Court by two veterans who had been denied educational benefits because they had failed to apply for them within 10 years after leaving military service. They pointed out that the law provides for an extension of the 10-year deadline if a veteran is diseased or handicapped during that period. They claimed that they did have a disease—alcoholism—during those 10 years but that they had now recovered and were well enough to attend college. After listening to many contradictory definitions of the terms *alcoholism* and *disease,* the Court ruled that under the veterans' benefit law alcoholism did not qualify as a disease.

Second, the "disease" concept of alcoholism implies that alcoholics gradually progress to drinking more and more. Supporters of this view hold that the only hope for an alcoholic lies in complete abstention from alcohol; one drink, or one sip, will cause a reformed alcoholic to revert to uncontrolled drinking (Peele, 1984). Many researchers regard that view as an overgeneralization, because different alcoholics deteriorate to different degrees (Vaillant, 1983). Most alcoholics who go on drinking eventually reach a stable level, though not necessarily a desirable level. Some actually cut back on their drinking even though they continue to drink to excess (Hodgson, Rankin, & Stockwell, 1979; Moos & Finney, 1983; Wanberg & Horn, 1983).

Finally, to regard alcoholism strictly as a disease ignores the possibility that environmental factors may have some influence on drinking behavior (Marlatt, 1978). Excessive drinking can sometimes be brought under control by altering the environment. One approach is to provide reinforcers that compete with the reinforcers provided by drinking. For example, a therapist might help an alcoholic to find a full-time job, provide marital counseling, and get the person interested in a social club or a hobby (Azrin, 1976).

Another Controversy:
Can Alcoholics Learn
to Drink in Moderation?

Most physicians agree with Alcoholics Anonymous that the only hope for an alcoholic is total abstinence. Drinking in moderation, they insist, is out of the question.

Not all psychologists agree. Some claim that at least some alcoholics can be trained to cut back on their drinking. They do not claim, however, that alcoholics can start drinking in moderation simply by deciding to do so. Nor do they claim that moderate drinking is an appropriate goal for all alcoholics, perhaps not even for very many.

Mark Sobell and Linda Sobell (1976) reported that they had trained some severe alcoholics to drink in a controlled manner. As part of the treatment, they had alcoholics watch videotapes of themselves drinking out of control. The investigators counseled each alcoholic on when, where, and how to drink in moderation. They reported that an experimental group of 20 alcoholics treated in this manner fared as well as or better than a control group of 20 alcoholics who received treatments that emphasized total abstinence.

Those claims were greeted with great skepticism. A follow-up study found that only 1 of the 20 alcoholics in the experimental group could be considered a "controlled" drinker 10 years later (Pendery, Maltzman, & West, 1982). Of the others, 8 were excessive drinkers, and 4 had died from alcohol-related causes. Six had been in and out of jails and hospitals because of alcohol problems until at last they gave up on controlled drinking and entered an abstinence program. The last person from the original study could not be found 10 years later, but was known to have been drinking excessively at last report.

The 20 alcoholics in the control group, whose treatment had centered on total abstinence, did just as poorly. After 10 years, 6 of them had died from alcohol-related causes and the rest were still drinking in excess (Sobell & Sobell, 1984). To ask which treatment is better for severe alcoholics, total abstinence or controlled drinking, is like asking whether aspirin or Tylenol is better for a broken leg. At this time, no known treatment offers severe alcoholics a high probability of recovery.

Treating Opiate Addiction

For a long time, opiate drugs such as morphine were considered far less dangerous than alcohol (Siegel, 1987). In fact, many medical doctors used to urge their alcoholic patients to switch from alcohol to morphine. Then, around 1900, the use of opiates was made illegal in the United States, except by prescription for relief from pain. Since then, research on opiate use has been limited by the fact that only law-breakers now use opiates.

One approach to the treatment of opiate dependence is for the user to go "cold turkey"—to abstain altogether until the withdrawal symptoms subside, generally under medical supervision. At the end of the treatment, the person might join Narcotics Anonymous, a self-help group similar to Alcoholics Anonymous. Many users who go through this procedure do manage to abandon their use of drugs.

Many others, however, especially those who have

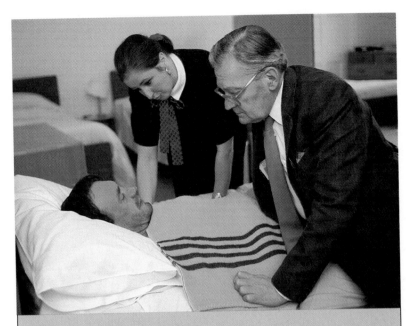

Going cold turkey: Heroin withdrawal resembles a severe bout of the flu, with aching limbs, intense chills, vomiting, and diarrhea; it lasts a week on average. Unfortunately, even after people have suffered through withdrawal, they are likely to experience periods of craving for the drug.

been using opiates for years, experience a recurring urge to take the drug, even long after the withdrawal symptoms have subsided. For those who cannot quit, researchers have sought to find a non-addictive substitute that would satisfy the craving for opiates without creating their harmful effects. Heroin was originally introduced as a substitute for morphine. Soon, however, physicians discovered that heroin is even more addictive and disruptive than morphine. Heroin enters the brain more swiftly than morphine does and once there is converted into morphine. So heroin is just a faster-acting form of morphine.

Today, the most common substitute for opiates is **methadone** (METH-uh-don). Methadone is chemically similar to both morphine and heroin and can itself be addictive. (Table 14.5 compares methadone and morphine.) When taken in pill form, however, it takes hours to enter and leave the bloodstream (Dole, 1980). (If morphine or heroin is taken as a pill, most of the drug is broken down in the digestive system and never reaches the brain.) Thus methadone does not produce the "rush" associated with intravenous injections of opiates; nor does it produce rapid withdrawal symptoms. Although methadone satisfies the craving for opiates without seriously disrupting the user's behav-

TABLE 14.5 Comparison of Methadone with Morphine		
	Morphine	Methadone
Addictive?	Yes	Yes
Administration	Usually by injection	Recommended for oral use
Onset	Rapid	Slow if taken orally
"Rush"?	Yes	Not if taken orally
Relieves craving?	Yes	Yes
Rapid withdrawal symptoms?	Yes	No

ior, it does not eliminate the addiction itself. Once the dosage is reduced, the craving returns.

Many addicts who stick to a methadone maintenance program are able to hold down a job and commit fewer crimes than they did when they were using heroin or morphine (Woody & O'Brien, 1986). Some of them, after discovering that they can no longer get a high from opiates, turn instead to the nonopiate drug cocaine (Kosten, Rounsaville, & Kleber, 1987). In other words, methadone maintenance programs do not eliminate the addictive behaviors. At present, there is no reliable cure for opiate dependence, just as there is none for severe alcoholism.

SUMMARY

1. People who find it difficult or impossible to stop using a substance are said to be dependent on it or addicted to it. (page 526)

2. Generally, the faster a substance enters the brain, the more likely it is to be addictive. For some people, however, almost any substance can be addictive. (page 526)

3. After using a drug, the user enters a rebound state known as withdrawal. After repeated use of certain drugs, withdrawal symptoms grow more severe. (page 527)

4. Drug users develop tolerance to a drug after repeated use. Tolerance is partly a form of classical conditioning in which the drug administration procedure becomes associated with the effects of the drug. (page 527)

5. Some people may be predisposed to become alcoholics for genetic or other reasons. People at risk for alcoholism find that alcohol relieves their stress more than it does for other people. They also tend to underestimate how intoxicated they are. (page 528)

6. The most common treatment for alcoholism in North America is provided by the self-help group called Alcoholics Anonymous. (page 531)

7. Some alcoholics are treated with Antabuse, a prescription drug that makes them ill if they drink alcohol. (page 532)

8. Whether or not alcoholism is a disease is controversial; calling it a disease may distract attention from the environmental factors that lead to drinking. (page 532)

9. Whether alcoholics can be trained to drink in moderation is also a controversial, unsettled question. For severe alcoholics, no known method of treatment offers a high probability of recovery. (page 532)

10. Some opiate users quit using opiates, suffer through the withdrawal symptoms, and manage to abstain from further use. Others substitute methadone under medical supervision. Although methadone has less destructive effects than morphine or heroin does, it does not eliminate the underlying dependence. (page 533)

SUGGESTIONS FOR FURTHER READING

Marlatt, G. A., & Baer, J. S. (1988). Addictive behaviors: Etiology and treatment. *Annual Review of Psychology, 39,* 223–252. A review of the literature on who becomes an alcoholic or drug addict, why, and what can be done to help.

Vaillant, G. E. (1983). *The natural history of alcoholism.* Cambridge, MA: Harvard University Press. A thorough study of what happens to alcoholics over the course of their lifetime.

MOOD DISORDERS

Why do people become depressed?
What can be done to relieve depression?
How are depression and suicide related?

Even when things are going badly, most people remain optimistic that all will be well in the end. After the hurt and disappointment we feel when a relationship breaks up, we say, "Oh, well, at least I learned something from the experience." When we lose money, we say, "It could have been worse. I still have my health."

But sometimes we feel depressed. Nothing seems as much fun as it used to be, and the future seems ominous. For some people, the depression is severe and long lasting. Why?

DEPRESSION

Depression has been called the common cold of psychology. Almost all of us suffer a bout of depression once in a while. Unlike the common cold, however, depression can become severe. At its worst, it can be persistent and disabling.

Depressed people take little pleasure in life. They tend to be slow and inactive; when they do engage in activity, it is usually unproductive. They have trouble concentrating. Their appetite and sex drive decline. Their facial expression is typically sad. They feel worthless, fearful, guilty, and powerless to control what happens to them. Most of them consider suicide and many attempt it.

Nearly all depressed people experience sleep abnormalities (Carroll, 1980; Healy & Williams, 1988). (See Figure 14.14.) They enter REM sleep (page 105) in less than 45 minutes after falling asleep (an unusually short time for most people). Most depressed people wake up too early and cannot

get back to sleep. When morning comes they feel poorly rested. In fact, early morning is usually the time when they feel most depressed. During most of the day they feel a little sleepy.

Depression comes in several forms. A **major depression** differs from other depressions in its severity and duration. Someone with major depression is almost constantly depressed for at least two weeks, perhaps months, and some people have recurring episodes throughout their lives. **Bipolar disorder**, also known as manic-depressive disorder, has two alternating extremes—mania and depression. We shall return to bipolar disorder later.

Many psychologists also distinguish between reactive and endogenous depressions (Zimmerman, Coryell, Pfohl, & Stangl, 1986). A **reactive depression** develops suddenly in reaction to a severe loss, such as the death of a spouse. An **endogenous depression** develops more gradually and cannot be traced to any single traumatic experience. Rather, it seems to result from internal, biological influences.

In practice, this distinction is difficult to draw. In many cases, depression apparently results from a combination of a biological predisposition and a history of unpleasant experiences. Moreover, classifying someone's depression as reactive or endog-

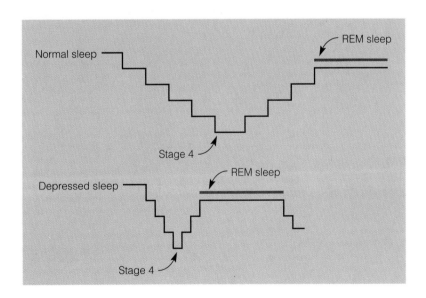

FIGURE 14.14

Most depressed people have abnormal sleep cycles. They enter REM sleep sooner than other people do after falling asleep. Later they may awaken sooner than they wished and find themselves unable to go back to sleep. (Adapted from Hobson, 1989.)

The appearance of depressed people mirrors their feelings of sadness and hopelessness, as this painting by Rafael Coronel shows. Downcast eyes and sagging head and shoulders accompany slow movement. Suggestions to "smile" or "cheer up" fall on deaf ears.

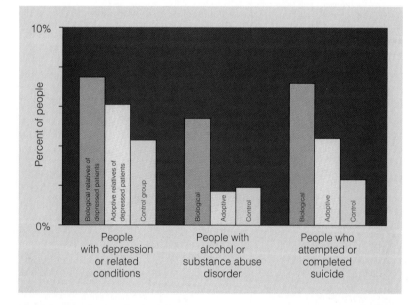

FIGURE 14.15

Family tendencies: When compared with incidences of depression in the general public, which is 5%, blood relatives of a depressed person are more likely to suffer depression themselves. The closer the genetic relationship is, the greater is the probability of depression.

enous is of little help in deciding how to treat it (Arana, Baldessarini, & Ornsteen, 1985; Keller et al., 1986). Depression is treated in a variety of ways as we shall see in Chapter 15.

About 5% of all people in the U.S. suffer from a major depression at some time during their life (Robins et al., 1984). For unknown reasons, depression is more common among women than among men (Nolen-Hoeksema, 1987). The most common age of onset for major depression is about 40; for bipolar disorder, about 30.

Biological Predispositions to Depression

The fact that depression tends to run in families suggests that some people have a biological predisposition to depression (see Figure 14.15). It is two to five times more common among the close relatives of a depressed person than it is in the population at large (Beardslee, Bemporad, Keller, & Klerman, 1983; Weissman, Kidd, & Prusoff, 1982). It is particularly common among the relatives of people who themselves became severely depressed before age 30 (Price, Kidd, & Weissman, 1987). Adopted children who become depressed usually have more biological relatives than adopting relatives who are depressed.

Depressed people also tend to have relatives who suffer from severe anxiety (Kendler, Heath, Martin, & Eaves, 1987). It is possible that anxiety and depression are associated with the same set of genes and that circumstances determine whether those genes will express themselves in one way or the other.

Fluctuations in the level of sex hormones and other hormones may trigger episodes of depression, especially in women. About 30% of all mothers experience a mild depression just after giving birth, a time of massive hormonal changes (Davenport & Adland, 1982). About one or two mothers per thousand enter a major depression at this time. However, it is doubtful that the hormonal swings actually *cause* depression. They may merely influence the timing of depression in a person who is already prone to depression (Schöpf, Bryois, Jonquière, & Le, 1984).

Other Risk Factors in Depression

What kind of person becomes depressed? Biological predisposition is only part of the answer. Another part is that people become depressed when bad things happen to them. But why do some people become deeply depressed after a loss that upsets other people only a little?

A severe loss early in life seems to make some people overresponsive to losses later on. For example, adolescents who lose a parent through death or divorce are particularly vulnerable to depression later in life (Roy, 1985). Breaking up with a boyfriend or girlfriend, or the death of another close relative, may bring back the feelings of desertion they felt over the loss of the parent.

People with poor social support also tend to be vulnerable to depression. As we saw in Chapter 12, social support helps people to cope with stress. People with a happy marriage and close friends are less likely to become depressed or to remain depressed than are people who have no one to talk to about their troubles (Barnett & Gotlib, 1988; Flaherty, Gaviria, Black, Altman, & Mitchell, 1983).

Finally, people who are undergoing severe pain are likely to become depressed (Katon, Egan, & Miller, 1985; Romano & Turner, 1985). However, the correlation between the two does not establish that pain leads to depression. Many people show signs of depression before complaining of pain.

COGNITIVE ASPECTS OF DEPRESSION

Most people believe that every cloud has a silver lining. Show depressed people a silver lining and they wrap it in a cloud. Somehow they think differently from people who are not depressed. Do their thoughts perhaps lead to their depression?

In one experiment, depressed and undepressed people were asked to imagine certain events that might happen to them and then to explain why those events might have happened (Peterson, 1983). The undepressed people often suggested explanations that turned bad events into good ones. For example, to the statement "You have a date that goes badly," they might explain that "the weather was bad, and I slipped in the mud and got my good clothes all messy. But then the two of us had a good laugh, I went back and changed clothes, and we ended up having a better time than ever." The depressed people suggested explanations that made the bad event even worse. For example, "The date went badly because I said something stupid and my date was embarrassed and refused to see me ever again." Even to good news like "you got rich," a depressed person might say, "I got rich because one of my favorite relatives died and left me some money. And then all my friends got jealous of my wealth and wouldn't talk to me anymore."

Why do some people see only the unpleasant side of life? According to the **learned-helplessness**

theory, their experiences have taught them that they have no control over what happens to them.

Learned Helplessness: Animal Experiments

The learned-helplessness theory of depression grew out of some experiments with animals. While testing theories about avoidance learning in animals, Steven Maier, Martin Seligman, and Richard Solomon (1969) trained some dogs in shuttle boxes. First, the dog hears a tone and then, five seconds later, it receives a five-second shock to its feet. Most dogs quickly learn to jump across the barrier as soon as they hear the tone and manage to avoid the shocks altogether.

In one variation of this procedure, the experimenters first strapped dogs with no previous experience into restraining harnesses and then repeatedly sounded a tone that was followed by a shock to the dogs' feet. The dogs soon learned that the tone predicted shock. They struggled to escape but could not. When the experimenters put the same dogs into the shuttle box the next day (without the harness), they discovered to their surprise that the dogs were extremely slow to learn the avoidance response. Most of them failed to learn it at all. Why? Besides learning on the first day that the tone predicted shock, the dogs had also learned that none of their actions could reduce the shock. On the second day, even though they were no longer restrained, the dogs did not jump when they received the shocks. They had learned that they were helpless to escape from shock.

These "helpless" dogs resembled depressed people in several respects. The dogs were inactive and slow to learn. Even their posture and "facial expressions" suggested sadness. The experimenters proposed that the same process might operate in humans: People who, despite their best efforts, meet only with defeat and loss may come to feel "helpless" and fall into depression.

Learned Helplessness: Studies with Humans

In later experiments (for example, Price, Tryon, & Raps, 1978), human subjects were asked to perform certain tasks. Some of them were given tasks that were much more difficult than they seemed to be—so difficult, in fact, that the subjects were bound to fail. Then they were given a second task, this one only moderately difficult. Those who had been forced to fail on the first task performed the second task worse than others who had never attempted

*L*ike thousands of others, this family of seven, refugees from drought-stricken Oklahoma, went to California during the Depression of the 1930s hoping to get work picking cotton. But no work, no home, and no prospects became their daily lessons in helplessness. They discovered what one character in John Steinbeck's book The Grapes of Wrath *says, "Okie use' to mean you was from Oklahoma. Now it means you're scum."*

FIGURE 14.16

The cycle of learned helplessness.

the first task (Figure 14.16). Apparently they had lost their self-esteem, felt "low," and were somewhat depressed. The depression was mild, however, and vanished as soon as the experimenter explained that they had not really "failed" on the first task. Experiments of this type suggest that the learned-helplessness theory may be applicable to humans.

Do Depressed People Underestimate Their Control of Events?

According to the learned-helplessness theory, some people become depressed because they believe they have little control over events. But do they really underestimate their control, or do they just *seem* to underestimate it, because everyone else *over*estimates it? Lauren Alloy and Lyn Abramson (1979) set up an experiment to answer those questions.

First, students were asked to fill out a questionnaire designed to measure depression. Those with higher-than-average scores were considered depressed; the others were considered undepressed.

(We do not know whether depressed college students are representative of other depressed people.)

Then the students were told to try to get a green light to come on, either by pressing a button or by not pressing it. Pressing the button might either increase or decrease the probability that the light would come on. Consequently, the students should try both pressing and not pressing to see what would happen. The apparatus was set up so that some students had a great deal of control: One response (either pressing or not pressing) would turn the light on 75% of the time, while the other response would never turn it on. Other students had less control, and some had no control at all.

Afterward, the experimenters asked subjects to estimate how much control they had had over the outcome. The depressed subjects estimated their control fairly accurately in each situation. The subjects who were not depressed estimated correctly when they had at least 25% control, but they seriously overestimated when they had no control (see Figure 14.17a). In other words, the depressed people did not underestimate their control over the light. On the contrary, the normal, undepressed people had an illusion of control when, in fact, they did not have control.

We could interpret that result in two ways (Schwartz, 1981). First, some people become depressed because they perceive—rightly or wrongly—that they have no control. And perhaps other people do *not* become depressed because they maintain an illusion of controlling their fate even when it is out of their hands. Depressed people say, "I'm not pessimistic, just realistic." Maybe they are right.

Second, perhaps people become depressed for other reasons, but after becoming depressed they begin to recognize their lack of control. We do not know which interpretation is correct.

For whatever reason, people who are not depressed tend to take an optimistic view of their ability to control events, and of their abilities in general. In another experiment, depressed and undepressed people were asked to guess how highly other people would rate their social qualities. The depressed people guessed pretty accurately (Figure 14.17b). Most of the undepressed people overestimated other people's ratings of them (Lewinsohn, Mischel, Chaplin, & Barton, 1980).

Concept Check

11. Why do most students predict that they will raise their grades in the future? And why does almost every sports coach predict that his or her team will

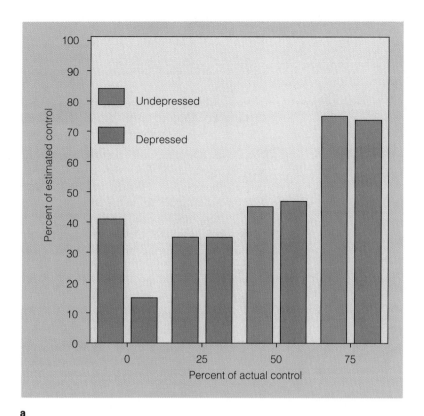

a

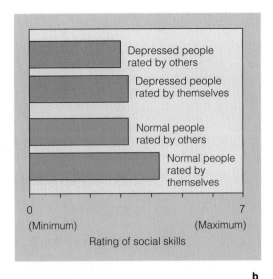

b

Figure 14.17

(a) Estimates of amount of control of a light by depressed and undepressed people in a situation in which actual control varied from 0% to 75%. Note the results when subjects had no control. Depressed subjects believe they have a slight amount of control; undepressed subjects believe they have more than 40% control! (Based on data of Alloy & Abramson, 1979.)
(b) Depressed people also seem to be more accurate in guessing what other people think of them than undepressed people are.

do better this year than last? Would depressed people be more or less likely than undepressed people to buy a lottery ticket or to bet on the horses? (Check your answers on page 555.)

Learned Helplessness and Attributions for Failure

Having an unpleasant experience is usually not enough in itself to make a person depressed. People become depressed only if they believe they are somehow to blame for the unpleasant experience. Suppose you fail a French test. How bad do you feel? The answer depends on why you think you failed. You might attribute your failure to any of a number of causes:

- I failed because the test was so hard. This prof always makes the first test of the semester extra difficult just to scare us into studying harder.

- I failed because I'm the only one in the class who didn't take French in high school.

- I failed because I was sick and didn't get a chance to study.

- I failed because I'm stupid.

With any of the first three attributions for failure, you probably wouldn't feel very depressed.

You would be attributing your failure to something that wasn't your fault. But the fourth attribution applies to you at all times in all situations. If you make that attribution—and if your French grade is important to you—you are likely to feel depressed. And if you are already depressed, you are likely to make that attribution (Abramson, Seligman, & Teasdale, 1978; Peterson, Bettes, & Seligman, 1985).

Depressed people tend to attribute their failures to factors that are stable (long-lasting), global (applicable to many situations), and internal (within themselves). However, they attribute their successes to external forces or to luck. In terms of the "locus of control" personality trait discussed in Chapter 13, depressed people tend to show an external locus of control (Benassi, Sweeney, & Dufour, 1988; Costello, 1982).

But which came first: the depression or the feeling of helplessness and the attribution of failure to personal inadequacies? It is difficult to determine what caused what, because many people become depressed and develop attitudes of helplessness at about the same time (Barnett & Gotlib, 1988; Silverman, Silverman, & Eardley, 1984).

Something to Think About

Are nations as well as individuals subject to learned helplessness? If so, might this principle explain why

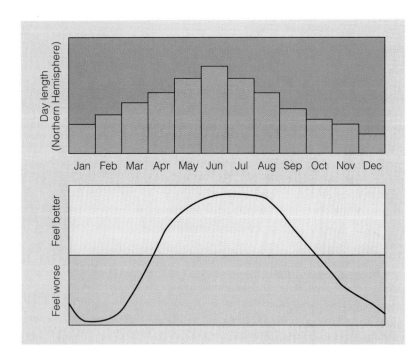

Figure 14.18

In June the number of hours of daylight is more than double the number during December in most of the United States. But for people with seasonal affective disorder, December 21st may feel like the longest day of the year. Such people swing from mild mania in summer to depression in winter because of changes in the amount of daylight.

some nations decide that it is pointless to negotiate with other nations? Can you think of other examples in an international setting?

Seasonal Affective Disorder

One variety of depression is known as **seasonal affective disorder**, or *depression with a seasonal pattern* (Figure 14.18). People with this disorder become seriously depressed every winter. In summer they are either normal or slightly manic (the opposite of depressed). Unlike most other depressed patients, they tend to sleep and eat excessively during their depressed periods (Jacobsen, Sack, Wehr, Rogers, & Rosenthal, 1987).

People with seasonal affective disorder respond to the amount of sunlight they see each day. Most of us are more cheerful when the sun is shining than we are on cloudy days, but these people are particularly sensitive to the effects of sunlight. Seasonal affective disorder can be relieved by sitting for a few hours each day in front of a bright light after the sun sets or before it rises—in effect, artificially lengthening the day (Wehr et al., 1986).

Concept Check

12. In which parts of the world should seasonal affective disorder be most common? (Check your answer on page 555.)

Bipolar Disorder

People with bipolar disorder alternate between the extremes of mania and depression. In most respects, **mania** is the opposite of depression. When people with bipolar disorder are in the depressed phase, they are slow, inactive, and inhibited. When they are in the manic phase, they are constantly active and uninhibited. When depressed, they feel helpless, guilt ridden, and sad. When manic, they are either happy or angry. About 1% of all adults in the United States suffer from bipolar disorder at some time during their life (Robins et al., 1984).

People in a manic phase follow their every impulse. Mental hospitals cannot install fire alarms in certain wards because manic patients cannot resist pulling the alarm every time they pass. Manic people make costly mistakes of judgment. Such a person might quit his job, mortgage his house, and withdraw all his money from the bank to raise money for an exciting new idea—perhaps the manufacture of solar-powered flashlights. His friends plead, "But there's no market for them. They only work when the sun is out, and people don't *need* flashlights when the sun is out." The manic person goes right ahead with the scheme: "After all, even if there is no market, a good salesperson can always *create* a market."

The rambling speech of a manic person has been described as a "flight of ideas." The person starts talking about one topic, which suggests another, which suggests another. Here is a quote from a manic patient:

I like playing pool a lot, that's one of my releases, that I play pool a lot. Oh what else? Bartend, bartend on the side, it's kind of fun to, if you're a bartender you can, you can see how people reacted, amounts of alcohol and different guys around, different chicks around, and different situations, if it's snowing outside, if it's cold outside, the weather conditions, all types of different types of environments and types of different types of people you'll usually find in a bar [Hoffman, Stopek, & Andreasen, 1986, page 835].

Some people experience a mild degree of mania ("hypomania") almost always. They are productive, popular, extroverted, "life-of-the-party" types. Mania may become so serious, however, that it makes normal life impossible.

The theatrical director Joshua Logan has described his own experiences with depression and mania (Fieve, 1975). A few excerpts follow.

A Self-Report: Depressive Phase

I had no faith in the work I was doing or the people I was working with. . . . It was a great burden to get up in the morning and I couldn't wait to go to bed at night, even though I started not sleeping well. . . . I thought I was well but feeling low because of a hidden personal discouragement of some sort—something I couldn't quite put my finger on. . . . I just forced myself to live through a dreary, hopeless existence that lasted for months on end. . . .

My depressions actually began around the age of thirty-two. I remember I was working on a play, and I was forcing myself to work. . . . I can remember that I sat in some sort of aggravated agony as it was read aloud for the first time by the cast. It sounded so awful that I didn't want to direct it. I didn't even want to see it. I remember feeling so depressed that I wished that I were dead without having to go through the shame and defeat of suicide. I couldn't sleep well at all, and sleep meant, for me, oblivion, and that's what I longed for and couldn't get. I didn't know what to do and I felt very, very lost [Fieve, 1975, pages 42–43].

A Self-Report: Manic Phase

Here, Logan (Fieve, pages 43–45) describes his manic experiences:

Finally, as time passed, the depression gradually wore off and turned into something else, which I didn't understand either. But it was a much pleasanter thing to go through, at least at first. Instead of hating everything, I started liking things—liking them too much, perhaps. . . . I put out a thousand ideas a minute: things to do, plays to write, plots to write stories about. . . .

I decided to get married on the spur of the moment. . . . I practically forced her to say yes. Suddenly we had a loveless marriage and that had to be broken up overnight. . . .

I can only remember that I worked constantly, day and night, never even seeming to need more than a few hours of sleep. I always had a new idea or another conference. . . . It was an exhilarating time for me.

It finally went too far. In the end I went over the bounds of reality, or law and order, so to say.

I don't mean that I committed any crimes, but I could easily have done so if anyone had crossed me. I flew into rages if contradicted. I began to be irritable with everyone. Should a man, friend or foe, object to anything I did or said, it was quite possible that I could poke him in the jaw. I was eventually persuaded by the doctors that I was desperately ill and should go into the hospital. But it was not, even then, convincing to me that I was ill.

There I was, on the sixth floor of a New York building that had special iron bars around it and an iron gate that had slid into place and locked me away from the rest of the world. . . . I looked about and saw that there was an open window. I leaped up on the sill and climbed out of the window on the ledge on the sixth floor and said, "Unless you open the door, I'm going to climb down the outside of this building." At the time, I remember feeling so powerful that I might actually be able to scale the building. . . . They immediately opened the steel door, and I climbed back in. That's where manic elation can take you.

Bipolar Cycles

A manic period or a depressed period may last for months or for just a day. Figure 14.19 shows the mood ratings for a manic-depressive woman over three weeks (Richter, 1938). Note that she alternated day by day. She slept more on her cheerful

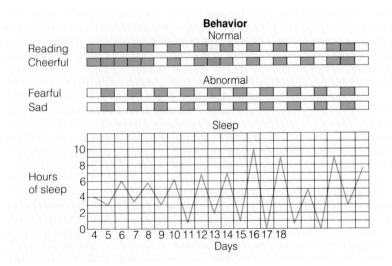

FIGURE 14.19

Riding an emotional roller coaster: Records for a woman who had one-day manic periods alternating with one-day depressed periods. Green means definitely, blue means somewhat, and white means no. Note that days of cheerfulness and reading alternated with days of fearfulness and sadness. (Based on Richter, 1938.)

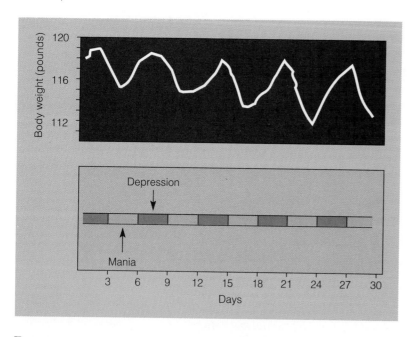

FIGURE 14.20

Records for a man who had three-day manic periods (light blue) alternating with three-day depressed periods (dark blue). Note that he loses weight during manic times because of his high activity level. (Based on Crammer, 1959.)

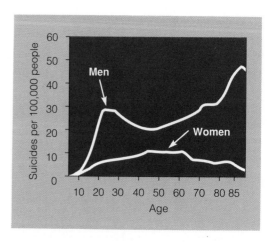

FIGURE 14.21

Annual suicide rates for men and women as a function of age. (Based on Boyd, 1983.)

days than on her sad days. Figure 14.20 shows the mood and body weight fluctuations for a manic-depressive man who had three-day manic periods and three-day depressed periods (Crammer, 1959). In many patients the depressed periods last longer than the manic periods.

SUICIDE

Résumé

Razors pain you;
Rivers are damp;
Acids stain you;
And drugs cause cramp.

Guns aren't lawful;
Nooses give;
Gas smells awful;
You might as well live.

DOROTHY PARKER
(1944)

Many psychologically disturbed people attempt suicide, especially those who are depressed. Suicide is one of the most common causes of death among young people. Figure 14.21 shows the estimated rates of suicide as a function of age (Boyd, 1983). Accurate records are hard to come by, because an unknown number of people disguise their suicides to look like accidents, either to reduce their family's anguish or to enable their survivors to collect life insurance.

Women make more suicide attempts than men, yet more men than women die by suicide (Cross & Hirschfeld, 1986). Most men who attempt suicide use guns or other violent means. Women are more likely to try poison, drugs, or other relatively slow, nonviolent, uncertain methods (Rich, Ricketts, Fowler, & Young, 1988). Many women who injure themselves in suicide attempts are believed to be crying out for help and not really trying to kill themselves (Barnes, 1985). That is particularly true of young women. Unfortunately, some of them actually die, and others are handicapped for life.

Warning Signs of Possible Suicide

Suicide follows no dependable pattern. There are no set clues that tell you someone is likely to attempt suicide. However, certain factors are associated with an increased probability of attempting suicide. Anyone working with troubled people should be aware of these warning signals. Suicide attempts are most common among the types of people in Table 14.6.

Some Questions and Answers About Suicide

If you suspect that someone you know is thinking about suicide, what should you do? Treat the person like a normal human being. Don't assume that the person is so fragile that one wrong word will be disastrous. Don't be afraid to ask, "You have been looking depressed. Have you been thinking about suicide?" You may do the person a favor by showing that you are not frightened by the thought and that you are willing to talk about it.

People think about suicide when they are in pain, either mental or physical. You may not be able to guess what kind of pain someone is feeling. Be prepared to listen.

Urge the person to get professional help. Most large cities have a suicide prevention hotline listed in the white pages of the telephone directory.

Is it true that someone who has attempted sui-

TABLE 14.6 People Most Likely to Attempt Suicide

- Depressed people, especially those with disordered thinking (Roose, Glassman, Walsh, Woodring, & Vital-Herne, 1983)

- People who have untreated psychological disorders (Brent et al., 1988)

- People who have recently suffered the death of a spouse and men who have recently been divorced or separated, especially those who have little social support from friends and family (Blumenthal & Kupfer, 1986)

- People who during their childhood or adolescence lost a parent through death or divorce (Adam, 1986)

- Drug and alcohol abusers (Rich, Fowler, Fogarty, & Young, 1988)

- Children and adolescents who are not living with both parents, who have a family history of psychiatric disorders, or who have a history of drug abuse (Garfinkel, Froese, & Hood, 1982)

- People with guns in their home, particularly those with a history of violent attacks on others (Brent et al., 1988)

- People whose relatives have suffered depression or who have committed suicide (Blumenthal & Kupfer, 1986)

- People with low activity of the neurotransmitter serotonin in the brain (Mann, McBride, & Stanley, 1986)

cide but survived will never actually commit suicide? No. In fact, about one third of those who survive one attempt eventually kill themselves (Blumenthal & Kupfer, 1986).

Is it true that people who talk about committing suicide will not really do so? Not necessarily. Threats of suicide should be taken seriously. Many people who talk about suicide are crying out for help. They are saying, "Please stop me." If they do not get the help they need, they may attempt suicide.

Is it true that most suicides are planned well in advance? People who are thinking about suicide usually send out warning signals well in advance. However, one study found that more than half of the people who make a serious suicide attempt do so on the spur of the moment; they decide on suicide less than 24 hours before making the attempt (Peterson, Peterson, O'Shanick, & Swann, 1985).

SUMMARY

1. A depressed person takes little interest or pleasure in life, feels worthless, powerless, and guilty, and may consider suicide. Such a person has trouble sleeping, loses interest in sex and eating, and cannot concentrate. A major depression is more severe and longer lasting than other depressions. (page 535)

2. Some people are predisposed to depression by genetic or other biological factors, by early experiences such as the loss of a parent, or by poor social support in adulthood. (page 536)

3. Depressed people interpret disappointing experiences as personal failures. They act as if they believe they are helpless in the face of adversity. (page 537)

4. Depressed people accurately assess their lack of control in situations in which they do have low control, while people who are not depressed generally believe they have more control than they do. (page 538)

5. Seasonal affective disorder is an uncommon condition in which people become depressed during the winter and somewhat manic during the summer. (page 540)

6. People with bipolar disorder alternate between periods of depression and periods of mania, in which they engage in constant, driven, uninhibited activity. (page 540)

7. Although it is difficult to know who will or will not attempt suicide, it is common among depressed people and people who show certain other warning signs. (page 542)

SUGGESTIONS FOR FURTHER READING

Beers, C. W. (1948). *A mind that found itself.* Garden City, NJ: Doubleday. (Original work published 1908). An autobiography of a man who recovered from a severe case of bipolar disorder.

Galton, L. (1979). *You may not need a psychiatrist.* New York: Simon & Schuster. Suggests that depression and other psychological disorders may be caused by improper diet, inappropriate sleep schedules, and other bad habits.

SCHIZOPHRENIA AND AUTISM

What is schizophrenia?
What causes it?
What can be done about it?
What is autism?

We all have strange dreams and fantasies at one time or another. I once dreamed that I saw a bird larger than an airplane. I have dreamed of being dead, of being a child again, of being able to fly. I have fantasized about being President of the United States and of being a famous athlete. And I have had other fantasies I keep to myself. You have your own dreams and fantasies. But most of us have no trouble distinguishing between fantasy and reality.

Some people do confuse fantasy with reality. They may claim that they are the President of the United States or a messenger from God, that they are receiving messages from outer space, or that everyone is persecuting them. Their speech may jump from one topic to another, rather like the events in a dream. They are suffering from a disorder called schizophrenia.

THE SYMPTOMS OF SCHIZOPHRENIA

Schizophrenia is a generally severe, widely misunderstood psychological disorder. It was once known as *dementia praecox,* a Latin term that translates loosely as "premature senility." The resemblance between schizophrenia and senility is superficial, however, and that term fell out of favor. The term *schizophrenia* is based on Greek roots meaning split mind. It does *not* refer to a split into two minds or personalities, but a split between the intellectual and emotional aspects of the person-

ality, as if the intellect and the emotions were no longer in contact with each other. (Television programs and movies sometimes confuse schizophrenia with *multiple personality.* A person with schizophrenia has an abnormal personality but has only one personality.)

A person suffering from schizophrenia may seem happy or sad without cause or may fail to show emotions in a situation that normally evokes them. Such a person may even report bad news cheerfully or good news sadly. To be diagnosed with **schizophrenia**, according to DSM III-R, a person must exhibit a deterioration of daily activities over a period of at least six months, including work, social relations, and self-care. He or she must *also* exhibit either hallucinations, delusions, flat or inappropriate emotions, certain movement disorders, or thought disorders. If the hallucinations are not prominent or the delusions are not bizarre, then the person must exhibit one of the other symptoms as well.

Hallucinations and Other Symptoms

A person subject to **hallucinations** has sensory experiences that do not correspond to anything in the outside world. Most commonly, people with schizophrenia hear voices and other sounds that no one else hears. Not all schizophrenic people hear voices, but most people who do are suffering from schizophrenia. The "voices" may speak only nonsense, or they may tell the person to carry out certain acts. Sometimes hallucinating people think the voices are real, sometimes they know the voices are coming from within their own head, and sometimes they are not sure (Junginger & Frame, 1985). Few people with schizophrenia have visual hallucinations, which are more characteristic of drug abusers. Occasionally, some have distorted or exaggerated visual experiences. (See Figure 14.22.)

There are several common types of **delusions,** which are unfounded beliefs. A **delusion of persecution** is a belief that "people are out to get me." A **delusion of grandeur** is a belief that one is a special messenger from God or that one has some other unusually exalted position in the world. A **delusion of reference** is a tendency to interpret all sorts of messages as if they were meant for oneself. Someone with a delusion of reference may interpret a headline in the morning newspaper as a coded message or may take a television announcer's comments as personal insults. People with delusions do not always hold them with great conviction (Rudden, Gilmore, & Allen, 1982), but they sometimes act on them nevertheless.

Many people with schizophrenia show little sign of emotion. Their faces seldom express emotion, and they speak without the inflections most people use for emphasis. When they do show emotions, the expressions are inappropriate, such as laughing for no reason.

Some people with schizophrenia have a movement disorder called catatonia. **Catatonia** may take the form of either rigid inactivity or excessive activity; in either case, the person's movements or lack of movements seem to be unrelated to stimuli in the outside world.

The Thought Disorder of Schizophrenia

One characteristic of schizophrenic thought is the use of *loose and idiosyncratic associations,* somewhat like the illogical leaps that occur in dreams. For example, one man used the words *Jesus, cigar,* and *sex* as synonyms. When he was asked to explain, he said they were all the same because Jesus has a halo around his head, a cigar has a band around it, and during sex people put their arms around each other.

Another characteristic of schizophrenic thought is *difficulty in using abstract concepts* (Wright, 1975). For instance, many people with schizophrenia have trouble sorting objects into categories. Many also give strictly literal responses when asked to interpret the meaning of proverbs. Here are some examples (Krueger, 1978, pages 196–197):

Proverb: People who live in glass houses shouldn't throw stones.
Interpretation: "It would break the glass."

Proverb: All that glitters is not gold.
Interpretation: "It might be brass."

Proverb: A stitch in time saves nine.
Interpretation: "If you take one stitch for a small tear now, it will save nine later."

Because of this tendency to interpret everything literally, people with schizophrenic thought disorder often misunderstand simple statements. On being taken to the admitting office of a hospital, one person said, "Oh, is this where people go to admit their faults?"

Many schizophrenic people use vague, roundabout ways of saying something simple. For instance, one such person said, "I was born with a male sense"

FIGURE 14.22

These portraits graphically illustrate their artist's progressive psychosis. When well-known animal artist Louis Wain (1860–1939) began suffering delusions of persecution, his drawings showed a schizophrenic's disturbing distortions in perception.

instead of "I'm a man." They often take many words to say almost nothing. They ramble aimlessly when they speak and write, as in this excerpt from a letter one man wrote to his mother:

I am writing on paper. The pen which I am using is from a factory called "Perry & Co." This factory is in England. I assume this. Behind the name of Perry Co. the city of London is inscribed; but not the city. The city of London is in England. I know this from my school-days. Then, I always liked geography. My last teacher in that subject was Professor August A. He was a man with black eyes. I also like black eyes. There are also blue and gray eyes and other sorts, too. I have heard it said that snakes have green eyes. All people have eyes. There are some, too, who are blind. These blind people are led about by a boy. It must be very terrible not to be able to see. There are people who can't see and, in addition, can't hear. I know some who hear too much [Bleuler, 1911, page 17].

The Distinction Between Positive and Negative Symptoms

Many investigators distinguish between positive symptoms and negative symptoms of schizophrenia (Andreasen & Olsen 1982; Crow, 1985). **Positive symptoms** are characteristics present in people with schizophrenia and absent in others—such as hallucinations, delusions, and thought disorder. **Negative symptoms** are behaviors that are present in other people—such as the ability to take care of themselves—but absent in schizophrenic people. Other common negative symptoms include the lack of emotional expression, a lack of social interaction, a deficit of speech, and a lack of pleasure.

Some patients have mostly positive symptoms; others have mostly negative symptoms. Investigators originally considered the possibility that the causes of positive symptoms might be different from those of negative symptoms and that patients with mostly positive symptoms might respond to treatment better than those with mostly negative symptoms. However, the research so far has not supported these hypotheses decisively (Crow, 1985; Farmer, Jackson, McGuffin, & Storey, 1987).

Types of Schizophrenia

In some schizophrenic patients, a particular set of symptoms may be especially prominent. Depending on which symptoms they exhibit, they are said to be suffering from one of four types of schizophrenia: undifferentiated, catatonic, paranoid, or disorganized schizophrenia.

Undifferentiated schizophrenia is characterized by the basic symptoms—a deterioration of daily activities, plus some combination of hallucinations, delusions, inappropriate emotions, movement disorders, and thought disorders. However, none of these symptoms is unusually pronounced or bizarre.

Catatonic schizophrenia is characterized by the basic symptoms plus prominent movement disorders. The affected person may go through periods of extremely rapid, mostly repetitive activity alternating with periods of total inactivity. During the inactive periods he or she may hold a given posture without moving and may resist attempts to alter that posture. Catatonic schizophrenia has become less

common over the years and is now fairly rare.

Disorganized schizophrenia is characterized by incoherent speech, extreme lack of social relationships, and "silly" or "odd" behavior. For example, one man gift-wrapped one of his feces and proudly presented it to his therapist. Here is a conversation with someone suffering from disorganized schizophrenia (Duke & Nowicki, 1979):

INTERVIEWER: *How does it feel to have your problems?*

PATIENT: *Who can tell me the name of my song? I don't know, but it won't be long. It won't be short, tall, none at all. My head hurts, my knees hurt— my nephew, his uncle, my aunt. My God, I'm happy . . . not a care in the world. My hair's been curled, the flag's unfurled. This is my country, land that I love, this is the country, land that I love.*

INTERVIEWER: *How do you feel?*

PATIENT: *Happy! Don't you hear me? Why do you talk to me? (barks like a dog) [Duke & Nowicki, 1979, page 162].*

Paranoid schizophrenia is characterized by the basic symptoms plus hallucinations and delusions, especially delusions of persecution and delusions of grandeur. Most people with paranoid schizophrenia have undergone less deterioration than have people suffering from other types of schizophrenia. They generally take better care of themselves and operate at a higher intellectual level. They can manage their own lives reasonably well, except for their constant suspicion that they are surrounded by spies or that evil forces from Mars are trying to control their minds.

Paranoid schizophrenia tends not to run in the same families as other types of schizophrenia do (Farmer, McGuffin, & Gottesman, 1987). In some ways, it resembles depression more than it resembles other types of schizophrenia (Zigler & Glick, 1988).

Although the distinctions among these types of schizophrenia are convenient, they are not absolute. Some people fall on the borderline of two or more types of schizophrenia, perhaps switching back and forth between them. Switching is especially common between undifferentiated schizophrenia and one of the other types (Kendler, Gruenberg, & Tsuang, 1985).

Concept Check

13. Why are people more likely to switch between undifferentiated schizophrenia and one of the other types than, say, between disorganized schizophrenia and one of the other types? (Check your answer on page 555.)

b

(a) A person suffering from catatonic
schizophrenia may hold a bizarre posture
for hours and alternate this rigid stupor
with equally purposeless, excited activity.
Such people may stubbornly resist attempts
to change their behavior, but they need
supervision to avoid hurting themselves or
others. (b) A patient with disorganized
schizophrenia.

a

Prevalence and Onset of Schizophrenia

Approximately 1 to 2% of Americans are afflicted with schizophrenia at some point in their life (Robins et al., 1984). The exact percentage may be slightly higher or lower, depending on how many "borderline" cases we include. Schizophrenia occurs in all countries and in all ethnic groups, although it is apparently rare in the tropics and especially prevalent in densely populated areas of cities. It is about as common among men as among women.

Schizophrenia is most frequently diagnosed in young adults in their teens or 20s. A first diagnosis is rare after age 30 and unheard of after age 45. The onset is sometimes sudden but is usually gradual.

Efforts at Early Diagnosis

Schizophrenia is difficult to diagnose. Suppose someone shows a slight thought disorder along with mild depression and moderate deterioration of everyday functioning. Should we treat that person for schizophrenia or depression or for both or neither? A mistake can be costly. The drugs used to combat schizophrenia are most effective for people who start taking them early. If a therapist postpones

drug treatment until the symptoms are full blown, it may be too late for the drugs to do much good. Yet prolonged use of the drugs can produce harmful side effects. So it is important to avoid giving the drugs to someone who does not need them.

Consequently, investigators are trying to diagnose schizophrenia as early and as accurately as possible. To some extent it is possible to do so by monitoring behavior, beginning in childhood. Most people with schizophrenia are described as having been "strange" children who had a short attention span, made few friends, often disrupted their classroom with "unusual" behaviors, and had mild thought disorders (Arboleda & Holzman, 1985; Parnas, Schulsinger, Schulsinger, Mednick, & Teasdale, 1982).

Another possible marker of schizophrenia is a test of eye movements. An examiner moves an object from side to side and asks people to keep their eyes on it. Although only about 8% of people without schizophrenia have trouble maintaining these **pursuit eye movements**, 80% of people with schizophrenia move their eyes in a series of rapid jerks instead of moving them smoothly (Holzman, 1985). The impairment of eye movements shows itself before the onset of schizophrenic behavior and persists even after successful drug therapy

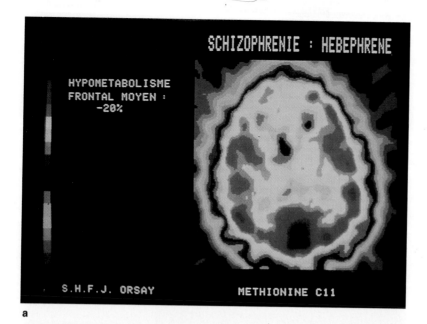

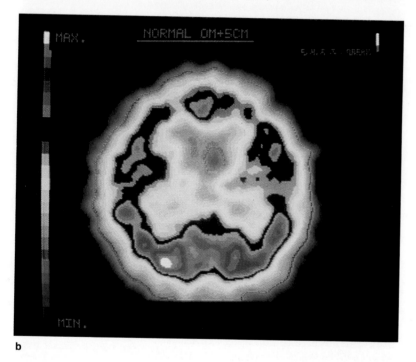

FIGURE 14.23

Positron emission tomography (PET) scans of the brain of (a) a person who has untreated schizophrenia and (b) a normal person. PET scans rely on the brain's use of glucose to fuel its activity. A person is injected with a minute dose of a radioactive chemical similar to glucose. That chemical tends to concentrate where there is increased activity (where the brain is using glucose), and it is detected by the radioactivity it emits. A computer processes the resulting signals to produce these maps showing what brain areas are most active. Red indicates the highest concentration of the radioactive chemical—and thus of brain activity. Certain areas of the brain, especially the frontal lobes, appear to be less active in many schizophrenic people than they are in people without schizophrenia.

(Holzman et al., 1988). In other words, it signals that a person is likely to develop schizophrenia. The eye-movement test is not sufficiently accurate by itself to diagnose an individual, but it can help to support a diagnosis in a marginal case (Lipton & Wong, 1989).

CAUSES OF SCHIZOPHRENIA

Most investigators now believe that schizophrenia is a biological disorder that can be either aggravated or relieved by various experiences. However, the nature of the biological disorder and the nature of the relevant experiences are both unclear.

Evidence of Brain Damage

Unlike people suffering from other psychological disorders, people suffering from schizophrenia show minor but widespread brain damage (see Figure 14.23). The cerebral cortex is somewhat shrunken in one fourth to one third of all schizophrenic patients, and the cerebral ventricles (fluid-filled spaces in the brain) are enlarged in about half of them (Pfefferbaum, 1988; Seidman, 1983; Smythies, 1982). People with schizophrenia generally perform as poorly on the same tasks as do people with damage to the frontal or temporal lobes of the cerebral cortex (Kolb & Whishaw, 1983; Weinberger, Berman, & Illowsky, 1988).

One hypothesis is that schizophrenic people, through some abnormal biochemical pathway, produce a chemical that gradually destroys their brain cells (Stein & Wise, 1971). This hypothesis fits the finding that brain damage in schizophrenic people increases over time. The longer people suffer from schizophrenia, the larger the ventricles in their brain and the smaller the space that is left for neurons (Woods & Wolf, 1983).

Concept Check

14. *Following a stroke a patient shows symptoms similar to schizophrenia. Where is the brain damage probably located? (Check your answer on page 555.)*

The Dopamine Theory of Schizophrenia

Schizophrenia is commonly treated with drugs. All the effective drugs share one characteristic: They block dopamine synapses in the brain. In fact, the therapeutic effectiveness of these drugs is nearly proportional to their tendency to block those synapses (Seeman & Lee, 1975). This relationship has led to the **dopamine theory of schizophrenia,** which holds that the underlying cause of schizophrenia is excessive stimulation of certain dopamine synapses. That stimulation may occur in part because other, competing synapses are being destroyed.

Genetic Factors

What causes the brain damage often associated with schizophrenia and the apparent overactivity of dopamine synapses? Perhaps a particular gene produces chemicals that damage certain neurons or that make certain neurons more active than others. Substantial evidence supports this genetic predisposition for schizophrenia.

If one member of a pair of identical twins develops schizophrenia, there is almost a 50% chance that the other will develop it too (Matthysse & Kidd, 1976). (See Figure 14.24.) That figure understates the role of genetics in schizophrenia, however, because a high percentage of the twins who do not develop schizophrenia will suffer from *other* serious psychological disturbances, including "borderline" schizophrenia (Farmer, McGuffin, & Gottesman, 1987; Kendler & Robinette, 1983). Furthermore, the schizophrenic twin and the non-schizophrenic twin run an equal risk of passing schizophrenia on to their children (Nicol & Gottesman, 1983). Apparently some gene or genes tend to increase the likelihood of schizophrenia. Although certain environmental factors determine whether those genes will lead to schizophrenia, some other disorder, or no disorder at all, the person still passes the genes to the next generation.

One massive study of adoption records in Denmark identified 34 adopted children who later became schizophrenic. Schizophrenia was much more common among their biological relatives than among their adoptive relatives (Kety, 1977, 1983; Lowing, Mirsky, & Pereira, 1983). That evidence indicates that either genetics or the prenatal environment has a strong influence on schizophrenia.

Something to Think About

People suffering from schizophrenia are less likely than others to have children. This is particularly true of schizophrenic men, partly because they have a weaker-than-average sex drive and partly because they are socially inept. So it is difficult to imagine how a gene that leads to schizophrenia could spread enough to affect 1% of the population. Can you imagine a possible explanation?

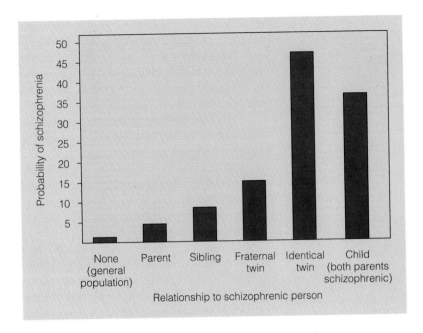

FIGURE 14.24

Schizophrenia in biological relatives. A concordance rate of 100% would mean that if one member of the biologically related pair is schizophrenic, the other person will be, too. Note that if a fraternal twin is schizophrenic, the concordance rate is close to that of any other sibling. But if an identical twin is schizophrenic, the concordance rate is far higher. (After Gottesman, 1978.)

The Role of Experience

Assuming that genes predispose certain people to schizophrenia, what environmental factors determine whether or not those genes will be expressed as schizophrenia? Some years ago, psychologists suggested that mothers who gave a confusing mixture of "come here" and "go away" signals were likely to induce schizophrenia in their children. That theory has been discarded, for several reasons.

One reason is that it does not fit the data on adoptions. The child of a schizophrenic parent who is adopted by normal parents has a high risk of developing schizophrenia, whereas other adopted children reared in the same family generally do not become schizophrenic. So it seems unlikely that confusing signals from the mother are responsible for schizophrenia.

Another reason is that the suggested cause does not seem sufficient to produce the effect. Even abused and battered children seldom develop schizophrenia. It is unlikely that confusing verbal signals would cause even greater damage.

Finally, the "bad mother" theory does not fit the course of the disorder over time. If the mother's behavior were the main cause of the problem, we would expect the child to improve when separated from her. In fact, schizophrenia usually develops in early adulthood—when most people become independent of their parents—and gradually grows more severe from then on unless drugs are administered.

A more reasonable hypothesis is that the onset of schizophrenia may be triggered by stress. Note the word *triggered*. Although stress probably does not *cause* schizophrenia, it may aggravate the symptoms. The effect of stress is difficult to measure, however, because the term *stress* is imprecise and subjective; events that are stressful for one person may not be stressful for another.

Judith Rabkin (1980) reviewed studies in which schizophrenic people were asked to report any stressful events that had occurred during the months just before they developed schizophrenia. The frequency of stressful events turned out to be only slightly higher than normal. This finding could mean any of several things: The schizophrenic people may have forgotten the stressful events they experienced; stress may not be particularly significant in the onset of schizophrenia; the critically stressful events may have occurred more than a few months before the onset of the disorder; or people who are susceptible to schizophrenia may overrespond to very mild stress. We shall need further studies, preferably longitudinal studies, to decide among these possibilities.

Infections During Early Development

A person born in the winter months is slightly more likely to develop schizophrenia than a person born at any other time (Bradbury & Miller, 1985). No other psychological disorder has this characteristic. Moreover, investigators have clearly demonstrated this **season of birth effect** only in the northern climates, not near the equator. Evidently, something about the weather at or near the time of birth contributes to some people's vulnerability to schizophrenia.

One possible explanation is that an infant born during the winter months is more likely to be infected by a virus or a bacterium that damages the brain. If so, the brain damage probably occurs at once, even though the person may not show clear signs of schizophrenia until many years later. If the damage occurs in the prefrontal cortex, few effects will be apparent during childhood, because that cortical area does not become fully functional until adolescence. As the brain begins to rely more and more on that area, the effects of the damage become more evident (Weinberger, 1987).

A damaging infection may exert its effects before birth. For example, a major influenza epidemic struck Helsinki, Finland, in October and November 1957. Women who were then in their second trimester of pregnancy gave birth to a large number of infants who eventually became schizophrenic adults (Mednick, Machon, Huttunen, & Bonett, 1988). Perhaps an illness during the middle of pregnancy damages critical areas of the infant's developing brain.

The causes of schizophrenia are still not understood; what is clear is that schizophrenia depends on a number of influences, not just a single cause. Genetics, stress, and prenatal exposure to illness are likely influences on schizophrenia, but exactly how these and other influences interact will be a topic of research for years to come.

AUTISM

Autism is a disorder that resembles schizophrenia in certain ways, although the underlying causes are apparently quite different. The term *autism* literally means self-ism. (It comes from the same Greek root as does *automobile,* which literally means self-mover.) Autistic children live in a world of their own, socially unresponsive to other people.

Both childhood autism and schizophrenia are characterized by extreme social isolation, repetitive movements, and a failure to communicate with others. Autism and schizophrenia do not as a rule run in the same families, however, and the drugs that are effective in treating schizophrenia do nothing to autistic children except sedate them.

A rare condition that affects only about 1 child in 2,500, autism has an early onset. Parents often recognize that "something is wrong" by the time the child is 6 months old and invariably by age 3 years. Autism usually persists for a lifetime, although some improvement may occur. More than 75% of all autistic children are boys. Because it is generally a lifelong disorder beginning in infancy, DSM III-R lists it on Axis 2.

Symptoms

The following list contains the main symptoms of autism (Creak, 1961; Kanner, 1943; Ornitz & Ritvo, 1976):

- *Social isolation.* Autistic children almost never seek social contact with others. They pay little attention to what others are doing and learn almost nothing by imitation (Varni, Lovaas, Koegel, & Everett, 1979).

- *Stereotyped behaviors.* Autistic children repeat movements such as biting the hands, rotating an object, or flapping the arms.

- *Resistance to change in routine.* Autistic children protest any change in daily activities.

- *Abnormal responses to sensory stimuli.* Autistic children ignore much of what they see and hear and are extremely unresponsive to painful stimuli. They focus their attention narrowly on one stimulus or one activity and ignore everything else (Lovaas, Koegel, & Schreibman, 1979).

- *Inappropriate emotional expressions.* Autistic children engage in occasional outbursts of laughter or crying for no apparent reason. Emotions seem to arise from internal rather than external sources.

- *Great fluctuations in activity level.* Autistic children have periods of either inactivity or uncontrollably high activity.

- *Poor development of language.* Autistic children are very slow in learning to speak and to understand language. Some learn to speak as a parrot does, showing little evidence of comprehension. Many confuse the pronouns *me* and *you.*

- *Wide variation in performance between one intellectual task and another.* Many autistic children perform extraordinarily well on one task, such as memorization or music or mathematical calculations, but perform at the level of retarded people on other tasks.

What is it like to be autistic? Most autistic people can never answer that question for us. However, one man made a substantial recovery and described the experience (White & White, 1987). He said that he often experienced stimuli as being extremely intense. Noises were so loud and lights were so bright that he retreated into a world of his own as a means of escape.

As with schizophrenics, autistic children and adults seem to be locked into a universe of one, and when they express emotions, they do so in an odd manner. The autistic are also absorbed in a single activity or preoccupation, essentially disregarding the outside world and other people.

Possible Causes

Autism was first described by the psychiatrist Leo Kanner in 1943. Early studies reported that the condition occurs most often in families with highly intellectual, emotionally cold mothers, giving rise to the theory that children become autistic in reaction to such mothers. That theory has been abandoned, for two main reasons. One is that autistic children have been identified in all kinds of families—rich and poor, educated and uneducated (DeMyer, 1979). The other is that 98% of the broth-

ers and sisters of autistic children are psychologically normal. If the behavior of the mother were really the cause of autism, we would expect all her children to be at least somewhat abnormal.

Genetic factors may contribute to autism (Folstein & Rutter, 1977), but the fact that only about 2% percent of the brothers and sisters of autistic children are affected indicates that no single gene contributes strongly to autism. If genetic factors have any influence at all, we must assume that the impact comes either from a combination of several genes or from the interaction of genes with abnormal factors in the environment.

Many autistic children have a history of complications during the mother's pregnancy or around the time of birth (Links, Stockwell, Abichandani, & Simeon, 1980). Those complications lead to a wide variety of physical disorders, sleep disorders, electroencephalogram abnormalities, and enlargement of the ventricles of the brain (DeMyer, 1979).

One biological abnormality may be particularly important: Many autistic children have unusually high levels of endorphins, the brain chemicals that resemble morphine and inhibit pain (Gillberg, Terenius, & Lönnerholm, 1985). Several of the symptoms of autism resemble those of morphine users, including social withdrawal, insensitivity to pain, and a tendency to overrespond to stimuli at some times and to ignore them at others (Kalat, 1978; Panksepp, Herman, & Vilberg, 1978).

Treatment and Outcome

A combination of methods is generally used to treat autism. Many drugs have been tried, but so far none has brought consistently encouraging results.

Special education has proved somewhat successful in the treatment of autistic children, who learn best in a highly structured environment with a highly predictable routine (Schopler, 1987). An autistic child will pay attention to another person only if that person constantly demands the child's attention on a one-to-one basis. Autistic children gradually learn language under careful tutoring that combines spoken language and sign language—much as one teaches deaf children (Barrera, Lobato-Barrera, & Sulzer-Azaroff, 1980). Even then, however, some autistic children use language as a "trick" that they employ only in the environment in which they learned it (Handleman, 1979). Stereotyped behaviors can be eliminated by reducing the sensory stimulation they produce (Rincover, 1978). For instance, a hand-biting habit can be suppressed by forcing the child to wear gloves.

What happens to autistic children when they reach adulthood? According to one follow-up study of 80 autistic children, more than half spent their adult lives in mental institutions. Some lived with their parents or other relatives; a few progressed far enough to live independently and hold jobs. All but a few had continuing problems, including poor development of speech (Wolf & Goldberg, 1986).

SUMMARY

1. A person with schizophrenia is someone whose everyday functioning has deteriorated over a period of at least six months and who shows at least one of the following symptoms: hallucinations (mostly auditory), delusions, weak or inappropriate emotional expression, catatonic movements, and thought disorder. (page 544)

2. The thought disorder of schizophrenia is characterized by loose associations, impaired use of abstract concepts, and vague, wandering speech that conveys little information. (page 545)

3. Psychologists distinguish four types of schizophrenia: undifferentiated, catatonic, disorganized, and paranoid. Some authorities believe paranoid schizophrenia resembles depression more than it does other types of schizophrenia. (page 546)

4. Schizophrenia is usually first diagnosed in young adults. However, certain signs are evident in children, including mild thought disorder, lack of emotional contact with others, and impaired pursuit eye movements. (page 547)

5. Many people with schizophrenia show indications of mild brain damage. (page 548)

6. Schizophrenia is relieved by various drugs that block dopamine synapses in the brain. For that reason, many people believe schizophrenia is due to overactivity at certain dopamine synapses. (page 548)

7. A predisposition to schizophrenia may be inherited. However, experience influences the timing and intensity of schizophrenic behavioral episodes. (page 549)

8. Schizophrenia is more common in people born in the winter months, especially in cold climates. For that reason, some investigators believe that some cases of schizophrenia may be caused by a virus or bacterium contracted before or shortly after birth. (page 550)

9. Autism is a childhood condition that resembles schizophrenia in certain ways. Autistic children fail to seek social contact with other people. The causes of autism are uncertain, and no treatment produces reliably good results. (page 550)

SUGGESTION FOR FURTHER READING

Fann, W. E., Karacan, I., Pokorny, A., & Williams, R. L. (Eds.). (1978). *Phenomenology and treatment of schizophrenia.* New York: Spectrum. A comprehensive account of research on schizophrenia.

TERMS TO REMEMBER

addiction the inability to stop using a substance that impairs a person's health or well-being

agoraphobia a fear of open places or public places

Alcoholics Anonymous (AA) a self-help group of people who are trying to abstain from drinking alcohol and who are trying to help others do the same

alcoholism the habitual overuse of alcohol

Antabuse disulfiram, a drug that blocks the breakdown of acetaldehyde into acetic acid

autism a lifelong condition beginning in childhood that is characterized by extreme social isolation, repetitive movements, and failure to communicate

bipolar disorder a disorder marked by alternation between two emotional extremes, depression and mania

catatonia a condition of either rigid inactivity or excessive activity unrelated to external stimuli

catatonic schizophrenia a condition marked by the basic symptoms of schizophrenia plus prominent movement disorders

compulsion a repetitive, almost irresistible action

conversion disorder a condition in which a person shows symptoms such as paralysis, blindness, or deafness, apparently for psychological rather than medical reasons

delusion an unfounded belief

delusion of grandeur a person's unfounded belief that he or she is extraordinarily important

delusion of persecution a person's unfounded belief that other people are trying to hurt him or her

delusion of reference a person's tendency to interpret all messages as if they referred to himself or herself

dependence the inability to stop using a substance that impairs a person's health or well-being

depression a condition in which a person takes little pleasure in life and experiences feelings of worthlessness, powerlessness, and guilt

detoxification a supervised period to remove drugs from the body

disorganized schizophrenia a condition marked by the basic symptoms of schizophrenia plus incoherent speech, extreme lack of social relationships, and odd behaviors

dissociation the separation of one set of memories from another for no discernible organic reason

dopamine theory of schizophrenia the theory that the underlying cause of schizophrenia is excessive stimulation of certain dopamine synapses in the brain

DSM III-R The *Diagnostic and statistical manual of mental disorders,* Third Edition-Revised—the standard reference work on the classification of psychological disorders

endogenous depression a depression that develops gradually and that reflects biological causes rather than traumatic experiences

flooding or **implosion** a method of reducing fear by suddenly exposing a person to the object of fear in reality or in imagination

generalized anxiety disorder a condition in which a person is constantly plagued by exaggerated worries

hallucination a sensory experience that does not correspond to anything that is happening in the outside world

hyperventilation prolonged deep breathing

hypochondriasis a condition in which a person exaggerates physical ailments or repeatedly complains of ailments that a physician cannot detect

implosion see **flooding**

learned-helplessness theory the theory that depression may result when people perceive that they have no control over the major events that affect them

major depression a long, severe depression

mania a condition marked by constant, driven activity and a lack of inhibitions

methadone an opiate sometimes prescribed because its effects on behavior are less disruptive than those of morphine or heroin

multiple personality disorder a condition in which a person alternates among two or more personalities

negative symptom a characteristic notable for its absence, such as a lack of emotional expression

obsession a repetitive, intrusive thought pattern

obsessive-compulsive disorder a condition marked by repetitive thought patterns and actions

panic disorder a condition in which a person experiences frequent attacks of severe anxiety, often including sweating, faintness, increased heart rate, difficulty in breathing, and chest pain

paranoid schizophrenia a condition marked by the basic symptoms of schizophrenia plus prominent, well-developed hallucinations or delusions (especially delusions of persecution or grandeur)

personality disorder a maladaptive, inflexible way of dealing with the environment and other people

phobia a fear so extreme that it interferes with normal living

positive symptom a characteristic notable for its presence, such as a hallucination

psychogenic fugue a condition in which a person wanders away from home and cannot remember his or her identity

pursuit eye movements eye movements to maintain constant focus on a moving object

reactive depression a depression that develops suddenly in response to a great loss

schizophrenia a condition characterized by deterioration of daily activities and by hallucinations, delusions, or thought disorder

season of birth effect the tendency for those born during the winter months in a northern climate to be at greater risk for schizophrenia than those born during other seasons

seasonal affective disorder a condition in which a person becomes depressed in winter and normal or manic in summer

secondary gain the indirect benefits a patient receives such as the attention and sympathy of others and an excuse for avoiding unpleasant activities

somatization disorder a condition in which a person suffers through a long series of pains and ailments with no apparent medical basis

somatoform disorder a disorder in which a person has physical symptoms that are based on psychological rather than medical factors

superstition a repeated behavior engaged in as a way of gaining good luck or avoiding bad luck

systematic desensitization a method of reducing fear by gradually exposing a person to the object of the fear

tolerance the weakened effect of a drug after repeated use

undifferentiated schizophrenia a type of schizophrenia that has the basic symptoms but no single symptom that is especially prominent

withdrawal the unpleasant effects of stopping the prolonged use of a drug

ANSWERS TO CONCEPT CHECKS

1. A personality disorder qualifies as abnormal by the third definition because society considers the behavior troublesome. Some personality disorders qualify as abnormal by the second definition because they lead to an increased risk of loss of freedom (through unemployment or imprisonment). As a rule, personality disorders do not qualify as abnormal by the first definition because people generally do not complain about their personality disorders. (page 511)

2. Alzheimer's disease is associated with brain deterioration. A disorder is considered "dissociative" only if it occurs for psychological rather than organic reasons. (page 513)

3. In a person in poor condition, even mild physical exertion may suddenly raise the carbon dioxide level in the blood. A sharp rise in the blood's carbon dioxide triggers a panic attack. (page 516)

4. The CS was the white rat. The US was the loud noise. The CR and the UR were crying and other reactions of fear. (page 518)

5. The method of extinguishing a learned shock-avoidance response is to prevent the response so that the animal learns that its failure to respond is not followed by shock. Similarly, in systematic desensitization the patient

is prevented from fleeing the feared stimulus; he or she therefore learns that the danger is not as great as imagined. (page 521)

6. The flooding procedure is compatible with the James-Lange theory of emotions, which holds that emotions follow from perceptions of body arousal. In flooding, as arousal of the autonomic nervous system decreases, the person perceives, "I am calming down. I must not be as frightened of this situation as I thought I was." (page 522)

7. Instead of taking a pill just before a meal, they should take it between meals, when they are not planning to eat right away or when they plan to skip a meal altogether. If they eat right after taking a pill, they soon develop a tolerance to its appetite-suppressing effects. (page 527)

8. The CS is the injection procedure. The US is the entry of the drug into the brain. Both the CR and the UR are the body's defenses against the drug. (page 528)

9. To extinguish tolerance, present the CS without the US. That is, go through the injection procedure (CS) without injecting the drug (US). (Inject just water or salt water.) Shepard Siegel (1977) has demonstrated that repeated injections of salt water do reduce tolerance to morphine in rats. (page 528)

10. They are less likely than others to become alcoholics. This gene is considered the probable reason why relatively few Asians become alcoholics (Harada et al., 1982; Reed, 1985). (page 532)

11. Most people who are not depressed overestimate their own positive qualities and their own control of the situation. That is why most students predict greater success in the future, even though the number of students who will get lower grades in the future is the same as the number who will get higher grades. The same is true of sports coaches. Depressed people are less likely than others to buy a lottery ticket or to make any other type of bet

because they would accurately perceive that their chance of success is low. (page 538)

12. Seasonal affective disorder is more common in areas close to the poles, where the days grow very short during the winter. It does not occur near the equator, where the days are about the same length throughout the year. (page 540)

13. With any disorder, symptoms are more severe at some times than at others. Whenever any of the special symptoms of catatonic, disorganized, or paranoid schizophrenia become less severe, the person is left with undifferentiated schizophrenia. To shift between any two of the other types, a person would have to lose the symptoms of one type and gain the symptoms of the other type. (page 546)

14. The damage is probably located in the frontal or temporal lobes of the cerebral cortex, the areas that are generally damaged in people with schizophrenia. (page 548)

ANSWERS TO OTHER QUESTIONS IN THE TEXT

Typical answers for obsessive-compulsive people (page 524): 1. T, 2. T, 3. T, 4. F, 5. F, 6. T, 7. F, 8. F, 9. T

CHAPTER

15

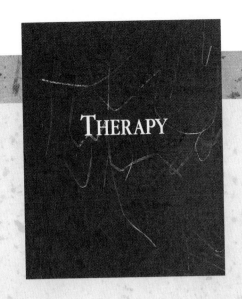

THERAPY

Deliria is sitting at the voice-activated monitor of the World's Greatest Computer. She says, "I feel vaguely dissatisfied with my life. Nothing serious; it just seems that I'm not living life to its fullest. What should I do?"

The computer asks her a few questions and then calls up its medical program. "Next to your chair you will find two devices. Attach the large one to your head and the small one to your wrist. They will feed me all the information I need for a quick but accurate diagnosis." Deliria attaches the devices and waits. A few minutes later the computer speaks again: "You're entirely healthy. I had to check your medical condition; sometimes people say they are unhappy because they are ill.

"Next, let's try education. For many people, education opens new horizons and leads to a fuller, more satisfying life. I could provide you with a computer-interactive tutorial course on any topic. How about the history of philosophy?"

"No thanks," says Deliria. "I'm taking five college courses right now. Interesting courses, too—especially my introduction to psychology course."

"Very good," says the computer. "Then perhaps what you need is a relationship with another per-

son. I can't provide the relationship myself—I do have a few limitations—but I can help you find the right person to talk to. Have you tried talking to your parents, your friends—someone who could be supportive and sympathetic?"

"Hmm," Deliria pauses.

"Is that part of the problem, perhaps?" the computer interjects. "Maybe you have trouble talking to them?"

"Uh huh. Oh, they try. But they don't really listen to me."

"Let me recommend a psychotherapist."

"A therapist? But I'm not . . ."

"I didn't mean to imply that anything is wrong with you," the computer says. "A good therapist is a little like a friend, a little like a parent, a little like an educator."

"Will seeing a therapist do me any good?" asks Deliria.

"Maybe."

"What do you mean, 'maybe'?"

"Even megacomputers can't be sure about everything. Therapy helps some people but not others. It's hard to predict who will benefit and who won't."

PSYCHOTHERAPY

into any set category. In fact, about a third of the people who consult psychotherapists have no psychological disorder (Shapiro et al., 1984). They are the "worried well" or the "nervous normals"—basically normal people seeking help with some aspect of their lives. They consult a therapist not like a sick person seeing a physician but like an athlete seeking advice from a coach.

What methods are used to help people overcome psychological disorders?
How effective are these methods?

Psychotherapy is a means of helping people to help themselves through interaction with a therapist. But psychotherapy does little good unless people give the proverbial damn.

Before the Second World War, almost all psychotherapists were psychiatrists, and most of them used Freudian methods. Since then, clinical psychologists, social workers, and others have begun to practice psychotherapy. Table 15.1 contrasts the practices of psychiatrists and clinical psychologists (Knesper, Belcher, & Cross, 1989).

Both the number of therapists and the variety of methods they use have increased enormously (Garfield, 1981). Well over 100 forms of psychotherapy are available today. Psychotherapy is used for certain well-defined disorders, such as phobia, depression, and addiction, and for a wide variety of adjustment and coping problems that do not fall

GENERAL PRINCIPLES OF THERAPY ... AND WHY MOST THERAPIES PRODUCE BENEFITS

In some types of psychotherapy, the therapist does most of the talking; in others, the therapist says little. Some emphasize past emotions; others emphasize current emotions; still others emphasize current behaviors. Some concentrate on helping clients understand the reasons behind their behaviors; others concentrate on changing the behaviors. Some focus on the problems of the individual; some focus on problems of families or whole communities. But whatever method is used, most clients show at least moderate improvement (Stiles, Shapiro, & Elliott, 1986).

If the various types of psychotherapy really are

Observation

If I don't drive around
the park,
I'm pretty sure to make
my mark.
If I'm in bed each night
by ten,
I may get back my
looks again.
If I abstain from fun
and such,
I'll probably amount to
much.
But I shall stay the way
I am,
Because I do not give a
damn.

DOROTHY PARKER
(1944)

Because psychotherapy can require a sizable commitment of time and money with no guarantee of change or improvement, trust is essential for success. Clients must feel their therapists care about them, can help them, and will accept them while they reveal failures, secrets, and inadequacies. For those deeply troubled by fears or depression, developing such trust may involve a major leap of faith. (Milton Avery, Interlude. *Oil on canvas.)*

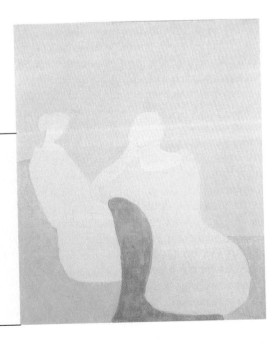

TABLE 15.1 Comparison of Psychiatrists and Clinical Psychologists

	Education	Mean Time Spent with Each Client per Month	Types of Patients Seen	Mean Fee per Hour (late 1980s)
Psychiatrist	M.D. degree plus residency in psychiatry	About 4 hours (some psychiatrists reported means less than 2 hours; some reported means above 6 hours)	Much diversity; includes some with severe disorders and some with minor disorders	$74
Clinical psychologist	Ph.D. degree with specialization in clinical psychology	About 4 hours (some reported means as low as 2 hours; some as high as 4.7 hours)	Less diversity; includes few patients with schizophrenia and other severe disorders	$58

Source: Adapted from data of Knesper, Belcher, & Cross, 1989.

as different as they seem, why do they all produce similar results? Perhaps their similarities are more important than their differences (Horvath, 1988; Strupp, 1986). For example, they all rely on the "therapeutic alliance"—a relationship between therapist and client that is characterized by acceptance, caring, respect, and attention. This relationship provides social support that helps clients deal with their problems and acquire social skills that they can apply to other relationships.

Moreover, in nearly all forms of therapy, clients talk about their beliefs and emotions, how they act, and why they act that way. They examine aspects of themselves that they ordinarily take for granted; in so doing, they gain self-understanding.

The mere fact of entering therapy, whatever the method, improves clients' morale. The therapist conveys the message, "You are going to get better." Clients begin to think of themselves as people who can cope with their problems and overcome them. Just expecting improvement can lead to improvement.

Finally, every form of therapy requires clients to commit themselves to making some sort of change in their lives (Klein, Zitrin, Woerner, & Ross, 1983). Simply by coming to the therapy session, they are reaffirming their commitment—to drink less, to feel less depressed, or to overcome a fear. They are also obliged to work on that change between sessions so that they can come to the next session and report, "I've been doing a little better lately." Improvement may depend as much on what clients do between sessions as on what happens in the sessions themselves.

Some therapists try to strengthen their clients'

sense of commitment by making the therapy a major "ordeal" (Haley, 1984). Once clients accept therapy as a demanding, time-consuming activity, it comes to symbolize a real change in their lives. For example, Alcoholics Anonymous asks new members to attend 90 meetings in the first 90 days. By attending one meeting per day, they are affirming, "This is serious business. I'm really going to quit drinking."

Something to Think About

A large wedding is another "ordeal" that symbolizes a major change in a person's life. So is an initiation ceremony for a fraternity or sorority. Can you think of other examples?

Here is how one therapist helps clients break a bad habit—by strengthening their commitment to change (Haley, 1984). Suppose the problem is cigarette smoking. After discussing the habit with the client, the therapist casually mentions a "guaranteed cure" and then changes the subject. The client asks skeptically about the guaranteed cure, and the therapist says that it is not for everyone. "You probably wouldn't be interested."

"What do you mean I wouldn't be interested? What is it?"

"Well," replies the therapist, "part of the deal is that I can't tell you what the method is unless you agree to follow it."

"But how can I do that if I don't know what it is?"

"You're absolutely right. As I said, I don't think you would be interested."

Over the next few weeks the client keeps

returning to the topic of the guaranteed cure, becoming more and more curious. Each time, the therapist refuses to describe it and tries to change the subject. Eventually the client says, "All right. Whatever this guaranteed cure thing is, I'll do it."

Even then the therapist does not agree: "This isn't a commitment you can enter into lightly. I know it will work, but it will be difficult. Go home and discuss it with your family and friends, and we'll talk about it next week."

The client returns. "Look, I've talked it over with my friends and relatives. I promise to do whatever you say. Now what is this guaranteed cure?"

"I want you to carry a little notebook with you and record every time you smoke a cigarette. When you come back next week I'll ask you to show it to me. For the first cigarette, you'll owe me a penny, in addition to my usual fee. For the second cigarette, you'll owe me two pennies. The next one will cost you four pennies, and so on. The price doubles for each cigarette. And you pay in cash. No checks."

The client leaves, disappointed by this unimpressive scheme but committed to follow it. The next week the client returns with $10.23, the charge for 10 cigarettes. "You dirty so-and-so! The first few cigarettes were cheap. But now they're getting expensive! I've smoked my last cigarette!"

The therapist pretends to be disappointed. "Nuts, there goes my trip to the Bahamas."

This treatment succeeds only because the client makes an irrevocable, public commitment to follow the therapist's plan. Once that commitment has been made, the battle is won. All forms of therapy require at least an implied commitment by the client to make some change. Without such a commitment, success would be doubtful.

In the following survey of the most common forms of therapy and some less common ones, we'll see how therapists use different methods depending on what they consider the central problem of troubled people.

PSYCHOANALYSIS

Psychoanalysis, Sigmund Freud's method of psychotherapy, was the first of the "talk" therapies. Psychoanalysts try to help clients achieve insight into why they do what they do and think what they think (Figure 15.1). Psychoanalysis is therefore described as an "insight-oriented therapy" in contrast to therapies that focus on changing thoughts and behaviors.

Freud believed that psychological problems were the result of unconscious thought processes and that the only way to control self-defeating behaviors was to make those processes conscious.

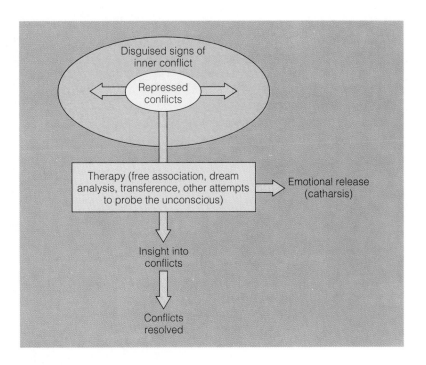

FIGURE 15.1

The goal of psychoanalysis is to resolve psychological problems by bringing to consciousness the unconscious thought processes that are responsible for the difficulty. *Analysis* literally means to loosen or break up, to look at the parts.

Bringing them to consciousness, he thought, would release pent-up emotion in a process called **catharsis**.

At first, Freud sought to gain access to his clients' unconscious through hypnosis. He abandoned that approach, however, after he discovered that many clients immediately forgot the insights they had gained while under hypnosis. He developed other methods of bringing unconscious material to consciousness: free association, dream analysis, and transference.

Free Association

Free association is a method that Freud and his patients developed together. (Actually, a more accurate translation of the German expression would be "free intrusion.") In **free association**, the client lies on a couch, starts thinking about a particular symptom or problem, and then reports everything that comes to mind—a word, a phrase, a visual image. The client is instructed not to omit anything, not to censor anything that might be embarrassing, and not to worry about trying to express everything in complete sentences.

The therapist listens for links and themes that might tie the patient's fragmentary remarks together. Freud believed that all behavior is determined, that

Freud's famous couch: In Freud's consulting room, patients reclining on a pile of pillows were surrounded by patterned rugs and ancient art, featuring Egyptian pictures and figurines. His 55-minute session cost $8.10 (Wilson et al., 1964).

nothing happens without a cause. (You will recall that behaviorists make the same assumption; see page 241.) Even when the client jumps from one thought to another, the thoughts must be related in some way.

Here is a paraphrased excerpt from a free-association session:

A man begins by describing a conference he had with his boss the previous day. He did not like the boss's policy, but he was in no position to contradict the boss. He had had a dream. It was something about an ironing board, but that was all he remembered of the dream. He comments that his wife has been complaining about the way their maid irons. He thinks his wife is being unfair; he hopes she does not fire the maid. He complains that his boss did not give him credit for some work he did recently. He recalls a childhood episode: He jumped off a cupboard and bounced off his mother's behind while she was leaning over to do some ironing. She told his father, who gave him a spanking. His father never let him explain; he was always too strict [Munroe, 1955, page 39].

The links in this story suggest that the man is associating his wife with his mother. His wife was unfair to the maid about the ironing, just as his mother had been unfair to him. Moreover, his boss is like his father, never giving him a chance to explain his errors and never giving him credit for what he did well.

Dream Analysis

For thousands of years, people have been trying to divine the meaning of dreams. Some have said that dreams predict the future, others that they reveal the dreamer's personality.

Freud (1900/1955) agreed that dreams reveal something about personality, but he rejected the view that each detail has the same meaning for everyone. To understand a dream, he said, one must determine what associations each detail has for the dreamer. Each dream has a **manifest content**—the content that appears on the surface—and a **latent content**—the hidden content that is represented only symbolically. The only way a psychoanalyst can discover the latent content of a dream is to ask what each detail of the manifest content means to the dreamer.

To illustrate, Freud (1900) interpreted one of his own dreams, in which he dreamed that one of his friends was his uncle. He worked out the following associations: Both this friend and another friend had been recommended for an appointment as professor at the university. Both had been turned down, probably because they were Jews. Freud himself had recently been recommended for the same appointment, but he feared he too would be turned down because he was a Jew. Freud's only uncle had once been convicted of illegal business dealings. Freud's father had said, however, that the uncle was not a bad man but just a simpleton.

What was the relationship between the two friends and the uncle? One of the friends was, in Freud's reluctant judgment, a bit simpleminded. The other had once been taken to court by a woman who accused him of sexual misconduct. Although the charges were dropped, some people might still feel that being accused was as bad as being convicted. By linking these two friends to his uncle, Freud interpreted the dream as meaning, "Maybe they didn't get rejected for the university appointment because they were Jews, but because one was a simpleton and the other was regarded as a criminal. If so, I still have a chance to get the appointment."

To Freud, every dream represents a wish fulfillment. The wish may be disguised, but it is always there. For example, in his dream Freud was not wishing that his friend were his uncle. Rather, he was wishing that he would get the university appointment, and he was wishing that his friends had been rejected for some reason other than for being Jews.

Freud's theory seems to apply to many dreams. For example, people who have been deprived of food and water—and who, presumably, are wishing for food and water—have more frequent and more elaborate dreams about eating and drinking than other people do (O'Nell, 1965). Most psychologists deny that Freud's theory applies to all dreams, however.

Concept Check

1. A popular paperback purports to tell you what your dreams mean. It says that every element of a dream has a symbolic meaning, in many cases a sexual meaning. A ballpoint pen represents a penis, for example, and walking up a flight of stairs represents sexual arousal. Do you think Freud would agree or disagree with this book? (Check your answer on page 591.)

Transference

Some clients show exaggerated love or hatred for their therapist that seems inappropriate under the circumstances. Psychoanalysts call this reaction **transference**, by which they mean that clients are transferring onto the therapist what they actually feel toward their father or mother or some other important figure. Transference often provides a clue to the client's feelings about those people.

Psychoanalysts are fairly active in **interpretation** of what the client says—that is, they explain the underlying meaning—and may even argue with the client about interpretations. They may regard the client's disagreement as **resistance**, continued repression that interferes with the therapy.

Although psychoanalysis has changed somewhat since Freud's time, its basic approach is still the same. Its goal is to bring about a major reorganization of personality over months or even years. Psychoanalysts try to change their clients from the inside out and pay more attention to their thoughts and emotions than to their actions.

Something to Think About

Recall from Chapter 13 that some critics have attacked Freud's theories for not being falsifiable. What would those critics probably say about the concept of resistance?

THERAPIES THAT FOCUS ON THOUGHTS AND BELIEFS

Someone says to you, "Look how messy your room is! Don't you ever clean it?" How do you react? You might say, "Big deal. Maybe I'll clean it tomorrow." Or you might feel worried, angry, even depressed. If you get upset, it is not merely because you were criticized but because you want everyone to believe that you are scrupulously clean and tidy at all times. Some therapists focus on the thoughts and beliefs that underlie people's emotional reactions. Unlike psychoanalysts, these therapists are more concerned about what people are thinking right now than about early experiences that may have led to their thoughts.

Rational-Emotive Therapy

Rational-emotive therapy is based on the assumption that people's emotions depend on their "internal sentences" such as "I can't be happy unless everyone thinks my room is clean" (Ellis & Harper, 1961). This therapy is called "rational-emotive" because it assumes that thoughts (rationality) lead to emotions.

Rational-emotive therapists (Ellis, 1987) hold that abnormal behavior often results from such irrational beliefs as these:

- I must perform certain tasks successfully.
- I must perform well at all times.
- I must have the approval of certain people at all times.
- Others must treat me fairly and with consideration.
- I must live under easy, gratifying conditions.

It is the word *must* that makes these beliefs irrational. Rational-emotive therapists try to identify people's irrational beliefs (which they may never have verbalized) and then contradict them. They urge clients to substitute other, more realistic "internal sentences." These therapists try to stop their clients from constantly evaluating their own performance and comparing themselves to others (Orth & Thebarge, 1984). Rational-emotive therapists intervene directly, instructing, persuading, and doing much of the talking. Here is an excerpt from a rational-emotive therapy session with a 25-year-old physicist:

CLIENT: *The whole trouble is that I am really a phony. I am living under false pretenses. And the longer it goes on, the more people praise me and make a fuss over my accomplishments, the worse I feel.*

THERAPIST: *What do you mean you are a phony? I thought that you told me, during our last session, that your work has been examined at another laboratory and that some of the people there think your ideas are of revolutionary importance.*

CLIENT: *But I have wasted so much time. I could be doing very much better. . . . Remember that book I told you I was writing . . . it's been three weeks now since I've spent any time on it. And this is simple stuff that I should be able to do with my left hand while I am writing a technical paper with my right. I have heard Bob Oppenheimer reel off stuff extemporaneously to a bunch of newspaper reporters that is twice as good as what I am mightily laboring on in this damned book!*

THERAPIST: *Perhaps so. And perhaps you're not quite as good—yet—as Oppenheimer or a few other outstanding people in your field. But the real point, it seems to me, is that . . . here you are, at just twenty-five, with a Ph.D. in a most difficult field, with an excellent job, much good work in process, and what well may be a fine professional paper and a good popular book also in progress. And just because you're not another Oppenheimer or Einstein quite yet, you're savagely berating yourself.*

CLIENT: *Well, shouldn't I be doing much better than I am?*

THERAPIST: *No, why the devil should you? As far as I can see, you are not doing badly at all. But your major difficulty—the main cause of your present unhappiness—is your utterly perfectionistic criteria for judging your performance [Ellis & Harper, 1961, pages 99–100].*

Concept Check

***2.** How does the idea behind rational-emotive therapy compare to the James-Lange theory of emotions, page 427? (Check your answer on page 591.)*

Cognitive Therapy

Cognitive therapy seeks to improve people's psychological well-being by changing their cognitions—their thoughts and beliefs. Cognitive therapy is best known through the work of Aaron Beck with depressed patients (Beck, 1976; Hollon & Beck, 1979). According to Beck, depressed people hold three kinds of discouraging beliefs, which he calls the "negative cognitive triad of depression": They regard themselves as deprived or defeated; they regard the world as full of obstacles; and they regard the future as devoid of hope. These beliefs lead to what Beck calls "automatic thoughts." From time to time depressed people suddenly think, "I'm a loser," or "Nothing ever works out right for me and it's all my fault," or "I never have a good time."

The task of a cognitive therapist is to help people substitute more favorable beliefs. Unlike rational-emotive therapists, who in many cases simply tell their clients what to think, cognitive therapists try to get their clients to make discoveries for themselves. The therapist focuses on one of the client's

beliefs such as "No one likes me." The therapist points out that this is a hypothesis, not an established fact, and invites the client to test the hypothesis as a scientist would: "What evidence do you have for this hypothesis?"

"Well," a client may reply, "when I arrive at work in the morning, hardly anyone says hello."

"Is there any other way of looking at that evidence?"

"Hmm. . . . I suppose it's possible that the others are busy."

"Does anyone ever seem happy to see you?"

"Well, maybe. I'm not sure."

"Then let's find out. For the next week, keep a notebook with you and record every time that anyone smiles or seems happy to see you. The next time I see you we'll discuss what you find."

The therapist's goal is to get depressed clients to discover that their automatic thoughts are incorrect, that things are not so bad as they seem, and that the future is not hopeless. If one of the client's thoughts does turn out to be correct—for example, "My boyfriend is interested in someone else"—then the therapist asks, "Even if it's true, is that the end of the world?"

HUMANISTIC THERAPY

As we saw in Chapter 13, humanistic psychologists believe that people can decide consciously and deliberately what kind of person to be and that people naturally strive to achieve their full potential. However, people sometimes learn to dislike themselves because others criticize and reject them. They become distressed by the **incongruence** (mismatch) between their self-concept and their ideal self (page 482). Humanistic therapists hold that once people are freed from the inhibiting influences of a rejecting society they can solve their own problems.

The best-known version of humanistic therapy is **person-centered therapy**, pioneered by Carl Rogers. It is also known as nondirective or client-centered therapy. The therapist listens to the client sympathetically, with total acceptance and *unconditional positive regard*, like the love of a parent for a child. Most of the time the therapist restates what the client has said in order to clarify it, conveying the message, "I'm trying to understand your experience from your point of view." The therapist strives to be genuine, empathic, and caring; rarely does he or she offer any interpretation or advice. Here is an example (shortened from Meador & Rogers, 1984, pages 187–189). A 30-year-old divorcee, Gloria, has always been honest with her 9-year-old daughter, Pammy, except that she has recently lied to conceal her sexual relationships with men:

GLORIA: *I almost want an answer from you. I want you to tell me if it would affect her wrong if I told her the truth, or what.*

ROGERS: *And it's this concern . . . that this open relationship that has existed between you, now you feel it's kind of vanished? . . . I sure wish I could give you the answer as to what you should tell her.*

GLORIA: *You're just going to sit there and let me stew in it and I want more.*

ROGERS: *No, I don't want to let you just stew in your feelings, but on the other hand, I also feel this is the kind of very private thing that I couldn't possibly answer for you. But I sure as anything will try to help you work toward your own answer.*

GLORIA: *I want you very much to give me a direct answer.*

ROGERS: *I am sure this will sound evasive to you, but it seems to me that perhaps the person you are not being fully honest with is you, because I was very much struck by the fact that you were saying, "If I feel all right about what I have done, whether it's going to bed with a man or what, then I do not have any concern about what I would tell Pam or my relationship with her."*

GLORIA: *All right. Now I hear what you are saying. Then all right, then I want to work on accepting me. That makes sense. Then that will come natural and I won't have to worry about Pammy.*

ROGERS: *I guess one thing that I feel very keenly is that it's an awfully risky thing to* live. *You'd be taking a chance on your relationship with her and taking a chance on letting her know who you are, really.*

GLORIA: *Now I feel like "now that's solved"—and I didn't even solve a thing; but I feel relieved. I do feel like you have been saying to me, "You know what pattern you want to follow, Gloria, and go ahead and follow it." I sort of feel a backing up from you.*

ROGERS: *I guess the way I sense it, you've been telling me that you know what you want to do, and yes, I do believe in backing up people in what they want to do.*

The therapist provides an atmosphere in which the client can freely explore feelings of guilt, anxiety, and hostility (Rogers, 1951). By accepting the client's feelings, the therapist conveys the message, "You can make your own decisions. Now that you are more aware of certain problems, you can deal with them constructively yourself."

BEHAVIOR THERAPY

Behavior therapists assume that human behavior is learned and that it can be unlearned. They identify the behavior that needs to be changed, such as a phobia or an addiction or a nervous twitch, and then set about changing it through reinforcement, punishment, and other principles of learning. They may try to understand the causes of the behavior as a first step toward changing it, but, unlike psychoanalysts, they are more interested in directly changing behaviors than in understanding their origins.

Behavior therapy begins with clear, well-defined goals, such as eliminating test anxiety or getting the client to quit smoking. Setting clear goals enables the therapist to judge whether or not the therapy is succeeding. If the client shows no improvement after a few sessions, the therapist tries a different procedure.

Systematic desensitization of phobias, which we examined in Chapter 14, is one example of behavior therapy. For other problems, behavior therapists use a variety of methods.

Behavior Modification for Anorexia Nervosa

One of the quickest and most successful ways of treating anorexia nervosa (Chapter 11) is behavior modification, a system in which the therapist provides reinforcement whenever the person exhibits a clearly defined target behavior. One woman with severe anorexia nervosa was isolated from her family and placed in a small, barren hospital room (Bachrach, Erwin, & Mohr, 1965). She was told that she could not leave the room and could see no one except the nurse who came at mealtimes. She could obtain privileges—such as having a radio, television, or reading material; the right to leave the room; or the right to have visitors—only as a reward for gaining weight. This method may seem heartless, but life-threatening cases like this one demand drastic measures. The woman gradually gained weight and was released from the hospital when she reached 77 pounds (35 kilograms). After leaving, she lost some of the weight she had gained but not enough to endanger her life.

Behavior modification can be combined with other therapeutic methods. In cases of anorexia nervosa, it is most effective when combined with

Although tube feeding may save this young woman's life, it will not solve her problems in the long run. In behavior modification to treat anorexia nervosa, the goals include altering eating habits and gaining weight. Family counseling can help uncover how the problem developed and prevent its recurrence.

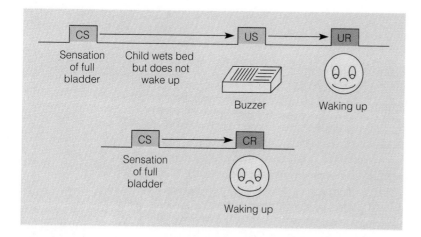

FIGURE 15.2

A child can be trained not to wet the bed through use of classical conditioning techniques. At first the sensation of a full bladder (the CS) produces no response, and the child wets the bed. This causes the buzzer to sound (the US), and the child wakes up (the UR). By associating the sensation of a full bladder with a buzzer, the child soon begins waking up to the sensation of a full bladder alone, and he or she will not wet the bed.

family counseling designed to alter the family interactions that may have led to the problem (Russell, Szmukler, Dare, & Eisler, 1987).

Behavior Therapy for Bed-Wetting

Some children continue to wet the bed long after the usual age of toilet training. Most of them outgrow the problem, but occasionally it lingers on to age 5, 10, or even into the teens.

We now know that most bed-wetters have small bladders and thus have difficulty getting through the night without urinating. We also know that they are unusually deep sleepers who do not wake up when they wet the bed (Stegat, 1975).

The most effective procedure uses a simple device, sold by Sears, that makes use of classical conditioning. It trains the child to wake up at night and go to the bathroom without wetting the bed (Hansen, 1979).

Here is how it works: Two thin pieces of metal foil separated by a piece of cloth are placed under the bottom sheet. The top piece of foil has holes in it, and wires connect the two pieces of foil to an alarm. If the child wets the bed, the moisture completes a circuit and triggers the alarm. In the early stages of conditioning, the alarm awakens both the child and the parents, and the child is taken to the bathroom to finish urinating.

The buzzer acts as an unconditioned stimulus (US) that evokes the unconditioned response (UR) of waking up. In this instance, the body itself generates the conditioned stimulus (CS): the sensation produced by a full bladder (Figure 15.2). Whenever that sensation is present, it serves as a signal that a buzzer will soon sound. After a few pairings (or more), the sensation of a full bladder is enough to wake the child.

Actually the situation is a little more complicated, because the child is positively reinforced with praise for waking up to go to the toilet. Training with this device enables most, but not all, bed-wetting children to cease bed-wetting after one to three months of treatment (Bollard, 1982; Dische, Yule, Corbett, & Hand, 1983).

Aversion Therapy

Although behavior therapists rely mostly on positive reinforcement, they occasionally use punishments to try to teach clients an aversion (dislike) of some stimulus. For example, they might ask someone who is trying to quit smoking to smoke twice as many cigarettes as usual for a few days, to inhale rapidly (one puff every six seconds), or to smoke nonstop in a small, airtight room with over-

Aversion therapy aims to condition negative reactions to specific stimuli to reduce or extinguish certain behavior. To discourage smoking, this woman receives an electric shock whenever she brings a cigarette to her mouth. Such therapy may succeed where other negative results—a persistent cough, stained fingers and teeth, the threat of cancer and emphysema—have failed.

flowing ash trays until there is little oxygen left to breathe. The goal is to teach the client an aversion to smoking. At the end of this treatment, most people stop smoking at least temporarily, although they are likely to start again within a year (Poole, Sanson-Fisher, & German, 1981). Apparently, it is difficult to undo years of enjoyable smoking with a few unpleasant sessions.

Concept Check

3. Answer the following questions with reference to psychoanalysis, cognitive therapy, humanistic therapy, and behavior therapy.
a. In which type of therapy is the therapist least likely to offer interpretations of behavior and advice?
b. Which type focuses more on changing what people do than on exploring what they think?
c. Which two types try to change what people think? (Check your answers on page 591.)

ECLECTIC THERAPY

In 1950, almost half of all the psychotherapists in the United States relied mostly on psychoanalysis or closely related methods. Since then, psychoanalysis has declined in popularity (Mahoney, 1988). (See Figure 15.3.) Today, almost half of all psychologists practice **eclectic therapy**, meaning that they use a combination of methods and approaches. For example, an eclectic therapist might use behavior modification, psychoanalysis, and rational-emo-

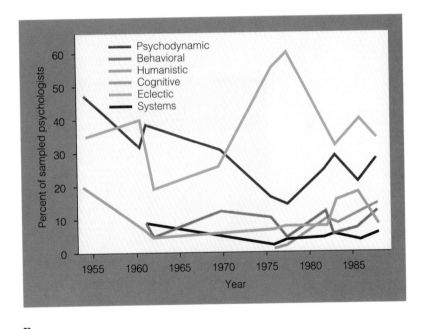

FIGURE 15.3

Theoretical orientation of American clinical psychologists. The psychodynamic approach includes psychoanalysis and related therapies. The systems approach includes family therapy and other therapies that focus on relationships among people. (From Mahoney, 1990.)

TABLE 15.2 Comparison of Some Major Types of Psychotherapy

Type of Psychotherapy	Theory of What Causes Psychological Disorders	Goal of Treatment	Therapeutic Methods	Role of the Therapist
Psychoanalysis	Unconscious thoughts and motivations	To bring unconscious thoughts to consciousness; to achieve insight	Free association, dream analysis, and other analysis, and other methods of probing the unconscious mind	To interpret associations
Rational-emotive and cognitive therapy	Irrational beliefs and unrealistic goals	To establish realistic goals and expectations	Dialogue with the therapist	To offer advice
Humanistic (person-centered) therapy	Reactions to a rejecting society; incongruence between self-concept and ideal self	To enable the client to make personal decisions; to promote self-acceptance	Client-centered interviews	To focus the client's attention; to provide "unconditional positive regard"
Behavior therapy	Learned inappropriate, maladaptive behaviors	To change behaviors	Behavior modification	To develop and direct the behavior modification program
Eclectic therapy	Different causes for different people	To alter beliefs or behaviors; to increase self-understanding	Whatever the therapist believes is appropriate for the client	The therapist's role varies, depending on the client's problems

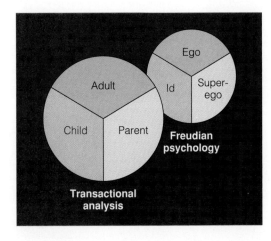

FIGURE 15.4

The three aspects of the personality in transactional analysis are analogous to the three aspects of the personality in Freudian psychology.

tive techniques in different combinations, depending on each client's needs (Garfield, 1980). Table 15.2 contrasts the major types of psychotherapy.

SOME LESS COMMON THERAPIES

Besides the common forms of therapy there are countless methods that come and go like fads, some of them rather bizarre (Appelbaum, 1979). To cure what ails you, you can climb naked into a hot tub to reenact the moment of birth, or you can sprawl on the floor and scream, or you can take LSD, or you can get "Rolfed," a treatment in which you are massaged until it hurts, according to the methods of Ida Rolf. Here is a look at three unusual but respectable forms of therapy.

Transactional Analysis

Transactional analysis, often abbreviated **TA,** attempts to analyze "transactions," or communication patterns (Berne, 1964). It assumes that each of us has three aspects of personality: a childlike aspect, a rational adult aspect, and a parenting aspect. These are analogous to the Freudian concepts of id, ego, and superego (see Chapter 13). (See Figure 15.4.)

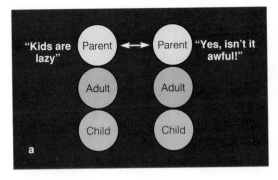 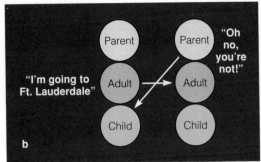

FIGURE 15.5

Clear lines and crossed wires: According to transactional analysis, "balanced" transactions occur when each person is talking to the aspect of the other person that is responding (a). "Crossed" transactions occur when a person is talking to one aspect and a different aspect is responding (b). Crossed transactions often lead to confusion.

When we speak, we speak either as a child, as an adult, or as a parent. Moreover, we speak *to* someone as if that person were a child, an adult, or a parent. A "transaction" (or communication) is "balanced" if each person is speaking to the same aspect of the other person who is replying. For example, if I ask you how to get downtown and you give me directions, our transaction is balanced. I speak to you as adult to adult, and you reply as adult to adult. If I say, "Kids nowadays are lazy," and you reply, "Yes, they're awful," both of us are speaking as parent to parent.

Problems arise when a transaction is "crossed." For example, you tell your parents, "Some of my friends and I are planning to go to Florida for spring break." But your father replies, "No way! I've heard about spring break in Florida. No child of mine is going to go down there and. . . ." You were trying for an adult-adult transaction, but your father came back with a parent-child transaction (Figure 15.5).

How do you respond? You might pick up the cue and respond as child to parent: "You never let me do anything! All my friends get to go except me!" Or you might continue to speak as adult to adult and try to get your father to do the same: "I understand how you feel. Let me reassure you that we're not going to drink and party with all those rowdies you've heard about. We're going to spend our time visiting the museums and sight-seeing. It will be very educational."

According to transactional analysts, many interpersonal conflicts develop because of crossed transactions. People make trouble for themselves because they are not really communicating. The analysts try to teach people to be aware of how

they are addressing each other and how they are being addressed, so that they can keep their transactions parallel.

Concept Check

4. Linda and Maria are shopping for a VCR. Linda says, "This is the nicest one, but you can't afford it." Maria replies, "Oh, yeah? Well, that's the one I'm going to buy." Is this a parallel transaction or a crossed transaction? (Check your answer on page 591.)

Gestalt Therapy

In Chapter 5 we considered *Gestalt psychology,* the study of how people integrate perceptions into a whole. **Gestalt therapy** (Perls, 1973) is loosely based on the same idea. It deals with the person "as a whole," including body as well as mind. For example, a Gestalt therapist, noticing a client's body language, might say, "You say you are no longer upset with your mother, but whenever you mention her you clench your fists."

Unlike psychoanalysts and many other therapists, Gestalt therapists discourage clients from dwelling on the past. They concentrate on the person's immediate experience and current behavior. They believe it does little good for you to discover that you are acting strangely because your mother was too harsh with you during toilet training. Instead, they urge you to accept responsibility for your own actions and find solutions to your problems here and now.

Here is an exchange between a married couple during a Gestalt therapy session (Perls, 1973, pages

Gestalt therapists focus on the here and now, paying special attention to what patients say with their bodies. Fritz Perls considered gestures and expressions more honest reflections of feelings than statements are. But such signs may be mixed. Are the crossed arms and posture of this woman consistent with her smile?

138–139). Note the attention to body cues, to the obvious, to the present:

ANN: *I'm aware of my heart pounding, and that I'm aware of the, sort of, sitting in this chair, sort of, very solidly back in the chair, with my arms kind of propped on each side. And I'm aware of you looking very, uh, intently into my eyes. And breathing more uh, quickly, uh, at least I'm aware of your breathing.*

BILL: *My heart is thumping. And I'm leaning a little bit on my left arm. The thing is, I seem to totally, to be settling, settling down, coming to the center. And I see you, Ann. I see your face as being soft, but a bit tense. And I see your right shoulder, just very slightly tensed and . . .*

THERAPIST: *Are you aware of what your eyes are doing?*

BILL: *They're wandering around.*

THERAPIST: *What are you avoiding when you look at her?*

BILL: *I'm trying to find myself, right now, I think. And I'm not prepared to deal with what's out there until I come back here.*

THERAPIST: *Very good. Close your eyes and withdraw. So, this is a very good example—he's not ready to cope, so he needs more time for withdrawing into himself, and to get support from within.*

Paradoxical Intervention

Sometimes psychotherapists have to cope with patients who have no interest in helping themselves and who *like* being considered "mentally ill." Their behavior wins them attention and sympathy and gives them an excuse for not carrying out their obligations at home or at work (Fontana, Marcus, Noel, & Rakusin, 1972). Others enjoy being told that they are a "juvenile delinquent" or "the thinnest anorexic I've ever seen."

You are a psychotherapist trying to deal with someone who does not want to change. What do you do? You might decide that the patient should be left free to make that choice. Or you might decide that people should *not* be permitted to engage in self-defeating behavior. If you chose the latter approach, how might you intervene?

One method is known as **paradoxical intervention**. A paradox is an apparently self-contradictory statement. Paradoxical intervention consists of telling a person to do something but giving such an undesirable reason for doing it that the person will want to stop.

For example, a school psychologist was trying to deal with a teenage student who seldom attended school and misbehaved when he did attend. After a long series of other approaches had failed, the psychologist told him:

Psychologists sometimes find that children, somewhat younger than you, go through a phase in which they like to misbehave before they are able to become mature young men. This pattern is sort of like a last fling. . . . It seems that you have not passed through this childish phase yet. It is expected that you will be misbehaving and getting into trouble for a while longer than your mature friends until you grow up like them. . . . It seems it would be best for you if you didn't go to school until you grow through this childish stage; we don't want you to fight the urge to misbehave because you apparently aren't mature enough to control it.

After this conversation, the student's attendance and grades improved and his misbehavior declined (Kolko & Milan, 1983, page 657).

Paradoxical intervention is used only as a last resort after more conventional forms of therapy have failed. Even then, it must be used with caution. Simply telling someone to continue some undesirable behavior may backfire and cause the person to increase the frequency of the behavior instead of abandoning it (Haley, 1984). As with any other treatment, the therapist must constantly monitor the effects of the treatment.

The Betty Ford Clinic has become known as a sort of celebrity camp for drink and drug abusers. The clinic does not pamper clients like Liza Minnelli and Elizabeth Taylor; all are assigned chores and required to participate in group activities. The idea is to recognize and take responsibility for personal behavior. Publicly admitting to a problem is considered therapeutic.

Group therapy offers opportunities to work on problems in relating to others—problems common among psychotherapy clients, who may also lack experience participating in any group. Psychiatrist Irvin D. Yalom (1985) notes, "To the extent that the group is a social microcosm, it contains the possibilities of satisfying virtually any social need in an individual's life."

TREATING PEOPLE IN GROUPS

Freud and the other early pioneers of psychotherapy dealt with their clients on a one-to-one basis. Individual psychotherapy has its advantages, most of all privacy. But for many purposes it is helpful to treat clients in groups.

Group Therapy

Group therapy is therapy that is administered to a group of people all at one time. It first came into vogue for economic reasons. Most psychotherapists charge substantial fees for the usual 50-minute session. (They have to charge more per patient than most medical practitioners simply because they see only one patient per hour.) Because middle-class and poor people in need of psychotherapy cannot afford those fees, some therapists began to treat small groups of people, spreading the cost among them.

Group therapy has other advantages as well.

Therapists typically try to set up a group of about seven or eight people who are about the same age with similar problems—people who have as much in common with one another as possible. They take comfort when they discover that others share their problems. They learn from each other and are encouraged by each other's successes.

Group therapy sessions give people an opportunity to explore how they relate to others. Clients become aware of how they irritate others and how they can be useful to others. They use group therapy to develop and practice social skills (Bloch, 1986).

Family Therapy

In **family therapy**, the group consists of members of one family. It is based on the assumption that many psychological disorders are related to problems of communication and interaction within a family. Family therapy is not exactly an alternative to other forms of therapy; a family therapist may use psychoanalysis, cognitive therapy, behavior therapy, or any other technique. What distinguishes family therapists is that they prefer to talk with two or more members of a family together; even when they talk with just one member they focus on how that individual fits into the family (Hazelrigg, Cooper, & Borduin, 1987).

For example, one young man who had been

The novelist Leo Tolstoy observed, "All happy families resemble one another, but each unhappy family is unhappy in its own way." While one family may be aware of shared problems, another may make one member the scapegoat. As impartial referees, family therapists can help people deal with what's wrong in their family even when some members refuse to participate in this form of "group" therapy.

Self-help groups operate on the assumption that people can help and be helped by others who share the same problem. The excuses and rationalizations an alcoholic might use in therapy are unlikely to get far with fellow alcoholics.

caught stealing a car was taken to a psychologist. The psychologist, a family therapist, asked to talk with the parents as well. As it turned out, the father had been a heavy drinker until his boss pressured him to quit drinking and join AA. Until that time, the mother had made most of the family decisions in close consultation with her son, who had become almost a substitute husband. When the father quit drinking, he began to assume more authority over the family, and his son came to resent him. The mother felt less needed and grew depressed.

Each member of the family had problems that could not be resolved by an individual. The therapist worked to help the father improve his relationship with both his son and his wife and to help all three find satisfying roles within the family (Foley, 1984). Because so many psychological problems arise from family relationships, family therapy has been growing more and more popular (Gurman, Kniskern, & Pinsof, 1986).

Self-Help Groups

Self-help groups, such as Alcoholics Anonymous (page 531), operate much like group-therapy sessions, except that they do not include a therapist. Everyone in the group both gives and receives help. Sometimes the people who understand a problem best are those who have experienced it themselves. Alcoholics and drug abusers can shout at a therapist, "You don't know what it's like, doc!" But they can't shout that at one another. Self-help groups have another advantage: The members are available whenever someone needs help—often or seldom, without appointment, without charge.

Some self-help groups are composed of current or former mental patients. The members feel a need to talk to others who have gone through a similar experience, either in addition to or instead of treatment by a therapist. The Mental Patients' Association in Canada was organized by former patients who were frustrated and angry at the treatment they had received (or failed to receive) from therapists, especially in mental hospitals (Chamberlin, 1978). Similar organizations in the United States and Europe enable former patients to share experiences with one another, provide support, and work together to defend the rights and welfare of mental patients.

BRIEF THERAPY

For many years, psychoanalysts expected to see each client for at least an hour a week for years. Even therapists who rejected the psychoanalytic approach

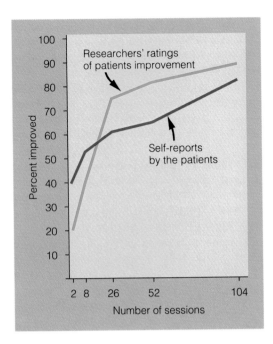

Figure 15.6

The relationship of the number of psychotherapy sessions and the percentage of patients improved. (From Howard et al., 1986.)

regarded psychotherapy as a long-term commitment. They regarded any client who quit after a few sessions as a dropout, a failure. Eventually they realized that some of the apparent "failures" were really "premature successes" who did not need further treatment (Rockwell & Pinkerton, 1982). In fact, about half of all the people who enter psychotherapy show significant improvement within 8 sessions, and three-fourths show improvement within 26 sessions (Howard, Kopta, Krause, & Orlinsky, 1986). (See Figure 15.6.)

Now, many therapists realize that it is sometimes desirable to limit the duration of therapy. At the start of **brief therapy**, or *time-limited* therapy (Clarkin & Frances, 1982), the therapist offers a contract outlining what therapist and client can expect from each other and how long the treatment will last—generally between two months and six months (Koss & Butcher, 1986).

As the deadline approaches, both the therapist and the client are strongly motivated to bring the therapy to a successful conclusion. How hard would you work on a term paper if you had no deadline to meet? When people know that their therapy may go on forever, they feel no need to come to grips with their problems quickly. They may even resist doing so for fear of breaking off a satisfying relationship with their therapist. When they know they

have a deadline, they deal with their main problems promptly.

Moreover, with a deadline agreed on in advance, clients do not feel "deserted" when the therapy ends. They may return for an occasional session months later (Bennett, 1983), but for a time they must get along without help. Any client who fails to make progress by the time the deadline nears should think about going to a different therapist.

Research has found that brief therapy is about as successful as long-term therapy for most clients. Brief therapy is least successful with clients who have complex, severe problems and clients who fail to form a working relationship with the therapist during the early sessions (DeLeon, VandenBos, & Cummings, 1983; Dush, Hirt, & Schroeder, 1983; Koss & Butcher, 1986). However, those clients are not likely to make great progress in long-term therapy either.

EVALUATING THE EFFECTIVENESS OF PSYCHOTHERAPY

How well does psychotherapy work? Hans Eysenck (1952b) called attention to this question by pointing out that about 65% of the people who never receive therapy for their psychological problems nevertheless improve in a year or two. According to the statistics available at that time, people who did receive therapy improved at about the same rate as those without therapy. Before Eysenck's article appeared, no scientifically sound study of the question had been made—that is, no study in which patients were randomly assigned to therapy groups and placebo groups.

Since then, researchers have made many serious studies comparing the effectiveness of various forms of psychotherapy. Some of these studies compared groups that received therapy to similar groups that did not. Many of these studies have been brought together in comprehensive reviews that evaluate all forms of psychotherapy and all types of disorder. According to most of those evaluations, the average client in psychotherapy shows greater improvement than do about 75 to 80% of all untreated people with similar problems (Landman & Dawes, 1982; Shapiro & Shapiro, 1982; Smith & Glass, 1977); one review concluded that the benefits of psychotherapy were somewhat less than that (Matt, 1989).

The effectiveness of psychotherapy depends in part on the nature of the client's disorder; it is generally more effective with clients who have specific, clear-cut problems than with clients who have vague, general complaints or all-pervasive problems (Singer, 1981).

To the embarrassment of some psychotherapists, several studies report that all forms of psychotherapy produce almost equally good results (Stiles, Shapiro, & Elliott, 1986). Even meeting regularly with untrained sympathetic listeners produces significant benefits (Strupp & Hadley, 1979). Given the sharp disagreements among therapists on how to treat clients, we might expect that some methods would prove clearly superior to others. Again, the effectiveness of psychotherapy seems more closely related to what all the therapies have in common—such as the client-therapist relationship—than to any specific technique.

No one as yet has been able to answer one very important question about psychotherapy (Dance & Neufeld, 1988): Do particular types of therapy work best with particular disorders or with particular clients? For analogy, in educational research it would be pointless to ask whether lectures are better than discussion classes; each has advantages for particular purposes. Similarly, medical researchers try to determine which treatment is best for patients with particular illnesses, not which treatment is best in general. Although most psychologists believe that different types of psychotherapy are best for different psychological disorders, they have had little success in demonstrating that specificity. We do know that for reducing phobias, breaking bad habits, and initiating other specific behavioral changes, behavior therapists and cognitive therapists achieve somewhat better results than most others do (Lambert, Shapiro, & Bergin, 1986; Shapiro & Shapiro, 1982). Beyond that, we know little about how to choose the best treatment for particular disorders or for particular clients. Research on this question is likely to become more prominent.

SUMMARY

1. A wide variety of therapies share certain features: All rely on a caring relationship between therapist and client. All promote a certain degree of self-understanding. All improve clients' morale. And all require a commitment by clients to try to make changes in their lives. Some therapists concentrate on strengthening that commitment. (page 559)

2. Psychoanalysts try to uncover the unconscious reasons behind self-defeating behaviors. To bring the unconscious to consciousness, they rely on free association, dream analysis, and transference. (page 561)

3. Rational-emotive therapists and cognitive therapists try to get clients to give up their irrational beliefs and unrealistic goals and to replace defeatist thinking with more favorable views of themselves and the world. (page 563)

4. Humanistic therapists, including person-centered therapists, assume that if people accept themselves as they are, they can solve their own problems. Person-centered therapists listen with unconditional positive regard but seldom offer interpretations or advice. (page 564)

5. Behavior therapists set specific goals for changing a client's behavior and use a variety of learning techniques to help a client achieve those goals. (page 565)

6. About half of all psychotherapists today call themselves "eclectic"—that is, they use a combination of methods, depending on the circumstances. (page 567)

7. Among the many other forms of psychotherapy available are transactional analysis, Gestalt therapy, and paradoxical intervention. (page 568)

8. Psychotherapy is sometimes provided to people in groups, often composed of people with similar problems or members of a family. Self-help groups provide sessions similar to group therapy but without a therapist. (page 571)

9. Many therapists set a time limit on the treatment, usually ranging from two to six months. Brief therapy is about as successful as long-term therapy if the goals are limited. (page 572)

10. Psychotherapy helps most of the people who seek it. Behavior therapy and cognitive therapy are most effective in producing specific changes in behavior. Beyond that, psychologists know little about which types of therapy are best for which types of clients. (page 573)

SUGGESTIONS FOR FURTHER READING

Goleman, D., & Speeth, K. R. (1982). *The essential psychotherapies.* New York: New American Library. Includes excerpts from the writings of pioneers in psychotherapy.

Haley, J. (1984). *Ordeal therapy.* San Francisco: Jossey-Bass. Describes a clever, inventive approach to therapy.

MEDICAL THERAPIES

How do drugs and other medical interventions alleviate psychological disorders?
How effective are medical therapies?
Under what circumstances should they be used?

The Russian novelist Fyodor Dostoyevsky once described what he experienced in the moments just before an epileptic seizure:

It seemed his brain was on fire, and in an extraordinary surge all his vital forces would be intensified. The sense of life, the consciousness of self were multiplied tenfold in these moments. . . . His mind and heart were flooded with extraordinary light; all torment, all doubt, all anxieties were relieved at once, resolved in a kind of lofty calm, full of serene, harmonious joy and hope, full of understanding and knowledge of the ultimate cause of things. . . . Thinking about this moment afterward, when he was again in health, he often told himself that all these gleams and flashes of superior self-awareness and, hence, of a "higher state of being" were nothing other than sickness. . . . And yet he came finally to an extremely paradoxical conclusion. "What if it is sickness?" he asked himself. "What does it matter if it is abnormal intensity, if the result . . . turns out to be the height of harmony and beauty, and gives an unheard-of and till then undreamed-of feeling of wholeness, of proportion, of reconciliation, and an ecstatic and prayer-like union in the highest synthesis of life?"

. . . In retrospect when he thought about that minute there was unquestionably a mistake in his conclusion [1868/1969, pages 245–246].

Does happiness really "count" if it is produced by an abnormal state of the brain? Dostoyevsky had mixed feelings about this question, as do most peo-

ple today. A few people with epilepsy experience the same ecstasy as Dostoyevsky did just before their seizures; yet no matter how great that ecstasy, physicians try to alleviate their disorder. Our society has passed laws to prevent people from achieving intense pleasure through drugs. We want people to be happy but not because their brain is in an abnormal state.

By contrast, how do we treat people who complain of severe anxiety or depression? We are not sure whether unpleasant experiences or an abnormal condition of the brain causes their distress. But to them it really doesn't matter. We can tell them that their happiness is not genuine if it depends on an altered state of the brain, but we can hardly tell them that their distress isn't genuine. Regardless of the cause, distress counts, and we want to do everything we can to alleviate it. Although we oppose using drugs to make normal people happy, we may support using drugs to make distressed people feel closer to normal.

What are the effects of drugs and other medical treatments on people with psychological disorders? Do they do more good than harm? And how do they work?

THE RATIONALE BEHIND MEDICAL THERAPIES

The therapies we have examined so far all try to change people's thoughts and actions by subjecting them to new experiences. They rely on conversations between the client and the therapist or among members of a therapy group. The clients must be committed, or at least willing, to change certain aspects of their lives.

Medical therapies differ from talk therapies in some important regards. They attempt to change brain functioning directly, rather than through experience. Once the physician and client have agreed to try a drug or some other medical treatment, there is no need for further talk. To be sure, they will meet periodically to evaluate the client's progress, but those discussions are not a necessary part of the therapy itself. Moreover, clients do not need to make a commitment to changing their lives. They must agree to receive the treatment—or, if they are considered legally incompetent to decide, a legal guardian must agree—but no additional cooperation is necessary. (Medical therapies are often, though not always, combined with some form of talk therapy.)

Medical therapies assume that abnormal behavior reflects a brain that is not functioning properly. Because of its great complexity, the brain is vulnerable to many kinds of physical impairment. Even subtle chemical imbalances in the brain can lead to significant changes in behavior. The goal of medical therapies is to restore the brain to a normal physiological state.

BIOLOGICAL THERAPIES FOR DEPRESSION

Two types of drugs are widely used as antidepressants: tricyclics and monoamine oxidase inhibitors. Both types act at dopamine, norepinephrine, and serotonin synapses in the brain. When one of these neurotransmitters is released from the terminal button at the end of an axon, it stimulates receptors on the postsynaptic cell. When it detaches from those receptors, some of the molecules are reabsorbed by the terminal button; others are converted into inactive molecules; and still others reattach to the receptors on the postsynaptic cell. **Tricyclic drugs** block the reabsorption of these neurotransmitters by the terminal button. **Monoamine** (MAHN-oh-ah-MEEN) **oxidase inhibitors** (**MAOIs**) block their conversion into inactive molecules.

The effect of either type of drug is to increase the number of neurotransmitter molecules available to stimulate the postsynaptic cell. Tricyclic drugs are more commonly used. MAOIs are used for patients who suffer from severe anxiety as well as depression and for those who do not respond to tricyclics (Joyce & Paykel, 1989).

The effects of antidepressant drugs build up slowly. Some depressed people begin to experience relief within one week; most people have to take the drugs for two to three weeks before they notice any effects. The relief from depression continues to increase over six to eight weeks (Blaine, Prien, & Levine, 1983). What is happening so gradually over that time?

Two changes are taking place: First, while the drugs increase the stimulation of certain synaptic receptors, they slowly decrease the sensitivity of those receptors (McNeal & Cimbolic, 1986; Sulser, Gillespie, Mishra, & Manier, 1984). Apparently, relief from depression requires both increased stimulation and decreased sensitivity. (Exactly *why* both are needed is a puzzle.)

Second, the prolonged use of antidepressant drugs gradually improves the timing of the person's sleep patterns. Most depressed people have disorders of their 24-hour cycles. They are not as alert as other people during the day and not as sleepy at night. They wake up too early and cannot get back to sleep. Antidepressant drugs slowly restore their 24-hour cycles to normal at about the same rate at which they relieve their depression (Healy & Williams, 1988).

Concept Check

5. *The drug* mianserin *prolongs the release of dopamine, norepinephrine, and serotonin from the terminal button (Leonard, 1982). Should mianserin increase or decrease the intensity of depression? (Check your answer on page 591.)*

The Pros and Cons of Antidepressant Drugs

Antidepressant drugs alleviate depression for most people. The drugs are convenient to use and relatively inexpensive. Double-blind studies consistently find that 50 to 70% of the people who take tricyclic drugs experience an improvement in their mood, as compared to 20 to 30% of people who take placebos (Blaine, Prien, & Levine, 1983; Gerson, Plotkin, & Jarvik, 1988; Morris & Beck, 1974).

These drugs do not work for all depressed people, however. At least 30% derive no benefit from them, and many others experience only partial relief. Moreover, about one third of the people who take the drugs experience dry mouth, dizziness, sweating, and constipation. A smaller number experience tremor, blurred vision, rapid heartbeat, impaired concentration, and other side effects (Blaine, Prien, & Levine, 1983). Some people experience no side effects or only minor ones; others experience such severe side effects that they have to stop using the drugs.

Drug Therapy and Cognitive Therapy for Depression

Like the antidepressant drugs, cognitive therapy helps some depressed people but not others. Overall, drugs and cognitive therapies seem to be about equally effective (Murphy, Simons, Wetzel, & Lustman, 1984). Although cognitive therapy has the advantage of producing no side effects, it has the disadvantage of being more expensive.

Some patients who fail to respond to antidepressant drugs do respond to cognitive therapy, and some who fail to respond to cognitive therapy respond to drugs. Unfortunately, no one can predict whether a given patient will respond better to cognitive therapy or to drugs. Although it seems likely that a combination of the two would be better than either one by itself, the evidence so far is inconclusive.

Electroconvulsive Shock Therapy

Another well-known but controversial treatment for depression is **electroconvulsive therapy**, abbreviated **ECT**. In ECT, a brief electrical shock is administered across the patient's head to induce a convulsion similar to epilepsy. First used in the 1930s, ECT became popular in the 1940s and 1950s as a treatment for schizophrenia, depression, and many other disorders. It then fell out of favor, partly because antidepressant drugs and other therapeutic methods had become available and partly because ECT had been widely abused. Some patients were subjected to ECT 100 times or more without their consent. In many cases it was used as a threat to enforce patients' cooperation.

Beginning in the 1970s, ECT has made a comeback in modified form. Today it is used more selectively than it was in the past, mostly for severely depressed people who fail to respond to antidepressant drugs, whose thinking is seriously disordered, or who have strong suicidal tendencies (Scovern & Kilmann, 1980). For suicidal patients, this treatment has the advantage of taking effect more quickly than antidepressant drugs do—in about one week instead of two or three. When a life is at stake, delaying the relief is risky. ECT also decreases the time that patients spend in a hospital.

ECT is now used only with patients who have given their informed consent, and its use is generally limited to six to eight applications on alternate days. The shock is less intense than it used to be, and the patient is given muscle relaxants and anesthetics to prevent injury and to reduce discomfort.

Exactly how ECT works is uncertain. Some have suggested that it relieves depression by causing people to forget certain depressing thoughts and memories. However, the data do not support that suggestion. Although ECT usually does impair memory, at least temporarily, there are ways to reduce the memory loss without lessening the antidepressant effect (Miller, Small, Milstein, Malloy, & Stout, 1981). Among the many effects of ECT on the brain, one may be of critical importance: By decreasing the sensitivity of synapses that inhibit certain neurons from releasing dopamine and norepinephrine, ECT increases the stimulation of those synapses (Chiodo & Antelman, 1980).

The use of ECT continues to be controversial. According to extensive reviews of the literature, ECT relieves depression for about 80% of the patients and generally produces fewer side effects than antidepressant drugs do (Fink, 1985; Janicak et al., 1985; Weiner, 1984). However, other researchers question those benefits and believe that the long-term side effects have been underestimated. Even if ECT is safe and effective, it *seems* barbaric. Patients' rights groups, aware of how ECT has been abused at times, generally oppose its use. Most psychiatrists recommend ECT only as a last resort after other treatments have failed.

LITHIUM THERAPY FOR BIPOLAR DISORDER

Many years ago, researcher J. F. Cade had the idea that uric acid might be effective in treating mania. To get the uric acid to dissolve in water, he mixed it with lithium salts. The resulting mixture proved effective, but eventually researchers discovered that the lithium salts, not the uric acid, were therapeutic.

Lithium salts were soon adopted in the Scandinavian countries, but they were slow to be accepted in the United States. One reason was that drug manufacturers had no interest in marketing lithium pills. (Lithium is a natural substance and cannot be patented.) A second reason was that lithium salts produce toxic side effects unless the dosage is carefully monitored. If the dose is too low, it does no good. If it is slightly higher than the recommended level, it produces nausea and blurred vision.

Properly regulated doses of lithium are the most effective known treatment for bipolar disorder. Lithium reduces mania and protects the patient from relapsing into either mania or depression. It does not provide a permanent "cure," however; the person must continue to take lithium pills every day. When someone whose mood has been normal for months decides to quit taking the pills, mania or depression is likely to return within a few weeks.

At this point, no one is certain what causes bipolar disorder or how lithium relieves its symptoms. One possibility is that the disorder is caused by "fluctuations" in the activity of certain synapses in the brain and that lithium "stabilizes" those synapses, preventing both increases and decreases in receptor sensitivity (Pert, Rosenblatt, Sivit, Pert, & Bunney, 1978; Treiser et al., 1981).

DRUG THERAPIES FOR SCHIZOPHRENIA

Before the discovery of effective drugs, the outlook for people with schizophrenia was bleak. Usually

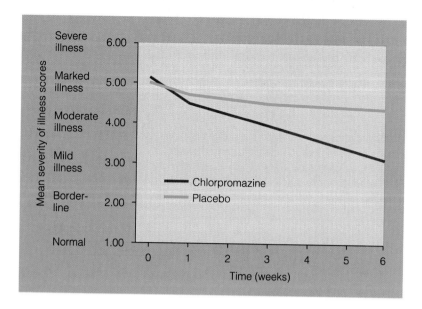

FIGURE 15.7

Antipsychotic drugs have different levels of effectiveness in treating individual schizophrenics. Such drugs reduce psychotic symptoms gradually over several weeks. Placebo pills are noticeably less effective. (Data from Cole, Goldberg, & Davis, 1966; Davis, 1985.)

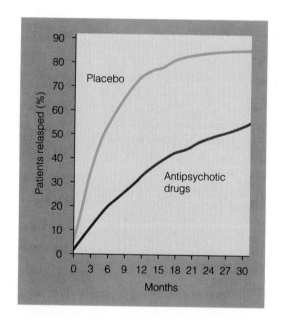

FIGURE 15.8

This graph indicates that during 2½ years, the percentage of schizophrenic patients who remained "improved" is higher in the group that received drug treatment than in the placebo group. But it also shows that antipsychotic drugs do not always prevent relapse. (Based on Baldessarini, 1984.) With these drugs, there are no quick or permanent fixes. A schizophrenic may sustain the initial improvement chlorpromazine provided by continuing to take it, but the drug will not continue improving the person's behavior.

During the 1950s, researchers discovered the first effective antischizophrenic drug: chlorpromazine (klor-PRAHM-uh-ZEEN, trade name: Thorazine). Drugs that relieve schizophrenia are known as **neuroleptic drugs**. Chlorpromazine and other neuroleptic drugs, including haloperidol (HAHL-o-PAIR-ih-doll, trade name: Haldol), have enabled many schizophrenic people to escape lifelong confinement in a mental hospital. Although these drugs do not "cure" the disorder, a daily dosage does control it, much as daily insulin shots control diabetes. Since the 1950s, a majority of people with schizophrenia have improved enough to leave mental hospitals or to avoid ever entering one (Harding et al., 1987).

All neuroleptic drugs block dopamine receptors in the brain, and their effectiveness in blocking those receptors is proportional to their effectiveness in relieving schizophrenia (Seeman, Lee, Chau-Wong, & Wong, 1976). Presumably neuroleptic drugs relieve a condition in which dopamine overstimulates certain synapses.

Neuroleptic drugs work gradually (Figure 15.7) and produce a variable degree of recovery. If treatment with neuroleptic drugs begins shortly after a rapid onset of schizophrenia, recovery is prompt and almost complete. If the onset is gradual, the recovery is also gradual. The greater the deterioration before drug treatment begins, the slighter the recovery. Most of the recovery that will ever take place emerges gradually during the first month (Szymanski, Simon, & Gutterman, 1983). Beyond that point, the drugs merely maintain behavior but do not improve it. If an affected person stops taking the drugs, the symptoms are likely to return and to grow worse, though in some cases they do not return (see Figure 15.8). For a given patient, it is difficult to predict what will happen (Lieberman et al., 1987).

Side Effects of Drug Therapies for Schizophrenia

Because of the side effects of neuroleptic drugs, psychiatrists are cautious in prescribing them. Prolonged use of these drugs leads to impotence in men (Mitchell & Popkin, 1982). They also produce a movement disorder, **tardive dyskinesia** (TAHRD-eev DIS-ki-NEE-zhuh), characterized by tremors and involuntary movements (Chouinard & Jones, 1980). Tardive dyskinesia is the result of increased sensitivity of the synapses to dopamine. After neuroleptic drugs have blocked someone's dopamine receptors for years, the brain builds additional dopamine receptors to compensate for the loss. Some dopamine receptors facilitate movement, and when those receptors become oversensitive, involuntary move-

they underwent a gradual deterioration interrupted by periods of partial recovery. Within a few years, most of them entered a mental hospital, where they spent the rest of their lives.

ments occur. Tardive dyskinesia is often a permanent condition, although a patient who quits taking neuroleptic drugs at an early age has a good chance of recovery (Smith & Baldessarini, 1980). So far, physicians are unable to predict which patients will develop tardive dyskinesia and which ones will not.

Concept Check

6. *In the previous chapter, we considered the efforts that are made to diagnose schizophrenia as early as possible. Given what we know about neuroleptic drugs, why is early diagnosis so important? (Check your answer on page 591.)*

Drug Therapy and Psychotherapy for Schizophrenia

The degree of recovery produced by antischizophrenic drugs varies, and drug therapy by itself is not a perfect solution. Some people with schizophrenia never have to enter a mental hospital, but others spend years in hospitals and still others are in and out of hospitals throughout their lives (Pokorny, 1978).

Highly stressful experiences sometimes aggravate schizophrenia and may cause a flare-up of problems that had been brought under control. If a patient faces constant criticism and hostility from relatives, the schizophrenic symptoms are likely to grow worse (Vaughn, Snyder, Jones, Freeman, & Falloon, 1984). In extreme cases, it may be necessary to separate the patient from the family scene. In other cases, psychotherapy for the family may improve the situation. Psychotherapy can be a valuable adjunct to drug therapies.

DRUG THERAPIES FOR OTHER DISORDERS

Drug therapies are also used to treat a number of other disorders. In Chapter 14, we considered the use of Antabuse for alcohol abuse and methadone for opiate abuse.

Tranquilizers are widely used to reduce anxiety. Benzodiazepine tranquilizers (including drugs with the trade names Valium, Librium, and Xanax) facilitate transmission at synapses that use the neurotransmitter GABA (Macdonald, Weddle, & Gross, 1986). Facilitation of those synapses decreases anxiety and promotes sleep. Tranquilizers also reduce anxiety indirectly: People who have tranquilizers available "as a crutch" are less worried about having an anxiety attack and are consequently less likely to have such an attack. Unfortunately, some people come to rely on tranquilizers for problems they could handle without drugs.

Drugs have been used experimentally in treating several other disorders. For example, a drug called clomipramine has helped some obsessive-compulsive people, especially those who also show signs of depression (Benkelfat et al., 1989). Clomipramine prolongs the effects of serotonin at its synapses by blocking the terminal button from absorbing it again.

The future of drug therapy is difficult to predict. The drugs currently available help many people but are far from being fully satisfactory. Researchers are searching for new drugs that will produce desirable effects with as few side effects as possible.

SUMMARY

1. Medical therapies are designed to alter brain activity directly. (page 575)

2. Tricyclic drugs and MAOIs are widely used to treat depression. Both types of drugs prolong the stimulation of synaptic receptors by dopamine, norepinephrine, and serotonin. (page 576)

3. The effects of antidepressant drugs build up slowly over weeks. About 50 to 70% of depressed people benefit from taking these drugs, as compared to 20 to 30% of those who take placebos. The drugs produce unpleasant side effects for some people. (page 576)

4. Electroconvulsive shock therapy has a long history of abuse; in modified form it has made a comeback and is now helpful to some depressed people who fail to respond to antidepressant drugs. (page 577)

5. Lithium salts are the most effective treatment for bipolar disorder. (page 577)

6. Drugs that block dopamine synapses often alleviate schizophrenia. Results are best if treatment begins before the person has suffered serious deterioration. (page 578)

7. Drug treatment for schizophrenia sometimes produces a movement disorder called tardive dyskinesia. (page 578)

8. Drugs are also used in the treatment of other disorders, including anxiety. Research continues to search for drugs that relieve psychological disorders without producing undesirable side effects. (page 579)

SUGGESTION FOR FURTHER READING

Solomon, S. H. (1980). *Biological aspects of mental disorder.* New York: Oxford University Press. Discussion of research on biological causes and treatments of psychological disorders.

SOCIAL AND
LEGAL ISSUES
IN THE
TREATMENT
OF
PSYCHOLOGICAL
DISORDERS

What should society do about psychological
disorders?
Can anything be done to prevent them?

———————

A group of nearsighted people, lost in the woods, were trying to find their way home. One of the few who wore glasses said, "I think I know the way. Follow me." The others burst into laughter. "That's ridiculous," said one. "How could anybody who needs glasses be our leader?"

In 1972, the Democratic Party nominated Senator Thomas Eagleton for vice president of the United States. Shortly after his nomination he revealed that he had once received psychiatric treatment for depression. He was subjected to merciless ridicule: "How could anybody who needs a psychiatrist be our leader?" In 1988, rumors circulated that the Democratic nominee for president, Michael Dukakis, had once received psychotherapy for depression. Although the rumors were apparently unfounded, they hurt Dukakis's standing in the polls.

About one fourth to one third of all Americans suffer from a psychological disorder at some time during their lives. Unfortunately, many people in our society consider it shameful to seek help for a psychological disorder. They struggle along on their own, like a nearsighted person who refuses to wear glasses, rather than admit they need help.

Suppose you never become a psychiatrist or a clinical psychologist and never go to one for treatment. And suppose that none of your relatives or friends ever suffer from any psychological disorder. (It's hard to imagine how that could happen. Maybe you don't have many friends.) As a citizen and voter, you will still have to deal with issues relating to psychological disorders and therapies: How should society treat current and former mental patients? Should we reject such people if they seek a job or public office? Who, if anyone, should be confined to a mental hospital? Under what circumstances, if any, should a criminal defendant be acquitted because of "insanity"? Should mental patients have the right to refuse treatment? Can society take steps to prevent certain types of psychological disorders?

MENTAL HOSPITALS VERSUS COMMUNITY-BASED CARE

About once every eight seconds someone in the United States is admitted to a hospital or a nursing home because of a psychological problem (Kiesler, 1982b). Most of those people stay less than a month, but some stay years, even a lifetime. Hospitalization for psychological problems accounts for 25% of hospitalizations for all types of illness in the United States.

Until the 1950s, people with severe psychological disturbances were generally confined in large mental hospitals supported by their state or county. At the time most of those hospitals were built, severely disturbed mental patients had little hope of ever returning to society. The hospitals, which were designed to provide long-term custodial care, were usually located in some remote country area far from the patients' homes. Ordinarily, they were constructed so that the patients could not escape or hurt one another. In other words, they resembled prisons (Okin, 1983). Patients were dependent on hospital attendants who cooked the food, did the laundry, and made all the decisions. Little thought was given to helping patients learn the skills they would need if they were ever to leave. State hospitals claimed to provide psychiatric care, but most patients seldom saw a psychiatrist or a psychologist. Moreover, state legislatures rarely furnished enough financial support to attract well-qualified, professional personnel. Some hospitals were better than others, but most of them were pretty grim places.

With the advent of antidepressant and antischizophrenic drugs in the 1950s and with subsequent changes in the commitment laws, the number of long-term residents in mental hospitals declined steadily. Today, those hospitals have less than one third the number of residents they had in 1950 (Pepper & Ryglewicz, 1982). The goal of men-

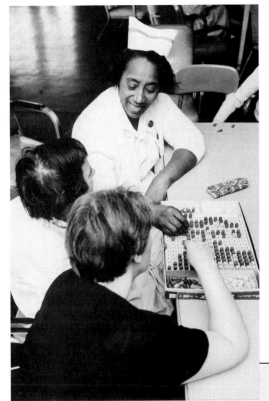

Until recently, conditions in mental hospitals, with their bleak, prisonlike environments, have done little to foster patients' improvement. The title of a 1948 book on state mental hospitals— The Shame of the States—*reflects the conditions the author found. Patients today are less likely to be abused but still likely to be neglected. While some mental institutions try to be more pleasant places, many of them provide only housing, not therapy.* Is There No Place on Earth for Me? *describes the frustrations of one frequently hospitalized schizophrenic (Sheehan, 1982).*

tal hospitals is no longer to provide long-term custody. Instead, it is to supply short-term care until a patient is ready to return home.

Unfortunately, however, most mental hospitals are still prisonlike institutions, ill suited to their new goals. Moreover, with the decline in mental-hospital populations, state legislatures have shown little interest in spending money on new, modern facilities. Since the 1950s, our understanding of psychological disorders has grown dramatically, but the settings and policies of mental hospitals have remained about the same.

Life in Mental Hospitals

To find out what life is like in mental hospitals, eight healthy adults—three psychologists, a psychiatrist, a psychology graduate student, and three others—each approached a different mental hospital and asked to be voluntarily committed (Rosenhan, 1973). Some repeated the experience until as a group they had entered 12 mental hospitals. When asked why

they thought they belonged in a mental hospital, they said, "Sometimes I hear voices. . . ." Apparently those were the magic words; each was admitted at once, generally with a diagnosis of schizophrenia. (One was given a diagnosis of bipolar disorder.)

D. L. Rosenhan reports that he and the other "patients" were immediately degraded to a status less than human. First they were given a physical examination in a semipublic room where a number of other people came and went. Then they were assigned to a ward where the staff paid little attention to them.

At first, the pseudopatients tried to conceal the fact that they were "spying" on the hospital and jotted down their notes in secret. Later, when they realized that none of the staff members were paying much attention, they grew bolder and bolder. Eventually they followed the staff around, taking notes on everything the staff did. Far from being intimidated by this behavior, the staff regarded this note taking as a "symptom" of the patients' "illness"!

One day a nurse unbuttoned her uniform to

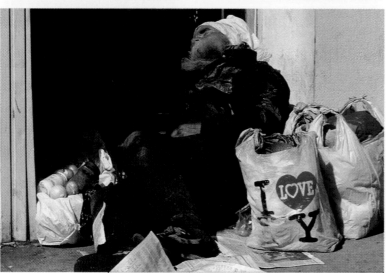

The San Mateo County program in California achieved much success in providing community mental health services but also encountered these problems: lack of attention to preventive care, inadequate services for children and the elderly, deficient 24-hour emergency care, limited availability of day hospitals and partial hospitalization, failure to evaluate policies' effectiveness, and difficulties in distinguishing short- and long-term patients when they are hospitalized. In addition, community services cope with some people who are severely disturbed and have little family and social support (Lamb, Heath, and Downing, 1969). The recent trend of deinstitutionalization has left many mentally ill people on the street, homeless and uncared for—a situation that can hardly improve anyone's mental health.

adjust her bra while standing in the middle of a men's ward. Rosenhan noted that she showed no embarrassment and paid no attention to the men. Her action told them that she did not regard them as *men*. They were just *mental patients*.

Eventually all the pseudopatients were discharged with a diagnosis of "schizophrenia in remission"—meaning that they still had schizophrenia but were no longer showing symptoms. None of the psychiatrists or other staff showed any suspicion that the pseudopatients were really healthy; none expressed any doubt about the diagnosis of schizophrenia. Actually, it is not surprising that the staff members were so easily taken in by the fake mental patients—healthy people rarely try to get admitted to mental hospitals. The significance of the report is that the hospitals showed scant respect for the privacy and self-respect of their patients.

When the staff at another mental hospital heard about these results and expressed doubt that they would ever admit a fake patient, Rosenhan arranged an experiment. He told them that one or more healthy people would attempt to be admitted to the hospital within the next three months, and he challenged the staff to identify the impostors. No pseudopatients actually showed up, but one or more staff members pointed out 41 new patients (from a total of 193) as "probable impostors." Evidently, even experienced professionals have trouble identifying who has a psychological disorder and who does not.

Deinstitutionalization: The Concept and the Reality

Many mental-health specialists believe that putting people in large institutions is not the best way to deal with their problems. Far too many mental hospitals are impersonal and degrading, hardly an ideal setting for overcoming psychological disorders. Critics claim that people with mild to moderate problems are better off in community mental-health centers close to their own homes. There they receive supervision and treatment, but they also enjoy some degree of independence, some freedom to come and go, and some contact with the "real world." Certain patients may even live at home, getting their professional care either by visiting a treatment center or by having a mental-health worker visit them at home. Still others may rely on a self-help group.

Several studies have compared these "alternate" forms of care with full-time confinement in mental hospitals. Every study has found that well-planned alternate care is as good as or better than care in mental hospitals in promoting psychological adjustment, in helping patients return to their school or job, and in restoring them to independent living (Braun et al., 1981; Kiesler, 1982a). Alternate care is also less expensive.

Such research prompted a movement toward **deinstitutionalization,** the removal of patients from mental hospitals. The idea is to give people the least restrictive care possible. Only those few patients who cannot care for themselves or who are considered dangerous to society would be confined to mental hospitals. The rest would live in their own homes or in group homes and would receive care at well-funded community mental-health centers.

Unfortunately, many states got only half the message. They discharged great numbers of patients from their mental hospitals *without* planning adequate alternatives for care and housing (Pepper & Ryglewicz, 1982). They unwittingly created a population of mentally disturbed people with no home, no job, and little opportunity for professional care (Teplin, 1983). One study found that about one fourth of the homeless people in Los Angeles were suffering from long-term psychological disorders (Koegel, Burnam, & Farr, 1988).

THE RIGHT TO REFUSE TREATMENT

A psychiatrist believes that Charles is severely schizophrenic. He cannot hold a job, he does not pay his bills or take care of his personal hygiene, and his neighbors consider him a nuisance. His family wants to commit him to a mental hospital, and the psychiatrist wants to give him drugs. But Charles refuses both courses. He claims that his family is "out to get him," and he does not want anyone to "control his mind" with drugs. Should he be permitted to refuse treatment?

We can argue this question either way. On the one hand, although most people with psychological disorders are harmless, except perhaps to themselves, a few are dangerous. Moreover, some seriously disordered people fail to recognize that there is anything wrong with them. On the other hand, some families have been known to commit aging or otherwise unwelcome relatives to mental hospitals just to get them out of the way. And some psychiatrists have given drugs and ECT treatments to people with only minor problems, doing them more harm than good. People need protection from inappropriate treatment.

Which people (if any) should be confined to a mental hospital against their will? In the United States, laws vary from state to state. The mere fact that psychiatrists believe a person "needs treat-

ment" is not enough. In some states, a court can commit patients to a mental hospital only if they are suffering from a mental disorder *and* are dangerous to themselves or others. The American Psychiatric Association has recommended that the laws be changed to allow commitment of any patient who "lacks capacity to make an informed decision concerning treatment" and who has a severe disorder that can be treated (Bloom & Faulkner, 1987; Hoge, Sachs, Appelbaum, Greer, & Gordon, 1988). That is, they would rely on a judgment of the patient's competence rather than on whether the patient was dangerous. Regardless of how the law is stated, a judge has to make the final decision after a court hearing. Because some judges are willing to accept a psychiatrist's opinion, while others are not, the outcome of such hearings varies haphazardly (Bloom & Faulkner, 1987).

Patients in a mental hospital have the right to refuse certain forms of treatment even if they have been involuntarily committed by a judge who decided that they needed those treatments (Appelbaum, 1988a). What patients are likely to refuse treatment? Many of them exhibit hostility, emotional withdrawal, and disorganized thinking (Marder et al., 1983). They may have serious disorders and may really need the help they refuse. Some of them, however, may have reason to be angry; they may be emotionally distressed because the hospital staff is trying to force them to submit to treatment. Figure 15.9 compares patients with schizophrenia who refused drug treatment and patients who agreed to drug treatment.

Thomas Szasz (1982) has proposed that psychologically "normal" people write a "psychiatric will" specifying what is to be done if they ever develop a psychological disorder that disqualifies them from making their own decisions. Such a will might state, "If Dr. Shrink decides that I am severely depressed, I may be given antidepressant drugs but not ECT. If I am judged schizophrenic, I may be given chlorpromazine or haloperidol only up to the following maximum doses. ... If there is any dispute over whether I should be confined to an institution, I authorize my sister Ellen to make the decision for me."

But such instructions might create more problems than they solve. How many people know enough to make an informed decision about every treatment that someone might recommend years in the future? What if you wrote such a will, and then, later on, while suffering from depression, decided that you *did* want ECT? Should your psychiatrist withhold treatment because of what you wrote when you were healthy? And what if sister Ellen decides to commit you to a mental hospital

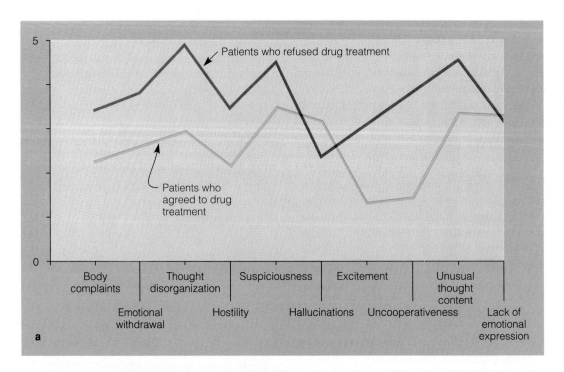

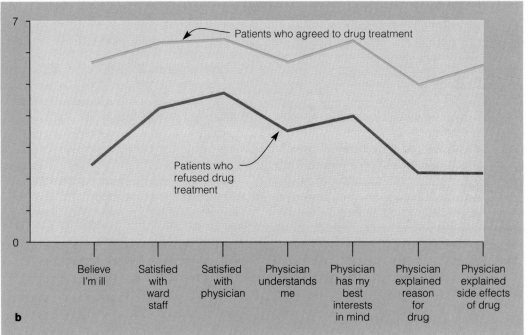

FIGURE 15.9

Comparison of schizophrenics who refused drug treatment and who agreed to drug treatment. (a) Physicians' ratings of their patients. High scores indicate greater disturbance. Those refusing treatment showed greater indications of disturbance on most scales. (b) Patients' self-ratings. The higher scores of patients who agreed to drug treatment indicate their higher satisfaction with how they have been treated. (Based on data from Marder et al., 1983.)

over your objections? The will, after all, takes effect only *after* you have been judged psychologically incompetent to make your own decisions. Who decides whether you have reached that point—you, Ellen, or a judge? As with so many other moral dilemmas, it is difficult to find a policy that is satisfactory in all cases.

THE INSANITY DEFENSE

British and American courts have traditionally accepted "insanity" as a defense against criminal charges, on the grounds that people who did not understand the act they committed, or who did not commit it voluntarily, cannot be held "morally blameworthy." But it is difficult to determine who is insane. *Insanity* is a legal term, not a psychological or medical one, and its definition has gone through many changes over the years (Shapiro, 1985). One definition, the **M'Naghten rule**, was written in Britain in 1843. It states:

To establish a defense on the ground of insanity, it must be clearly proved that, at the time of the committing of the act, the party accused was laboring under such a defect of reason, from disease of the mind, as not to know the nature and quality of the act he was doing; or if he did know it, that he did not know he was doing what was wrong [Shapiro, 1985].

In other words, to be regarded as insane under the M'Naghten rule, people must be so disordered that they do not realize they are committing a crime.

In the late 1800s, the rule was broadened slightly to include the concept of "irresistible impulse." Under that rule, a defendant who knew an act was wrong could not be held criminally responsible if he or she was unable to prevent the act. In practice, this rule is difficult to apply. What is the difference between an *irresistible* impulse to commit a criminal act and an impulse that is merely *not resisted*? (Some states have ruled that an act is irresistible if the person would have committed the act even with a policeman standing by.)

The next attempt was the **Durham rule**, established by a U.S. court in 1954 in the case of a man named Durham. The court held that a defendant is not criminally responsible if the activity was "a product of mental disease or defect." That rule confused more than it clarified. Almost anything can be considered a mental disease or defect. And what does it mean to say that an act is a "product" of such a defect?

The **Model Penal Code**, written in the 1950s, attempted to clarify the definition of insanity:

A person is not responsible for criminal conduct if at the time of such conduct as a result of mental disease or defect he lacks substantial capacity either to appreciate the criminality (wrongfulness) of his conduct or to conform his conduct to the requirements of law [Shapiro, 1985].

The Model Penal Code further excludes any disorder whose *only* manifestation is criminal activity: The defense cannot argue that "obviously the defendant must have been insane, because the crime itself was so bizarre." In other words, there must be evidence of insanity other than the criminal act itself.

The rules on the determination of insanity differ from country to country and from state to state within the United States. In any event, less than 1% of people accused of felonies in the United States are acquitted by reason of insanity (Insanity Defense Work Group, 1983).

One question under debate is whether the prosecution or the defense should bear the "burden of proof" in establishing insanity. When John Hinckley, Jr., was tried in 1981 for attempting to assassinate President Ronald Reagan, the judge instructed the jury that, in order to convict the defendant, the prosecution had to prove that he was sane. In other cases, the defense has had to prove that the defendant was insane in order to win an acquittal.

When John Hinckley, Jr., was found not guilty by reason of insanity in 1982, laws were revised across the country to limit the insanity defense—despite the fact that it is not often used and is successful even less often. In 1981, "only four federal defendants were acquitted of charges on the basis of a successful insanity defense"; of those four, one was charged with murder (Caplan, 1984, page 104).

A second question is whether those who are called to give "expert testimony" should state their opinion of the defendant's sanity or just describe the defendant's mental condition. A growing number of lawyers, psychiatrists, and psychologists would prefer to limit expert testimony to descriptive statements, leaving the legal question of insanity to the judge and jury (Insanity Defense Work Group, 1983). Many psychiatrists and psychologists prefer that policy because they view mental health as a matter of degree, while the courts insist on a yes or no answer to questions of insanity. They want to avoid the confusion that results when one "expert" insists that a defendant is insane and another insists just as firmly that the defendant is sane (Faust & Ziskin, 1988).

How easy would it be for a criminal to "fake" a psychological disorder? It is difficult to say. In many cases, two or more qualified therapists have examined the same defendant and have come to entirely different judgments on the person's mental status. In the two cases that follow, the therapists and the courts had trouble deciding but eventually concluded that the defendant was only pretending to be psychologically disordered.

The Bianchi Case

In 1979, Kenneth Bianchi was arrested for raping and strangling two women. He was suspected of raping and strangling many others in similar fashion—of being the "Hillside Strangler" who had been terrifying the Los Angeles area. While he was awaiting trial, a psychiatrist hypnotized him and claimed to uncover a second personality, "Steve Walker," who had first appeared at age 9 and who had, Bianchi said, actually committed the crimes. Bianchi pleaded not guilty by reason of insanity.

Six psychiatrists were asked to decide whether Bianchi really had two personalities, or was faking, or was responding to the hypnotist's suggestion. It is generally difficult for therapists to determine whether someone is pretending to have a psychological disorder, because most of them have had little experience with pretenders. (Few healthy people pretend to be severely disturbed.)

Finally, one psychiatrist, Martin Orne, managed to convince a majority of the others that Bianchi was not a true case of multiple personality (Orne, Dinges, & Orne, 1984). Among Orne's reasons were the following:

1. None of Bianchi's acquaintances recalled his ever changing his personality drastically or asking them to call him by a different name.

2. Bianchi was known to have seen the movie, *The Three Faces of Eve* (which portrayed a case of multiple personality; page 512), and to have read a magazine article about a murderer who was found not guilty because of multiple personalities that had begun at age 9.

3. At one point Orne told Bianchi that he doubted Bianchi was a true case of multiple personality because "real" multiple personalities have three personalities, not just two. (This is not true; Orne just wanted to see what would happen.) Later that day, Bianchi developed a third personality.

4. Bianchi had held many jobs, none for long. One of them was as a psychologist (!). To get a diploma to hang on his wall, he advertised that he was opening a practice in clinical psychology and invited applications from other psychologists who might like to join him. He then took the name Steve Walker from one of the applications and wrote to Walker's university, claiming to be Walker and asking for a second copy of his diploma. He asked that they leave the name blank, because he wanted to have someone inscribe it with fancy calligraphy. The university promptly sent Bianchi a blank diploma, on which he inserted his own name. Bianchi clearly got the name Steve Walker from this experience, not from a second personality that emerged at age 9.

After Orne had uncovered these facts, Bianchi agreed to plead guilty in return for the state's dropping its request for the death penalty. He also stopped claiming to have multiple personalities.

The "Son of Sam" Case

In 1977, David Berkowitz was arrested for a series of murders in New York. He had shot a number of young women in cars, and sometimes their dates as well, leaving messages saying the murderer was the "Son of Sam." When arrested, he claimed that he was acting on orders from his neighbor's dog, Sam. Berkowitz described hallucinations and delusions; two psychiatrists concluded that he was suffering from paranoid schizophrenia.

A third psychologist, David Abrahamsen (1985), pointed out that in many ways Berkowitz's reports did not resemble true hallucinations. For example, they occurred only while he was at home. Moreover, Abrahamsen was able to trace Berkowitz's violent behavior to earlier experiences. Berkowitz had had a stormy relationship with his adoptive parents. As a child, he had committed many acts of vandalism for which he was rarely caught and never disciplined. He had a long history of hating girls and women. When he eventually met his biological mother, he was deeply disappointed to find that she did not live up to his idealized image of her. He was even more disturbed to learn that although she had put him up for adoption, she had kept his half-sister. Enraged, he committed many acts of arson and then went on to commit the murders, almost all of them in the Queens, New York, neighborhood where his half-sister now lived. Eventually, he guaranteed his own arrest by leaving a trail of clues, such as parking his car in front of a fire hydrant while committing a murder. Clearly Berkowitz was disturbed; clearly he was abnormal. But was he insane in the legal sense? No. He was not schizophrenic, and he knew that what he was doing was wrong. He was found guilty of murder and sentenced to prison.

The point of these cases is *not* that we should disbelieve every criminal defendant who pleads insanity. The point is simply that psychologists and the courts must look for solid evidence to support or refute such claims.

ARE MENTAL PATIENTS DANGEROUS?

The widespread concern about the insanity defense seems to imply that mental patients are dangerous. Are they? Suppose you were told that the house next to yours was about to be converted to a community mental-health center, a halfway house for former mental patients. How would you feel? Many people would be afraid. Television and films contribute to this fear by featuring stories about mentally deranged mass murderers. The impression of danger is compounded by selective reporting—we hear about the few mental patients who commit crimes and never about the many who do not. As a result, we perceive an *illusory correlation*, an apparent relationship between two unrelated variables.

That fear of mental patients is mostly unjustified. A small number of people who are arrested for a crime get sent to a mental hospital instead of a prison. When released, they have a high probability of committing further crimes. Other patients who are sent to a mental hospital—those who have *not* been arrested—are nearly always harmless. After their release, they are no more likely than any other citizen to become a suspect in a crime (Cocozza, Melick, & Steadman, 1978; Rabkin, 1979; Teplin, 1985). (See Figure 15.10.)

However, many cities have homeless mentally

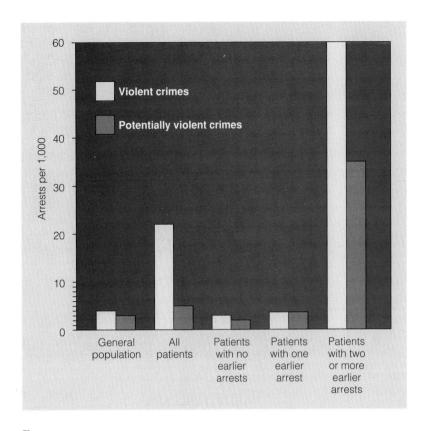

FIGURE 15.10

These arrest rates compare levels of violent crimes among the general population and mental patients. (After data reported by Cocozza, Melick, & Steadman, 1978.) A few mental patients with a previous criminal history continue to be dangerous. The others are no more dangerous than anyone else.

ill people whom no one knows how to handle. Many of them are arrested and jailed for minor offenses that the police ordinarily ignore such as public drunkenness, panhandling, or jaywalking. In other words, society uses the legal system to get people off the streets instead of relying on psychological or medical reasons (Teplin, 1984).

Under a practice known as **preventive detention**, psychologically disturbed people who are considered dangerous to society can be involuntarily committed to a mental hospital to prevent them from committing crimes, even though it is practically impossible to decide who is dangerous. Someone tells a therapist, "Sometimes I feel like going out and killing someone." In fact, many normal people sometimes feel that way. But very few people who *feel* like killing someone ever do it. So therapists do not necessarily consider such statements as serious threats, and most would prefer to avoid using preventive detention.

However, several courts have ruled that if a

therapist does not take a murder threat seriously and the patient does commit a murder, the therapist can be held legally responsible. In other words, the therapist has a "duty to warn." Those rulings have put therapists in an awkward position. Suppose you are a therapist and one of your clients expresses an urge to kill someone. You doubt that your client will do anything of the sort, but do you take the chance? If your client does commit murder, you could be in serious legal trouble. Many therapists deal with this situation by ordering such a client committed to a mental hospital, even if hospitalization is clearly not in the client's best interests (Appelbaum, 1988b). (Moral of the story: Legal decisions sometimes have unintended consequences.)

Concept Check

7. *Why is it probably true that the mental hospitals in some states contain more dangerous people than in other states? (Check your answer on page 591.)*

PREDICTING AND PREVENTING MENTAL ILLNESS

Early in his career, Sigmund Freud wrote that psychological disorders were the result of sexual abuse early in childhood (Freud & Breuer, 1893). We now recognize that early sexual abuse, especially abuse by a father or stepfather, can indeed increase the probability of later psychological disorders (Browne & Finkelhor, 1986; Herman, Russell, & Trocki, 1986). If psychologists had taken Freud's early writings seriously, they might have taken steps to reduce the incidence of sexual abuse and consequently the incidence of psychological disorders. At the very least they might have identified some of the children who were most vulnerable to later disorders and who were most likely to need psychological attention.

When Freud changed his theory and said that psychological disorders are the result of childhood sexual *fantasies,* he implied that psychological disorders are unpredictable and unpreventable. Since then, most psychotherapists have waited for disorders to emerge before trying to treat them and have made few attempts at prevention.

Some psychologists, especially community psychologists, have begun to pay more attention to prevention. **Community psychologists** focus on the needs of large groups rather than on individuals. They distinguish between **primary prevention**, preventing a disorder from starting, and **secondary prevention**, identifying a disorder in its early stages and preventing it from becoming more serious.

Methods of Prevention

Just as our society puts fluoride into drinking water to prevent tooth decay and immunizes people against contagious diseases, it can take action to prevent certain types of psychological disorder (Albee, 1986; Goldston, 1986; Long, 1986). For example, it can take the following actions:

- Banning toxins: The sale of lead-based paint has been banned because children who eat flakes of lead-based paint sustain brain damage. Other toxins in the air and water have yet to be controlled.

- Educating pregnant women about prenatal care: For example, women need to be informed that the use of alcohol or other drugs during pregnancy may cause brain damage to the fetus and that certain bacterial and viral infections during pregnancy may impair fetal brain development and increase the risk of psychological disorders.

- Support groups: Alcoholics Anonymous and other support groups help people to cope with a variety of problems. Even if they do not prevent problems altogether, they may prevent moderate problems from growing more serious.

- Jobs: Helping people who lose their jobs to find new work enables them to regain their self-esteem.

- Child care: Providing better day-care facilities would contribute to the psychological health of both parents and children.

Besides these techniques, which are aimed at many segments of the population, society can also support efforts to identify and treat people who seem likely to develop particular disorders. In earlier chapters, we found that some people are more likely than others to develop violent behavior (page 439), alcoholism (page 528), depression (page 536), and schizophrenia (page 549). Through genetic testing, behavioral observations, and biological tests, psychologists and psychiatrists may be able to identify such people early enough to prevent the problem from developing or at least to limit its severity—provided that we can find ways to intervene without stigmatizing people as "future mental patients."

Can the Media Cause or Prevent Suicide? What's the Evidence?

During late 1984 and early 1985, the U.S. television networks broadcast four programs in well-meaning attempts to discourage suicide, partly by dramatizing the pain that suicide causes to families. What effect, if any, might those shows have had on the suicide rate? Although the networks did not intend this as a scientific study, Madelyn Gould and David Shaffer (1986) analyzed the results as if it were one.

Hypothesis   The suicide rate will either increase or decrease—we do not know which—during the two weeks after a fictional suicide is portrayed on television.

Method   Gould and Shaffer (1986) collected data about suicides and suicide attempts by teenagers who had been admitted to six hospitals in the New York City area. (They concentrated on teenagers because the TV programs portrayed teenagers.) They determined the teenage suicide rates for the two weeks immediately after each of the four TV shows on suicide, when viewers were most likely to be influenced by them. They then compared those rates to the rates during other weeks in the fall and winter of 1984–1985.

Results   During the two weeks just after each show, teenagers in the area committed a mean of 1.6 suicides per week plus 11 uncompleted attempts. During *other* weeks in the fall and winter of 1984–1985, the means were 1.1 suicides and 7.8 attempts. The increase in suicide attempts was statistically significant ($p < .05$), but the increase in completed suicides was not.

Interpretation   The publicity had backfired. There were more suicide attempts just after the shows than at other times. Evidently some people who attempt suicide are responding to suggestion. Knowing that someone else has taken that action may make it seem more acceptable to them, and they may imagine that their own act will receive similar publicity. ■

David Phillips and Lundie Carstensen (1986) reported similar results in a study on the effects of reports of actual suicides. From 1973 to 1979, the teenage suicide rate generally went up during the week after a news story about a teenage suicide. (This was true for both newspaper and TV accounts.) The greater the publicity, the greater the increase in the suicide rate. Phillips (1974) reported similar results for adults.

These results suggest that society could help reduce the suicide rate by urging the media to give less publicity to suicides. Still, it is difficult to interpret before-and-after studies like these. Perhaps the suicide rates went up or down at particular times for reasons unrelated to the TV programs.

Two other studies attempted to replicate Gould and Shaffer's results. Gould and Shaffer had limited their study to hospital records in the New York City area. David Phillips and Daniel Paight (1987) examined records in Pennsylvania and California, and A. L. Berman (1988) looked at suicide rates throughout the United States. Neither study found a significant change in suicide rates after the broadcast of the same programs that Gould and Shaffer had studied. In fact, they found slightly fewer suicides during the two weeks after each program than during the two weeks before.

Another study examined suicide rates throughout the country following TV news stories about actual (not fictional) suicides (Kessler, Downey, Milafsky, & Stipp, 1988). This study confirmed the finding by Phillips and Carstensen (1986) that between 1973 and 1980 the teenage suicide rate rose during the weeks following the airing of such stories. However, between 1981 and 1984 the teenage suicide rate *decreased* during the weeks following the broadcast of similar stories.

What conclusions can we draw? First, it is hard to draw any conclusion about whether televised stories about suicide, either fictional or factual, will lead to an increase or a decrease in the suicide rate. However, there does seem to be evidence that some people copy the *method* of suicide described in such stories. For example, after a story about suicide by carbon monoxide poisoning, the use of that method shows a temporary increase (Berman, 1988).

A second conclusion is that efforts to prevent psychological disorders through education do not always succeed. We probably would have guessed that stories about suicide would discourage suicide. We now see that it is not that easy. We must evaluate the success of any effort to use education and information to discourage drug abuse, anorexia nervosa, or behaviors that lead to AIDS to see whether the effect is succeeding, backfiring, or having no effect.

Third, the results underline an important point about the scientific method: the need for replication. Even when a study has been carefully conducted, other investigators must repeat the procedures to see whether they get the same results in other times and places. As we have seen, the results of studies on suicide publicity could not be replicated elsewhere. It may be that the effect of publicity about suicide really does vary from one time and place to another. Or perhaps some of the results represent random fluctuations or the effects of events other than the TV programs. In any event, we must be cautious about drawing conclusions from a study before its results have been replicated.

SUMMARY

1. Most mental hospitals were designed and built at a time when society expected mental patients to remain in them for a long time, even for a lifetime. Today, most patients stay a month or less. Large mental hospitals are not well designed to help restore people to society. In many of them, patients receive little attention and little respect. (page 580)

2. Community mental-health centers provide psychological care while permitting people some measure of freedom. The care they provide is equal or superior to the care provided by large mental hospitals. However, many states have released patients from mental hospitals without supplying adequate community mental-health facilities. (page 582)

3. Laws on involuntary commitment to mental hospitals vary. In some states people can be committed only if they are dangerous; in others, people can be committed if they are judged incompetent to decide about their own treatment. It is difficult to frame laws that ensure treatment for those who need it, while also protecting the rights of those who have good reasons for refusing it. (page 583)

4. Some defendants accused of a crime are acquitted for reasons of insanity, which is a legal rather than a medical or psychological concept. The criteria for establishing insanity are vague and controversial. (page 585)

5. Some defendants who have pleaded insanity have turned out to be pretenders. It is often difficult to determine whether a defendant is suffering from a psychological disorder or only pretending to be. (page 586)

6. Mental patients are rarely dangerous, except for those few who had committed crimes before being admitted to a mental hospital. Yet some mental patients are arrested to keep them off the streets, and others are involuntarily committed to mental hospitals to prevent them from committing crimes, even when it is highly unlikely that they will do so. (page 587)

7. Psychologists and psychiatrists are increasingly concerned about preventing psychological disorders. Many preventive measures require the cooperation of society as a whole. (page 588)

8. It may be possible to lower suicide rates by curtailing media publicity about suicide, although the evidence is not conclusive. (page 589)

SUGGESTIONS FOR FURTHER READING

Ewing, C. P. (Ed.). (1985). *Psychology, psychiatry, and the law: A clinical and forensic handbook.* Sarasota, FL: Professional Resource Exchange. A review of procedures governing commitment to mental hospitals, the insanity defense, the right to refuse treatment, and other legal issues.

Sheehan, S. (1982). *Is there no place on earth for me?* Boston: Houghton Mifflin. The story of a young woman with schizophrenia and her life in and out of mental hospitals.

TERMS TO REMEMBER

behavior therapy a form of therapy in which the therapist and client agree on specific behavioral goals and set up learning experiences to achieve those goals, using positive reinforcement, classical conditioning, and sometimes punishment

brief therapy therapy that begins with an agreement to restrict its duration, generally to six months or less

catharsis the release of pent-up emotions

cognitive therapy a form of therapy that seeks to improve people's well-being by encouraging them to seek evidence that either supports or refutes their beliefs

community psychologist a psychologist who focuses on the needs of large groups rather than those of individuals

deinstitutionalization the removal of large numbers of patients from mental hospitals

Durham rule a rule that states that criminal defendants are insane if their acts were a product of mental disease or defect

eclectic therapy therapy that uses a combination of methods and approaches

electroconvulsive therapy (ECT) treatment in which a brief electrical shock is administered across the patient's head to induce a convulsion similar to epilepsy

family therapy therapy provided to a family, generally focusing on communications within the family

free association a procedure in which someone reports everything that comes to mind, without omission or censorship

Gestalt therapy a form of therapy that deals with the client's immediate experience and current behavior, attending to body language as well as spoken language

group therapy therapy provided to a group of people rather than to an individual

incongruence in person-centered therapy, a mismatch between the self-concept and the ideal self

interpretation in psychoanalysis, an explanation of the underlying meaning of someone's thoughts, words, or actions

latent content the hidden content of a dream that is represented only symbolically

manifest content the content of a dream as the person experiences it

M'Naghten Rule a rule that states that criminal defendants are insane if they did not know what they were doing at the time of the crime or did not know that it was wrong

Model Penal Code a rule that states that criminal defendants are insane if their conduct was a result of a mental disease or defect that reduced their capacity to appreciate the wrongfulness of their conduct or to conform to the requirements of law

monoamine oxidase inhibitors (MAOIs) drugs that block the conversion of dopamine, norepinephrine, and serotonin into inactive molecules

neuroleptic drugs drugs that relieve schizophrenia

paradoxical intervention a form of therapy in which a therapist tells a person to continue to do something, but gives an undesirable reason for doing it in the hope that the person will stop that behavior

person-centered therapy a type of therapy in which the therapist provides unconditional positive regard and supports the client's efforts to make his or her own decisions

preventive detention the commitment of people to a mental hospital to prevent them from committing crimes

primary prevention preventing a disorder from developing

psychoanalysis a method of psychotherapy that attempts to bring unconscious thoughts and motivations to consciousness so that they can be dealt with rationally

rational-emotive therapy a form of therapy that focuses on the thoughts and beliefs that lead to people's emotions and attempts to replace irrational beliefs with rational ones

resistance in psychoanalysis, continued repression that interferes with the therapy

secondary prevention identifying a disorder in its early stage and preventing it from becoming more serious

tardive dyskinesia a movement disorder characterized by tremors and involuntary movements

transactional analysis (TA) a form of treatment that focuses on how people communicate with one another—for example, as adult to adult or as parent to child

transference reacting toward a therapist as if he or she were a parent or some other important figure in one's life

tricyclic drugs drugs that block the reabsorption of dopamine, norepinephrine, and serotonin by the terminal button

Answers to Concept Checks

1. Freud would disagree with the premise of this paperback. Freud believed that the symbolism of dream elements differed from one person to another. (page 563)

2. The assumptions of rational-emotive therapy are contrary to the James-Lange theory, which argues that changes in the body give rise to the thoughts that we experience as emotion. (page 564)

3. (a) Humanistic therapy; (b) behavior therapy; (c) psychoanalysis and cognitive therapy. (page 567)

4. This is a parallel transaction. Linda is speaking as parent to child and Maria is responding as child to parent. (page 569)

5. Mianserin should relieve depression. Although it acts by a different route from that of the tricyclics and MAOIs, it prolongs the stimulation of dopamine, norepinephrine, and serotonin receptors. Mianserin has been used as an antidepressant in Europe. (page 576)

6. Neuroleptics are more helpful to people in the early stages of schizophrenia than to those who have deteriorated severely. However, psychiatrists do not want to administer neuroleptics to people who do not need them because of the risk of tardive dyskinesia. Consequently, early and accurate diagnosis of schizophrenia is important. (page 579)

7. In some states, people can be involuntarily committed to mental hospitals only if they are dangerous. In other states, they can be committed if they are judged incompetent to make their own decisions. (page 588)

CHAPTER

16

by Richard A. Lippa
and James W. Kalat

SOCIAL PSYCHOLOGY

In the *Communist Manifesto,* Karl Marx and Friedrich Engels wrote, "Mankind are more disposed to suffer, while evils are sufferable, than to right themselves by abolishing the forms to which they are accustomed. But when a long train of abuses and usurpations, pursuing invariably the same object, evinces a design to reduce them under absolute despotism, it is their right, it is their duty, to throw off such government." Vladimir Lenin later wrote, "A little rebellion, now and then, is a good thing."

Do you agree with those statements? Why or why not? Can you think of anything that would change your mind?

Oh, pardon. . . . That first statement was not from the *Communist Manifesto*—it was from the United States' *Declaration of Independence.* Sorry. And that second statement was a quote from Thomas Jefferson, not Lenin.

Do you agree with these statements more now that you know they were written by the founding fathers of the United States rather than by the founding fathers of communism? When are you likely to be persuaded by the arguments of others? When are you unlikely to be persuaded? Such questions are typical of the questions asked by **social psychologists**—the psychologists who study social behavior and how an individual's behavior is influenced by other people.

In this chapter, we shall focus on four topics that social psychologists study: social cognition and perception, attitudes and attitude change, interpersonal attraction, and groups and group influence. We shall also consider applications of social psychology to the behavior of people at work.

In contrast to this New York anti-apartheid rally, an anti-apartheid rally in South Africa is a dangerous act for participants, who risk beatings, arrest, and death. Yet people who would never take action on their own may join a protesting group. Often we decide what to do by observing others.

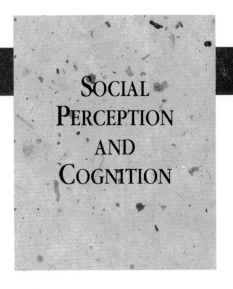

SOCIAL PERCEPTION AND COGNITION

How do we form impressions of other people?
How do we decide why someone behaves
in a certain way?

In 1988, Lieutenant Colonel Oliver North was accused of illegally selling U.S. weapons to Iran and then sending the profits to military forces opposing the government of Nicaragua. He was also accused of lying to Congress and of destroying government documents. After he defended his actions at a congressional hearing, people were divided in their perceptions of him. Some thought he was a villain; others thought he was a hero.

During the televised congressional hearings, viewers saw Oliver North either as sincere or as manipulative. Different people can form entirely different impressions of the same individual.

Every day people try to make a good impression on you: an alleged criminal who denies wrongdoing, a candidate for public office, a classmate who wants you to go on a date, a used-car salesperson. How do you decide what you think of these people, whether you like or dislike them, trust or distrust them? That is, how do you form **social perceptions**—interpretations of the feelings, intentions, and personalities of other people?

FIRST IMPRESSIONS

When you talk to someone you have never met before—say, the student sitting next to you in class—you begin to form an impression of how intelligent he or she is, how friendly, how energetic. Right or wrong, many people trust their first impressions. What information do we use in forming first impressions?

Physical Characteristics

Many people hold strong (and often incorrect) beliefs that physical characteristics are related to psychological traits (Bradshaw, 1969; Secord, Dukes, & Bevan, 1954). You may believe that hairy men are aggressive or that blondes are vivacious and sociable (see Figure 16.1). According to one study, we tend to believe that people with childlike facial features (big eyes, large foreheads) are more submissive, honest, and naive than other people are (Berry & McArthur, 1986).

Moreover, we tend to believe that physically attractive people have more desirable traits than unattractive people do (Hatfield & Sprecher, 1986). One group of experimenters asked subjects to rate the personality and intelligence of students in a series of yearbook photographs (Dion, Bersheid, & Walster, 1972). The photographs had been selected to include equal numbers of attractive, average-looking, and homely students. The subjects rated the attractive students as more sensitive, kind, poised, and sociable than the others. They also predicted that the more attractive students would enjoy better careers and happier marriages than would the less attractive students.

Physical characteristics have a great deal to do with how people are treated in various settings. Other things being equal, teachers expect better performance from attractive children than from

SOCIAL PERCEPTION AND COGNITION 595

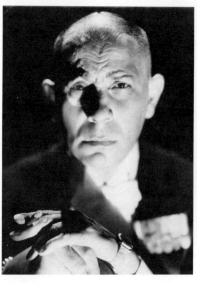

FIGURE 16.1

Bad guys wear black: The movies often rely on simple stereotypes based on physical appearance to express character. Judy Holliday was just one of a long string of dumb, innocent blondes, while Theda Bara typified the dark, sultry vamp. Hollywood, which perpetuates this link of light with good and dark with evil, also popularizes the concept that heroes are handsome and villains are not. Eric von Stroheim was so typecast as the cold, ruthless foreigner that his character was established with his first line of dialog—he just looked and sounded like a bad guy, as did outlaw Lee Van Cleef. Such stereotypes reduce people to a handful of symbols. But this visual shorthand succeeds in part because it confirms age-old notions, such as the idea that attractive people are inherently more virtuous. Literature is full of tales of the ugly who unjustly suffer rejection because of their appearance. They are usually drawn to gorgeous women: Beauty and the Beast, Esmerelda (the gypsy) and Quasimodo (the hunchback of Notre Dame), Roxanne and Cyrano de Bergerac. The enduring appeal of these stories suggests that they speak to common beliefs.

unattractive children (Clifford & Walster, 1973). Attractive people are on average paid higher salaries than unattractive people are (Quinn, 1978). Juries often treat attractive defendants less harshly than unattractive defendants, unless the jury believes a defendant used his or her good looks to gain people's trust and then swindle them (Sigall & Ostrove, 1975; Stewart, 1980). Even clinical psychologists and counselors tend to be more attentive and empathetic to attractive clients than to unattractive clients (Hatfield & Sprecher, 1986).

Nonverbal Behavior

We also form impressions of others simply by watching them. For example, we judge people's emotions and personality traits by observing their facial expressions and their body movements (Lippa, 1983). You may infer that one woman is introverted because she makes small, tight gestures and that another is extraverted because she makes large, expansive gestures. You decide that one man is anxious and "uptight" because he twitches, fidgets, and trembles and that another is calm and composed because he makes smooth, controlled gestures.

Research suggests that when nonverbal information conflicts with verbal information, we are more likely to trust the nonverbal information (Mehrabian & Wiener, 1967). When a friend says, "I love you," but frowns, stands far away, and refuses to look at you, which do you believe—the verbal statement or the nonverbal statement?

The Primacy Effect

Our first impressions of others, correct or incorrect, are influential simply because they are first. Other things being equal, the first information we learn about someone influences us more than later information does (Belmore, 1987; Jones & Goethals, 1972). This tendency is known as the **primacy effect**.

Subjects in one study read two paragraphs about a character named Jim. One paragraph described Jim as friendly and sociable, and the other described him as reserved and introverted. Some of the subjects read one paragraph first; the others read the other paragraph first. Most of them based their opinion of Jim mainly on the first paragraph they read (Luchins, 1957).

In another study, subjects watched a man answer 30 questions on an intelligence test. All the subjects saw him answer 15 questions correctly and 15 incorrectly. However, some saw him answer most of the early questions correctly, while the others

"*Actions speak louder than words*": According to Jacob Bronowski, *"The hand is the cutting edge of the mind."* Hand gestures, crude or subtle, can be quicker than the tongue and clearer for self-expression. When gangster Frank Costello testified during congressional crime investigations in 1951, he refused to let his face be shown on camera. So millions of Americans saw only his nervous hands on TV; his fidgety digits may have been more incriminating for Costello, and they illustrate how we form impressions on the basis of nonverbal behavior.

saw him miss most of the early ones and then answer most of the last questions correctly. Those who saw him start off strong judged him to be significantly more intelligent than did those who saw him start off weak (Jones et al., 1968). When the subjects were asked to guess how many questions the man got right, those who saw him answer the first ones correctly guessed his total was about 21. Those who saw him miss the first ones but finish strong guessed his total was about 13. (Remember, both groups saw him answer 15 questions correctly.)

Why does the primacy effect color our first impressions? People pay more attention to the first information they receive about someone than they do to information they receive later. Moreover, the first information they receive influences their interpretation of later information (Anderson & Hubert, 1963; Zanna & Hamilton, 1977). Compare these two pairs of sentences:

a. Today I saw Julie kick a dog. Julie is usually kind to animals.

b. Julie is usually kind to animals. Today I saw Julie kick a dog.

In a, the first thing we learn about Julie is that she kicked a dog. The second statement doesn't improve her image very much because it sounds as though someone were trying to make excuses for her. In b, the first thing we learn about Julie is that she is usually kind to animals. When we hear that she kicked a dog, we try to reconcile that information with what we already know. We think, "Maybe it was just a little playful kick. Or maybe the dog had attacked Julie's pet hamster. There must be some reason."

The primacy effect is strongest when we judge people hastily or when we have no particular rea-

son to try to judge them accurately (Kruglanski & Freund, 1983). For example, you probably rely heavily on your first impression in deciding what you think of someone you meet briefly at a party.

Something to Think About

In a criminal trial, the prosecution presents its evidence first. Might that give the jury an unfavorable first impression of the defendant and increase the probability of a conviction?

Concept Check

1. Why do some professors avoid looking at students' names when they grade essay exams? Why is it more important for them to do so on the tests later in the semester than on the first test? (Check your answer on page 649.)

SOCIAL COGNITION

Eventually we progress beyond first impressions. **Social cognition** is the process by which we combine and remember information about others and make inferences based on that information (Sherman, Judd, & Park, 1989).

Impression Formation

Suppose I say to you, "My friend Dave is intelligent, skillful, and industrious. He's also warm, determined, practical, and cautious." How do you combine those pieces of information to form an overall impression of Dave?

In early research on impression formation, Solomon Asch (1946) proposed that when people try

Impression formation: What's in a word? During his presidential campaign, George Bush labeled Michael Dukakis a liberal; it became known as "the L word," suggesting that liberal *is a "dirty" word. With that label, whatever Dukakis did or said then seemed more liberal.*

to organize a list of traits into an integrated pattern, certain traits are more influential than others; these *central traits* serve to organize the total list. They may even influence the meaning or connotation of the other traits. For example, compare the expression "warm and determined" to the expression "cold and determined." Does the implication of *determined* change from one expression to the other?

Asch found that changing "warm" to "cold" in a list of traits drastically changed people's impression of a person. Changing other traits in the list had less effect. So Asch identified "warm" and "cold" as central traits.

Other researchers suggest that we form our impressions of others simply by averaging the information we have about them (Anderson, 1974). Suppose I ask you how likable you think Dave is based on the traits listed at the start of this section. You might assign a likability score to each trait, ranging from highly positive to highly negative, and then average all the scores.

But you would probably do more than just determine the average likability. Suppose I tell you Ruth is "intelligent, generous, and honest." All three of those traits are extremely likable, so her average is very high. Now I add that "Ruth is cautious." Because that is not particularly good or bad, you might assign her cautiousness a likability score near zero. But there is no reason why you should average that zero with her other scores; in fact, it should hardly affect your opinion at all.

Generally, we determine likability by taking a *weighted average* of a person's traits. For example, we may ascribe more importance to warmth and honesty than we do to cautiousness. Moreover, the first traits in a list carry more weight than do later traits. (Here we see the primacy effect again.)

We also pay more attention to unusual information than we do to ordinary information (Skowronski & Carlston, 1987). Suppose I write a letter of recommendation for a student who is applying to medical school. If I say the student is "bright, motivated, and neat," I doubt the admissions committee will be very impressed. If I say the student wrote the longest, most thorough term paper I have ever seen and turned it in a week before it was due, the admissions committee is likely to pay attention to that unusual information.

Because most people try to describe others in favorable terms, any unfavorable comments tend to catch our attention (Kanouse & Hanson, 1972). If I included in my letter of recommendation such phrases as "socially inept" or "not always reliable," the admissions committee would probably pay more attention to those comments than to any of my favorable comments.

Schematic Processing of Information

Social psychologists also study the ways in which our prior knowledge alters the impressions we form of people. **Schemas** are the information and expectations we have about people.

In one study, white college students watched a videotape of an argument between a white student and a black student (Duncan, 1976). The argument grew heated and at last one student shoved the other. In one version of the videotape, the white student shoved the black student; in another version, the black student shoved the white student. Subjects who saw the white student shove the black student described the action as "playing around" or "dramatizing"; those who saw the black student shove the white student described the action as "violent." Schemas sometimes lead us to perceive what we expect to perceive—because of prejudice or other factors—instead of what is really happening.

Schemas may also influence our memory of the information we acquire about others. Claudia Cohen (1981) showed subjects a videotape of a woman having dinner with her husband. Some of the subjects were told that she was a waitress; others were told that she was a librarian. The videotape showed the woman doing certain things that fit popular expectations of a waitress (drinking beer, listening

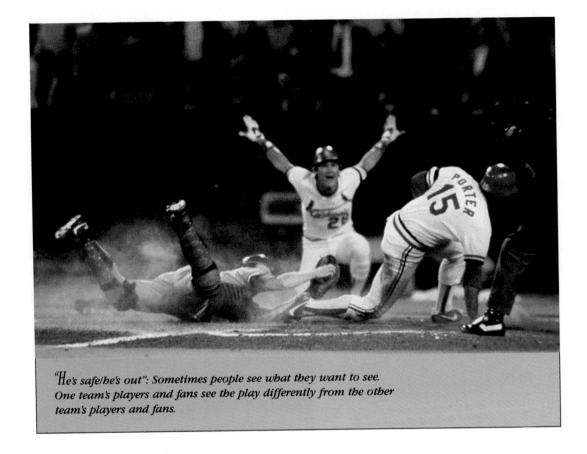

"He's safe/he's out": Sometimes people see what they want to see. One team's players and fans see the play differently from the other team's players and fans.

to popular music) and doing other things that fit common expectations of a librarian (wearing glasses, reading historical novels). When the subjects were later tested on their memory of what they had seen, they chiefly remembered the facts that matched their expectations. For example, those who had been told the woman was a waitress were more likely to remember that she drank beer; those who were told she was a librarian were more likely to remember that she read historical novels. In short, schemas have a strong effect on what we perceive and remember about other people.

Stereotypes

Our schemas are not always accurate because we recall some events more readily than others. You are more likely to recall the three times your next-door neighbors were rude to you than the thousands of times they were not. You therefore form an inaccurate schema about your neighbors.

Schemas about groups of people are called **stereotypes**. For example, some people believe that Germans are hard-working, the Irish are temperamental, and Japanese people are polite. Stereotypes are at best overgeneralizations and often just plain wrong.

How do stereotypes get started? Many grow out of the illusory correlations that arise because we

remember unusual events more clearly than ordinary events (see Chapter 2). For example, if you are white and 90% of the people you ordinarily see in the course of a day are white, you will probably remember what black people do more readily than what white people do. If, in addition to *looking* different from the majority, a few members of a minority group *do* something unusual, the combination is likely to make an especially strong impression (Hamilton & Gifford, 1976). Moreover, as we have seen, we usually look for an explanation of unusual behavior and tend to attribute it to whatever we notice most clearly about the person who engages in it.

How can stereotypes be broken down? A moderate amount of contact with members of the stereotyped group is not enough. When the U.S. federal government decided to integrate the public schools, many people expected that daily contact between black children and white children would weaken racial stereotypes and the prejudice they nourish. In some areas, as it turned out, the stereotypes actually became more firmly established. One reason is that schools are competitive places, and when students compete for grades and recognition, the members of one group tend to view members of the competing group unfavorably. However, when schools encourage black children and white children to cooperate in working toward their goals,

These politicians look appropriate for a reviewing stand—except for one. We don't expect this "pucker up" expression and so we attribute it to an internal cause (a puckish sense of humor?) rather than an external one.

the groups grow in their respect for each other (Aronson, 1987).

Sometimes people hold stereotypes so firmly that they ignore all evidence against them. As we saw in Chapter 9, when people learn about a category, they also learn about members that constitute exceptions. Suppose Joe Bigot has a stereotype of black people that includes the characteristic *poorly educated*. Now he meets a successful black chemist with a Ph.D. degree from a prestigious university. Instead of discarding his stereotype of blacks, he will probably regard this particular black person as an exception to the rule (Rothbart & John, 1985). Unfortunately, it takes a good many "exceptions to the rule" for most people to abandon their stereotypes.

ATTRIBUTION

We often try to figure out why the people we observe behave as they do. Yesterday you won a million dollars in the state lottery. Today a classmate who had never seemed to notice you before asks you for a date. You wonder whether this sudden interest is the result of your charming personality or your new wealth. When we are not sure what is causing the behavior of someone we are observing, we *attribute* causes that seem appropriate. **Attribution** is the set of thought processes we use to assign causes to our own behavior and the behavior of others.

Internal Causes Versus External Causes

Fritz Heider, the founder of attribution theory, maintained that people often try to decide whether someone's behavior is the result of internal causes or external causes (Heider, 1958). Internal causes come from the person's stable characteristics, such as attitudes, traits, or abilities. External causes come from the situation, such as stimuli in the environment, the events of the day, and the rewards and penalties associated with certain acts. For example, your brother decides to walk to work every morning instead of driving. You could attribute his action to an internal cause ("He likes fresh air and exercise") or to an external cause ("He saves money" or "It allows him to walk past the house of that woman he's trying to meet").

We look for internal causes when someone does

something unexpected, something that makes us say, "I wouldn't have done that." For example, if someone laughs and talks boisterously at a funeral, we look for an internal cause, such as "immaturity and lack of respect" (Jones & Davis, 1965). But if someone laughs and talks boisterously at a party, we attribute the behavior to the situation.

Harold Kelley (1967) offered a more complex explanation. He proposed that we use three kinds of information when making attributions: **consistency information** (how much the person's behavior varies over time and in different situations), **consensus information** (how the person's behavior compares with other people's behavior), and **distinctiveness information** (how much the person's behavior depends on the object of the behavior—who or what the person is relating to). (See Figure 16.2.) Suppose you see your classmate frowning. If you know that she frowns all the time and in many situations (consistency information), that she frowns more than any other person you know (consensus information), and that she frowns at almost everybody she sees (distinctiveness information), you will probably decide that the cause of her frowning is internal: unfriendliness. However, if she frowns in just one setting, no more than most other people, and only when she is with one particular person (her ex-boyfriend), you will probably decide that the cause is external.

Something to Think About

Try to explain these examples of behavior:

- Why did you choose to go to the college you are attending?

- Why did your mother marry your father?

- Why did you go out with your last date?

- Why is President Bush against burning the American flag?

Did you attribute internal causes or external causes to these behaviors? Did you rely more on external causes to explain other people's behavior or to explain your own?

The Discounting Principle

Kelley's theory of attribution suggests that we usually engage in fairly complex thought processes when we search for the cause of another person's behavior. Sometimes, however, we use simple rules of thumb. According to Kelley's (1972) **discounting principle**, when we attribute a person's behavior to one obvious cause, we tend to discount the likeli-

a. Consistency of behavior under the same circumstances

b. Comparison of behavior with consensus of others' behavior in the same circumstances

c. Distinctiveness of behavior in different circumstances

FIGURE 16.2

We consider three types of data when making attributions about behavior: consistency, consensus, and distinctiveness. We compare the person against herself, others, and the context of the action. (The person being scrutinized is yellow.)

hood of other possible causes. For example, you learn that Senator Philip Buster, who voted against gun-control legislation last month, received a $100,000 donation from the National Rifle Association a while back. So you attribute his vote to an external cause (the large donation) rather than to an internal cause (his opposition to gun control). In other words, the clear external cause leads you to discount the less certain internal cause (Kruglanski, 1970; Strickland, 1958).

Sometimes the discounting principle operates when we attribute causes to our own behavior. Imagine that after graduation you receive several job offers and accept the one with the highest salary. Because you attribute your acceptance of the job to the salary, you may discount the importance of your interest in the job.

As we saw in Chapter 11, receiving a reward sometimes undermines a person's intrinsic motivation to perform a task. In one study, children in nursery school were given felt-tip pens and blank sheets of paper to play with, a task that children ordinarily enjoy. Children in one group were told beforehand that they would receive an award for playing with the pens and paper. A second group received an unexpected award after playing, and a third group received no award. A week later, the

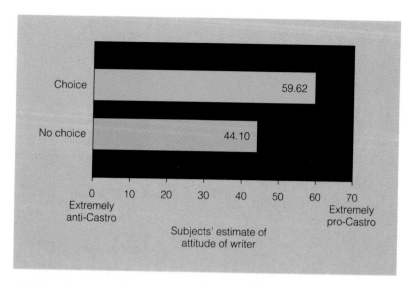

FIGURE 16.3

When subjects were told that a person chose to write a pro-Castro essay, they attributed pro-Castro attitudes to the writer. Even when they were told that the writer had been required to write the essay, they still attributed mildly pro-Castro attitudes to the writer. (Based on data from Jones & Harris, 1967.)

Many people assume that actors behave in real life like the TV or movie characters they portray. The actors may view this as a tribute to their acting skills; the viewers may think the actors "aren't really acting." Those who assume that Leonard Nimoy, who played Mr. Spock in Star Trek, *is cold, logical, and unemotional credit his behavior in* Star Trek *to internal causes. They are making a fundamental attribution error. Out of exasperation with this common misperception, Nimoy wrote a book titled* I Am Not Spock.

children were again given felt-tip pens and paper to play with. Those who had received the awards they had been promised after the first session spent less time playing during the second session. According to the discounting principle, those children reasoned that they had played with the pens during the first session mostly because of the promised award (an external attribution), not just because they enjoyed the task (Lepper, Greene, & Nisbett, 1973).

Still, people do not always discount internal causes completely. In one experiment, subjects were asked to read an essay another student had written, which either praised Fidel Castro, the communist leader of Cuba, or criticized him. The subjects were then asked to judge the writer's real attitude toward Castro. It might seem natural for them to assume that the writer meant what he or she said—that is, to attribute the content of the essays to internal causes (Jones & Harris, 1967).

But the investigators told some of the subjects that the writer of the pro- or anti-Castro essay had been assigned, almost forced, to write it. Did the revelation of that strong external cause lead those subjects to discount the internal cause? Not completely. Most of the subjects still thought the writer was pro-Castro. Figure 16.3 shows the results.

Errors and Biases

As the preceding experiment suggests, we often assume that people's behavior results from internal causes even when we know that some strong external cause may have been operating. Lee Ross (1977) calls this tendency to overemphasize internal explanations of behavior the **fundamental attribution error.**

Moreover, people are more likely to attribute internal causes to other people's behavior than they are to their own behavior (Jones & Nisbett, 1972). This tendency is called the **actor-observer effect.** You are an "actor" when you try to explain the causes of your own behavior and an "observer" when you try to explain someone else's behavior.

The actor-observer effect has been demonstrated in a number of studies (Watson, 1982). In one of them, Richard Nisbett and his colleagues (1973) asked college students to rate themselves, their fathers, their best friends, and the TV newscaster Walter Cronkite on a number of traits. For each trait, the subjects had three choices: (1) the person possesses the trait, such as "leniency," (2) the person possesses the opposite trait, such as "firmness," and (3) the person's behavior "depends on the situation." Subjects checked "depends on the situation" most frequently when they were rating themselves, less frequently when they were rating their fathers and friends, and least often when they were rating Walter Cronkite. These results are consistent with the actor-observer effect; subjects described their own behavior more often in external terms ("depends on the situation") and others' behavior more often in internal terms ("they possess certain traits"). Figure 16.4 shows the results.

Why do we tend to explain our own behavior differently from that of others? There are several possibilities (Jones & Nisbett, 1972; Watson, 1982). First, the person we have the most information about is ourselves. Because we observe ourselves in many different situations, we realize how much our behavior varies from one situation to another. (Recall Kelley's theory: You make external attributions when someone's behavior varies across time and across situations.) If we possessed as much information about others as we do about ourselves, we might be more likely to attribute their behavior to external causes, too. (Ironically, we are confident in attributing the behavior of public figures such as Leonard Nimoy and Walter Cronkite to internal causes even though we have observed them in very limited situations.)

A second possible reason is that, as we have seen, we tend to attribute unexpected, surprising behavior to internal causes. Our own behavior seldom surprises us, so we do not attribute it to internal causes. Someone else's behavior often surprises us, because we know we would have behaved differently. So we attribute the other person's behavior to some internal characteristic.

A third reason is perceptual. We do not see ourselves as objects, because our eyes look outward and focus on our environment. We see other people, however, as objects in our visual field. Thus, when we explain the causes of our own behavior, we tend to focus on our environment, but when we explain the behavior of others, we focus on their personality and their behavior.

The perceptual explanation for the actor-observer effect has an interesting implication: If you could somehow become an object in your own visual field, then you might explain your own behavior in terms of internal traits, just as you tend to explain the behavior of others. In one clever study, Michael Storms (1973) videotaped several subjects as they carried on a conversation. Before showing them the videotape, he asked them why they had said certain things and why they thought the others had said what they had. At first, most of the subjects attributed their own remarks to external causes ("I was responding to what the other person said") and attributed what the other people had said to internal causes ("He was showing off"

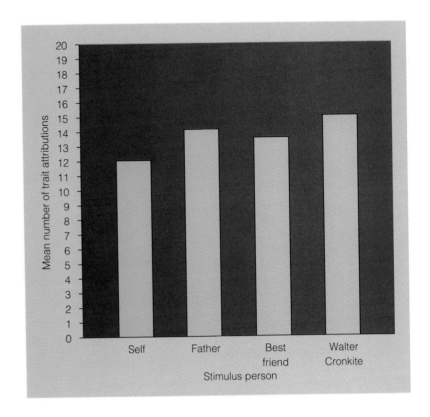

FIGURE 16.4

Attributions for one's own and for others' behavior. Subjects were asked whether certain people had certain traits, such as "leniency," or the opposite traits, such as "firmness," or whether "it depended on the situation." They attributed the most traits to news announcer Walter Cronkite (the person they knew least) and the fewest to themselves. That is, they were most likely to say their own behavior depended on the situation. (Based on data of Nisbett et al., 1973.)

or "She always says things like that"). Then Storms showed them the videotape and asked them the same questions. This time, many of them attributed their own behavior more to internal causes ("I was being smart-alecky.... I was trying to act friendly").

Concept Check

2. You go along with a crowd to see Return of the Son of Sequel Strikes Back, Part 2. *Are you more likely to think that you really want to see the movie or that the others do? (Check your answer on page 649.)*

Ways We Use Attributions to Protect Our Self-Esteem

Although we generally attribute our own behavior more to external causes than we attribute the behavior of others, we sometimes make exceptions to that rule to protect our self-esteem. You attribute your own good grades to intelligence and hard work; you may attribute someone else's good grades to

The performer who does poorly at an audition may attribute this result to external circumstances to maintain self-esteem: "She must have slept with the director," "They only wanted a certain type," or "The whole show was cast beforehand."

taking easy courses. This is an example of a **self-serving bias** in attribution—a tendency to attribute your successes to skill and your failures to external forces beyond your control (Miller & Ross, 1975; Van Der Pligt & Eiser, 1983). Self-serving biases help us feel better about ourselves and present ourselves in a better light to others (Miller, 1978).

Another way in which we sometimes protect our self-esteem is to adopt **self-handicapping strategies.** We create external causes as "decoys" for our failures so we can avoid attributing them to internal causes. Suppose you expect to do poorly on your midterm exam in calculus tomorrow. You go to a party tonight and stay out until three in the morning. Now you can blame your low score on your lack of sleep and avoid having to admit that you would have done poorly anyway.

In an experiment on self-handicapping strategies, Steven Berglas and Edward Jones (1978) had college students work on problems; some of these problems could be solved, some could not. Then they told all the subjects that they had done well. They wanted the subjects who had been given solvable problems to believe that they had performed skillfully and the subjects who had been given unsolvable problems to believe that they had been

lucky. (It had to be luck because those subjects knew they had not understood the problems!)

Next they told the subjects that the experiment's purpose was to investigate the effects of drugs on problem solving and that they were now going to pass out another set of problems. The subjects could choose between taking a drug that supposedly impaired problem solving and another drug that supposedly improved it. The subjects who had worked on unsolvable problems the first time were more likely than the others were to choose the drug that supposedly impaired performance. Because they did not expect to do well on the second set of problems anyway, they provided themselves with a convenient excuse.

Misattribution

People sometimes make **misattributions**—incorrect inferences about behavior—particularly when they try to identify the cause of emotional arousal (Reisenzein, 1983). For example, you feel your heart pounding and your stomach fluttering. Rightly or wrongly, you may attribute it to the attractive person you are with and decide you are in love.

In one experiment, college students were asked

to deliver a speech in front of a video camera. Most of them felt nervous about giving the speech. Some were told beforehand that they would be bombarded with "subliminal noises" that would make them feel "unpleasantly aroused." Others were not. Those who could misattribute their arousal to the subliminal noise gave their speeches more confidently and more fluently than the others did (Olson, 1988). Apparently they said to themselves, "I'm feeling agitated because of the subliminal noise," rather than, "I'm feeling aroused because I'm a nervous wreck."

SUMMARY

1. We form first impressions of others on the basis of their appearance and their nonverbal behavior. (page 595)

2. Other things being equal, we pay more attention to the first information we learn about someone than to later information. (page 596)

3. People organize the information they have about other people into an overall impression. They ascribe greater weight to certain central traits, such as "warmness" or "coldness," than they do to other traits, and they weigh some kinds of information more heavily than others. (page 598)

4. People tend to perceive and remember other people's behavior in ways that match their expectations. (page 598)

5. Stereotypes are generalized beliefs about groups of people. They are sometimes illusory correlations that arise from people's tendency to remember unusual actions clearly, especially unusual actions by members of minority groups. People often hold on to a stereotype despite evidence against it. (page 599)

6. Attribution is the set of thought processes by which we assign causes to behavior. We attribute behavior either to internal causes or to external causes. According to Harold Kelley, we are likely to attribute behavior to an internal cause if it is consistent over time, different from most other people's behavior, and directed toward a variety of other people or objects. (page 600)

7. We tend to discount one possible cause for behavior when we become aware of a more obvious cause for it. (page 601)

8. We are more likely to attribute the behavior of other people to internal causes than we are to attribute our own behavior to internal causes. (page 602)

9. We sometimes try to protect our self-esteem by attributing our successes to skill and our failures to outside influences. (page 604)

10. Occasionally people misattribute their behavior, ascribing their excitement or nervousness to a reason other than the real one. (page 604)

"Nothing but blue skies": When they develop from misattribution, holiday romances last about as long as the holiday. Having met while vacationing in the Caribbean, this couple think they're falling in love, but they're actually in love with a beautiful location, the freedom from everyday routine, and the idea of romance. Next week, when he's in a Chicago blizzard and she's back reviewing insurance claims in Indianapolis, their romance may fade as quickly as their tans.

SUGGESTION FOR FURTHER READING

Fiske, S. T., & Taylor, S. E. (1984). *Social cognition.* New York: Random House. A discussion of research on how people perceive, process, and remember information about others.

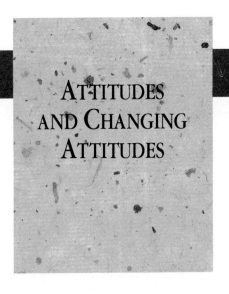

ATTITUDES AND CHANGING ATTITUDES

What are attitudes?
How do attitudes affect behavior?
What are the most effective means of persuading
people to change their attitudes?

"If you want to change people's behavior, first you have to change their attitudes." Do you agree?

Suppose you say yes. Now answer two more questions:

What is your attitude toward paying higher taxes? If you're like most people, you will say your attitude is unfavorable. The government has just passed a law requiring you to pay higher taxes. Will you pay them? You will answer yes, I assume. If I am right, the government apparently has succeeded in changing your behavior without changing your attitude. Indeed, it is fairly easy to change your tax-paying behavior and almost impossible to change your attitude toward paying taxes.

So what effects *do* attitudes have on behavior? And what leads people to change their attitudes?

ATTITUDES AND THEIR INFLUENCE

An **attitude** is a learned like or dislike of something or somebody that influences our behavior toward that thing or person (Allport, 1935; Bem, 1970; Petty & Cacciopo, 1981). You probably hold attitudes toward all sorts of things and people: capital punishment, the Soviet Union, your psychology instructor, the New York Yankees, yogurt. Your attitudes include an emotional component (the way you feel about something), a cognitive component (what you know or believe), and a behavioral component (what you are likely to do).

A common way of measuring attitudes is through the use of attitude scales, such as Likert scales, also known as summated rating scales (Dawes & Smith, 1985). On a **Likert scale** (named after the psychologist Rensis Likert), a person checks some point along a line ranging from 1, meaning "strongly disagree," to 5 or 7, meaning "strongly agree" on each of several statements about some topic (see Figure 16.5). Then someone adds all the numerical values. The higher the total, the more favorable the person's attitude toward the topic.

The Development of Attitudes

We are not born with attitudes; they develop from our experiences and from the information we receive from others (McGuire, 1985). For example, you may have an unfavorable attitude toward dogs because a dog attacked you once. Your attitude toward the use of alcohol may be modeled on the attitudes of your parents and friends. You express a positive attitude toward the United Way (a charitable fund) because people praise you for doing so. You develop a negative attitude toward eating red meat because you learned in a health class that red meat is high in saturated fats and that excessive consumption of saturated fats contributes to heart disease. In short, all the kinds of learning that we considered in Chapter 7 enter into the development of attitudes.

Attitudes as Predictors of Behavior

It may seem obvious that attitudes influence behavior. If you have a positive attitude toward a certain brand of soap, you will probably buy it. If you have a negative attitude toward your senator, you will probably vote for the opposition candidate.

Surprisingly, however, many studies suggest that people's behavior is only weakly related to their attitudes in many cases (McGuire, 1985; Wicker, 1969). Why might that be? One reason is that many variables other than attitudes also influence our behavior (Fishbein & Ajzen, 1975). For example, you may have a very favorable attitude toward new Porsches, but you buy a used Plymouth because you can afford it.

Attitudes that develop through direct experience seem to predict behavior better than do attitudes that develop indirectly (Fazio & Zanna, 1981).

Please indicate your level of agreement with the items below using the following scale:

1	2	3	4	5
Strongly agree		Neutral		Strongly disagree

1. I would not mind having homosexual friends.
2. Finding out that an artist was gay would have no effect on my appreciation of his/her work.
3. I won't associate with known homosexuals if I can help it.
4. I would look for a new place to live if I found out my roommate was gay.
5. Homosexuality is a mental illness.
6. I would not be afraid for my child to have a homosexual teacher.
7. Gays dislike members of the opposite sex.
8. I do not really find the thought of homosexual acts disgusting.
9. Homosexuals are more likely to commit deviant sexual acts, such as child molestation, rape, and voyeurism (Peeping Toms), than are heterosexuals.
10. Homosexuals should be kept separate from the rest of society (i.e., separate housing, restricted employment).
11. Two individuals of the same sex holding hands or displaying affection in public is revolting.
12. The love between two males or two females is quite different from the love between two persons of the opposite sex.
13. I see the gay movement as a positive thing.
14. Homosexuality, as far as I'm concerned, is not sinful.
15. I would not mind being employed by a homosexual.
16. Homosexuals should be forced to have psychological treatment.
17. The increasing acceptance of homosexuality in our society is aiding in the deterioration of morals.
18. I would not decline membership in an organization just because it had homosexual members.
19. I would vote for a homosexual in an election for public office.
20. If I knew someone were gay, I would still go ahead and form a friendship with that individual.
21. If I were a parent, I could accept my son or daughter being gay.

Note: Items 1, 2, 6, 8, 13, 14, 15, 18, 19, 20, and 21 are reverse-scored.

FIGURE 16.5

Attitude assessment: Your *attitude,* which comes from Latin for "fitness," may not fit the facts in some instances. But some issues simply have two sides—which is right or wrong depends on your attitude. Likert scales—such as this one assessing attitudes toward homosexuals—are commonly used in attitude research. Subjects rate the degree to which they agree or disagree with items; these items are selected to be clear and to measure the same attitude. A subject's score on a Likert scale is the sum of his or her responses, thus the term *summated rating scale.* (From Kite & Deaux, 1986.)

If you have a favorable attitude toward a Pontiac because you have driven one for some time, you will probably buy another Pontiac when the time comes. But if your attitude is based only on something you read in the newspaper, it is less likely to predict what car you will buy next.

The more aware people are of their attitudes, the more likely it is that their behavior will be consistent with their attitudes (Carver & Scheier, 1981). And attitudes are most likely to predict behavior accurately when the behavior is voluntary and under the person's direct control. For example, do students' attitudes toward getting good grades predict whether or not they will get good grades? Yes, but only to a limited extent (Ajzen & Madden, 1986). Some students with highly positive attitudes toward scholastic achievement simply lack the ability to be straight-A students.

The behavior of some people is more consistent with their attitudes than is the behavior of others. For example, low self-monitors (Chapter 13) tend to behave in ways that are consistent with their attitudes, whereas high self-monitors tend to behave more as the social setting dictates.

Finally, attitudes are better predictors of people's overall behavior than they are of any specific behavior (Ajzen & Fishbein, 1980; Fishbein & Ajzen, 1975). For example, people's attitudes toward religion correlate poorly with any single religious behavior (such as praying before meals, donating money to religious institutions, or attending religious services). However, their attitudes correlate highly with a composite measure of 70 religious behaviors (Fishbein & Ajzen, 1974). That is, people with a more positive attitude toward religion participate in more kinds of religious behavior than do people with a less positive attitude.

ATTITUDE CHANGE AND PERSUASION

According to a survey of people who watched one of the 1980 presidential debates between Jimmy Carter and Ronald Reagan, most of those who planned to vote for Carter thought Carter won the debate, and most of those who planned to vote for Reagan thought Reagan won (Bothwell & Brigham, 1983). Few people changed their attitudes toward the candidates as a result of watching the debate.

In fact, it is difficult to change people's attitudes, especially deeply held attitudes. Still, political candidates try to convince us to vote for them, and advertisers try to induce us to buy their products.

What are the most effective ways of persuading people to change their attitudes? The effectiveness of persuasion depends on *who* says *what, how* he or she says it, and to *whom* (Hovland, Janis, & Kelley, 1953; Hovland, Lumsdaine, & Sheffield, 1949).

Persuasive Speakers

Let's start with *who* does the talking. Persuasion depends in large measure on the characteristics of the person who delivers the message. Credible speakers—speakers who are perceived to be trustworthy, expert, and believable—are more persuasive than speakers without such credentials are (Hovland & Weiss, 1951). That finding is hardly surprising, but it suggests that we may sometimes be persuaded more by the reputation and appeal of the person delivering the message than we are by the logic and rationality of the message itself. If the president of the United States recommends a new policy toward the Middle East, you may think it is a good idea. If a congressional candidate makes the same recommendation, you may be less sure about it. If your nitwit next-door neighbor suggests the same idea, you probably would dismiss it as ridiculous.

Not surprisingly, physically attractive people are more persuasive than unattractive people are, and famous people are more persuasive than unknowns. That is why advertisers pay celebrities and models to endorse their products. However, the persuasive power of such speakers tends to fade quickly (Chaiken, 1987). You may be impressed that the entire backfield of the San Francisco 49ers use Eau Gallie deodorant, but you may choose a different brand when you go to the drugstore a week later.

Although we may not be persuaded initially by a message from a poorly qualified speaker or an unattractive speaker, we may be persuaded by it later. Over time we sometimes forget the source of a message and remember only the message itself. If it makes sense, we begin to consider it seriously (Hovland & Weiss, 1951; Pratkanis, Greenwald, Leippe, & Baumgardner, 1988). The tendency of a message from a questionable source to exert little effect at first but a greater effect later is called the **sleeper effect**.

Something to Think About

Most people regard textbooks as highly credible sources. Do you believe everything you read in this book, even statements you would question if they came from some other source? (Maybe this text is wrong when it says that people tend to believe what

Persuasive speakers are not always photogenic—Hitler and Churchill are two examples—but as noted earlier in this chapter, we tend to put more confidence in physically attractive people than in unattractive people. Although their politics and speaking styles are polar opposites, both Ronald Reagan and Jesse Jackson are good examples of political careers built on the individuals' powers of persuasion. Supporters of either man may have difficulty identifying his stands on various issues; they may simply like his attitude.

they hear from credible sources. Maybe this sentence is wrong when it suggests you should question even your textbook. Maybe. . . .)

Persuasion by the Minority

Suppose you want to persuade some group to take a certain action, but you know you will be outvoted. Should you just give up and keep quiet? Not necessarily.

From 1900 through the 1950s, the Socialist party of the United States ran candidates for president and other elective offices. The party made its best showing in 1912 when it received 6% of the vote in the presidential election. The Socialists never carried a single state and never won a single electoral vote. None of their candidates was ever elected senator or governor; only a few were elected to the House of Representatives (Shannon, 1955). Beginning in the 1930s the party's membership and support began to dwindle, until eventually the party stopped nominating candidates. Was that because the Socialists had given up? No. It was because *they had already accomplished many of their original goals.* Most of the major points in the party's 1900 platform had been enacted into law (see Table 16.1). Of course, the Democrats and Republicans who voted for these changes always claimed the ideas were their own. Still, the Socialist party, though always a minority, had exerted an enormous influence on the majority.

TABLE 16.1 The Political Platform of the U.S. Socialist Party, 1900

Proposal	Eventual Fate of Proposal
Women's right to vote	Established by 19th amendment to U.S. Constitution, ratified 1920
Old-age pensions	Included in the Social Security Act of 1935
Unemployment insurance	Included in the Social Security Act of 1935; also guaranteed by other state and federal legislation
Health and accident insurance	Included in part in Social Security Act of 1935 and in Medicare Act of 1965
Increased wages, including minimum wage	First minimum-wage law passed in 1938; periodically updated since then
Reduction of working hours	Maximum 40-hour work week (with exceptions) established by Fair Labor Standards Act of 1938
Public ownership of electric, gas, and other utilities and of the means of transportation and communication	Utilities not owned by government, but heavily regulated by federal and state governments since the 1930s
Initiative, referendum, and recall (mechanisms for private citizens to push for changes in legislation and for removal of elected officials)	Adopted by most state governments at various times

Source: Foster, 1968, and Leuchtenburg, 1963.

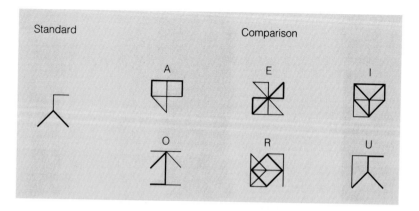

Standard   Comparison

FIGURE 16.6

An observer of the British political party system said it is just "a convenient device to enable the majority to have their way and the minority to have their say." Sometimes having its say enables the minority to gets its way. These simple figures embedded in patterns were a stimulus Nemeth (1986) used in his research on minority influence. At first people saw only one answer. When a minority pointed out a second answer, others began to recognize that answer and other answers as well.

The power of persistence: Mahatma Gandhi (1869–1948). With the ambitious goal of unifying a vast nation divided by social and religious differences and using unconventional methods of nonviolent resistance, Gandhi managed gradually to free India from its position as the jewel in the crown of the British Empire. Beginning as a minority of one, he developed a huge following, the respect of his opponents, and worldwide admiration for his steadfastness. Other minority leaders, most notably Martin Luther King, Jr., have effectively drawn from Gandhi's examples of active but peaceful protest.

People generally accept the majority position as correct, at least at first. But if the minority keeps repeating a single, simple message and if its members seem to be united, eventually it has a good chance of influencing the majority position (Moscovici & Mugny, 1983; Nemeth, 1986). (That chance is improved if the minority's message is reasonable and practical.)

By expressing its views, a minority can even prompt the majority to generate new ideas of its own. Suppose you are a member of a group assigned to solve a problem like the one shown in Figure 16.6. The instructions are to find all the patterns in which a simple figure is embedded. At first, almost everyone says, "The figure is embedded in U and only in U." Just as your group leader is about to write that down as the group consensus, one person says, "Wait. I see the figure in E and I, upside-down." The others not only accept this minority viewpoint; one of them also notices the figure in R, this time on its side (Nemeth, 1986).

Concept Check

3. You belong to a social club that is planning its annual dance. You and a few of your friends say, "No, let's hold a bridge tournament instead." How will the majority probably respond to your unexpected suggestion? (Check your answer on page 650.)

Ways of Presenting Persuasive Messages

In the presidential campaign of 1964, Lyndon Johnson claimed that the election of his opponent, Barry Goldwater, would mean extremist policies and an increased probability of war. Johnson's tactics succeeded and he won a landslide victory. In the campaign of 1980, Jimmy Carter claimed that the election of his opponent, Ronald Reagan, would mean extremist policies and an increased probability of war. This time the scare tactics failed, and Reagan defeated Carter handily. Why does fear help to persuade people sometimes and not at other times?

Fear messages are effective only if they generate real fear and only if they convince people that the danger is real (Leventhal, 1970). Most voters in 1964 knew little about Goldwater and were prepared to believe he was an extremist. Reagan had been a familiar face for years, and most voters did not believe he would do anything rash. Johnson's charges seemed realistic; Carter's did not.

Moreover, a fear message is effective only if people believe they can do something to prevent the threatened disaster. Frightening messages about AIDS have changed many people's sex practices.

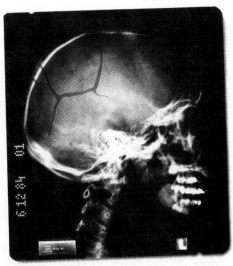

Some men break more than their girlfriends' hearts.

A bad relationship can hurt more than your feelings.

Developed by the Family Violence Project of San Francisco · 1987
1001 Potrero Ave., Building One, Suite 200, San Francisco, CA 94110

Yolanda Bako

Family Violence Project 1982

The impact of a fear message depends on context and on the person receiving it as much as on the strength of its packaging and content. For someone who has been battered, such messages as these may strike home with a palpable force. Yet the cycle of family violence—in which abused children grow up to abuse their spouses and kids—indicates that fear messages have limits to their ability to alter certain behaviors.

Frightening messages about the "greenhouse effect" have proved less persuasive because most people do not see what, if anything, they can do about it.

Finally, if a message is too frightening, people may reject it or ignore it altogether (Chaiken, 1987). If the consequences of AIDS or the greenhouse effect strike people as too extreme, they simply stop listening.

Of the various ways in which persuasive messages can be delivered—face-to-face communication, newspapers, magazines, radio, and television—face-to-face communication tends to be the most effective (Katz & Lazarsfeld, 1955). However, because the mass media reach millions of people at once, advertisers and political candidates rely heavily on media messages.

The visual media (television and films) focus attention more on superficial variables like physical attractiveness and likability, whereas the print media (newspapers and magazines) focus attention more on logic and evidence (Chaiken & Eagly, 1983). Thus a charismatic speaker with little information might be more persuasive on TV, while an unattractive speaker with solid evidence might be more persuasive in a newspaper article.

Audience Variables

Finally, some people are more easily persuaded than others are. Would you guess that highly intelligent people are persuaded more easily, or less easily,

than less intelligent people are? Actually, it depends on the message (McGuire, 1968; Petty & Cacioppo, 1981). It is easier to persuade highly intelligent people to accept a new, complex scientific theory because they can understand the evidence better than less intelligent people can. Because less intelligent people are less likely to evaluate the evidence critically, it is easier to persuade them to accept a poorly supported idea (Eagly & Warren, 1976).

COGNITIVE RESPONSES AND PERSUASION

Most of the studies we have considered so far overlook the active thought processes people use in mulling over persuasive messages, relating them to prior knowledge, and reviewing arguments for or against them (Petty & Cacioppo, 1981, 1986). *Cognitive responses* are the arguments people generate for or against a persuasive message. These responses have a strong influence on attitude change (Greenwald, 1968).

When people have a chance to think of their own arguments against a persuasive message ahead of time, the message is less persuasive than it would otherwise be. For example, simply informing subjects a few minutes ahead of time that they are about to hear a persuasive speech on a certain topic weakens the effect of the talk on their attitudes (Petty & Cacioppo, 1977); this is called the **forewarning effect**.

In the **inoculation effect**, the force of a persuasive message also is weakened when subjects are first exposed to a weaker persuasive message arguing the same position. In one experiment, subjects were exposed to a persuasive message that attacked the belief that people should brush their teeth after every meal. This topic was chosen because most Americans believe that brushing their teeth is a good idea, but they are not accustomed to defending that belief (McGuire & Papageorgis, 1961). First, the experimenters exposed one group of subjects to arguments supporting their belief and another group to weak attacks on that belief. A control group heard nothing at this time. Two days later, all the subjects heard a strong attack on frequent toothbrushing (for example, "Brushing your teeth too frequently wears away tooth enamel, leading to serious disease"). The subjects who had previously heard weak attacks on toothbrushing resisted the persuasive message more strongly than did those who had previously heard arguments supporting their belief in toothbrushing. Indeed, those who had previously heard arguments supporting their belief were persuaded almost as much as the control group was.

According to research on the forewarning and inoculation effects, people tend to mull over persuasive messages and come up with arguments for or against them. Recall, however, that people are sometimes persuaded for superficial reasons, such as the fact that an attractive person has endorsed a product or a course of action. Is there a contradiction in these findings?

Richard Petty and John Cacioppo (1981, 1986) propose that there are two main routes to persuasion, which they term the *central route* and the *peripheral route*. People who think carefully about a persuasive message and evaluate the logic and evidence behind it follow the central route to persuasion. People who respond to such superficial factors as the speaker's appearance or the sheer number of arguments presented, ignoring their merits, follow the peripheral route to persuasion.

What determines which route people follow? Petty and Cacioppo suggest that when the persuasive message is personally relevant, people are more likely to invest time and effort in evaluating it and are more likely to follow the central route. When the message is of little relevance to them, they are more likely to follow the peripheral route.

Concept Checks

4. *If you want your children to preserve the beliefs and attitudes you try to teach them, should you give them only arguments that support those beliefs or should you also expose them to attacks on those beliefs? Why? (Check your answers on page 650.)*

5. *You are debating whether to change your major from astrology to psychology. Your future success may depend on making the right decision. You attend a speech on the advantages of majoring in psychology. Do you follow the central route or the peripheral route to persuasion? Later, you listen to someone explain why a trip to the Bahamas is better than a trip to the Fiji Islands. You had no intention of going to either place. Will you follow the central route or the peripheral route? (Check your answers on page 650.)*

COGNITIVE DISSONANCE

A few pages back, we considered whether people's behavior will change when their attitudes change. The theory of cognitive dissonance reverses the direction: It holds that when people's behavior changes, their attitudes will change (Festinger, 1957).

Cognitive dissonance is a state of unpleasant tension that people experience when they hold contradictory attitudes or when they behave in a way that is inconsistent with their attitudes. People try to reduce that tension in several ways: They can change their behavior to match their attitudes, change their attitudes to match their behavior, or adopt a new attitude that justifies their behavior under the circumstances (Wicklund & Brehm, 1976). (See Figure 16.7.) For example, Jane, a heavy smoker, believes that cigarette smoking is bad because it causes lung cancer and heart disease. Yet she smokes two packs a day. The inconsistency between her attitudes and her behavior creates dissonance, an unpleasant state of arousal. To reduce the dissonance, Jane can stop smoking, she can change her attitude—by deciding that cigarette smoking is not really dangerous after all—or she can adopt a new attitude, such as "smoking reduces my tension and keeps me from gaining weight."

Evidence Favoring Cognitive Dissonance Theory

Leon Festinger and J. Merrill Carlsmith (1959) carried out a classic experiment demonstrating that cognitive dissonance can lead to attitude change. They created dissonance in college students by inducing them to lie to another student. Here's how the experiment worked: Seventy-one male undergraduates were invited to take part in an experiment on "motor behavior." Each subject was individually asked to perform a boring task—for example, rotating pegs on a board over and over again—for an hour. (The task was made as boring as possible, for reasons you will learn in a moment.) Afterward, the experimenter thanked each subject and explained that the study's actual purpose was to see whether the subjects' performance was affected by their attitudes toward the task. (This was not in fact the purpose.) The experimenter further explained that some subjects and not others were told that the experiment would be fun and interesting before starting.

As a matter of fact, the experimenter continued, right now the research assistant is supposed to inform the next subject, a young woman waiting in the next room, that the experiment will be fun and interesting. The experimenter excused himself to find the research assistant and then returned distraught a few minutes later. The assistant was nowhere to be found, he said. He turned to the subject and asked, "Would you be willing to tell the next subject that you thought this was an interesting, enjoyable experiment? If so, I will pay you."

Some students were offered $1; others were offered $20. Most of them, regardless of how much they were offered, agreed to tell the woman in the next room that the experiment was interesting. Presumably they experienced cognitive dissonance as they told this whopper of a lie. As they left, thinking the experiment was over, they were met by a representative of the psychology department who explained that the department wanted to find out what kinds of experiments were being conducted and whether they were educationally worthwhile. (The answers to these questions were the real point of the experiment.) Each subject was asked how enjoyable he considered the experiment and whether he would be willing to participate in a similar experiment later.

Which subjects do you think said they liked the experiment more, those who were paid $20 or those who were paid only $1? The students who received $20 said they thought the experiment was boring and that they wanted nothing to do with another such experiment. Those who received just $1 said they enjoyed the experiment and would be glad to participate again (see Figure 16.8).

Why? According to the theory of cognitive dissonance, those who accepted $20 to tell a lie experienced little conflict. They knew they were lying, but they also knew why: for the $20. (In the 1950s, when this experiment took place, $20 was worth more than three times what it is worth now.) They had no reason to change their original opinion of the experiment—that they were bored to tears.

However, the students who had told a lie for

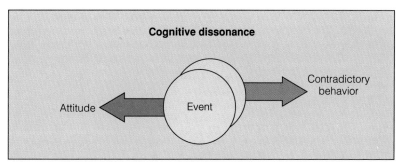

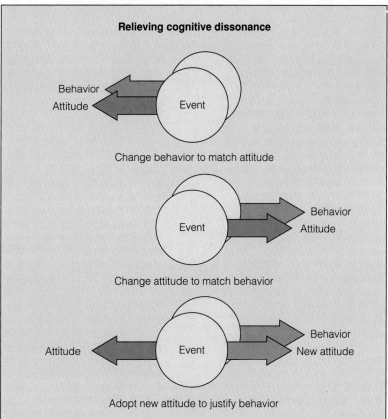

FIGURE 16.7

Cognitive dissonance and strategies for relieving the stress it causes.

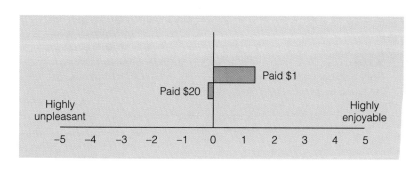

FIGURE 16.8

The size of the prize: The effect of the amount of the reward on subjects' enjoyment of an experiment. (Based on data from Festinger & Carlsmith, 1959.)

The glamour of emphysema: Cigarette ads aimed at women portray smoking as sophisticated or fun—something active people enjoy— a message some tobacco companies reinforce by sponsoring tennis and golf tournaments. But cigarette ads also contain warnings from the surgeon general, setting up a clear signal of cognitive dissonance. Another message in ads: "Smoking by pregnant women may result in fetal injury, premature birth, and low birth weight." Are such warnings effective fear messages?

only $1 felt a conflict between their true attitude toward the boring experiment and what they had said about it. The small payment did not provide them with a good reason for lying, so they experienced cognitive dissonance. Because it was too late to take back their lie, the only way they could reduce their dissonance was to change their attitude, to decide that the experiment really *was* interesting after all. ("I learned a lot of interesting things about myself, like . . . uh . . . how good I am at rotating pegs.")

In a second experiment (Aronson & Carlsmith, 1963), 4-year-old children (one at a time) were shown five toys: a tank, a steam shovel, plastic gears, a fire engine, and a set of dishes and pans. Each child was asked which toy looked like the best one, the second best, and so on. Then the experimenter said he would have to leave the room. He invited the child to play with the toys while he was gone, except, he insisted, "I don't want you to play with the _____," filling in whichever toy the child had ranked second. To some of the children he made a mild threat: "If you played with it, I would be annoyed." To others he made a more severe threat: "If you played with it, I would be very angry. I would have to take all my toys and go home and never come back again. . . . I would think you were just a baby."

The experimenter left for 10 minutes and watched each child through a one-way mirror. All the children dutifully avoided the forbidden toy. Then he returned and asked each child to tell him again which was the best toy, the second best, and so on.

All the children who had received the severe threat ranked the forbidden toy either first or second. They knew why they had avoided the toy, and they had no reason to change their mind about how much they wished they could play with it. However, almost half the children who had heard the mild threat lowered their evaluation of the forbidden toy. They had dissonant beliefs: "I really like that toy" and "I didn't play with it." Why hadn't they played with it? They didn't know. Was it because a man they had never met before said he would be "annoyed"—whatever *that* means? That didn't sound like much of a reason. The only way they could relieve their dissonance was to convince themselves that they did not really like the toy very much.

Whether or not cognitive dissonance arises during the course of an experiment depends on some subtle points of procedure. For example, subjects who behave in ways inconsistent with their attitudes are most likely to experience dissonance if they believe they have chosen their actions freely.

They also experience more dissonance if they believe they cannot undo their actions. Subjects in one experiment were asked to say unkind things to another student (Davis & Jones, 1960). Some of them were told they could withdraw from the experiment if they chose; others were told they must perform the task. Independently, some of the subjects were told that they could meet the other student later on and take back the unkind things they had said; other subjects were told that they would have no opportunity to apologize.

Which subjects experienced the greatest amount of dissonance? Those who believed that they had freely chosen to say unkind things and that they could not retract their statements (Figure 16.9). They were also the subjects who changed their attitudes the most during the experiment. In order to justify their actions and relieve their dissonance, they decided that the other student was in fact unlikable and deserved their unkind comments.

Concept Check

6. *Suppose your parents pay you to make good grades. According to cognitive dissonance theory, are you more likely to develop a positive attitude toward your studies if your parents pay you $10 or $100 for each A you get? Would the theory of intrinsic and extrinsic motivation, discussed in Chapter 11, lead to the same prediction or a different one? (Check your answers on page 650.)*

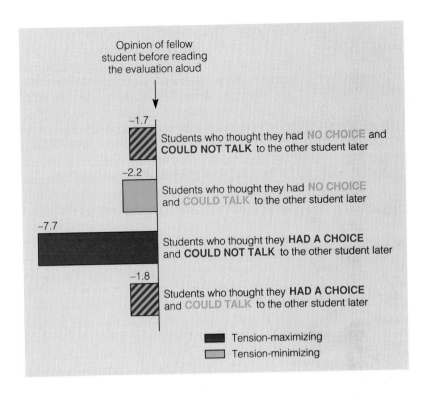

FIGURE 16.9

Saying is believing? Changes in subjects' attitudes toward a fellow student after telling the other student, "My first impression of you ... was not too favorable. ... Your general interests and so on just strike me as those of a pretty shallow person. ... Frankly, I just wouldn't know how much I could trust you." Students who were told participation was optional but an apology was not possible felt the worst and changed their attitudes the most. (Based on data from Davis & Jones, 1960.)

Self-Perception Theory

According to cognitive dissonance theory, people change their attitudes to reduce the tension they experience when their attitudes do not match their behavior. Self-perception theory explains the change in attitude in a different manner. According to **self-perception theory**, subjects in dissonance experiments are simply trying to attribute their behavior to reasonable causes (Bem, 1967, 1972).

For example, in the experiment in which students lied about the boring experiment, they heard themselves saying, "This was a fun experiment," and then asked themselves why they had said that. Those who were paid $20 attributed their behavior to an external cause—they had told a lie for the money. (In other words, they discounted any internal cause for their behavior.) But those who were paid only a dollar for telling the lie could not attribute their behavior to any strong external cause. The only way they could explain their behavior was to attribute it to an internal cause—they must have really enjoyed the experiment.

Cognitive dissonance theory assumes that arousal is necessary for changes in attitude to take place, whereas self-perception theory assumes that people simply observe their behavior and try to infer logically what their attitude must be. One way to compare the two theories is to ask subjects to behave in ways inconsistent with their attitudes and then measure their heart rate and other physiological indicators of arousal. Such studies find, as cognitive dissonance theory predicts, that situations designed to provoke dissonance do produce heightened arousal (Croyle & Cooper, 1983; Elkin & Leippe, 1986).

A further test: According to dissonance theory, if we could somehow *reduce* the subjects' arousal in dissonance experiments, the subjects should not alter their attitudes much, whereas if we could *increase* their arousal, they should alter their attitudes to a greater degree than usual. In one experiment, subjects in one group were given tranquilizers (to reduce their arousal), and subjects in a second group were given amphetamines (to heighten it). Subjects in a third group were given a placebo. All the subjects were then asked to write an essay in favor of a position the experimenters knew they disagreed with. Writing such an essay produces cognitive dissonance; the subjects think, "Why am I writing this? I thought I disagreed with this." Frequently subjects relieve their dissonance by changing their attitudes to match what they are writing. In this experiment, as predicted, the subjects who had received amphetamines changed their attitudes the most, and the subjects who had received tranquilizers changed them the least. In short, the greater the tension, the greater the attitude change.

Does this result mean that self-perception theory is wrong? No. Self-perception theory can explain some phenomena that dissonance theory cannot. For example, when you are rewarded for doing something you enjoy, your behavior is fully consistent with your attitudes and dissonance theory does not apply. However, self-perception theory correctly predicts that when you are rewarded for doing something enjoyable, you discount the internal cause of your behavior and enjoy the activity less than usual.

One suggestion is that dissonance theory and self-perception theory apply to different situations (Fazio, Zanna, & Cooper, 1977). We feel strong dissonance when our behavior is highly inconsistent with our firmly established attitudes. We are influenced by self-perception when our behavior is only mildly inconsistent with our attitudes or when our attitudes were not clearly formed to begin with (Fazio, 1987).

SUMMARY

1.   An attitude is a learned like or dislike of something or somebody that influences our behavior toward that thing or person. (page 606)

2.   Attitudes are rather poor predictors of behavior, especially a single behavior in a single situation, because many other factors influence behavior. (page 606)

3.   Attractive and apparently well-qualified speakers are generally more persuasive than other speakers are and may succeed in getting listeners to change their attitudes. (page 608)

4.   Although a minority may have little influence at first, it may, through persistent repetition of its message, eventually persuade the majority to adopt its position or to consider other alternatives. (page 609)

5.   Whether or not messages that appeal to fear prove effective depends on whether people perceive the danger as real and on whether they think they can do anything about it. (page 610)

6.   People evaluate the reasoning behind the persuasive messages they hear. If they have been warned that someone will try to persuade them of something, or if they have previously heard a weak version of the persuasive argument, they tend to resist the persuasive argument more strongly than they otherwise would have. (page 611)

7.   Cognitive dissonance is a state of unpleasant tension that arises from contradictory attitudes or from behavior that conflicts with a person's attitudes. When people behave in a way that does not match their attitudes, they reduce the inconsistency by changing either their behavior or their attitudes. (page 612)

8.   Self-perception theory holds that people try to find reasonable causes to which they can attribute their behavior. (page 615)

SUGGESTION FOR FURTHER READING

Petty, R. E., & Cacioppo, J. T. (1981). *Attitudes and persuasion: Classic and contemporary approaches.* Dubuque, Iowa: Wm. C. Brown. A complete yet readable review of research on attitudes and attitude change.

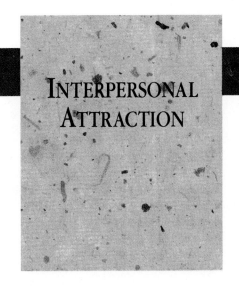

INTERPERSONAL ATTRACTION

Why do we like some people better than others?
Why are we more eager to be with other people
at some times than at other times?
What is the difference between loving and liking?

William Proxmire, a former U.S. senator, used to give "Golden Fleece Awards" to those who, in his opinion, were most flagrant in wasting the taxpayers' money. He once bestowed an award on some psychologists who had received a federal grant to study how people fall in love. He declared that their experimental design was flawed. (It is not clear what his qualifications were for judging that.) Anyway, he went on, it is pointless to study love because people do not want to understand love. They prefer, he said, to let such matters remain a mystery, and therefore psychologists should stop doing research on love.

This section is about the information Senator Proxmire did not want you to know.

AFFILIATION

Affiliation is the motivation to be with others. Most of us like to be with other people, though not with just anyone. Suppose you are looking for someone to go to the movies with you or to be your lab partner in chemistry. How do you decide whom to ask? Four important influences on your decision are similarity, proximity, mere exposure, and physical attractiveness.

The Similarity Principle

If you could travel back in time and become close friends with any famous historical figure you chose,

whom would you choose? Benjamin Franklin, Martin Luther King, Jr., Marie Curie, Agatha Christie, Confucius, Chief Sitting Bull, Susan B. Anthony, Joan of Arc, Sigmund Freud? Those are just suggestions; choose anyone you wish. How would you decide? Many historical figures would probably be interesting to meet, but in choosing a *friend*, you would probably look for someone similar to you or someone you would like to resemble.

How about your close friends? Do they resemble you in ethnic background, political and religious beliefs, academic interests, and attitudes toward sex and drugs? Most people choose friends who resemble themselves in many ways. This tendency is known as the **similarity principle**.

In one study, researchers at the University of Michigan surveyed 1,000 men living in or around Detroit. They asked the men to list their three closest friends and to provide information about themselves and about their friends, including age, occupation, religious affiliation, and political leanings. It turned out that the friends resembled the men on every variable that was measured in the study (Laumann, 1969).

Moreover, most people choose romantic partners who resemble them in various ways. Both dating couples and married couples tend to resemble each other in age, physical appearance, social class, ethnic identity, religion, intelligence, attitudes and values, and use of or abstention from alcohol and tobacco (Burgess & Wallin, 1943; Buss, 1985; Osborne et al., 1978). Well-matched couples are more likely to stay together than are couples who are not well matched (Hill, Rubin, & Peplau, 1976).

In a number of experiments to determine what role similar attitudes play in the attraction between people, pairs of subjects have filled out attitude questionnaires and then been shown what was said to be the other's responses. Actually, the experimenter falsified the responses in order to suggest a greater or lesser degree of similarity between the two. Then each subject has been asked how much he or she liked the other person. The results have consistently shown that subjects like partners whose attitudes resemble their own (Byrne, 1971).

Is it ever true that "opposites attract"? Sometimes, perhaps, but not often. Some psychologists report that people do occasionally seek friends or partners with opposite personality traits and motivational needs (Winch, 1958). For example, a dominant person may choose a submissive friend, or a

Like makes right: The similarity principle in action among New Zealand lawn bowlers. We like other people like ourselves because we think their attitudes and interests are right—in harmony with ours.

nurturing woman may choose a husband who likes to be "babied." But the notion that opposites attract has not received much research support (Hill, Rubin, & Peplau, 1976; Levinger, 1983; Murstein, 1976).

Misery Loves Company:
WHAT'S THE EVIDENCE?

Tomorrow you have to do something you dread. Perhaps you have to give a speech to a hundred strangers or go to the dentist to have a tooth pulled. What do you do? If you are like most people, you seek out the company of sympathetic friends. As people say, "Misery loves company."

What's the evidence for that statement? Is it always true or only under certain circumstances? Stanley Schachter (1959) conducted a study to find out.

EXPERIMENT 1

Hypothesis People who are fearful or anxious are more likely to seek the company of others than are people who feel calm and secure.

Method Subjects were told that the purpose of the experiment was to measure the effects of electric shock on heart rate and blood pressure. The experimenter gave one group instructions designed to

make them anxious: "I feel I must be completely honest with you and tell you exactly what you are in for. These shocks will hurt; they will be painful. As you can guess, if, in research of this sort, we're to learn anything at all that will really help humanity, it is necessary that our shocks be intense." Another group received instructions designed to minimize anxiety: "Do not let the word *shock* trouble you: I am sure that you will enjoy the experiment. . . . I assure you that what you will feel will not in any way be painful. It will resemble more a tickle or a tingle than anything unpleasant."

Then the subjects in both groups were told, "Before we begin with the shocking proper there will be about a 10-minute delay while we get this room in order. We have several pieces of equipment to bring in and get set up. With this many people in the room, this would be very difficult to do, so we will have to ask you to be kind enough to leave this room." The subjects were then given a choice between waiting alone in a room or waiting in a room with other subjects in the same experiment. The purpose of the experiment was to see where the subjects would choose to wait. (They were never actually given any shocks.)

Comment In experiments like this, the instructions are critical. A slight change in the wording can change people's responses. So the experimenters either read their instructions from a prepared script (sometimes committed to memory) or play them on a tape recorder. They do not ad lib.

Results The high-anxiety subjects showed a much stronger preference for waiting with others than the low-anxiety subjects did, as shown in Figure 16.10.

Interpretation Besides demonstrating that misery loves company, this experiment illustrates two important points about psychological research. First, in some studies, especially in social psychology, experimenters begin by misleading the subjects about the purpose of the experiment. In this study, the experimenter falsely told the subjects they would be receiving shocks. If the subjects knew exactly what the experimenter was going to do and why, the experiment might be ruined. (Recall the problem of demand characteristics from Chapter 2.)

Is it unethical to deceive subjects? Sometimes yes, sometimes no. Before psychologists begin a study, they submit the procedures to a committee that determines whether the procedures pose any ethical problems. It would be unethical to tell subjects that they were just going to fill out a questionnaire and then to give them painful electric shocks. Most psychologists see less harm in telling subjects they are going to receive electric shocks and then not delivering any. (None of Schachter's subjects complained.)

Second, even when a study supports a commonsense conclusion, as this one did, it may open the way for other studies that go beyond common sense. Once Schachter had demonstrated that misery loves company, he could go on to find out whether misery loves some kinds of company more than others.

EXPERIMENT 2

Hypothesis People who feel anxiety prefer to be with others, but only if those others also are anxious.

Method Two groups were given the same instructions as the high-anxiety group in Experiment 1. Subjects in one group were then given a choice between waiting alone and waiting with others who were taking part in the same experiment. Subjects in a second group were given a choice between waiting alone and waiting with students who were waiting to talk with their academic advisers.

Results The subjects chose to wait with others who were waiting for the same experiment. They were indifferent toward waiting with others who were waiting for their advisers and presumably feeling no anxiety (Figure 16.11).

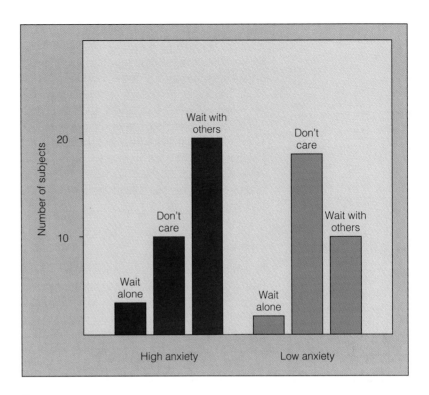

FIGURE 16.10

High-anxiety subjects strongly prefer the company of others to being alone.

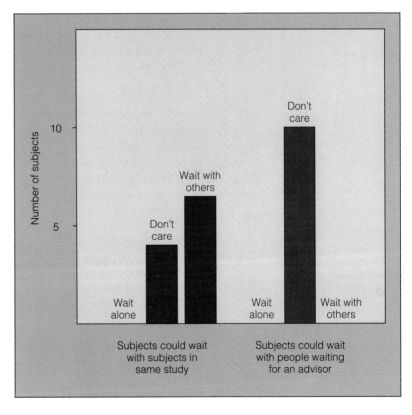

FIGURE 16.11

In the same boat: Subjects preferred to wait with those who shared their anxiety.

Interpretation Misery does not love any and all company; it loves only *miserable* company. Schachter proposed two explanations: First, people who are suffering anxiety may find some relief from just being with other people who share their experience. Second, being with others who are anxious helps people to judge whether their own anxiety is greater or less than normal. Note that Schachter's findings offer additional support for the similarity principle: When we are anxious, we want to be with others who are anxious—that is, with people who are similar to us. ■

Proximity

Proximity means closeness. (It comes from the same root as *approximate*.) We tend to choose as friends people who are in close proximity to us, who cross our path frequently. In one study, residents of a graduate housing project at the Massachusetts Institute of Technology were asked to list their three closest friends (Festinger, Schachter, & Back, 1950). The residents lived in two-story buildings with five apartments on each floor (Figure 16.12). On the average, they reported that about two thirds of their closest friends lived in the same building, and of those about two thirds lived on the same floor. Residents who lived near the middle of a floor or near the staircases connecting the first and second floors (and who therefore came in contact with more passersby) had more friends than did those who lived at the end of a hall.

In another study, college dormitory residents reported that they were more likely to be friends with students who lived one door away than with students who lived two doors away (Priest & Sawyer, 1967). At the start of a school year, Robert Hays (1985) asked college students to name two other students with whom they thought they might become friends. After three months, he found that more of the potential friends who lived close together had become friends than had those who lived farther apart.

Proximity influences romantic relationships as well. In an early study, James Bossard (1931) analyzed 5,000 marriage-license applications in Philadelphia and observed a clear relationship between proximity and marriage rates. More couples who lived one block apart got married than those who lived two blocks apart, and so forth. People tend to be more mobile today than they were when this study was conducted in 1931, but people are still more likely to marry someone who lives in the same part of town, or at least in the same city, than someone who lives farther away.

Effects of Mere Exposure on Liking

Proximity promotes liking by increasing the number of opportunities two people have to discover what they have in common. But it also promotes liking just by increasing familiarity. The more often we come in contact with another person—or with an inanimate object such as a food or a painting—the more likely we are to like that person or object (Saegert, Swap, & Zajonc, 1973; Zajonc, 1968). This tendency is known as the **mere-exposure effect**. (There are exceptions, of course. Some college roommates become almost homicidal by the end of a semester.)

Physical Attractiveness

What characteristics do you look for in a person you date and perhaps eventually marry? If you are like most college students, you say you want "a person who is intelligent, honest, easy to talk to, . . . and who has a good sense of humor."

A friend of yours says, "Hey, you're not doing anything this weekend, are you? How about going out on a blind date? My cousin is visiting here for the weekend."

"Well, I don't know," you reply. "Tell me about your cousin."

"My cousin is intelligent, honest, easy to talk to, . . . has a good sense of humor."

Do you go on the date? Probably not. Your friend just described your "dream date," but you are thinking, "Didn't say anything about appearance . . . that cousin must be ugly."

Some time ago Elaine Walster and her colleagues (1966) set up "computer dates" for over 700 freshmen at the University of Minnesota. All the participants were asked to complete attitude scales, personality tests, and academic aptitude tests.

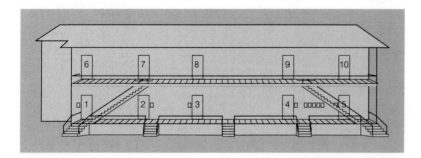

FIGURE 16.12

Near and dear: Housing developments. The graduate housing used in a study of friendship formation. (From Festinger, Schachter, & Back, 1950.)

The burdens of being beautiful: While attractiveness has its advantages, there are disadvantages as well. Research indicates that extremely attractive people have fewer friends of the same sex than people of average appearance do (Krebs & Adinolfi, 1975). Perhaps attractive people arouse feelings of competitiveness or jealousy in potential friends. Moreover, many people perceive uncommonly attractive people as conceited, vain, adulterous, and unsympathetic (Dermer & Thiel, 1975). Finally, very attractive people may not know whether others like them for their looks or "for themselves" (Hatfield & Sprecher, 1986).

Unknown to the subjects, Walster's research assistants rated the physical attractiveness of each subject while he or she was filling in the forms.

Actually, the dates were assigned at random, with no regard for the information the students had provided about themselves. The researchers then organized a big dance at the university gymnasium. During an intermission, they asked the students to fill out a questionnaire that asked how much they liked their dates.

The students with physically attractive dates liked their dates much more than did those with less attractive dates. How much they liked their dates had almost nothing to do with their dates' attitudes or personality. In a way, that result is not surprising. After an hour or two of dancing to the music of a loud rock band, couples probably knew little about each other and could state only their first impression.

Still, first impressions are important. Couples seldom date at all unless they find each other attractive. Moreover, most couples are similar to each other in physical attractiveness (McKillip & Riedel,

1983; Silverman, 1971). The most attractive people date other highly attractive people, average-looking people date average-looking people, and less attractive people date unattractive people. Again we see the similarity principle at work.

Some studies report that women's popularity with men depends more on physical attractiveness than does men's popularity with women (Berscheid et al., 1971). Men's popularity with women depends on a wider variety of factors, including wealth and athletic ability (Buss & Barnes, 1986). Figure 16.13 summarizes the influences on affiliation.

Concept Check

7. An attractive person your own age from another country moves in next door to you. Neither of you speaks the other's language. Are you likely to become friends? What factors will tend to strengthen the likelihood of your becoming friends? What factors will tend to weaken it? (Check your answers on page 650.)

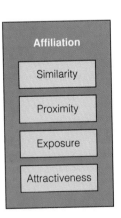

FIGURE 16.13

Influences on affiliation.

Love or lust? As expressed in Auguste Rodin's The Kiss *(1886), passion is one of the three key aspects of romantic love. But physical closeness does not always include the other two dimensions—intimacy, or emotional closeness, and commitment. According to La Rochefoucauld (1613–1680), "The happiest liaisons are based on mutual misunderstandings," but contemporary research doesn't back up his piquant observation that love should be blind.*

ROMANTIC AND PASSIONATE LOVE

So far we have focused mostly on what attracts people to each other on their first meeting or during the early stages of a relationship. As a relationship develops, other forces come into play (Kelley et al., 1983). Researchers ask questions like these: How can we conceptualize and measure romantic love? What is the nature of passionate love, and what influence does it have on a romantic relationship? Can we predict which relationships will endure and which will not?

Defining and Measuring Love

The poet Elizabeth Barrett Browning once asked, "How do I love thee? Let me count the ways." How do social psychologists count the ways of love?

In one of the first attempts to measure love, Zick Rubin (1970, 1973) developed scales of liking and loving. According to Rubin, liking includes a feeling of respect and admiration for someone. Two items from his liking scale are "In my opinion, __ is an exceptionally mature person" and "_____ is one of the most likable people I know." (Fill in the name of a friend or romantic partner in the blank spaces.) Loving has to do with feelings of intimacy, absorption, and possessiveness. Sample items are "I feel that I can confide in _____ about virtually everything" and "It would be hard for me to get along without _____ ."

In one study, Rubin (1973) asked 182 college couples to rate their dating partners and their best friends on his liking and loving scales. Not surprisingly, the subjects rated both friends and romantic partners high on the liking scale, but they rated their romantic partners significantly higher on the loving scale. The scores on the two scales were positively correlated, though not perfectly. Apparently, you like almost all the people you love, but you may not love all the people you like.

When Rubin asked the subjects how likely they were to marry their dating partner, they reported high probabilities only if they both liked and loved their partner. Six months later, Rubin contacted the same subjects and found that the couples with high liking and loving scores were more likely to have strengthened their relationship, while many of those with low scores on either scale had broken up.

Is love a single experience or does it have multiple dimensions? Robert Sternberg (1986; Sternberg & Grajek, 1984) asked subjects questions about their experience of love and then analyzed the results to see whether the answers to each question correlated with the answers to others. He concluded that love has three main dimensions: *intimacy* (how well you can talk with and confide in your partner), *passion* (erotic attraction and the feeling of being in love), and *commitment* (an intention to continue in the relationship).

According to Sternberg, these three dimensions are somewhat independent. For example, a passionate relationship might be low in intimacy and commitment. And a marriage high in intimacy and commitment might be low in passion. (Such a "companionate" marriage resembles a solid friendship.) Some people remain committed to a marriage in which they find neither intimacy nor passion. Most of us aspire to romantic relationships that are high on all counts: intimacy, passion, and commitment. Sternberg terms such ideal relationships "consummate loves."

Clyde and Susan Hendrick (1986) have identified three primary styles of love: *eros* (passionate, erotic love), *ludus* (uncommitted, game-playing love), and *storge* (friendship love). (The strange-sounding labels are borrowed from Greek.) Hendrick and Hendrick also describe three secondary styles of love: *mania* (possessive and obsessive love), *pragma* (practical, list-of-benefits love), and *agape* (ah-GAH-pay; selfless, spiritual love). Table 16.2

Modern love: Romantic love may not endure without intimacy and commitment. Reflecting the importance of these elements is the popular catchphrase "a willingness to make a commitment to a relationship." Some people cannot decide whether to marry. As Irvin Yalom (1989, page 10) notes in Love's Executioner, *"Decision invariably involves renunciation: for every yes there must be a no, each decision eliminating or killing other options (the root of the word* decide *means 'flay,' as in* homicide *or* suicide*)."*

TABLE 16.2 Example Items from a Questionnaire to Identify Types of Love

Eros	My lover and I have the right physical "chemistry" between us.
Ludus	I enjoy playing the "game of love" with a number of different partners.
Storge	My most satisfying love relationships have developed from good friendships.
Pragma	I consider what a person is going to become in life before I commit myself to him/her.
Mania	When my lover doesn't pay attention to me, I feel sick all over.
Agape	I cannot be happy unless I place my lover's happiness before my own.

Source: Hendrick & Hendrick, 1986.

shows some of the items used on a questionnaire to measure these six styles of love.

Hendrick and Hendrick (1986) also found that men tend to be more ludic (game playing and uncommitted), whereas women tend to be more storgic and pragmatic (inclined to see love as friendship or as a relationship based on practical considerations). Couples tend to share the same love style—that is, erotic partners choose erotic partners, and storgic partners choose storgic partners (Hendrick, Hendrick, & Adler, 1988). Relationships in which both partners share the same view of love tend to be more successful than relationships in which the partners have different views. A person who views love as friendship would probably be incompatible with a partner who takes an uncommitted, game-playing approach to love.

Passionate Love and Theories of Emotion

You will recall that according to Schachter and Singer's theory of emotion (Chapter 12), emotions result from autonomic arousal and cognitive attri-

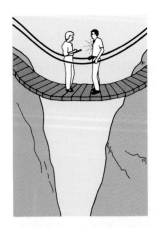

FIGURE 16.14

Sex, lies, and shaky bridges: Arousal actually due to the precariousness of the bridge on the left might be attributed to physical attraction. The sturdiness of the bridge on the right provoked no arousal and no emotion.

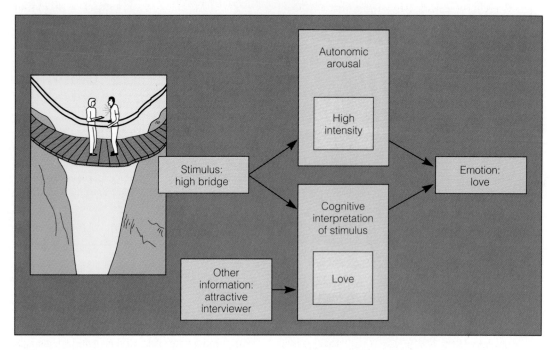

FIGURE 16.15

Schachter and Singer's theory of emotions (see page 430), as applied to the misattribution experiment on the bridge.

butions. We can apply that theory to passionate love: To fall in love, you must be physiologically aroused, and you must attribute your arousal to love (Berscheid & Walster, 1974). An interesting implication is that if people become excited without knowing why, they may misattribute their arousal to a romantic partner.

In one experiment, an attractive young woman stopped men ages 18 to 35 as they walked across one of two bridges in Vancouver, British Columbia, and asked them to tell her a story about one of the cards in the Thematic Apperception Test (Dutton & Aron, 1974). One bridge was wide and sturdy and ran 10 feet above a small stream. The other

was a long, rickety bridge with low handrails 230 feet above a canyon. The researcher told the men that she was conducting an experiment on "the effects of scenic attractions on creative expression." She gave each man her phone number in case he wanted to find out more about the experiment later.

The men who were interviewed on the high, rickety bridge told stories that were rich in romantic and sexual themes, and 39% of them phoned the woman within a few days. Few of the men who were interviewed on the low, sturdy bridge told romantic or sexual stories, and only 9% of them called the woman (Dutton & Aron, 1974). Presumably, the men on the rickety bridge felt strong arousal (fear), but some of them misattributed their arousal to the presence of the researcher: "Wow! What an exciting woman! My heart has never pounded like this for any woman before!" (see Figure 16.14).

The results of this experiment are consistent with Schachter and Singer's theory of emotion (see Figure 16.15). To feel a romantic attraction, the men had to be aroused, and they had to be aroused in a situation where they could attribute their arousal to a romantic partner. If they had been approached by an ill-mannered man instead of by an attractive woman, they might have interpreted their arousal as anger.

Other experiments have shown that anything that increases physiological arousal—such as physical exercise or the threat of electric shock—can strengthen a person's attraction to a potential romantic partner (Carducci et al., 1978; White & Knight, 1984). Couples who like to go to rock concerts, horror movies, and amusement parks may have discovered that "adrenaline makes the heart grow fonder" (Walster & Berscheid, 1971).

The Life Cycle of Romantic Relationships

Romantic relationships have a beginning, a middle, and sometimes an intentional end. George Levinger (1980, 1983) suggests that relationships go through five stages: initial attraction, buildup, continuation and consolidation, deterioration, and ending (see Figure 16.16). Not all relationships, of course, go through all five stages. Here are some of the factors that affect each stage.

We have already considered the variables that influence *initial attraction*: similarity, proximity, exposure, and physical attractiveness. Generally, we form relationships with people we meet at school, at work, or near where we live and who are similar to us in age, socioeconomic status, ethnic background, and physical appearance.

The emotional excitement that often develops during initial attraction tends to fade over time (Berscheid, 1983; Solomon & Corbit, 1974). As couples enter the *buildup* stage, partners learn new things about each other. In a good relationship, self-disclosure increases over time—the partners feel freer to reveal intimate, sometimes embarrassing information about themselves (Altman, Vinsel, & Brown, 1981). They substitute realistic views of each other for their first impressions.

They also establish the give and take of the relationship. According to some social psychological theories—called **exchange** or **equity theories**—all social relationships are transactions in which partners exchange goods and services. In general, relationships are healthier when both partners receive nearly equal costs and rewards.

In one study, Caryl Rusbult (1980) asked over a hundred University of North Carolina students to rate the rewards and costs of current or past romantic relationships. The rewards included the physical attractiveness of the partner, similarity of attitudes, and sexual satisfaction. The costs included monetary expenses, annoying habits of the partner, and the partner's lack of faithfulness. Using a mathematical model based on exchange theory, Rusbult rated the subjects' overall degree of satisfaction and commitment. If the rewards seemed equal to or greater than the costs, the subject was generally satisfied with the relationship.

Something to Think About

Does exchange theory help to explain the similarity principle? If so, how? (*Hint:* Would it be easier to "balance the books" in a relationship with a person who is similar to yourself or with someone who differs from you in many ways?)

In the *continuation* stage, the relationship reaches a stable "middle age." By this time the partners have worked out a complex system of shared work and understandings. The excitement of constantly discovering new things about each other is over, and the partners may not arouse each other's emotions as intensely or as frequently as before (Berscheid, 1983). This does not mean that they no longer love each other. The emotion that persists in a mature relationship may become apparent only when the relationship is terminated by the death or departure of one of the partners.

Although the partners in a successful mature relationship may not live in a constant state of rapturous passion, they enjoy their intimacy and their ease in communicating with each other. John Gottman (1979) notes that the partners in a successful marriage listen to each other and validate each other's opinions, whereas the partners in an unsuccessful marriage engage in "cross complaining," nagging and criticizing each other without really listening to what the other is saying.

As time passes, some relationships enter a stage of *deterioration*. Why? Exchange theories offer one explanation (Levinger, 1976). When people grow dissatisfied with the rewards and costs of a relationship, they may consider withdrawing from it. Whether they actually do depends on what alternatives they think they have (Thibault & Kelley, 1959). For example, some people remain in an unsatisfying marriage because they think that noth-

No dating

Dating ends

Meeting: initial attraction

Dating: emotional excitement

Buildup: self-disclosure, realistic
views, commitment

ing better is available, and they prefer what they have to no relationship at all.

According to one survey of 2,000 married people, the subjects who felt they were not getting their fair share out of the relationship were more likely to engage in extramarital affairs, apparently to even the score (Walster, Traupman, & Walster, 1978). (Or was it the other way around? Did they first commit adultery and then justify their behavior by saying that their marriage was unrewarding?)

When problems arise in a relationship, how do the partners deal with them? In one study, 50 college students described how they reacted when they confronted problems in their romantic relationships (Rusbult & Zembrodt, 1983). Most of their responses fell into one of four categories: *voice* (talking about the problems and trying to work

them out), *loyalty* (passively waiting and hoping things will improve), *neglect* (allowing the relationship to deteriorate), and *exit* (withdrawing from the relationship).

Some relationships finally arrive at an *ending*. One partner may decide to end the relationship before the other partner is even aware that a problem exists (Vaughan, 1986). It is rare that both partners decide to end a relationship at the same time. As a rule, college men are less sensitive to problems in their relationships than college women are, and men are less likely to foresee a breakup (Rubin, Peplau, & Hill, 1981). When the breakup comes, the men usually seem more upset than the women do (Bloom, White, & Asher, 1979). Perhaps women monitor relationships more carefully and prepare themselves for what lies ahead.

Continuation: problems, lack of communication, misunderstanding, dissatisfaction, deterioration

Relationship ends

FIGURE 16.16

"They're playing our song": Relationships are rarely static. Instead, they involve a fairly consistent pattern of five stages: the first attraction, buildup of interaction, consolidation, deterioration, and termination. Tune in a radio and you'll hear songs celebrating or complaining about every stage of romance: "I Should Have Known Better," "Respect," "Everytime You Go Away," "Let's Stay Together," "I Heard It Through the Grapevine," "Maybe I'm Amazed."

Continuation: problems, communication, resolution, new understanding, consolidation

Reaffirmation of commitment, contentment

SUMMARY

1. People generally choose friends and romantic partners who are similar to themselves in many ways. When people are frightened or anxious, they choose to be with other people who are facing the same problem. (page 617)

2. People tend to choose partners from people with whom they come in frequent contact and whom they regard as about as physically attractive as they are themselves. (page 620)

3. Although people generally like the people they love, loving and liking can be measured separately. (page 622)

4. Love has several dimensions, including intimacy, passion, and commitment. Psychologists distinguish several types of love. (page 622)

5. When people feel physiologically aroused for nonsocial reasons, they sometimes misattribute their arousal to a potential romantic partner. (page 624)

6. Romantic relationships go through some or all of five stages: initial attraction, buildup, continuation and consolidation, deterioration, and ending. (page 625)

SUGGESTIONS FOR FURTHER READING

Brehm, S. S. (1985). *Intimate relationships*. New York: Random House. A readable discussion of research on close relationships.

Duck, S. (1988). *Relating to others*. Chicago: Dorsey. A short survey of research on attraction and social interaction.

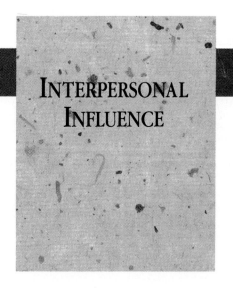

INTERPERSONAL INFLUENCE

CONFORMITY

Social psychologists define a **group** as two or more people who are united by some common characteristic or interest and who act together in some way. A group may be temporary and informal, such as a few people who go to the movies together, or permanent and well organized, such as the Republican party or the United Methodist Church.

Membership in a group can exert strong influences on the behavior of an individual. **Conformity** means maintaining or changing one's behavior in order to be consistent with group standards. Sometimes conformity is good, as when everyone agrees to drive on the right side of the road. Sometimes conformity is neither good nor bad, as when people dress like their friends. Sometimes conformity is dangerous, as when someone uses drugs because "everyone else is doing it."

Do people conform more in some situations than in others? Early research suggested that people conform strongly when they are not confident of their own opinions and look to others for guidance (Sherif, 1935). Do people conform even when they are confident of their own opinions? To answer that question, Solomon Asch (1951, 1956) carried out a now-famous series of experiments.

Asch showed bars like those in Figure 16.17 to college students in groups of 8 to 10. He told them he was studying visual perception and that their task was to decide which of the bars on the right was the same length as the one on the left. As you can see, the task is simple, and the correct answer is obvious. Asch asked the students to give their answers aloud. He repeated the procedure with 18 sets of bars.

Only one student in each group was a real subject. All the others were confederates who had been instructed to give incorrect answers on 12 of the 18 trials. Asch arranged for the real subject to be the next-to-the-last person in the group to announce his answer so that he would hear most of the confederates' incorrect responses before giving his own (Figure 16.18). Would he go along with the crowd?

To Asch's surprise, 37 of the 50 subjects conformed to the majority at least once, and 14 of them conformed on more than 6 of the 12 trials. When faced with a unanimous wrong answer by the other group members, the mean subject conformed on

Under what circumstances do we conform
to the behavior of others?
Under what circumstances
do we behave as others tell us to?
Why do people act differently in groups
from when they are alone?

In the spring of 1983, a strange epidemic swept through a Palestinian village in one of the territories occupied by Israel. The hospitals were flooded with people, mostly adolescents, complaining of headaches, dizzy spells, stomach pains, blurred vision, and difficulty breathing. The Palestinians accused the Israelis of poisoning the air or the water, perhaps in an effort to sterilize the young Palestinian women. The Israelis replied with heated denials.

Meanwhile, although physicians conducted extensive tests on all the patients, they could find nothing medically wrong. They studied the food, the air, the water, every possible source of poison or of contagious disease. They found no signs of anything that could cause illness. Finally they concluded that all the symptoms were the result of anxiety, coupled with the power of suggestion (Paicheler, 1988). The Palestinians were understandably nervous about the political tensions in the region; as soon as one person reported symptoms of poisoning, other people experienced the same symptoms.

Most people are strongly influenced by what other people say and do. What have social psychologists learned about interpersonal influence?

FIGURE 16.17

Choosing conformity: In Asch's conformity studies, subjects asked to match a line with one of three other lines on another card were surrounded by experimental accomplices who gave obviously wrong answers.

We get our chief notions of who we are from our most intimate groups, our families. Membership in other groups—a sports team, a labor union, or a church choir—can boost our self-esteem, broaden our network of friends, and improve our social skills. But belonging to a group may also require substantial conformity in which the individual both gains and loses identity. A life restricted to one group may be secure—a safe haven—but also stifling. Some groups have thrived with restrictions on their settlements; some have not. Native Americans, such as these Hopi, have been relegated to reservations; ghettos originally referred to city sections that Jews were required to live in. These Lubovitch Jews in New York City can reside where they want, but they derive a sense of community by associating with members of their group.

FIGURE 16.18

Group pressure: Three of the eight subjects in Asch's experiment on conformity. The one in the middle is the real subject; the others are the experimenter's confederates. (From Asch, 1951.) In this test of group pressure's power to induce conformity, people had only to disagree with strangers for a short time. The correct answers were clear—yet most subjects denied them, simply to avoid being different. Of those who consistently refused to accept the group's mistakes, some apologized for disagreeing, while others responded in a progressively louder voice. Some were confident; others wondered what was wrong with them.

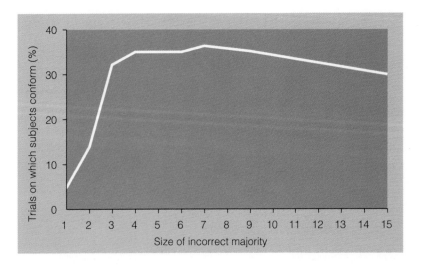

FIGURE 16.19

Conformity, group size, and cohesiveness: Asch (1955) found that conformity became more frequent as group size increased up to about three and then leveled off. But when subjects had an "ally," conformity decreased considerably.

Totalitarian governments have always realized that to tolerate one nonconformist is to encourage others to become noncomformists as well. When the Soviet Union, after suppressing all dissent for decades, began to permit freer expression of opinions during the 1980s, political turmoil spread throughout the country. After nearly 40 turbulent years of communism, the Chinese government, like the Soviet Union, began allowing modest entrepreneurial experiments, a form of economic dissent. But when students occupied Tiananmen Square in 1989, calling for government reforms, the People's Army was turned against protesters armed with rocks. To emphasize that nonconformity would not be tolerated, the government executed captured leaders.

4 of the 12 trials. Asch was disturbed by these results: "That we have found the tendency to conformity in our society so strong that reasonably intelligent and well-meaning young people are willing to call white black is a matter of concern. It raises questions about our ways of education and about the values that guide our conduct" (Asch, 1955, page 34).

Why did the subjects conform so readily? When they were interviewed after the experiment, most of them said that they did not really believe their conforming answers, but had gone along with the group for fear of being ridiculed or thought "peculiar." A few of them said that they really did believe the group's answers were correct.

Asch conducted a revised version of his experiment to find out whether the subjects truly did not believe their incorrect answers. When they were permitted to write down their answers after hearing the answers of the others, their level of conformity declined to about one third what it had been in the original experiment.

Apparently, people conform for two main reasons: because they want to be liked by the group and because they believe the group is better informed than they are (Deutsch & Gerard, 1955; Insko et al., 1985). Suppose you go to a fancy dinner party and notice to your dismay that there are four forks beside your plate. When the first course arrives, you are not sure which fork to use. If you are like most people, you look around and use the fork everyone else is using. You do this because you want to be accepted by the group and because you assume the others know more about table etiquette than you do.

Asch (1951) found that one of the situational factors that influence conformity is the size of the opposing majority. In a series of studies, he varied the number of confederates who gave incorrect answers from 1 to 15. He found that the subjects conformed to a group of 3 or 4 as readily as they did to a larger group (see Figure 16.19). However, the subjects conformed much less if they had an "ally." In some of his experiments, Asch instructed one of the confederates to give correct answers. In the presence of this nonconformist, the real subjects conformed only one fourth as much as they did in the original experiment. There were several reasons: First, the real subject observed that the majority did not ridicule the dissenter for his answers. Second, the dissenter's answers made the subject more certain that the majority was wrong. Third, the real subject now experienced social pressure from the dissenter as well as from the majority. Many of the real subjects later reported that they had liked their nonconformist partner (the similarity principle again). Apparently, it is difficult to be a minority of one but not so difficult to be part of a minority of two.

COMPLIANCE

Compliance is the tendency to do what someone asks us to do. For example, you may comply with someone's request to vote for a candidate, to contribute to a nonprofit organization, or to buy a product.

There are several techniques for increasing the likelihood that people will comply with a request. (These are worth knowing about so that you can avoid being tricked into doing something you don't want to do.) One technique is to make a modest request at first and then to follow it up with a much larger second request. This is called the **foot-in-the-door technique.** When Jonathan Freedman and Scott Fraser (1966) asked suburban residents in Palo Alto, California, to put a small "Drive Safely" sign in their window, most of them agreed to do so. A couple of weeks later, other researchers asked the same residents to let them set up a large, unsightly "Drive Safely" billboard in their front yard for 10 days. They made the same request to a group of residents whom the first group of researchers had not approached. Of those who had already been asked to display the small sign, 76% agreed to let them set up the billboard. Only 17% of the others agreed. Even agreeing to make such a small commitment as signing a petition to support a cause significantly increases the probability that people will later donate money to that cause (Schwarzwald, Bizman, & Raz, 1983).

Another technique for gaining compliance is the **door-in-the-face technique** (Cialdini et al., 1975). In this technique, someone follows an outrageous initial request with a much more reasonable second one. Imagine, for example, that someone comes to your door and asks you to donate $50 to the fund to Protect Endangered Species of Ticks. You refuse. Then she says, "Okay. But would you at least buy a box of oatmeal cookies? Part of the money goes to support the cause." You feel a little guilty about refusing her first request and now she is asking for so little. Even if you don't particularly like oatmeal cookies, how can you possibly refuse?

Robert Cialdini and his colleagues (1975) demonstrated the power of the door-in-the-face technique with a clever experiment. They asked college students to agree to spend two hours a week for two years working as counselors to juvenile delinquents. Not surprisingly, every student refused. Then the researchers asked, "If you won't do that, would you chaperone a group from the juvenile detention center for one trip to the zoo?" Half the subjects complied with this more modest request, as compared to only 17% of the subjects who had not first been asked to make the larger commitment.

Why did presenting the larger request first make the students more willing to comply with the smaller request? Apparently they felt that the researchers were conceding a great deal and that it was only fair to meet them halfway.

Another approach is the **that's-not-all technique.** In this one, someone makes an offer and then, before the other person has a chance to reply, makes a better offer. The television announcer says, "Here's your chance to buy this amazing combination paper shredder and coffee maker for only $39.95. But wait, there's more! We'll throw in a can of dog deodorant! And this handy windshield-wiper cleaner and a subscription to *Modern Lobotomist*! And if you act now, you can get this amazing offer, which usually costs $39.95, for only $19.95! Call this number!" People who hear the first offer and then the "improved" offer are more likely to comply than are people who begin with the "improved" offer (Burger, 1986).

Concept Check

8. Identify each of the following as an example of the foot-in-the-door technique, the door-in-the-face technique, or the that's-not-all technique.

a. Your boss says, "We need to cut costs drastically around here. I'm afraid I'm going to have to cut your salary by 50%." You protest vigorously. Your boss replies, "Well, I suppose we could cut expenses some other way. Maybe I can give you just a 5% cut." "Thanks," you reply. "I can live with that."

b. A store marks its prices "25% off," then scratches that out and marks them "50% off!" Though the prices are now about the same as at competing stores, customers flock in to buy.

c. A friend asks you to help carry some supplies over to the elementary school for an afternoon tutoring program. When you get there, the principal says that one of the tutors is late and asks whether you could take her place until she arrives. You agree and spend the rest of the afternoon tutoring. The principal then talks you into coming back every week as a tutor.

(Check your answers on page 650.)

A cult group started in California, the People's Temple led by Reverend Jim Jones, turned into a bizarre tragedy ending in mass suicide and murder in 1978. Some 1,000 people looking for some group to be part of followed their leader to South America to found Jonestown, an agricultural commune. In a dramatic show of group conformity and obedience to authority, nearly everyone drank poison when told to do so.

OBEDIENCE TO AUTHORITY

Obedience means following a direct command from someone in authority: a parent, boss, teacher, or government official. When are people most likely to obey commands? When are they not?

When the Nazi concentration camps were exposed after the Second World War, those who had committed the atrocities defended themselves by saying they were only obeying orders. International courts rejected that defense, and outraged people throughout the world told themselves, "If I had been there, I would have refused to follow such orders" and "It couldn't happen here."

What do you think? Could it happen here? Stanley Milgram (1974) set up an experiment to discover under what conditions people would obey apparently dangerous orders. Here is how the experiment worked: Two adult male subjects arrived at the experimental room—the real subject and a confederate of the experimenter pretending to be a subject. The experimenter told them that this was an experiment on learning and that one subject would be the "teacher" and the other the "learner." The teacher would read lists of words through a microphone to the learner, who would sit in a nearby room. The teacher would then test the learner's memory for the words. Every time the learner made a mistake, the teacher was to deliver an electric shock as punishment.

The experiment was rigged so that the real subject was always the teacher and the confederate was always the learner. The teacher watched as the learner was strapped into the shock device, so he knew that the learner could not escape (Figure 16.20). In one version of the experiment, the learner was a middle-age man who said he had a heart condition. The learner never actually received any shocks, but the teacher was led to believe that he did.

The experiment began uneventfully. The teacher read the words and tested the learner's memory for them. The learner made many mistakes. The teacher sat at a shock generator that had levers to deliver shocks ranging from 15 volts up to 450 volts, in 15-volt increments. The experimenter instructed the teacher to deliver a shock every time the learner made a mistake, beginning with the 15-volt switch and raising the voltage by 15 volts for each successive mistake.

As the voltage went up, the learner in the next room cried out in pain and even kicked the wall. Typically, the teachers grew upset as they delivered what they believed were more and more painful shocks, but the experimenter kept ordering them to continue. If a teacher asked who would take responsibility for any harm to the learner, the experimenter replied that he would take responsibility, but he insisted that "while the shocks may be painful, they are not dangerous." When the shock reached 150 volts, the learner called out in pain and begged to be let out of the experiment, complaining that his heart was bothering him. Beginning at 270, he responded to shocks with agonized screams. At 300 volts he shouted that he would no longer answer any questions. After 330 volts he made no response at all. Still, the experimenter ordered the teacher to continue asking questions and delivering shocks. (Remember, the learner was not really being shocked. The screams of pain were played on a tape recorder.)

How many subjects, if any, would you guess continued to deliver shocks? Of 40 subjects, 25 continued to deliver shocks all the way up to 450 volts. Milgram replicated his results in somewhat modified experiments: He conducted the experiment in a rundown office building in Bridgeport, Connecticut, instead of on the campus of Yale University. He recruited a different man to play the role of learner and had women serve as teachers. In each case, about half the teachers continued to give shocks all the way to 450 volts.

Many students who hear about this experiment exclaim, "There must have been something wrong with those people! Maybe they were sadists." They were not. They were normal adults, recruited from

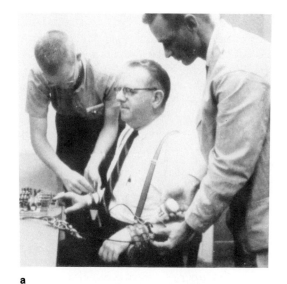

a

b

FIGURE 16.20

(a) The "learner" in Milgram's experiment on obedience, being attached to the shock device. (b) The shock box that the "teacher" used in the same experiment. (From Milgram, 1974.)

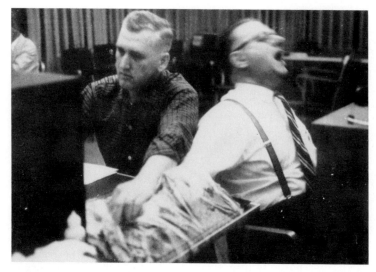

FIGURE 16.21

An obedient subject presses a "learner's" hand on the shock electrode. (From Stanley Milgram's 1965 film *Obedience*.) This physical contact with the learner caused obedience to fall to less than half that when learners were only overheard.

the community through newspaper ads. (They were not college students.) They were paid a few dollars for their services, and those who asked were told that they could keep the money even if they quit. (Not many asked.) People from all walks of life obeyed the experimenter's orders, including blue-collar workers, white-collar workers, and professionals. Most of them grew quite upset and agitated while they were supposedly delivering shocks to the screaming learner, but they kept right on.

What may have promoted obedience in this experiment? One factor is that the teacher was in another room and could not see the learner. In another version of the experiment, both were in the same room and the teacher could see the learner's expressions of pain as well as hear his cries. Under those conditions, fewer subjects (40%) obeyed. In yet another version, Milgram asked the teacher to force the learner's hand down on a shock

plate when he tried to quit (Figure 16.21). Obedience then dropped to 30%. (It may be easier to press a button to fire a missile that will kill a million people you don't see than to plunge a bayonet into one person you do see.)

In further experiments, Milgram added the pressure to conform to the pressure to obey. Now the real subject acting as teacher was joined by two other teachers who were Milgram's confederates. Each one had a specific duty to perform, such as reading the list of words or flipping the switches on the shock generator. So long as the two confederates followed all the orders without protest, 93% of the real subjects followed suit. But when the confederates rebelled and refused to go on, only 10% of the real subjects continued to obey orders. Figure 16.22 shows the results under a variety of conditions.

Something to Think About

Here is a version of the experiment that Milgram never tried: At the start of the experiment, we announce that the teacher and the learner will trade places halfway through the experiment. How do you think the teachers would behave then? What other changes in procedure might influence the degree of obedience?

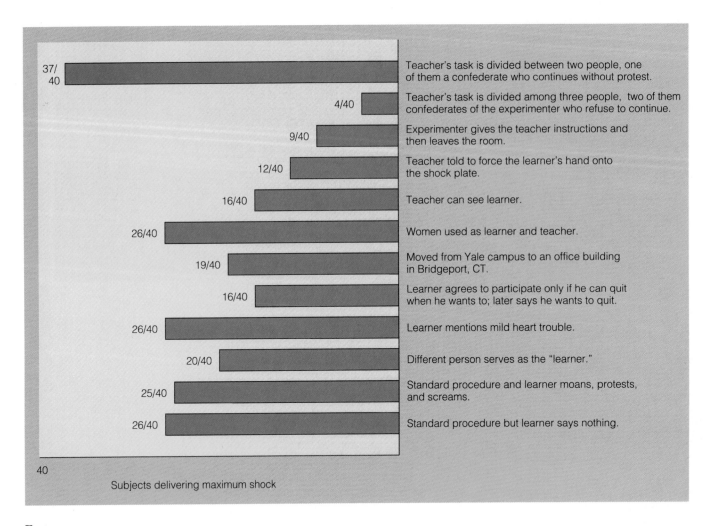

37/40 | Teacher's task is divided between two people, one of them a confederate who continues without protest.

4/40 | Teacher's task is divided among three people, two of them confederates of the experimenter who refuse to continue.

9/40 | Experimenter gives the teacher instructions and then leaves the room.

12/40 | Teacher told to force the learner's hand onto the shock plate.

16/40 | Teacher can see learner.

26/40 | Women used as learner and teacher.

19/40 | Moved from Yale campus to an office building in Bridgeport, CT.

16/40 | Learner agrees to participate only if he can quit when he wants to; later says he wants to quit.

26/40 | Learner mentions mild heart trouble.

20/40 | Different person serves as the "learner."

25/40 | Standard procedure and learner moans, protests, and screams.

26/40 | Standard procedure but learner says nothing.

40

Subjects delivering maximum shock

FIGURE 16.22

Compliance by "teachers" in various forms of Milgram's experiment on obedience. Note that unlike Nazi soldiers, who might have been shot for not following orders, these people simply risked displeasing some strangers.

DIFFUSION OF RESPONSIBILITY

Who do you think would be more likely to go to the aid of someone in distress: someone in a group or a lone individual? Late one night in March, 1964, Kitty Genovese was stabbed to death near her apartment in Queens, New York. For 30 minutes, 38 of her neighbors listened to her screams. A few stood at their windows watching. None of them came to her aid or called the police. Why?

Bibb Latané and John Darley (1969) proposed that one reason the neighbors failed to help was **diffusion of responsibility**—the fact that we feel less responsibility for helping when other people are around than when we know that no one else can help. Latané and Darley suggest that no one

helped Kitty Genovese because everyone knew that there were many other people on the scene who *could* help her.

In an experiment designed to test this hypothesis, a young woman ushered either one student or two students into a room and asked them to wait a few minutes for the start of a market research study (Latané & Darley, 1968, 1969). She then went into the next room, closing the door behind her. There she played a tape recording that made it sound as if she had climbed onto a chair and had fallen off. For about two minutes she could be heard crying and moaning, "Oh ... my foot ... I can't move it. Oh ... my ankle. ..." Of the subjects who were waiting alone, 70% went next door and offered to help. Of the subjects who were waiting with someone else, only 13% offered to help.

"It's not my problem," "Why doesn't the government help street people?" "I've got to look out for number one first." These are some of the excuses we may use to avoid taking responsibility for helping others. For decades, Mother Teresa has aided people some would consider beyond help: Calcutta's poorest sick and dying.

Diffusion of responsibility is one possible explanation. Each person thinks, "It's not my responsibility to help any more than it is the other person's. And if we get blamed for not helping, it's as much that person's fault as it is mine." A second possible explanation is that the presence of another person changes the way we react to an ambiguous situation: "Does that woman need help or not? I'm not really sure. This other person isn't doing anything, so maybe she doesn't."

Note the similarity between the results of this study and the results of Milgram's obedience experiment: In both cases, people followed social pressures instead of their own conscience.

GROUP DECISION MAKING

To determine whether or not a defendant is guilty of a criminal offense, we present the evidence to a jury of up to 12 people. An organization that has to make a decision will often appoint a committee to gather information and make recommendations. Do people in a group make better decisions than an individual does? Do groups always make better decisions?

We trust a group to make a decision because a group has more time and knowledge than a given individual and a greater chance of being representative of the whole population. An individual may come up with a brilliant idea, but is just as likely to come up with an impractical or obviously flawed idea.

But recall the phenomenon of diffusion of responsibility: A member of a group feels less responsibility than an individual acting alone. Might that tendency lead a group to make some irresponsible or extreme decisions?

Group Polarization

Groups are more likely to make extreme decisions than most isolated individuals are (Lamm & Myers, 1978). This phenomenon, **group polarization**, does not mean that a group fragments into opposing factions. Rather, it means that the members of a group, after discussing the issues, move together toward one *pole* (extreme position) or the other.

In one study, French students were asked in one session to report their attitudes toward Americans and toward Charles de Gaulle, then president of France. Most of them expressed negative atti-

Group polarization in a jury means coming to a verdict of guilty or not guilty. A jury gets no thanks for failing to reach a verdict. Groupthink, extreme polarization, refers to groups in which dissent is suppressed. It is common in religious groups that insist on absolute harmony, where a true believer is an unquestioning believer.

tudes toward Americans and positive attitudes toward de Gaulle. After discussing the questions as a group, most of them became more extreme in their anti-American and pro–de Gaulle attitudes (Moscovici & Zavalloni, 1969).

Group polarization occurs for at least two reasons: increased information and the pressure to conform (Isenberg, 1986). During the group discussion, the members become aware of new arguments and new information. If most of the members were leaning in one direction at the start, the group hears arguments mostly favoring that side of the issue (Burnstein & Vinokur, 1973, 1977). And as the members of the group become aware of the consensus during the discussion, they feel pressure to conform. They are praised for supporting the consensus and perhaps scowled at for criticizing it. In fact, just hearing how other group members feel about the issue, even when they offer no explanation or defense of their position, impels most people to move toward the majority position (Goethals & Zanna, 1979).

Concept Check

9. *Is group polarization more likely to occur if the majority of the group members were in agreement at the start of the discussion or if the group was about evenly divided? Why? (Check your answers on page 650.)*

Groupthink

An extreme form of group polarization is known as **groupthink**, in which the members of a group actively silence all dissenters and move quickly toward a decision that may be ill conceived (Janis, 1972, 1985). Groupthink is most likely to occur in a highly cohesive group, such as a fraternal or religious organization, in which the members think it would be rude to criticize one another's views. Rather than spoil the harmony, they keep silent and pretend to agree. Groupthink also occurs when the group leaders make it clear that they do not wish to hear objections to their plans.

One dramatic example of groupthink led to the Bay of Pigs fiasco of 1962 (Janis, 1972). U.S. President John F. Kennedy and his advisers were considering a plan to support a small-scale invasion of Cuba at the Bay of Pigs. The assumption was that a small group of Cuban exiles could overwhelm the Cuban army and trigger a spontaneous rebellion of the Cuban people against Fidel Castro and the communist government. Kennedy's advisers raised few questions to challenge that assumption. When one adviser expressed doubts, he was told that he was being disloyal and that he should support the president, who had already made up his mind. Within a few hours after the invasion began, all the invaders were killed or captured. The decision makers (and everyone else) wondered how they could have made such a stupid decision.

Another example of groupthink was NASA's decision to launch the space shuttle *Challenger* on a cold morning in 1986 despite protests from the project engineers that the rocket booster was unsafe at low temperatures. The top decision makers let it be known that there were strong economic and public-relations reasons for launching the shuttle on schedule and that they wanted to hear no objections. Seventy-three seconds after the launch, the *Challenger* exploded, killing all seven people on board.

In both cases, a cohesive group under strong leadership made a disastrous decision. The leaders and some of the group members discouraged dissent and created an illusion of unanimous support.

Irving Janis (1985) suggests several techniques for reducing the likelihood of groupthink: Leaders should encourage dissent. The group can be divided into subgroups to see whether, in independent discussions, they arrive at the same conclusions. Leaders should consult their advisers one by one in private. The group should seek the advice of outside experts, including those with dissenting opinions. One or more members might be assigned the role of devil's advocate to point out possible weaknesses in the majority position.

COOPERATION AND UNCOOPERATIVE BEHAVIOR

Suppose we were to turn the government over to private contractors. You can join the government of your choice and pay only the taxes that government charges. Government A charges high taxes, but provides services that benefit everyone, including highway construction and protection of the environment. Government B charges low taxes, but builds no highways and does nothing to protect the environment. Which government do you hope most people join? Which one do you *think* most people will join? And which one will you join yourself?

Sometimes when people consider a decision from the standpoint of their own immediate interests they make a choice (such as joining Government B) that is clearly harmful to the group in the long run. They behave in an uncooperative manner because the situation itself evokes that behavior.

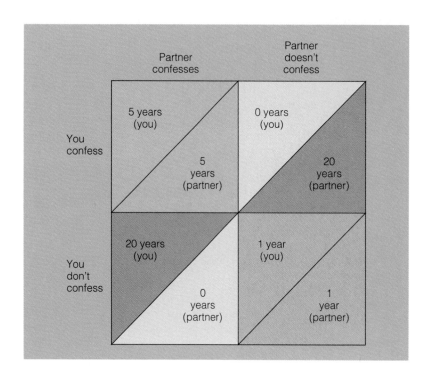

FIGURE 16.23

The prisoner's dilemma: Truth and consequences.

The Prisoner's Dilemma

Here is one situation that evokes uncooperative behavior, the **prisoner's dilemma:** You and a friend are arrested and charged with armed robbery. The police take each of you into separate rooms and ask you to confess. If neither of you confesses, the police will not have enough evidence to convict you of armed robbery, but they can convict you of a lesser offense that carries a sentence of one year in prison. If either of you confesses and testifies against the other, the one who confesses will go free and the other will get 20 years in prison. If you both confess, you will each get 5 years in prison. Figure 16.23 illustrates your choices.

If your friend does not confess, it is to your own advantage to confess—you go free instead of spending a year in prison. (Your friend will get 20 years in prison, but let's assume you are much more interested in your own welfare than in that of your friend.) If your friend does confess, it is still to your advantage to confess—you get only 5 years in prison instead of 20. So you confess. Your friend, reasoning the same way, also confesses, and you both get 5 years in prison. You both would have been better off if you had both kept quiet. Again the situation has fostered uncooperative behavior because each person decides what is best for himself or herself,

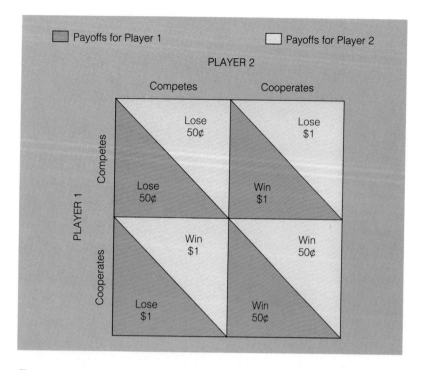

PLAYER 2

Competes   Cooperates

PLAYER 1

Competes

Lose 50¢
Lose 50¢
Lose $1
Win $1

Cooperates

Win $1
Lose $1
Win 50¢
Win 50¢

FIGURE 16.24

In this game based on the prisoner's dilemma, each player can choose the cooperative move or the competitive move. If both cooperate, each wins 50 cents; in other choices, one or both players lose money.

and the resulting decisions are harmful to the group—in this case, a group of two people.

It is hard to persuade people to behave cooperatively in a situation like this. If you and your friend could have talked things over in advance, you would have agreed not to confess. Then when the police took you to separate rooms, you would each hope that the other would keep the bargain. And if your friend did keep the bargain, what should you do? Confess, of course! We're back where we started.

The two of you will behave cooperatively only if you can stay in constant communication with each other (Nemeth, 1972). If you and your friend agree not to confess and then listen to everything the other one says, you both keep the bargain. You know that if one confesses, the other will retaliate immediately.

For experiments on the prisoner's dilemma, social psychologists have invented games in which each player chooses between two moves, one cooperative and the other competitive. The moves the players make determine their costs and rewards (see Figure 16.24). To complicate matters (and make them more interesting), the game continues for many trials. If one player chooses the competitive response on one trial, the player can retaliate on the next trial. Players earn the most rewards if both choose the cooperative move. Frequently, however, one

player chooses the competitive response, the other retaliates, both begin making only the competitive response, and both players lose rewards (Brickman, Becker, & Castle, 1979).

The prisoner's dilemma is analogous to many actual situations in which people have to decide whether to compete or to cooperate. For example, the United States and Japan might agree to cooperate by creating a free market for each other's exports. If, however, one country switches to the competitive strategy of restricting imports while the other continues with a cooperative policy, the competitive country will prosper at the other's expense. But if both countries adopt a competitive strategy, both will suffer. The payoffs are similar to those in the prisoner's dilemma.

Something to Think About

The arms race between the United States and the Soviet Union also resembles the prisoner's dilemma: Each country reasons, "If they stop building new weapons, we can gain an advantage by building more. If they build more, we'll still be better off if we build more than if we let them get ahead." So both countries go on producing more weapons, even if they both wish they could put an end to the arms race. What steps would help to end this version of the prisoner's dilemma?

The Commons Dilemma

The commons dilemma is another example of how the immediate interests of the individual conflict with the long-term interests of the group (Hardin, 1968). The **commons dilemma** takes its name from this parable: You are a shepherd in a small village with a piece of land—the commons—that everyone is free to share. Most of the time, your sheep graze on your own land, but when a few of them need a little extra grass, you are free to take them to the commons. There are 50 shepherds in the village, and the commons can support about 50 sheep a day. So if each shepherd takes an average of one sheep a day to the commons, everything works out fine. But suppose a few shepherds decide to take several sheep a day to the commons and save the grass on their own land. Not to be outdone, other shepherds do the same. Soon the commons is barren.

The same holds true for any situation in which people overuse a resource that has a fixed rate of replacement: harvesting whales, cutting down forests, burning fossil fuels, or tapping underground water supplies. The whole world is our "com-

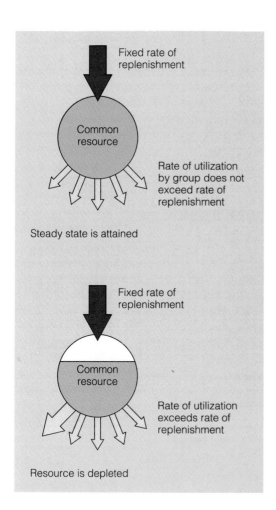

Fixed rate of replenishment

Common resource

Rate of utilization by group does not exceed rate of replenishment

Steady state is attained

Fixed rate of replenishment

Common resource

Rate of utilization exceeds rate of replenishment

Resource is depleted

FIGURE 16.25

The commons dilemma: Unless the users agree to moderate their utilization of a resource, it will soon be used up. This dilemma is occurring on a global scale now, as 50 million acres of tropical rain forest disappear each year—100 acres a minute. Caught between exploiters and environmentalists in the remaining Amazon rain forest are the poor and landless. Some have long depended on tapping latex sap from wild rubber trees, which are being cleared; others want to mine for gold or farm where the forest has been burned away (Caufield, 1989).

mons," and the tragedy of the commons is that short-term profits for the individual lead to long-term losses for everyone (see Figure 16.25).

The commons dilemma, like the prisoner's dilemma, has been simulated in laboratory games. In one study, college students were asked to sit around a bowl that contained 10 nuts (Edney, 1979). They were told that they could take as many nuts as they wanted any time they chose. Every 10 seconds, the number of nuts remaining in the bowl would be doubled. The object of the game was to collect as many nuts as possible. Clearly, the rational strategy is to let the nuts double every 10 seconds for a while and then to "harvest" some and divide them among the participants. But what actually happened? Most of the groups never made it past the first 10 seconds. The subjects simply plunged in and grabbed as many nuts as they could, immediately exhausting the resources.

People acting as a group behave more competitively than individuals do (Komorita & Lapworth, 1982). For example, when people hunt whales in groups, they kill even more irresponsibly than usual, because of the diffusion of responsibility.

Fortunately, there are ways to avoid the tragedy of the commons. In some experiments (as in some real situations), people have resisted the temptation to gobble up resources for short-term profits by talking over the situation and agreeing on a sensible method for distributing the available resources (Messick et al., 1983; Samuelson et al., 1984). By studying group behavior, social psychologists may find ways to help preserve our air, water, forests, petroleum, and all the other resources of our worldwide commons.

SUMMARY

1. Many people conform to the majority view even when they are confident that the majority is wrong. An individual is as likely to conform to a group of three as to a larger group, but an individual who has an ally is less likely to conform to the majority. (page 628)

2. The likelihood that people will comply with the requests of others is increased when someone starts with a small request that is accepted and then makes a large request or if someone starts with a large request that is refused and then makes a small request. (page 631)

3. Many people obey the orders of a person in authority even if they believe their action will injure someone else. They are less likely to obey if they can see the person who would be injured. They are more likely to obey if other people are following orders without protest. (page 632)

4. People in groups are less likely than an isolated individual to come to the aid of another because they experience a diffusion of responsibility. (page 634)

5. Groups of people who lean mostly in the same direction on a given issue often make decisions that are more extreme than the decisions most individuals would have made on their own. (page 635)

6. Groupthink occurs when members of a cohesive group fail to express their opposition to a decision or when the leaders of the group try to silence dissent. (page 636)

7. In certain situations, people compete instead of cooperate because what is in their own best interests individually is not in the best interests of the group. (page 637)

SUGGESTIONS FOR FURTHER READING

Cialdini, R. B. (1985). *Influence: Science and practice.* Glenview, IL: Scott, Foresman. A book full of instructive and entertaining examples on how people try to influence one another. Highly recommended.

Janis, I. (1982). *Groupthink: Psychological studies of policy decisions and fiascoes.* (2nd ed.) Boston: Houghton Mifflin. Gives fascinating examples of how groups sometimes make disastrous decisions by stifling dissent.

Milgram, S. (1975). *Obedience to authority.* New York: Harper & Row. Describes Milgram's classic experiments on obedience.

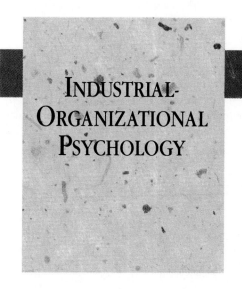

INDUSTRIAL-ORGANIZATIONAL PSYCHOLOGY

How do psychologists help employers select
among job applicants?
Why are some people satisfied and other people
dissatisfied with their jobs?
How do psychologists
help employers design jobs
to increase productivity and satisfaction?

Suppose you have to choose one thing to do and one place to do it. Once you have chosen, you will have to spend most of your waking hours doing that one thing in that one place for the rest of your life. You will, I hope, choose very carefully.

Guess what. You really do have to make that choice when you choose your job. True, your decision does not bind you for life; most people change jobs several times along the way. But even when you change jobs, you will probably continue doing a similar kind of work. So choosing a job is an important matter.

Industrial-organizational psychology—that is, the psychology of work—is not exactly an area of social psychology, but much of it illustrates social psychology in action. Employees have to work together as a group. Someone has to give orders, and others have to obey orders. The employer hopes employees will maintain a favorable attitude toward their work.

About a third of industrial and organizational psychologists, sometimes referred to as I-O psychologists, are employed by business and industry to help workers become more effective, productive, and satisfied. Another third are employed as college professors. The rest work in research and consulting firms, in government agencies, and in the military (Thayer, 1983).

Industrial and organizational psychologists try to improve the productivity and job satisfaction of workers by developing better ways for employers to select and train new employees. They try to devise systems of pay incentives to encourage high productivity among workers. And they help employers design and enrich jobs to increase the satisfaction of workers (Hunter & Schmidt, 1983).

SELECTION AND TRAINING

Universal Generic, Inc., advertises for someone to fill a newly created position: that of supervisor of its solar-powered flashlight division. Thirty people apply. The company will have to choose one applicant and then train him or her to do the job. The applicants report a wide range of education and experience, but none of them has had a job exactly like this before. Trying applicants out on the job is a valid way to predict performance, but it is too time consuming and costly for most jobs (Hunter & Hunter, 1984). How can the company identify the applicant who is likely to do the best job?

Cognitive Tests and Alternative Methods of Selection

One way is to test the applicants on their cognitive ability and perceptual-motor skills, using tests that are similar to the IQ tests we examined in Chapter 10. People who score high on such tests generally turn out to be good workers. According to Frank Schmidt and John Hunter (1981, page 1128), "Professionally developed cognitive ability tests are valid predictors of performance on the job . . . for all jobs . . . in all settings." That is probably an overstatement. (It could hardly be an understatement!) Still, for many jobs, cognitive tests are the *only* valid predictors known, and using them to select employees increases the company's productivity and saves money. It is also beneficial to employees, because those who are hired are likely to succeed at their job.

On most cognitive tests, however, black and Hispanic applicants receive lower scores on the average than white applicants receive. Consequently, the use of such tests has an adverse impact on those groups by making it less likely that they will get the most desirable jobs.

The courts have ruled that employers can use cognitive tests for selecting employees only if they can demonstrate that the test scores are valid predictors of performance for a particular job in a particular company. Although most studies have found that the commonly used tests are valid predictors, many employers have stopped using them because they cannot afford to conduct the research needed to prove validity for their particular jobs (Grant, 1980).

Several alternatives are available to employers who want to hire qualified minority applicants without abandoning cognitive tests. One way is to use test scores to eliminate the least qualified applicants and then to choose randomly among the rest. For example, an employer might select randomly among all the applicants who make test scores above the lowest 25%. However, this method generally proves unsatisfactory to all concerned. Random choice means that the employer inevitably passes up some of the best qualified applicants (including some blacks and Hispanics) in favor of less qualified applicants. Moreover, it does not fully balance the hiring of white applicants and minority applicants.

A second alternative is for the employer to use **quotas**—that is, to fill a fixed percentage of available jobs from members of each group. Under the quota system, the employer can use test scores to select the best qualified applicants from each group (Hunter & Hunter, 1984). But some observers question whether the use of quotas is ethically fair (Hunter & Schmidt, 1976). The willingness of employers to rely on quotas depends to some extent on the nature of the job. (Most employers are more willing to take a chance on a poorly qualified taxi driver than on a poorly qualified airplane pilot.)

Interviews

The most common, and probably the least valid, method of choosing among applicants for a job is the interview. Typically, the interviewer has only a foggy notion of what the job requires, puts different questions to different applicants, and takes few if any notes on what the applicants say (Schmitt, 1976; Thayer, 1983). An interviewer who is favorably impressed by an applicant spends most of the session talking about the job and asks the applicant only a few easy questions (Dipboye, 1982). An interviewer who forms a bad first impression of an applicant tends to ask "no-win" questions: "What aspects of this job do you think will be most difficult for you?" "What troubles do you have in getting along with other people?" "What did you like least about your last job?" Because many interviews are so unsystematic, interviewers may differ widely on

their evaluations of the same applicant (Carlson, Thayer, Mayfield, & Peterson, 1971).

Something to Think About

How would you respond to an interviewer who asked you only "no-win" questions?

Biographical Data

I-O psychologists continue to search for other ways of predicting job performance. Using biographical data is valid for some jobs (Owens, 1976). For example, the manager of a sporting-goods store might discover that the best salespeople are 20- to 28-year-olds who have played on at least one high school team, who like to watch sports on television, and who subscribe to at least one sports magazine. To glean such biographical information, the manager could ask each applicant to fill out a detailed questionnaire.

Physical Standards

Suppose you apply for a job and are turned down without an explanation. You ask why. The employer says, "Because you're too short. We never hire anyone who is shorter than five-feet-ten."

Can employers do that? Employers who set physical standards for employees, such as a minimum height, have been challenged in the courts. For example, women's groups have claimed that a minimum-height standard discriminates unfairly against women. Employers have defended themselves, saying that tall people (or thin people or heavy people) perform certain jobs better than other people do.

Police departments sometimes insist on a minimum height. Imagine a thief who hears, "Drop your gun!" The thief turns and sees the police officer. According to many police departments, the thief is more likely to drop the gun and go quietly if the police officer is tall and more likely to shoot it out if the police officer is short.

So they say, at any rate. U.S. courts have ruled that police and fire departments and other employers can set physical standards for employees only if they demonstrate conclusively that people who meet those standards make better employees than those who do not (Hogan & Quigley, 1986). The rule for physical standards is the same as the rule for cognitive tests: Any employer who sets such standards must be able to demonstrate that they lead to the selection of better employees.

Concept Check

10. *To use cognitive tests, physical standards, or any other criteria for selecting employees, an employer must demonstrate that those criteria are valid. It is easier to validate criteria for jobs that have clear standards for success and failure (such as a sales job) than for jobs that are hard to evaluate (such as most desk jobs). Why? (Check your answer on page 650.)*

Orienting New Employees to the Job

Most companies make some effort to acquaint new employees with their job in an effort to promote their job satisfaction later. To make the job sound good, many companies tell applicants and new employees only about the benefits of the job; they ignore or distort its disadvantages. Sooner or later, however, employees discover that the work is tiring, that some of the clients are rude, that the supervisor is obnoxious, or that raises are hard to come by. They may feel that they have been betrayed and may have no way to deal with their disappointment except to quit.

To avoid that possibility, some companies give job applicants and new employees a **realistic job preview** in which they honestly describe both the good and the bad features of the job (Figure 16.26). Employees who hear the bad news at the outset are about as likely as others to accept the job and are less likely to quit after a short time (Premack & Wanous, 1985). Many of those who refuse the job after learning about its real advantages and disadvantages would probably have been ill suited to the job anyway. In other words, a realistic job preview enables applicants to decide for themselves whether or not they are suited to the job.

The realistic job preview is more appropriate in dealing with new employees in higher-level jobs than it is in dealing with new employees in such jobs as bank teller. Presumably applicants for the lower-level jobs already have a reasonably accurate idea of what to expect on the job (Dean & Wanous, 1984; Reilly, Brown, Blood, & Malatesta, 1981). Moreover, a realistic job preview may be more helpful to workers with high self-efficacy than to those with low self-efficacy. As we saw in Chapter 7, self-efficacy is confidence in your own ability to perform a task. Once workers with high self-efficacy have been given a realistic description of a job, they tend to take the initiative in devising better ways of doing it. Workers with low self-efficacy prefer to perform routine duties; when they are told about all the things that can go wrong, they feel

FIGURE 16.26

Why they call it work: Which job would you prefer to take? Which would you be more likely to keep after experiencing frustration? Knowing what you're getting into can be helpful.

threatened rather than challenged (Jones, 1986; Pond & Hay, 1989).

The realistic job preview sometimes serves as a selection device, though that is not its primary purpose. C. Northcote Parkinson (1957) suggests that describing a job accurately discourages ill-suited people from applying. For example:

Wanted: Acrobat capable of crossing a slack wire 200 feet above raging furnace. Twice nightly, three times on Saturday. $250 per week. No health or accident insurance provided. Apply in person at Daredevil Circus.

Only someone who is thoroughly qualified for that job will even consider applying, Parkinson predicts, and no tests will be necessary. If more than one acrobat applies, Parkinson suggests (half seriously) that the salary offered must be too high.

Money isn't everything: Many people find satisfaction in work that is personally important but pays poorly in monetary terms. This famine relief volunteer finds rewards in directly helping to alleviate a life-or-death problem. To her, a high-paid job as an advertising executive has no appeal; promoting scented toilet paper or microwave pudding would offer no pride of accomplishment or other valued motivation.

Something to Think About

Do your professors provide a realistic course preview at the first meeting of the class? Would a realistic course preview provide the same benefits as a realistic job preview?

Job Training

I-O psychologists often conduct training programs for employees or help companies set up such programs. Over 90% of private corporations have a systematic training program. The format may range from lectures to role playing, encounter groups, or computer-assisted instruction. Some of the techniques used in these programs are little more than fads whose effectiveness is uncertain (Goldstein, 1980).

Many training programs, especially those intended to teach new skills to experienced workers, fail for lack of worker motivation. Paul Thayer and William McGehee (1977) report that one way to overcome worker apathy is to avoid training pro-

grams altogether. In helping a company to improve its training techniques, they announced that employees would take an "open book" test on certain information to see what they already knew "before starting the training course" (which never took place). The employee who received the highest score would win a free steak dinner, and the employees were encouraged to bet on who would win. Although the test was extremely detailed, all the employees earned a perfect or near-perfect score. The company bought steak dinners for everyone and considered it a bargain. The workers had mastered the material much more swiftly and more cheaply than they would have in a formal training course.

PAY AND WORK MOTIVATION

I-O psychologists like to quote this formula: "Performance is a function of ability times motivation." But what motivates people to work? "They work for money, of course," you reply. "Everyone knows that!" True, but "everyone" also knows that money is not the whole story. Given a choice among jobs, not everyone takes the job that offers the highest pay. Most people say that even if they suddenly became rich, they would continue to work (Vroom, 1964). Moreover, doubling the salary for a given job does not make employees twice as satisfied with their work or make them work twice as hard.

People work for a variety of motives (Locke, 1976; Vroom, 1964). One is money. A second is status. Many jobs provide prestige, and even the lowliest job is more prestigious than no job at all. A third motive is social interaction. Most workers enjoy dealing with co-workers, clients, and supervisors. A fourth motive is pride of accomplishment. Most people believe their work contributes in some way to the betterment of society. A fifth motive is physical activity. Although people dislike jobs that drain their energies, many workers welcome a moderate amount of physical exertion on the job.

The influence of pay on performance is complex. Performance generally improves when pay is related to the level of performance, either by paying for units of output (piecework) or by granting a bonus for high productivity. Yet most workers prefer to be paid by the hour rather than by the piece (Lawler, 1971). When they are paid by the piece, they tend to resent the workers who work the hardest, partly because they fear that management will cut the piece rate to compensate for the increased production. Moreover, in certain settings, piecework pay encourages workers to neglect important but unrewarded chores. For example, when salespeople are paid strictly on commission, they tend to compete for customers and to ignore such activities as checking stock and arranging displays (Vroom, 1964).

Most of all, workers do not want to feel cheated. When employers grant bonuses to the best workers ("merit pay increases"), those who fail to receive a bonus may resent being overlooked, especially if they believe their employer failed to evaluate their performance fairly and accurately (Thayer, 1987). In many jobs, such as teaching in public schools, evaluating the contributions and merits of employees is extremely difficult.

According to J. Stacy Adams (1963), workers like to think they are being paid what they are worth. They want to be paid as much as possible, but they also want to believe they are earning their pay. How would a worker react to an apparent discrepancy between those two desires? What would be the effect of telling a worker that he or she is overpaid or underpaid? Adams (1963) measured that effect with college students hired for temporary jobs as interviewers. Those in the control group were told their

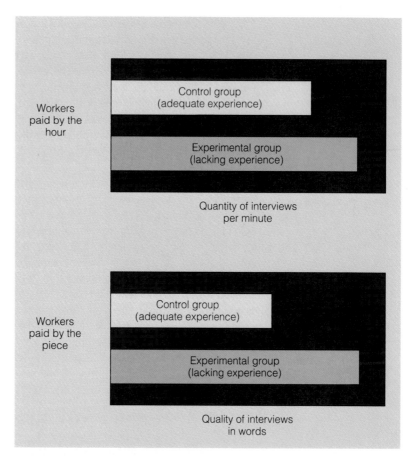

qualifications were exactly what the "employer" (the experimenter) was looking for. Those in the experimental group were told that they lacked the necessary experience for the job. The employer complained to each of the experimental subjects that the Placement Service had fouled up, muttered a little, called the Placement Service to find out what had gone wrong, got a busy signal, and finally said, "I guess I'll have to hire you anyway." He added that he would have to pay the same rate he was paying other, better-qualified employees.

Some employees in both the control group and the experimental group were paid by the hour. Others were paid a fixed amount for each interview they completed (piecework).

Subjects in the experimental group (those who had been told they were unqualified) worked harder than did subjects in the control group. Those in the experimental group who were being paid by the hour completed more interviews per hour than did subjects in the control group who were paid by the hour—that is, they produced a higher quantity of work. Those in the experimental group who were paid a fixed amount for each interview completed fewer interviews per hour (and thereby lowered their income) but recorded more information per interview— that is, they produced higher-quality work (see Figure 16.27).

FIGURE 16.27

Workers who thought they were unqualified for a job as an interviewer actually outperformed those who believed they had adequate experience.

In short, the workers who had been told they were unqualified tried to demonstrate either to themselves or to their employer (we cannot say which) that they were earning their pay. Those who were paid by the hour kept their output high, and those who were paid by the interview completed fewer but more detailed interviews. By forgoing the higher income to keep the quality of their work high, they presumably felt they were giving the employer more for the money.

The results are different, however, when the experiment is changed in either of two respects (Goodman & Friedman, 1971): First, if the salary is low, telling workers they are poorly qualified has little effect on their performance. They seem to think, "That employer has a lot of nerve complaining about my qualifications while offering only the minimum wage!" Second, telling workers they are being overpaid has little effect on their performance if they believe that everyone else is being overpaid, too. For example, if the employer says that everyone is being paid more than the job is worth because there was a misprint in the job advertisement, workers feel no obligation to work extra hard.

JOB DESIGN AND JOB ENRICHMENT

Despite their efforts to select the best applicants, some employers find that many of their employees fail to perform well. They might ask themselves whether the job is at fault rather than the employees. For example, no matter how employees are selected, few perform well at jobs that pay a low starting salary, jobs that pay only a commission on sales rather than a salary, and jobs that require new employees to reach a high level of performance in an unreasonably short time. Such conditions are characteristic of jobs in the life-insurance business, for example, in which many employees quit or get fired within the first year or two. The reason probably lies not in the method the companies use to select agents but in the conditions of the job itself (Thayer, 1977).

In one job in a plywood plant, workers had to align strips of wood on a moving belt (Campion & Thayer, 1985). They had to bend over and reach out to move the strips while balancing on one leg and operating a foot pedal with the other. The supervisor was dissatisfied with their performance and grumbled that all workers today are lazy and inefficient. In fact, given the way the job was designed, no one could perform it without expe-

riencing constant discomfort. After I-O psychologists helped the company redesign the equipment, workers were able to perform the task more effectively and with fewer complaints.

On other jobs, workers perform poorly because the work is boring and provides no sense of accomplishment. For many years, job design, especially in factories, was based on the **scientific-management approach**, also known as **Theory X**, which holds that employees are lazy, indifferent, and uncreative: "More people want to have a job than want to do a job." According to that approach, jobs should be made simple and routine so that employees will make few decisions and even the dullest worker can do the work with a minimum of errors (McGregor, 1960).

Practitioners of the scientific-management approach carried out *time and motion studies* to determine how each job could be done with the greatest speed, least fatigue, and fewest accidents. Figure 16.28 shows, for example, the "right" and "wrong" ways to lift a brick.

An alternative to the scientific-management approach is the **human-relations approach** to job design, also known as **Theory Y**, which holds that employees like to take responsibility for their work, like to use a variety of skills, and like to see the results of their labor and feel a sense of accomplishment. According to this approach, jobs should be expanded rather than simplified and made more challenging rather than made foolproof (McGregor, 1960).

Proponents of the human-relations approach use **job enrichment**, which takes several forms to increase employees' satisfaction and sense of accomplishment (Hackman, 1980). For example, a small group of workers may build a large component together. When they finish, they can see the results of their efforts. Or workers may rotate from one job to another in order to enjoy variety and avoid boredom.

Job enrichment can benefit both the employees and the company. At one company, the clerks who punched computer cards received no feedback on how well they were doing, were forbidden to correct even obvious errors, and had no opportunity for advancement. Morale was low and absenteeism was high. I-O psychologists redesigned the job so that each clerk had control over a single account and was authorized to correct obvious errors. The clerks were told of the mistakes they made and were given a chance to repair them. Those who did well were given added responsibility in handling their accounts. The quality of work rose dramatically and absenteeism dropped abruptly (Hackman, Oldham, Janson, & Purdy, 1975).

FIGURE 16.28

Right and wrong ways to lift a brick, according to Gilbreth (1911). Can you guess which is which? (Check your answer on page 650.)

Job enrichment has its trade-offs, however (Campion & Thayer, 1985). Although it generally increases workers' motivation and morale, only carefully selected, well-trained employees manage to perform the most highly enriched jobs with a low rate of errors. Moreover, job enrichment is more appropriate for some employees than for others. Some workers thrive on a challenging job; others, especially those who have been doing a simple job for many years, are more content with a routine job (Arnold & House, 1980; Hackman & Lawler, 1971). It is difficult to predict whether or not job enrichment will increase overall productivity and satisfaction in a given setting (Roberts & Glick, 1981).

Concept Check

11. *"I want my employees to enjoy their work and to feel pride in their achievements." Does that statement reflect a belief in Theory X or Theory Y? (Check your answer on page 650.)*

JOB SATISFACTION

"A happy worker is a productive worker." Right? It sounds as if it should be. And yet most studies show that the correlation between job satisfaction and productivity is low, around +0.17 (Iaffaldano & Muchinsky, 1985).

In a way, that lack of strong correlation should not be surprising. Although it seems reasonable to assume that workers who do a job well must like what they are doing, some of the most productive workers are dissatisfied because they believe (justifiably) that they could get a better job or that they are overdue for a promotion. Moreover, some of the least productive workers are satisfied with their job because they know it is the best they will ever get.

The Mennonites, of which these Amish are part, first settled in Pennsylvania more than 300 years ago, and they continue to live in much the same way as their ancestors. They acquire and pass on skills in such community work projects as barn raising and quilting bees. When everyone pitches in, the job passes quickly, and participants have the satisfaction of knowing they have made a valued contribution. Neighbors helping neighbors in this way built the log cabins and sod houses of pioneer America. Such work was a practical necessity, using the skills and raw material available. The housing was manufactured—that is, made by hand. Although homes are still built by hand, few Americans have jobs that manufacture anything in which they can take pride.

Nevertheless, workers who are satisfied with their job, for whatever reason, show better "citizenship" than do less satisfied workers in their willingness to help co-workers, accept extra duties when necessary, keep the workplace clean, conserve resources, and perform other unpaid tasks for the benefit of the organization (Bateman & Organ, 1983). For example, both satisfied and dissatisfied workers usually show up for work on time, but right after a blizzard, only the most satisfied workers make the effort to get to work (Smith, 1977).

SUMMARY

1.   Industrial and organizational psychologists study the behavior of people at work. They try to improve the productivity and satisfaction of workers by devising more effective methods of selection and training, pay incentives, and job design and job enrichment. (page 641)

2.   To choose among job applicants, employers use cognitive tests, interviews, biographical information, and physical standards. Each method has its advantages and disadvantages. If challenged in court, employers must be able to demonstrate that their methods are valid predictors of job performance. (page 641)

3.   Many employers provide new workers with a realistic job preview that explains both the desirable and the undesirable aspects of the job. Workers who receive such previews are less likely than other workers are to quit when problems arise. (page 643)

4.   Workers like to believe they are receiving fair pay for their work. Workers who believe they are being overpaid adjust either the quality or the quantity of their work to make it appear that they are earning their pay. (page 645)

5.   Some employers try to provide simple, foolproof jobs. Others try to make the jobs interesting and challenging. Some workers perform better on simple jobs; others do best with interesting jobs. (page 646)

6.   The correlation between satisfaction and productivity is low. However, satisfied workers are more likely than others are to perform citizenship tasks to help the organization. (page 647)

SUGGESTIONS FOR FURTHER READING

Blanchard, K. H. (1982). *The one minute manager.* New York: Morrow. A short, informative book on how to manage employees.

Glaser, R., & Bond, L. (Eds.). Testing: Concepts, policy, practice, and research. [Special issue.] *American Psychologist, 36*(10), 997–1206. A collection of articles concerning the use of tests, including their use for selecting people for jobs.

TERMS TO REMEMBER

actor-observer effect the tendency for people to be more likely to attribute internal causes to other people's behavior than they are to their own behavior

affiliation the motivation to be with others

attitude a learned like or dislike of something or somebody that influences behavior toward that thing or person

attribution the set of thought processes we use to assign causes to our own behavior and the behavior of others

cognitive dissonance a state of unpleasant tension that people experience when they hold contradictory attitudes or when they behave in a way that is inconsistent with their attitudes

commons dilemma a situation in which people may choose to deplete common resources for their own advantage faster than the resources can be replenished

compliance the tendency to do what someone asks us to do

conformity maintaining or changing one's behavior to be consistent with group standards

consensus information input about how a person's behavior compares with other people's behavior

consistency information information about how much a person's behavior varies over time and in different situations

diffusion of responsibility the tendency for people to feel less responsibility for helping when other people are around than when they know that no one else can help

discounting principle the tendency for people to discount the likelihood of one cause for a behavior when they are strongly aware of another cause

distinctiveness information information about how much a person's behavior depends on who or what the person is relating to

door-in-the-face technique a way to gain compliance in which someone follows an outrageous initial request with a much more reasonable second request

equity theory a theory that holds that all social relationships are transactions in which partners exchange goods and services; people strive for a fair exchange of such goods

exchange theory see **equity theory**

foot-in-the-door technique a way to gain compliance in which someone makes a modest request at first and then follows it up with a much larger second request

forewarning effect the tendency for a warning that people are about to hear a persuasive speech to weaken the talk's persuasive impact

fundamental attribution error the tendency to overemphasize internal explanations of behavior and underemphasize external explanations

group two or more people united by some common characteristic or interest and acting together in some way

group polarization the tendency for groups to make more extreme decisions than isolated individuals would, on the average

groupthink an extreme form of group polarization in which a cohesive group with leaders intolerant of dissent actively silences all dissenters and moves quickly toward a decision that may be ill conceived

human-relations approach see Theory Y

industrial-organizational (I-O) psychology branch of psychology that studies the behavior of people at work

inoculation effect the tendency for exposure to a weak persuasive message to weaken a subsequent stronger message's effect on people's attitudes

job enrichment an increase in the complexity and challenge of a job

Likert scale a scale on which a person checks some point along a line ranging from 1, meaning "strongly disagree," to 5 or 7, meaning "strongly agree," on each of several statements about some topic; ratings are summed over items

mere-exposure effect the tendency of people to come to like objects or people more as a result of coming into contact with them frequently

misattributions incorrect inferences about behavior

obedience following a direct command from someone in authority

primacy effect the tendency for the first information we learn about someone to influence us more than later information does

prisoner's dilemma a situation in which each person must choose between two actions, one a competitive response that benefits the person at another's expense, the other a cooperative response that brings less immediate benefit to the individual but benefits both people

proximity closeness

quota in employment, a rule for offering a fixed percentage of available jobs to each group of candidates

realistic job preview an orientation for a new worker in which the employer honestly describes the job's good and bad features

schemas the information and expectations we have about a person or groups of people

scientific-management approach see Theory X

self-handicapping strategies the use of external causes as "decoys" for our failures so we can avoid attributing them to internal causes

self-perception theory the theory that subjects attribute their behavior to situational factors such as rewards

self-serving bias the tendency to attribute your successes to internal factors such as skill and your failures to external forces beyond your control

similarity principle the tendency for people to choose friends who resemble themselves in many ways

sleeper effect the tendency of a message from a questionable source to exert little effect at first but a greater effect later

social cognition the process by which we combine and remember information about others and make inferences based on that information

social perception interpretation of the feelings, intentions, and personalities of other people

social psychologist a psychologist who studies social behavior and how an individual's behavior is influenced by other people

stereotypes schemas about groups of people

that's-not-all technique a way to gain compliance in which someone makes an offer and then, before the other person has a chance to reply, makes a better offer

Theory X an approach to job design that holds that employees are lazy, indifferent, and uncreative and that jobs should be made simple and routine

Theory Y an approach to job design that maintains that employees like to take responsibility for their work, like to use a variety of skills, and like to see the results of their labor and feel a sense of accomplishment

ANSWERS TO CONCEPT CHECKS

1. They want to avoid being biased by their first impressions of the students. That procedure is less important on the first test because they do not yet have a strong impression of the students. (page 597)

2. You are likely to think that the others really want to go to the movie (an internal attribution) and that you are going because of the external situation (peer pressure). (page 604)

3. Chances are, they will vote it down. If you and your friends continue to make the same suggestion at later meetings, they may eventually agree to give it a try. Or they may decide on some other activity that would never have occurred to them had it not been for your suggestion. (page 610)

4. You should expose them to weak attacks on their beliefs so that they will learn how to resist such attacks. Otherwise, they will be like children who grow up in a germ-free environment: They will develop no "immunity" and will be vulnerable when their beliefs are attacked. (page 612)

5. You will follow the central route to persuasion about your major and the peripheral route to persuasion about the advantages of a trip to the Bahamas. (page 612)

6. You will come to like your studies more if you are paid $10 than if you are paid $100. If you are paid only $10, you won't be able to tell yourself you are doing it only for the money. Instead, you will tell yourself that you must be really interested. The theory of intrinsic and extrinsic motivation leads to the same prediction: If you study hard in the absence of any strong external reason, you will perceive that you have internal reasons for studying. (page 615)

7. Three factors will strengthen the likelihood of your becoming friends: proximity, exposure, and attractiveness. The similarity principle will weaken it. Because of the difference in languages, you will have little chance, at least at first, to discover any similarities in interests or attitudes. In fact, proximity will probably not be a potent force because it serves largely as a means of enabling people to discover what they have in common. (page 621)

8. (a) Door-in-the-face technique; (b) that's-not-all technique; (c) foot-in-the-door technique. (page 631)

9. Group polarization is more likely to occur if the majority was in agreement at the start of the discussion. The members would be exposed to a barrage of arguments favoring the majority position and would be subjected to a pressure to conform. Neither factor would operate if the group was about evenly divided at first. (page 636)

10. To determine the validity, the employer may compute the correlation between score on a test (or height or any other criterion) and performance on the job. An employer who cannot accurately measure performance on the job cannot compute a meaningful correlation. (page 643)

11. Theory Y. (page 647)

ANSWERS TO OTHER QUESTIONS IN THE TEXT

In Figure 16.28 (page 647) the drawing on the left shows the correct way to lift a brick.

REFERENCES*

Aarons, L. (1976). Sleep-assisted instruction. *Psychological Bulletin, 83,* 1–40. (4)

Abelson, R. P. (1981). Psychological status of the script concept. *American Psychologist, 36,* 715–729. (13)

Abrahamsen, D. (1985). *Confessions of Son of Sam.* New York: Columbia University Press. (15)

Abramson, L. Y., Seligman, M. E. P., & Teasdale, J. D. (1978). Learned helplessness in humans: Critique and reformulation. *Journal of Abnormal Psychology, 87,* 49–74. (14)

Adam, K. (1980). Sleep as a restorative process and a theory to explain why. In P. S. McConnell, G. J. Boer, H. J. Romijn, N. E. van de Poll, & M. A. Corner (Eds.), *Progress in brain research: Vol. 53, Adaptive capabilities of the nervous system* (pp. 289–305). Amsterdam: Elsevier/North Holland Biomedical. (4)

Adam, K. S. (1986). Early family influences on suicidal behavior. *Annals of the New York Academy of Sciences, 487,* 63–76. (14)

Adams, J. S. (1963). Wage inequities, productivity, and work quality. *Industrial Relations, 3,* 9–16. (16)

Adler, A. (1927). *Understanding human nature.* New York: Greenberg. (13)

Adler, A. (1928/1964). Brief comments on reason, intelligence, and feeble-mindedness. In H. L. Ansbacher & R. R. Ansbacher (Eds.), *Superiority and social interest* (pp. 41–49). New York: Viking. (Original work published 1928) (13)

Adler, A. (1932/1964). The structure of neurosis. In H. L. Ansbacher & R. R. Ansbacher (Eds.), *Superiority and social interest* (pp. 83–95). New York: Viking. (Original work published 1932) (13)

Ajzen, I., & Fishbein, M. (1980). *Understanding attitudes and predicting social behavior.* Englewood Cliffs, NJ: Prentice-Hall. (16)

Ajzen, I., & Madden, T. (1986). Prediction of goal-directed behavior: Attitudes, intentions, and perceived behavioral control. *Journal of Experimental Social Psychology, 22,* 453–474. (16)

Albee, G. W. (1986). Toward a just society: Lessons from observations on the primary prevention of psychopathology. *American Psychologist, 41,* 891–898. (15)

Alexander, I. E. (1982). The Freud-Jung relationship—the other side of Oedipus and countertransference. *American Psychologist, 37,* 1009–1018. (13)

Allgeier, E. R. (1987). Coercive versus consensual sexual interactions. *The G. Stanley Hall Lecture Series, 7,* 11–63. (11)

Alloy, L. B., & Abramson, L. Y. (1979). Judgment of contingency in depressed and nondepressed students: Sadder but wiser? *Journal of Experimental Psychology: General, 108,* 441–485. (14)

Allport, G. W. (1935). Attitudes. In C. Murchison (Ed.), *A handbook of social psychology* (pp. 798–844). Worcester, MA: Clark University.

Allport, G. W. (1966). Traits revisited. *American Psychologist, 21,* 1–10. (13)

Allport, G. W., & Odbert, H. S. (1936). Trait-names: A psycholexical study. *Psychological Monographs, 47* (Whole No. 211). (13)

Alston, W. P. (1970). Toward a logical geography of personality: Traits and deeper lying personality characteristics. In H. E. Kiefer & M. K. Munitz (Eds.), *Mind, science, and history* (pp. 59–92). Albany, NY: State University of New York Press. (13)

Altman, I., Vinsel, A., & Brown, B. A. (1981). Dialectic conceptions in social psychology: An application to social penetration and privacy regulation. In L. Berkowitz (Ed.), *Advances in experimental social psychology* (Vol. 14, pp., 107–160). New York: Academic Press. (16)

American Medical Association. (1986). Council Report: Scientific status of refreshing recollection by the use of hypnosis. *International Journal of Clinical and Experimental Hypnosis, 34,* 1–12. (4)

American Psychiatric Association. (1987). *Diagnostic and statistical manual of mental disorders* (Third edition–Revised.) Washington, DC: Author. (14)

American Psychological Association. (1982). *Ethical principles in the conduct of research with human participants.* Washington, DC: Author. (2)

Anastasi, A. (1988). *Psychological testing* (6th ed.). New York: Macmillan. (10, 13)

Andersen, B. L. (1983). Primary orgasmic dysfunction: Diagnostic considerations and review of treatment. *Psychological Bulletin, 93,* 105–136. (11)

Anderson, C. D., Warner, J. L., & Spencer, C. C. (1984). Inflation bias in self-assessment examinations: Implications for valid employee selection. *Journal of Applied Psychology, 69,* 574–580. (13)

Anderson, N. H. (1974). Cognitive algebra: Integration theory applied to social attribution. In L. Berkowitz (Ed.), *Advances in experimental social psychology* (Vol. 7, pp. 1–101). New York: Academic Press. (16)

Anderson, N. H., & Hubert, S. (1963). Effects of concomitant verbal recall on order effects in personality impression formation. *Journal of Verbal Learning and Verbal Behavior, 2,* 379–391. (16)

Andreasen, N. C., & Olsen, S. (1982). Negative v. positive schizophrenia. Definition and validation. *Archives of General Psychiatry, 39,* 789–794. (14)

Angoff, W. H. (1988). The nature-nurture debate, aptitudes, and group differences. *American Psychologist, 43,* 713–720. (10)

Anisman, H., & Zacharko, R. M. (1983). Stress and neoplasia: Speculations and caveats. *Behavioral Medicine Update, 5,* 27–35. (12)

Anonymous. (1955). *Alcoholics anonymous* (2nd ed.). New York: Alcoholics Anonymous World Services. (14)

Appelbaum, P. S. (1988a). The right to refuse treatment with antipsychotic medications: Retrospect and prospect. *American Journal of Psychiatry, 145,* 413–419. (15)

Appelbaum, P. S. (1988b). The new preventive detention: Psychiatry's problematic responsibility for the control of violence. *American Journal of Psychiatry, 145,* 779–785. (15)

Appelbaum, S. A. (1979). *Out in inner space.* Garden City, NY: Anchor Press/Doubleday. (15)

Arana, G. W., Baldessarini, R. J., & Ornsteen, M. (1985). The dexamethasone suppression test for diagnosis and prognosis in psychiatry. *Archives of General Psychiatry, 42,* 1193–1204. (14)

Arboleda, C., & Holzman, P. S. (1985). Thought disorder in children at risk for psychosis. *Archives of General Psychiatry, 42,* 1004–1013. (14)

Arbour, K. J., & Wilkie, D. M. (1988). Rodents' (*Rattus, Mesocricetus,* and *Meriones*) use of learned caloric information in diet selection. *Journal of Comparative Psychology, 102,* 177–181. (7)

Argyle, N. (1988). The nature of cognitions in panic disorder. *Behaviour Research & Therapy, 26,* 261–264. (14)

Arkin, A. M. (1978). Sleeptalking. In A. M. Arkin, J. S. Antrobus, & S. J. Ellman (Eds.), *The mind in sleep* (pp. 513–532). Hillsdale, NJ: Lawrence Erlbaum. (4)

Arkin, A. M., & Antrobus, J. S. (1978). The effects of external stimuli applied prior to and during sleep on sleep experience. In A. M. Arkin, J. S. Antrobus, & S. J. Ellman (Eds.), *The mind in sleep* (pp. 351–391). Hillsdale, NJ: Lawrence Erlbaum. (4)

Arnold, H. J., & House, R. J. (1980). Methodological and substantive extensions to the job characteristics model of motivation. *Organizational Behavior and Human Performance, 25,* 161–183. (16)

Arnold, M. B. (1970). Perennial problems in the field of emotion. In M. B. Arnold (Ed.), *Feelings and emotions* (pp. 169–185). New York: Academic Press. (12)

Aronson, E. (1987). Teaching students what they think they already know about prejudice and desegregation. *The G. Stanley Hall Lecture Series, 7,* 69–84. (16)

Aronson, E., & Carlsmith, J. M. (1963). Effect of the severity of threat on the devaluation of forbidden behavior. *Journal of Abnormal and Social Psychology, 66,* 584–588. (16)

Asch, S. E. (1946). Forming impressions of personality. *Journal of Abnormal and Social Psychology, 41,* 258–290. (16)

Asch, S. E. (1951). Effects of group pressure upon the modification and distortion of judgments. In H. Guetzkow (Ed.), *Groups, leadership, and men* (pp. 177–190). Pittsburgh, PA: Carnegie Press. (16)

Asch, S. E. (1955, November). Opinions and social pressure. *Scientific American, 193*(5), 31–35. (16)

Asch, S. E. (1956). Studies of independence and conformity: I. A minority of one against a unanimous majority. *Psychological Monographs, 70*(9, Whole No. 416). (16)

Ash, R. (1986, August). An anecdote submitted by Ron Ash. *The Industrial-Organizational Psychologist, 23*(4), 8. (7)

Aslin, R. N. (1985). Oculomotor measures of visual development. In G. Gottlieb & N. A. Krasnegor (Eds.), *Measurement of audition and vision in the first year of postnatal life* (pp. 391–417). Norwood, NJ: Ablex. (6)

Atchley, R. C. (1980). *The social forces in later life* (3rd ed.). Belmont, CA: Wadsworth. (6)

Atkinson, J. W. (1957). Motivational determinants of risk taking behavior. *Psychological Review, 64,* 359–372. (11)

---

*The number in parentheses after each entry is the chapter in which the reference appears.

Atkinson, J. W., & Birch, D. (1978). *Introduction to motivation* (2nd ed.). New York: D. Van Nostrand. (11)

Averill, J. R. (1983). Studies on anger and aggression: Implications for theories of emotion. *American Psychologist, 38,* 1145–1160. (12)

Azrin, N. H. (1976). Improvements in the community-reinforcement approach to alcoholism. *Behaviour Research and Therapy, 14,* 339–348. (14)

Azrin, N. H., & Nunn, R. G. (1973). Habit-reversal: A method of eliminating nervous habits and tics. *Behaviour Research & Therapy, 11,* 619–628. (7)

Bachevalier, J., & Mishkin, M. (1984). An early and a late developing system for learning and retention in infant monkeys. *Behavioral Neuroscience, 98,* 770–778. (8)

Bachevalier, J., & Mishkin, M. (1986). Visual recognition impairment follows ventromedial but not dorsolateral prefrontal lesions in monkeys. *Behavioral Brain Research, 20,* 249–261. (3)

Bachrach, A. J., Erwin, W. J., & Mohr, J. P. (1965). The control of eating behavior in an anoretic by operant conditioning techniques. In L. P. Ullmann & L. Krasner (Eds.), *Case studies in behavior modification* (pp. 153–163). New York: Holt, Rinehart, & Winston. (11, 15)

Backlund, E.-O., Granberg, P. O., Hamberger, B., Sedvall, G., Seiger, A., & Olson, L. (1985). Transplantation of adrenal medullary tissue to striatum in Parkinsonism. In A. Björklund & U. Stenevi (Eds.), *Neural grafting in the mammalian CNS* (pp. 551–556). Amsterdam: Elsevier. (3)

Baddeley, A., & Wilson, B. (1986). Amnesia, autobiographical memory, and confabulation. In D. C. Rubin (Ed.), *Autobiographical memory* (pp. 225–252). Cambridge, England: Cambridge University Press. (8)

Bahrick, H. (1984). Semantic memory content in permastore: 50 years of memory for Spanish learned in school. *Journal of Experimental Psychology: General, 113,* 1–29. (8)

Baird, J. C. (1982). The moon illusion: A reference theory. *Journal of Experimental Psychology: General, 111,* 304–315. (5)

Baker, G. H. B. (1987). Invited review: Psychological factors and immunity. *Journal of Psychosomatic Research, 31,* 1–10. (12)

Baker, T. B., & Tiffany, S. T. (1985). Morphine tolerance as habituation. *Psychological Bulletin, 92,* 78–108. (14)

Balay, J., & Shevrin, H. (1988). The subliminal psychodynamic activation method: A critical review. *American Psychologist, 43,* 161–174. (5)

Baldessarini, R. J. (1984). Antipsychotic drugs. In T. B. Karasu (Ed.), *The psychiatric therapies. I. The somatic therapies* (pp. 119–170). Washington, DC: American Psychiatric Press. (15)

Baldwin, J. D., & Baldwin, J. I. (1988). Factors affecting AIDS-related sexual risk-taking behavior among college students. *Journal of Sex Research, 25,* 181–196. (11)

Bandura, A. (1977). *Social learning theory.* Englewood Cliffs, NJ: Prentice-Hall. (7)

Bandura, A. (1986). *Social foundations of thought and action.* Englewood Cliffs, NJ: Prentice-Hall. (7)

Bandura, A., Ross, D., & Ross, S. A. (1963). Imitation of film-mediated aggressive models. *Journal of Abnormal and Social Psychology, 66,* 3–11. (7)

Barber, T. X. (1979). Suggested ("hypnotic") behavior: The trance paradigm versus an alternative paradigm. In E. Fromm & R. E. Shor (Eds.), *Hypnosis: Developments in research and new perspectives* (2nd ed.) (pp. 217–271). New York: Aldine. (4)

Bard, P. (1934). On emotional expression after decortication with some remarks on certain theoretical views. *Psychological Review, 41,* 309–329. (12)

Barnes, C. A., & McNaughton, B. L. (1985). An age comparison of the rates of acquisition and forgetting of spatial information in relation to long-term

enhancement of hippocampal synapses. *Behavioral Neuroscience, 99,* 1040–1048. (8)

Barnes, R. (1985). Women and self-injury. *International Journal of Women's Studies, 8,* 465–474. (14)

Barnett, P. A., & Gotlib, I. H. (1988). Psychosocial functioning and depression: Distinguishing among antecedents, concomitants, and consequences. *Psychological Bulletin, 104,* 97–126. (14)

Barrera, R. D., Lobato-Barrera, D., & Sulzer-Azaroff, B. (1980). A simultaneous treatment comparison of three expressive language training programs with a mute autistic child. *Journal of Autism and Developmental Disorders, 10,* 21–37. (14)

Barron, F., & Harrington, D. M. (1981). Creativity, intelligence, and personality. *Annual Review of Psychology, 32,* 439–476. (9)

Bass, B. M., & Ryterband, E. C. (1979). *Organizational psychology* (2nd ed.). Boston: Allyn & Bacon. (6)

Bassok, M., & Holyoak, K. J. (1989). Interdomain transfer between isomorphic topics in algebra and physics. *Journal of Experimental Psychology: Learning, Memory, and Cognition, 15,* 153–166. (9)

Bateman, T. S., & Organ, D. W. (1983). Job satisfaction and the good soldier: The relationship between affect and employee "citizenship." *Academy of Management Journal, 26,* 587–595. (16)

Bates, J. A. (1979). Extrinsic reward and intrinsic motivation: A review with implications for the classroom. *Review of Educational Research, 49,* 557–576. (11)

Baum, A., Gatchel, R. J., & Schaeffer, M. A. (1983). Emotional, behavioral, and physiological effects of chronic stress at Three Mile Island. *Journal of Consulting and Clinical Psychology, 51,* 565–572. (12)

Baylor, D. A., Lamb, T. D., & Yau, K.-W. (1979). Responses of retinal rods to single photons. *Journal of Physiology* (London), *288,* 613–634. (5)

Beardslee, W. R., Bemporad, J., Keller, M. B., & Klerman, G. L. (1983). Children of parents with major affective disorder: A review. *American Journal of Psychiatry, 140,* 825–832. (14)

Beauchamp, G. K. (1987). The human preference for excess salt. *American Scientist, 75,* 27–33. (11)

Beck, A. T. (1976). *Cognitive therapy and the emotional disorders.* New York: New American Library. (15)

Beck, S. J. (1960). *The Rorschach experiment: Ventures in blind diagnosis.* New York: Grune & Stratton. (13)

Beech, H. R., & Vaughan, M. (1978). *Behavioural treatment of obsessional states.* Chichester, England: Wiley. (14)

Belmore, S. M. (1987). Determinants of attention during impression formation. *Journal of Experimental Psychology: Learning, Memory and Cognition, 13,* 480–489. (16)

Bem, D. J. (1967). Self-perception: An alternative interpretation of cognitive dissonance phenomena. *Psychological Review, 74,* 183–200. (16)

Bem, D. J. (1970). *Beliefs, attitudes, and human affairs.* Pacific Grove, CA: Brooks/Cole. (16)

Bem, D. J. (1972). Self-perception theory. *Advances in Experimental Social Psychology, 6,* 1–62. (16)

Bem, D. J., & Allen, A. (1974). On predicting some of the people some of the time. *Psychological Review, 81,* 506–520. (13)

Bem, S. L. (1974). The measurement of psychological androgyny. *Journal of Consulting and Clinical Psychology, 42,* 155–162. (13)

Benassi, V. A., Sweeney, P. D., & Dufour, C. L. (1988). Is there a relation between locus of control orientation and depression? *Journal of Abnormal Psychology, 97,* 357–367. (14)

Benkelfat, C., Murphy, D. L., Zohar, J., Hill, J. L., Grover, G., & Insel, T. R. (1989). Clomipramine in obsessive-compulsive disorder. *Archives of General Psychiatry, 46,* 23–28. (14)

Bennett, M. J. (1983). Focal psychotherapy—terminable and interminable. *American Journal of Psychotherapy, 37,* 365–375. (15)

Bennett, W. (1980). The cigarette century. *Science 80, 1*(6), 36–43. (14)

Benson, H. (1977). Systemic hypertension and the relaxation response. *New England Journal of Medicine, 296,* 1152–1156. (12)

Benson, H. (1985). Stress, health, and the relaxation response. In W. D. Gentry, H. Benson, & C. J. de Wolff (Eds.), *Behavioral medicine: Work, stress and health* (pp. 15–32). Dordrecht, Netherlands: Martinus Nijhoff. (12)

Benton, A. L. (1980). The neuropsychology of facial recognition. *American Psychologist, 35,* 176–186. (3)

Berglas, S., & Jones, E. E. (1978). Drug choice as a self-handicapping strategy in response to noncontingent success. *Journal of Personality and Social Psychology, 36,* 405–417. (4, 16)

Berkow, R. (Ed.) (1987). *The Merck Manual* (15th ed.). Rahway, NJ: Merck Sharp & Dohme Research Laboratories. (11)

Berkowitz, L. (1983). Aversively stimulated aggression: Some parallels and differences in research with animals and humans. *American Psychologist, 38,* 1135–1144. (12)

Berlyne, D. E. (1981). Humanistic psychology as a protest movement. In J. R. Royce & L. P. Mos (Eds.), *Humanistic psychology: Concepts and criticisms* (pp. 261–293). New York: Plenum. (13)

Berman, A. L. (1988). Fictional depiction of suicide in television films and imitation effects. *American Journal of Psychiatry, 145,* 982–986. (15)

Berne, E. (1964). *Games people play.* New York: Grove. (15)

Bernstein, I. L. (1985). Learned food aversions in the progression of cancer and its treatment. *Annals of the New York Academy of Sciences, 443,* 365–380. (11)

Bernstein, I. L., & Borson, S. (1986). Learned food aversion: A component of anorexia syndromes. *Psychological Review, 93,* 462–472. (11)

Berry, D. S., & McArthur, L. Z. (1986). Perceiving character in faces: The impact of age-related craniofacial changes in social perception. *Psychological Bulletin, 100,* 3–18. (16)

Berscheid, E. (1983). Emotion. In H. H. Kelley, E. Berscheid. A. Christensen, J. H. Harvey, T. L. Huston, G. Levinger, E. McClintock, L. A. Peplau, & D. R. Peterson, *Close relationships* (pp. 110–168). New York: W. H. Freeman. (16)

Berscheid, E. (1985). Interpersonal attraction. In G. Lindzey & E. Aronson, (Eds.), *Handbook of social psychology* (Vol. 2, pp. 413–484). New York: Random House. (16)

Berscheid, E., Dion, K., & Walster, E. (1971). Physical attractiveness and dating choice: A test of the matching hypothesis. *Journal of Experimental Social Psychology, 7,* 173–189. (16)

Berscheid, E., & Walster, E. (1974). A little bit about love. In T. L. Huston (Ed.), *Foundations of interpersonal attraction* (pp. 355–381). New York: Academic Press. (16)

Binet, A., & Simon, T. (1905). Méthodes nouvelles pour le diagnostic du niveau intellectuel des anormaux [New methods for the measurement of the intellectual level of the abnormal]. *L'Année Psychologique, 11,* 191–244. (10)

Björklund, A., Stenevi, U., Dunnett, S. B., & Gage, F. H. (1982). Cross-species neural grafting in a rat model of Parkinson's disease. *Nature, 298,* 652–654. (3)

Black, I. B., Adler, J. E., Dreyfus, C. F., Jonakait, G. M., Katz, D. M., LaGamma, E. F., & Markey, K. M. (1984). Neurotransmitter plasticity at the molecular level. *Science, 225,* 1266–1270. (3)

Blaine, J. D., Prien, R. F., & Levine, J. (1983). The role of antidepressants in the treatment of affective disorders. *American Journal of Psychotherapy, 37,* 502–520. (15)

Blakemore, C., & Sutton, P. (1969). Size adaptation: A new aftereffect. *Science, 166,* 245–247. (5)

Blanchard, D. C., & Blanchard, R. J. (1984). Inadequacy of pain-aggression hypothesis revealed in naturalistic settings. *Aggressive Behavior, 10,* 33–46. (12)

Blanchard, E. B., & Young, L. D. (1973). Self-control of cardiac functioning: A promise as yet unfulfilled. *Psychological Bulletin, 79,* 145–163. (12)

Blanchard, E. B., & Young, L. D. (1974). Clinical applications of biofeedback training: A review of evidence. *Archives of General Psychiatry, 30,* 573–589. (12)

Blaney, P. H. (1986). Affect and memory: A review. *Psychological Bulletin, 99,* 229–246. (8)

Bleuler, E. (1911/1950). *Dementia praecox, or the group of schizophrenias* (J. Zinkin, Trans.). New York: International Universities Press. (Original work published 1911) (14)

Bloch, S. (1986). Group psychotherapy. In S. Bloch (Ed.), *An introduction to the psychotherapies* (pp. 80–112). Oxford, England: Oxford University Press. (15)

Bloom, B. L., White, S. W., & Asher, S. J. (1979). Marital disruption as a stressful life event. In G. Levinger & O. C. Moles (Eds.), *Divorce and separation* (pp. 184–200). New York: Basic Books. (16)

Bloom, J. D., & Faulkner, L. R. (1987). Competency determinations in civil commitment. *American Journal of Psychiatry, 144,* 193–196. (15)

Blum, G. S., & Barbour, J. S. (1979). Selective inattention to anxiety-linked stimuli. *Journal of Experimental Psychology: General, 108,* 182–224. (5)

Blumenthal, S. J., & Kupfer, D. J. (1986). Generalizable treatment strategies for suicidal behavior. *Annals of the New York Academy of Sciences, 487,* 327–340. (14)

Blundell, J. E. (1987). Nutritional manipulations for altering food intake. *Annals of the New York Academy of Sciences, 499,* 144–155. (11)

Bollard, J. (1982). A 2-year follow-up of bedwetters treated by dry-bed training and standard conditioning. *Behavior Research and Therapy, 20,* 571–580. (15)

Bond, J. A. (1986). Inconsistent responding to repeated MMPI items: Is its major cause really carelessness? *Journal of Personality Assessment, 50,* 50–64. (13)

Booth-Kewley, S., & Friedman, H. S. (1987). Psychological predictors of heart disease: A quantitative review. *Psychological Bulletin, 101,* 343–362. (12)

Bores, L. D. (1983). Historical review and clinical results of radial keratotomy. *International Ophthalmology Clinics, 23,* 93–118. (5)

Boring, E. G. (1930). A new ambiguous figure. *American Journal of Psychology, 42,* 444–445. (5)

Bornstein, M. H., & Sigman, M. D. (1986). Continuity in mental development from infancy. *Child Development, 57,* 251–274. (10)

Bosard, J. H. S. (1931). Residential propinquity as a factor in marriage selection. *American Journal of Sociology, 38,* 219–224. (16)

Bothwell, R. K., & Brigham, J. C. (1983). Selective evaluation and recall during the 1980 Reagan-Carter debate. *Journal of Applied Social Psychology, 13,* 427–442. (16)

Bouchard, T. J., Jr., & McGue, M. (1981). Familial studies of intelligence: A review. *Science, 212,* 1055–1059. (10)

Bourne, P. G. (1971). Altered adrenal function in two combat situations in Viet Nam. In B. E. Eleftheriou & J. P. Scott (Eds.), *The physiology of aggression and defeat* (pp. 265–290). New York: Plenum. (12)

Bower, T. G. R., & Wishart, J. G. (1972). Effects of motor skill on object permanence. *Cognition, 1,* 165–172. (6)

Bowlby, J. (1952). *Maternal care and mental health.* Geneva: World Health Organization. (6)

Boyd, J. H. (1983). The increasing rate of suicide by firearms. *New England Journal of Medicine, 308,* 872–874. (14)

Boynton, R. M. (1988). Color vision. *Annual Review of Psychology, 39,* 69–100. (5)

Brabeck, M. (1983). Moral judgment: Theory and research on differences between males and females. *Developmental Psychology, 3,* 274–291. (6)

Bradburn, N. M., Rips, L. J., & Shevell, S. K. (1987). Answering autobiographical questions: The impact of memory and inference on surveys. *Science, 236,* 157–161. (8)

Bradbury, T. N., & Miller, G. A. (1985). Season of birth in schizophrenia: A review of evidence, methodology, and etiology. *Psychological Bulletin, 98,* 569–594. (14)

Bradshaw, J. L. (1969). The information conveyed by varying dimensions of features in human outline faces. *Perception and Psychophysics, 6,* 5–9. (16)

Brady, J. V., Porter, R. W., Conrad, D. G., & Mason, J. W. (1958). Avoidance behavior and the development of gastroduodenal ulcers. *Journal of the Experimental Analysis of Behavior, 1,* 69–72. (12)

Bransford, J. D., & Johnson, M. K. (1972). Contextual prerequisites for understanding: Some investigations of comprehension and recall. *Journal of Verbal Learning and Verbal Behavior, 11,* 717–726. (8)

Bransford, J. D., & Stein, B. S. (1984). *The ideal problem solver.* New York: W. H. Freeman. (9)

Braun, P., Kochansky, G., Shapiro, R., Greenberg, S., Gudeman, J. E., Johnson, S., & Shore, M. F. (1981). Overview: Deinstitutionalization of psychiatric patients: A critical review of outcome studies. *American Journal of Psychiatry, 138,* 736–749. (15)

Bregman, A. S. (1981). Asking the "what for" question in auditory perception. In M. Kubovy & J. R. Pomerantz (Eds.), *Perceptual organization* (pp. 99–118). Hillsdale, NJ: Lawrence Erlbaum. (5)

Brent, D. A., Perper, J. A., Goldstein, C. E., Kolko, D. J., Allan, M. J., Allman, C. J. & Zelenak, J. P. (1988). Risk factors for adolescent suicide. *Archives of General Psychiatry, 45,* 581–588. (14)

Breslau, N., & Prabucki, K. (1987). Siblings of disabled children. *Archives of General Psychiatry, 44,* 1040–1046. (6)

Brewer, W. F., & Treyens, J. C. (1981). Role of schemata in memory for places. *Cognitive Psychology, 13,* 207–230. (8)

Brickman, P., Becker, L. J., & Castle, S. (1979). Making trust easier and harder through forms of sequential interaction. *Journal of Personality and Social Psychology, 37,* 515–521. (16)

Brickman, P., Coates, D., & Janoff-Bulman, R. (1978). Lottery winners and accident victims: Is happiness relative? *Journal of Personality and Social Psychology, 36,* 917–927. (12)

Brierley, J. B. (1977). The neuropathology of amnesic states. In C. W. M. Whitty & O. L. Zangwill (Eds.), *Amnesia* (2nd ed.) (pp. 199–223). New York: Appleton-Century-Crofts. (1)

Briggs, S. R. (1985). A trait account of social shyness. *Review of Personality and Social Psychology, 6,* 35–64. (13)

Brooks-Gunn, J., & Furstenberg, F. F., Jr. (1989). Adolescent sexual behavior. *American Psychologist, 44,* 249–257. (11)

Brophy, J. (1987). Socializing students' motivation to learn. *Advances in Motivation and Achievement, 5,* 181–210. (11)

Brower, K. J., & Anglin, M. D. (1987). Adolescent cocaine use: Epidemiology, risk factors, and prevention. *Journal of Drug Education, 17,* 163–180. (4)

Brown, N. R., Shevell, S. K., & Rips, L. J. (1986). Public memories and their personal context. In D. C. Rubin (Ed.), *Autobiographical memory* (pp. 137–158). Cambridge, England: Cambridge University Press. (8)

Brown, R., & Kulik, J. (1977). Flashbulb memories. *Cognition, 5,* 73–99. (8)

Brown, R., & McNeill, D. (1966). The "tip of the tongue." *Journal of Verbal Learning and Verbal Behavior, 5,* 325–337. (8)

Brown, R. J., & Donderi, D. C. (1986). Dream content and reported well-being among recurrent dreamers, past-recurrent dreamers, and nonrecurrent dreamers. *Journal of Personality and Social Psychology, 50,* 612–623. (4)

Browne, A., & Finkelhor, D. (1986). Impact of child sexual abuse: A review of the research. *Psychological Bulletin, 99,* 66–77. (15)

Brownell, K. D. (1982). Obesity: Understanding and treating a serious, prevalent, and refractory disorder. *Journal of Consulting & Clinical Psychology, 50,* 820–840. (11)

Brownell, K. D., Marlatt, G. A., Lichtenstein, E., & Wilson, G. T. (1986). Understanding and preventing relapse. *American Psychologist, 41,* 765–782. (14)

Bruch, H. (1980). Preconditions for the development of anorexia nervosa. *American Journal of Psychoanalysis, 40,* 169–172. (11)

Buell, S. J., & Coleman, P. D. (1981). Quantitative evidence for selective growth in normal human aging but not in senile dementia. *Brain Research, 214,* 23–41. (3)

Burchfield, S. R. (1979). The stress response: A new perspective. *Psychosomatic Medicine, 41,* 661–672. (12)

Burger, J. M. (1986). Desire for control and the illusion of control: The effects of familiarity and sequence of options. *Journal of Research in Personality, 20,* 66–76. (13)

Burger, J. M. (1986). Increasing compliance by improving the deal: The that's-not-all technique. *Journal of Personality and Social Psychology, 51,* 277–283. (16)

Burgess, A. W., Hazelwood, R. R., Rokous, F. E., Hartman, C. R., & Burgess, A. G. (1988). Serial rapists and their victims: Reenactment and repetition. *Annals of the New York Academy of Sciences, 528,* 277–295. (11)

Burgess, E. W., & Wallin, P. (1953). *Engagement and marriage.* Philadelphia: Lippincott. (16)

Burke, H. R. (1985). Raven's Progressive Matrices (1938): More on norms, reliability, and validity. *Journal of Clinical Psychology, 41,* 231–235. (10)

Burnstein, E., & Vinokur, A. (1973). Testing two classes of theories about group-induced shifts in individual choice. *Journal of Experimental Social Psychology, 9,* 123–137. (16)

Burnstein, E., & Vinokur, A. (1977). Persuasive arguments and social comparison as determinants of attitude polarization. *Journal of Experimental Social Psychology, 13,* 315–332. (16)

Buss, D. M. (1985). Human mate selection. *American Scientist, 73,* 47–51. (16)

Buss, D. M., & Barnes, M. (1986). Preferences in human mate selection. *Journal of Personality and Social Psychology, 50,* 559–570. (16)

Butcher, J. (1989). The MMPI—a classic revised. Presentation at Carolinas Psychology Conference, Raleigh, NC. (13)

Byrne, D. (1971). *The attraction paradigm.* New York: Academic Press. (16)

Cahalan, D. (1978). Subcultural differences in drinking behavior in U.S. national surveys and selected European studies. In P. E. Nathan, G. A. Marlatt, & T. Løberg (Eds.), *Alcoholism: New directions in behavioral research and treatment* (pp. 235–253). New York: Plenum. (14)

Caltabiano, M. L., & Smithson, M. (1983). Variables affecting the perception of self-disclosure appropriateness. *Journal of Social Psychology, 120,* 119–128. (6)

Camara, W. J. (1988). Reagan signs ban of polygraph testing for job applicants. *The Industrial-Organizational Psychologist, 26,* 39–41. (12)

Camel, J. E., Withers, G. S., & Greenough, W. T. (1986). Persistence of visual cortex dendritic alterations induced by postweaning exposure to a "superenriched" environment in rats. *Behavioral Neuroscience, 100,* 810–813. (3)

Campbell, S. S., & Tobler, I. (1984). Animal sleep: A review of sleep duration across phylogeny. *Neuroscience & Biobehavioral Reviews, 8,* 269–300. (4)

Campion, J., Latto, R., & Smith, Y. M. (1983). Is blindsight an effect of scattered light, spared cortex, and near-threshold vision? *Behavioral and Brain Sciences, 6,* 423–486. (3)

Campion, M. A., & Thayer, P. W. (1985). Development and field evaluation of an interdisciplinary measure of job design. *Journal of Applied Psychology, 70,* 29–43. (16)

Cannon, W. B. (1927). The James-Lange theory of emotion. *American Journal of Psychology, 39,* 106–124. (12)

Cannon, W. B. (1929). Organization for physiological homeostasis. *Physiological Reviews, 9,* 399–431. (11)

Caplan, L. (1984). *The insanity defense and the trial of John W. Hinckley, Jr.* Boston: Godine.

Caporael, L. R. (1976). Ergotism: The Satan loosed in Salem? *Science, 192,* 21–26. (3)

Carducci, B. J., Cozby, P. C., & Ward, C. D. (1978). Sexual arousal and interpersonal evaluations. *Journal of Experimental Social Psychology, 14,* 449–457. (16)

Carey, S. (1978). The child as word learner. In M. Halle, J. Bresnan, & G. A. Miller (Eds.), *Linguistic theory and psychological reality* (pp. 264–293). Cambridge, MA: MIT Press. (6)

Carlson, R. E., Thayer, P. W., Mayfield, E. C., & Peterson, D. A. (1971). Improvements in the selection interview. *Personnel Journal, 50,* 268–275, 317. (16)

Carroll, B. J. (1980). Implications of biological research for the diagnosis of depression. In J. Mendlewicz (Ed.), *New advances in the diagnosis and treatment of depressive illness* (pp. 85–107). Amsterdam: Excerpta medica. (14)

Carver, C. S., & Scheier, M. F. (1981). *Attention and self-regulation: A control theory approach to human behavior.* New York: Springer-Verlag. (16)

Castleman, M. (1989, July 2). Mellow fellows. *San Jose Mercury News: West,* pp. 18–27. (12)

Cattell, R. B. (1965). *The scientific analysis of personality.* Chicago: Aldine. (13)

Cattell, R. B. (1987). *Intelligence: Its structure, growth and action.* Amsterdam: North-Holland. (10)

Caufield, C. (1989, October 1). Paradise lost. *San Francisco Chronicle: This world* (Sunday magazine), p. 7.

Ceci, S. J., Ross, D. F., & Toglia, M. P. (1987). Suggestibility of children's memory: Psycholegal implications. *Journal of Experimental Psychology: General, 116,* 38–49. (8)

Chaiken, S. (1987). The heuristic model of persuasion. In M. P. Zanna, J. M. Olson, & C. P. Herman (Eds.), *Social influence: The Ontario symposium* (Vol. 5, pp. 3–39). Hillsdale, NJ: Lawrence Erlbaum. (16)

Chaiken, S., & Eagly, A. H. (1983). Communication modality as a determinant of persuasion: The role of communicator salience. *Journal of Personality and Social Psychology, 45,* 241–256. (16)

Chamberlin, J. (1978). *On our own.* New York: Hawthorn. (15)

Charlton, S. G. (1983). Differential conditionability: Reinforcing grooming in golden hamsters. *Animal Learning & Behavior, 11,* 27–34. (7)

Chase, T. N., Wexler, N. S., & Barbeau, A. (Eds.) (1979). *Advances in Neurology: Vol. 23, Huntington's disease.* New York: Raven Press. (1)

Cheetham, E. (1973). *The prophecies of Nostradamus.* New York: Putnam's. (2)

Chiodo, L. A., & Antelman, S. M. (1980). Electroconvulsive shock: Progressive dopamine autoreceptor subsensitivity independent of repeated treatment. *Science, 210,* 799–801. (15)

Chiueh, C. C. (1988). Dopamine in the extrapyramidal motor function. *Annals of the New York Academy of Sciences, 515,* 226–238. (3)

Chodoff, P. (1982). Hysteria and women. *American Journal of Psychiatry, 139,* 545–551. (14)

Chomsky, N. (1980). *Rules and representations.* New York: Columbia University Press. (6)

Chouinard, G., & Jones, B. D. (1980). Neuroleptic-induced supersensitivity psychosis: Clinical and pharmacological characteristics. *American Journal of Psychiatry, 137,* 16–21. (15)

Christopher, F. S., & Cate, R. M. (1985). Premarital sexual pathways and relationship development. *Journal of Social and Personal Relationships, 2,* 271–288. (6, 11)

Cialdini, R. B. (1985). *Influence: Science and practice.* Glenview, IL: Scott, Foresman. (7)

Cialdini, R. B., Vincent, J. E., Lewis, S. K., Catalan, J., Wheeler, D., & Darby, B. L. (1975). Reciprocal concessions procedure for inducing compliance: The door-in-the-face technique. *Journal of Personality and Social Psychology, 31,* 206–215. (16)

Cines, B. M., & Rozin, P. (1982). Some aspects of the liking for hot coffee and coffee flavor. *Appetite: Journal for Intake Research, 3,* 23–34. (4)

Cirignotta, F., Tedesco, C. V., & Lugaresi, E. (1980). Temporal lobe epilepsy with ecstatic seizures (so-called Dostoevsky epilepsy). *Epilepsia, 21,* 705–710. (3)

Clarke, A. M., & Clarke, A. D. B. (1976). *Early experience: Myth and evidence.* New York: Free Press. (6)

Clarke-Stewart, K. A. (1989). Infant day care: Maligned or malignant? *American Psychologist, 44,* 266–273. (6)

Clarkin, J. F., & Frances, A. (1982). Selection criteria for the brief psychotherapies. *American Journal of Psychotherapy, 36,* 166–180. (15)

Clifford, M. M., & Walster, E. (1973). The effect of physical attractiveness on teacher expectation. *Sociology of Education, 46,* 248–258. (16)

Clifton, R., Siqueland, E. R., & Lipsitt, L. P. (1972). Conditioned head-turning in human newborns as a function of conditioned response requirements and states of wakefulness. *Journal of Experimental Child Psychology, 13,* 43–57. (6)

"Clinicopathologic conference." (1967). *Johns Hopkins Medical Journal, 120,* 186–199. (12)

Cloninger, C. R. (1987). Neurogenetic adaptive mechanisms in alcoholism. *Science, 236,* 410–416. (14)

Cloninger, C. R., Bohman, M., & Sigvardsson, S. (1981). Inheritance of alcohol abuse: Cross-fostering analysis of adopted men. *Archives of General Psychiatry, 38,* 861–868. (3, 14)

Cocozza, J., Melick, M., & Steadman, H. (1978). Trends in violent crime among ex-mental patients. *Criminology, 16,* 317–334. (15)

Cohen, C. E. (1981). Person categories and social perception: Testing some boundaries of the processing effects of prior knowledge. *Journal of Personality and Social Psychology, 40,* 441–452. (16)

Cohen, N. J., & Squire, L. R. (1980). Preserved learning and retention of pattern-analyzing skill in amnesia: Dissociation of knowing how and knowing that. *Science, 210,* 207–211. (8)

Cohen, S. L., & Cohen, R. (1985). The role of activity in spatial cognition. In R. Cohen (Ed.), *The development of spatial cognition* (pp. 199–223). Hillsdale, NJ: Lawrence Erlbaum. (9)

Coile, D. C., & Miller, N. (1984). How radical animal activists try to mislead humane people. *American Psychologist, 39,* 700–701. (2)

Cole, J. O., Goldberg, S. C., & Davis, J. M. (1966). Drugs in the treatment of psychosis. In P. Solomon (Ed.), *Psychiatric drugs* (pp. 153–180). New York: Grune & Stratton. (15)

Cole, N. S. (1981). Bias in testing. *American Psychologist, 36,* 1067–1077. (10)

Cole, R. A., & Rudnicky, A. I. (1983). What's new in speech perception? The research and ideas of William Chandler Bagley, 1874–1946. *Psychological Review, 90,* 94–101. (5)

Collins, A. M., & Loftus, E. F. (1975). A spreading-activation theory of semantic processing. *Psychological Review, 82,* 407–428. (9)

Collins, A. M., & Quillian, M. R. (1969). Retrieval time from semantic memory. *Journal of Verbal Learning and Verbal Behavior, 8,* 240–247. (9)

Collins, A. M., & Quillian, M. R. (1970). Does category size affect categorization time? *Journal of Verbal Learning and Verbal Behavior, 9,* 432–438. (9)

Collins, R. L., & Marlatt, G. A. (1981). Social modeling as a determinant of drinking behavior: Implications for prevention and treatment. *Addictive Behaviors, 6,* 233–239. (7)

Colwill, R. M., & Rescorla, R. A. (1985). Post-conditioning devaluation of a reinforcer affects instrumental responding. *Journal of Experimental Psychology: Animal Behavior Processes, 11,* 120–132. (7)

Cook, J. O. (1953). A gradient theory of multiple-choice learning. *Psychological Review, 60,* 15–22. (7)

Cook, T. D., Kendzierski, D. A., & Thomas, S. V. (1983). The implicit assumptions of television research: An analysis of the 1982 NIMH report on *Television and Behavior. Public Opinion Quarterly, 47,* 161–201. (2)

Coombs, R. H., & Fawzy, F. I. (1982). The effect of marital status on stress in medical school. *American Journal of Psychiatry, 139,* 1490–1493. (12)

Corkin, S. (1984). Lasting consequences of bilateral medial temporal lobectomy: Clinical course and experimental findings in H. M. *Seminars in Neurology, 4,* 249–259. (8)

Costello, E. J. (1982). Locus of control and depression in students and psychiatric outpatients. *Journal of Clinical Psychology, 38,* 340–343. (14)

Cowan, N. (1988). Evolving conceptions of memory storage, selective attention, and their mutual constraints within the human information-processing system. *Psychological Bulletin, 104,* 163–191. (8)

Cowan, P. A. (1978). *Piaget with feeling.* New York: Holt, Rinehart, Winston. (6)

Coyle, J. T., Price, D. L., & DeLong, M. R. (1983). Alzheimer's disease: A disorder of cortical cholinergic innervation. *Science, 219,* 1184–1190. (8)

Craik, F. I. M., & Lockhart, R. S. (1972). Levels of processing: A framework for memory research. *Journal of Verbal Learning and Verbal Behavior, 11,* 671–684. (8)

Craik, F. I. M., & Watkins, M. J. (1973). The role of rehearsal in short-term memory. *Journal of Verbal Learning and Verbal Behavior, 12,* 599–607. (8)

Cramer, J. (1989, Sept. 11). Where did the gung-ho go? *Time,* pp. 52–56. (7)

Crammer, J. L. (1959). Water and sodium in two psychotics. *Lancet, 1*(7083), 1122–1126. (14)

Creak, M. (1961). Schizophrenic syndrome in childhood. *British Medical Journal, 2,* 889–890. (14)

Creed, T. L. (1987). Subliminal deception: Pseudoscience on the college lecture circuit. *Skeptical Inquirer, 11,* 358–366. (5)

Crews, D. J., & Landers, D. M. (1987). A meta-analytic review of aerobic fitness and reactivity to psychosocial stressors. *Medicine & Science in Sports & Exercise, 19,* S114-S120. (12)

Cross, C. K., & Hirschfeld, R. M. A. (1986). Psychosocial factors and suicidal behavior. *Annals of the New York Academy of Sciences, 487,* 77–89. (14)

Crovitz, H. F., & Schiffman, H. (1974). Frequency of episodic memories as a function of their age. *Bulletin of the Psychonomic Society, 4,* 517–518. (8)

Crow, T. J. (1985). The two-syndrome concept: Origins and current status. *Schizophrenia Bulletin, 11,* 471–486. (14)

Croyle, R. T., & Cooper, J. (1983). Dissonance arousal: Physiological evidence. *Journal of Personality and Social Psychology, 45,* 782–791. (16)

Cummings, N. A. (1979). Turning bread into stones: Our modern antimiracle. *American Psychologist, 34,* 1119–1129. (11, 14)

Curry, S., Marlatt, A., & Gordon, J. R. (1987). Abstinence violation effect: Validation of an attributional construct with smoking cessation. *Journal of Consulting and Clinical Psychology, 55,* 145–149. (7)

Czeisler, C. A., Moore-Ede, M. C., & Coleman, R. M. (1982). Rotating shift work schedules that disrupt sleep are improved by applying circadian principles. *Science, 217,* 460–463. (4)

Dackis, C. A., Pottash, A. L. C., Annitto, W., & Gold, M. S. (1982). Persistence of urinary marijuana levels after supervised abstinence. *American Journal of Psychiatry, 139,* 1196–1198. (4)

Dallenbach, K. M. (1951). A puzzle picture with a new principle of concealment. *American Journal of Psychology, 54,* 431–433. (5)

Daly, M., Wilson, M., & Weghorst, S. J. (1982). Male sexual jealousy. *Ethology & Sociobiology, 3,* 11–27. (11, 12)

Damaser, E. C., Shor, R. E., & Orne, M. E. (1963). Physiological effects during hypnotically requested emotions. *Psychosomatic Medicine, 25,* 334–343. (4)

Damasio, A. (1979). The frontal lobes. In K. M. Heilman & E. Valenstein (Eds.), *Clinical neuropsychology* (pp. 360–412). New York: Oxford University Press. (3)

Dance, K. A., & Neufeld, R. W. J. (1988). Aptitude-treatment interaction research in the clinical setting: A review of attempts to dispel the "patient uniformity" myth. *Psychological Bulletin, 104,* 192–213. (15)

Darwin, C. (1871). *The descent of man.* New York: D. Appleton. (7)

Darwin, C. (1872/1965). *The expression of emotions in man and animals.* Chicago: University of Chicago Press. (Original work published 1872) (12)

Davenport, D., & Foley, J. M. (1979). Fringe benefits of cataract surgery. *Science, 204,* 454–457. (5)

Davenport, W. H. (1977). Sex in cross-cultural perspective. In F. A. Beach (Ed.), *Human sexuality in four perspectives* (pp. 62–86). Baltimore: Johns Hopkins University Press. (11)

Davenport, Y. B., & Adland, M. L. (1982). Postpartum psychoses in female and male bipolar manic-depressive patients. *American Journal of Orthopsychiatry, 52,* 288–297. (14)

Davidson, R. J. (1978). Specificity and patterning in biobehavioral systems: Implications for behavior change. *American Psychologist, 33,* 430–436. (12)

Davidson, R. J. (1984). Affect, cognition, and hemispheric specialization. In C. E. Izard, J. Kagan, & R. B. Zajonc (Eds.), *Emotions, cognition, & behavior* (pp. 320–365). Cambridge, England: Cambridge University Press. (12)

Davis, K. E., & Jones, E. E. (1960). Changes in interpersonal perception as a means of reducing cognitive dissonance. *Journal of Abnormal and Social Psychology, 61,* 402–410. (16)

Dawes, R. M., & Smith, T. L. (1985). Attitude and opinion measurement. In G. Lindzey & E. Aronson (Eds.), *Handbook of social psychology* (Vol. 1, pp. 509–566). New York: Random House. (1)

Day, R. H. (1972). Visual spatial illusions: A general explanation. *Science, 175,* 1335–1340. (5)

Dean, R. A., & Wanous, J. P. (1984). Effects of realistic job previews on hiring bank tellers. *Journal of Applied Psychology, 69,* 61–68. (16)

Deaux, K., & Major, B. (1987). Putting gender into context: An interactive model of gender-related behavior. *Psychological Review, 94,* 369–389. (6)

DeCasper, A. J., & Fifer, W. P. (1980). Of human bonding: Newborns prefer their mothers' voices. *Science, 208,* 1174–1177. (6)

Deci, E. L. (1971). Effects of externally mediated rewards on intrinsic motivation. *Journal of Personality and Social Psychology, 18,* 105–115. (11)

deGroot, A. D. (1966). Perception and memory versus thought: Some old ideas and recent findings. In B. Kleinmuntz (Ed.), *Problem solving* (pp. 19–50). New York: Wiley. (9)

DeKoninck, J., Gagnon, P., & Lallier, S. (1983). Sleep positions in the young adult and their relationship with the subjective quality of sleep. *Sleep, 6,* 52–59. (4)

DeLeon, P. H., Vanden Bos, G. R., & Cummings, N. A. (1983). Psychotherapy—Is it safe, effective, and appropriate? *American Psychologist, 38,* 907–911. (15)

Delgado, J. M. R. (1969). *Physical control of the mind.* New York: Harper & Row. (1)

DeLuise, M., Blackburn, G. L., & Flier, J. S. (1980). Reduced activity of the red-cell sodium-potassium pump in human obesity. *New England Journal of Medicine, 303,* 1017–1022. (11)

Dement, W. (1960). The effect of dream deprivation. *Science, 131,* 1705–1707. (4)

Dement, W. C. (1972). *Some must watch while some must sleep.* Stanford, CA: Stanford Alumni Association. (4)

Dement, W., & Kleitman, N. (1957a). Cyclic variations in EEG during sleep and their relation to eye movements, body motility, and dreaming. *Electroencephalography and Clinical Neurophysiology, 9,* 673–690. (4)

Dement, W., & Kleitman, N. (1957b). The relation of eye movements during sleep to dream activity: An objective method for the study of dreaming. *Journal of Experimental Psychology, 53,* 339–346. (4)

Dement, W., & Wolpert, E. A. (1958). The relation of eye movements, body motility, and external stimuli to dream content. *Journal of Experimental Psychology, 55,* 543–553. (4)

DeMyer, M. K. (1979). *Parents and children in autism.* Washington, DC: V. H. Winston. (14)

Dermer, M., & Thiel, D. L. (1975). When beauty may fail. *Journal of Personality and Social Psychology, 31,* 1168–1176. (16)

Derogatis, L. (1986). Psychology in cancer medicine: A perspective and overview. *Journal of Consulting and Clinical Psychology, 54,* 632–638. (12)

Desiderato, O., MacKinnon, J. R., & Hissom, H. (1974). Development of gastric ulcers in rats following stress termination. *Journal of Comparative and Physiological Psychology, 87,* 208–214. (12)

Desimone, R., Albright, T. D., Gross, C. G., & Bruce, C. (1984). Stimulus-selective properties of inferior temporal neurons in the macaque. *Journal of Neuroscience, 4,* 2051–2062. (5)

Detterman, D. K. (1979). Detterman's laws of individual differences research. In R. J. Sternberg & D. K. Detterman (Eds.), *Human intelligence* (pp. 165–175). Norwood, NJ: Ablex. (10)

Deutsch, A. (1948). *The shame of the states.* New York: Harcourt and Brace. (15)

Deutsch, J. A. (1983). Dietary control and the stomach. *Progress in Neurobiology, 20,* 313–332. (11)

Deutsch, J. A., Young, N. G., & Kalogeris, T. J. (1978). The stomach signals satiety. *Science, 201,* 165–167. (11)

Deutsch, M., & Gerard, H. B. (1955). A study of normative and informational social influences upon individual judgment. *Journal of Abnormal and Social Psychology, 51,* 629–636. (16)

DeValois, R. L. (1965). Behavioral and electrophysiological studies of primate vision. In W. D. Neff (Ed.), *Contributions to sensory physiology* (Vol. 1, pp. 137–178). New York: Academic. (5)

deWolff, C. J. (1985). Stress and strain in the work environment: Does it lead to illness? In W. D. Gentry, H. Benson, & C. J. deWolff (Eds.), *Behavioral medicine: Work, stress, and health* (pp. 33–43). Dordrecht, Netherlands: Martinus Nijhoff. (12)

Dick, M., Ullman, S., & Sagi, D. (1987). Parallel and serial processes in motion detection. *Science, 237,* 400–402. (5)

Diener, E. (1984). Subjective well-being. *Psychological Bulletin, 95,* 542–575. (12)

Dion, K. E., Berscheid, E., & Walster, E. (1972). What is beautiful is good. *Journal of Personality and Social Psychology, 24,* 285–290. (16)

Dipboye, R. L. (1982). Self-fulfilling prophecies in the selection-recruitment interview. *Academy of Management Review, 7,* 579–586. (16)

Dische, S., Yule, W., Corbett, J., & Hand, D. (1983). Childhood nocturnal enuresis: Factors associated with outcome of treatment with an enuresis alarm. *Developmental Medicine and Child Neurology, 25,* 67–80. (15)

Dixon, N. F. (1981). *Preconscious processing.* New York: Wiley. (5)

Dobrzecka, C., Szwejkowska, G., & Konorski, J. (1966). Qualitative versus directional cues in two forms of differentiation. *Science, 153,* 87–89. (7)

Döhl, J. (1970). Zielorientiertes Verhalten beim Schimpansen [Goal-oriented behavior in the chimpanzee]. *Naturwissenschaft und Medizin, 7,* 43–57. (9)

Dole, V. P. (1978). A clinician's view of addiction. In J. Fishman (Ed.), *The bases of addiction* (pp. 37–46). Berlin: Dahlem Konferenzen. (14)

Dole, V. P. (1980). Addictive behavior. *Scientific American, 243*(6), 138–154. (14)

Dollard, J., Miller, N. E., Doob, L. W., Mowrer, O. H., & Sears, R. R. (1939). *Frustration and aggression.* New Haven, CT: Yale University Press. (12)

Dostoyevsky, F. (1862/1986). *The house of the dead.* London: Penguin. (Original work published 1862) (12)

Dostoyevsky, F. (1868/1969). *The idiot.* New York: New American Library. (Original work published 1868) (15)

Druckman, D., & Swets, J. A. (1988). *Enhancing human performance.* Washington: National Academy Press. (2)

Duda, R. O., & Shortliffe, E. H. (1983). Expert system research. *Science, 220,* 261–268. (9)

Duke, M., & Nowicki, S., Jr. (1979). *Abnormal psychology: Perspectives on being different.* Monterey, CA: Brooks/Cole. (14)

Duncan, B. L. (1976). Differential social perception and attribution of intergroup violence: Testing the lower limits of stereotyping of blacks. *Journal of Personality and Social Psychology, 34,* 590–598. (16)

Dush, D. M., Hirt, M. L., & Schroeder, H. (1983). Self-statement modification with adults: A meta-analysis. *Psychological Bulletin, 94,* 408–422. (5)

Dutton, D. G., & Aron, A. P. (1974). Some evidence for heightened sexual attraction under conditions of high anxiety. *Journal of Personality and Social Psychology, 30,* 510–517. (16)

Duvoisin, R. C., Eldridge, R., Williams, A., Nutt, J., & Calne, D. (1981). Twin study of Parkinson disease. *Neurology, 31,* 77–80. (3)

Dworkin, B. R., & Miller, N. E. (1986). Failure to replicate visceral learning in the acute curarized rat preparation. *Behavioral Neuroscience, 100,* 299–314. (7)

Dwyman, J., & Bowers, K. (1983). The use of hypnosis to enhance recall. *Science, 222,* 184–185. (4)

Eagly, A. H., & Crowley, M. (1986). Gender and helping behavior: A meta-analytic review of the social psychological literature. *Psychological Bulletin, 100,* 283–308. (6)

Eagly, A. H., & Steffen, V. J. (1986). Gender and aggressive behavior: A meta-analytic review of the social psychological literature. *Psychological Bulletin, 100,* 309–330. (6)

Eagly, A. H., & Warren, R. (1976). Intelligence, comprehension, and opinion change. *Journal of Personality, 44,* 226–242. (16)

Earls, C. M. (1988). Aberrant sexual arousal in sexual offenders. *Annals of the New York Academy of Sciences, 528,* 41–48. (11)

Eaton, W. W., Holzer, C. E., von Korff, M., Anthony, J. C., Helzer, J. E., George, L., Burnam, A., Boyd, J. H., Kessler, L. G., & Locke, B. Z. (1984). The design of the epidemiologic catchment area surveys. *Archives of General Psychiatry, 41,* 942–948. (14)

Ebbinghaus, H. (1913). *Memory.* New York: Teachers College. (Original work published 1885) (8)

Edelman, B. (1981). Binge eating in normal weight and overweight individuals. *Psychological Reports, 49,* 739–746. (10)

Edney, J. H. (1979). The nuts game: A concise commons dilemma analog. *Environmental Psychology and Nonverbal Behavior, 3,* 252–254. (16)

Eibl-Eibesfeldt, I. (1973). *Der vorprogrammierte Mensch.* Vienna: Verlag Fritz Molden. (12)

Eibl-Eibesfeldt, I. (1974). *Love and hate.* New York: Schocken. (12)

Eikelboom, R., & Stewart, J. (1982). Conditioning of drug-induced physiological responses. *Psychological Review, 89,* 507–528. (14)

Eimas, P. D., Siqueland, E. R., Jusczyk, P., & Vigorito, J. (1971). Speech perception in infants. *Science, 171,* 303–306. (6)

Einstein, G. O., & Hunt, R. R. (1980). Levels of processing and organization: Additive effects of individual item and relational processing. *Journal of Experimental Psychology: Human Learning and Memory, 6,* 588–598. (8)

Ekman, P. (1972). Universals and cultural differences in facial expressions of emotion. In J. K. Cole (Ed.), *Nebraska symposium on motivation 1971* (pp. 207–283). Lincoln, NE: University of Nebraska Press. (12)

Ekman, P., Friesen, W. V., & Ancoli, S. (1980). Facial signs of emotional experience. *Journal of Personality and Social Psychology, 39,* 1125–1134. (12)

Ekman, P., Friesen, W. V., O'Sullivan, M., Chan, A., Diacoyanni-Tarlatzis, I., Heider, K., Krause, R., LeCompte, W. A., Pitcairn, T., Ricci-Bitti, P. E., Scherer, K., Tomita, M., & Tzavaras, A. (1987). Universals and cultural differences in the judgments of facial expressions of emotion. *Journal of Personality and Social Psychology, 53,* 712–717. (12)

Ekman, P., Levenson, R. W., & Friesen, W. V. (1983). Autonomic nervous system activity distinguishes among emotions. *Science, 221,* 1208–1210. (12)

Ekman, P., Sorenson, E. R., & Friesen, W. V. (1969). Pan-cultural elements in facial displays of emotion. *Science, 164,* 86–88. (12)

Ekstrand, L. H. (1979). Replacing the critical period and optimum age theories of second language acquisition with a theory of ontogenetic development beyond puberty. *Educational & Psychological Interactions, 69,* 1–83. (6)

Elkin, R. A., & Leippe, M. R. (1986). Physiological arousal, dissonance, and attitude change: Evidence for a dissonance-arousal link and a "don't remind me" effect. *Journal of Personality and Social Psychology, 51,* 55–65. (16)

Elkind, D. (1984). *All grown up and no place to go.* Reading, MA: Addison-Wesley. (6)

Ellis, A. (1987). The impossibility of achieving consistently good mental health. *American Psychologist, 42,* 364–375. (15)

Ellis, A., & Harper, R. A. (1961). *A guide to rational living.* Englewood Cliffs, NJ: Prentice-Hall. (15)

Ellis, L., & Ames, M. A. (1987). Neurohormonal functioning and sexual orientation: A theory of homosexuality-heterosexuality. *Psychological Bulletin, 101,* 233–258. (11)

Ellis, L., Ames, M. A., Peckham, W., & Burke, D. (1988). Sexual orientation of human offspring may be altered by severe maternal stress during pregnancy. *Journal of Sex Research, 25,* 152–157. (11)

Ellman, S. J., Spielman, A. J., Luck, D., Steiner, S. S., & Halperin, R. (1978). REM deprivation: A review. In A. M. Arkin, J. S. Antrobus, & S. J. Ellman (Eds.), *The mind in sleep* (pp. 419–457). Hillsdale, NJ: Lawrence Erlbaum. (4)

Emery, R. W. (1982). Interparental conflict and the children of discord and divorce. *Psychological Bulletin, 92,* 310–330. (6)

Emrick, C. D. (1987). Alcoholics Anonymous: Affiliation processes and effectiveness as treatment. *Alcoholism: Clinical & Experimental Research, 11,* 416–423. (14)

Epstein, L. H., & Wing, R. R. (1987). Behavioral treatment of childhood obesity. *Psychological Bulletin, 101,* 331–342. (11)

Epstein, L. H., Wing, R. R., Koeske, R., & Valoski, A. (1984). Effects of diet plus exercise on weight change in parents and children. *Journal of Consulting and Clinical Psychology, 52,* 429–437. (11)

Epstein, S. (1979). The stability of behavior: I. On predicting most of the people much of the time. *Journal of Personality and Social Psychology, 37,* 1097–1126. (13)

Epstein, S., & O'Brien, E. J. (1985). The person-situation debate in historical and current perspective. *Psychological Bulletin, 98,* 513–537. (13)

Epstein, Y. M. (1982). Crowding stress and human behavior. In G. W. Evans (Ed.), *Environmental stress* (pp. 133–148). Cambridge, England: Cambridge University Press. (12)

Ericsson, K. A., Chase, W. G., & Falcon, S. (1980). Acquisition of a memory skill. *Science, 208,* 1181–1182. (8)

Erikson, E. H. (1963). *Childhood and society* (2nd ed.). New York: Norton. (6)

Ernhart, C. B., Sokol, R. J., Martier, S., Moron, P., Nadler, D., Ager, J. W., & Wolf, A. (1987). Alcohol teratogenicity in the human: A detailed assessment of specificity, critical period, and threshold. *American Journal of Obstetrics and Gynecology, 156,* 33–39. (12)

Ernst, C., & Angst, J. (1983). *Birth order: Its influence on personality.* New York: Springer-Verlag. (6)

Eron, L. D. (1987). The development of aggressive behavior from the perspective of a developing behaviorism. *American Psychologist, 42,* 435–442. (12)

Eysenck, H. J. (1952a). *The scientific study of personality.* New York: Macmillan. (13)

Eysenck, H. J. (1952b). The effects of psychotherapy: An evaluation. *Journal of Consulting Psychology, 16,* 319–324. (15)

Fagerström, K.-O. (1981). A comparison of psychological and pharmacological treatment in smoking cessation. *Uppsala Psychological Reports,* No. 302. (4)

Falk, J. R., Halmi, K. A., & Tryon, W. W. (1985). Activity measures in anorexia nervosa. *Archives of General Psychiatry, 42,* 811–814. (11)

Fallon, A. E., & Rozin, P. (1985). Sex differences in perceptions of desirable body shape. *Journal of Abnormal Psychology, 94,* 102–105. (11)

Fantz, R. L. (1963). Pattern vision in newborn infants. *Science, 140,* 296–297. (6)

Farah, M. J. (1988). Is visual imagery really visual? Overlooked evidence from neuropsychology. *Psychological Review, 95,* 307–317. (9)

Farber, S. L. (1981). *Identical twins reared apart: A reanalysis.* New York: Basic. (10)

Farell, B. (1985). "Same"-"different" judgments: A review of current controversies in perceptual comparisons. *Psychological Bulletin, 98,* 419–456. (9)

Farmer, A., Jackson, R., McGuffin, P., & Storey, P. (1987). Cerebral ventricular enlargement in chronic schizophrenia: Consistencies and contradictions. *British Journal of Psychiatry, 150,* 324–330. (14)

Farmer, A. E., McGuffin, P., & Gottesman, I. I. (1987). Twin concordance for DSM-III schizophrenia. *Archives of General Psychiatry, 44,* 634–641. (14)

Farmer, H. (1983). Career and homemaking plans for high school youth. *Journal of Counseling Psychology, 30,* 40–45. (11)

Farmer, H. S. (1987). Female motivation and achievement: Implications for interventions. *Advances in Motivation and Achievement, 5,* 51–97. (11)

Farmer, H., & Bohn, M. (1970). Home-career conflict reduction and the level of career interest in women. *Journal of Counseling Psychology, 17,* 228–232. (11)

Faust, D., & Ziskin, J. (1988). The expert witness in psychology and psychiatry. *Science, 241,* 31–35. (15)

Fausto-Sterling, A. (1985). *Myths of gender.* New York: Basic Books. (2)

Fawzy, F. I., Coombs, R. H., & Gerber, B. (1983). Generational continuity in the use of substances: The impact of parental substance use on adolescent substance use. *Addictive Behaviors, 8,* 109–114. (4)

Fay, R. E., Turner, C. F., Klassen, A. D., & Gagnon, J. H. (1989). Prevalence and patterns of same-gender sexual contact among men. *Science, 243,* 338–348. (11)

Fazio, R. H. (1987). Self-perception theory: A current perspective. In M. Zanna, J. M. Olson, & C. P. Herman (Eds.), *Social influence: The Ontario symposium* (Vol. 5, pp. 129–150). Hillsdale, NJ: Lawrence Erlbaum. (16)

Fazio, R. H., & Zanna, M. P. (1981). Direct experience and attitude-behavior consistency. In L. Berkowitz (Ed.), *Advances in experimental social psychology* (Vol. 14, pp. 161–202). New York: Academic Press. (16)

Fazio, R. H., Zanna, M. P., & Cooper, J. (1977). Dissonance and self-perception: An integrative view of each theory's proper domain of application. *Journal of Experimental Social Psychology, 13,* 464–479. (16)

Feeney, D. M. (1987). Human rights and animal welfare. *American Psychologist, 42,* 593–599. (2)

Fehrenbach, P. A., & Thelen, M. H. (1982). Behavioral approaches to the treatment of aggressive disorders. *Behavior Modification, 6,* 465–497. (12)

Feingold, A. (1988). Cognitive gender differences are disappearing. *American Psychologist, 43,* 95–103. (10)

Feist, J., & Brannon, L. (1988). *Health psychology.* Belmont, CA: Wadsworth. (12)

Fernald, D. (1984). *The Hans legacy: A story of science.* Hillsdale, NJ: Lawrence Erlbaum. (2)

Festinger, L. (1957). *A theory of cognitive dissonance.* Stanford, CA: Stanford University Press. (16)

Festinger, L., & Carlsmith, J. M. (1959). Cognitive consequences of forced compliance. *Journal of Abnormal and Social Psychology, 58,* 203–210. (16)

Festinger, L., Schachter, S., & Back, K. (1950). *Social pressures in informal groups: A study of human factors in housing.* New York: Harper. (16)

Fieve, R. R. (1975). *Moodswing.* New York: William Morrow. (14)

Finger, S., & Stein, D. G. (1982). *Brain damage and recovery.* New York: Academic Press. (3)

Fink, M. (1985). Convulsive therapy: Fifty years of progress. *Convulsive Therapy, 1,* 204–216. (15)

Fishbein, M., & Ajzen, I. (1974). Attitudes towards objects as predictors of single and multiple behavioral criteria. *Psychological Review, 81,* 59–74. (16)

Fishbein, M., & Ajzen, I. (1975). *Belief, attitude, intention and behavior: An introduction to theory and research.* Reading, MA: Addison–Wesley. (16)

Fisher, S., & Greenberg, R. P. (1977). *The scientific credibility of Freud's theories and therapy.* New York: Basic Books. (13)

Flaherty, J. A., Gaviria, F. M., Black, E. M., Altman, E., & Mitchell, T. (1983). The role of social support in the functioning of patients with unipolar depression. *American Journal of Psychiatry, 140,* 473–476. (14)

Flavell, J. (1986). The development of children's knowledge about the appearance-reality distinction. *American Psychologist, 41,* 418–425. (6)

Fletcher, R., & Voke, J. (1985). *Defective colour vision.* Bristol, England: Adam Hilger. (5)

Flynn, J. R. (1984). The mean IQ of Americans: Massive gains 1932 to 1978. *Psychological Bulletin, 95,* 29–51. (10)

Flynn, J. R. (1987). Massive IQ gains in 14 nations: What IQ tests really measure. *Psychological Bulletin, 101,* 171–191. (10)

Foley, V. D. (1984). Family therapy. In R. J. Corini (Ed.), *Current psychotherapies* (3rd ed.) (pp. 447–490). Itasca, IL: F. E. Peacock Publishers. (15)

Folstein, S., & Rutter, M. (1977). Infantile autism: A genetic study of 21 twin pairs. *Journal of Child Psychology and Psychiatry, 18,* 297–321. (14)

Fontana, A. F., Marcus, J. L., Noel, B., & Rakusin, J. M. (1972). Prehospitalization coping styles of psychiatric patients: The goal-directedness of life events. *Journal of Nervous and Mental Disease, 155,* 311–321. (15)

Forer, B. R. (1949). The fallacy of personal validation: A classroom demonstration of gullibility. *Journal of Abnormal and Social Psychology, 44,* 118–123. (13)

Forsberg, L. K., & Goldman, M. S. (1987). Experience-dependent recovery of cognitive deficits in alcoholics: Extended transfer of training. *Journal of Abnormal Psychology, 96,* 345–353. (4)

Försterling, F. (1985). Attributional retraining: A review. *Psychological Bulletin, 98,* 495–512. (12)

Foster, W. Z. (1968). *History of the Communist Party of the United States.* New York: Greenwood Press. (16)

Fowler, M. J., Sullivan, M. J., & Ekstrand, B. R. (1973). Sleep and memory. *Science, 179,* 302–304. (4)

Fox, B. H. (1983). Current theory of psychogenic effects on cancer incidence and prognosis. *Journal of Psychosocial Oncology, 1,* 17–31. (12)

Frankenhaeuser, M. (1980). Psychoneuroendocrine approaches to the study of stressful person-environment transactions. In H. Selye (Ed.), *Selye's guide to stress research* (pp. 46–70). New York: Van Nostrand Reinhold. (12)

Frankmann, S. P., & Green, B. G. (1988). Differential effects of cooling on the intensity of taste. *Annals of the New York Academy of Sciences, 510,* 300–303. (5)

Freedman, J. L. (1984). Effect of television violence on aggressiveness. *Psychological Bulletin, 96,* 227–246. (2)

Freedman, J. L. (1986). Television violence and aggression: A rejoinder. *Psychological Bulletin, 100,* 372–378. (2)

Freedman, J. L., & Fraser, S. C. (1966). Compliance without pressure: The foot in the door technique. *Journal of Personality and Social Psychology, 4,* 195–202. (16)

Freedman, M., & Oscar-Berman, M. (1986). Bilateral frontal lobe disease and selective delayed response deficits in humans. *Behavioral Neuroscience, 100,* 337–342. (3)

Freud, S. (1900/1955). *The interpretation of dreams* (J. Strachey, Trans.). New York: Basic. (Original work published 1900) (15)

Freud, S. (1905/1925). *Three contributions to the theory of sex* (A. A. Brill, Trans.). New York: Nervous and Mental Disease Pub. Co. (Original work published 1905) (13)

Freud, S. (1908/1963). "Civilized" sexual morality and modern nervousness. In P. Rieff (Ed.), *Freud: Sexuality and the psychology of love* (pp. 20–40). New York: Collier Books. (Original work published 1908) (11)

Freud, S. (1927/1953). *The future of an illusion* (J. Strachey, Trans.). New York: Liveright. (Original work published 1927) (13)

Freud, S., & Breuer, J. (1893). Neurologisches Zentralblatt, Nos. 1 and 2 (Collected papers, vol. 1). (15)

Frick, R. W. (1988). The role of memory in attenuations of the suffix effect. *Memory & Cognition, 16,* 15–22. (8)

Frick, W. B. (1983). The symbolic growth experience. *Journal of Humanistic Psychology, 23,* 108–125. (13)

Friedman, H. S., & Booth-Kewley, S. (1988). Validity of the Type A construct: A reprise. *Psychological Bulletin, 104,* 381–384. (12)

Friedman, M., & Rosenman, R. H. (1974). *Type-A behavior and your heart.* New York: Knopf. (12)

Friedman, M. I., & Stricker, E. M. (1976). The physiological psychology of hunger: A physiological perspective. *Psychological Review, 83,* 409–431. (11)

Friedman, R., & Iwai, J. (1976). Genetic predisposition and stress-induced hypertension. *Science, 193,* 161–162. (11)

Friedrich-Cofer, L., & Huston, A. C. (1986). Television violence and aggression: The debate continues. *Psychological Bulletin, 100,* 364–371. (2)

Frieze, I. H., Parsons, J. E., Johnson, P. B., Ruble, D. N., & Zellman, G. L. (1978). *Women and sex roles.* New York: Norton. (6)

Frijda, N. H. (1988). The laws of emotion. *American Psychologist, 45,* 349–358. (12)

Frishhoff, B., & Beyth-Marom, R. (1983). Hypothesis evaluation from a Bayesian perspective. *Psychological Review, 90,* 239–260. (9)

Fuller, R. K., & Roth, H. P. (1979). Disulfiram for the treatment of alcoholism: An evaluation in 128 men. *Annals of Internal Medicine, 90,* 901–904. (14)

Gabrieli, J. D. E., Cohen, N. J., & Corkin, S. (1988). The impaired learning of semantic knowledge following bilateral medial temporal-lobe resection. *Brain and Cognition, 7,* 157–177. (8)

Gabrielli, W. F., Jr., & Plomin, R. (1985). Drinking behavior in the Colorado adoptee and twin sample. *Journal of Studies on Alcohol, 46,* 24–31. (14)

Galanter, E. (1962). Contemporary psychophysics. In R. Brown, E. Galanter, E. H. Hess, & G. Mander, *New directions in psychology* (pp. 87–156). New York: Holt, Rinehart, & Winston. (5)

Gallup, G. G., Jr., & Suarez, S. D. (1980). On the use of animals in psychological research. *Psychological Record, 30,* 211–218. (2)

Gallup, G. G., Jr., & Suarez, S. D. (1985). Alternatives to the use of animals in psychological research. *American Psychologist, 40,* 1104–1111. (2)

Gallup, G. H. (1976–77). Human needs and satisfactions: A global survey. *Public Opinion Quarterly, 40,* 459–467. (12)

Galper, R. E., & Hochberg, J. (1971). Recognition memory for photographs of faces. *American Journal of Psychology, 84,* 351–354. (5)

Galton, F. (1869/1978). *Hereditary genius.* New York: St. Martin's. (10)

Gangestad, S., & Snyder, M. (1985). On the nature of self-monitoring. *Review of Personality and Social Psychology, 6,* 65–85. (13)

Gantt, W. H. (1973). Reminiscences of Pavlov. *Journal of the Experimental Analysis of Behavior, 20,* 131–136. (7)

Garcia, J., Ervin, F. R., & Koelling, R. A. (1966). Learning with prolonged delay of reinforcement. *Psychonomic Science, 5,* 121–122. (7)

Garcia, J., & Koelling, R. A. (1966). *Psychonomic Science, 4,* 123–124. (7)

Gardner, H. (1985). *Frames of mind.* New York: Basic Books. (10)

Gardner, R. A., & Gardner, B. T. (1969). Teaching sign language to a chimpanzee. *Science, 165,* 664–672. (6)

Gardner, M. (1978). Mathematical games. *Scientific American, 239*(5), 22–32. (9)

Garfield, B. D., Froese, A., & Hood, J. (1982). Suicide attempts in children and adolescents. *American Journal of Psychiatry, 139,* 1257–1261. (14)

Garfield, S. L. (1980). *Psychotherapy: An eclectic approach.* New York: Wiley. (15)

Garfield, S. L. (1981). Psychotherapy: A 40-year appraisal. *American psychologist, 36,* 174–183. (15)

Gash, D. M., Collier, T. J., & Sladek, J. R., Jr. (1985). Neural transplantation: A review of recent developments and potential applications to the aged brain. *Neurobiology of Aging, 6,* 131–150. (3)

Gawin, F. H., & Kleber, H. D. (1986). Abstinence symptomatology and psychiatric diagnosis in cocaine abusers. *Archives of General Psychiatry, 43,* 107–113. (14)

Gazzaniga, M. S. (1970). *The bisected brain.* New York: Appleton-Century-Crofts. (3)

Gebhard, P. H., Gagnon, J. H., Pomeroy, W. B., & Christenson, C. V. (1965). *Sex offenders: An analysis of types.* New York: Harper & Row. (11)

Geer, S., Morris, T., & Pettingale, K. W. (1979). Psychological response to breast cancer: Effect on outcome. *Lancet, ii*(8146), 785–787. (12)

Gelb, S. A. (1986). Henry H. Goddard and the immigrants, 1910–1917: The studies and their social context. *Journal of the History of the Behavioral Sciences, 22,* 324–332. (10)

Gellhorn, E. (1970). The emotions and the ergotropic and trophotropic systems. *Psychologische Forschung, 34,* 48–94. (12)

Gelman, R. (1982). Accessing one-to-one correspondence: Still another paper about conservation. *British Journal of Psychology, 73,* 209–220. (6)

Gelman, R., & Baillargeon, R. (1983). A review of some Piagetian concepts. In P. H. Mussen (Ed.), *Handbook of child psychology* (4th ed.) (Vol. 3, pp. 167–230). New York: Wiley. (6)

Gerson, S. C., Plotkin, D. A., & Jarvik, L. F. (1988). Antidepressant drug studies, 1964 to 1986: Empirical evidence for aging patients. *Journal of Clinical Pharmacology, 8,* 311–322. (15)

Geschwind, N. (1979). Specializations of the human brain. In Scientific American (Ed.), *The brain: A Scientific American book.* San Francisco: Freeman. (3)

Gibson, H. B. (1982). The use of hypnosis in police investigations. *Bulletin of the British Psychological Society, 35,* 138–142. (4)

Gibson, J. J. (1968). What gives rise to the perception of movement? *Psychological Review, 75,* 335–346. (5)

Gick, M. L., & Holyoak, K. J. (1983). Schema induction and analogical transfer. *Cognitive Psychology, 15,* 1–38. (9)

Giebel, H. D. (1958). Visuelles Lernvermögen bei Einhufern [Visual learning capacity in hoofed animals]. *Zoologisches Jahrbücher Abteilung für Allgemeine Zoologie, 67,* 487–520. (7)

Gigerenzer, G., Hell, W., & Blank, H. (1988). Presentation and context: The use of base rates as a continuous variable. *Journal of Experimental Psychology: Human Perception and Performance, 14,* 513–525. (9)

Gilbert, D. G. (1979). Paradoxical tranquilizing and emotion-reducing effects of nicotine. *Psychological Bulletin, 86,* 643–661. (4)

Gillberg, C., Terenius, L., & Lönnerholm, G. (1985). Endorphin activity in childhood psychosis. *Archives of General Psychiatry, 42,* 780–783. (14)

Gilliam, T. C., Bucan, M., MacDonald, M. E., Zimmer, M., Haines, J., Cheng, S. V., Pohl, T. M., Meyers, R. H., Whaley, W. L., Allitto, B. A., Faryniarz, A., Wasmuth, J. J., Frischauf, A.-M., Conneally, P. M., Lehrach, H., & Gusella, J. F. (1987). A DNA segment encoding two genes very tightly linked to Huntington's disease. *Science, 238,* 950–952. (3)

Gilligan, C. (1977). In a different voice: Women's conceptions of self and morality. *Harvard Educational Review, 47,* 481–517. (6)

Gilligan, C. (1979). Woman's place in man's life cycle. *Harvard Educational Review, 49,* 431–446. (6)

Glass, D. C., Singer, J. E., & Pennebaker, J. W. (1977). Behavioral and physiological effects of uncontrollable environmental events. In D. Stokols (Ed.), *Perspectives on environment and behavior* (pp. 131–151). New York: Plenum. (12)

Glenberg, A. M., Sanocki, T., Epstein, W., & Morris, C. (1987). Enhancing calibration of comprehension. *Journal of Experimental Psychology: General, 116,* 119–136. (8)

Godden, D. R., & Baddeley, A. D. (1975). Context-dependent memory in two natural environments: On land and underwater. *British Journal of Psychology, 66,* 325–331. (8)

Goethals, G. P., & Zanna, M. P. (1979). The role of social comparison in choice shifts. *Journal of Personality and Social Psychology, 37,* 1469–1476. (16)

Gogel, W. C., & Mershon, D. H. (1977). Local autonomy in visual space. *Scandinavian Journal of Psychology, 18,* 237–250. (5)

Golani, I., Wolgin, D. L., & Teitelbaum, P. (1979). A proposed natural geometry of recovery from akinesia in the lateral hypothalamic rat. *Brain Research, 164,* 237–267. (3)

Goldgaber, D., Lerman, M. I., McBride, O. W., Saffiotti, U., & Gajdusek, D. C. (1987). Characterization and chromosomal localization of a cDNA encoding brain amyloid of Alzheimer's disease. *Science, 235,* 877–880. (3)

Goldin-Meadow, S. (1985). Language development under atypical learning conditions: Replication and implications of a study of deaf children of hearing parents. In K. E. Nelson (Ed.), *Children's language* (Vol. 5, pp. 197–245). Hillsdale, NJ: Lawrence Erlbaum. (6)

Goldstein, A. (1980). Thrills in response to music and other stimuli. *Physiological Psychology, 8,* 126–129. (12)

Goldstein, E. B. (1989). *Sensation and perception* (3rd ed.). Belmont, CA: Wadsworth. (5)

Goldstein, I. L. (1980). Training and organizational psychology. *Professional Psychology, 11,* 421–427. (16)

Goldstein, M. J. (1981). Family factors associated with schizophrenia and anorexia nervosa. *Journal of Youth and Adolescence, 10,* 385–405. (11)

Goldston, S. E. (1986). Primary prevention. *American Psychologist, 41,* 453–460. (15)

Goodman, P. S., & Friedman, A. (1971). An examination of Adams' theory of inequity. *Administration Science Quarterly, 16,* 271–288. (16)

Goodwin, D. W. (1978). Adoption studies of alcoholism. In J. Fishman (Ed.), *The bases of addiction* (pp. 81–88). Berlin: Dahlem Konferenzen. (3)

Gorman, J. M., Cohen, B. S., Liebowitz, M. R., Fyer, A. J., Ross, D., Davies, S. O., & Klein, D. R. (1986). Blood gas changes and hypophosphatemia in lactate-induced panic. *Archives of General Psychiatry, 43,* 1067–1071. (14)

Gottesman, I. I. (1978). Schizophrenia and genetics: Where are we? Are you sure? In L. C. Wynne, R. L. Cromwell, & S. Matthysse (Eds.), *The nature of schizophrenia: New approaches to research and treatment* (pp. 59–69). New York: Wiley. (14)

Gottfredson, L. S., & Crouse, J. (1986). Validity versus utility of mental tests: Example of the SAT. *Journal of Vocational Behavior, 29,* 363–378. (10)

Gottman, J. M. (1979). *Marital interaction: Experimental investigations.* New York: Academic Press. (16)

Gould, M. S., & Shaffer, D. (1986). The impact of suicide in television movies. *New England Journal of Medicine, 315,* 690–694. (15)

Graf, P., & Mandler, G. (1984). Activation makes words more accessible, but not necessarily more retrievable. *Journal of Verbal Learning and Verbal Behavior, 23,* 553–568. (8)

Graham, J. R. (1977). *The MMPI: A practical guide.* New York: Oxford Universityy Press. (13)

Grant, D. L. (1980). Issues in personnel selection. *Professional Psychology, 11,* 369–384. (16)

Greene, R. L. (1987). Effects of maintenance rehearsal on human memory. *Psychological Bulletin, 102,* 403–413. (8)

Greene, R. L. (1988). Stimulus suffix effects in recognition memory. *Memory & Cognition, 16,* 206–209. (8)

Greenough, W. T. (1975). Experiential modification of the developing brain. *American Scientist, 63,* 37–46. (3)

Greenwald, A. G. (1968). Cognitive learning, cognitive responses to persuasion, and attitude change. In A. G. Greenwald, T. C. Brock, & T. M. Ostrom (Eds.), *Psychological foundation of attitudes* (pp. 147–170). New York: Academic Press. (16)

Greenwald, A. G., Pratkanis, A. R., Leippe, M. R., & Baumgardner, M. H. (1986). Under what conditions does theory obstruct research progress? *Psychological Review, 93,* 216–229. (2)

Groth, A. N. (1979). *Men who rape: The psychology of the offender.* New York: Plenum. (11)

Grünbaum, A. (1986). Précis of *The Foundations of Psychoanalysis:* A philosophical critique. *Behavioral and Brain Sciences, 9,* 217–284. (13)

Guilford, J. P. (1973). Theories of intelligence. In B. B. Wolman (Ed.), *Handbook of general psychology* (pp. 630–643). Englewood Cliffs, NJ: Prentice-Hall. (10)

Gurman, A. S., Kniskern, D. P., & Pinsof, W. M. (1986). Research on the process and outcome of marital and family therapy. In S. L. Garfield & A. E. Bergin (Eds.), *Handbook of psychotherapy and behavior change* (pp. 565–624). New York: Wiley. (15)

Gusella, J. F., Wexler, N. S., Conneally, P. M., Naylor, S. L., Anderson, M. A., Tanzi, R. E., Watkins, P. C., Ottina, K., Wallace, M. R., Sakachi, A. Y., Young, A. B., Shoulson, I., Bonilla, E., & Martin, J. B. (1983). A polymorphic DNA marker genetically linked to Huntington's disease. *Nature, 306,* 234–238. (12)

Gustavson, A. R., Dawson, M. E., & Bonett, D. G. (1987). Androstenol, a putative human phero-mone, affects human *(Homo sapiens)* male choice performance. *Journal of Comparative Psychology, 101,* 210–212. (5)

Haber, R. N. (1979). Twenty years of haunting eidetic imagery: Where's the ghost? *Behavioral and Brain Sciences, 2,* 583–629. (8)

Hackman, J. R. (1980). Work redesign and motivation. *Professional Psychology, 11,* 445–455. (16)

Hackman, J. R., & Lawler, E. E., III. (1971). Employee reactions to job characteristics. *Journal of Applied Psychology, 55,* 259–286. (16)

Hackman, J. R., Oldham, G., Janson, R., & Purdy, K. (1975). A new strategy for job enrichment. *California Management Review, 17*(4), 57–71. (16)

Hahn, W. K. (1987). Cerebral lateralization of function: From infancy through childhood. *Psychological Bulletin, 101,* 376–392. (3)

Hakuta, K., & Diaz, R. M. (1985). The relationship between degree of bilingualism and cognitive ability: A critical discussion and some new longitudinal data. In K. E. Nelson (Ed.), *Children's language* (Vol. 5, pp. 319–344). Hillsdale, NJ: Lawrence Erlbaum. (6)

Haley, J. (1984). *Ordeal therapy.* San Francisco: Jossey-Bass. (15)

Hall, J. A. (1978). Gender effects in decoding nonverbal cues. *Psychological Bulletin, 85,* 845–857. (12)

Hall, R. C. W., Gardner, E. R., Perl, M., Stickney, S. K., & Pfefferbaum, B. (1978). Psychiatric and physiological reactions produced by over-the-counter medications. *Journal of Psychedelic Drugs, 10,* 243–249. (14)

Hamilton, D. L. (1979). A cognitive-attributional analysis of stereotyping. *Advances in Experimental Social Psychology, 12,* 53–84. (13)

Hamilton, D. L., & Gifford, R. K. (1976). Illusory correlation in interpersonal perception: A cognitive basis of stereotypic judgments. *Journal of Experimental Social Psychology, 12,* 392–407. (16)

Handleman, J. S. (1979). Generalization by autistic-type children of verbal responses across settings. *Journal of Applied Behavior Analysis, 12,* 273–282. (14)

Hannah, B. (1976). *Jung: His life and work.* New York: G. P. Putnam's Sons. (13)

Hansel, C. E. M. (1966). *ESP: A scientific evaluation.* New York: Charles Scribner's Sons. (2)

Hansen, G. D. (1979). Enuresis control through fading, escape, and avoidance training. *Journal of Applied Behavior Analysis, 12,* 303–307. (15)

Harada, S., Agarwal, D. P. Goedde, H. W., Tagaki, S., & Ishikawa, B. (1982). Possible protective role against alcoholism for aldehyde dehydrogenase isozyme deficiency in Japan. *Lancet, ii,* 827. (11)

Hardin, G. (1968). The tragedy of the commons. *Science, 162,* 1243–1248. (16)

Harding, C. M., Brooks, G. W., Ashikaga, T., Straus, J. S., & Breier, A. (1987). The Vermont longitudinal study of persons with severe mental illness, II: Long-term outcome of subjects who retrospectively met DSM-III criteria for schizophrenia. *American Journal of Psychiatry, 144,* 727–735. (15)

Harlow, H. F. (1958). The nature of love. *American Psychologist, 13,* 673–685. (6)

Harlow, H. F., & Harlow, M. K. (1965). The affectional systems. In A. M. Schrier, H. F. Harlow, & F. Stollnitz (Eds.), *Behavior of nonhuman primates* (Vol. 2, pp. 287–334). New York: Academic Press. (6)

Harlow, H. F., Harlow, M. K., & Meyer, D. R. (1950). Learning motivated by a manipulative drive. *Journal of Experimental Psychology, 40,* 228–234. (11)

Harlow, H. F., Harlow, M. K., & Suomi, S. J. (1971). From thought to therapy: Lessons from a primate laboratory. *American Scientist, 59,* 538–549. (6)

Harmon, L. D., & Julesz, B. (1973). Masking in visual recognition: Effects of two-dimensional filtered noise. *Science, 180,* 1194–1197. (5)

Harris, B. (1979). What ever happened to little Albert? *American Psychologist, 34,* 151–160. (14)

Harris, T. (1967). *I'm OK—You're OK.* New York: Avon. (13)

Hart, B. L. (Ed.). (1976). *Experimental psychobiology.* San Francisco: Freeman. (11)

Hartmann, E. (1983). Two case reports: Night terrors with sleepwalking—a potentially lethal disorder. *Journal of Nervous and Mental Disease, 171,* 503–505. (4)

Hashtroudi, S., & Parker, E. S. (1986). Acute alcohol amnesia: What is remembered and what is forgotten. *Research Advances in Alcohol and Drug Problems, 9,* 179–209. (4)

Hatfield, E., & Sprecher, S. (1986). *Mirror, mirror . . . The importance of looks in everyday life.* Albany, NY: State University of New York Press. (16)

Hathaway, S. R., & McKinley, J. C. (1940). A multiphasic personality schedule (Minnesota): I. Construction of the schedule. *Journal of Psychology, 10,* 249–254. (13)

Hay, D., & Oken, D. (1977). The psychological stresses of intensive care unit nursing. In A. Monat & R. S. Lazarus (Eds.), *Stress and coping* (pp. 118–140). New York: Columbia University Press. (12)

Hayes, C. (1951). *The ape in our house.* New York: Harper. (6)

Hays, R. B. (1985). A longitudinal study of friendship development. *Journal of Personality and Social Psychology, 48,* 909–924. (16)

Hazelrigg, M. D., Cooper, H. M., & Borduin, C. M. (1987). Evaluating the effectiveness of family therapies: An integrative review and analysis. *Psychological Bulletin, 101,* 428–442. (15)

Healy, D., & Williams, J. M. G. (1988). Dysrhythmia, dysphoria, and depression: The interaction of learned helplessness and circadian dysrhythmia in the pathogenesis of depression. *Psychological Bulletin, 103,* 163–178. (14, 15)

Heckhausen, H. (1984). Emergent achievement behavior: Some early developments. *Advances in Motivation and Achievement, 3,* 1–32. (11)

Heffner, R. S., & Heffner, H. E. (1982). Hearing in the elephant *(Elephas maximus):* Absolute sensitivity, frequency discrimination, and sound localization. *Journal of Comparative and Physiological Psychology, 96,* 926–944. (5)

Heider, F. (1958). *The psychology of interpersonal relations.* New York: Wiley. (16)

Heilman, K. M. (1979). Neglect and related disorders. In K. M. Heilman & E. Valenstein (Eds.), *Clinical neuropsychology* (pp. 268–307). New York: Oxford University Press. (3)

Held, R., & Hein, A. (1963). Movement-produced stimulation in the development of visually guided behavior. *Journal of Comparative and Physiological Psychology, 56,* 872–876. (6)

Helzer, J. E., Robins, L. N., & McEnvoy, L. (1987). Post-traumatic stress disorder in the general population. *New England Journal of Medicine, 317,* 1630–1634. (12)

Hendrick, C., & Hendrick, S. (1986). A theory and method of love. *Journal of Personality and Social Psychology, 50,* 392–402. (16)

Hendrick, C., Hendrick, S., & Adler, N. L. (1988). Romantic relationships: Love, satisfaction, and staying together. *Journal of Personality and Social Psychology, 54,* 980–988. (16)

Hendrick, S., Hendrick, C., Slapion-Foote, M. J., & Foote, F. H. (1985). Gender differences in sexual attitudes. *Journal of Personality and Social Psychology, 48,* 1630–1642. (16)

Henry, R. M. (1983). The cognitive versus psychodynamic debate about morality. *Human Development, 26,* 173–179. (6)

Herman, J., Roffwarg, H., & Tauber, E. S. (1968). Color and other perceptual qualities of REM and NREM sleep. *Psychophysiology, 5,* 223. (4)

Herman, J., Russell, D., & Trocki, K. (1986). Long-term effects of incestuous abuse in childhood. *American Journal of Psychiatry, 143,* 1293–1296. (15)

Herman, L. M., Richards, D. G., & Qolz, J. P. (1984). Comprehension of sentences by bottlenosed dolphins. *Cognition, 16,* 129–219. (6)

Herz, A., & Schulz, R. (1978). Changes in neuronal sensitivity during addictive processes. In J. Fishman (Ed.), *The bases of addiction* (pp. 375–394). Berlin: Dahlem Konferenzen. (14)

Hetherington, E. M., Cox, M., & Cox, R. (1982). Effects of divorce on parents and children. In M. E. Lamb (Ed.), *Nontraditional families* (pp. 233–288). Hillsdale, NJ: Lawrence Erlbaum. (6)

Hetherington, E. M., Stanley-Hagan, M., & Anderson, E. R. (1989). Marital transitions: A child's perspective. *American Psychologist, 44,* 303–312. (6)

Hilgard, E. R. (1979). Divided consciousness in hypnosis: The implications of the hidden observer. In E. Fromm & R. E. Shor (Eds.), *Hypnosis: Developments in research and new perspectives* (2nd ed.) (pp. 45–79). New York: Aldine. (4)

Hill, C., Rubin, Z., & Peplau, L. A. (1976). Breakups before marriage: The end of 103 affairs. *Journal of Social Issues, 32,* 147–167. (6)

Hines, M. (1982). Prenatal gonadal hormones and sex differences in human behavior. Psychological Bulletin, 92, 56–80. (11)

Hobson, J. A. (1988). *The dreaming brain.* New York: Basic Books. (4)

Hobson, J. A., & McCarley, R. W. (1977). The brain as a dream state generator: An activation-synthesis hypothesis of the dream process. *American Journal of Psychiatry, 134,* 1335–1348. (4)

Hobson, J. A., Spagna, T., & Malenka, R. (1978). Ethology of sleep studied with time-lapse photography: Postural immobility and sleep-cycle phase in humans. *Science, 201,* 1251–1253. (4)

Hochberg, J., & Galper, R. E. (1967). Recognition of faces: I. An exploratory study. *Psychonomic Science, 9,* 619–620. (5)

Hodgson, R., Rankin, H., & Stockwell, T. (1979). Alcohol dependence and the priming effect. *Behaviour Research and Therapy, 17,* 379–387. (14)

Hoff-Ginsberg, E., & Shatz, M. (1982). Linguistic input and the child's acquisition of language. *Psychological Bulletin, 92,* 3–26. (6)

Hoffer, A. (1973). Mechanism of action of nicotinic acid and nicotinamide in the treatment of schizophrenia. In D. Hawkins & L. Pauling (Eds.), *Orthomolecular psychiatry* (pp. 202–262). San Francisco: W. H. Freeman. (1)

Hoffman, L. W. (1989). Effects of maternal employment in the two-parent family. *American Psychologist, 44,* 283–292. (6)

Hoffman, M. (1977). Homosexuality. In F. A. Beach (Ed.), *Human sexuality in four perspectives* (pp. 164–189). Baltimore, MD: Johns Hopkins University Press. (11)

Hoffman, R. E., Stopek, S., & Andreasen, N. C. (1986). A comparative study of manic vs. schizophrenic speech disorganizaion. *Archives of General Psychiatry, 43,* 831–838. (14)

Hogan, J., & Quigley, A. M. (1986). Physical standards for employment and the courts. *American Psychologist, 11,* 1193–1217. (16)

Hogan, J. A. (1980). Homeostasis and behaviour. In F. M. Toates & T. R. Halliday (Eds.), *Analysis of motivational processes* (pp. 3–21). London: Academic Press. (11)

Hogan, R. A., & Kirchner, J. H. (1967). Preliminary report of the extinction of learned fears via short-term implosive therapy. *Journal of Abnormal Psychology, 72,* 106–109. (14)

Hogarth, R. M. (1981). Beyond discrete biases: Functional and dysfunctional aspects of judgmental heuristics. *Psychological Bulletin, 90,* 197–217. (9)

Hoge, S. K., Sachs, G., Appelbaum, P. S., Greer, A., & Gordon, C. (1988). Limitations on psychiatrists' discretionary civil commitment authority by the Stone and dangerousness criteria. *Archives of General Psychiatry, 45,* 764–769. (15)

Holden, C. (1986). Researchers grapple with problems of updating classic psychological test. *Science, 233,* 1249–1251. (13)

Hollandsworth, S. (1989, August-October). Have you exercised your mind today? *Special reports: Health,* pp. 18–26. (12)

Hollister, L. E. (1986). Health aspects of cannabis. *Pharmacological Reviews, 38,* 1–20. (4)

Hollon, S. D., & Beck, A. T. (1979). Cognitive therapy of depression. In P. C. Kendall & S. D. Hollon (Eds.), *Cognitive-behavioral interventions* (pp. 153–203). New York: Academic Press. (15)

Holmes, D. S. (1978). Projection as a defense mechanism. *Psychological Bulletin, 85,* 677–688. (13)

Holmes, T., & Rahe, R. (1967). The social readjustment rating scale. *Journal of Psychosomatic Research, 11,* 213–218. (12)

Holzman, P. S. (1985). Eye movement dysfunctions and psychosis. *International Review of Neurobiology, 27,* 179–205. (14)

Honer, W. G., Gewirtz, G., & Turey, M. (1987). Psychosis and violence in cocaine smokers. *Lancet, ii*(8556), 451. (4)

Honig, A. S. (1983). Sex role socialization in early childhood. *Young Children, 38,* 57–70. (11)

Honzik, M. P. (1974). The development of intelligence. In B. B. Wolman (Ed.), *Handbook of general psychology* (pp. 644–655). Englewood Cliffs, NJ: Prentice-Hall. (10)

Horn, J. L., & Donaldson, G. (1976). On the myth of intellectual decline in adulthood. *American Psychologist, 31,* 701–719. (10)

Horne, J. A., & Minard, A. (1985). Sleep and sleepiness following a behaviorally "active" day. *Ergonomics, 28,* 567–575. (4)

Horner, M. S. (1972). Toward an understanding of achievement-related conflicts in women. *Journal of Social Issues, 28,* 157–175. (11)

Horvath, P. (1988). Placebos and common factors in two decades of psychotherapy research. *Psychological Bulletin, 104,* 214–225. (15)

Hovland, C. I. (1937). The generalization of conditioned responses: I. The sensory generalization of conditioned responses with varying frequencies of tone. *Journal of General Psychology, 17,* 125–148. (7)

Hovland, C. I., Janis, I. L., & Kelley, H. H. (1953). Communication and persuasion. New Haven: Yale University Press. (16)

Hovland, C. I., Lumsdaine, A. A., & Sheffield, F. D. (1949). *Studies in social psychology in World War II: Vol. 3, Experiments on mass communications.* Princeton, NJ: Princeton University Press. (16)

Hovland, C. I., & Weiss, W. (1951). The influences of source credibility on communication effectiveness. *Public Opinion Quarterly, 15,* 635–650. (16)

Howard, K. I., Kopta, S. M., Krause, M. S., & Orlinsky, D. E. (1986). The dose-effect relationship in psychotherapy. *American Psychologist, 41,* 159–164. (15)

Hoyt, M. F., & Singer, J. L. (1978). Psychological effects of REM ("dream") deprivation upon waking mentation. In A. M. Arkin, J. S. Antrobus, & S. J. Ellman (Eds.), *The mind in sleep* (pp. 487–510). Hillsdale, NJ: Lawrence Erlbaum. (4)

Hubel, D. H., & Wiesel, T. N. (1968). Receptive fields and functional architecture of monkey striate cortex. *Journal of Physiology* (London), *195,* 215–243. (5)

Hull, C. L. (1943). *Principles of behavior: An introduction to behavior theory.* New York: D. Appleton. (11)

Hull, J. G., & Bond, C. F., Jr. (1986). Social and behavioral consequences of alcohol consumption and expectancy: A meta-analysis. *Psychological Bulletin, 99,* 347–360. (4)

Hull, J. G., & Van Treuren, R. R. (1986). Experimental social psychology and the causes and effects of alcohol consumption. *Research Advances in Alcohol and Drug Problems, 9,* 211–244. (4)

Hunter, I. M. (1977). An exceptional memory. *British Journal of Psychology, 68,* 155–164. (8)

Hunter, J. E., & Hunter, R. F. (1984). Validity and utility of alternative predictors of job performance. *Psychological Bulletin, 96,* 72–98. (16)

Hunter, J. E., & Schmidt, F. L. (1976). A critical analysis of the statistical and ethical implications of five definitions of test fairness. *Psychological Bulletin, 83,* 1053–1071. (16)

Hunter, J. E., & Schmidt, F. L. (1983). Quantifying the effects of psychological interventions on employee job performance and work-force productivity. *American Psychologist, 83,* 473–478. (16)

Hyde, J. S., & Linn, M. C. (1988). Gender differences in verbal ability. A meta-analysis. *Psychological Bulletin, 104,* 53–69. (10)

Iafaldano, M. T., & Muchinsky, P. M. (1985). Job satisfaction and job performance. *Psychological Bulletin, 97,* 251–273. (16)

Iggo, A., & Andres, K. H. (1982). Morphology of cutaneous receptors. *Annual Review of Neuroscience, 5,* 1–31. (5)

Infurna, R. N. (1981). Daily biorhythmicity influences homing behavior, psychopharmacological responsiveness, learning, and retention of suckling rats. *Journal of Comparative and Physiological Psychology, 95,* 896–914. (8)

Insanity defense work group. (1983). American Psychiatric Association statement on the insanity defense. *American Journal of Psychiatry, 140,* 681–688. (15)

Insko, C. A., Smith, R. H., Alicke, M. D., Wade, J., & Taylor, S. (1985). Conformity and group size: The concern with being right and the concern with being liked. *Personality and Social Psychology Bulletin, 11,* 41–50. (16)

Intons-Peterson, M. J., & Fournier, J. (1986). External and internal memory aids: When and how often do we use them? *Journal of Experimental Psychology: General, 115,* 267–280. (8)

Isaacs, E. A., & Clark, H. H. (1987). References in conversation between experts and novices. *Journal of Experimental Psychology: General, 116,* 26–37. (1)

Isenberg, D. J. (1986). Group polarization: A critical review and meta-analysis. *Journal of Personality and Social Psychology, 50,* 1141–1151. (16)

Izard, C. E. (1977). *Human emotions.* New York: Plenum. (12)

Jacobs, B. L. (1987). How hallucinogenic drugs work. *American Scientist, 75,* 386–392. (4)

Jacobs, B. L., & Trulson, M. E. (1979). Mechanisms of action of LSD. *American Scientist, 67,* 396–404. (3)

Jacobs, G. H. (1981). *Comparative color vision.* New York: Academic Press. (5)

Jacobsen, F. M., Sack, D. A., Wehr, T. A., Rogers, S., & Rosenthal, N. E. (1987). Neuroendocrine 5-hydroxytryptophan in seasonal affective disorder. *Archives of General Psychiatry, 44,* 1086–1091. (14)

James, W. (1884). What is an emotion? *Mind, 9,* 188–205. (12)

James, W. (1899/1962). *Talks to teachers on psychology.* New York: Dover. (Original work published 1899) (9)

Janicak, P. G., Davis, J. M., Gibbons, R. D., Ericksen, S., Chang, S., & Gallagher, P. (1985). Efficacy of ECT: A meta-analysis. *American Journal of Psychiatry, 142,* 297–302. (15)

Janis, I. L. (1972). *Victims of groupthink.* Boston: Houghton Mifflin. (16)

Janis, I. L. (1983). Stress inoculation in health care. In D. Meichenbaum & M. E. Jaremko (Eds.), *Stress reduction and prevention* (pp. 67–99). New York: Plenum. (12)

Janis, I. L. (1985). Sources of error in strategic decision making. In J. M. Pennings and associates (Eds.), *Organizational strategy and change* (pp. 157–197). San Francisco: Jossey-Bass. (16)

Janson, P., & Martin, J. K. (1982). Job satisfaction and age: A test of two views. *Social Forces, 60,* 1089–1102. (6)

Jaremko, M. E. (1983). Stress inoculation training for social anxiety, with emphasis on dating anxiety. In D. Meichenbaum & M. E. Jaremko (Eds.), *Stress reduction and prevention* (pp. 419–450). New York: Plenum. (12)

Jarvis, M. (1983). The treatment of cigarette dependence. *British Journal of Addiction, 78,* 125–130. (4)

Jasnos, T. M., & Hakmiller, K. L. (1975). Some effects of lesion level and emotional cues on affective expression in spinal cord patients. *Psychological Reports, 37,* 859–870. (12)

Jensen, A. R. (1969). How much can we boost I.Q. and scholastic achievement? *Harvard Educational Review, 39,* 1–123. (10)

Jensen, A. R. (1980). *Bias in mental testing.* New York: Free Press. (6)

Jéquier, E. (1987). Energy utilization in human obesity. *Annals of the New York Academy of Sciences, 499,* 73–83. (11)

Johanssen, H. S., & Victor, C. (1986). Visual information processing in the left and right hemispheres during unilateral tachistoscopic stimulation of stutterers. *Journal of Fluency Disorders, 11,* 285–291. (6)

Johnson, L. C. (1969). Physiological and psychological changes following total sleep deprivation. In A. Kales (Ed.), *Sleep: Physiology & pathology* (pp. 206–220). Philadelphia: J. B. Lippincott. (4)

Johnson, W. G., & Wildman, H. E. (1983). Influence of external and covert food stimuli on insulin secretion in obese and normal subjects. *Behavioral Neuroscience, 97,* 1025–1028. (11)

Johnston, J. C., & McClelland, J. L. (1974). Perception of letters in words: Seek not and ye shall find. *Science, 184,* 1192–1194. (9)

Johnston, J. J. (1975). Sticking with first responses on multiple-choice exams: For better or for worse? *Teaching of Psychology, 2,* 178–179. (Preface)

Jones, E. E., & Berglas, S. (1978). Control of attributions about the self through self-handicapping strategies: The appeal of alcohol and the role of underachievement. *Personality and Social Psychology Bulletin, 4,* 200–206. (4)

Jones, E. E., & Davis, K. E. (1965). From acts to dispositions: The attribution process in person perception. In L. Berkowitz (Ed.), *Advances in Experimental Social Psychology* (Vol. 2, pp. 219–266). New York: Academic Press. (16)

Jones, E. E., & Goethals, G. R. (1972). Order effects in impression formation: Attribution context and the nature of the entity. In E. Jones, D. Kanouse, H. Kelley, R. Nisbett, S. Valins, & B. Wiener (Eds.), *Attribution: Perceiving the causes of behavior* (pp. 27–46). Morristown, NJ: General Learning Press. (16)

Jones, E. E., & Harris, V. A. (1967). The attribution of attitudes. *Journal of Experimental Social Psychology, 13,* 1–24. (16)

Jones, E. E., & Nisbett, R. E. (1972). The actor and the observer: Divergent perception of the causes of behavior. In E. Jones, D. Kanouse, H. Kelley, R. Nisbett, S. Valins, & B. Wiener (Eds.), *Attribution: Perceiving the causes of behavior* (pp. 79–94). Morristown, NJ: General Learning Press. (16)

Jones, E. E., Rock, L., Shaver, K. G., Goethals, G. R., & Ward, L. M. (1968). Pattern of performance and ability attribution: An unexpected primacy effect. *Journal of Personality and Social Psychology, 10,* 317–340. (16)

Jones, G. R. (1986). Socialization tactics, self-efficacy, and newcomers' adjustments to organizations. *Academy of Management Journal, 29,* 262–279. (16)

Jones, H. E., & Kaplan, O. J. (1945). Psychological aspects of mental disorders in later life. In O. J. Kaplan (Ed.), *Mental disorders in later life* (pp. 69–115). Stanford, CA: Stanford University Press. (6)

Jones, L. V. (1984). White-black achievement differences: The narrowing gap. *American Psychologist, 39,* 1207–1213. (10)

Jones, R. A., Scott, J., Solernou, J., Noble, A., Fiala, J., & Miller, K. (1977). Availability and formation of stereotypes. *Perceptual and motor skills, 44,* 631–638. (9)

Jones, R. K. (1966). Observations on stammering after localized cerebral injury. *Journal of Neurology, Neurosurgery, and Psychiatry, 29,* 192–195. (6)

Jouvet, M., & Delorme, F. (1965). Locus coeruleus et sommeil paradoxal [Locus coeruleus and paradoxical sleep]. *Comptes Rendus des Séances de la Société de Biologie, 159,* 895–899. (4)

Jouvet, M., Michel, F., & Courjon, J. (1959). Sur un stade d'activité électrique cérébrale rapide au cours du sommeil physiologique [On a state of rapid electrical cerebral activity during physiological sleep]. *Comptes Rendus des Séances de la Société de Biologie, 153,* 1024–1028. (4)

Joyce, P. R., & Paykel, E. S. (1989). Predictors of drug response in depression. *Archives of General Psychiatry, 46,* 89–99. (15)

Jung, C. G. (1965). *Memories, dreams, reflections* (A. Jaffe, Ed.). New York: Random House. (13)

Junginger, J., & Frame, C. L. (1985). Self-report of the frequency and phenomenology of verbal hallucinations. *Journal of Nervous and Mental Disease, 173,* 149–155. (14)

Jurkovic, G. J. (1980). The juvenile delinquent as a moral philosopher: A structural-developmental perspective. *Psychological Bulletin, 88,* 709–727. (6)

Jusczyk, P. W. (1985). The high-amplitude sucking technique as a methodological tool in speech perception research. In G. Gottlieb & N. A. Krasnegor (Eds.), *Measurement of audition and vision in the first year of postnatal life* (pp. 195–222). Norwood, NJ: Ablex. (5)

Just, M. A., & Carpenter, P. A. (1985). Cognitive coordinate systems: Accounts of mental rotation and individual differences in spatial ability. *Psychological Review, 92,* 137–172. (9)

Kaas, J. H. (1983). What, if anything, is SI? Organization of first somatosensory area of cortex. *Physiological Reviews, 63,* 206–231. (5)

Kadden, R. M. (1973). Facilitation and suppression of responding under temporally defined schedules of negative reinforcement. *Journal of the Experimental Analysis of Behavior, 19,* 469–480. (14)

Kagan, J. (1984). *The nature of the child.* New York: Basic Books. (6)

Kagan, J., Reznick, J. S., & Snidman, N. (1988). Biological bases of childhood shyness. *Science, 240,* 167–171. (6)

Kahneman, D., & Tversky, A. (1973). On the psychology of prediction. *Psychological Review, 80,* 237–251. (9)

Kail, R., & Strauss, M. S. (1984). The development of human memory: An historical overview. In R. Kail & N. E. Spear (Eds.), *Comparative perspectives on the development of memory* (pp. 3–22). Hillsdale, NJ: Lawrence Erlbaum. (8)

Kaiser, M. K., Jonides, J., & Alexander, J. (1986). Intuitive reasoning about abstract and familiar physics problems. *Memory & Cognition, 14,* 308–312. (9)

Kalat, J. W. (1977). Status of "learned safety" or "learned noncorrelation" as a mechanism in taste-aversion learning. In L. M. Barker, M. R. Best, & M. Domjan (Eds.), *Learning mechanisms in food selection* (pp. 273–293). Waco, TX: Baylor University Press. (7)

Kalat, J. W. (1978). Letter to the editor: Speculations on similarities between autism and opiate addiction. *Journal of Autism and Childhood Schizophrenia, 8,* 477–479. (14)

Kalat, J. W. (1983). Evolutionary thinking in the history of the comparative psychology of learning. *Neuroscience & Biobehavioral Reviews, 7,* 309–314. (7)

Kalat, J. W. (1988). *Biological Psychology* (3rd ed.). Belmont, CA: Wadsworth. (3)

Kamin, L. J. (1969). Predictability, surprise, attention, and conditioning. In B. A. Campbell & R. M. Church (Eds.), *Punishment and aversive behavior*

(pp. 279–296). New York: Appleton-Century-Crofts. (7)

Kamin, L. J. (1974). *The science and politics of IQ.* New York: Wiley. (10)

Kandel, D. (1975). Stages in adolescent involvement in drug use. *Science, 190,* 912–914. (4)

Kandel, D. B., Davies, M., Karus, D., & Yamaguchi, K. (1986). The consequences in young adulthood of adolescent drug involvement. *Archives of General Psychiatry, 43,* 746–753. (4)

Kandel, E. R., & Schwartz, J. H. (1982). Molecular biology of learning: Modulation of transmitter release. *Science, 218,* 433–443. (7)

Kanizsa, G. (1979). *Organization in vision.* New York: Praeger. (5)

Kanner, L. (1943). Autistic disturbances of affective contact. *Nervous Child, 2,* 217–250. (14)

Kanouse, D. E., & Hanson, L. R., Jr. (1972). Negativity in evaluations. In E. Jones, D. Kanouse, H. Kelley, R. Nisbett, S. Valins, & B. Wiener (Eds.), *Attribution: Perceiving the causes of behavior* (pp. 47–62). Morristown, NJ: General Learning Press. (16)

Kaplan, E. H. (1988). Crisis? A brief critique of Masters, Johnson and Kolodny. *Journal of Sex Research, 25,* 317–322. (11)

Kapur, N., Heath, P., Meudell, P., & Kennedy, P. (1986). Amnesia can facilitate memory performance: Evidence from a patient with dissociated retrograde amnesia. *Neuropsychologia, 24,* 215–221. (8)

Karlin, R. A., Rosen, L. S., & Epstein, Y. M. (1979). Three into two doesn't go: A follow-up on the effects of overcrowded dormitory rooms. *Personality and Social Psychology Bulletin, 5,* 391–395. (12)

Karno, M., Golding, J. M., Sorenson, S. B., & Burnam, A. (1988). The epidemiology of obsessive-compulsive disorder in five US communities. *Archives of General Psychiatry, 45,* 1094–1099. (14)

Kassin, S. M., & Lepper, M. R. (1984). Oversufficient and insufficient justification effects: Cognitive and behavioral development. *Advances in Motivation and Achievement, 3,* 73–106. (11)

Katon, W., Egan, K., & Miller, D. (1985). Chronic pain: Lifetime psychiatric diagnoses and family history. *American Journal of Psychiatry, 142,* 1156–1160. (14)

Katz, E., & Lazarsfeld, P. F. (1955). *Personal influence.* Glencoe, IL: Free Press. (16)

Keane, T. M., Wolfe, J., & Taylor, K. L. (1987). Posttraumatic stress disorder: Evidence for diagnostic validity and methods of psychological assessment. *Journal of Clinical Psychology, 43,* 32–43. (12)

Keil, F. C. (1981). Constraints on knowledge and cognitive development. *Psychological Review, 88,* 197–227. (9)

Keith-Lucas, T., & Guttman, N. (1975). Robust-single-trial delayed backward conditioning. *Journal of Comparative and Physiological Psychology, 88,* 468–476. (7)

Keller, M. B., Lavori, P. W., Klerman, G. L., Andreason, N. C., Endicott, J., Coryell, W., Fawcett, J., Rice, J. P., & Hirschfeld, R. M. A. (1986). Low levels and lack of predictors of somatotherapy and psychotherapy received by depressed patients. *Archives of General Psychiatry, 43,* 458–466. (14)

Kelley, H. H. (1967). Attribution theory in social psychology. In D. Levine (Ed.), *Nebraska symposium on motivation* (Vol. 15, pp. 192–238). Lincoln, NE: University of Nebraska Press. (16)

Kelley, H. H. (1972). Causal schemata and the attribution process. In E. Jones, D. Kanouse, H. Kelley, R. Nisbett, S. Valins, & B. Wiener (Eds.), *Attribution: Perceiving the causes of behavior* (pp. 151–174). Morristown, NJ: General Learning Press. (16)

Kelley, H. H., Berscheid, E., Christensen, A., Harvey, J. H., Huston, T. L., Levinger, G., McClintock, E., Peplau, L. A., & Peterson, D. R. (1983). *Close relationships.* New York: W. H. Freeman. (16)

Kellogg, W. N., & Kellogg, L. A. (1933). *The ape and the child.* New York: McGraw-Hill. (6)

Kendler, K. S., Gruenberg, A. M., & Tsuang, M. T. (1985). Subtype stability in schizophrenia. *American Journal of Psychiatry, 142,* 827–832. (14)

Kendler, K. S., Heath, A. C., Martin, N. G., & Eaves, L. J. (1987). Symptoms of anxiety and symptoms of depression: Same genes, different environments? *Archives of General Psychiatry, 122,* 451–457. (14)

Kendler, K. S., & Robinette, C. D. (1983). Schizophrenia in the National Academy of Sciences–National Research Council twin registry—A 16-year update. *American Journal of Psychiatry, 140,* 1551–1563. (14)

Kenrick, D. T., & Stringfield, D. O. (1980). Personality traits and the eye of the beholder: Crossing some traditional philosophical boundaries in the search for consistency in all of the people. *Psychological Review, 87,* 88–104. (13)

Keon, T. L., & McDonald, B. (1982). Job satisfaction and life satisfaction: An empirical evaluation of their interrelationship. *Human Relations, 35,* 167–180. (6)

Kerzendorfer, M. (1977). Diagnostic usefulness of Cattell's 16PF. *Zeitschrift für Klinische Psychologie, 6,* 259–280. (13)

Kessler, R. C., Downey, G., Milafsky, J. R., & Stipp, H. (1988). Clustering of teenage suicides after television news stories about suicides: A reconsideration. *American Journal of Psychiatry, 145,* 1379–1383. (15)

Kety, S. S. (1977). Genetic aspects of schizophrenia: Observations on the biological and adoptive relatives of adoptees who became schizophrenic. In E. S. Gershon, R. H. Belmaker, S. S. Kety, & M. Rosenbaum (Eds.), *The impact of biology on modern psychiatry* (pp. 195–206). New York: Spectrum. (14)

Kety, S. S. (1983). Mental illness in the biological and adoptive relatives of schizophrenic adoptees: Findings relevant to genetic and environmental factors in etiology. *American Journal of Psychiatry, 140,* 720–727. (14)

Khantzian, E. J., & Treece, C. (1985). DSM-III psychiatric diagnosis of narcotic addicts. *Archives of General Psychiatry, 42,* 1067–1071. (4)

Kiesler, C. A. (1982a). Mental health and alternative care. *American Psychologist, 37,* 349–360. (15)

Kiesler, C. A. (1982b). Public and professional myths about mental hospitalization. *American Psychologist, 37,* 1323–1339. (15)

Kihlstrom, J. F. (1979). Hypnosis and psychopathology: Retrospect and prospect. *Journal of Abnormal Psychology, 88,* 459–473. (4)

Kimble, G. A. (1961). *Hilgard and Marquis' Conditioning and Learning* (2nd ed.). New York: Appleton-Century-Crofts. (7)

Kimble, G. A. (1981). Biological and cognitive constraints on learning. *The G. Stanley Hall Lecture Series, 1,* 11–60. (7)

Kimble, G. A., & Garmezy, N. (1968). *Principles of general psychology* (3rd ed.). New York: Ronald. (13)

King, B. M., Smith, R. L., & Frohman, L. A. (1984). Hyperinsulinemia in rats with ventromedial hypothalamic lesions: Role of hyperphagia. *Behavioral Neuroscience, 98,* 152–155. (14)

Kinsey, A. C., Pomeroy, W. B., & Martin, C. E. (1948). *Sexual behavior in the human male.* Philadelphia: W. B. Saunders. (11)

Kinsey, A. C., Pomeroy, W. B., Martin, C. E., & Gebhard, P. H. (1953). *Sexual behavior in the human female.* Philadelphia: W. B. Saunders. (11)

Kite, M. E., & Deaux, K. (1986). Attitudes toward homosexuality: Assessment and behavioral consequences. *Basic and Applied Social Psychology, 7,* 137–162.

Klatzky, R. L., Lederman, S., & Reed, C. (1987). There's more to touch than meets the eye: The salience of object attributes for haptics with and without vision. *Journal of Experimental Psychology: General, 116,* 356–369. (5)

Klayman, J., & Ha, Y.-W. (1987). Confirmation, disconfirmation, and information in hypothesis testing. *Psychological Review, 94,* 211–228. (9)

Klein, D. F., Zitrin, C. M., Woerner, M. G., & Ross, D. C. (1983). Treatment of phobias. II. Behavior therapy and supportive psychotherapy: Are there any specific ingredients? *Archives of General Psychiatry, 40,* 139–145. (15)

Klein, S. B., & Kihlstrom, J. F. (1986). Elaboration, organization, and the self-reference effect in memory. *Journal of Experimental Psychology: General, 115,* 26–38. (8)

Kleinmuntz, B., & Szucko, J. J. (1984). Lie detection in ancient and modern times. *American Psychologist, 39,* 766–776. (12)

Kleitman, N. (1963). *Sleep and wakefulness* (revised and enlarged edition). Chicago: University of Chicago Press. (4)

Klineberg, O. (1938). Emotional expression in Chinese literature. *Journal of Abnormal and Social Psychology, 33,* 517–520. (12)

Knesper, D. J., Belcher, B. E., & Cross, J. G. (1989). A market analysis comparing the practices of psychiatrists and psychologists. *Archives of General Psychiatry, 46,* 305–314. (15)

Knowlton, C. (1988, March 28). What America makes best. *Fortune,* p. 45. (9)

Koegel, P., Burnam, A., & Farr, R. K. (1988). The prevalence of specific psychiatric disorders among homeless individuals in the inner city of Los Angeles. *Archives of General Psychiatry, 45,* 1085–1092. (15)

Koh, T.-H., Abbatiello, A., & McLoughlin, C. S. (1984). Cultural bias in WISC subtest items: A response to Judge Grady's suggestion in relation to the *PASE* case. *School Psychology Review, 13,* 89–94. (10)

Kohlberg, L. (1969). Stage and sequence: The cognitive-developmental approach to socialization. In D. A. Goslin (Ed.), *Handbook of socialization theory and research.* Chicago: Rand McNally (6)

Kohlberg, L. (1981). *The meaning and measurement of moral development.* Worcester, MA: Clark University Press. (6)

Kohlberg, L., & Hersh, R. H. (1977). Moral development: A review of the theory. *Theory into Practice, 16,* 53–59. (6)

Kolata, G. (1989a, July 19). A new toll of alcohol abuse: The Indians' next generation. *New York Times* (national edition), pp. 1, 12. (6)

Kolata, G. (1989b, August 24). Experts finding new hope on treating crack addicts. *New York Times,* pp. A1, A12. (national edition). (14)

Kolb, B., & Whishaw, I. Q. (1983). Performance of schizophrenic patients on tests sensitive to left or right frontal, temporal, or parietal function in neurological patients. *Journal of Nervous and Mental Disease, 171,* 435–443. (14)

Kolko, D. J., & Milan, M. A. (1983). Reframing and paradoxical instruction to overcome "resistance" in the treatment of delinquent youths: A multiple baseline analysis. *Journal of Consulting and Clinical Psychology, 51,* 655–660. (15)

Komaki, J., Barwick, K. D., & Scott, L. R. (1978). A behavioral approach to occupational safety: Pinpointing and reinforcing safe performance in a food manufacturing plant. *Journal of Applied Psychology, 63,* 434–445. (7)

Komorita, S. S., & Lapworth, C. W. (1982). Cooperative choice among individuals versus groups in a N-person dilemma situation. *Journal of Personality and Social Psychology, 42,* 487–496. (16)

Koppenaal, R. J. (1963). Time changes in the strengths of A-B, A-C lists; spontaneous recovery? *Journal of Verbal Learning and Verbal Behavior, 2,* 310–319. (8)

Kornhuber, H. H. (1974). Cerebral cortex, cerebellum, and basal ganglia: An introduction to their motor functions. In F. O. Schmitt & F. G. Worden (Eds.), *The neurosciences: Third study program* (pp. 267–280). Cambridge, MA: MIT Press. (3)

Koss, M. P., & Butcher, J. N. (1986). Research on brief psychotherapy. In S. L. Garfield & A. E. Bergin (Eds.), *Handbook of psychotherapy and behavior change* (pp. 627–670). New York: Wiley. (15)

Koss, M. P., & Dinero, T. E. (1988). Predictors ual aggression among a national sample of

college students. *Annals of the New York Academy of Sciences, 528,* 133–147. (11)

Koss, M. P., Gidycz, C. A., & Wisniewski, N. (1987). The scope of rape: Incidence and prevalence of sexual aggression and victimization in a national sample of higher education students. *Journal of Consulting and Clinical Psychology, 55,* 162–170. (11)

Kosslyn, S. M. (1988). Aspects of a cognitive neuroscience of mental imagery. *Science, 240,* 1621–1626. (9)

Kosslyn, S. M., Ball, T. M., & Reiser, B. J. (1978). Visual images preserve metric spatial information: Evidence from studies of image scanning. *Journal of Experimental Psychology: Human Perception and Performance, 4,* 47–60. (9)

Kosten, T. R., Rounsaville, B. J., & Kleber, H. D. (1987). A 2.5-year follow-up of cocaine use among treated opioid addicts. *Archives of General Psychiatry, 44,* 281–284. (14)

Kozel, N. J., & Adams, E. H. (1986). Epidemiology of drug abuse: An overview. *Science, 234,* 970–974. (4)

Krebs, D., & Adinolfi, A. A. (1975). Physical attractiveness, social relations, and personality style. *Journal of Personality and Social Psychology, 31,* 245–253. (16)

Krueger, D. W. (1978). The differential diagnosis of proverb interpretation. In W. E. Fann, I. Karacan, A. D. Pokorny, & R. L. Williams (Eds.), *Phenomenology and treatment of schizophrenia* (pp. 193–201). New York: Spectrum. (14)

Krug, S. E. (1978). Reliability and scope in personality assessment: A comparison of the Cattell and Eysenck inventories. *Multivariate Experimental Clinical Research, 3,* 195–204. (13)

Kruglanski, A. W. (1970). Attributing trustworthiness in supervisor-worker relations. *Journal of Experimental Social Psychology, 6,* 214–232. (16)

Kruglanski, A. W., & Freund, T. (1983). The freezing and unfreezing of lay-inferences: Effects of impressional primacy, ethnic stereotyping, and numerical anchoring. *Journal of Experimental Social Psychology, 19,* 448–468. (16)

Kübler-Ross, E. (1969). *On death and dying.* New York: Macmillan. (6)

Kübler-Ross, E. (1975). *Death: The final stage of growth.* Englewood Cliffs, NJ: Prentice-Hall. (6)

Kulik, J. A., Bangert-Drowns, R. L., & Kulik, C. C. (1984). Effectiveness of coaching for aptitude tests. *Psychological Bulletin, 95,* 179–188. (10)

Kumar, J. (1975). The recent level of age at menarche and the effect of nutrition level and socioeconomic status on menarche: A comparative study. *Eastern Anthropologist, 28,* 99–131. (11)

Kumar, R., Cooke, E. C., Lader, M. H., & Russell, M. A. H. (1977). Is nicotine important in tobacco smoking? *Clinical Pharmacology & Therapeutics, 21,* 520–529. (4)

Laird, J. D. (1974). Self-attribution of emotion: The effects of expressive behavior on the quality of emotional experience. *Journal of Personality and Social Psychology, 29,* 475–486. (12)

Lakoff, G. (1987). *Women, fire, and dangerous things.* Chicago: University of Chicago. (9)

Lamb, H. R., Heath, D., and Downing, J. J. (Eds.). (1969). *Handbook of community mental health practice.* San Francisco: Jossey-Bass. (15)

Lamb, M. (1974). Paternal influences and the father's role. *American Psychologist, 34,* 938–943. (6)

Lamb, M. E., Frodi, A. M., Hwang, C.-P., & Frodi, M. (1982). Varying degrees of paternal involvement in infant care: Attitudinal and behavioral correlates. In M. E. Lamb (Ed.), *Nontraditional families* (pp. 117–137). Hillsdale, NJ: Lawrence Erlbaum. (6)

Lambert, M. J., Shapiro, D. A., & Bergin, A. E. (1986). The effectiveness of psychotherapy. In S. L. Garfield & A. E. Bergin (Eds.), *Handbook of psychotherapy and behavior change* (pp. 157–211). New York: Wiley. (15)

Lambert, N. M. (1981). Psychological evidence in Larry P. v. Wilson Riles: An evaluation by a witness for the defense. *American Psychologist, 36,* 937–952. (10)

Lamm, H., & Myers, D. G. (1978). Group-induced polarization of attitudes and behavior. *Advances in Experimental Social Psychology, 11,* 145–195. (16)

Lancet, D., Chen, Z., Ciobotairu, A., Eckstein, F., Khen, M., Heldman, J., Ophir, D., & Shafir, I. (1987). Toward a comprehensive molecular analysis of olfactory transduction. *Annals of the New York Academy of Sciences, 510,* 27–32. (5)

Land, E. H., Hubel, D. H., Livingstone, M. S., Perry, S. H., & Burns, M. M. (1983). Colour-generating interactions across the corpus callosum. *Nature, 303,* 616–618. (5)

Land, E. H., & McCann, J. J. (1971). Lightness and retinex theory. *Journal of the Optical Society of America, 61,* 1–11. (5)

Lande, S. D. (1982). Physiological and subjective measures of anxiety during flooding. *Behaviour Research and Therapy, 20,* 81–88. (14)

Landman, J. T., & Dawes, R. M. (1982). Psychotherapy outcome. *American Psychologist, 37,* 504–516. (15)

Langer, E. J. (1975). The illusion of control. *Journal of Personality and Social Psychology, 32,* 311–328. (13)

Larkin, J., McDermott, J., Simon, D. P., & Simon, H. A. (1980). Expert and novice performance in solving physics problems. *Science, 208,* 1335–1342. (9)

Lashley, K. S. (1951). The problem of serial order in behavior. In L. A. Jeffress (Ed.), *Cerebral mechanisms in behavior* (pp. 112–146). New York: Wiley. (6)

Latané, B., & Darley, J. M. (1968). Group inhibition of bystander intervention in emergencies. *Journal of Personality and Social Psychology, 10,* 215–221. (16)

Latané, B., & Darley, J. M. (1969). Bystander "apathy." *American Scientist, 57,* 244–268. (16)

Laumann, E. O. (1969). Friends of urban men: An assessment of accuracy in reporting their socio-economic attributes, mutual choice, and attitude development. *Sociometry, 32,* 54–69. (16)

Lavine, R., Buchsbaum, M. S., & Poncy, M. (1976). Auditory analgesia: Somatosensory evoked response and subjective pain rating. *Psychophysiology, 13,* 140–148. (5, 12)

Lawler, E. E., III. (1971). *Pay and organizational effectiveness.* New York: McGraw-Hill. (16)

Layman, S., & Greene, E. (1988). The effects of stroke on object recognition. *Brain and Cognition, 7,* 87–114. (1, 3)

Lazarus, R. S. (1977). Cognitive and coping processes in emotion. In A. Monat & R. S. Lazarus (Eds.) *Stress and coping* (pp. 145–158). New York: Columbia University Press. (12)

Lazarus, R. S., Averill, J. R., & Opton, E. M., Jr. (1970). Towards a cognitive theory of emotion. In M. B. Arnold (Ed.), *Feelings and emotions* (pp. 207–232). New York: Academic Press. (12)

Lê, A. D., Poulos, C. X., & Cappell, H. (1979). Conditioned tolerance to the hypothermic effect of ethyl alcohol. *Science, 206,* 1109–1110. (14)

LeBlanc, J., & LeBlanc, R. D. (1978). *Suddenly rich.* Englewood Cliffs, NJ: Prentice-Hall. (11)

Ledwidge, B. (1980). Run for your mind: Aerobic exercise as a means of alleviating anxiety and depression. *Canadian Journal of Behavioral Science, 12,* 126–140. (14)

Lefcourt, H. M. (1976). *Locus of control: Current trends in theory and research.* New York: Wiley. (13)

Leff, J. (1981). *Psychiatry around the globe.* New York: Marcel Dekker. (14)

LeMagnen, J. (1981). The metabolic basis of dual periodicity of feeding in rats. *Behavioral and Brain Sciences, 4,* 561–607. (11)

Lenneberg, E. H. (1967). *Biological foundations of language.* New York: Wiley. (6)

Lenneberg, E. H. (1969). On explaining language. *Science, 164,* 635–643. (6)

Leonard, B. E. (1982). On the mode of action of mianserin. In E. Costa & G. Racagni (Eds.), *Typical and atypical antidepressants: Molecular mechanisms: Vol. 31, Advances in Biochemical Psychopharmacology* (pp. 301–319). New York: Raven Press. (15)

Lepper, M. R., Greene, D., & Nisbett, R. E. (1973). Undermining children's intrinsic interest with external rewards: A test of the overjustification hypothesis. *Journal of Personality and Social Psychology, 28,* 129–137. (16)

Lester, J. T. (1983). Wrestling with the self on Mount Everest. *Journal of Humanistic Psychology, 23,* 31–41. (13)

Leuchtenburg, W. E. (1963). *Franklin D. Roosevelt and the New Deal 1932–1940.* New York: Harper & Row. (16)

Levenson, R. W., Oyama, O. N., & Meek, P. S. (1987). Greater reinforcement from alcohol for those at risk: Parental risk, personality risk, and sex. *Journal of Abnormal Psychology, 96,* 242–253. (14)

Leventhal, H. (1970). Findings and theory in the study of fear communication. In L. Berkowitz (Ed.), *Advances in Experimental Social Psychology* (Vol. 5, pp. 119–186). New York: Academic Press. (16)

LeVere, N. D., & LeVere, T. E. (1982). Recovery of function after brain damage: Support for the compensation theory of the behavioral deficit. *Physiological Psychology, 10,* 165–174. (3)

Levinger, G. (1976). A social psychological perspective on marital dissolution. *Journal of Social Issues, 32,* 21–47. (16)

Levinger, G. (1980). Toward the analysis of close relationships. *Journal of Experimental Social Psychology, 16,* 510–544. (16)

Levinger, G. (1983). Development and change. In H. H. Kelley, E. Berscheid, A. Christensen, J. H. Harvey, T. L. Huston, G. Levinger, E. McClintock, L. A. Peplau, & D. R. Peterson, *Close relationships* (pp. 315–359). New York: W. H. Freeman. (16)

Levinson, D. J. (1977). The mid-life transition: A period in adult psychosocial development. *Psychiatry, 40,* 99–112. (6)

Levinson, D. J. (1978). *The seasons of a man's life.* New York: Ballantine. (6)

Levy-Agresti, J., & Sperry, R. W. (1968). Differential perceptual capacities in major and minor hemispheres. *Proceedings of the National Academy of Sciences (U.S.A.), 61,* 1151. (3)

Levy, J., & Kueck, L. (1986). A right hemispatial field advantage on a verbal free-vision task. *Brain and Language, 27,* 24–37. (3)

Lewin, R. (1988). Cloud over Parkinson's therapy. *Science, 240,* 390–392. (3)

Lewinsohn, P. M., Mischel, W., Chaplin, W., & Barton, R. (1980). Social competence and depression: The role of illusory self-perceptions. *Journal of Abnormal Psychology, 89,* 203–212. (14)

Lewis, D. O., Moy, E., Jackson, L. D., Aaronson, R., Restifo, N., Serra, S., & Simos, A. (1985). Biopsychosocial characteristics of children who later murder: A prospective study. *American Journal of Psychiatry, 142,* 1161–1167. (12)

Lewis, D. O., Pincus, J. H., Lovly, R., Spitzer, E., & Moy, E. (1987) Biopsychosocial characteristics of matched samples of delinquents and nondelinquents. *Journal of the American Academy of Child and Adolescent Psychiatry, 26,* 744–752. (12)

Lewis, D. O., Shanok, S. S., Grant, M., & Ritvo, E. (1983). Homicidally aggressive young children: Neuropsychiatric and experiential correlates. *American Journal of Psychiatry, 140,* 148–153. (12)

Lichtenstein, E. (1982). The smoking problem: A behavioral perspective. *Journal of Consulting & Clinical Psychology, 50,* 804–819. (4)

Lieberman, J. A., Kane, J. M., Sarantakos, S., Gadaleta, D., Woerner, M., Alvir, J., & Ramos-Lorenzi, J. (1987). Prediction of relapse in schizophrenia. *Archives of General Psychiatry, 44,* 597–603. (15)

Liebeskind, J. C., & Paul, L. A. (1977). Psychological and physiological mechanisms of pain. *Annual Review of Psychology, 28,* 41–60. (5)

Lindberg, N. O., Coburn, C., & Stricker, E. M. (1984). Increased feeding by rats after subdiabetogenic streptozotocin treatment: A role for insulin in satiety. *Behavioral Neuroscience, 98,* 138–145. (11)

Link, N. F., Sherer, S. E., & Byrne, P. N. (1977). Moral judgment and moral conduct in the psychopath. *Canadian Psychiatric Association Journal, 22,* 341–346. (6)

Links, P. S., Stockwell, M., Abichandi, F., & Simeon, J. (1980). Minor physical anomalies in childhood autism. Part I. Their relationship to pre- and perinatal complications. *Journal of Autism and Developmental Disorders, 10,* 273–285. (14)

Linton, M. (1982). Transformations of memory in everyday life. In U. Neisser (Ed.), *Memory observed* (pp. 77–91). San Francisco: W. H. Freeman. (8)

Lippa, R. (1983). Expressive behavior. In L. Wheeler & P. Shaver (Eds.), *Review of personality and social psychology* (Vol. 4, pp. 181–205). Beverly Hills, CA: Sage. (16)

Lipsitt, L. P. (1963). Learning in the first year of life. *Advances in Child Development and Behavior, 1,* 147–195. (6)

Lipton, R. B., & Wong, M.-L. (1989). Eye-tracking disturbance and EEG. *Neuropsychiatry, Neuropsychology, and Behavioral Neurology, 2,* 61–66. (14)

Lisak, D., & Roth, S. (1988). Motivational factors in nonincarcerated sexually aggressive men. *Journal of Personality and Social Psychology, 55,* 795–802. (11)

Locke, E. A. (1976). The nature and causes of job satisfaction. In M. D. Dunnette (Ed.), *Handbook of industrial and organizational psychology* (pp. 1297–1349). Chicago: Rand McNally. (16)

Locke, E. A., Shaw, K. N., Saari, L. M., & Latham, G. P. (1981). Goal setting and task performance: 1969–1980. *Psychological Bulletin, 90,* 125–152. (11)

Loehlin, J. C., Willerman, L., & Horn, J. M. (1988). Human behavior genetics. *Annual Review of Psychology, 39,* 101–133. (3)

Loftus, E. F. (1975). Leading questions and the eyewitness report. *Cognitive Psychology, 7,* 560–572. (8)

Long, B. B. (1986). The prevention of mental-emotional disabilities. *American Psychologist, 41,* 825–829. (15)

Longstreth, L. E. (1981). Revisiting Skeels' final study: A critique. *Developmental Psychology, 17,* 620–625. (10)

Lorenz, K. (1950). The comparative method in studying innate behaviour patterns. *Symposia of the Society for Experimental Biology, 4,* 221–268. (11)

Lovaas, O. I., Koegel, R. L., & Schreibman, L. (1979). Stimulus overselectivity in autism: A review of research. *Psychological Bulletin, 86,* 1236–1254. (14)

Lowe, G. (1986). State-dependent learning effects with a combination of alcohol and nicotine. *Psychopharmacology, 89,* 105–107. (8)

Lowe, J., & Carroll, D. (1985). The effects of spinal injury on the intensity of emotional experience. *British Journal of Clinical Psychology, 24,* 135–136. (12)

Lowing, P. A., Mirsky, A. F., & Pereira, R. (1983). The inheritance of schizophrenia spectrum disorders: A reanalysis of the Danish adoptee study plan. *American Journal of Psychiatry, 140,* 1167–1171. (14)

Luchins, A. S. (1957). Primacy-recency in impression formation. In C. Hovland (Ed.), *The order of presentation in persuasion* (pp. 33–61). New Haven, CT: Yale University Press. (16)

Ludwick-Rosenthal, R., & Neufeld, R. W. J. (1988). Stress management during noxious medical procedures: An evaluative review of outcome studies. *Psychological Bulletin, 104,* 326–342. (12)

Lundy, A. (1985). The reliability of the thematic apperception test. *Journal of Personality Assessment, 49,* 141–145. (13)

Lykken, D. T. (1979). The detection of deception. *Psychological Bulletin, 86,* 47–53. (12)

Lykken, D. T. (1982). Research with twins: The concept of emergenesis. *Psychophysiology, 19,* 361–373. (3)

Macdonald, R. L., Weddle, M. G., & Gross, R. A. (1986). Benzodiazepine, beta-carboline, and barbiturate actions on GABA responses. *Advances in Biochemical Psychopharmacology, 41,* 67–78. (15)

MacDonald, W. S., & Oden, C. W., Jr. (1973). Effects of extreme crowding on the performance of five married couples during twelve weeks of intensive training. *Proceedings of the 81st Annual Convention of the American Psychological Association,* 209–210. (12)

Mackintosh, N. J. (1973). Stimulus selection: Learning to ignore stimuli that predict no change in reinforcement. In R. A. Hinde & J. Stevenson-Hinde (Eds.), *Constraints on learning* (pp. 75–100). London: Academic Press. (7)

MacLean, P. D. (1970). The limbic brain in relation to the psychoses. In P. Black (Ed.), *Physiological correlates of emotion* (pp. 129–146). New York: Plenum. (12)

MacLean, P. D. (1977). The triune brain in conflict. *Psychotherapy and Psychosomatics, 28,* 207–220. (3)

MacLean, P. D. (1980). Sensory and perceptive factors in emotional functions of the triune brain. In A. O. Rorty (Ed.), *Explaining emotions* (pp. 9–36). Berkeley, CA: University of California Press. (12)

MacLeod, C. M. (1988). Forgotten but not gone: Savings for pictures and words in long-term memory. *Journal of Experimental Psychology: Learning, Memory, and Cognition, 14,* 195–212. (8)

Macphail, E. M. (1987). The comparative psychology of intelligence. *Behavioral and Brain Sciences, 10,* 645–695. (7)

Maddahian, E., Newcomb, M. D., & Bentler, P. M. (1988). Risk factors for substance use: Ethnic differences among adolescents. *Journal of Substance Abuse, 1,* 11–23. (14)

Madsen, K. B. (1959). *Theories of motivation.* Copenhagen: Munksgaard. (11)

Mahoney, M. J. (1990). *Human change processes.* New York: Basic Books.

Maier, N. R. F., & Schneirla, T. C. (1964). *Principles of animal psychology* (enlarged edition). New York: Dover. (7)

Maier, S. F., Seligman, M. E. P., & Solomon, R. L. (1969). Pavlovian fear conditioning and learned helplessness: Effects on escape and avoidance behavior of (a) the CS-US contingency and (b) the independence of the US and voluntary responding. In B. A. Campbell and R. M. Church (Eds.), *Punishment and aversive behavior* (pp. 299–342). New York: Appleton-Century-Crofts. (14)

Maki, R., & Berry, S. (1984). Metacomprehension of text material. *Journal of Experimental Psychology: Learning, Memory, and Cognition, 10,* 663–679. (8)

Malamuth, N. M., & Donnerstein, E. (1982). The effects of aggressive-pornographic mass media stimuli. In L. Berkowitz (Ed.), *Advances in experimental social psychology* (Vol. 15, pp. 103–136). New York: Academic Press. (11)

Malinowski, B. (1929). *The sexual life of savages in North-western Melanesia.* New York: Harcourt, Brace, & World. (2)

Mann, J. J., McBride, P. A., & Stanley, M. (1986). Postmortem monoamine receptor and enzyme studies in suicide. *Annals of the New York Academy of Sciences, 487,* 114–121. (14)

Mansky, P. A. (1978). Opiates: Human psychopharmacology. In L. L. Iversen, S. D. Iversen, & S. H. Snyder (Eds.), *Handbook of psychopharmacology:*

Vol. 12, Drugs of abuse (pp. 95–185). New York: Plenum. (14)

Marcia, J. E. (1980). Identity in adolescence. In J. Adelson (Ed.), *Handbook of adolescent psychology* (pp. 159–187). New York: Wiley. (6)

Marder, S. R., Mebane, A., Chien, C., Winslade, W. J., Swann, E., & Van Putten, T. (1983). A comparison of patients who refuse and consent to neuroleptic treatment. *American Journal of Psychiatry, 140,* 470–472. (15)

Marek, G. R. (1975). *Toscanini.* London: Vision. (8)

Margraf, J., Ehlers, A., & Roth, W. T. (1986). Biological models of panic disorder and agoraphobia: A review. *Behaviour Research and Therapy, 24,* 553–567. (14)

Mark, V. H., & Ervin, F. R. (1970). *Violence and the brain.* New York: Harper & Row. (3)

Markman, E. M., & Hutchinson, J. E. (1984). Children's sensitivity to constraints on word meaning: Taxonomic versus thematic relations. *Cognitive Psychology, 16,* 1–27. (6)

Marks, D., & Kammann, R. (1980). *The psychology of the psychic.* Buffalo, NY: Prometheus. (2, 13)

Marks, I. M. (1981). Review of behavioral psychotherapy, I: Obsessive-compulsive disorders. *American Journal of Psychiatry, 138,* 584–592. (14)

Marlatt, G. A. (1978). Craving for alcohol, loss of control, and relapse: A cognitive-behavioral analysis. In P. E. Nathan, G. A. Marlatt, & T. Løberg (Eds.), *Alcoholism: New directions in behavioral research and treatment* (pp. 271–314). New York: Plenum. (14)

Marriott, F. H. C. (1976). Abnormal colour vision. In H. Davson (Ed.), *The eye* (2nd ed.) (pp. 533–547). New York: Academic Press. (5)

Marshall, G. D., & Zimbardo, P. G. (1979). Affective consequences of inadequately explained physiological arousal. *Journal of Personality and Social Psychology, 37,* 970–988. (12)

Marshall, W. L. (1988). The use of sexually explicit stimuli by rapists, child molesters, and nonoffenders. *Journal of Sex Research, 25,* 267–288. (11)

Martin, B. R. (1986). Cellular effects of cannabinoids. *Pharmacological Reviews, 38,* 45–74. (4)

Martin, C. E. (1981). Factors affecting sexual functioning in 60–79-year-old married males. *Archives of Sexual Behavior, 10,* 399–420. (11)

Maslach, C. (1979). Negative emotional biasing of unexplained arousal. *Journal of Personality and Social Psychology, 37,* 953–969. (12)

Maslow, A. H. (1962). *Toward a psychology of being.* Princeton, NJ: Van Nostrand. (13)

Maslow, A. H. (1970). *Motivation and personality* (2nd ed.). New York: Harper & Row. (11)

Maslow, A. H. (1971). *The farther reaches of human nature.* New York: Viking. (13)

Massaro, D. W. (1988). Some criticisms of connectionist models of human performance. *Journal of Memory and Language, 27,* 213–234. (8)

Masson, J. M. (1984). *The assault on truth.* New York: Farrar, Straus, and Giroux. (13)

Masters, W. H., & Johnson, V. E. (1966). *Human sexual response.* Boston: Little, Brown. (11)

Matossian, M. K. (1982). Ergot and the Salem witchcraft affair. *American Scientist, 70,* 355–357. (3)

Matsui, T., Okada, A., & Kakuyama, T. (1982). Influence of goal setting, performance, and feedback effectiveness. *Journal of Applied Psychology, 67,* 645–648. (11)

Matt, G. E. (1989). Decision rules for selecting effect sizes in meta-analysis: A review and reanalysis of psychotherapy outcome studies. *Psychological Bulletin, 105,* 106–115. (15)

Mattes, R. D. (1988). Blocking learned food aversions in cancer patients receiving chemotherapy. *Annals of the New York Academy of Sciences, 510,* 478–479. (11)

Matthews, K. A. (1988). Coronary heart disease and Type A behaviors: Update on and alternative to the Booth-Kewley and Friedman (1987) quantitative review. *Psychological Review, 104,* 373–380. (12)

Matthysse, S. W., & Kidd, K. K. (1976). Estimating the genetic contribution to schizophrenia. *American Journal of Psychiatry, 133,* 185–191. (14)

McCaul, K. D., & Malott, J. M. (1984). Distraction and coping with pain. *Psychological Bulletin, 95,* 516–533. (5, 12)

McClelland, D. C. (1958). Risk taking in children with high and low need for achievement. In J. W. Atkinson (Ed.), *Motives in fantasy, action, and society* (pp. 306–321). Princeton, NJ: Van Nostrand. (11)

McClelland, D. C. (1985). How motives, skills, and values determine what people do. *American Psychologist, 40,* 812–825. (11)

McClelland, D. C., Atkinson, J. W., Clark, R. A., & Lowell, E. L. (1953). *The achievement motive.* New York: Appleton-Century-Crofts. (11)

McClelland, J. L. (1985). Putting knowledge in its place: A scheme for programming parallel processing structures on the fly. *Cognitive Science, 9,* 113–146. (8)

McClelland, J. L. (1988). Connectionist models and psychological evidence. *Journal of Memory and Language, 27,* 107–123. (8)

McClelland, J. L., & Rumelhart, D. E. (1981). An interactive activation model of context effects in letter perception: Part 1. An account of basic findings. *Psychological Review, 88,* 375–407. (9)

McCornack, R. L. (1983). Bias in the validity of predicted college grades in four ethnic minority groups. *Educational & Psychological Measurement, 43,* 517–522. (10)

McCrae, R. R., & Costa, P. T., Jr. (1987). Validation of the five-factor model of personality across instruments and observers. *Journal of Personality and Social Psychology, 52,* 81–90. (13)

McDaniel, M. A., Einstein, G. O., & Lollis, T. (1988). Qualitative and quantitative considerations in encoding difficulty effects. *Memory & Cognition, 16,* 8–14. (8)

McDougall, W. (1932). *The energies of men.* New York: Charles Scribner's Sons. (11)

McGowan, J., & Gormly, J. (1976). Validation of personality traits: A multicriteria approach. *Journal of Personality and Social Psychology, 34,* 701–795. (13)

McGregor, D. M. (1960). *The human side of enterprise.* New York: McGraw-Hill. (16)

McGuire, W. J. (1968). Personality and attitude change: An information-processing theory. In A. G. Greenwald et al. (Eds.), *Psychological foundations of attitudes* (pp. 171–196). New York: Academic Press. (16)

McGuire, W. J. (1985). Attitudes and attitude change. In G. Lindzey & E. Aronson (Eds.), *Handbook of social psychology* (Vol. 2, pp. 233–346). New York: Random House. (16)

McGuire, W. J., & Papageorgis, D. (1961). The relative efficacy of various types of prior belief-defense in producing immunity against persuasion. *Journal of Abnormal and Social Psychology, 62,* 327–337. (16)

McKillip, J., & Riedel, S. L. (1983). External validity of matching on physical attractiveness for same and opposite sex couples. *Journal of Applied Social Psychology, 13,* 328–337. (16)

McLean, S., Skirboll, L. R., & Pert, C. B. (1985). Comparison of substance P and enkephalin distribution in rat brain: An overview using radioimmunocytochemistry. *Neuroscience, 14,* 837–852. (5)

McMahon, C. E. (1975). The wind of the cannon ball: An informative anecdote from medical history. *Psychotherapy & Psychosomatics, 26,* 125–131. (12)

McMorrow, M. J., & Foxx, R. M. (1983). Nicotine's role in smoking: An analysis of nicotine regulation. *Psychological Bulletin, 93,* 302–327. (4)

McNeal, E. T., & Cimbolic, P. (1986). Antidepressants and biochemical theories of depression. *Psychological Bulletin, 99,* 361–374. (14)

McReynolds, P. (1985). Psychological assessment and clinical practice: Problems and prospects. *Advances in Personality Assessment, 4,* 1–30. (13)

Meador, B. D., & Rogers, C. R. (1984). Person-centered therapy. In R. J. Corsini (Ed.), *Current psychotherapies* (3rd ed.). (pp. 142–195). Itasca, IL: F. E. Peacock Publishers. (15)

Meddis, R., Pearson, A. J. D., & Langford, G. (1973). An extreme case of healthy insomnia. *EEG and Clinical Neurophysiology, 35,* 213–214. (4)

Mednick, S. A., Machon, R. A., Huttunen, M. O., & Bonett, D. (1988). Adult schizophrenia following prenatal exposure to an influenza epidemic. *Archives of General Psychiatry, 45,* 189–192. (14)

Mehrabian, A., & Wiener, M. (1967). Decoding of inconsistent communication. *Journal of Personality and Social Psychology, 6,* 108–114. (16)

Meichenbaum, D. (1985). *Stress inoculation training.* New York: Pergamon. (12)

Meichenbaum, D., & Cameron, R. (1983). Stress inoculation training. In D. Meichenbaum & M. E. Jaremko (Eds.), *Stress reduction and prevention* (pp. 115–154). New York: Plenum. (12)

Meichenbaum, D. H., & Goodman, J. (1971). Training impulsive children to talk to themselves: A means of developing self-control. *Journal of Abnormal Psychology, 77,* 115–126. (12)

Mello, N. K., & Mendelson, J. H. (1978). Behavioral pharmacology of human alcohol, heroin and marihuana use. In J. Fishman (Ed.), *The bases of addiction* (pp. 133–158). Berlin: Dahlem Konferenzen. (14)

Meltzoff, A. N., & Moore, M. K. (1977). Imitation of facial and manual gestures by human neonates. *Science, 198,* 75–78. (6)

Melzack, R., & Wall, P. D. (1965). Pain mechanisms: A new theory. *Science, 150,* 971–979. (5)

Melzack, R., & Wall, P. D. (1983). *The challenge of pain.* New York: Basic. (5)

Melzack, R., Weisz, A. Z., & Sprague, L. T. (1963). Stratagems for controlling pain: Contributions of auditory stimulation and suggestion. *Experimental Neurology, 8,* 239–247. (12)

Mershon, D. H., Desaulniers, D. H., Amerson, T. L., Jr., & Kiefer, S. A. (1980). Visual capture in auditory distance perception: Proximity image effect reconsidered. *Journal of Auditory Research, 20,* 129–136. (5)

Mesmer, F. A. (1980). *Mesmerism: A translation of the original medical and scientific writings of F. A. Mesmer.* Los Altos, CA: William Kaufmann. (4)

Messenger, J. C. (1971). Sex and repression in an Irish folk community. In D. S. Marshall & R. C. Suggs (Eds.), *Human sexual behavior: Variations in the ethnographic spectrum* (pp. 3–37). New York: Basic Books. (11)

Messick, D. M., Wilke, H., Brewer, M. B., Krammer, R. M., Zemke, P. E., & Lui, L. (1983). Individual adaptations and structural change as solutions to social dilemmas. *Journal of Personality and Social Psychology, 44,* 294–309. (16)

Messick, S., & Jungeblut, A. (1981). Time and method in coaching for the SAT. *Psychological Bulletin, 89,* 191–216. (10)

Metcalfe, J., & Wiebe, D. (1987). Intuition in insight and noninsight problem solving. *Memory & Cognition, 15,* 238–246. (9)

Michael, C. R. (1978). Color vision mechanisms in monkey striate cortex: Dual-opponent cells with concentric receptive fields. *Journal of Neurophysiology, 41,* 572–588. (5)

Milgram, S. (1974). *Obedience to authority.* New York: Harper & Row. (16)

Miller, D. T. (1978). What constitutes a self-serving attributional bias? *Journal of Personality and Social Psychology, 36,* 1211–1223. (16)

Miller, D. T., & Ross, M. (1975). Self-serving biases in the attribution of causality: Fact or fiction? *Psychological Bulletin, 82,* 213–225. (16)

Miller, G. A. (1956). The magical number seven, plus or minus two: Some limits on our capacity for processing information. *Psychological Review, 63,* 81–97. (8)

Miller, L. L., & Branconnier, R. J. (1983). Cannabis: Effects on memory and the cholinergic limbic system. *Psychological Bulletin, 93,* 441–456. (4)

Miller, M. J., Small, I. F., Milstein, V., Malloy, F., & Stout, J. R. (1981). Electrode placement and cognitive change with ECT: Male and female response. *American Journal of Psychiatry, 138,* 384–386. (15)

Miller, N. E. (1969). Learning of visceral and glandular responses. *Science, 163,* 434–445. (7)

Miller, N. E. (1985). The value of behavioral research on animals. *American Psychologist, 40,* 423–440. (2)

Miller, R. J., Hennessy, R. T., & Leibowitz, H. W. (1973). The effect of hypnotic ablation of the background on the magnitude of the Ponzo perspective illusion. *International Journal of Clinical and Experimental Hypnosis, 21,* 180–191. (4)

Miller, R. R., & Spear, N. E. (Eds.) (1985). *Information processing in animals: Conditioned inhibition.* Hillsdale, NJ: Lawrence Erlbaum. (7)

Miller, R. S. (1986). Embarrassment: Causes and consequences. In W. Jones, J. Cheek, & S. Briggs (Eds.), *Shyness: Perspectives on research and treatment* (pp. 295–311). New York: Plenum. (12)

Miller, S., & Peacock, R. (1982). Evidence for the uniqueness of eidetic imagery. *Perceptual and Motor Skills, 55,* 1219–1233. (8)

Miller, W. R., & Hester, R. K. (1986). Inpatient alcohol treatment: Who benefits? *American Psychologist, 41,* 794–805. (14)

Milner, B. (1959). The memory defect in bilateral hippocampal lesions. *Psychiatric Research Reports, 11,* 43–52. (8)

Mineka, S. (1985). The frightful complexity of the origin of fears. In F. R. Brush & J. B. Overmier (Eds.), *Affect, conditioning, and cognition* (pp. 55–73). Hillsdale, NJ: Lawrence Erlbaum. (14)

Mineka, S. (1987). A primate model of phobic fears. In H. Eysenck & I. Martin (Eds.), *Theoretical foundations of behavior therapy* (pp. 81–111). New York: Plenum. (14)

Mineka, S., & Cook, M. (1986). Immunization against the observational conditioning of snake fear in rhesus monkeys. *Journal of Abnormal Psychology, 95,* 307–318. (14)

Mineka, S., Cook, M., & Miller, S. (1984). Fear conditioned with escapable and inescapable shock: The effects of a feedback stimulus. *Journal of Experimental Psychology: Animal Behavior Processes, 10,* 307–323. (14)

Mineka, S., Davidson, M., Cook, M., & Keir, R. (1984). Observational conditioning of snake fear in rhesus monkeys. *Journal of Abnormal Psychology, 93,* 355–372. (14)

Mischel, W. (1973). Toward a cognitive social learning reconceptualization of personality. *Psychological Review, 80,* 252–283. (13)

Mischel, W. (1981). Current issues and challenges in personality. In L. T. Benjamin, Jr. (Ed.). *The G. Stanley Hall Lecture Series* (Vol. 1, pp. 81–99). Washington, DC: American Psychological Association. (13)

Mitchell, J. E., & Eckert, E. D. (1987). Scope and significance of eating disorders. *Journal of Consulting and Clinical Psychology, 55,* 628–634. (11)

Mitchell, J. E., & Popkin, M. K. (1982). Antipsychotic drug therapy and sexual dysfunction in men. *American Journal of Psychiatry, 139,* 633–637. (15)

Moar, I., & Bower, G. H. (1983). Inconsistency in spatial knowledge. *Memory & Cognition, 11,* 107–113. (9)

Mobily, K. (1982). Using physical therapy activity and recreation to cope with stress and anxiety: A review. *American Corrective Therapy Journal, 36,* 77–81. (12)

Moely, B. E., Olson, F. A., Halwes, T. G., & Flavell, J. H. (1969). Production deficiency in young children's clustered recall. *Developmental Psychology, 1,* 26–34. (8)

Monahan, J. (1984). The prediction of violent behavior: Toward a second generation of theory and policy. *American Journal of Psychiatry, 141,* 10–15. (12)

Money, J. (1983). The genealogical descent of sexual psychoneuroendocrinology from sex and health theory: The eighteenth to the twentieth centuries. *Psychoneuroendocrinology, 8,* 391–400. (11)

Money, J., & Ehrhardt, A. A. (1972). *Man and woman, boy and girl.* Baltimore, MD: Johns Hopkins University Press. (6, 11)

Moore, V. (1986). The relationship between children's drawings and preferences for alternative depictions of a familiar object. *Journal of Experimental Child Psychology, 42,* 187–198. (6)

Moos, R. H., & Finney, J. W. (1983). The expanding scope of alcoholism treatment evaluation. *American Psychologist, 38,* 1036–1044. (14)

Moray, N. (1959). Attention in dichotic listening: Affective cues and the influence of instructions. *Quarterly Journal of Experimental Psychology, 11,* 56–60. (5)

Morris, J. B., & Beck, A. T. (1974). The efficacy of antidepressant drugs. *Archives of General Psychiatry, 30,* 667–674. (15)

Morrison, D. B. (1985). Adolescent contraceptive behavior: A review. *Psychological Bulletin, 98,* 538–568. (6)

Morrow, R. S., & Morrow, S. (1974). The measurement of intelligence. In B. B. Wolman (Ed.), *Handbook of general psychology* (pp. 656–670). Englewood Cliffs, NJ: Prentice-Hall. (10)

Moscovici, S., & Mugny, G. (1983). Minority influence. In P. B. Paulus (Ed.), *Basic group processes* (pp. 41–64). New York: Springer-Verlag. (16)

Moscovici, S., & Zavalloni, M. (1969). The group as a polarizer of attitudes. *Journal of Personality and Social Psychology, 12,* 125–135. (16)

Moscovitch, M. (1985). Memory from infancy to old age: Implications for theories of normal and pathological memory. *Annals of the New York Academy of Sciences, 444,* 78–96. (8)

Moskowitz, B. A. (1978). The acquisition of language. *Scientific American, 239*(5), 92–108. (6)

Moskowitz, D. S. (1982). Coherence and cross-situational generality in personality: A new analysis of old problems. *Journal of Personality and Social Psychology, 43,* 754–768. (13)

Motley, M. T., & Baars, B. J. (1979). Effects of cognitive set upon laboratory induced verbal (Freudian) slips. *Journal of Speech and Hearing Research, 22,* 421–432. (13)

Mumford, M. D., & Gustafson, S. B. (1988). Creativity syndrome: Integration, application, and innovation. *Psychological Bulletin, 103,* 27–43. (9)

Munro, J. F., Stewart, I. C., Seidelin, P. H., Mackenzie, H. S., & Dewhurst, N. G. (1987). Mechanical treatment for obesity. *Annals of the New York Academy of Sciences, 499,* 305–312. (11)

Munroe, R. (1955). *Schools of psychoanalytic thought.* New York: Dryden. (15)

Murphy, G. E., Simons, A. D., Wetzel, R. D., & Lustman, P. J. (1984). Cognitive therapy and pharmacotherapy. *Archives of General Psychiatry, 41,* 33–41. (15)

Murphy, G. L., & Medin, D. L. (1985). The role of theories in conceptual coherence. *Psychological Review, 92,* 289–316. (1)

Murray, H. A. (1938). *Explorations in personality.* New York: Oxford University Press. (11)

Murray, H. A. (1943). *Thematic Apperception Test manual.* Cambridge, MA: Harvard University Press. (13)

Murstein, B. I. (1976). *Who will marry whom? Theories and research in marital choice.* New York: Springer Publishing Co. (16)

Myers, J. K., Weissman, M. M., Tischler, G. L., Holzer, C. E., III, Leaf, P. J., Orvaschel, H., Anthony, J. C., Boyd, J. H., Burke, J. D., Jr., Kramer, M., & Stoltzman, R. (1984). Six-month prevalence of psychiatric disorders in three communities. *Archives of General Psychiatry, 41,* 959–967. (14)

Myles-Worsley, M., Johnston, W. A., & Simons, M. A. (1988). The influence of expertise on x-ray image processing. *Journal of Experimental Psychology: Learning, Memory, and Cognition, 14,* 553–557. (9)

Nagera, H. (1976). *Obsessional neuroses.* New York: Jason Aronson. (14)

Nash, M. (1987). What, if anything, is regressed about hypnotic age regression? A review of the empirical literature. *Psychological Bulletin, 102,* 42–52. (4)

Nash, M. R., Johnson, L. S., & Tipton, R. D. (1979). Hypnotic age regression and the occurrence of transitional object relationships. *Journal of Abnormal Psychology, 88,* 547–555. (4)

Nash, M. R., Lynn, S. J., Stanley, S., & Carlson, V. (1987). Subjectively complete hypnotic deafness and auditory priming. *International Journal of Clinical and Experimental Hypnosis, 35,* 32–40. (4)

National Center for Health Statistics (1988). *Vital Statistics of the United States, 1984* (Vol. 3). Washington: U.S. Government Printing Office. (11)

National Institute of Mental Health. (1982). *Television and behavior: Ten years of scientific progress and implications for the eighties.* Rockville, MD: Author. (2)

Nebes, R. D. (1974). Hemispheric specialization in commissurotomized man. *Psychological Bulletin, 81,* 1–14. (3)

Neiss, R. (1988). Reconceptualizing arousal: Psychobiological stakes in motor performance. *Psychological Bulletin, 103,* 345–366. (12)

Nelson, K. (1981). Individual differences in language development: Implications for development and language. *Developmental Psychology, 17,* 170–187. (6)

Nelson, K. (1985). *Making sense: The acquisition of shared meaning.* Orlando, FL: Academic Press. (6)

Nelson, K. E., Baker, N. D., Denninger, M., Bonvillian, J. D., & Kaplan, B. J. (1985). Cookie versus Do-it-again: Imitative-referential and personal-social-syntactic-initiating language styles in young children. *Linguistics, 23,* 433–454. (6)

Nemeth, C. (1972). A critical analysis of research utilizing the prisoner's dilemma paradigm for the study of bargaining. In L. Berkowitz (Ed.), *Advances in Experimental Social Psychology* (Vol. 6, pp. 203–234). New York: Academic Press. (16)

Nemeth, C. J. (1986). Differential contributions of majority and minority influence. *Psychological Review, 93,* 23–32. (16)

Netter, F. H. (1965). *The CIBA collection of medical illustrations: Vol. 2, Reproductive system.* Summit, NJ: CIBA. (11)

Newman, S. E. (1987). Ebbinghaus' *On memory:* Some effects on early American research. In D. S. Gorfein & R. R. Hoffman (Eds.), *Memory and learning: The Ebbinghaus centennial conference* (pp. 77–87). Hillsdale, NJ: Lawrence Erlbaum. (8)

Newman, S. E., Cooper, M. H., Parker, K. O., Sidden, J. A., Gonder-Frederick, L. A., Moorefield, K. M., & Nelson, P. A. (1982). Some tests of the encoding specificity and semantic integration hypotheses. *American Journal of Psychology, 95,* 103–123. (6)

Nickerson, R. S., & Adams, M. J. (1979). Long-term memory for a common object. *Cognitive Psychology, 11,* 287–307. (8)

Nicol, S. E., & Gottesman, I. I. (1983). Clues to the genetics and neurobiology of schizophrenia. *American Scientist, 71,* 398–404. (14)

Nietzel, M. T., & Bernstein, D. A. (1987). *Introduction to clinical psychology.* Englewood Cliffs, NJ: Prentice-Hall. (10)

Nisbett, R. E., Fong, G. T., Lehman, D. R., & Cheng, P. W. (1987). Teaching reasoning. *Science, 238,* 625–631. (9)

Nisbett, R. E., & Schachter, S. (1966). Cognitive manipulation of pain. *Journal of Experimental Social Psychology, 2,* 227–236. (9)

Nisbett, R. E., & Wilson, T. D. (1977). Telling more than we can know: Verbal reports on mental processes. *Psychological Review, 84,* 231–259. (9)

Nolen-Hoeksema, S. (1987). Sex differences in unipolar depression: Evidence and theory. *Psychological Bulletin, 101,* 259–282. (14)

Norman, D. A. (1981). Categorization of action slips. *Psychological Review, 88,* 1–15. (13)

Nosofsky, R. M. (1986). Attention, similarity, and the identification-categorization relationship. *Journal of Experimental Psychology: General, 115,* 39–57. (9)

Noyes, R. J., Jr., Crowe, R. R., Harris, E. L., Hamra, B. J., McChesney, C. M., & Chaudhry, D. R. (1986). Relationship between panic disorder and agoraphobia. *Archives of General Psychiatry, 43,* 227–232. (14)

Nygard, R. (1982). Achievement motives and individual differences in situational specificity of behavior. *Journal of Personality and Social Psychology, 43,* 319–327. (11)

O'Brien, M., & Nagle, K. J. (1987). Parents' speech to toddlers: The effect of play context. *Journal of Child Language, 14,* 269–279. (6)

Okin, R. L. (1983). The future of state hospitals: Should there be one? *American Journal of Psychiatry, 140,* 577–581. (15)

Olds, J. (1958). Satiation effects in self-stimulation of the brain. *Journal of Comparative and Physiological Psychology, 51,* 675–678. (1)

Olds, J. (1962). Hypothalamic substrates of reward. *Psychological Review, 42,* 554–604. (1)

Olson, J. M. (1988). Misattribution, preparatory information, and speech anxiety. *Journal of Personality and Social Psychology, 54,* 758–767. (16)

O'Malley, S. S., & Maisto, S. A. (1985). Effects of family drinking history and expectancies on responses to alcohol in men. *Journal of Studies on Alcohol, 46,* 289–297. (14)

O'Nell, C. W. (1965). A cross-cultural study of hunger and thirst motivation manifested in dreams. *Human Development, 8,* 181–193. (15)

Orne, M. T. (1951). The mechanisms of hypnotic age regression: An experimental study. *Journal of Abnormal and Social Psychology, 46,* 213–225. (4)

Orne, M. T. (1959). The nature of hypnosis: Artifact and essence. *Journal of Abnormal and Social Psychology, 58,* 277–299. (4)

Orne, M. T. (1969). Demand characteristics and the concept of quasi-controls. In R. Rosenthal & R. L. Rosnow (Eds.), *Artifact in behavioral research* (pp. 143–179). (2)

Orne, M. T. (1979). On the simulating subject as a quasi-control group in hypnosis research: What, why, and how. In E. Fromm & R. E. Shor (Eds.), *Hypnosis: Developments in research and new perspectives* (2nd ed.) (pp. 519–565). New York: Aldine. (4)

Orne, M. T., Dinges, D. F., & Orne, E. C. (1984). On the differential diagnosis of multiple personality in the forensic context. *International Journal of Clinical and Experimental Hypnosis, 32,* 118–169. (15)

Orne, M. T., & Evans, F. J. (1965). Social control in the psychological experiment: Antisocial behavior and hypnosis. *Journal of Personality and Social Psychology, 1,* 189–200. (4)

Orne, M. T., & Scheibe, K. E. (1964). The contribution of nondeprivation factors in the production of sensory deprivation effects: The psychology of the "panic button." *Journal of Abnormal and Social Psychology, 68,* 3–12. (2)

Ornitz, E. M., & Ritvo, E. R. (1976). Medical assessment. In E. R. Ritvo (Ed.), *Autism* (pp. 7–23). New York: Spectrum. (14)

Orth, J. E., & Thebarge, R. W. (1984). Helping clients reduce self-evaluative beliefs: Consider the consequences. *Cognitive Therapy and Research, 8,* 13–18. (15)

Osborne, R. T., Noble, C. E., & Wey, N. J. (Eds.) (1978). *Human variation: Biopsychology of age, race, and sex.* New York: Academic Press. (16)

Oscar-Berman, M. (1980). Neuropsychological consequences of long-term chronic alcoholism. *American Scientist, 68,* 410–419. (8)

Öst, L.-G., & Hugdahl, K. (1981). Acquisition of phobias and anxiety response patterns in clinical patients. *Behaviour Research and Therapy, 19,* 439–447. (14)

O'Sullivan, M., Ekman, P., Friesen, W., & Scherer, K. (1985). What you say and how you say it: The contribution of speech content and voice quality to judgments of others. *Journal of Personality and Social Psychology, 48,* 54–62. (12)

Owens, W. A. (1976). Background data. In M. D. Dunnette (Ed.), *Handbook of industrial and organizational psychology* (pp. 609–644). Chicago: Rand McNally. (16)

Padgham, C. A. (1975). Colours experienced in dreams. *British Journal of Psychology, 66,* 25–28. (4)

Paicheler, G. (1988). *The psychology of social influence.* Cambridge, England: Cambridge University Press. (16)

Panksepp, J., Herman, B., & Villberg, T. (1978). An opiate excess model of childhood autism. *Neuroscience Abstracts, 4*(Abstract 1601), 500. (14)

Parke, R. D., & Asher, S. R. (1983). Social and personality development. *Annual Review of Psychology, 34,* 465–509. (6)

Parke, R. D., Berkowitz, L., Leyens, J. P., West, S. G., & Sebastian, R. J. (1977). Some effects of violent and nonviolent movies on the behavior of juvenile delinquents. In L. Berkowitz (Ed.), *Advances in experimental social psychology* (Vol. 10, pp. 135–172). New York: Academic Press. (2)

Parker, D. (1944). *The portable Dorothy Parker.* New York: Viking. (14, 15)

Parker, D. F., & DeCotiis, T. A. (1983). *Organizational determinants of job stress. Organizational Behavior and Human Performance, 32,* 160–177. (12)

Parker, K. (1983). A meta-analysis of the reliability and validity of the Rorschach. *Journal of Personality Assessment, 47,* 227–231. (13)

Parkinson, C. N. (1957). *Parkinson's law.* Boston: Houghton Mifflin. (16)

Parmeggiani, P. L. (1982). Regulation of physiological functions during sleep in mammals. *Experientia, 38,* 1405–1408. (4)

Parnas, J., Schulsinger, F., Schulsinger, H., Mednick, S. A., & Teasdale, T. W. (1982). Behavioral precursors of schizophrenia spectrum. *Archives of General Psychiatry, 39,* 658–664. (14)

Parsons, H. M. (1974). What happened at Hawthorne? *Science, 183,* 922–932. (2)

Pate, J. L., & Rumbaugh, D. M. (1983). The language-like behavior of Lana chimpanzee: Is it merely discrimination and paired-associate learning? *Animal Learning & Behavior, 11,* 134–138. (6)

Pavlov, I. P. (1927/1960). *Conditioned reflexes.* New York: Dover. (Original work published 1927) (7)

Peachey, J. E., & Naranjo, C. A. (1983). The use of disulfiram and other alcohol-sensitizing drugs in the treatment of alcoholism. *Research Advances in Alcohol and Drug Problems, 7,* 397–431. (14)

Pearce, J. M. (1987). A model for stimulus generalization in Pavlovian conditioning. *Psychological Review, 94,* 61–73. (7)

Peele, S. (1984). The cultural context of psychological approaches to alcoholism. *American Psychologist, 39,* 1337–1351. (14)

Pendery, M. L., Maltzman, I. M., & West, L. J. (1982). Controlled drinking by alcoholics? New findings and a reevaluation of a major affirmative study. *Science, 217,* 169–175. (14)

Pepper, B., & Ryglewicz, H. (1982). Testimony for the neglected: The mentally ill in the post-deinstitutionalized age. *American Journal of Orthopsychiatry, 52,* 388–392. (15)

Perls, F. (1973). *The Gestalt approach and eye witness to therapy.* Ben Lomond, CA: Science and Behavior Books. (15)

Perry, D. G., & Bussey, K. (1979). The social learning theory of sex differences: Imitation is alive and well. *Journal of Personality and Social Psychology, 37,* 1699–1712. (7)

Pert, A., Rosenblatt, J. E., Sivit, C., Pert, C. B., & Bunney, W. E., Jr. (1978). Long-term treatment with lithium prevents the development of dopamine receptor supersensitivity. *Science, 201,* 171–173. (15)

Pervin, L. A. (1983). The stasis and flow of behavior: Toward a theory of goals. In M. M. Page (Ed.), *Nebraska symposium on motivation 1982* (pp. 1–53). Lincoln, NE: University of Nebraska Press. (11)

Peterson, C. (1983). Clouds and silver linings: Depressive symptoms and causal attributions about ostensibly "good" and "bad" events. *Cognitive Therapy and Research, 7,* 575–578. (14)

Peterson, C., Bettes, B. A., & Seligman, M. E. P. (1985). Depressive symptoms and unprompted causal attributions: Content analysis. *Behavior Research and Therapy, 23,* 379–382. (14)

Peterson, L. G., Peterson, M., O'Shanick, G. J., & Swann, A. (1985). Self-inflicted gunshot wounds: Lethality of method versus intent. *American Journal of Psychiatry, 142,* 228–231. (14)

Peterson, L. R., & Peterson, M. J. (1959). Short-term retention of individual verbal items. *Journal of Experimental Psychology, 58,* 193–198. (8)

Petty, R. E., & Cacioppo, J. T. (1977). Effects of forewarning of persuasive intent and involvement on cognitive responses and persuasion. *Personality and Social Psychology Bulletin, 5,* 173–176. (16)

Petty, R. E., & Cacioppo, J. T. (1981). *Attitudes and persuasion: Classic and contemporary approaches.* Dubuque, IA: Wm. C. Brown. (16)

Petty, R. E., & Cacioppo, J. T. (1986). *Communication and persuasion: Central and peripheral routes to attitude change.* New York: Springer-Verlag. (16)

Pfefferbaum, A., Zipursky, R. B., Lim, K. O., Zatz, L. M., Stahl, S. M., & Jernigan, T. L. (1988). Computed tomographic evidence for generalized sulcal and ventricular enlargement in schizophrenia. *Archives of General Psychiatry, 45,* 633–640. (14)

Pfungst, O. (1911). *Clever Hans.* New York: Holt. (2)

Phillips, D. P. (1974). The influence of suggestion on suicide: Substantive and theoretical implications of the Werther effect. *American Sociological Review, 39,* 340–354. (15)

Phillips, D. P., & Carstensen, L. L. (1986). Clustering of teenage suicides after television news stores about suicide. *New England Journal of Medicine, 315,* 685–689. (15)

Phillips, D. P., & Paight, D. J. (1987). The impact of televised movies about suicide. *New England Journal of Medicine, 317,* 809–811. (15)

Piaget, J. (1923/1957). *The language and thought of the child* (M. Gabain & R. Gabain, Trans.). New York: Humanities. (Original work published 1923) (6)

Piaget, J. (1937/1954). *The construction of reality in the child* (M. Cook, Trans.). New York: Basic Books. (Original work published 1937) (6)

Pichot, P. (1984). Centenary of the birth of Hermann Rorschach. *Journal of Personality Assessment, 48,* 591–596. (13)

Pierrot-Deseilligny, C., Gray, F., & Brunet, P. (1986). Infarcts of both inferior parietal lobules with impairment of visually guided eye movements, peripheral visual inattention and optic ataxia. *Brain, 109,* 81–97. (1)

Pinsky, S. D., & McAdam, D. W. (1980). Electroencephalographic and dichotic indices of cerebral laterality in stutterers. *Brain and Language, 11,* 374–397. (6)

Pi-Sunyer, F. X. (1987). Exercise effects on calorie intake. *Annals of the New York Academy of Sciences, 499,* 94–103. (11)

Pitman, R. K., Orr, S. P., Forgue, D. F., deJong, J. B., & Claiborn, N. M. (1987). Psychophysiologic assessment of posttraumatic stress disorder imagery in Vietnam combat veterans. *Archives of General Psychiatry, 44,* 970–975. (12)

Plomin, R., & DeFries, J. C. (1980). Genetics and intelligence: Recent data. *Intelligence, 4,* 15–24. (10)

Plomin, R., DeFries, J. C., & Roberts, M. K. (1977). Assortative mating by unwed biological parents of adopted children. *Science, 196,* 449–450. (6)

Plutchik, R. (1982). A psychoevolutionary theory of emotions. *Social Science Information, 21,* 529–553. (12)

Plutchik, R., & Ax, A. F. (1967). A critique of "determinants of emotional state" by Schachter and Singer (1962). *Psychophysiology, 4,* 79–82. (12)

Pokorny, A. D. (1978). The course and prognosis of schizophrenia. In W. E. Fann, I. Karacan, A. D. Pokorny, & R. L. Williams (Eds.), *Phenomenology and treatment of schizophrenia* (pp. 21–37). New York: Spectrum. (15)

Polivy, J., Heatherton, T. F., & Herman, C. P. (1988). Self-esteem, restraint, and eating behavior. *Journal of Abnormal Psychology, 97,* 354–356. (11)

Polivy, J., & Herman, C. P. (1985). Dieting and binging: A causal analysis. *American Psychologist, 40,* 193–201. (11)

Polivy, J., & Herman, C. P. (1987). Diagnosis and treatment of normal eating. *Journal of Consulting and Clinical Psychology, 55,* 635–644. (11)

Pollak, J. M. (1979). Obsessive-compulsive personality: A review. *Psychological Bulletin, 86,* 225–241. (14)

Polya, G. (1957). *How to solve it.* Garden City, NY: Doubleday Anchor. (9)

Pomeroy, W. B. (1972). Dr. Kinsey and the Institute for Sex Research. New York: Harper & Row. (11)

Pond, S. B., III, & Hay, M. S. (1989). The impact of task preview information as a function of recipient self-efficacy. *Journal of Vocational Behavior, 35,* 17–29. (16)

Poole, A. D., Sanson-Fisher, R. W., & German, G. A. (1981). The rapid-smoking technique: Therapeutic effectiveness. *Behaviour Research and Therapy, 19,* 389–397. (15)

Popper, K. (1986). Predicting overt behavior versus predicting hidden states. *Behavioral and Brain Sciences, 9,* 254–255. (13)

Poulos, C. X., Wilkinson, D. A., & Cappell, H. (1981). Homeostatic regulation and Pavlovian conditioning in tolerance to amphetamine-induced anorexia. *Journal of Comparative and Physiological Psychology, 95,* 735–746. (14)

Powers, S., Barkan, J. H., & Jones, P. B. (1986). Reliability of the Standard Progressive Matrices Test for Hispanic and Anglo-American children. *Perceptual & Motor Skills, 62,* 348–350. (10)

Pratkanis, A. R., Greenwald, A. G., Leippe, M. R., & Baumgardner, M. H. (1988). In search of reliable persuasion effects: III. The sleeper effect is dead. Long live the sleeper effect. *Journal of Personality and Social Psychology, 54,* 203–218. (16)

Premack, A. J., & Premack, D. (1972). Teaching language to an ape. *Scientific American, 227* (4), 92–99. (6)

Premack, D. (1965). Reinforcement theory. In D. Levine (Ed.), *Nebraska symposium on motivation* (pp. 123–188). Lincoln, NE: University of Nebraska Press. (7)

Premack, S. L., & Wanous, J. P. (1985). A meta-analysis of realistic job preview experiments. *Journal of Applied Psychology, 70,* 706–719. (16)

Prentky, R. A., Knight, R. A., & Rosenberg, R. (1988). Validation analyses on a taxonomic system for rapists: Disconfirmation and reconceptualization. *Annals of the New York Academy of Sciences, 528,* 21–40. (11)

Price, K. P., Tryon, W. W., & Raps, C. S. (1978). Learned helplessness and depression in a clinical population: A test of two behavioral hypotheses. *Journal of Abnormal Psychology, 87,* 113–121. (14)

Price, L. H., Ricaurte, G. A., Krystal, J. H., & Heninger, G. R. (1989). Neuroendocrine and mood responses to intravenous L-tryptophan in 3,4-methylene dioxymethamphetamine (MDMA) users. *Archives of General Psychiatry, 46,* 20–22. (4)

Price, R. A., Kidd, K. K., & Weissman, M. M. (1987). Early onset (under age 30 years) and panic disorder as markers for etiologic homogeneity in major depression. *Archives of General Psychiatry, 44,* 434–440. (14)

Priest, R. F., & Sawyer, J. (1967). Proximity and peership: Bases of balance in interpersonal attraction. *American Journal of Sociology, 72,* 633–649. (16)

Probst, T., Krafczyk, S., Brandt, T., & Wist, E. R. (1984). Interaction between perceived self-motion and object-motion impairs vehicle guidance. *Science, 225,* 536–538. (5)

Provine, R. R., & Westerman, J. A. (1979). Crossing the midline: Limits of early eye-hand behavior. *Child Development, 50,* 437–441. (6)

Psychology today (4th ed.). (1979). New York: Random House. (10)

Purves, D., & Hadley, R. D. (1985). Changes in the dendritic branching of adult mammalian neurons revealed by repeated imaging *in situ. Nature, 315,* 404–406. (3)

Quinn, R. P. (1978). Physical deviance and occupational mistreatment: The short, the fat, and the ugly. Master's thesis, University of Michigan Survey Research Center, University of Michigan, Ann Arbor. (16)

Rabkin, J. G. (1979). Criminal behavior of discharged mental patients: A critical appraisal of the research. *Psychological Bulletin, 86,* 1–27. (15)

Rabkin, J. G. (1980). Stressful life events and schizophrenia: A review of the research literature. *Psychological Bulletin, 87,* 408–425. (14)

Rachman, S. (1969). Treatment by prolonged exposure to high intensity stimulation. *Behaviour Research and Therapy, 7,* 295–302. (14)

Rachman, S. J., & Hodgson, R. J. (1980). *Obsessions and compulsions.* Englewood Cliffs, NJ: Prentice-Hall. (14)

Radin, N. (1982). Primary caregiving and role-sharing fathers. In M. E. Lamb (Ed.), *Nontraditional families* (pp. 173–204). Hillsdale, NJ: Lawrence Erlbaum. (6)

Ransdell, S. E., & Fischler, I. (1987). Memory in a monolingual mode: When are bilinguals at a disadvantage? *Journal of Memory and Language, 26,* 392–405. (6)

Ratcliff, R. (1985). Theoretical interpretations of the speed and accuracy of positive and negative responses. *Psychological Review, 92,* 212–225. (9)

Ravussin, E., Lillioja, S., Knowler, W. C., Christin, L., Freymona, D., Abbott, W. G. H., Boyce, V., Howard, B. V., & Bogardus, C. (1988). Reduced rate of energy expenditure as a risk factor for body-weight gain. *New England Journal of Medicine, 318,* 467–472. (11)

Rechtschaffen, A., & Kales, A. (Eds.) (1968). *A manual of standardized terminology, techniques, and scoring system for sleep stages of human subjects.* Washington, DC: U.S. Government Printing Office. (4)

Redican, W. K. (1982). An evolutionary perspective on human facial displays. In P. Ekman (Ed.), *Emotion in the human face* (pp. 212–280). Cambridge, England: Cambridge University Press. (12)

Reed, T. E. (1985). Ethnic differences in alcohol use, abuse, and sensitivity: A review with genetic interpretation. *Social Biology, 32,* 195–209. (11)

Regier, D. A., Myers, J. K., Kramer, M., Robins, L. N., Blazer, D. G., Hough, R. L., Eaton, W. W., & Locke, B. Z. (1984). The NIMH epidemiologic catchment area program. *Archives of General Psychiatry, 41,* 934–941. (14)

Reich, J. (1986). The epidemiology of anxiety. *Journal of Nervous and Mental Disease, 174,* 129–136. (14)

Reicher, G. M. (1969). Perceptual recognition as a function of meaningfulness of stimulus material. *Journal of Experimental Psychology, 81,* 275–280. (9)

Reilly, R. R., Brown, B., Blood, M. R., & Malatesta, C. Z. (1981). The effects of realistic previews: A study and discussion of the literature. *Personnel Psychology, 34,* 823–834. (16)

Reisenzein, R. (1983). The Schachter theory of emotion: Two decades later. *Psychological Bulletin, 94,* 239–264. (16)

Renner, M. J., & Rosenzweig, M. R. (1987). *Enriched and impoverished environments: Effects on brain and behavior.* London: Springer-Verlag. (6)

Rensch, B., & Döhl, J. (1968). Wahlen zwischen zwei überschaubaren Labyrinthwegen durch einen

Schimpansen [Choice between two surveyable maze routes by a chimpanzee]. *Zeitschrift für Tierpsychologie, 25,* 216–231. (9)

Rensch, B. & Dücker, G. (1963). Haptisches Lern- und Unterscheidungs-Vermögen bei einem Waschbären. *Zeitschrift für Tierpsychologie, 20,* 608–615. (5)

Rescorla, R. A. (1968). Probability of shock in the presence and absence of CS in fear conditioning. *Journal of Comparative and Physiological Psychology, 66,* 1–5. (7)

Rescorla, R. (1985). Associationism in animal learning. In L.-G. Nilsson & T. Archer (Eds.), *Perspectives on learning and memory* (pp. 39–61). Hillsdale, NJ: Lawrence Erlbaum. (7)

Rescorla, R. A. (1988). Pavlovian conditioning: It's not what you think it is. *American Psychologist, 43,* 151–160. (7)

Rest, J. R. (1983). Morality. In P. H. Mussen (Ed.), *Handbook of child psychology* (4th ed.) (Vol. 3, pp. 556–629). New York: Wiley. (6)

Restle, F. (1970). Moon illusion explained on the basis of relative size. *Science, 167,* 1092–1096. (5)

Rhine, J. B. (1947). *The reach of the mind.* New York: William Sloane. (2)

Rice, M. L. (1989). Children's language acquisition. *American Psychologist, 44,* 149–156. (6)

Rich, C. L., Fowler, R. C., Fogarty, L. A., & Young, D. (1988). San Diego suicide study: III. Relationships between diagnoses and stressors. *Archives of General Psychiatry, 45,* 589–592. (14)

Rich, C. L., Ricketts, J. E., Fowler, R. C., & Young, D. (1988). Some differences between men and women who commit suicide. *American Journal of Psychiatry, 145,* 718–722. (14)

Richardson-Klavehn, A., & Bjork, R. A. (1988). Measures of memory. *Annual Review of Psychology, 39,* 475–543. (8)

Richter, C. P. (1929). Physiological factors involved in the electrical resistance of the skin. *American Journal of Physiology, 88,* 596–615. (12)

Richter, C. P. (1938). Two-day cycles of alternating good and bad behavior in psychotic patients. *Archives of Neurology and Psychiatry, 39,* 587–598. (14)

Richwald, G. A., Morisky, D. E., Kyle, G. R., Kristal, A. R., Gerber, M. M., & Friedland, J. M. (1988). Sexual activities in bathhouses in Los Angeles county: Implications for AIDS prevention education. *Journal of Sex Research, 25,* 169–180. (11)

Riley, J. N., & Walker, D. W. (1978). Morphological alterations in hippocampus after long-term alcohol consumption in mice. *Science, 201,* 646–648. (3)

Riley, V. (1981). Psychoneuroendocrine influences on immunocompetence and neoplasia. *Science, 212,* 1100–1109. (12)

Rincover, A. (1978). Sensory extinction: A procedure for eliminating self-stimulatory behavior in developmentally disabled children. *Journal of Abnormal Child Psychology, 6,* 299–310. (14)

Rips, L. J., Shoben, E. J., & Smith, E. E. (1973). Semantic distance and the verification of semantic relations. *Journal of Verbal Learning and Verbal Behavior, 12,* 1–20. (9)

Ritz, M. C., Lamb, R. J., Goldberg, S. R., & Kuhar, M. J. (1987). Cocaine receptors on dopamine transporters are related to self-administration of cocaine. *Science, 237,* 1219–1223. (4)

Roberts, A. H. (1985). Biofeedback: Research, training, and clinical roles. *American Psychologist, 40,* 938–941. (12)

Roberts, K. H., & Glick, W. (1981). The job characteristics approach to task design: A critical review. *Journal of Applied Psychology, 66,* 193–217. (16)

Roberts, S. B., Savage, J., Coward, W. A., Chew, B., & Lucas, A. (1988). Energy expenditure and intake in infants born to lean and overweight mothers. *New England Journal of Medicine, 318,* 461–466. (11)

Robins, L. N., Helzer, J. E., Weissman, M. M., Orvaschel, H., Gruenberg, E., Burke, J. D., Jr., & Regier, D. A. (1984). Lifetime prevalence of specific psychiatric disorders in three sites. *Archives of General Psychiatry, 41,* 949–958. (14)

Rock, I., & Kaufman, L. (1962). The moon illusion, II. *Science, 136,* 1023–1031. (5)

Rockwell, W. J. K., & Pinkerton, R. S. (1982). Single-session psychotherapy. *American Journal of Psychotherapy, 36,* 32–40. (15)

Rodin, J. (1986). Aging and health: Effects of the sense of control. *Science, 233,* 1271–1276. (6)

Roediger, H. L., III, & Crowder, R. G. (1976). A serial position effect in recall of United States presidents. *Bulletin of the Psychonomic Society, 8,* 275–278. (8)

Roediger, H. L., & Neely, J. H. (1982). Retrieval blocks in episodic and semantic memory. *Canadian Journal of Psychology, 36,* 213–242. (8)

Roffwarg, H. P., Muzio, J. N., & Dement, W. C. (1966). Ontogenetic development of human sleep-dream cycle. *Science, 152,* 604–609. (4)

Rogers, C. (1951). *Client-centered therapy.* Boston: Houghton Mifflin. (15)

Rogers, C. (1977). *On personal power.* New York: Delacorte. (13)

Rogers, C. (1980). *A way of being.* Boston: Houghton Mifflin. (13)

Romano, J. M., & Turner, J. A. (1985). Chronic pain and depression: Does the evidence support a relationship? *Psychological Bulletin, 97,* 18–34. (14)

Roose, S. P., Glassman, A. H., Walsh, B. T., Woodring, S., & Vital-Herne, J. (1983). Depression, delusions, and suicide. *American Journal of Psychiatry, 140,* 1159–1162. (14)

Rosch, E. (1978). Principles of categorization. In E. Rosch & B. B. Lloyd (Eds.), *Cognition and categorization* (pp. 27–48). Hillsdale, NJ: Lawrence Erlbaum. (9)

Rosch, E., & Mervis, C. B. (1975). Family resemblances: Studies in the internal structure of categories. *Cognitive Psychology, 7,* 573–605. (9)

Rose, J. E., Brugge, J. F., Anderson, D. J., & Hind, J. E. (1967). Phase-locked response to low-frequency tones in single auditory nerve fibers of the squirrel monkey. *Journal of Neurophysiology, 30,* 769–793. (5)

Rose, S. A., & Wallace, I. F. (1985). Cross-modal and intramodal transfer as predictors of mental development in full-term and preterm infants. *Developmental Psychology, 21,* 949–962. (10)

Rosenbaum, M., & Smira, K. B. (1986). Cognitive and personality factors in the delay of gratification of hemodialysis patients. *Journal of Personality and Social Psychology, 51,* 357–364. (7)

Rosenbaum, M. E. (1980). Cooperation and competition. In P. B. Paulus (Ed.), *The psychology of group influence.* Hillsdale, NJ: Lawrence Erlbaum. (16)

Rosenhan, D. L. (1973). On being sane in insane places. *Science, 179,* 250–258. (15)

Rosenman, A. A. (1987). The relationship between auditory discrimination and oral production of Spanish sounds in children and adults. *Journal of Psycholinguistic Research, 16,* 517–534. (6)

Rosenthal, R., & Rubin, D. B. (1978). Interpersonal expectancy effects: The first 345 studies. *Behavioral and Brain Sciences, 3,* 377–415. (1)

Ross, L. (1977). The intuitive psychologist and his shortcomings: Distortions in the attribution process. In L. Berkowitz (Ed.), *Advances in experimental social psychology* (Vol. 10, pp. 173–220). New York: Academic Press. (16)

Rothbart, M., Fulero, S., Jensen, C., Howard, J., & Birrell, P. (1978). From individual to group impressions: Availability heuristics in stereotype formation. *Journal of Experimental Social Psychology, 14,* 237–255. (9)

Rothbart, M., & John, O. P. (1985). Social categorization and behavioral episodes: A cognitive analysis of the effects of intergroup contact. *Journal of Social Issues, 41,* 81–104. (16)

Rotter, J. B. (1966). Generalized expectancies for internal versus external control of reinforcement. *Psychological Monographs, 80*(Whole No. 603). (13)

Rotton, J., & Kelly, I. W. (1985). Much ado about the full moon: A meta-analysis of lunar-lunacy research. *Psychological Bulletin, 97,* 286–306. (2)

Rovee-Collier, C. (1984). The ontogeny of learning and memory in human infancy. In R. Kail & N. E. Spear (Eds.), *Comparative perspectives on the development of memory* (pp. 103–134). Hillsdale, NJ: Lawrence Erlbaum. (6)

Rowe, J. W., & Kahn, R. L. (1987). Human aging: Usual and successful. *Science, 237,* 143–149. (6)

Rowland, C. V., Jr. (Ed.) (1970). *Anorexia and obesity.* Boston: Little, Brown. (11)

Roy, A. (1985). Early parental separation and adult depression. *Archives of General Psychiatry, 42,* 987–991. (14)

Royce, J. R., & Powell, A. (1983). *Theory of personality and individual differences: Factors, systems, and processes.* Englewood Cliffs, NJ: Prentice-Hall. (13)

Rozin, P. (1968). Specific aversions and neophobia as a consequence of vitamin deficiency and/or poisoning in half-wild and domestic rats. *Journal of Comparative and Physiological Psychology, 66,* 82–88. (11)

Rozin, P. (1969). Central or peripheral mediation of learning with long CS-US intervals in the feeding system. *Journal of Comparative and Physiological Psychology, 67,* 421–429. (7)

Rozin, P., & Fallon, A. E. (1987). A perspective on disgust. *Psychological Review, 94,* 23–41. (11)

Rozin, P., Fallon, A., & Augustoni-Ziskind, M. L. (1986). The child's conception of food: The development of categories of acceptable and rejected substances. *Journal of Nutrition Education, 18,* 75–81. (11)

Rozin, P., Hammer, L., Oster, H., Horowitz, T., & Marmora, V. (1986). The child's conception of food: Differentiation of categories of rejected substances in the 16 months to 5 year age range. *Appetite, 7,* 141–151. (11)

Rozin, P., & Kalat, J. W. (1971). Specific hungers and poison avoidance as adaptive specializations of learning. *Psychological Review, 78,* 459–486. (11)

Rozin, P., Millman, L., & Nemeroff, C. (1986). Operation of the laws of sympathetic magic in disgust and other domains. *Journal of Personality and Social Psychology, 50,* 703–712. (11)

Rubenstein, J. L. (1985). The effects of maternal employment on young children. *Applied Developmental Psychology, 2,* 99–128. (6)

Rubenstein, R., & Newman, R. (1954). The living out of "future" experiences under hypnosis. *Science, 119,* 472–473. (4)

Rubin, D. C. (1977). Very long-term memory for prose and verse. *Journal of Verbal Learning and Verbal Behavior, 16,* 611–621. (8)

Rubin, D. C., Wetzler, S. E., & Nebes, R. D. (1986). Autobiographical memory across the lifespan. In D. C. Rubin (Ed.), *Autobiographical memory* (pp. 202–221). Cambridge, England: Cambridge University Press. (8)

Rubin, Z. (1970). Measurement of romantic love. *Journal of Personality and Social Psychology, 16,* 265–273. (16)

Rubin, Z. (1973). *Liking and loving: An invitation to social psychology.* New York: Holt, Rinehart, & Winston. (16)

Rubin, Z. (1974). Lovers and other strangers: The development of intimacy in encounters and relationships. *American Scientist, 62,* 182–190. (16)

Rubin, Z., Hill, C. T., Peplau, L. A., & Dunkel-Schetter, C. (1980). Self-disclosure in dating couples: Sex roles and the ethic of openness. *Journal of Marriage and the Family, 42,* 305–317. (6)

Rubin, Z., Peplau, L. A., & Hill, C. T. (1981). Loving and leaving: Sex differences in romantic attachments. *Sex Roles, 7,* 821–835. (16)

Ruch, J. (1984). *Psychology: The personal science.* Belmont, CA: Wadsworth. (3)

Rudden, M., Gilmore, M., & Allen, F. (1982). Delusions: When to confront the facts of life? *American Journal of Psychiatry, 139,* 929–932. (14)

Ruderman, A. J. (1986). Dietary restraint: A theoretical and empirical review. *Psychological Review, 99*, 247–262. (11)

Ruderman, A. J., & Christensen, H. C. (1983). Restraint theory and its applicability to overweight individuals. *Journal of Abnormal Psychology, 92*, 210–215. (11)

Rumelhart, D. E., & McClelland, J. L. (1982). An interactive activation model of context effects in letter perception: Part 2, The contextual enhancement effect and some tests and extensions of the model. *Psychological Review, 89*, 60–94. (9)

Rumelhart, D. E., McClelland, J. L., & the PDP Research Group. (1986). *Parallel distributed processing.* Cambridge, MA: MIT Press. (8)

Rusbult, C. E. (1980). Commitment and satisfaction in romantic associations: A test of the investment model. *Journal of Experimental Social Psychology, 16*, 172–186. (16)

Rusbult, C. E., & Zembrodt, I. M. (1983). Response to dissatisfaction in romantic involvements: A multidimensional scaling analysis. *Journal of Experimental Social Psychology, 19*, 274–293. (16)

Rushing, W. J. (1986). Ritual and myth: Native American culture and abstract expressionism. In *The spiritual in art: Abstract painting 1890–1985* (pp. 273–295). New York: Abbeville Press; Los Angeles: Los Angeles County Museum of Art. (13)

Russell, G. F. M., Szmukler, G. I., Dare, C., & Eisler, I. (1987). An evaluation of family therapy in anorexia nervosa and bulimia nervosa. *Archives of General Psychiatry, 44*, 1047–1056. (11)

Russell, M. J., Switz, G. M., & Thompson, K. (1980). Olfactory influences on the human menstrual cycle. *Pharmacology, Biochemistry, and Behavior, 13*, 737–738. (5)

Saarinen, T. F. (1973). The use of projective techniques in geographic research. In W. H. Ittelson (Ed.), *Environment and cognition* (pp. 29–52). New York: Seminar Press. (9)

Sabo, K. T., & Kirtley, D. D. (1982). Objects and activities in the dreams of the blind. *International Journal of Rehabilitation Research, 5*, 241–242. (4)

Sachs, J. S. (1967). Recognition memory for syntactic and semantic aspects of connected discourse. *Perception and Psychophysics, 2*, 437–442. (6)

Sadger, J. (1941). Preliminary study of the psychic life of the fetus and the primary germ. *Psychoanalytic Review, 28*, 327–358. (2)

Saegert, S., Swap, W., & Zajonc, R. B. (1973). Exposure, context, and interpersonal attraction. *Journal of Personality and Social Psychology, 25*, 234–242. (16)

Sakurai, Y., & Sugimoto, S. (1986). Multiple unit activity of prefrontal cortex and dorsomedial thalamus during delayed go/no-go alternation in the rat. *Behavioural Brain Research, 20*, 295–301. (3)

Salzarulo, P., & Chevalier, A. (1983). Sleep problems in children and their relationship with early disturbances of the waking-sleeping rhythms. *Sleep, 6*, 47–51. (4)

Samelson, F. (1980). J. B. Watson's little Albert, Cyril Burt's twins, and the need for a critical science. *American Scientist, 35*, 619–625. (14)

Samuelson, C. D., Messick, D. M., Rutte, C. G., & Wilke, H. (1984). Individual and structural solutions to resource dilemmas in two cultures. *Journal of Personality and Social Psychology, 47*, 94–104. (16)

Santrock, J. W., Warshak, R. A., & Elliott, G. L. (1982). Social development and parent-child interaction in father-custody and stepmother families. In M. E. Lamb (Ed.), *Nontraditional families* (pp. 289–314). Hillsdale, NJ: Lawrence Erlbaum. (6)

Satinoff, E. (1983). A reevaluation of the concept of the homeostatic organization of temperature regulation. In E. Satinoff & P. Teitelbaum (Eds.), *Handbook of behavioral neurobiology: Vol. 6, Motivation* (pp. 443–472). New York: Plenum. (11)

Sattler, J. M., & Gwynne, J. (1982). White examiners generally do not impede the intelligence test performance of black children: To debunk a myth. *Journal of Consulting and Clinical Psychology, 50*, 196–208. (10)

Savage-Rumbaugh, E. W., Rumbaugh, D. M., Smith, S. T., & Lawson, J. (1980). Reference: The linguistic essential. *Science, 210*, 922–925. (6)

Savage-Rumbaugh, S., McDonald, K., Sevcik, R. A., Hopkins, W. D., & Rubert, E. (1986). Spontaneous symbol acquisition and communicative use by pygmy chimpanzees *(Pan paniscus). Journal of Experimental Psychology: General, 115*, 211–235. (6)

Scarborough, E., & Furomoto, L. (1987). *Untold lives: The first generation of American women psychologists.* New York: Columbia University Press. (1)

Scarr, S. (1968). Environmental bias in twin studies. *Eugenics Quarterly, 15*, 34–40. (10)

Scarr, S., & Carter-Saltzman, L. (1979). Twin method: Defense of a critical assumption. *Behavior Genetics, 9*, 527–542. (10)

Scarr, S., Pakstis, A. J., Katz, S. H., & Barker, W. B. (1977). The absence of a relationship between degree of white ancestry and intellectual skills within a black population. *Human Genetics, 39*, 69–86. (10)

Scarr, S., & Weinberg, R. A. (1976). IQ test performance of black children adopted by white families. *American Psychologist, 31*, 726–739. (10)

Schachter, D. L. (1983). Amnesia observed: Remembering and forgetting in a natural environment. *Journal of Abnormal Psychology, 92*, 236–242. (8)

Schachter, D. L. (1986a). Amnesia and crime: How much do we really know? *American Psychologist, 41*, 286–295. (8)

Schachter, D. L. (1986b). Feeling-of-knowing ratings distinguish between genuine and simulated forgetting. *Journal of Experimental Psychology: Learning, Memory, & Cognition, 12*, 30–41. (8)

Schachter, D. L. (1987a). Implicit memory: History and current status. *Journal of Experimental Psychology: Learning, Memory, & Cognition, 13*, 501–518. (8)

Schachter, D. L. (1987b). Memory, amnesia, and frontal lobe dysfunction. *Psychobiology, 15*, 21–36. (8)

Schachter, S. (1959). *The psychology of affiliation.* Stanford, CA: Stanford University Press. (16)

Schachter, S. (1968). Obesity and eating. *Science, 161*, 751–756. (11)

Schachter, S. (1971). Some extraordinary facts about obese humans and rats. *American Psychologist, 26*, 129–144. (11)

Schachter, S. (1982). Recidivism and self-cure of smoking and obesity. *American Psychologist, 37*, 436–444. (11, 14)

Schachter, S., & Rodin, J. (1974). *Obese humans and rats.* New York: Wiley. (11)

Schachter, S., & Singer, J. (1962). Cognitive, social, and physiological determinants of emotional state. *Psychological Review, 69*, 379–399. (12)

Schaie, K., & Strother, C. (1968). A cross-sequential study of age changes in cognitive behavior. *Psychological Bulletin, 70*, 671–680. (6)

Schallert, T. (1983). Sensorimotor impairment and recovery of function in brain-damaged rats: Reappearance of symptoms during old age. *Behavioral Neuroscience, 97*, 159–164. (3)

Schank, R. C. (1984). *The cognitive computer.* Reading, MA: Addison-Wesley. (9)

Schiffman, S. S. (1983). Taste and smell in disease. *New England Journal of Medicine, 308*, 1275–1279, 1337–1343. (5)

Schiffman, S. S., Diaz, C., & Beeker, T. G. (1986). Caffeine intensifies taste of certain sweeteners: Role of adenosine receptor. *Pharmacology, Biochemistry, & Behavior, 24*, 429–432. (5)

Schiffman, S. S., & Erickson, R. P. (1971). A psychophysical model for gustatory quality. *Physiology & Behavior, 7*, 617–633. (5)

Schiffman, S. S., Simon, S. A., Gill, J. M., & Beeker, T. G. (1988). Bretylium tosylate enhances salt taste

via amiloride-sensitive pathway. *Annals of the New York Academy of Sciences, 510*, 584–586. (5)

Schlesier-Stropp, B. (1984). Bulimia: A review of the literature. *Psychological Review, 95*, 247–257. (11)

Schlossberg, N. K. (1984). Exploring the adult years. The *G. Stanley Hall Lecture Series, 4*, 101–154. (6)

Schmidt, F. L., & Hunter, J. E. (1981). Employment testing: Old theories and new research findings. *American Psychologist, 36*, 1128–1137. (16)

Schmitt, N. (1976). Social and situational determinants of interview decisions: Implications for the employment interview. *Personnel Psychology, 29*, 79–101. (16)

Schneck, M. K., Reisberg, B., & Ferris, S. H. (1982). An overview of current concepts of Alzheimer's disease. *American Journal of Psychiatry, 139*, 165–173. (3)

Schneider, C. J. (1987). Cost effectiveness of biofeedback and behavioral medicine treatments: A review of the literature. *Biofeedback and Self-Regulation, 12*, 71–92. (12)

Schneider, K. (1984). The cognitive basis of task choice in preschool children. *Advances in Motivation and Achievement, 3*, 57–72. (11)

Schoenfeld, A. H. (1985). *Mathematical problem solving.* Orlando, FL: Academic Press. (9)

Schooler, C. (1972). Birth order effects: Not here, not now! *Psychological Bulletin, 78*, 161–175. (6)

Schöpf, J., Bryois, C., Jonquière, M., & Le, P. K. (1984). On the nosology of severe psychiatric post-partum disorders. *European Archives of Psychiatry and Neurological Sciences, 234*, 54–63. (14)

Schopler, E. (1987). Specific and nonspecific factors in the effectiveness of a treatment system. *American Psychologist, 42*, 376–383. (14)

Schuckit, M. A. (1985). Ethanol-induced changes in body sway in men at high alcoholism risk. *Archives of General Psychiatry, 42*, 375–379. (14)

Schulsinger, F., Knop, J., Goodwin, D. W., Teasdale, T. W., & Mikkelsen, U. (1986). A prospective study of young men at high risk for alcoholism. *Archives of General Psychiatry, 43*, 755–760. (14)

Schuman, H., & Scott, J. (1987). Problems in the use of survey questions to measure public opinion. *Science, 236*, 957–959. (2)

Schusterman, R. J., & Krieger, K. (1986). Artificial language comprehension and size transposition by a California sea lion *(Zalophus californianus). Journal of Comparative Psychology, 100*, 348–355. (6)

Schwartz, B. (1981). Does helplessness cause depression, or do only depressed people become helpless? Comment on Alloy and Abramson. *Journal of Experimental Psychology: General, 110*, 429–435. (14)

Schwartz, F. N. (1989, January-February). Management women and the new facts of life. *Harvard Business Review*, 65–76. (11)

Schwartz, G. E. (1975). Biofeedback, self-regulation, and the patterning of physiological processes. *American Scientist, 63*, 314–324. (12)

Schwartz, G. E. (1982). Psychophysiological patterning and emotion revisited: A systems perspective. In C. E. Izard (Ed.), *Measuring emotions in infants and children* (pp. 67–93). Cambridge, England: Cambridge University Press. (12)

Schwartz, G. E. (1987). Personality and health: An integrative health science approach. *G. Stanley Hall Lecture Series, 7*, 125–157. (12)

Schwarzwald, J., Bizman, A., & Raz, M. (1983). The foot-in-the-door paradigm: Effects of second request size on donation probability and donor generosity. *Personality and Social Psychology Bulletin, 9*, 443–450. (16)

Schweder, R. (1982). Fact and artifact in trait perception: The systematic distortion hypothesis. *Progress in Experimental Personality Research, 11*, 65–100. (13)

Sclafani, A., & Springer, D. (1976). Dietary obesity in adult rats: Similarities to hypothalamic and human obesity syndromes. *Physiology & Behavior, 17*, 461–471. (11)

Scott, W. E. (1976). The effects of extrinsic rewards on "intrinsic motivation." *Organizational Behavior & Human Performance, 15*, 117–129. (11)

Scovern, A. W., & Kilmann, P. R. (1980). Status of electroconvulsive therapy: Review of the outcome literature. *Psychological Bulletin, 87*, 260–303. (15)

Scribner, S. (1986). Thinking in action: Some characteristics of practical thought. In R. J. Sternberg & R. K. Wagner (Eds.), *Practical intelligence* (pp. 13–30). Cambridge, England: Cambridge University Press. (10)

Secord, P. F., Dukes, W. F., & Bevan, W. (1954). Personalities in face: I. An experiment in social perceiving. *Genetic Psychology Monographs, 49*, 231–279. (16)

Seeman, P., & Lee, T. (1975). Antipsychotic drugs: Direct correlation between clinical potency and presynaptic action on dopamine neurons. *Science, 188*, 1217–1219. (14)

Seeman, P., Lee, T., Chau-Wong, M., & Wong, K. (1976). Antipsychotic drug doses and neuroleptic/dopamine receptors. *Nature, 261*, 717–719. (15)

Segal, N. (1985). Monozygotic and dizygotic twins: A comparative analysis of mental ability profiles. *Child Development, 56*, 1051–1058. (3)

Seidman, L. J. (1983). Schizophrenia and brain dysfunction: An integration of recent neurodiagnostic findings. *Psychological Bulletin, 94*, 195–238. (14)

Selfridge, O. (1959). Pandemonium: A paradigm for learning. In *Symposium on the mechanisation of thought processes* (Vol. 1, pp. 513–526). London: H. M. Stationery Office. (5)

Seligman, M. E. P. (1970). On the generality of the laws of learning. *Psychological Review, 77*, 406–418. (7)

Seligman, M. E. P. (1971). Phobias and preparedness. *Behavior Therapy, 2*, 307–320. (11)

Selye, H. (1979). Stress, cancer, and the mind. In J. Taché, H. Selye, & S. B. Day (Eds.), *Cancer, stress, and death* (pp. 11–27). New York: Plenum. (12)

Semeonoff, B. (1976). *Projective techniques*. London: Wiley. (13)

Shannon, D. A. (1955). *The Socialist Party of America*. New York: Macmillan. (16)

Shapiro, D. A., & Shapiro, D. (1982). Meta-analysis of comparative therapy outcome studies: A replication and refinement. *Psychological Bulletin, 92*, 581–604. (15)

Shapiro, D. L. (1985). Insanity and the assessment of criminal responsibility. In C. P. Ewing (Ed.), *Psychology, psychiatry, and the law: A clinical and forensic handbook* (pp. 67–94). Sarasota, FL: Professional Resource Exchange. (15)

Shapiro, S., Skinner, E. A., Kessler, L. G., Von Korff, M., German, P. S., Tischler, G. L., Leaf, P. J., Benham, L., Cottler, L., & Regier, D. A. (1984). Utilization of health and mental health services. *Archives of General Psychiatry, 41*, 971–978. (14, 15)

Shavit, Y., Terman, G. W., Martin, F. C., Lewis, J. W., Liebeskind, J. C., & Gale, R. P. (1985). Stress, opioid peptides, the immune system, and cancer. *Journal of Immunology, 135*, 834S–837S. (12)

Shepard, R. N., & Metzler, J. N. (1971). Mental rotation of three-dimensional objects. *Science, 171*, 701–703. (9)

Shepher, J. (1971). Mate selection among second generation kibbutz adolescents and adults: Incest avoidance and negative imprinting. *Archives of Sexual Behavior, 1*, 293–307. (6)

Sher, K. J., Frost, R. O., Kushner, M., Crews, T. M., & Alexander, J. E. (1989). Memory deficits in compulsive checkers: Replication and extension in a clinical sample. *Behaviour Research and Therapy, 27*, 65–69. (14)

Sher, K. J., Frost, R. O., & Otto, R. (1983). Cognitive deficits in compulsive checkers: An exploratory study. *Behaviour Research and Therapy, 21*, 357–363. (14)

Sherif, M. (1935). A study of some social factors in perception. *Archives of Psychology, 27*, 1–60. (16)

Sherman, S. J., Judd, C. M., & Park, B. (1989). Social cognition. In M. R. Rosenzweig & L. W. Porter (Eds.) *Annual Review of Psychology* (Vol. 40, pp. 281–326). Palo Alto, CA: Annual Reviews. (16)

Sherrod, D. R., Hage, J. N., Halpern, P. L., & Moore, B. S. (1977). Effects of personal causation and perceived control on responses to an aversive environment: The more control, the better. *Journal of Experimental Social Psychology, 13*, 14–27. (12)

Sherwood, G. G. (1981). Self-serving biases in person perception: A reexamination of projection as a mechanism of defense. *Psychological Bulletin, 90*, 445–459. (13)

Shields, R. B. (1978). The usefulness of the Rorschach Prognostic Rating Scale: A rebuttal. *Journal of Personality Assessment, 42*, 579–582. (13)

Sidman, M., Herrnstein, R. J., & Conrad, D. G. (1957). Maintenance of avoidance behavior by unavoidable shocks. *Journal of Comparative and Physiological Psychology, 50*, 553–557. (14)

Siegel, S. (1977). Morphine tolerance as an associative process. *Journal of Experimental Psychology: Animal Behavior Processes, 3*, 1–13. (14)

Siegel, S. (1983). Classical conditioning, drug tolerance, and drug dependence. *Research Advances in Alcohol and Drug Problems, 7*, 207–246. (14)

Siegel, S. (1987). Alcohol and opiate dependence: Reevaluation of the Victorian perspective. *Research Advances in Alcohol and Drug Problems, 9*, 279–314. (14)

Siegelman, M. (1974). Parental background of male homosexuals and heterosexuals. *Archives of Sexual Behavior, 3*, 3–18. (11)

Siegler, R. S., & Richards, D. D. (1982). The development of intelligence. In R. J. Sternberg (Ed.), *Handbook of human intelligence* (pp. 897–971). Cambridge, England: Cambridge University Press. (10)

Sigall, H., & Ostrove, N. (1975). Beautiful but dangerous: Effects of offender attractiveness and nature of the crime on juridic judgment. *Journal of Personality and Social Psychology, 31*, 410–414. (16)

Silverman, I. (1971). Physical attractiveness. *Sexual Behavior*, September, 22–25. (16)

Silverman, J. S., Silverman, J. A., & Eardley, D. A. (1984). Do maladaptive attitudes cause depression? *Archives of General Psychiatry, 41*, 28–30. (14)

Silverstein, A. (1988). An Aristotelian resolution of the idiographic versus nomothetic tension. *American Psychologist, 43*, 425–430. (13)

Simmons, E. J. (1949). *Leo Tolstoy*. London: John Lehmann. (14)

Simonton, D. K. (1988). Age and outstanding achievement: What do we know after a century of research? *Psychological Bulletin, 104*, 251–267. (9)

Sines, J. O. (1979). Non-pharmacological and non-surgical resistance to stress ulcers in temperamentally and physiologically susceptible rats. *Journal of Psychosomatic Research, 23*, 77–82. (12)

Sinex, F. M., & Myers, R. H. (1982). Alzheimer's disease, Down's syndrome, and aging: The genetic approach. *Annals of the New York Academy of Sciences, 396*, 3–13. (3)

Singer, J. L. (1981). Clinical intervention: New developments in methods and evaluation. *G. Stanley Hall Lecture Series, 1*, 101–128. (15)

Siqueland, E. R., & Lipsitt, L. P. (1966). Conditioned head-turning in human newborns. *Journal of Experimental Child Psychology, 3*, 356–376. (6)

Sizemore, C. C., & Pittillo, E. S. (1977). *I'm Eve*. Garden City, NY: Doubleday. (14)

Skeels, H. M. (1966). Adult status of children with contrasting early life experiences. *Monographs of the Society for Research in Child Development, 31*, 1–65. (10)

Skeptical Inquirer (1978a). Psychic vibrations. *Skeptical Inquirer, 3*(2), 13. (2)

Skeptical Inquirer (1978b). Psychic vibrations. *Skeptical Inquirer, 2*(2), 23. (2)

Skinner, B. F. (1938). *The behavior of organisms*. New York: D. Appleton-Century. (7)

Skinner, B. F. (1956). A case history in scientific method. *American Psychologist, 11*, 221–233. (7)

Skinner, B. F. (1960). Pigeons in a pelican. *American Psychologist, 15*, 28–37. (7)

Skinner, B. F. (1961, November). Teaching machines. *Scientific American*.

Skinner, B. F. (1983). Intellectual self-management in old age. *American Psychologist, 38*, 239–244. (8)

Skowronski, J. J., & Carlston, D. E. (1987). Social judgment and social memory: The role of cue diagnosticity in negativity, positivity, and extremity biases. *Journal of Personality and Social Psychology, 52*, 689–699. (16)

Slamecka, N. J. (1968). An examination of trace storage in free recall. *Journal of Experimental Psychology, 76*, 504–513. (8)

Slobin, D. I. (1979). *Psycholinguistics* (2nd ed.). Glenview, IL: Scott, Foresman. (6)

Smith, E. E., Shoben, E. J., & Rips, L. J. (1974). Structure and process in semantic memory: A featural model for semantic decisions. *Psychological Review, 81*, 214–241. (9)

Smith, F. J. (1977). Work attitudes as predictors of attendance on a specific day. *Journal of Applied Psychology, 62*, 16–19. (16)

Smith, G. P., & Gibbs, J. (1987). The effect of gut peptides on hunger, satiety, and food intake in humans. *Annals of the New York Academy of Sciences, 499*, 132–136. (14)

Smith, J. M., & Baldessarini, R. J. (1980). Changes in prevalence, severity, and recovery in tardive dyskinesia with age. *Archives of General Psychiatry, 37*, 1368–1373. (15)

Smith, M. L. (1988). Recall of spatial location by the amnesic patient H. M. *Brain and Cognition, 7*, 178–183. (8)

Smith, M. L., & Glass, G. V. (1977). Meta-analysis of psychotherapy outcome studies. *American Psychologist, 32*, 752–760. (15)

Smith, S., & Haythorn, W. (1972). Effects of compatibility, crowding, group size, and leadership seniority on stress, anxiety, hostility, and annoyance in isolated groups. *Journal of Personality and Social Psychology, 22*, 67–79. (12)

Smythies, J. R. (1982). Biological markers for the schizophrenic and atypical psychoses. *Journal of Nervous and Mental Disease, 170*, 732–736. (14)

Snyder, G. L., & Stricker, E. M. (1985). Effects of lateral hypothalamic lesions on food intake of rats during exposure to cold. *Behavioral Neuroscience, 99*, 310–322. (3)

Snyder, M. (1979). Self-monitoring process. *Advances in Experimental Social Psychology, 12*, 85–128. (13)

Snyder, M., Gangestad, S., & Simpson, J. A. (1983). Choosing friends as activity partners: The role of self-monitoring. *Journal of Personality and Social Psychology, 45*, 1061–1072. (13)

Snyder, M., & Uranowitz, S. W. (1978). Reconstructing the past: Some cognitive consequences of person perception. *Journal of Personality and Social Psychology, 36*, 941–950. (8)

Snyder, S. H. (1984). Drug and neurotransmitter receptors in the brain. *Science, 224*, 22–31. (3)

Snyderman, M., & Herrnstein, R. J. (1983). Intelligence tests and the Immigration Act of 1924. *American Psychologist, 38*, 986–995. (10)

Snyderman, M., & Rothman, S. (1987). Survey of expert opinion on intelligence and aptitude testing. *American Psychologist, 42*, 137–144. (10)

Sobell, M. B., & Sobell, L. C. (1976). Second-year treatment outcome of alcoholics treated by individualized behavior therapy: Results. *Behaviour Research and Therapy, 14*, 195–215. (14)

Sobell, M. B., & Sobell, L. C. (1984). The aftermath of heresy: A response to Pendery et al.'s (1982) critique of "individualized behavior therapy for alcoholics." *Behaviour Research and Therapy, 22*, 413–440. (14)

Soldatos, C. R., & Kales, A. (1982). Sleep disorders: Research in psychopathology and its practical implications. *Acta Psychiatrica Scandinavica, 65,* 381–387. (4)

Solomon, R. L. (1980). The opponent-process theory of acquired motivation. *American Psychologist, 35,* 691–712. (12, 14)

Solomon, R. L., & Corbit, J. D. (1974). An opponent-process theory of motivation: I. Temporal dynamics of affect. *Psychological Review, 81,* 119–145. (12, 14, 16)

Solomon, R. S., & Solomon, V. (1982). Differential diagnosis of the multiple personality. *Psychological Reports, 51,* 1187–1194. (14)

Solomon, Z., Mikulincer, M., & Flum, H. (1988). Negative life events, coping responses, and combat-related psychopathology: A prospective study. *Journal of Abnormal Psychology, 97,* 302–307. (12)

Sonenstein, F. L., Pleck, J. H., & Ku, L. C. (1989). Sexual activiy, condom use and AIDS awareness among adolescent men. *Family Planning Perspectives, 21,* 152–158. (11)

Spanos, N. P. (1987–88). Past-life hypnotic regression: A critical view. *Skeptical Inquirer, 12,* 174–180. (4)

Spearman, C. (1904). "General intelligence," objectively determined and measured. *American Journal of Psychology, 15,* 201–293. (10)

Spence, J. T. (1984). Masculinity, femininity, and gender-related traits: A conceptual analysis and critique of current research. *Progress in Experimental Personality Research, 13,* 1–97. (13)

Sperling, G. (1960). The information available in brief visual presentations. *Psychological Monographs, 74*(11), Whole No. 498). (8)

Sperry, R. W. (1967). Split-brain approach to learning problems. In G. C. Quarton, T. Melnechuk, & F. O. Schmitt (Eds.), *The neurosciences: A study program* (pp. 714–722). New York: Rockefeller University Press. (3)

Spitz, R. A. (1945). Hospitalism: An inquiry into the genesis of psychiatric conditions in early childhood. *Psychoanalytic Study of the Child, 1,* 53–74. (6)

Spitz, R. A. (1946). Hospitalism: A follow-up report. *Psychoanalytic Study of the Child, 2,* 113–117. (6)

Spring, B., Chiodo, J., & Bowen, D. J. (1987). Carbohydrates, tryptophan, and behavior: A methodological review. *Psychological Bulletin, 102,* 234–256. (3)

Squire, L. R. (1982). The neuropsychology of human memory. *Annual Review of Neuroscience, 5,* 241–273. (8)

Squyres, E. M., & Craddick, R. A. (1982). A measure of time perspective with the TAT and some measures of reliability. *Journal of Personality Assessment, 46,* 257–259. (13)

Stager, G. L., & Lundy, R. M. (1985). Hypnosis and the learning and recall of visually presented material. *International Journal of Clinical and Experimental Hypnosis, 33,* 27–39. (4)

Stanford, L. R. (1987). Conduction velocity variations minimize conduction time differences among retinal ganglion cell axons. *Science, 238,* 358–360. (5)

Stanovich, K. E. (1986). *How to think straight about psychology.* Glenview, IL: Scott, Foresman. (2)

Stapp, J., Tucker, A. M., & VandenBos, G. R. (1985). Census of psychological personnel: 1983. *American Psychologist, 40,* 1317–1351. (1)

Stark, R. (1989). *Sociology* (3rd ed.). Belmont, CA: Wadsworth. (6, 12)

Starr, C., & Taggart, R. (1989). *Biology: The unity and diversity of life* (5th ed.). Belmont, CA: Wadsworth.

Stegat, H. (1975). Die Verhaltenstherapie der Enuresis und Enkopresis [Behavior therapy for enuresis and encopresis]. *Zeitschrift für Kinder- und Jugend-psychiatrie, 3,* 149–173. (3)

Stein, J. A., Newcomb, M. D., & Bentler, P. M. (1986). Stability and change in personality: A longitudinal study from early adolescence to young adulthood. *Journal of Research in Personality, 20,* 276–291. (13)

Stein, L., & Wise, C. D. (1971). Possible etiology of schizophrenia: Progressive damage to the noradrenergic reward system by 6-hydroxydopamine. *Science, 171,* 1032–1036. (14)

Sternberg, R. J. (1985). *Beyond IQ.* Cambridge, England: Cambridge University Press. (10)

Sternberg, R. (1986). A triangular theory of love. *Psychological Review, 93,* 119–135. (16)

Sternberg, R. J., & Grajek, S. (1984). The nature of love. *Journal of Personality and Social Psychology, 47,* 312–329. (16)

Sternberg, S. (1967). Two operations in character recognition: Some evidence from reaction-time measurements. *Perception and Psychophysics, 2,* 45–53. (9)

Stevens, A., & Coupe, P. (1978). Distortions in judged spatial relations. *Cognitive Psychology, 10,* 422–437. (9)

Stevens, S. S. (1961). To honor Fechner and repeal his law. *Science, 133,* 80–86. (5)

Stewart, J. E. (1980). Defendant's attractiveness as a factor in the outcome of criminal trials: An observational study. *Journal of Applied Social Psychology, 10,* 348–361. (16)

Stiles, W. B., Shapiro, D. A., & Elliott, R. (1986). "Are all psychotherapies equivalent?" *American Psychologist, 41,* 165–180. (15)

Stipek, D. J. (1984). Young children's performance expectations: Logical analysis or wishful thinking? *Advances in Motivation and Achievement, 3,* 33–56. (11)

Stoffregen, T. A., & Riccio, G. E. (1988). An ecological theory of orientation and the vestibular system. *Psychological Review, 95,* 3–14. (5)

Storms, M. D. (1973). Videotape and the attribution process: Reversing actors' and observers' points of view. *Journal of Personality and Social Psychology, 27,* 165–175. (16)

Strack, F., Martin, L. L., & Stepper, S. (1988). Inhibiting and facilitating conditions of the human smile: A nonobtrusive test of the facial feedback hypothesis. *Journal of Personality and Social Psychology, 54,* 768–777. (12)

Streather, A., & Hinson, R. E. (1985). Neurochemical and behavioral factors in the development of tolerance to anorectics. *Behavioral Neuroscience, 99,* 842–852. (14)

Streissguth, A. P., Barr, H. M., & Martin, D. C. (1983). Maternal alcohol use and neonatal habituation assessed with the Brazelton scale. *Child Development, 54,* 1109–1118. (6)

Strickland, L. H. (1958). Surveillance and trust. *Journal of Personality, 26,* 200–215. (16)

Striegel-Moore, R. H., Silberstein, L. R., & Rodin, J. (1986). Toward an understanding of risk factors for bulimia. *American Psychologist, 41,* 246–263. (11)

Stromeyer, C. F., III. (1970, December). Eidetikers. *Psychology Today,* pp. 76–80. (8)

Strupp, H. H. (1986). Psychotherapy: Research, practice, and public policy (How to avoid dead ends). *American Psychologist, 41,* 120–130. (15)

Strupp, H. H., & Hadley, S. W. (1979). Specific vs. nonspecific factors in psychotherapy. *Archives of General Psychiatry, 36,* 1125–1136. (15)

Stunkard, A. J., Sørensen, T. I. A., Hanis, C., Teasdale, T. W., Chakraborty, R., Shull, W. J., & Schulinger, F. (1986). An adoption study of human obesity. *New England Journal of Medicine, 314,* 193–198. (11)

Stuss, D. T., & Benson, D. F. (1984). Neuropsychological studies of the frontal lobes. *Psychological Bulletin. 95,* 3–28. (3)

Sudzak, P. D., Glowa, J. R., Crawley, J. N., Schwartz, R. D., Skolnick, P., & Paul, S. M. (1986). A selective imidazobenzodiazepine antagonist of ethanol in the rat. *Science, 234,* 1243–1247. (4)

Suinn, R. M., & Oskamp, S. (1969). *The predictive validity of projective measures.* Springfield, IL: Charles C. Thomas. (13)

Sulser, F., Gillespie, D. D., Mishra, R., & Manier, D. H. (1984). Desensitization by antidepressants of central norepinephrine receptor systems coupled to adenylate cyclase. *Annals of the New York Academy of Sciences, 430,* 91–101. (14)

Sussman, H. M., & MacNeilage, P. F. (1975). Hemispheric specialization for speech production and perception in stutterers. *Neuropsychologia, 13,* 19–26. (6)

Sutton, P. M., & Swensen, C. H. (1983). The reliability and concurrent validity of alternative methods for assessing ego development. *Journal of Personality Assessment, 47,* 468–475. (13)

Svanum, S., & Bringle, R. G. (1982). Race, social class, and predictive bias: An evaluation using the WISC, WRAT, and teacher ratings. *Intelligence, 6,* 275–286. (10)

Swash, M. (1972). Released involuntary laughter after temporal lobe infarction. *Journal of Neurology, Neurosurgery, and Psychiatry, 35,* 108–113. (3)

Szasz, T. S. (1982). The psychiatric will. *American Psychologist, 37,* 762–770. (15)

Szenthágothai, J. (1983). Modular architectonic principle of neural centers. *Reviews of Physiology, Biochemistry, and Pharmacology, 98,* 11–61. (3)

Szymanski, H. V., Simon, J. C., & Gutterman, N. (1983). Recovery from schizophrenic psychosis. *American Journal of Psychiatry, 140,* 335–338. (15)

Tallman, J. F., Paul, S. M., Skolnick, P., & Gallager, D. W. (1980). Receptors for the age of anxiety: Pharmacology of the benzodiazepines. *Science, 207,* 274–281. (4)

Tanzi, R. E., Gusella, J. F., Watkins, P. C., Bruns, G. A. P., St. George-Hyslop, P., VanKeuren, M. L., Patterson, D., Pagan, S., Kurnit, D. M., & Neve, R. L. (1987). Amyloid beta protein gene: cDNA, mRNA distribution, and genetic linkage near the Alzheimer's locus. *Science, 235,* 880–884. (3)

Taylor, H. G. (1984). Early brain injury and cognitive development. In C. R. Almli & S. Finger (Eds.), *Early brain damage* (pp. 325–345). Orlando, FL: Academic Press. (3)

Taylor, S. E. (1983). Adjustment to threatening events: A theory of cognitive adaptation. *American Psychologist, 38,* 1161–1173. (12)

Taylor, S. E., & Brown, J. D. (1988). Illusion and well-being: A social psychological perspective on mental health. *Psychological Bulletin, 103,* 193–210. (12)

Teasdale, T. W., & Owen, D. R. (1984). Heredity and familial environment in intelligence and educational level: A sibling study. *Nature, 309,* 620–622. (10)

Teitelbaum, P. (1955). Sensory control of hypothalamic hyperphagia. *Journal of Comparative and Physiological Psychology, 48,* 156–163. (11)

Teplin, L. A. (1983). The criminalization of the mentally ill: Speculation in search of data. *Psychological Bulletin, 94,* 54–67. (15)

Teplin, L. A. (1984). Criminalizing mental disorder: The comparative arrest rate of the mentally ill. *American Psychologist, 39,* 794–803. (15)

Teplin, L. A. (1985). The criminality of the mentally ill: A dangerous misconception. *American Journal of Psychiatry, 142,* 593–599. (15)

Terrace, H. S., Petitto, L. A., Sanders, R. J., & Bever, T. G. (1979). Can an ape create a sentence? *Science, 206,* 891–902. (6)

Thayer, F. C. (1987). Performance appraisal and merit pay systems: The disasters multiply. *Review of Public Personnel Administration, 7,* 36–53. (16)

Thayer, P. W. (1977). "Somethings old, somethings new." *Personnel Psychology, 30,* 513–524. (16)

Thayer, P. W. (1983). Industrial/organizational psychology: Science and application. *G. Stanley Hall Lecture Series, 3,* 5–30. (16)

Thayer, P. W., & McGehee, W. (1977). On the effectiveness of not holding a formal training course. *Personnel Psychology, 30,* 455–456. (16)

Theorell, T. (1985). Relationships between critical life events, job stress, and cardiovascular illness. In W. D. Gentry, H. Benson, & C. J. de Wolff (Eds.),

Behavioral medicine: Work, stress and health (pp. 81–99). Dordrecht, Netherlands: Martinus Nijhoff. (12)

Thibault, J. W., & Kelley, H. (1959). *The social psychology of groups.* New York: Wiley. (16)

Thieman, T. J. (1984). A classroom demonstration of encoding specificity. *Teaching of Psychology, 11,* 101–102. (8)

Thigpen, C., & Cleckley, H. (1957). *The three faces of Eve.* New York: McGraw-Hill. (14)

Thomas, A., & Chess, S. (1980). *The dynamics of psychological development.* New York: Brunner/Mazel. (6)

Thomas, A., Chess, S., & Birch, H. G. (1968). *Temperament and behavior disorders in children.* New York: New York University Press. (6)

Thompson, C. R., & Church, R. M. (1980). An explanation of the language of a chimpanzee. *Science, 208,* 313–314. (6)

Thompson, S. C. (1981). Will it hurt less if I can control it? A complex answer to a simple question. *Psychological Bulletin, 90,* 89–101. (12)

Thorndike, E. L. (1898). Animal intelligence: An experimental study of the associative processes in animals. *Psychological Monographs, 2*(No. 8). (7)

Thorndike, E. L. (1911/1970). *Animal Intelligence.* Darien, CT: Hafner. (Original work published 1911) (7)

Thorndyke, P. W. (1981). Distance estimation from cognitive maps. *Cognitive Psychology, 13,* 526–550. (9)

Thurstin, A. H., Alfano, A. M., & Nerviano, V. J. (1987). The efficacy of AA attendance for aftercare of inpatient alcoholics: Some follow-up data. *International Journal of the Addictions, 22,* 1083–1090. (14)

Tiffany, S. T., & Baker, T. B. (1981). Morphine tolerance in rats: Congruence with a Pavlovian paradigm. *Journal of Comparative and Physiological Psychology, 95,* 747–762. (14)

Time. (April 22, 1974). Alcoholism. (4)

Tinbergen, N. (1958). *Curious naturalists.* New York: Basic Books. (3)

Tolman, E. C. (1932). *Purposive behavior in animals and men.* New York: Century. (7)

Tolman, E. C., & Honzik, C. H. (1930). Introduction and removal of reward, and maze performance in rats. *University of California Publications in Psychology, 4,* 257–275. (7)

Tolstedt, B. E., & Stokes, J. P. (1984). Self-disclosure, intimacy, and the depenetration process. *Journal of Personality and Social Psychology, 46,* 84–90. (6)

Torrance, E. P. (1980). Growing up creatively gifted: A 22-year longitudinal study. *Creative Child and Adult Quarterly, 5,* 148–159. (9)

Torrance, E. P. (1981). Empirical validation of criterion-referenced indicators of creative ability through a longitudinal study. *Creative Child and Adult Quarterly, 6,* 136–140. (9)

Torrance, E. P. (1982). "Sounds and images" productions of elementary school pupils as predictors of the creative achievements of young adults. *Creative Child and Adult Quarterly, 7,* 8–14. (9)

Treiser, S. L., Cascio, C. S., O'Donohue, T. L., Thoa, N. B., Jacobowitz, D. M., & Kellar, K. J. (1981). Lithium increases serotonin release and decreases serotonin receptors in the hippocampus. *Science, 213,* 1529–1532. (15)

Treisman, A., & Souther, J. (1985). Search asymmetry: A diagnostic for preattentive processing of separable features. *Journal of Experimental Psychology: General, 114,* 285–310. (5)

Tulving, E. (1972). Episodic and semantic memory. In E. Tulving & W. Donaldson (Eds.), *Organization of memory* (pp. 381–403). New York: Academic. (8)

Tulving, E. (1985). How many memory systems are there? *American Psychologist, 40,* 385–398. (8)

Tulving, E., & Thomson, D. M. (1973). Encoding specificity and retrieval processes in episodic memory. *Psychological Review, 80,* 352–373. (8)

Tversky, A., & Kahneman, D. (1981). The framing of decisions and the psychology of choice. *Science, 211,* 453–458. (9)

Tversky, B. (1981). Distortions in memory for maps. *Cognitive Psychology, 13,* 407–433. (9)

U. S. Bureau of the Census (1982). *Statistical abstract of the United States: 1982–83* (103rd ed.). Washington, DC: U.S. Government Printing Office. (6)

U.S. Department of Labor. (1989, April). *Employment and Earnings* (Vol. 36, No. 4). Washington, DC: U.S. Government Printing Office. (6)

Udolf, R. (1981). *Handbook of hypnosis for professionals.* New York: Van Nostrand Reinhold. (4)

Ulrich, R. E., Stachnik, T. J., & Stainton, N. R. (1963). Student acceptance of generalized personality interpretations. *Psychological Reports, 13,* 831–834. (13)

Ulrich, R. E., Wolff, P. C., & Azrin, N. H. (1964). Shock as an elicitor of intra- and inter-species fighting behavior. *Animal Behavior, 12,* 14–15. (12)

Ulrich, R. S. (1984). View through a window may influence recovery from surgery. *Science, 224, 420–421.* (5)

Vaillant, G. E. (1983). *The natural history of alcoholism.* Cambridge, MA: Harvard University Press. (14)

Vaillant, G. E., & Milofsky, E. S. (1982). The etiology of alcoholism: A prospective viewpoint. *American Psychologist, 37,* 494–503. (1, 3, 14)

Valenstein, E. S. (1986). *Great and desperate cures.* New York: Basic Books. (3)

Van Der Pligt, J., & Eiser, J. R. (1983). Actors' and observers' attributions, self-serving bias, and positivity. *European Journal of Social Psychology, 13,* 95–104. (16)

van Dyke, C., & Byck, R. (1982). Cocaine. *Scientific American, 246*(3), 128–141. (3)

Varni, J. W., Lovaas, O. I., Koegel, R. L., & Everett, N. L. (1979). An analysis of observational learning in autistic and normal children. *Journal of Abnormal Child Psychology, 7,* 31–43. (14)

Vaughan, D. (1986). *Uncoupling.* New York: Vintage Books. (16)

Vaughn, C. E., Snyder, K. S., Jones, S., Freeman, W. B., & Falloon, I. R. H. (1984). Family factors in schizophrenia relapse. *Archives of General Psychiatry, 41,* 1169–1177. (15)

Vernon, M. (1967). Relationship of language to the thinking process. *Archives of General Psychiatry, 16,* 325–333. (10)

Vogel, G. W., Thompson, F. C., Jr., Thurmond, A., & Rivers, B. (1973). The effect of REM deprivation on depression. In W. P. Koella & P. Levin (Eds.), *Sleep: Physiology, biochemistry, psychology, pharmacology, clinical implications* (pp. 191–195). Basel, Switzerland: Karger. (4)

Vokey, J. R., & Read, J. D. (1985). Subliminal messages: Between the devil and the media. *American Psychologist, 40,* 1231–1239. (5)

von Baeyer, C. (1988, September/October). How Fermi would have fixed it. *The Sciences, 28*(5), 2–4. (9)

Vroom, V. H. (1964). *Work and motivation.* New York: Wiley. (16)

Wadden, T. A., & Stunkard, A. J. (1987). Psychopathology and obesity. *Annals of the New York Academy of Sciences, 499,* 55–65. (11)

Wagenaar, W. A. (1986). My memory: A study of autobiographical memory over six years. *Cognitive Psychology, 18,* 225–252. (8)

Wahba, M. A., & Bridwell, L. G. (1976). Maslow reconsidered: A review of research on the need hierarchy theory. *Organizational Behavior & Human Performance, 15,* 212–240. (11)

Waid, W. M., & Orne, M. T. (1982). The physiological detection of deception. *American Scientist, 70,* 402–409. (12)

Wakeling, A. (1979). A general psychiatric approach to sexual deviation. In I. Rosen (Ed.), *Sexual deviation* (2nd ed.) (pp. 1–28). Oxford: Oxford University Press. (11)

Wald, G. (1968). Molecular basis of visual excitation. *Science, 162,* 230–239. (5)

Walk, R. D., & Gibson, E. J. (1961). A comparative and analytical study of visual depth perception. *Psychological Monographs, 75*(Whole No. 519). (6)

Walster, E., Aronson, E., Abrahams, D., & Rottman, L. (1966). Importance of physical attractiveness in dating behavior. *Journal of Personality and Social Psychology, 4,* 508–516. (16)

Walster, E., & Berscheid, E. (1971). Adrenaline makes the heart grow fonder. *Psychology Today, 5,* 46–50. (16)

Walster, E., Traupman, J., & Walster, G. W. (1978). Equity and extramarital sexuality. *Archives of Sexual Behavior, 7,* 127–142. (16)

Walters, G. C., & Grusec, J. E. (1977). *Punishment.* San Francisco: W. H. Freeman. (7)

Wanberg, K. W., & Horn, J. L. (1983). Assessment of alcohol use with multidimensional concepts and measures. *American Psychologist, 38,* 1055–1069. (14)

Warburton, C. M., Wesnes, K., Shergold, K., & James, M. (1986). Facilitation of learning and state dependency with nicotine. *Psychopharmacology, 89,* 55–59. (8)

Ward, I. L. (1972). Prenatal stress feminizes and demasculinizes the behavior of males. *Science, 175,* 82–84. (11)

Ward, I. L. (1977). Exogenous androgen activates female behavior in noncopulating, prenatally stressed male rats. *Journal of Comparative and Physiological Psychology, 91,* 465–471. (11)

Ward, I. L., & Reed, J. (1985). Prenatal stress and prepubertal social rearing conditions interact to determine sexual behavior in male rats. *Behavioral Neuroscience, 99,* 301–309. (11)

Waring, G. O., III, Lynn, M. J., Culbertson, W., Laibson, P. R., Lindstrom, R. D., McDonald, M. B., Myers, W. D., Obstbaum, S. A., Rowsey, J. J., & Schanzlin, D. J. (1987). Three-year results of the prospective evaluation of radial keratotomy (PERK) study. *Ophthalmology, 94,* 1339–1354. (5)

Warren, R. M. (1970). Perceptual restoration of missing speech sounds. *Science, 167,* 392–393. (5)

Wason, P. C. (1960). On the failure to eliminate hypotheses in a conceptual task. *Quarterly Journal of Experimental Psychology, 12,* 129–140. (9)

Watson, D. (1982). The actor and the observer: How are their perceptions of causality divergent? *Psychological Bulletin, 92,* 682–700. (16)

Watson, J. B. (1913). Psychology as the behaviorist views it. *Psychological Review, 20,* 158–177. (7)

Watson, J. B. (1925). *Behaviorism.* New York: Norton. (7)

Watson, J. B., & Rayner, R. (1920). Conditioned emotional reactions. *Journal of Experimental Psychology, 3,* 1–14. (14)

Weaver, C. N. (1980). Job satisfaction in the United States in the 1970s. *Journal of Applied Psychology, 65,* 364–367. (6)

Webb, W. B. (1979). Theories of sleep functions and some clinical implications. In R. Drucker-Colín, M. Shkurovich, & M. B. Sterman (Eds.), *The functions of sleep* (pp. 19–35). New York: Academic Press. (4)

Wegner, D. M., Schneider, D. J., Carter, S. R., III, & White, T. L. (1987). Paradoxical effects of thought suppression. *Journal of Personality and Social Psychology, 53,* 5–13. (14)

Wehr, T. A., Jacobsen, F. M., Sack, D. A., Arendt, J., Tamarkin, L., & Rosenthal, N. E. (1986). Phototherapy of seasonal affective disorder. *Archives of General Psychiatry, 43,* 870–875. (14)

Weil, A. T., Zinberg, N. E., & Nelson, J. M. (1968). Clinical and psychological effects of marihuana in man. *Science, 162,* 1234–1242. (4)

Weinberg, R. A. (1989). Intelligence and IQ: Landmark issues and great debates. *American Psychologist, 44,* 98–104. (10)

Weinberger, D. R. (1987). Implications of normal brain development for the pathogenesis of schizophrenia. *Archives of General Psychiatry, 44,* 660–669. (14)

Weinberger, D. R., Berman, K. F., & Illowsky, B. P. (1988). Physiological dysfunction of dorsolateral prefrontal cortex in schizophrenia. III. A new cohort and evidence for a monoaminergic mechanism. *Archives of General Psychiatry, 45,* 609–615. (14)

Weiner, R. D. (1984). Does electroconvulsive therapy cause brain damage? *Behavioral and Brain Sciences, 7,* 1–53. (15)

Weinstock, C. (1984). Further evidence on psychobiological aspects of cancer. *International Journal of Psychosomatics, 31,* 20–22. (12)

Weiss, J. M. (1970). Somatic effects of predictable and unpredictable shock. *Psychosomatic Medicine, 32,* 397–408. (12)

Weiss, J. M. (1972). Psychological factors in stress and disease. *Scientific American, 226*(6), 104–113. (12)

Weiss, J. M., Poherecky, L. A., Salman, S., & Gruenthal, M. (1976). Attenuation of gastric lesions by psychological aspects of aggression in rats. *Journal of Comparative and Physiological Psychology, 90,* 252–259. (12)

Weissman, M. M., Kidd, K. K., & Prusoff, B. A. (1982). Variability in rates of affective disorders in relatives of depressed and normal probands. *Archives of General Psychiatry, 39,* 1397–1403. (14)

Weitzman, E. D. (1981). Sleep and its disorders. *Annual Review of Neuroscience, 4,* 381–417. (4)

Weitzman, R. A. (1982). The prediction of college achievement by the Scholastic Aptitude Test and the high school record. *Journal of Educational Measurement, 19,* 179–191. (10)

Wender, P. H., Kety, S. S., Rosenthal, D., Schulsinger, F., Ortmann, J., & Lunde, I. (1986). Psychiatric disorders in the biological and adoptive families of adopted individuals with affective disorders. *Archives of General Psychiatry, 43,* 923–929. (1, 14)

Wenger, J. R., Tiffany, T. M., Bombardier, C., Nicholls, K., & Woods, S. C. (1981). Ethanol tolerance in the rat is learned. *Science, 213,* 575–576. (14)

West, D. J. (1962). *Psychical research today.* Harmondsworth, England: Penguin. (2)

West, J. R., Hodges, C. A., & Black, A. C., Jr. (1981). Prenatal exposure to ethanol alters the organization of hippocampal mossy fibers in rats. *Science, 211,* 957–959. (3)

Wetzer, S. E., & Sweeney, J. A. (1986). Childhood amnesia: An empirical demonstration. In D. C. Rubin (Ed.), *Autobiographical memory* (pp. 191–201). Cambridge, England: Cambridge University Press. (8)

Whaley, D. L., & Malott, R. W. (1971). *Elementary principles of behavior.* Englewood Cliffs, NJ: Prentice-Hall. (7)

Wheeler, D. D. (1970). Processes in word recognition. *Cognitive Psychology, 1,* 59–85. (9)

White, B. B., & White, M. S. (1987). Autism from the inside. *Medical Hypotheses, 24,* 223–229. (14)

White, G. L., & Knight, T. D. (1984). Misattribution of arousal and attraction: Effects of salience of explanations for arousal. *Journal of Experimental Social Psychology, 20,* 55–64. (16)

Wicker, A. W. (1969). Attitudes vs. action: The relation of verbal and overt behavioral responses to attitude objects. *Journal of Social Issues, 25*(4), 47–78. (16)

Wicklund, R. A., & Brehm, J. W. (1976). *Perspectives on cognitive dissonance.* Hillsdale, NJ: Lawrence Erlbaum. (16)

Wild, H. M., Butler, S. R., Carden, D., & Kulikowski, J. J. (1985). Primate cortical area V4 important for colour constancy but not wavelength discrimination. *Nature, 313,* 133–135. (5)

Wilkins, L., & Richter, C. P. (1940). A great craving for salt by a child with corticoadrenal insufficiency. *Journal of the American Medical Association, 114,* 866–868. (11)

William, D. C. (1984). The prevention of AIDS by modifying sexual behavior. *Annals of the New York Academy of Sciences, 437,* 283–285. (11)

Williams, R. B., Jr., Lane, J. D., Kuhn, C. M., Melosh, W., White, A. D., & Schanberg, S. M. (1982). Type A behavior and elevated physiological and neuroendocrine responses to cognitive tasks. *Science, 218,* 483–485. (12)

Wilson, E. O. (1975). *Sociobiology: The new synthesis.* Cambridge, England: Belknap. (3)

Wilson, J. R., and the editors of *Life.* (1964). *The mind.* New York: Time. (5, 10)

Winch, R. (1958). *Mate-selection: A study of complementary needs.* New York: Harper. (16)

Winner, E. (1986, August). Where pelicans kiss seals. *Psychology Today,* 24–35. (6)

Winocur, G., Moscovitch, M., & Witherspoon, D. (1987). Contextual cuing and memory performance in brain-damaged amnesics and old people. *Brain and Cognition, 6,* 129–141. (8)

Winograd, E., & Church, V. E. (1988). Role of spatial location in learning face-name associations. *Memory & Cognition, 16,* 1–7. (8)

Winograd, E., & Soloway, R. M. (1986). On forgetting the locations of things stored in special places. *Journal of Experimental Psychology: General, 115,* 366–372. (8)

Wise, R. A., & Bozarth, M. A. (1987). A psychomotor stimulant theory of addiction. *Psychological Review, 94,* 469–492. (14)

Wolf, L., & Goldberg, B. (1986). Autistic children grow up: An eight to twenty-four year follow-up study. *Canadian Journal of Psychiatry, 31,* 550–556. (14)

Wolitzky, D. L., & Wachtel, P. L. (1973). Personality and perception. In B. B. Wolman (Ed.), *Handbook of general psychology* (pp. 826–857). Englewood Cliffs, NJ: Prentice-Hall. (5)

Wolman, B. B. (1989). *Dictionary of behavioral science* (2nd ed.). San Diego, CA: Academic Press. (10)

Wolpe, J. (1961). The systematic desensitization treatment of neuroses. *Journal of Nervous and Mental Disease, 132,* 189–203. (14)

Wolpe, J., & Rowan, V. C. (1988). Panic disorder: A product of classical conditioning. *Behaviour Research and Therapy, 26,* 441–450. (14)

Woods, B. T., & Wolf, J. (1983). A reconsideration of the relation of ventricular enlargement to duration of illness in schizophrenia. *American Journal of Psychiatry, 140,* 1564–1570. (14)

Woods, C. W., Charney, D. S., Loke, J., Goodman, W. K., Redmond, E. E., Jr., & Heninger, G. R. (1986). Carbon dioxide sensitivity in panic anxiety. *Archives of General Psychiatry, 43,* 900–909. (14)

Woody, G. E., & O'Brien, C. P. (1986). Update on methadone maintenance. *Research Advances in Alcohol and Drug Problems, 9,* 261–277. (14)

Wright, D. M. (1975). Impairment in abstract conceptualization in schizophrenia. *Psychological Bulletin, 82,* 120–127. (14)

Wurtman, J. J. (1985). Neurotransmitter control of carbohydrate consumption. *Annals of the New York Academy of Sciences, 443,* 145–151. (11)

Yalom, I. D. (1985.) *The theory and practice of group psychotherapy* (3rd ed.). New York: Basic Books. (15)

Yalom, I. D. (1989). *Love's executioner and other tales of psychotherapy.* New York: Basic Books. (16)

Yamaguchi, S., & Komata, Y. (1988). Independence and primacy of umami as compared with the four basic tastes. *Annals of the New York Academy of Sciences, 510,* 725–726. (5)

Yamamoto, T. (1987). Cortical organization in gustatory perception. *Annals of the New York Academy of Sciences, 510,* 49–54. (5)

Yarsh, T. L., Farb, D. H., Leeman, S. E., & Jessell, T. M. (1979). Intrathecal capsaicin depletes substance P in the rat spinal cord and produces prolonged thermal analgesia. *Science, 206,* 481–483. (5)

Yates, B. (1984). *Self-management.* Belmont, CA: Wadsworth. (7)

Yonas, A., & Granrud, C. E. (1985). Reaching as a measure of infants' spatial perception. In G. Gottlieb & N. A. Krasnegor (Eds.), *Measurement of audition and vision in the first year of postnatal life* (pp. 301–322). Norwood, NJ: Ablex. (6)

Young, P. T. (1936). *Motivation of behavior.* New York: Wiley. (7)

Young-Ok, K., & Stevens, J. H., Jr. (1987). The socialization of prosocial behavior in children. *Childhood Education, 63,* 200–206. (7)

Zabrucky, K., Moore, D., & Schultz, N. R., Jr. (1987). Evaluation of comprehension in young and old adults. *Developmental Psychology, 23,* 39–43. (8)

Zajonc, R. B. (1968). Attitudinal effects of mere exposure. *Journal of Personality and Social Psychology, 9,* Monograph Supplement 2, part 2. (16)

Zanna, M., & Hamilton, D. L. (1977). Further evidence for meaning change in impression formation. *Journal of Experimental Social Psychology, 13,* 224–238. (16)

Zaragoza, M. S., McCloskey, M., & Jamis, M. (1987). Misleading postevent information and recall of the original event: Further evidence against the memory impairment hypothesis. *Journal of Experimental Psychology: Learning, Memory, and Cognition, 13,* 36–44. (8)

Zelnik, M., & Kantner, J. F. (1977). Sexual and contraceptive experience of young unmarried women in the United States, 1976 and 1971. *Family Planning Perspectives, 9,* 55–71. (6)

Zelnik, M., & Kantner, J. F. (1978). Contraceptive patterns and premarital pregnancy among women aged 15–19 in 1976. *Family Planning Perspectives, 10,* 135–142. (6)

Zepelin, H., & Rechtschaffen, A. (1974). Mammalian sleep, longevity, and energy metabolism. *Brain, Behavior, and Evolution, 10,* 425–470. (4)

Zigler, E., & Glick, M. (1988). Is paranoid schizophrenia really camouflaged depression? *American Psychologist, 43,* 284–290. (14)

Zimmerman, M., Coryell, W., Pfohl, B., & Stangl, D. (1986). The validity of four definitions of endogenous depression. II. Clinical, demographic, familial, and psychosocial correlates. *Archives of General Psychiatry, 43,* 234–244. (14)

Zucker, R. A., & Gomberg, E. S. L. (1986). Etiology of alcoholism reconsidered. *American Psychologist, 41,* 783–793. (14)

Zuckerman, M., Buchsbaum, M. S., & Murphy, D. L. (1980). Sensation seeking and its biological correlates. *Psychological Bulletin, 88,* 187–214. (11)

Zuckerman, M., Koestner, R., & Alton, A. O. (1984). Learning to detect deception. *Journal of Personality and Social Psychology, 46,* 519–528. (12)

Zuckerman, M., & Wheeler, L. (1975). To dispel fantasies about the fantasy-based measure of fear of success. *Psychological Bulletin, 82,* 932–946. (11)

Zwislocki, J. J. (1981). Sound analysis in the ear: A history of discoveries. *American Scientist, 69,* 184–192. (5)

CREDITS

PHOTO, ILLUSTRATION, AND EXCERPT CREDITS

Page 3: Leonardo da Vinci, *Autoritratto.* Torino, Biblioteca Reale. Art Resource.

Page 5: Photo from Bruce Coleman Ltd.

Page 7: Photo from Rex Features.

Page 8: Photo from Science Photo Library.

Page 11: Photo courtesy of Wellesley College.

Page 13: Photo at left from Rex Features. Photo at right from Science Photo Library.

Page 15: Photo from Rex Features.

Page 19: Leonardo da Vinci, *Male profile and proportional schema.* Venice, Academy. Art Resource.

Page 24: Photo from Rex Features.

Page 26: Figure 2.5: photo from Photofest.

Page 29: Figure 2.7: photo by Bohdan Hrynewych/Stock Boston.

Page 30: Figure 2.8: photo by Sally and Richard Greenhill.

Page 31: Photo by MCX Terman/Gamma/Frank Spooner Pictures.

Page 36: Photo by B. Prince/Format.

Page 43: Figure 2.18: photo by David Reed/Impact Photos.

Page 55: Leonardo da Vinci, *The Human proportions reconstructed according to Vitruvius.* Venice, Academia. SCALA/Art Resource.

Page 56: Photo from ZEFA/The Stock Market.

Page 58: Figure 3.2: photo from Science Photo Library.

Page 59: Figure 3.5: photo from ZEFA.

Page 60: Figure 3.6 from *Psychology* by John C. Ruch. Copyright © 1984 by Wadsworth, Inc. Used by permission of the publisher.

Page 61: Figure 3.7: top photo by David Muscroft/Rex Features; bottom photo from Rex Features/SIPA. Photos at bottom of page by Michael Nichols/Magnum Photos.

Page 63: Figure 3.9: photo from Bruce Coleman Ltd.

Page 64: Figure 3.10: photos from Oxford Scientific.

Page 65: Top photo from Colorific! Bottom photo from Stockphotos, Inc.

Page 68: Figure 3.12b from J. G. Brandon and R. G. Coss, *Brain Research,* 252:51–61, 1982. Used by permission of R. G. Coss. Figure 3.13b: photo by McCoy/Scheilbel/Rainbow.

Page 69: Figure 3.14 from *Biology: The Unity and Diversity of Life* (5th ed.) by Cecie Starr and Ralph Taggart. Copyright © 1989 by Wadsworth, Inc. Used by permission of the publisher.

Page 70: Figure 3.15: photo by D. D. Kunkel, University of Washington/Biological Photo Service.

Page 76: Figure 3.19: illustration from Mary Evans Picture Library.

Page 77: Figure 3.20a: photo by Burt Glinn/Magnum Photos. Figure 3.20b: photo by Karen Ber-

man and Daniel Weinberger, National Institute of Mental Health.

Page 82: Photo from Science Photo Library.

Page 83: Figure 3.29: photos by Dr. Colin Chumbley/Science Photo Library.

Page 84: Figure 3.30 from Norman Geschwind, "Specializations of the Human Brain," September, 1979. Copyright © 1979 by Scientific American. All rights reserved.

Page 85: Figure 3.31 from *Clinical Neuropsychology* by Kenneth M. Heilman and Edward Valenstein. Copyright © 1979 by Oxford University Press, Inc. Used by permission.

Page 87: Figure 3.33: photo by Hans Reinhard/Bruce Coleman Ltd.

Page 90: Figure 3.38: photos from ZEFA.

Page 91: Figure 3.39: photo by Dr. John Mazziotti et al./Neurology/Science Photo Library.

Page 92: Figure 3.40 courtesy of Dr. Jerre Levy, University of Chicago. Figure 3.41: photos courtesy of Dana Copeland.

Page 93: Photo from Rex Features.

Page 99: Leonardo da Vinci, *Testa di donna.* Firenze-Uffizi, Gabinetto dei disegni. Art Resource.

Page 100: Photo by Penny Tweedie/Impact Photos.

Page 101: Figure 4.1: photo by Dennis di Cicco.

Page 102: Photo at left by Chris Steele-Perkins/Magnum Photos. Figure 4.2: photo from Wide World Photos.

Page 104: Figure 4.5: photo by Paul Conklin/Colorific!

Page 105: Figure 4.6: photos by Dr. J. Allan Hobson, Harvard Medical School.

Page 106: Figure 4.7: photo by Richard Nowitz/Black Star/Colorific! Figure 4.8: EEG records provided by T. E. LeVere.

Page 107: Figure 4.9 from *Some Must Watch While Some Must Sleep* by William C. Dement. Copyright © 1972, 1974, 1976 by William C. Dement. Used by permission of William C. Dement and the Stanford Alumni Association.

Page 108: Photos by Allan Hobson/Science Photo Library. Figure 4.10 from "Ontogenetic Development of Human Sleep-Dream Cycle" by H. P. Roffwarg, J. N. Muzio, and W. C. Dement, *Science,* 152:604–609, 1966. Copyright © 1966 by the American Association for the Advancement of Science. Used by permission of William C. Dement.

Page 109: Painting by David Gifford/Science Photo Library.

Page 110: Illustration from Colorific!

Page 112: Photo from Colorific!

Page 113: From *Key to Physick* by E. Sibly/Mary Evans Picture Library.

Page 114: Figure 4.11: photo from Science Photo Library. Photo at right by Sally and Richard Greenhill.

Page 116: Figure 4.13: photo by Mario Cabera/Wide World Photos.

Page 123: Photo at left from Science Photo Library. Photo at right from the Archive for Research in Archetypal Symbolism, San Francisco.

Page 124: Photo by Sally and Richard Greenhill.

Page 127: Leonardo da Vinci, *Canon.* Codex Atlanticus f. 9v. Art Resource.

Page 128: Photo from Bruce Coleman Ltd.

Page 131: Top photo by Dr. Ralph Eagle/Science Photo Library. Bottom photo from CNRI/Science Photo Library.

Page 132: Photos from ZEFA.

Page 133: Figure 5.5b: photo by Dr. Ralph Eagle/Science Photo Library. Figure 5.5c: photo by E. M. de Monasterio/Petit Format/Science Photo Library.

Page 135: Photo from The Image Bank.

Page 137: Painting by Georges Seurat, *Sunday Afternoon on the Island of La Grande Jatte,* 1884–86. Oil on canvas, 81 × 120⅜ in. © 1989 The Art Institute of Chicago. All rights reserved.

Page 139: Figure 5.13: photo by Klaus Benser/ZEFA.

Pages 141, 142: Figures 5.16 and 5.17b reproduced from *Ishihara's Test for Colour Blindness,* Kanehara & Co., Ltd., Tokyo, Japan. A test for color blindness cannot be conducted with this material. Used by permission.

Page 145: Top left photo by Hans Reinhard/Bruce Coleman Ltd. Top right photo from Rex Features. Bottom photo by Gilles Mermet/Gamma/Frank Spooner Pictures.

Page 146: Photo by B. Lewis/Network.

Page 148: Photo at left from The Image Bank. Photo at right from NASA.

Page 149: Photo by John Cole/Network.

Page 150: Photo from ZEFA.

Page 151: Photo from Omikron/Science Photo Library.

Page 152: Photo by Trevor Wood/The Image Bank.

Page 153: Figure 5.26: photo courtesy of Dana Copeland. Bottom photo by Louise Psimoyos/Contact Press Images/Colorific!

Page 158: Photo at left by Chuck Fishman/Woodfin Camp/Colorific! Figure 5.30: photo by Van Bucher, University of Florida, Department of Clinical Psychology/Photo Researchers, Inc.

Page 159: Photo courtesy of American Association of Advertising Agencies.

Page 160: Painting by Robert William Vonnoh, *Spring in France,* 1890. Oil on canvas, 15³⁄₁₆ × 22 in., Wirt D. Walker Fund, 1982.272. © 1989 The Art Institute of Chicago. All rights reserved. Figure 5.31 from *Organization in Vision* by Gaetano Kanizsa. Copyright © 1979 by Gaetano Kanizsa. Used by permission of Praeger Publishers.

Page 161: Figure 5.32 from "Asking the 'What For' Question in Auditory Perception" by A. S. Bregman in *Perceptual Organization* by M. Kubovy and J. R. Pomerantz (eds.), 1981. Used by permis-

673

Page 357: Photo by Sally Fear/Impact Photos.

Page 358: Figures 10.6 and 10.7 from *Psychology Today*, 4th ed. Copyright © 1979 by Random House, Inc.

Page 361: Photo by Jim Pickerell/Colorific!

Page 362: Photo at left by David Moore/Colorific! Photo at right by Isa Bradshaw/Colorific!

Page 364: Top left photo from ZEFA/The Stock Market. Top right photo by Mike Powell/Allsport. Bottom photos from ZEFA.

Page 367: Photo from Frank Spooner Pictures.

Page 368: Left photo by Paul Schutzer/*Life* Magazine/Colorific! Right photo by Rick Friedman/Black Star/Colorific!

Page 369: Figure 10.10 adapted from "Familial Studies of Intelligence: A Review," T. Bouchard et al., *Science,* 212:1055–1059, 1981. Copyright 1981 by the AAAS. Used by permission of the AAAS and T. Bouchard.

Page 370: Photo by Ros Drinkwater/Rex Features.

Page 375: Leonardo da Vinci, Codex Atlanticus f. 387r. Art Resource.

Page 376: Photo from Agence Vertical/Colorific!

Page 382: Figure 11.3: Top photo by Sally and Richard Greenhill. Middle photo by Jim Pickerell/Colorific! Bottom left photo from Rex Features. Bottom right photo from AP/World Wide Photos.

Page 383: Figure 11.3, continued: photo by David Burnett/Contact Press Images/Colorific!

Page 387: Top photo and photo in Figure 11.7 by Yoav Levy/Colorific!

Page 388: Photo from Rex Features.

Page 389: Photo by Sally and Richard Greenhill.

Page 390: Top photo by Butch Martin/The Image Bank. Bottom photo by Ethan Hoffman/Colorific!

Page 391: Top photo by Mike McQueen/Impact Photos. Bottom photo by Penny Tweedie/Impact Photos.

Page 392: Photo from ZEFA.

Page 393: Photo at left by G. Rogers/The Image Bank. Photo at right from ZEFA.

Page 394: Top photo by Sally and Richard Greenhill. Bottom photo by Yoav Levy/Phototake/Colorific!

Page 395: Photo from ZEFA.

Page 397: Figure 11.12: photos from "The Control of Eating Behavior in an Anorectic by Operant Conditioning Techniques" by A. J. Bachrach, W. J. Erwin, and J. P. Mohr in *Case Studies in Behavior Modification,* L. P. Ullmann and L. Krasner (eds.), 1965. Used by permission of L. Krasner.

Page 398: Photo by Davies/Network.

Page 400: Photo by Caroline Abitbol/SIPA/Rex Features.

Page 401: Figure 11.13a from *Sexual Behavior in the Human Male* by A. C. Kinsey, W. B. Pomeroy, and C. E. Martin, 1948, W. B. Saunders Company. Reprinted by permission of The Kinsey Institute for Research in Sex, Gender, and Reproduction, Inc. Figure 11.13b from *Sexual Behavior in the Human Female* by A. C. Kinsey, W. B. Pomeroy, C. E. Martin, and P. H. Gebhard, 1953, W. B. Saunders Company. Reprinted by permission of The Kinsey Institute for Research in Sex, Gender, and Reproduction, Inc.

Page 403: Top photo by Mario Ruiz/Picture Group/Colorific! Bottom photo by Rasmussen/SIPA/Rex Features.

Page 407: Photo by Foulon/SIPA/Rex Features.

Page 409: Photo from ZEFA.

Page 411: Photo from TDY/Today Sport/Rex Features.

Page 412: Figure 11.18: photo © Elizabeth Crews.

Page 414: Photo from ZEFA.

Page 415: Photo by Schaefer/ZEFA.

Page 416: Photo at left by Wally McNamee/Woodfin Camp and Assoc./Colorific! Photo at right from Gamma.

Page 421: Leonardo da Vinci, *Mary and Anne cartoon.* National Gallery, London. Art Resource.

Page 422: Photo by Jim Anderson/Colorific!

Page 424: Photo at left from SPP/Rex Features. Photo at right by Schneiders/ZEFA.

Page 425: Figure 12.2: top photo from UPI/Bettman Newsphoto; lower photo from Animals Animals/Stouffer Productions, Ltd.

Page 426: Figure 12.4: photo by Alon Reiniger/Contact Press Images/Colorific!

Page 430: Photo from Culver Pictures, Inc.

Page 433: Figure 12.10 based on "An Opponent-Process Theory of Motivation: I. Temporal Dynamics of Affect" by R. L. Solomon and J. D. Corbit, *Psychological Review,* 81:119–145, 1974. Copyright 1974 by the American Psychological Association. Reprinted by permission of the publisher and R. L. Solomon.

Page 434: Figure 12.11: photos by Gary Mcdonald. Figure 12.12: bottom left photo by Chanloup/TV Magazine/Frank Spooner Pictures; bottom right photo by Yann Arthus/Bertrand/Impact Photos.

Page 435: Figure 12.13: photos from *Der Vorprogrammierte Mensch* by I. Eibl-Eibesfeldt, 1973. Used by permission of I. Eibl-Eibesfeldt.

Page 436: Figure 12.14: photos from *Unmasking the Face* (2d ed.) by P. Ekman and W. Friesen, 1984. Used by permission of P. Ekman. Figures 12.15 and 12.16: photos from *Der Vorprogrammierte Mensch* by I. Eibl-Eibesfeldt, 1973. Used by permission of I. Eibl-Eibesfeldt.

Page 437: Photo by Alan LeGarsmeur/Impact Photos.

Page 438: Top photo by Alex Webb/Magnum Photos. Bottom photo by Jim Howard/Colorific!

Page 439: Photo by John Sturrock/Network/J. B. Pictures.

Page 441: Photos from Comstock, Inc.

Page 444: Figure 12.19 from "Psychoneuroendocrine Approaches to the Study of Stressful Person-Environment Transactions" by M. Frankenhauser in *Selye's Guide to Stress Research,* H. Selye (ed.). Copyright © 1980 by Van Nostrand Reinhold Company Inc. All rights reserved. Used by permission. Photo from St. Bartholomew's Hospital, London/Science Photo Library.

Page 445: Photo by Frankee (Jim Lenoir).

Page 446: Photo at left by Lewis/Network. Photo at right by Kalvzny/Liaison/Gamma. Table 12.2 from "The Social Readjustment Rating Scale" by T. H. Holmes and R. H. Rahe in *Journal of Psychosomatic Research,* 11:213–218, 1967. Copyright 1967 by Pergamon Press, Ltd. Reprinted by permission of Pergamon Press and T. H. Holmes.

Page 449: Photo by Katherine Lambert/Black Star/Colorific!

Page 450: Figure 12.21 from *Type-A Behavior and Your Heart* by Meyer Friedman, M.D. and Ray H. Rosenman, M.D. Copyright © 1974 by Meyer Friedman. Reprinted by permission of Alfred A. Knopf, Inc.

Page 451: Figure 12.22: photo by Marc St. Gil/The Image Bank.

Page 453: Photo by Zao/Grimberg/The Image Bank.

Page 454: Top photo by M. Daly/ZEFA. Bottom photo from ZEFA.

Page 455: Photo by William Strode/Black Star/Colorific!

Page 456: Photo by Joseph Rodriquez/Black Star/Colorific!

Page 295: Photo by U. Schreiber/Frank Spooner Pictures.

Page 301: Figure 8.18 from "Evidence for the Uniqueness of Eidetic Imagery" by S. Miller and R. Peacock, *Perceptual and Motor Skills,* 55:1219–1233, 1982. Used by permission of S. Miller, R. Peacock, and the publisher.

Page 302: Figure 8.19 from "Semantic Memory Content in Permastore: Fifty Years of Memory for Spanish Learned in School" by Harry P. Bahrick, *Journal of Experimental Psychology: General,* 113:1–29, 1984. Copyright 1984 by the American Psychological Association, Inc. Used by permission of the author.

Page 303: Photos in top row: left and center, from Rex Features; right, by P. F. Bentley/Photo Reporters. Photos in bottom row: left, by Sten Rosenlund/Rex Features; center, from Rex Features; right, from SIPA/Trippett/Rex Features.

Page 304: Painting by Salvador Dali, *The Persistence of Memory,* 1931, from Bridgeman Art Library. © DEMART PRO ARTE BV/DACS 1990.

Page 305: Photo by Brian T. Gooding.

Page 306: Photo by Jim Howard/Colorific! Figure 8.22 adapted from *Children's Eyewitness Memory* edited by Stephen J. Ceci et al., 1987, Springer-Verlag New York, Inc. Used by permission of Stephen J. Ceci and the publisher.

Page 309: Figure 8.25: photos from Laboratory of Neuroscience, National Institute on Aging. Lower photo by Lynn Johnson/Colorific!

Page 315: Leonardo da Vinci, *Ornothopter wings.* Codex Atlanticus fol. 311v. Art Resource.

Page 316: Photo from ZEFA/The Stock Market.

Page 317: Photo from Woods Hole Oceanographic Institution.

Page 320: Figure 9.5: photo from "Zielorientiertes Verhalten beim Schimpansen" by J. Döhl, *Naturwissenschaft und Medizin,* 1970, 7:43–57.

Page 321: Left photo by Sally and Richard Greenhill. Right photo by Joop Grijpink/ZEFA.

Page 322: Figure 9.6 from "Mental Rotation of Three-Dimensional Objects" by R. N. Shepard and J. N. Metzler, *Science,* 171:701–703, 1971. Copyright 1971 by the AAAS. Used by permission of the AAAS and R. N. Shepard.

Page 325: Photo from ZEFA/Voight.

Page 326: Photo by Sally and Richard Greenhill.

Page 329: Photo by Gary Mcdonald.

Page 331: Figure 9.16: photo by Gary Mcdonald.

Page 336: Photo by Margaret W. Peterson/The Image Bank.

Page 338: Photo by Sally and Richard Greenhill.

Page 341: Photo from Comstock, Inc.

Page 347: Leonardo da Vinci, *Due disegni di architettura.* Paris, Institut de France. Art Resource.

Page 351: Photo by Will and Deni McIntyre/Science Photo Library/Moor.

Page 353: Figure 10.1 from Wechsler Intelligence Scale for Children—Revised. Copyright © 1974 by The Psychological Corporation. Reproduced by permission of The Psychological Corporation and William Erchul. All rights reserved. Photo by Enrico Ferorelli/Colorific!

Page 355: Figure 10.4: SAT questions reprinted by permission of the Educational Testing Service. Permission to reprint the material does not constitute review or endorsement by Educational Testing Service or the College Board of this publication as a whole or of any other questions or testing information it may contain. Photo by Sally and Richard Greenhill.

tion.) Copyright 1986 by MIT Press. Used by permission of the publisher.

Page 457: Photo by Homer Sykes/Daily Telegraph Colour Library.

Page 458: Top photo from ZEFA. Bottom photo by Burt Glinn/Magnum Photos.

Page 459: Photo from Fotos International.

Page 460: Photo by Duclos-Guichard-Couver/Gamma.

Page 461: Photo by David Lawrence/Stockphotos, Inc.

Page 462: Photo by Alan Carruthers/Wheeler Pictures/Colorific!

Page 465: Leonardo da Vinci, *San Pietro*. Wein-Albertina. Art Resource.

Page 466: Painting by Frederick Brown, *Geronimo with His Spirit*, 1984. Oil on linen, 80 × 80 in. Collectio Fondacion Culturaltelevisa. Marlborough Gallery, New York.

Page 468: Figure 13.2: Illustration from the Granger Collection. Painting by Frida Kahlo, *Self-Portrait*, 1940. Oil on canvas, 24½ × 18¾ in. Harry Ransom Humanities Research Center Art Collection, The University of Texas at Austin.

Page 469: Photo from Mary Evans Picture Library.

Page 470: Painting by Jackson Pollock, *Convergence*, 1952. Oil on canvas, 93½ × 155 in. Wadsworth Atheneum, Hartford. Gift of Susan Morse Hilles.

Page 471: Photo at left by Kindra Clineff/Picture Cube. Photo at right by Carol Palmer/Picture Cube.

Page 472: Top left photo by Stacy Pick/Stock Boston. Top right photo by Kindra Clineff/Picture Cube. Lower photo by David Schaefer/Picture Cube.

Page 475: Photo by Robin Anderson/Rex Features.

Page 478: Top photo from Bettman Archive, New York. Bottom photo from Culver Pictures, Inc.

Page 479: Figure 13.6: photo of Chartres Cathedral window by Stephanie Dinkins/Photo Researchers, Inc. Hindu mandala from The Granger Collection. All other photos from the Archive for Research in Archetypal Symbolism, San Francisco.

Page 480: Photo from AP/Wide World Photos.

Page 481: Photo by Flip and Debra Schulke/Black Star.

Page 482: Photo from Bettman Archive, New York.

Page 483: Top left photo from Bettman Archive, New York. Top right photo from the Sophia Smith Collection/Smith College. Bottom photo from Rex Features.

Page 487: Top left photo by Sally and Richard Greenhill. Top right photo by Diane Enkelis/Stock Boston/Colorific! Bottom left photo by Penny Tweedie/Impact Photos. Middle right photo by Derek Berwin/The Image Bank. Bottom right photo by Barth Falkenberg/Stock Boston.

Page 489: Photo by Yves-Guy Berges/SIPA-Press/Rex Features.

Page 491: Photo by Sally and Richard Greenhill.

Page 498: Figure 13.13 adapted from Raymond B. Cattell, *Handbook for the Sixteen Personality Factors*. Copyright 1970, 1988 by the Institute for Personality and Ability Testing, Inc. All rights reserved. Reproduced by permission. Figure 13.14 from *The Scientific Analysis of Personality* by Raymond B. Cattell, 1965, Penguin Library.

Page 499: Photo from Science Photo Library.

Page 501: Figure 13.16 from *Thematic Apperception Test* by Henry A. Murray. Copyright 1943 by the President and Fellow of Harvard College, © 1971 by Henry A. Murray. Reprinted by permission of Harvard University Press.

Page 505: Leonardo da Vinci (facsimile), *Volto grottesco*. Firenze, Gabinetto dei disegni. Art Resource.

Page 506: Photo from Stills/Lynn Goldsmith, Inc./Rex Features.

Page 508: *Three Miracles of S. Zenobius* (detail) by Botticelli/The National Gallery, London.

Page 509: Figure 14.1 adapted from Meyers et al. and Robins et al., *Archives of General Psychiatry*, 41:949–967, 1984. Copyright 1984 by the American Medical Association.

Page 513: Figure 14.2: photo from AP/Wide World Photos. Figure 14.3 from *I'm Eve* by Chris Costner Sizemore and Élen Sain Pittillo. Copyright © 1977 by Chris Costner Sizemore and Élen Sain Pittillo.

Page 517: Photo TM & © Lucasfilm Ltd. (LFL) 1989. All rights reserved. Courtesy of Lucasfilm Ltd.

Page 519: Figure 14.7: photo courtesy of Professor Benjamin Harris, Department of Psychology, University of Wisconsin.

Page 521: Figure 14.9: photo by Don Hogan Charles/NYT Pictures.

Page 524: Tables 14.3 and 14.4 from *Obsessions and Compulsions* by Stanley J. Rachman and Ray J. Hodgson. Copyright © 1980. Reprinted by permission of Prentice-Hall, Inc., Englewood Cliffs, NJ.

Page 525: Photo by Omar Bradley/Picture Group/Colorific!

Page 526: Photo by Chuck Nacke/Picture Group.

Page 529: Photo at left by Julian Calder/Impact Photos. Photo at right from Rex Features.

Page 530: Figure 14.13 adapted from Levenson et al., "Greater Reinforcement from Alcohol for Those at Risk: Parental Risk, Personality Risk, and Sex," *Journal of Abnormal Psychology*, 96:242–253, 1987. Used by permission of the author.

Page 531: Photo by Jim McHugh/Visages/Colorific!

Page 533: Photo by Mike Goldwater/Network.

Page 535: Figure 14.14 adapted from *Sleep* by J. Allan Hobson. Copyright © 1989 by J. Allan Hobson. Reprinted by permission of W. H. Freeman and Co.

Page 536: Painting by Rafael Coronel, *Mujer*. Courtesy B. Lewin Galleries.

Page 538: Photo by Dorothea Lange/Gamma/Frank Spooner Pictures.

Page 541: Excerpts from Joshua Logan in *Moodswing* by Ronald R. Fieve. Copyright © 1975 by Ronald R. Fieve. Used by permission of William Morrow & Co. Figure 14.19 based on "Two-Day Cycles of Alternating Good and Bad Behavior in Psychotic Patients" by C. P. Richter in *Archives of Neurology and Psychology*, 39:587–598, 1938. Copyright 1938 by the American Medical Association.

Page 542: Figure 14.20 based on "Water and Sodium in Two Psychotics" by J. L. Crammer in *Lancet*, 1(7083):1122–1126, 1959. Used by permission of Lancet Ltd. Figure 14.21 from "The Increasing Rate of Suicide by Firearms" by J. H. Boyd in *New England Journal of Medicine*, 308:872–874, 1983. Used by permission.

Page 545: Figure 14.22: photos of Wain's paintings by Derek Bayes/*Life* Magazine, © Time, Inc.

Page 547: Photo at left by Grunnitos/Monkmeyer Press. Photo at right by Benyas-Kaugman/Black Star.

Page 548: Figure 14.23: photos from Science Photo Library/Photo Researchers, Inc.

Page 549: Figure 14.24 based on "Schizophrenia and Genetics: Where Are We? Are You Sure?" by

I. I. Gottesman in *The Nature of Schizophrenia: New Approaches to Research and Treatment*, Wynne et al. (eds.). Copyright © 1978 by John Wiley & Sons, Inc. Reprinted by permission.

Page 551: Photo by Jack Moss/Colorific!

Page 557: Leonardo da Vinci, *Due testa*. Firenze, Gabinetto dei disegni. Art Resource.

Page 559: Painting by Milton Avery, *Interlude*, 1960. Oil on canvas, 68 × 58 in. Philadelphia Museum of Art. Given by the Woodward Foundation Centennial Gifts.

Page 562: Photo from Historical Pictures, Chicago.

Page 566: Photo by Paul Fusco/Magnum Photos.

Page 567: Photo by Korody/Sygma. Figure 15.3 from a figure by Michael J. Mahoney, University of California, Santa Barbara. Copyright © 1989 by Michael J. Mahoney.

Page 570: Photo by Nancy Bates/The Picture Cube.

Page 571: Photo at left by Mark Hanauer/SIPA-Press/Rex Features. Photo at right by Mike Goldwater/Network.

Page 572: Top photo by Scott Witte/Third Coast Stock Source. Bottom photo by E. Sander/Liaison/Gamma/Frank Spooner Pictures.

Page 573: Figure 15.6 based on "The Dose-Effect Relationship in Psychotherapy" by Kenneth I. Howard et al., in *American Psychologist*, 41:159–164, 1986. Used by permission of Kenneth I. Howard.

Page 578: Figure 15.7 from "Drugs in the Treatment of Psychosis" by J. O. Cole et al., in *Psychiatric Drugs*, P. Solomon (ed.), 1966, Grune & Stratton. Used by permission.

Page 581: Top left photo by Ken Heyman. Top right photo by Jack Sprat/Black Star. Lower photo by John Moss/Colorific!

Page 582: Top photo by Stacy Pick/Stock Boston. Bottom photo by Andrew Holbrooke/Black Star/Colorific!

Page 585: Photo by D. Halstear/Frank Spooner Pictures.

Page 593: Leonardo da Vinci (facsimile), *Disegno del montaggio di un cannone nel cortile di una fonderia*. Firenze, Gabinetto dei disegni. Art Resource.

Page 594: Photo by Paul Weinberg/Contact Press Images/Colorific!

Page 595: Photo from AP/Wide World Photos.

Page 596: Top photos and bottom left photo from Culver Pictures, Inc. Bottom right photo from Photofest.

Page 597: Photo from AP/Wide World Photos.

Page 598: Photo by Roger Sandler/Black Star.

Page 599: Photo by Lewis Portnoy/The Stock Market.

Page 600: Photo by Robert Frank, *City Fathers, Hoboken, New Jersey*, 1955. From *The Americans*, 1959. Gelatin Silver Print, 9¾ × 13 in. San Francisco Museum of Modern Art, Byron Meyer Fund Purchase.

Page 602: Photo from Photofest.

Page 604: Photo from Photofest.

Page 605: Photo from ZEFA.

Page 607: Figure 16.5 is an adaptation of a Likert scale assessing attitudes toward homosexuals from M. E. Kite and K. Deaux in "Attitudes Toward Homosexuality: Assessment & Behavioral Consequences," in *Basic and Applied Social Psychology*, 7:137-162, 1986. Used by permission of Lawrence Erlbaum Associates, Inc.

Page 609: Photo at left by Luongo/Liaison/Frank Spooner Pictures. Photo at right from AP/Wide World Photos.

Page 610: Figure 16.6 from C. J. Nemeth, "Differential Contributions of Majority and Minority Influence," *Psychological Review*, 93:23–32, 1986. Copyright 1986 by the American Psychological Association. Reprinted by permission. Photo from Paul Popper, Ltd.

Page 611: Photo at left from San Francisco Family Violence Project. Artwork at right from Yolanda Bako and the San Francisco Family Violence Project.

Page 614: Photo by Brad Bower/Picture Group/Colorific!

Page 618: Photo by Heinz Stucke/Frank Spooner Pictures.

Page 620: Figure 16.12 from *Social Pressures in Informal Groups: A Study of Human Factors in Housing* by Leon Festinger, Stanley Schachter, and Kurt Back, 1950. Reprinted with permission of the publishers, Stanford University Press, and the authors. Copyright © 1950.

Page 621: Photo by William Kennedy/The Image Bank.

Page 622: Rodin, *The Kiss*, Paris, Musée Rodin. Photo by Giraudon/Art Resource.

Page 623: Photo at left by Barbara Filet/Click Chicago Ltd. Photo at right by Nathaniel Antman/The Image Works.

Page 626: Left photos by Lawrence Migdale/Color 2000. Top right photo by Richard Hutchings/Infoedit. Middle right photo by Henley & Savage/Click Chicago Ltd. Bottom right photo by John Reis/The Stock Market.

Page 627: Top left photo by Jeff Albertson/The Picture Cube. Bottom left photo by Barbara Filet/Click Chicago Ltd. Photo at right by Paul Fusco/Magnum Photos.

Page 629: Top photo by John Running/Colorific! Lower photo by Sally Fear/Impact Photos. Figure 16.18: photos by William Vandivert.

Page 630: Figure 16.19 adapted from "Opinion and Social Pressure" by Solomon Asch, *Scientific American*, November, 1955, from illustration by Sara Love on pages 32 and 35. Copyright © 1955 by Scientific American, Inc. All rights reserved. Photo by Fallander/SIPA-Press/Rex Features.

Page 632: Photo by Tim Chapman/Black Star.

Page 633: Figures 16.20 and 16.21: photos © 1965 · by Stanley Milgram. From *Obedience*, distributed by the New York University Film Library.

Page 635: Photo at left by Frilbt/SIPA-Press/Rex Features. Photo at right by Gian Franco Gorgoni/Contact Press Images/Colorific!

Page 636: Top photo by Jim Howard/Colorific! Bottom photo by David Reed/Impact Photos.

Page 639: Figure 16.25: photo by Stephen Ferry/J. B. Pictures.

Page 644: Photo by D. Willets/Gamma/Frank Spooner Pictures.

Page 647: Photo by Jerry Irwin/Photo Researchers.

ILLUSTRATORS' CREDITS

John and Judy Waller. Figures 1.1, 2.17, 3.1, 3.3, 3.11, 3.12, 3.13a, 3.16, 3.17, 3.18, 3.21, 3.23, 3.26, 3.30, 3.35, 4.3, 5.2, 5.3, 5.4, 5.11, 5.14, 5.21, 5.36, 5.42, 6.13, 6.14, 7.1, 7.2, 7.4, 7.12, 7.13, 8.17, 9.14, 9.17, 9.18, 9.24, 11.2, 11.5, 11.6, 11.10, 14.4, 14.8, 14.14, 16.15 left, 16.28. Illustration on page 325 at bottom.

Carlyn Iverson. Figures 5.5a, 5.19, 5.22, 5.23, 5.24, 5.25, 7.10, 11.4, 11.8, 11.16.

Beck Visual Communication. Figures 3.24, 3.27, 3.28, 3.32, 3.34, 5.7, 8.24.

Darwen Hennings: Figure 13.4

Jeanne Schreiber: Figures 5.34, 5.53, 9.10, 9.15, 9.20.

Jeanne Schreiber and Graphic Typesetting Service: Figure 9.21.

Graphic Typesetting Service: Figures 1.2, 1.3, 2.1, 2.2, 2.4, 2.9, 2.10, 2.11, 2.12, 2.13, 2.14, 2.15, 2.16, 2.19, 2.20, 2.21, 2.22, 2.23, 2.24, 3.4, 3.7, 3.8, 3.14, 3.25, 4.4, 4.5, 4.9, 4.10, 4.12, 4.15, 5.1, 5.6, 5.9, 5.10, 5.18, 5.20, 5.27, 5.28, 5.29, 5.32, 5.33, 5.35, 5.37, 5.38, 5.41c, 5.44, 5.45, 5.49, 5.55b and c, 5.57, 6.5, 6.6, 6.7, 6.18, 6.19, 6.20, 6.23, 6.24, 6.25, 6.26, 7.5b, 7.6, 7.7, 7.8, 7.9, 7.11, 7.18, 7.19b, 7.20, 7.21, 7.22, 8.1, 8.2, 8.3, 8.4, 8.6, 8.7, 8.8, 8.10, 8.11, 8.12, 8.13, 8.14, 8.15, 8.16, 8.18, 8.19, 8.20, 8.21, 8.22, 8.23, 9.1, 9.2, 9.3, 9.7, 9.9, 9.11, 9.13, 9.25, 9.26, 9.27, 9.28, 9.30, 10.3, 10.4, 10.5, 10.8, 10.10, 10.11, 11.1, 11.3, 11.9, 11.11, 11.13, 11.14, 11.15, 11.17, 11.19, 11.20, 12.3, 12.4b, 12.5, 12.6, 12.7, 12.8, 12.9, 12.10, 12.17, 12.18, 12.19, 12.20, 12.21, 12.22b, 13.1, 13.3, 13.5, 13.8, 13.9, 13.10, 13.11, 13.12, 13.13, 13.14, 14.1, 14.5, 14.6, 14.10, 14.11, 14.12, 14.13, 14.14, 14.15, 14.16, 14.17, 14.18, 14.19, 14.20, 14.21, 14.24, 15.1, 15.2, 15.3, 15.4, 15.5, 15.6, 15.7, 15.8, 15.9, 15.10, 15.11, 16.2, 16.3, 16.4, 16.5, 16.6, 16.7, 16.8, 16.9, 16.10, 16.11, 16.12, 16.13, 16.15 right, 16.16, 16.17, 16.19, 16.22, 16.23, 16.24, 16.25 left, 16.27. Illustrations on pages 9, 197, 345 at right, 431, 433 and 461.

Heatherton, T. F., 397
Heckhausen, H., 413, 414, 415
Heffner, H. E., 144
Heffner, R. S., 144
Heider, F., 600
Heider, K., 435
Heilman, K. M., 84, 85
Held, R., 191
Heldman, J., 152
Hell, W., 342
Helzer, J. E., 444, 508, 509, 512, 515, 536, 540, 547
Hendrick, C., 228, 622–23
Hendrick, S., 228, 622–23
Heninger, G. R., 123
Hennessy, R. T., 115
Henry, R. M., 203
Hering, E., 138–39
Herman, B., 552
Herman, C. P., 396, 397, 399
Herman, J., 111, 588
Herman, L. M., 214
Herrnstein, R. J., 366, 517
Hersh, R. H., 202
Hertz, H., 144
Herz, A., 527
Hester, R. K., 531
Hetherington, E. M., 223
Hilgard, E. R., 115
Hill, C., 617, 618
Hill, C. T., 228, 627
Hill, J. L., 579
Hinckley, J., Jr., 585
Hind, J. E., 145
Hines, M., 406
Hinson, R. E., 527
Hirschfeld, R. M. A., 536, 542
Hirt, M. L., 573
Hissom, H., 449
Hitchcock, A., 430
Hitler, A., 51
Hobbes, T., 467, 484
Hobson, J. A., 110, 111
Hochberg, J., 161
Hockney, D., 164
Hodges, C. A., 69
Hodgson, R., 532
Hodgson, R. J., 523, 524
Hoffer, A., 13
Hoff-Ginsberg, E., 209
Hoffman, L. W., 222
Hoffman, M., 406
Hoffman, R. E., 540
Hogan, J., 642
Hogan, J. A., 378
Hogan, R. A., 521
Hogarth, R. M., 342
Hoge, S. K., 583
Holden, C., 496
Hollandsworth, S., 451
Hollister, L. E., 122
Hollon, S. D., 564
Holmes, D. S., 475
Holmes, T., 445, 446
Holyoak, K. J., 333
Holzer, C. E., 508
Holzer, C. E., III, 509, 512, 515, 518
Holzman, P. S., 547, 548
Honer, W. G., 123
Honig, A. S., 415
Honzik, C. H., 261
Honzik, M. P., 351
Hood, J., 543
Hopkins, W. D., 214
Horn, J. L., 363, 532
Horn, J. M., 60
Horne, J. A., 102
Horner, M. S., 416–17
Horney, K., 477–78
Horowitz, T., 389
Horvath, P., 560
Hough, R. L., 508
House, R. J., 647
Hovland, C. I., 246, 608

Howard, B. V., 394
Howard, J., 343
Howard, K. I., 573
Hoyt, M. F., 107
Hubel, D. H., 140, 162
Hubert, S., 597
Hugdahl, K., 519
Hull, C. L., 378, 384
Hull, J. G., 120, 124
Humphrey, H. H., 476
Hunt, R. R., 296
Hunter, I. M., 299
Hunter, J. E., 641, 642
Hunter, R. F., 641, 642
Huston, A. C., 39
Huston, T. L., 622
Hutchinson, J. E., 209
Huttunen, M. O., 550
Hwang, C.-P., 223
Hyde, J. S., 367

Iafaldano, M. T., 647
Iggo, A., 149
Illowsky, B. P., 548
Infurna, R. N., 298
Insanity defense work group, 585, 586
Insel, T. R., 579
Insko, C. A., 630
Institute for Personality and Ability Testing, Inc., 498
Intons-Peterson, M. J., 298
Isenberg, D. J., 636
Ishikawa, B., 555
Issacs, E. A., 14
Iwai, J., 447
Izard, C. E., 437

Jackson, J., 609
Jackson, L. D., 439
Jackson, R., 546
Jacobowitz, D. M., 577
Jacobs, B. L., 74, 123
Jacobs, G. H., 133, 134
Jacobsen, F. M., 540
James, M., 298
James, W., 317, 427, 429, 430, 431, 442, 463, 591
Jamis, M., 307
Janicak, P. G., 577
Janis, I. L., 457, 608, 636, 637
Janoff-Bulman, R., 440
Janson, P., 230
Janson, R., 646
Jaremko, M. E., 457
Jarvik, L. F., 576
Jarvis, M., 123
Jasnos, T. M., 428
Jefferson, T., 594
Jensen, A. R., 192, 371
Jensen, C., 343
Jéquier, E., 388
Jernigan, T. L., 548
Jessell, T. M., 150
Johanssen, H. S., 215
John, O. P., 600
Johnson, L., 610
Johnson, L. C., 102
Johnson, L. S., 118
Johnson, M. K., 284, 285
Johnson, P. B., 225
Johnson, S., 583
Johnson, V. E., 404
Johnson, W. G., 386
Johnston, J. C., 336
Johnston, W. A., 336
Jonakait, G. M., 67
Jones, B. D., 578
Jones, E. E., 124, 596, 601, 602, 603, 604, 615
Jones, G. R., 597, 643
Jones, L. V., 368
Jones, P. B., 354

Jones, R. A., 343
Jones, R. K., 215
Jones, S., 579
Jonides, J., 333
Jonquière, M., 536
Jouvet, M., 105, 111
Joyce, P. R., 576
Judd, C. M., 597
Julesz, B., 164
Jung, C. G., 478–79, 480, 484
Jungeblut, A., 356
Junginger, J., 544
Jurkovic, G. J., 203
Jusczyk, P., 188, 189
Jusczyk, P. W., 189
Just, M. A., 322

Kaas, J. H., 149
Kadden, R. M., 517
Kael, P., 430
Kagan, J., 185, 203
Kahlo, F., 468
Kahn, R. L., 231
Kahneman, D., 342, 343
Kail, R., 310
Kaiser, M. K., 333
Kakuyama, T., 413
Kalat, J. W., 73, 241, 244, 389, 522
Kales, A., 110
Kalogeris, T. J., 388
Kamin, L. J., 248, 249, 369, 370
Kammann, R., 26, 27, 28, 493
Kandel, D., 124
Kandel, D. B., 124
Kandel, E. R., 248
Kane, J. M., 578
Kanizsa, G., 160
Kanner, L., 550, 551
Kanouse, D. E., 597
Kant, I., 183
Kantner, J. F., 228
Kaplan, B. J., 211
Kaplan, E. H., 404
Kapur, N., 309
Karlin, R. A., 456
Karno, M., 523
Karus, D., 124
Kassin, S. M., 380
Katon, W., 537
Katz, D. M., 67
Katz, E., 611
Katz, S. H., 371
Keane, T. M., 444
Keil, F. C., 193
Keir, R., 519
Keith-Lucas, T., 247
Kellar, K. J., 577
Keller, M. B., 536
Kelley, H., 625
Kelley, H. H., 601, 608, 622
Kellogg, L. A., 212
Kellogg, W. N., 212
Kelly, I. W., 361
Kendler, K. S., 536, 546, 549
Kendzierski, D. A., 39
Kennedy, J. F., 51, 636
Kennedy, P., 309
Kennedy, R. F., 51
Kenrick, D. T., 492
Keon, T. L., 230
Kerner, J., 499
Kerzendorfer, M., 497
Kessler, L. G., 508, 559
Kessler, R. C., 589
Kety, S. S., 12, 549
Khantzian, E. J., 124
Khen, M., 152
Kidd, K. K., 536, 549
Kiefer, S. A., 147
Kiesler, C. A., 580
Kihlstrom, J. F., 117
Kilmann, P. R., 577
Kimble, G. A., 250, 258, 501

King, B. M., 386
King, M. L., Jr., 231, 438, 481, 507
Kinsey, A. C., 400–402, 409
Kirchner, J. H., 521
Kirtley, D. D., 112
Kite, 607
Klassen, A. D., 401, 406, 407
Klatzky, R. L., 149
Klayman, J., 341
Kleber, H. D., 527, 534
Klein, D. F., 560
Klein, D. R., 516
Klein, S. B., 296
Kleinmuntz, B., 426
Kleitman, N., 101, 103, 105
Klerman, G. L., 536
Klineberg, O., 435
Knesper, D. J., 559, 560
Knight, R. A., 409
Knight, T. D., 625
Kniskern, D. P., 572
Knop, J., 529
Knowler, W. C., 394
Knowlton, L. C., 329
Kochansky, G., 583
Koegel, P., 583
Koegel, R. L., 550, 551
Koelling, R. A., 250, 251
Koeske, R., 395
Koestner, R., 426
Koh, T.-H., 366
Kohlberg, L., 202, 203, 204, 205, 206
Kolata, G., 186
Kolb, B., 548
Kolko, D. J., 543, 570
Komaki, J., 272
Komata, Y., 151
Komorita, S. S., 639
Konorski, J., 255
Koppenaal, R. J., 303
Kopta, S. M., 573
Kornhuber, H. H., 81
Koss, M. P., 408, 573
Kosslyn, S. M., 323, 324
Kosten, T. R., 534
Kozel, N. J., 122
Krafczyk, S., 170
Kramer, M., 508, 509, 512, 515, 518
Krammer, R. M., 639
Krause, M. S., 573
Krause, R., 435
Kreskin, 26–27, 116
Krieger, K., 214
Kristal, A. R., 404
Krueger, D. W., 545
Krug, S. E., 497
Kruglanski, A. W., 597, 601
Krystal, J. H., 123
Ku, 403
Kübler-Ross, E., 231–32
Kueck, L., 91, 92
Kuhar, M. J., 122
Kuhn, C. M., 450
Kulik, C. C., 356
Kulik, J., 284
Kulik, J. A., 356
Kulikowski, J. J., 140
Kumar, J., 403
Kumar, R., 123
Kupfer, D. J., 543
Kurnit, D. M., 57
Kushner, M., 523
Kyle, G. R., 404

Ladd-Franklin, C., 11
Lader, M. H., 123
LaGamma, E. F., 67
Laibson, P. R., 132
Laird, J. D., 433–34
Lakoff, G., 325
Lallier, S., 110
Lamb, M., 222
Lamb, M. E., 223

Murphy, G. L., 14
Murray, H. A., 381, 500
Murstein, B. I., 618
Muzio, J. N., 108
Myers, D. G., 635
Myers, J. K., 508, 509, 512, 515, 518
Myers, R. H., 57
Myers, W. D., 132
Myles-Worsley, M., 336

Nagera, H., 522
Nagle, K. J., 225
Naranjo, C. A., 532
Nash, M. R., 115, 118
Nathanson, D., 260
National Center for Health Statistics, 403
National Institute of Mental Health, 39
Navratilova, M., 411
Naylor, S. L., 456
Neal, P., 93
Nebes, R. D., 88
Neely, J. H., 304
Neiss, R., 428
Nelson, J. M., 121
Nelson, K. E., 211
Nelson, P. A., 279
Nemeth, C., 638
Nemeth, C. J., 610
Nerviano, V. J., 531
Netter, F. H., 405
Neufeld, R. W. J., 455, 574
Neve, R. L., 57
Newcomb, M. D., 490, 529
Newman, R., 118
Newman, S. E., 279
Nicholls, K., 527
Nickerson, R. S., 286, 287
Nicol, S. E., 549
Nietzel, M. T., 350
Nimoy, L., 602
Nisbett, R. E., 317, 318, 333, 602, 603
Noble, A., 343
Noble, C. E., 617
Noel, B., 570
Nolen-Hoeksema, S., 536
Norman, D. A., 476
North, O., 595
Nosofsky, R. M., 328
Nostradamus, 26, 51
Nowicki, S., Jr., 517, 546
Noyes, R. J., Jr., 518
Nunn, R. G., 266
Nutt, J., 73
Nygard, R., 413

O'Brien, C. P., 534
O'Brien, E. J., 492
O'Brien, M., 225
O'Connor, S. D., 416
O'Donohue, T. L., 577
O'Malley, S. S., 530
O'Nell, C. W., 563
O'Shanick, G. J., 543
O'Sullivan, M., 435
Obstbaum, S. A., 132
Oden, C. W., Jr., 455
Okada, A., 413
Oken, D., 457
Okin, R. L., 580
Oldham, G., 646
Olds, J., 6
Olsen, S., 546
Olson, F. A., 310
Olson, J. M., 605
Olson, L., 93
Ophir, D., 152
Opton, E. M., Jr., 437, 453
Organ, D. W., 648
Orlinsky, D. E., 573
Orne, E. C., 586
Orne, M. E., 116

Orne, M. T., 40, 116, 117, 118, 426, 586
Ornitz, E. M., 550
Ornsteen, M., 536
Orr, S. P., 444
Orth, J. E., 563
Ortmann, J., 12
Orvaschel, H., 509, 512, 515, 518, 536, 540, 547
Osborne, R. T., 617
Oscar-Berman, M., 85, 308
Oskamp, S., 501
Öst, L.-G., 519
Oster, H., 389
Ostrove, N., 596
Ottina, K., 456
Otto, R., 523
Owen, D. R., 370
Owens, W. A., 642
Oyama, O. N., 529, 530

Padgham, C. A., 111
Pagan, S., 57
Paicheler, G., 628
Paight, D. J., 589
Pakstis, A. J., 371
Panksepp, J., 552
Papageorgis, D., 612
Park, B., 597
Parke, R. D., 39, 185
Parker, D., 542, 559
Parker, D. F., 461
Parker, E. S., 120
Parker, K., 500
Parker, K. O., 279
Parkinson, C. N., 643
Parmeggiani, P. L., 105
Parnas, J., 547
Parsons, H. M., 41
Parsons, J. E., 225
Pate, J. L., 214
Patterson, D., 57
Paul, L. A., 150
Paul, S. M., 120
Pavlov, I. P., 242–250, 252, 253, 279, 335
Paykel, E. S., 576
PDP Research Group, 293
Peachey, J. E., 532
Peacock, R., 301
Pearce, J. M., 246
Pearson, A. J. D., 102
Peckham, W., 407
Peele S., 532
Pendery, M. L., 533
Pennebaker, J. W., 455
Peplau, 228, 627
Peplau, L. A., 617, 618, 622
Pepper, B., 580, 583
Pereira, R., 549
Perl, M., 508
Perls, F., 569
Perper, J. A., 543
Perry, D. G., 269
Perry, S. H., 140
Pert, A., 577
Pert, C. B., 150, 577
Pervin, L. A., 383
Peterson, C., 537, 539
Peterson, D. A., 642
Peterson, D. R., 622
Peterson, L. G., 543
Peterson, L. R., 289, 290
Peterson, M., 543
Peterson, M. J., 289, 290
Petitto, L. A., 213–14
Pettingale, K. W., 450
Petty, R. E., 606, 611, 612
Pfefferbaum, A., 548
Pfefferbaum, B., 508
Pfohl, B., 535
Pfungst, O., 25
Phillips, D. P., 589
Piaget, J., 192–202, 206, 211, 233, 234
Picasso, P., 316

Pichot, P., 499
Pierrot-Deseilligny, C., 13
Pincus, J. H., 439
Pinkerton, R. S., 573
Pinsky, S. D., 215
Pinsof, W. M., 572
Pi-Sunyer, F. X., 395
Pitcairn, T., 435
Pitman, R. K., 444
Pittillo, E. S., 512
Pleck, J. H., 403
Plomin, R., 228, 369, 529
Plotkin, D. A., 576
Plutchik, R., 423, 432
Poherecky, L. A., 449
Pohl, T. M., 59
Pokorny, A. D., 579
Polivy, J., 396, 397, 399
Pollak, J. M., 523
Pollock, J., 470
Polya, G., 330
Pomeroy, W. B., 400, 401, 409
Poncy, M., 150, 459
Pond, S. B., III, 643
Poole, A. D., 567
Popkin, M. K., 578
Popper, K., 473
Porter, R. W., 444
Pottash, A. L. C., 121
Poulos, C. X., 528
Powell, A., 486
Powers, S., 354
Prabucki, K., 224
Pratkanis, A. R., 23, 608
Premack, A. J., 213
Premack, D., 213, 260
Premack, S. L., 643
Prentky, R. A., 409
Price, D. L., 308
Price, K. P., 537
Price, L. H., 123
Price, R. A., 536
Prien, R. F., 576
Priest, R. F., 620
Probst, T., 170
Provine, R. R., 196
Proxmire, W., 617
Prusoff, B. A., 536
Purdy, K., 646
Purves, D., 67

Quigley, A. M., 642
Quillian, M. R., 326
Quinn, R. P., 596

Rabkin, J. G., 550, 587
Rachman, S., 521
Rachman, S. J., 523, 524
Radin, N., 223
Rahe, R., 445, 446
Rakusin, J. M., 570
Ramos-Lorenzi, J., 578
Rankin, H., 532
Ransdell, S. E., 215
Raps, C. S., 537
Ratscliff, R., 320
Raven, J. C., 353, 354
Ravussin, E., 394
Rayner, R., 518, 519
Raz, M., 631
Read, J. D., 159
Reagan, R., 585, 608, 609, 610
Rechtschaffen, A., 103
Redican, W. K., 434
Reed, C., 149
Reed, J., 407
Reed, T. E., 555
Regier, D. A., 508, 509, 512, 515, 536, 540, 547, 559
Reich, J., 518
Reicher, G. M., 336
Reilly, R. R., 643

Reisberg, B., 57
Reisenzein, R., 604
Reiser, B. J., 323, 324
Renner, M. J., 189
Rensch, B., 149, 321
Rescorla, R., 252
Rescorla, R. A., 249, 261
Rest, J. R., 203
Restifo, N., 439
Restle, F., 176
Reznick, J. S., 185
Rhine, J. B., 25, 27
Ricaurte, G. A., 123
Ricci-Bitti, P. E., 435
Riccio, G. E., 149
Rice, J. P., 536
Rice, M. L., 211
Rich, C. L., 542, 543
Richards, D. D., 359
Richards, D. G., 214
Richardson-Klavehn, A., 282
Richter, C. P., 389, 426, 541
Richwald, G. A., 404
Ricketts, J. E., 542
Riedel, S. L., 621
Riley, J. N., 69
Riley, V., 443
Rincover, A., 552
Rips, L. J., 304, 305, 327
Ritvo, E., 439
Ritvo, E. R., 550
Ritz, M. C., 122
Rivers, B., 107
Roberts, A. H., 452
Roberts, K. H., 647
Roberts, M. K., 228
Roberts, S. B., 394
Robinette, C. D., 549
Robins, L. N., 444, 508, 509, 512, 515, 536, 540, 547
Rock, I., 176
Rockwell, W. J. K., 573
Rodin, J., 231, 393, 399
Roediger, H. L., III, 283
Roffwarg, H., 111
Roffwarg, H. P., 108
Rogers, C., 467, 482, 484, 564–65
Rogers, S., 540
Rokous, F. E., 409
Rolf, I., 568
Romano, J. M., 537
Roose, S. P., 543
Roosevelt, E., 288
Roosevelt, F., 30
Rorschach, H., 499
Rosch, E., 325, 328
Rose, J. E., 145
Rose, S. A., 351
Rosen, L. S., 456
Rosenbaum, M., 272
Rosenbaum, M. E., 638
Rosenberg, R., 409
Rosenblatt, J. E., 577
Rosenhan, D. L., 581–82
Rosenman, A. A., 215
Rosenman, R. H., 449, 450
Rosenthal, D., 12
Rosenthal, N. E., 540
Rosenthal, R., 14
Rosenzweig, M. R., 189
Ross, D., 269, 516
Ross, D. C., 560
Ross, D. F., 306
Ross, L., 602
Ross, M., 604
Ross, S. A., 269
Rosslyn, 323
Roth, H. P., 532
Roth, S., 409
Roth, W. T., 518
Rothbart, M., 343, 600
Rothman, S., 361, 370
Rotter, J. B., 488, 489
Rottman, L., 620

GLOSSARY / SUBJECT INDEX

A

abnormal behavior, 504–555

absolute threshold the sensory threshold at a time of maximum sensory adaptation. 156, 157

abstract concepts, 199–201

accommodation Piaget's term for the modification of an established schema to fit new objects. 194

acetylcholine, 73, 121

achievement. *See* need for achievement.

Acquired Immune Deficiency Syndrome (AIDS) a disease often transmitted sexually that gradually destroys the body's immune system. 403, 404

acquisition the process by which a conditioned response is established or strengthened. 244

action potential a sudden decrease or reversal in electrical charge across the membrane of an axon. 69, 70, 72

activation-synthesis theory of dreams the theory that parts of the brain are spontaneously activated during REM sleep and that a dream is the brain's attempt to synthesize that activation into a coherent pattern. 111

active versus passive movement, 190, 191

actor-observer effect the tendency for people to be more likely to attribute internal causes to other people's behavior than they are to their own behavior. 602–604

adaptation (sensory), 134, 135, 156, 157

addiction the inability to stop using a substance that impairs a person's health or well-being. 525–534

adolescence, 217–219, 226–228

adopted children, 62, 370–371

adrenal gland, 80, 81, 389, 407

adrenalin. *See* epinephrine.

adulthood, 219, 228–231

adverse impact, 641, 642

affiliation the motivation to be with others. 617–620

afterimage. *See* negative afterimage.

agape love, 622, 623

age differences:
    in brain, 57, 69
    in intelligence, 185, 186, 350, 351, 363
    in job satisfaction, 230
    in learning and memory, 310
    in muscle control, 187
    in need for achievement, 414, 415
    in recovery from brain damage, 94
    in sensation, 130
    in sleep, 107, 108
    in thought processes, 192–202

aging. *See* development.

aggressive behavior, 30, 31, 73, 85, 269, 408, 409, 437–439

agoraphobia a fear of open places or public places. 518

agreeableness, 486

AIDS, 403, 404

alcohol a class of carbon-based molecules that include an –OH group. 69, 94, 120–122, 124, 187, 526, 527

Alcoholics Anonymous (AA) a self-help group of people who are trying to abstain from drinking alcohol and who are trying to help others do the same. 457, 531, 560

alcoholism the habitual overuse of alcohol. 12, 62, 74, 528–533

algorithm a mechanical, repetitive mathematical procedure for solving a problem. 331, 332

altered states, 98–125

Alzheimer's disease a degenerative condition of old age marked by gradual damage to the brain leading to the gradual loss of memory and other abilities. 57, 308, 309

ambition. *See* goal setting.

American Psychological Association, 42

Ames room, 174, 175

amiloride, 152

amnesia a severe loss of memory. 291, 307–310

amphetamine, 121, 122

amplitude of sound, 143

amygdala, 82, 83

anal stage Freud's second stage of psychosexual development, in which psychosexual pleasure is focused on the anus. 471, 472

androgyny a combination of the features of masculinity and femininity. 486–488

anecdotes, 26

anesthetics, 70

angel dust, 74

anger, 423, 429–432, 437–439

animal experiments (ethics of), 43

animal learning, 239–243, 248–265

animal magnetism, 113

animal training, 265

anorexia nervosa a condition in which a person refuses to eat adequate food and steadily loses weight. 397, 398, 565, 566

Antabuse disulfiram, a drug that blocks the breakdown of acetaldehyde into acetic acid. 532

anterograde amnesia the inability to form new long-term memories. 307–309

anthropology. *See* cultural differences.

antidepressant drugs, 10, 109, 576

antisocial personality disorder, 511

anvil (bone), 144

anxiety, 73, 515, 516

apnea, 109

apparent movement, 170, 171

approaches to psychology, 12–16

arousal, 81, 423–433, 459

art, 183–185

artificial intelligence, 335, 339, 340

artificial mother experiment, 220, 221

artificial selection the purposeful selection, by humans, of certain animals for breeding purposes. 62

assessment. *See* tests.

assimilation Piaget's term for the application of an established schema to new objects. 194

association, 279, 280

attachment a long-term feeling of closeness between people, such as a child and a caregiver. 219–222

attention, 158, 167, 168

attention-deficit disorder, 510

attentive process paying attention to only one part of a visual field at a time. 168, 171

attitude a learned like or dislike of something or somebody that influences behavior toward that thing or person. 606–616

attraction, 228–230, 617–627

attractive people, 595, 596, 608, 620, 621

attribution the set of thought processes we use to assign causes to our own behavior and the behavior of others. 539, 600–605

attributional bias, 602, 603

audition. *See* hearing.

autism a lifelong condition beginning in childhood that is characterized by extreme social isolation, repetitive movements, and failure to communicate. 550–552

autokinetic effect the illusory perception that a point of light in a darkened room is in motion. 160, 161

autonomic nervous system a set of neurons lying in and alongside the spinal cord, which receives information from and sends information to the internal organs such as the heart. 78, 80, 81, 423–433, 449, 459

autonomy versus shame and doubt the conflict between independence and doubt about one's abilities. 216

autosomal chromosomes the chromosomes other than the sex chromosomes. 60

availability heuristic the strategy of assuming that the number of available memories of an event indicates how common the event actually is. 342, 343

average. *See* mean.

aversion therapy, 566, 567

avoidance learning, 259, 516, 517, 521

687

avoidant personality disorder, 511

axes of DSM III-R, 509–511

axon a single long, thin fiber that transmits impulses from a neuron to other neurons or to muscle cells. 67–70, 72, 73, 88

B

babbling, 210, 211

babies, 187–189, 195, 196, 210, 211, 219, 220, 471, 472

backward conditioning presenting the unconditioned stimulus before the conditioned stimulus. 246, 247

bait shyness. *See* conditioned taste aversion.

balance, 147–149

barbiturate, 120, 121

basal ganglia, 74, 82, 83

base-rate information information about the frequency or probability of a given item. 341, 342

basic trust versus mistrust the conflict between trusting and mistrusting that one's parents and other key figures will meet one's basic needs; first conflict in Erikson's eight ages of human development. 216, 220

basilar membrane a thin membrane in the cochlea that vibrates after sound waves strike the eardrum. 144, 145, 147

bat, 103

Bay of Pigs, 636, 637

bed-wetting, 566

bee, 63, 130

behaviorist a psychologist who tries to explain the causes of behavior by studying only those behaviors that he or she can observe and measure, without reference to unobservable mental processes. 13–15, 241, 242, 253

behavior modification a procedure for modifying behavior by setting specific behavior goals and reinforcing the subject for successive approximations to those goals. 265, 565, 566

behavior therapy a form of therapy in which the therapist and client agree on specific behavioral goals and set up learning experiences to achieve those goals, using positive reinforcement, classical conditioning, and sometimes punishment. 565–567

belongingness the concept that certain stimuli are readily associated with each other and that certain responses are readily associated with certain outcomes. 255

benzodiazepine, 120, 121

Bianchi case, 586

bias a systematic underestimation or overestimation of the performance of a given group in a certain activity. 365–367

binge eating, 395–397, 399

binocular cues visual cues that depend on the action of both eyes. 169

biofeedback a method for providing constant information about physiological processes in order to gain voluntary control over processes that people cannot ordinarily control. 451, 452

biographical information, 439, 642

biological cycles, 101, 104, 105

biological (or **physiological**) **psychologist** a psychologist who tries to relate behavior to activities of the brain and other organs. 12, 13

biological psychology, 54–97

biorhythms, 20

bipolar cells, 135, 138, 139

bipolar disorder a disorder marked by alternation between two emotional extremes, depression and mania. 540–542, 577

bird, 63–65

birth order, 223, 224

black children. *See* race differences.

bladder control, 566

blindness, 112, 435, 436

blind observer an observer who does not know which subjects are in which group or what results are expected. 31

blind spot the area of the retina through which the optic nerve exits. 131, 135, 136

blind study, 31

blood pressure, 426

blood types, 371, 372

bonding. *See* attachment.

borderline personality disorder, 511

bottom-up processing, 167

braille, 149

brain, 78–94

and aging, 57, 69

damage, 13, 92–94, 308, 548

electrical stimulation of, 6, 7

maturation, 67, 69, 78, 79

species differences in, 79

transplant (partial), 93

waves, 106

breathing, 81, 426

brief therapy therapy that begins with an agreement to restrict its duration, generally to 6 months or less. 572, 573

brightness contrast, 140

bulimia a condition in which people have periods of excessive eating. 399

bystander apathy, 634, 635

C

cabin fever, 455

caffeine, 121, 122

cancer, 391, 450, 451, 459, 460

Cannon-Bard theory of emotions theory that certain areas of the brain evaluate sensory information and, when appropriate, send one set of impulses to the autonomic nervous system and another set to the forebrain, which is responsible for the subjective and cognitive aspects of emotion. 428, 429, 431

capacity of memory, 288, 289

capsaicin, 150

carbohydrate, 392

case history a thorough description of a single individual, including information on both past experiences and current behavior. 32

cat, 103, 107, 162, 190, 191, 253, 254

cataract, 130

catatonia a condition of either rigid inactivity or excessive activity unrelated to external stimuli. 545

catatonic schizophrenia a condition marked by the basic symptoms of schizophrenia plus prominent movement disorders. 546

categorization, 325–328

by features, 327, 328

by levels, 326, 327

by prototypes, 328

catharsis the release of pent-up tension. 469, 561

caudal locus coeruleus, 111

causation, 36, 37

cell body the part of the neuron that includes the nucleus. 67, 68, 70

central nervous system the brain and the spinal cord. 78–94

central route to persuasion, 612

central traits, 598

cerebellum (Latin for "little brain") a hindbrain structure. 81–83

cerebral cortex the outer surface of the forebrain, consisting of six distinct layers of cells and fibers. 82–92

cerebral ventricles, 548

chaining a procedure for developing a sequence of behaviors in which the reinforcement for one response is the opportunity to engage in the next response. 257, 258

Challenger disaster, 637

checking, 523

chemical receptors the receptors that respond to the chemicals that come into contact with the nose and mouth. 151–154

chemotherapy, 391

chess, 335, 336

chewing, 81

chewing gum, 123

child abuse, 439

child psychology. *See* developmental psychology.

child-rearing practices, 222–224

children's language, 209–212

chimpanzee, 212–214, 320, 321

chlorpromazine, 578

chromosome a strand of hereditary material found in the nucleus of a cell. 57–60

chunking the process of grouping letters or digits into meaningful sequences that can be easily remembered. 289

cigarette, 121, 123, 124, 187, 526, 566, 567

circadian rhythms, 101, 104, 105

clairvoyance, 25

classical conditioning or **Pavlovian conditioning** the process by which an organism learns a new association between two stimuli paired with each other—a neutral stimulus and one that already evokes a reflexive response. 239–252, 255, 256, 518, 527, 528, 566

classification of disorders, 509–511

cleaning, 522, 523

Clever Hans, 24, 25

client-centered therapy. *See* person-centered therapy.

clinical psychologist psychologist who specializes in identifying and treating psychological disorders. 8–10

closure in Gestalt psychology, the tendency to imagine the rest of an incomplete familiar figure. 166

cocaine, 121, 122, 526

cochlea the snail-shaped, fluid-filled structure that contains the receptors for hearing. 144

coffee, 122, 404

cognition the processes that enable us to imagine, to gain knowledge, to reason about knowledge, and to judge its meaning. 14, 312–347

cognitive dissonance a state of unpleasant tension that people experience when they hold contradictory attitudes or when they behave in a way that is inconsistent with their attitudes. 612–616

cognitive map a mental representation of a spatial arrangement. 324, 325

cognitive psychologist a psychologist who studies thought processes and the acquisition of knowledge. 14

cognitive responses to persuasion, 611, 612

cognitive tests (in job selection), 641, 642

cognitive therapy a form of therapy that seeks to improve people's well-being by encouraging them to seek evidence that either supports or refutes their beliefs. 564, 576

cohort a group of people born at a particular time (as compared to people born at a different time). 185, 186

cold remedies, 74

collective unconscious according to Jung, an inborn level of the unconscious that symbolizes the collective experience of the human species. 478, 479

color blindness, 60, 141, 142

color constancy the tendency of an object to appear nearly the same color under a variety of lighting conditions. 139

color vision, 136–142

commons dilemma a situation in which people may choose to deplete common resources for their own advantage faster than the resources can be replenished. 638, 639

common sense, 4, 5

communication. *See* language.

community psychologist a psychologist who focuses on the needs of large groups rather than those of individuals. 588

comparative psychology the branch of psychology that compares the behaviors of various animal species. 9, 63, 64, 239–242

competency interpretation, 413

compliance the tendency to do what someone asks us to do. 631

compulsion a repetitive, almost irresistible action. 522–524

computers. *See* artificial intelligence.

concrete-operations stage according to Piaget, the third stage of intellectual development, in which children can deal with the properties of concrete objects but cannot readily deal with hypothetical or abstract questions. 198, 199

concurrent validity the relationship between a test's scores and performances outside the test at approximately the same time. 359

conditioned inhibitor a stimulus that inhibits the conditioned response because of past experiences in which it predicted the absence of the unconditioned stimulus. 247

conditioned response (CR) a response that the conditioned stimulus elicits only because it has previously been paired with the unconditioned stimulus. 243

conditioned stimulus (CS) a stimulus that comes to evoke a particular response after being paired with the unconditioned stimulus. 243

conditioned taste aversion or **bait shyness** the tendency to avoid eating a substance that has been followed by illness when eaten in the past. 250–252, 391, 392

conduction velocity of axon, 69, 136

conductive deafness hearing loss that results if the bones connected to the eardrum fail to transmit sound waves properly to the cochlea. 144

cone the type of visual receptor that is adapted for color vision, daytime vision, and detailed vision. 132–141

conformity maintaining or changing one's behavior to be consistent with group standards. 124, 628–631

connectionist model a model that represents memory as a set of links among units. 293

conscientiousness, 486

consciousness. *See* sleep.

consensus information input about how a person's behavior compares with other people's behavior. 601

conservation the concept that objects retain their weight, volume, and certain other properties in spite of changes in their shape or arrangement. 196–198, 201, 202

consistency information information about how much a person's behavior varies over time and in different situations. 601

consolidation the transfer of information from short-term memory to long-term memory. 290

constancies, 139, 168

construct validity the degree to which the properties of a test correspond to a theoretical concept. 359

contact comfort, 220

content validity the degree to which the questions on a test represent the information that the test is supposed to measure. 359

context-dependent memory a memory that is easier to recall in the environment in which it was formed than in some other environment. 298

contingency the degree to which the occurrence of one stimulus predicts the occurrence of a second stimulus. 250

continuation in Gestalt psychology, the tendency to fill in the gaps in an interrupted line. 166

continuous reinforcement reinforcement for every response. 262, 263

contraceptives, 228

contrast in vision, 140, 176

control group the group that is subjected to the same procedures as the experimental group except for the treatment that is being tested. 38

controlled drinking, 532, 533

control of events, 455–457, 538

convergence the turning in of the eyes as they focus on close objects. 168, 169

conversion disorder a condition in which a person shows symptoms such as paralysis, blindness, or deafness, apparently for psychological rather than medical reasons. 512

cooperation, 637–639

coping with stress, 453–462

cornea a rigid, transparent structure in the eye. 130, 131

corpus callosum a large set of axons connecting the left and right hemispheres of the cerebral cortex and enabling the two hemispheres to communicate with each other. 86–91, 196

correlation a measure of the relationship between two variables, neither of which is controlled by the investigator. 33–37

correlation coefficient a mathematical estimate of the relationship between two variables, ranging from +1 (perfect positive relationship) to 0 (no linear relationship) to −1 (perfect negative relationship). 34, 35, 53

cortex. *See* cerebral cortex.

Cotard's syndrome, 32

counseling psychologist, 9

cow, 103

CR. *See* conditioned response.

crack, 122, 123, 526

creativity the development of novel, socially valued products. 329, 330, 334, 335

crime, 439, 587, 588

cross-culture comparisons. *See* cultural differences.

crossed transactions, 569

cross-sectional study a study of individuals of different ages all at the same time. 183–186

crowding, 455, 456

crystallized intelligence acquired skills and knowledge and the application of that knowledge to specific content in a person's experience. 362, 363

CS. *See* conditioned stimulus.

cued recall a method of testing the persistence of memory by asking someone to remember a certain item after being given a hint. 281

cultural differences:
in abnormal behavior, 508
in alcohol use, 529, 532
in art and folklore, 479
in facial expressions, 434–437
in food choice, 390, 391
in sexual behavior, 401, 402

culture-fair tests, 353, 354

cumulative record a method of recording responses in which a recording pen moves up one notch for each response. 261, 262, 264

curiosity, 379

cutaneous senses the skin senses, including pressure, warmth, cold, pain, vibration, movement across the skin, and stretch of the skin. 149, 150

D

daily rhythms, 101, 104, 105

dangerousness, 439, 587, 588

dark adaptation a gradual improvement in the ability to see under dim light. 134, 135

dating, 228–230

dating anxiety, 457

day care, 222

deafness, 144, 214, 435, 436

death anxiety, 231–233

decay of memory traces, 289, 290

deception, 426, 427, 496

deep structure the logic of the language underlying a sentence. 209

defense mechanism a method of protecting oneself against anxiety caused by conflict between the id's demands and the superego's constraints. 473–476

deinstitutionalization the removal of large numbers of patients from mental hospitals. 583

delayed conditioning, 246, 247

delayed response, 239, 240

delinquency, 39

delusion an unfounded belief. 544, 545

delusion of grandeur a person's unfounded belief that he or she is extraordinarily important. 544

delusion of persecution a person's unfounded belief that other people are trying to hurt him or her. 544

delusion of reference a person's tendency to interpret all messages as if they referred to himself or herself. 544

demand characteristics cues that reveal to the participants what results the experimenter expects. 40, 42, 434

dementia praecox, 544

dendrite one of the widely branching structures of a neuron that generally receive transmission from other neurons. 67–70, 72, 189

denial the refusal to believe information that provokes anxiety. 475

deoxyribonucleic acid (DNA) the chemical that makes up a chromosome. 57, 58

dependence the inability to stop using a substance that impairs a person's health or well-being. 525–534

dependent personality disorder, 511

dependent variable the variable the experimenter measures to see how changes in the independent variable affect it. 37, 38

depressant drug, 121

depression a condition in which a person takes little pleasure in life and experiences feelings of worthlessness, powerlessness, and guilt. 12, 107, 450, 535–540, 576, 577

deprivation of sleep, 102, 103

depth-of-processing principle the principle that a memory can be stored either superficially or at various depths, depending on how deeply a person thinks about it and how many associations he or she forms with it. 296

depth perception the perception of distance. 168–170, 172, 175, 176

descriptive statistics mathematical summaries of results, such as measures of the central score and the amount of variation. 45–48

desensitization, 521

determinism the view that all behavior has a physical cause. 5, 6, 241, 481

detour, 240

detoxification a supervised period to remove drugs from the body. 531

deuteranopia, 141

development:

of brain, 78, 79

of language, 209–212

of learning, 187–189

of moral reasoning, 202–206

of muscle control, 187, 190, 191

of sensory organs, 187, 188

of sleep, 107, 108

of social and emotional behavior, 216–233

of thinking, 192–202

developmental psychology, 180–235

diabetes, 386

diet and behavior, 13, 74

dieting, 394–397

differential survival the tendency for some people to remain in an experiment longer than others. 41, 42

diffusion of responsibility the tendency for people to feel less responsibility for helping when other people are around than when they know that no one else can help. 634, 635

digestion, 425

disabled people, 462

discounting principle the tendency for peole to discount the likelihood of one cause for a behavior when they are strongly aware of another cause. 601, 602

discrimination making different responses to different stimuli that have been followed by different outcomes; in operant conditioning, the learning of different behaviors in response to stimuli associated with different levels of reinforcement. 246

disgust, 423

disorganized schizophrenia a condition marked by the basic symptoms of schizophrenia plus incoherent speech, extreme lack of social relationships, and odd behaviors. 546

displacement the diversion of a thought or action away from its natural target toward a less threatening target. 475

dissociation the separation of one set of memories from another for no discernible organic reason. 512, 513

dissonance. *See* cognitive dissonance.

distance (auditory), 147

distinctiveness (in memory) the quality of being different from other elements in a list. 284

distinctiveness information (social behavior) information about how much a person's behavior depends on who or what the person is relating to. 601

distortion of memory, 304–307, 491

distraction, 458, 459

distributed practice practice of something one is trying to learn spread over a period of time. 295

disulfiram, 532

divorce, 223

dizygotic twins (literally, two-egg twins) fraternal twins who develop from two ova fertilized by different sperm. 60, 61, 369, 370

DNA, 57, 58

dog, 242, 243, 537

dolphin, 214

dominant gene a gene that will exert its effects on development even in a person who is heterozygous for that gene. 59

door-in-the-face technique a way to gain compliance in which someone follows an outrageous initial request with a much more reasonable second request. 631

DOPA. *See* L-DOPA.

dopamine a neurotransmitter that promotes activity levels and facilitates movement. 73, 74, 121, 122, 526

dopamine theory of schizophrenia the theory that the underlying cause of schizophrenia is excessive stimulation of certain dopamine synapses in the brain. 548, 549

Dostoyevskian epilepsy, 85

double-blind study a study in which neither the observer nor the subjects know which subjects received which treatment. 31

dove, 63

drawing, 183–185

dream analysis, 112, 562, 563

dreaming, 107–112

drive an internal state of unrest that energizes learned behaviors. 378

drugs:

abuse, 525–534

effects, 120–125

medical uses, 122

therapies, 575–579

tolerance, 527, 528

withdrawal, 526, 527

DSM III-R *Diagnostic and Statistical Manual of Mental Disorders,* Third Edition—Revised, the standard reference work on the classification of psychological disorders. 509–511

Durham rule a rule that states that criminal defendants are insane if their acts were a product of mental disease or defect. 585

duty to warn, 588

dying, 231–233

E

ear, 143–147

eardrum, 144

early experience, 189–191

eating, 385–399

eating disorders, 392–399

eclectic therapy therapy that uses a combination of methods and approaches. 567, 568

"ecstasy," 73, 121, 123

ECT. *See* electroconvulsive therapy.

education, 202

educational psychologist, 9

EEG. *See* electroencephalograph.

effectiveness of psychotherapy, 573, 574

ego according to Freud, the rational, decision-making aspect of personality. 473, 474

egocentric thinking an inability to take the perspective of another person; a tendency to view the world as centered around oneself. 193, 194

ego integrity versus despair the conflict between satisfaction and dissatisfaction with one's life; the final conflict in Erikson's eight ages of human development. 219

eidetic imagery the ability to look at a large, complicated picture or pattern and later recall its contents in detail. 299, 301

Electra complex according to Freud, a young girl's romantic attraction toward her father and hostility toward her mother. 473

electrical stimulation of brain, 6, 7

electroconvulsive therapy (ECT) treatment in which a brief electrical shock is administered across the patient's head to induce a convulsion similar to epilepsy. 577

electroencephalograph (EEG) a device that measures and amplifies slight electrical changes on the scalp that reflect brain activity. 106

electromagnetic spectrum the continuum of all the frequencies of radiated energy. 129, 130

embarrassment, 433

emotion, 82, 420–463, 623–625

emotional expression, 86, 433–437

employment, 641–648

encoding specificity principle the principle that memory is strengthened by using the same retrieval cues when recovering a memory as when storing it. 297, 298

endocrine system a set of glands producing hormones and releasing them into the blood. 80, 81

endogenous depression a depression that develops gradually and that reflects biological causes rather than traumatic experiences. 535, 536

endorphin a neurotransmitter that inhibits the sensation of pain. 73, 74, 120, 121, 150, 459

engineering psychology. *See* ergonomics.

enriched environment, 67, 69, 189

enuresis. *See* bed-wetting.

environmental psychology, 9

epilepsy a disease characterized by abnormal rhythmic activity of some neurons in the brain. 85, 86

epinephrine, 81, 425, 429, 430, 444

episodic memory a person's memory of particular events in his or her life. 291, 292

equity theory a theory that holds that all social relationships are transactions in which partners exchange goods and services; people strive for a fair exchange of such goods. 625–627

ergonomics, 8, 9

ergot, 74, 75

Erikson's ages of development, 216–219

eros love, 622, 623

error of the mean, 49, 53

ESP. *See* extrasensory perception.

estrogen a hormone present in higher quantities in females than in males. 406

ethanol. *See* alcohol.

ethics. *See* moral reasoning.

ethics in research, 42, 43, 619

ethnic differences. *See* cultural differences.

ethology the branch of biology that studies animal behavior under natural or nearly natural conditions. 63, 64

euphoria, 429–432

Eve, 512, 513

evolution a change in the gene frequencies of a species. 62–64

evolutionary theory of sleep the theory that sleep evolved primarily as a means of forcing animals to conserve their energy when they are relatively inefficient. 103

exceptional memory, 299, 301

exchange theory. *See* equity theory.

excitation of neurons, 70, 72, 138

executive monkey experiment, 448, 449

exercise and energy expenditure, 393–395, 398, 454, 455, 516

expectancy the perceived probability of achieving a goal. 412

expectancy effect, 14

expectancy-value interpretation, 412, 413

experiment, 37–43

experimental group the group that receives the treatment that an experiment is designed to test. 38

expert performance, 14, 335–339

expert testimony, 310, 586

explicit memory tests, 282

exposure effects, 620

expression of emotions, 433–437

external cause of behavior, 600–604

externality hypothesis hypothesis that overweight people are motivated more strongly by external cues (such as the aroma and taste of food) than by internal cues (the physiological mechanisms that control hunger). 392, 393

external locus of control belief that outside forces are responsible for most of the important events in one's life. 488–490

extinction in classical conditioning, the dying out of the conditioned response after repeated presentations of the conditioned stimulus unaccompanied by the conditioned stimulus; in operant conditioning, the weakening of a response after a period of no reinforcement. 245, 255, 256, 264

extrasensory perception the alleged ability of certain people to obtain information without using any sense organ and without receiving any form of energy. 25–28

extraversion, 486

extrinsic motivation a motivation based on rewards and punishments separate from the act itself. 379, 380, 411

eye, 87, 88

eyebrow-raising greeting, 435

eye movement, 547, 548

eyewitness report, 305–307

F

face recognition, 161

facial expression, 433–437

factor analysis, 486

factual memory the ability to remember facts. 291

falsifiable capable of being contradicted by imaginable evidence. 23

familiar foods, 390, 392

familiar stimuli, 244

families, 222–224

family therapy therapy provided to a family, generally focusing on communications within the family. 571, 572

farsightedness, 130, 132

father, 222, 223

fear of failure a preoccupation with avoiding failure, rather than taking risks in order to succeed. 413, 423, 610. *See also* phobia.

fear of success, 416, 417

feature detector a neuron in the visual system of the brain that responds to particular lines or other features of a visual stimulus. 161–164, 167

femininity, 486–488

fetal alcohol syndrome a condition marked by decreased alertness and other signs of impaired development, caused by exposure to alcohol prior to birth. 187

fetus an individual at an early stage of development—in humans, an offspring more than 8 weeks after conception. 186, 187, 406

fight-or-flight activities, 80

figure and ground an object and its background. 165

finger-to-nose test a test to assess possible damage to the cerebellum, in which a person is asked to hold one arm straight out and then to touch the nose as quickly as possible. 82

firstborn, 223, 224

first impressions, 595–597

fish, 64, 65, 79, 143, 377

fixation in Freud's theory, a persisting preoccupation with an immature psychosexual interest as a result of frustration at that stage of psychosexual development. 471

fixed-interval schedule a rule for delivering reinforcement for the first response the subject makes after a specified period of time has passed. 263, 264

fixed-ratio schedule a rule for delivering reinforcement only after the subject has made a certain number of responses. 263, 264

flight of ideas, 540

flooding a method of reducing fear by suddenly exposing a person to the object of fear in reality or in imagination. 521

fluctuations in performance, 360

fluid intelligence the basic power of reasoning and using information, including the ability to perceive relationships, deal with unfamiliar problems, and gain new types of knowledge. 362, 363

food selection, 389–392

foot-in-the-door technique a way to gain compliance in which someone makes a modest request at first and then follows it up with a much larger second request. 631

forebrain the most anterior (forward) part of the brain, including the cerebral cortex and the limbic system. 78, 79

forewarning effect the tendency for a warning that people are about to hear a persuasive speech to weaken the talk's persuasive impact. 612

forgetting, 245, 301–303

formal-operations stage according to Piaget, the fourth and final stage of intellectual development, in which people use logical, deductive reasoning and systematic planning. 199–201

fovea the central part of the retina that consists solely of cones. 131, 133

framing of questions, 343, 344

fraternal twins. *See* dizygotic twins.

free association a procedure in which someone reports everything that comes to mind, without omission or censorship. 561, 562

free recall remembering a list of items in any order. 280

free will the alleged ability of an individual to make decisions that are not determined by heredity, past experience, or the environment. 5, 6

frequency of sound waves, 143

Freudian slip, 476, 477

frontal lobe the anterior portion of each hemisphere of the cerebral cortex, containing the motor cortex and the prefrontal cortex. 85, 548

frowning, 433–437

frustration-aggression hypothesis the theory that frustration leads to aggressive behavior. 438

F scale of MMPI, 496

fugue, 512

full moon (effects on behavior), 36

fundamental attribution error the tendency to overemphasize internal explanations of behavior and underemphasize external explanations. 602, 603

G

g Spearman's "general" factor that all IQ tests and all parts of an IQ test are believed to have in common. 362, 365

GABA, 73, 121

galvanic skin response (GSR) a brief increase in the electrical conductivity of the skin, indicating increased arousal of the sympathetic nervous system. 426

gambling, 264

ganglion cells neurons in the eye that receive input from the visual receptors and send impulses via the optic nerve to the brain. 135, 138

Garcia effect. *See* conditioned taste aversion.

gate theory a theory that pain messages have to pass through a gate in the spinal cord on their way to the brain and that messages from the brain can open or close that gate. 150

gender roles the different behaviors that society generally expects of women and men. 224–226, 269

gene a segment of a chromosome that indirectly controls development. 12, 57, 58

general adaptation syndrome a reaction to severe and prolonged stress, marked by fatigue, loss of interest, and increased vulnerability to illness. 443

generalization. *See* stimulus generalization.

generalized anxiety disorder a condition in which a person is constantly plagued by exaggerated worries. 515

generativity versus stagnation the conflict between a productive life and an unproductive life. 219

genetics, 57–62
  of alcoholism, 528, 529
  of autism, 551
  of depression, 536
  of intelligence, 368–372
  of schizophrenia, 549

genitals, 405, 406

genital stage Freud's final stage of psychosexual development, in which sexual pleasure is focused on sexual intimacy with others. 471, 473

genotype the entire set of genes within an individual. 62

German measles, 187

Gestalt psychology an approach to psychology that seeks explanations of how we perceive overall patterns. 164–167

Gestalt therapy a form of therapy that deals with the client's immediate experience and current behavior, attending to body language as well as spoken language. 569, 570

Gilles de la Tourette's syndrome, 510

glaucoma, 121, 122, 133

glia a cell of the nervous system that insulates neurons, removes waste materials (such as dead cells), and performs other supportive functions. 67

glucose a sugar, the main source of nutrition for the brain. 74, 386

goal setting, 412–414

goat, 103

good figure in Gestalt psychology, the tendency to perceive simple, symmetrical figures. 166

grammatical rules, 208, 211, 212

gray matter, 82

group two or more people united by some common characteristic or interest and acting together in some way. 628

group decision making, 635–637

group polarization the tendency for groups to make more extreme decisions than isolated individuals would, on the average. 635, 636

group therapy therapy provided to a group of people rather than to an individual. 571

groupthink an extreme form of group polarization in which a cohesive group with leaders intolerant of dissent actively silences all dissenters and moves quickly toward a decision that may be ill conceived. 636, 637

guilty-knowledge test a test that uses the polygraph to measure whether a person has information that only someone guilty of a certain crime could know. 427

gull, 63, 64

H

habit, 266, 267

habituate to decrease a person's response to a stimulus when it is presented repeatedly. 187, 189

hair cells, 144, 145, 147

hallucination a sensory experience that does not correspond to reality, such as seeing or hearing something that is not present or failing to see or hear something that is present. 115, 121, 527

hallucinogens drugs that induce delusions or sensory distortions. 74, 85, 121, 123, 544, 545

haloperidol, 74

hammer (bone), 144

hamster, 241

handicapped people, 462

Hans. *See* Clever Hans.

happiness, 6, 440, 441

Hawthorne effect the tendency for people's performance to improve not because of the independent variable but simply because they know a change has occurred in some procedure or because they know they are being observed. 41, 42

health psychology a field of psychology that deals with how people's behavior can enhance health and prevent illness and how behavior contributes to recovery from illness. 443–452

hearing, 81, 143–147, 166

heart disease, 449, 450

heart rate, 425, 426

hebephrenic schizophrenia. *See* disorganized schizophrenia.

helplessness. *See* learned-helplessness theory.

hemisphere the left or the right half of the brain. 82, 85–91

heredity. *See* genetics and nature-nurture issue.

heroin, 74, 120, 121, 533

hertz a unit of frequency representing one cycle per second. 144, 145

heterozygous having different genes on a pair of chromosomes. 59

heuristics strategies for simplifying a problem, or for guiding an investigation. 331, 332

hierarchy of needs Maslow's categorization of human motivations, ranging from basic physiological needs at the bottom to the need for self-actualization at the top. 380–382

high self-monitors people who constantly monitor their own behavior and change it readily to make a good impression. 490, 608

hindbrain the most posterior (hind) part of the brain, including the medulla, pons, and cerebellum. 78, 79, 81, 82

hippocampus a forebrain structure believed to be important for certain aspects of memory. 82, 83, 308

history of psychology, 8, 10, 11

histrionic personality disorder, 511

homeostasis the maintenance of biological conditions within an organism in a state of equilibrium. 378, 379

homosexuality, 404–408

homozygous having the same gene on both members of a pair of chromosomes. 59

hormone a chemical released by a gland and conveyed by the blood to other parts of the body, where it alters activity. 80, 81, 406–408, 536

horse, 103

humanistic psychologist a psychologist who stresses the human potential to make conscious, deliberate decisions about one's life. 15

humanistic psychology a branch of psychology that emphasizes the capacity of people to make conscious decisions about their own lives. 481–484

humanistic therapy, 564, 565

human-relations approach. *See* Theory Y.

Human Subjects Committee, 42

hunger, 385–399

Huntington's disease, 12, 456, 457

hyperactivity, 510

hyperventilation prolonged deep breathing. 515, 516

hypnosis a condition of increased suggestibility that occurs in the context of a special hypnotist-subject relationship. 113–119
  hypnotic regression, 118, 119
  and memory, 117–119
  and pain, 115
  and perception, 115
  and posthypnotic suggestion, 117
hypochondriasis a condition in which a person exaggerates physical ailments or repeatedly complains of ailments that a physician cannot detect. 510, 512
hypothalamus, 80, 82, 83
hypothesis a preliminary, testable prediction of what will happen under certain conditions. 21, 330–332, 340, 341
hysteria, 512
Hz. *See* hertz.

I

iconic store. *See* sensory store.
id according to Freud, the aspect of personality that consists of biological drives and demands for immediate gratification. 473, 474
ideal self a person's image of what he or she would like to be. 482
identical twins. *See* monozygotic twins.
identity achievement the deliberate choice of a role or identity. 227
identity crisis the search for self-understanding. 226, 227
identity foreclosure the acceptance of a role that a person's parents prescribe. 226, 227
identity versus role confusion the conflict between the sense of self and confusion over one's identity. 217–219
idiographic laws laws that apply to individual differences. 485
idiosyncratic associations, 545
illogical reasoning, 340–344
illusion, 459–461
illusory correlation an apparent relationship between two variables based on casual observation, even though the variables are actually unrelated. 36
imitation copying a behavior or custom. 188, 189, 225, 268, 269
immigration, 366
immunization. *See* inoculation.
implicit memory tests, 282
implosion a method of reducing fear by suddenly exposing a person to the object of fear in reality or in imagination. 521
impression formation, 597, 598
impulse control disorders, 510
incentive an external stimulus that pulls people toward certain actions. 379
incongruence in person-centered therapy, a mismatch between the self-concept and the ideal self. 564
incus, 144
independent variable the variable the experimenter manipulates to see how it affects the dependent variable. 37, 38
individual differences, 12–16
individual psychology the psychology of the person as an indivisible whole, as formulated by Adler. 480, 481

induced movement a perception that an object is moving and the background is stationary when in fact the object is stationary and the background is moving. 170
industrial-organizational (I-O) psychology branch of psychology that studies the behavior of people at work. 641–648
industry versus inferiority the conflict between feelings of accomplishment and feelings of worthlessness. 217, 218
infancy, 187–189, 195, 196, 210, 211, 219–220, 471, 472
infant amnesia the relative lack of memory for experiences that occurred before the age of about 5 years. 310
infections, 550
inferential statistics statements about large groups based on inferences from small samples. 48, 49
inferiority complex an exaggerated feeling of weakness, inadequacy, and helplessness. 480, 481
information-processing model the procedure by which either a computer or a person codes, stores, and retrieves information. 285–292
informed consent a subject's agreement to take part in an experiment after being informed about what will happen. 42
inhibition of neurons, 70, 72, 138
initiative versus guilt the conflict between independent behavior and behavior inhibited by guilt. 217
injection procedure, 527, 528
inkblots, 499, 500
inoculation protection against the harmful effects of stress (or an infectious agent) by earlier exposure to a small amount of it. 457
inoculation effect the tendency for exposure to a weak persuasive message to weaken a subsequent stronger message's effect on people's attitudes. 612
insanity defense, 585–587
insight thinking of an answer suddenly and unpredictably. 332
insomnia difficulty in getting to sleep or in staying asleep. 104, 105, 109
instinctive behavior, 63, 377, 378
institutionalized infants, 221
instrumental conditioning. *See* operant conditioning.
insulin a hormone released by the pancreas that increases the entry of glucose into the cells and increases the amount of food that is stored as fats. 81, 386
intelligence, 346–373
intelligence in animals, 239–242
intelligence quotient (IQ) a measure of an individual's probable performance in school and in similar settings. 349–351
intelligence testing, 185, 186, 349–357, 365–372
interference competition among related memories. 302, 303
internal cause of behavior, 600–604
internal locus of control belief that one's own efforts control most of the important events in one's life. 488–490
interneuron a neuron that carries information from one neuron to another. 67

interpersonal attraction, 228–230, 617–627
interpersonal influence, 628–640
interpretation in psychoanalysis, an explanation of the underlying meaning of someone's thoughts, words, or actions. 563
interview, 642
intimacy versus isolation the conflict between establishing a long-term relationship with another person and remaining alone. 219
intrinsic motivation a motivation to engage in an act for its own sake. 379, 380, 411
introversion, 486
intuitive thinking, 192, 193
I-O psychology. *See* industrial-organizational psychology.
IQ tests, 185, 186, 349–357, 365–377
iris, 131
isolation. *See* social isolation.

J

jalapeño pepper, 150
James-Lange theory the theory that emotion is merely our perception of autonomic changes and movements evoked directly by various stimuli. 427–429, 431
jet lag, 104, 105
JND, 156
job design, 646, 647
job enrichment an increase in the complexity and challenge of a job. 646, 647
job satisfaction, 230, 646, 647
job selection, 497, 641, 642
job training, 644
just noticeable difference (JND) the minimum change that a person can detect in the intensity of a physical stimulus. 156
juvenile delinquency, 39

K

kitten. *See* cat.
kittiwake, 63, 64
knowledge-acquisition components, 363
Korsakoff's syndrome a condition caused by prolonged deficiency of vitamin B$_1$, which results in a combination of both retrograde amnesia and anterograde amnesia. 74, 308

L

Laboratory Animal Care Committees, 43
language, 207–215
  in chimpanzees, 212–214
  development, 209–212
latent content the hidden content of a dream that is represented only symbolically. 562
latent period according to Freud, a period in which psychosexual interest is suppressed or dormant. 471, 473
lateral hypothalamus an area of the brain that contributes to the control of hunger. 386
lateral line system, 143
laughter, 85

law of effect Thorndike's theory that a response that is followed by favorable consequences becomes more probable and a response that is followed by unfavorable consequences becomes less probable. 254

L-DOPA, 73, 74

learned avoidance, 516, 517, 521

learned-helplessness theory the theory that depression may result when people perceive that they have no control over the major events that affect them. 537–540

learning, 236–275
  while asleep, 110

left hemisphere of brain, 88, 89

lens a structure that varies its thickness to enable the eye to focus on objects at different distances. 88, 130, 131

lesbians, 408

libido according to Sigmund Freud, a sexual energy. 377, 471

Librium, 120, 121

lie-detector test, 426, 427

life insurance industry, 646

light, 129, 130

Likert scale a scale on which a person checks some point along a line ranging from 1, meaning "strongly disagree," to 5 or 7, meaning "strongly agree," on each of several statements about some topic; ratings are summed over items. 606, 607

liking, 622

limbic system forebrain structures below the cerebral cortex that are important for motivated and emotional behaviors such as eating, mating, and fighting. 82, 85, 428

lion, 65

lithium, 577

lobes of cerebral cortex, 82–86

lobotomy. *See* prefrontal lobotomy.

localization of sound, 147

locus coeruleus, 111

locus of control, 488–490

logical reasoning, 199, 201, 330–334

longitudinal study a study of a single group of individuals over time. 183–186, 401, 402

long-term memory memory that lasts indefinitely. 287–292

loose associations, 545

loudness a perception closely related to the amplitude of sound waves. 143

love, 622–627

low self-monitors people who make relatively little effort to mold their behavior to the expectations of others. 490, 608

LSD. *See* lysergic acid diethylamide.

ludus love, 622, 623

lysergic acid diethylamide (LSD) a chemical that can affect the brain, sometimes producing hallucinations. 73–75, 121, 123

M

magic tricks, 26, 27, 166

maintenance insomnia trouble staying asleep, with a tendency to awaken briefly but frequently. 109

major depression a long, severe depression. 535

malleus, 144

mania a condition marked by constant, driven activity and a lack of inhibitions. 540–542

mania form of love, 622, 623

manic-depressive disorder. *See* bipolar disorder.

manifest content the content of a dream as the person experiences it. 562

many-door problem, 240

MAOIs. *See* monoamine oxidase inhibitors.

marijuana, 121, 122, 527

marriage, 229, 230

masculinity, 486–488

Maslow's hierarchy of needs, 380–382

massed practice practice of something one is trying to learn by means of many repetitions in a short time. 295

mathematics, 338, 339

maturation. *See* development.

MDMA, 121, 123

mean the sum of all the scores reported in a study divided by the number of scores. 45, 46

meaningfulness the ability of a person to fit a given item into a known pattern of information. 284, 285

measurement. *See* tests.

mechanoreceptors receptors that respond to mechanical stimulation. 147

media, 22, 30, 37–40, 589, 590

median the middle score in a list of scores arranged from highest to lowest. 45, 46

medical therapies, 575–579

meditation, 454

medulla a structure just above the spinal cord that controls many of the muscles of the head and several life-preserving functions such as breathing. 81

membrane of neuron, 69, 70

memory, 276–312
  and aging, 310
  and drugs, 298
  and hypnosis, 117–119
  and means of testing, 280–283
  and neurotransmitters, 73
  and obsessive-compulsive disorder, 523
  and sleep, 108, 109
  of stories, 304, 305

menstruation, 153

mental age a measurement of an individual's intelligence, expressed as an age. Someone who performs as well as the average child of age *x* has a mental age of *x* years. 350

mental hospitals, 580–583

mental illness, 504–555

mental imagery, 320–324

Mental Patients' Association, 572

mental retardation, 212, 511

mental rotation, 322, 323

mere-exposure effect the tendency of people to come to like objects or people more as a result of coming into contact with them frequently. 620

mescaline, 74, 121, 123

Mesmerism. *See* hypnosis.

metacomponents, 363

methadone an opiate sometimes prescribed because its effects on behavior are less disruptive than those of morphine or heroin. 533, 534

method of loci a mnemonic device that calls for linking the items on a list with a memorized list of places. 299, 300

midbrain the middle part of the brain, more prominent in birds and reptiles than in mammals. 78, 79, 82, 111

middle adulthood, 219, 230, 231

midlife transition a time of reassessment of one's goals. 230, 231

mind-brain problem the philosophical question of how the conscious mind is related to the physical brain. 6, 7

Minnesota Multiphasic Personality Inventory (MMPI) a true-false standardized personality test. 494–497

minority groups, 10, 11, 599, 600, 609, 610, 641, 642. *See also* race differences.

misattribution an incorrect inference about behavior. 604, 605, 624, 625

misery loves company, 618–620

MMPI. *See* Minnesota Multiphasic Personality Inventory.

M'Naghten Rule a rule that states that criminal defendants are insane if they did not know what they were doing at the time of the crime or did not know that it was wrong. 585

mnemonic device any technique for aiding memory by encoding each item in some special way. 298–300

mode the score that occurs most frequently in a distribution of scores. 46

modeling copying a behavior or custom. 268, 269

Model Penal Code a rule that states that criminal defendants are insane if their conduct was a result of a mental disease or defect that reduced their capacity to appreciate the wrongfulness of their conduct or to conform to the requirements of law. 585

monkey, 6, 79, 103, 162, 220, 221, 379, 448, 519, 520

monoamine oxidase inhibitors (MAOIs) drugs that block the conversion of dopamine, norepinephrine, and serotonin into inactive molecules. 576

monocular cues visual cues that are just as effective with one eye as with both. 169

monozygotic twins (literally, one-egg twins) identical twins who develop from a single fertilized ovum. 60, 61, 212, 369, 370

mood disorders, 535–543

moon (effects on behavior), 36

moon illusion the apparent difference between the size of the moon at the horizon and its size higher in the sky. 175, 176

moral behavior, 203

moral dilemma a problem that pits one moral value against another. 203, 204

moral reasoning, 202–206

moratorium a delay in resolving an identity crisis. 227

morpheme a unit of meaning. 207, 208

morphine, 74, 120, 121

motion parallax the apparently swift motion of objects close to a moving observer and the apparently slow motion of objects farther away. 169

motion pictures, 171

motivation, 374–419
  and dream content, 111

motor cortex a strip of cerebral cortex in the rear of the frontal lobe, critical for fine control of the muscles. 84, 85

motor nerves nerves that convey impulses from the spinal cord to the muscles and glands. 79

motor neuron a neuron that transmits impulses from the central nervous system to the muscles or glands. 67, 68, 73

motor skills, 81

movement, 85, 187, 190, 191

movement perception, 170, 171

MPPP and MPTP, 74

Müller-Lyer illusion, 172

multiple-choice problem, 240

multiple intelligences Gardner's theory that intelligence is composed of numerous unrelated forms of intelligent behavior. 365

multiple personality disorder a condition in which a person alternates among two or more personalities. 512, 513, 586

muscle control, 187

music, 458, 459

mutation a random change in the structure of a gene. 59, 62

myopia nearsightedness; the inability to focus on distant objects. 82, 130, 132

N

naloxone, 150

narcissistic personality disorder, 511

narcolepsy a condition characterized by sudden attacks of sleep. 109

natural selection the tendency in nature of individuals with certain genetically controlled characteristics to reproduce more successfully than others do. 62

nature-nurture issue the question of the relative roles played by heredity (nature) and environment (nurture) in determining differences in behavior. 7, 57, 62, 368–372

nausea, 121, 122

nearsightedness, 130, 132

Necker cube, 165

need for achievement a striving for competitive success and accomplishment. 411–417

negative afterimage a color that a person sees after staring at its opposite color for a while. 138, 139, 172

negative correlation a relationship in which increases in one variable are associated with decreases in another variable. 34–36

negative punishment the weakening of a response by the omission of a favorable stimulus. 259

negative reinforcement escape from an unfavorable event. 258, 259

negative symptom a characteristic notable for its absence, such as a lack of emotional expression. 546

neglect, 84

neo-Freudians personality theorists who have remained faithful to parts of Freud's theory while modifying other parts. 477, 478

nerve a bundle of axons carrying messages from the sense organs to the central nervous system or from the central nervous system to the muscles and glands. 78

nerve deafness hearing loss that results from damage to the cochlea, the hair cells, or the auditory nerve. 144

nerve impulse. *See* action potential.

nervous system, 78–94

neuroleptic drugs drugs that relieve schizophrenia. 578

neuron a cell of the nervous system that receives information and transmits it to other cells by conducting electrochemical impulses. 67–75

neuropeptides, 73

neuroticism, 486

neurotransmitter a chemical that is released by a neuron and then diffuses across a narrow gap to excite or inhibit another neuron. 70–75, 80, 121

newborn, 187–189, 216

nicotine, 121, 123

nightmare, 110

night terror, 110

noise, 455

nomothetic laws laws intended to apply to all individuals. 485

nondirective therapy. *See* person-centered therapy.

non-REM (NREM) sleep all stages of sleep other than REM sleep. 105, 107

nonsense syllable a meaningless syllable, such as JID, sometimes used in studies of memory. 279, 280

nontraditional family, 222, 223

nonverbal communication, 596

norepinephrine, 70, 73

normal distribution a symmetrical frequency of scores produced by many factors, each of which produces small, random variations. 45–48, 356

norms descriptions of the frequencies at which particular scores occur. 356

Novocain, 70

NREM sleep. *See* non-REM sleep.

nucleus, 57

nursing, 244

nymphomaniac, 402

O

obedience following a direct command from someone in authority. 632, 633

obesity the excessive accumulation of body fat. 392–397

object permanence the concept that an object continues to exist even when one does not see, hear, or otherwise sense it. 195, 196

obsession a repetitive, intrusive thought pattern. 522

obsessive-compulsive disorder a condition marked by repetitive thought patterns and actions. 522–524

occipital lobe the rear portion of each hemisphere of the cerebral cortex, critical for vision. 84

occupations in psychology, 10

oddity, 240

odor. *See* olfaction.

Oedipal complex according to Freud, a young boy's sexual interest in his mother accompanied by competitive aggression toward his father. 472, 473

old age, 57, 94, 231

olfaction the sense of smell, the detection of chemicals in contact with the membranes inside the nose. 152–154

olfactory bulb, 83

onset insomnia trouble falling asleep. 109

openness to new experiences, 486

operant conditioning or **instrumental conditioning** the process of changing behavior by following a response with reinforcement. 253–267

operation according to Piaget, a mental process that can be reversed. 196

operational definition a definition that specifies the procedures used to measure some variable or to produce some phenomenon. 29, 30, 242

opiates drugs that are either derived from the opium poppy or that resemble drugs so derived. 120, 121, 526, 527, 533, 534

opponent-process principle of emotions principle that the removal of a stimulus that excites one emotion causes a swing to an opposite emotion. 432, 433, 527

opponent-process theory (of color vision) the theory that we perceive color in terms of a system of paired opposites: red versus green, yellow versus blue, and white versus black. 138, 139

optical illusion a misinterpretation of a visual stimulus as being larger or smaller or straighter or more curved than it really is. 171–176

optic chiasm the location at which half of the axons from each eye cross to the opposite side of the brain. 88

optic nerve a set of axons that extend from the ganglion cells of the eye to the thalamus and several other areas of the brain. 88, 135, 136

oral stage Freud's first stage of psychosexual development, in which psychosexual pleasure is focused on the mouth. 471, 472

organizational interventions, 461, 462

organization of memory, 296

orgasm, 401, 405

otolith, 147–149

ovary, 80

overjustification effect the tendency for intrinsic motivation to decline after people have been given more extrinsic motivation than necessary to perform a task. 380

overweight, 392–397

P

$p < .05$ an expression meaning that the probability of accidentally getting results equal to the reported results is less than 5%. 49

pain, 73, 120, 121, 149, 150

paired-associates learning memorization of pairs of items. 11, 280

pancreas, 80, 81

panic disorder a condition in which a person experiences frequent attacks of severe anxiety, often including sweating, faintness, increased heart rate, difficulty in breathing, and chest pain. 515, 516, 518

preventive detention the commitment of people to a mental hospital to prevent them from committing crimes. 587, 588

primacy effect the tendency for the first information we learn about someone to influence us more than later information does. 596, 597

primary motivation motivation that serves an obvious biological need. 380

primary prevention preventing a disorder from developing. 588–590

primary reinforcer an event that satisfies a biological need. 260, 261

prisoners, 455, 456

prisoner's dilemma a situation in which each person must choose between two actions, one a competitive response that benefits the person at another's expense, the other a cooperative response that brings less immediate benefit to the individual but benefits both people. 637, 638

proactive interference the interference produced by an older memory on a newer one. 302, 303

problem solving, 330–335, 338, 339

procedural memory the ability to remember how to perform acquired skills. 291

Progressive Matrices an IQ test that attempts to measure abstract reasoning and is designed to be as fair as possible to people from a variety of cultures and backgrounds. 353, 354, 362

projection the attribution of one's own undesirable characteristics to other people. 475

projective test a test designed to encourage people to project their personality characteristics onto ambiguous stimuli. 499–501

protanopia, 141

protein, 57, 58

prototype a highly typical member of a category. 328

proximity in Gestalt psychology, the tendency to perceive objects that are close together as belonging to a group; in social behavior, closeness. 165, 166, 620

psychiatric will, 583

psychiatry the branch of medicine that specializes in identifying and treating psychological disorders. 8, 10

psychics, 26, 27

psychoactive substance dependence, 525–534

psychoanalysis a mental-health profession that treats psychological disorders by focusing on underlying, unconscious motives and thoughts, based on Freud's theory of the interplay of conscious and unconscious forces. 8, 10, 14, 15, 469–478, 561–563

psychodynamic theory a theory that relates personality to the interplay of conflicting forces within the individual, including some that are unconscious. 469–479

psychogenic fugue a condition in which a person wanders away from home and cannot remember his or her identity. 512

psychokinesis, 25

psychological disorders, 504–555

psychological test. *See* tests.

psychology (defined) the systematic study of behavior and experience. 5

psychometric the measurement of individual differences in abilities and behaviors. 9, 362

psychophysical function a mathematical function that relates the physical intensity of a stimulus to its perceived intensity— for example, luminous energy to brightness. 155

psychophysics the study of the relationship between the properties of physical stimuli and our perception of those stimuli. 155–159

psychosexual development in Freud's theory, progression through a series of developmental periods, each with a characteristic psychosexual focus that leaves its mark on adult personality. 471–473

psychosexual pleasure according to Freud, any enjoyment arising from stimulation of part of the body. 471

psychosomatic illness an illness that is influenced by a person's experiences or reactions to experiences. 447–451

psychotherapy, 559–574

PTC, 59

puberty the time of onset of sexual maturation. 227

punishment an event that decreases the probability that the preceding response will be repeated in the future. 259, 439

pupil the opening in the eye through which light enters. 88, 130, 131

pursuit eye movements eye movements to maintain constant focus on a moving object. 547, 548

pygmy chimpanzee, 213, 214

Q

quantitative psychologist a psychologist who measures individual differences in behavior and applies statistical procedures to analyze those measurements. 12

quota in employment, a rule for offering a fixed percentage of available jobs to each group of candidates. 642

R

rabbit, 103

raccoon, 149

race differences, 366–368, 371, 372, 398. *See also* minority groups.

racial prejudice. *See* stereotype.

radial keratotomy, 130

random assignment assignment of subjects to groups by means of some chance procedure, to make sure that every subject has the same probability as any other subject has of being assigned to a given group. 38, 39

random sample a group of people picked in such a way that every individual in the population has an equal chance of being selected. 30, 31

range a statement of the highest and lowest scores in a distribution of scores. 46, 47

rape sexual contact obtained through violence, threats, or intimidation. 408, 409, 444

rapid-eye-movement (REM) sleep a stage of sleep characterized by rapid eye movements, a high level of brain activity, and deep relaxation of the postural muscles; also known as paradoxical sleep. 105, 111

rational-emotive therapy a form of therapy that focuses on the thoughts and beliefs that lead to people's emotions and attempts to replace irrational beliefs with rational ones. 563, 564

rationalization attempting to prove that one's actions are rational and justifiable and thus worthy of approval. 475

Raven's Progressive Matrices, 353, 354, 362

rCBF. *See* regional cerebral blood flow.

reaction formation presenting oneself as the opposite of what one really is in an effort to reduce anxiety. 475, 476

reaction time the delay between a stimulus and the subject's response to it. 318–320

reactive depression a depression that develops suddenly in response to a great loss. 535, 536

reading, 336–338

realistic job preview an orientation for a new worker in which the employer honestly describes the job's good and bad features. 643

reasoning, 199, 201, 330–334, 340–344

rebound effects, 425, 426, 432, 433, 449. *See also* opponent-process theory.

recall a method of testing the persistence of memory by asking someone to produce a certain item (such as a word). 281

receptor a specialized cell that responds to a particular form of energy and conveys its response to other cells in the nervous system. 129, 132–139, 144, 145, 147, 151–154

recessive gene a gene that will affect development only in a person who is homozygous for that gene. 59

recognition a method of testing the persistence of memory by asking someone to choose the correct item from several items. 281

reconstruction filling in the gaps in a memory with what seems reasonable. 304, 305

recovery from brain damage, 92–94

red-green color blindness the inability to distinguish between red and green. 141

reductionism the attempt to explain complex phenomena in terms of simpler components or events. 67, 481

regional cerebral blood flow (rCBF) a technique for estimating the level of activity in an area of the brain by dissolving radioactive xenon in the blood and measuring the radioactivity emitted in that area. 77

regression the return to a more juvenile level of functioning as a means of reducing anxiety or in response to emotionally trying circumstances. 475

reinforcement an event that increases the probability that the response that preceded it will be repeated in the future. 254, 255, 258–261

relaxation, 453, 454
relearning method. *See* savings method.
reliability the repeatability of a set of test scores. 358, 359
REM deprivation, 107
REM sleep. *See* rapid-eye-movement sleep.
repair and restoration theory the theory that the purpose of sleep is to enable the body to recover from the wear and tear of the day. 102, 103
replicable result a result that can be repeated (at least approximately) by any competent investigator who follows the original procedure. 22
representativeness heuristic the tendency to assume that if an item is similar to members of a particular category, it is probably a member of that category itself. 341, 342
representative sample a selection of the population chosen to match the overall population with regard to specific variables. 30, 31
repression motivated forgetting; the relegation of unacceptable impulses or memories to the unconscious. 474, 475
research ethics, 42, 43, 619
resistance in psychoanalysis, continued repression that interferes with the therapy. 563
retardation. *See* mental retardation.
reticular formation a diffuse set of neurons, extending from the medulla into the forebrain, that is largely responsible for variations in the level of arousal of the brain. 81
retina the rear surface of the eye, lined with visual receptors. 88, 130–136
retinal disparity the difference in the apparent position of an object as seen by the left retina and by the right retina. 168
retinex theory the theory that color perception results from the cerebral cortex's comparison of various retinal patterns. 139–141
retirement, 231
retrieval an association that facilitates retrieval of information from long-term memory. 287, 288, 292, 293, 297
retroactive interference the interference produced by a newer memory on an older one. 302, 303
retrograde amnesia loss of memory for events that occurred during a time just prior to the onset of the amnesia. 307
reversible figure a stimulus that a person can perceive in more than one way. 165
rhesus. *See* monkey.
ribonucleic acid, 57, 58
right hemisphere of brain, 90, 91
right to refuse treatment, 583–585
RNA, 57, 58
rod the type of visual receptor that is adapted for dim light. 132, 134, 135
role confusion experimentation with various roles or identities. 217, 218, 226, 227
Rorschach Inkblot Test a set of 10 inkblots used as a projective test of personality. 499, 500
Rosenthal effect. *See* expectancy effect.
rubella, 187

S

Salem witch trials, 74, 75
salivation, 242, 243
salt deficiency, 389
salt taste preference, 389, 391
SAT. *See* Scholastic Aptitude Test.
satiety the experience of being full, of feeling no hunger. 388
savant, 365
savings method a method of testing the persistence of memory by measuring how much faster someone can relearn something learned in the past than something being learned for the first time. 281
scapegoat food, 391
scatterplot, 35
Schachter and Singer's theory of emotions theory that emotions are our interpretation of autonomic arousal in light of all the information we have about ourselves and the situation. 429–432, 623–625
schedule of reinforcement a rule for the delivery of reinforcement following various patterns of responding. 262–264
schema (plural: schemata or schemas) in Piaget's theory, an organized way of interacting with objects in the world; in social behavior, the information and expectations we have about a person or groups of people. 194, 598, 599
schizophrenia a condition characterized by deterioration of daily activities and by hallucinations, delusions, or thought disorder. 73, 77, 544–550, 577–579
Scholastic Aptitude Test (SAT) a test of students' likelihood of performing well in college. 47, 48, 355, 356, 366, 368
school psychologist, 9
science, 21–23, 28
scientific-management approach. *See* Theory X.
script a set of rules governing what people do in a certain setting. 339, 340, 491
sea lion, 214
seasonal affective disorder a condition in which a person becomes depressed in winter and normal or manic in summer. 540
season of birth effect the tendency for those born during the winter months in a northern climate to be at greater risk for schizophrenia than those born during other seasons. 550
secondary gain the indirect benefits a person receives from a disability, such as the attention and sympathy of others and an excuse for avoiding unpleasant activities. 512
secondary motivation a motivation that develops as a result of specific experiences and that does not directly serve any biological need. 380
secondary prevention, 588
secondary reinforcer an event that becomes reinforcing when it is associated with a primary reinforcer. 260, 261
second language learning, 214, 215
sedative. *See* tranquilizers.
selection of employees, 497, 641, 642
selective memory, 304, 305

selective reporting publishing results that match researchers' expectations and neglecting results that do not match expectations. 22, 23
self-actualization the need to achieve one's full potential. 381, 382, 482
self-actualized personality, 482–484
self-centeredness, 227
self-concept a person's image of what he or she really is. 482
self-efficacy the perception of one's own ability to perform a task successfully. 271, 272
self-fulfilling prophecy, 14, 41
self-handicapping strategies the use of external causes as "decoys" for our failures so we can avoid attributing them to internal causes. 124, 604
self-help groups, 531, 572
self-monitoring
    as personality variable, 490, 608
    of reading comprehension, 296, 297
self-perception theory the theory that subjects attribute their behavior to situational factors such as rewards. 615, 616
self-reinforcement, 266, 267, 272
self-serving bias the tendency to attribute your successes to internal factors such as skill and your failures to external forces beyond your control. 604
self-stimulation of brain, 6
semantic memory memory of facts, ideas, or general principles. 291, 292
semantics a set of rules for deriving meaning. 208
semicircular canal, 147, 148
senility, 69
sensation the conversion of energy from the environment into a pattern of response by the nervous system. 127–154
sensation seeking, 378
sensorimotor stage according to Piaget, the first stage of intellectual development, in which an infant's behavior is limited to making simple motor responses to sensory stimuli. 195, 196
sensory adaptation the tendency of a sensory threshold to fall after a period when the sensory receptors have not been stimulated and to rise after exposure to intense stimuli. 156, 157
sensory deprivation temporary reduction of visual, auditory, and other stimulation of senses. 40, 41
sensory neglect, 84
sensory nerves nerves that carry information from the sense organs to the spinal cord. 79
sensory neuron a neuron that conveys sensory information to the central nervous system. 67, 68, 79
sensory store the very brief storage of information derived from the senses. 285–287
sensory threshold the minimum intensity at which an individual can detect a sensory stimulus 50% of the time; a low threshold indicates ability to detect faint stimuli. 156–159
serial learning memorization of a series of items in order. 280
serial-order effect the tendency of people to remember items at the beginning and the

end of a list better than those in the middle. 283, 284

serotonin a neurotransmitter that plays an important role in sleep and mood changes. 73, 74, 121, 123

set point a level (such as a weight level) that the body attempts to maintain. 388–392

sex chromosomes the chromosomes that determine whether an individual will develop as a female or as a male. 60

sex differences:
  desire to be thin, 395–398
  detecting emotions, 433
  genetics of, 60
  intellectual abilities, 367
  moral reasoning, 203, 206
  need for achievement, 415, 417
  psychological disorders, 536, 550
  reaction to divorce, 223
  sexual behaviors, 65, 401, 404, 405
  social behaviors, 224–226
  suicide attempts, 542

sex-limited gene a gene that exerts its effects on one sex only or on one sex more than on the other, even though both sexes have the gene. 60

sex-linked gene a gene found on the X chromosome. 60

sex stereotypes, 269
sexual abuse, 409
sexual arousal, 404, 405
sexual behavior, 227, 228, 400–410
sexual fantasies, 470, 471

sexual identity the sex a person regards himself or herself as being. 405–408

sexual orientation a person's preference for male or female sex partners. 405–408

shape constancy, 168

shaping a technique for establishing a new response by reinforcing successive approximations to it. 256, 257

sheep, 103
shift work, 105
shock avoidance, 516, 517, 521
shock treatment. *See* electroconvulsive therapy.

short-term memory memory that forms instantaneously but lasts only until a person's attention is distracted. 287–291

shyness, 185
siblings, 223, 224
sight. *See* vision.

signal-detection theory the study of people's tendencies to make correct judgments, misses, and false alarms. 157

sign language, 212, 213

similarity in Gestalt psychology, the tendency to perceive related objects as belonging to a group. 166

similarity principle (in interpersonal attraction) the tendency for people to choose friends who resemble themselves in many ways. 617, 618

simple schizophrenia. *See* undifferentiated schizophrenia.

single-blind study a study in which either the observer or the subjects are unaware of which subjects received one treatment and which received another treatment. 31

situational differences in learning, 250–252

16-PF Test a standardized personality test that measures 16 personality traits. 497, 498

size constancy, 168
size perception, 172, 175, 176

skeletal pertaining to the muscles that move the limbs, trunk, and head. 255

sleep:
  abnormalities, 109, 110
  cycles, 101, 106, 109
  and depression, 107
  deprivation, 102, 103
  and dreams, 107–112
  good versus poor sleepers, 110
  and memory, 107–109
  need for, 102, 103
  position, 109, 110
  schedule, 101, 104, 105
  stages, 105–109

sleep apnea a condition in which a person has trouble breathing while asleep. 109

sleeper effect the tendency of a message from a questionable source to exert little effect at first but a greater effect later. 608

sleeptalking, 109, 110
sleepwalking, 110
slip of the tongue, 476, 477
slow-wave sleep, 106
smell. *See* olfaction.
smiling, 433–437
smoking. *See* cigarette.
snake phobia, 519, 520

social cognition the process by which we combine and remember information about others and make inferences based on that information. 595–605

social development, 216–233

social interest a sense of solidarity and identification with other people. 481

social isolation, 220–221, 550
Socialist Party, 609

social-learning theory the view that people learn by observing and imitating the behavior of others and by imagining the consequences of their own behavior. 268–273

social perception interpretation of the feelings, intentions, and personalities of other people. 595–605

social psychologist, 14

social psychology the study of social behavior and how an individual's behavior is influenced by other people. 14, 592–651

Social Readjustment Rating Scale, 445–447
social support, 457, 458, 527

sociobiology a field that tries to explain the social behaviors of animals in terms of their survival and reproductive advantages. 64–66

sociopathic personality. *See* antisocial personality disorder.
sodium, 69, 70, 72, 389
sodium lauryl sulfate, 152

somatic nervous system the nerves that control the muscles. 78

somatization disorder a condition in which a person suffers through a long series of pains and ailments with no apparent medical basis. 512

somatoform disorder a disorder in which a person has physical symptoms that are based on psychological rather than medical factors. 512

somatosensory cortex a strip of cerebral cortex in the parietal lobe that is specialized for touch and related information. 84

somatosensory system, 149, 150

Son of Sam case, 586, 587
sound localization, 147

sound waves vibrations of the air or of some other medium. 143, 144

SPAR method a self-monitoring method of study based on these steps: survey, process meaningfully, ask questions, review and self-test. 297

species differences:
  in brain, 79
  in hearing, 144
  in learning, 239–242
  in sleep, 103
  in vision, 132–134

species-specific behavior a particular behavior that is widespread in one animal species but not in others. 63

specific hungers, 389
speech. *See* language.
speed of action potential, 69, 136

spinal cord the part of the central nervous system that communicates with sense organs and muscles below the level of the head. 78, 79, 428

split brain, 86–91
spontaneous firing, 70

spontaneous recovery the return of an extinguished response after a delay. 245, 303

Spoonerism an exchange of parts of two or more words, usually the initial sounds. 208

SQ3R method a self-monitoring method of study based on these steps: survey, question, read, recite, review. 297

S-R psychology, 242

stage of concrete operations according to Piaget, the third stage of intellectual development, in which children can deal with the properties of concrete objects but cannot readily deal with hypothetical or abstract questions. 198, 199

stage of formal operations according to Piaget, the fourth and final stage of intellectual development, in which people use logical, deductive reasoning and systematic planning. 199–201

stage performers, 26, 27
stages:
  of adjustment to dying, 231–233
  of intellectual development, 194–202
  of language development, 209–212
  of moral reasoning development, 202–206
  of psychosexuality, 471–473
  of romantic relationships, 625–627
  of sleep, 105–107
  of social and emotional behavior, 216–219

standard deviation a measurement of the amount of variation among scores in a normal distribution. 47, 48, 52

standard error of the mean, 49, 53

standardization the process of selecting items for a test, determining its mean and standard deviation, and determining what various scores on the test mean. 356, 357

standardized test a test that is administered according to specified rules and whose scores are interpreted in a prescribed fashion. 494

Stanford-Binet IQ test a test of intelligence; the first important IQ test in the English language. 350, 351, 366

stapes, 144
starling, 65

state a temporary activation of a particular personality tendency. 485

state-dependent memory a memory that is easiest to recall when a person is in the same physiological state as when the memory was formed. 298

states of consciousness. *See* hypnosis.

statistically significant results results that have a low probability of having arisen by chance. 48, 49, 53

statistical reasoning, 332, 333

statistics, 45–49

stereotype a schema about a group of people. 269, 342, 343, 599, 600

stereotyped movements, 551

stickleback fish, 64

stimulant drug, 109, 121, 122, 527

stimulus an energy in the environment that can influence action. 129

stimulus generalization the extension of a learned response from the original stimulus to similar stimuli; in operant conditioning, the tendency to make a similar response to a stimulus that resembles one that has been associated with reinforcement. 245, 246, 255, 256

stimulus-response psychology, 242

stirrup (bone), 144, 145

stomach, 388, 449

storge love, 622, 623

story memory, 304, 305

stress according to Selye, the nonspecific response of the body to any demand made upon it. 407, 408, 443–452, 530, 550

striving for superiority according to Adler, a universal desire to seek a personal feeling of excellence and fulfillment. 480

stroboscopic movement an illusion of movement created by a rapid succession of stationary images. 171

stroke an interruption of blood flow, and thus of oxygen supply, to part of the brain. 92

Stroop effect the difficulty of naming the colors in which words are written instead of reading the words themselves. 337, 338

stuttering, 215

style of life according to Adler, a person's master plan for achieving a sense of superiority. 480

subcortical areas of brain, 82

sublimation the transformation of an unacceptable impulse into an acceptable, even an admirable, behavior. 476

subliminal perception the alleged influence on behavior of a stimulus that is below the threshold for conscious recognition. 157–159

substance abuse disorders, 525–534

substance P, 150

substantia nigra, 74, 82

suicide, 542, 543, 589, 590

superego according to Freud, the aspect of personality that consists of memories of rules put forth by one's parents. 473, 474

superior colliculus, 135

superstition a repeated behavior engaged in as a way of gaining good luck or avoiding bad luck. 516, 517

surface structure the structure of a sentence as it is actually spoken or written. 209

survey a study of the prevalence of certain beliefs, attitudes, or behaviors based on

people's responses to specific questions. 30–33

swallowing, 81

sweating, 425, 426

sympathetic nervous system a system composed of two chains of neuron clusters lying just to the left and right of the spinal cord; the neurons send messages to the internal organs to prepare them for a burst of vigorous activity. 80, 81, 424–426, 449, 453, 454

synapse the specialized junction at which one neuron releases a neurotransmitter, which excites or inhibits another neuron. 70–75, 189, 378

synaptic vesicles, 70, 71

syntax a set of rules for linking words into sentences. 208

systematic desensitization a method of reducing fear by gradually exposing a person to the object of the fear. 521

T

TA. *See* transactional analysis.

tabula rasa, 183

tardive dyskinesia a movement disorder characterized by tremors and involuntary movements. 578, 579

taste the sensory system that responds to chemicals on the tongue. 81, 151, 152, 389, 392, 393

taste-aversion learning. *See* conditioned taste aversion.

taste bud the site of the taste receptors, located in one of the folds on the surface of the tongue. 151

TAT. *See* Thematic Apperception Test.

teenagers, 226–228

telepathy, 25

televised violence, 22, 30, 37–40

temperament, 183–185

temporal contiguity being close together in time. 247–250

temporal lobe a portion of each hemisphere of the cerebral cortex that is critical for hearing, complex aspects of vision, and emotional behavior. 85, 88, 548

terminal button a bulge at the end of an axon from which the axon releases a neurotransmitter. 70, 72

termination insomnia a tendency to awaken early and to be unable to get back to sleep. 109

territoriality the tendency to fight to defend the area where one builds a nest and raises young. 437

testis, 80

testosterone a hormone present in higher quantities in males than in females. 80, 81, 153, 406–408

test-retest reliability the reliability of a test, as determined by comparing scores on an initial test with scores on a retest. 358

tests, of

intelligence, 185, 186, 349–357, 365–372

personality, 493–501

tetrahydrocannabinol, 121

thalamus, 82, 83, 135

that's-not-all technique a way to gain compliance in which someone makes an offer and then, before the other person

has a chance to reply, makes a better offer. 631

THC. *See* tetrahydrocannabinol.

Thematic Apperception Test (TAT) a projective personality test in which people are asked to make up stories about a series of pictures. 412, 500, 501

theory a comprehensive explanation of natural phenomena that leads to accurate predictions. 23

Theory X an approach to job design that holds that employees are lazy, indifferent, and uncreative and that jobs should be made simple and routine. 646

Theory Y an approach to job design that maintains that employees like to take responsibility for their work, like to use a variety of skills, and like to see the results of their labor and feel a sense of accomplishment. 646

therapy:

for alcoholism, 530–532

for autism, 552

for bipolar disorder, 577, 578

for brain damage, 93, 94

for depression, 576, 577

medical therapy, 575–579

for obsessive-compulsive disorder, 523, 524

for opiate abuse, 533, 534

for panic disorder, 516

for phobia, 521

psychotherapy, 559–574

for schizophrenia, 578, 579

social and legal issues in, 580–590

thiamine, 74

thinking. *See* cognition.

thought disorder, 545–546

Three Faces of Eve, 512, 513, 586

threshold, 156–159

thyroid gland, 80

tip-of-the-tongue phenomenon the experience of knowing something but being unable to produce it. 303, 304

toddler, 211, 216, 217

tolerance the weakened effect of a drug after repeated use. 527, 528

tongue, 151

top-down processing, 167

touch sensation, 81, 84, 149

Tourette's disorder, 510

trace conditioning, 247

training, 644

trait a relatively permanent personality tendency. 485–492

tranquilizers drugs that help people to relax. 10, 73, 120, 121, 392, 527, 579

transactional analysis (TA) a form of treatment that focuses on how people communicate with one another—for example, as adult to adult or as parent to child. 568, 569

transference reacting toward a therapist as if he or she were a parent or some other important figure in one's life. 563

transformational grammar the theory that we transform the underlying logic of the language, the deep structure, into a spoken surface structure. 209

treatment. *See* therapy.

triarchic theory Sternberg's theory that intelligence is governed by three types of processes, which he refers to as metacomponents, performance components, and knowledge-acquisition components. 363–365

trichromatic theory the theory that color vision depends on the relative rate of response of three types of cones. 136, 137

tricyclic drugs drugs that block the reabsorption of dopamine, norepinephrine, and serotonin by the terminal button. 576

tritanopia, 141
Trobriand Islanders, 24
tryptophan, 392
t-test, 53
tumor, 85
Turing test, 340
twins, 60, 61, 212, 369, 370
two-paycheck families, 222

Type A personality a personality characterized by impatience, hostility, and intense striving for achievement. 449, 450

Type B personality a personality characterized by less impatience, less hostility, and less competitiveness than a Type A personality. 449, 450

U

UFOs, 175

ulcer an open sore on the lining of the stomach or duodenum. 448, 449, 455

unconditional positive regard complete, unqualified acceptance of another person as he or she is. 482

unconditioned reflex an automatic connection between a stimulus and a response. 242

unconditioned response (UR) an automatic response to an unconditioned stimulus. 243

unconditioned stimulus (US) a stimulus that automatically elicits an unconditioned response. 243

unconscious according to Freud, an aspect of the mind that influences behavior, although we are not directly aware of it. 469, 470, 476, 477

undifferentiated schizophrenia a type of schizophrenia that has the basic symptoms but no single symptom that is especially prominent. 546

utility usefulness of a test for a practical purpose. 359, 360

V

validity the degree to which a test measures what it is intended to measure. 359, 497, 500, 501

Valium, 120, 121

variable. *See* dependent variable, independent variable.

variable-interval schedule a rule for delivering reinforcement after varying amounts of time. 264

variable-ratio schedule a rule for delivering reinforcement after varying numbers of responses. 263, 264

variance, 47, 52
velocity of action potential, 69, 136

venereal disease a disease that is spread through sexual contact. 404

ventricles, 548
ventriloquism, 147

ventromedial hypothalamus an area of the brain, in which damage leads to weight gain via an increase in the secretion of insulin. 386

vesicle. *See* synaptic vesicles.

vestibular sense a sense that detects the direction of tilt and amount of acceleration of the head. 111, 147–149, 170

vicarious reinforcement or **punishment** reinforcement or punishment observed to have been experienced by someone else. 270, 271

Vietnam veterans, 444
violent behavior. *See* aggressive behavior.

visceral pertaining to the internal organs. 255
vision, 84, 85, 87, 88, 129–142, 160–179
visual capture, 147

visual cliff an apparatus that makes one side of a table appear to drop sharply in depth, as if off a cliff. 190, 191

visual constancy the tendency to perceive objects as unchanging in shape, size, and color, despite variations in what actually reaches the retina. 168

visual cortex, 88, 135, 162, 163

visual field what you see. 84, 88, 89
vitamin B_1, 74
vitreous humor, 130
volley principle in hearing, 145

von Restorff effect the tendency to remember the most unusual items on a list better than other items. 284

W

WAIS-R. *See* Wechsler Adult Intelligence Scale—Revised.
walking, 82, 89
warm-up effect, 94
waterfall illusion, 162
Weber's law, 156

Wechsler Adult Intelligence Scale— Revised (WAIS-R) an IQ test commonly used with adults. 351, 352, 353, 356

Wechsler Intelligence Scale for Children—Revised (WISC-R) an IQ test commonly used with children, which yields a verbal score and a performance score as well as an overall IQ. 351, 352, 353, 356

weight loss, 394–397
weight regulation, 388
what-the-heck effect, 396, 399
white matter, 82
WISC-R. *See* Wechsler Intelligence Scale for Children—Revised.
wish fulfillment, 562

withdrawal the unpleasant effects of stopping the prolonged use of a drug. 526
women. *See* sex differences.
women in psychology, 10, 11

word superiority effect greater ease of identifying a letter when it is part of a whole word than when it is presented by itself. 336–338

working mothers, 222
work motivation, 644–646
work safety, 272
work shifts, 105

X

Xanax, 120, 121

X chromosome a sex chromosome of which females have two per cell and males have one. 60

xenon, 77
X rays, 250, 251, 336

Y

Y chromosome a sex chromosome found in males but not in females. 60

yellow-blue color blindness, 141
young adulthood, 219

Young-Helmholtz theory. *See* trichromatic theory.

Z

zebra, 241

TO THE OWNER OF THIS BOOK:

I hope that you have enjoyed *Introduction to Psychology*, Second Edition as much as I enjoyed writing it. I would like to know as much about your experience as you would care to offer. Only through your comments and those of others can I learn how to make this a better text for future readers.

School _____ Your instructor's name _____

1. What did you like the most about *Introduction to Psychology*, Second Edition? _____

_____

_____

_____

2. Do you have any recommendations for ways to improve the next edition of this text? _____

_____

_____

_____

3. In the space below or in a separate letter, please write any other comments you have about the book. (For example, were any chapters or concepts particularly difficult?) I'd be delighted to hear from you! _____

_____

_____

_____

_____

_____

_____

_____

_____

_____

_____

_____

_____

Optional:

Your name _____ Date _____

May Wadsworth quote you, either in promotion for *Introduction to Psychology* or in future publishing ventures?

Yes ☐   No ☐

Thanks!

FOLD HERE

CUT PAGE OUT

FOLD HERE

NO POSTAGE
NECESSARY
IF MAILED
IN THE
UNITED STATES

BUSINESS REPLY MAIL
FIRST CLASS   PERMIT NO. 34   BELMONT, CA

Postage will be paid by addressee

James W. Kalat
Wadsworth Publishing Company
10 Davis Drive
Belmont, CA 94002